Sixth Edition

CompTIA Linux+ and LPIC-1

Guide to Linux Certification

Jason W. Eckert
triOS College

Cengage

Australia • Brazil • Canada • Mexico • Singapore • United Kingdom • United States

**CompTIA Linux+ and LPIC-1: Guide to
Linux Certification, Sixth Edition**
Jason W. Eckert and triOS College

SVP, Product: Erin Joyner

VP, Product: Thais Alencar

Senior Product Director: Mark Santee

Portfolio Product Manager: Natalie Onderdonk

Product Assistant: Ethan Wheel

Learning Designer: Carolyn Mako

Content Manager: Marlena Sullivan

Digital Project Manager: Jim Vaughey

Technical Editor: Danielle Shaw

Developmental Editor: Lisa Ruffolo

VP, Product Marketing: Jason Sakos

Director, Product Marketing: Danaë April

Product Marketing Manager: Mackenzie Paine

Content Acquisition Analyst: Ann Hoffman

Production Service: Straive

Senior Designer: Erin Griffin

Cover Image Source: sollia/Shutterstock.com

For product information and technology assistance, contact us at
**Cengage Customer & Sales Support, 1-800-354-9706 or
support.cengage.com.**

For permission to use material from this text or product, submit all
requests online at **www.copyright.com.**

Library of Congress Control Number: 2023902115

SE ISBN: 979-8-214-00080-0

LLF ISBN: 979-8-214-00085-5

Cengage

200 Pier 4 Boulevard

Boston MA 02210

USA

Cengage is a leading provider of customized learning solutions. Our
employees reside in nearly 40 different countries and serve digital
learners in 165 countries around the world. Find your local representative
at **www.cengage.com.**

To learn more about Cengage platforms and services, register or access
your online learning solution, or purchase materials for your course, visit
www.cengage.com.

Notice to the Reader

Printed in the United States of America

Print Number: 01   Print Year: 2023

Brief Contents

Table of Contents

Introduction

> "In a future that includes competition from open source, we can expect that the eventual destiny of any software technology will be to either die or become part of the open infrastructure itself."
>
> Eric S. Raymond, The Cathedral and the Bazaar

As Eric S. Raymond reminds us, open source software will continue to shape the dynamics of the computer software industry for the next long while, just as it has for the last three decades. Coined and perpetuated by hackers, the term "open source software" refers to software in which the source code is freely available to anyone who wants to improve it (usually through collaboration). At the heart of the open source software movement lies Linux—an operating system whose rapid growth has shocked the world by demonstrating the nature and power of the open source model.

However, as Linux continues to grow, so must the number of Linux-educated users, administrators, developers, and advocates. We now find ourselves in a time in which Linux education is of great importance to the information technology industry. Key to demonstrating Linux skills and knowledge is the certification process. This book, *Linux+ and LPIC-1 Guide to Linux® Certification,* uses carefully constructed examples, questions, and practical exercises to prepare readers with the necessary information to achieve the latest version of the sought-after Linux+ certification from CompTIA, as well as the latest version of the LPIC-1 certification from the Linux Professional Institute (LPI). Whatever your ultimate goal, you can be assured that reading this book in combination with study, creativity, and practice will make the open source world come alive for you as it has for many others.

Intended Audience

Simply put, this book is intended for those who want to learn the Linux operating system and master the topics tested on the Linux+ certification exam from CompTIA or the LPIC-1 certification exams from LPI. It does not assume any prior knowledge of Linux. Although the topics introduced in this book and associated certification exams are geared toward systems administration, they are also well suited for those who will use or develop programs for Linux systems, or want to pursue a career in cloud computing, supercomputing, cybersecurity, web development, cloud development, or Internet of Things (IoT) technology, where Linux knowledge is a prerequisite.

Chapter Descriptions

Chapter 1, "Introduction to Linux," introduces operating systems as well as the features, benefits, and uses of the Linux operating system. This chapter also discusses the history and development of Linux and open source software, as well as the xrole that Linux plays in the cloud.

Chapter 2, "Linux Installation and Usage," outlines the procedures necessary to prepare for and install Linux on a typical computer system. This chapter also describes how to interact with a Linux system via a terminal and enter basic commands into a Linux shell, such as those used to obtain help and to properly shut down the system.

Chapter 3, "Exploring Linux Filesystems," outlines the Linux filesystem structure and the types of files that you find within it. This chapter also discusses commands you can use to view and edit the content of those files.

Chapter 4, "Linux Filesystem Management," covers the commands you can use to locate and manage files and directories on a Linux filesystem. This chapter also discusses how to link files, as well as interpret and set file and directory permissions, special permissions, and attributes.

Chapter 5, "Linux Filesystem Administration," discusses how to create, mount, and manage filesystems in Linux. This chapter also discusses the files that identify storage devices, the various filesystems available for Linux systems, as well as the partitions and logical volumes used to host filesystems.

Chapter 6, "Linux Server Deployment," introduces the types of hardware and storage configurations used within server environments, as well as the considerations for installing a Linux server. This chapter also discusses device driver support, common problems that may occur during installation, system rescue, as well as configuring Linux server storage (SAN, RAID, ZFS, and BTRFS).

Chapter 7, "Working with the Shell," covers the major features of the BASH and Z shells, including redirection, piping, variables, aliases, and environment files. This chapter also explores the syntax of basic shell scripts and the use of Git to provide version control for shell scripts.

Chapter 8, "System Initialization, X Windows, and Localization," covers the GRUB bootloader that you use to start the Linux kernel. This chapter also discusses how to start daemons during system initialization as well as how to start and stop them afterwards. Finally, this chapter discusses the structure and configuration of Linux graphical user interfaces, as well as setting up time, time zone, and locale information.

Chapter 9, "Managing Linux Processes," covers types of processes as well as how to view their attributes, run them in the background, change their priority, and kill them. This chapter also discusses how to schedule processes to occur in the future using various utilities.

Chapter 10, "Common Administrative Tasks," details three important areas of system administration: printer administration, log file administration, and user administration.

Chapter 11, "Compression, System Backup, and Software Installation," describes utilities that are commonly used to compress and back up files on a Linux filesystem. This chapter also discusses how to install software from source code, how to use the Red Hat Package Manager and the Debian Package Manager, as well as how to install and manage sandboxed applications.

Chapter 12, "Network Configuration," introduces networks, network utilities, and the IP protocol, as well as how to configure the IP protocol on a network interface. This chapter also explains how to set up name resolution, IP routing, network services, and the technologies you can use to administer Linux servers remotely.

Chapter 13, "Configuring Network Services and Cloud Technologies," details the configuration of key infrastructure, web, file sharing, email, and database network services. This chapter also examines how virtualization and containers are used within cloud environments, as well as the configuration and usage of the Docker container runtime and Kubernetes orchestrator.

Chapter 14, "Security, Troubleshooting, and Performance," discusses the utilities and processes used to provide security for Linux systems. This chapter also explores the utilities used to monitor system performance, as well as the troubleshooting procedures for solving performance, hardware, application, filesystem, and network problems.

Additional information is contained in the appendices at the rear of the book. Appendix A discusses the certification process, with emphasis on the Linux+ and LPIC-1 certifications. It also explains how the objective lists for the Linux+ and LPIC-1 certifications match each chapter in the textbook. Appendix B explains how to find Linux resources on the Internet and lists some common resources by category. Appendix C applies the Linux concepts introduced within this book to the macOS operating system from Apple, while Appendix D applies these same concepts to the FreeBSD UNIX operating system.

Features

To ensure a successful learning experience, this book includes the following pedagogical features:

- *Chapter objectives*: Each chapter in this book begins with a detailed list of the concepts to be mastered within the chapter. This list provides you with a quick reference to chapter contents as well as a useful study aid.

- *Illustrations and tables*—Numerous illustrations of server screens and components aid you in visualizing common setup steps, theories, and concepts. In addition, many tables provide details and comparisons of both practical and theoretical information and can be used for a quick review of topics.
- *End-of-chapter material*—The end of each chapter includes the following features to reinforce the material covered in the chapter:
  - *Summary*—A bulleted list gives a brief but complete summary of the chapter.
  - *Key Terms list*—This section lists all new terms in the chapter. Definitions for each key term can be found in the Glossary.
  - *Review Questions*—A list of review questions tests your knowledge of the most important concepts covered in the chapter.
  - *Hands-On Projects*—Hands-On Projects help you to apply the knowledge gained in the chapter.
  - *Discovery Exercises*—Additional projects guide you through real-world scenarios and advanced topics.

New to This Edition

This edition has been updated to include the concepts and procedures tested on the latest certification exams from CompTIA and the Linux Professional Institute (LPI). More specifically, this edition contains:

- Content that maps to the latest CompTIA Linux+ (XK0-005) and LPIC-1: System Administrator (101-500, 102-500) certification exams
- Updated information pertinent to the latest Linux distributions and technologies
- New and expanded material related to security tools and configuration, Git, cloud technologies, Docker containers, and Kubernetes
- Continued focus on Linux server administration, including key network services (FTP, NFS, Samba, Apache, DNS, DHCP, NTP, Postfix, SSH, VNC, and SQL)
- Hands-On Projects that configure modern Fedora and Ubuntu Linux, using steps that will work on either a Windows or macOS PC (Intel or Apple Silicon)
- A GitHub resource that outlines modifications to Hands-On Project steps that result from changes made by future Linux releases to ensure that you can always use the latest versions of Fedora and Ubuntu
- Appendices that map the latest Linux+ and LPIC-1 certification objectives to each chapter, identify key Linux-related Internet resources, and apply the Linux administration topics covered within the book to Apple macOS and FreeBSD UNIX

Text and Graphic Conventions

Wherever appropriate, additional information and exercises have been added to this book to help you better understand what is being discussed in the chapter. Special boxes throughout the text alert you to additional materials:

Note

The Note box is used to present additional helpful material related to the subject being described.

Hands-On Projects

The Hands-On Projects box indicates that the projects it contains give you a chance to practice the skills you learned in the chapter and acquire hands-on experience.

Discovery Exercises

The Discovery Exercises box contains exercises that guide you to explore real-world scenarios and advanced topics.

MindTap

MindTap for *CompTIA Linux+ and LPIC-1: Guide to Linux Certification* is an online learning solution designed to help you master the skills needed in today's workforce. Research shows employers need critical thinkers, troubleshooters, and creative problem-solvers to stay relevant in our fast-paced, technology-driven world. MindTap helps you achieve this with assignments and activities that provide hands-on practice, real-life relevance, and mastery of difficult concepts. Students are guided through assignments that progress from basic knowledge and understanding to more challenging problems. MindTap activities and assignments are tied to learning objectives. MindTap features include the following:

- *Live Virtual Machine labs* allow you to practice, explore, and try different solutions in a safe sandbox environment. Each module provides you with an opportunity to complete an in-depth project hosted in a live virtual machine environment. You implement the skills and knowledge gained in the chapter through real design and configuration scenarios in a private cloud created with OpenStack.
- *Simulations* allow you to apply concepts covered in the chapter in a step-by-step virtual environment and receive immediate feedback.
- *Linux for Life* assignments encourage you to stay current with what's happening in the Linux field.
- *Reflection* activities encourage classroom and online discussion of key issues covered in the chapters.
- *Pre- and Post-Quizzes* assess your understanding of key concepts at the beginning and end of the course and emulate the CompTIA Linux+ XK0-005 and LPIC-1 101-500 and 102-500 Certification Exam.

Instructors, MindTap is designed around learning objectives and provides analytics and reporting so you can easily see where the class stands in terms of progress, engagement, and completion rates. Use the content and learning path as is or pick and choose how your materials will integrate with the learning path. You control what the students see and when they see it. Learn more at https://www.cengage.com/mindtap/.

Instructor Resources

Instructors, please visit cengage.com and sign in to access instructor-specific resources, which include the instructor manual, solutions manual, and PowerPoint presentations.

- *Instructor's Manual*—The Instructor's Manual that accompanies this book includes additional instructional material to assist in class preparation, including items such as overviews, chapter objectives, teaching tips, quick quizzes, class discussion topics, additional projects, additional resources, and key terms. A sample syllabus is also available.

- *Test bank*—Cengage Testing Powered by Cognero is a flexible, online system that allows you to do the following:
  - Author, edit, and manage test bank content from multiple Cengage solutions.
  - Create multiple test versions in an instant.
  - Deliver tests from your LMS, your classroom, or wherever you want.
- *PowerPoint presentations*—This book provides PowerPoint slides to accompany each chapter. Slides can be used to guide classroom presentations, to make available to students for chapter review, or to print as classroom handouts. Files are also supplied for every figure in the book. Instructors can use these files to customize PowerPoint slides, illustrate quizzes, or create handouts.
- *Solution and Answer Guide*—Solutions to all end-of-chapter review questions and projects are available.

Student Resources

MindTap for Linux+ and LPIC-1 Guide to Linux Certification, Sixth Edition, helps you learn on your terms.

- Instant access in your pocket: Take advantage of the MindTap Mobile App to learn on your terms. Read or listen to textbooks and study with the aid of instructor notifications, flashcards, and practice quizzes.
- MindTap helps you create your own potential. Gear up for ultimate success: Track your scores and stay motivated toward your goals. Whether you have more work to do or are ahead of the curve, you'll know where you need to focus your efforts. The MindTap Green Dot will charge your confidence along the way.
- MindTap helps you own your progress. Make your textbook yours; no one knows what works for you better than you. Highlight key text, add notes, and create custom flashcards. When it's time to study, everything you've flagged or noted can be gathered into a guide you can organize.

About the Author

Jason W. Eckert is an experienced technical trainer, consultant, and best-selling author in the Information Technology (IT) industry. With over three decades of IT experience, 45 industry certifications, 4 published apps, and 25 published textbooks covering topics such as UNIX, Linux, Security, Windows Server, Microsoft Exchange Server, PowerShell, BlackBerry Enterprise Server, and Video Game Development, Mr. Eckert brings his expertise to every class that he teaches at triOS College, and to his role as the Dean of Technology. He was named 2019 Outstanding Train-the-Trainer from the Computing Technology Industry Association (CompTIA) for his work providing Linux training to other educators. For more information about Mr. Eckert, visit jasoneckert.net.

Acknowledgments

Firstly, I would like to thank the staff at Cengage for an overall enjoyable experience writing a textbook on Linux that takes a fundamentally different approach than traditional textbooks. Additionally, I wish to thank Lisa Ruffolo, Danielle Shaw, Marlena Sullivan, Carolyn Mako, and Natalie Onderdonk for working extremely hard to pull everything together and ensure that the book provides a magnificent Linux experience. I also wish to thank Frank Gerencser of triOS College for providing me, over the past two decades, with the opportunity to write six editions of a book on a topic about which I'm very passionate. Finally, I wish to thank the Starbucks Coffee Company for keeping me ahead of schedule, and my dog Pepper for continually reminding me that taking a break is always a good idea. Readers are encouraged to email comments, questions, and suggestions regarding *Linux+ and LPIC-1 Guide to Linux® Certification* to Jason W. Eckert: jason.eckert@trios.com.

Dedication

This book is dedicated to my grandson Chase, who was no help at all.

Before You Begin

Linux can be a large and intimidating topic if studied in a haphazard way. So, as you begin your study of Linux, keep in mind that each chapter in this book builds on the preceding one. To ensure that you gain a solid understanding of core Linux concepts, read the chapters in consecutive order and complete the Hands-On Projects. You should also participate in a local Linux Users Group (LUG) and explore the Internet for websites, forums, YouTube videos, and social media articles that will expand your knowledge of Linux.

Lab Requirements

The following hardware is required at minimum for the Hands-On Projects at the end of each chapter:

- A Windows or macOS PC with a 64-bit Intel, AMD, ARM, or Apple Silicon CPU
- 8 GB RAM (16 GB RAM or greater recommended)
- 500 GB hard disk or SSD (SSD strongly recommended)
- A network that provides Internet access

Similarly, the following lists the software required for the Hands-On Projects at the end of each chapter:

- Latest version of Fedora Workstation installation media
- Latest version of Ubuntu Server installation media

Chapter 1

Introduction to Linux

Chapter Objectives

1   Explain the purpose of an operating system.

2   Outline the key features of the Linux operating system.

3   Describe the origins of the Linux operating system.

4   Identify the characteristics of various Linux distributions and where to find them.

5   Explain the common uses of Linux in industry today.

6   Describe how Linux is used in the cloud.

Linux technical expertise is essential in today's computer workplace as more and more companies switch to Linux to meet their computing needs. Thus, it is important to understand how Linux can be used, what benefits Linux offers to a company, and how Linux has developed and continues to develop. In the first half of this chapter, you learn about operating system terminology and features of the Linux operating system, as well as the history and development of Linux. Later in this chapter, you learn about the various types of Linux, as well as the situations and environments in which Linux is used. Finally, you explore the ways that Linux can be hosted in the cloud, as well as the process and technologies used to add web apps to cloud-based Linux systems.

Operating Systems

Every computer has two fundamental types of components: hardware and software. You are probably familiar with these terms, but it's helpful to review their meanings so you can more easily understand how Linux helps them work together.

Hardware consists of the physical components inside a computer that are electrical in nature; they contain a series of circuits that manipulate the flow of information. A computer can contain many different pieces of hardware, including the following:

- A processor (also known as the central processing unit or CPU), which computes information
- Physical memory (also known as random access memory or RAM), which stores information needed by the processor
- Hard disk drives (HDDs) and solid state drives (SSDs), which store most of the information that you use
- CD/DVD drives, which read and write information to and from CD/DVD discs

- Flash memory card readers, which read and write information to and from removable memory cards, such as Secure Digital (SD) cards
- Sound cards, which provide audio to external speakers
- Video cards (also known as graphics processing units or GPUs), which display results to the computer monitor
- Network adapter cards, which provide access to wired and wireless (Wi-Fi or Bluetooth) networks
- Ports (such as USB, eSATA, GPIO, and Thunderbolt), which provide access to a wide variety of external devices including keyboards, mice, printers, and storage devices
- Mainboards (also known as motherboards), which provide the circuitry (also known as a bus) for interconnecting all other components

Software, on the other hand, refers to the sets of instructions or programs that allow the hardware components to manipulate data (or files). When a bank teller types information into the computer behind the counter at a bank, for example, that bank teller is using a program that understands what to do with your bank records. Programs and data are usually stored on hardware media, such as hard disk drives or SSDs, although they can also be stored on removable media or even embedded in computer chips. These programs are loaded into parts of your computer hardware (such as your computer's memory and processor) when you first turn on your computer and when you start additional software, such as word processors or Internet browsers. After a program is executed on your computer's hardware, that program is referred to as a process. In other words, a program is a file stored on your computer, whereas a process is that file in action, performing a certain task.

There are two types of programs. The first type, applications (apps), includes those programs designed for a specific use and with which you commonly interact, such as word processors, computer games, graphical manipulation programs, and computer system utilities. The second type, operating system software, consists of a set of software components that control the hardware of your computer. Without an operating system, you would not be able to use your computer. Turning on a computer loads the operating system into computer hardware, which then loads and centrally controls all other application software in the background. At this point, the user (the person using the computer) is free to interact with the applications, perhaps by typing on the keyboard or clicking a mouse. Applications take the information the user supplies and relay it to the operating system. The operating system then uses the computer hardware to carry out the requests. The relationship between users, application software, operating system software, and computer hardware is illustrated in Figure 1-1.

The operating system carries out many tasks by interacting with different types of computer hardware. For the operating system to accomplish the tasks, it must contain the appropriate device driver software for every hardware device in your computer. Each device driver tells the operating system how to use that specific device. The operating system also provides a user interface, which is a program that accepts user input indicating what to do, forwards this input to the operating system for completion, and, after it is completed, gives the results back to the user. The user interface can be a command-line prompt, in which the user types commands, or it can be a graphical user interface (GUI), which consists of menus, dialog boxes, and symbols (known as icons) that the user can interact with via the keyboard or the mouse. A typical Linux GUI that also provides a command-line interface via an app is shown in Figure 1-2.

Figure 1-1 The role of operating system software

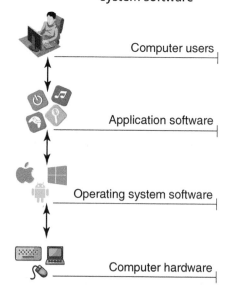

Finally, operating systems offer services, which are applications that handle system-related tasks, such as printing, scheduling programs, and network access. These services determine most of the functionality in an operating system. Different operating systems offer different services, and many operating systems allow users to customize the services they offer.

Figure 1-2   A Linux graphical and command-line user interface

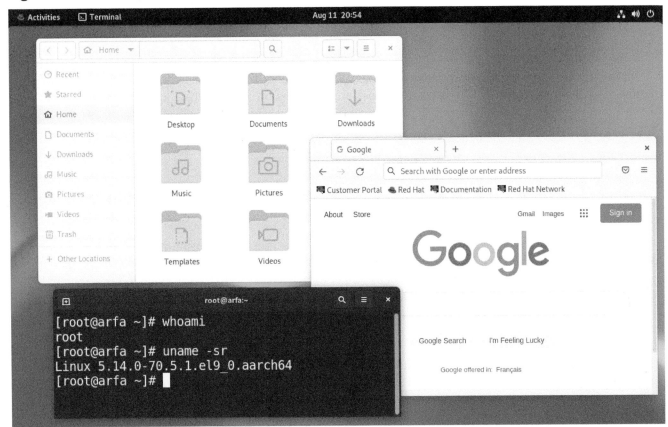

The Linux Operating System

Linux (pronounced "Lih-nucks") is an operating system that is used today to run applications on a variety of hardware. Similar to other operating systems, the Linux operating system loads into computer memory when you first power on your computer and initializes (or activates) all of the hardware components. Next, it loads the programs that display the interface. From within the interface, you can execute commands that tell the operating system and other applications to perform specific tasks. The operating system then uses the computer hardware to perform the tasks required by the applications.

Versions of the Linux Operating System

The core component of the Linux operating system is called the Linux kernel. The Linux kernel and supporting software (called function libraries) are written almost entirely in the C programming language, which is one of the most common languages that software developers use when creating programs.

Although a variety of software can be used to modify the appearance of Linux, the underlying kernel is common to all types of Linux. The Linux kernel is developed continuously; thus, you should understand the different version numbers of the Linux kernel to decide which kernel version is appropriate for your needs. Because the Linux kernel is directly responsible for controlling the computer's hardware (via device drivers), you might sometimes need to upgrade the Linux kernel after installing Linux to take advantage of new technologies or to fix problems (also known as bugs) related to your computer's hardware. Consequently, a good understanding of your system's hardware is important in deciding which kernel to use.

> **Note 1**
>
> For a complete list of kernels, kernel versions, and their improvements, see kernel.org.

In some cases, you can use updates in the form of a kernel module or a kernel patch to provide or fix hardware supported by the kernel. Kernel modules and kernel patches are discussed later in this book.

Identifying Kernel Versions

Linux kernel versions are made up of the following three components:

- Major number
- Minor number
- Revision number

Let's look at a sample Linux kernel version, 5.18.16. In this example, the major number is the number 5, which indicates the major version of the Linux kernel. The minor number, represented by the number 18, indicates the minor revision of the Linux kernel. As new features are added to the Linux kernel over time, the minor number is incremented. The major number is usually incremented when a major kernel feature is implemented, when the minor number versioning reaches a high number, or to signify a major event; for example, the 3.0 kernel was introduced to commemorate the twentieth anniversary of Linux.

Linux kernel changes occur frequently. Those changes that are very minor are represented by a revision number indicating the most current changes to the version of the particular kernel that is being released. For example, a 5.18.16 kernel has a revision number of 16. This kernel is the sixteenth release of the 5.18 kernel. Some kernels have over 100 revisions as a result of developers making constant improvements to the kernel code.

> **Note 2**
>
> Sometimes, a fourth number is added to a kernel version to indicate a critical security or bug patch. For example, a 5.18.16.1 kernel is a 5.18.16 kernel with a critical patch number of 1.

Modern Linux kernels that have a major, minor, and revision number are referred to as production kernels; they have been thoroughly tested by several Linux developers and are declared stable. Development kernels are not fully tested and imply instability; they are tested for vulnerabilities by people who develop Linux software. Most development kernels append the minor number with the letters -rc (release candidate) followed by a number that represents the version of the development kernel. For example, the 5.19-rc8 development kernel is the eighth release candidate for the 5.19 kernel; if Linux developers declare it stable after being thoroughly tested, it will become the 5.19.0 production kernel.

> **Note 3**
>
> Until Linux kernel 2.6.0, an odd-numbered minor number was used to denote a development kernel, and an even-numbered minor number was used to denote a production kernel.

> **Note 4**
>
> When choosing a kernel for a mission-critical computer such as a server, ensure that you choose a production kernel. This reduces the chance that you will encounter a bug in the kernel, which saves you the time needed to change kernels.

Table 1-1 shows some sample kernel versions released since the initial release of Linux.

Table 1-1   Sample Linux Kernel version history

Kernel Version	Date Released	Type
0.01	September 1991	First Linux kernel
0.12	January 1992	Production (stable)
0.99.15	March 1994	Development
1.0.8	April 1994	Production (stable)
1.3.100	May 1996	Development
2.0.36	November 1998	Production (stable)
2.3.99	May 2000	Development
2.4.17	December 2001	Production (stable)
2.5.75	July 2003	Development
2.6.35	August 2010	Production (stable)
3.0.0	July 2011	Production (stable)
3.15.10	August 2014	Production (stable)
4.0.0	April 2015	Production (stable)
4.12.5	August 2017	Production (stable)
5.0.0	March 2019	Production (stable)
5.19-rc8	July 2022	Development

Licensing Linux

Companies often choose Linux as their operating system because of the rules governing Linux licensing. Unlike most other operating systems, Linux is freely developed and continuously improved by a large community of software developers. For this reason, it is referred to as open source software (OSS).

To understand OSS, you must first understand how source code is used to create programs. Source code refers to the list of instructions that a software developer writes to make up a program; an example of source code is shown in Figure 1-3.

Figure 1-3   Source code

```
#define MODULE
#include <linux/module.h>
int init_module(void){
        printk("My module has been activated.\n");
        return 0;
}
void cleanup_module(void){
        printk("My module has been deactivated.");
}
```

After the software developer finishes writing the instructions, the source code is compiled into a format that your computer's processor can understand and execute directly or via an interpreter program. To edit an existing program, the software developer must edit the source code and then recompile it.

The format and structure of source code follows certain rules defined by the programming language in which it was written. Programmers write Linux source code in many programming languages. After being compiled, all programs look the same to the computer operating system, regardless of the programming language in which they were written. As a result, software developers choose a programming language to create source code based on ease of use, functionality, and comfort level.

The fact that Linux is an open source operating system means that software developers can read other developers' source code, modify that source code to make the software better, and redistribute that source code to other developers who might improve it further. Like all OSS, Linux source code must be distributed free of charge, regardless of the number of modifications made to it. People who develop OSS commonly use the Internet to share their source code, manage software projects, and submit comments and fixes for bugs (flaws). In this way, the Internet acts as the glue that binds together Linux developers in particular and OSS developers in general.

> **Note 5**
>
> To read the complete open source definition, visit opensource.org.

> **Note 6**
>
> OSS is also called free and open source software (FOSS) or free/libre and open source software (FLOSS).

Here are some implications of the OSS way of developing software:

- Software is developed rapidly through widespread collaboration.
- Software bugs (errors) are noted and promptly fixed.
- Software features evolve quickly, based on users' needs.
- The perceived value of the software increases because it is based on usefulness and not on price.

As you can imagine, the ability to share ideas and source code is beneficial to software developers. However, a software company's business model changes drastically when OSS enters the picture. The main issue is this: How can a product that is distributed freely generate revenue? After all, without revenue any company will go out of business.

The OSS process of software development was never intended to generate revenue directly. Its goal was to help people design better software by eliminating many of the problems associated with traditional software development, which is typically driven by predefined corporate plans and rigid schedules. By contrast, OSS development relies on the unsystematic contributions of several software developers that have a direct need for the software that they are developing. While this process may seem haphazard, it ensures that software is constantly developed to solve real-world needs. Because the source code is scrutinized and improved by different developers, OSS often solves problems in the best possible way. Each developer contributes their strengths to a project, while learning new techniques from other developers at the same time.

By leveraging existing OSS, organizations can develop software much faster than they could otherwise. A typical software app today contains dozens or hundreds of well-designed OSS software components that the organization's developers didn't have to create themselves. To support this ecosystem, organization developers contribute improvements to existing OSS, as well as create and maintain OSS software components that they'd like other developers to evolve through contributions. In short, OSS saves companies a large amount of time and money when developing software.

Other companies make money by selling computer hardware that runs OSS, by selling customer support for OSS, or by creating closed source software programs that run on open source products such as Linux.

The OSS development process is, of course, not the only way to develop and license software. Table 1-2 summarizes the types of software you are likely to encounter. The following section explains these types in more detail.

Table 1-2 Software types

Type	Description
Open source	Software in which the source code and software can be obtained free of charge and optionally modified to suit a particular need
Closed source	Software in which the source code is not available; although this type of software might be distributed free of charge, it is usually quite costly and commonly referred to as commercial software
Freeware	Closed source software that is given out free of charge; it is sometimes referred to as freemium software
Shareware	Closed source software that is initially given out free of charge but that requires payment after a certain period of use

Types of Open Source Licenses

Linux adheres to the **GNU General Public License (GPL)**, which was developed by the **Free Software Foundation (FSF)**. The GPL stipulates that the source code of any software published under its license must be freely available. If someone modifies that source code, that person must also redistribute that source code freely, thereby keeping the source code free forever.

Note 7

"GNU" stands for "GNUs Not UNIX."

Note 8

The GPL is freely available at gnu.org.

The GPL is an example of a **copyleft license** as it contains strict restrictions on how the source code can be used in derivative software. To encourage adoption in software projects, most OSS instead use a **permissive license** that contains far fewer restrictions. The BSD, MIT, and Apache licenses are examples of permissive open source licenses.

Note 9

For a list of copyleft and permissive open source licenses, visit opensource.org.

Types of Closed Source Licenses

Closed source software can be distributed for free or for a cost; either way, the source code for the software is unavailable from the original developers. The majority of closed source software is sold commercially and bears the label of its manufacturer. Each of these software packages can contain a separate license that restricts free distribution of the program and its source code in many ways.

> **Note 10**
>
> Examples of closed source software are software created by companies such as Microsoft, Apple, and Electronic Arts (EA).

Another type of closed source software is freeware, in which the software program is distributed free of charge, yet the source code is unavailable. Freeware might also contain licenses that restrict the distribution of source code. Another approach to this style of closed source licensing is shareware, which is distributed free of charge, yet after a certain number of hours of usage or to gain certain features of the program, payment is required. Although freeware and shareware do not commonly distribute their source code under an open source license, some people incorrectly refer to them as OSS, assuming that the source code is freely shared as well.

Linux Advantages

The main operating systems in use today include Linux, Microsoft Windows, UNIX, and macOS. Notably, Linux is the fastest growing operating system released to date. Although Linux was only created in 1991, the number of Linux users estimated by Red Hat in 1998 was 7.5 million, and the number of Linux users estimated by Google in 2010 was over 40 million (including the number of Linux-based Android smartphone and device users). In 2013, LinuxCounter.net estimated that the number of Linux users was over 70 million, and Google estimated that over 900 million Linux-based Android devices had shipped by then. In 2018, Linux ran on the top 500 supercomputers, 60 percent of the computers purchased by schools in North America (due to widespread adoption of Linux-based Chromebooks), as well as nearly all web servers and Internet-connected hardware devices. In 2021, Gartner estimated that nearly half of the global population (3.5 billion people) were Linux users, whether they realized it or not.

Organizations have adopted Linux for many reasons. The following advantages are examined in the sections that follow:

- Risk reduction
- Meeting business needs
- Stability and security
- Support for different hardware
- Ease of customization
- Ease of obtaining support
- Cost reduction

Risk Reduction

Companies need software to perform mission-critical tasks, such as managing business operations and providing valuable services to customers over the Internet. However, changes in customer needs and market competition can cause the software a company uses to change frequently. Keeping the software up to date can be costly and time-consuming but is a risk that companies must take. Imagine that a fictitious company, ABC Inc., buys a piece of software from a fictitious software vendor, ACME Inc., to integrate its sales and accounting information with customers via the Internet. What would happen if ACME went out of business or stopped supporting the software due to lack of sales? In either case, ABC would be using a product that had no software support, and any problems that ABC had with the software after that time would go unsolved and could result in lost revenue. In addition, all closed source software is eventually retired after it is purchased, forcing companies to buy new software every so often to obtain new features and maintain software support.

If ABC instead chose to use an OSS product and the original developers became unavailable to maintain it, then ABC would be free to take the source code, add features to it, and maintain it themselves provided the source code was redistributed free of charge. Also, most OSS does not retire after a short period of time because collaborative open source development results in constant software improvement geared to the needs of the users.

Meeting Business Needs

Recall that Linux is merely one product of open source development. Many thousands of OSS programs are available, and new ones are created daily by software developers worldwide. Most open source Internet tools have been developed for quite some time now, and the focus in the Linux community in the past few years has been on developing application software, cloud technologies, and security-focused network services that run on Linux. Almost all of this software is open source and freely available, compared to other operating systems, in which most software is closed source and costly.

OSS is easy to locate on the web, at sites such as SourceForge (sourceforge.net), GitHub (github. com), GitLab (gitlab.com), and GNU Savannah (savannah.gnu.org). New software is published to these sites daily. SourceForge alone hosts over 500,000 software development projects.

Common software available for Linux includes but is not limited to the following:

- Scientific and engineering software
- Software emulators
- Web servers, web browsers, and e-commerce suites
- Desktop productivity software (e.g., word processors, presentation software, spreadsheets)
- Graphics manipulation software
- Database software
- Security software

In addition, companies that run the UNIX operating system (including macOS, which is a flavor of UNIX) might find it easy to migrate to Linux. For those companies, Linux supports most UNIX commands and standards, which eases a transition to Linux because the company likely would not need to purchase additional software or retrain staff. For example, suppose a company that tests scientific products has spent time and energy developing custom software that runs on the UNIX operating system. If this company transitioned to another operating system, its staff would need to be retrained or hired, and much of the custom software would need to be rewritten and retested, which could result in a loss of customer confidence. If, however, that company transitions to Linux, the staff would require little retraining, and little of the custom software would need to be rewritten and retested, hence saving money and minimizing impact on consumer confidence.

Companies that need to train staff on Linux usage and administration can take advantage of several educational resources and certification exams for various Linux skill levels. Certification benefits as well as the CompTIA Linux+ and LPIC-1 certifications are discussed in this book's Appendix A, "Certification."

In addition, for companies that require a certain development environment or need to support custom software developed in the past, Linux provides support for nearly all programming languages and software development frameworks.

Stability and Security

OSS is developed by people who have a use for it. This collaboration among software developers with a common need speeds up the software creation, and when bugs in the software are found, bug fixes are created quickly. Often, the users who identify the bugs can fix the problem because they have the source code, or they can provide detailed descriptions of their problems so that other developers can fix them.

By contrast, customers using closed source operating systems must rely on the operating system vendor to fix any bugs. Users of closed source operating systems must report the bug to the manufacturer and wait for the manufacturer to develop, test, and release a bug fix. This process might take weeks or even months, which is slow and costly for most companies and individuals. The thorough and collaborative open source approach to testing software and fixing software bugs increases the stability of Linux; it is not uncommon to find a Linux system that has been running continuously for months or even years without being turned off.

Security, a vital concern for most companies and individuals, is another Linux strength. Because Linux source code is freely available and publicly scrutinized, security loopholes are quickly identified and fixed by developers. In contrast, the source code for closed source operating systems is not released to the public for scrutiny, which means customers must rely on the operating system vendor to detect and fix security loopholes. A security loophole unnoticed by the vendor can be exploited by the wrong person. Every day, new malicious software (such as viruses and malware) is unleashed on the Internet with the goal of infiltrating operating systems and other software. However, most malicious software targets closed source operating systems and software. As of April 2008, Linux had fewer than 100 known viruses, whereas Windows had more than 1,000,000 known viruses. Compared to other systems, the amount of malicious software for Linux systems remains incredibly low.

Note 11

For a list of recent malicious software, visit cisecurity.org.

Support for Different Hardware

Another important feature of Linux is that it can run on a wide variety of hardware. Although Linux is most commonly installed on workstations and server systems that use an Intel CPU platform, it can also be installed on supercomputers that use an IBM POWER CPU or high-performance cloud servers that use an ARM CPU, such as Amazon's Graviton EC2. Linux can also be installed on other systems, such as point-of-sale terminals and sales kiosks that use an Intel CPU, as well as small custom hardware devices that use an ARM, MIPS, or RISC-V CPU. Small hardware devices that can connect to the Internet are collectively called the Internet of Things (IoT).

The open source nature of Linux combined with the large number of OSS developers at work today makes Linux an attractive choice for manufacturers of mobile, custom, and IoT devices. NASA spacecrafts, Internet routers and firewalls, Google Android smartphones and tablets, Amazon Kindle eBook readers, GPS navigation systems, smart speakers, home automation equipment, and Wi-Fi access points all run Linux.

Few other operating systems run on more than two CPU platforms, making Linux the ideal choice for companies that use and support many different types of hardware. Here is a partial list of CPU platforms on which Linux can run:

- Intel x86/x86_64 (also implemented by AMD)
- ARM/ARM64
- MIPS/MIPS64
- RISC-V
- PPC (PowerPC, POWER)
- Mainframe (S/390, z/Architecture)

Ease of Customization

The ease of controlling the inner workings of Linux is another attractive feature, particularly for companies that need their operating system to perform specialized functions. If you want to use Linux as a web server, you can recompile the Linux kernel to include only the support needed to be a web server. This results in a much smaller and faster kernel.

Note 12

A small kernel performs faster than a large kernel because it contains less code for the processor to analyze. On high performance systems, you should remove any unnecessary features from the kernel to improve perfomance.

Today, customizing and recompiling the Linux kernel is a well-documented and easy process; however, it is not the only way to customize Linux. Only software packages necessary to perform certain tasks need to be installed; thus, each Linux system can have a unique configuration and set of applications available to the user. Linux also supports several system programming languages, such as shell and PERL, which you can use to automate tasks or create custom tasks.

Consider a company that needs an application to copy a database file from one computer to another computer, yet also needs to manipulate the database file (perhaps by checking for duplicate records), summarize the file, and finally print it as a report. This might seem like a task that would require expensive software; however, in Linux, you can write a short shell script that uses common Linux commands and programs to perform these tasks. This type of customization is invaluable to companies because it allows them to combine several existing applications to perform a certain task, which might be specific only to that company and, hence, not previously developed by another free software developer. Most Linux configurations present hundreds of small utilities, which, when combined with shell or PERL programming, can make new programs that meet many business needs.

Ease of Obtaining Support

For those who are new to Linux, the Internet offers a world of Linux documentation. A search of the word "Linux" on a typical Internet search engine such as google.com displays thousands of results, including Linux-related guides, information portals, and video tutorials.

In addition, several Internet forums allow Linux users to post messages and reply to previously posted messages. If you have a specific problem with Linux, you can post your problem on an Internet forum and receive help from those who know the solution. Linux forums are posted to frequently; thus, you can usually expect a solution to a problem within hours. You can find Linux-related forums on several different websites, including linux.org, linuxquestions.org, facebook.com (called groups), discord.com (called servers), and reddit.com (called subreddits).

> **Note 13**
>
> Appendix C, "Finding Linux Resources on the Internet," describes how to navigate Internet resources and lists some resources that you might find useful.

Although online support is the typical method of getting help, other methods are available, including **Linux User Groups (LUGs)**. LUGs are groups of Linux users who meet regularly to discuss Linux-related issues and problems. An average LUG meeting consists of several new Linux users (also known as Linux newbies), administrators, developers, and experts (also known as Linux gurus). LUG meetings are a resource to solve problems and learn about the local Linux community. Most LUGs host websites that contain a multitude of Linux resources, including summaries of past meetings and discussions. One common activity seen at a LUG meeting is referred to as an Installfest; several members bring in their computer equipment to install Linux and other Linux-related software. This approach to transferring knowledge is very valuable to LUG members because concepts can be demonstrated and the solutions to problems can be modeled by more experienced Linux users.

> **Note 14**
>
> To find a list of available LUGs in your region, search for the words "LUG cityname" on an Internet search engine such as google.com (substituting your city's name for "cityname"). When searching for a LUG, keep in mind that LUGs might go by several different names; for example, the LUG in the Kitchener-Waterloo area of Ontario, Canada is known as KW-LUG (Kitchener-Waterloo Linux Users Group). Many LUGs today are managed using custom websites, Facebook groups, or meeting sites such as meetup.com.

Cost Reduction

Linux is less expensive than other operating systems such as Windows because there is no cost associated with acquiring the software. In addition, a wealth of OSS can run on different hardware platforms running Linux, and a large community of developers is available to diagnose and fix bugs in a short period of time for free. While Linux and the Linux source code are distributed freely, implementing Linux is not cost free. Costs include purchasing the computer hardware necessary for the computers hosting Linux, hiring people to install and maintain Linux, and training users of Linux software.

The largest costs associated with Linux are the costs associated with hiring people to maintain the Linux system. However, closed source operating systems have this cost in addition to the cost of the operating system itself. The overall cost of using a particular operating system is known as the total cost of ownership (TCO). Table 1-3 shows an example of the factors involved in calculating the TCO for operating systems.

Table 1-3   Calculating the total cost of ownership

Costs	Linux	Closed Source Operating System
Operating system cost	$0	Greater than $0
Cost of administration	Low: Stability is high and bugs are fixed quickly by open source developers.	Moderate/high: Bug fixes are created by the vendor of the operating system, which could result in costly downtime.
Cost of additional software	Low/none: Most software available for Linux is also open source.	Moderate/high: Most software available for closed source operating systems is also closed source.
Cost of software upgrades	Low/none	Moderate/high: Closed source software is eventually retired, and companies must buy upgrades or new products to gain functionality and stay competitive.

The History of Linux

Linux is based on the UNIX operating system developed by Ken Thompson and Dennis Ritchie of AT&T Bell Laboratories in 1969 and was developed through the efforts of many people as a result of the hacker culture that formed in the 1980s. Therefore, to understand how and why Linux emerged on the operating system market, you must first understand UNIX and the hacker culture. Figure 1-4 illustrates a timeline representing the history of the UNIX and Linux operating systems.

UNIX

The UNIX operating system has roots running back to 1965, when the Massachusetts Institute of Technology (MIT), General Electric, and AT&T Bell Laboratories began developing an operating system called Multiplexed Information and Computing Service (MULTICS). MULTICS was a test project intended to reveal better ways of developing time-sharing operating systems, in which the operating system regulates the amount of time each process has to use the processor. The project was abandoned in 1969. However, Ken Thompson, who had worked on the MULTICS operating system, continued to experiment with operating systems. In 1969, he developed an operating system called UNIX that ran on the DEC (Digital Equipment Corporation) PDP-7 computer.

Figure 1-4 Timeline of UNIX and Linux development

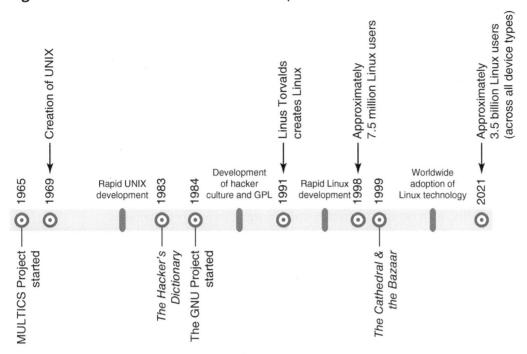

Shortly thereafter, Dennis Ritchie invented the C programming language that was used on Ken Thompson's UNIX operating system. The C programming language was a revolutionary language. Most programs at the time needed to be written specifically for the hardware of the computer, which involved referencing volumes of information regarding the hardware in order to write a simple program. However, the C programming language was much easier to use to write programs, and it was possible to run a program on different machines without having to rewrite the code. The UNIX operating system was rewritten in the C programming language, and by the late 1970s, the UNIX operating system ran on different hardware platforms, something that the computing world had never seen until that time. Hence, people called UNIX a portable operating system.

Unfortunately, the company Ken Thompson and Dennis Ritchie worked for (AT&T) was restricted by a federal court order from marketing UNIX. In an attempt to keep UNIX viable, AT&T sold the UNIX source code to several companies, encouraging them to agree to standards among them. Each of these companies developed its own variety, or **flavor**, of UNIX yet adhered to standards agreed upon by all. AT&T also gave free copies of the UNIX source code to certain universities to promote widespread development of UNIX. One result was a UNIX version developed at the University of California, Berkeley in the early 1980s known as BSD (Berkeley Software Distribution). In 1982, one of the companies to whom AT&T sold UNIX source code (Sun Microsystems) marketed UNIX on relatively inexpensive hardware and sold thousands of computers that ran UNIX to companies and universities.

Throughout the 1980s, UNIX found its place primarily in large corporations that had enough money to purchase the expensive computing equipment needed to run UNIX (usually a DEC PDP-11, VAX, or Sun Microsystems computer). A typical UNIX system in the 1980s could cost over $100,000, yet it performed thousands of tasks for client computers (also known as dumb terminals). Today, UNIX still functions in that environment; many large companies employ different flavors of UNIX for their heavy-duty, mission-critical tasks, such as e-commerce and database hosting. Common flavors of UNIX today include FreeBSD, OpenBSD, NetBSD, HP-UX, Solaris, AIX, macOS, and iOS.

The Hacker Culture

The term hacker refers to a person who attempts to expand their knowledge of computing through experimentation. It should not be confused with the term cracker, which refers to someone who illegally uses computers for personal benefit or to cause damage.

In the early days of UNIX, hackers came primarily from engineering or scientific backgrounds, because those were the fields in which most UNIX development occurred. Fundamental to hacking was the idea of sharing knowledge. A famous hacker, Richard Stallman, promoted the free sharing of ideas while he worked at the Artificial Intelligence Laboratory at MIT. He believed that free sharing of all knowledge in the computing industry would promote development. In the mid-1980s, Stallman formed the Free Software Foundation (FSF) to encourage free software development. This movement was quickly accepted by the academic community in universities around the world, and many university students and other hackers participated in making free software, most of which ran on UNIX. As a result, the hacker culture was commonly associated with the UNIX operating system.

Unfortunately, UNIX was not free software, and by the mid-1980s some of the collaboration seen earlier by UNIX vendors diminished and UNIX development fragmented into different streams. As a result, UNIX did not represent the ideals of the FSF, and so Stallman founded the GNU Project in 1984 to promote free development for a free operating system that was not UNIX.

Note 15

For a description of the FSF and GNU, visit gnu.org.

This development eventually led to the publication of the GNU Public License (GPL), which legalized free distribution of source code and encouraged collaborative development. Any software published under this license must be freely available with its source code; any modifications made to the source code must then be redistributed free as well, keeping the software development free forever.

As more and more hackers worked together developing software, a hacker culture developed with its own implied rules and conventions. Most developers worked together without ever meeting each other; they communicated primarily via online forums and email. *The Hacker's Dictionary*, published by MIT in 1983, detailed the terminology regarding computing and computing culture that had appeared since the mid-1970s. Along with the FSF, GNU, and GPL, it served to codify the goals and ideals of the hacker culture. But it wasn't until the publication of Eric S. Raymond's *The Cathedral and the Bazaar*, in 1999, that the larger world was introduced to this thriving culture. Raymond, a hacker himself, described several aspects of the hacker culture:

- Software users are treated as codevelopers.
- Software is developed primarily for peer recognition and not for money.
- The original author of a piece of software is regarded as the owner of that software and coordinates the cooperative software development.
- The use of a particular piece of software determines its value, not its cost.
- Attacking the author of source code is never done. Instead, bug fixes are either made or recommended.
- Developers must understand the implied rules of the hacker culture before being accepted into it.

This hacker culture proved to be very productive, with several thousand free tools and applications created in the 1980s, including the famous Emacs editor, which is a common tool used in Linux today. During this time, many programming function libraries and UNIX commands also appeared because of the work on the GNU Project. Hackers became accustomed to working together via online forum and email correspondence. In short, the UNIX hacker culture, which supported free sharing of source code and collaborative development, set the stage for Linux.

Linux

Although Richard Stallman started the GNU Project to make a free operating system, the GNU operating system never took off. Much of the experience gained by hackers developing the GNU Project was later pooled into Linux. A Finnish student named Linus Torvalds first developed Linux in 1991 when he was experimenting with improving MINIX (Mini-UNIX, a small educational version of UNIX developed by Andrew Tannenbaum) for his Intel x86-based computer. The Intel x86 platform was fast becoming standard in homes and businesses around the world and was a good choice for any free development at the time. The key feature of the Linux operating system that attracted the development efforts of the hacker culture was that Torvalds had published Linux under the GNU Public License.

Since 1991, when the source code for Linux was released, the number of software developers dedicated to improving Linux has increased each year. The Linux kernel was developed collaboratively and was centrally managed; however, many Linux add-on packages were developed freely worldwide by those members of the hacker culture who were interested in their release. Linux was a convenient focal point for free software developers. During the early- to mid-1990s, Linux development proceeded at full speed, with hackers contributing their time to what turned into a large-scale development project. All of this effort resulted in several distributions of Linux. A distribution (distro) of Linux is a collection or bundle of software containing the commonly developed Linux operating system kernel and libraries, combined with add-on software specific to a certain use. Well-known distributions of Linux include Red Hat, openSUSE, Debian, Ubuntu, Gentoo, Linux Mint, Kali, and Arch.

This branding of Linux did not imply the fragmentation that UNIX experienced in the late-1980s. All distributions of Linux had a common kernel and utilities. Their blend of add-on packages simply made them look different on the surface. Linux still derived its usefulness from collaborative development.

Linux development continued to expand throughout the late-1990s as more developers grew familiar with the form of collaborative software development advocated by the hacker culture. By 1998, when the term "OSS" first came into use, there were already many thousands of OSS developers worldwide. Small companies formed to offer Linux solutions for business. People invested in these companies by buying stock in them. Unfortunately, this trend was short-lived. By the year 2000, most of these companies had vanished. At the same time, the OSS movement caught the attention and support of large companies (including IBM, Compaq, Dell, and Hewlett-Packard), and there was a shift in Linux development over the following decade to support the larger computing environments and mobile devices.

It is important to note that Linux is a by-product of OSS development. Recall that OSS developers are still members of the hacker culture and, as such, are intrinsically motivated to develop software that has an important use. Thus, OSS development has changed over time; in the 1980s, the hacker culture concentrated on developing Internet and programming tools, whereas in the 1990s, it focused on developing the Linux operating system. Since 2000, interest has grown in embedded Linux (Linux systems that run on custom, mobile, and IoT devices) and developing cloud- and security-focused software for use on the Linux operating system. As cloud computing and security continue to grow in importance, even more development in these areas can be expected from the OSS community over the next decade.

Note 16

For more information on the free software movement and the early development of Linux, watch the 2001 television documentary *Revolution OS* (available on YouTube). It features interviews with Linus Torvalds, Richard Stallman, and Eric S. Raymond.

Linux Distributions

It is time-consuming and inefficient to obtain Linux by first downloading and installing the Linux kernel and then adding desired OSS packages. Instead, it's more common to download a distribution of Linux containing the Linux kernel, common function libraries, and a series of OSS packages.

Note 17

Remember that although Linux distributions appear different on the surface, they run the same kernel and contain many of the same packages.

Despite the fact that varied distributions of Linux are essentially the same under the surface, they do have important differences. Different distributions might support different hardware platforms. Also, Linux distributions include predefined sets of software; some Linux distributions include many server-related software applications, such as web servers and database servers, whereas others include numerous workstation and development software applications. Others might include a set of open source tools that you can use to analyze and test the security of other systems on a network.

While Linux distributions use the same Linux kernel versions that are community developed, they can modify those kernels to provide fixes and optimizations that are specific to the distribution and used for long-term support. These are called **distribution kernels**, and list a patch version and distribution identifier following the major, minor, and revision number. For example, the 5.14.0-70.5.1.el9_0.aarch64 kernel is distribution release 70.5.1 of the Linux 5.14.0 production kernel used on a 64-bit ARM (aarch64) version of the Red Hat Enterprise Linux 9.0 distribution (el9_0).

Linux distributions that include many specialized tools might not contain a GUI; an example of this is a Linux distribution that fits within a single small flash memory chip and can be used as a home Internet router. Similarly, Linux distributions used by servers usually do not include a GUI. Workstation-focused distributions, however, do include a GUI that can be further customized to suit the needs of the user.

The core component of the GUI in Linux is referred to as **X Windows**. The original implementation of X Windows on Linux was called XFree86 but has since been replaced by X.org and Wayland. X.org is the latest implementation of X Windows based on the original MIT X Windows project that was released as OSS in 2004, and Wayland is an alternative to X.org that was designed to be easier to develop and maintain. In addition to X Windows, several Linux **desktop environments** are available, which provide for the look and feel of the Linux GUI. The two main competing desktop environments available in Linux are the **GNU Network Object Model Environment (GNOME)** and the **K Desktop Environment (KDE)**. These two desktop environments are comparable in functionality, although users might have a personal preference for one over the other. GNOME closely resembles the macOS desktop, while KDE closely resembles the Windows desktop. Most Linux distributions will ship with either GNOME or KDE but allow you to download and install other desktop environments. Figures 1-5 and 1-6 compare the GNOME and KDE desktop environments.

Note 18

In addition to GNOME and KDE, several other desktop environments are available to Linux systems. One example is Cinnamon, which is a desktop derived from GNOME that is particularly easy to use. Another example is XFCE, which is a lightweight desktop environment designed for Linux systems with few CPU and RAM resources.

Although the differences between Linux distributions can help narrow the choice of Linux distributions to install, one of the most profound reasons companies choose one distribution over another is support for package managers. A **package manager** is a software system that installs and maintains

Figure 1-5   The GNOME desktop environment

Figure 1-6   The KDE desktop environment

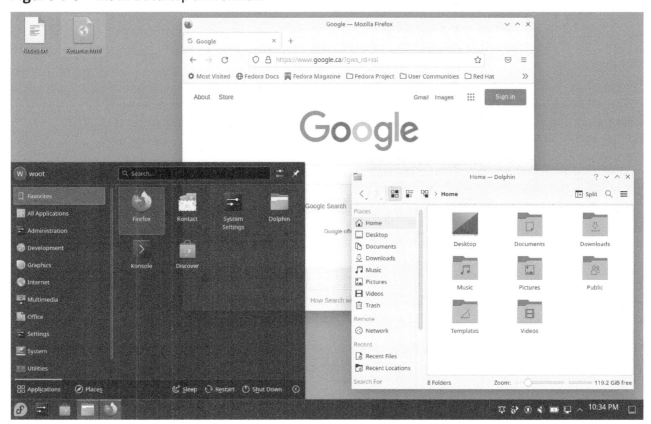

software. It keeps track of installed software, requires a standard format and documentation, and can manage and remove software from a system by recording all relevant software information in a central software database on your computer.

> **Note 19**
>
> A package manager in Linux is similar to the Apps and Features section within the Windows Settings app on a Windows system.

One of the most widely supported package managers is the Red Hat Package Manager (RPM). Most Linux software is available in RPM format, and the RPM is standard on many Linux distributions that were originally derived from the Red Hat Linux distribution. The Debian Package Manager (DPM) is also very common today; it offers the same advantages as the RPM but for systems that were originally derived from the Debian Linux distribution. Other, less common package managers available for Linux include Pacman (Arch Linux), Zypper (openSUSE Linux), and Portage (Gentoo Linux). There are even some package managers that install all related software components as a single unit (called a sandbox) for security and reliability. Snap, Flatpak, and AppImage are examples of sandbox-based packaged managers.

In addition to obtaining software in package manager format, you can download software in tarball format. A tarball is a compressed archive of files, like WinZip or RAR files, usually containing scripts that install the software contents to the correct location on the system, or source code that can be compiled into a working program and copied to the system. Unfortunately, tarballs do not update a central software database and, as a result, are very difficult to manage, upgrade, or remove from the system. Traditionally, most Linux software was available in tarball format, but package managers have since become the standard method for installing software.

> **Note 20**
>
> For a comprehensive list of Linux distributions, visit distrowatch.com.

Anyone can create a Linux distribution by packaging OSS with the Linux kernel. As a result, over 600 Linux distributions are publicly registered. Many are small, specialized distributions designed to fulfill certain functions, but some are mainstream Linux distributions used widely throughout the computing world. Typically, a distribution is associated with a website from which the distribution can be downloaded for free.

Table 1-4 describes some common mainstream Linux distributions, their features, and where to find them on the Internet.

Common Uses of Linux

As discussed earlier, an important feature of Linux is its versatility. Linux can provide apps and services to meet the needs of differing companies in a variety of situations. Some Linux configurations commonly used today include:

- Workstations
- Servers
- Supercomputers
- Network Devices
- Mobile and IoT Devices

Table 1-4 Common Linux distributions

Distribution	Features	Platforms	Location
Red Hat	One of the most used distributions within organizations today. Two distributions of Red Hat are available: the Red Hat Enterprise Linux (RHEL) distribution geared for enterprise environments and the Fedora distribution geared for all environments (servers, desktops, laptops, etc.).	Intel x86_64 ARM/ARM64 MIPS/MIPS64 RISC-V PPC Mainframe	redhat.com getfedora.org
openSUSE	Originally developed primarily in Europe, openSUSE is the oldest business-focused distribution. Like Red Hat, it is commonly used within many organizations today.	Intel x86/x86_64 ARM/ARM64 RISC-V PPC Mainframe	opensuse.org
Debian	One of the earliest distributions, Debian focuses on stability in its structure, release cycle, and available OSS packages. For these reasons, there are many other mainstream distributions based on Debian.	Intel x86/x86_64 ARM/ARM64 MIPS/MIPS64 RISC-V PPC Mainframe	debian.org
Ubuntu	A Debian-based distribution that is widely used in many cloud computing environments, Ubuntu is also commonly used on desktop and mobile devices.	Intel x86_64 ARM/ARM64 RISC-V PPC Mainframe	ubuntu.com
Kali	A Debian-based distribution that is designed for security monitoring, digital forensics, and penetration testing.	Intel x86/x86_64 ARM	kali.org
Gentoo	A distribution that focuses on hardware and software optimization. Each Gentoo component is compiled and optimized specifically for the hardware on the system.	Intel x86/x86_64 PPC/POWER ARM/ARM64	gentoo.org
Linux Mint	A distribution based on Ubuntu that is focused on providing a simple and intuitive desktop experience for novice Linux users.	Intel x86/x86_64	linuxmint.com
Arch	A very lightweight and customizable distribution designed for advanced Linux users that prefer to shape all aspects of their operating system.	Intel x86_64 ARM64 RISC-V PPC	archlinux.org

Workstations

While Windows and macOS remain the most common workstation operating systems today, cybersecurity professionals and software developers often choose to install Linux on their desktop or laptop workstation instead.

Cybersecurity professionals must use specialized tools to scan computers and networks for security vulnerabilities as well as attempt to break into systems to test the strength of their security measures (often called a penetration test). Additionally, cybersecurity professionals must continually monitor the security of systems and networks to determine when a system has been breached, as well as perform forensic analysis to investigate the nature of the breach and the damage incurred. Most of the tools used to perform these activities are available exclusively for Linux systems and preinstalled on cybersecurity-focused Linux distributions, such as Kali Linux.

The rich set of OSS development tools and frameworks available for Linux also makes Linux the preferred choice for software development workstations. For this reason, most major computer vendors provide a developer-focused laptop model that comes preinstalled with a Linux distribution instead of Windows. Some common examples include the HP Dev One, Dell XPS Developer Edition, and Lenovo ThinkPad (Linux Edition).

Modern Linux distributions contain drivers for nearly all desktop and laptop hardware, and often run faster than Windows and macOS on the same system. Consequently, organizations that have a limited budget for computer upgrades (e.g., elementary and secondary schools) often install Linux on legacy systems to extend their useful life.

Note 21

Many open source alternatives to common closed source software can also be installed on Linux workstations. For example, LibreOffice is an open source equivalent to Microsoft Office, and Krita is an open source equivalent to Adobe Photoshop.

Servers

Linux hosts a wide range of services that can be made available to other systems across a network such as the Internet. A computer that hosts one or more services that can be accessed by other systems across a network is commonly referred to as a server.

Note 22

On Linux systems, services are often called daemons.

Servers typically use more powerful hardware compared to workstations and may be located within your organization or in the cloud. While you can install Linux directly onto server hardware (called a bare metal installation), most organizations today run multiple server operating systems concurrently on the same server hardware for cost and power efficiency using virtualization software (also called a hypervisor). There are many different hypervisors available for servers, including the following:

- Hyper-V, a closed source hypervisor developed by Microsoft
- Elastic Sky X Integrated (ESXi), a closed source hypervisor developed by VMWare
- Kernel-based Virtual Machine (KVM), a hypervisor built into the Linux kernel
- Quick Emulator (QEMU), an open source hypervisor that is often used alongside KVM to provide fast access to hardware
- Xen, an open source hypervisor developed by the Linux Foundation

Each operating system that is run using a hypervisor is called a virtual machine. Modern server hardware can run dozens or hundreds of virtual machines, with each virtual machine hosting a separate Linux server.

Linux servers may also be hosted within a container. Containers are like virtual machines but lack an operating system kernel. Consequently, containers must use the kernel on an underlying operating system that has container runtime software installed. Docker, Podman, and LXC are common examples of container runtime software. Additionally, containers are usually smaller than virtual machines because they are configured with just enough filesystem, software libraries and supporting programs to run a particular service or app. This makes containers ideal for running in the cloud; a typical cloud server today can run thousands of small Linux containers.

Regardless of whether they are installed bare metal or hosted within a virtual machine or container, Linux servers can be configured to provide many different services to other systems on a network. The most common services found on Linux servers include the following:

- Web services
- DNS services
- DHCP services
- Time services
- Mail services
- File and print services
- Database services
- Authentication services
- Certificate services

Many of these services are discussed in more detail later in this course.

Web Services

The most popular tool for accessing resources on the Internet is the web browser, which can connect computers to web servers worldwide hosting information of many types: text, pictures, music, binary data, video, and much more. On a basic level, a web server is just a server using Hypertext Transfer Protocol (HTTP) to provide information to requesting web browsers running on other computers. However, web servers can also run Common Gateway Interface (CGI) programs to perform processing and access other resources, as well as encrypt communication using Secure Sockets Layer (SSL) or Transport Layer Security (TLS) to protect the information entered and shown within the web browser. You can tell SSL/TLS is in use when the *http://* in the browser's address bar changes to *https://*. While there are many open source web server software packages available for Linux, the two most common are Apache and Nginx.

DNS Services

Each computer on the Internet needs a unique way to identify itself and to refer to other computers. This is accomplished by assigning each computer a number called an Internet Protocol (IP) address. An IP address is a string of numbers that would be difficult for the typical person to remember. Thus, IP addresses are often associated with more user-friendly names. In particular, servers are identified by names like www.linux.org, which are known as fully qualified domain names (FQDNs). When you use a web browser such as Google Chrome or Mozilla Firefox to request information from a web server, you typically type the web server's FQDN (e.g., www.linux.org) into your browser's address bar. However, FQDNs exist only for the convenience of the human beings who use computer networks. The computers themselves rely on IP addresses. Thus, before your browser can retrieve the requested information from the web server, it needs to know the IP address associated with the FQDN you typed into the address bar. Your web browser gets this information by contacting a server hosting a Domain Name Space (DNS) service. The server running the DNS service maintains a list of the proper FQDN to IP mappings, and quickly returns the requested IP address to your browser. Your browser can then use this IP address to connect to the target website.

For companies wanting to create a DNS server, Linux is an inexpensive solution, as many distributions of Linux ship with a DNS service known as BIND (Berkeley Internet Name Daemon).

DHCP Services

Recall that each computer on the Internet must have an IP address. While an administrator typically configures this address on servers, it is impractical to do the same to the plethora of workstations and other systems on the Internet. As a result, most computers on the Internet automatically receive an IP address and related configuration from a Dynamic Host Configuration Protocol (DHCP) server by broadcasting an IP address request on the network. This is normally performed at system startup and periodically afterwards. Any Linux computer can function as a DHCP server by adding and configuring the DHCP daemon, dhcpd.

Time Services

Most system components and network services require the correct date and time in order to function properly. The BIOS on each computer contains a system clock that stores the current date and time. Operating systems can choose to use the time from this system clock or obtain time information from other servers on the Internet or local network using the Network Time Protocol (NTP). A Linux system can obtain time information from an NTP server or provide time information to other systems using NTP via the NTP daemon (ntpd) or Chrony NTP daemon (chronyd).

Mail Services

In the 1980s and early 1990s, email was a service that was found primarily in universities. Today, almost every Internet user has an email account and uses email on a regular basis. Email addresses are easy to acquire and can be obtained free of charge. Email is distributed via a network of email server services, also known as Mail Transfer Agents (MTAs). Many MTAs are freely available for Linux, including sendmail, postfix, and exim.

File and Print Services

The most common and efficient method for transferring files over the Internet is by using the File Transfer Protocol (FTP). Most FTP servers available on the Internet allow any user to connect and are, hence, called anonymous FTP servers. Furthermore, web browsers and FTP client programs that allow users to connect to these FTP servers are freely available for Linux, UNIX, Windows, and macOS systems. Although several FTP services are available for Linux, the most used is the Very Secure FTP Server daemon, vsftpd.

Most organizations use private networks to share resources, primarily printers and files. In business, it is not cost effective to purchase and install a printer next to the computer of every user who needs to print. It is far easier and cheaper to install one central printer on a server and let multiple users print to it across the computer network. Additionally, files must also be available to multiple users on the network to allow them to collaborate on projects or perform their daily jobs. By centrally storing these files on a server, users can access data regardless of the computer that they log into. Central storage also allows a company to safeguard its information by using devices to back up or make copies of stored data on a regular basis in case of computer failure. Most companies perform backups of data at least every week to ensure that if data is lost on the central server, it can be restored from a backup copy quickly.

Linux is well suited to the task of centrally sharing file and print resources on a corporate network to other Linux, UNIX, Windows, and macOS machines using services such as Network File System (NFS), Common UNIX Printing System (CUPS), and Samba.

Database Services

Most data used by applications is organized into tables of related information and stored in a database, where it is accessible via database management system (DBMS) software. Applications on workstations and other systems interact with a DBMS on a database server to create, manage, and retrieve the data stored within the database. Several free open and closed source DBMS software packages are available for Linux. The most popular open source DBMS packages include PostgreSQL, MySQL (My Structured Query Language), and MariaDB (based on MySQL), while the most popular closed source DBMS packages include Microsoft SQL Server and Oracle Database.

Authentication Services

To access any computer securely, you must log in using a valid username and password before gaining access to the user interface. This process is called authentication. However, users today often need to securely access resources on several servers within their organization, and each of these computers requires that you authenticate before access is granted. To ensure that you do not need to enter your username and password on every network computer that you access within your organization, you can configure your computer to log into an authentication service on a network server using a protocol, such as Kerberos. Once you log into an authentication service using Kerberos successfully, you receive a Kerberos ticket that your computer presents to all other computers within your organization to prove your identity. Microsoft Active Directory is one of the most common Kerberos-based authentication services, and every Linux computer can be easily configured to log into it. However, organizations can install alternate authentication services on Linux servers, including the Kerberos-based Apache Directory.

Note 23

You can learn more about Apache Directory at directory.apache.org.

Certificate Services

Since data is frequently passed across networks to other computers, the data within them could easily be intercepted and read by crackers. To prevent this, many technologies use an encryption algorithm to protect the data before it is transmitted on the network. An encryption algorithm uses a series of mathematical steps in sequence to scramble data. Because the steps within encryption algorithms are widely known, nearly all encryption algorithms use a random component called a key to modify the steps within the algorithm. Symmetric encryption algorithms are reversible; data can be decrypted by reversing the algorithm using the same key that was used to encrypt it. Unfortunately, it is difficult for two computers on a network to communicate this key. As a result, network technologies typically use asymmetric encryption to protect the data that travels across the network. Asymmetric encryption uses a pair of keys that are uniquely generated on each system: a public key and a private key. You can think of a public key as the opposite of a private key. If you encrypt data using a public key, that data can only be decrypted using the matching private key. Alternatively, if you encrypt data using a private key, that data can only be decrypted using the matching public key. Each system must contain at least one public/private key pair. The public key is freely distributed to any other host on the network, whereas the private key is used only by the system and never distributed.

Say, for example, that you want to send an encrypted message from your computer (host A) to another computer (host B). Your computer would first obtain the public key from host B and use it to encrypt the message. Next, your computer will send the encrypted message across the network to host B, at which point host B uses its private key to decrypt the message. Because host B is the only computer on the network with the private key that matches the public key you used to encrypt the message, host B is the only computer on the network that can decrypt the message.

You can also use private keys to authenticate a message. If host A encrypts a message using its private key and sends that message to host B, host B (and any other host on the network) can easily obtain the matching public key from host A to decrypt the message. By successfully decrypting the message, host B has proved that it must have been encrypted using host A's private key. Because host A is the only computer on the network that possesses this private key, host B has proven that the message was sent by host A and not another computer that has impersonated the sender.

Note 24

A message that has been encrypted using a private key is called a **digital signature**.

Note 25

Most network technologies use symmetric encryption to encrypt data that is sent on a network, and asymmetric encryption to securely communicate the symmetric encryption key between computers on the network.

Note 26

Common symmetric encryption algorithms include AES, 3DES, and RC4. Common asymmetric encryption algorithms include DH, RSA, and ECC.

Because public keys are transmitted across a network, a cracker could substitute their own public key in place of another public key to hijack encrypted communications. To prevent this, nearly all public keys are digitally signed by a trusted third-party computer called a **Certification Authority (CA)**. While some commercial CAs digitally sign certificates for a fee (e.g., DigiCert), others do it free of charge (e.g., Let's Encrypt). Alternatively, an organization can install their own CA to digitally sign public keys for use by their own computers when communicating across networks and the Internet. Common CA software packages for Linux include OpenSSL and OpenXPKI.

Note 27

A public key that has been digitally signed by a CA is called a **certificate**.

Note 28

An organization that installs one or more CAs is said to have a **Public Key Infrastructure (PKI)**.

Note 29

You can learn more about OpenSSL at openssl.org. To learn more about OpenXPKI, visit openxpki.org.

Supercomputers

Many companies and institutions use computers to perform extraordinarily large calculations for which most servers would be unsuitable. To accomplish these tasks, companies use specialized services to combine several servers in a way that allows them to function as one large supercomputer. Combining multiple computers to function as a single unit is called **clustering**.

Although it might seem logical to instead purchase computers with many processors, the performance of a computer relative to the number of processors decreases as you add processors to a computer. In other words, a computer with 64 processors does not handle 64 times as much work as one processor because of physical limitations within the computer hardware itself; a computer with 64 processors might only perform 50 times as much work as a single processor. The ability for a computer to increase workload as the number of processors increases is known as scalability, and most computers, regardless of the operating system used, do not scale well with more than 32 processors. Clustering, however, results in much better scalability; 64 computers with one processor each working toward a common goal can handle close to 64 times as much as a single processor.

The supercomputing community has focused on Linux when developing clustering technology, and the most common method of Linux clustering is known as Beowulf clustering. One way to implement a Beowulf cluster is to have one main computer send instructions to several other computers, which compute parts of the calculation concurrently and send their results back to the main computer using a Message Passing Interface (MPI) software framework such as OpenMPI. This type of supercomputing breaks tasks into smaller units and executes them in parallel on many machines at once; thus, it is commonly referred to as parallel supercomputing. Beowulf parallel supercomputer technology has been aggressively developed since the mid-1990s and has been tested in various environments; currently, institutions, companies, and universities host thousands of Beowulf clusters worldwide.

> **Note 30**
>
> You can find more information about OpenMPI at open-mpi.org.

Network Devices

Specialized network devices are used to ensure that information can be sent between different networks and the Internet, as well as prevent malicious software from propagating to systems on the network. Most network devices are specialized Linux computers that provide key network-focused services, including the following:

- Routing services
- Firewall and proxy services
- Advanced security services

Routing Services

Routing is a core service that is necessary for the Internet to function. The Internet is merely a large network of interconnected networks; in other words, it connects company networks, home networks, and institutional networks so that they can communicate with each other. A router is a computer or special hardware device that provides this interconnection; it contains information regarding the structure of the Internet and sends information from one network to another. Companies can use routers to connect their internal networks to the Internet as well as to connect their networks together inside the company. Linux is a good choice for this service as it provides support for routing and is easily customizable; many small Linux distributions, each of which can fit within a few hundred megabytes of flash storage, provide routing capabilities.

Firewall and Proxy Services

The term firewall describes the structures that prevent a fire from spreading. In the automobile industry, a firewall protects the passengers in a car if a fire breaks out in the engine compartment. Just as an automobile firewall protects passengers, a computer firewall protects companies from outside intruders on the Internet. Most firewalls are routers that are placed between the company network and the company's connection to the Internet; all traffic must then pass through this firewall, allowing the company to control traffic at the firewall, based on a complex set of rules. Linux has firewall support built directly into the kernel. Utilities such as iptables and nftables are included with nearly all Linux distributions, and can be used to configure the rules necessary to make a router a firewall.

Because firewalls are usually located between a company's internal network and the Internet, they often provide other services that allow computers inside the company easy access to the Internet. The most common of these services are known as proxy services. A proxy server requests Internet resources, such as websites and FTP sites, on behalf of the computer inside the company. In other words, a workstation computer inside the company sends a request to the proxy server connected to the Internet. The proxy server then obtains and returns the requested information to the workstation computer. One proxy server can allow thousands of company workstation computers access to the Internet simultaneously without lengthy configuration of the workstation computers; proxy servers keep track of the information passed to each client by maintaining a Network Address Translation (NAT) table. Although routers and firewalls can be configured to perform NAT capabilities, Squid is the most common fully featured proxy server used on Linux. Squid retains (or caches) a copy of any requested Internet resources so that it can respond more quickly to future requests for the same resources.

Advanced Security Services

Today, most organizations use specialized server hardware running Linux to provide routing, firewall, and proxy services alongside additional advanced security services. These servers are called security appliances and are typically used to provide security between an organization's network and the Internet. Many Linux-based security appliances and security appliance software suites provide one or more of the following advanced security services:

- Malware, virus, and spam filtering
- Bot and intrusion prevention
- Advanced traffic throttling
- Virtual private network (VPN) functionality
- Centralized event logging for network devices using Simple Network Management Protocol (SNMP)
- Security Information and Event Management (SIEM) for centralized network and security monitoring

Note 31

Security appliances that provide multiple security functions are often called Next Generation Firewall (NGFW) or Unified Threat Management (UTM) appliances.

Note 32

A common Linux-based SIEM security appliance software suite is Alienvault OSSIM, which is available at cybersecurity.att.com/products/ossim.

Note 33

Some routers, firewalls, and security appliances can also separate requests for a specific resource, such as a website, across several servers that provide the same service; this feature is called load balancing, and can be used to provide fast, fault-tolerant access to specific services on other servers.

Mobile and IoT Devices

Over the past two decades, mobile devices such as tablets and smartphones have grown tremendously in popularity. Today, most of these devices are custom built to run either the UNIX-based Apple iOS or Linux-based Google Android operating system. However, some tablet and smartphone device models allow for the installation of other Linux-based mobile operating systems that have greater customization and privacy options. Some examples of Linux-based operating systems designed as an alternative to Android include postmarketOS, Ubuntu Touch, Mobian, and Manjaro.

Similarly, embedded technology advances in recent years have led to a wide range of IoT devices, such as personal fitness trackers and smart door locks. To avoid software licensing fees and remain cost-competitive on the market, IoT device manufacturers typically use a custom Linux operating system on these devices. This has led to a rich and well-documented IoT OSS ecosystem that anyone can take advantage of using general purpose IoT hardware devices, such as the Raspberry Pi. For example, computer hobbyists can configure Linux software on a Raspberry Pi to drive robotics, monitor agriculture, as well as perform a wide range of home and industrial automation tasks.

Linux in the Cloud

Many different types of cloud configurations and technologies are available today. To understand Linux's role in the cloud, you must first have a solid understanding of cloud concepts. More specifically, you should be able to define the cloud, as well as various cloud types and delivery models. Additionally, you should understand the process used to deploy new versions of web apps on cloud servers.

Defining the Cloud

In the early 1990s, the US government-funded Advanced Research Projects Agency Network (ARPANET) and National Science Foundation Network (NSFNET) infrastructures were sold to different companies to create the commercial Internet. These companies were called Internet Service Providers (ISPs) and provided Internet access to individuals and organizations for a fee.

However, aside from providing physical network access to other computers, ISPs provided no resources for users to consume. Instead, most resources available on the Internet in the 1990s consisted of websites that contained webpages with information and media (e.g., pictures, music, video) for different topics and organizations. These websites were hosted on web servers and accessed using the HTTP or HTTPS protocols from a web browser on a user's computer. As shown in Figure 1-7, the worldwide collection of web servers on the Internet was called World Wide Web (WWW).

Figure 1-7   The World Wide Web of the 1990s

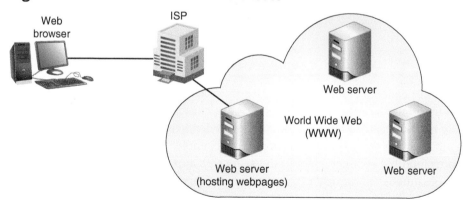

Today, most web servers contain one or more web apps that process and communicate both data and media to users in complex ways. Search engines (e.g., Google), Office 365, video streaming services (e.g., Netflix), personal banking, social media websites, and the software on the Internet that smartphones and smart assistants (e.g., Amazon Alexa) communicate with are all examples of web apps. Web apps are software programs on web servers that can be accessed by other computers and IoT devices across the Internet via a program, web browser, or mobile app. Each web server that runs a web app is called a cloud server, and the worldwide collection of cloud servers is called the cloud, as shown in Figure 1-8.

Figure 1-8   The cloud

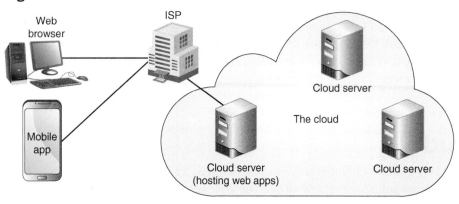

Note 34

Most web apps are accessed from a website on a web server. In this case, the website is said to provide the "front end" for the web app. Computer programs and mobile apps can also be used as the front end for web apps, either by connecting to a website using the HTTP or HTTPS protocol, or by communicating directly to a web app on a cloud server using a custom protocol.

The rapid growth of the WWW in the 1990s was largely due to the open source Apache web server software that ran on the open source Linux operating system. Apache and Linux allowed anyone with a computer and Internet access to host a web server to serve webpages without any software costs. Consequently, web technologies have evolved using the open source ecosystem since the 1990s, and most web apps in the cloud today run on Linux systems using open source **web app frameworks**. A web app framework is a collection of software packages or modules that allow software developers to write web apps using a programming language without having to implement many underlying system functionalities, such as network protocol usage and process management. For example, the Django web app framework allows programmers to easily write web apps using the Python programming language, whereas the React framework allows programmers to easily write web apps using JavaScript.

Cloud Types

Any organization that hosts cloud servers is called a **cloud provider**. A **public cloud** consists of cloud servers on the Internet that can be rented by others, whereas a **private cloud** consists of cloud servers that are used exclusively by the organization that owns them. **Hybrid cloud** refers to using both a public and private cloud together for a specific purpose. For example, you could provide access to a web app in a private cloud but redirect users to the same web app in a public cloud when your web app receives a large number of requests that consume too many hardware resources.

Note 35

There are many public clouds available on the Internet, including Amazon Web Services, Google Cloud Platform, Salesforce Cloud, Digital Ocean, and Microsoft Azure.

Note 36

Private clouds vary in size from one organization to another; they may consist of many cloud servers in a data center or a single cloud server within an organization.

Cloud Delivery Models

Regardless of whether you are using a public or private cloud, you can host web apps on a cloud server using different methods. These methods are called cloud delivery models and include Infrastructure as a Service (IaaS), Platform as a Service (PaaS), and Software as a Service (SaaS).

With IaaS, the cloud provider offers a cloud platform that provides Internet access, IP addressing, and FQDN name resolution to virtual machines that you create on their hypervisor. You must manage each virtual machine as you would any other operating system, including installing and managing the web apps that users will access from across the Internet. This structure is shown in Figure 1-9.

PaaS allows you to run web app containers in the cloud. Recall that containers do not contain a full operating system. As a result, they must be run using container runtime software that allows access to a kernel on an underlying operating system (or "platform"), as shown in Figure 1-10.

Figure 1-9 A sample IaaS structure

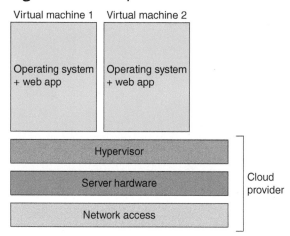

Note 37

IaaS and PaaS can be used together. In this case, containers are run on the operating system in a virtual machine hosted on a cloud provider.

Unlike IaaS and PaaS, SaaS is not used to configure virtual machines or containers. Instead, the SaaS cloud provider maintains all aspects of the network, hardware, and operating system; it merely executes the web app that you provide. This structure is shown in Figure 1-11.

Because Linux is OSS and doesn't require expensive licensing, it is often used as the underlying operating system for SaaS, as well as the operating system used for containers (PaaS) and virtual machines (IaaS). In fact, Linux comprised over 90 percent of the public cloud in 2020, which is often reflected by posts on websites and social media sites as shown in Figure 1-12.

Figure 1-10 A sample PaaS structure

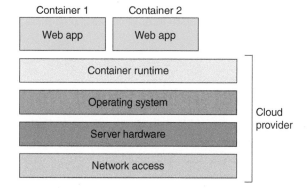

Figure 1-11 A sample SaaS structure

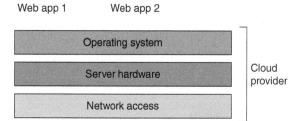

Note 38

Most public cloud providers allow you to choose between SaaS, PaaS, and IaaS.

Figure 1-12 A Reddit post regarding Linux cloud market share

> **Note 39**
>
> The words "as a service" are commonly used for marketing purposes. For example, Mobile as a Service (MaaS) can be used to describe web apps that manage smartphone devices, whereas Database as a Service (DBaaS) can be used to describe web apps that provide access to a database. These terms are collectively referred to as Anything as a Service (XaaS), and represent specific uses of either SaaS, PaaS, or IaaS.

Understanding Cloud Workflows

The prevalence of Linux in the cloud means that most web apps that software developers create are implemented using open source frameworks and developed on Linux workstations, or on Windows or macOS workstations that run a Linux virtual machine. These web apps must be revised on a continual basis to fix bugs and incorporate new features. While developers can create new versions of the web app on their workstation, they need to test these new versions on the cloud provider to ensure that they work as expected before replacing the existing web app with the new version. As part of the development process, new versions of the web app may need to be tested on a cloud provider several times per day. Each new version will require that a new container or virtual machine be created with the correct settings for the web app using **build automation** software. Additional software is required to move the web app from the developer workstation to the new container or virtual machine on the cloud provider, as well as ensure that the web app is ready for execution. This entire process is called a **continuous deployment (CD)** workflow, and the people that manage this workflow are called **DevOps** because they are system operators (ops) that support web app development (dev). Figure 1-13 illustrates a sample CD workflow that allows developers to push new versions of a web app to virtual machines in the cloud.

The first step shown in Figure 1-13 involves developers pushing a new version of their web app code to a **code repository** server, where it is peer-reviewed and eventually approved for use; a process called **continuous integration (CI)**. Next, **orchestration** software running on a server at the cloud provider obtains the new version of the web app from the code repository server (step 2) and compiles it to executable form. The web app is then sent to a build automation server (step 3),

Figure 1-13   A sample CD workflow

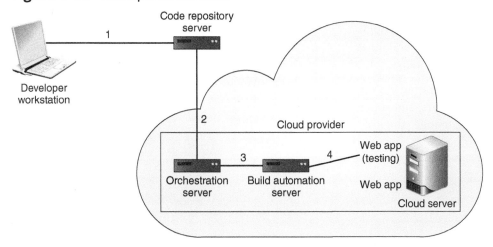

which creates a new container or virtual machine on the cloud server and adds the web app to it for testing (step 4). At this point, the new version of the web app can be tested by the web app developers or automated testing software. If this new version doesn't work as expected, the container or virtual machine is removed and the whole process is repeated for another new version of the web app. However, if this new version of the web app works as expected, the container or virtual machine used to test the web app will replace the publicly accessible container or virtual machine running the old version of the web app, and Internet users will immediately have access to the new version.

Note 40

As with developer workstations and cloud servers, the code repository, orchestration, and build automation servers shown in Figure 1-13 almost always run the Linux operating system.

Note 41

Hundreds of different software packages are available for implementing CD workflows. Today, Git is the most common code repository software used for CI, while Kubernetes is most used for orchestration. Ansible, Puppet, Chef, Terraform, and SaltStack are commonly used for build automation.

Summary

- Linux is an operating system whose kernel and associated software packages are freely developed and improved upon by a large community of software developers in collaboration. It is based on the UNIX operating system and has roots in the hacker culture perpetuated by the Free Software Foundation.

- Because Linux is published under the GNU Public License, it is referred to as open source software (OSS). Most additional software that is run on Linux is also OSS.

- Companies find Linux a stable, low-risk, and flexible alternative to other operating systems; it can be installed on several hardware platforms to meet business needs and results in a lower TCO.

- The Linux operating system is available in various distributions, all of which have a common kernel but are packaged with different OSS applications. Distributions, documentation, and other Linux resources are freely available online.

- Linux is an extremely versatile operating system that is used on workstations, servers, and supercomputers, as well as network, mobile, and IoT devices.

- The cloud is an evolution of the World Wide Web that includes complex web apps. Most of these web apps are hosted on Linux servers using the SaaS, PaaS, or IaaS cloud delivery models and updated frequently using a continuous deployment workflow.

Key Terms

application (app)	Free Software Foundation (FSF)	Platform as a Service (PaaS)
asymmetric encryption	freeware	private cloud
authentication	fully qualified domain name	private key
bare metal	(FQDN)	process
Beowulf clustering	GNU General Public License (GPL)	production kernel
build automation	GNU Network Object Model	program
certificate	Environment (GNOME)	programming language
Certification Authority (CA)	GNU Project	proxy server
closed source software	graphical user interface (GUI)	public cloud
cloud delivery model	hacker	public key
cloud provider	hardware	Public Key Infrastructure (PKI)
clustering	hybrid cloud	revision number
code repository	Hypertext Transfer Protocol (HTTP)	router
Common Gateway Interface (CGI)	Infrastructure as a Service (IaaS)	sandbox
container	Internet of Things (IoT)	scalability
container runtime	Internet Protocol (IP) address	Secure Sockets Layer (SSL)
continuous deployment (CD)	Internet Service Provider (ISP)	security appliance
continuous integration (CI)	K Desktop Environment (KDE)	server
copyleft license	Kerberos	service
cracker	kernel	shareware
daemon	key	software
database	Linus Torvalds	Software as a Service (SaaS)
database management system	Linux	source code
(DBMS)	Linux User Group (LUG)	symmetric encryption
desktop environment	load balancing	tarball
development kernel	Mail Transfer Agent (MTA)	total cost of ownership (TCO)
device driver	major number	Transport Layer Security (TLS)
DevOps	Message Passing Interface (MPI)	UNIX
digital signature	minor number	user
distribution (distro)	Multiplexed Information and	user interface
distribution kernel	Computing Service (MULTICS)	virtual machine
Domain Name Space (DNS)	Network Address Translation (NAT)	virtualization software (hypervisor)
Dynamic Host Configuration	Network Time Protocol (NTP)	web app
Protocol (DHCP)	open source software (OSS)	web app framework
File Transfer Protocol (FTP)	operating system	World Wide Web (WWW)
firewall	orchestration	X Windows
flavor	package manager	
forum	permissive license	

Review Questions

1. Which of the following components comprise an operating system? (Choose all that apply.)

    a. user interface

    b. kernel

    c. device drivers

    d. services

2. Which of the following kernels are development kernels? (Choose all that apply.)

    a. 2.3.4

    b. 4.5.5

    c. 5.10-rc5

    d. 6.0.0

3. Many types of software are available today. Which type of software does Linux represent?

    a. open source

    b. closed source

    c. freeware

    d. shareware

4. Which of the following are characteristics of OSS? (Choose all that apply.)

    a. The value of the software is directly related to its price.

    b. The software is developed collaboratively.

    c. The source code for software is available for a small fee.

    d. Bugs are fixed quickly.

5. To which license does Linux adhere?

    a. BSD

    b. MIT

    c. GNU GPL

    d. Apache

6. What are some good reasons for using Linux in a corporate environment? (Choose all that apply.)

    a. Linux software is unlikely to be abandoned by its developers.

    b. Linux is secure and has a lower total cost of ownership than other operating systems.

    c. Linux is widely available for many hardware platforms and supports many programming languages.

    d. Most Linux software is closed source.

7. Which of the following are common methods for gaining support for Linux?

    a. websites

    b. Linux User Groups

    c. online forums

    d. all these methods

8. Which two people are credited with creating the UNIX operating system? (Choose two answers.)

    a. Dennis Ritchie

    b. Richard Stallman

    c. Linus Torvalds

    d. Ken Thompson

9. On which types of systems can Linux be installed? (Choose all that apply.)

    a. IoT devices

    b. supercomputers

    c. servers

    d. workstations

10. Who formed the Free Software Foundation to promote open development?

    a. Dennis Ritchie

    b. Richard Stallman

    c. Linus Torvalds

    d. Ken Thompson

11. Which culture embraced the term "GNU" (GNU's Not UNIX) and laid the free software groundwork for Linux?

    a. the hacker culture

    b. the BSD culture

    c. the cracker culture

    d. the artificial intelligence culture

12. Linux was developed by _____ to resemble the _____ operating system.

    a. Linus Torvalds, MINIX

    b. Linus Torvalds, GNU

    c. Richard Stallman, GNU

    d. Richard Stallman, MINIX

13. When the core components of the Linux operating system are packaged together with other OSS, it is called a _____.

    a. new kernel

    b. new platform

    c. Linux distribution

    d. GNU Project

14. Which common desktop environments are available in most Linux distributions? (Choose all that apply.)

    a. GNOME

    b. CDE

    c. KDE

    d. RPM

15. Which of the following are factors that determine which Linux distribution a user will use? (Choose all that apply.)
    a. package manager support
    b. hardware platform
    c. kernel features
    d. language support

16. What is a common open source web server available for Linux?
    a. Samba
    b. Apache
    c. Squid
    d. NFS

17. Which of the following components is required to run Linux virtual machines?
    a. container runtime
    b. desktop environment
    c. hypervisor
    d. orchestration software

18. Which of the following Linux distributions is likely to be used by a cybersecurity worker?
    a. Fedora
    b. Ubuntu
    c. Kali
    d. Gentoo

19. When Linux is hosted within a container on a cloud provider, what cloud delivery model is being used?
    a. IaaS
    b. PaaS
    c. XaaS
    d. SaaS

20. What component within a CD workflow creates a new virtual machine or container to host the web app?
    a. orchestration server
    b. testing server
    c. code repository server
    d. build automation server

Discovery Exercises

Discovery Exercise 1-1

Estimated Time: 20 minutes

Objective: Detail the considerations and advantages for a Linux migration.

Description: You work for a large manufacturing company that is considering Linux as a solution for some or all servers in its IT Department. The company hosts an Oracle database on UNIX, and the UNIX servers that host this database contain several small programs that were custom made. Furthermore, Windows 11 is currently used on desktops throughout the company, and users store their data on Windows Server 2019 file servers. What considerations must you keep in mind before migrating your company's servers to Linux? Which distribution(s) and OSS would you choose to accomplish this? If you need to create a report detailing the benefits of moving to an open source solution using Linux, what benefits would you list in the report to persuade others in the company that Linux lowers the total cost of ownership?

Discovery Exercise 1-2

Estimated Time: 20 minutes

Objective: Outline the benefits of OSS.

Description: At a local Linux User Group (LUG) meeting, some people who are unfamiliar with Linux ask you to explain what the GPL is and how it relates to OSS. These people also don't understand how OSS generates profit and are under the impression that the quality of OSS is poor compared to commercial software. They suggest that the potential for OSS in the future might be limited. How do you reply? Include examples to demonstrate your points. To which websites can you direct them for further information?

Discovery Exercise 1-3

Estimated Time: 30 minutes

Objective: Describe the features and usage of permissive open source licenses.

Description: As a software developer working for a large clothing store chain, you are responsible for creating software used to connect retail store computers to a central database at the head office. Recently, some friends of yours suggested that you publish your software under a permissive open source license. What are some direct benefits to publishing your software under a permissive open source license? To publish software made for a company under any open source license, you need the company's permission because the company owns all software that it pays developers to create. When you approach people in your company regarding OSS and explain how companies benefit from releasing software as open source, you are asked what benefits the company will receive from funding an open source project over time. Your company also wants to know what the procedure is for releasing and maintaining OSS. What benefits will you offer them? Where could you send them to gain more information on procedures involved in the open source community?

Discovery Exercise 1-4

Estimated Time: 40 minutes

Objective: Detail the steps needed to implement Kerberos authentication on a network.

Description: You are a network administrator who oversees a medium-sized network consisting of Linux servers, as well as Linux, macOS, and Windows clients. The company you work for asks you to implement Kerberos authentication in the network, a topic with which you are unfamiliar. Where could you go to learn what you must obtain to enable Kerberos on your network? Provided that you have a functional web browser and an Internet connection, explore this topic on the Internet and list the websites that you used to obtain the information required. This information might range from broad descriptions of what you need to do to accomplish a certain task to detailed guides and instructions on putting your plan into action. From these sources of information, devise a report outlining the major steps necessary to implement Kerberos on your network.

Discovery Exercise 1-5

Estimated Time: 15 minutes

Objective: Describe how Linux reduces the total cost of ownership for an organization.

Description: At a company function, a top executive corners you and complains that your department is wasting too much money. The executive demands to know why the company must spend so much money on computers and software, especially operating systems and related licenses (for closed source programs and operating systems). Write a report that defends your department by explaining the nature of hardware, software, and operating systems. In the report, be sure to explain how OSS and the Linux operating system can be used to reduce these costs in the long term.

Discovery Exercise 1-6

Estimated Time: 35 minutes

Objective: Illustrate the features and evolution of OSS and Linux.

Description: You are contacted by a project organizer for a university computer science fair. The project organizer asks you to hold a forum that discusses the origins of the Linux operating system, including how it has evolved and continues to develop. The main focus of this forum is to encourage university students toward participating in the open source community; therefore, it should detail the philosophy, major features, and methods of the hacker culture. Prepare a bulleted list of the major topics that you will discuss and write some sample questions that you anticipate from the participants as well as your responses.

Discovery Exercise 1-7

Estimated Time: 35 minutes

Objective: Outline the features of different Linux distributions.

Description: Research three different distributions of Linux on the Internet that were not mentioned in this chapter. Record where you went to obtain your information. Compare and contrast the distributions with regard to their strengths and the packages available for each. After you finish, visit two Linux forums. How did you locate them and where did you obtain the information? What are the topics specific to each? Find two questions per forum posted by a user in need of a solution to a problem and follow the thread of responses suggested by others to find possible solutions to that problem.

Chapter 2

Linux Installation and Usage

Chapter Objectives

1 Prepare for and install Fedora Linux using good practices.

2 Outline the structure of the Linux interface.

3 Enter basic shell commands and find command documentation.

4 Properly shut down the Linux operating system.

This chapter explores the concepts and procedures needed to install a Fedora Linux system. The latter half of the chapter presents an overview of the various components that you will use when interacting with the operating system, as well as how to enter basic shell commands, obtain help, and properly shut down the Linux system.

Installing Linux

Installing Linux requires careful planning as well as configuring parts of the Linux operating system via an installation program.

Preparing for Installation

An operating system is merely a series of software programs that interact with and control the computer hardware. Thus, all operating systems have a certain minimum set of computer hardware requirements to function properly. Although most up-to-date hardware is sufficient to run the Linux operating system, it is, nonetheless, important to ensure that a computer meets the minimum hardware requirements before performing an installation.

These minimum installation requirements for each CPU platform can be obtained from the vendor's website. For the Fedora Workstation Linux operating system on the Intel x86_64 platform, you can find the minimum hardware requirements at docs.fedoraproject.org or in Table 2-1.

Understanding Installation Media

Before performing a Linux installation, you must choose the source of the Linux packages and the installation program itself. The most common source of these packages is removeable media, such as a DVD or USB flash drive.

To perform a bare metal Linux installation from DVD or USB flash drive, you turn on the computer after placing the Linux DVD into the DVD drive or inserting the USB flash drive into a USB port. Most computers automatically search for a startup program on removeable media immediately after being

Table 2-1   Minimum hardware requirements for Fedora workstation Linux on x86_64

Type of Hardware	Requirement
Central processing unit (CPU)	2 GHz dual-core 64-bit Intel or AMD CPU (quad core recommended)
Random access memory (RAM)	2 GB (4 GB recommended)
Free disk space (permanent storage)	15 GB free space (20 GB recommended)
Additional drives	DVD drive (for DVD-based installation)
Graphics processing unit (GPU)	Intel GMA9xx, Nvidia GeForce FX5xxx, or AMD Radeon 9500 (older models will work but may not support 3D-accelerated desktop graphics)

turned on; the computer can then use this program to start the Linux installation. Alternatively, you can manually select the boot device on your computer using a special manufacturer-specific key, such as F12, during the startup sequence.

Note 1

Turning on a computer to load an operating system is commonly referred to as booting a computer. DVDs and USB flash drives that contain a program that can be loaded when you first turn on the computer are commonly called bootable devices.

Note 2

If a server on your network has been configured to share Linux installation files and your computer has a network adapter card that supports **Preboot eXecution Environment (PXE)** you can instead choose the network adapter card as your boot device during the startup sequence to install Linux.

Nearly all Linux distributions provide a website from which you can download DVD images (called ISO images) that have an .iso file extension. These ISO images can be written to a blank writable DVD or USB flash drive and then used to boot your computer to start the Linux installation.

In addition to a standard Linux installation ISO image, many Linux distribution websites allow you to download a bootable live media ISO image. If you write a live media ISO image to a blank DVD or USB flash drive and boot your computer with it, a fully functional graphical Linux operating system that you can use will be loaded into RAM. This allows you to test the operating system on your computer to ensure that all hardware drivers were detected properly before installing it to permanent storage, such as a hard disk drive or SSD. After you are satisfied with the functionality of your Linux system loaded from live media, you can select the appropriate icon on the desktop to start the installation program that will install Linux to permanent storage.

Note 3

To obtain a standard or live media ISO image of Fedora Linux, you can visit getfedora.org.

To write an ISO image to a blank writable DVD, you can use the built-in disc burning software on an existing Windows, macOS, or Linux system. To write an ISO image to a USB flash drive, you can download and use an image writing tool, such as balenaEtcher. To make this process easier, many distributions provide a user-friendly tool that downloads and writes ISO images to USB flash drives. For Fedora Linux, you can download and install the Fedora Media Writer tool on a Windows or macOS system, as shown in Figure 2-1. The default selection shown in Figure 2-1 downloads the ISO image for the latest version of Fedora Workstation and writes it to a USB flash drive. However, you can instead choose to select an already-downloaded ISO image.

Note 4

You can download the Fedora Media Writer tool from getfedora.org/workstation/download/.

Figure 2-1   The Fedora Media Writer tool

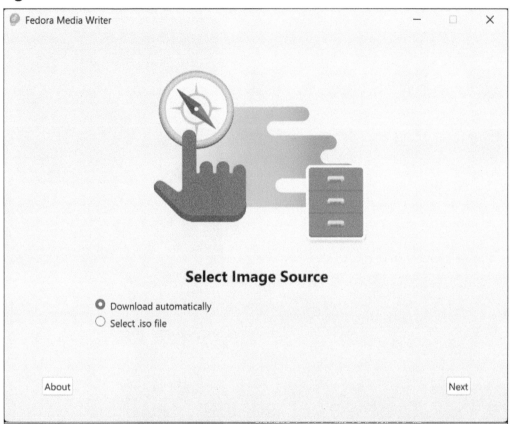

Recall from Chapter 1 that virtualization software (also called a hypervisor) is commonly used to run multiple operating systems (called virtual machines) concurrently on server hardware. You can also use virtualization software to run multiple operating systems concurrently on a workstation. Consequently, there are several workstation-focused virtualization software products available on the market today, including the following:

- Microsoft Hyper-V, which is included in Windows 10 and Windows 11 (Professional, Enterprise, or Education editions) available from microsoft.com.
- VMWare Workstation Pro, which can be purchased from vmware.com and installed on Windows 10, Windows 11, and Linux systems.
- Parallels Desktop, which can be purchased from parallels.com and installed on Intel- and Apple Silicon-based macOS systems.
- Universal Turing Machine (UTM), which is an open source hypervisor based on QEMU that can be freely downloaded from mac.getutm.app and installed on Apple Silicon-based macOS systems.
- Oracle VM VirtualBox, which is an open source hypervisor that can be freely downloaded from virtualbox.org and installed on Windows 7 (and later), Linux, Solaris UNIX, and Intel-based macOS systems.

System administrators, cybersecurity professionals, and software developers often run one or more Linux virtual machines on a Windows or macOS workstation to test or run Linux-based software. Figure 2-2 shows a Fedora Linux virtual machine running on the Windows 11 operating system using the Microsoft Hyper-V virtualization software.

Figure 2-2   Fedora Linux running as a virtual machine on the Windows 11 operating system

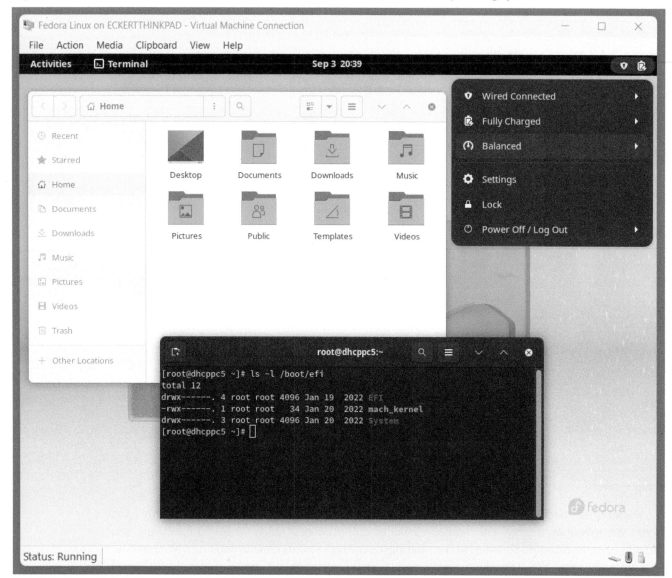

To install Linux as a virtual machine, you need to first download the standard or live media ISO image to a directory on your system (e.g., Windows). When you open the configuration program for your virtualization software and choose to create a new virtual machine, you can specify the file location of the appropriate ISO image, and the virtualization software will boot from the ISO image directly, without requiring you to write the ISO image to a DVD or USB flash drive. Figure 2-3 shows the page of the Hyper-V New Virtual Machine Wizard that allows you to specify the location of an ISO image containing the Fedora Workstation installation media.

Figure 2-3   Selecting installation media within the Hyper-V New Virtual Machine Wizard

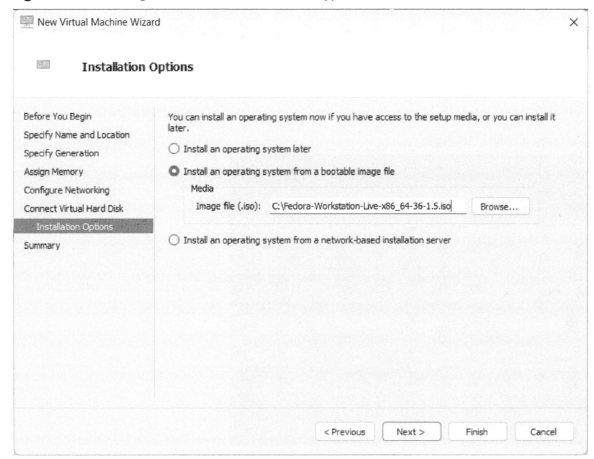

Performing the Installation

Installing the Linux operating system involves interacting with an installation program, which prompts you for information regarding the nature of the Linux system being installed. More specifically, the installation program for Fedora Workstation involves the following general stages:

- Starting the installation
- Choosing an installation language, localization, and system options
- Configuring disk partitions and filesystems
- Configuring user accounts

Starting the Installation

As mentioned earlier, to perform an installation of Fedora Linux, you can boot your computer or virtual machine using Fedora installation media. If you are booting your system from standard Fedora installation media, you will be prompted to start the installation or perform troubleshooting actions. However, if you boot your system from Fedora live media, you will instead be prompted to start a live Fedora system (which later allows you to install Fedora), test your installation media, and then start a live Fedora system, or perform troubleshooting actions, as shown in Figure 2-4.

Figure 2-4   Beginning a Fedora installation

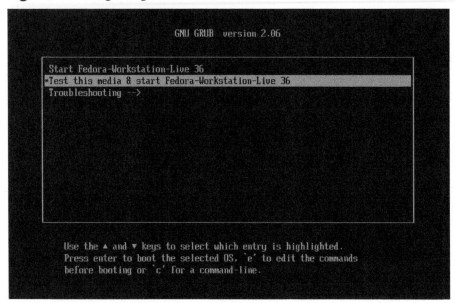

If you select the *Troubleshooting* option shown in Figure 2-4, you will be presented with the option to start the live Fedora system in basic graphics mode, as shown in Figure 2-5. This option uses only generic video drivers and low resolution, which is useful in the rare event that the live Fedora system doesn't detect the correct driver for your video card and cannot display a graphical desktop as a result.

Figure 2-5   Starting a Fedora installation using basic graphics mode

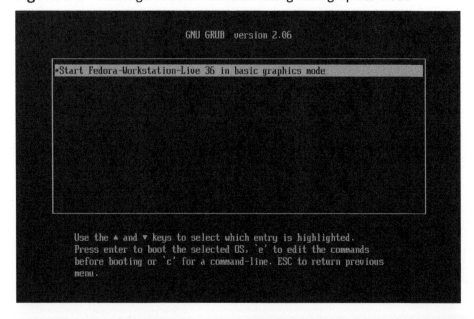

After the live Fedora system has loaded, you will be presented with a welcome screen that prompts you to install Fedora Linux on permanent storage or continue using the live Fedora system loaded from your installation media, as shown in Figure 2-6.

Figure 2-6   The Welcome to Fedora screen

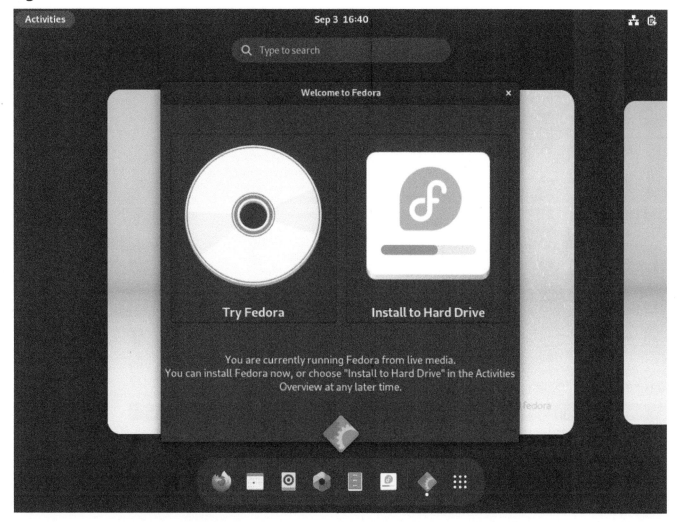

If you choose *Install to Hard Drive* in Figure 2-6, the Fedora installation program will start. Alternatively, if you choose *Try Fedora*, you will be able to explore the desktop of a live Fedora system and can later select *Install to Hard Drive* from the Activities menu in the upper-left corner of the desktop to start the Fedora installation program.

Choosing an Installation Language, Localization, and System Options

After you start a Fedora installation, you will be prompted to select a language that is used during the installation program, as shown in Figure 2-7. If you click *Continue*, you will be prompted to configure the keyboard layout, time and date, and installation destination as shown in Figure 2-8.

You can click each of the localization and system option icons in Figure 2-8 to modify the configuration. By default, your keyboard layout is automatically detected, your network interface is set to obtain network configuration using the DHCP protocol, and the date and time are obtained from the Internet using NTP if your network has Internet connectivity. However, you must manually review the installation destination settings before the installation can continue (hence the warning shown in Figure 2-8). The installation destination is a permanent storage device that will contain the Linux operating system; it is often a hard disk drive or SSD.

Figure 2-7 Selecting an installation language

Figure 2-8 Configuring localization and system options

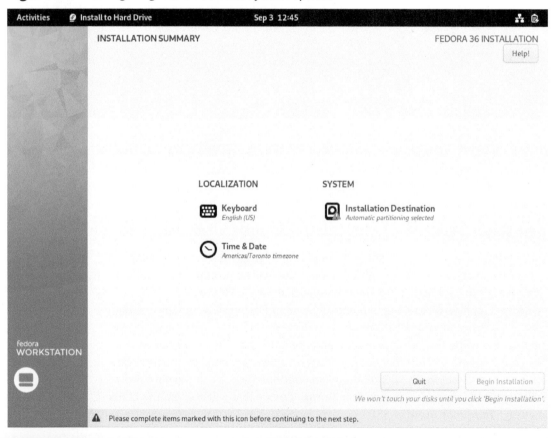

Older systems may use Parallel Advanced Technology Attachment (PATA) hard disk drives that physically connect to the computer in one of four configurations. As shown in Table 2-2, Linux refers to each of these disks according to its configuration on your computer.

> **Note 7**
>
> In the past, PATA hard disk drives were referred to as Integrated Drive Electronics (IDE) or Advanced Technology Attachment (ATA) hard disk drives.

> **Note 8**
>
> You can verify your PATA hard disk drive configuration by accessing your computer's Basic Input/Output System (BIOS) configuration. You can access your BIOS configuration by pressing the appropriate manufacturer-specific key, such as F10, during system startup.

Table 2-2   PATA hard disk drive configurations

Description	Linux Name
Primary master PATA hard disk drive	hda
Primary slave PATA hard disk drive	hdb
Secondary master PATA hard disk drive	hdc
Secondary slave PATA hard disk drive	hdd

Newer systems typically use Serial Advanced Technology Attachment (SATA) hard disk drives or SSDs, or Non-Volatile Memory Express (NVMe) SSDs. Server systems have traditionally used Small Computer Systems Interface (SCSI) hard disk drives. However, modern server systems typically use Serial Attached SCSI (SAS) hard disk drives or SSDs, or NVMe SSDs. Unlike PATA, you can have more than four SATA, NVMe, SCSI, and SAS hard disk drives or SSDs within a system. The first SATA/SCSI/SAS hard disk drive or SSD is referred to as sda, the second SATA/SCSI/SAS hard disk drive or SSD is referred to as sdb, and so on. The first NVMe SSD is referred to as nvme0, the second NVMe SSD is referred to as nvme1, and so on.

If you click the installation destination icon shown in Figure 2-8, you will be presented with a list of the permanent storage devices in your system. The system shown in Figure 2-9 contains a single SAS hard disk drive (sda).

If you have multiple storage devices, you can select the device that will be used to contain the Fedora Linux operating system and then click *Done*. Normally, this is a local hard disk drive or SSD, but you can also install Linux on an external iSCSI or FCoE Storage Area Network (SAN), non-volatile DIMM (NVDIMM), Multipath IO (MPIO), or firmware Redundant Array of Inexpensive Disks (RAID) device if you select *Add a disk* shown in Figure 2-9 and supply the appropriate configuration information. You can optionally choose to encrypt all of the data on the storage device using Linux Unified Key Setup (LUKS); a technology that will be discussed later in Chapter 14.

Configuring Disk Partitions and Filesystems

Regardless of type, each hard disk drive or SSD is divided into sections called partitions. Before you can store files in a partition, you must format it with a filesystem. A filesystem is a structure that specifies how data should physically reside in the partition on the hard disk drive or SSD.

Figure 2-9   Configuring an installation destination

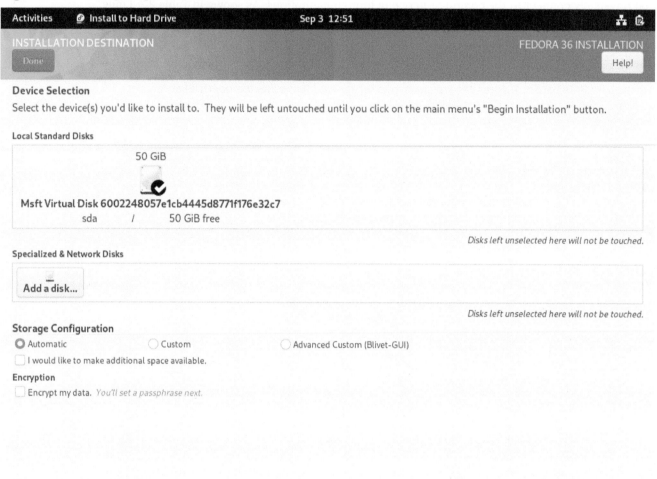

> ### Note 9
>
> In the Windows operating system, each drive letter (e.g., C:, D:, E:) can correspond to a separate filesystem that resides on a partition on your hard disk drive or SSD.

There are limits to the number and types of partitions into which a hard disk drive or SSD can be divided. On hard disk drives and SSDs that store partition configuration in a **Master Boot Record (MBR)**, you can create a maximum of four major partitions (called **primary partitions**). To overcome this limitation, you can optionally label one of these primary partitions as "extended"; this **extended partition** can then contain an unlimited number of smaller partitions called **logical drives**. Each logical drive within the extended partition and all other primary partitions can contain a filesystem and be used to store data. The MBR is limited to devices that are less than 2TB in size. Newer devices and devices larger than 2TB use a **GUID Partition Table (GPT)** instead of an MBR and can contain up to 128 primary partitions, eliminating the need for extended partitions and logical drives altogether.

> ### Note 10
>
> The MBR and GPT are functionally equivalent.

Recall that, in Linux, the first SATA/SCSI/SAS device in your system is referred to as sda, the first primary partition on this device is labeled sda1, the second sda2, and so on. Because only four primary partitions are allowed in an MBR device, logical drives inside the extended partition are labeled sda5, sda6, and so on. An example of this partition strategy is listed in Table 2-3.

Table 2-3 Example MBR partitioning scheme for the first SATA/SCSI/SAS device

Description	Linux Name	Windows Name
First primary partition on the first SATA/SCSI/SAS device	sda1	C:
Second primary partition on the first SATA/SCSI/SAS device	sda2	D:
Third primary partition on the first SATA/SCSI/SAS device	sda3	E:
Fourth primary partition on the first SATA/SCSI/SAS device (EXTENDED)	sda4	F:
First logical drive in the extended partition on the first SATA/SCSI/SAS device	sda5	G:
Second logical drive in the extended partition on the first SATA/SCSI/SAS device	sda6	H:
Third logical drive in the extended partition on the first SATA/SCSI/SAS device	sda7	I:

Note 11

For the primary master PATA device, replace sda with hda in Table 2-3. NVMe devices can use **namespace** divisions in addition to partitions. As a result, the first NVMe partition (p1) within the first namespace (n1) on the first NVMe SSD (nvme0) would be called nvme0n1p1.

Note 12

For devices that use a GPT instead of an MBR, the sda1 through sda7 partitions shown in Table 2-3 would refer to the first through seventh primary partitions on the GPT device.

Note 13

When Linux is run in a QEMU-based virtual machine, a separate virtualization driver is used to access the underlying storage, regardless of the storage technology used. In this case, Linux uses vda in place of sda for the partitions shown in Table 2-3.

Partitioning divides a storage device into sections, each of which can contain a separate filesystem used to store data. Each of these filesystems can then be accessed by Linux if it is attached (or mounted) to a certain directory. When data is stored in that directory, it is physically stored on the respective filesystem on the storage device. The Fedora installation program can automatically create partitions based on common configurations; however, it is generally good practice to manually partition to suit the needs of the specific Linux system.

At minimum, Linux workstations require two partitions to be created: a partition that is mounted to the root directory in Linux (/) and that can contain all of the files used by the operating system, applications, and users, and a partition that is mounted to /boot and that can contain the files needed to boot the Linux kernel.

Note 14

If your system has a **Unified Extensible Firmware Interface (UEFI)** BIOS on the motherboard, the Linux installation program will create a small **UEFI System Partition**. This partition is mounted to /boot/efi and stores UEFI-related information needed to boot the system.

Note 15

If your system has a hard disk drive or SSD that uses a GPT instead of an MBR and does not contain an UEFI BIOS on the motherboard, the Linux installation program will create a small **BIOS Boot partition**. This partition does not contain a filesystem and is not mounted in Linux.

Although you might choose to create only / and /boot partitions, extra partitions make Linux more robust against filesystem errors. For example, if the filesystem on one partition encounters an error, only data on one part of the system is affected and not the entire system (i.e., other filesystems). Because some common directories in Linux are used vigorously and, as a result, are more prone to failure, it is good practice to mount these directories to their own filesystems. Table 2-4 lists directories that are commonly mounted from separate partitions as well as their recommended sizes.

Table 2-4   Common Linux filesystems and sizes

Directory	Description	Recommended Size
/	Contains all directories not present on other filesystems	Depends on the size and number of other filesystems present, but is typically 20 GB or more
/boot	Contains the Linux kernel and boot-related files	1 GB
/home	Default location for user home directories	500 MB per user
/usr	System commands and utilities	Depends on the packages installed—typically 30 GB or more
/usr/local	Location for most additional programs	Depends on the packages installed—typically 30 GB or more
/opt	An alternate location for additional programs	Depends on the packages installed—typically 30 GB or more
/var	Contains log files and spools	Depends on whether the Linux system is used as a print server (which contains a large spool). For print servers, 30 GB or more is typical. For other systems, 5 GB or more is usually sufficient.
/tmp	Holds temporary files created by programs	1 GB

Each of these filesystems can be of a different type. The most common types used today are the ext2, ext3, ext4, vfat, exfat, and xfs filesystems, although Linux can support upward of 50 filesystems. Each filesystem essentially performs the same function, which is to store files on a partition; however, each filesystem offers different features and is specialized for different uses. The ext2 filesystem is the traditional filesystem, the vfat filesystem is compatible with the Microsoft FAT and FAT32 filesystems, and the exfat filesystem is compatible with the Microsoft exFAT filesystem. Because they perform a function called journaling, the ext3, ext4, and xfs filesystems are much more robust than the ext2, vfat, and exfat filesystems. A journaling filesystem uses a journal to keep track of the information written to the storage device. If you copy a file on the filesystem from one directory to another, that file must pass into RAM and then be written to the new location. If the power to the computer is turned off during this process, information might not be transmitted as expected and data might be lost or corrupted. With a journaling filesystem, each step required to copy the file to the new location is first written to a journal; this means the system can retrace the steps the system took prior to a power outage and complete the file copy. These filesystems also host a variety of additional improvements compared to ext2, vfat, and exfat, including faster data transfer and indexing, which makes them common choices for Linux servers today.

You can also create a partition used for virtual memory (also known as swap memory). Virtual memory consists of an area on the hard disk drive or SSD that can be used to store information that would normally reside in physical memory (RAM) if the physical memory was being used excessively. When programs are executed that require a great deal of resources on the computer, information is continuously swapped from physical memory to virtual memory, and vice versa. Linux swap partitions are usually made to be 4 GB in size or smaller. A swap partition does not contain a filesystem and is never mounted to a directory because the Linux operating system is ultimately responsible for swapping information.

Note 16

If you do not create a swap partition during installation, most Linux distributions will either create a file that is used for virtual memory or allocate a compressed area of RAM for virtual memory using the zswap feature of the Linux kernel. On modern systems, zswap often provides better virtual memory performance compared to using a swap partition or file.

After you have selected the appropriate hard disk drive or SSD as an installation destination during the Fedora Linux installation shown in Figure 2-9, you must also choose whether the installation program should create partitions for you (*Automatic*), or whether you want to configure partitions manually (*Custom*) or manually using an advanced interface (*Advanced Custom*). If you choose *Custom* shown in Figure 2-9 and click *Done*, you will be prompted to choose the partitioning scheme, and optionally create a default partition layout that you can modify to suit your needs. If you choose a Standard partitioning scheme on a system with a UEFI BIOS, this default partition layout will consist of / and /boot partitions with ext4 filesystems, as well as a UEFI System Partition with a vfat filesystem mounted to /boot/efi, as shown in Figure 2-10.

Figure 2-10   Configuring disk partitions and filesystems

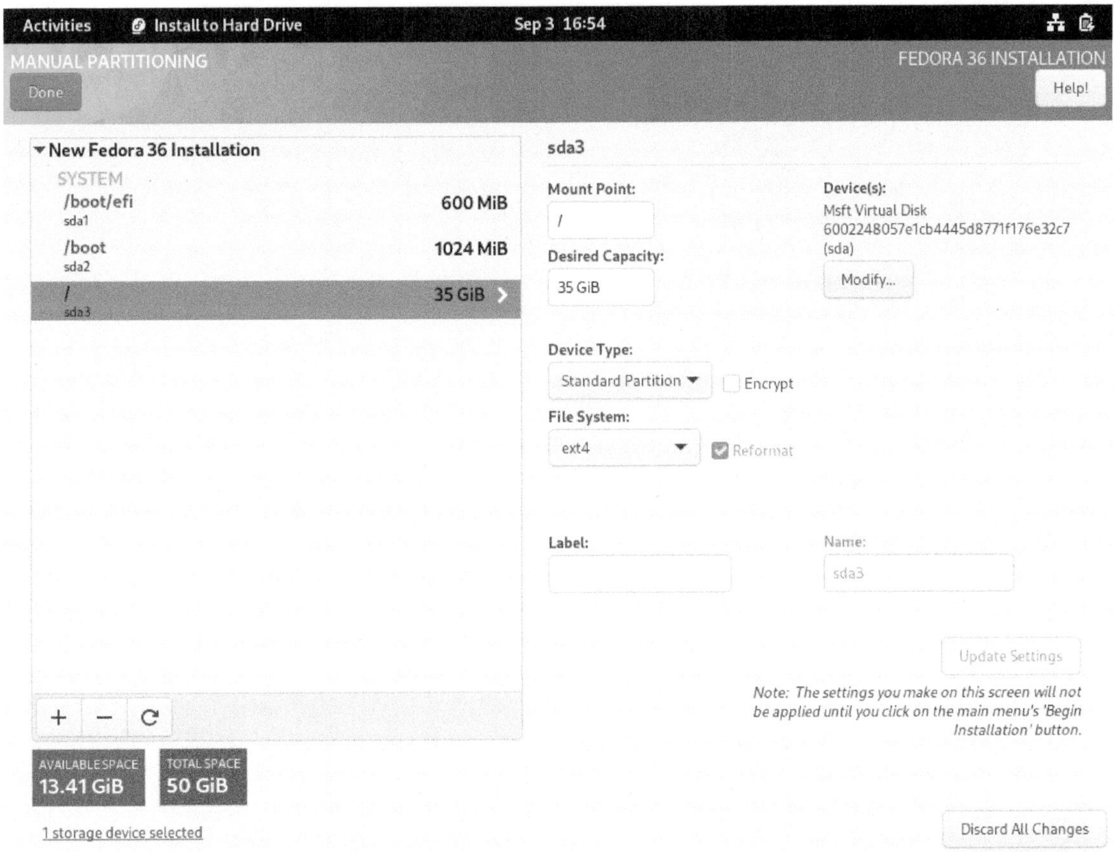

In addition to the standard partitions that we have discussed already, you can instead choose a partition scheme that creates logical volumes for your Linux filesystems using the **Logical Volume Manager (LVM)** or partitions that support the new btrfs filesystem. LVM and btrfs are discussed in Chapters 5 and 6. To allow for easier system recovery, it is good form to choose a standard partition scheme and ensure that contents of disk partitions are not encrypted.

After you are satisfied with your partition and filesystem configuration, you can click *Done* shown in Figure 2-10, confirm your changes in the dialog box that appears, and return to the localization and system options configuration screen shown in Figure 2-8. If you click the *Begin Installation* button in Figure 2-8, partition changes will be written to your storage device and the Fedora system packages will be installed from the installation media to the appropriate filesystems. This process will take some time to complete. After it has completed, you can click the *Finish Installation* button that appears to exit the installation program. Next, you can shut down your live Fedora system, remove the installation media from your computer, and boot your computer into your new Fedora system.

Configuring User Accounts

All Linux systems require secure authenticated access, which means that each user must log in with a valid user name and password before gaining access to a user interface. Two user accounts must be created at minimum: the administrator account (root), which has full rights to the system, as well as a regular user account; the root user account should only be used when performing system administration tasks.

On the first boot following a Fedora installation, you will be required to complete a Setup wizard. This wizard allows you to disable location services and automatic error reporting, optionally integrate your online social media accounts, as well as configure a single regular user account for yourself, as shown in Figure 2-11. You can optionally click *Enterprise Login* in Figure 2-11 to join your Linux system to an Active Directory or Kerberos domain. After you click *Next* in Figure 2-11, you will be prompted to supply a password for your newly created user account and the Setup wizard will then continue to boot into your system.

Figure 2-11   Choosing a regular user account user name during the Setup wizard

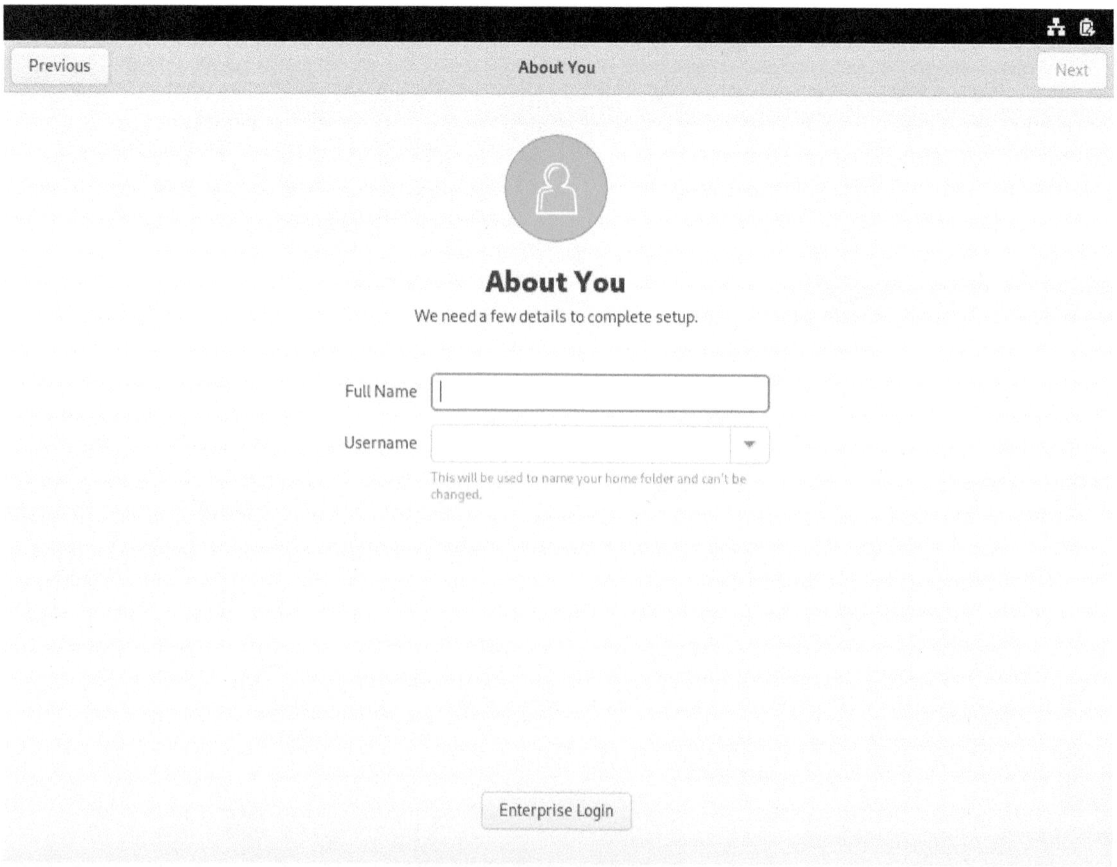

By default, a root user is created during the installation process but not assigned a valid password. The regular user account that you create during the Setup wizard is given special rights that allows it to set a valid password for the root user using the `sudo password root` command following installation.

Basic Linux Usage

After the Linux operating system has been installed, you must log in to the system with a valid user name and password and interact with the user interface to perform tasks. To do this, it is essential to understand the Linux user interfaces, as well as basic tasks, such as command execution, obtaining online help, and shutting down the Linux system.

Shells, Terminals, and the Kernel

Recall that an operating system is merely a collection of software that allows you to use your computer hardware in a meaningful fashion. Every operating system has a core component, which loads all other components and serves to centrally control the activities of the computer. This component is known as the kernel, and in Linux it is simply a file, usually called vmlinuz-*version*, that is located in the /boot directory and loaded when you first turn on your computer.

When you interact with a computer, you are ultimately interacting with the kernel of the computer's operating system. However, this interaction cannot happen directly; it must have a channel through which it can access the kernel as well as a user interface that passes user input to the kernel for processing. The channel that allows you to log in is called a **terminal**. Linux can have many terminals that allow you to log in to the computer locally or across a network. After you log in to a terminal, you receive a user interface called a **shell**, which then accepts your input and passes it to the kernel for processing. The shell that is used by default on most Linux systems is the **BASH shell** (short for Bourne Again Shell), which is an improved version of the Bourne shell from AT&T and is the shell that is used throughout most of this book. The whole process looks similar to that shown in Figure 2-12.

Linux can allow for thousands of terminals. Each terminal could represent a separate logged-in user that has its own shell. The four different "channels" shown in Figure 2-12 could be different users logged in to the same Linux server, for example. Two users could be logged in locally to the server (seated at the server itself), and the other two could be logged in across a network, such as the Internet.

By default, when you log in to a terminal, you receive a command-line shell (e.g., BASH shell), which prompts you to type commands to tell the Linux kernel what to do. However, Linux workstation users often prefer to use a graphical desktop in which they can use a pointing device such as a mouse to navigate and start tasks. In this case, you can choose to start a desktop environment on top of your shell after you are logged in to a command-line terminal, or you can switch to a graphical terminal, which allows users to log in and immediately receive a desktop environment. A typical command-line terminal login prompt looks like the following:

Figure 2-12 Shells, terminals, and the kernel

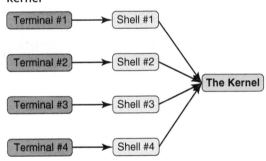

```
Fedora Linux 36 (Workstation Edition)
Kernel 5.17.5-300.fc36.x86_64 on an x86_64 (tty3)

server1 login:
```

A typical graphical terminal login for Fedora Linux (called the GNOME Display Manager or GDM) is shown in Figure 2-13.

Figure 2-13   The GNOME Display Manager (GDM)

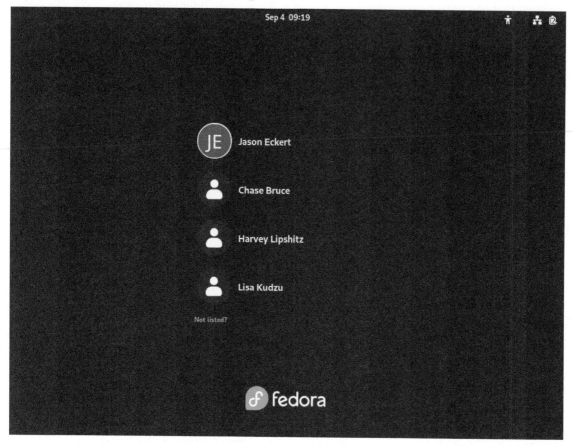

To access a terminal device at the local server, you can press a combination of keys, such as Ctrl+Alt+F2, to change to a separate terminal. If you are logging in across the network, you can use a variety of programs that connect to a terminal on the Linux computer. A list of local Linux terminals, along with their names and types, is shown in Table 2-5.

Table 2-5   Common Linux terminals

Terminal Name	Key Combination	Login Type
tty1	Ctrl+Alt+F1	graphical (GDM)
tty2	Ctrl+Alt+F2	command-line
tty3	Ctrl+Alt+F3	command-line
tty4	Ctrl+Alt+F4	command-line
tty5	Ctrl+Alt+F5	command-line
tty6	Ctrl+Alt+F6	command-line

After you are logged in to a command-line terminal, you receive a prompt at which you can enter commands. The following example shows the user logging in as the root (administrator) user. As you can see in this example, after you log in as the root user, you see a # prompt:

```
Fedora Linux 36 (Workstation Edition)
Kernel 5.17.5-300.fc36.x86_64 on an x86_64 (tty3)

server1 login: root
Password:
```

```
Last login: Mon Aug 16 09:45:42 from tty5
[root@server1 ~]#_
```

However, if you log in as a regular user to a command-line terminal (e.g., user1), you see a $ prompt, as follows:

```
Fedora Linux 36 (Workstation Edition)
Kernel 5.17.5-300.fc36.x86_64 on an x86_64 (tty3)

server1 login: user1
Password:
Last login: Mon Aug 16 11:15:06 from tty3
[user1@server1 ~]$_
```

When you log in to a graphical terminal, the desktop environment of your choice is started; the default desktop environment in Fedora Linux is GNOME on Wayland, but you can instead select GNOME on X.org (shown as X11) from the settings icon next to the Sign In button within the GDM. On most legacy Linux systems, the desktop environment replaces the GDM on tty1. However, on modern Linux systems, the desktop environment is typically loaded on tty2, and the GDM remains available on tty1 to allow for additional graphical logins for different users. Each additional graphical login results in an additional desktop environment loaded on the next available terminal (tty3, tty4, and so on.).

After the desktop environment starts, you can access a command-line terminal by accessing the Activities menu in the upper left of the desktop and navigating to Show Applications, Utilities, Terminal to start the Terminal app. This will start a command-line terminal within your GNOME desktop, as shown in Figure 2-14. You can open multiple, separate Terminal apps within a single desktop environment or click the icon in the upper-left corner of the Terminal app to create additional tabs that allow

Figure 2-14   Using a command-line terminal within the GNOME desktop

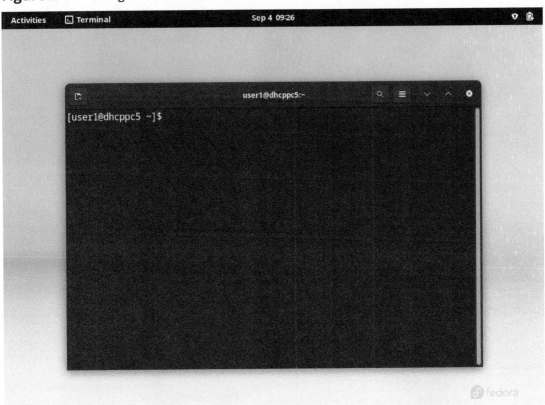

you to access multiple, separate command-line terminals. Similarly, you can access several different shells within a single command-line terminal (e.g., tty3) using an interactive terminal program such as screen or tmux. A sample tmux session started by the root user with three shells on tty3 is shown in Figure 2-15. The shell that is currently active (i.e., accepts commands that the user types in on the keyboard) is outlined in green.

Figure 2-15   Accessing multiple BASH windows within a single command-line terminal using tmux

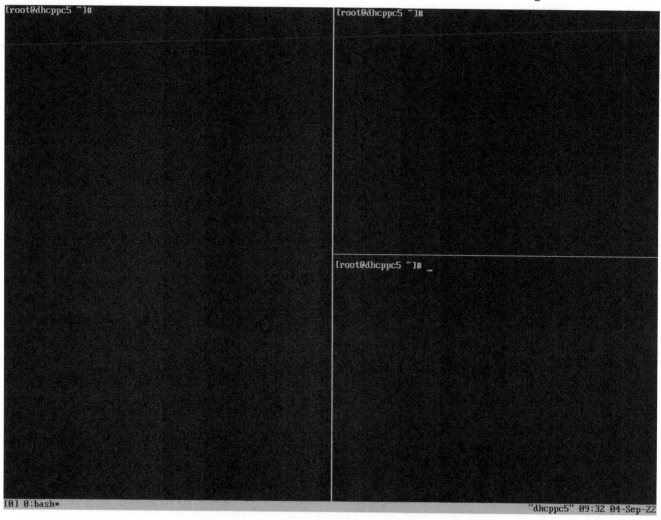

Basic Shell Commands

When using a command-line terminal, the shell ultimately interprets all information you enter into the command line. This information includes the command itself, as well as options and arguments. Commands indicate the name of the program to execute. Options are specific letters that start with a dash (-) and appear after the command name to alter the way the command works. Options are specific to the command in question; the persons who developed the command determined which options to allow for that command.

> **Note 18**
>
> Some options start with two dashes (--); these options are referred to as POSIX options and are usually composed of a whole word, not just a letter. Portable Operating System Interface (POSIX) is a family of UNIX standards that is also implemented by Linux.

Arguments also appear after the command name, yet they do not start with a dash. They specify the parameters that tailor the command to your particular needs. Suppose, for example, that you want to list all of the files in the /etc/rpm directory on the filesystem. You could use the ls command with the -a option (which tells the ls command to list all files, including hidden files) and the /etc/rpm argument (which tells ls to look in the /etc/rpm directory), as shown in the following example:

```
[root@server1 root]# ls -a /etc/rpm
.      macros.color  macros.fjava   macros.imgcreate
..     macros.dist   macros.gconf2  macros.jpackage
[root@server1 root]#_
```

After you type the command and press Enter in the preceding output, the ls command shows that there are six files in the /etc/rpm directory (macros.color, macros.fjava, and so on). The command prompt then reappears, so that you can enter another command.

> **Note 19**
>
> Commands, options, and arguments are case sensitive; an uppercase letter (A), for instance, is treated differently than a lowercase letter (a).

> **Note 20**
>
> Always put a space between the command name, options, and arguments; otherwise, the shell does not understand that they are separate, and your command might not work as expected.

Although you can pass options and arguments to commands, not all commands need to have arguments or options to work properly. The date command, which prints the current date and time by default, is an example:

```
[root@server1 root]# date
Sun Aug 19 08:46:57 EDT 2023
[root@server1 root]#_
```

Table 2-6 lists some common commands that you can use without specifying any options or arguments.

Table 2-6 Some common Linux commands

Command	Description
clear	Clears the terminal screen
reset	Resets your terminal to use default terminal settings
who	Displays currently logged-in users
w	Displays currently logged-in users and their tasks
whoami	Displays your login name
id	Displays the numbers associated with your user account name and group names; these are commonly referred to as User IDs (UIDs) and Group IDs (GIDs)
date	Displays the current date and time
cal	Displays the calendar for the current month
uname -a	Displays system information
ls	Lists files
exit	Exits out of your current shell

If the output of a certain command is too large to fit on the terminal screen, press the Shift+Page Up keys simultaneously to view previous screens of information. Press Shift+Page Down simultaneously to navigate in the opposite direction.

You can recall commands previously entered in the shell using the keyboard arrow keys (the up, down, right, and left arrow keys). Thus, if you want to enter the same command again, cycle through the list of available commands with the keyboard up and down arrow keys and press Enter to re-execute that command.

As a Linux administrator, you will regularly run commands that only the root user can run to perform system configuration. Even if you are logged in to the system as a regular user account, you can easily switch to the root user to perform any administrative tasks using the su (switch user) command. To switch to the root user and load the root user's environment variables, you can run the su command with the – option and supply the root user's password when prompted:

```
[user1@server1 ~]$ su - root
Password:
Last login: Mon Aug 16 09:45:42 EDT 2023 from tty3
[root@server1 root]#_
```

Alternatively, to run a single command as the root only, you can run su -c "command" root and specify the root user's password when prompted.

If you do not specify the user name when using the su command, the root user is assumed. Additionally, the root user can use the su command to switch to any other user account without specifying a password:

```
[root@server1 root]# su - user1
Last login: Mon Aug 16 10:22:21 EDT 2023 from tty5
[user1@server1 ~]$_
```

Shell Metacharacters

Another important part of the shell are shell metacharacters, which are keyboard characters that have special meaning. One of the most commonly used metacharacters is the $ character, which tells the shell that the following text refers to a variable. A variable is a piece of information that is stored in memory; variable names are typically uppercase words, and most variables are set by the Linux system when you log in. An example of how you might use the $ metacharacter to refer to a variable is by using the echo command (which prints text to the terminal screen):

```
[root@server1 root]# echo Hi There!
Hi There!
[root@server1 root]# echo My shell is $SHELL
My Shell is /bin/bash
[root@server1 root]#_
```

Notice from the preceding output that $SHELL was translated into its appropriate value from memory (/bin/bash, the BASH shell). The shell recognized SHELL as a variable because it was prefixed by the $ metacharacter. Table 2-7 presents a list of common shell metacharacters that are discussed throughout this book.

Table 2-7   Common shell metacharacters

Metacharacter(s)	Description
$	Shell variable
~	Special home directory variable
#	Shell script comment
&	Background command execution
;	Command termination
< << > >>	Input/Output redirection
|	Command piping
* ? [ ]	Shell wildcards
' " \	Metacharacter quotes
`	Command substitution
( ) { }	Command grouping

It is good practice to avoid metacharacters when typing commands unless you need to take advantage of their special functionality, as the shell readily interprets them, which might lead to unexpected results.

Note 21

If you accidentally use one of these characters and your shell does not return you to the normal prompt, press the Ctrl+c keys to cancel and your current command.

In some circumstances, you might need to use a metacharacter in a command and prevent the shell from interpreting its special meaning. To do this, enclose the metacharacters in single quotation marks ('). Single quotation marks protect those metacharacters from being interpreted specially by the shell (that is, a $ is interpreted as a $ character and not a variable identifier). You can also use double quotation marks (") to perform the same task; however, double quotation marks do not protect $, \, and ` characters. If only one character needs to be protected from shell interpretation, you can precede that character by a backslash (\ ) rather than enclosing it within quotation marks. An example of this type of quoting follows:

```
[root@server1 root]# echo My Shell is $SHELL
My Shell is /bin/bash
[root@server1 root]# echo 'My Shell is $SHELL'
My Shell is $SHELL
[root@server1 root]# echo "My Shell is $SHELL"
My Shell is /bin/bash
[root@server1 root]# echo My Shell is \$SHELL
My Shell is $SHELL
[root@server1 root]#_
```

As shown in Table 2-7, not all quotation characters protect characters from the shell. The back quotation character (` ) can be used to perform command substitution; anything between back quotes is treated as another command by the shell, and its output is substituted in place of the back quotes. Take the expression `date` as an example:

```
[root@server1 root]# echo Today is `date`
Today is Tue Mar 29 09:28:11 EST 2023
[root@server1 root]#_
```

Getting Command Help

Most distributions of Linux contain more than 5,000 Linux commands in their standard configurations, and thus it is impractical to memorize the syntax and use of each command. Fortunately, Linux stores documentation for each command in central locations so that it can be accessed easily. The most common form of documentation for Linux commands is **manual pages** (commonly referred to as **man pages**). Type the man command followed by a command name to display extensive page-by-page information about that Linux command on the terminal screen. This information includes a description of the command and its syntax, as well as available options, related files, and related commands. For example, to receive information on the format and usage of the whoami command, you can use the following command:

```
[root@server1 root]# man whoami
```

The manual page is then displayed page-by-page on the terminal screen. You can use the arrow keys on the keyboard to scroll though the information or press q to quit. The manual page for whoami is similar to the following:

```
WHOAMI(1)                  User Commands                  WHOAMI(1)


NAME
       whoami - print effective user name

SYNOPSIS
       whoami [OPTION]...

DESCRIPTION
       Print the user name associated with the current effective
       user ID. Same as id -un.

       --help display this help and exit

       --version
              output version information and exit
```

```
AUTHOR
      Written by Richard Mlynarik.

REPORTING BUGS
      GNU coreutils home page:<https://www.gnu.org/software/coreutils/>
      Report translation bugs to <https://translationproject.org/team>

COPYRIGHT
      Copyright©2021 Free Software Foundation, Inc. License GPLv3+: GNU
      GPL version 3 or later <https://gnu.org/licenses/gpl.html>.
      This is free software: you are free to change and redistribute it.
      There is NO WARRANTY, to the extent permitted by law.

SEE ALSO
      Full documentation:<https://www.gnu.org/software/coreutils/whoami>
      or available locally via: info '(coreutils) whoami invocation'

GNU coreutils 9.0              March 2022              WHOAMI(1)
[root@server1 root]#_
```

Notice that the `whoami` command is displayed as WHOAMI(1) at the top of the preceding manual page output. The (1) denotes a section of the manual pages; section (1) means that `whoami` is a command that can be executed by any user. All manual pages contain certain section numbers that describe the category of the command in the manual page database; Table 2-8 lists the manual page section numbers.

Table 2-8   Manual page section numbers

Manual Page Section	Description
1	Commands that any user can execute
2	Linux system calls
3	Library routines
4	Special device files
5	File formats
6	Games
7	Miscellaneous
8	Commands that only the root user can execute
9	Linux kernel routines
n	New commands not categorized yet

Note 22

Manual page sections may also have a letter appended to them to indicate a specific version. For example, 1p refers to the POSIX version of the manual page from section 1.

Sometimes, more than one command, library routine, or file has the same name. If you run the man command with that name as an argument, Linux returns the manual page with the lowest section number. For example, if there is a file called whoami as well as a command named whoami and you type man whoami, the manual page for the whoami command (section 1 of the manual pages) is displayed. To display the manual page for the whoami file format instead, you type man 5 whoami to display the whoami file format (section 5 of the manual pages).

Recall that many commands are available to the Linux user; thus, it might be cumbersome to find the command that you need to perform a certain task without using a Linux command dictionary. Fortunately, you can search the manual pages by keyword. To find all of the commands that have the word "usb" in their names or descriptions, type the following:

```
[root@server1 root] # man -k usb
```

This command produces the following output:

```
cyrusbdb2current (8)          -  command-line utility converting the SASLDB...
flatpak-create-usb (1)        -  Copy apps and/or runtimes onto removable...
lsusb (8)                     -  list USB devices
ostree-create-usb (1)         -  Put the given refs on an external drive for...
sane-canon630u (5)            -  SANE backend for the Canon 630u USB scanner
sane-canon_lide70 (5)         -  SANE backend for the Canon LiDE 70 and 600...
sane-cardscan (5)             -  SANE backend for Corex CardScan usb scanners
sane-epjitsu (5)              -  SANE backend for Epson-based Fujitsu USB...
sane-find-scanner (1)         -  find SCSI and USB scanners and their device...
sane-genesys (5)              -  SANE backend for GL646, GL841, GL843, GL847...
sane-gt68xx (5)               -  SANE backend for GT-68XX based USB flatbed...
sane-kvs1025 (5)              -  SANE backend for Panasonic KV-S102xC USB ADF...
sane-kvs20xx (5)              -  SANE backend for Panasonic KV-S20xxC USB/SCSI...
sane-kvs40xx (5)              -  SANE backend for Panasonic KV-S40xxC USB/SCSI...
sane-ma1509 (5)               -  SANE backend for Mustek BearPaw 1200F USB...
sane-mustek_usb (5)           -  SANE backend for Mustek USB flatbed scanners
sane-mustek_usb2 (5)          -  SANE backend for SQ113 based USB flatbed...
sane-pieusb (5)               -  SANE backend for USB-connected PIE PowerSlide...
sane-plustek (5)              -  SANE backend for LM983[1/2/3] based USB scanners
sane-sm3600 (5)               -  SANE backend for Microtek scanners with M011...
sane-sm3840 (5)               -  SANE backend for Microtek scanners with...
sane-u12 (5)                  -  SANE backend for Plustek USB flatbed scanners...
sane-usb (5)                  -  USB configuration tips for SANE
usb-devices (1)               -  print USB device details
usb_modeswitch (1)            -  control the mode of 'multi-state' USB devices
usb_modeswitch_dispatcher (1) -  Linux wrapper for usb_modeswitch...
usbhid-dump (8)               -  dump USB HID device report descriptors and...
usbmuxd (8)                   -  Expose a socket to multiplex connections from...
virkeycode-usb (7)            -  Key code values for usb
[root@server1 root]#_
```

After you find the command needed, you can run the man command on that command without the -k option to find out detailed information about the command.

Note 23

You can also use the `apropos usb` command to perform the same function as the `man -k usb` command. Both commands yield the exact same output on the terminal screen.

Note 24

If you do not see any output from the `man -k` or `apropos` command following a Linux installation, you might need to run the `mandb` command to index the manual page database.

Note 25

If you want to only view a short description of a command (for example, to see what the command does), you can use the `whatis` command. For example, the `whatis whoami` command will only display the name and description from the `whoami` manual page.

Another utility, originally intended to replace the man command in Linux, is the GNU **info pages**. You can access this utility by typing the `info` command followed by the name of the command in question. The `info` command returns an easy-to-read description of each command and contains links to other information pages (called hyperlinks). Today, however, both the info pages and the manual pages are used to find documentation because manual pages have been used in Linux since its conception, and for over two decades in the UNIX operating system. An example of using the info utility to find information about the `whoami` command follows:

```
[root@server1 root]# info whoami
```

The info page is then displayed interactively:

```
Next: groups invocation, Prev: logname invocation, Up: User information

20.3 'whoami': Print effective user ID
========================================

'whoami' prints the user name associated with the current effective user ID. It is
equivalent to the command 'id -un'.

   The only options are '--help' and '--version'. *Note Common options::.

   An exit status of zero indicates success, and a nonzero value indicates failure

-----Info: (coreutils)whoami invocation, 14 lines -All----------
Welcome to Info version 6.8. Type H for help, h for tutorial.
[root@server1 root]#_
```

Note 26

While in the info utility, press the H key to display a help screen that describes the usage of info. As with the `man` command, you can use the q key to quit.

Some commands do not have manual pages or info pages. These commands are usually functions that are built into the shell itself. To find help on these commands, you must use the `help` command, as follows:

```
[root@server1 root]# help echo
echo: echo [-neE] [arg ...]
  Write arguments to the standard output.

  Display the ARGs, separated by a single space character and
  followed by a newline, on the standard output.

  Options:
    -n    do not append a newline
    -e    enable interpretation of the following backslash escapes
    -E    explicitly suppress interpretation of backslash escapes

  'echo' interprets the following backslash-escaped characters:
    \a    alert (bell)
    \b    backspace
    \c    suppress further output
    \e    escape character
    \E    escape character
    \f    form feed
    \n    new line
    \r    carriage return
    \t    horizontal tab
    \v    vertical tab
    \\    backslash
    \0nnn the character whose ASCII code is NNN (octal).  NNN can be
          0 to 3 octal digits
    \xHH  the eight-bit character whose value is HH (hexadecimal). HH
          can be one or two hex digits
    \uHHHH the Unicode character whose value is the hexadecimal
          value HHHH. HHHH can be one to four hex digits.
    \UHHHHHHHH the Unicode character whose value is the hexadecimal
          value HHHHHHHH. HHHHHHHH can be one to eight hex digits.

  Exit Status:
  Returns success unless a write error occurs.
[root@server1 root]#_
```

Shutting Down the Linux System

Because the operating system handles writing data from computer memory to the disk drives in a computer, turning off the power to the computer might result in damaged user and system files. Thus, it is important to prepare the operating system for shutdown before turning off the power to the hardware components of the computer. To do this, you can issue the `shutdown` command, which can power off or reboot (restart) your computer after a certain period of time. To power off your system in 15 minutes, for example, you could type:

```
[root@server1 root] # shutdown -P +15
```

This produces output similar to the following:

```
Shutdown scheduled for Wed 2023-09-17 15:51:48 EDT, use 'shutdown -c' to cancel.
```

Before scheduling a system shutdown, it is good form to advise users who are currently logged in to the system such that they can save their work and log off beforehand. You can do this using the `wall` (warn all) command followed by the message to send to users on the system:

```
[root@server1 root] # wall The system is shutting down in 15 min - ensure that you save your work and log off before then.
```

To power off your system now, you could type:

```
[root@server1 root] # poweroff
```

Other examples of the `shutdown` command and their descriptions are shown in Table 2-9.

Table 2-9   Commands to shut down and reboot the Linux operating system

Command	Description
`shutdown -P +4` `shutdown -h +4`	Powers off your system in four minutes
`shutdown -H +4`	Halts the operating system from executing in four minutes, but does not invoke the ACPI function in your BIOS to turn off power to your computer
`shutdown -r +4`	Reboots your system in four minutes
`shutdown -P now` `shutdown -h now`	Powers off your system immediately
`shutdown -r now`	Reboots your system immediately
`shutdown -c`	Cancels a scheduled shutdown
`halt`	Halts your system immediately, but does not power it off
`poweroff`	Powers off your system immediately
`reboot`	Reboots your system immediately

Summary

- Prior to installation, you should verify hardware requirements and compatibility.
- You can obtain Linux installation media by downloading an ISO image from the Internet that can be written to a DVD or USB flash drive or can be used directly by virtualization software.
- A typical Linux installation prompts the user for information such as language, date, time zone, keyboard layout, user account configuration, and permanent storage configuration.
- Users must log in to a terminal and receive a shell before they can interact with the Linux system and kernel. A single user can log in several times simultaneously to different terminals locally or across a network.
- Regardless of the type of terminal that you use (graphical or command-line), you can enter commands, options, and arguments at a shell prompt to perform system tasks, obtain command help, or shut down the Linux system. The shell is case sensitive and understands a variety of special characters called shell metacharacters, which should be protected if their special meaning is not required.

Key Terms

Advanced Technology Attachment (ATA)
arguments
BASH shell
Basic Input/Output System (BIOS)
BIOS Boot Partition
command
extended partition
filesystem
GUID Partition Table (GPT)
info page
Integrated Drive Electronics (IDE)
ISO image
journaling
live media

logical drive
Logical Volume Manager (LVM)
man (manual) page
Master Boot Record (MBR)
metacharacter
namespace
Non-Volatile Memory Express (NVMe)
option
Parallel Advanced Technology Attachment (PATA)
partition
Portable Operating System Interface (POSIX)
Preboot eXecution Environment (PXE)

primary partition
Serial Advanced Technology Attachment (SATA)
Serial Attached SCSI (SAS)
shell
Small Computer Systems Interface (SCSI)
swap memory
terminal
UEFI System Partition
Unified Extensible Firmware Interface (UEFI)
virtual memory
zswap

Review Questions

1. What is the default shell on most Linux systems called?
   a. SH
   b. BSH
   c. CSH
   d. BASH

2. What equivalent to the man command generally provides an easier-to-read description of the queried command and contains links to other related information?
   a. who
   b. man help
   c. man -descriptive
   d. info

3. What command can you use to safely shut down the Linux system immediately?
   a. shutdown -c
   b. shutdown -r
   c. down
   d. halt

4. What command is equivalent to the man -k keyword command?
   a. find keyword
   b. man keyword
   c. apropos keyword
   d. appaloosa keyword

5. Which of the following is not a piece of information that the Fedora installation program prompts you for?
   a. time zone

   b. installation destination
   c. firewall settings
   d. installation language

6. Linux commands entered via the command line are not case sensitive.
   a. True
   b. False

7. Which command blanks the terminal screen, erasing previously displayed output?
   a. erase
   b. clean
   c. blank
   d. clear

8. When sitting at a computer running Linux, what key combination do you press to switch to a graphical login screen?
   a. Ctrl+Alt+F1
   b. Ctrl+Alt+F4
   c. Ctrl+Alt+F2
   d. Ctrl+Alt+F7

9. To install Linux within a virtual machine, you can specify the path to an ISO image that contains the Linux installation media within virtualization software without having to first write the ISO image to a DVD or USB flash drive.
   a. True
   b. False

10. After you log in to a terminal, you receive a user interface called a _____.
   a. GUID
   b. shell
   c. text box
   d. command screen

11. Users enter commands directly to the kernel of the Linux operating system.
   a. True
   b. False

12. How can you protect a metacharacter (such as the $ character) from shell interpretation?
   a. Precede it with a /.
   b. Precede it with a \.
   c. Precede it with a $.
   d. It cannot be done because metacharacters are essential.

13. You know a Linux command will perform a desired function for you, but you cannot remember the full name of the command. You do remember it will flush a variable from your system. Which command typed at a command prompt displays a list of commands that would likely contain the command you desire?
   a. man -k flush
   b. man -k find all
   c. man flush
   d. man -key flush

14. Which command displays the users who are currently logged in to the Linux system?
   a. finger
   b. who
   c. id
   d. date

15. Which prompt does the root user receive when logged in to the system?
   a. $
   b. @
   c. #
   d. !

16. Which prompt do regular users receive when logged in to the system?
   a. $
   b. @
   c. #
   d. !

17. Which of the following refers to the third primary partition on the second SAS hard disk drive within Linux?
   a. hdb2
   b. sda3
   c. hdb3
   d. sdb3

18. Which three partitions are typically created at minimum during a Fedora Workstation Linux installation on a system with a UEFI BIOS? (Choose three answers.)
   a. /
   b. /boot
   c. swap
   d. /boot/efi

19. If you boot your computer from Linux live media, you will be able to use a fully functional Linux system prior to installing Linux on permanent storage.

20. Which of the following is *not* an example of virtualization software that can be used to install Linux within another operating system?
   a. Oracle VirtualBox
   b. Microsoft Hyper-V
   c. Spiceworks
   d. UTM

Hands-On Projects

These projects should be completed in the order given and should take a total of three hours to complete. The software and hardware requirements for these projects include the following:

- A 64-bit computer with at least 8 GB of RAM, at least 250 GB of permanent disk storage, and a DVD drive
- A Windows or macOS operating system that contains a virtualization software product, a web browser, and an Internet connection
- The latest live media ISO image of Fedora Workstation Linux for your computer platform (Intel or ARM)

Note 27

New versions of each Linux distribution are released frequently. While nearly all steps within the Hands-On Projects in this book will remain the same for newer versions of Linux, some steps may need to be modified. To view steps that need to be modified for each future Linux version, you can visit github.com/jasoneckert/CengageLinux.

Project 2-1

Estimated Time: 50 minutes

Objective: Install Fedora Workstation Linux on a Windows or macOS system.

Description: In this hands-on project, you install Fedora Workstation Linux within a virtual machine on a Windows or macOS computer.

1. In your virtualization software, create a new virtual machine called **Fedora Linux** that has the following characteristics:

   - 4 GB of memory (not dynamically allocated)
   - An Internet connection via your PC's network card (preferably using an external virtual switch or bridged mode)
   - A 50 GB SATA/SAS/SCSI virtual hard disk drive (dynamically allocated)
   - The virtual machine DVD drive attached to the live media ISO image of Fedora Workstation Linux

Note 28

If your hypervisor supports secure boot (e.g., Hyper-V), deselect this feature within the settings of your virtual machine prior to Step 2.

2. Start and then connect to your Fedora Linux virtual machine using your virtualization software.

3. At the GNU GRUB screen, press **Enter** to test your installation media and boot Fedora Live.

4. After the graphical desktop and Welcome to Fedora screen has loaded, select the option **Install to Hard Drive** to start the Fedora installation program.

5. At the Welcome to Fedora screen, select **English (United States)** and click **Continue**.

6. On the Installation Summary screen, click **Time & Date**, select your time zone (and time if necessary), and click **Done**.

7. On the Installation Summary screen, click **Installation Destination**. You should see that your 50 GB virtual disk is already selected and called sda. Select **Custom** under Storage Configuration and click **Done** when finished.

8. At the Manual Partitioning screen, choose a partition scheme of **Standard Partition** from the list box and select the link **Click here to create them automatically**. This will create several partitions.

   a. Highlight the **/ (sda3)** partition, reduce the Desired Capacity to **35 (35 GiB)**, and click **Update Settings**. This will leave some free unpartitioned space on your first disk for a later exercise.

   b. Click **Done** and then click **Accept Changes** when prompted.

9. At the Installation Summary screen, click **Begin Installation**.

10. When the installation has finished, click **Finish Installation**. This will return you to your Fedora live desktop.

11. Click the icon in the upper-right corner of the Fedora live desktop, click the **Power Off/Log Out** drop-down menu and select **Power Off**. Click **Power Off** to shut down your Fedora Live installation image.

12. In the Settings for your virtual machine in your virtualization software, ensure that the virtual DVD drive is no longer attached to the live media ISO image of Fedora Workstation Linux.

13. Finally, start your Fedora Linux virtual machine using your virtualization software to boot into your new operating system.

14. At the Setup wizard, click **Start Setup**.

    a. At the Privacy page, disable Location Services and Automatic Problem Reporting using the sliders and click **Next**.

    b. At the Third-Party Repositories page, click **Enable Third-Party Repositories** and click **Next**.

    c. At the Online Accounts page, click **Skip**.

    d. On the About You page, supply your full name in the Full Name text box, the name **user1** in the Username text box, and then click **Next**.

    e. At the Password page, supply a password of **LINUXrocks!** in both text boxes. Click **Next** and then click **Start Using Fedora Linux**.

15. At the Welcome to GNOME wizard, click **Take Tour**. Navigate through the wizard using the arrow icons and close the window when finished.

Project 2-2

Estimated Time: 30 minutes
Objective: Examine Linux terminals and run shell commands.
Description: In this hands-on project, you set a password for the root user, explore some command-line terminals on a Linux system, and enter some basic commands into the BASH shell.

1. After your Linux system has been loaded following installation and the completion of the Welcome wizard, you are placed at a graphical terminal (tty1). Instead of logging in to this graphical terminal, press **Ctrl+Alt+F3** to switch to a command-line terminal (tty3) and then log in to the terminal using the user name of **user1** and the password of **LINUXrocks!**. Which prompt did you receive and why?

> **Note 29**
>
> If you are using a laptop computer, you may need to hold down the Function (Fn) key on your keyboard when pressing Ctrl+Alt+F3.

2. At the command prompt, type `sudo passwd root` and press **Enter** to set the root user password. When prompted, enter your password **LINUXrocks!**, and then enter the desired root password of **LINUXrocks!** twice to set the root user password to LINUXrocks!

3. At the command prompt, type `date` and press **Enter** to view the current date and time. Now, type `Date` and press **Enter**. Why did you receive an error message? Can you tell which shell gave you the error message?

4. Switch to a different command-line terminal (tty5) by pressing **Ctrl+Alt+F5** and log in to the terminal using the user name of **root** and the password of **LINUXrocks!**. Which prompt did you receive and why?

5. At the command prompt, type `who` and press **Enter** to view the users logged in to the system. Who is logged in and on which terminal?

6. Switch back to the terminal tty3 by pressing **Ctrl+Alt+F3**. Did you need to log in? Are the outputs from the `date` and `Date` commands still visible?

7. Try typing each command listed in Table 2-6 in order (pressing **Enter** after each) and observe the output. What did the last command (`exit`) do?

8. Switch to the terminal tty5 by pressing **Ctrl+Alt+F5** and type `exit` to log out of your shell.

Project 2-3

Estimated Time: 50 minutes
Objective: Use Linux desktop environments.
Description: In this hands-on project, you log in to a graphical terminal in Fedora Linux and interact with the GNOME and KDE desktops.

1. Switch to the graphical terminal (tty1) by pressing **Ctrl+Alt+F1**, click your name (which is the display name for the user account named user1), supply the password of **LINUXrocks!**, and click **Sign In**. Close the Getting Started window. By default, the GNOME desktop environment is started using Wayland.

2. Observe the GNOME desktop. Use your mouse to select the **Activities** menu in the upper-left corner of your screen, select the **Show Applications** icon (at the bottom of the application panel), and then navigate to **Terminal** to open a BASH shell prompt. What prompt do you receive and why?

3. At the command prompt, type `who` and press **Enter** to view the users logged in to the system. Note that you are currently logged into tty2.

4. Switch to the terminal tty1 by pressing **Ctrl+Alt+F1**. Is the GDM still available? Switch back to your GNOME desktop on tty2 by pressing **Ctrl+Alt+F2**.

5. At the command prompt, type `su  –` and press **Enter** to switch to the root user. Supply the root user password **LINUXrocks!** when prompted.

6. By default, the KDE desktop is not installed in Fedora Linux. To download and install the KDE desktop (the latest edition is called Plasma Workspaces), type `dnf groupinstall "KDE Plasma Workspaces"` and press **Enter** when finished. Press **y** when prompted to download and install the required packages from the Internet, which could take several minutes, depending on your Internet speed. The `dnf` command will be discussed in more detail in Chapter 11.

7. Type `reboot` to restart Fedora Linux. After the system has rebooted, click your name at the GDM screen and then click the settings (cog wheel) icon in the lower-right corner. Note that you can start different desktop environments using either Wayland or X.org (X11). Select **Plasma (X11)** to start the KDE desktop on X.org, supply your password (**LINUXrocks!**), and click **Sign In**.

8. Click the Fedora start button in the lower-left of the desktop and navigate to **System**, **Terminal** to start a command-line shell. How does application navigation in the KDE desktop differ from the GNOME desktop?

9. At the command prompt, type `who` and press **Enter**. While your desktop environment is still loaded on tty2, the `who` command lists display 0 (:0) as your terminal. This is because X.org uses different display numbers to denote different desktops that users can connect to locally, or from across a network. Additionally, any command-line BASH shells that you open within a desktop environment on X.org are started as pseudo terminal sessions (pts); the first pseudo terminal session is called pts/0, the second pseudo terminal session is called pts/1, and so on.

10. Click the **File** menu in your terminal window and select **New Tab**. At the command prompt in this new window, type `who` and press **Enter**. Do you see an additional pseudo terminal session for this new tab?

11. Click the Fedora start button, navigate to **Leave** (the icon next to Shut Down), **Log Out**, and click **OK** to exit the KDE desktop.

Project 2-4

Estimated Time: 10 minutes
Objective: Use multiple shells within a terminal.
Description: In this hands-on project, you work with multiple BASH windows within a single terminal using the `screen` and `tmux` tools.

1. Switch to a command-line terminal (tty5) by pressing **Ctrl+Alt+F5** and log in to the terminal using the user name of **root** and the password of **LINUXrocks!**.

2. At the command prompt, type `screen` and press **Enter**. When prompted to install the command, press **y** (twice). Next, type `screen` and press **Enter** to open a new window within the `screen` tool.

3. At the command prompt in this new window, type `who` and press **Enter**. Note that the `screen` tool turns your tty5 terminal into a pseudo terminal session in order to provide additional BASH windows.

4. Press the **Ctrl+a** keys and then immediately press **c** to create a new BASH window. At the command prompt in this new window, type `who` and press **Enter**. Note that you see an additional pseudo terminal session for the current window.

5. Press the **Ctrl+a** keys again and then immediately press **c** to create a third BASH window. At the command prompt in this new window, type `who` and press **Enter**. You should now see three pseudo terminal sessions within the tty5 terminal.

6. Press the **Ctrl+a** keys and then immediately press **p** to switch to the previous BASH window. Next, press the **Ctrl+a** keys and then immediately press **n** to switch to the next BASH window.

7. Type `exit` and press **Enter** to log out of your current BASH window.

8. Repeat Step 7 twice more to log out of the remaining two BASH windows and the `screen` tool. Type `who` and press **Enter** to verify that you are within your original tty5 terminal.

9. At the command prompt, type `tmux` and press **Enter** to start the `tmux` tool. Next, type `who` and press **Enter**. Does the `tmux` tool turn your tty5 terminal into a pseudo terminal session?

10. Press the **Ctrl+b** keys and then immediately press **%** (percent) to create a new BASH window split horizontally. Next, press the **Ctrl+b** keys again and then immediately press **"** (double quote) to create a third BASH window split vertically.

11. Press the **Ctrl+b** keys and then use a keyboard arrow key (**up**, **down**, **left**, **right**) of your choice to navigate between the windows. Repeat this step to navigate among all three BASH windows within your tty5 terminal.

12. Type `exit` and press **Enter** to log out of your current BASH window.

13. Repeat Step 7 twice more to log out of the remaining two BASH windows and the `tmux` tool. Finally, type `exit` and press **Enter** to log out of your shell.

Project 2-5

Estimated Time: 20 minutes
Objective: Use shell metacharacters.
Description: In this hands-on project, you use and protect shell metacharacters.

1. Switch to a command-line terminal (tty5) by pressing **Ctrl+Alt+F5** and log in to the terminal using the user name of **root** and the password of **LINUXrocks!**.

2. At the command prompt, type `date;who` and press **Enter** to run the `date` command immediately followed by the `who` command. Use the information in Table 2-7 to describe the purpose of the ; metacharacter.

3. At the command prompt, type `echo This is OK` and press **Enter** to display a message on the terminal screen.

4. At the command prompt, type `echo Don't do this` and press **Enter**. Which character needs to be protected in the previous command? Press the **Ctrl+c** keys to cancel your command and return to a BASH shell prompt.

5. At the command prompt, type `echo "Don't do this"` and press **Enter**. What is displayed on the terminal screen?

6. At the command prompt, type `echo Don\'t do this` and press **Enter**. What is displayed on the terminal screen?

7. At the command prompt, type `echo $SHELL` and press **Enter** to view the expansion of a variable using a shell metacharacter. What is displayed on the terminal screen? Next, type `echo $TEST` and press **Enter** to find out what happens when a variable that does not exist is used in a command. What is displayed?

8. At the command prompt, type `echo You have $4.50` and press **Enter**. What is displayed? Why? Which character needs to be protected in the previous command? What are two different ways that you can protect this character from interpretation by the shell?

9. At the command prompt, type `echo 'You have $4.50'` and press **Enter**. What is displayed on the terminal screen? Did the single quotation marks protect this metacharacter from shell interpretation?

10. At the command prompt, type echo "You have $4.50" and press **Enter**. What is displayed on the terminal screen? Did the double quotation marks protect this metacharacter from shell interpretation?

11. At the command prompt, type echo You have \$4.50 and press **Enter**. What is displayed on the terminal screen? Did the backslash protect this metacharacter from shell interpretation?

12. At the command prompt, type echo My name is `whoami` and press **Enter**. What function do back quotes perform?

13. Type exit and press **Enter** to log out of your shell.

Project 2-6

Estimated Time: 15 minutes
Objective: Obtain command help.
Description: In this hands-on project, you find information about commands using help utilities.

1. Press **Ctrl+Alt+F5** to switch to a command-line terminal (tty5), and then log in to the terminal using the user name of **root** and the password of **LINUXrocks!**.

2. At the command prompt, type man -k cron and press **Enter** to view a list of manual pages that have the word "cron" in the name or description. Use Table 2-8 to determine what type of manual pages are displayed. How many manual pages are there for crontab? Are they different types of manual pages?

> **Note 30**
>
> If you do not see any output from the man -k command, run the mandb command to generate the manual pages index.

3. At the command prompt, type man crontab and press **Enter** to view the manual page for the crontab command. Observe the syntax of the crontab command and press **q** when finished to quit the manual page and return to your command prompt.

4. At the command prompt, type man 5 crontab and press **Enter** to view the manual page for the crontab file format. Observe the syntax of the crontab file format and press **q** when finished to quit the manual page and return to your command prompt.

5. At the command prompt, type info and press **Enter** to view a list of available GNU info pages. When finished, press **q** to quit the info utility.

6. At the command prompt, type info date and press **Enter** to view syntax information regarding the date command, and press **q** to quit the info utility when finished.

7. At the command prompt, type help to view a list of BASH shell functions that have documentation. If the list is too long for your terminal, press the **Shift+Page Up** keys to shift one page up to view the top of the list. Then press the **Shift+Page Down** keys to shift one page down to view your command prompt again.

8. At the command prompt, type help exit to view information on the exit command, a function of your BASH shell.

9. Type exit and press **Enter** to log out of your shell.

Project 2-7

Estimated Time: 5 minutes
Objective: Power down your Linux system.
Description: In this hands-on project, you properly shut down your Linux system.

1. Press **Ctrl+Alt+F5** to switch to a command-line terminal (tty5), and then log in to the terminal using the user name of **root** and the password of **LINUXrocks!**.

2. At the command prompt, type poweroff to shut down your Linux system immediately. Which commands from Table 2-9 can also be used to shut down your Linux system?

Discovery Exercises

Discovery Exercise 2-1

Estimated Time: 30 minutes

Objective: Use Linux help utilities.

Description: You are the network administrator for Slimjim, a peripheral device company. The network uses Linux, and you need information on some commands to perform your job. Open the manual pages and find all the commands that have the word "copy" in their name or description. What command did you use to accomplish this task? Are there any commands in this list that only a root user can execute? How are they indicated? Select any two of them and compare their info and manual pages. Access and read the manual pages on three other commands that interest you either by using the command name or searching for them by related keyword (try using `apropos`).

Discovery Exercise 2-2

Estimated Time: 20 minutes

Objective: Describe common Linux command syntax errors.

Description: Identify the errors with the following commands and indicate possible solutions. (*Hint:* Try typing them at a shell prompt to view the error message.)

```
Echo "This command does not work properly"
date -z
apropos man -k
help date
shutdown -c now
echo "I would like lots of $$$"
man 8 date
```

Discovery Exercise 2-3

Estimated Time: 15 minutes

Objective: Use the `cheat` command to obtain common command usage.

Description: While the manual pages are the standard way to obtain help on Linux commands, it often takes a while to find the information necessary to run a particular command in the way that you would like. To find useful examples (or "cheat sheets") for common Linux commands, you can instead use the `cheat` command. Use the `dnf install cheat` command to install this command on your system and then run the **cheat date** and **cheat uname** commands to view cheat sheets for the `date` and `uname` commands, respectively. Optionally run some of the commands suggested in these cheat sheets.

Chapter 3

Exploring Linux Filesystems

Chapter Objectives

1 Navigate the Linux directory structure using relative and absolute pathnames.

2 Describe the various types of Linux files.

3 View filenames and file types.

4 Use shell wildcards to specify multiple filenames.

5 Display the contents of text files and binary files.

6 Search text files for regular expressions using `grep`.

7 Use the vi editor to manipulate text files.

8 Identify common alternatives to the vi editor.

An understanding of the structure and commands surrounding the Linux filesystem is essential for effectively using Linux to manipulate data. In the first part of this chapter, you explore the Linux filesystem hierarchy by changing your position in the filesystem tree and listing filenames of various types. Next, you examine the shell wildcard metacharacters used to specify multiple filenames as well as view the contents of files using standard Linux commands. You then learn about the regular expression metacharacters used when searching for text within files and are introduced to the vi text editor and its alternatives.

The Linux Directory Structure

Fundamental to using the Linux operating system is an understanding of how Linux stores files on the filesystem. Typical Linux systems could have thousands of data and program files; thus, a structure that organizes those files is necessary to make it easier to find and manipulate data and run programs. Recall from the previous chapter that Linux uses a logical directory tree to organize files into **directories** (also known as folders). When a user stores files in a certain directory, the files are physically stored in the filesystem of a certain partition on a storage device (e.g., hard disk drive or SSD) inside the computer. Most people are familiar with the Windows operating system directory tree structure as shown in Figure 3-1; each filesystem on a storage device partition is referred to by a drive letter (such as C: or D:) and has a root directory (indicated by the \ character) containing subdirectories that together form a hierarchical tree.

It is important to describe directories in the directory tree properly; the **absolute pathname** to a file or directory is the full pathname of a certain file or directory starting from the root directory. In Figure 3-1, the absolute pathname for the color directory is C:\windows\color and the absolute

Figure 3-1   The Windows filesystem structure

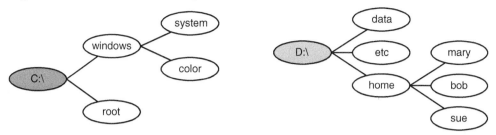

pathname for the sue directory is D:\home\sue. In other words, you refer to C:\windows\color as the color directory below the windows directory below the root of C drive. Similarly, you refer to D:\home\sue as the sue directory below the home directory below the root of D drive.

Linux uses a similar directory structure, but with no drive letters. The structure contains a single root (referred to using the / character), with different filesystems on storage device partitions mounted (or attached) to different directories on this directory tree. The directory that each filesystem is mounted to is transparent to the user. An example of a sample Linux directory tree equivalent to the Windows sample directory tree shown in Figure 3-1 is shown in Figure 3-2. Note that the subdirectory named "root" in Figure 3-2 is different from the root (/) directory. You'll learn more about the root subdirectory in the next section.

Figure 3-2   The Linux filesystem structure

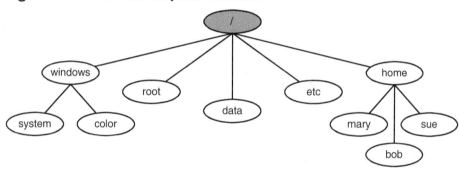

In Figure 3-2, the absolute pathname for the color directory is /windows/color and the absolute pathname for the sue directory is /home/sue. In other words, you refer to the /windows/color directory as the color directory below the windows directory below the root of the system (the / character). Similarly, you refer to the /home/sue directory as the sue directory below the home directory below the root of the system.

Changing Directories

When you log into a Linux system, you are placed in your **home directory**, which is a place unique to your user account for storing personal files. Regular users usually have a home directory named after their user account under the /home directory, as in /home/sue. The root user, however, has a home directory called root under the root directory of the system (/root), as shown in Figure 3-2. Regardless of your user name, you can always refer to your own home directory using the ~ **metacharacter**.

To confirm the system directory that you are currently in, simply observe the name at the end of the shell prompt or run the pwd **(print working directory) command** at a command-line prompt. If you are logged in as the root user, the following output is displayed on the terminal screen:

```
[root@server1 ~]# pwd
/root
[root@server1 ~]#_
```

However, if you are logged in as the user sue, you see the following output:

```
[sue@server1 ~]$ pwd
/home/sue
[sue@server1 ~]$_
```

To change directories, you can issue the cd (change directory) command with an argument specifying the destination directory. If you do not specify a destination directory, the cd command returns you to your home directory:

```
[root@server1 ~]# cd /home/mary
[root@server1 mary]# pwd
/home/mary
[root@server1 mary]# cd /etc
[root@server1 etc]# pwd
/etc
[root@server1 etc]# cd
[root@server1 ~]# pwd
/root
[root@server1 ~]#_
```

You can also use the ~ metacharacter to refer to another user's home directory by appending a user name at the end:

```
[root@server1 ~]# cd ~mary
[root@server1 mary]# pwd
/home/mary
[root@server1 mary]# cd ~
[root@server1 ~]# pwd
/root
[root@server1 ~]#_
```

In many of the examples discussed earlier, the argument specified after the cd command is an absolute pathname to a directory, meaning that the system has all the information it needs to find the destination directory because the pathname starts from the root (/) of the system. However, in most Linux commands, you can also use a relative pathname in place of an absolute pathname to reduce typing. A relative pathname is the pathname of a target file or directory relative to your current directory in the tree. To specify a directory below your current directory, refer to that directory by name (do not start the pathname with a / character). To refer to a directory one step closer to the root of the tree (also known as a parent directory), use two dots (..). An example of using relative pathnames to move around the directory tree is shown next:

```
[root@server1 ~]# cd /home/mary
[root@server1 mary]# pwd
/home/mary
[root@server1 mary]# cd ..
[root@server1 home]# pwd
/home
[root@server1 home]# cd mary
[root@server1 mary]# pwd
/home/mary
[root@server1 mary]#_
```

The preceding example used ".." to move up one parent directory and then used the word "mary" to specify the mary subdirectory relative to the current location in the tree; however, you can also move more than one level up or down the directory tree:

```
[root@server1 ~]# cd /home/mary
[root@server1 mary]# pwd
/home/mary
[root@server1 mary]# cd ../..
[root@server1 /]# pwd
/
[root@server1 /]# cd home/mary
[root@server1 mary]# pwd
/home/mary
[root@server1 mary]#_
```

Note 1

You can also use one dot (.) to refer to the current directory. Although this is not useful when using the cd command, you do use one dot later in this book.

Although absolute pathnames are straightforward to use as arguments to commands when specifying the location of a certain file or directory, relative pathnames can save you a great deal of typing and reduce the potential for error if your current directory is far away from the root directory. Suppose, for example, that the current directory is /home/sue/projects/acme/plans and you need to change to the /home/sue/projects/acme directory. Using an absolute pathname, you would type cd /home/sue/projects/acme; however, using a relative pathname, you only need to type cd .. to perform the same task because the /home/sue/projects/acme directory is one parent directory above the current location in the directory tree.

An alternate method for saving time when typing pathnames as arguments to commands is to use the **Tab-completion feature** of the BASH shell. To do this, type enough unique letters of a directory and press the Tab key to allow the BASH shell to find the intended file or directory being specified and fill in the appropriate information. If there is more than one possible match, the Tab-completion feature alerts you with a beep; pressing the Tab key again after this beep presents you with a list of possible files or directories.

Observe the directory structure in Figure 3-2. To use the Tab-completion feature to change the current directory to /home/sue, you type cd /h and then press the Tab key. This changes the previous characters on the terminal screen to display cd /home/ (the BASH shell was able to fill in the appropriate information because the /home directory is the only directory under the / directory that starts with the letter "h"). Then, you could add an s character to the command, so that the command line displays cd /home/s, and press the Tab key once again to allow the shell to fill in the remaining letters. This results in the command cd /home/sue/ being displayed on the terminal screen (the sue directory is the only directory that begins with the s character under the /home directory). At this point, you can press Enter to execute the command and change the current directory to /home/sue.

Note 2

In addition to directories, the Tab-completion feature of the BASH shell can be used to specify the pathname to files and executable programs.

Viewing Files and Directories

The point of a directory structure is to organize files into an easy-to-use format. In order to locate the file you need to execute, view, or edit, you need to be able to display a list of the contents of a particular directory. You'll learn how to do that shortly, but first you need to learn about the various types of files and filenames, as well as the different commands used to select filenames for viewing.

File Types

Fundamental to viewing files and directories is a solid understanding of the various types of files present on most Linux systems. A Linux system can have several types of files; the most common include the following:

- Text files
- Binary data files
- Executable program files
- Directory files
- Linked files
- Special device files
- Named pipes and sockets

Most files on a Linux system that contain configuration information are text files. Another type of file is a program that exists on the filesystem before it is executed in memory to become a process. A program is typically associated with several supporting binary data files that store information such as common functions and graphics. In addition, directories themselves are actually files; they are special files that serve as placeholders to organize other files. When you create a directory, a file is placed on the filesystem to represent that directory.

Linked files are files that have an association with one another; they can represent the same data or they can point to another file (also known as a shortcut file). Special device files are less common than the other file types that have been mentioned, yet they are important for managing Linux because they represent different devices on the system, such as hard disk drives and SSDs. These device files are used in conjunction with commands that manipulate devices on the system; special device files are typically found only in the /dev directory and are discussed in later chapters of this book. As with special device files, named pipe files are less commonly used. Named pipes are files that pass information from one process in memory to another. One process writes to the file while another process reads from it to achieve this passing of information. Another variant of a named pipe file is a socket file, which allows a process on another computer to write to a file on your computer while another process on your computer reads from that file.

Filenames

Files are recognized by their filenames, which can include up to 255 characters, yet are rarely longer than 20 characters on most Linux systems. Filenames are typically composed of alphanumeric characters, the underscore (_) character, the dash (-) character, and the period (.) character.

Note 3

It is important to avoid using the shell metacharacters discussed in the previous chapter when naming files. Using a filename that contains a shell metacharacter as an argument to a Linux command might produce unexpected results.

Note 4

Filenames that start with a period (.) are referred to as hidden files. You need to use a special command to display them in a file list. This command is discussed later in this chapter.

Filenames used by the Windows operating system typically end with a period and three characters that identify the file type—for example, document.txt (a text file) and program.exe (an executable program file). While most files on a Linux filesystem do not follow this pattern, some do contain characters at the end of the filename that indicate the file type. These characters are commonly referred to as filename extensions. Table 3-1 lists common examples of filename extensions and their associated file types.

Table 3-1 Common filename extensions

Metacharacter	Description
.bin	Binary executable program files (similar to .exe files within Windows)
.c	C programming language source code files
.cc, .cpp	C++ programming language source code files
.html, .htm	HTML (Hypertext Markup Language) files
.ps	Files formatted for printing with postscript
.txt	Text files
.tar	Archived files (contain other files within)
.gz, .bz2, .xz, .Z	Compressed files
.tar.gz, .tgz, .tar.bz2, .tar.xz, .tar.Z	Compressed archived files
.conf, .cfg	Configuration files (contain text)
.so	Shared object (programming library) files
.o, ko	Compiled object files
.pl	PERL (Practical Extraction and Report Language) programs
.tcl	Tcl (Tool Command Language) programs
.jpg, .jpeg, .png, .tiff, .xpm, .gif	Binary files that contain graphical images
.sh	Shell scripts (contain text that is executed by the shell)

Listing Files

Linux hosts a variety of commands that can be used to display files and their types in various directories on filesystems. By far, the most common method for displaying files is to use the `ls` command. Following is an example of a file listing in the root user's home directory:

```
[root@server1 ~]# pwd
/root
[root@server1 ~]# ls
current myprogram project project12 project2 project4
Desktop myscript project1 project13 project3 project5
[root@server1 ~]#_
```

Note 5

The files listed previously and discussed throughout this chapter are for example purposes only. The hands-on projects use different files.

The `ls` command displays all the files in the current directory in columnar format; however, you can also pass an argument to the `ls` command indicating the directory to list if the current directory listing is not required. In the following example, the files are listed under the /home/bob directory without changing the current directory.

```
[root@server1 ~]# pwd
/root
[root@server1 ~]# ls /home/bob
```

```
assignment1 file1 letter letter2 project1
[root@server1 ~]#_
```

Note 6

When running the `ls` command, you will notice that files of different types are often represented as different colors; however, the specific colors used to represent files of certain types might vary depending on your terminal settings. As a result, do not assume color alone indicates the file type.

Note 7

Windows uses the `dir` command to list files and directories; to simplify the learning of Linux for Windows users, there is a `dir` command in Linux, which is either a copy of, or shortcut to, the `ls` command.

Recall from the previous chapter that you can use options to alter the behavior of commands. To view a list of files and their type, use the `-F` option to the `ls` command:

```
[root@server1 ~]# pwd
/root
[root@server1 ~]# ls -F
current@  myprogram*  project    project12  project2  project4
Desktop/  myscript*   project1   project13  project3  project5
[root@server1 ~]#_
```

The `ls -F` command appends a special character at the end of each filename displayed to indicate the type of file. In the preceding output, note that the filenames current, Desktop, myprogram, and myscript have special characters appended to their names. The @ symbol indicates a symbolically linked file (a shortcut to another file), the * symbol indicates an executable file, the / indicates a subdirectory, the = character indicates a socket, and the | character indicates a named pipe. Other file types do not have a special character appended to them and could be text files, binary data files, or special device files.

Note 8

It is a common convention to name directories starting with an uppercase letter, such as the D in the Desktop directory shown in the preceding output. This allows you to quickly determine which names refer to directories when running the `ls` command without any options that specify file type.

Although the `ls -F` command is a quick way of getting file type information in an easy-to-read format, at times you need to obtain more detailed information about each file. The `ls -l` command can be used to provide a long listing for each file in a certain directory.

```
[root@server1 ~]# pwd
/root
[root@server1 ~]# ls -l
total 548
lrwxrwxrwx   1 root     root              9 Apr  7 09:56 current -> project12
drwx------   3 root     root           4096 Mar 29 10:01 Desktop
-rwxr-xr-x   1 root     root         519964 Apr  7 09:59 myprogram
-rwxr-xr-x   1 root     root             20 Apr  7 09:58 myscript
-rw-r--r--   1 root     root             71 Apr  7 09:58 project
-rw-r--r--   1 root     root             71 Apr  7 09:59 project1
-rw-r--r--   1 root     root             71 Apr  7 09:59 project12
-rw-r--r--   1 root     root              0 Apr  7 09:56 project13
```

```
-rw-r--r--    1 root    root         71 Apr   7 09:59 project2
-rw-r--r--    1 root    root         90 Apr   7 10:01 project3
-rw-r--r--    1 root    root         99 Apr   7 10:01 project4
-rw-r--r--    1 root    root        108 Apr   7 10:01 project5
[root@server1 ~]#_
```

Each file listed in the preceding example has eight components of information listed in columns from left to right:

1. A file type character:
   - The d character represents a directory.
   - The l character represents a symbolically linked file (discussed in Chapter 4).
   - The b or c character represents a special device file (discussed in Chapter 5).
   - The n character represents a named pipe.
   - The s character represents a socket.
   - The – character represents all other file types (text files, binary data files).
2. A list of permissions on the file (also called the mode of the file and discussed in Chapter 4).
3. A hard link count (discussed in Chapter 4).
4. The owner of the file (discussed in Chapter 4).
5. The group owner of the file (discussed in Chapter 4).
6. The file size.
7. The most recent modification time of the file (or creation time if the file was not modified following creation).
8. The filename. Some files are shortcuts or pointers to other files and indicated with an arrow, as with the file called "current" in the preceding output; these are known as symbolic links and are discussed in Chapter 4.

For the file named "project" in the previous example, you can see that this file is a regular file because its long listing begins with a – character, the permissions on the file are rw-r--r--, the hard link count is 1, the owner of the file is the root user, the group owner of the file is the root group, the size of the file is 71 bytes, and the file was modified last on April 7 at 9:58 a.m.

Note 9

If SELinux is enabled on your system, you may also notice a period (.) immediately following the permissions on a file or directory that is managed by SELinux. SELinux will be discussed in Chapter 14.

Note 10

On most Linux systems, a shortcut to the ls command can be used to display the same columns of information as the ls -l command. Some users prefer to use this shortcut, commonly known as an alias, which is invoked when a user types ll at a command prompt. This is known as the ll command.

The ls -F and ls -l commands are valuable to a user who wants to display file types; however, neither of these commands can display all file types using special characters. To display the file type of any file, you can use the file command; you give the file command an argument specifying what file to analyze. You can also pass multiple files as arguments or use the * metacharacter to refer to all files in the current directory. An example of using the file command in the root user's home directory is:

```
[root@server1 ~]# pwd
/root
```

```
[root@server1 ~]# ls
current   myprogram  project    project12   project2   project4
Desktop   myscript   project1   project13   project3   project5
[root@server1 ~]# file Desktop
Desktop:   directory
[root@server1 ~]# file project Desktop
project:   ASCII text
Desktop:   directory
[root@server1 ~]# file *
Desktop:   directory
current:   symbolic link to project12
myprogram: ELF 64-bit LSB pie executable, x86_64, version 1 (SYSV),
dynamically linked, for GNU/Linux 3.2.0, stripped
myscript:  Bourne-Again shell script text executable
project:   ASCII text
project1:  ASCII text
project12: ASCII text
project13: empty
project2:  ASCII text
project3:  ASCII text
project4:  ASCII text
project5:  ASCII text
[root@server1 ~]#_
```

As shown in the preceding example, the `file` command can also identify the differences between types of executable files. The myscript file is a text file that contains executable commands (also known as a **shell script**), whereas the myprogram file is a 64-bit executable compiled program for the x86_64 CPU platform. The `file` command also identifies empty files such as project13 in the previous example.

You can also use the `stat` **command** to display additional details for a file, including the date and time a file was created (the birth time), as well as the last time the file was accessed, or its contents modified, or file information changed. Following is an example of using the `stat` command to view these details for the project file:

```
[root@server1 ~]# stat project
  File: project
  Size: 71          Blocks: 2          IO Block: 4096    regular file
Device: 8,3    Inode: 1179655    Links: 1
Access: (0644/-rw-r--r--) Uid: (0/root) Gid: (0/root)
Context: system_u:object_r:admin_home_t:s0
Access: 2023-09-03 12:15:40.462610154 -0400
Modify: 2023-09-02 22:00:11.840345812 -0400
Change: 2023-09-02 22:00:11.840345812 -0400
 Birth: 2023-09-01 16:55:46.462610154 -0400
[root@server1 ~]#_
```

Some filenames inside each user's home directory represent important configuration files or program directories. Because these files are rarely edited by the user and can clutter the listing of files, they are normally hidden from view when using the `ls` and `file` commands. Recall that filenames for hidden files start with a period character (.). To view them, pass the –a option to the `ls` command. Some hidden files that are commonly seen in the root user's home directory are shown next:

```
[root@server1 ~]# ls
current   myprogram  project    project12   project2   project4
```

```
Desktop  myscript   project1   project13   project3   project5
[root@server1 ~]# ls -a
.                    .bash_profile   current     project     project2    .pki
..                   .bashrc         Desktop     project1    project3    .tcshrc
.bash_history   .cache          myprogram   project12   project4
.bash_logout    .config         myscript    project13   project5
[root@server1 ~]#_
```

As discussed earlier, the (.) character refers to the current working directory and the (..) character refers to the parent directory relative to your current location in the directory tree. Each of these pointers is seen as a special (or fictitious) file when using the ls -a command, as each starts with a period.

You can also specify several options simultaneously for most commands on the command line and receive the combined functionality of all the options. For example, to view all hidden files and their file types, you could combine the -a and -F options:

```
[root@server1 ~]# ls -aF
.                    .bash_profile   current@    project     project2    .pki/
..                   .bashrc         Desktop/    project1    project3    .tcshrc
.bash_history   .cache/         myprogram   project12   project4
.bash_logout    .config/        myscript    project13   project5
[root@server1 ~]#_
```

To view files and subdirectories under a directory, you can add the recursive (-R) option to the to the ls command, or use the `tree` command. The following example uses these commands to display the files and subdirectories underneath the Desktop directory:

```
[root@server1 ~]# ls -R Desktop
Desktop/:
project-tracking   social   stuff

Desktop/project-tracking:
project1.xlsx   project2.xlsx   project3.xlsx

Desktop/social:
confirmations.docx   event-poster.pdf   events-calendar.cip

Desktop/stuff:
quotes.txt  todo.txt
[root@server1 ~]# tree Desktop
Desktop/
├── project-tracking
│   ├── project1.xlsx
│   ├── project2.xlsx
│   └── project3.xlsx
├── social
│   ├── confirmations.docx
│   ├── event-poster.pdf
│   └── events-calendar.cip
└── stuff
    ├── quotes.txt
    └── todo.txt

3 directories, 8 files
[root@server1 ~]#_
```

Note 11

To instead display only the subdirectories under the Desktop directory, you could add the –d option to the ls and tree commands shown in the previous example.

While the ls options discussed in this section (–l, –F, –a, –R, –d) are the most common you would use when navigating the Linux directory tree, there are many more available. Table 3-2 lists the most common of these options and their descriptions.

Table 3-2   Common options to the ls command

Option	Description
-a --all	Lists all filenames
-A --almost-all	Lists most filenames (excludes the . and .. special files)
-C	Lists filenames in column format
--color=none	Lists filenames without color
-d --directory	Lists directory names instead of their contents
-f	Lists all filenames without sorting
-F --classify	Lists filenames classified by file type
--full-time	Lists filenames in long format and displays the full modification time
-l	Lists filenames in long format
-lhs -l --human- readable --size	Lists filenames in long format with human-readable (easy-to-read) file sizes
-lG -l --no-group -o	Lists filenames in long format but omits the group information
-r --reverse	Lists filenames reverse sorted
-R --recursive	Lists filenames in the specified directory and all subdirectories
-s --size	Lists filenames and their associated sizes in blocks (on most systems, each block is 1 KB)
-S	Lists filenames sorted by file size (largest first)
-t	Lists filenames sorted by modification time (newest first)
-U	Lists selected filenames without sorting
-x	Lists filenames in rows rather than in columns

Wildcard Metacharacters

In the previous section, you saw that the * metacharacter matches all the files in the current directory, much like a wildcard matches certain cards in a card game. As a result, the * metacharacter is called a wildcard metacharacter. Wildcard metacharacters can simplify commands that specify more than one filename on the command line, as you saw with the file command earlier. They match certain portions of filenames or the entire filename itself. Because they are interpreted by the shell, they can be used with most common Linux filesystem commands, including those that have already been mentioned (ls, file, stat, tree, and cd). Table 3-3 displays a list of wildcard metacharacters and their descriptions.

Table 3-3   Wildcard Metacharacters

Metacharacter	Description
*	Matches 0 or more characters in a filename
?	Matches 1 character in a filename
[aegh]	Matches 1 character in a filename—provided this character is either an a, e, g, or h
[a-e]	Matches 1 character in a filename—provided this character is either an a, b, c, d, or e
[!a-e]	Matches 1 character in a filename—provided this character is NOT an a, b, c, d, or e

Wildcards can be demonstrated using the ls command. Examples of using wildcard metacharacters to narrow the listing produced by the ls command are shown next.

```
[root@server1 ~]# ls
current     myprogram  project    project12   project2   project4
document1  myscript    project1   project13   project3   project5
[root@server1 ~]# ls project*
project  project1  project12  project13  project2  project3  project4  project5
[root@server1 ~]# ls project?
project1  project2  project3  project4  project5
[root@server1 ~]# ls project??
project12  project13
[root@server1 ~]# ls project[135]
project1  project3  project5
[root@server1 ~]# ls project[!135]
project2  project4
[root@server1 ~]#_
```

Note 12

Using wildcards to match multiple files or directories within a command is often called file globbing.

Displaying the Contents of Text Files

So far, this chapter has discussed commands that can be used to navigate the Linux directory structure and view filenames and file types; it is usual now to display the contents of these files. By far, the most common file type that Linux users display is text files. These files are usually shell scripts, source code files, user documents, or configuration files for Linux components or services. To view an entire text file on the terminal screen (also referred to as concatenation), you can use the cat command. The following is an example of using the cat command to display the contents of the fictitious file project4:

```
[root@server1 ~]# ls
current     myprogram  project    project12  project2   project4
document1   myscript   project1   project13  project3   project5
[root@server1 ~]# cat project4
Hi there, I hope this day finds you well.

Unfortunately, we were not able to make it to your dining
room this year while vacationing in Algonquin Park - I
especially wished to see the model of the Highland Inn
and the train station in the dining room.

I have been reading on the history of Algonquin Park but
nowhere could I find a description of where the Highland
Inn was originally located on Cache Lake.

If it is no trouble, could you kindly let me know such that
I need not wait until next year when I visit your lodge?

Regards,
Mackenzie Elizabeth
[root@server1 ~]#_
```

You can also use the cat command to display the line number of each line in the file in addition to the contents by passing the –n option to the cat command. In the following example, the number of each line in the project4 file is displayed:

```
[root@server1 ~]# cat -n project4
     1  Hi there, I hope this day finds you well.
     2
     3  Unfortunately, we were not able to make it to your dining
     4  room this year while vacationing in Algonquin Park - I
     5  especially wished to see the model of the Highland Inn
     6  and the train station in the dining room.
     7
     8  I have been reading on the history of Algonquin Park but
     9  nowhere could I find a description of where the Highland
    10  Inn was originally located on Cache Lake.
    11
    12  If it is no trouble, could you kindly let me know such that
    13  I need not wait until next year when I visit your lodge?
    14
    15  Regards,
    16  Mackenzie Elizabeth
[root@server1 ~]#_
```

In some cases, you might want to display the contents of a certain text file in reverse order, which is useful when displaying files that have text appended to them continuously by system services. These files, also known as log files, contain the most recent entries at the bottom of the file. To display a file in reverse order, use the tac command (tac is cat spelled backwards), as shown next with the file project4:

```
[root@server1 ~]# tac project4
Mackenzie Elizabeth
Regards,
```

```
I need not wait until next year when I visit your lodge?
If it is no trouble, could you kindly let me know such that

Inn was originally located on Cache Lake.
nowhere could I find a description of where the Highland
I have been reading on the history of Algonquin Park but

and the train station in the dining room.
especially wished to see the model of the Highland Inn
room this year while vacationing in Algonquin Park - I
Unfortunately, we were not able to make it to your dining

Hi there, I hope this day finds you well.
[root@server1 ~]#_
```

If the file displayed is very large and you only want to view the first few lines of it, you can use the head **command**. The head command displays the first 10 lines (including blank lines) of a text file to the terminal screen but can also take a numeric option specifying a different number of lines to display. The following shows an example of using the head command to view the top of the project4 file:

```
[root@server1 ~]# head project4
Hi there, I hope this day finds you well.

Unfortunately, we were not able to make it to your dining
room this year while vacationing in Algonquin Park - I
especially wished to see the model of the Highland Inn
and the train station in the dining room.

I have been reading on the history of Algonquin Park but
nowhere could I find a description of where the Highland
Inn was originally located on Cache Lake.
[root@server1 ~]# head -3 project4
Hi there, I hope this day finds you well.

Unfortunately, we were not able to make it to your dining
[root@server1 ~]#_
```

Just as the head command displays the beginning of text files, the tail **command** can be used to display the end of text files. By default, the tail command displays the final 10 lines of a file, but it can also take a numeric option specifying the number of lines to display on the terminal screen, as shown in the following example with the project4 file:

```
[root@server1 ~]# tail project4

I have been reading on the history of Algonquin Park but
nowhere could I find a description of where the Highland
Inn was originally located on Cache Lake.

If it is no trouble, could you kindly let me know such that
I need not wait until next year when I visit your lodge?

Regards,
Mackenzie Elizabeth
[root@server1 ~]# tail -2 project4
```

```
Regards,
Mackenzie Elizabeth
[root@server1 ~]#_
```

> **Note 13**
>
> The -f option to the tail command displays the final 10 lines of a file but keeps the file open so that you can see when additional lines are added to the end of the file. This is especially useful when viewing log files while troubleshooting a system problem. For example, you could run the tail -f logfile command in one terminal while performing troubleshooting actions in another terminal. After performing each troubleshooting action, the associated events will be displayed in the terminal running the tail command.

Although some text files are small enough to be displayed completely on the terminal screen, you might encounter text files that are too large to fit in a single screen. In this case, the cat command sends the entire file contents to the terminal screen; however, the screen only displays as much of the text as it has room for. To display a large text file in a page-by-page fashion, you need to use the more and less commands.

The more command gets its name from the pg command once used on UNIX systems. The pg command displayed a text file page-by-page on the terminal screen, starting at the beginning of the file; pressing the spacebar or Enter key displays the next page, and so on. The more command does more than pg did, because it displays the next complete page of a text file if you press the spacebar but displays only the next line of a text file if you press Enter. In that way, you can browse the contents of a text file page-by-page or line-by-line. The fictitious file project5 is an excerpt from Shakespeare's tragedy *Macbeth* and is too large to be displayed fully on the terminal screen using the cat command. Using the more command to view its contents results in the following output:

```
[root@server1 ~]# more project5
Go bid thy mistress, when my drink is ready,
She strike upon the bell. Get thee to bed.
Is this a dagger which I see before me,
The handle toward my hand? Come, let me clutch thee.
I have thee not, and yet I see thee still.
Art thou not, fatal vision, sensible
To feeling as to sight? or art thou but
A dagger of the mind, a false creation,
Proceeding from the heat-oppressed brain?
I see thee yet, in form as palpable
As this which now I draw.
Thou marshall'st me the way that I was going;
And such an instrument I was to use.
Mine eyes are made the fools o' the other senses,
Or else worth all the rest; I see thee still,
And on thy blade and dudgeon gouts of blood,
Which was not so before. There's no such thing:
It is the bloody business which informs
Thus to mine eyes. Now o'er the one halfworld
Nature seems dead, and wicked dreams abuse
The curtain'd sleep; witchcraft celebrates
Pale Hecate's offerings, and wither'd murder,
Alarum'd by his sentinel, the wolf,
--More--(71%)
```

As you can see in the preceding output, the more command displays the first page without returning you to the shell prompt. Instead, the more command displays a prompt at the bottom of the terminal screen that indicates how much of the file is displayed on the screen as a percentage of the total file size. In the preceding example, 71 percent of the project5 file is displayed. At this prompt, you can press the spacebar to advance one whole page, or you can press the Enter key to advance to the next line. In addition, the more command allows other user interactions at this prompt. Pressing the h character at the prompt displays a help screen, which is shown in the following output, and pressing the q character quits the more command completely without viewing the remainder of the file.

```
--More--(71%)
Most commands optionally preceded by integer argument k. Defaults in
brackets. Star (*) indicates argument becomes new default.
-------------------------------------------------------------------
<space>                 Display next k lines of text
z                       Display next k lines of text
<return>                Display next k lines of text [1]
d or ctrl-D             Scroll k lines [current scroll size, initially 11]
q or Q or <interrupt>   Exit from more
s                       Skip forward k lines of text [1]
f                       Skip forward k screenfuls of text [1]
b or ctrl-B             Skip backward k screenfuls of text [1]
'                       Go to place where previous search started
=                       Display current line number
/<regular expression>   Search for kth occurrence of expression [1]
n                       Search for kth occurrence of last r.e [1]
!<cmd> or :!<cmd>       Execute <cmd> in a subshell
v                       Start up /usr/bin/vi at current line
ctrl-L                  Redraw screen
:n                      Go to kth next file [1]
:p                      Go to kth previous file [1]
:f                      Display current filename and line number
.                       Repeat previous command
-------------------------------------------------------------------
--More—(71%)
```

Just as the more command was named for allowing more user functionality, the less command is named for doing more than the more command (remember that "less is more," more or less). Like the more command, the less command can browse the contents of a text file page-by-page by pressing the spacebar and line-by-line by pressing the Enter key; however, you can also use the arrow keys on the keyboard to scroll up and down the contents of the file. The output of the less command, when used to view the project5 file, is as follows:

```
[root@server1 ~]# less project5
Go bid thy mistress, when my drink is ready,
She strike upon the bell. Get thee to bed.
Is this a dagger which I see before me,
The handle toward my hand? Come, let me clutch thee.
I have thee not, and yet I see thee still.
Art thou not, fatal vision, sensible
To feeling as to sight? or art thou but
A dagger of the mind, a false creation,
Proceeding from the heat-oppressed brain?
I see thee yet, in form as palpable
As this which now I draw.
```

```
Thou marshall'st me the way that I was going;
And such an instrument I was to use.
Mine eyes are made the fools o' the other senses,
Or else worth all the rest; I see thee still,
And on thy blade and dudgeon gouts of blood,
Which was not so before. There's no such thing:
It is the bloody business which informs
Thus to mine eyes. Now o'er the one halfworld
Nature seems dead, and wicked dreams abuse
The curtain'd sleep; witchcraft celebrates
Pale Hecate's offerings, and wither'd murder,
Alarum'd by his sentinel, the wolf,
Whose howl's his watch, thus with his stealthy pace.
project5
```

Like the more command, the less command displays a prompt at the bottom of the file using the : character or the filename of the file being viewed (project5 in our example), yet the less command contains more keyboard shortcuts for searching out text within files. At the prompt, you can press the h key to obtain a help screen or the q key to quit. The first help screen for the less command is shown next:

```
                SUMMARY OF LESS COMMANDS


  Commands marked with * may be preceded by a number, N.
  Notes in parentheses indicate the behavior if N is given.
  A key preceded by a caret indicates the Ctrl key; thus ^K is ctrl-K.


h  H                    Display this help.
q  :q  Q  :Q  ZZ        Exit.
--------------------------------------------------------------------


                      MOVING


e   ^E   j   ^N  CR  * Forward  one line   (or N lines).
y   ^Y   k   ^K  ^P  * Backward one line   (or N lines).
f   ^F   ^V  SPACE   * Forward  one window (or N lines).
b   ^B   ESC-v       * Backward one window (or N lines).
z                   * Forward  one window (and set window to N).
w                   * Backward one window (and set window to N).
ESC-SPACE           * Forward  one window, but don't stop at end-of-file.
d   ^D              * Forward  one half-window (and set half-window to N).
u   ^U              * Backward one half-window (and set half-window to N).
ESC-) RightArrow    * Right one half screen width (or N positions).


HELP -- Press RETURN for more, or q when done
```

The more and less commands can also be used in conjunction with the output of commands if that output is too large to fit on the terminal screen. To do this, use the | metacharacter after the command, followed by either the more or less command, as follows:

```
[root@server1 ~]# cd /etc
[root@server1 etc]# ls -l | more
total 3688
-rw-r--r--   1 root     root       15276 Mar 22 12:20 a2ps.cfg
```

```
-rw-r--r--   1 root     root         2562 Mar 22 12:20 a2ps-site.cfg
drwxr-xr-x   4 root     root         4096 Jun 11 08:45 acpi
-rw-r--r--   1 root     root           46 Jun 16 16:42 adjtime
drwxr-xr-x   2 root     root         4096 Jun 11 08:47 aep
-rw-r--r--   1 root     root          688 Feb 17 00:35 aep.conf
-rw-r--r--   1 root     root          703 Feb 17 00:35 aeplog.conf
drwxr-xr-x   4 root     root         4096 Jun 11 08:47 alchemist
-rw-r--r--   1 root     root         1419 Jan 26 10:14 aliases
-rw-r-----   1 root     smmsp       12288 Jun 17 13:17 aliases.db
drwxr-xr-x   2 root     root         4096 Jun 11 11:11 alternatives
drwxr-xr-x   3 amanda   disk         4096 Jun 11 10:16 amanda
-rw-r--r--   1 amanda   disk            0 Mar 22 12:28 amandates
-rw-------   1 root     root          688 Mar  4 22:34 amd.conf
-rw-r-----   1 root     root          105 Mar  4 22:34 amd.net
-rw-r--r--   1 root     root          317 Feb 15 14:33 anacrontab
-rw-r--r--   1 root     root          331 May  5 08:07 ant.conf
-rw-r--r--   1 root     root         6200 Jun 16 16:42 asound.state
drwxr-xr-x   3 root     root         4096 Jun 11 10:37 atalk
-rw-------   1 root     root            1 May  5 13:39 at.deny
-rw-r--r--   1 root     root          325 Apr 14 13:39 auto.master
-rw-r--r--   1 root     root          581 Apr 14 13:39 auto.misc
--More--
```

In the preceding example, the output of the `ls  -l` command was redirected to the `more` command, which displays the first page of output on the terminal. You can then advance through the output page-by-page or line-by-line. This type of redirection is discussed in Chapter 7.

> **Note 14**
>
> You can also use the `diff command` to identify the content differences between two text files, which is often useful when comparing revisions of source code or configuration files on a Linux system. For example, the `diff file1 file2` command would list the lines that are different between file1 and file2.

Displaying the Contents of Binary Files

It is important to employ text file commands, such as `cat`, `tac`, `head`, `tail`, `more`, and `less`, only on files that contain text; otherwise, you might find yourself with random output on the terminal screen or even a dysfunctional terminal. To view the contents of binary files, you typically use the program that was used to create the file. However, some commands can be used to safely display the contents of most binary files. The `strings command` searches for text characters in a binary file and outputs them to the screen. In many cases, these text characters might indicate what the binary file is used for. For example, to find the text characters inside the /bin/echo binary executable program page-by-page, you could use the following command:

```
[root@server1 ~]# strings /bin/echo | more
/lib/ld-linux.so.2
PTRh|
<nt7<e
|[^_]
[^_]
[^_]
Try '%s --help' for more information.
Usage: %s [OPTION]... [STRING]...
```

```
Echo the STRING(s) to standard output.
  -n          do not output the trailing newline
  -e          enable interpretation of the backslash-escaped characters
              listed below
  -E          disable interpretation of those sequences in STRINGs
  --help      display this help and exit
  --version   output version information and exit
Without -E, the following sequences are recognized and interpolated:
  \NNN    the character whose ASCII code is NNN (octal)
  \\      backslash
--More--
```

Although this output might not be easy to read, it does contain portions of text that can point a user in the right direction to find out more about the /bin/echo command. Another command that is safe to use on binary files and text files is the od command, which displays the contents of the file in octal format (numeric base 8 format). An example of using the od command to display the first five lines of the file project4 is shown in the following example:

```
[root@server1 ~]# od project4 | head -5
0000000 064510 072040 062550 062562 020054 020111 067550 062560
0000020 072040 064550 020163 060544 020171 064546 062156 020163
0000040 067571 020165 062567 066154 006456 006412 052412 063156
0000060 071157 072564 060556 062564 074554 073440 020145 062567
0000100 062562 067040 072157 060440 066142 020145 067564 066440
[root@server1 ~]#_
```

> **Note 15**
>
> You can use the −x option to the od command to display a file in hexadecimal format (numeric base 16 format).

Searching for Text within Files

Recall that Linux was modeled after the UNIX operating system. The UNIX operating system is often referred to as the "grandfather" of all operating systems because it is over 40 years old and has formed the basis for most advances in computing technology. The major use of the UNIX operating system in the past 40 years involved simplifying business and scientific management through database applications. As a result, many commands (referred to as text tools) were developed for the UNIX operating system that could search for and manipulate text, such as database information, in many advantageous ways. A set of text wildcards was also developed to ease the searching of specific text information. These text wildcards are called regular expressions (regexp) and are recognized by text tools, as well as most modern programming languages, such as Python and C++.

Because Linux is a close relative of the UNIX operating system, these text tools and regular expressions are available to Linux as well. By combining text tools, a typical Linux system can search for and manipulate data in almost every way possible (as you will see later). As a result, regular expressions and the text tools that use them are frequently used today.

Regular Expressions

As mentioned earlier, regular expressions allow you to specify a certain pattern of text within a text document. They work similarly to wildcard metacharacters in that they are used to match characters, yet they have many differences:

- Wildcard metacharacters are interpreted by the shell, whereas regular expressions are interpreted by a text tool program.

- Wildcard metacharacters match characters in filenames (or directory names) on a Linux filesystem, whereas regular expressions match characters *within* text files on a Linux filesystem.
- Wildcard metacharacters typically have different definitions than regular expression metacharacters.
- More regular expression metacharacters are available than wildcard metacharacters.

In addition, regular expression metacharacters are divided into two categories: common (basic) regular expressions and extended regular expressions. Common regular expressions are available to most text tools; however, extended regular expressions are less common and available in only certain text tools. Table 3-4 shows definitions and examples of some common and extended regular expressions.

Table 3-4 Regular expressions

Regular Expression	Description	Example	Type
*	Matches 0 or more occurrences of the previous character	letter* matches lette, letter, letterr, letterrrr, letterrrrr, and so on	Common
?	Matches 0 or 1 occurrences of the previous character	letter? matches lette, letter	Extended
+	Matches 1 or more occurrences of the previous character	letter+ matches letter, letterr, letterrrr, letterrrrr, and so on	Extended
. (period)	Matches 1 character of any type	letter. matches lettera, letterb, letterc, letter1, letter2, letter3, and so on	Common
[...]	Matches one character from the range specified within the braces	letter[1238] matches letter1, letter2, letter3, and letter8; letter[a-c] matches lettera, letterb, and letterc	Common
[^...]	Matches one character NOT from the range specified within the braces	letter[^1238] matches letter4, letter5, letter6, lettera, letterb, and so on (any character except 1, 2, 3, or 8)	Common
{ }	Matches a specific number or range of the previous character	letter{3} matches letterrr, whereas letter {2,4} matches letterr, letterrr, and letterrrr	Extended
^	Matches the following characters if they are the first characters on the line	^letter matches letter if letter is the first set of characters in the line	Common
$	Matches the previous characters if they are the last characters on the line	letter$ matches letter if letter is the last set of characters in the line	Common
(... | ...)	Matches either of two sets of characters	(mother|father) matches the word "mother" or "father"	Extended

The grep Command

The most common way to search for information using regular expressions is the grep command. The grep command (the command name is short for global regular expression print) is used to display lines in a text file that match a certain common regular expression. To display lines of text that match extended regular expressions, you must use the egrep command (or the –E option to the grep command). In addition, the fgrep command (or the –F option to the grep command) does not interpret any regular expressions and consequently returns results much faster. Take, for example, the project4 file shown earlier:

```
[root@server1 ~]# cat project4
Hi there, I hope this day finds you well.
```

```
Unfortunately, we were not able to make it to your dining
room this year while vacationing in Algonquin Park - I
especially wished to see the model of the Highland Inn
and the train station in the dining room.

I have been reading on the history of Algonquin Park but
nowhere could I find a description of where the Highland
Inn was originally located on Cache Lake.

If it is no trouble, could you kindly let me know such that
I need not wait until next year when I visit your lodge?

Regards,
Mackenzie Elizabeth
[root@server1 ~]#_
```

The `grep` command requires two arguments at minimum, the first argument specifies which text to search for, and the remaining arguments specify the files to search. If a pattern of text is matched, the `grep` command displays the entire line on the terminal screen. For example, to list only those lines in the file project4 that contain the words "Algonquin Park," enter the following command:

```
[root@server1 ~]# grep "Algonquin Park" project4
room this year while vacationing in Algonquin Park - I
I have been reading on the history of Algonquin Park but
[root@server1 ~]#_
```

To return the lines that do not contain the text "Algonquin Park," you can use the –v option of the `grep` command to reverse the meaning of the previous command:

```
[root@server1 ~]# grep -v "Algonquin Park" project4
Hi there, I hope this day finds you well.

Unfortunately, we were not able to make it to your dining
especially wished to see the model of the Highland Inn
and the train station in the dining room.

nowhere could I find a description of where the Highland
Inn was originally located on Cache Lake.

If it is no trouble, could you kindly let me know such that
I need not wait until next year when I visit your lodge?

Regards,
Mackenzie Elizabeth
[root@server1 ~]#_
```

Keep in mind that the text being searched is case sensitive; to perform a case-insensitive search, use the –i option to the `grep` command:

```
[root@server1 ~]# grep "algonquin park" project4
[root@server1 ~]#_
[root@server1 ~]# grep -i "algonquin park" project4
room this year while vacationing in Algonquin Park - I
I have been reading on the history of Algonquin Park but
[root@server1 ~]#_
```

Another important note to keep in mind regarding text tools such as grep is that they match only patterns of text; they are unable to discern words or phrases unless they are specified. For example, if you want to search for the lines that contain the word "we," you can use the following grep command:

```
[root@server1 ~]# grep "we" project4
Hi there, I hope this day finds you well.
Unfortunately, we were not able to make it to your dining
[root@server1 ~]#_
```

However, notice from the preceding output that the first line displayed does not contain the word "we"; the word "well" contains the text pattern "we" and is displayed as a result. To display only lines that contain the word "we," you can type the following to match the letters "we" surrounded by space characters:

```
[root@server1 ~]# grep " we " project4
Unfortunately, we were not able to make it to your dining
[root@server1 ~]#_
```

All of the previous grep examples did not use regular expression metacharacters to search for text in the project4 file. Some examples of using regular expressions (see Table 3-4) when searching this file are shown throughout the remainder of this section.

To view lines that contain the word "toe" or "the" or "tie," you can enter the following command:

```
[root@server1 ~]# grep " t.e " project4
especially wished to see the model of the Highland Inn
and the train station in the dining room.
I have been reading on the history of Algonquin Park but
nowhere could I find a description of where the Highland
[root@server1 ~]#_
```

To view lines that start with the word "I," you can enter the following command:

```
[root@server1 ~]# grep "^I " project4
I have been reading on the history of Algonquin Park but
I need not wait until next year when I visit your lodge?
[root@server1 ~]#_
```

To view lines that contain the text "lodge" or "Lake," you need to use an extended regular expression and the egrep command, as follows:

```
[root@server1 ~]# egrep "(lodge|Lake)" project4
Inn was originally located on Cache Lake.
I need not wait until next year when I visit your lodge?
[root@server1 ~]#_
```

Editing Text Files

Recall that most system configuration is stored in text files, as are shell scripts and program source code. Consequently, most Linux distributions come with an assortment of text editor programs that you can use to modify the contents of text files. Text editors come in two varieties: editors that can be used on the command line, including vi (vim), nano, and Emacs, and editors that can be used in a desktop environment, including Emacs (graphical version) and gedit.

The vi Editor

The **vi editor** (pronounced "vee eye") is one of the oldest and most popular visual text editors available for UNIX operating systems. Its Linux equivalent (known as vim, which is short for "vi improved") is equally popular and widely considered the standard Linux text editor. Although the vi editor is not the easiest of the editors to use when editing text files, it has the advantage of portability. A Fedora Linux user who is proficient in using the vi editor will find editing files on all other UNIX and Linux systems easy because the interface and features of the vi editor are nearly identical across Linux and UNIX systems. In addition, the vi editor supports regular expressions and can perform over 1,000 different functions for the user.

To open an existing text file for editing, you can type vi filename (or vim filename), where *filename* specifies the file to be edited. To open a new file for editing, type vi or vim at the command line:

```
[root@server1 ~]# vi
```

The vi editor then runs interactively and replaces the command-line interface with the following output:

```
~
~
~
~                           VIM - Vi IMproved
~
~                             version 8.2.4621
~                          by Bram Moolenaar et al.
~                       Modified by <bugzilla@redhat.com>
~                   Vim is open source and freely distributable
~
~                          Sponsor Vim development!
~           type   :help sponsor<Enter>    for information
~
~           type   :q<Enter>                to exit
~           type   :help<Enter>  or  <F1>  for on-line help
~           type   :help version8<Enter>   for version info
~
~
~
```

The tilde (~) characters on the left indicate the end of the file; they are pushed further down the screen as you enter text. The vi editor is called a bimodal editor because it functions in one of two modes: **command mode** and **insert mode**. The vi editor opens command mode, in which you must use the keyboard to perform functions, such as deleting text, copying text, saving changes to a file, and exiting the vi editor. To insert text into the document, you must enter insert mode by typing one of the characters listed in Table 3-5. One such method to enter insert mode is to type the i key while in command mode; the vi editor then displays INSERT at the bottom of the screen and allows the user to enter a sentence such as the following:

```
This is a sample sentence.
~
~
~
~
~
~
~
~
~
-- INSERT --
```

When in insert mode, you can use the keyboard to type text as required, but when finished you must press the Esc key to return to command mode to perform other functions via keys on the keyboard. Table 3-6 provides a list of keys useful in command mode and their associated functions. After you are in command mode, to save the text in a file called samplefile in the current directory, you need to type the : (colon) character (by pressing the Shift and ; keys simultaneously) to reach a : prompt where you can enter a command to save the contents of the current document to a file, as shown in the following example and in Table 3-7.

```
This is a sample sentence.
~
~
~
~
~
~
~
~
~
:w samplefile
```

As shown in Table 3-7, you can quit the vi editor by typing the : character and entering q!, which then returns the user to the shell prompt:

```
This is a sample sentence.
~
~
~
~
~
~
~
~
~
:q!
[root@server1 ~]#_
```

Table 3-5   Common keyboard keys used to change to and from insert mode

Key	Description
i	Changes to insert mode and places the cursor before the current character for entering text
a	Changes to insert mode and places the cursor after the current character for entering text
o	Changes to insert mode and opens a new line below the current line for entering text
r	Changes to insert mode to replace the current character only (once this character has been replaced with another one you supply, the editor switches back to command mode)
I	Changes to insert mode and places the cursor at the beginning of the current line for entering text
A	Changes to insert mode and places the cursor at the end of the current line for entering text
O	Changes to insert mode and opens a new line above the current line for entering text
Esc	Changes back to command mode while in insert mode

Table 3-6   Key combinations commonly used in command mode

Key	Description
w, W	Moves the cursor forward one word to the beginning of the next word
e, E	Moves the cursor forward one word to the end of the next word
b, B	Moves the cursor backward one word
53G	Moves the cursor to line 53
G	Moves the cursor to the last line in the document
0, ^	Moves the cursor to the beginning of the line
$	Moves the cursor to the end of the line
X	Deletes the character the cursor is on
3x	Deletes three characters starting from the character the cursor is on
dw	Deletes one word starting from the character the cursor is on
d3w, 3dw	Deletes three words starting from the character the cursor is on
dd	Deletes one whole line starting from the line the cursor is on
d3d, 3dd	Deletes three whole lines starting from the line the cursor is on
d$	Deletes from the cursor character to the end of the current line
d^, d0	Deletes from the cursor character to the beginning of the current line
yw	Copies one word (starting from the character the cursor is on) into a temporary buffer in memory for later use
y3w, 3yw	Copies three words (starting from the character the cursor is on) into a temporary buffer in memory for later use
yy	Copies the current line into a temporary buffer in memory for later use
y3y, 3yy	Copies three lines (starting from the current line) into a temporary buffer in memory for later use
y$	Copies the current line from the cursor to the end of the line into a temporary buffer in memory for later use
y^, y0	Copies the current line from the cursor to the beginning of the line into a temporary buffer in memory for later use
p	Pastes the contents of the temporary memory buffer underneath the current line
P	Pastes the contents of the temporary memory buffer above the current line
J	Joins the line below the current line to the current line
Ctrl+g	Displays current line statistics
Ctrl+w followed by s	Splits the screen horizontally
Ctrl+g followed by v	Splits the screen vertically
Ctrl+ww	Move to the next screen
Ctrl+w followed by _	Minimize current screen
Ctrl+w followed by =	Restore a minimized screen
u	Undoes the last function (undo)
.	Repeats the last function (repeat)
/pattern	Searches for the first occurrence of pattern in the forward direction
?pattern	Searches for the first occurrence of pattern in the reverse direction
n	Repeats the previous search in the forward direction
N	Repeats the previous search in the reverse direction

Table 3-7   Key combinations commonly used at the command mode : prompt

Function	Description
:q	Quits from the vi editor if no changes were made
:q!	Quits from the vi editor and does not save any changes
:wq	Saves any changes to the file and quits from the vi editor
:w filename	Saves the current document to a file called filename
:!date	Executes the date command using a BASH shell
:r !date	Reads the output of the date command into the document under the current line
:r filename	Reads the contents of the text file called filename into the document under the current line
:set all	Displays all vi environment options
:set option	Sets a vi environment option
:s/the/THE/g	Searches for the regular expression "the" and replaces each occurrence globally throughout the current line with the word "THE"
:1,$ s/the/THE/g	Searches for the regular expression "the" and replaces each occurrence globally from line 1 to the end of the document with the word "THE"
:split proposal1	Creates a new screen (split horizontally) to edit the file "proposal1"
:vsplit proposal1	Creates a new screen (split vertically) to edit the file "proposal1"
:tabe notes	Creates a new tab called "notes"
:tabs	Displays all tabs
:tabn	Moves to the next tab
:tabp	Moves to the previous tab
:help p	Displays help for vi commands that start with p
:help holy-grail	Displays help for all vi commands

The vi editor also offers some advanced features to Linux users, as explained in Table 3-7. Examples of some of these features are discussed next, using the project4 file shown earlier in this chapter. To edit the project4 file, type vi project4 and view the following screen:

```
Hi there, I hope this day finds you well.

Unfortunately, we were not able to make it to your dining
room this year while vacationing in Algonquin Park - I
especially wished to see the model of the Highland Inn
and the train station in the dining room.

I have been reading on the history of Algonquin Park but
nowhere could I find a description of where the Highland
Inn was originally located on Cache Lake.

If it is no trouble, could you kindly let me know such that
I need not wait until next year when I visit your lodge?

Regards,
Mackenzie Elizabeth
~
```

```
~
~
~
~
~
~
```
```
"project4" 17L, 583C
```

Note that the name of the file as well as the number of lines and characters in total are displayed at the bottom of the screen (project4 has 17 lines and 583 characters in this example). To insert the current date and time at the bottom of the file, you can move the cursor to the final line in the file and type the following at the : prompt while in command mode:

```
Hi there, I hope this day finds you well.

Unfortunately, we were not able to make it to your dining
room this year while vacationing in Algonquin Park - I
especially wished to see the model of the Highland Inn
and the train station in the dining room.

I have been reading on the history of Algonquin Park but
nowhere could I find a description of where the Highland
Inn was originally located on Cache Lake.

If it is no trouble, could you kindly let me know such that
I need not wait until next year when I visit your lodge?

Regards,
Mackenzie Elizabeth
~
~
~
~
~
~
~
~
```
```
:r !date
```

When you press Enter, the output of the date command is inserted below the current line:

```
Hi there, I hope this day finds you well.

Unfortunately, we were not able to make it to your dining
room this year while vacationing in Algonquin Park - I
especially wished to see the model of the Highland Inn
and the train station in the dining room.

I have been reading on the history of Algonquin Park but
nowhere could I find a description of where the Highland
Inn was originally located on Cache Lake.

If it is no trouble, could you kindly let me know such that
I need not wait until next year when I visit your lodge?
```

```
Regards,
Mackenzie Elizabeth
Sat Aug 7 18:33:10 EDT 2023
~
~
~
~
~
~
```

To change all occurrences of the word "Algonquin" to "ALGONQUIN," you can type the following at the : prompt while in command mode:

```
Hi there, I hope this day finds you well.

Unfortunately, we were not able to make it to your dining
room this year while vacationing in Algonquin Park - I
especially wished to see the model of the Highland Inn
and the train station in the dining room.

I have been reading on the history of Algonquin Park but
nowhere could I find a description of where the Highland
Inn was originally located on Cache Lake.

If it is no trouble, could you kindly let me know such that
I need not wait until next year when I visit your lodge?

Regards,
Mackenzie Elizabeth
Sat Aug 7 18:33:10 EDT 2023
~
~
~
~
~
~
```

```
:1,$ s/Algonquin/ALGONQUIN/g
```

The output changes to the following:

```
Hi there, I hope this day finds you well.

Unfortunately, we were not able to make it to your dining
room this year while vacationing in ALGONQUIN Park - I
especially wished to see the model of the Highland Inn
and the train station in the dining room.

I have been reading on the history of ALGONQUIN Park but
nowhere could I find a description of where the Highland
Inn was originally located on Cache Lake.

If it is no trouble, could you kindly let me know such that
I need not wait until next year when I visit your lodge?
```

```
Regards,
Mackenzie Elizabeth
Sat Aug 7 18:33:10 EDT 2023
~
~
~
~
~
~
~
```

Another attractive feature of the vi editor is its ability to customize the user environment through settings that can be altered at the : prompt while in command mode. Type set all at this prompt to observe the list of available settings and their current values:

```
:set all
--- Options ---
  aleph=224          fileencoding=      menuitems=25      swapsync=fsync
noarabic             fileformat=unix    modeline          switchbuf=
  arabicshape        filetype=          modelines=5       syntax=
noallowrevins      nofkmap              modifiable        tabstop=8
noaltkeymap          foldclose=         modified          tagbsearch
  ambiwidth=single   foldcolumn=0       more              taglength=0
noautoindent         foldenable         mouse=            tagrelative
noautoread           foldexpr=0         mousemodel=extend tagstack
noautowrite          foldignore=#       mousetime=500     term=xterm
noautowriteall       foldlevel=0      nonumber            notermbidi
-- More --
```

Note in the preceding output that, although some settings have a configured value (e.g., fileformat=unix), most settings are set to either on or off; those that are turned off are prefixed with a "no." In the preceding example, line numbering is turned off (nonumber in the preceding output); however, you can turn it on by typing set number at the : prompt while in command mode. This results in the following output in vi:

```
 1 Hi there, I hope this day finds you well.
 2
 3 Unfortunately, we were not able to make it to your dining
 4 room this year while vacationing in ALGONQUIN Park - I
 5 especially wished to see the model of the Highland Inn
 6 and the train station in the dining room.
 7
 8 I have been reading on the history of ALGONQUIN Park but
 9 nowhere could I find a description of where the Highland
10 Inn was originally located on Cache Lake.
11
12 If it is no trouble, could you kindly let me know such that
13 I need not wait until next year when I visit your lodge?
14
15 Regards,
16 Mackenzie Elizabeth
17 Sat Aug 7 18:33:10 EDT 2023
18
```

```
~
~
~
~
~
~
```

`:set number`

Conversely, to turn off line numbering, you could type `set nonumber` at the : prompt while in command mode.

> **Note 16**
>
> Most Linux distributions ship with the vim-minimal package, which provides a smaller version of the vi editor. You can install the vim-enhanced package to obtain full vi editor functionality. To do this on Fedora Linux, you can run the `dnf install vim-enhanced` command.

Other Common Text Editors

Although the vi editor is the most common text editor used on Linux and UNIX systems, you can instead choose a different text editor.

An alternative to the vi editor that offers an equal set of functionalities is the GNU **Emacs (Editor MACroS) editor**. Emacs is not installed by default on most Linux distributions. To install it on a Fedora system, you can run the command `dnf install emacs` at a command prompt to obtain Emacs from a free software repository on the Internet. Next, to open the project4 file in the Emacs editor in a command-line terminal, type `emacs project4` and the following is displayed on the terminal screen:

```
File  Edit  Options  Buffers  Tools  Conf Help
Hi there, I hope this day finds you well.

Unfortunately, we were not able to make it to your dining
room this year while vacationing in Algonquin Park - I
especially wished to see the model of the Highland Inn
and the train station in the dining room.

I have been reading on the history of Algonquin Park but
nowhere could I find a description of where the Highland
Inn was originally located on Cache Lake.

If it is no trouble, could you kindly let me know such that
I need not wait until next year when I visit your lodge?

Regards,
Mackenzie Elizabeth




-UU-:----F1  project4   Top L1    (Conf[Space])-------------------
For information about GNU Emacs and the GNU system, type C-h C-a.
```

The Emacs editor uses the Ctrl key in combination with certain letters to perform special functions, can be used with the LISP (LISt Processing) artificial intelligence programming language, and supports hundreds of keyboard functions, similar to the vi editor. Table 3-8 shows a list of some common keyboard functions used in the Emacs editor.

Table 3-8   Keyboard functions commonly used in the GNU Emacs editor

Key	Description
Ctrl+a	Moves the cursor to the beginning of the line
Ctrl+e	Moves the cursor to the end of the line
Ctrl+h	Displays Emacs documentation
Ctrl+d	Deletes the current character
Ctrl+k	Deletes all characters between the cursor and the end of the line
Esc+d	Deletes the current word
Ctrl+x + Ctrl+c	Exits the Emacs editor
Ctrl+x + Ctrl+s	Saves the current document
Ctrl+x + Ctrl+w	Saves the current document as a new filename
Ctrl+x + u	Undoes the last change

Another text editor that uses Ctrl key combinations for performing functions is the nano editor (based on the Pine UNIX editor). Unlike vi or Emacs, nano is a very basic and easy-to-use editor that many Linux administrators use to quickly modify configuration files if they don't need advanced functionality. As a result, nano is often installed by default on most modern Linux distributions. If you type nano project4, you will see the following displayed on the terminal screen:

```
GNU nano 6.0                          project4
Hi there, I hope this day finds you well.

Unfortunately, we were not able to make it to your dining
room this year while vacationing in Algonquin Park - I
especially wished to see the model of the Highland Inn
and the train station in the dining room.

I have been reading on the history of Algonquin Park but
nowhere could I find a description of where the Highland
Inn was originally located on Cache Lake.

If it is no trouble, could you kindly let me know such that
I need not wait until next year when I visit your lodge?


Regards,
Mackenzie Elizabeth



                         [ Read 16 lines ]
^G Help ^O WriteOut  ^W Where Is ^K Cut    ^T Execute ^C Location
^X Exit ^R Read File ^\ Replace  ^U Paste ^J Justify ^_ Go To Line
```

The bottom of the screen lists common Ctrl key combinations. The ^ symbol represents the Ctrl key. This means that, to exit nano, you can press Ctrl+x (^X = Ctrl+x).

If you are using a desktop environment, there is often a graphical text editor provided by your desktop environment, as well as others that can be optionally installed. The **gedit editor** is one of the most common Linux graphical text editors, and functionally analogous to the Windows WordPad and Notepad editors. If you type `gedit project4` within a desktop environment, you will be able to edit the project4 file content graphically, as well as access any gedit functionality from the drop-down menu shown in Figure 3-3.

Figure 3-3   The gedit text editor

Summary

- The Linux filesystem is arranged hierarchically using a series of directories to store files. The location of these directories and files can be described using a relative or absolute pathname. The Linux filesystem can contain many types of files, such as text files, binary data, executable programs, directories, linked files, and special device files.

- The `ls` command can be used to view filenames and offers a wide range of options to modify this view.

- Wildcard metacharacters are special keyboard characters. They can be used to simplify the selection of several files when using common Linux file commands.

- Text files are the most common file type whose contents can be viewed by several utilities, such as `head`, `tail`, `cat`, `tac`, `more`, and `less`.

- Regular expression metacharacters can be used to specify certain patterns of text when used with certain programming languages and text tool utilities, such as `grep`.

- Although many command-line and graphical text editors exist, vi (vim) is a powerful, bimodal text editor that is standard on most UNIX and Linux systems.

Key Terms

~ metacharacter
absolute pathname
binary data file
`cat` command
`cd (change directory)` command
command mode
concatenation
`diff` command
directory
`egrep` command
Emacs (Editor MACroS) editor
executable program
`fgrep` command
`file` command
file globbing
filename
filename extension

gedit editor
`grep` command
`head` command
home directory
insert mode
`less` command
linked file
`ll` command
log file
`ls` command
`more` command
named pipe file
nano editor
`od` command
parent directory
`pwd` (print working
    directory) command

regular expressions (regexp)
relative pathname
shell script
socket file
special device file
`stat` command
`strings` command
subdirectory
Tab-completion feature
`tac` command
`tail` command
text file
text tool
`tree` command
vi editor
wildcard metacharacter

Review Questions

1. A directory is a type of file.
   a. True
   b. False

2. Which command would a user type on the command line to find out the current directory in the directory tree?
   a. pd
   b. cd
   c. where
   d. pwd

3. Which of the following is an absolute pathname? (Choose all that apply.)
   a. C:\myfolder\resume
   b. resume
   c. /home/resume
   d. C:home/resume

4. A special device file is used to _____.
   a. enable proprietary custom-built devices to work with Linux
   b. represent hardware devices
   c. keep a list of device settings specific to each individual user
   d. do nothing in Linux

5. If a user's current directory is /home/mary/project1, which command could they use to move to the etc directory directly under the root?
   a. cd ..
   b. cd etc

   c. cd /etc
   d. cd \etc

6. After typing the `ls -a` command, you notice a file whose filename begins with a period (.). What does this mean?
   a. It is a binary file.
   b. It is a system file.
   c. It is a file in the current directory.
   d. It is a hidden file.

7. After typing the `ls -F` command, you notice a filename that ends with an * (asterisk) character. What does this mean?
   a. It is a hidden file.
   b. It is a linked file.
   c. It is a special device file.
   d. It is an executable file.

8. The vi editor can function in which two of the following modes? (Choose both that apply.)
   a. Command
   b. Input
   c. Interactive
   d. Insert

9. The `less` command offers less functionality than the `more` command.
   a. True
   b. False

10. Which command searches for and displays any text contents of a binary file?
    a. `text`
    b. `strings`
    c. `od`
    d. `less`

11. How can a user switch from insert mode to command mode when using the vi editor?
    a. Press the Ctrl+Alt+Del keys simultaneously.
    b. Press the Del key.
    c. Type a : character.
    d. Press the Esc key.

12. If "resume" is the name of a file in the home directory off the root of the filesystem and your present working directory is home, what is the relative name for the file named resume?
    a. /home/resume
    b. /resume
    c. resume
    d. \home\resume

13. What will the following wildcard expression return: `file[a-c]`?
    a. `filea-c`
    b. `filea, filec`
    c. `filea, fileb, filec`
    d. `fileabc`

14. What will typing `q!` at the : prompt in command mode do when using the vi editor?
    a. Quit as no changes were made.
    b. Quit after saving any changes.
    c. Nothing because the ! is a metacharacter.
    d. Quit without saving any changes.

15. A user types the command `head /poems/mary`. What will be displayed on the terminal screen?
    a. The first line of the file mary
    b. The first 10 lines of the file mary
    c. The header for the file mary
    d. The first 20 lines of the file mary

16. The `tac` command _____.
    a. displays the contents of a file in reverse order, last line first and first line last
    b. displays the contents of hidden files
    c. displays the contents of a file in reverse order, last word on the line first and first word on the line last
    d. is not a valid Linux command

17. How can you specify a text pattern that must be at the beginning of a line of text using a regular expression?
    a. Precede the string with a /.
    b. Follow the string with a \.
    c. Precede the string with a $.
    d. Precede the string with a ^.

18. Linux has only one root directory per directory tree.
    a. True
    b. False

19. Using a regular expression, how can you indicate a character that is *not* an a or b or c or d?
    a. `[^abcd]`
    b. `not [a-d]`
    c. `[!a-d]`
    d. `!a-d`

20. A user typed the command `pwd` and saw the output: /home/jim/sales/pending. How could that user navigate to the /home/jim directory?
    a. `cd ..`
    b. `cd /jim`
    c. `cd ../..`
    d. `cd ./.`

Hands-On Projects

These projects should be completed in the order given. The hands-on projects presented in this chapter should take a total of three hours to complete. The requirements for this lab include:

- A computer with Fedora Linux installed according to Hands-On Project 2-1.

Project 3-1

Estimated Time: 30 minutes
Objective: Navigate the Linux filesystem.
Description: In this hands-on project, you log in to the computer and navigate the file structure.

1. Boot your Fedora Linux virtual machine. After your Linux system has been loaded, switch to a command-line terminal (tty5) by pressing **Ctrl+Alt+F5** and log in to the terminal using the user name of **root** and the password of **LINUXrocks!**.

2. At the command prompt, type **pwd** and press **Enter** to view the current working directory. What is your current working directory?

3. At the command prompt, type **cd** and press **Enter**. At the command prompt, type **pwd** and press **Enter** to view the current working directory. Did your current working directory change? Why or why not?

4. At the command prompt, type **cd .** and press **Enter**. At the command prompt, type **pwd** and press **Enter** to view the current working directory. Did your current working directory change? Why or why not?

5. At the command prompt, type **cd ..** and press **Enter**. At the command prompt, type **pwd** and press **Enter** to view the current working directory. Did your current working directory change? Why or why not?

6. At the command prompt, type **cd root** and press **Enter**. At the command prompt, type **pwd** and press **Enter** to view the current working directory. Did your current working directory change? Where are you now? Did you specify a relative or absolute pathname to your home directory when you used the **cd root** command?

7. At the command prompt, type **cd etc** and press **Enter**. What error message did you receive and why?

8. At the command prompt, type **cd /etc** and press **Enter**. At the command prompt, type **pwd** and press **Enter** to view the current working directory. Did your current working directory change? Did you specify a relative or absolute pathname to the /etc directory when you used the **cd /etc** command?

9. At the command prompt, type **cd /** and press **Enter**. At the command prompt, type **pwd** and press **Enter** to view the current working directory. Did your current working directory change? Did you specify a relative or absolute pathname to the / directory when you used the **cd /** command?

10. At the command prompt, type **cd ~user1** and then press **Enter**. At the command prompt, type **pwd** and press **Enter** to view the current working directory. Did your current working directory change? Which command discussed earlier performs the same function as the **cd ~** command?

11. At the command prompt, type **cd Desktop** and press **Enter** (be certain to use a capital D). At the command prompt, type **pwd** and press **Enter** to view the current working directory. Did your current working directory change? Where are you now? What kind of pathname did you use here (absolute or relative)?

12. Currently, you are in a subdirectory of user1's home folder, three levels below the root. To go up three parent directories to the / directory, type **cd ../../..** and press **Enter** at the command prompt. Next, type **pwd** and press **Enter** to ensure that you are in the / directory.

13. At the command prompt, type **cd /etc/samba** and press **Enter** to change the current working directory using an absolute pathname. Next, type **pwd** and press **Enter** at the command prompt to ensure that you have changed to the /etc/samba directory. Now, type the command **cd ../sysconfig** at the command prompt and press **Enter**. Type **pwd** and press **Enter** to view your current location. Explain how the relative pathname seen in the **cd ../sysconfig** command specified your current working directory.

14. At the command prompt, type **cd ../../home/user1/Desktop** and press **Enter** to change your current working directory to the Desktop directory under user1's home directory. Verify that you are in the target directory by typing the **pwd** command at a command prompt and press **Enter**. Would it have been more advantageous to use an absolute pathname to change to this directory instead of the relative pathname that you used?

15. Type **exit** and press **Enter** to log out of your shell.

Project 3-2

Estimated Time: 10 minutes
Objective: Use the BASH Tab-completion feature.
Description: In this hands-on project, you navigate the Linux filesystem using the Tab-completion feature of the BASH shell.

1. Switch to a command-line terminal (tty5) by pressing **Ctrl+Alt+F5** and log in to the terminal using the user name of **root** and the password of **LINUXrocks!**.

2. At the command prompt, type **cd /** and press **Enter**.

3. Next, type `cd ro` at the command prompt and press **Tab**. What is displayed on the screen and why? How many subdirectories under the root begin with "ro"?

4. Press the **Ctrl+c** keys to cancel the command and return to an empty command prompt.

5. At the command prompt, type `cd b` and press **Tab**. Did the display change?

6. Press the **Tab** key again. How many subdirectories under the root begin with "b"?

7. Type the letter **i**. Notice that the command now reads "cd bi." Press the **Tab** key again. Which directory did it expand to? Why? Press the **Ctrl+c** keys to cancel the command and return to an empty command prompt.

8. At the command prompt, type `cd m` and press **Tab**. Press **Tab** once again after hearing the beep. How many subdirectories under the root begin with "m"?

9. Type the letter **e**. Notice that the command now reads "cd me." Press **Tab**.

10. Press **Enter** to execute the command at the command prompt. Next, type the `pwd` command and press **Enter** to verify that you are in the /media directory.

11. Type `exit` and press **Enter** to log out of your shell.

Project 3-3

Estimated Time: 20 minutes
Objective: View Linux filenames and types.
Description: In this hands-on project, you examine files and file types using the `ls` and `file` commands.

1. Switch to a command-line terminal (tty5) by pressing **Ctrl+Alt+F5** and log in to the terminal using the user name of **root** and the password of **LINUXrocks!**.

2. At the command prompt, type `cd /etc` and press **Enter**. Verify that you are in the /etc directory by typing `pwd` at the command prompt and press **Enter**.

3. At the command prompt, type `ls` and press **Enter**. What do you see listed in the four columns? Do any of the files have extensions? What is the most common extension you see and what does it indicate? Is the list you are viewing on the screen the entire contents of /etc?

4. At the command prompt, type `ls | more` and then press **Enter** (the | symbol is usually near the Enter key on the keyboard and is obtained by pressing the Shift and \ keys in combination). What does the display show? Notice the highlighted --More-- prompt at the bottom of the screen. Press **Enter**. Press **Enter** again. Press **Enter** once more. Notice that each time you press Enter, you advance one line further into the file. Now, press the **spacebar**. Press the **spacebar** again. Notice that with each press of the spacebar, you advance one full page into the displayed directory contents. Press the **h** key to get a help screen. Examine the command options.

5. Press the **q** key to quit the `more` command and return to an empty command prompt.

6. At the command prompt, type `ls | less` and then press **Enter**. What does the display show? Notice the : at the bottom of the screen. Press **Enter**. Press **Enter** again. Press **Enter** once more. Notice that each time you press Enter, you advance one line further into the file. Now press the **spacebar**. Press the **spacebar** again. Notice that with each press of the spacebar, you advance one full page into the displayed directory contents. Press the **h** key to get a help screen. Examine the command options, and then press **q** to return to the command output.

7. Press the ↑ (up arrow) key. Press ↑ again. Press ↑ once more. Notice that each time you press the ↑ key, you go up one line in the file display toward the beginning of the file. Now, press the ↓ (down arrow) key. Press ↓ again. Press ↓ once more. Notice that each time you press the ↓ key, you move forward into the file display.

8. Press the **q** key to quit the `less` command and return to a shell command prompt.

9. At the command prompt, type `cd` and press **Enter**. At the command prompt, type `pwd` and press **Enter**. What is your current working directory? At the command prompt, type `ls` and press **Enter**.

10. At the command prompt, type `ls /etc` and press **Enter**. How does this output compare with what you saw in Step 9? Has your current directory changed? Verify your answer by typing `pwd` at the command prompt and press **Enter**. Notice that you were able to list the contents of another directory by giving the absolute name of it as an argument to the `ls` command without leaving the directory in which you are currently located.

11. At the command prompt, type `ls /etc/skel` and press **Enter**. Did you see a listing of any files? At the command prompt, type `ls -a /etc/skel` and press **Enter**. What is special about these files? What do the first two entries in the list (. and ..) represent?

12. At the command prompt, type `ls -aF /etc/skel` and press **Enter**. Which file types are available in the /etc/skel directory?

13. At the command prompt, type `ls -F /bin/*` and press **Enter**. What file types are present in the /bin directory?

14. At the command prompt, type `ls -R /etc/ssh` and press **Enter**. Note the files and subdirectories listed. Type `tree /etc/ssh` and press **Enter** and note the same output in a more friendly format. Next, type `tree -d /etc/ssh` and press **Enter**. What does the -d option specify?

15. At the command prompt, type `ls /boot` and press **Enter**. Next, type `ls -l /boot` and press **Enter**. What additional information is available on the screen? What types of files are available in the /boot directory? At the command prompt, type `ll /boot` and press **Enter**. Is the output any different from that of the `ls -l /boot` command you just entered? Why or why not?

16. At the command prompt, type `file /boot/*` to see the types of files in the /boot directory. Is this information more specific than the information you gathered in Step 15?

17. At the command prompt, type `file /etc` and press **Enter**. What kind of file is etc?

18. At the command prompt, type `file /etc/issue` and press **Enter**. What type of file is /etc/issue?

19. At the command prompt, type `stat /etc/issue` and press **Enter**. Note the time this file was last accessed.

20. Type `exit` and press **Enter** to log out of your shell.

Project 3-4

Estimated Time: 20 minutes
Objective: View the contents of text files.
Description: In this hands-on project, you display file contents using the `cat`, `tac`, `head`, `tail`, `strings`, and `od` commands.

1. Switch to a command-line terminal (tty5) by pressing **Ctrl+Alt+F5,** and then log in to the terminal using the user name of **root** and the password of **LINUXrocks!**.

2. At the command prompt, type `cat /etc/hosts` and press **Enter** to view the contents of the file hosts, which reside in the directory /etc. Next, type `cat -n /etc/hosts` and press **Enter**. How many lines does the file have? At the command prompt, type `tac /etc/hosts` and press **Enter** to view the same file in reverse order.

3. To see the contents of the same file in octal format instead of ASCII text, type `od /etc/hosts` at the command prompt and press **Enter**.

4. At the command prompt, type `cat /etc/services` and press **Enter**.

5. At the command prompt, type `head /etc/services` and press **Enter**. How many lines are displayed, and why?

6. At the command prompt, type `head -5 /etc/services` and press **Enter**. How many lines are displayed and why? Next, type `head -3 /etc/services` and press **Enter**. How many lines are displayed and why?

7. At the command prompt, type `tail /etc/services` and press **Enter**. What is displayed on the screen? How many lines are displayed and why?

8. At the command prompt, type `tail -5 /etc/services` and press **Enter**. How many lines are displayed and why? Type the `cat -n /etc/services` command at a command prompt and press **Enter** to justify your answer.

9. At the command prompt, type `file /bin/nice` and press **Enter**. What type of file is it? Should you use a text tool command on this file?

10. At the command prompt, type `strings /bin/nice` and press **Enter**. Notice that you can see some text within this binary file. Next, type `strings /bin/nice | less` to view the same content page-by-page. When finished, press **q** to quit the `less` command.

11. Type `exit` and press **Enter** to log out of your shell.

Project 3-5

Estimated Time: 50 minutes
Objective: Use the vi editor.
Description: In this hands-on project, you create and edit text files using the vi editor.

1. Switch to a command-line terminal (tty5) by pressing **Ctrl+Alt+F5** and log in to the terminal using the user name of **root** and the password of **LINUXrocks!**.

2. At the command prompt, type `dnf install vim-enhanced` and press **Enter**. Press **y** when prompted to install the vim-enhanced package.

3. At the command prompt, type `pwd`, press **Enter**, and ensure that /root is displayed, showing that you are in the root user's home folder. At the command prompt, type `vi sample1` and press **Enter** to open the vi editor and create a new text file called sample1. Notice that this name appears at the bottom of the screen along with the indication that it is a new file.

4. At the command prompt, type `My letter` and press **Enter**. Why was nothing displayed on the screen? To switch from command mode to insert mode so you can type text, press **i**. Notice that the word Insert appears at the bottom of the screen. Next, type `My letter` and notice that this text is displayed on the screen. What types of tasks can be accomplished in insert mode?

5. Press **Esc**. Did the cursor move? What mode are you in now? Press ← two times until the cursor is under the last t in letter. Press **x**. What happened? Next, press **i** to enter insert mode, then type the letter **h**. Was the letter h inserted before or after the cursor?

6. Press **Esc** to switch back to command mode and then move your cursor to the end of the line. Next, press **o** to open a line underneath the current line and enter insert mode.

7. Type the following:

    It might look like I am doing nothing, but at the cellular level I
    can assure you that I am quite busy.

8. Type `dd` to delete the line in the file.

9. Press **i** to enter insert mode, and then type:

    Hi there, I hope this day finds you well.

    and press **Enter**. Press **Enter** again. Type:

    Unfortunately, we were not able to make it to your dining

    and press **Enter**. Type:

    room this year while vacationing in Algonquin Park - I

    and press **Enter**. Type:

    especially wished to see the model of the Highland Inn

and press **Enter**. Type:

```
and the train station in the dining room.
```

and press **Enter**. Press **Enter** again. Type:

```
I have been reading on the history of Algonquin Park but
```

and press **Enter**. Type:

```
nowhere could I find a description of where the Highland
```

and press **Enter**. Type:

```
Inn was originally located on Cache Lake.
```

and press **Enter**. Press **Enter** again. Type:

```
If it is no trouble, could you kindly let me know such that
```

and press **Enter**. Type:

```
I need not wait until next year when I visit your lodge?
```

and press **Enter**. Press **Enter** again. Type:

```
Regards,
```

and press **Enter**. Type:

```
Mackenzie Elizabeth
```

and press **Enter**. You should now have the sample letter used in this chapter on your screen. It should resemble the letter in Figure 3-3.

10. Press **Esc** to switch to command mode. Next press the **Shift** and ; keys together to open the : prompt at the bottom of the screen. At this prompt, type **w** and press **Enter** to save the changes you have made to the file. What is displayed at the bottom of the file when you are finished?

11. Press the **Shift** and ; keys together again to open the : prompt at the bottom of the screen, type **q**, and then press **Enter** to exit the vi editor.

12. At the command prompt, type `ls` and press **Enter** to view the contents of your current directory. Notice that there is now a file called sample1 listed.

13. Next, type `file sample1` and press **Enter**. What type of file is sample1? At the command prompt, type `cat sample1` and press **Enter**.

14. At the command prompt, type `vi sample1` and press **Enter** to open the letter again in the vi editor. What is displayed at the bottom of the screen? How does this compare with Step 10?

15. Use the cursor keys to navigate to the bottom of the document. Press the **Shift** and ; keys together to open the : prompt at the bottom of the screen again, type `!date` and press **Enter**. The current system date and time appear at the bottom of the screen. As indicated, press **Enter** to return to the document.

16. Press the **Shift** and ; keys together to open the : prompt at the bottom of the screen again, type `r !date` and press **Enter**. What happened and why?

17. Use the cursor keys to position your cursor on the line in the document that displays the current date and time, and type **yy** to copy it to the buffer in memory. Next, use the cursor keys to position your cursor on the first line in the document, and type **P** (capitalized) to paste the contents of the memory buffer above your current line. Does the original line remain at the bottom of the document?

18. Use the cursor keys to position your cursor on the line at the end of the document that displays the current date and time, and type **dd** to delete it.

19. Use the cursor keys to position your cursor on the "t" in the word "there" on the second line of the file that reads **Hi there, I hope this day finds you well.**, and type `dw` to delete the word. Next, press **i** to enter insert mode, type the word `Bob`, and then press **Esc** to switch back to command mode.

20. Press the **Shift** and **;** keys together to open the : prompt at the bottom of the screen, type `w sample2` and press **Enter**. What happened?

21. Press **i** to enter insert mode, and type the word `test`. Next, press **Esc** to switch to command mode. Press the **Shift** and **;** keys together to open the : prompt at the bottom of the screen, type `q`, and press **Enter** to quit the vi editor. Were you able to quit? Why not?

22. Press the **Shift** and **;** keys together to open the : prompt at the bottom of the screen, type `q!`, and press **Enter** to quit the vi editor and discard any changes since the last save.

23. At the command prompt, type `ls` and press **Enter** to view the contents of your current directory. Notice it now includes a file called sample2, which was created in Step 20. Type `diff sample1 sample2` and press **Enter** to view the difference in content between the two files you created.

24. At the command prompt, type `vi sample2` and press **Enter** to open the letter again in the vi editor.

25. Use the cursor keys to position your cursor on the line that reads **Hi Bob, I hope this day finds you well.**

26. Press the **Shift** and **;** keys together to open the : prompt at the bottom of the screen, type `s/Bob/Barb/g`, and press **Enter** to change all occurrences of "Bob" to "Barb" on the current line.

27. Press the **Shift** and **;** keys together to open the : prompt at the bottom of the screen, type `1,$ s/to/TO/g`, and press **Enter** to change all occurrences of the word "to" to "TO" for the entire file.

28. Press the **u** key. What happened?

29. Press the **Shift** and **;** keys together to open the : prompt at the bottom of the screen, type `wq`, and press **Enter** to save your document and quit the vi editor.

30. At the command prompt, type `vi sample3` and press **Enter** to open a new file called sample3 in the vi editor. Press **i** to enter insert mode. Next, type `P.S. How were the flies this year?` Press the **Esc** key when finished.

31. Press the **Shift** and **;** keys together to open the : prompt at the bottom of the screen, type `wq`, and press **Enter** to save your document and quit the vi editor.

32. At the command prompt, type `vi sample1`, press **Enter** to open the file sample1 again, and use the cursor keys to position your cursor on the line that reads "Mackenzie Elizabeth."

33. Press the **Shift** and **;** keys together to open the : prompt at the bottom of the screen, type `r sample3`, and press **Enter** to insert the contents of the file sample3 below your current line.

34. Press the **Shift** and **;** keys together to open the : prompt at the bottom of the screen, type `s/flies/flies and bears/g` and press **Enter**. What happened and why?

35. Press the **Shift** and **;** keys together to open the : prompt at the bottom of the screen, type `set number`, and press **Enter** to turn on line numbering.

36. Press the **Shift** and **;** keys together to open the : prompt at the bottom of the screen, type `set nonumber`, and press **Enter** to turn off line numbering.

37. Press the **Shift** and **;** keys together to open the : prompt at the bottom of the screen, type `set all`, and press **Enter** to view all vi parameters. Press **Enter** to advance through the list, and press **q** when finished to return to the vi editor.

38. Press the **Shift** and **;** keys together to open the : prompt at the bottom of the screen again, type `wq`, and press **Enter** to save your document and quit the vi editor.

39. Type `exit` and press **Enter** to log out of your shell.

Project 3-6

Estimated Time: 20 minutes

Objective: Use wildcard metacharacters.

Description: In this hands-on project, you use the `ls` command alongside wildcard metacharacters in your shell to explore the contents of your home directory.

1. Switch to a command-line terminal (tty5) by pressing **Ctrl+Alt+F5** and log in to the terminal using the user name of **root** and the password of **LINUXrocks!**.

2. At the command prompt, type `pwd`, press **Enter**, and ensure /root is displayed showing that you are in the root user's home folder. At the command prompt, type `ls`. How many files with a name beginning with the word "sample" exist in **/root**?

3. At the command prompt, type `ls *` and press **Enter**. What is listed and why?

4. At the command prompt, type `ls sample*` and press **Enter**. What is listed?

5. At the command prompt, type `ls sample?` and press **Enter**. What is listed and why?

6. At the command prompt, type `ls sample??` and press **Enter**. What is listed and why?

7. At the command prompt, type `ls sample[13]` and press **Enter**. What is listed and why?

8. At the command prompt, type `ls sample[!13]` and press **Enter**. What is listed and why?

9. At the command prompt, type `ls sample[1-3]` and press **Enter**. What is listed and why?

10. At the command prompt, type `ls sample[!1-3]` and press **Enter**. What is listed and why?

11. Type `exit` and press **Enter** to log out of your shell.

Project 3-7

Estimated Time: 30 minutes

Objective: Use regular expressions.

Description: In this hands-on project, you use the `grep` and `egrep` commands alongside regular expression metacharacters to explore the contents of text files.

1. Switch to a command-line terminal (tty5) by pressing **Ctrl+Alt+F5** and log in to the terminal using the user name of **root** and the password of **LINUXrocks!**.

2. At the command prompt, type `grep "Inn" sample1` and press **Enter**. What is displayed?

3. At the command prompt, type `grep -v "Inn" sample1` and press **Enter**. What is displayed?

4. At the command prompt, type `grep "inn" sample1` and press **Enter**. What is displayed and why?

5. At the command prompt, type `grep -i "inn" sample1` and press **Enter**. What is displayed?

6. At the command prompt, type `grep "I" sample1` and press **Enter**. What is displayed?

7. At the command prompt, type `grep " I " sample1` and press **Enter**. What is displayed?

8. At the command prompt, type `grep "t.e" sample1` and press **Enter**. What is displayed?

9. At the command prompt, type `grep "w...e" sample1` and press **Enter**. What is displayed?

10. At the command prompt, type `grep "^I" sample1` and press **Enter**. What is displayed?

11. At the command prompt, type `grep "^I " sample1` and press **Enter**. What is displayed?

12. At the command prompt, type `grep "(we|next)" sample1` and press **Enter**. What is displayed? Why?

13. At the command prompt, type `egrep "(we|next)" sample1` and press **Enter**. What is displayed?

14. At the command prompt, type `grep "Inn$" sample1` and press **Enter**. What is displayed?

15. At the command prompt, type `grep "?$" sample1` and press **Enter**. What is displayed and why? Does the ? metacharacter have special meaning here? Why?

16. At the command prompt, type `grep "^$" sample1` and press **Enter**. Is anything displayed? (*Hint:* Be certain to look closely!) Can you explain the output?

17. Type `exit` and press **Enter** to log out of your shell.

Discovery Exercises

Discovery Exercise 3-1

Estimated Time: 30 minutes

Objective: Detail the commands used to navigate and view files.

Description: You are the systems administrator for a scientific research company that employs over 100 scientists who write and run Linux programs to analyze their work. All of these programs are stored in each scientist's home directory on the Linux system. One scientist has left the company, and you are instructed to retrieve any work from that scientist's home directory. When you enter the home directory for that user, you notice that there are very few files and only two directories (one named Projects and one named Lab). List the commands that you would use to navigate through this user's home directory and view filenames and file types. If there are any text files, what commands could you use to view their contents?

Discovery Exercise 3-2

Estimated Time: 20 minutes

Objective: Explain relative and absolute pathnames.

Description: When you type the `pwd` command, you notice that your current location on the Linux filesystem is the /usr/local directory. Answer the following questions, assuming that your current directory is /usr/local for each question.

    a. Which command could you use to change to the /usr directory using an absolute pathname?

    b. Which command could you use to change to the /usr directory using a relative pathname?

    c. Which command could you use to change to the /usr/local/share/info directory using an absolute pathname?

    d. Which command could you use to change to the /usr/local/share/info directory using a relative pathname?

    e. Which command could you use to change to the /etc directory using an absolute pathname?

    f. Which command could you use to change to the /etc directory using a relative pathname?

Discovery Exercise 3-3

Estimated Time: 30 minutes

Objective: Identify wildcard metacharacters.

Description: Using wildcard metacharacters and options to the `ls` command, view the following:

    a. All the files that end with .cfg under the /etc directory

    b. All hidden files in the /home/user1 directory

    c. The directory names that exist under the /var directory

    d. All the files that start with the letter "a" under the /bin directory

    e. All the files that have exactly three letters in their filename in the /bin directory

    f. All files that have exactly three letters in their filename and end with either the letter "t" or the letter "h" in the /bin directory

Discovery Exercise 3-4

Estimated Time: 40 minutes

Objective: Obtain command help.

Description: Explore the manual pages for the `ls`, `grep`, `cat`, `od`, `tac`, `head`, `tail`, `diff`, `pwd`, `cd`, `strings`, and `vi` commands. Experiment with what you learn using the file sample1 that you created earlier.

Discovery Exercise 3-5

Estimated Time: 20 minutes

Objective: Explain regular expressions.

Description: The famous quote from Shakespeare's Hamlet "To be or not to be" can be represented by the following regular expression:

```
(2b|[^b]{2})
```

If you used this expression when searching a text file using the egrep command (egrep "(2b|[^b]{2})" filename), what would be displayed? Try this command on a file that you have created. Why does it display what it does? That is the question.

Discovery Exercise 3-6

Estimated Time: 30 minutes

Objective: Use the vi editor.

Description: The vim-enhanced package you installed earlier in Hands-On Project 3-5 comes with a short 30-minute tutorial on its usage. Start this tutorial by typing vimtutor at a command prompt and then follow the directions.

Discovery Exercise 3-7

Estimated Time: 40 minutes

Objective: Use the vi editor.

Description: Enter the following text into a new document called question7 using the vi editor. Next, use the vi editor to fix the mistakes in the file using the information in Tables 3-5, 3-6, and 3-7 as well as the examples provided in this chapter.

```
Hi there,
Unfortunately we were not able to make it to your dining room
Unfortunately we were not able to make it to your dining room
this year while vacationing in Algonuin Park - I especially wished
to see the model of the highland inn and the train station in the
dining rooms.

I have been readng on the history of Algonuin Park but
no where could I find a description of where the Highland Inn was
originally located on Cache lake.

If it is not trouble, could you kindly let me that I need
not wait until next year when we visit Lodge?

I hope this day finds you well.
Regard
Elizabeth Mackenzie
```

Discovery Exercise 3-8

Estimated Time: 40 minutes

Objective: Use the Emacs editor.

Description: The knowledge gained from using the vi editor can be transferred easily to the Emacs editor. Perform Discovery Exercise 3-7 using the Emacs editor instead of the vi editor.

Discovery Exercise 3-9

Estimated Time: 20 minutes

Objective: Configure persistent vi environment settings.

Description: When you use the vi editor and change environment settings at the : prompt, such as `:set number` to enable line numbering, those changes are lost when you exit the vi editor. To continuously apply the same environment settings, you can choose to put any vi commands that can be entered at the : prompt in a special hidden file in your home directory called either .vimrc or .exrc. Each time the vi (vim) editor is opened, it looks for these files and automatically executes the commands within. Enter the vi editor and find two environment settings that you want to change in addition to line numbering. Then create a new file called .exrc in your home directory and enter the three lines changing these vi environment settings (do not start each line with a : character, just enter the `set` command—e.g., `set number`). When finished, open the vi editor to edit a new file and test to see whether the settings were applied automatically.

Chapter 4

Linux Filesystem Management

Chapter Objectives

1   Find files and directories on the filesystem.

2   Describe and create linked files.

3   Explain the function of the Filesystem Hierarchy Standard.

4   Use standard Linux commands to manage files and directories.

5   Modify file and directory ownership.

6   Define and change Linux file and directory permissions.

7   Identify the default permissions created on files and directories.

8   Apply special file and directory permissions.

9   Modify the default access control list (ACL).

10   View and set filesystem attributes.

In the previous chapter, you learned about navigating the Linux filesystem as well as viewing and editing files. This chapter focuses on the organization of files on the Linux filesystem as well as their linking and security. First, you explore standard Linux directories using the Filesystem Hierarchy Standard. Next, you explore common commands used to manage files and directories as well as learn methods that are used to find files and directories on the filesystem. Finally, you learn about file and directory linking, permissions, special permissions, and attributes.

The Filesystem Hierarchy Standard

The many thousands of files on a typical Linux system are organized into directories in the Linux directory tree. It's a complex system, made even more complex in the past by the fact that different Linux distributions were free to place files in different locations. This meant that you could waste a great deal of time searching for a configuration file on a Linux system with which you were unfamiliar. To simplify the task of finding specific files, the Filesystem Hierarchy Standard (FHS) was created.

FHS defines a standard set of directories for use by all Linux and UNIX systems as well as the file and subdirectory contents of each directory. Because the filename and location follow a standard convention, a Fedora Linux user will find the correct configuration file on an Arch Linux or macOS UNIX computer with little difficulty. The FHS also gives Linux software developers the ability to locate files on a Linux system regardless of the distribution, allowing them to create software that is not distribution-specific.

A comprehensive understanding of the standard types of directories found on Linux systems is valuable when locating and managing files and directories; some standard UNIX and Linux directories defined by FHS and their descriptions are listed in Table 4-1. These directories are discussed throughout this chapter and subsequent chapters.

Note 1

To read the complete Filesystem Hierarchy Standard definition, go to www.pathname.com/fhs.

Table 4-1   Linux directories defined by the Filesystem Hierarchy Standard

Directory	Description
/bin	Contains binary commands for use by all users (on most Linux systems, this directory is a shortcut to /usr/bin)
/boot	Contains the Linux kernel and files used by the boot loader
/dev	Contains device files
/etc	Contains system-specific configuration files
/home	Is the default location for user home directories
/lib /lib64	Contains shared program libraries (used by the commands in /bin and /sbin) as well as kernel modules (on most Linux systems, /lib is a shortcut to /usr/lib and /lib64 is a shortcut to /usr/lib64)
/media	A directory that contains subdirectories used for accessing (mounting) filesystems on removable media devices, such as DVDs and USB flash drives
/mnt	An empty directory used for temporarily accessing filesystems on removable media devices
/opt	Stores additional software programs
/proc	Contains process and kernel information
/root	Is the root user's home directory
/sbin	Contains system binary commands used for administration (on most Linux systems, this directory is a shortcut to /usr/sbin)
/sys	Contains configuration information for hardware devices on the system
/tmp	Holds temporary files created by programs
/usr	Contains most system commands and utilities—contains the following directories: /usr/bin—User binary commands /usr/games—Educational programs and games /usr/include—C program header files /usr/lib and /usr/lib64—Libraries /usr/local—Local programs /usr/sbin—System binary commands /usr/share—Files that are architecture independent /usr/share/X11—The X Window system (sometimes replaced by /etc/X11) /usr/src—Source code
/usr/local	Is the location for most additional programs
/var	Contains log files and spools

Managing Files and Directories

As mentioned earlier, using a Linux system involves navigating several directories and manipulating the files inside them. Thus, an efficient Linux user must understand how to create directories as needed, copy or move files from one directory to another, and delete files and directories. These tasks are commonly referred to as file management tasks.

Following is an example of a directory listing from the root user:

```
[root@server1 ~]# pwd
/root
[root@server1 ~]# ls -F
myprogram*  project   project12  project2  project4
myscript*   project1  project13  project3  project5
[root@server1 ~]#_
```

As shown in the preceding output, two executable files (myprogram and myscript), and several project-related files (project*) exist on this example system. Although this directory structure is not cluttered, typical home directories on a Linux system contain many more files. As a result, it is good practice to organize these files into subdirectories based on file purpose. Because several project files are in the root user's home directory in the preceding output, you could create a subdirectory called proj_files to contain the project-related files and decrease the size of the directory listing. To do this, you use the mkdir (make directory) command, which takes arguments specifying the absolute or relative pathnames of the directories to create. To create a proj_files directory under the current directory, you can use the mkdir command with a relative pathname:

```
[root@server1 ~]# mkdir proj_files
[root@server1 ~]# ls -F
myprogram* project   project12  project2  project4   proj_files/
myscript*  project1 project13  project3  project5
[root@server1 ~]#_
```

Now, you can move the project files into the proj_files subdirectory by using the mv (move) command. The mv command requires two arguments at minimum: the source file/directory and the target file/directory. For example, to move the /etc/sample1 file to the /root directory, you could use the command mv /etc/sample1 /root.

If you want to move several files, you include one source argument for each file you want to move and then include the target directory as the last argument. For example, to move the /etc/sample1 and /etc/sample2 files to the /root directory, you could use the command mv /etc/sample1 /etc/sample2 /root.

Note that both the source (or sources) and the destination can be absolute or relative pathnames and the source can contain wildcards if several files are to be moved. For example, to move all of the project files to the proj_files directory, you could type mv with the source argument project* (to match all files starting with the letters "project") and the target argument proj_files (relative pathname to the destination directory), as shown in the following output:

```
[root@server1 ~]# mv project* proj_files
[root@server1 ~]# ls -F
myprogram*  myscript*  proj_files/
[root@server1 ~]# ls -F proj_files
project   project12  project2  project4
project1 project13  project3  project5
[root@server1 ~]#_
```

In the preceding output, the current directory listing does not show the project files anymore, yet the listing of the proj_files subdirectory indicates that they were moved successfully.

Note 2

If the target is the name of a directory, the mv command moves those files to that directory. If the target is a filename of an existing file in a certain directory and there is one source file, the mv command overwrites the target with the source. If the target is a filename of a nonexistent file in a certain directory, the mv command creates a new file with that filename in the target directory and moves the source file to that file.

Another important use of the mv command is to rename files, which is simply moving a file to the same directory but with a different filename. To rename the myscript file from earlier examples to myscript2, you can use the following mv command:

```
[root@server1 ~]# ls -F
myprogram*  myscript*  proj_files/
[root@server1 ~]# mv myscript myscript2
[root@server1 ~]# ls -F
myprogram*  myscript2*  proj_files/
[root@server1 ~]#_
```

Similarly, the mv command can rename directories. If the source is the name of an existing directory, it is renamed to whatever directory name is specified as the target.

The mv command works similarly to a cut-and-paste operation in which the file is copied to a new directory and deleted from the source directory. In some cases, however, you might want to keep the file in the source directory and instead insert a copy of the file in the target directory. You can do this using the **cp (copy) command**. Much like the mv command, the cp command takes two arguments at minimum. The first argument specifies the source file/directory to be copied and the second argument specifies the target file/directory. If several files need to be copied to a destination directory, specify several source arguments, with the final argument on the command line serving as the target directory. Each argument can be an absolute or relative pathname and can contain wildcards or the special metacharacters "." (which specifies the current directory) and ".." (which specifies the parent directory). For example, to make a copy of the file /etc/hosts in the current directory (/root), you can specify the absolute pathname to the /etc/hosts file (/etc/hosts) and the relative pathname indicating the current directory (.):

```
[root@server1 ~]# cp /etc/hosts .
[root@server1 ~]# ls -F
hosts  myprogram*  myscript2*  proj_files/
[root@server1 ~]#_
```

You can also make copies of files in the same directory. For example, to make a copy of the hosts file called hosts2 in the current directory and view the results, you can run the following commands:

```
[root@server1 ~]# cp hosts hosts2
[root@server1 ~]# ls -F
hosts hosts2 myprogram* myscript2* proj_files/
[root@server1 ~]#_
```

Despite their similarities, the mv and cp commands work on directories differently. The mv command renames a directory, whereas the cp command creates a whole new copy of the directory and its contents. To copy a directory full of files in Linux, you must tell the cp command that the copy will be **recursive** (involve files and subdirectories too) by using the −r option. The following example demonstrates copying the proj_files directory and all of its contents to the /home/user1 directory without and with the −r option:

```
[root@server1 ~]# ls -F
hosts  myprogram*  myscript2*  proj_files/
[root@server1 ~]# ls -F /home/user1
Desktop/
[root@server1 ~]# cp proj_files /home/user1
cp: -r not specified; omitting directory 'proj_files'
[root@server1 ~]# ls -F /home/user1
Desktop/
[root@server1 ~]# cp -r proj_files /home/user1
[root@server1 ~]# ls -F /home/user1
```

```
Desktop/  proj_files/
[root@server1 ~]#_
```

If the target is a file that exists, both the mv and cp commands warn the user that the target file will be overwritten and will ask whether to continue. This is not a feature of the command as normally invoked, but it is a feature of the default configuration in Fedora Linux because the BASH shell in Fedora Linux contains aliases to the cp and mv commands.

> **Note 3**
>
> Aliases are special variables in memory that point to commands; they are fully discussed in Chapter 7.

When you type mv, you are actually running the mv command with the –i option without realizing it. If the target file already exists, both the mv command and the mv command with the –i option interactively prompt the user to choose whether to overwrite the existing file. Similarly, when you type the cp command, the cp –i command is actually run to prevent the accidental overwriting of files. To see the aliases in your current shell, type alias, as shown in the following output:

```
[root@server1 ~]# alias
alias cp='cp -i'
alias egrep='egrep --color=auto'
alias fgrep='fgrep --color=auto'
alias grep='grep --color=auto'
alias l.='ls -d .* --color=auto'
alias ll='ls -l --color=auto'
alias ls='ls --color=auto'
alias mv='mv -i'
alias rm='rm -i'
alias which='(alias; declare -f) | /usr/bin/which --tty-only --read-
alias --read-functions --show-tilde --show-dot'
alias xzegrep='xzegrep --color=auto'
alias xzfgrep='xzfgrep --color=auto'
alias xzgrep='xzgrep --color=auto'
alias zegrep='zegrep --color=auto'
alias zfgrep='zfgrep --color=auto'
alias zgrep='zgrep --color=auto'
[root@server1 ~]#_
```

If you want to override this interactive option, which is known as interactive mode, use the –f (force) option to override the choice, as shown in the following example. In this example, the root user tries to rename the hosts file using the name "hosts2," a name already assigned to an existing file. The example shows the user attempting this task both without and with the –f option to the mv command:

```
[root@server1 ~]# ls -F
hosts   hosts2  myprogram*  myscript2*  proj_files/
[root@server1 ~]# mv hosts hosts2
mv: overwrite 'hosts2'? n
[root@server1 ~]# mv -f hosts hosts2
[root@server1 ~]# ls -F
hosts2  myprogram*  myscript2*  proj_files/
[root@server1 ~]#_
```

Creating directories, copying, and moving files are file management tasks that preserve or create data on the filesystem. To remove files or directories, you must use either the rm command or the rmdir command.

The rm (remove) command takes a list of arguments specifying the absolute or relative path-names of files to remove. As with most commands, wildcards can be used to simplify the process of removing multiple files. After a file has been removed from the filesystem, it cannot be recovered. As a result, the rm command is aliased in Fedora Linux to the rm command with the -i option, which interactively prompts the user to choose whether to continue with the deletion. Like the cp and mv commands, the rm command accepts the -f option to override this choice and immediately delete the file. An example demonstrating the use of the rm and rm -f commands to remove the current and hosts2 files is shown here:

```
[root@server1 ~]# ls -F
hosts2  myprogram*  myscript2*  proj_files/
[root@server1 ~]# rm myprogram
rm: remove regular file 'myprogram'? y
[root@server1 ~]# rm -f hosts2
[root@server1 ~]# ls -F
myscript2*  proj_files/
[root@server1 ~]#_
```

To remove a directory, you can use the rmdir (remove directory) command; however, the rmdir command only removes a directory if it contains no files. To remove a directory and the files inside, you must use the rm command and specify that a directory full of files should be removed. As explained earlier in this chapter, you need to use the recursive option (-r) with the cp command to copy directories; to remove a directory full of files, you can also use a recursive option (-r) with the rm command. In the following example, the proj_files subdirectory and all of the files within it are removed without being prompted to confirm each file deletion by the rm -rf proj_files command:

```
[root@server1 ~]# ls -F
myscript2*  proj_files/
[root@server1 ~]# rmdir proj_files
rmdir: failed to remove 'proj_files': Directory not empty
[root@server1 ~]# rm -rf proj_files
[root@server1 ~]# ls -F
myscript2*
[root@server1 ~]#_
```

Note 4

In many commands, such as rm and cp, both the -r and the -R options have the same meaning (recursive).

Note 5

The recursive (-r or -R) option to the rm command is dangerous if you are not certain which files exist in the directory to be deleted recursively. As a result, this option to the rm command is commonly referred to as the résumé option; if you use it incorrectly in a production server environment, you might need to prepare your résumé, as there is no Linux command to restore deleted files.

Note 6

An alternative to the rm command is the unlink command. However, the unlink command can be used to remove files only (not directories).

The aforementioned file management commands are commonly used by Linux users, developers, and administrators alike. Table 4-2 shows a summary of these common file management commands.

Table 4-2   Common linux file management commands

Command	Description
mkdir	Creates directories
rmdir	Removes empty directories
mv	Moves/renames files and directories
cp	Copies files and directories full of files (with the –r or –R option)
alias	Displays BASH shell aliases
rm	Removes files and directories full of files (with the –r or –R option)
unlink	Removes files

Finding Files

Before using the file management commands mentioned in the preceding section, you must know the locations of the files involved. The fastest method to search for files in the Linux directory tree is to use the **locate command**. For example, to view all of the files under the root directory with the text "inittab" or with "inittab" as part of the filename, you can type locate inittab at a command prompt, which produces the following output:

```
[root@server1 ~]# locate inittab
/etc/inittab
/usr/share/augeas/lenses/dist/inittab.aug
/usr/share/vim/vim90/syntax/inittab.vim
[root@server1 ~]#_
```

The locate command looks in a premade database that contains a list of all the files on the system. This database is indexed much like a textbook for fast searching, yet it can become outdated as files are added and removed from the system, which happens on a regular basis. As a result, the database used for the locate command (/var/lib/plocate/plocate.db) is updated each day automatically and can be updated manually by running the updatedb command at a command prompt. You can also exclude specific directories, file extensions, and whole filesystems from being indexed by the updatedb command by adding them to the /etc/updatedb.conf file; this is called **pruning**. For example, to exclude the /etc directory from being indexed by the updatedb command, add the line PRUNEPATHS=/etc to the /etc/updatedb.conf file.

As the locate command searches all files on the filesystem, it often returns too much information to display on the screen. To make the output easier to read, you can use the more or less command to pause the output; if the locate inittab command produced too many results, you could run the command locate inittab | less. To prevent the problem entirely, you can do more specific searches.

A slower, yet more versatile, method for locating files on the filesystem is to use the **find command**. The find command does not use a premade index of files; instead, it searches the directory tree recursively, starting from a certain directory, for files that meet a certain criterion. The format of the find command is as follows:

```
find  <start directory>  -criterion  <what to find>
```

For example, to find any files named "inittab" under the /etc directory, you can use the command find /etc -name inittab and receive the following output:

```
[root@server1 ~]# find /etc -name inittab
/etc/inittab
[root@server1 ~]#_
```

You can also use wildcard metacharacters with the `find` command; however, these wildcards must be protected from shell interpretation, as they must only be interpreted by the `find` command. To do this, ensure that any wildcard metacharacters are enclosed within quote characters. An example of using the `find` command with wildcard metacharacters to find all files that start with the letters "host" underneath the /etc directory is shown in the following output:

```
[root@server1 ~]# find /etc -name "host*"
/etc/hosts
/etc/host.conf
/etc/avahi/hosts
/etc/hostname
[root@server1 ~]#_
```

Although searching by name is the most common criterion used with the `find` command, many other criteria can be used with the `find` command as well. To find all files starting from the /var directory that have a size greater than 8192K (kilobytes), you can use the following command:

```
[root@server1 ~]# find /var -size +8192k
/var/lib/rpm/Packages
/var/lib/rpm/Basenames
/var/lib/PackageKit/system.package-list
/var/log/journal/034ec8ccdf4642f7a2493195e11d7df6/user-1000.journal
/var/log/journal/034ec8ccdf4642f7a2493195e11d7df6/user-42.journal
/var/log/journal/034ec8ccdf4642f7a2493195e11d7df6/system.journal
/var/cache/PackageKit/36/updates/gen/prestodelta.xml
/var/cache/PackageKit/36/updates/gen/primary_db.sqlite
/var/cache/PackageKit/36/updates/gen/filelists_db.sqlite
/var/cache/PackageKit/36/updates/gen/updateinfo.xml
/var/cache/PackageKit/36/updates/gen/other_db.sqlite
/var/cache/PackageKit/36/fedora-filenames.solvx
/var/cache/dnf/x86_64/36/fedora.solv
/var/cache/dnf/x86_64/36/updates-filenames.solvx
/var/tmp/kdecache-user1/plasma_theme_internal-system-colors.kcache
/var/tmp/kdecache-user1/plasma_theme_Heisenbug_v19.90.2.kcache
/var/tmp/kdecache-user1/icon-cache.kcache
[root@server1 ~]#_
```

As well, if you want to find all the directories only under the /boot directory, you can type the following command:

```
[root@server1 ~]# find /boot -type d
/boot
/boot/extlinux
/boot/lost+found
/boot/grub2
/boot/grub2/fonts
/boot/efi
/boot/efi/EFI
/boot/efi/EFI/BOOT
/boot/efi/EFI/fedora
/boot/efi/System
/boot/efi/System/Library
/boot/efi/System/Library/CoreServices
/boot/loader
/boot/loader/entries
[root@server1 ~]#_
```

Table 4-3 provides a list of some common criteria used with the find command.

Table 4-3 Common criteria used with the find command

Criteria	Description
-amin -x	Searches for files that were accessed less than x minutes ago
-amin +x	Searches for files that were accessed more than x minutes ago
-atime -x	Searches for files that were accessed less than x days ago
-atime +x	Searches for files that were accessed more than x days ago
-empty	Searches for empty files or directories
-fstype x	Searches for files if they are on a certain filesystem x (where x could be ext2, ext3, and so on)
-group x	Searches for files that are owned by a certain group or GID (x)
-inum x	Searches for files that have an inode number of x
-mmin -x	Searches for files that were modified less than x minutes ago
-mmin +x	Searches for files that were modified more than x minutes ago
-mtime -x	Searches for files that were modified less than x days ago
-mtime +x	Searches for files that were modified more than x days ago
-name x	Searches for a certain filename x (x can contain wildcards)
-regex x	Searches for certain filenames using regular expressions instead of wildcard metacharacters
-size -x	Searches for files with a size less than x
-size x	Searches for files with a size of x
-size +x	Searches for files with a size greater than x
-type x	Searches for files of type x where x is: b for block files c for character files d for directory files p for named pipes f for regular files l for symbolic links (shortcuts) s for sockets
-user x	Searches for files owned by a certain user or UID (x)

Although the find command can be used to search for files based on many criteria, it might take several minutes to complete the search if the number of directories and files being searched is large. To reduce the time needed to search, narrow the directories searched by specifying a subdirectory when possible. It takes less time to search the /usr/local/bin directory and its subdirectories, compared to searching the /usr directory and all of its subdirectories. As well, if the filename that you are searching for is an executable file, that file can likely be found in less time using the which command. The which command only searches directories that are listed in a special variable called the PATH variable in the current BASH shell. Before exploring the which command, you must understand the usage of PATH.

Executable files can be stored in directories scattered around the directory tree. Recall from FHS that most executable files are stored in directories named bin or sbin, yet there are over 20 bin and sbin directories scattered around the directory tree after a typical Fedora Linux installation. To ensure that users do not need to specify the full pathname to commands such as ls (which is the executable file /usr/bin/ls), a special variable called PATH is placed into memory each time a user logs in to the Linux system. Recall that you can see the contents of a certain variable in memory by using the $ metacharacter with the echo command:

```
[root@server1 ~]# echo $PATH
/root/.local/bin:/root/bin:/usr/local/sbin:
/usr/local/bin:/usr/sbin:/usr/bin
[root@server1 ~]#_
```

The PATH variable lists directories that are searched for executable files if a relative or absolute pathname was not specified when executing a command on the command line. Assuming the PATH variable in the preceding output, if a user types the ls command on the command line and presses Enter, the system recognizes that the command was not an absolute pathname (e.g., /usr/bin/ls) or relative pathname (e.g., ../../usr/bin/ls) and then proceeds to look for the ls executable file in the /root/.local/bin directory, then the /root/bin directory, then the /usr/local/sbin directory, then the /usr/local/bin directory, then the /usr/sbin directory, and finally the /usr/bin directory. If all the directories in the PATH variable are searched and no ls command is found, the shell gives an error message to the user stating that the command was not found. In the preceding output, the /usr/bin directory is in the PATH variable and, thus, the ls command is found and executed, but not until the previous directories in the PATH variable are searched first.

To search the directories in the PATH variable for the file called "grep," you could use the word "grep" as an argument for the which command and receive the following output:

```
[root@server1 ~]# which grep
alias grep='grep --color=auto'
        /usr/bin/grep
[root@server1 ~]#_
```

As shown in the previous output, the which command will also list any command aliases for a particular command. In this example, the grep command has the path /usr/bin/grep, but it also has an alias that ensures that each time the user runs the grep command, it runs it using the --color=auto option.

If the file being searched does not exist in the PATH variable directories, the which command lets you know in which directories it was not found, as shown in the following output:

```
[root@server1 ~]# which grepper
/usr/bin/which: no grepper in
(/root/.local/bin:/root/bin:/usr/local/sbin:/usr/local/bin:
/usr/sbin:/usr/bin)
[root@server1 ~]#_
```

There are two alternatives to the which command: the type command displays only the first result normally outputted by the which command, and the whereis command displays the location of the command as well as any associated man and info pages, as shown in the following output:

```
[root@server1 ~]# type grep
grep is aliased to 'grep --color=auto'
[root@server1 ~]# whereis grep
grep: /usr/bin/grep /usr/share/man/man1/grep.1.gz
/usr/share/man/man1p/grep.1p.gz /usr/share/info/grep.info.gz
[root@server1 ~]#_
```

Linking Files

Files can be linked to one another in two ways. In a **symbolic link**, one file is a pointer, or shortcut, to another file. In a **hard link**, two files share the same data.

To better understand how files are linked, you must understand how files are stored on a filesystem. On a structural level, a filesystem has three main sections:

- Superblock
- Inode table
- Data blocks

The **superblock** is the section that contains information about the filesystem in general, such as the number of inodes and data blocks, as well as how much data a data block stores, in kilobytes. The **inode table** consists of several **inodes** (information nodes); each inode describes one file or directory on the filesystem and contains a unique inode number for identification. What is more important, the inode stores information such as the file size, data block locations, last date modified, permissions, and ownership. When a file is deleted, only its inode (which serves as a pointer to the actual data) is deleted. The data that makes up the contents of the file as well as the filename are stored in **data blocks**, which are referenced by the inode. In filesystem-neutral terminology, blocks are known as allocation units because they are the unit by which disk space is allocated for storage.

> **Note 7**
>
> Each file and directory must have an inode. All files except for special device files also have data blocks associated with the inode. Special device files are discussed in Chapter 5.

> **Note 8**
>
> Recall that directories are simply files that are used to organize other files; they too have an inode and data blocks, but their data blocks contain a list of filenames that are located within the directory.

Hard-linked files share the same inode and inode number. As a result, they share the same inode number and data blocks, but the data blocks allow for multiple filenames. Thus, when one hard-linked file is modified, the other hard-linked files are updated as well. This relationship between hard-linked files is shown in Figure 4-1. You can hard-link a file an unlimited number of times; however, the hard-linked files must reside on the same filesystem.

Figure 4-1   The structure of hard-linked files

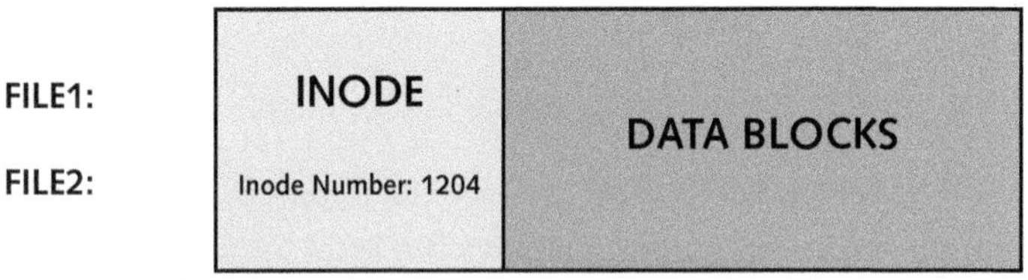

To create a hard link, you must use the `ln (link) command` and specify two arguments: the existing file to hard-link and the target file that will be created as a hard link to the existing file. Each argument can be the absolute or relative pathname to a file. Take, for example, the following contents of the root user's home directory:

```
[root@server1 ~]# ls -l
total 520
drwx------    3 root      root           4096 Apr  8 07:12 Desktop
-rwxr-xr-x    1 root      root         519964 Apr  7 09:59 file1
-rwxr-xr-x    1 root      root           1244 Apr 27 18:17 file3
[root@server1 ~]#_
```

Suppose you want to make a hard link to file1 and call the new hard link file2. To accomplish this, you issue the command `ln file1 file2` at the command prompt; a file called file2 is created and hard-linked to file1. To view the hard-linked filenames after creation, you can use the `ls -l` command:

```
[root@server1 ~]# ln file1 file2
[root@server1 ~]# ls -l
total 1032
drwx------     3 root      root           4096 Apr  8 07:12 Desktop
-rwxr-xr-x     2 root      root         519964 Apr  7 09:59 file1
-rwxr-xr-x     2 root      root         519964 Apr  7 09:59 file2
-rwxr-xr-x     1 root      root           1244 Apr 27 18:17 file3
[root@server1 ~]#_
```

Notice from the preceding long listing that file1 and file2 share the same inode and data section, as they have the same size, permissions, ownership, modification date, and so on. Also note that the link count (the number after the permission set) for file1 has increased from the number one to the number two in the preceding output. A link count of one indicates that only one inode is shared by the file. A file that is hard-linked to another file shares two inodes and, thus, has a link count of two. Similarly, a file that is hard-linked to three other files shares four inodes and, thus, has a link count of four.

Although hard links share the same inode and data section, deleting a hard-linked file does not delete all the other hard-linked files; it simply removes one filename reference. Removing a hard link can be achieved by removing one of the files, which then lowers the link count.

To view the inode number of hard-linked files to verify that they are identical, you can use the `-i` option to the `ls` command in addition to any other options. The inode number is placed on the left of the directory listing on each line, as shown in the following output:

```
[root@server1 ~]# ls -li
total 1032
 37595 drwx------     3 root      root           4096 Apr  8 07:12 Desktop
  1204 -rwxr-xr-x     2 root      root         519964 Apr  7 09:59 file1
  1204 -rwxr-xr-x     2 root      root         519964 Apr  7 09:59 file2
 17440 -rwxr-xr-x     1 root      root           1244 Apr 27 18:17 file3
[root@server1 ~]#_
```

Note 9

Directory files are not normally hard-linked on modern Linux systems, as the result would consist of two directories that contain the same contents. However, the root user has the ability to hard-link directories, using the −F or −d option to the `ln` command.

Symbolic links (shown in Figure 4-2) are different from hard links because they do not share the same inode and data blocks with their target file; one is merely a pointer to the other, thus both files have different sizes. The data blocks in a symbolically linked file contain only the pathname to the target file. When a user edits a symbolically linked file, the user is actually editing the target file. Thus, if the target file is deleted, the symbolic link serves no function, as it points to a nonexistent file.

Note 10

Symbolic links are sometimes referred to as "soft links" or "symlinks"

Figure 4-2   The structure of symbolically linked files

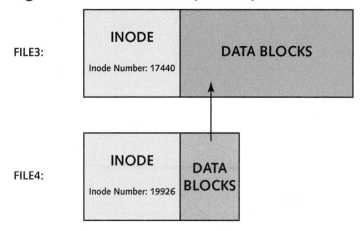

To create a symbolic link, you use the -s option to the ln command. For example, to create a symbolic link to file3 called file4 you can type ln -s file3 file4 at the command prompt. As with hard links, the arguments specified can be absolute or relative pathnames. To view the symbolically linked filenames after creation, you can use the ls -l command, as shown in the following example:

```
[root@server1 ~]# ln -s file3 file4
[root@server1 ~]# ls -l
total 1032
drwx------    3 root        root           4096 Apr  8 07:12 Desktop
-rwxr-xr-x    2 root        root         519964 Apr  7 09:59 file1
-rwxr-xr-x    2 root        root         519964 Apr  7 09:59 file2
-rwxr-xr-x    1 root        root           1244 Apr 27 18:17 file3
lrwxrwxrwx    1 root        root              5 Apr 27 19:05 file4 -> file3
[root@server1 ~]#_
```

Notice from the preceding output that file4 does not share the same inode, because the permissions, size, and modification date are different from file3. In addition, symbolic links are easier to identify than hard links; the file type character (before the permissions) is l, which indicates a symbolic link, and the filename points to the target using an arrow. The ls -F command also indicates symbolic links by appending an @ symbol, as shown in the following output:

```
[root@server1 ~]# ls -F
Desktop/  file1*  file2*  file3*  file4@
[root@server1 ~]#_
```

Another difference between hard links and symbolic links is that symbolic links need not reside on the same filesystem as their target. Instead, they point to the target filename and do not require the same inode number, as shown in the following output:

```
[root@server1 ~]# ls -li
total 1032
37595 drwx------    3 root    root       4096 Apr  8 07:12 Desktop
 1204 -rwxr-xr-x    2 root    root     519964 Apr  7 09:59 file1
 1204 -rwxr-xr-x    2 root    root     519964 Apr  7 09:59 file2
17440 -rwxr-xr-x    1 root    root       1244 Apr 27 18:17 file3
19926 lrwxrwxrwx    1 root    root          5 Apr 27 19:05 file4 -> file3
[root@server1 ~]#_
```

Note 11

Unlike hard links, symbolic links are commonly made to directories to simplify navigating the filesystem tree. Also, symbolic links made to directories are typically used to maintain FHS compatibility with other UNIX and Linux systems. For example, on Fedora Linux, the /usr/tmp directory is symbolically linked to the /var/tmp directory for this reason.

File and Directory Permissions

Recall that all users must log in with a user name and password to gain access to a Linux system. After logging in, a user is identified by their user name and group memberships; all access to resources depends on whether the user name and group memberships have the required permissions. Thus, a firm understanding of ownership and permissions is necessary to operate a Linux system in a secure manner and to prevent unauthorized users from having access to sensitive files, directories, and commands.

File and Directory Ownership

When a user creates a file or directory, that user's name and primary group becomes the owner and group owner of the file, respectively. This affects the permission structure, as you see in the next section; however, it also determines who has the ability to modify file and directory permissions and ownership. Only two users on a Linux system can modify permissions on a file or directory or change its ownership: the owner of the file or directory and the root user.

To view your current user name, you can use the whoami command. To view your group memberships and primary group, you can use the groups command. An example of these two commands when logged in as the root user is shown in the following output:

```
[root@server1 ~]# whoami
root
[root@server1 ~]# groups
root bin daemon sys adm disk wheel
[root@server1 ~]#_
```

Notice from the preceding output that the root user is a member of seven groups, yet the root user's primary group is also called "root," as it is the first group mentioned in the output of the groups command.

Note 12

On Fedora Linux, the root user is only a member of one group by default (the "root" group).

If the root user creates a file, the owner is "root" and the group owner is also "root." To quickly create an empty file, you can use the touch command:

```
[root@server1 ~]# touch file1
[root@server1 ~]# ls -l
total 4
drwx------    3 root      root           4096 Apr  8 07:12 Desktop
-rw-r--r--    1 root      root              0 Apr 29 15:40 file1
[root@server1 ~]#_
```

Note 13

Although the main purpose of the touch command is to update the modification date on an existing file to the current time, it will create a new empty file if the file specified as an argument does not exist.

Notice from the preceding output that the owner of file1 is "root" and the group owner is the "root" group. To change the ownership of a file or directory, you can use the chown (change owner) command, which takes two arguments at minimum: the new owner and the files or directories to change. Both arguments can be absolute or relative pathnames, and you can also change permissions recursively throughout the directory tree using the −R option to the chown command. To change the ownership of file1 to the user user1 and the ownership of the directory Desktop and all of its contents to user1 as well, you can enter the following commands:

```
[root@server1 ~]# chown user1 file1
[root@server1 ~]# chown -R user1 Desktop
[root@server1 ~]# ls -l
total 4
drwx------   3 user1   root    4096 Apr  8 07:12 Desktop
-rw-r--r--   1 user1   root       0 Apr 29 15:40 file1
[root@server1 ~]# ls -l Desktop
total 16
-rw-------   1 user1   root     163 Mar 29 09:58 Work
-rw-r--r--   1 user1   root    3578 Mar 29 09:58 Home
-rw-r--r--   1 user1   root    1791 Mar 29 09:58 Start Here
drwx------   2 user1   root    4096 Mar 29 09:58 Trash
[root@server1 ~]#_
```

Recall that the owner of a file or directory and the root user can change ownership of a particular file or directory. If a regular user changes the ownership of a file or directory that they own, that user cannot gain back the ownership. Instead, the new owner of that file or directory must change it to the original user. However, the root user always has the ability to regain the ownership:

```
[root@server1 ~]# chown root file1
[root@server1 ~]# chown -R root Desktop
[root@server1 ~]# ls -l
total 4
drwx------   3 root    root    4096 Apr  8 07:12 Desktop
-rw-r--r--   1 root    root       0 Apr 29 15:40 file1
[root@server1 ~]# ls -l Desktop
total 16
-rw-------   1 root    root     163 Mar 29 09:58 Work
-rw-r--r--   1 root    root    3578 Mar 29 09:58 Home
-rw-r--r--   1 root    root    1791 Mar 29 09:58 Start Here
drwx------   2 root    root    4096 Mar 29 09:58 Trash
[root@server1 ~]#_
```

Just as the chown (change owner) command can be used to change the owner of a file or directory, you can use the chgrp (change group) command to change the group owner of a file or directory. The chgrp command takes two arguments at minimum: the new group owner and the files or directories to change. As with the chown command, the chgrp command also accepts the −R option to change group ownership recursively throughout the directory tree. To change the group owner of file1 and the Desktop directory recursively throughout the directory tree, you can execute the following commands:

```
[root@server1 ~]# chgrp sys file1
[root@server1 ~]# chgrp -R sys Desktop
[root@server1 ~]# ls -l
total 4
drwx------   3 root    sys     4096 Apr  8 07:12 Desktop
-rw-r--r--   1 root    sys        0 Apr 29 15:40 file1
```

```
[root@server1 ~]# ls -l Desktop
total 16
-rw-------    1 root     sys       163 Mar 29 09:58 Work
-rw-r--r--    1 root     sys      3578 Mar 29 09:58 Home
-rw-r--r--    1 root     sys      1791 Mar 29 09:58 Start Here
drwx------    2 root     sys      4096 Mar 29 09:58 Trash
[root@server1 ~]#_
```

Note 14

Regular users can change the group of a file or directory only to a group to which they belong.

Normally, you change both the ownership and group ownership on a file when that file needs to be maintained by someone else. As a result, you can change both the owner and the group owner at the same time using the chown command. To change the owner to user1 and the group owner to root for file1 and the directory Desktop recursively, you can enter the following commands:

```
[root@server1 ~]# chown user1.root file1
[root@server1 ~]# chown -R user1.root Desktop
[root@server1 ~]# ls -l
total 4
drwx------    3 user1    root     4096 Apr  8 07:12 Desktop
-rw-r--r--    1 user1    root        0 Apr 29 15:40 file1
[root@server1 ~]# ls -l Desktop
total 16
-rw-------    1 user1    root      163 Mar 29 09:58 Work
-rw-r--r--    1 user1    root     3578 Mar 29 09:58 Home
-rw-r--r--    1 user1    root     1791 Mar 29 09:58 Start Here
drwx------    2 user1    root     4096 Mar 29 09:58 Trash
[root@server1 ~]#_
```

Note that there must be no spaces before and after the . character in the chown commands shown in the preceding output.

Note 15

You can also use the : character instead of the . character in the chown command to change both the owner and group ownership (e.g., chown -R user1:root Desktop).

To protect your system's security, you should ensure that most files residing in a user's home directory are owned by that user; some files in a user's home directory (especially the hidden files and directories) require this to function properly. To change the ownership back to the root user for file1 and the Desktop directory to avoid future problems, you can type the following:

```
[root@server1 ~]# chown root.root file1
[root@server1 ~]# chown -R root.root Desktop
[root@server1 ~]# ls -l
total 4
drwx------    3 root     root     4096 Apr  8 07:12 Desktop
-rw-r--r--    1 root     root        0 Apr 29 15:40 file1
[root@server1 root]# ls -l Desktop
total 16
-rw-------    1 root     root      163 Mar 29 09:58 Work
```

```
-rw-r--r--    1 root      root      3578 Mar 29 09:58 Home
-rw-r--r--    1 root      root      1791 Mar 29 09:58 Start Here
drwx------    2 root      root      4096 Mar 29 09:58 Trash
[root@server1 ~]#_
```

Note 16

You can override who is allowed to change ownership and permissions using a kernel setting. Many Linux distributions, including Fedora Linux, use this kernel setting by default to restrict regular (non-root) users from changing the ownership and group ownership of files and directories. This prevents these users from bypassing disk quota restrictions, which rely on the ownership of files and directories to function properly. Disk quotas are discussed in Chapter 5.

Managing File and Directory Permissions

Every file and directory file on a Linux filesystem contains information regarding permissions in its inode. The section of the inode that stores permissions is called the **mode** of the file and is divided into three sections based on the user(s) who receive the permissions to that file or directory:

- User (owner) permissions
- Group (group owner) permissions
- Other (everyone else on the Linux system) permissions

Furthermore, you can assign to each of these users the following regular permissions:

- Read
- Write
- Execute

Interpreting the Mode

Recall that the three sections of the mode and the permissions that you can assign to each section are viewed when you perform an `ls -l` command; a detailed depiction of this is shown in Figure 4-3. Note that the root user supersedes all file and directory permissions; in other words, the root user has all permissions to every file and directory regardless of what the mode of the file or directory indicates.

Figure 4-3   The structure of a mode

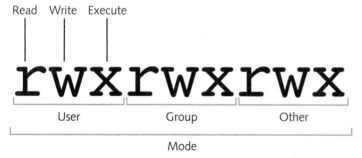

Consider the root user's home directory listing shown in the following example:

```
[root@server1 ~]# ls -l
total 28
drwx------    3 root      root      4096 Apr  8 07:12 Desktop
-r---w---x    1 bob       proj       282 Apr 29 22:06 file1
-------rwx    1 root      root       282 Apr 29 22:06 file2
```

```
-rwxrwxrwx    1 root      root            282 Apr 29 22:06 file3
----------    1 root      root            282 Apr 29 22:06 file4
-rw-r--r--    1 root      root            282 Apr 29 22:06 file5
-rw-r--r--    1 user1     sys             282 Apr 29 22:06 file6
[root@server1 ~]#_
```

Note from the preceding output that all permissions (as shown in Figure 4-3) need not be on a file or directory; if the permission is unavailable, a dash character (-) replaces its position in the mode. Be certain not to confuse the character to the left of the mode (which determines the file type) with the mode, as it is unrelated to the permissions on the file or directory. From the preceding output, the Desktop directory gives the **user** or **owner** of the directory (the root user) read, write, and execute permission, yet members of the **group** (the root group) do not receive any permissions to the directory. Note that **other** (everyone on the system) does not receive permissions to this directory either.

Permissions are not additive; the system assigns the first set of permissions that are matched in the mode order: user, group, other. Let us assume that the bob user is a member of the proj group. In this case, the file called file1 in the preceding output gives the user or owner of the file (the bob user) read permission, gives members of the group (the proj group) write permission, and gives other (everyone else on the system) execute permission only. Because permissions are not additive, the bob user will only receive read permission to file1 from the system.

Linux permissions should not be assigned to other only. Although file2 in our example does not give the user or group any permissions, all other users receive read, write, and execute permission via the other category. Thus, file2 should not contain sensitive data because many users have full access to it. For the same reason, it is bad form to assign all permissions to a file that contains sensitive data, as shown with file3 in the preceding example.

On the contrary, it is also possible to have a file that has no permissions assigned to it, as shown in the preceding example with respect to file4. In this case, the only user who has permissions to the file is the root user.

The permission structure that you choose for a file or directory might result in too few or too many permissions. You can follow some general guidelines to avoid these situations. The owner of a file or directory is typically the person who maintains it; members of the group are typically users in the same department or project and must have limited access to the file or directory. As a result, most files and directories that you find on a Linux filesystem have more permissions assigned to the user of the file/directory than to the group of the file/directory, and the other category has either the same permissions or less than the group of the file/directory, depending on how private that file or directory is. The file file5 in the previous output depicts this common permission structure. In addition, files in a user's home directory are typically owned by that user; however, you might occasionally find files that are not owned by that user. For these files, their permission definition changes, as shown in the previous example with respect to file1 and file6. The user (or owner) of file6 is user1, who has read and write permissions to the file. The group owner of file6 is the sys group; thus, any members of the sys group have read permission to the file. Finally, everyone on the system receives read permission to the file via the other category. Regardless of the mode, the root user receives all permissions to this file.

Interpreting Permissions

After you understand how to identify the permissions that are applied to user, group, and other on a certain file or directory, you can then interpret the function of those permissions. Permissions for files are interpreted differently than those for directories. Also, if a user has a certain permission on a directory, that user does not have the same permission for all files or subdirectories within that directory; file and directory permissions are treated separately by the Linux system. Table 4-4 shows a summary of the different permissions and their definitions.

Table 4-4 Linux permissions

Permission	Definition for Files	Definition for Directories
Read	Allows a user to open and read the contents of a file	Allows a user to list the contents of the directory (if the user has also been given execute permission)
Write	Allows a user to open, read, and edit the contents of a file	Allows a user to add or remove files to and from the directory (if the user has also been given execute permission)
Execute	Allows a user to execute the file in memory (if it is a program file or script)	Allows a user to enter the directory and work with directory contents

The implications of the permission definitions described in Table 4-4 are important to understand. If a user has the read permission to a text file, that user can use, among others, the `cat`, `more`, `head`, `tail`, `less`, `strings`, and `od` commands to view its contents. That same user can also open that file with a text editor such as vi; however, the user does not have the ability to save any changes to the document unless that user has the write permission to the file as well.

Recall from earlier that some text files contain instructions for the shell to execute and are called shell scripts. Shell scripts can be executed in much the same way that binary compiled programs are; the user who executes the shell script must then have execute permission to that file to execute it as a program.

> **Note 17**
>
> Avoid giving execute permission to files that are not programs or shell scripts. This ensures that these files will not be executed accidentally, causing the shell to interpret the contents.

Remember that directories are simply special files that have an inode and a data section, but what the data section contains is a list of that directory's contents. If you want to read that list (using the `ls` command for example), then you require the read permission to the directory. To modify that list by adding or removing files, you require the write permission to the directory. Thus, if you want to create a new file in a directory with a text editor such as vi, you must have the write permission to that directory. Similarly, when a source file is copied to a target directory with the `cp` command, a new file is created in the target directory. You must have the write permission to the target directory for the copy to be successful. Conversely, to delete a certain file, you must have the write permission to the directory that contains that file. A user who has the write permission to a directory can delete all files and subdirectories within it.

The execute permission on a directory is sometimes referred to as the search permission, and it works similarly to a light switch. When a light switch is turned on, you can navigate a room and use the objects within it. However, when a light switch is turned off, you cannot see the objects in the room, nor can you walk around and view them. A user who does not have the execute permission to a directory is prevented from listing the directory's contents, adding and removing files, and working with files and subdirectories inside that directory, regardless of what permissions the user has to them. In short, a quick way to deny a user from accessing a directory and all of its contents in Linux is to take away the execute permission on that directory. Because the execute permission on a directory is crucial for user access, it is commonly given to all users via the other category, unless the directory must be private.

Changing Permissions

To change the permissions for a certain file or directory, you can use the `chmod` (change mode) command. The `chmod` command takes two arguments at minimum; the first argument specifies the criteria used to change the permissions (see Table 4-5), and the remaining arguments indicate the filenames to change.

Table 4-5 Criteria used within the chmod command

Category	Operation	Permission
u (user)	+ (adds a permission)	r (read)
g (group)	- (removes a permission)	w (write)
o (other)	= (makes a permission equal to)	x (execute)
a (all categories)		

Take, for example, the directory list used earlier:

```
[root@server1 ~]# ls -l
total 28
drwx------     3 root      root          4096 Apr  8 07:12 Desktop
-r---w---x     1 bob       proj           282 Apr 29 22:06 file1
-------rwx     1 root      root           282 Apr 29 22:06 file2
-rwxrwxrwx     1 root      root           282 Apr 29 22:06 file3
----------     1 root      root           282 Apr 29 22:06 file4
-rw-r--r--     1 root      root           282 Apr 29 22:06 file5
-rw-r--r--     1 user1     sys            282 Apr 29 22:06 file6
[root@server1 ~]#_
```

To change the mode of file1 to rw-r--r--, you must add the write permission to the user of the file, add the read permission and take away the write permission for the group of the file, and add the read permission and take away the execute permission for other.

From the information listed in Table 4-5, you can use the following command:

```
[root@server1 ~]# chmod u+w,g+r-w,o+r-x file1
[root@server1 ~]# ls -l
total 28
drwx------     3 root      root          4096 Apr  8 07:12 Desktop
-rw-r--r--     1 bob       proj           282 Apr 29 22:06 file1
----r--rwx     1 root      root           282 Apr 29 22:06 file2
-rwxrwxrwx     1 root      root           282 Apr 29 22:06 file3
----------     1 root      root           282 Apr 29 22:06 file4
-rw-r--r--     1 root      root           282 Apr 29 22:06 file5
-rw-r--r--     1 user1     sys            282 Apr 29 22:06 file6
[root@server1 ~]#_
```

Note 18

You should ensure that there are no spaces between any criteria used in the chmod command because all criteria make up the first argument only.

You can also use the = criteria from Table 4-5 to specify the exact permissions to change. To change the mode on file2 in the preceding output to the same as file1 (rw-r--r--), you can use the following chmod command:

```
[root@server1 ~]# chmod u=rw,g=r,o=r file2
[root@server1 ~]# ls -l
total 28
drwx------     3 root      root          4096 Apr  8 07:12 Desktop
-rw-r--r--     1 bob       proj           282 Apr 29 22:06 file1
```

```
-rw-r--r--    1 root      root            282 Apr 29 22:06 file2
-rwxrwxrwx    1 root      root            282 Apr 29 22:06 file3
----------    1 root      root            282 Apr 29 22:06 file4
-rw-r--r--    1 root      root            282 Apr 29 22:06 file5
-rw-r--r--    1 user1     sys             282 Apr 29 22:06 file6
[root@server1 ~]#_
```

If the permissions to change are identical for the user, group, and other categories, you can use the "a" character to refer to all categories, as shown in Table 4-5 and in the following example, when adding the execute permission to user, group, and other for file1:

```
[root@server1 ~]# chmod a+x file1
[root@server1 ~]# ls -l
total 28
drwx------    3 root      root           4096 Apr  8 07:12 Desktop
-rwxr-xr-x    1 bob       proj            282 Apr 29 22:06 file1
-rw-r--r--    1 root      root            282 Apr 29 22:06 file2
-rwxrwxrwx    1 root      root            282 Apr 29 22:06 file3
----------    1 root      root            282 Apr 29 22:06 file4
-rw-r--r--    1 root      root            282 Apr 29 22:06 file5
-rw-r--r--    1 user1     sys             282 Apr 29 22:06 file6
[root@server1 ~]#_
```

However, if there is no character specifying the category of user to affect, all users are assumed, as shown in the following example when adding the execute permission to user, group, and other for file2:

```
[root@server1 ~]# chmod +x file2
[root@server1 ~]# ls -l
total 28
drwx------    3 root      root           4096 Apr  8 07:12 Desktop
-rwxr-xr-x    1 bob       proj            282 Apr 29 22:06 file1
-rwxr-xr-x    1 root      root            282 Apr 29 22:06 file2
-rwxrwxrwx    1 root      root            282 Apr 29 22:06 file3
----------    1 root      root            282 Apr 29 22:06 file4
-rw-r--r--    1 root      root            282 Apr 29 22:06 file5
-rw-r--r--    1 user1     sys             282 Apr 29 22:06 file6
[root@server1 ~]#_
```

All of the aforementioned chmod examples use the symbols listed in Table 4-5 as the criteria for changing the permissions on a file or directory. You might instead choose to use numeric criteria with the chmod command to change permissions. All permissions are stored in the inode of a file or directory as binary powers of two:

- read = 2^2 = 4
- write = 2^1 = 2
- execute = 2^0 = 1

Thus, the mode of a file or directory can be represented using the numbers 421421421 instead of rwxrwxrwx. Because permissions are grouped into the categories user, group, and other, you can then simplify this further by using only three numbers, one for each category that represents the sum of the permissions, as shown in Figure 4-4.

Figure 4-4   Numeric representation of the mode

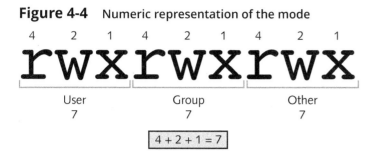

Similarly, to represent the mode rw-r--r--, you can use the numbers 644 because user has read and write (4 + 2 = 6), group has read (4), and other has read (4). The mode rwxr-x--- can also be represented by 750 because user has read, write, and execute (4 + 2 + 1 = 7), group has read and execute (4 + 1 = 5), and other has nothing (0). Table 4-6 provides a list of the different permissions and their corresponding numbers.

Table 4-6   Numeric representations of the permissions in a mode

Mode (One Section Only)	Corresponding Number
rwx	4 + 2 + 1 = **7**
rw-	4 + 2 = **6**
r-x	4 + 1 = **5**
r--	4
-wx	2 + 1 = **3**
-w-	2
--x	1
---	0

To change the mode of the file1 file used earlier to r-xr-----, you can use the command chmod 540 file1, as shown in the following example:

```
[root@server1 ~]# chmod 540 file1
[root@server1 ~]# ls -l
total 28
drwx------   3 root     root         4096 Apr  8 07:12 Desktop
-r-xr-----   1 bob      proj          282 Apr 29 22:06 file1
-rwxr-xr-x   1 root     root          282 Apr 29 22:06 file2
-rwxrwxrwx   1 root     root          282 Apr 29 22:06 file3
----------   1 root     root          282 Apr 29 22:06 file4
-rw-r--r--   1 root     root          282 Apr 29 22:06 file5
-rw-r--r--   1 user1    sys           282 Apr 29 22:06 file6
[root@server1 ~]#_
```

Similarly, to change the mode of all files in the directory that start with the word "file" to 644 (which is common permissions for files), you can use the following command:

```
[root@server1 ~]# chmod 644 file*
[root@server1 ~]# ls -l
total 28
drwx------   3 root     root         4096 Apr  8 07:12 Desktop
-rw-r--r--   1 bob      proj          282 Apr 29 22:06 file1
```

```
-rw-r--r--      1 root      root            282 Apr 29 22:06 file2
-rw-r--r--      1 root      root            282 Apr 29 22:06 file3
-rw-r--r--      1 root      root            282 Apr 29 22:06 file4
-rw-r--r--      1 root      root            282 Apr 29 22:06 file5
-rw-r--r--      1 user1     sys             282 Apr 29 22:06 file6
[root@server1 ~]#_
```

Like the `chown` and `chgrp` commands, the `chmod` command can be used to change the permission on a directory and all of its contents recursively by using the `–R` option, as shown in the following example when changing the mode of the Desktop directory:

```
[root@server1 ~]# chmod –R 755 Desktop
[root@server1 ~]# ls -l
total 28
drwxr-xr-x      3 root      root           4096 Apr  8 07:12 Desktop
-rw-r--r--      1 bob       proj            282 Apr 29 22:06 file1
-rw-r--r--      1 root      root            282 Apr 29 22:06 file2
-rw-r--r--      1 root      root            282 Apr 29 22:06 file3
-rw-r--r--      1 root      root            282 Apr 29 22:06 file4
-rw-r--r--      1 root      root            282 Apr 29 22:06 file5
-rw-r--r--      1 user1     sys             282 Apr 29 22:06 file6
[root@server1 ~]# ls -l Desktop
total 16
-rwxr-xr-x      1 root      root            163 Mar 29 09:58 Work
-rwxr-xr-x      1 root      root           3578 Mar 29 09:58 Home
-rwxr-xr-x      1 root      root           1791 Mar 29 09:58 Start Here
drwxr-xr-x      2 root      root           4096 Mar 29 09:58 Trash
[root@server1 ~]#_
```

Default Permissions

Recall that permissions provide security for files and directories by allowing only certain users access, and that there are common guidelines for setting permissions on files and directories, so that permissions are not too strict or too permissive. Also important to maintaining security are the permissions that are given to new files and directories after they are created. New files are given rw-rw-rw- by the system when they are created (because execute should not be given unless necessary), and new directories are given rwxrwxrwx by the system when they are created (because execute needs to exist on a directory for other permissions to work). These default permissions are too permissive for most files, as they allow other full access to directories and nearly full access to files. Hence, a special variable on the system called the **umask** (user mask) takes away permissions on new files and directories immediately after they are created. The most common umask that you will find is 022, which specifies that nothing (0) is taken away from the user, write permission (2) is taken away from members of the group, and write permission (2) is taken away from other on new files and directories when they are first created and given permissions by the system.

> **Note 19**
>
> Keep in mind that the umask applies only to newly created files and directories; it is never used to modify the permissions of existing files and directories. You must use the `chmod` command to modify existing permissions.

An example of how a umask of 022 can be used to alter the permissions of a new file or directory after creation is shown in Figure 4-5.

Figure 4-5   Performing a umask 022 calculation

	New Files	New Directories
Permissions assigned by system	rw-rw-rw-	rwxrwxrwx
- umask	0 2 2	0 2 2
= resulting permissions	rw-r--r--	rwxr-xr-x

To verify the umask used, you can use the `umask command` and note the final three digits in the output. To ensure that the umask functions as shown in Figure 4-5, create a new file using the `touch` command and a new directory using the `mkdir` command, as shown in the following output:

```
[root@server1 ~]# ls -l
total 28
drwx------      3 root       root             4096 Apr   8 07:12 Desktop
[root@server1 ~]# umask
0022
[root@server1 ~]# mkdir dir1
[root@server1 ~]# touch file1
[root@server1 ~]# ls -l
total 8
drwx------      3 root       root             4096 Apr   8 07:12 Desktop
drwxr-xr-x      2 root       root             4096 May   3 21:39 dir1
-rw-r--r--      1 root       root                0 May   3 21:40 file1
[root@server1 ~]#_
```

Because the umask is a variable stored in memory, it can be changed. To change the current umask, you can specify the new umask as an argument to the `umask` command. Suppose, for example, you want to change the umask to 007; the resulting permissions on new files and directories is calculated in Figure 4-6.

Figure 4-6   Performing a umask 007 calculation

	New Files	New Directories
Permissions assigned by system	rw-rw-rw-	rwxrwxrwx
- umask	0 0 7	0 0 7
= resulting permissions	rw-rw----	rwxrwx---

To change the umask to 007 and view its effect, you can type the following commands on the command line:

```
[root@server1 ~]# ls -l
total 8
drwx------      3 root       root             4096 Apr   8 07:12 Desktop
```

```
drwxr-xr-x     2 root      root        4096 May  3 21:39 dir1
-rw-r--r--     1 root      root           0 May  3 21:40 file1
[root@server1 ~]# umask 007
[root@server1 ~]# umask
0007
[root@server1 ~]# mkdir dir2
[root@server1 ~]# touch file2
[root@server1 ~]# ls -l
total 12
drwx------     3 root      root        4096 Apr  8 07:12 Desktop
drwxr-xr-x     2 root      root        4096 May  3 21:39 dir1
drwxrwx---     2 root      root        4096 May  3 21:41 dir2
-rw-r--r--     1 root      root           0 May  3 21:40 file1
-rw-rw----     1 root      root           0 May  3 21:41 file2
[root@server1 ~]#_
```

Special Permissions

Read, write, and execute are the regular file permissions that you would use to assign security to files; however, you can optionally use three more special permissions on files and directories:

- SUID (Set User ID)
- SGID (Set Group ID)
- Sticky bit

Defining Special Permissions

The SUID has no special function when set on a directory; however, if the SUID is set on a file and that file is executed, the person who executed the file temporarily becomes the owner of the file while it is executing. Many commands on a typical Linux system have this special permission set; the `passwd` command (/usr/bin/passwd) that is used to change your password is one such file. Because this file is owned by the root user, when a regular user executes the `passwd` command to change their own password, that user temporarily becomes the root user while the `passwd` command is executing in memory. This ensures that any user can change their own password because a default kernel setting on Linux systems only allows the root user to change passwords. Furthermore, the SUID can only be applied to binary compiled programs. The Linux kernel will not interpret the SUID on an executable text file, such as a shell script, because text files are easy to edit and, thus, pose a security hazard to the system.

Contrary to the SUID, the SGID has a function when applied to both files and directories. Just as the SUID allows regular users to execute a binary compiled program and become the owner of the file for the duration of execution, the SGID allows regular users to execute a binary compiled program and become a member of the group that is attached to the file. Thus, if a file is owned by the group "sys" and also has the SGID permission, any user who executes that file will be a member of the group "sys" during execution. If a command or file requires the user executing it to have the same permissions applied to the sys group, setting the SGID on the file simplifies assigning rights to the file for user execution.

The SGID also has a special function when placed on a directory. When a user creates a file, recall that that user's name and primary group become the owner and group owner of the file, respectively. However, if a user creates a file in a directory that has the SGID permission set, that user's name becomes the owner of the file and the directory's group owner becomes the group owner of the file.

Finally, the sticky bit was used on files in the past to lock them in memory; however, today the sticky bit performs a useful function only on directories. As explained earlier in this chapter, the write permission applied to a directory allows you to add and remove any file to and from that directory. Thus, if you have the write permission to a certain directory but no permission to files within it, you could delete all of those files. Consider a company that requires a common directory that gives all employees the ability to add files; this directory must give everyone the write permission. Unfortunately, the write permission also gives all employees the ability to delete all files and directories within, including the ones that others have added to the directory. If the sticky bit is applied to this common directory in addition to the write permission, employees can add files to the directory but only delete those files that they have added and not others.

> **Note 20**
>
> Note that all special permissions also require the execute permission to work properly; the SUID and SGID work on executable files, and the SGID and sticky bit work on directories (which must have execute permission for access).

Setting Special Permissions

The mode of a file that is displayed using the `ls -l` command does not have a section for special permissions. However, because special permissions require execute, they mask the execute permission when displayed using the `ls -l` command, as shown in Figure 4-7.

Figure 4-7   Representing special permissions in the mode

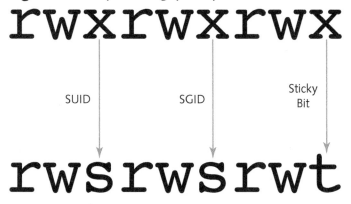

The system allows you to set special permissions even if the file or directory does not have execute permission. However, the special permissions will not perform their function. If the special permissions are set on a file or directory without execute permissions, then the ineffective special permissions are capitalized as shown in Figure 4-8.

Figure 4-8   Representing special permission in the absence of the execute permission

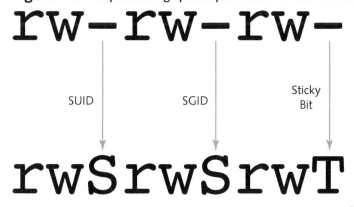

To set the special permissions, you can visualize them to the left of the mode, as shown in Figure 4-9.

Figure 4-9   Numeric representation of regular and special permissions

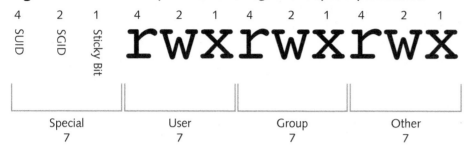

Thus, to set all of the special permissions on a certain file or directory, you can use the command chmod 7777 name, as indicated from Figure 4-9. However, the SUID and SGID bits are typically set on files. To change the permissions on the file1 file used earlier such that other can view and execute the file as the owner and a member of the group, you can use the command chmod 6755 file1, as shown in the following example:

```
[root@server1 ~]# ls -l
total 12
drwx------    3 root      root          4096 Apr  8 07:12 Desktop
drwxr-xr-x    2 root      root          4096 May  3 21:39 dir1
drwx------    2 root      root          4096 May  3 21:41 dir2
-rw-r--r--    1 root      root             0 May  3 21:40 file1
-rw-------    1 root      root             0 May  3 21:41 file2
[root@server1 ~]# chmod 6755 file1
[root@server1 ~]# ls -l
total 12
drwx------    3 root      root          4096 Apr  8 07:12 Desktop
drwxr-xr-x    2 root      root          4096 May  3 21:39 dir1
drwx------    2 root      root          4096 May  3 21:41 dir2
-rwsr-sr-x    1 root      root             0 May  3 21:40 file1
-rw-------    1 root      root             0 May  3 21:41 file2
[root@server1 ~]#_
```

Similarly, to set the sticky bit permission on the directory dir1 used earlier, you can use the command chmod 1777 dir1, which allows all users (including other) to add files to the dir1 directory. This is because you gave the write permission; however, users can only delete the files that they own in dir1 because you set the sticky bit. This is shown in the following example:

```
[root@server1 ~]# ls -l
total 12
drwx------    3 root      root          4096 Apr  8 07:12 Desktop
drwxr-xr-x    2 root      root          4096 May  3 21:39 dir1
drwx------    2 root      root          4096 May  3 21:41 dir2
-rwsr-sr-x    1 root      root             0 May  3 21:40 file1
-rw-------    1 root      root             0 May  3 21:41 file2
[root@server1 ~]# chmod 1777 dir1
[root@server1 ~]# ls -l
total 12
drwx------    3 root      root          4096 Apr  8 07:12 Desktop
drwxrwxrwt    2 root      root          4096 May  3 21:39 dir1
drwx------    2 root      root          4096 May  3 21:41 dir2
-rwsr-sr-x    1 root      root             0 May  3 21:40 file1
-rw-------    1 root      root             0 May  3 21:41 file2
[root@server1 ~]#_
```

Also, remember that assigning special permissions without execute renders those permissions useless. For example, you may forget to give execute permission to user, group, or other, and the long listing covers the execute permission with a special permission. In that case, the special permission is capitalized, as shown in the following example when dir2 is not given execute underneath the position in the mode that indicates the sticky bit (t):

```
[root@server1 ~]# ls -l
total 12
drwx------     3 root      root          4096 Apr  8 07:12 Desktop
drwxrwxrwt     2 root      root          4096 May  3 21:39 dir1
drwx------     2 root      root          4096 May  3 21:41 dir2
-rwsr-sr-x     1 root      root             0 May  3 21:40 file1
-rw-------     1 root      root             0 May  3 21:41 file2
[root@server1 ~]# chmod 1770 dir2
[root@server1 ~]# ls -l
total 12
drwx------     3 root      root          4096 Apr  8 07:12 Desktop
drwxrwxrwt     2 root      root          4096 May  3 21:39 dir1
drwxrwx--T     2 root      root          4096 May  3 21:41 dir2
-rwsr-sr-x     1 root      root             0 May  3 21:40 file1
-rw-------     1 root      root             0 May  3 21:41 file2
[root@server1 ~]#_
```

Setting Custom Permissions in the Access Control List (ACL)

An access control list (ACL) is a list of users or groups that you can assign permissions to. As discussed earlier, the default ACL used in Linux consists of three entities: user, group, and other. However, there may be situations where you need to assign a specific set of permissions on a file or directory to an individual user or group.

Take, for example, the file doc1:

```
[root@server1 ~]# ls -l doc1
-rw-rw----     1 user1     acctg            0 May  2 22:01 doc1
[root@server1 ~]#_
```

The owner of the file (user1) has read and write permission, the group (acctg) has read and write permission, and everyone else has no access to the file.

Now imagine that you need to give read permission to the bob user without giving permissions to anyone else. The solution to this problem is to modify the ACL on the doc1 file and add a special entry for bob only. This can be accomplished by using the following setfacl (set file ACL) command:

```
[root@server1 ~]# setfacl -m u:bob:r-- doc1
[root@server1 ~]#_
```

The –m option in the preceding command modifies the ACL. You can use g instead of u to add a group to the ACL.

Now, when you perform a long listing of the file doc1, you will see a + symbol next to the mode to indicate that there are additional entries in the ACL for this file. To see these additional entries, use the getfacl (get file ACL) command:

```
[root@server1 ~]# ls -l doc1
-rw-rw----+    1 user1     acctg            0 May  2 22:01 doc1
 [root@server1 ~]# getfacl doc1
# file: doc1
# owner: user1
```

```
# group: acctg
user::rw-
user:bob:r--
group::rw-
mask::rw-
other::---
[root@server1 ~]#_
```

After running the getfacl command, you will notice an extra node in the output: the mask. The mask is compared to all additional user and group permissions in the ACL. If the mask is more restrictive, it takes precedence when it comes to permissions. For example, if the mask is set to r-- and the user bob has rw-, then the user bob actually gets r-- to the file. When you run the setfacl command, the mask is always made equal to the least restrictive permission assigned so that it does not affect additional ACL entries. The mask was created as a mechanism that could easily revoke permissions on a file that had several additional users and groups added to the ACL.

To remove all extra ACL assignments on the doc1 file, use the –b option to the setfacl command:

```
[root@server1 ~]# setfacl -b doc1
[root@server1 ~]# ls -l doc1
-rw-rw----   1 user1      acctg           0 May  2 22:01 doc1
[root@server1 ~]#_
```

Managing Filesystem Attributes

As with the Windows operating system, Linux has file attributes that can be set, if necessary. These attributes work outside Linux permissions and are filesystem-specific. This section examines attributes for the ext4 filesystem that you configured for your Fedora Linux system during Hands-On Project 2-1. Filesystem types will be discussed in more depth in Chapter 5.

To see the filesystem attributes that are currently assigned to a file, you can use the lsattr (list attributes) command, as shown here for the doc1 file:

```
[root@server1 ~]# lsattr doc1
--------------e---- doc1
[root@server1 ~]#_
```

By default, all files have the e attribute, which writes to the file in "extent" blocks (rather than immediately in a byte-by-byte fashion). If you would like to add or remove attributes, you can use the chattr (change attributes) command. The following example assigns the immutable attribute (i) to the doc1 file and displays the results:

```
[root@server1 ~]# chattr +i doc1
[root@server1 ~]# lsattr doc1
----i---------e---- doc1
[root@server1 ~]#_
```

The immutable attribute is the most commonly used filesystem attribute and prevents the file from being modified in any way. Because attributes are applied at a filesystem level, not even the root user can modify a file that has the immutable attribute set.

Note 21

Most filesystem attributes are rarely set, as they provide for low-level filesystem functionality. To view a full listing of filesystem attributes, visit the manual page for the chattr command.

Similarly, to remove an attribute, use the `chattr` command with the – option, as shown here with the doc1 file:

```
[root@server1 ~]# chattr -i doc1
[root@server1 ~]# lsattr doc1
--------------e---- doc1
[root@server1 ~]#_
```

Summary

- The Linux directory tree obeys the Filesystem Hierarchy Standard, which allows Linux users and developers to locate system files in standard directories.

- Many file management commands are designed to create, change the location of, or remove files and directories. The most common of these include cp, mv, rm, rmdir, and mkdir.

- You can find files on the filesystem using an indexed database (the locate command) or by searching the directories listed in the PATH variable (the which command). However, the most versatile command used to find files is the find command, which searches for files based on a wide range of criteria.

- Files can be linked two ways. In a symbolic link, one file serves as a pointer to another file. In a hard link, one file is a linked duplicate of another file.

- Each file and directory has an owner and a group owner. In the absence of system restrictions, the owner of the file or directory can change permissions and give ownership to others.

- File and directory permissions can be set for the owner (user), group owner members (group), as well as everyone else on the system (other).

- There are three regular file and directory permissions (read, write, execute) and three special file and directory permissions (SUID, SGID, sticky bit). The definitions of these permissions are different for files and directories.

- Permissions can be changed using the chmod command by specifying symbols or numbers.

- To ensure security, new files and directories receive default permissions from the system, less the value of the umask variable.

- The root user has all permissions to all files and directories on the Linux filesystem. Similarly, the root user can change the ownership of any file or directory on the Linux filesystem.

- The default ACL (user, group, other) on a file or directory can be modified to include additional users or groups.

- Filesystem attributes can be set on Linux files to provide low-level functionality such as immutability.

Key Terms

access control list (ACL)

chattr (change attributes) command

chgrp (change group) command

chmod (change mode) command

chown (change owner) command

cp (copy) command

data blocks

Filesystem Hierarchy Standard (FHS)

find command

getfacl (get file ACL) command

group

hard link

inode

inode table

interactive mode

ln (link) command

locate command

lsattr (list attributes) command

mkdir (make directory) command

mode

mv (move) command

other

owner

passwd command

PATH variable

permission

primary group

pruning

recursive

rm (remove) command

rmdir (remove directory)
  command

setfacl (set file ACL) command

source file/directory

superblock

symbolic link

target file/directory

touch command

type command

umask

umask command

unlink command

user

whereis command

which command

Review Questions

1. A symbolic link is depicted by an @ symbol appearing at the beginning of the filename when viewed using the ls -l command.

   a. True
   b. False

2. What was created to define a standard directory structure and common file location for UNIX and Linux systems?

   a. POSIX
   b. X.500
   c. FHS
   d. OOBLA

3. There is no real difference between the "S" and "s" special permissions when displayed using the ls -l command. One just means it is on a file, and the other means that it is on a directory.

   a. True
   b. False

4. The default permissions given by the system prior to analyzing the umask are _____ for newly created directories and _____ for newly created files.

   a. rw-rw-rw- and rw-rw-rw-
   b. rw-rw-rw- and r--r--r--
   c. rw-rw-rw- and rwxrwxrwx
   d. rwxrwxrwx and rw-rw-rw-

5. What must a Fedora Linux user do to run cp or mv interactively and be asked whether to overwrite an existing file?

   a. Just run cp or mv because they run in interactive mode by default.
   b. Run interactive cp or interactive mv.
   c. Run cp -i or mv -i.
   d. Run cp -interactive or mv -interactive.

6. The root user utilizes the chown command to give ownership of a file to another user. What must the root user do to regain ownership of the file?

   a. Have the new owner run chgrp and list the root user as the new owner.
   b. Run chgrp again listing the root user as the new owner.

   c. Nothing, because this is a one-way, one-time action.
   d. Run chown and list the root user as the new owner.

7. After typing the ls -F command, you see the following line in the output:

   -rw-r-xr-- 1 user1 root 0 Apr 29 15:40 file1

   How do you interpret the mode of file1?

   a. User1 has read and write, members of the root group have read and execute, and all others have read permissions to the file.
   b. Members of the root group have read and write, user1 has read and execute, and all others have read permissions to the file.
   c. All users have read and write, members of the root group have read and execute, and user1 has read permissions to the file.
   d. User1 has read and write, all others have read and execute, and members of the root group have read permissions to the file.

8. After typing the command umask 731, the permissions on all subsequently created files and directories will be affected. In this case, what will be the permissions on all new files?

   a. rw-rw-rw-
   b. rwxrw-r--
   c. ---r--rw-
   d. ----wx--x

9. You noticed a file in your home directory that has a + symbol appended to the mode. What does this indicate?

   a. Special permissions have been set on the file.
   b. The file has one or more files on the filesystem that are hard linked to it.
   c. The sticky bit directory permission has been set on the file and will remain inactive as a result.
   d. Additional entries exist within the ACL of the file that can be viewed using the getfacl command.

10. When you change the data in a file that is hard-linked to three others, _____.

    a. the data in the file you modified and the data in all hard-linked files are modified because they have different inodes

b. the data in the file you modified as well as the data in all hard-linked files are modified because they share the same data and inode

c. only the data in the file you modified is affected

d. only the data in the file you modified and any hard-linked files in the same directory are affected

11. The command `chmod 317 file1` would produce which of the following lines in the `ls` command?

   a. -w-r--rwx 1 user1 root 0 Apr 29 15:40 file1

   b. -wx--xrwx 1 user1 root 0 Apr 29 15:40 file1

   c. -rwxrw-r-x 1 user1 root 0 Apr 29 15:40 file1

   d. --w-rw-r-e 1 user1 root 0 Apr 29 15:40 file1

12. Which of the following commands will change the user ownership and group ownership of *file1* to user1 and root, respectively?

   a. `chown user1:root file1`

   b. `chown user1 : root file1`

   c. `chown root:user1 file1`

   d. `chown root : user1 file1`

13. What does the /var directory contain?

   a. various additional programs

   b. log files and spool directories

   c. temporary files

   d. files that are architecture-independent

14. What does the `mv` command do? (Choose all that apply.)

   a. It renames a file.

   b. It renames a directory.

   c. It moves a directory to another location on the filesystem.

   d. It moves a file to another location on the filesystem.

15. A file has the following permissions: *r----x-w-*. The command `chmod 143 file1` would have the same effect as the command _____. (Choose all that apply.)

   a. `chmod u+x-r,g+r-x,o+x file1`

   b. `chmod u=w,g=rw,o=rx file1`

   c. `chmod u-r-w,g+r-w,o+r-x file1`

   d. `chmod u=x,g=r,o=wx file1`

   e. `chmod u+w,g+r-w,o+r-x file1`

16. The `which` command _____.

   a. can only be used to search for aliases

   b. searches for a file in all directories, starting from the root

   c. is not a valid Linux command

   d. searches for a file only in directories that are in the PATH variable

17. Hard links need to reside on the same filesystem, whereas symbolic links need not be on the same filesystem as their target.

   a. True

   b. False

18. When applied to a directory, the SGID special permission _____.

   a. allows users the ability to use more than two groups for files that they create within the directory

   b. causes all new files created in the directory to have the same group membership as the directory, and not the entity that created them

   c. causes users to have their permissions checked before they are allowed to access files in the directory

   d. cannot be used because it is applied only to files

19. Given the following output from the `ls` command, how many other files are hard linked with file3?

```
drwxr-xr-x  3  root   root  4096 Apr 8  07:12  Desktop
-rw-r--r--  3  root   root  282  Apr 29 22:06  file1
-rw-r--r--  1  root   root  282  Apr 29 22:06  file2
-rw-r--r--  4  root   root  282  Apr 29 22:06  file3
-rw-r--r--  2  root   root  282  Apr 29 22:06  file4
-rw-r--r--  1  root   root  282  Apr 29 22:06  file5
-rw-r--r--  1  user1  sys   282  Apr 29 22:06  file6
```

   a. one

   b. two

   c. three

   d. four

20. Only the root user can modify a file that has the immutable attribute set.

   a. True

   b. False

Hands-On Projects

These projects should be completed in the order given. The hands-on projects presented in this chapter should take a total of three hours to complete. The requirements for this lab include:

- A computer with Fedora Linux installed according to Hands-On Project 2-1
- Completion of all hands-on projects in Chapter 3

Project 4-1

Estimated Time: 10 minutes
Objective: Create directories.
Description: In this hands-on project, you log in to the computer and create new directories.

1. Boot your Fedora Linux virtual machine. After your Linux system has loaded, switch to a command-line terminal (tty5) by pressing **Ctrl+Alt+F5**. Log in to the terminal using the user name of **root** and the password of **LINUXrocks!**.

2. At the command prompt, type `ls -F` and press **Enter**. Note the contents of your home folder.

3. At the command prompt, type `mkdir mysamples` and press **Enter**. Next type `ls -F` at the command prompt, and press **Enter** to verify the creation of the subdirectory.

4. At the command prompt, type `cd mysamples` and press **Enter**. Next, type `ls -F` at the command prompt and press **Enter**. What are the contents of the subdirectory mysamples?

5. At the command prompt, type `mkdir undermysamples` and press **Enter**. Next, type `ls -F` at the command prompt and press **Enter**. What are the contents of the subdirectory mysamples?

6. At the command prompt, type `mkdir todelete` and press **Enter**. Next, type `ls -F` at the command prompt and press **Enter**. Does the subdirectory todelete you just created appear listed in the display?

7. At the command prompt, type `cd ..` and press **Enter**. Next, type `ls -R` and press **Enter**. Notice that the subdirectory mysamples and its subdirectory undermysamples are both displayed.

8. At the command prompt, type `cd ..` and press **Enter**. At the command prompt, type `pwd` and press **Enter**. What is your current directory?

9. At the command prompt, type `mkdir foruser1` and press **Enter**. At the command prompt, type `ls -F` and press **Enter**. Does the subdirectory you just created appear listed in the display?

10. Type `exit` and press **Enter** to log out of your shell.

Project 4-2

Estimated Time: 15 minutes
Objective: Copy files and directories.
Description: In this hands-on project, you copy files and directories using the `cp` command.

1. Switch to a command-line terminal (tty5) by pressing **Ctrl+Alt+F5** and log in to the terminal using the user name of **root** and the password of **LINUXrocks!**.

2. Next, type `ls -F` at the command prompt and press **Enter**. Note the contents of your home folder.

3. At the command prompt, type `cp sample1` and press **Enter**. What error message was displayed and why?

4. At the command prompt, type `cp sample1 sample1A` and press **Enter**. Next, type `ls -F sample*` at the command prompt and press **Enter**. How many files are there and what are their names?

5. At the command prompt, type `cp sample1 mysamples/sample1B` and press **Enter**. Next, type `ls -F sample*` at the command prompt and press **Enter**. How many files are there and what are their names?

6. At the command prompt, type `cd mysamples` and press **Enter**. Next, type `ls -F` at the command prompt and press **Enter**. Was sample1B copied successfully?

7. At the command prompt, type `cp /root/sample2 .` and press **Enter**. Next, type `ls -F` at the command prompt and press **Enter**. How many files are there and what are their names?

8. At the command prompt, type `cp sample1B ..` and press **Enter**. Next, type `cd ..` at the command prompt and press **Enter**. At the command prompt, type `ls -F sample*` and press **Enter**. Was the sample1B file copied successfully?

9. At the command prompt, type `cp sample1 sample2 sample3 mysamples` and press **Enter**. What message do you get and why? Choose **y** and press **Enter**. Next, type `cd mysamples` at the command prompt and press **Enter**. At the command prompt, type `ls -F` and press **Enter**. How many files are there and what are their names?

10. At the command prompt, type `cd ..` and press **Enter**. Next, type `cp mysamples mysamples2` at the command prompt and press **Enter**. What error message did you receive? Why?

11. At the command prompt, type `cp -R mysamples mysamples2` and press **Enter**. Next, type `ls -F` at the command prompt, and press **Enter**. Was the directory copied successfully? Type `ls -F mysamples2` at the command prompt and press **Enter**. Were the contents of mysamples successfully copied to mysamples2?

12. Type `exit` and press **Enter** to log out of your shell.

Project 4-3

Estimated Time: 20 minutes
Objective: Organize files and directories.
Description: In this hands-on project, you use the `mv` command to rename and move files and directories.

1. Switch to a command-line terminal (tty5) by pressing **Ctrl+Alt+F5** and log in to the terminal using the user name of **root** and the password of **LINUXrocks!**.

2. Next, type `ls -F` at the command prompt and press **Enter**. Note the contents of your home folder.

3. At the command prompt, type `mv sample1` and press **Enter**. What error message was displayed and why?

4. At the command prompt, type `mv sample1 sample4` and press **Enter**. Next, type `ls -F sample*` at the command prompt and press **Enter**. How many files are listed and what are their names? What happened to sample1?

5. At the command prompt, type `mv sample4 mysamples` and press **Enter**. Next, type `ls -F sample*` at the command prompt and press **Enter**. How many files are there and what are their names? Where did sample4 go?

6. At the command prompt, type `cd mysamples` and press **Enter**. Next, type `ls -F sample*` at the command prompt and press **Enter**. Notice that the sample4 file you moved in Step 5 was moved here.

7. At the command prompt, type `mv sample4 ..` and press **Enter**. Next, type `ls -F sample*` at the command prompt and press **Enter**. How many files are there and what are their names? Where did the sample4 file go?

8. At the command prompt, type `cd ..` and press **Enter**. Next, type `ls -F` at the command prompt and press **Enter** to view the new location of sample4.

9. At the command prompt, type `mv sample4 mysamples/sample2` and press **Enter**. What message appeared on the screen and why?

10. Type **y** and press **Enter** to confirm you want to overwrite the file in the destination folder.

11. At the command prompt, type `mv sample? mysamples` and press **Enter**. Type **y** and press **Enter** to confirm you want to overwrite the file sample3 in the destination folder.

12. At the command prompt, type `ls -F sample*` and press **Enter**. How many files are there and why?

13. At the command prompt, type `mv sample1* mysamples` and press **Enter**. Type **y** and press **Enter** to confirm you want to overwrite the file sample1B in the destination directory.

14. At the command prompt, type `ls -F sample*` and press **Enter**. Notice that there are no sample files in the /root directory.

15. At the command prompt, type `cd mysamples` and press **Enter**. Next, type `ls -F` at the command prompt and press **Enter**. Notice that all files originally in /root have been moved to this directory.

16. At the command prompt, type `cd ..` and press **Enter**. Next, type `ls -F` at the command prompt and press **Enter**. Type `mv mysamples samples` and press **Enter**. Next, type `ls -F` at the command prompt and press **Enter**. Why did you not need to specify the recursive option to the `mv` command to rename the mysamples directory to samples?

17. Type `exit` and press **Enter** to log out of your shell.

Project 4-4

Estimated Time: 20 minutes
Objective: Create hard and symbolic links.
Description: In this hands-on project, you make and view links to files and directories.

1. Switch to a command-line terminal (tty5) by pressing **Ctrl+Alt+F5** and log in to the terminal using the user name of **root** and the password of **LINUXrocks!**.

2. At the command prompt, type `cd samples` and press **Enter**. Next, type `ls -F` at the command prompt and press **Enter**. What files do you see? Next, type `ls -l` at the command prompt and press **Enter**. What is the link count for the sample1 file?

3. At the command prompt, type `ln sample1 hardlinksample` and press **Enter**. Next, type `ls -F` at the command prompt and press **Enter**. Does anything in the terminal output indicate that sample1 and hardlinksample are hard-linked? Next, type `ls -l` at the command prompt and press **Enter**. Does anything in the terminal output indicate that sample1 and hardlinksample are hard-linked? What is the link count for sample1 and hardlinksample? Next, type `ls -li` at the command prompt and press **Enter** to view the inode numbers of each file. Do the two hard-linked files have the same inode number?

4. At the command prompt, type `ln sample1 hardlinksample2` and press **Enter**. Next, type `ls -l` at the command prompt and press **Enter**. What is the link count for the files sample1, hardlinksample, and hardlinksample2? Why?

5. At the command prompt, type `vi sample1` and press **Enter**. Enter a sentence of your choice into the vi editor, and then save your document and quit the vi editor.

6. At the command prompt, type `cat sample1` and press **Enter**. Next, type `cat hardlinksample` at the command prompt and press **Enter**. Next, type `cat hardlinksample2` at the command prompt and press **Enter**. Are the contents of each file the same? Why?

7. At the command prompt, type `ln -s sample2 symlinksample` and press **Enter**. Next, type `ls -F` at the command prompt and press **Enter**. Does anything in the terminal output indicate that sample2 and symlinksample are symbolically linked? Next, type `ls -l` at the command prompt and press **Enter**. Does anything in the terminal output indicate that sample2 and symlinksample are symbolically linked? Next, type `ls -li` at the command prompt and press **Enter** to view the inode numbers of each file. Do the two symbolically linked files have the same inode number?

8. At the command prompt, type `vi symlinksample` and press **Enter**. Enter a sentence of your choice into the vi editor, and then save your document and quit the vi editor.

9. At the command prompt, type `ls -l` and press **Enter**. What is the size of the symlinksample file compared to sample2? Why? Next, type `cat sample2` at the command prompt and press **Enter**. What are the contents and why?

10. At the command prompt, type `ln -s /etc/samba samba` and press **Enter**. Next, type `ls -F` at the command prompt and press **Enter**. What file type is indicated for samba? Next, type `cd samba` at the command prompt and press **Enter**. Type `pwd` at the command prompt and press **Enter** to view your current directory. What is your current directory? Next, type `ls -F` at the command prompt and press **Enter**. What files are listed? Next, type `ls -F /etc/samba` at the command prompt and press **Enter**.

    Note that your samba directory is merely a pointer to the /etc/samba directory. How can this type of linking be useful?

11. Type `exit` and press **Enter** to log out of your shell.

Project 4-5

Estimated Time: 15 minutes
Objective: Find system files.
Description: In this hands-on project, you find files on the filesystem using the `find`, `locate`, `which`, `type`, and `whereis` commands.

1. Switch to a command-line terminal (tty5) by pressing **Ctrl+Alt+F5** and log in to the terminal using the user name of **root** and the password of **LINUXrocks!**.

2. At the command prompt, type `touch newfile` and press **Enter**. Next, type `locate newfile` at the command prompt and press **Enter**. Did the `locate` command find the file you just created? Why?

3. At the command prompt, type `updatedb` and press **Enter**. When the command is finished, type `locate newfile` at the command prompt and press **Enter**. Did the `locate` command find the file? If so, how quickly did it find it? Why?

4. At the command prompt, type `find / -name "newfile"` and press **Enter**. Did the `find` command find the file? If so, how quickly did it find it? Why?

5. At the command prompt, type `find /root -name "newfile"` and press **Enter**. Did the `find` command find the file? How quickly did it find it? Why?

6. At the command prompt, type `which newfile` and press **Enter**. Did the `which` command find the file? Type `echo $PATH` at the command prompt and press **Enter**. Is the /root directory listed in the PATH variable? Is the /usr/bin directory listed in the PATH variable?

7. At the command prompt, type `which grep` and press **Enter**. Did the `which` command find the file? Why?

8. At the command prompt, type `type grep` and press **Enter**. Next, type `whereis grep` and press **Enter**. Do these commands return less or more than the `which` command did in the previous step? Why?

9. At the command prompt, type `find /root -name "sample*"` and press **Enter**. What files are listed?

10. At the command prompt, type `find /root -type l` and press **Enter**. What files are listed?

11. At the command prompt, type `find /root -size 0` and press **Enter**. What types of files are listed? Type `find / -size 0 | less` to see all of the files of this type on the system.

12. Type `exit` and press **Enter** to log out of your shell.

Project 4-6

Estimated Time: 10 minutes

Objective: Remove files and directories.

Description: In this hands-on project, you delete files and directories using the `rmdir` and `rm` commands.

1. Switch to a command-line terminal (tty5) by pressing **Ctrl+Alt+F5** and log in to the terminal using the user name of **root** and the password of **LINUXrocks!**.

2. At the command prompt, type `cd samples` and press **Enter**. At the command prompt, type `ls -R` and press **Enter**. Note the two empty directories todelete and undermysamples.

3. At the command prompt, type `rmdir undermysamples todelete` and press **Enter**. Next, type `ls -F` at the command prompt and press **Enter**. Were both directories deleted successfully? Why?

4. At the command prompt, type `rm sample1*` and press **Enter**. What message is displayed? Answer **n** to all three questions.

5. At the command prompt, type `rm -f sample1*` and press **Enter**. Why were you not prompted to continue? Next, type `ls -F` at the command prompt and press **Enter**. Were all three files deleted successfully? What other command may be used to delete a file within Linux?

6. At the command prompt, type `cd ..` and press **Enter**. Next, type `rmdir samples` at the command prompt and press **Enter**. What error message do you receive and why?

7. At the command prompt, type `rm -rf samples` and press **Enter**. Next, type `ls -F` at the command prompt and press **Enter**. Was the samples directory and all files within it deleted successfully?

8. Type `exit` and press **Enter** to log out of your shell.

Project 4-7

Estimated Time: 30 minutes

Objective: Set access permissions.

Description: In this hands-on project, you apply and modify access permissions on files and directories and test their effects.

1. Switch to a command-line terminal (tty5) by pressing **Ctrl+Alt+F5** and log in to the terminal using the user name of **root** and the password of **LINUXrocks!**.

2. At the command prompt, type `touch permsample` and press **Enter**. Next, type `chmod 777 permsample` at the command prompt and press **Enter**.

3. At the command prompt, type `ls -l` and press **Enter**. Who has read, write, and execute permissions to this file?

4. At the command prompt, type `chmod 000 permsample` and press **Enter**. Next, type `ls -l` at the command prompt and press **Enter**. Who has read, write, and execute permissions to this file?

5. At the command prompt, type `rm -f permsample` and press **Enter**. Were you able to delete this file? Why?

6. At the command prompt, type `cd /` and press **Enter**. Next, type `pwd` at the command prompt and press **Enter**. Type `ls -F` at the command prompt and press **Enter**. Note the directories you see under the /.

7. At the command prompt, type `ls -l` and press **Enter** to view the owner, group owner, and permissions on the foruser1 directory created in Hands-On Project 4-1. Who is the owner and group owner? If you were logged in as the user user1, in which category would you be placed (user, group, other)? What permissions do you have as this category (read, write, execute)?

8. At the command prompt, type `cd /foruser1` and press **Enter** to enter the foruser1 directory. Next, type `ls -F` at the command prompt and press **Enter**. Are there any files in this directory? Type `cp /etc/hosts .`

at the command prompt and press **Enter**. Next, type `ls -F` at the command prompt and press **Enter** to ensure that a copy of the hosts file was made in your current directory.

9. Switch to a different command-line terminal (tty3) by pressing **Ctrl+Alt+F3** and log in to the terminal using the user name of **user1** and the password of **LINUXrocks!**.

10. At the command prompt, type `cd /foruser1` and press **Enter**. Were you successful? Why? Next, type `ls -F` at the command prompt and press **Enter**. Were you able to see the contents of the directory? Why? Next, type `rm -f hosts` at the command prompt and press **Enter**. Why did you receive an error message?

11. Switch back to your previous command-line terminal (tty5) by pressing **Ctrl+Alt+F5**. Note that you are logged in as the root user on this terminal and within the /foruser1 directory.

12. At the command prompt, type `chmod o+w /foruser1` and press **Enter**. Were you able to change the permissions on the /foruser1 directory successfully? Why?

13. Switch back to your previous command-line terminal (tty3) by pressing **Ctrl+Alt+F3**. Note that you are logged in as the user1 user on this terminal and within the /foruser1 directory.

14. At the command prompt, type `rm -f hosts` at the command prompt and press **Enter**. Were you successful now? Why?

15. Switch back to your previous command-line terminal (tty5) by pressing **Ctrl+Alt+F5**. Note that you are logged in as the root user on this terminal.

16. At the command prompt, type `cp /etc/hosts .` at the command prompt and press **Enter** to place another copy of the hosts file in your current directory (/foruser1).

17. At the command prompt, type `ls -l` and press **Enter**. Who is the owner and group owner of this file? If you were logged in as the user user1, in which category would you be placed (user, group, other)? What permissions does user1 have as this category (read, write, execute)?

18. Switch back to your previous command-line terminal (tty3) by pressing **Ctrl+Alt+F3**. Note that you are logged in as the user1 user on this terminal and in the /foruser1 directory.

19. At the command prompt, type `cat hosts` at the command prompt and press **Enter**. Were you successful? Why? Next, type `vi hosts` at the command prompt to open the hosts file in the vi editor. Delete the first line of this file and save your changes. Were you successful? Why? Exit the vi editor and discard your changes.

20. Switch back to your previous command-line terminal (tty5) by pressing **Ctrl+Alt+F5**. Note that you are logged in as the root user on this terminal and in the /foruser1 directory.

21. At the command prompt, type `chmod o+w hosts` and press **Enter**.

22. Switch back to your previous command-line terminal (tty3) by pressing **Ctrl+Alt+F3**. Note that you are logged in as the user1 user on this terminal and in the /foruser1 directory.

23. At the command prompt, type `vi hosts` at the command prompt to open the hosts file in the vi editor. Delete the first line of this file and save your changes. Why were you successful this time? Exit the vi editor.

24. At the command prompt, type `ls -l` and press **Enter**. Do you have permission to execute the hosts file? Should you make this file executable? Why? Next, type `ls -l /usr/bin` at the command prompt and press **Enter**. Note how many of these files to which you have execute permission. Type `file /usr/bin/* | more` at the command prompt and press **Enter** to view the file types of the files in the /bin directory. Should these files have the execute permission?

25. Type `exit` and press **Enter** to log out of your shell.

26. Switch back to your previous command-line terminal (tty5) by pressing **Ctrl+Alt+F5**. Note that you are logged in as the root user on this terminal.

27. Type `exit` and press **Enter** to log out of your shell.

Project 4-8

Estimated Time: 15 minutes
Objective: Set default permissions.
Description: In this hands-on project, you view and manipulate the default file and directory permissions using the umask variable.

1. Switch to a command-line terminal (tty5) by pressing **Ctrl+Alt+F5** and log in to the terminal using the user name of **user1** and the password of **LINUXrocks!**.

2. At the command prompt, type `umask` and press **Enter**. What is the default umask variable?

3. At the command prompt, type `touch utest1` and press **Enter**. Next, type `ls -l` at the command prompt and press **Enter**. What are the permissions on the utest1 file? Do these agree with the calculation in Figure 4-4? Create a new directory by typing the command `mkdir udir1` at the command prompt and pressing **Enter**. Next, type `ls -l` at the command prompt and press **Enter**. What are the permissions on the udir1 directory? Do these agree with the calculation in Figure 4-4?

4. At the command prompt, type `umask 007` and press **Enter**. Next, type `umask` at the command prompt and press **Enter** to verify that your umask variable has been changed to 007.

5. At the command prompt, type `touch utest2` and press **Enter**. Next, type `ls -l` at the command prompt and press **Enter**. What are the permissions on the utest2 file? Do these agree with the calculation in Figure 4-5? Create a new directory by typing the command `mkdir udir2` at the command prompt and pressing **Enter**. Next, type `ls -l` at the command prompt and press **Enter**. What are the permissions on the udir2 directory? Do these agree with the calculation in Figure 4-5?

6. Type `exit` and press **Enter** to log out of your shell.

Project 4-9

Estimated Time: 15 minutes
Objective: Set file and directory ownership.
Description: In this hands-on project, you view and change file and directory ownership using the `chown` and `chgrp` commands.

1. Switch to a command-line terminal (tty5) by pressing **Ctrl+Alt+F5** and log in to the terminal using the user name of **root** and the password of **LINUXrocks!**.

2. At the command prompt, type `touch ownersample` and press **Enter**. Next, type `mkdir ownerdir` at the command prompt and press **Enter**. Next, type `ls -l` at the command prompt and press **Enter** to verify that the file ownersample and directory ownerdir were created and that root is the owner and group owner of each.

3. At the command prompt, type `chgrp sys owner*` and press **Enter** to change the group ownership to the sys group for both ownersample and ownerdir. Why were you successful?

4. At the command prompt, type `chown user1 owner*` and press **Enter** to change the ownership to the user1 user for both ownersample and ownerdir. Why were you successful?

5. At the command prompt, type `chown root.root owner*` and press **Enter** to change the ownership and group ownership back to the root user for both ownersample and ownerdir. Although you are not the current owner of these files, why did you not receive an error message?

6. At the command prompt, type `mv ownersample ownerdir` and press **Enter**. Next, type `ls -lR` at the command prompt and press **Enter** to note that the ownersample file now exists within the ownerdir directory and that both are owned by root.

7. At the command prompt, type `chown -R user1 ownerdir` and press **Enter**. Next, type `ls -lR` at the command prompt and press **Enter**. Who owns the ownerdir directory and ownersample file?

8. At the command prompt, type `rm -Rf ownerdir` and press **Enter**. Why were you able to delete this directory without being the owner of it?

9. Type `exit` and press **Enter** to log out of your shell.

Project 4-10

Estimated Time: 15 minutes
Objective: Set special permissions and ACL entries.
Description: In this hands-on project, you view and set special permissions on files and directories as well as modify the default ACL on a file.

1. Switch to a command-line terminal (tty3) by pressing **Ctrl+Alt+F3** and log in to the terminal using the user name of **user1** and the password of **LINUXrocks!**.

2. At the command prompt, type `touch specialfile` and press **Enter**. Next, type `ls -l` at the command prompt and press **Enter** to verify that specialfile was created successfully. Who is the owner and group owner of specialfile?

3. At the command prompt, type `chmod 4777 specialfile` and press **Enter**. Next, type `ls -l` at the command prompt and press **Enter**. Which special permission is set on this file? If this file were executed by another user, who would that user be during execution?

4. At the command prompt, type `chmod 6777 specialfile` and press **Enter**. Next, type `ls -l` at the command prompt and press **Enter**. Which special permissions are set on this file? If this file were executed by another user, who would that user be during execution and which group would that user be a member of?

5. At the command prompt, type `chmod 6444 specialfile` and press **Enter**. Next, type `ls -l` at the command prompt and press **Enter**. Can you tell if execute is not given underneath the special permission listings? Would the special permissions retain their meaning in this case?

6. Switch to a command-line terminal (tty5) by pressing **Ctrl+Alt+F5** and log in to the terminal using the user name of **root** and the password of **LINUXrocks!**.

7. At the command prompt, type `mkdir /public` and press **Enter**. Next, type `chmod 1777 /public` at the command prompt and press **Enter**. Which special permission is set on this directory? Who can add or remove files to and from this directory?

8. At the command prompt, type `touch /public/rootfile` and press **Enter**.

9. Type `exit` and press **Enter** to log out of your shell.

10. Switch back to your previous command-line terminal (tty3) by pressing **Ctrl+Alt+F3**. Note that you are logged in as the user1 user on this terminal.

11. At the command prompt, type `touch /public/user1file` and press **Enter**. Next, type `ls -l /public` at the command prompt and press **Enter**. What files exist in this directory and who are the owners?

12. At the command prompt, type `rm /public/user1file` and press **Enter**. Were you prompted to confirm the deletion of the file?

13. At the command prompt, type `rm /public/rootfile` and press **Enter**. Note the error message that you receive because of the sticky bit.

14. Type `exit` and press **Enter** to log out of your shell.

15. Switch to a command-line terminal (tty5) by pressing **Ctrl+Alt+F5** and log in to the terminal using the user name of **root** and the password of **LINUXrocks!**.

16. At the command prompt, type `touch aclfile` and press **Enter**. Next, type `getfacl aclfile` at the command prompt and press **Enter**. Are there any additional entries beyond user, group, and other?

17. At the command prompt, type `setfacl -m u:user1:r-- aclfile` and press **Enter**. Next, type `ls -l aclfile` at the command prompt and press **Enter**. Is there a + symbol following the mode? Next, type `getfacl aclfile` at the command prompt and press **Enter**. Explain the permissions. When would this permission set be useful?

18. At the command prompt, type `setfacl -b aclfile` and press **Enter**. Next, type `ls -l aclfile` at the command prompt and press **Enter**. Is there a + symbol following the mode?

19. Type `exit` and press **Enter** to log out of your shell.

Project 4-11

Estimated Time: 15 minutes

Objective: Set filesystem attributes.

Description: In this hands-on project, you configure and research filesystem attributes.

1. Switch to a command-line terminal (tty5) by pressing **Ctrl+Alt+F5** and log in to the terminal using the user name of **root** and the password of **LINUXrocks!**.

2. At the command prompt, type `touch toughfile` and press **Enter**. Next, type `lsattr toughfile` at the command prompt and press **Enter**. What filesystem attributes are set on toughfile by default?

3. At the command prompt, type `chattr +i toughfile` and press **Enter**. Next, type `lsattr toughfile` at the command prompt and press **Enter**. Is the immutable attribute set on toughfile?

4. At the command prompt, type `vi toughfile` and press **Enter**. Does the vi editor warn you that the file is read-only? Add a line of text of your choice in the vi editor and attempt to save your changes using `w!` at the `:` prompt. Were you successful? Quit the vi editor using `q!` at the `:` prompt.

5. At the command prompt, type `rm -f toughfile` and press **Enter**. Were you successful? Why?

6. At the command prompt, type `chattr -i toughfile` and press **Enter**. Next, type `rm -f toughfile` and press **Enter**. Were you successful this time? Why?

7. At the command prompt, type `man chattr` and press **Enter**. Search the manual page for other filesystem attributes. Which attribute tells the Linux kernel to automatically compress/decompress the file as it is written and read from the filesystem? Which attribute causes the data blocks of a file to be immediately overwritten once the file has been deleted? Type `q` and press **Enter** to quit out of the manual page when finished.

8. Type `exit` and press **Enter** to log out of your shell.

Discovery Exercises

Discovery Exercise 4-1

Estimated Time: 30 minutes

Objective: Explore FHS directories.

Description: Use the `ls` command with the `-F` option to explore directories described in the Filesystem Hierarchy Standard starting with /bin. Do you recognize any of the commands in /bin? Explore several other FHS directories and note their contents. Refer to Table 4-1 for a list of directories to explore. Further, visit www.pathname.com/fhs and read about the Filesystem Hierarchy Standard. What benefits does it offer Linux?

Discovery Exercise 4-2

Estimated Time: 35 minutes

Objective: Compose file management commands.

Description: Write the commands required for the following tasks. Try out each command on your system to ensure that it is correct:

a. Make a hierarchical directory structure under /root that consists of one directory containing three subdirectories.

b. Copy two files into each of the subdirectories.

c. Create one more directory with three subdirectories beneath it and move files from the subdirectories containing them to the counterparts you just created.

d. Hard-link three of the files. Examine their inodes.

e. Symbolically link two of the files and examine their link count and inode information.

f. Make symbolic links from your home directory to two directories in this structure and examine the results.

g. Delete the symbolic links in your home directory and the directory structure you created under /root.

Discovery Exercise 4-3

Estimated Time: 35 minutes

Objective: Compose file search commands.

Description: Write the command that can be used to answer the following questions. (*Hint:* Try each on the system to check your results.)

a. Find all files on the system that have the word "test" as part of their filename.

b. Search the PATH variable for the pathname to the `awk` command.

c. Find all files in the /usr directory and subdirectories that are larger than 50 kilobytes in size.

d. Find all files in the /usr directory and subdirectories that are less than 70 kilobytes in size.

e. Find all files in the / directory and subdirectories that are symbolic links.

f. Find all files in the /var directory and subdirectories that were accessed less than 60 minutes ago.

g. Find all files in the /var directory and subdirectories that were accessed less than six days ago.

h. Find all files in the /home directory and subdirectories that are empty.

i. Find all files in the /etc directory and subdirectories that are owned by the group bin.

Discovery Exercise 4-4

Estimated Time: 10 minutes

Objective: Express permission sets numerically.

Description: For each of the following modes, write the numeric equivalent (e.g., 777):

a. rw-r--r--

b. r--r--r--

c. ---rwxrw-

d. -wxr-xrw-

e. rw-rw-rwx

f. -w-r-----

Discovery Exercise 4-5

Estimated Time: 15 minutes

Objective: Explain permissions.

Description: Fill in the permissions in Table 4-7 with checkmarks, assuming that all four files are in the directory /public, which has a mode of rwxr-xr-x.

Table 4-7   Permissions table for Discovery Exercise 4-5

Filename	Mode		Read	Edit	Execute	List	Delete
sample1	rw-rw-rw-	User					
		Group					
		Other					
sample2	r--r-----	User					
		Group					
		Other					
sample3	rwxr-x---	User					
		Group					
		Other					
sample4	r-x------	User					
		Group					
		Other					

Discovery Exercise 4-6

Estimated Time: 15 minutes
Objective: Explain permissions.
Description: Fill in the permissions in Table 4-8 with checkmarks, assuming that all four files are in the directory /public, which has a mode of rwx--x---.

Table 4-8   Permissions table for Discovery Exercise 4-6

Filename	Mode		Read	Edit	Execute	List	Delete
sample1	`rwxr--r--`	User					
		Group					
		Other					
sample2	`r-xr--rw-`	User					
		Group					
		Other					
sample3	`--xr-x---`	User					
		Group					
		Other					
sample4	`r-xr--r--`	User					
		Group					
		Other					

Discovery Exercise 4-7

Estimated Time: 15 minutes
Objective: Calculate default permissions.
Description: For each of the following umasks, calculate the default permissions given to new files and new directories:

a. 017

b. 272

c. 777

d. 000

e. 077

f. 027

Discovery Exercise 4-8

Estimated Time: 10 minutes
Objective: Outline secure umasks.
Description: For each of the umasks in Discovery Exercise 4-7, list the umasks that are reasonable to use to increase security on your Linux system and explain why.

Discovery Exercise 4-9

Estimated Time: 30 minutes
Objective: Configure umasks.
Description: Starting from the Linux default permissions for file and directories, what umask would you use to ensure that for all new_____?

a. directories, the owner would have read, write, and execute; members of the group would have read and execute; and others would have read

b. files, the owner would have read and execute; the group would have read, write, and execute; and others would have execute

c. files, the owner would have write; the group would have read, write, and execute; and others would have read and write

d. directories, the owner would have read, write, and execute; the group would have read, write, and execute; and others would have read, write, and execute

e. directories, the owner would have execute; the group would have read, write, and execute; and others would have no permissions

f. files, the owner would have read and write; the group would have no permissions; and others would have write

g. directories, the owner would have read, write, and execute; the group would have read; and others would have read and execute

h. directories, the owner would have write; the group would have read, write, and execute; and others would have read, write, and execute

i. files, the owner would have no permissions; the group would have no permissions; and others would have no permissions

Discovery Exercise 4-10

Estimated Time: 30 minutes
Objective: Configure permissions.
Description: What permissions argument to the chmod command would you use to impose the following permissions?

a. on a directory such that: the owner would have read, write, and execute; the group would have read and execute; and others would have read

b. on a file such that: the owner would have read and write; the group would have no permissions; and others would have write

c. on a file such that: the owner would have write; the group would have read, write, and execute; and others would have read and write

d. on a file such that: the owner would have read and execute; the group would have read, write, and execute; and others would have execute

e. on a directory such that: the owner would have execute; the group would have read, write, and execute; and others would have no permissions

f. on a directory such that: the owner would have write; the group would have read, write, and execute; and others would have read, write, and execute

g. on a directory such that: the owner would have read, write, and execute; the group would have read; and others would have read and execute

h. on a directory such that: the owner would have read, write, and execute; the group would have read, write, and execute; and others would have read, write, and execute

i. on a file such that: the owner would have no permissions; the group would have no permissions; and others would have no permissions

Chapter 5

Linux Filesystem Administration

Chapter Objectives

1   Identify the structure and types of device files in the /dev directory.

2   Identify common filesystem types and their features.

3   Mount and unmount filesystems to and from the Linux directory tree.

4   Create and manage filesystems on hard disk drives, SSDs, and removable media storage devices.

5   Create and use ISO images.

6   Use the LVM to create and manage logical volumes.

7   Monitor free space on mounted filesystems.

8   Check filesystems for errors.

9   Use disk quotas to limit user space usage.

Navigating the Linux directory tree and manipulating files are common tasks that are performed daily by all users. However, administrators must provide this directory tree for users, as well as manage and fix the storage devices that support it. In this chapter, you learn about the various device files that represent storage devices and the different filesystems that can be placed on those devices. Next, you learn how to create and manage filesystems on a wide variety of different storage devices, as well as learn standard disk partitioning, LVM configuration, and filesystem management. The chapter concludes with a discussion of disk usage, filesystem errors, and restricting the ability of users to store files.

The /dev Directory

Fundamental to administering the disks used to store information is an understanding of how these disks are specified by the Linux operating system. Most standard devices on a Linux system (such as hard disk drives, SSDs, terminals, and serial ports) are represented by a file on the filesystem called a **device file**. There is one file per device, and these files are typically found in the **/dev directory**. This allows you to specify devices on the system by using the pathname to the file that represents it in the /dev directory.

   Recall from Chapter 2 that the first partition on the first SATA/SCSI/SAS hard disk drive or SSD is identified by the installation program as sda1. When working with Linux utilities, you can specify the pathname to the file /dev/sda1 to refer to this partition.

Furthermore, each device file specifies how data should be transferred to and from the device. There are two methods for transferring data to and from a device. The first method involves transferring information character-by-character to and from the device. Devices that transfer data in this fashion are referred to as character devices. The second method transfers chunks or blocks of information at a time by using physical memory to buffer the transfer. Devices that use this method of transfer are called block devices; they can transfer information much faster than character devices. Device files that represent storage, such as CDs, DVDs, USB flash drives, hard disk drives, and SSDs, are typically block device files because they are formatted with a filesystem that organizes the available storage into discrete blocks that can be written to. Tape drives and most other devices, however, are typically represented by character device files.

To see whether a particular device transfers data character-by-character or block-by-block, recall that the ls -l command displays a c or b character in the type column indicating the type of device file. To view the type of the file /dev/sda1, you can use the following command:

```
[root@server1 ~]# ls -l /dev/sda1
brw-rw----   1 root      disk     8,   1 Feb 23 16:02 /dev/sda1
[root@server1 ~]#_
```

From the leftmost character in the preceding output, you can see that the /dev/sda1 file is a block device file. Table 5-1 lists common device files that you may find on your Linux system and their types.

Table 5-1   Common device files

Device File	Description	Block or Character
/dev/hda1	First partition on the first PATA hard disk drive (primary master)	Block
/dev/hdb1	First partition on the second PATA hard disk drive (primary slave)	Block
/dev/hdc1	First partition on the third PATA hard disk drive (secondary master)	Block
/dev/hdd1	First partition on the fourth PATA hard disk drive (secondary slave)	Block
/dev/sda1	First partition on the first SATA/SCSI/SAS hard disk drive or SSD	Block
/dev/sdb1	First partition on the second SATA/SCSI/SAS hard disk drive or SSD	Block
/dev/vda1	First partition on the first QEMU virtual disk	Block
/dev/vdb1	First partition on the second QEMU virtual disk	Block
/dev/nvme0n1p1	First partition in the first namespace on the first NVMe SSD	Block
/dev/nvme1n1p1	First partition in the first namespace on the second NVMe SSD	Block
/dev/zram0	First RAM disk used by zswap for virtual memory	Block
/dev/zram1	Second RAM disk used by zswap for virtual memory	Block
/dev/sr0	First writeable SATA CD or DVD device in the system	Block
/dev/loop0	First loopback interface	Block
/dev/tty1	First local terminal on the system (Ctrl+Alt+F1)	Character
/dev/tty2	Second local terminal on the system (Ctrl+Alt+F2)	Character
/dev/ttyS0	First serial port on the system (COM1)	Character
/dev/ttyS1	Second serial port on the system (COM2)	Character
/dev/psaux	PS/2 mouse port	Character
/dev/lp0	First parallel port on the system (LPT1)	Character
/dev/null	Device file that represents nothing; any data sent to this device is discarded	Character

(continues)

Table 5-1   Common device files (continued)

Device File	Description	Block or Character
/dev/zero	Device file that produces NULL (empty) characters; it can be used within commands to generate sample input	Character
/dev/random /dev/urandom	Device file that produces pseudorandom numbers; it can be used to provide random numbers for use within commands	Character
/dev/st0	First SCSI tape device in the system	Character
/dev/bus/usb/*	USB device files	Block or Character

Note 1

If a device file is not present on your system, the underlying hardware was not detected by the **udev daemon**, which is responsible for automatically creating device files as necessary.

After a typical Fedora Linux installation, you will find several hundred different device files in the /dev directory that represent devices on the system. This large number of device files on a Linux system does not require much disk space because all device files consist of inodes and no data blocks; as a result, the entire contents of the /dev directory is 0 KB in size unless other regular files are stored within it. When using the `ls -l` command to view device files, the portion of the listing describing the file size is replaced by two numbers: the major number and the minor number. The **major number** of a device file points to the device driver for the device in the Linux kernel; several devices can share the same major number if they are of the same general type (i.e., two different SATA devices might share the same major number as they use the same driver in the Linux kernel). The **minor number** indicates the particular device itself; in the case of storage devices, different minor numbers are used to represent different partitions as shown in the following output:

```
[root@server1 ~]# ls -l /dev/sda*
brw-rw----. 1 root disk 8,  0 Sep  7 09:41 /dev/sda
brw-rw----. 1 root disk 8,  1 Sep  7 09:41 /dev/sda1
brw-rw----. 1 root disk 8,  2 Sep  7 09:41 /dev/sda2
brw-rw----. 1 root disk 8,  3 Sep  7 09:41 /dev/sda3
[root@server1 ~]# ls -l /dev/sdb*
brw-rw----. 1 root disk 8, 16 Sep  7 10:18 /dev/sdb
brw-rw----. 1 root disk 8, 17 Sep  7 10:18 /dev/sdb1
brw-rw----. 1 root disk 8, 18 Sep  7 10:18 /dev/sdb2
brw-rw----. 1 root disk 8, 19 Sep  7 10:18 /dev/sdb3
[root@server1 ~]#_
```

Note 2

In the previous output, note that /dev/sdb* shares the same major number as /dev/sda* because they use the same driver in the Linux kernel. Because it is rare to create more than 15 partitions on a single device, Linux starts minor numbers for additional devices of the same type in increments of 16; thus, the minor number for /dev/sdb is 16, and the minor number for /dev/sdc is 32, and so on. If you create more than 15 partitions on a single device, this minor numbering scheme is automatically adjusted by the udev daemon.

Together, the device file type (block or character), the major number (device driver), and the minor number (specific device) make up the unique characteristics of each device file. To create a device file, you need to know these three pieces of information.

If a device file becomes corrupted, it is usually listed as a regular file instead of a block or character special file. Recall from Chapter 4 that you can use the `find /dev -type f` command to search for regular files under the /dev directory to identify whether corruption has taken place. If you find a corrupted device file or accidentally delete a device file, the mknod command can be used to re-create the device file if you know the type and major and minor numbers. An example of re-creating the /dev/sda1 block device file used earlier with a major number of 8 and a minor number of 1 is shown in the following example:

```
[root@server1 ~]# mknod /dev/sda1 b 8 1
[root@server1 ~]# ls -l /dev/sda1
brw-rw----. 1 root disk 8, 1 Oct  9 15:02 /dev/sda1
[root@server1 ~]#_
```

To see a list of block and character devices that are currently used on the system and their major numbers, you can view the contents of the /proc/devices file. To view the block devices on the system, you can view the contents of the /sys/block directory or run the lsblk command. These methods are shown below:

```
[root@server1 ~]# cat /proc/devices
Character devices:
  1 mem
  4 /dev/vc/0
  4 tty
  4 ttyS
  5 /dev/tty
  5 /dev/console
  5 /dev/ptmx
  7 vcs
 10 misc
 13 input
 14 sound
 21 sg
 29 fb
116 alsa
128 ptm
136 pts
162 raw
180 usb
188 ttyUSB
189 usb_device
202 cpu/msr
203 cpu/cpuid
240 usbmon

Block devices:
  8 sd
  9 md
 11 sr
 65 sd
128 sd
252 zram
253 device-mapper
254 mdp
259 blkext
```

```
[root@server1 ~]#_
[root@server1 ~]# ls /sys/block
sda  sdb  sr0
[root@server1 ~]# lsblk
NAME    MAJ:MIN RM   SIZE RO TYPE MOUNTPOINTS
sda       8:0    0    50G  0 disk
├─sda1    8:1    0   600M  0 part /boot/efi
├─sda2    8:2    0     1G  0 part /boot
└─sda3    8:3    0    35G  0 part /
sdb       8:16   0    40G  0 disk
├─sdb1    8:17   0     5G  0 part /var
├─sdb2    8:18   0    20G  0 part /var/spool
└─sdb3    8:19   0    15G  0 part /var/log
sr0      11:0    1  1024M  0 rom
zram0   252:0    0   3.8G  0 disk [SWAP]
[root@server1 ~]#_
```

Note 3

You can also use the `udevadm command` to view detailed information for a particular device file. For example, `udevadm info /dev/sda` will display details for the first SATA/SCSI/SAS storage device on the system, and `udevadm info /dev/sda1` will display details for the first partition on that storage device.

Filesystems

Recall from Chapter 2 that files must be stored within a partition on the hard disk drive or SSD in a defined format called a filesystem so that the operating system can work with them. The type of filesystem used determines how files are managed on the physical storage device. Each filesystem can have different methods for storing files and features that make the filesystem robust against errors. Although many types of filesystems are available, all filesystems share three common components, as discussed in Chapter 4: the superblock, the inode table, and the data blocks. On a structural level, these three components work together to organize files and allow rapid access to, and retrieval of, data. As discussed in Chapter 2, journaling filesystems contain a fourth component called a journal that keeps track of changes that are to be written to the filesystem. In the event of a power outage, the filesystem can check the journal to complete any changes that were not performed to prevent filesystem errors related to the power outage. All storage media, such as hard disk drives, SSDs, USB flash drives, and DVDs, need to contain a filesystem before they can be used by the Linux operating system.

Note 4

Creating a filesystem on a device is commonly referred to as **formatting**.

Filesystem Types

As mentioned, many filesystems are available for use in the Linux operating system. Each has its own strengths and weaknesses; thus, some are better suited to some tasks and not as well suited to others. One benefit of Linux is that you need not use only one type of filesystem on the system; you can use several partitions formatted with different filesystems under the same directory tree. In addition, files and directories appear the same throughout the directory tree regardless of whether there is one filesystem or 20 filesystems in use by the Linux system. Table 5-2 lists some common filesystems available for use in Linux.

Table 5-2 Common Linux filesystems

Filesystem	Description
btrfs	B-tree File System—A new filesystem for Linux systems that includes many features that are geared toward large-scale storage, including compression, subvolumes, quotas, snapshots, and the ability to span multiple devices. While relatively new and still in development, it is envisioned to be a replacement for the ext4 filesystem in the long term. Its name is commonly pronounced as "Butter F S." You will learn how to configure btrfs in Chapter 6.
exFAT	Extended FAT filesystem—An improved version of the FAT filesystem with large file support. It is the most common filesystem used on removeable storage devices such as USB flash drives and portable USB hard drives, as it has full support on modern Linux, macOS, and Windows operating systems.
ext2	Second extended filesystem—The traditional filesystem used on Linux, it supports access control lists (individual user permissions). In addition, it retains its name from being the new version of the original extended filesystem, based on the Minix filesystem.
ext3	Third extended filesystem—A variation on ext2 that allows for journaling and, thus, has a faster startup and recovery time.
ext4	Fourth extended filesystem—A variation on ext3 that has larger filesystem support and speed enhancements.
iso9660	ISO 9660 filesystem—A filesystem that originated from the International Standards Organization recommendation 9660 that is used by ISO images, CDs, and DVDs.
msdos, fat	File Allocation Table (FAT) filesystem. It can use a 12, 16, or 32-bit table to store file locations.
ntfs	New Technology File System (NTFS)—A Microsoft proprietary filesystem developed for its Windows operating systems. Due to license restrictions, Linux systems can read from, but not write to, NTFS filesystems.
udf	Universal Disk Format (UDF) filesystem—A DVD filesystem originally intended as a modern replacement for the ISO 9660 filesystem.
vfat	FAT filesystem with long filename support.
xfs	X File System (XFS)—A very high-performance filesystem created by Silicon Graphics for use on their IRIX UNIX systems. Many Linux administrators prefer to use xfs on systems that need to quickly write large numbers of files to the filesystem.
zfs	Zettabyte File System (ZFS)—A very high-performance filesystem and volume manager originally created by Sun Microsystems that protects against data corruption and has features that support very large distributed storage systems. Many large-scale Linux server systems in industry use the zfs filesystem to store and manage large amounts of data. You will learn how to configure zfs in Chapter 6.

Note 5

Filesystem support is typically built into the Linux kernel or added as a package on most distributions.

Mounting

The term **mounting** originated in the 1960s when information was stored on large tape reels that had to be mounted on computers to make the data available. Today, mounting still refers to making data available. More specifically, it refers to the process whereby a device is made accessible to users via the logical directory tree. This device is attached to a certain directory on the directory tree called a **mount point**. Users can then create files and subdirectories in this mount point directory, which are then stored on the filesystem that was mounted to that particular directory.

Remember that directories are merely files that do not contain data; instead, they contain a list of files and subdirectories organized within them. Thus, it is easy for the Linux system to cover up directories to prevent user access to that data. This is essentially what happens when a device is mounted to a certain directory; the mount point directory is temporarily covered up by that device while the device remains mounted. Any file contents that were present in the mount point directory prior to mounting are not lost; when the device is unmounted, the mount point directory is uncovered, and the previous file contents are revealed. Suppose, for example, that you mount a USB flash drive that contains a filesystem to the /mnt directory. The /mnt directory is an empty directory that is commonly used as a temporary mount point for mounting removable media devices. Before mounting, the directory structure would resemble that depicted in Figure 5-1. After the USB flash drive is mounted to the /mnt directory, the contents of the /mnt directory would be covered up by the filesystem on the USB flash drive, as illustrated in Figure 5-2.

Figure 5-1   The directory structure prior to mounting

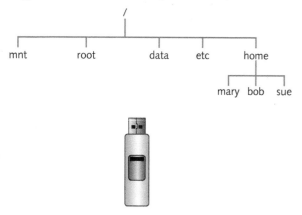

Figure 5-2   The directory structure after mounting a USB flash drive

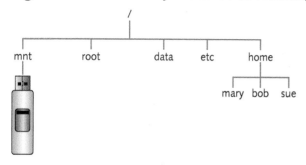

If a user then stores a file in the /mnt directory, as shown in Figure 5-2, that file will be stored in the filesystem on the USB flash drive. Similarly, if a user creates a subdirectory under the /mnt directory depicted in Figure 5-2, that subdirectory will be made in the filesystem on the USB flash drive.

Any existing directory can be used as a mount point. If a user mounts a USB flash drive to the /usr/bin directory, all files in the /usr/bin directory are covered up during the time the drive is mounted, including the command used to unmount the drive. Thus, it is safe practice to create empty directories used specifically for mounting devices to avoid making existing files inaccessible to users.

> ### Note 6
>
> Most systems today have several removable media devices such as CDs, DVDs, USB flash drives, and USB hard drives that may be connected to the computer for long periods of time. As a result, it is considered good form to create subdirectories under the /media directory on your Linux system to mount these removable media devices and only use the /mnt directory to temporarily mount devices. For example, you could mount your USB flash drive to the /media/USBdrive directory and your DVD to the /media/DVD directory. You can then access the files on your USB flash drive by navigating to the /media/USBdrive directory, as well as access the files on your DVD by navigating to the /media/DVD directory.

When the Linux system is first turned on, a filesystem on the hard drive is mounted to the / directory. This is referred to as the **root filesystem** and contains most of the operating system files. Other filesystems on storage devices inside the computer can also be mounted to various mount point directories under the / directory at boot time, as well as via entries in the filesystem table (**/etc/fstab**) discussed in the following sections.

The `mount command` is used to mount devices to mount point directories, and the `umount command` is used to unmount devices from mount point directories; both of these commands are discussed throughout the remainder of this chapter.

Working with USB Flash Drives

The most common type of removable media used to store files that need to be transferred from computer to computer are USB flash drives. USB flash drives are recognized as SCSI drives by operating systems, and often ship with a single partition formatted with the DOS FAT or exFAT filesystem. However, you can reformat the filesystem on this partition with a different filesystem of your choice after determining the appropriate device file. If your system has a single SATA hard disk drive (/dev/sda), the first USB flash drive inserted into your system will be recognized as /dev/sdb, and the partition on it can be represented by /dev/sdb1. To verify that your USB flash drive model (e.g., Kingston DataTraveler) was recognized by the system after inserting it, you can use the `lsusb command`:

```
[root@server1 ~]# lsusb
Bus 001 Device 003: ID 0930:6545 Toshiba Corp. Kingston DataTraveler
Bus 001 Device 002: ID 80ee:0021 VirtualBox USB Tablet
Bus 001 Device 001: ID 1d6b:0001 Linux Foundation 1.1 root hub
[root@server1 ~]#_
```

To verify the device file used to represent the partition on your USB flash drive, you can use the **lsblk** command; a number 1 in the RM column indicates that the device is removable storage. The **lsblk** output shown below indicates that the first partition on the first removeable storage device is /dev/sdb1, and that it is not currently mounted to a directory:

```
[root@server1 ~]# lsblk
NAME    MAJ:MIN RM   SIZE RO TYPE MOUNTPOINTS
sda       8:0    0    50G  0 disk
├─sda1    8:1    0   600M  0 part /boot/efi
├─sda2    8:2    0     1G  0 part /boot
└─sda3    8:3    0    35G  0 part /
sdb       8:16   1     8G  0 disk
└─sdb1    8:17   1     8G  0 part
sr0      11:0    1  1024M  0 rom
zram0   252:0    0   3.8G  0 disk [SWAP]
[root@server1 ~]#_
```

To create a new filesystem on a USB flash drive, you can use the `mkfs` **(make filesystem)** **command** and specify the filesystem type using the `-t` switch and the device file representing the partition. Thus, to format /dev/sdb1 with the ext2 filesystem you can type the following command:

```
[root@server1 ~]# mkfs -t ext2 /dev/sdb1
mke2fs 1.46.5 (30-Dec-2023)
Creating filesystem with 1952512 4k blocks and 488640 inodes
Filesystem UUID: 95b7fdcd-8baa-4e3f-ad6b-1ff5b5ba1f2f
Superblock backups stored on blocks:
        32768, 98304, 163840, 229376, 294912, 819200, 884736, 1605632

Allocating group tables: done
Writing inode tables: done
Writing superblocks and filesystem accounting information: done
[root@server1 ~]#_
```

Note 7

Note from the previous output that each newly formatted Linux filesystem is given a **Universally Unique Identifier (UUID)** that can be used to identify the filesystem. This UUID can be used to identify filesystems that need to be mounted at boot time, as discussed later in this chapter.

Alternatively, you can specify a different filesystem after the `-t` option, such as the FAT filesystem with long filename support (vfat). This results in output different from the `mkfs` command, as shown in the following example:

```
[root@server1 ~]# mkfs -t vfat /dev/sdb1
mkfs.fat 4.2 (2023-01-31)
[root@server1 ~]#_
```

Because the FAT filesystem is universally supported by Windows, macOS, UNIX, and Linux systems, it is often used on removable media. However, the maximum size of a FAT filesystem is 32 GB. For USB flash drives and USB hard disk drives or SSDs larger than 32 GB, you should instead use the exFAT filesystem, which has a maximum filesystem size of 128 PB (petabytes) and is universally supported by modern versions of Windows, macOS, UNIX, and Linux. To format /dev/sdb1 with the exFAT filesystem, you can run the following command:

```
[root@server1 ~]# mkfs -t exfat /dev/sdb1
Creating exFAT filesystem(/dev/sdb1, cluster size=32768)

Writing volume boot record: done
Writing backup volume boot record: done
Fat table creation: done
Allocation bitmap creation: done
Upcase table creation: done
Writing root directory entry: done
Synchronizing...

exFAT format complete!
[root@server1 ~]#_
```

If you do not specify the filesystem using the `mkfs` command, the default filesystem assumed is the ext2 filesystem as shown below:

```
[root@server1 ~]# mkfs /dev/sdb1
mke2fs 1.46.5 (30-Dec-2023)
Creating filesystem with 1952512 4k blocks and 488640 inodes
```

```
Filesystem UUID: 95b7fdcd-8baa-4e3f-ad6b-1ff5b5ba1f2f
Superblock backups stored on blocks:
        32768, 98304, 163840, 229376, 294912, 819200, 884736, 1605632

Allocating group tables: done
Writing inode tables: done
Writing superblocks and filesystem accounting information: done
[root@server1 ~]#_
```

Although the most common command to create filesystems is the mkfs command, you can use other variants and shortcuts to the mkfs command. For example, to create an ext2 filesystem, you could type mke2fs /dev/sdb1 on the command line. Other alternatives to the mkfs command are listed in Table 5-3.

Table 5-3   Commands used to create filesystems

Command	Filesystem It Creates
mkfs	Filesystems of most types
mkdosfs mkfs.msdos mkfs.fat mkfs.vfat	FAT (12, 16, or 32-bit, depending on the size of the filesystem)
mkfs.ext2 mke2fs	ext2
mkfs.ext3 mke2fs -t ext3	ext3
mkfs.ext4 mke2fs -t ext4	ext4
mkisofs	ISO 9660
mkfs.xfs	XFS
mkudffs mkfs.udf	UDF
mkntfs mkfs.ntfs	NTFS
mkexfatfs mkfs.exfat	exFAT

After a USB flash drive has been formatted with a filesystem, it must be mounted to the directory tree before it can be used. A list of currently mounted filesystems can be obtained by using the mount command with no options or arguments, which reads the information listed in the **/etc/mtab** (mount table) file. On modern systems, the output of this command is quite lengthy as it contains many special filesystems and filesystem parameters. Consequently, it is much easier to see a list of currently mounted filesystems using the lsblk command or the df (disk free space) command. The -T option to the df command will also print the filesystem type, and the -h option displays friendly (human readable) size formats, as shown in the following sample output:

```
[root@server1 ~]# df -hT
Filesystem      Type       Size  Used Avail Use% Mounted on
devtmpfs        devtmpfs   4.0M     0  4.0M   0% /dev
```

```
tmpfs           tmpfs       2.0G     0   2.0G   0%  /dev/shm
tmpfs           tmpfs       784M  1.2M   783M   1%  /run
/dev/sda3       ext4         35G  8.9G    24G  28%  /
tmpfs           tmpfs       2.0G  8.0K   2.0G   1%  /tmp
/dev/sda2       ext4        974M  150M   757M  17%  /boot
/dev/sda1       vfat        599M   14M   585M   3%  /boot/efi
tmpfs           tmpfs       392M   92K   392M   1%  /run/user/42
tmpfs           tmpfs       392M   76K   392M   1%  /run/user/0
tmpfs           tmpfs       392M   76K   392M   1%  /run/user/1000
[root@server1 ~]#_
```

From the preceding example output, you can see that the ext4 filesystem on /dev/sda3 is mounted to the / directory, the ext4 filesystem on /dev/sda2 is mounted to the /boot directory, and the vfat filesystem on /dev/sda1 is mounted to the /boot/efi directory. The other filesystems listed are special filesystems that are used by the system; these filesystems are called virtual filesystems or pseudo filesystems and are discussed later in this book.

To mount a device on the directory tree, you can use the mount command with options and arguments to specify the filesystem type, the device to mount, and the directory on which to mount the device (mount point). It is important to ensure that no user is currently using the mount point directory; otherwise, the system gives you an error message and the device is not mounted. To check whether the /media/USBdrive directory is being used by any users, you can use the fuser command with the −u option, as shown in the following output:

```
[root@server1 ~]# fuser -u /media/USBdrive
[root@server1 ~]#_
```

The preceding output indicates the /media/USBdrive directory is not being used by any user processes; to mount a USB flash drive (/dev/sdb1) formatted with the ext2 filesystem to this directory, you could run the following command:

```
[root@server1 ~]# mount -t ext2 /dev/sdb1 /media/USBdrive
[root@server1 ~]# df -hT
Filesystem      Type        Size  Used  Avail Use%  Mounted on
devtmpfs        devtmpfs    4.0M     0   4.0M   0%  /dev
tmpfs           tmpfs       2.0G     0   2.0G   0%  /dev/shm
tmpfs           tmpfs       784M  1.2M   783M   1%  /run
/dev/sda3       ext4         35G  8.9G    24G  28%  /
tmpfs           tmpfs       2.0G  8.0K   2.0G   1%  /tmp
/dev/sda2       ext4        974M  150M   757M  17%  /boot
/dev/sda1       vfat        599M   14M   585M   3%  /boot/efi
tmpfs           tmpfs       392M   92K   392M   1%  /run/user/42
tmpfs           tmpfs       392M   76K   392M   1%  /run/user/0
tmpfs           tmpfs       392M   76K   392M   1%  /run/user/1000
/dev/sdb1       ext2        7.9G   24K   7.5G   1%  /media/USBdrive
[root@server1 ~]#_
```

Note 8

If you omit the −t option to the mount command, it attempts to automatically detect the filesystem on the device. Thus, the command mount /dev/sdb1 /media/USBdrive will perform the same action as the mount command shown in the preceding output.

Notice that /dev/sdb1 is mounted to the /media/USBdrive directory in the preceding output of the mount command. To access and store files on the USB flash drive, you can now treat the /media/USBdrive directory as the root of the USB flash drive. When an ext2, ext3, or ext4 filesystem is created on a device, one directory called lost+found is created by default and used by the fsck command discussed later in this chapter. To explore the recently mounted filesystem, you can use the following commands:

```
[root@server1 ~]# cd /media/USBdrive
[root@server1 USBdrive]# pwd
/media/USBdrive
[root@server1 USBdrive]# ls -F
lost+found/
[root@server1 USBdrive]#_
```

To copy files to the USB flash drive, specify the /media/USBdrive directory as the target for the cp command, as follows:

```
[root@server1 USBdrive]# cd /etc
[root@server1 etc]# cat issue
\S
Kernel \r on an \m (\l)
[root@server1 etc]# cp issue /media/USBdrive
[root@server1 etc]# cd /media/USBdrive
[root@server1 USBdrive]# ls -F
issue  lost+found/
[root@server1 USBdrive]# cat issue
\S
Kernel \r on an \m (\l)
[root@server1 USBdrive]#_
```

Similarly, you can also create subdirectories under the USB flash drive to store files; these subdirectories are referenced under the mount point directory. To make a directory called workfiles on the USB flash drive mounted in the previous example and copy the /etc/inittab file to it, you can use the following commands:

```
[root@server1 USBdrive]# pwd
/media/USBdrive
[root@server1 USBdrive]# ls -F
issue  lost+found/
[root@server1 USBdrive]# mkdir workfiles
[root@server1 USBdrive]# ls -F
issue  lost+found/  workfiles
[root@server1 USBdrive]# cd workfiles
[root@server1 workfiles]# pwd
/media/USBdrive/workfiles
[root@server1 workfiles]# cp /etc/inittab .
[root@server1 workfiles]# ls
inittab
[root@server1 workfiles]#_
```

Even though you can remove a USB flash drive without permission from the system, doing so is likely to cause error messages to appear on the terminal screen. Before a USB flash drive is removed, it must be properly unmounted using the umount command. The umount command can take the name of the device to unmount or the mount point directory as an argument. Similar to mounting a device, unmounting a device requires that the mount point directory has no users using it. If you try to unmount the USB flash drive mounted to the /media/USBdrive directory while it is being used, you receive an error message similar to the one in the following example:

```
[root@server1 USBdrive]# pwd
/media/USBdrive
[root@server1 USBdrive]# umount /media/USBdrive
umount: /media/USBdrive: target is busy.
[root@server1 USBdrive]# fuser -u /media/USBdrive
/media/USBdrive:         17368c(root)
[root@server1 USBdrive]# cd /root
[root@server1 ~]# umount /media/USBdrive
[root@server1 ~]# df -hT
Filesystem      Type      Size  Used Avail Use% Mounted on
devtmpfs        devtmpfs  4.0M     0  4.0M   0% /dev
tmpfs           tmpfs     2.0G     0  2.0G   0% /dev/shm
tmpfs           tmpfs     784M  1.2M  783M   1% /run
/dev/sda3       ext4       35G  8.9G   24G  28% /
tmpfs           tmpfs     2.0G  8.0K  2.0G   1% /tmp
/dev/sda2       ext4      974M  150M  757M  17% /boot
/dev/sda1       vfat      599M   14M  585M   3% /boot/efi
tmpfs           tmpfs     392M   92K  392M   1% /run/user/42
tmpfs           tmpfs     392M   76K  392M   1% /run/user/0
tmpfs           tmpfs     392M   76K  392M   1% /run/user/1000
[root@server1 ~]#_
```

Notice from the preceding output that you were still using the /media/USBdrive directory because it was the current working directory. The fuser command also indicated that the root user had a process using the directory. After the current working directory was changed, the umount command was able to unmount the USB flash drive from the /media/USBdrive directory, and the output of the mount command indicated that it was no longer mounted.

Recall that mounting simply attaches a disk device to the Linux directory tree so that you can treat the device like a directory full of files and subdirectories. A device can be mounted to any existing directory. However, if the directory contains files, those files are inaccessible until the device is unmounted. Suppose, for example, that you create a directory called /USBdrive for mounting USB flash drives and a file inside called samplefile, as shown in the following output:

```
[root@server1 ~]# mkdir /USBdrive
[root@server1 ~]# touch /USBdrive/samplefile
[root@server1 ~]# ls /USBdrive
samplefile
[root@server1 ~]#_
```

If the USB flash drive used earlier is mounted to the /USBdrive directory, a user who uses the /USBdrive directory will be using the filesystem on the USB flash drive; however, when nothing is mounted to the /USBdrive directory, the previous contents are available for use:

```
[root@server1 ~]# mount /dev/sdb1 /USBdrive
[root@server1 ~]# df -hT
Filesystem      Type      Size  Used Avail Use% Mounted on
devtmpfs        devtmpfs  4.0M     0  4.0M   0% /dev
tmpfs           tmpfs     2.0G     0  2.0G   0% /dev/shm
tmpfs           tmpfs     784M  1.2M  783M   1% /run
/dev/sda3       ext4       35G  8.9G   24G  28% /
tmpfs           tmpfs     2.0G  8.0K  2.0G   1% /tmp
/dev/sda2       ext4      974M  150M  757M  17% /boot
```

```
/dev/sda1       vfat        599M    14M    585M    3%  /boot/efi
tmpfs           tmpfs       392M    92K    392M    1%  /run/user/42
tmpfs           tmpfs       392M    76K    392M    1%  /run/user/0
tmpfs           tmpfs       392M    76K    392M    1%  /run/user/1000
/dev/sdb1       ext2        7.9G    24K    7.5G    1%  /USBdrive
[root@server1 ~]# ls -F /USBdrive
issue  lost+found/  workfiles
[root@server1 ~]# umount /USBdrive
[root@server1 ~]# ls /USBdrive
samplefile
[root@server1 ~]#_
```

The mount command used in the preceding output specifies the filesystem type, the device to mount, and the mount point directory. To save time typing on the command line, you can alternatively specify one argument and allow the system to look up the remaining information in the /etc/fstab (filesystem table) file. The /etc/fstab file has a dual purpose; it is used to mount devices at boot time and is consulted when a user does not specify enough arguments on the command line when using the mount command.

The /etc/fstab file has six fields:

<device to mount> <mount point> <type> <mount options> <dump#> <fsck#>

The device to mount can be the path to a device file (e.g., /dev/sda1), the filesystem UUID (e.g., UUID=db545f1d-c1ee-4b70-acbe-3dc61b41db20), the GPT partition UUID (e.g., PARTUUID=ed835873-01), or the filesystem label (e.g., LABEL=BackupDisk). The mount point specifies the directory to which the device should be mounted. The type can be a specific value (such as ext4) or can be automatically detected. The mount options are additional options that the mount command accepts when mounting the volume (such as read only, or "ro"). Any filesystems with the mount option "noauto" are not automatically mounted at boot time; a complete list of options that the mount command accepts can be found by viewing the manual page for the mount command.

The dump# is used by the dump command (discussed in Chapter 11) when backing up filesystems; a 1 in this field indicates that the filesystem should be backed up, whereas a 0 indicates that no backup is necessary. The fsck# is used by the fsck command discussed later in this chapter when checking filesystems at boot time for errors; any filesystems with a 1 in this field are checked before any filesystems with a number 2, and filesystems with a number 0 are not checked.

Note 9

You can use the blkid command to display the filesystem and partition UUIDs on your system. You can also use the lsblk --fs command to display filesystem UUIDs and labels.

Note 10

Filesystem labels are optional; to set a label on a filesystem, you must use a command for the filesystem type. For example, the e2label command can be used to set a label on an ext2/ext3/ext4 filesystem, the fatlabel command can be used to set a label on a FAT filesystem, the exfatlabel command can be used to set a label on an exFAT filesystem, and the xfs_admin command can be used to set a label on an XFS filesystem.

Note 11

To easily associate filesystem UUIDs and labels with their device files, the udev daemon creates symbolic links for each UUID and label in subdirectories under /dev/disk that point to the correct device file (e.g., /dev/sdb1); /dev/disk/by-uuid stores symbolic links by filesystem UUID, /dev/disk/by-partuuid stores symbolic links by GPT partition UUID, and /dev/disk/by-label stores symbolic links by filesystem label. You can also find symbolic links for each disk by Linux kernel identifier under /dev/disk/by-id and by PCI bus identifier under /dev/disk/by-path.

Note 12

To mount all filesystems in the /etc/fstab file that are intended to mount at boot time, you can type the mount -a command.

The following output displays the contents of a sample /etc/fstab file:

```
[root@server1 ~]# cat /etc/fstab
# Accessible filesystems, by reference, are maintained under
# '/dev/disk/'. See man pages fstab(5), findfs(8), mount(8) and/or
# blkid(8) for more info.
#
# After editing this file, run 'systemctl daemon-reload' to update
# systemd units generated from this file.
#
UUID=e8ffcefc-8a11-474e-b879-d7adb1fd1e94 /          ext4 defaults 1 1
UUID=c203af16-e9b2-4577-aab5-5f353f0f2074 /boot      ext4 defaults 1 2
UUID=F4D6-9E57                            /boot/efi vfat umask=077 0 2
/dev/sdb1                                 /USBdrive auto noauto    0 0
[root@server1 ~]#_
```

Thus, to mount the first USB flash drive (/dev/sdb1) to the /USBdrive directory and automatically detect the type of filesystem on the device, specify enough information for the mount command to find the appropriate line in the /etc/fstab file:

```
[root@server1 ~]# mount /dev/sdb1
[root@server1 ~]# df -hT
Filesystem      Type      Size  Used Avail Use% Mounted on
devtmpfs        devtmpfs  4.0M     0  4.0M   0% /dev
tmpfs           tmpfs     2.0G     0  2.0G   0% /dev/shm
tmpfs           tmpfs     784M  1.2M  783M   1% /run
/dev/sda3       ext4       35G  8.9G   24G  28% /
tmpfs           tmpfs     2.0G  8.0K  2.0G   1% /tmp
/dev/sda2       ext4      974M  150M  757M  17% /boot
/dev/sda1       vfat      599M   14M  585M   3% /boot/efi
tmpfs           tmpfs     392M   92K  392M   1% /run/user/42
tmpfs           tmpfs     392M   76K  392M   1% /run/user/0
tmpfs           tmpfs     392M   76K  392M   1% /run/user/1000
/dev/sdb1       ext2      7.9G   24K  7.5G   1% /USBdrive
[root@server1 ~]# umount /dev/sdb1
[root@server1 ~]#_
```

The mount command in the preceding output succeeded because a line in /etc/fstab described the mounting of the /dev/sdb1 device. Alternatively, you could specify the mount point as an argument to the mount command to mount the same device via the correct entry in /etc/fstab:

```
[root@server1 ~]# mount /USBdrive
[root@server1 ~]# df -hT
Filesystem      Type      Size  Used Avail Use% Mounted on
devtmpfs        devtmpfs  4.0M     0  4.0M   0% /dev
tmpfs           tmpfs     2.0G     0  2.0G   0% /dev/shm
tmpfs           tmpfs     784M  1.2M  783M   1% /run
/dev/sda3       ext4       35G  8.9G   24G  28% /
tmpfs           tmpfs     2.0G  8.0K  2.0G   1% /tmp
/dev/sda2       ext4      974M  150M  757M  17% /boot
```

```
/dev/sda1        vfat        599M    14M    585M    3% /boot/efi
tmpfs            tmpfs       392M    92K    392M    1% /run/user/42
tmpfs            tmpfs       392M    76K    392M    1% /run/user/0
tmpfs            tmpfs       392M    76K    392M    1% /run/user/1000
/dev/sdb1        ext2        7.9G    24K    7.5G    1% /USBdrive
[root@server1 ~]# umount /USBdrive
[root@server1 ~]#_
```

Table 5-4 lists commands that are useful when mounting and unmounting USB flash drives.

Table 5-4   Useful commands when mounting and unmounting filesystems

Command	Description

`mount`
`df -hT`
`lsblk --fs`
	Displays mounted filesystems and their type

`mount -t <type> <device> <mount point>`	Mounts a `<device>` of a certain `<type>` to a `<mount point>` directory
`fuser -u <directory>`	Displays the users using a particular directory
`umount <mount point>` or `umount <device>`	Unmounts a `<device>` from its `<mount point>` directory

Working with CDs, DVDs, and ISO Images

CDs and DVDs are another form of removeable media used by some systems today. Like USB flash drives, CDs and DVDs can be mounted with the `mount` command and unmounted with the `umount` command, as shown in Table 5-4; however, the device file used with these commands is different. The device files used by CD and DVD drives depend on the technology used by the drive itself. To make the identification of your CD or DVD drive easier, Linux creates a symbolic link to the correct device file for your first CD or DVD drive called /dev/cdrom. For example, if your system contains a writable SATA CD/DVD drive, a long listing of /dev/cdrom may show the following:

```
[root@server1 ~]# ls -l /dev/cdrom
lrwxrwxrwx. 1 root root 3 Jul 19 07:51 /dev/cdrom -> sr0
[root@server1 ~]#_
```

In this case, you could use /dev/cdrom or /dev/sr0 to mount CDs or DVDs. To write to a CD or DVD in this same drive, however, you must use disc burning software that knows how to write data to /dev/cdrom or /dev/sr0.

Note 13

Nearly all DVD drives can also work with CDs.

Note 14

Many OSS disc burning software applications are available for Linux. One example is the graphical Brasero Disc Burner program that you can install by running the command `dnf install brasero` as the root user.

In addition, CDs and DVDs typically use either the ISO 9660 or UDF filesystem type and are read-only when accessed using Linux (recall that you must use disc burning software to record to a CD or DVD). Thus, to mount a CD or DVD to a directory, you should use the −r (read-only) option to the mount command to avoid warnings. To mount a sample CD to the /media/CD directory and view its contents, you could use the following commands:

```
[root@server1 ~]# mount -r /dev/cdrom /media/CD
[root@server1 ~]# df -hT
Filesystem      Type       Size  Used Avail Use% Mounted on
devtmpfs        devtmpfs   4.0M     0  4.0M   0% /dev
tmpfs           tmpfs      2.0G     0  2.0G   0% /dev/shm
tmpfs           tmpfs      784M  1.2M  783M   1% /run
/dev/sda3       ext4        35G  8.9G   24G  28% /
tmpfs           tmpfs      2.0G  8.0K  2.0G   1% /tmp
/dev/sda2       ext4       974M  150M  757M  17% /boot
/dev/sda1       vfat       599M   14M  585M   3% /boot/efi
tmpfs           tmpfs      392M   92K  392M   1% /run/user/42
tmpfs           tmpfs      392M   76K  392M   1% /run/user/0
tmpfs           tmpfs      392M   76K  392M   1% /run/user/1000
/dev/sr0        iso9660    430M  430M    0M 100% /media/CD
[root@server1 ~]# ls -F /media/CD
autorun.inf*    install*   graphics/   jungle/   jungle.txt*   joystick/
[root@server1 ~]# umount /media/CD
[root@server1 ~]#_
```

As with USB flash drives, you can modify the /etc/fstab file such that you can specify only a single argument to the mount command to mount a CD or DVD. Also remember that the mount point directory must not be in use to successfully mount or unmount CDs and DVDs; the fuser command can be used to verify this.

Unlike USB flash drives, CDs and DVDs cannot be ejected from the drive until they are properly unmounted, because the mount command locks the CD/DVD drive as a precaution. Alternatively, you can use the eject command, which unmounts the filesystem and forces the CD or DVD drive to physically eject the disc.

The ISO 9660 filesystem type is not limited to CDs and DVDs. ISO images, like the one you installed a Fedora Linux virtual machine with Hands-On Project 2-1, also contain an ISO 9660 filesystem. These files can be easily written to a CD or DVD using disc burning software or mounted and accessed by your Linux system. If you download an ISO image called sample.iso, you can mount it to the /mnt directory as a read-only loopback device. This allows your system to access the contents of the sample.iso file, as shown here:

```
[root@server1 ~]# mount -o loop -r -t iso9660 sample.iso /mnt
[root@server1 ~]# df -hT
Filesystem      Type       Size  Used Avail Use% Mounted on
devtmpfs        devtmpfs   4.0M     0  4.0M   0% /dev
tmpfs           tmpfs      2.0G     0  2.0G   0% /dev/shm
tmpfs           tmpfs      784M  1.2M  783M   1% /run
/dev/sda3       ext4        35G  8.9G   24G  28% /
tmpfs           tmpfs      2.0G  8.0K  2.0G   1% /tmp
/dev/sda2       ext4       974M  150M  757M  17% /boot
/dev/sda1       vfat       599M   14M  585M   3% /boot/efi
tmpfs           tmpfs      392M   92K  392M   1% /run/user/42
tmpfs           tmpfs      392M   76K  392M   1% /run/user/0
tmpfs           tmpfs      392M   76K  392M   1% /run/user/1000
/dev/loop0      iso9660    364M  364M     0 100% /mnt
```

```
[root@server1 ~]# ls /mnt
setup.exe       tools       binaries
[root@server1 ~]#_
```

You can then view or execute files within the /mnt directory or copy files from the /mnt directory to another directory to extract the contents of the ISO image.

To create a new ISO image from a directory of files, you can use the mkisofs command. The following command creates an ISO image called newimage.iso that contains all of the files and subdirectories under the /data directory with additional support for the Rock Ridge (-R) and Joliet (-J) standards:

```
[root@server1 ~]# mkisofs -RJ -o newimage.iso /data
I: -input-charset not specified, using utf-8 (detected in locale settings)
Total translation table size: 0
Total rockridge attributes bytes: 256
Total directory bytes: 0
Path table size(bytes): 10
Max brk space used 0
182 extents written (0 MB)
[root@server1 ~]#_
```

Working with Removeable Media within a Desktop Environment

Because of their large capacity and portability, removable storage devices often store copies of data, pictures, music, movies, programs, and documents that users regularly use within a desktop environment. When working within a desktop environment, a process automatically mounts removeable media to a directory so that you can work with it immediately, much like on a Windows or macOS computer. When you insert a USB flash drive, CD, or DVD while in a desktop environment, it is automatically mounted by the system to the /run/media/*username*/*label* directory, where *username* is the name of the user logged into the desktop environment and *label* is the filesystem label on the removeable media. For example, if you insert a DVD with a filesystem label of "Fedora-Workstation-Live-x86_64" into your system while logged into a desktop environment as user1, the system will automatically create a /run/media/user1/Fedora-Workstation-Live-x86_64 directory and mount the DVD to it. Similarly, if you insert a USB flash drive with a filesystem label of "KINGSTON" into your system while logged into a desktop environment as user1, the system will automatically create a /run/media/user1/KINGSTON directory and mount the USB flash drive to it. This is shown in the following output:

```
[root@server1 ~]# df -hT
Filesystem      Type       Size  Used Avail Use% Mounted on
devtmpfs        devtmpfs   4.0M     0  4.0M   0% /dev
tmpfs           tmpfs      2.0G     0  2.0G   0% /dev/shm
tmpfs           tmpfs      784M  1.2M  783M   1% /run
/dev/sda3       ext4        35G  8.9G   24G  28% /
tmpfs           tmpfs      2.0G  8.0K  2.0G   1% /tmp
/dev/sda2       ext4       974M  150M  757M  17% /boot
/dev/sda1       vfat       599M   14M  585M   3% /boot/efi
tmpfs           tmpfs      392M   92K  392M   1% /run/user/42
tmpfs           tmpfs      392M   76K  392M   1% /run/user/0
tmpfs           tmpfs      392M   76K  392M   1% /run/user/1000
/dev/sr0        iso9660    3.8G  3.8G    0M 100% /run/media/user1/
Fedora-Workstation-Live-x86_64
/dev/sdb1       exfat       64G  506M 63.5G   1% /run/media/user1/KINGSTON
[root@server1 ~]#_
```

In addition, the system will also display filesystem label shortcuts to the /run/media/user1/ Fedora-Workstation-Live-x86_64 and /run/media/user1/KINGSTON directories in the Files application within the desktop environment so that you can easily access the contents of your removeable media, as shown in Figure 5-3.

Figure 5-3   Accessing removeable media within the GNOME desktop

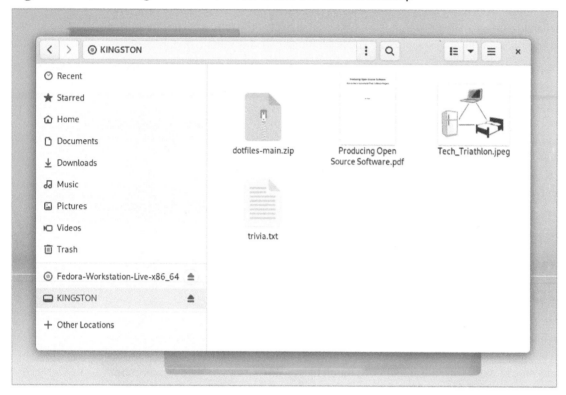

When you are finished accessing the files on the removeable media, you can click the eject icon next to the filesystem label shortcuts shown in Figure 5-3 to unmount the removeable media device, and, in the case of a CD or DVD, eject the physical disk as well.

Removeable media is not limited to USB flash drives, CDs, and DVDs; you can use many other types of removeable media devices on Linux, including SD memory cards, smartphones, external hard disk drives, and external SSDs. Most removeable storage device manufacturers emulate the SCSI protocol in the firmware of the device itself, much like a USB flash drive.

When working with removeable media devices within a desktop environment, understanding the device names and mount point directories used by the devices themselves is often irrelevant. You can work with the files on removeable media devices by accessing the appropriate icons in the Files application that represent the devices in the desktop environment. However, if you are working in a command-line terminal on a Linux server that does not have a desktop environment, you must manually mount and manage removeable storage devices.

Working with Hard Disk Drives and SSDs

Hard disk drives typically come in three flavors: PATA, SATA, and SCSI/SAS. PATA hard disk drives must be set to one of four configurations, each of which has a different device file:

- Primary master (/dev/hda)
- Primary slave (/dev/hdb)
- Secondary master (/dev/hdc)
- Secondary slave (/dev/hdd)

SATA and SCSI/SAS hard disk drives typically have faster data transfer speeds than PATA hard disk drives, and most systems allow for the connection of more than four SATA or SCSI/SAS hard disk drives. As a result of these benefits, both SATA and SCSI/SAS hard disk drives are well suited to Linux servers that require a great deal of storage space for programs and user files. However, SATA and SCSI/SAS hard disk drives have different device files associated with them:

- First SATA/SCSI/SAS hard disk drive (/dev/sda)
- Second SATA/SCSI/SAS hard disk drive (/dev/sdb)
- Third SATA/SCSI/SAS hard disk drive (/dev/sdc)
- And so on

SSDs are a newer technology that use much faster NAND flash storage. PATA, SATA, and SCSI/SAS SSDs provide a hard disk compatible interface so that they can function as a drop-in replacement for hard disk drives. Most SSDs of this type on the market are SATA or SAS; as a result, /dev/sda could refer to the first hard disk drive or the first SSD, /dev/sdb could refer to the second hard disk drive or second SSD, and so on. NVMe SSDs are often faster than SATA and SAS SSDs as they provide an SSD-only architecture that directly connects to the PCIe bus on a computer. As a result, NVMe SSDs use different device files; /dev/nvme0 is the first NVMe SSD, /dev/nvme1 is the second NVMe SSD, and so on. Unlike other SSDs or hard disk drives, NVMe SSDs can be divided into namespaces, and each namespace can then be further subdivided into partitions that contain a filesystem. The device files for NVMe SSDs reflect this; the first partition on the first namespace on the first NVMe SSD is /dev/nvme0n1p1, the second partition on the first namespace on the first NVMe SSD is /dev/nvme0n1p2, and so on.

Note 15

For simplicity, this book will refer primarily to hard disk drives when discussing permanent storage from now on. However, all of the concepts related to hard disk drives apply equally to SSDs.

Standard Hard Disk Drive Partitioning

Recall that hard disk drives have the largest storage capacity of any device that you use to store information on a regular basis. As helpful as this storage capacity can be, it also poses some problems; as the size of a disk increases, organization becomes more difficult and the chance of error increases. To solve these problems, Linux administrators divide a hard disk drive into smaller partitions. Each partition can contain a separate filesystem and can be mounted to different mount point directories. Recall from Chapter 2 that Linux requires two partitions at minimum: a partition that is mounted to the / directory (the root partition) and a partition that is mounted to the /boot directory. You can optionally create a swap partition, but the system will automatically create a swap file or compressed zswap RAM disk (/dev/zram0) for virtual memory if you do not.

It is a good practice to use more than just two partitions on a Linux system. This division allows you to do the following:

- Segregate different types of data—for example, home directory data is stored on a separate partition mounted to /home.
- Allow for the use of more than one type of filesystem on one hard disk drive—for example, some filesystems are tuned for database use.
- Reduce the chance that filesystem corruption will render a system unusable; if the partition that is mounted to the /home directory becomes corrupted, it does not affect the system because operating system files are stored on a separate partition mounted to the / directory.
- Speed up access to stored data by keeping filesystems as small as possible.
- Allow for certain operating system features—for example, a /boot/efi partition is required to boot systems that use a UEFI BIOS.

On a physical level, hard disk drives contain circular metal platters that spin at a fast speed. Data is read off these disks in concentric circles called **tracks**; each track is divided into **sectors** of information, and sectors are combined into more usable **blocks** of data, as shown in Figure 5-4. Most hard disk drives contain several platters organized on top of each other such that they can be written to simultaneously to speed up data transfer. A series consisting of the same concentric track on all of the metal platters inside a hard disk drive is known as a **cylinder**.

Figure 5-4   The physical areas of a hard disk drive

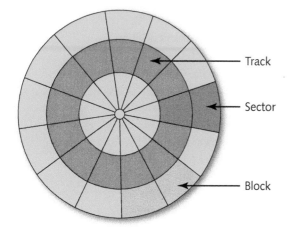

Track

Sector

Block

> **Note 16**
>
> SSDs use circuitry within the drive itself to map data to logical tracks, sectors, blocks, and cylinders to ensure that the OS can work with SSDs like any hard disk drive. This allows you to create partitions and filesystems on an SSD in the same way that you would a hard disk drive. Because SSDs are much faster at reading and writing data compared to hard disk drives, they are typically used on production Linux servers today.

Partition definitions are stored in the first readable sector of the hard disk drive known as the Master Boot Record (MBR). Large hard disk drives (>2 TB) and newer hard disk drives use a GUID Partition Table (GPT) in place of an MBR to allow for the additional addressing of sectors. If the MBR or GPT area of the hard disk drive becomes corrupted, the entire contents of the hard disk drive might be lost.

> **Note 17**
>
> It is common for Linux servers to have several hard disk drives. In these situations, it is also common to configure one partition on each hard disk drive and mount each partition to different directories on the directory tree. Thus, if one partition fails, an entire hard disk drive can be replaced with a new one and the data retrieved from a back-up source.

Recall from Chapter 2 that hard disk drives with an MBR normally contain up to four primary partitions; to overcome this limitation, you can use an extended partition in place of one of these primary partitions. An extended partition can then contain many more subpartitions called logical drives; each logical drive can be formatted with a filesystem. Partition device files start with the name of the hard disk drive (e.g., /dev/sda) and append a number indicating the partition on that hard disk drive. The first primary partition is given the number 1, the second primary partition is given the number 2, the third primary partition is given the number 3, and the fourth primary partition is given the number 4. If any one of these primary partitions is labeled as an extended partition, the logical drives within are named starting with number 5. Unlike hard disk drives that use an MBR, GPT hard disk drives don't need to adhere to the limitation of four primary partitions. Instead, you can create as many as 128 partitions (e.g., /dev/sda1 to /dev/sda128). Consequently, a hard disk drive that uses a GPT has no need for extended partitions or logical drives. Table 5-5 lists some common hard disk drive partition names.

Table 5-5   Common MBR partition device files for /dev/hda and /dev/sda

MBR Partition	GPT Partition	PATA Device Name (assuming /dev/hda)	SATA/SCSI/SAS Device Name (assuming /dev/sda)	NVMe Device Name (assuming /dev/ nvme0)
1st primary partition	1st partition	/dev/hda1	/dev/sda1	/dev/nvme0p1
2nd primary partition	2nd partition	/dev/hda2	/dev/sda2	/dev/nvme0p2
3rd primary partition	3rd partition	/dev/hda3	/dev/sda3	/dev/nvme0p3
4th primary partition	4th partition	/dev/hda4	/dev/sda4	/dev/nvme0p4
1st logical drive	5th partition	/dev/hda5	/dev/sda5	/dev/nvme0p5
2nd logical drive	6th partition	/dev/hda6	/dev/sda6	/dev/nvme0p6
3rd logical drive	7th partition	/dev/hda7	/dev/sda7	/dev/nvme0p7
nth logical drive	nth partition	/dev/hda$n$	/dev/sda$n$	/dev/nvme0pn

Note from Table 5-5 that any one of the MBR primary partitions can be labeled as the extended partition and contain the logical drives. Also, for hard disk drives other than those listed in Table 5-5 (e.g., /dev/sdc), the partition numbers remain the same (e.g., /dev/sdc1, /dev/sdc2, and so on).

An example Linux MBR hard disk drive structure for the first SATA/SCSI/SAS hard disk drive (/dev/sda) can contain a partition for the /boot filesystem (/dev/sda1), a partition for the root filesystem (/dev/sda2), as well as an extended partition (/dev/sda3) that further contains a swap partition (/dev/sda5), a /home filesystem partition (/dev/sda6), and some free space, as shown in Figure 5-5.

Figure 5-5   A sample MBR partitioning strategy

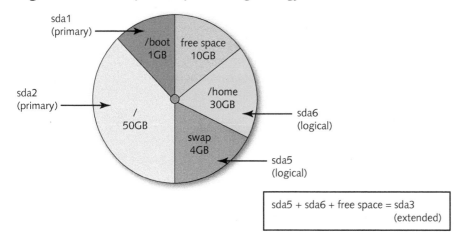

A more complicated example Linux GPT hard disk drive structure for the first SATA/SCSI/SAS hard disk drive might involve preserving the Windows operating system partition, allowing a user to boot into and use the Linux operating system or boot into and use the Windows operating system. This is known as dual booting and is discussed in Chapter 8. Recall from Chapter 2 that systems that have a UEFI BIOS create a small UEFI System Partition; this partition is formatted with the FAT filesystem and used to store boot-related information for one or more operating systems. If Windows has created this partition, Linux will modify and use it to store the information needed to dual boot both operating systems.

In Figure 5-6, a UEFI System Partition was created as /dev/sda1 because the system had a UEFI BIOS, and the Windows partition was created as /dev/sda2. Linux mounted the UEFI System Partition to the /boot/efi directory and created a separate partition for the /boot filesystem (/dev/sda3), the root filesystem (/dev/sda4), and the /home filesystem (/dev/sda5).

Figure 5-6   A sample dual-boot GPT partitioning strategy

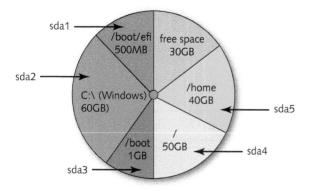

Working with Standard Hard Disk Drive Partitions

Recall that you can create partitions at installation using the graphical installation program. To create partitions after installation, you can use the `fdisk command` to create partitions that will be stored in the MBR or GPT on the hard disk drive. To use the `fdisk` command, specify the hard disk drive to partition as an argument. An example of using `fdisk` to work with the first SATA hard disk drive (/dev/sda) is shown in the following output:

```
[root@server1 ~]# fdisk /dev/sda
Welcome to fdisk (util-linux 2.38).
Changes will remain in memory only, until you decide to write them.
Be careful before using the write command.

Command (m for help):
```

Note from the preceding output that the `fdisk` command displays a prompt for the user to accept commands; a list of possible `fdisk` commands can be seen if the user types m at this prompt, as shown in the following example:

```
Command (m for help): m
Help:

  DOS (MBR)
   a   toggle a bootable flag
   b   edit nested BSD disklabel
   c   toggle the dos compatibility flag
```

```
Generic
  d   delete a partition
  F   list free unpartitioned space
  l   list known partition types
  n   add a new partition
  p   print the partition table
  t   change a partition type
  v   verify the partition table
  i   print information about a partition

Misc
  m   print this menu
  u   change display/entry units
  x   extra functionality (experts only)

Script
  I   load disk layout from sfdisk script file
  O   dump disk layout to sfdisk script file

Save & Exit
  w   write table to disk and exit
  q   quit without saving changes

Create a new label
  g   create a new empty GPT partition table
  G   create a new empty SGI (IRIX) partition table
  o   create a new empty DOS partition table
  s   create a new empty Sun partition table
Command (m for help):_
```

To print a list of the partitions currently set on /dev/sda, you could type p at the prompt:

```
Command (m for help): p
Disk /dev/sda: 50 GiB, 53687091200 bytes, 104857600 sectors
Disk model: Virtual Disk
Units: sectors of 1 * 512 = 512 bytes
Sector size (logical/physical): 512 bytes / 4096 bytes
I/O size (minimum/optimal): 4096 bytes / 4096 bytes
Disklabel type: gpt
Disk identifier: 6DE393B9-5DBA-466F-AF72-1D79894BBFEB

Device        Start       End   Sectors  Size Type
/dev/sda1      2048   1230847   1228800  600M EFI System
/dev/sda2   1230848   3327999   2097152    1G Linux filesystem
/dev/sda3   3328000  76728319  73400320   35G Linux filesystem
/dev/sda4  76728320 104855551  28127232 13.4G Linux filesystem
Command (m for help):_
```

Notice the Disklabel type of gpt, indicating that /dev/sda uses a GPT. For MBR storage devices, the Disklabel type will list msdos. The device names for each partition appear on the left side of the preceding output, including the number of sectors used by each partition (including the start and end sectors), partition size and type (/dev/sda1 is the UEFI System Partition while the remaining partitions contain Linux filesystems). To remove the /dev/sda4 partition and all the data contained on the filesystem within, you could type d at the prompt:

```
Command (m for help): d
Partition number (1-4, default 4): 4
Partition 4 has been deleted.

Command (m for help): p
Disk /dev/sda: 50 GiB, 53687091200 bytes, 104857600 sectors
Disk model: Virtual Disk
Units: sectors of 1 * 512 = 512 bytes
Sector size (logical/physical): 512 bytes / 4096 bytes
I/O size (minimum/optimal): 4096 bytes / 4096 bytes
Disklabel type: gpt
Disk identifier: 6DE393B9-5DBA-466F-AF72-1D79894BBFEB

Device        Start       End   Sectors  Size Type
/dev/sda1      2048   1230847   1228800  600M EFI System
/dev/sda2   1230848   3327999   2097152    1G Linux filesystem
/dev/sda3   3328000  76728319  73400320   35G Linux filesystem
Command (m for help):_
```

To create two additional partitions (/dev/sda4 and /dev/sda5), you could type n at the prompt and specify the partition to create, the starting sector on the hard disk drive, and the size in blocks (+5G makes a 5 GB partition):

```
Command (m for help): n
Partition number (4-128, default 4): 4
First sector (76728320-104857566, default 76728320): 76728320
Last sector, +/-sectors or +/-size{K,M,G,T,P} (76728320-104857566,
default 104855551): +5G

Created a new partition 4 of type 'Linux filesystem' and of size 5 GiB.

Command (m for help): n
Partition number (5-128, default 5): 5
First sector (87214080-104857566, default 87214080): 87214080
Last sector, +/-sectors or +/-size{K,M,G,T,P} (87214080-104857566,
default 104855551): 104855551

Created a new partition 5 of type 'Linux filesystem' and of size 8.4 GiB.

Command (m for help): p
Disk /dev/sda: 50 GiB, 53687091200 bytes, 104857600 sectors
Disk model: Virtual Disk
Units: sectors of 1 * 512 = 512 bytes
Sector size (logical/physical): 512 bytes / 4096 bytes
I/O size (minimum/optimal): 4096 bytes / 4096 bytes
Disklabel type: gpt
Disk identifier: 6DE393B9-5DBA-466F-AF72-1D79894BBFEB

Device        Start       End   Sectors  Size Type
/dev/sda1      2048   1230847   1228800  600M EFI System
/dev/sda2   1230848   3327999   2097152    1G Linux filesystem
```

```
/dev/sda3   3328000   76728319  73400320    35G Linux filesystem
/dev/sda4  76728320   87214079  10485760     5G Linux filesystem
/dev/sda5  87214080  104855551  17641472   8.4G Linux filesystem
Command (m for help):_
```

Note 18

Instead of entering the first sector for a new partition in the examples above, you can press Enter to accept the default value of the next available sector. Similarly, you can press Enter to accept the default value of the last sector (the last available sector on the hard disk drive) to create a partition that uses the remaining available space.

Note 19

When you create a new partition on an MBR storage device, `fdisk` will first prompt you to choose the partition type (primary, extended, or logical drive).

Notice from the preceding output that the default type for new partitions created with `fdisk` is "Linux filesystem." The partition type describes the use of the partition; while it doesn't restrict partition functionality in any way, you should choose a type that allows others to easily identify its usage. To change a partition type, you can type `t` at the prompt, and then choose the partition number and type code. Typing `L` at the prompt will list all 199 available type codes using the `less` command. For example, to change the /dev/sda4 partition to type 19 (Linux swap) and the /dev/sda5 partition to type 21 (Linux server data), you can type the following at the prompt:

```
Command (m for help): t
Partition number (1-5, default 5): 4
Partition type or alias (type L to list all): L
   1 EFI System                    C12A7328-F81F-11D2-BA4B-00A0C93EC93B
   2 MBR partition scheme          024DEE41-33E7-11D3-9D69-0008C781F39F
   3 Intel Fast Flash              D3BFE2DE-3DAF-11DF-BA40-E3A556D89593
   4 BIOS boot                     21686148-6449-6E6F-744E-656564454649
   5 Sony boot partition           F4019732-066E-4E12-8273-346C5641494F
   6 Lenovo boot partition         BFBFAFE7-A34F-448A-9A5B-6213EB736C22
   7 PowerPC PReP boot             9E1A2D38-C612-4316-AA26-8B49521E5A8B
   8 ONIE boot                     7412F7D5-A156-4B13-81DC-867174929325
   9 ONIE config                   D4E6E2CD-4469-46F3-B5CB-1BFF57AFC149
  10 Microsoft reserved            E3C9E316-0B5C-4DB8-817D-F92DF00215AE
  11 Microsoft basic data          EBD0A0A2-B9E5-4433-87C0-68B6B72699C7
  12 Microsoft LDM metadata        5808C8AA-7E8F-42E0-85D2-E1E90434CFB3
  13 Microsoft LDM data            AF9B60A0-1431-4F62-BC68-3311714A69AD
  14 Windows recovery environment  DE94BBA4-06D1-4D40-A16A-BFD50179D6AC
  15 IBM General Parallel Fs       37AFFC90-EF7D-4E96-91C3-2D7AE055B174
  16 Microsoft Storage Spaces      E75CAF8F-F680-4CEE-AFA3-B001E56EFC2D
  17 HP-UX data                    75894C1E-3AEB-11D3-B7C1-7B03A0000000
  18 HP-UX service                 E2A1E728-32E3-11D6-A682-7B03A0000000
  19 Linux swap                    0657FD6D-A4AB-43C4-84E5-0933C84B4F4F
  20 Linux filesystem              0FC63DAF-8483-4772-8E79-3D69D8477DE4
  21 Linux server data             3B8F8425-20E0-4F3B-907F-1A25A76F98E8
:q
Partition type or alias (type L to list all): 19
Changed type of partition 'Linux filesystem' to 'Linux swap'.
```

```
Command (m for help): t
Partition number (1-5, default 5): 5
Partition type or alias (type L to list all): 21
Changed type of partition 'Linux filesystem' to 'Linux server data'.

Command (m for help): p
Disk /dev/sda: 50 GiB, 53687091200 bytes, 104857600 sectors
Disk model: Virtual Disk
Units: sectors of 1 * 512 = 512 bytes
Sector size (logical/physical): 512 bytes / 4096 bytes
I/O size (minimum/optimal): 4096 bytes / 4096 bytes
Disklabel type: gpt
Disk identifier: 6DE393B9-5DBA-466F-AF72-1D79894BBFEB

Device        Start       End  Sectors  Size Type
/dev/sda1      2048   1230847  1228800  600M EFI System
/dev/sda2   1230848   3327999  2097152    1G Linux filesystem
/dev/sda3   3328000  76728319 73400320   35G Linux filesystem
/dev/sda4  76728320  87214079 10485760    5G Linux swap
/dev/sda5  87214080 104855551 17641472  8.4G Linux server data
Command (m for help):_
```

Finally, to save partition changes to the hard disk drive and exit fdisk, you can type w at the prompt:

```
Command (m for help): w
The partition table has been altered.
Syncing disks. [root@server1 ~]#_
```

If you modify the hard disk drive that also hosts the Linux operating system (as in the preceding example), you can either run the partprobe command or reboot your system to ensure that your partition changes are seen by the Linux kernel. Following this, you can use the mkfs, mount, and umount commands discussed earlier, specifying the partition device file as an argument. To create an ext4 filesystem on the /dev/sda5 partition created earlier, you can use the following command:

```
[root@server1 ~]# mkfs -t ext4 /dev/sda5
mke2fs 1.46.5 (30-Dec-2023)
Discarding device blocks: done
Creating filesystem with 2205184 4k blocks and 551616 inodes
Filesystem UUID: eab39f1b-8e60-4d2a-9baf-fdfede1fe189
Superblock backups stored on blocks:
        32768, 98304, 163840, 229376, 294912, 819200, 884736, 1605632

Allocating group tables: done
Writing inode tables: done
Creating journal (16384 blocks): done
Writing superblocks and filesystem accounting information: done
[root@server1 ~]#_
```

To mount this ext4 filesystem to a new mount point directory called /data and view the contents, you can use the following commands:

```
[root@server1 ~]# mkdir /data
[root@server1 ~]# mount /dev/sda5 /data
[root@server1 ~]# df -hT
Filesystem      Type     Size  Used Avail Use% Mounted on
devtmpfs        devtmpfs 4.0M     0  4.0M   0% /dev
```

```
tmpfs           tmpfs       2.0G      0   2.0G    0%  /dev/shm
tmpfs           tmpfs       784M   1.2M   783M    1%  /run
/dev/sda3       ext4         35G   8.9G    24G   28%  /
tmpfs           tmpfs       2.0G   8.0K   2.0G    1%  /tmp
/dev/sda2       ext4        974M   150M   757M   17%  /boot
/dev/sda1       vfat        599M    14M   585M    3%  /boot/efi
tmpfs           tmpfs       392M    92K   392M    1%  /run/user/42
tmpfs           tmpfs       392M    76K   392M    1%  /run/user/0
tmpfs           tmpfs       392M    76K   392M    1%  /run/user/1000
/dev/sda5       ext4        8.2G    24K   7.8G    1%  /data
[root@server1 ~]# ls -F /data
lost+found/
[root@server1 ~]#_
```

To allow the system to mount this filesystem automatically at every boot, you can edit the /etc/fstab file such that it has the following entry for /dev/sda5:

```
[root@server1 ~]# cat /etc/fstab
# Accessible filesystems, by reference, are maintained under
# '/dev/disk/'. See man pages fstab(5), findfs(8), mount(8) and/or
# blkid(8) for more info.
#
# After editing this file, run 'systemctl daemon-reload' to update
# systemd units generated from this file.
#
UUID=e8ffcefc-8a11-474e-b879-d7adb1fd1e94  /          ext4 defaults  1 1
UUID=c203af16-e9b2-4577-aab5-5f353f0f2074  /boot      ext4 defaults  1 2
UUID=F4D6-9E57                             /boot/efi  vfat umask=077  0 2
/dev/sdb1                                  /USBdrive  auto noauto     0 0
/dev/sda5                                  /data      ext4 defaults   0 0
[root@server1 ~]#_
```

Although swap partitions do not contain a filesystem, you must still prepare swap partitions and activate them for use on the Linux system. To do this, you can use the mkswap command to prepare the swap partition and the swapon command to activate it. To prepare and activate the /dev/sda4 partition created earlier as virtual memory, you can use the following commands:

```
[root@server1 ~]# mkswap /dev/sda4
Setting up swapspace version 1, size = 5 GiB (5368705024 bytes)
no label, UUID=1932ddbf-8c5b-4936-9588-3689a9b25e74
[root@server1 ~]# swapon /dev/sda4
[root@server1 ~]#_
```

Note 20

You can also use the swapoff command to deactivate a swap partition.

Next, you can edit the /etc/fstab file to ensure that the new /dev/sda4 partition is activated as virtual memory at boot time, as shown here:

```
[root@server1 ~]# cat /etc/fstab
# Accessible filesystems, by reference, are maintained under
# '/dev/disk/'. See man pages fstab(5), findfs(8), mount(8) and/or
# blkid(8) for more info.
```

```
#
# After editing this file, run 'systemctl daemon-reload' to update
# systemd units generated from this file.
#
UUID=e8ffcefc-8a11-474e-b879-d7adb1fd1e94 /          ext4 defaults  1 1
UUID=c203af16-e9b2-4577-aab5-5f353f0f2074 /boot      ext4 defaults  1 2
UUID=F4D6-9E57                            /boot/efi vfat umask=077 0 2
/dev/sdb1                                 /USBdrive auto noauto     0 0
/dev/sda5                                 /data      ext4 defaults  0 0
/dev/sda4                                 swap       swap defaults  0 0
[root@server1 ~]#_
```

Note 21

You can create and activate multiple swap partitions, even if your system already uses a swap file or compressed zswap RAM disk (e.g., /dev/zram0) for virtual memory. In this case, the sum total of all swap partitions, swap files, and zswap RAM disks will comprise the virtual memory on the system.

An easier alternative to fdisk is the cfdisk command. If you run the cfdisk /dev/sda command following the creation of the partitions you examined earlier, you will see the interactive graphical utility shown in Figure 5-7. You can use this utility to quickly create, manipulate, and delete partitions using choices at the bottom of the screen that you can navigate using your cursor keys.

Figure 5-7 The cfdisk utility

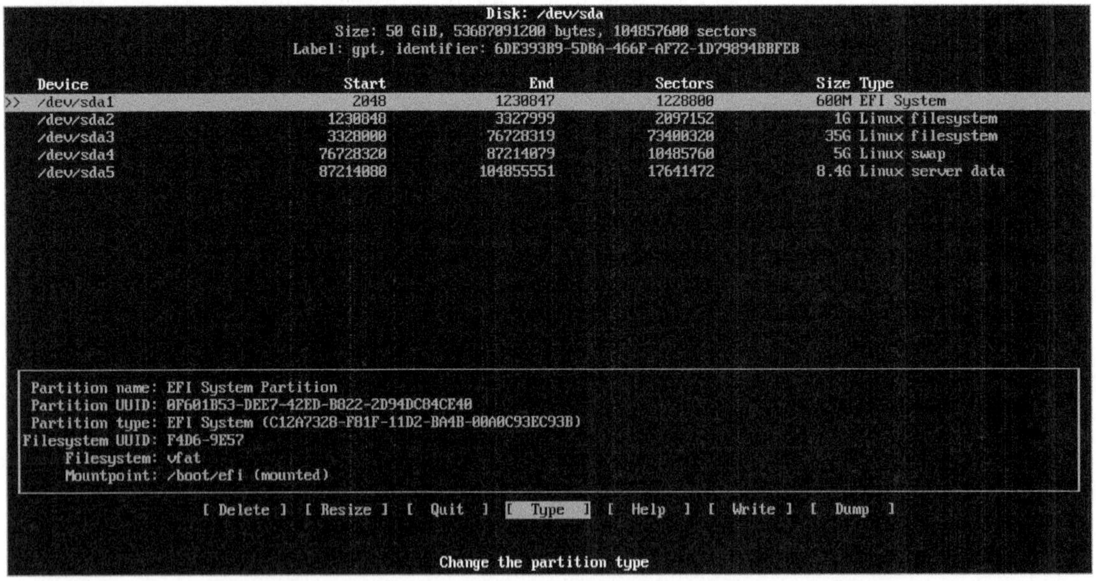

While fdisk and cfdisk can be used to create or modify both MBR and GPT partitions, there are many other partitioning commands that you can use. For example, the gdisk (GPT fdisk) command can create and work with GPT partitions using an interface that is nearly identical to fdisk. If your hard disk drive has an MBR, gdisk will first prompt you to convert the MBR to a GPT, which will destroy all existing MBR partitions on the disk.

Many Linux distributions also contain the `parted` (GNU Parted) command, which can be used to create and modify partitions on both MBR and GPT hard disk drives. Once in the GNU Parted utility, you can type help to obtain a list of valid commands, or type print to print the existing partitions, as shown here:

```
[root@server1 ~]# parted /dev/sdb
GNU Parted 3.4
Using /dev/sdb
Welcome to GNU Parted! Type 'help' to view a list of commands.
(parted) print
Model: Msft Virtual Disk (scsi)
Disk /dev/sdb: 8590MB
Sector size (logical/physical): 512B/4096B
Partition Table: msdos
Disk Flags:

Number  Start    End     Size    Type     File system  Flags
 1      1049kB   8590MB  8589MB  primary  xfs
(parted)_
```

Note from the previous output that /dev/sdb uses an MBR (msdos) partition table and contains a single 8589 MB partition (/dev/sdb1) that contains an xfs filesystem type. In the following example, this partition is removed and two additional primary partitions are created: a 5 GB partition with an ext4 filesystem type (/dev/sdb1) and a 3 GB partition with an xfs filesystem type (/dev/sdb1).

```
(parted) rm 1
(parted) mkpart
Partition type?  primary/extended? primary
File system type?  [ext2]? ext4
Start? 0GB
End? 5GB
(parted) mkpart
Partition type?  primary/extended? primary
File system type?  [ext2]? xfs
Start? 5GB
End? 8GB
(parted) print
Model: Msft Virtual Disk (scsi)
Disk /dev/sdb: 8590MB
Sector size (logical/physical): 512B/4096B
Partition Table: msdos
Disk Flags:

Number  Start    End     Size    Type     File system  Flags
 1      1049kB   5000MB  4999MB  primary  ext4         lba
 2      5000MB   8000MB  3000MB  primary  xfs          lba

(parted) quit
Information: You may need to update /etc/fstab.
[root@server1 ~]#_
```

As with the partition types shown in other tools, such as fdisk, the ext4 and xfs filesystem types specified in the previous example provide descriptive information only. After creating a partition in the parted command, you must still format it with a filesystem using the mkfs command and mount it to the directory tree using the mount command, like you did earlier after creating partitions with fdisk. Alternatively, you can prepare the partition for swap using the mkswap command and activate it using the swapon command. Finally, you can update the /etc/fstab file to mount new filesystems and activate new swap partitions automatically at boot time.

> **Note 22**
>
> As with *fdisk*, after making changes to the hard disk drive that hosts the Linux operating system using *cfdisk*, *gdisk*, or *parted*, you should run *partprobe* or reboot your system.

Working with the LVM

In the previous section, you learned how to create standard hard disk drive partitions on an MBR or GPT hard disk drive. You also learned how to create filesystems on those partitions and mount the filesystems to a directory within the Linux filesystem hierarchy.

Instead of creating and mounting filesystems that reside on standard partitions, recall from Chapter 2 that you can use the Logical Volume Manager (LVM) to create logical volumes that can be mounted to directories within the Linux filesystem hierarchy. Using volumes to host filesystems is far more flexible than using standard partitions because it allows you to select free space from unused partitions across multiple hard disk drives in your computer. This free space is then pooled together into a single group from which volumes can be created. These volumes can be formatted with a filesystem and mounted to a directory on the Linux filesystem hierarchy. Furthermore, additional hard disk drives can easily be added to the LVM, where existing volumes can be extended to take advantage of the additional storage space.

The LVM consists of several different components:

- **Physical Volumes (PVs)** are unused partitions on hard disk drives that the LVM can use to store information.
- **Volume Groups (VGs)** contain one or more PVs. They represent the pools of storage space that are available to the LVM for creating logical volumes. Additional PVs can easily be added to a VG after creation.
- **Logical Volumes (LVs)** are the usable volumes that are created by the LVM from the available storage space within a VG. LVs contain a filesystem and are mounted to a directory in the Linux filesystem hierarchy. In addition, LVs can be resized easily by the LVM to use more or less storage space.

The LVM subsystem in Linux manages the storage of all data that is saved to LVs. The physical location of the data is transparent to the user. Furthermore, the LVM has error correction abilities that minimize the chance that data will become corrupted or lost. Figure 5-8 illustrates the relationships among LVM components in a sample LVM configuration that creates four PVs from the standard partitions on three hard disk drives. These PVs are added to a VG divided into three LVs that are each mounted to a directory on the Linux filesystem hierarchy (/directory1, /directory2, and /directory3).

To configure the LVM, you must first create one or more PVs that reference an unused partition on a hard disk drive in your computer. Say, for example, that you recently created a new partition called /dev/sda4. Rather than placing a filesystem on /dev/sda4, you could instead allow the LVM to use the /dev/sda4 partition using the pvcreate command, as shown here:

```
[root@server1 ~]# pvcreate /dev/sda4
  Physical volume "/dev/sda4" successfully created
[root@server1 ~]#_
```

Figure 5-8   A sample LVM configuration

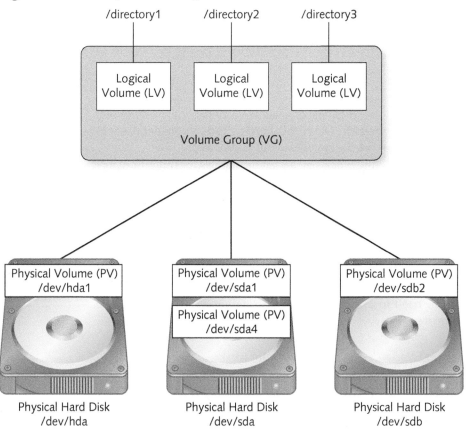

Note 23

You should use the `pvcreate` command to create PVs for each unused partition that you want the LVM to use. For simplicity, this section begins with how to create a single PV to demonstrate the configuration of LVM.

The `pvdisplay command` can be used to display detailed information about each PV. The following `pvdisplay` command indicates that /dev/sda4 has 13.41 GB of available space:

```
[root@server1 ~]# pvdisplay
  "/dev/sda4" is a new physical volume of "13.41 GiB"
  --- NEW Physical volume ---
  PV Name               /dev/sda4
  VG Name
  PV Size               13.41 GiB
  Allocatable           NO
  PE Size               0
  Total PE              0
  Free PE               0
  Allocated PE          0
  PV UUID               R6Q0ei-urbT-p6nB-HpXj-CB5u-sLeG-eNVlwm
[root@server1 ~]#_
```

After you have created PVs, you can create a VG that uses the space in the PVs by using the `vgcreate` command. For example, to create a VG called vg00 that uses the /dev/sda4 PV, you could use the following `vgcreate` command:

```
[root@server1 ~]# vgcreate vg00 /dev/sda4
  Volume group "vg00" successfully created
[root@server1 ~]#_
```

To create a VG that uses multiple PVs, add multiple device arguments to the `vgcreate` command. For example, the `vgcreate vg00 /dev/sda5 /dev/sdb1 /dev/sdc3` command would create a VG called vg00 that uses three PVs (/dev/sda5, /dev/sdb1, and /dev/sdc3).

When creating a VG, it is important to choose the block size for saving data as it cannot be safely changed later. This is called the **physical extent (PE) size** of the VG. A large PE size results in larger write operations and a larger maximum filesystem size for LVs. For example, a PE size of 32 MB will allow for a maximum LV size of 2TB.

By default, the `vgcreate` command chooses an appropriate PE size according to the current sizes of the PVs that are associated with the VG, but you can use the `-s` or `--physicalextent-size` options with the `vgcreate` command to select a different PE size during VG creation. This is important if you plan on adding a large amount of additional storage to the VG later.

The `vgdisplay` command can be used to display detailed information about each VG. The following `vgdisplay` command indicates that vg00 has access to 13.41 GB of storage using a PE size of 4 MB:

```
[root@server1 ~]# vgdisplay
  --- Volume group ---
  VG Name               vg00
  System ID
  Format                lvm2
  Metadata Areas        1
  Metadata Sequence No  1
  VG Access             read/write
  VG Status             resizable
  MAX LV                0
  Cur LV                0
  Open LV               0
  Max PV                0
  Cur PV                1
  Act PV                1
  VG Size               13.41 GiB
  PE Size               4.00 MiB
  Total PE              3433
  Alloc PE / Size       0 / 0
  Free  PE / Size       3433 / 13.41 GiB
  VG UUID               MfwlOf-nwbN-jW3s-9cNK-TFB6-M2Hw-xAF476
[root@server1 ~]#_
```

Next, you can create LVs from the available space in your VG using the `lvcreate` command and view your results using the `lvdisplay` command. The following commands create an LV called data1 that uses 10 GB of space from vg00 as well as an LV called data2 that uses 3.41 GB of space from vg00, displaying the results afterwards.

```
[root@server1 ~]# lvcreate -L 10GB -n data1 vg00
  Logical volume "data1" created
[root@server1 ~]# lvcreate -L 3.41GB -n data2 vg00
  Logical volume "data2" created
```

```
[root@server1 ~]# lvdisplay
  --- Logical volume ---
  LV Path                /dev/vg00/data1
  LV Name                data1
  VG Name                vg00
  LV UUID                BbZUcM-Rqf7-1ic0-U1Ew-5DKN-CXjt-IskCLR
  LV Write Access        read/write
  LV Creation host, time server1, 2023-09-06 20:14:34 -0400
  LV Status              available
  # open                 0
  LV Size                10.00 GiB
  Current LE             2560
  Segments               1
  Allocation             inherit
  Read ahead sectors     auto
  - currently set to     256
  Block device           253:0

  --- Logical volume ---
  LV Path                /dev/vg00/data2
  LV Name                data2
  VG Name                vg00
  LV UUID                CWjWz2-2qL8-z1Hf-qrzW-WU40-vE3j-PA3Uuf
  LV Write Access        read/write
  LV Creation host, time server1, 2023-09-06 20:14:45 -0400
  LV Status              available
  # open                 0
  LV Size                3.41 GiB
  Current LE             873
  Segments               1
  Allocation             inherit
  Read ahead sectors     auto
  - currently set to     256
  Block device           253:1
[root@server1 ~]#_
```

Notice from the preceding output that the new VGs can be accessed using the device files /dev/vg00/data1 and /dev/vg00/data2. You can also refer to your new VGs using the device files /dev/mapper/vg00-data1 and /dev/mapper/vg00-data2, which are used by the system when accessing the filesystems on your VGs. These device files are created by the device mapper framework within the Linux kernel, which maps physical block devices such as /dev/sda4 to logical devices within the LVM; as a result, these device files are merely shortcuts to device mapper device files (/dev/dm-*), as shown below:

```
[root@server1 ~]# ll /dev/vg00/data*
total 0
lrwxrwxrwx. 1 root root 7 Sep  6 20:14 data1 -> ../dm-0
lrwxrwxrwx. 1 root root 7 Sep  6 20:14 data2 -> ../dm-1
[root@server1 ~]# ll /dev/mapper/vg00*
lrwxrwxrwx. 1 root root 7 Sep  6 20:14 vg00-data1 -> ../dm-0
lrwxrwxrwx. 1 root root 7 Sep  6 20:14 vg00-data2 -> ../dm-1
[root@server1 ~]#_
```

Note 24

The device mapper files shown in the previous output reflect the identifiers that the Linux kernel uses when working with LVs, as the kernel stores configuration for each LV within the associated /sys/block/ dm-*/ directories. However, Linux administrators need only refer to VG and LV names (such as vg00 and data1) when working with LVM commands, as these names are automatically mapped to the appropriate device mapper file.

You can work with these device files as you would normally work with any other hard disk drive partition device file. For example, to create an ext4 filesystem on these devices and mount them to the appropriate directories on the filesystem, you could use the following commands:

```
[root@server1 ~]# mkfs -t ext4 /dev/vg00/data1
mke2fs 1.46.5 (30-Dec-2023)
Discarding device blocks: done
Creating filesystem with 2621440 4k blocks and 655360 inodes
Filesystem UUID: 3e77d984-fdd6-461e-aab3-b2e83cd17f1b
Superblock backups stored on blocks:
    32768, 98304, 163840, 229376, 294912, 819200, 884736, 1605632

Allocating group tables: done
Writing inode tables: done
Creating journal (16384 blocks): done
Writing superblocks and filesystem accounting information: done
[root@server1 ~]# mkfs -t ext4 /dev/vg00/data2
mke2fs 1.46.5 (30-Dec-2023)
Discarding device blocks: done
Creating filesystem with 893952 4k blocks and 223552 inodes
Filesystem UUID: 5afb6dc6-d283-4413-a2a5-c7d84333096a
Superblock backups stored on blocks:
    32768, 98304, 163840, 229376, 294912, 819200, 884736

Allocating group tables: done
Writing inode tables: done
Creating journal (16384 blocks): done
Writing superblocks and filesystem accounting information: done
[root@server1 ~]# mkdir /data1
[root@server1 ~]# mkdir /data2
[root@server1 ~]# mount /dev/vg00/data1 /data1
[root@server1 ~]# mount /dev/vg00/data2 /data2
[root@server1 ~]# df -hT
Filesystem          Type      Size  Used Avail Use% Mounted on
devtmpfs            devtmpfs  4.0M     0  4.0M   0% /dev
tmpfs               tmpfs     2.0G   12K  2.0G   1% /dev/shm
tmpfs               tmpfs     784M  1.2M  783M   1% /run
/dev/sda3           ext4       35G  8.9G   24G  28% /
tmpfs               tmpfs     2.0G  8.0K  2.0G   1% /tmp
/dev/sda2           ext4      974M  150M  757M  17% /boot
/dev/sda1           vfat      599M   14M  585M   3% /boot/efi
tmpfs               tmpfs     392M   92K  392M   1% /run/user/42
tmpfs               tmpfs     392M   76K  392M   1% /run/user/0
tmpfs               tmpfs     392M   76K  392M   1% /run/user/1000
```

```
/dev/mapper/vg00-data1 ext4      9.8G   24K  9.3G   1% /data1
/dev/mapper/vg00-data2 ext4      3.3G   24K  3.1G   1% /data2
[root@server1 ~]#_
```

Next, you can edit the /etc/fstab file to ensure that your new logical volumes are automatically mounted at system startup, as shown here:

```
[root@server1 ~]# cat /etc/fstab
# Accessible filesystems, by reference, are maintained under
# '/dev/disk/'. See man pages fstab(5), findfs(8), mount(8) and/or
# blkid(8) for more info.
#
# After editing this file, run 'systemctl daemon-reload' to update
# systemd units generated from this file.
#
UUID=e8ffcefc-8a11-474e-b879-d7adb1fd1e94 /        ext4 defaults  1 1
UUID=c203af16-e9b2-4577-aab5-5f353f0f2074 /boot    ext4 defaults  1 2
UUID=F4D6-9E57                            /boot/efi vfat umask=077 0 2
/dev/vg00/data1                           /data1   ext4 defaults  0 0
/dev/vg00/data2                           /data2   ext4 defaults  0 0
[root@server1 ~]#_
```

As files are added over time, you may find that additional capacity is needed in your filesystems. With the LVM, you can easily add additional storage devices and extend the capacity of existing LVs and their associated filesystems. After adding an additional storage device, you create a new PV for the partition using the pvcreate command, add the new PV to your existing VG using the vgextend command, and then extend the size of your LV and filesystem to use the additional space from the VG using the lvextend command. Say, for example, that you wish to extend the size of the data2 LV and associated ext4 filesystem created in the previous example by 5 GB. To do this, you could add a new hard drive to your computer (e.g., /dev/sdb) and create a /dev/sdb1 partition that spans that entire hard drive using the fdisk /dev/sdb command. Next, you could run the following commands to extend the data2 LV and filesystem while it remains mounted and accessible by users:

```
[root@server1 ~]# pvcreate /dev/sdb1
  Physical volume "/dev/sdb1" successfully created.
[root@server1 ~]# vgextend vg00 /dev/sdb1
  Volume group "vg00" successfully extended
[root@server1 ~]# lvextend -L +5GB -r /dev/vg00/data2
  Size of logical volume vg00/data2 changed from 3.41 GiB (873 extents)
  to 8.41 GiB (2153 extents).

  Logical volume vg00/data2 successfully resized.
  resize2fs 1.46.5 (30-Dec-2023)
  Filesystem at /dev/mapper/vg00-data2 is mounted on /data2
  on-line resizing required; old_desc_blocks = 1, new_desc_blocks = 2
  The filesystem on /dev/mapper/vg00-data2 is now 2204672 (4k) blocks
  long.
[root@server1 ~]# df -hT
Filesystem              Type      Size  Used Avail Use% Mounted on
devtmpfs                devtmpfs  4.0M     0  4.0M   0% /dev
tmpfs                   tmpfs     2.0G   12K  2.0G   1% /dev/shm
tmpfs                   tmpfs     784M  1.2M  783M   1% /run
/dev/sda3               ext4       35G  8.9G   24G  28% /
tmpfs                   tmpfs     2.0G  8.0K  2.0G   1% /tmp
```

```
/dev/sda2              ext4       974M   150M   757M   17%  /boot
/dev/sda1              vfat       599M    14M   585M    3%  /boot/efi
tmpfs                  tmpfs      392M    92K   392M    1%  /run/user/42
tmpfs                  tmpfs      392M    76K   392M    1%  /run/user/0
tmpfs                  tmpfs      392M    76K   392M    1%  /run/user/1000
/dev/mapper/vg00-data1 ext4       9.8G    24K   9.3G    1%  /data1
/dev/mapper/vg00-data2 ext4       8.3G    24K   7.9G    1%  /data2
[root@server1 ~]#_
```

Note 25

If you don't use the `-r` option to the `lvextend` command to resize the existing filesystem when extending an LV, your system will not be able to use the additional space. In this case, you can use a command to resize your filesystem after extending your LV. For example, to extend an ext2/ext3/ext4 filesystem, you can use the `resize2fs command`, and to extend an XFS filesystem, you can use either the `xfs_info command` or `xfs_growfs command`.

In addition to those discussed in this section, there are many other useful commands that can list and configure PVs, VGs, and LVs. Table 5-6 summarizes these commands.

Table 5-6   Common LVM Commands

Command	Description
pvdisplay pvscan pvs	Displays PV configuration
vgdisplay vgscan vgs	Displays VG configuration
lvdisplay lvscan lvs	Displays LV configuration
pvcreate	Creates a PV
vgcreate	Creates a VG that includes one or more PVs
lvcreate	Creates a LV from available space within a VG
pvremove	Removes a PV
vgremove	Removes a VG
lvremove	Removes a LV
vgextend	Adds additional PVs to a VG
vgreduce	Removes PVs from a VG
lvextend	Expands the size of a LV using free storage in a VG
lvreduce	Reduces the size of a LV, returning freed space to the VG
lvresize	Performs the same functions as lvextend and lvreduce
pvchange	Modifies settings for an existing PV
vgchange	Modifies settings for an existing VG
lvchange	Modifies settings for an existing LV

Monitoring Filesystems

After filesystems are created on devices and those devices are mounted to the directory tree, they should be checked periodically for errors, disk space usage, and inode usage. This minimizes the problems that can occur as a result of a damaged filesystem and reduces the likelihood that a file cannot be saved due to insufficient disk space.

Disk Usage

Several filesystems can be mounted to the directory tree. As mentioned earlier, the more filesystems that are used, the less likely a corrupted filesystem will interfere with normal system operations. Conversely, more filesystems typically result in less space per filesystem and frequent monitoring is necessary to ensure that adequate space is always available to each filesystem. In addition to the /boot and root filesystems, many Linux administrators create /home, /usr, and /var filesystems during installation. The available space in the /home filesystem reduces as users store more data, and the available space in the /usr filesystem reduces as additional programs are added to the system. Moreover, log files and print queues in the /var filesystem grow in size continuously unless they are cleared periodically. The root filesystem, however, is the most vital to monitor; it should always contain a great deal of free space used as working space for the operating system. If free space on the root filesystem falls below 10 percent, the system might suffer from poorer performance or cease to operate.

The easiest method for monitoring free space by mounted filesystems is to use the df command discussed earlier alongside the -h option at minimum to list human readable size formats:

```
[root@server1 ~]# df -h
Filesystem               Size  Used Avail Use% Mounted on
devtmpfs                 4.0M     0  4.0M   0% /dev
tmpfs                    2.0G   12K  2.0G   1% /dev/shm
tmpfs                    784M  1.2M  783M   1% /run
/dev/sda3                 35G  8.9G   24G  28% /
tmpfs                    2.0G  8.0K  2.0G   1% /tmp
/dev/sda2                974M  150M  757M  17% /boot
/dev/sda1                599M   14M  585M   3% /boot/efi
tmpfs                    392M   92K  392M   1% /run/user/42
tmpfs                    392M   76K  392M   1% /run/user/0
tmpfs                    392M   76K  392M   1% /run/user/1000
/dev/mapper/vg00-data1   9.8G   24K  9.3G   1% /data1
/dev/mapper/vg00-data2   8.3G   24K  7.9G   1% /data2
[root@server1 ~]#_
```

From the preceding output, the only filesystems used alongside the root filesystem are the /boot, /boot/efi, /data1, and /data2 filesystems; the /home, /usr, and /var directories are simply directories on the root filesystem, which increases the importance of monitoring the root filesystem. Because the root filesystem is 28 percent used in the preceding output, there is no immediate concern. However, log files and software installed in the future will increase this number and might warrant the purchase of additional storage devices for data to reside on.

> **Note 26**
>
> The df command only views mounted filesystems; thus, to get disk free space statistics for a USB flash drive filesystem, you should mount it prior to running the df command.

If a filesystem is approaching full capacity, it might be useful to examine which directories on that filesystem are taking up the most disk space. You can then remove or move files from that directory to another filesystem that has sufficient space. To view the size of a directory and its contents, you can use the du (directory usage) command. As with the df command, the du command also accepts the –h option to make size formats more human readable. For directories that have a large number of files and subdirectories, you should use either the more or less command to view the output page-by-page, as shown with the following /usr directory:

```
[root@server1 ~]# du -h /usr | more
72K     /usr/lib/sysusers.d
8.0K    /usr/lib/sddm/sddm.conf.d
12K     /usr/lib/sddm
44K     /usr/lib/sysctl.d
4.0K    /usr/lib/kde3/plugins
8.0K    /usr/lib/kde3
244K    /usr/lib/tmpfiles.d
62M     /usr/lib/jvm/java-17-openjdk-17.0.2.0.8-7.fc36.x86_64/lib/server
76K     /usr/lib/jvm/java-17-openjdk-17.0.2.0.8-7.fc36.x86_64/lib/jfr
194M    /usr/lib/jvm/java-17-openjdk-17.0.2.0.8-7.fc36.x86_64/lib
194M    /usr/lib/jvm
4.0K    /usr/lib/games
48K     /usr/lib/kdump
64K     /usr/lib/abrt-java-connector
--More--
```

To view only a summary of the total size of a directory, add the –s switch to the du command, as shown in the following example with the /usr directory:

```
[root@server1 ~]# du -hs /usr
6.9G    /usr
[root@server1 ~]#_
```

Recall that every filesystem has an inode table that contains the inodes for the files and directories on the filesystem; this inode table is made during filesystem creation and is usually proportionate to the size of the filesystem. Each file and directory uses one inode; thus, a filesystem with several small files might use up all of the inodes in the inode table and prevent new files and directories from being created on the filesystem. To view the total number of inodes and free inodes for mounted filesystems on the system, you can add the -i option to the df command, as shown in the following output:

```
[root@server1 ~]# df -i
Filesystem               Inodes  IUsed    IFree IUse% Mounted on
devtmpfs                1048576    466  1048110    1% /dev
tmpfs                    501506      4   501502    1% /dev/shm
tmpfs                    819200    875   818325    1% /run
/dev/sda3               2293760 238184  2055576   11% /
tmpfs                   1048576     34  1048542    1% /tmp
/dev/sda2                 65536     91    65445    1% /boot
/dev/sda1                     0      0        0    - /boot/efi
tmpfs                    100301     75   100226    1% /run/user/42
tmpfs                    100301     56   100245    1% /run/user/0
tmpfs                    100301     57   100244    1% /run/user/1000
/dev/mapper/vg00-data1   655360     11   655349    1% /data1
/dev/mapper/vg00-data2   542912     11   542901    1% /data2
[root@server1 ~]#_
```

The preceding output shows that the inode table for the root filesystem has 2293760 inodes and only 238184 (or 11%) of them are currently used.

Checking Filesystems for Errors

Filesystems themselves can accumulate errors over time. These errors are often referred to as filesystem corruption and are common on most filesystems. Those filesystems that are accessed frequently are more prone to corruption than those that are not. As a result, such filesystems should be checked regularly for errors.

The most common filesystem corruption occurs because a system was not shut down properly using the shutdown, poweroff, halt, or reboot commands. Data is stored in memory for a short period of time before it is written to a file on the filesystem. This process of saving data to the filesystem is called syncing. If the computer's power is turned off, data in memory might not be synced properly to the filesystem, causing corruption.

Filesystem corruption can also occur if the storage devices are used frequently for time-intensive tasks such as database access. As the usage of any system increases, so does the possibility for operating system errors when writing to storage devices. Along the same lines, physical hard disk drives and SSDs themselves can wear over time with heavy usage. Some parts of a hard disk drive platter may cease to hold a magnetic charge and some of the NAND flash memory cells in an SSD may cease to function properly; these areas are known as bad blocks. When the operating system finds a bad block, it puts a reference to the block in the bad blocks table on the filesystem. Any entries in the bad blocks table are not used for any future storage.

To check a filesystem for errors, you can use the fsck (filesystem check) command, which can check filesystems of many different types. The fsck command takes an option specifying the filesystem type and an argument specifying the device to check; if the filesystem type is not specified, the filesystem is automatically detected. The filesystem being checked must be unmounted beforehand for the fsck command to work properly, as shown next:

```
[root@server1 ~]# fsck /dev/vg00/data1
fsck from util-linux 2.38
e2fsck 1.46.5 (30-Dec-2023)
/dev/mapper/vg00-data1 is mounted.
e2fsck: Cannot continue, aborting.
[root@server1 ~]# umount /dev/vg00/data1
[root@server1 ~]# fsck /dev/vg00/data1
fsck from util-linux 2.38
e2fsck 1.46.5 (30-Dec-2023)
/dev/mapper/vg00-data1: clean, 11/655360 files, 66753/2621440 blocks
[root@server1 ~]#_
```

Note 27

Because the root filesystem cannot be unmounted, you should only run the fsck command on the root filesystem from single-user mode (discussed in Chapter 8) or from a system booted from live installation media (discussed in Chapter 6).

Notice from the preceding output that the fsck command does not display lengthy output when checking the filesystem; this is because the fsck command only performs a quick check for errors unless the -f option is used to perform a full check, as shown in the following example:

```
[root@server1 ~]# fsck -f /dev/vg00/data1
fsck from util-linux 2.38
e2fsck 1.46.5 (30-Dec-2023)
```

```
Pass 1: Checking inodes, blocks, and sizes
Pass 2: Checking directory structure
Pass 3: Checking directory connectivity
Pass 4: Checking reference counts
Pass 5: Checking group summary information
/dev/mapper/vg00-data1: 11/655360 files (0.0% non-contiguous), 66753/2621440 blocks
[root@server1 ~]#_
```

Table 5-7 displays a list of common options used with the fsck command.

Table 5-7   Common Options to the `fsck` Command

Option	Description
-f	Performs a full filesystem check
-y	Allows fsck to automatically repair any errors (if not run in interactive mode)
-A	Checks all filesystems in /etc/fstab that have a 1 or 2 in the sixth field
-Cf	Performs a full filesystem check and displays a progress line
-AR	Checks all filesystems in /etc/fstab that have a 1 or 2 in the sixth field but skips the root filesystem
-V	Displays verbose output

If the fsck command finds a corrupted file, it displays a message to the user asking whether to fix the error; to avoid these messages, you may use the -y option listed in Table 5-7 to specify that the fsck command should automatically repair any corruption. If the fsck command finds files it cannot repair, it places them in the lost+found directory on that filesystem and renames the file to the inode number.

To view the contents of the lost+found directory, mount the device and view the contents of the lost+found directory immediately under the mount point. Because it is difficult to identify lost files by their inode number, most users delete the contents of this directory periodically. Recall that the lost+found directory is automatically created when an ext2, ext3, or ext4 filesystem is created.

Just as you can use the mke2fs command to make an ext2, ext3, or ext4 filesystem, you can use the e2fsck command to check an ext2, ext3, or ext4 filesystem. The e2fsck command accepts more options and can check a filesystem more thoroughly than fsck. For example, by using the -c option to the e2fsck command, you can check for bad blocks on the underlying storage device and add them to a bad block table on the filesystem so that they are not used in the future, as shown in the following example:

```
[root@server1 ~]# e2fsck -c /dev/vg00/data1
e2fsck 1.46.5 (30-Dec-2023)
Checking for bad blocks (read-only test): done
/dev/vg00/data1: Updating bad block inode.
Pass 1: Checking inodes, blocks, and sizes
Pass 2: Checking directory structure
Pass 3: Checking directory connectivity
Pass 4: Checking reference counts
Pass 5: Checking group summary information

/dev/vg00/data1: ***** FILE SYSTEM WAS MODIFIED *****
/dev/vg00/data1: 11/655360 files (0.0% non-contiguous), 66753/2621440 blocks
[root@server1 ~]#_
```

Note 28

The `badblocks` command can be used to perform the same function as the `e2fsck` command with the `-c` option.

Note 29

You cannot use the `fsck` command to check and repair an XFS filesystem. Instead, you can use the `xfs_db` command to examine an XFS filesystem for corruption, the `xfs_repair` command to check and repair an XFS filesystem, as well as the `xfs_fsr` command to optimize an XFS filesystem and minimize the chance of future corruption.

Recall from earlier in this chapter that the `fsck` command is run at boot time when filesystems are mounted from entries in the /etc/fstab file. Any entries in /etc/fstab that have a 1 in the sixth field are checked first, followed by entries that have a 2 in the sixth field. However, on many Linux systems, a full filesystem check is forced periodically each time an ext2, ext3, or ext4 filesystem is mounted. This might delay booting for several minutes, depending on the size of the filesystems being checked. To change this interval to a longer interval, such as 20 days, you can use the `-i` option to the `tune2fs` command, as shown next:

```
[root@server1 ~]# tune2fs -i 20d /dev/vg00/data1
tune2fs 1.46.5 (30-Dec-2023)
Setting interval between checks to 1728000 seconds
[root@server1 ~]#_
```

The `tune2fs` command can be used to change or "tune" filesystem parameters after a filesystem has been created. Changing the interval between automatic filesystem checks to 0 disables filesystem checks altogether.

Disk Quotas

If there are several users on a Linux system, the system must have enough free space to support the files that each user expects to store on each filesystem. To prevent users from using unnecessary space, you can impose limits on filesystem usage. These restrictions, called disk quotas, can be applied to users or groups of users. Furthermore, quotas can restrict how many files and directories a user can create (i.e., restrict the number of inodes created) on a particular filesystem or the total size of all files that a user can own on a filesystem. Two types of quota limits are available: soft limits and hard limits. Soft limits are disk quotas that the user can exceed for a certain period of time with warnings (seven days by default), whereas hard limits are rigid quotas that the user cannot exceed. Quotas are typically enabled at boot time if there are quota entries in /etc/fstab, but they can also be turned on and off afterward by using the `quotaon` command and `quotaoff` command, respectively.

To set up quotas for the /data1 filesystem and restrict the user user1, you can perform the following steps:

1. Edit the /etc/fstab file to add the usrquota and grpquota mount options for the /data1 filesystem. The resulting line in /etc/fstab file should look like the following:

```
[root@server1 ~]# grep data1 /etc/fstab
/dev/vg00/data1    /data1  ext4    defaults,usrquota,grpquota  0 0
[root@server1 ~]#_
```

Note 30

You can also use journaled quotas on modern Linux kernels, which protects quota data during an unexpected shutdown. To use journaled quotas, replace the mount options of `defaults,usrquota,grpquota` in Step 1 with: `defaults,usrjquota=aquota.user,grpjquota=aquota.group,jqfmt=vfsv0`.

2. Remount the /data1 filesystem as read-write to update the system with the new options from /etc/fstab, as follows:

```
[root@server1 ~]# mount /data1 -o remount,rw
[root@server1 ~]#_
```

3. Run the `quotacheck -mavugf -F vfsv0` command, which looks on the system for file ownership and creates the quota database (`-f`) using the default quota format (`-F vfsv0`) for all filesystems with quota options listed in /etc/fstab (`-a`), giving verbose output (`-v`) for all users and groups (`-u` and `-g`) even if the filesystem is used by other processes (`-m`). Normally, this creates and places information in the /data/aquota.user and /data/aquota .group files. However, if your Linux kernel has been compiled using ext4 quota support, the quota information will be stored in a hidden inode on the ext4 filesystem itself. Sample output from the `quotacheck` command is shown here:

```
[root@server1 ~]# quotacheck -mavugf -F vfsv0
quotacheck: Scanning /dev/mapper/vg00-data1 [/data1] done
quotacheck: Checked 3 directories and 2 files
[root@server1 ~]#_
```

Note 31

If you receive any warnings at the beginning of the `quotacheck` output at this stage, you can safely ignore them because they are the result of newly created aquota.user and aquota.group files that have not been used yet, or the ext4 quota support feature of your Linux kernel.

4. Turn user and group quotas on for all filesystems that have quotas configured using the `quotaon -avug` command:

```
[root@server1 ~]# quotaon -avug
/dev/mapper/vg00-data1 [/data1]: group quotas turned on
/dev/mapper/vg00-data1 [/data1]: user quotas turned on
[root@server1 ~]#_
```

Note 32

You can also enable and disable quotas for individual filesystems. For example, you can use the `quotaon /data1` command to enable quotas for the /data1 filesystem and the `quotaoff /data1` command to disable them.

5. Edit the quotas for certain users by using the `edquota command` as follows: `edquota -u username`. This brings up the nano editor and allows you to set soft and hard quotas for the number of blocks a user can own on the filesystem (typically, 1 block = 1 kilobyte) and the total number of inodes (files and directories) that a user can own on the filesystem. A soft limit and hard limit of zero (0) indicates that there is no limit. To set a hard limit

of 20 MB (=20480KB) and 1000 inodes, as well as a soft limit of 18 MB (=18432KB) and 900 inodes, you can run the edquota -u user1 command to open the quota table for user1 in the nano editor:

```
Disk quotas for user user1 (uid 1000):
Filesystem              blocks   soft   hard   inodes   soft   hard
/dev/mapper/vg001-data1 1188        0      0      326      0      0
```

Next, you can place the appropriate values in the columns provided and then save and quit the nano editor:

```
Disk quotas for user user1 (uid 1000):
Filesystem             blocks   soft   hard   inodes   soft   hard
/dev/mapper/vg00-data1  1188  18432  20480      326    900   1000
```

6. Edit the time limit for which users can go beyond soft quotas by using the edquota -u -t command, which opens the nano editor for you to change the default of seven days, as shown here:

```
Grace period before enforcing soft limits for users:
Time units may be: days, hours, minutes, or seconds
Filesystem             Block grace period      Inode grace period
/dev/mapper/vg00-data1      7days                   7days
```

7. Ensure that quotas were updated properly by gathering a report for quotas by user on the /data1 filesystem using the repquota command, as shown in the following output:

```
[root@server1 ~]# repquota /data1
*** Report for user quotas on device /dev/mapper/vg00-data1
Block grace time: 7days; Inode grace time: 7days
                        Block limits              File limits
User           used    soft   hard  grace   used  soft  hard  grace
----------------------------------------------------------------------
root     --     573       0      0            20     0     0
user1    --    1188   18432  20480           326   900  1000
[root@server1 ~]#_
```

8. The aforementioned commands are only available to the root user; however, regular users can view their own quota using the quota command. The root user can use the quota command but can also use it to view quotas of other users:

```
[root@server1 ~]# quota
Disk quotas for user root (uid 0): none
[root@server1 ~]# quota -u user1
Disk quotas for user user1 (uid 500):
Filesystem        blocks  quota  limit  grace  files  quota  limit grace
/dev/mapper/vg00-data1
                    1188  18432  20480           326    900   1000
[root@server1 ~]#_
```

Note 33

To configure and manage quotas for an XFS filesystem, you must use the xfs_quota command.

Summary

- Disk devices are represented by device files that reside in the /dev directory. These device files specify the type of data transfer, the major number of the device driver in the Linux kernel, and the minor number of the specific device.

- Each disk device must contain a filesystem, which is then mounted to the Linux directory tree for usage with the mount command. The filesystem can later be unmounted using the umount command. The directory used to mount the device must not be in use by any logged-in users for mounting and unmounting to take place.

- Storage devices, such as hard disk drives and SSDs, must be partitioned into distinct sections before filesystems are created on those partitions. To partition a storage device, you can use a wide variety of tools including fdisk, cfdisk, gdisk, and parted.

- Many filesystems are available to Linux; each filesystem is specialized for a certain purpose, and several filesystems can be mounted to different mount points on the directory tree. You can create a filesystem on a device using the mkfs command and its variants.

- The LVM can be used to create logical volumes from the free space within multiple partitions on the various storage devices within your system. Like partitions, logical volumes can contain a filesystem and be mounted to the Linux directory tree. They allow for the easy expansion and reconfiguration of storage.

- Most removeable media devices are recognized as SCSI disks by the Linux system and are automounted by desktop environments.

- It is important to monitor disk usage using the df and du commands to avoid running out of storage space and inodes. Similarly, it is important to check disks for errors using the fsck command and its variants.

- You can use disk quotas to limit the space that each user has on filesystems.

Key Terms

/dev directory
/etc/fstab
/etc/mtab
/proc/devices
bad blocks
blkid command
block
block devices
cfdisk command
character devices
cylinder
device file
df (disk free space) command
disk quotas
du (directory usage) command
e2label command
edquota command
eject command
exfatlabel command
fatlabel command
fdisk command
filesystem corruption
formatting
fsck (filesystem check) command
fuser command
gdisk (GPT fdisk) command
hard limit

Logical Volume (LV)
lsblk command
lsusb command
lvcreate command
lvdisplay command
lvextend command
major number
minor number
mkfs (make filesystem) command
mkisofs command
mknod command
mkswap command
mount command
mount point
mounting
parted (GNU Parted) command
partprobe command
physical extent (PE) size
Physical Volume (PV)
pseudo filesystem
pvcreate command
pvdisplay command
quota command
quotaoff command
quotaon command
quotas
repquota command

resize2fs command
root filesystem
sector
soft limit
swapoff command
swapon command
syncing
track
tune2fs command
udev daemon
udevadm command
umount command
Universally Unique Identifier (UUID)
vgcreate command
vgdisplay command
vgextend command
virtual filesystem
Volume Group (VG)
xfs_admin command
xfs_db command
xfs_fsr command
xfs_growfs command
xfs_info command
xfs_quota command
xfs_repair command

Review Questions

1. Which of the following commands can only be used to create partitions on a GPT storage device?

   a. `gdisk`

   b. `cfdisk`

   c. `fdisk`

   d. `parted`

2. After a partition on a storage device is formatted with a filesystem, all partitions on that storage device must use the same filesystem.

   a. True

   b. False

3. You want to see the filesystems that are in use on the system. What command could you use? (Choose all that apply.)

   a. `cat /etc/fstab`

   b. `df -hT`

   c. `cat /etc/mtab`

   d. `ls /sys/block`

4. Jaime has just installed two new SAS SSDs in his system. He properly installs the hardware in his machine. Before he can use them for data storage and retrieval, what must he do? (Choose all that apply.)

   a. Mount the two SSDs so they are accessible by the operating system.

   b. Mount a filesystem to each of the SSDs.

   c. Create one or more partitions on each of the SSDs.

   d. Use the vi editor to edit /etc/mtab and create an entry for the SSDs.

   e. Mount any partitions created on the two SSDs such that they are accessible by the operating system.

   f. Format any partitions created on the SSDs with a valid filesystem recognized by Linux.

5. Given the following output from /etc/fstab, which filesystems will be automatically checked on boot by the `fsck` command?

   ```
   /dev/sda1 /boot       ext4    defaults    1 1
   /dev/sda2 swap        swap    defaults    1 0
   /dev/sda3 /           ext4    defaults    0 1
   /dev/sda4 /var        ext4    defaults    1 0
   /dev/sda1 /home       ext4    defaults    0 1
   /dev/sr0  /media/dvd iso9660 noauto,ro   0 0
   ```

   a. none, as `fsck` must be run manually for each filesystem

   b. /, swap, and /var

   c. /, /boot, and /home

   d. all of them, as `fsck` is run automatically at boot for all filesystems

6. A user mounts a device to a mount point directory and realizes afterward they need files previously found within the mount point directory. What should this user do?

   a. Nothing; the files are lost and cannot ever be accessed.

   b. Nothing; the files could not have been there because you can only mount to empty directories.

   c. Unmount the device from the directory.

   d. Run the `fsck` command to recover the files.

   e. Look in the lost+found directory for the files.

7. Which command is used to display the amount of free space that exists on a filesystem?

   a. `fsck`

   b. `quota`

   c. `du`

   d. `df`

8. What must you do to successfully run the `fsck` command on a filesystem?

   a. Run the `fsck` command with the `-u` option to automatically unmount the filesystem first.

   b. Choose yes when warned that running `fsck` on a mounted filesystem can cause damage.

   c. Unmount the filesystem.

   d. Ensure that the filesystem is mounted.

9. Character devices typically transfer data more quickly than block devices.

   a. True

   b. False

10. What does the `du -hs /var` command do?

    a. shows the users connected to the /var directory

    b. shows the size of all directories within the /var directory

    c. dumps the /var directory

    d. displays the total size of the /var directory

11. What does the command `df -i` do?

    a. displays mounted filesystems using human-readable size formats

    b. displays the number of used and available inodes on each mounted filesystem

    c. displays mounted filesystems interactively, line by line

    d. nothing; it is not a valid command

12. Which command can be used to repair an XFS filesystem?

    a. `fsck -t xfs /dev/sdb1`
    b. `e2fsck /dev/sdb1`
    c. `fsck.xfs /dev/sdb1`
    d. `xfs_repair /dev/sdb1`

13. Which of the following statements are true? (Choose all that apply.)

    a. Quotas can only limit user space.
    b. Quotas can only limit the number of files a user can own.
    c. Quotas can limit both user space and the number of files a user can own.
    d. Hard limits can never be exceeded.
    e. Hard limits allow a user to exceed them for a certain period of time.
    f. Soft limits can never be exceeded.
    g. Soft limits allow a user to exceed them for a certain period of time.
    h. Either a hard limit or a soft limit can be set, but not both concurrently.

14. A device file _____. (Choose all that apply.)

    a. has no inode section
    b. has no data section
    c. displays a major and minor number in place of a file size
    d. has a fixed size of 300 KB

15. Which of the following statements regarding LVM structure is correct?

    a. PVs are collections of VGs.
    b. LVs are created from the free space available within PVs.
    c. VGs are comprised of one or more PVs.
    d. PVs use the space within LVs to create VGs.

16. The `lvextend` command can be used to add unused space within a volume group to an existing logical volume.

    a. True
    b. False

17. You plug a USB flash drive into a system that has two SATA hard disk drives. How will the partition on this USB flash drive be identified by Linux?

    a. /dev/sda1
    b. /dev/sda2
    c. /dev/sdb1
    d. /dev/sdc1

18. Which command mounts all existing filesystems in /etc/fstab?

    a. `mount -f`
    b. `mount -a`
    c. `mount /etc/fstab`
    d. `mount /etc/mtab`

19. A user runs the `fsck` command with the `-f` option on an ext4 filesystem that is showing signs of corruption. How would that user locate any files the system was unable to repair?

    a. Look in the root of the filesystem.
    b. The system prompts the user for a target location when it comes across a file it cannot repair.
    c. Mount the filesystem and check the lost+found directory underneath the mount point.
    d. View the contents of the directory /lost+found.

20. Which command is used to format a partition on a hard disk drive with the ext4 filesystem?

    a. `e2mkfs -t ext4 device`
    b. `makeext4FS device`
    c. `format_ext4 device`
    d. `ext4mkfs device`

Hands-On Projects

These projects should be completed in the order given. The hands-on projects presented in this chapter should take a total of three hours to complete. The requirements for this lab include:

- A computer with Fedora Linux installed according to Hands-On Project 2-1

Project 5-1

Estimated Time: 15 minutes
Objective: Create device files.
Description: In this hands-on project, you view and create device files.

1. Boot your Fedora Linux virtual machine. After your Linux system has loaded, switch to a command-line terminal (tty5) by pressing **Ctrl+Alt+F5**. Log in to the terminal using the user name of **root** and the password of **LINUXrocks!**.

2. At the command prompt, type `ls -l /dev/tty6` and press **Enter**. What device does /dev/tty6 represent? Is this file a block or character device file? Why? What are the major and minor numbers for this file?

3. At the command prompt, type `rm -f /dev/tty6` and press **Enter**. Next, type `ls -l /dev/tty6` at the command prompt and press **Enter**. Was the file removed successfully?

4. Switch to tty6 by pressing **Ctrl+Alt+F6** and attempt to log in to the terminal using the user name of **root** and the password of **LINUXrocks!**. Were you successful?

5. Switch back to tty5 by pressing **Ctrl+Alt+F5**, type the command `mknod /dev/tty6 c 4 6` at the command prompt, and press **Enter**. What did this command do? Next, type `ls -l /dev/tty6` at the command prompt and press **Enter**. Was the file re-created successfully?

6. Switch back to tty6 by pressing **Ctrl+Alt+F6** and log in to the terminal using the user name of **root** and the password of **LINUXrocks!**. Why were you successful?

7. At the command prompt, type `ls -l /dev/tty?` and press **Enter**. What is similar about all of these files? Is the major number different for each file? Is the minor number different for each file? Why?

8. At the command prompt, type `find /dev` and press **Enter** to list all of the filenames under the /dev directory. Are there many files? Next, type `du -hs /dev` at the command prompt and press **Enter**. How large in KB are all files within the /dev directory? Why?

9. At the command prompt, type `less /proc/devices` and press **Enter**. Note the devices and major numbers present on your system. What character devices have a major number of 4? How does this compare with what you observed in Step 2? Press `q` to exit the less utility when finished.

10. Type `exit` and press **Enter** to log out of your shell.

Project 5-2

Estimated Time: 15 minutes
Objective: Mount removeable media.
Description: In this hands-on project, you practice mounting and viewing removeable DVD media.

1. Switch to the graphical terminal (tty1) by pressing **Ctrl+Alt+F1** and log in to the GNOME desktop using your user account and the password of **LINUXrocks!**.

2. In your virtualization software, attach the ISO image for Fedora Linux to the virtual DVD drive for the virtual machine. After you have completed this action, view your Files application. Is there an icon that represents your Fedora Live installation media in the left pane? Place your mouse over this icon to view the mount point directory. Which directory was your ISO image automatically mounted to? Take a few moments to explore the contents of the ISO image within the Files application. When finished, close the Files application.

3. Switch to a command-line terminal (tty5) by pressing **Ctrl+Alt+F5**. Log in to the terminal using the user name of **root** and the password of **LINUXrocks!**.

4. At the command prompt, type `du -hT` and press **Enter**. Is your ISO image still mounted? What filesystem type is used? What device file is used? Next, type `ls -l /dev/cdrom` and press **Enter**. Is /dev/cdrom a symbolic link to this device file?

5. At the command prompt, type `umount /dev/cdrom` and press **Enter** to unmount your Fedora DVD. Next, type `du -hT` and press **Enter** to verify that it is no longer mounted.

6. At the command prompt, type `cp /etc/hosts /mnt` and press **Enter**. Next, type `ls /mnt` and press **Enter** to verify that the /etc/hosts file was successfully copied to the /mnt directory.

7. At the command prompt, type `mount /dev/cdrom /mnt` and press **Enter**. What warning did you receive? Next, type `du -hT` and press **Enter** to verify that your ISO image is mounted to the /mnt directory.

8. At the command prompt, type `mount` and press Enter and view the output. Next, type `cat /etc/mtab` and press Enter. Is the output shown by these commands more verbose than in Step 7?

9. At the command prompt, type `cd /mnt` and press **Enter**. Next, type `ls -F` and press **Enter**. Are the contents of the ISO image the same as Step 2?

10. At the command prompt, type `umount /mnt` and press **Enter**. What error did you receive? Next, type `fuser -u /mnt` and press **Enter.** Note that you are currently using the /mnt directory, which prevents unmounting.

11. At the command prompt, type `cd` and press **Enter** to return to your home directory and then type `umount /mnt` and press **Enter** to unmount your ISO image.

12. At the command prompt, type `ls /mnt` and press **Enter**. Is the copy of /etc/hosts available again after the ISO image was unmounted?

13. Type `exit` and press **Enter** to log out of your shell.

Project 5-3

Estimated Time: 45 minutes
Objective: Create partitions and ext4 filesystems.
Description: In this hands-on project, you work with partitions. You will first create a partition using the `fdisk` utility. Next, you create an ext4 filesystem on the partition and mount it to the directory tree. Finally, you use the /etc/fstab file to automatically mount the partition at boot time.

1. Switch to a command-line terminal (tty5) by pressing **Ctrl+Alt+F5** and log in to the terminal using the user name of **root** and the password of **LINUXrocks!**.

2. At the command prompt, type `lsblk` and press **Enter**. Note the storage device file that holds the partitions that you created during Fedora installation. Also note the partitions under this storage device.

3. At the command prompt, type `fdisk device` and press **Enter**, where *device* is the storage device file from Step 2 (e.g., /dev/sda). At the `fdisk` prompt, type `m` and press **Enter** to view the various `fdisk` commands.

4. At the `fdisk` prompt, type `p` and press **Enter** to view the partition table on your storage device. Do the partitions match the output from Step 2? Note whether your storage device uses an MBR or GPT.

5. If your storage device uses an MBR, perform the following. Otherwise, proceed to Step 6.

   a. At the `fdisk` prompt, type `n` and press **Enter** to create a new partition.

   b. Type `e` to select an extended partition and press **Enter**. When prompted for the start sector, observe the valid range within the brackets and press **Enter** to select the default (the first available sector). When prompted for the end cylinder, observe the valid range within the brackets and press **Enter** to select the default (the last available sector).

   c. Type `p` and press **Enter** to view the partition table on your storage device, noting the new extended partition and the device file it uses.

6. At the `fdisk` prompt, type `n` and press **Enter** to create a new partition. If your storage device uses an MBR, you may be prompted to create a logical drive or primary partition if there are primary partitions available for use; in this case, type `l` to create a logical drive. Otherwise, when prompted for the start sector, observe the valid range within the brackets and press **Enter** to select the default (the first available sector). When prompted for the end cylinder, type `+1GB` and press **Enter**.

7. At the `fdisk` prompt, type `p` and press **Enter** to view the partition table on your storage device. Note the partitions present and the device file for the 1 GB partition that you created in Step 6.

8. At the `fdisk` prompt, type `l` and press **Enter** to view the different partition types and press `q` when finished. Which character would you type at the fdisk prompt to change the type of partition?

9. At the `fdisk` prompt, type `w` and press **Enter** to save the changes to the storage device and exit the fdisk utility.

10. At the command prompt, type `partprobe` and press **Enter**.

11. At the command prompt, type `mkfs -t ext4` *device* and press **Enter** where *device* is the partition device file from Step 7 (e.g., /dev/sda4).

12. At the command prompt, type `mkdir /newmount` and press **Enter**.

13. At the command prompt, type `mount -t ext4` *device* `/newmount` and press **Enter** where *device* is the partition device file from Step 7 (e.g., /dev/sda4). Next, type the `df -hT` command and press **Enter** to verify that the filesystem was mounted correctly.

14. At the command prompt, type `ls -F /newmount` and press **Enter**. Is the lost+found directory present? Next, type `cp /etc/hosts /newmount` at the command prompt and press **Enter** to copy the hosts file to the new partition. Verify that the copy was successful by typing the `ls -F /newmount` command at the command prompt again, and press **Enter**.

15. At the command prompt, type `umount /newmount` and press **Enter**. Next, type the `df -hT` command and press **Enter** to verify that the filesystem was unmounted correctly.

16. At the command prompt, type `vi /etc/fstab` and press **Enter**. Observe the contents of the file. Add a line to the bottom of the file as follows (where *device* is the partition device file from Step 7):

    device `/newmount ext4 defaults 0 0`

17. Save your changes and quit the vi editor.

18. At the command prompt, type `reboot` and press **Enter**. After your Linux system has been loaded, switch to a command-line terminal (tty5) by pressing **Ctrl+Alt+F5** and log in to the terminal using the user name of **root** and the password of **LINUXrocks!**.

19. At the command prompt, type `df -hT` and press **Enter**. Is your new filesystem mounted?

20. At the command prompt, type `umount /newmount` and press **Enter**. Next, type the `df -hT` command to verify that the filesystem was unmounted correctly.

21. At the command prompt, type `mount -a` and press **Enter**. Next, type the `df -hT` command and press **Enter**. Is your new filesystem mounted again to /newmount? Why?

22. Type `exit` and press **Enter** to log out of your shell.

Project 5-4

Estimated Time: 45 minutes
Objective: Configure the LVM.
Description: In this hands-on project, you create two new partitions using the GNU Parted utility and configure the LVM to host an LV using the space within. During this process, you will learn how to create PVs, VGs, and LVs, as well as add storage to extend a VG and LV. Finally, you will edit the /etc/fstab file to ensure that your LV is mounted at boot time.

1. Switch to a command-line terminal (tty5) by pressing **Ctrl+Alt+F5** and log in to the terminal using the user name of **root** and the password of **LINUXrocks!**.

2. At the command prompt, type `parted` *device* and press **Enter** where *device* is the storage device file from Step 2 of Hands-On Project 5-3 (e.g., /dev/sda). At the parted prompt, type `help` and press **Enter** to view the available commands.

3. At the parted prompt, type `print` and press **Enter**. Write down the End value for the partition you created and mounted to /newmount in Hands-On Project 5-3: _____ (A). Next, write down the maximum size of your storage device (listed below the model in the output): _____ (B). These two values represent the start and end of the remainder of the free space on your storage device.

4. At the parted prompt, type `mkpart` and press **Enter**. Press **Enter** again to accept the default partition type. When prompted for the Start of the new partition, enter the (A) value you recorded in Step 3 and press **Enter**. When prompted for the End of the new partition, enter the (A) value you recorded in Step 3 plus 1 GB and press **Enter** to create a 1 GB partition.

5. At the parted prompt, type p and press **Enter** to view the partition table on your storage device. Note the device file for the 1 GB partition you created in Step 4. Next, note the End value for the 1 GB partition you created in Step 4: _____ (C).

6. At the parted prompt, type mkpart and press **Enter**. Press **Enter** again to accept the default partition type (Linux ext2). When prompted for the Start of the new partition, enter the (C) value you recorded in Step 5 and press **Enter**. When prompted for the End of the new partition, enter the (C) value you recorded in Step 5 plus 1 GB and press **Enter** to create another 1 GB partition.

7. At the parted prompt, type p and press **Enter** to view the partition table on your storage device. Note the device file for the 1 GB partition you created in Step 6.

8. At the parted prompt, type quit and press **Enter** to save the changes to the storage device and exit the GNU Parted utility.

9. At the command prompt, type partprobe and press **Enter**.

10. At the command prompt, type pvcreate *device* and press **Enter**, where *device* is the device file for the 1 GB partition that you created in Step 4. Next, type pvdisplay and press **Enter** to view the details for your PV.

11. At the command prompt, type vgcreate vg00 /dev/sda6 and press **Enter**. Next, type vgdisplay and press **Enter** to view the details for your VG.

12. At the command prompt, type lvcreate -L 0.9GB -n newdata vg00 and press **Enter** to create a 0.9 GB LV called newdata from the vg00 VG. Next, type lvdisplay and press **Enter** to view the path and size of your new LV.

13. At the command prompt, type mkfs -t ext4 /dev/vg00/newdata and press **Enter** to format the newdata LV using the ext4 filesystem. Next, type mkdir /newdata and press **Enter** to create a mount point for the newdata LV. Following this, type mount /dev/vg00/newdata /newdata and press **Enter** to mount the newdata LV to the /newdata directory.

14. At the command prompt, type df -hT and press **Enter** to verify that your LV is mounted via the device mapper. Next, type ls -l /dev/vg00/newdata and press **Enter,** noting it is a symbolic link to a device mapper device file. Following this, type lsblk and press **Enter to note the relationship between your LV and your PV.**

15. At the command prompt, type ls -F /newdata and press **Enter**. Is there a lost+found directory available? Why?

16. At the command prompt, type pvcreate *device* and press **Enter**, where *device* is the device file for the 1 GB partition that you created in Step 6. Next, type pvdisplay and press **Enter** to view the details for your PV.

17. At the command prompt, type vgextend vg00 *device* and press **Enter**, where *device* is the device file for the 1 GB partition that you created in Step 6. Next, type vgdisplay and press **Enter**. Note that the total size of your VG reflects both PVs.

18. At the command prompt, type lvextend -L +0.9GB -r /dev/vg00/newdata and press **Enter** to extend your newdata LV by another 0.9 GB. Next, type lvdisplay and press **Enter,** noting the size has doubled. Following this, type df -hT and press **Enter,** noting the ext4 filesystem was automatically resized to match the new LV capacity.

19. At the command prompt, type lsblk and press Enter to note the relationship between your LV and your two PVs.

20. At the command prompt, type vi /etc/fstab and press **Enter**. Add the following line to the bottom of the file to ensure that the newdata LV is mounted at boot time:

    /dev/vg00/newdata /newdata ext4 defaults 0 0

21. Save your changes and quit the vi editor.

22. At the command prompt, type `reboot` and press **Enter**. After your Linux system has been loaded, switch to a command-line terminal (tty5) by pressing **Ctrl+Alt+F5** and log in to the terminal using the user name of **root** and the password of **LINUXrocks!**.

23. At the command prompt, type `df -hT` and press **Enter** to verify that your LV was automatically mounted at boot time.

24. Type `exit` and press **Enter** to log out of your shell.

Project 5-5

Estimated Time: 20 minutes
Objective: Troubleshoot filesystems.
Description: In this hands-on project, you view disk usage and check filesystems for errors.

1. Switch to a command-line terminal (tty5) by pressing **Ctrl+Alt+F5** and log in to the terminal using the user name of **root** and the password of **LINUXrocks!**.

2. At the command prompt, type `df -hT` and press **Enter**. What non-virtual filesystems are displayed?

3. At the command prompt, type `df -i` and press **Enter**. Note how many inodes are available for use by filesystem.

4. At the command prompt, type `fsck /dev/vg00/newdata` and press **Enter**. What error message do you receive and why?

5. At the command prompt, type `umount /newdata` and press **Enter**. Next, type `fsck /dev/vg00/newdata` and press **Enter**. How long did the filesystem check take and why?

6. At the command prompt, type `fsck -f /dev/vg00/newdata` and press **Enter**. How long did the filesystem check take and why?

7. At the command prompt, type `e2fsck -c /dev/vg00/newdata` and press **Enter**. What does this command do?

8. At the command prompt, type `tune2fs -i 0 /dev/vg00/newdata` and press **Enter** to change the interval for forced checks such that they are avoided. Is this a good idea for the ext4 filesystem? Why?

9. At the command prompt, type `mount /dev/vg00/newdata` and press **Enter**. Next, type the `df -hT` command and press **Enter** to verify that the filesystem was mounted correctly. Why did the `mount` command work even though you didn't specify the mount point directory?

10. Type `exit` and press **Enter** to log out of your shell.

Project 5-6

Estimated Time: 20 minutes
Objective: Configure disk quotas.
Description: In this hands-on project, you enable, set, and view disk quotas for the /newmount filesystem created earlier in Project 5-3.

1. Switch to a command-line terminal (tty5) by pressing **Ctrl+Alt+F5** and log in to the terminal using the user name of **root** and the password of **LINUXrocks!**.

2. At the command prompt, type `chmod 777 /newmount` to give all users the ability to create files within the /newmount directory.

3. Switch to tty6 by pressing **Ctrl+Alt+F6** and log in to the terminal using the user name of **user1** and the password of **LINUXrocks!**.

4. At the command prompt, type `touch /newmount/samplefile` and press **Enter** to create a file in /newmount that is owned by the user user1.

5. Type `exit` and press **Enter** to log out of your shell.

6. Switch back to tty5 by pressing **Ctrl+Alt+F5** and note that you are still logged in as the root user on this terminal.

7. At the command prompt, type `vi /etc/fstab` and press **Enter**. Observe the options for the /new-mount filesystem. Change the /newmount line to the following (where *device* is the existing device file specified):

    ```
    device  /newmount  ext4  defaults,usrquota,grpquota  0  0
    ```

8. Save your changes and quit the vi editor.

9. Remount the filesystem as read-write by typing the command `mount /newmount -o remount,rw` and press **Enter**.

10. At the command prompt, type `quotacheck -mavugf -F vfsv0` and press **Enter**. Ignore any warnings that appear. What does this command do? Next, type `ls -l /newmount` and press **Enter**. What are the sizes of the aquota.user and aquota.group files? What are these files used for?

11. At the command prompt, type `quotaon -avug` and press **Enter** to activate quotas for all partitions that have quota options defined within /etc/fstab.

12. At the command prompt, type `edquota -u user1` and press **Enter**. Are there any quota limits applied to the user user1 by default? Change the value of the soft quota for blocks to `50000` and the value of the hard quota for blocks to `60000`. Similarly, change the value of the soft quota for inodes to `300` and the value of the hard quota for inodes to `400`. How many files and directories can user1 create on this partition? How much space can user1 use in total on this partition?

13. Save your changes and quit the nano editor.

14. At the command prompt, type `edquota -u -t` and press **Enter**. Change the time limit for users who extend the soft limit to `5 days` for both inodes and blocks.

15. Save your changes and quit the nano editor.

16. At the command prompt, type `repquota /newmount` and press **Enter**. Are the quota changes you made for the user user1 visible? How many files has user1 stored on this volume so far? What is the total size of those files (in 1KB blocks) and why?

17. At the command prompt, type `quota -u user1` and press **Enter**. How do the values compare with those from the previous step?

18. Type `exit` and press **Enter** to log out of your shell.

Project 5-7

Estimated Time: 20 minutes
Objective: Create and manage XFS filesystems.
Description: In this hands-on project, you create a new partition using the `cfdisk` utility, format and check an XFS filesystem on that partition, as well as mount the filesystem using a GUID at boot time.

1. Switch to a command-line terminal (tty5) by pressing **Ctrl+Alt+F5** and log in to the terminal using the user name of **root** and the password of **LINUXrocks!**.

2. At the command prompt, type `cfdisk device` and press **Enter** where *device* is the block device file from Step 2 of Hands-On Project 5-3 (e.g., /dev/sda). Highlight the **Free space** within the `cfdisk` utility and select **New**. Specify a partition size of `2G` and press **Enter**. Note the device file for your new partition.

3. Select **Write** to save your changes; type `yes` and press **Enter** when prompted to confirm. Next, select **Quit** to save your changes and exit the `cfdisk` utility.

4. At the command prompt, type `partprobe` and press **Enter**.

5. At the command prompt, type `mkfs -t xfs device` and press **Enter**, where *device* is the device file for the partition you created in Step 2. Next, type `mkdir /xfsmount` and press **Enter** to create a mount point directory for your filesystem. Following this, type `mount device /xfsmount` and press **Enter**, where *device* is the device file for the partition you created in Step 2.

6. At the command prompt, type `df -hT` and press **Enter** to verify that your XFS filesystem was mounted successfully. Next, type `ls /xfsmount` and press **Enter**. Why is there no lost+found directory?

7. At the command prompt, type `umount /xfsmount` and press **Enter**. Next, type `fsck -f device` and press **Enter**, where *device* is the device file for the partition you created in Step 2. Why did you receive an error? Following this, type `xfs_repair device` and press **Enter**, where *device* is the device file for the partition you created in Step 2.

8. At the command prompt, type `blkid` and press **Enter**. Record the UUID of your XFS filesystem: _____.

9. At the command prompt, type `vi /etc/fstab` and press **Enter**. Add the following line to the bottom of the file, where *filesystemUUID* is the UUID that you recorded in the previous step:

   ```
   UUID="filesystemUUID"   /xfsmount   xfs      defaults   0  0
   ```

10. Save your changes and quit the vi editor.

11. At the command prompt, type `reboot` and press **Enter** to reboot your machine and ensure that the partition table was read into memory correctly. After your Linux system has been loaded, switch to a command-line terminal (tty5) by pressing **Ctrl+Alt+F5** and log in to the terminal using the user name of **root** and the password of **LINUXrocks!**.

12. At the command prompt, type `df -hT` and press **Enter**. Is your XFS filesystem mounted?

13. Type `exit` and press **Enter** to log out of your shell.

Discovery Exercises

Discovery Exercise 5-1

Estimated Time: 30 minutes

Objective: View filesystem configuration.

Description: Answer the following questions regarding your system by using the commands listed in this chapter. For each question, write the command you used to obtain the answer. If there are multiple commands that can be used to obtain the answer, list all of the commands available.

    a. What are the total number of inodes in the root filesystem? How many are currently utilized? How many are available for use?

    b. What filesystems are currently mounted on your system?

    c. What filesystems are available to be mounted on your system?

    d. What filesystems will be automatically mounted at boot time?

Discovery Exercise 5-2

Estimated Time: 40 minutes

Objective: Configure additional hard disk drive storage.

Description: Power off your virtual machine. Next, use your virtualization software to add a second 8 GB virtual hard disk drive to your virtual machine (e.g., /dev/sdb). Create two 4 GB partitions on this device.

    a. For the first partition, use the appropriate commands to add the available space to the vg00 VG that you created in Project 5-4, and extend your newdata LV to use the additional space.

b. For the second partition, create an exFAT filesystem and mount it to the /exFATdata directory. Modify the /etc/fstab file to mount the filesystem automatically at boot time by label. Finally, perform a filesystem check on your new exFAT filesystem.

Discovery Exercise 5-3

Estimated Time: 20 minutes

Objective: Configure USB storage.

Description: Provided that your virtualization software allows for USB device pass-through, connect a USB flash drive to your system. Use the appropriate commands to locate the device file used by the device, mount the filesystem to a directory of your choice, and check the filesystem for errors. Finally, add a line to /etc/fstab to ensure that the filesystem can be easily mounted in the future (this line should not automount the filesystem at boot time).

Discovery Exercise 5-4

Estimated Time: 30 minutes

Objective: Configure NVMe storage.

Description: Provided that your virtualization software supports the creation of NVMe SSDs, attach an NVMe controller and SSD to your virtual machine and create a partition within the first namespace that is formatted using XFS. Next, create a mount point directory for it called /SSD and mount your new filesystem to this directory, ensuring that it is mounted automatically by UUID at boot time from the appropriate entry within /etc/fstab. Note that Oracle VirtualBox requires that you first download and install the Oracle VirtualBox Extension Pack in order to obtain NVMe support.

Discovery Exercise 5-5

Estimated Time: 30 minutes

Objective: Research filesystems.

Description: Use the Internet to gather information on four filesystems compatible with Linux. For each filesystem, list the situations for which the filesystem was designed and the key features that the filesystem provides.

Discovery Exercise 5-6

Estimated Time: 30 minutes

Objective: Plan storage configuration.

Description: You have a Linux system that has a 2 TB SSD, which has a 90 GB partition containing an ext4 filesystem mounted to the / directory and a 4 GB swap partition. Currently, this Linux system is only used by a few users for storing small files; however, the department manager wants to upgrade this system and use it to run a database application that will be used by 100 users. The database application and the associated data will take up over 600 GB of hard disk drive space. In addition, these 100 users will store their personal files on the hard disk drive of the system. Each user must have a maximum of 5 GB of storage space. The department manager has made it very clear that this system must not exhibit any downtime as a result of storage device errors. How much space will you require, and what partitions would you need to ensure that the system will perform as needed? Where would these partitions be mounted? What quotas would you implement? What commands would you need to run and what entries to /etc/fstab would you need to create? Justify your answers.

Discovery Exercise 5-7

Estimated Time: 20 minutes

Objective: Troubleshoot storage issues.

Description: You have several filesystems on your hard disk drive that are mounted to separate directories on the Linux directory tree. The /dev/sdc6 filesystem was unable to be mounted at boot time. What could have caused this? What commands could you use to find more information about the nature of the problem?

Chapter 6

Linux Server Deployment

Chapter Objectives

1 Identify the types of hardware present in most server systems.

2 Outline different Linux server virtualization options.

3 Describe the configuration of SCSI devices and SANs.

4 Explain the different levels of RAID and types of RAID configurations.

5 Configure the ZFS and BTRFS filesystems.

6 Install a Linux server distribution.

7 Troubleshoot the Linux server installation process.

8 Identify and resolve issues related to hardware device driver support.

9 Access an installed system using system rescue.

In Chapter 2, you examined a standard Linux workstation installation process using common hardware components and practices. This chapter examines the specialized hardware, software, and storage configurations that are used by Linux servers. In addition, you install the Ubuntu Server Linux distribution and learn how to deal with common installation problems. Finally, this chapter discusses how to access and use system rescue.

Understanding Server Hardware

Recall from Chapter 2 that the minimum hardware requirements for Fedora Linux include a meager 2 GHz CPU, 2 GB of RAM, and 15 GB of disk space, which is far lower than most modern operating systems. However, Linux is incredibly scalable and often configured to work with far more hardware to perform a specialized set of tasks. For example, a Linux computer used as a desktop workstation usually requires enough RAM to run GNOME and desktop applications smoothly, as well as a modern CPU and plenty of disk space to store files, pictures, movies, and so on. An Intel Core i5 system with 16 GB of RAM and a 500 GB SSD is typical hardware for a Linux desktop workstation. If the workstation is for personal use or gaming, expect to add a high-end graphics card supported by game platforms, such as Steam. For server computers, the amount of hardware should adequately support its intended use. A Linux web server that handles e-commerce and a database engine may require 128 GB of RAM, multiple CPUs, and high-capacity SSDs to host the operating system, web server software, and database engine.

Nearly all standard server hardware is supported by Linux. If you have recently purchased modern server hardware, most likely your Linux distribution has all of the drivers that you need. However, if your system has specialized hardware (e.g., a specific Fibre Channel controller), first verify with the hardware vendor that it has an adequate driver included for your Linux distribution (or available for download).

The form factor for server hardware is different from other computers. Nearly all servers within an organization are housed within a rackmount case mounted alongside other servers on a vertical server storage rack. Consequently, these servers are called **rackmount servers**.

> **Note 1**
>
> Some rackmount server enclosures contain two or more smaller, removeable servers. These smaller servers are called **blade servers**.

Each rackmount server may contain a different operating system (or multiple operating systems if virtualization software is used) and connect to a shared monitor/keyboard/mouse. The shared monitor/keyboard/mouse often folds into the rack for storage and is used for initial configuration tasks such as server installation. All other server administration is performed remotely using the remote administration methods discussed in Chapter 12.

Most racks also contain one or more **storage area network (SAN)** devices that provide a large amount of hard disk drive or SSD storage for the servers within the rack. They also include one or more **uninterruptible power supply (UPS)** devices to provide backup battery power to servers and SANs within the rack in the event of a power loss.

The minimum height of a rackmount server is 1.75 inches; this is called a **1U server**. Most 1U servers can contain up to 4 hard disk drives, 10 SATA/SAS SSDs, 36 NVMe SSDs, and 2 CPUs. Other rackmount servers take up more than one spot on the rack. Their height is a multiple of a 1U server. For example, a 2U server is twice as high as a 1U server and can contain double the hardware as a result. Rackmount servers rarely exceed 4U, but SAN devices are often 4U or more.

Figure 6-1 shows a sample server rack configuration that hosts three 1U servers (web server, file server, and firewall server), two 2U servers (database server and email server), a 2U UPS, a 4U SAN, and a management station with a shared monitor/keyboard/mouse.

Figure 6-1   A sample server rack

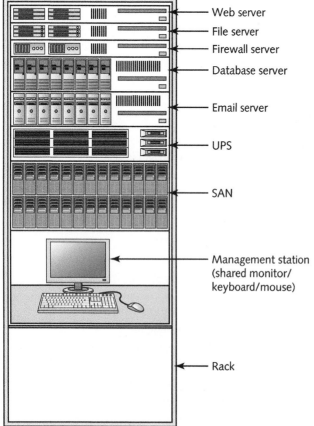

Web server
File server
Firewall server
Database server
Email server
UPS
SAN
Management station (shared monitor/keyboard/mouse)
Rack

Understanding Server Virtualization

Virtualization is the process of running more than one operating system at the same time on a single computer and has been used in various capacities since the dawn of computing in the 1960s. To perform virtualization, you must use software that allows the hardware to host multiple operating systems. Recall from Chapter 1 that this software is called a hypervisor and serves to efficiently handle simultaneous requests for underlying hardware. Type 2 hypervisors are designed to run on an existing workstation operating system (referred to as the host operating system). All additional operating systems are called virtual machines and access the hardware through the hypervisor and the underlying host operating system. Type 2 hypervisors are common today for software testing and development. For example, a software developer can test a specific application or web app on a variety of operating systems without requiring separate computers. Many college technology courses also take advantage of Type 2 hypervisors to run multiple operating systems within a classroom or lab environment.

Note 2

Virtual machines are sometimes referred to as guest operating systems.

Note 3

Common Type 2 hypervisors include VMWare Workstation Pro, Oracle VM VirtualBox, and Parallels Desktop.

By the mid-2000s, a typical server closet or data center contained many individual rackmount servers. To maintain security and stability, each rackmount server contained a single (or small number) of separate server software applications. Often, one rackmount server hosted web server software, while another hosted file sharing services, and so on. Unfortunately, most of these server software applications used only a small fraction of the actual rackmount server hardware. Supplying power and cooling the rackmount servers was expensive. To solve these problems, many IT administrators turned to server virtualization, but with a Type 1 hypervisor to ensure that each virtual machine would run as efficiently as possible. A Type 1 hypervisor interacts with the hardware directly and contains a small operating system to manage the hypervisor configuration and virtual machines. Figure 6-2 shows the difference between Type 1 and Type 2 hypervisors.

Note 4

Common Type 1 hypervisors include VMWare ESXi, Microsoft Hyper-V, Linux KVM/QEMU, and Xen. Each of these hypervisors can be used to provide IaaS within a public or private cloud.

Note 5

Nearly all hypervisors today require that your CPU supports hypervisor acceleration; for the x86_64 CPU platform, these extensions are called Intel VT-x (for Intel CPUs) and AMD-V (for AMD CPUs).

Figure 6-2   Comparing Type 1 and Type 2 hypervisors

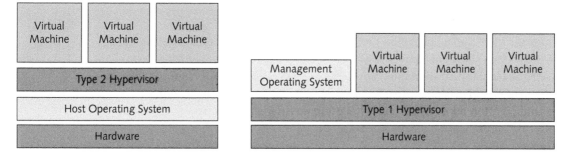

The Linux kernel has built-in hypervisor functionality called **Kernel-based Virtual Machine (KVM)**. In most configurations, KVM works with another open source hypervisor software package called **Quick Emulator (QEMU)** to provide near native speed for virtual machines using a process called binary translation. You can use KVM and QEMU to run virtual machines of other Linux and non-Linux operating systems on a Linux desktop workstation or server. In this configuration, KVM/QEMU provide a Type 1 hypervisor, and the remainder of the Linux system is merely used to manage the hypervisor functionality.

Regardless of the hypervisor used, all virtual machines store their configuration in a small configuration file specific to the hypervisor. The actual operating system data for the virtual machine is stored in a separate virtual hard disk file. When you create a virtual machine, you must choose the size of this virtual hard disk file. You must also specify whether the space allocated for the virtual hard disk file is set to a fixed size during creation (called **thick provisioning**) or dynamically allocated as the virtual machine uses the space (called **thin provisioning**). For example, if you create a 250 GB fixed sized virtual disk, then 250 GB is reserved on the storage device immediately; however, if you create a disk with thin provisioning, it uses a small virtual disk file that can grow up to 250 GB as the virtual machine stores more data. Thin provisioning is often preferred for server virtualization as it conserves space on the underlying server storage hardware.

Note 6

Hyper-V virtual hard disk files have a `.vhdx` extension while VMWare virtual hard disk files have a `.vmdk` extension. KVM/QEMU and Xen virtual hard disk files have either a `.qcow2` extension or omit the extension altogether.

Note 7

All Type 1 hypervisors support virtual machine **snapshots** (also called **checkpoints**). If you take a snapshot of a virtual machine, it creates a second virtual hard disk file that stores any changes to the operating system after the time the snapshot was taken. This is useful before testing a risky software configuration; if the software configuration fails, the snapshot can be used to roll back the operating system to the state it was at before the software configuration was applied.

To create and manage KVM/QEMU virtual machines, a Linux system must have virtualization libraries (libvirt) installed as well as a program that can use these libraries to perform virtualization functions. On Fedora Linux, KVM and QEMU can be easily configured and managed using a program called **Boxes** within the GNOME desktop. By default, Boxes can manage multiple KVM/QEMU virtual machines hosted on the local computer or on other computers across the network using the **Simple Protocol for Independent Computing Environments (SPICE)** protocol and related QXL graphical driver framework. Figure 6-3 shows a SPICE connection to an Ubuntu Linux virtual machine.

Note 8

While most Linux guest operating systems already contain SPICE and QXL support, you should install the guest tools from spice-space.org on other guest operating systems, such as Windows, to obtain full remote management functionality within Boxes.

To configure and manage virtual machines, you can navigate to Activities, Show Applications, Boxes to open the Boxes interface shown in Figure 6-4. Click the + button shown in Figure 6-4 to create a new KVM/QEMU virtual machine. At minimum, you must choose the installation source files, as well as the amount of memory and disk space to allocate to the virtual machine. By default, Boxes stores virtual machine configuration information in the ~/.config/libvirt/qemu directory and virtual hard disk files in the ~/.local/share/gnome-boxes/images directory. Virtual hard disk files created by

Figure 6-3   Managing an Ubuntu Linux virtual machine using Boxes

Figure 6-4   The Boxes application

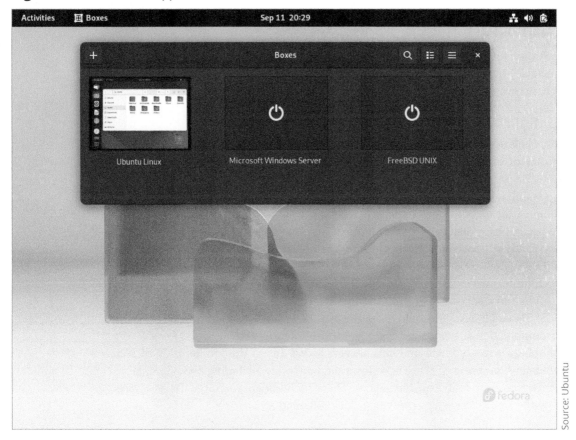

Boxes are thin provisioned by default. After a virtual machine has been created in Boxes, you can double-click its icon to connect to it using SPICE, or right-click its icon to manage it. If you right-click a virtual machine icon in Boxes and choose Preferences, you'll be able to modify its configuration, add additional storage devices, or configure snapshots.

There are also other virtual machine creation and management tools that you can install and use instead of Boxes to create and manage KVM/QEMU virtual machines. For example, the graphical Virtual Machine Manager program provides an interface that is very similar to that within Hyper-V Manager, VMWare Workstation Pro, or Parallels Desktop. To install the Virtual Machine Manager on Fedora, you can use the `dnf install virt-manager` command. Another example is the `virsh command`, which can be used to create and manage virtual machines on Linux systems without a desktop environment installed, such as a server. You can install `virsh` on Fedora Linux by running the `dnf install libvirt-client` command.

Configuring Server Storage

During the Fedora installation process, described in Chapter 2, one of the most important configuration tasks involves configuring the permanent storage devices that will host the Linux operating system. This task involves selecting the storage devices and creating partitions and filesystems. The storage that you configure during installation depends on your specific storage technologies and the space needs of your Linux system. In this section, you examine the configuration of advanced storage technologies commonly used on Linux servers, including SCSI, RAID, SAN storage, ZFS, and BTRFS.

> **Note 9**
>
> You can choose from many different advanced storage technologies available for server systems. However, because many of these technologies involve proprietary hardware and are used primarily on specialized systems, this section is limited to common general-use technologies.

SCSI Configuration

The Small Computer System Interface (SCSI) was designed as a way to connect multiple peripherals to the system in a scalable, high-speed manner. In most systems, a SCSI device is connected to a controller card, which, in turn, connects all devices attached to it to the system.

Legacy SCSI Configuration

SCSI technology dates back to 1986 and originally relied on ribbon cables to transmit information between a SCSI hard disk drive and SCSI controller in a parallel fashion; this type of SCSI is called parallel SCSI. Parallel SCSI hard disk drives are often connected to a single SCSI controller via a single cable in a daisy-chain fashion. To prevent signals from bouncing back and forth on the cable, each end of the cable contains a terminator device that stops signals from being perpetuated.

Each SCSI controller and hard disk drive has a unique ID number known as a SCSI ID or target ID. SCSI controllers typically support up to 15 devices for a total of 16 SCSI IDs (0–15). Moreover, some SCSI devices act as a gateway to other devices; in this case, each device is associated with a unique Logical Unit Number (LUN).

SCSI controllers often add a second SCSI BIOS to your system that is started after the system BIOS. To configure SCSI IDs and LUNs, you could enter the SCSI BIOS configuration tool by pressing a vendor-specific key combination at boot time.

Parallel SCSI technology is rarely found on Linux servers today due to the proliferation of SAS. However, many technologies based on SCSI are in widespread use today, including SAS, iSCSI, Fibre Channel, and most USB-based removeable media devices. These technologies use SCSI IDs and LUNs and are represented by the same device files (/dev/sda, /dev/sdb, and so on).

SAS Configuration

Serial Attached SCSI (SAS) is a newer SCSI technology designed in 2005 to replace parallel SCSI that can transfer data at up to 22.5 Gb/s. Up to 65,535 SAS hard disk drives or SSDs can be connected to a single SCSI controller via serial cables with small serial connectors; many types of SAS connectors are available, including one that is compatible with SATA devices.

Before you install Linux on a system that includes SAS devices, you must first connect them to the SCSI controller via the correct serial cable. Then, you must ensure that the hard disk drives are detected properly by the system or SCSI BIOS. All other SAS configuration (SCSI ID, LUN, etc.) is performed automatically by the SCSI controller but can be changed manually if you access the SCSI BIOS.

RAID Configuration

Recall that you typically create several partitions during installation to decrease the likelihood that the failure of a filesystem on one partition will affect the rest of the system. These partitions can be spread across several hard disk drives to minimize the impact of a hard disk drive failure; if one hard disk drive fails, the data on the other hard disk drives is unaffected.

If a hard disk drive failure occurs, you must power down the computer, replace the failed hard disk drive, power on the computer, and restore the data that was originally on the hard disk drive from a backup copy. The whole process can take several minutes or hours. However, for many server systems, no amount of downtime is acceptable. For these systems, you can use a **fault tolerant** hard disk drive configuration, which has traditionally been implemented by a **Redundant Array of Independent Disks (RAID)**. Note that RAID has other uses besides creating a fault tolerant system. It can be used to speed up access to hard disk drives or combine multiple hard disk drives into a single volume.

> **Note 10**
>
> Most SAN devices use RAID internally to provide both speed and fault tolerance for data.

Seven basic RAID configurations, ranging from level 0 to level 6, are available. RAID level 0 is not fault tolerant.

In RAID level 0, called **disk striping**, an individual file is divided into sections and saved concurrently on two or more hard disk drives, one section per disk. For example, suppose you have a disk striping configuration made up of three hard disk drives. In that case, when you save a file, it is divided into three sections, with each section written to separate hard disk drives concurrently, in a third of the amount of time it would take to save the entire file on one hard disk drive. Note that the system can also read the same file in one-third the time it would take if the file were stored on a single hard disk drive. Disk striping is useful when you need to speed up disk access, but it is not fault tolerant. If one hard disk drive fails in a RAID level 0 configuration, all data is lost.

> **Note 11**
>
> An alternative to RAID level 0 is **spanning** or **Just a Bunch of Disks (JBOD)**. In this configuration, two or more hard disk drives are configured as one large volume, but files are not divided up between the hard disk drives. Instead, files are written to the first hard disk drive, and when the capacity of that first hard disk drive is exhausted, subsequent files are written to the second hard disk drive, and so on.

RAID level 1, which is often referred to as **disk mirroring**, provides fault tolerance in the case of a hard disk drive failure. In this RAID configuration, the same data is written to two separate hard disk drives at the same time. This results in two hard disk drives with identical information. If one fails, the copy can replace the failed hard disk drive in a short period of time. The only drawback to RAID level 1 is the cost, because you need to purchase twice the hard disk drive space needed for a given computer.

RAID level 2 is no longer used and was a variant of RAID 0 that allowed for error and integrity checking on hard disk drives. Modern hard disk drives do this intrinsically.

RAID level 3 is disk striping with a parity bit, or marker, which indicates what data is where. It requires a minimum of three hard disk drives to function, with one of the hard disk drives used to store the parity information. Should one of the hard disk drives containing data fail, you can replace the hard disk drive and regenerate the data using the parity information stored on the parity hard disk drive. If the parity hard disk drive fails, the system must be restored from a backup device.

RAID level 4 is only a slight variant on RAID level 3. RAID level 4 offers greater access speed than RAID level 3, because it can store data in blocks and, thus, does not need to access all hard disk drives in the array at once to read data.

RAID level 5 replaces RAID levels 3 and 4; it is the most common RAID configuration used today and is called **disk striping with parity**. As with RAID levels 3 and 4, it requires a minimum of three hard disk drives; however, the parity information is not stored on a separate hard disk drive but is intermixed with data on the hard disk drives that make up the set. This offers better performance and fault tolerance; if any hard disk drive in the RAID configuration fails, the information on the other hard disk drives can be used to regenerate the lost information such that users can still access their data. After the failed hard disk drive has been replaced, the data can automatically be rebuilt on the new hard disk drive, returning the RAID configuration to its original state. However, if two hard disk drives fail at the same time, the data must be restored from a backup copy. Figure 6-5 shows how data can be calculated on a RAID level 5 using parity information. The parity bits shown in the figure are a sum of the information on the other two disks $(22 + 12 = 34)$. If the third hard disk drive fails, the information can be regenerated because only one element is missing from each equation:

$22 + 12 = 34$
$68 - 65 = 3$
$13 - 9 = 4$

Figure 6-5   Organization of data on RAID level 5

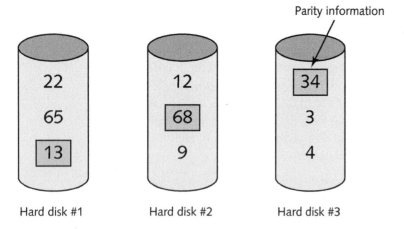

Parity information

22   12   34

65   68   3

13   9   4

Hard disk #1   Hard disk #2   Hard disk #3

RAID level 6 is basically the same as RAID level 5, but it adds a second set of parity bits for added fault tolerance and allows up to two simultaneous hard disk drive failures while remaining fault tolerant. As a result, RAID level 6 requires a minimum of four hard disk drives.

Note 12

RAID levels are often combined; for example, RAID level 10 refers to a stripe set (RAID level 0) that is mirrored (RAID level 1) to another stripe set. Similarly, RAID level 15 refers to a stripe set with parity (RAID level 5) that is mirrored (RAID level 1) to another stripe set with parity.

While RAID configurations can be handled by the hardware contained within a hard disk drive controller (called hardware RAID) or BIOS chipset (called firmware RAID), most modern RAID configurations are provided by software running on an operating system (called software RAID).

Note 13

Only some server grade SCSI/SAS/SATA hard disk drive controllers support hardware RAID. Furthermore, most BIOS chipsets that implement firmware RAID only support RAID level 0 and 1.

To configure and manage hardware RAID, you must use the RAID setup utility for your specific hard disk drive controller. You can access this setup utility by entering a manufacturer-specific key combination at system startup, or by using a manufacturer-supplied program. After you have configured a hardware RAID volume within the setup utility, it will automatically appear as a single hard disk drive to the Linux operating system or Linux installation program if you are installing Linux to a RAID volume. For example, if you configure three hard disk drives in a RAID level 5 volume using the RAID setup utility prior to installing the Linux operating system, the Linux installation program will see the RAID level 5 volume as a single hard disk drive (e.g., /dev/sda). You can then partition and place filesystems on /dev/sda as you would any other physical hard disk drive.

While firmware RAID functions identically to hardware RAID, you must configure and manage firmware RAID using the RAID setup utility within the system BIOS.

Unlike hardware or firmware RAID, software RAID is performed entirely by the Linux operating system; as a result, it can be configured within the Linux installation program during a Linux installation, or afterwards using the appropriate utilities. Your first RAID volume will use a multiple disk (md) device file called /dev/md0 that uses multiple disk files for the RAID level chosen. For example, /dev/md0 can be used to refer to a RAID 5 volume that spans the /dev/sdb, /dev/sdc, /dev/sdd, and /dev/sde devices as shown in the contents of the /proc/mdstat file below:

```
[root@server1 ~]# cat /proc/mdstat
Personalities: [linear] [multipath] [raid0] [raid1] [raid6] [raid5]
              [raid4] [raid10]

md0: active raid5 sde[4] sdd[2] sdc[1] sdb[0]
    322122547200 blocks super 1.2 level 5, 512k chunk, algorithm 2
    [4/4] [UUUU]

unused devices: <none>
[root@server1 ~]#_
```

You can create a filesystem on /dev/md0 and mount it to a directory as you would any other device. The output of the lsblk command below indicates that the RAID 5 volume shown earlier was mounted to the /data directory:

```
[root@server1 ~]# lsblk
NAME                       MAJ:MIN RM   SIZE RO TYPE  MOUNTPOINTS
loop0                          7:0  0    62M  1 loop  /snap/core20/1587
loop1                          7:1  0  79.9M  1 loop  /snap/lxd/22923
loop2                          7:2  0    47M  1 loop  /snap/snapd/16292
loop3                          7:3  0  63.2M  1 loop  /snap/core20/1623
sda                            8:0  0    50G  0 disk
├─sda1                         8:1  0     1G  0 part  /boot/efi
├─sda2                         8:2  0     2G  0 part  /boot
└─sda3                         8:3  0  46.9G  0 part
  └─ubuntu--vg-ubuntu--lv    253:0  0  46.9G  0 lvm   /
sdb                           8:16  0   100G  0 disk
```

```
└─md0                          9:0     0   300G   0 raid5 /data
sdc                            8:32    0   100G   0 disk
└─md0                          9:0     0   300G   0 raid5 /data
sdd                            8:48    0   100G   0 disk
└─md0                          9:0     0   300G   0 raid5 /data
sde                            8:64    0   100G   0 disk
└─md0                          9:0     0   300G   0 raid5 /data
sr0                            11:0    1  1024M   0 rom
[root@server1 ~]#_
```

The specific structure of software RAID volumes is autodetected at boot time but can be written to /etc/mdadm/mdadm.conf to ensure correctness. Additionally, RAID filesystems can be mounted at boot time via entries within /etc/fstab; however, you should list the filesystem UUID instead of the /dev/md0 device file within /etc/fstab to avoid problems should the udev daemon on the system rename the /dev/md0 device file.

To create and manage software RAID configuration after installation, you can use the `mdadm` command. For example, you can use the command `mdadm --create /dev/md0 --level=5 --raid-devices=4 /dev/sdb /dev/sdc /dev/sdd /dev/sde` to create a RAID level 5 called /dev/md0 from the /dev/sdb, /dev/sdc, /dev/sdd and /dev/sde storage devices. Next, you can view detailed information about the RAID volume using the following command:

```
[root@server1 ~]# mdadm --detail /dev/md0
/dev/md0:
             Version : 1.2
       Creation Time : Sat Sep 10 23:16:37 2023
          Raid Level : raid5
          Array Size : 322122547200 (300 GB)
       Used Dev Size : 107374182400 (100 GB)
        Raid Devices : 4
       Total Devices : 4
         Persistence : Superblock is persistent

         Update Time : Sat Sep 10 23:19:44 2023
               State : clean
      Active Devices : 4
     Working Devices : 4
      Failed Devices : 0
       Spare Devices : 0

              Layout : left-symmetric
          Chunk Size : 512K

  Consistency Policy : resync

                Name : ubuntu:0  (local to host ubuntu)
                UUID : 4f7dfff4:17842b43:8a126155:a8624183
              Events : 18

     Number   Major   Minor   RaidDevice State
        0        8       16        0      active sync   /dev/sdb
        1        8       32        1      active sync   /dev/sdc
        2        8       48        2      active sync   /dev/sdd
        4        8       64        3      active sync   /dev/sde
[root@server1 ~]#_
```

SAN Storage Configuration

Many rackmount servers today contain only enough storage to host the Linux operating system and associated server programs. All other data files, databases, web content, virtual hard disk files, and so on are stored on an external SAN device on the server rack that is connected to the Linux operating system using a SAN protocol. The two most common SAN protocols today include iSCSI and Fibre Channel. You can also use DM-MPIO to provide multiple connections to one or more SANs.

iSCSI Configuration

Internet SCSI (iSCSI) is a technology that uses Ethernet network cables to transfer data to and from a SAN device, either on the local network or across the Internet, using the SCSI protocol. The software component within the operating system that connects to the SAN device via iSCSI is referred to as an iSCSI initiator, and the storage that is made available to iSCSI initiator on the SAN is called the iSCSI target. A single iSCSI target typically contains multiple hard disk drives or SSDs that are combined using fault-tolerant hardware RAID (e.g., RAID 5) on the SAN device itself. As a result, the iSCSI initiator and Linux operating system will see the iSCSI target as a single device file (e.g., /dev/sdb).

Note 14

iSCSI is simply a transfer protocol used between a server and a SAN device. The SAN device itself can use different storage technologies to physically store the data, including NVMe SSDs, or SATA/SAS hard disk drives or SSDs.

Note 15

SAN devices contain many hard disk drives and SSDs to provide fast, fault-tolerant, and high-capacity storage for servers on a server rack. A single iSCSI SAN device can host multiple iSCSI targets that are accessed by the iSCSI initiators on different servers; each of these servers that access the iSCSI SAN device are said to be part of a "storage area network."

To connect a Linux server to an iSCSI SAN, you must first ensure that the appropriate iSCSI targets have been configured via the configuration tools provided by the iSCSI SAN device manufacturer. Next, you must connect an iSCSI-compatible Ethernet cable from an iSCSI-compliant network interface on your Linux server to an Ethernet port on your iSCSI SAN device. Finally, you must configure the iSCSI initiator on your Linux server using the iscsiadm command. For example, to configure the iSCSI initiator to connect to a target available on the SAN device with the IP address 192.168.1.1, you could use the following commands (and optionally specifying the iSCSI target password, if one was configured on the SAN device):

```
[root@server1 ~]# iscsiadm -m discovery -t st -p 192.168.1.1
192.168.1.1:3260,1 iqn.2001-05.com.equallogic:0-8a0120425dbe
[root@server1 ~]# iscsiadm -m node --login
Enter password: **********
[root@server1 ~]#_
```

Following this, the iSCSI target should be identified by the Linux system as the next available SCSI device (e.g., /dev/sdb). You can partition and format it as you would any other SCSI hard disk drive, as well as mount any filesystems on it to a mount point directory and update the /etc/fstab to ensure that the filesystems are mounted automatically at boot time. Additionally, you must configure the node.startup = automatic line within the /etc/iscsi/iscsid.conf file to ensure that the iSCSI initiator software is loaded at boot time; otherwise, the filesystems on the SAN device will not be accessible.

You can also configure an iSCSI initiator during a Linux installation. For example, to configure an iSCSI initiator during a Fedora installation, select Add a disk shown in Figure 2-9. This will allow you to select advanced storage options, as shown in Figure 6-6. You can then click the Add iSCSI Target button shown in Figure 6-6 and supply the IP address and password for your iSCSI SAN device.

Figure 6-6   Configuring advanced storage options during a Fedora installation

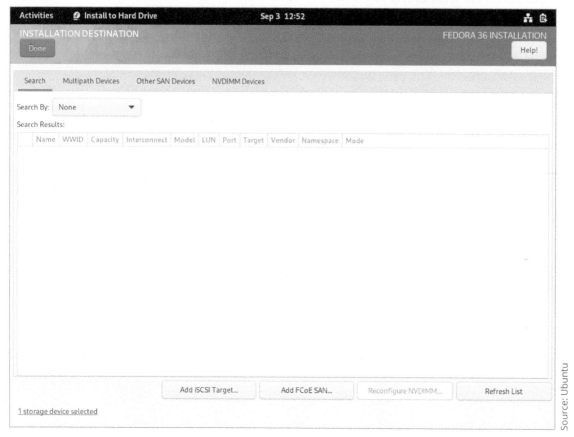

Fibre Channel Configuration

Fibre Channel (FC) is a technology that can be used to transport SCSI data to local FC-capable hard disk drives or SSDs or to a remote FC SAN device, across an Ethernet or fiber optic cable at speeds of up to 128 Gb/s. A server typically uses a FC controller called a FC **Host Bus Adapter (HBA)** that connects to one or more local FC-capable storage devices (hard disk drives or SSDs), or to a FC SAN that contains many FC-capable storage devices connected via a FC switch. All FC-capable storage devices must have a **World Wide Name (WWN)** identifier that is normally assigned by the FC HBA in order to function with the FC protocol.

> **Note 16**
>
> WWN identifiers are not specific to FC; they are storage-specific identifiers that can optionally be given to SATA and SAS devices.

> **Note 17**
>
> A FC HBA can also be a FC-capable 10 Gb (or faster) Ethernet network interface if the FC SAN uses FC over Ethernet (FCoE).

Most FC HBAs contain proprietary firmware that cannot be bundled within a Linux distribution due to GPL license incompatibility. As a result, to configure FC devices on a Linux system, you must first obtain and install the firmware package for your FC HBA from the manufacturer. Manufacturers often make their firmware available for installation from a private software repository and list instructions needed to install it on different Linux distributions. After installing the appropriate firmware package, you should see your FC HBA listed in the output of the `lspci` command, as follows:

```
[root@server1 ~]# lspci
0000:00:01.0 SCSI storage controller: LSI Logic / Symbios Logic 53c875 (rev 04)
0001:00:01.0 Ethernet controller: Oracle Corporation GEM 10/100/1000
Ethernet [ge] (rev 01)
0001:00:02.0 SCSI storage controller: QLogic Corp. QLA2200 64-bit Fibre
Channel Adapter (rev 05)
0003:01:04.0 SCSI storage controller: QLogic Corp. QLA2200 64-bit
Fibre Channel Adapter (rev 05)
0003:01:05.0 SCSI storage controller: QLogic Corp. QLA2200 64-bit
Fibre Channel Adapter (rev 05)
0003:02:04.0 SCSI storage controller: QLogic Corp. QLA2200 64-bit Fibre
Channel Adapter (rev 05)
0003:02:05.0 SCSI storage controller: QLogic Corp. QLA2200 64-bit Fibre
Channel Adapter (rev 05)
[root@server1 ~]#_
```

The FC HBA provides the same functionality as an iSCSI initiator; if connected properly, the FC HBA should detect and make any FC storage devices available to the Linux system. The /dev/disk/by-id directory should contain an entry for each FC SCSI device, as well as a matching WWN entry as shown in the output below. Each of these entries is a symbolic link to the appropriate device file (/dev/sdb, /dev/sdc, and so on) that you can use to create partitions and filesystems. You can then mount these filesystems and modify the /etc/fstab to mount them at boot time like any other disk device.

```
[root@server1 ~]# ls /dev/disk/by-id
lrwxrwxrwx 1 root root   9 Jul 24 scsi-320000004cf4cfb8f -> ../../sdb
lrwxrwxrwx 1 root root   9 Jul 24 scsi-32000000c507aa387 -> ../../sde
lrwxrwxrwx 1 root root   9 Jul 24 scsi-32000000c507aa421 -> ../../sdd
lrwxrwxrwx 1 root root   9 Jul 24 scsi-32000000c507aa43c -> ../../sdg
lrwxrwxrwx 1 root root   9 Jul 24 scsi-32000000c507aa50b -> ../../sdc
lrwxrwxrwx 1 root root   9 Jul 24 scsi-32000000c507aa5c0 -> ../../sdf
lrwxrwxrwx 1 root root   9 Jul 24 wwn-0x20000004cf4cfb8f -> ../../sdb
lrwxrwxrwx 1 root root   9 Jul 24 wwn-0x2000000c507aa387 -> ../../sde
lrwxrwxrwx 1 root root   9 Jul 24 wwn-0x2000000c507aa421 -> ../../sdd
lrwxrwxrwx 1 root root   9 Jul 24 wwn-0x2000000c507aa43c -> ../../sdg
lrwxrwxrwx 1 root root   9 Jul 24 wwn-0x2000000c507aa50b -> ../../sdc
lrwxrwxrwx 1 root root   9 Jul 24 wwn-0x2000000c507aa5c0 -> ../../sdf
[root@server1 ~]#_
```

Note 18

Like iSCSI SAN devices, FC SAN devices often use hardware RAID to create fault tolerant volumes; in this case, each SCSI (and associated WWN) identifier shown in the previous output may refer to a different RAID volume on the FC SAN itself.

Note 19

Most storage devices that support FC are either SCSI or SAS hard disk drives or SSDs. However, FC can also be used to transport data to and from NVMe devices that do not use the SCSI protocol; in this case, the /dev/disk/by-id directory will list both nvme and wwn identifiers.

> **Note 20**
>
> You can also configure FC HBAs during a Linux installation. For example, to configure a FCoE SAN during a Fedora installation, click the Add FCoE SAN button shown in Figure 6-6 and select the appropriate FC-capable network interface. To configure a different FC HBA, select the Other SAN Devices tab shown in Figure 6-6, choose the associated FC HBA, and supply the firmware, if necessary.

Configuring DM-MPIO

Data center server environments often have several iSCSI or FC SAN devices. Additionally, each server within a data center can have multiple connections to a single SAN for fault tolerance in case a single connection becomes unavailable, or to load balance requests across multiple connections for greater speed. Larger data centers often have multiple SANs that host the same information; in this case, servers can have multiple connections to different SANs to provide fault tolerance in case a single SAN becomes unavailable, or to load balance requests across multiple SANs for greater speed.

This configuration is called Multipath Input Output (MPIO). On Linux systems, it is implemented by the same device mapper used to map LVM logical volumes to physical devices; as a result, Linux often refers to this configuration as Device Mapper MPIO (DM-MPIO).

Before you configure DM-MPIO, each server must have multiple iSCSI targets or FC HBAs configured, and the associated SAN volumes represented by a device file (/dev/sdb, /dev/sdc, and so on). Following this, you can configure DM-MPIO using the `mpathconf` command, which autodetects your SAN configuration, creates the appropriate configuration entries within the /etc/multipath.conf file and starts the multipath daemon (multipathd). The following is an example of this command that scans for available SANs and configures them for DM-MPIO fault tolerance:

```
[root@server1 ~]# mpathconf --enable --with_multipathd y
[root@server1 ~]#_
```

After DM-MPIO has been configured, the device mapper will create a device mapping file that refers to two or more device files; for example, the /dev/mapper/mpath1 device mapping file may refer to the /dev/sdb and /dev/sdc iSCSI targets. You can then use this device mapping file when mounting and accessing your SAN filesystems.

You can also run the `multipathd -k` command to interact with the multipath daemon directly. This will open a multipathd prompt that you can use to type commands to view and manage the multipath daemon; to see a list of available commands at this prompt, you can type the `?` or `help` command. Alternatively, you can use the `multipath` command to view and manage the multipath daemon. For example, `multipath show config` will display the current multipath configuration, including all active devices.

> **Note 21**
>
> You can also configure DM-MPIO during a Linux installation. For example, if you add multiple iSCSI targets or FB HBAs during a Fedora installation, you can configure them to use DM-MPIO by selecting the Multipath Devices tab shown in Figure 6-6.

ZFS Configuration

The Zettabyte File System (ZFS) is a high-performance filesystem and volume management software that was designed for large-scale Linux systems that need to store data on multiple disks, SANs, and remote systems. You can create RAID-like ZFS volumes that span thousands of local and network storage devices, such as local hard disk drives, local SSDs, SANs, and remote file shares, as well as resize volumes, while the filesystem is mounted. Moreover, the ZFS filesystem detects and repairs data errors automatically as data is read and written, as well as protects against problems that are commonly seen on systems that write large amounts of data to a non-ZFS filesystem, including:

- Silent data corruption
- Bit rot
- Disk firmware bugs
- Phantom writes
- Misdirected writes
- Driver and kernel buffer errors
- Accidental driver overwrites

ZFS caches frequently accessed information in RAM and on faster storage devices such as SSDs to provide ultra-fast performance. ZFS also supports advanced filesystem features, including deduplication (storing one copy of a file that is located in multiple directories until one of the files change), snapshots, cloning, compression, encryption, NFSv4, volume management, and more.

> ### Note 22
>
> ZFS was initially created by Sun Microsystems in 2001 and is often used by the largest Linux and UNIX systems in the world. It is available for Solaris UNIX, Mac OSX, Linux, FreeBSD, FreeNAS, and more. Because ZFS does not currently have a GPL-compatible license, it cannot be bundled within a Linux distribution, but it can be easily added afterwards. On Linux, ZFS support is maintained by zfsonlinux.org.

Although ZFS is primarily used on large Linux systems that may have hundreds or thousands of storage devices, it is also used within small and medium-sized organizations that require flexible volume management for data that is easy to configure.

ZFS pools are groups of physical disks that ZFS can manage (local disks, SANs, shared devices, large raw files, remote shares, etc.), and **ZFS volumes** are ZFS-managed filesystems that are created from ZFS pools and mounted to a directory on the system.

Take, for example, a system that hosts several hard disk drives, with the Linux OS installed on /dev/sda. To create a simple ZFS pool called data1 from the second SATA/SCSI/SAS hard disk drive, you could use the following `zpool command`:

```
[root@server1 ~]# zpool create data1 /dev/sdb
[root@server1 ~]#_
```

This will also create a new ZFS volume called data1 and mount it to /data1, as shown here in the last line of the `mount` command output:

```
[root@server1 ~]# df -hT
Filesystem                           Type  Size Used Avail Use% Mounted on
tmpfs                                tmpf  191M 1.1M  190M   1% /run
/dev/mapper/ubuntu--vg-ubuntu--lv    ext4   46G 4.9G   39G  12% /
/dev/sda2                            ext4  2.0G 128M  1.7G   7% /boot
/dev/sda1                            vfat  1.1G 5.3M  1.1G   1% /boot/efi
data1                                zfs   880M    0  880M   0% /data1
[root@server1 ~]#_
```

You can also use the `zpool` command to view the details for your data1 volume:

```
[root@server1 ~]# zpool list
NAME   SIZE  ALLOC  FREE  CKPOINT  EXPANDSZ  FRAG  CAP  DEDUP  HEALTH  ALTROOT
data1  960G  372K   960G     -        -       0%   0%  1.00x  ONLINE   -
[root@server1 ~]#_
```

Note 23

You can remove a ZFS volume using the `zpool` command. For example, `zpool destroy data1` would remove the ZFS volume and pool created in the previous output.

If you specify multiple devices when creating a simple ZFS volume, then those devices are automatically added to the ZFS pool and a ZFS volume is created from their contents. For example, if you run the following command, the /dev/sdc and /dev/sdd hard disk drives would be added to the data2 pool, and a ZFS volume called data2 would be created (with a capacity of both hard disk drives combined) and mounted to the /data2 directory. This would act as the equivalent of a RAID 0 volume, but with the file corruption prevention benefits of ZFS.

```
[root@server1 ~]# zpool create data2 /dev/sdc /dev/sdd
[root@server1 ~]#_
```

To create a ZFS pool and mirrored ZFS volume called data3 from the /dev/sde and /dev/sdf hard disk drives and mount the volume to /data3, you specify the `mirror` keyword during creation, as shown here:

```
[root@server1 ~]# zpool create data3 mirror /dev/sde /dev/sdf
[root@server1 ~]#_
```

The data3 volume is the equivalent of RAID 1 but resizable under ZFS, and the total size of the volume is identical to the size of one of the hard disk drives.

Note 24

To create a ZFS mirrored volume, you need to specify a minimum of two hard disk drives to protect against a single hard disk drive failure.

To view the status of the disks that are part of the data3 pool, you can use the following command:

```
[root@server1 ~]# zpool status data3
  pool: data3
 state: DEGRADED
status: One or more devices has experienced an unrecoverable error. An
        attempt was made to correct the error.  Applications are
        unaffected.
action: Determine if the device needs to be replaced, and clear the
        errors using 'zpool clear' or replace the device with 'zpool
        replace'.
   see: https://openzfs.github.io/openzfs-docs/msg/ZFS-8000-9P
  scan: scrub repaired 340K in 00:00:00 with 0 errors on Sat Sep 10
        23:46:23 2023
config:
        NAME          STATE     READ WRITE CKSUM
        data3.        DEGRADED     0     0     0
          mirror-0    DEGRADED     0     0     0
            sde       UNAVAIL      0     0     0  corrupted data
            sdf       ONLINE       0     0     0

errors: No known data errors
[root@server1 ~]#_
```

Notice from the preceding example that one of the disks in the mirror has failed (/dev/sde). In this case, you should detach the device from the pool using the `zpool detach data3 /dev/sde` command, replace the failed hard disk drive, and reattach the disk to the mirror using the `zpool attach data3 /dev/sdf /dev/sde` command. During this process, the filesystem is still available to users for reading and writing data. After reattaching the new hard disk drive, the output of the `zpool status data3` command should resemble the following output:

```
[root@server1 ~]# zpool status data3
  pool: data3
 state: ONLINE
  scan: resilvered 1020K in 00:00:00 with 0 errors on Sat Sep 10
        23:47:19 2023
config:

        NAME            STATE     READ WRITE CKSUM
        data3           ONLINE       0     0     0
          mirror-0      ONLINE       0     0     0
            sde         ONLINE       0     0     0
            sdf         ONLINE       0     0     0

errors: No known data errors
[root@server1 ~]#_
```

To create a ZFS pool and RAID-Z volume (the equivalent of a RAID-5 volume with a variable-sized stripe) called data4 from the /dev/sdg, /dev/sdh, and /dev/sdi hard disk drives and mount it to /data4, specify the `raidz` keyword during creation, as shown here:

```
[root@server1 ~]# zpool create data4 raidz /dev/sdg /dev/sdh /dev/sdi
[root@server1 ~]#_
```

Note 25

A RAID-Z volume needs a minimum of three hard disk drives to protect against a single disk failure, and a minimum of seven hard disk drives to protect against a multidisk failure.

Note 26

You can also use `raidz2` (double parity like RAID-6) and `raidz3` (triple parity) in place of `raidz` in the previous command. You need a minimum of four devices for `raidz2` and a minimum of five devices for `raidz3`.

Note 27

Because ZFS writes parity info with a variable-sized stripe, performance is maximized, and there is virtually no chance of the infamous "RAID 5 Hole" (data loss in the event of a power failure) that plagues traditional RAID systems.

Following this, you can view the state and performance of the RAID-Z volume using the `zpool status` and `zpool iostat -v` commands:

```
[root@server1 ~]# zpool status data4
  pool: data4
 state: ONLINE
config:
```

```
            NAME           STATE      READ WRITE CKSUM
            data4          ONLINE        0     0     0
              raidz1-0     ONLINE        0     0     0
                sdg        ONLINE        0     0     0
                sdh        ONLINE        0     0     0
                sdi        ONLINE        0     0     0

errors: No known data errors
root@server1:~# zpool iostat -v data4
                 capacity       operations       bandwidth
pool          alloc   free    read  write     read   write
----------    -----   -----   ----- -----     -----  -----
data4         220K    8.6T        0    11      701   10.5K
  raidz1      220K    8.6T        0    11      701   10.5K
    /dev/sdg     -       -        0    10    25.2K   83.6K
    /dev/sdh     -       -        0    10    25.1K   83.6K
    /dev/sdi     -       -        0    10    1.48K   83.6K
----------    -----   -----   ----- -----     -----  -----

[root@server1 ~]#_
```

For more granular management of ZFS, you can use the `zfs command` to manage the specific features of the ZFS filesystem stored within ZFS volumes. The `zfs` command allows you to set a wide variety of ZFS-specific functionality, including directory size quotas, automatic compression, as well as many more file- and directory-specific features and performance options. Moreover, you can configure specific subdirectories on an existing ZFS volume that are managed as separate ZFS volumes. These subdirectories are called **ZFS datasets** and can be configured with unique ZFS filesystem settings and features. For example, if you create a directory under /data4 called research, you can run the following command to specify that the research subdirectory should be treated as a ZFS dataset:

```
[root@server1 ~]# zfs create data4/research
[root@server1 ~]#_
```

To see a list of ZFS datasets that are available for ZFS management, you can run the `zfs list` command:

```
[root@server1 ~]# zfs list
NAME                  USED   AVAIL   REFER   MOUNTPOINT
data4                 286K    8.6T   42.6K   /data4
data4/research       38.6K    8.6T   38.6K   /data4/research
[root@server1 ~]#_
```

Note that the `zfs list` output includes the data4 ZFS volume. This is because the data4 volume is also considered a dataset to ensure that it can be managed separately from other datasets in the volume. To list the specific configuration parameters that you can modify for the data4/research dataset, you can use the `zfs get all` command:

```
[root@server1 ~]# zfs get all data4/research | less
NAME             PROPERTY       VALUE                SOURCE
data4/research   type           filesystem           -
data4/research   creation       Sat Sep 10 23:48 2023 -
data4/research   used           38.6K                -
data4/research   available      214M                 -
data4/research   referenced     38.6K                -
data4/resear0h   compressratio  1.00x                -
```

```
data4/research mounted        yes                       -
data4/research quota          none                      default
data4/research reservation    none                      default
data4/research recordsize     128K                      default
data4/research mountpoint     /data4/research.          default
data4/research sharenfs       off                       default
data4/research checksum       on                        default
data4/research compression    off                       default
data4/research atime          on                        default
data4/research devices        on                        default
data4/research exec           on                        default
data4/research setuid         on                        default
data4/research readonly       off                       default
:
```

You can modify the settings for the research dataset to suit your needs. For example, to limit the total size of files within the research dataset to 500 GB, you could use the zfs set quota=500G data4/research command, or to ensure that the contents of the research dataset are read-only, you could run the zfs set readonly=on data4/research command.

ZFS volumes store their configuration within the volume itself and are mounted by the ZFS system software and not via entries within the /etc/fstab file. By default, the ZFS system software searches for and mounts all ZFS volumes on the system, but this can be disabled by modifying the ZFS_MOUNT='yes' line within the /etc/default/zfs file; in this case, you will need to run the zfs mount data4 command to manually mount the data4 ZFS filesystem, or the zfs mount -a command to manually mount all ZFS filesystems after boot time.

BTRFS Configuration

The B-tree File System (BTRFS) has many features that are similar to those found in ZFS, and is currently being developed to become a replacement for ext4. Currently, BTRFS isn't as fast or robust as ZFS; it does not detect and repair data errors automatically as data is read and written. However, it can be used to create volumes that span multiple storage devices using RAID 0, RAID 1, RAID 10, RAID 5, and RAID 6. It also supports some of the enterprise features available in ZFS, including compression, deduplication, snapshots, resizing, quotas, and datasets (called BTRFS subvolumes).

> **Note 28**
>
> BTRFS is still in development; as a result, many features of BTRFS, including RAID 5/6 and quotas, are not recommended for production use at the time of this writing.

BTRFS uses three terms to refer to its filesystem structure: data refers to the blocks available for data storage, metadata refers to the inode table, and system refers to the superblock. All BTRFS metadata is stored in B-tree structures for fast access. In addition, you can specify whether the data and metadata can be fault tolerant when creating a BTRFS filesystem that spans multiple storage devices; for example, to create a BTRFS filesystem that spans /dev/sdb and /dev/sdc, as well as uses RAID 1 for the system and metadata (-m) and data (-d), you could use the following mkfs.btrfs command:

```
[root@server1 ~]# mkfs.btrfs -m raid1 -d raid1 /dev/sdb /dev/sdc
btrfs-progs v5.16.2
See http://btrfs.wiki.kernel.org for more information.

Performing full device TRIM /dev/sdb (2.00TiB) ...
```

```
NOTE: several default settings have changed in version 5.15, please make sure
      this does not affect your deployments:
      - DUP for metadata (-m dup)
      - enabled no-holes (-O no-holes)
      - enabled free-space-tree (-R free-space-tree)

Performing full device TRIM /dev/sdc (1.00GiB) ...
Label:              (null)
UUID:               bfafccc8-7b1f-4e87-8f7f-a1ab672621f0
Node size:          16384
Sector size:        4096
Filesystem size:    4.00TiB
Block group profiles:
   Data:            RAID1            102.38MiB
   Metadata:        RAID1            102.38MiB
   System:          RAID1              8.00MiB
SSD detected:       no
Zoned device:       no
Incompat features:  extref, skinny-metadata, no-holes
Runtime features:   free-space-tree
Checksum:           crc32c
Number of devices:  2
Devices:
   ID        SIZE   PATH
    1     2.00TiB   /dev/sdb
    2     2.00TiB   /dev/sdc
[root@server1 ~]#_
```

Note 29

If you omit the -m and -d options to the mkfs.btrfs command, the default is to use RAID 0 for the data and RAID 1 for the metadata.

You can then mount the filesystem to a mount point directory by using any device file within the filesystem; in this example, you could use either the mount /dev/sdb /storage command or the mount /dev/sdc /storage command to mount the BTRFS filesystem to the /storage directory. Similarly, you could add either the /dev/sdb /storage btrfs defaults 0 0 line or the /dev/sdc /storage btrfs defaults 0 0 line to /etc/fstab to ensure that the BTRFS filesystem is mounted at boot time.

BRFS filesystem compression is enabled using a mount option. For example, the mount -o compress=lzo /dev/sdb /storage command would mount the BTRFS filesystem in our example using LZO compression, and the /dev/sdb /storage btrfs defaults,compress=lzo 0 0 line in /etc/fstab would ensure that it is mounted with LZO compression at boot time.

Note 30

While both ZFS and BTRFS support multiple compression algorithms, Lempel–Ziv–Oberhumer (LZO) is the preferred one for automatic filesystem compression within production environments due to its speed.

After a BRFS filesystem has been created, it can be managed using the btrfs command. Because BTRFS does not have the automatic repair functionality that ZFS has, you can check the unmounted

BTRFS filesystem in the previous example and automatically repair any errors using the following command:

```
[root@server1 ~]# btrfs check /dev/sdb
Opening filesystem to check...
Checking filesystem on /dev/sdb
UUID: bfafccc8-7b1f-4e87-8f7f-a1ab672621f0
[1/7] checking root items
[2/7] checking extents
[3/7] checking free space tree
[4/7] checking fs roots
[5/7] checking only csums items (without verifying data)
[6/7] checking root refs
[7/7] checking quota groups skipped (not enabled on this FS)
found 147456 bytes used, no error found
total csum bytes: 0
total tree bytes: 147456
total fs tree bytes: 32768
total extent tree bytes: 16384
btree space waste bytes: 132336
file data blocks allocated: 0
 referenced 0
[root@server1 ~]#_
```

Note 31

The `btrfsck` command can be used instead of the `btrfs check` command. For example, `btrfsck /dev/sdb` performs the same check as the `btrfs` command in the previous example.

The `btrfs` command can also be used to display BTRFS configuration and usage. For example, the `btrfs filesystem show /dev/sdb` command can be used to show the configuration of the BTRFS filesystem that includes the /dev/sdb device, while the `btrfs filesystem df /storage` command will show usage information for the BTRFS filesystem mounted to the /storage directory.

BTRFS subvolumes function similar to ZFS datasets and can be mounted separately to their own mount point directory with different options. To create a subvolume called backup on the BTRFS filesystem mounted to the storage directory, you could use the `btrfs subvolume create /storage/backup` command, and to mount it to the /backup directory using compression, you could use the `mount -o subvol=backup,compress=lzo /dev/sdb /backup` command, if one of the devices in the BTRFS filesystem is /dev/sdb.

You can also add devices and extend BTRFS filesystems while the BTRFS filesystem is mounted and online. For example, to add the /dev/sdd and /dev/sde devices to the RAID 1 BTRFS filesystem created earlier and mounted to /storage, as well as view the resulting configuration, you can use the following commands:

```
[root@server1 ~]# btrfs device add /dev/sdd /dev/sde /storage
Performing full device TRIM /dev/sdd (2.00TiB) ...
Performing full device TRIM /dev/sde (2.00TiB) ...
[root@server1 ~]# btrfs filesystem balance /storage
Done, had to relocate 3 out of 3 chunks
[root@server1 ~]# btrfs filesystem show /dev/sdb
Label: none  uuid: bfafccc8-7b1f-4e87-8f7f-a1ab672621f0
        Total devices 4 FS bytes used 144.00KiB
```

```
        devid     1 size 2.00TiB used 288.00MiB path /dev/sdb
        devid     2 size 2.00TiB used 288.00MiB path /dev/sdc
        devid     3 size 2.00TiB used 416.00MiB path /dev/sdd
        devid     4 size 2.00TiB used 416.00MiB path /dev/sde
[root@server1 ~]#_
```

Server Storage Configuration Scenarios

For a Linux workstation, fault tolerance for storage is rarely configured; however, for a Linux server, keeping the operating system, applications, and data fault tolerant is key to ensuring that the server can continue to provide services on the network. On most servers, two fault-tolerant storage approaches are used simultaneously; one to protect the operating system and applications, and another to protect the data that is used by the applications. Consequently, most rackmount servers on the market today come standard with two hard disk drives or SSDs for hosting the operating system and applications in a RAID 1 configuration. The administrator must choose whether to add local storage or an iSCSI-capable network interface or FC HBA for connection to a SAN.

Although the specific storage configuration of a rackmount server varies widely depending on the intended use of the server, some common fault-tolerant storage configurations for the operating system and applications include:

- Two hard disk drives or SSDs in a hardware RAID 1 configuration
- Two hard disk drives or SSDs in a firmware RAID 1 configuration
- Two hard disk drives or SSDs in a software RAID 1 configuration (configured during Linux installation)
- Two hard disk drives or SSDs in a BTRFS RAID 1 configuration (configured during Linux installation)

Additionally, some common fault-tolerant storage configurations used to host application data and virtual hard disk files include:

- Multiple hard disk drives or SSDs in a hardware RAID 5, 6, 10, or 15 configuration
- Multiple hard disk drives or SSDs in a software RAID 5, 6, 10, or 15 configuration
- A connection to an iSCSI or FC SAN (which uses fault-tolerant hardware RAID 5, 6, 10, or 15 on the SAN device)
- Multiple hard disk drives, SSDs, or SANs in a ZFS raidz, raidz2, or raidz3 configuration
- Multiple hard disk drives or SSDs in a BTRFS RAID 5, 6, or 10 configuration

Note 32

Of the fault-tolerant storage configurations for data listed, SAN and ZFS configurations are the most commonly implemented today.

Installing a Linux Server Distribution

Any Linux distribution can be used as a server if the necessary packages are installed that provide for server services on the network. However, many Linux distributions also provide a version that is geared for Linux servers. These Linux server distributions do not have a desktop environment installed by default, because administration of Linux installed on a rackmount server is often performed using commands within a BASH terminal on a remote computer across the network. Although most Linux software is normally obtained from Internet software repositories, many Linux server distributions ship with a set of server software packages that you can optionally select during the installation process.

Note 33

Remote administration methods are discussed in Chapter 12.

Note 34

The configuration of common server software packages is covered in Chapter 13.

The installation process for a Linux server distribution may differ from a standard or live Linux installation process. While some Linux server distributions offer a live desktop and graphical installer, others do not load a desktop environment at all. In this case, you must navigate through a text installer interface to install the Linux system. Additionally, Linux server distributions often allow you to configure additional systems settings during the installation process so that you don't need to configure that same information afterwards, including:

- *The host name and IP configuration of the server*—For a desktop system, the default hostname (localhost) will often suffice. However, for a server system, the host name is often used by the configuration of server services and should match the name that other computers on the network will use when contacting the server. Additionally, many Linux administrators prefer to configure a static IP address on server systems rather than obtain an IP address automatically. This ensures that the IP address of the server cannot change over time.
- *Whether to allow for automatic updating*—Most Linux systems are configured by default to download important OS and application updates periodically. However, for a Linux server, an update could potentially cause problems with software that is currently running on the server. As a result, most Linux administrators prefer to manually update software after testing the update on a non-production computer that contains the same software as the server. Application updates will be discussed in more depth in Chapter 11.
- *Package selection*—While most Linux workstation distributions automatically install a predefined set of software packages during installation without user input, Linux server distributions often prompt you to select the specific software packages that will be needed on the Linux server. This prevents unnecessary packages from being installed and space from being wasted on the server filesystems.
- *Server service configuration*—Some server service packages that are installed require additional configuration in order to provide functionality. The installation program for a Linux server distribution may prompt you for that information during the installation so that you don't need to configure it afterwards.
- *Root user password*—While most Linux workstation distributions prompt you to create a regular user account during the installation that can optionally set a password for the root user using the sudo passwd root command, some Linux server distributions allow you to configure the root user password during the installation program itself, saving you the time to do so afterwards.

Note 35

In Hands-On Project 6-1, you install the Ubuntu Server Linux distribution. In addition to providing the opportunity to apply concepts in later chapters to more than one Linux distribution, this allows you to configure Linux components that are not found in Fedora Linux, such as the Debian Package Manager.

Because servers provide a critical role within the organization, it is important to verify that the installation process has completed successfully and that all hardware components are working properly with the OS after installation.

Dealing with Problems during Installation

Most problems that occur during a Linux installation are related to faulty hardware or an incorrect device driver for a hardware component. In both cases, the installation may end abnormally and a "fatal signal 11" error message may appear on the screen. This indicates an error, known as a segmentation fault, in which a program accesses an unassigned area of RAM. If a segmentation fault occurs when you are installing Linux, first check the PC hardware vendor's website to determine if an updated chipset or storage controller driver is available for your distribution of Linux. If one is available that is needed during the installation process, the manufacturer will often provide instructions that allow you to specify the new driver during the installation process. This often involves switching to another terminal during installation (e.g., tty5), mounting a USB flash memory drive that contains the drivers, and running a manufacturer-provided driver installation script.

You can also experience a segmentation fault during installation if your CPU is overclocked or some hardware component is faulty. Zeroing in on the right piece of hardware can be tricky, and most often it is CPU, RAM, or storage related. Some segmentation faults can be fixed by turning off the CPU cache memory, disabling power management functionality, or by increasing the number of memory wait states in the BIOS/UEFI. Segmentation faults caused by storage device failures can sometimes be solved by disabling the associated storage controller in the BIOS/UEFI and using an alternate storage device on a different controller.

> **Note 36**
>
> An **overclocked** CPU is a CPU that is faster than the speed for which the processor was designed. Although this might lead to increased performance, it also makes the processor hotter and can result in intermittent computer crashes.

> **Note 37**
>
> If the installation fails with an error other than fatal signal 11, consult the support documentation for your distribution of Linux, or check the associated Internet forums.

Dealing with Problems after Installation

Even after a successful Linux installation, problems might arise if an installation task, such as an application installation or configuration task, failed to execute during installation or a system process failed to load successfully at boot time. Additionally, hardware components may not be recognized or function properly when used by applications if the system does not have the correct Linux device drivers configured for each hardware device within the system.

Viewing Installation Logs

To see whether all installation tasks performed successfully, you should check the installation log files immediately following installation; these are created by the installation program, and record the events that occurred during installation, including errors. For Fedora Linux, these log files are stored in the /var/log/anaconda directory; and for Ubuntu Server Linux, these log files are stored in the /var/log/installer directory. To search these files for errors and warnings, you should use the grep command, as their contents are often quite lengthy. For example, the egrep -i "(error|warn)" /var/log/anaconda/* command can be used to search for any errors or warnings within the log files in the /var/log/anaconda directory.

Understanding Linux Device Drivers

For the Linux kernel to work with any hardware device, it must have the correct device driver software for the device. After the Linux kernel is loaded into memory at the beginning of the boot process, it detects the hardware devices within the system. For hardware devices that are essential at the beginning of the boot process, such as storage devices, the associated device drivers are often compiled into the Linux kernel and referenced by a device file in the /dev directory, as discussed earlier in Chapter 5. Other devices (such as video cards, motherboard chipsets, network interface cards, FC HBAs, and so on) typically have a device driver loaded into the Linux kernel as a `module`.

Modules end with the .ko (kernel object) extension and are typically stored within subdirectories under the /lib/modules/*kernelversion* or /usr/lib/modules/*kernelversion* directory. They can be manually loaded into the Linux kernel using the `insmod command` or the `modprobe command`. To see a list of modules that are currently loaded into the Linux kernel, you can use the `lsmod command`. You can also view detailed information about a particular module using the `modinfo command`, or remove a module from the Linux kernel using the `rmmod command`.

Note 38

Some Linux distributions, such as Fedora, compress kernel modules; as a result, these modules will end with a longer extension, such as .ko.xz. Compression is discussed in Chapter 11.

As the Linux kernel detects each hardware component at boot time, it loads the associated module. However, for some hardware devices, the Linux kernel cannot detect them at all; for others, it cannot detect them properly. In these cases, the system can load the module manually at boot time via entries in a configuration file. Legacy Linux distributions list modules to load manually within the /etc/modprobe.conf, /etc/modules.conf, or /etc/modules text files, depending on the distribution. Modern Linux distributions list modules to load manually at boot time within text files located under the /etc/modprobe.d or /etc/modules-load.d directories. Software packages often add files to these directories when they are installed if they require a module to be loaded into the Linux kernel manually.

Note 39

Not all modules are used to provide device drivers for hardware; many software components, such as ZFS, are implemented by modules that are loaded manually into the Linux kernel at boot time.

Hardware components are also detected as part of the Linux installation process. If the Linux installation program finds that a particular piece of hardware is not automatically detectable by the Linux kernel, it will create or modify the appropriate file to ensure that the module is loaded manually at boot time. However, if no module is available for the hardware device, or the Linux installation program cannot successfully detect the hardware, you need to identify the hardware component that requires the device driver after installation, and then search for and install the associated module. Most hardware vendors provide a Linux software package with device drivers for their products. Installing this software package adds the module to a subfolder under the /lib/modules/*kernelversion* or /usr/lib/modules/*kernelversion* directory, as well as adds a file within the /etc/modprobe.d or /etc/modules-load.d directory to ensure that the module is loaded manually at boot time.

Note 40

Vendor websites list the instructions necessary to install Linux device drivers for their hardware. Software installation will be discussed in depth within Chapter 11.

Note 41

Some modules depend on other modules. After installing a new module by adding a Linux device driver package to the system, you should run the `depmod command` to update the module dependency database.

If you are running Linux as a virtual machine, it needs the appropriate modules loaded to interact with the virtualized hardware provided by the hypervisor. Most modern Linux distributions ship with the modules needed to interact with most mainstream hypervisors used within server environments, including Hyper-V, VMWare ESXi, KVM/QEMU, and Xen. For example, if you run Linux as a virtual machine on Hyper-V, you will see several modules that start with "hv_" in the output of the lsmod command. These modules provide the necessary support for the virtualized hardware provided by Hyper-V. Similarly, lsmod will list several modules that start with "vmw" on a VMWare ESXi hypervisor, "virtio" on a KVM/QEMU hypervisor, and "xen" on a Xen hypervisor. If you do not see these modules running on your Linux distribution, you can download and install the appropriate guest driver package for your Linux distribution from the hypervisor vendor's website.

Verifying Hardware Configuration

After a Linux installation, you should ensure that all your hardware has been detected and is functioning properly; if it is not, you may need to make configuration changes to your system or install the appropriate device driver software as described in the previous section. You can use many methods to view and verify your hardware configuration, including the /proc directory, the /sys directory, hardware commands, and startup logs.

The /proc directory is mounted to a pseudo filesystem (procfs) contained within RAM that lists system information made available by the Linux kernel. The following sample listing of the /proc directory shows many file and subdirectory contents:

```
[root@server1 ~]# ls -F /proc
1/      1171/   171/    3/      415/    48/     801/        kallsyms    softirqs
10/     12/     172/    300/    417/    484/    9/          kcore       stat
1018/   1224/   173/    334/    418/    485/    acpi/       keys        swaps
1020/   1239/   174/    361/    419/    49/     buddyinfo   key-users   sys/
1024/   1257/   175/    362/    422/    5/      bus/        kmsg        sysrq
1028/   1266/   176/    364/    424/    548/    cgroups     kpagecount  sysvipc/
1038/   1282/   177/    365/    425/    550/    cmdline     kpageflags  timer
1068/   1284/   178/    367/    426/    58/     consoles    loadavg     timer_s
1074/   1288/   179/    368/    428/    59/     cpuinfo     locks       tty/
1077/   13/     18/     369/    434/    6/      crypto      mdstat      uptime
1084/   1317/   180/    371/    436/    60/     devices     meminfo     version
1090/   14/     187/    372/    437/    62/     diskstats   misc        vmallocin
11/     15/     188/    373/    449/    624/    dma         modules     vmstat
1106/   16/     19/     383/    45/     64/     driver/     mounts@     zoneinfo
1109/   163/    190/    384/    455/    7/      execdomains mtrr
1112/   165/    2/      385/    456/    72/     fb          net@
1117/   166/    20/     392/    459/    748/    filesystems pagetypeinfo
1137/   167/    203/    393/    46/     751/    fs/         partitions
1141/   168/    204/    394/    460/    752/    interrupts  sched_debug
1159/   169/    205/    399/    462/    755/    iomem       scsi/
1165/   17/     287/    410/    47/     758/    ioports     self@
1168/   170/    297/    413/    478/    8/      irq/        slabinfo
[root@server1 ~]#_
```

The subdirectories that start with a number in the preceding output are used to display process information; other directories can contain kernel parameters. The files listed in the preceding output are text representations of various parts of the Linux system; they are updated continuously by the Linux kernel and can be viewed using standard text commands, such as cat or less. For example, you could view the output of the less /proc/cpuinfo command to see the information Linux has detected regarding the CPUs in the system, or you could view the output of the less /proc/meminfo command to see the information Linux has detected regarding the RAM in the system.

If this information is incorrect because Linux failed to detect the CPU or RAM information properly, you might need to change a setting in the BIOS/UEFI, update your Linux kernel, or install the correct device driver for your motherboard chipset.

The /proc directory contains many more files that you will find useful when examining a system after installation; Table 6-1 describes the most common of these files.

Table 6-1 Files commonly found in the /proc directory

Filename	Contents
cmdline	Lists the command used to load the current Linux kernel during the most recent system startup
cpuinfo	Information regarding the processors in the computer
devices	List of the character and block devices that are currently in use by the Linux kernel
execdomains	List of execution domains for processes on the system; execution domains allow a process to execute in a specific manner
fb	List of framebuffer devices in use on the Linux system; typically, these include video adapter card devices
filesystems	List of filesystems supported by the Linux kernel
interrupts	List of IRQs in use on the system
iomem	List of memory addresses currently used
ioports	List of memory address ranges reserved for device use
kcore	A representation of the physical memory inside the computer; this file should not be viewed
kmsg	Temporary storage location for messages from the kernel
loadavg	Statistics on the performance of the processor
locks	List of files currently locked by the kernel
mdstat	Configuration of RAID volumes
meminfo	Information regarding physical and virtual memory on the Linux system
misc	List of miscellaneous devices and their minor numbers (major number = 10)
modules	List of currently loaded modules in the Linux kernel
mounts	List of currently mounted filesystems
partitions	Information regarding partition tables loaded in memory on the system
swaps	Information on virtual memory utilization
version	Version information for the Linux kernel and libraries

Like the /proc directory, the /sys directory is also mounted to a special filesystem (sysfs) contained within RAM. However, it primarily lists the detailed configuration of different types of devices on the system for use by commands and other software. The following output shows the major subdirectories under /sys, the block devices that were detected on the system, as well as the detailed configuration (including partition names) for sda:

```
[root@server1 ~]# ls -F /sys
block/   class/   devices/   fs/          kernel/   power/
bus/     dev/     firmware/  hypervisor/  module/
[root@server1 ~]# ls /sys/block
dm-0   nvme0n1   sda   sdb   sdc   sr0
```

```
[root@server1 ~]# ls /sys/block/sda
alignment_offset   events            inflight   ro     sda6     subsys
bdi                events_async      integrity  sda1   sda7     trace
capability         events_poll_msecs power      sda2   sda8     uevent
dev                ext_range         queue      sda3   size
device             hidden            range      sda4   slaves
discard_alignment  holders           removable  sda5   stat
[root@server1 ~]#_
```

While the /proc and /sys directories contain the most detailed hardware information, their contents are often difficult to interpret. However, you can use many Linux commands to display key hardware information as shown in Table 6-2.

Table 6-2   Linux Commands that Display Hardware Information

Command	Description
lscpu	Displays system CPU information
lsmem	Displays system RAM information
lsdev	Displays interrupts, IO ports, and DMA channels used by hardware devices on the system
lspci	Displays information about connected PCI controllers and devices on the system
lsusb	Displays information about connected USB controllers and devices on the system
lsscsi	Displays information about connected parallel SCSI, SAS, iSCSI, and Fibre Channel controllers and devices on the system
lsblk	Displays information about connected block storage devices on the system
lshw	Displays general hardware information for the entire system as detected by the Linux kernel
dmidecode	Displays hardware information detected by the BIOS/UEFI
hwinfo	Probes hardware devices on the system and displays the related information
dmesg	Displays the kernel ring buffer (an area of RAM that stores kernel messages since system startup)

The lshw command shown in Table 6-2 is the most versatile; it can display hardware information regarding the motherboard, firmware, RAM, CPU, storage, network, video, PCI, and USB hardware devices within your system in an easy-to-read format. When run without options, it displays all information, but you can specify a class (type) of hardware; for example, the lshw -class video command would only list installed video display adapter hardware, and the lshw -class network command would only list installed network hardware. If the output from these commands does not list the correct video display adapter or network hardware in your system, you will need to install the appropriate device driver software.

If the lshw command does not display any information regarding a particular hardware device in your system, you instead can use the hwinfo command to probe for the hardware. While the hwinfo probes for and displays a detailed list of all hardware devices by default, you can instead summarize the results for a specific area. For example, hwinfo --short --storage will probe for and display a summary of all storage-related hardware detected on the system.

The dmidecode command can be also used to determine whether the Linux kernel detected the same hardware configuration as the BIOS/UEFI. For example, if the output of dmidecode -t processor and dmidecode -t memory does not display the same CPU and RAM configuration shown by lshw -class cpu and lshw -class memory, you may need to change a setting in the BIOS/UEFI, update the Linux kernel to a newer version, or install the correct device driver for your motherboard chipset. You can use `dmidecode -t baseboard` command to list the model and revision of your motherboard for use when searching for a chipset driver.

You can also view the hardware detected by the Linux kernel during boot time using the `dmesg command` after system startup, as shown in the following output:

```
[root@server1 ~]# dmesg | less
[0.000000] Linux version 5.15.0-47-generic (buildd@lcy02-amd64-060)
(gcc (Ubuntu 11.2.0-19ubuntu1) 11.2.0, GNU ld (GNU Binutils for Ubuntu)
2.38) #51-Ubuntu SMP Thu Aug 11 07:51:15 UTC 2022 (Ubuntu 5.15.0-47.51-
generic 5.15.46)
[0.000000] Command line: BOOT_IMAGE=/vmlinuz-5.15.0-47-generic
root=/dev/mapper/ubuntu--vg-ubuntu--lv ro
[0.000000] KERNEL supported cpus:
[0.000000]    Intel GenuineIntel
[0.000000]    AMD AuthenticAMD
[0.000000]    Hygon HygonGenuine
[0.000000]    Centaur CentaurHauls
[0.000000]    zhaoxin    Shanghai
[0.000000] x86/fpu: Supporting XSAVE feature 0x001: 'x87 floating point registers'
[0.000000] x86/fpu: Supporting XSAVE feature 0x002: 'SSE registers'
[0.000000] x86/fpu: Supporting XSAVE feature 0x004: 'AVX registers'
[0.000000] x86/fpu: xstate_offset[2]:  576, xstate_sizes[2]:  256
[0.000000] x86/fpu: Enabled xstate features 0x7, context size is 832 bytes, using
'compacted' format.
[0.000000] signal: max sigframe size: 1776
[0.000000] BIOS-provided physical RAM map:
[0.000000] BIOS-e820: [mem 0x0000000000000-0x000000000009ffff] usable
[0.000000] BIOS-e820: [mem 0x00000000c0000-0x00000000000fffff] reserved
[0.000000] BIOS-e820: [mem 0x0000000100000-0x000000007ff40fff] usable
:
```

> ### Note 42
>
> Modern Linux systems that include Systemd use a database system called **journald** to store system events; to view these events, you can use the `journalctl command`. On these systems, the `journalctl -k` command will display the same information shown by the dmesg command, but in a searchable format that is easy to read. Systemd is discussed in Chapter 8.

If `dmesg` reports that the hardware device was detected at boot time, but other hardware commands do not list the hardware device, then the device driver for that hardware was not available on the system and must be installed. Alternatively, `dmesg` may report that a particular hardware device is unavailable for other reasons. For example, if `dmesg` reports that a Wi-Fi network interface was detected but not loaded due to a chipset restriction, the Wi-Fi functionality may have been disabled by a keyboard combination, which is common on laptop computers.

Verifying System Processes

After installing a Linux system, several system processes will be loaded during each boot process. If a software component is missing or misconfigured, one or more of these system processes may fail during the boot process. You can view the system processes that started successfully or unsuccessfully during boot time by viewing the contents of the /var/log/boot.log, /var/log/bootstrap.log, /var/

log/messages, or /var/log/syslog file on most Linux distributions. A sample boot.log file from a Fedora system that indicates the CUPS daemon failed to load is shown in the following output:

```
[root@server1 ~]# tail /var/log/boot.log
[  OK  ] Starting systemd-user-sess…vice - Permit User Sessions...
[  OK  ] Starting virtqemud.service…0m - Virtualization qemu daemon...
[  OK  ] Started rpc-statd-notify.s…m - Notify NFS peers of a restart.
[  OK  ] Finished systemd-user-sess…ervice - Permit User Sessions.
[  OK  ] Started atd.service - Deferred execution scheduler.
[  OK  ] Started crond.service - Command Scheduler.
[FAILED] Failed to start cups.service - CUPS Scheduler.
[  OK  ] Starting plymouth-quit-wai… until boot process finishes up...
[  OK  ] Started gdm.service - GNOME Display Manager.
[  OK  ] Started virtqemud.service - Virtualization qemu daemon.
[root@server1 ~]#_
```

On modern Linux systems that include Systemd, you can instead use the journalctl -b command to display the system process that started or failed to start at boot time. Because the journalctl command will display entries for multiple system boots, it is important to narrow down the time frame. The following command only displays boot information from the current day:

```
[root@server1 ~]# journalctl -b --since=today | less
Aug 01 20:44:12 server1 systemd[1]: Starting Virtual Machine and
Container Registration Service...
Aug 01 20:44:12 server1 systemd[1]: Starting Avahi mDNS/DNS-SD Stack...
Aug 01 20:44:12 server1 systemd[1]: Starting Login Service...
Aug 01 20:44:12 server1 systemd[1]: Starting Disk Manager...
Aug 01 20:44:12 server1 systemd[1]: Started D-Bus System Message Bus.
Aug 01 20:44:12 server1 systemd[1]: Starting firewalld...
Aug 01 20:44:12 server1 systemd[1]: Starting GSSAPI Proxy Daemon...
Aug 01 20:44:12 server1 systemd-logind[647]: New seat seat0.
Aug 01 20:44:12 server1 systemd[1]: Started Switcheroo Control Proxy.
:
```

If a system process fails to load, it may be because it has misconfigured settings that are specific to the service, or that it was not installed properly during the Linux installation; in the latter case, you can often remove and reinstall the process to remedy the problem.

System Rescue

Recall from Chapter 2 that you can start a Linux installation by booting from DVD or USB live media, or a live media ISO image. Booting a system from live media offers several benefits to Linux administrators when repairing a damaged Linux system. The live media contains a small bootable Linux kernel and virtual filesystem that are loaded into RAM and have access to the filesystems on the underlying hard disk drive. As a result, you can use the utilities on the Linux system booted from live media to fix problems that prevent a Linux installation on the hard disk drive from booting, such as:

- Boot loader problems
- Filesystem/partition problems
- Configuration file problems
- Driver problems

All live media contain several utilities for fixing system problems, including fdisk, parted, e2mkfs, fsck, and several more that will be introduced in later modules. Recall from the previous module that the `fsck` command can only be run on an unmounted filesystem. If the root filesystem becomes corrupted, you can boot your system using live media for your Linux distribution and use the `fsck` command to check the root filesystem on the hard disk drive as it is not mounted by the live media Linux system by default.

> **Note 43**
>
> The process of using the Linux system on live media to repair problems on another Linux system installed on the hard disk drive is commonly called **system rescue**.

You can also configure the live media Linux system to use the root filesystem on the hard disk drive. To do this, mount the root filesystem on your local hard disk drive under an empty directory on the live media Linux system (e.g., /mnt) and then type `chroot  /mnt` at the command prompt. The `chroot command` will then change the root of the live media Linux system to the /mnt directory, which is actually the root filesystem on the local hard disk drive. From this point, you will have root user access to any commands on your root filesystem as you normally would if you had booted your Linux system on the hard disk drive. For example, if you run the `passwd` command (used for changing user passwords), you'll actually be changing the password for the root user on the Linux system installed on the hard disk drive. This is often used to recover a locally accessible Linux system if the root password has been lost or forgotten.

This feature is not limited to live media. If you install Linux from standard installation media, the welcome screen often provides a system rescue option for booting a small live Linux system that does not contain a desktop environment. This small live Linux system contains the same recovery utilities (fdisk, parted, e2mkfs, fsck, etc.) and will allow you to mount the root filesystem on your hard disk drive as well as run the `chroot` command to switch your live Linux system to it.

Summary

- Linux servers typically use far more hardware than desktop systems. This hardware is installed in a rack using a rackmount form factor.

- SCSI storage (specifically SAS) is common on Linux servers, as are connections to SAN storage devices using the iSCSI or Fibre Channel protocols. DM-MPIO can be optionally used to provide multiple redundant connections to one or more SANs.

- RAID is often used within Linux servers to combine several hard disk drives into a single volume for speed or fault tolerance. It can be implemented by software that runs within the OS, hardware on a hard disk drive controller card, or by the system firmware.

- ZFS is a high-performance, fault tolerant filesystem that is commonly installed on Linux servers. ZFS provides much of the same functionality as RAID, using storage space that spans a wide range of storage devices, including local disks, SANs, shared devices, large raw files, and remote shares.

- Although it is still being developed, BTRFS is designed to be a replacement for the ext4

- filesystem that offers some of the volume and RAID features of ZFS.

- Linux server distributions do not contain a desktop environment and are often administered remotely. They have an installation process that prompts for additional information compared to other Linux distributions.

- Unsupported or defective hardware is the most common cause of a failed Linux installation. Improper or missing device drivers are the most common cause of issues immediately following a Linux installation.

- Following a Linux installation, you should check installation logs, examine the files within the /proc and /sys directories, view the output of hardware-related commands, as well as view system logs created during boot time.

- You can use the bootable Linux found on standard and live Linux installation media to access and repair a damaged Linux installation.

Key Terms

1U server	iSCSI target	rmmod command
blade server	iscsiadm command	SCSI ID
Boxes	journalctl command	segmentation fault
B-tree File System (BTRFS)	journald	Simple Protocol for Independent
btrfs command	Just a Bunch of Disks (JBOD)	Computing Environments
BTRFS subvolume	Kernel-based Virtual Machine	(SPICE)
btrfsck command	(KVM)	snapshot
checkpoint	Linux server distribution	software RAID
chroot command	Logical Unit Number (LUN)	spanning
data	lshw command	storage area network (SAN)
depmod command	lsmod command	system
Device Mapper MPIO (DM-MPIO)	lspci command	system rescue
disk mirroring	mdadm command	target ID
disk striping	metadata	terminator
disk striping with parity	mkfs.btrfs command	thick provisioning
dmesg command	modinfo command	thin provisioning
dmidecode command	modprobe command	Type 1 hypervisor
fault tolerant	module	Type 2 hypervisor
Fibre Channel (FC)	mpathconf command	uninterruptible power supply (UPS)
firmware RAID	multipath command	virsh command
guest operating system	multipath daemon (multipathd)	Virtual Machine Manager
hardware RAID	Multipath Input Output (MPIO)	virtualization
Host Bus Adapter (HBA)	overclocked	World Wide Name (WWN)
host operating system	parallel SCSI	Zettabyte File System (ZFS)
hwinfo command	Quick Emulator (QEMU)	zfs command
insmod command	rackmount server	ZFS dataset
installation log files	RAID-Z	ZFS pool
Internet SCSI (iSCSI)	Redundant Array of Independent	ZFS volume
iSCSI initiator	Disks (RAID)	zpool command

Review Questions

1. BTRFS filesystems do not need to be checked for errors as they are resilient to data corruption.

   a. True

   b. False

2. Which of the following describes a computer that is used to access iSCSI storage across the network?

   a. iSCSI target

   b. iSCSI requestor

   c. iSCSI initiator

   d. iSCSI terminator

3. You want to view log files to get information about a problem that occurred during a Linux installation. In which directory will you likely find the log files?

   a. /root/log

   b. /sys/log

   c. /var/log

   d. /etc/log

4. Which of the following RAID levels is not fault tolerant?

   a. RAID 0

   b. RAID 1

   c. RAID 4

   d. RAID 5

5. Which command can you use during a system rescue to switch from the root of the live Linux system to the root of the Linux system installed on the hard disk drive?

   a. mount

   b. sysimage

   c. chroot

   d. rescue

6. Which of the following is not a type of RAID?

   a. hardware RAID

   b. software RAID

   c. firmware RAID

   d. serial RAID

7. Where is the /proc filesystem stored?

    a. in RAM
    b. on the hard disk drive in the / directory
    c. on the hard disk drive in the /etc directory
    d. on the hard disk drive in the /var directory

8. When configuring a virtual hard disk file, which term refers to the feature that allows the virtual hard disk file to expand dynamically as space is requested by the guest operating system?

    a. thick provisioning
    b. Type 1
    c. thin provisioning
    d. Type 2

9. DM-MPIO can be configured to provide multiple, redundant connections to data stored on a SAN.

    a. True
    b. False

10. What component of a Linux server is used to connect to a Fibre Channel SAN?

    a. FC initiator
    b. FC target
    c. FC HBA
    d. WWPN

11. Which type of RAID can be entirely configured during the Linux installation process?

    a. hardware RAID
    b. software RAID
    c. firmware RAID
    d. serial RAID

12. What command can be used to create a ZFS volume called test from the space on /dev/sdb and /dev/sdc that functions like RAID level 1?

    a. `zpool create test /dev/sdb /dev/sdc`
    b. `zpool create test mirror /dev/sdb /dev/sdc`
    c. `zpool create test raidz /dev/sdb /dev/sdc`
    d. `zpool create test raidz2 /dev/sdb /dev/sdc`

13. To which directory will the test ZFS volume from the previous question be mounted by the ZFS system?

    a. /mnt/test
    b. /media/test
    c. /zfs/test
    d. /test

14. Linux servers are typically installed in a rack using rackmount server hardware. Which of the following describes the minimum height of a rackmount server?

    a. 1U
    b. Series A
    c. Type A
    d. Level 5

15. Which of the following commands can quickly determine whether your network hardware was detected properly following a Linux installation?

    a. `cat /proc/modules/network`
    b. `lspci`
    c. `lshw -class network`
    d. `dmesg`

16. ZFS volumes are mounted at boot time from entries within /etc/fstab by default.

    a. True
    b. False

17. Which of the following could result in a segmentation fault (fatal signal 11) during a Fedora installation?

    a. RAM problems
    b. overclocked CPU
    c. faulty hardware components
    d. all of these

18. When viewing the output of the `lsmod` command, you notice several modules that start with vmw. What does this indicate?

    a. Linux is running as a guest operating system.
    b. Device drivers need to be installed on your system.
    c. There is no virtual memory in your system.
    d. The system is running the KVM/QEMU hypervisor.

19. What type of redundant storage configuration is most common for hosting the operating system and applications on a server?

    a. RAID 5
    b. ZFS
    c. RAID 1
    d. SAN + DM-MPIO

20. Which of the following commands can be used on a modern Linux system to view hardware information that was captured at the beginning of the boot process?

    a. `less /var/log/boot.log`
    b. `less /var/log/messages`
    c. `less /var/log/syslog`
    d. `journalctl -k`

Hands-On Projects

These projects should be completed in the order given. The hands-on projects presented in this chapter should take a total of three hours to complete. The requirements for this lab include:

- A computer with Fedora Linux installed according to Hands-On Project 2-1
- The latest live media ISO image of Ubuntu Server Linux for your computer platform (Intel or ARM)

Project 6-1

Estimated Time: 40 minutes
Objective: Install Ubuntu Server.
Description: In this hands-on project, you install Ubuntu Server Linux within a virtual machine on a Windows or macOS computer and examine the LVM partition configuration afterwards.

1. In your virtualization software, create a new virtual machine called **Ubuntu Linux** that has the following characteristics:

   a. 2 GB of memory (not dynamically allocated)

   b. An Internet connection via your PC's network card (preferably using an external virtual switch or bridged mode)

   c. A 50 GB SATA/SAS/SCSI virtual hard disk drive (dynamically allocated)

   d. The virtual machine DVD drive attached to the live media ISO image of Ubuntu Server Linux

> **Note 44**
>
> If your hypervisor supports secure boot (e.g., Hyper-V), deselect this feature within the settings of your virtual machine prior to Step 2.

2. Start and then connect to your Ubuntu Linux virtual machine using your virtualization software.

3. At the GNU GRUB screen, ensure that **Try or Install Ubuntu Server** is selected and press **Enter**.

> **Note 45**
>
> The Ubuntu Server Linux installation program does not use a graphical desktop. As a result, you must switch between buttons shown on the screen using the Tab key and then press Enter to make your selections.

4. At the Welcome screen, ensure that **English** is selected and press **Enter**.

5. At the Keyboard configuration screen, select the correct keyboard layout and select **Done**. For most keyboards this layout will be English (US).

6. At the Choose the type of install screen, ensure that **Ubuntu Server** is checked and select **Done**.

7. At the Network connections screen, note that your network interface is set to obtain an IP address from a DHCP server by default and select **Done**.

8. At the Configure proxy screen, optionally supply the URL address of your classroom proxy (if your classroom uses one) and select **Done**.

9. At the Configure Ubuntu archive mirror screen, select **Done**.

10. At the Guided storage configuration screen, ensure that **Use an entire disk** and **Set up this disk as an LVM group** are checked and select **Done**.

11. At the Storage configuration screen, view the partition and LVM configuration. Note that the root file system (ubuntu-lv) does not utilize all the remaining space available. Select **ubuntu-lv**, choose **Edit**,

enter the maximum size into the Size dialog box and select **Save**. Review your configuration, select **Done**, and then select **Continue**.

12. At the Profile setup screen, supply the following information and select **Done** when finished:

    a. Your name = supply your real name

    b. Your server's name = **ubuntu**

    c. Username = **user1**

    d. Password = **LINUXrocks!**

13. At the SSH setup screen, check **Install OpenSSH server** and select **Done**.

14. At the Featured Server Snaps screen, select **Done**.

15. At the Install complete screen, select **Reboot Now**. When prompted to remove your installation medium, use your virtualization software to disconnect your live media ISO image of Ubuntu Server from the virtual DVD drive and press **Enter**.

16. After the system has booted, note that a graphical login is not available. Log into tty1 as **user1** with the password **LINUXrocks!**.

17. At the command prompt, type `sudo passwd root` and press **Enter** to set the root user password. When prompted, enter your password (**LINUXrocks!**), and then enter the desired root password of **LINUXrocks!** twice to set the root user password to LINUXrocks!.

18. At the command prompt, type `su -` and press **Enter** to switch to the root user. Supply the root user password (**LINUXrocks!**) when prompted.

19. At the command prompt, type the following commands in turn and press **Enter**. Examine and interpret the output of each one:

    a. `df -hT`

    b. `fdisk -l`

    c. `lvdisplay`

    d. `lsblk`

    e. `blkid`

    f. `ls -l /dev/disk/by-uuid`

    g. `ls -l /dev/disk/by-partuuid`

    h. `ls -l /dev/disk/by-id`

    i. `ls -l /dev/disk/by-path`

    j. `cat /etc/fstab` (note that Ubuntu Server creates a /swap.img file for use as virtual memory instead of using zswap)

20. Type `exit` and press **Enter** to log out of your shell.

Project 6-2

Estimated Time: 30 minutes
Objective: Configure software RAID.
Description: In this hands-on project, you add virtual hard disk files to your Ubuntu Linux virtual machine, configure a software RAID 5 volume, and simulate a hard disk drive failure and recovery. At the end of this project, you will remove your RAID configuration.

1. On your Ubuntu Linux virtual machine, log into the command-line terminal (tty1) using the user name of **root** and the password of **LINUXrocks!**.

2. At the command prompt, type `poweroff` and press **Enter** to power down your virtual machine. In your virtualization software, add four new 1 GB dynamically allocated SATA/SAS virtual hard disk files to your virtual machine configuration. When finished, boot your Ubuntu Linux virtual machine.

3. After your Ubuntu Linux virtual machine has booted, log into the command-line terminal (tty1) using the user name of **root** and the password of **LINUXrocks!**.

4. At the command prompt, type `lsblk` and press **Enter**. Note that the names of the additional disk devices are sdb, sdc, sdd, and sde.

5. At the command prompt, type `mdadm --create /dev/md0 --level=5 --raid-devices=4 /dev/sdb /dev/sdc /dev/sdd /dev/sde --verbose` and press **Enter**.

6. At the command prompt, type `cat /proc/mdstat` and press **Enter**. Was your RAID 5 volume created successfully?

7. At the command prompt, type `cat /etc/mdadm/mdadm.conf` and press **Enter**. Is your RAID 5 volume listed within this configuration file by default?

8. At the command prompt, type `mdadm --detail --scan --verbose >/etc/mdadm/mdadm.conf` and press **Enter**. Next, type `cat /etc/mdadm/mdadm.conf` and press **Enter** and view your startup configuration.

9. At the command prompt, type `mkfs -t ext4 /dev/md0` and press **Enter** to format your RAID 5 volume with the ext4 filesystem.

10. At the command prompt, type `mkdir /data` and press **Enter** to create a mount point for your RAID 5 volume, and then type `mount /dev/md0 /data` and press **Enter** to mount your RAID 5 volume to it.

11. At the command prompt, type `cp /etc/hosts /data` and press **Enter**. Next, type `ls -F /data` and press **Enter** to verify that the hosts file was copied to your filesystem. What other directory was created on this filesystem and why?

12. At the command prompt, type `df -hT` and press **Enter**. What is the total size of your RAID 5 volume? Why is it not 4 GB (4 x 1 GB disks)?

13. At the command prompt, type `lsblk` and press **Enter**. Note the md0 device associations for each of your disks. Next, type `blkid` and press **Enter**. Does /dev/md0 have a filesystem UUID that can be used within /etc/fstab to automount the RAID volume at boot time?

14. At the command prompt, type `mdadm --detail /dev/md0` and press **Enter**. Are all of your four devices within the RAID volume active and working?

15. At the command prompt, type `mdadm --manage --set-faulty /dev/md0 /dev/sdc` and press **Enter** to simulate disk corruption on /dev/sdc. Next, type `mdadm --detail /dev/md0` and press **Enter** to view the failed device. Also note that the state of the RAID volume is listed as *clean* (working) and *degraded* (not fully functional).

16. Type `ls -F /data` and press **Enter**. Are your files still available and accessible? Why?

17. At the command prompt, type `mdadm --manage /dev/md0 --remove /dev/sdc` and press **Enter** to remove the /dev/sdc device from the RAID volume. In a production environment, this is when you would physically remove the hard disk drive from the server and replace it with a working one.

18. At the command prompt, type `mdadm --manage /dev/md0 --add /dev/sdc` and press **Enter** to add the /dev/sdc device to the RAID volume again. Next, type `mdadm --detail /dev/md0` and press **Enter**. Note that the state of the drive is listed as *spare rebuilding* as the RAID volume is rebuilding the data on this drive. After a few minutes, rerun your previous command. The state should list *active sync*, which indicates that the newly added device is now fully functional and part of your RAID volume.

19. At the command prompt, type `umount /data` and press **Enter** to unmount your RAID volume. Next, type `mdadm --stop /dev/md0` and press **Enter** to remove your RAID volume.

20. At the command prompt, type `fdisk /dev/sdb` and press **Enter**. Next, type w and press **Enter** to save your changes, which will remove the existing RAID signature from the /dev/sdb device file. Repeat this step three more times for /dev/sdc, /dev/sdd, and /dev/sde.

21. Finally, type `rm -f /etc/mdadm/mdadm.conf` to remove the RAID configuration file.

22. Type `exit` and press **Enter** to log out of your shell.

Project 6-3

Estimated Time: 30 minutes
Objective: Configure ZFS.
Description: In this hands-on project, you install and configure the ZFS filesystem on your Ubuntu Linux virtual machine. At the end of this project, you will remove your ZFS configuration.

1. On your Ubuntu Linux virtual machine, log into the command-line terminal (tty1) using the user name of **root** and the password of **LINUXrocks!**.

2. At the command prompt, type `apt install zfsutils-linux` and press **Enter** to install ZFS support on your Ubuntu system.

> ## Note 46
>
> Ubuntu Server Linux uses a different package manager than Fedora Linux. The `apt` command is functionally equivalent to the `dnf` command that you used in previous chapters to download and install software from Internet repositories. Both `apt` and `dnf` are discussed in Chapter 11.

3. At the command prompt, type `zpool create data /dev/sdb -f` and press **Enter** to create a simple ZFS volume called data from the space on /dev/sdb (the `-f` option is necessary because /dev/sdb still has a RAID signature from Project 6-2). Next, type `zpool list` at the command prompt and press **Enter** to view your configuration.

4. At the command prompt, type `df -hT` and press **Enter**. Note that the data ZFS volume was mounted to /data automatically. Next, type `lsblk` at the command prompt and press **Enter**. Note that ZFS created a single partition for the data (/dev/sdb1) as well as a partition for the ZFS configuration (/dev/sdb9).

5. At the command prompt, type `cp /etc/hosts /data` and press **Enter** to copy the /etc/hosts file to the new ZFS filesystem. Next, type `ls -F /data` to verify that the hosts file was copied successfully.

6. At the command prompt, type `zpool destroy data` and press **Enter** to remove the data volume.

7. At the command prompt, type `zpool create data mirror /dev/sdb /dev/sdc -f` and press **Enter** to create a mirrored ZFS volume called data from the space on /dev/sdb and /dev/sdc that is mounted to the /data directory. Next, type `zpool list` at the command prompt and press **Enter** to view your configuration. Following this, type `zpool status data` at the command prompt and press **Enter**. Does your mirror have any problems listed?

8. At the command prompt, type `lsblk` and press **Enter**. Note that ZFS created partitions for the data on each hard disk drive (/dev/sdb1 and /dev/sdc1) as well as partitions for the ZFS configuration (/dev/sdb9 and /dev/sdc9).

9. At the command prompt, type `dd if=/dev/zero of=/dev/sdb1 count=1000000` and press **Enter** to overwrite a portion of /dev/sdb1 using the `dd` command, simulating disk corruption. Next, type `zpool scrub data` at the command prompt and press **Enter** to update the status of the ZFS filesystem, and then type `zpool status data` at the command prompt and press **Enter**. Does your mirror have any problems listed?

10. At the command prompt, type `zpool detach data /dev/sdb` and press **Enter** to remove the bad disk (/dev/sdb) from the mirror. Type `zpool status data` at the command prompt and press **Enter** to verify that it is no longer listed.

11. At the command prompt, type `zpool attach data /dev/sdc /dev/sdd -f` and press **Enter** to mirror the data on /dev/sdc to a new disk (/dev/sdd), and then type `zpool status data` at the command prompt and press **Enter**. Is the mirror fully functional using /dev/sdc and /dev/sdd?

12. At the command prompt, type `zpool iostat -v data` and press **Enter** to view the input and output statistics for your mirror. Next, type `zpool destroy data` and press **Enter** to remove the data mirror.

13. At the command prompt, type `zpool create data raidz /dev/sdb /dev/sdc /dev/sdd /dev/sde -f` and press **Enter** to create a RAID-Z volume called data using /dev/sdb, /dev/sdc, /dev/sdd, and /dev/sde, and then type `zpool status data` at the command prompt and press **Enter** to verify the results. Next, type `zpool iostat -v data` and press **Enter** to view the input and output statistics for your RAID-Z volume.

14. At the command prompt, type each of the following commands in turn and press **Enter** to create three subdirectories under /data:

    ```
    mkdir /data/webstorage
    mkdir /data/databases
    mkdir /data/filestorage
    ```

15. At the command prompt, type `zfs list` and press **Enter**. Are the webstorage, databases, and filestorage directories listed? Why? Next, type each of the following commands in turn and press **Enter** to create three datasets for each of these directories:

    ```
    zfs create data/webstorage
    zfs create data/databases
    zfs create data/filestorage
    ```

16. At the command prompt, type `zfs list` and press **Enter**. Are the webstorage, databases, and filestorage directories listed? Why?

17. At the command prompt, type `zfs get all data/webstorage | less` and press **Enter** to view the available options for the webstorage dataset page by page. Next, type `zfs set quota=1G data/webstorage` at the command prompt and press **Enter** to set a quota of 1 GB for the dataset. Next, type `zfs set compression=lz4 data/webstorage` at the command prompt and press **Enter** to enable automatic lz4 compression for files stored within the dataset. Finally, type `zfs get all data/webstorage | less` and press **Enter** to verify that your settings were changed.

18. At the command prompt, type `zpool destroy data` and press **Enter** to remove the data volume.

19. At the command prompt, type `fdisk /dev/sdb` and press **Enter**. Next, type d and press **Enter** and **Enter** again to delete the ZFS configuration partition. Next, type d and press **Enter** to delete the ZFS data partition. Finally, type w and press **Enter** to save your changes. Repeat this step three more times for /dev/sdc, /dev/sdd, and /dev/sde.

20. Type `exit` and press **Enter** to log out of your shell.

Project 6-4

Estimated Time: 30 minutes
Objective: Configure BTRFS.
Description: In this hands-on project, you configure the BTRFS filesystem on your Ubuntu Linux virtual machine. At the end of this project, you will remove your BTRFS configuration.

1. On your Ubuntu Linux virtual machine, log into the command-line terminal (tty1) using the user name of **root** and the password of **LINUXrocks!**.

2. At the command prompt, type `mkfs.btrfs -m raid0 -d raid0 /dev/sdb /dev/sdc /dev/sdd -f` and press **Enter** to create a RAID 0 BTRFS volume that spans the three disks (the -f option is necessary because /dev/sdb, /dev/sdc, and /dev/sdd still have a ZFS signature from Project 6-3). Note from the output that the system configuration, data, and filesystem metadata are not fault tolerant (RAID 0). Next, type `btrfs filesystem show /dev/sdb` and press **Enter**. Note the output.

3. At the command prompt, type `mkdir /data` and press **Enter** to create the /data directory again (it was removed by ZFS when no longer used). Next, type `mount /dev/sdb /data` and press **Enter** to mount your new BTRFS volume to the /data directory.

4. At the command prompt, type `df -hT` and press **Enter**. Note that the entire volume size is 3 GB. Next, type `lsblk` and press **Enter**. Note that, while the BTRFS filesystem spans the three 1 GB sdb, sdc, and sdd devices, only sdb is shown to be mounted to the /data directory. Finally, type `btrfs filesystem df /data` and press **Enter**. Note the output.

5. At the command prompt, type `btrfs device add -f /dev/sde /data` and press **Enter** to add /dev/sde to your BTRFS volume. Next, type `btrfs filesystem balance /data` and press **Enter** to extend the existing data, system, and metadata structures to the new device.

6. At the command prompt, type `df -hT` and press **Enter**. Note that the entire volume size is 4 GB. Next, type `btrfs filesystem df /data` and press **Enter**. Note the output.

7. At the command prompt, type `btrfs subvolume list /data` and press **Enter**. Are any subvolumes listed? Next, type `btrfs subvolume create /data/archive` and press **Enter** to create a subvolume and subdirectory under /data called archive. Finally, type `btrfs subvolume list /data` and press **Enter** to view your new subvolume.

8. At the command prompt, type `cp /etc/hosts /data/archive` and press **Enter** to create a copy of the hosts file within the archive subvolume.

9. At the command prompt, type `mkdir /archive` and press **Enter**. Next, type `mount -o subvol=archive,compress=lzo /dev/sdb /archive` and press **Enter** to mount your archive subvolume to the /archive directory with automatic compression enabled.

10. At the command prompt, type `df -hT` and press **Enter**. Next, type `ls -F /archive` and press **Enter**. Is your hosts file listed?

11. Next, type `umount /archive ; umount /data` and press **Enter** to unmount your BTRFS subvolume and volume.

12. At the command prompt, type `mkfs.btrfs -m raid1 -d raid1 /dev/sdb /dev/sdc /dev/sdd /dev/sde -f` and press **Enter** to create a RAID 1 BTRFS volume that spans the four disks. Note from the output that the system configuration, data, and filesystem metadata are fault tolerant (RAID 1). Next, type `btrfs filesystem show /dev/sdb` and press **Enter**. Note the output.

13. At the command prompt, type `mount /dev/sdb /data` and press **Enter** to mount your new BTRFS volume to the /data directory.

14. At the command prompt, type the following commands in turn and press **Enter**. Compare the output to the output you saw earlier in Step 4:

    a. `df -hT`

    b. `lsblk`

    c. `btrfs filesystem df /data`

15. Next, type `umount /data` and press **Enter** to unmount your BTRFS volume.

16. At the command prompt, type `mkfs.btrfs -m raid5 -d raid5 /dev/sdb /dev/sdc /dev/sdd /dev/sde -f` and press **Enter** to create a RAID 5 BTRFS volume that spans the four disks. Note from the output that the system configuration, data, and filesystem metadata are fault tolerant (RAID 5). Next, type `btrfs filesystem show /dev/sdb` and press **Enter**. Note the output.

17. At the command prompt, type `mount /dev/sdb /data` and press **Enter** to mount your new BTRFS volume to the /data directory.

18. At the command prompt, type the following commands in turn and press **Enter**. Compare the output to the output you saw earlier in Step 4:

    a. `df -hT`

    b. `lsblk`

    c. `btrfs filesystem df /data`

19. Next, type `umount /data` and press **Enter** to unmount your BTRFS volume.

20. At the command prompt, type `btrfs check /dev/sdb` and press **Enter** to check your BTRFS file-system for errors. What other command can be used to perform the same check?

21. Type `exit` and press **Enter** to log out of your shell.

Project 6-5

Estimated Time: 30 minutes

Objective: View system and hardware configuration.

Description: In this hands-on project, you examine installation log files and system information on your Ubuntu Linux virtual machine.

1. On your Ubuntu Linux virtual machine, log into the command-line terminal (tty1) using the user name of **root** and the password of **LINUXrocks!**.

2. At the command prompt, type `ls /var/log/installer` and press **Enter**. Note the different log files in this directory. Next, type `less /var/log/installer/installer-journal.txt` and press **Enter**. Briefly examine the entries within this file to see each action taken during the installation process, and then type q to quit the less utility. Finally, type `egrep -i "(error|warn)" /var/log/installer/installer-journal.txt` and press **Enter**. View any warnings or errors that the installation program generated during your installation.

3. At the command prompt, type `ls -F /proc` and press **Enter** to view the file and directory contents of the proc filesystem.

4. At the command prompt, type `less /proc/cpuinfo` and press **Enter**. Did the installation detect your CPU correctly? Type q to quit the less utility. Use the less command to examine some of the other files within the /proc directory listed in Table 6-1.

5. At the command prompt, type `lshw | less` and press **Enter**. Examine the entries for your system hardware and type q to quit the less utility when finished. Next, type `apt install procinfo lsscsi hwinfo` to install the hardware commands listed in Table 6-2 that are not already present on the system. Following this, explore the commands listed in Table 6-2, viewing the manual pages as necessary.

6. At the command prompt, type `lsmod | less` and press **Enter**. Spend a few moments to examine the modules that are loaded into your kernel in depth, Googling their names if necessary. Can you match them to the hardware devices you saw in the previous step? Do you see modules that are used to interact with virtualized hardware? Do you see modules that are used to provide software feature or filesystem support? Type q to quit the less utility when finished.

7. At the command prompt, type `modinfo dummy` and press **Enter** to view the information about the dummy module.

8. At the command prompt, type `modprobe dummy` and press **Enter** to insert the dummy module into your Linux kernel. Next, type `lsmod | less` and press **Enter**. Is the dummy module listed? Type q to quit the less utility, and then type `rmmod dummy` and press **Enter** to remove the dummy module from the Linux kernel.

9. At the command prompt, type `ls /etc/modprobe.d` and press **Enter**. Next, type `ls /etc/modules-load.d` and press **Enter**. Observe the entries. What are the files within these directories used for?

10. At the command prompt, type `vi /etc/modules-load.d/modules.conf` and press **Enter**. Add the line `dummy` to the end of this file, save your changes, and quit the vi editor. Next, type `reboot` and press **Enter** to reboot your virtual machine.

11. After Ubuntu Linux has booted, log into the command-line terminal (tty1) using the user name of **root** and the password of **LINUXrocks!**. At the command prompt, type `lsmod | less` and press **Enter**. Is the dummy module listed? Type q to quit the less utility.

12. At the command prompt, type `dmesg | less` and press **Enter**. Observe the entries. How do they correspond with the hardware information that you saw within this project? Type `q` to quit the less utility.

13. At the command prompt, type `journalctl -k | less` and press **Enter**. How does the information compare to the previous step? Type `q` to quit the less utility.

14. At the command prompt, type `less /var/log/syslog` and press **Enter**. What does each entry represent? Type `q` to quit the less utility.

15. At the command prompt, type `journalctl -b | less` and press **Enter**. How does the information compare to the previous step? Type `q` to quit the less utility.

16. Type `poweroff` and press **Enter** to power off your Ubuntu Linux virtual machine.

Project 6-6

Estimated Time: 20 minutes
Objective: Perform system rescue.
Description: In this hands-on project, you use system rescue on your Fedora Linux virtual machine using your live installation media to check your root filesystem for errors and change the root user's password.

1. In your virtualization software, ensure that the virtual DVD drive for your **Fedora Linux** virtual machine is attached to the live media ISO image of Fedora Workstation Linux and that it is listed at the top of the boot order. Next, start and then connect to your Fedora Linux virtual machine using your virtualization software.

2. At the Fedora Live welcome screen, select **Start Fedora-Workstation-Live** and press **Enter**.

3. After the graphical desktop and Welcome to Fedora screen have loaded, select the option **Try Fedora** and click **Close** when prompted.

4. Navigate to **Activities**, **Show Applications**, **Terminal** within the GNOME desktop to open a BASH terminal.

5. At the command prompt, type `su - root` and press **Enter** to switch to the root user.

6. At the command prompt, type `df -hT` and press **Enter** to view the mounted filesystems. Is the root filesystem on your hard disk drive mounted?

7. At the command prompt, type `fdisk -l device` where *device* is the storage device file from Step 2 of Hands-On Project 5-3 (e.g., /dev/sda). Note the device files for the partition that contains the root filesystem (it should be 35 GB), /boot filesystem (it should be 1 GB), and UEFI System Partition (if used).

8. At the command prompt, type `fsck -f device` where *device* is the partition device file from Step 7 for the root filesystem and press **Enter**. This will check your root filesystem for errors and prompt you to fix any that are found.

9. At the command prompt, type `mount device /mnt` where *device* is the partition device file from Step 7 for the root filesystem and press **Enter**. This will mount the root filesystem on your hard disk drive to the /mnt directory on the live Fedora system. Next, type `mount device /mnt/boot` where *device* is the partition device file from Step 7 for the /boot filesystem and press **Enter**. This will mount the /boot filesystem on your hard disk drive to the /mnt/boot directory on the live Fedora system. If your system has a UEFI System Partition, type `mount device /mnt/boot` where *device* is the partition device file from Step 7 for the UEFI System Partition and press **Enter**. This will mount the UEFI System Partition to /mnt/boot/efi on the live Fedora system.

10. At the command prompt, type `mount -t proc proc /proc` and press **Enter** to mount the /proc filesystem.

11. At the command prompt, type `chroot /mnt` and press **Enter** to switch from the root filesystem on your Live Fedora system to the root filesystem on your hard disk drive (ignore any warnings). Next, type `ls /root` and press **Enter**. Do you recognize the files?

12. At the command prompt, type `passwd root` and press **Enter**. Supply a new root user password of **Secret123** and press **Enter** when prompted (twice). What warning did you receive regarding the Secret123 password?

13. Click the power icon in the upper-right corner, select the power icon that appears, and click **Power Off** to shut down your Fedora Live installation image.

14. In the Settings for your virtual machine in your virtualization software, ensure that the virtual DVD drive is no longer attached to the Fedora live media ISO image.

15. Finally, start your Fedora Linux virtual machine using your virtualization software. After the system has loaded, switch to a command-line terminal (tty5) by pressing **Ctrl+Alt+F5** and log in to the terminal using the user name of **root** and the password of **Secret123**. Were you successful?

16. At the command prompt, type `passwd root` and press **Enter**. Supply a new root user password of `LINUXrocks!` and press **Enter** when prompted (twice).

17. At the command prompt, type `poweroff` and press **Enter** to shut down your Fedora Linux virtual machine.

Discovery Exercises

Discovery Exercise 6-1

Estimated Time: 30 minutes
Objective: View system and hardware configuration.
Description: Project 6-5 was performed on your Ubuntu Linux virtual machine. Perform the same project using your Fedora Linux virtual machine and note any differences.

Discovery Exercise 6-2

Estimated Time: 60 minutes
Objective: Configure BTRFS during Linux installation.
Description: Modern Linux distributions often allow you to create fault tolerant BTRFS volumes during installation to host the Linux operating system and applications. Provided that you have adequate storage space on your host operating system, create a new virtual machine called Fedora BTRFS that has the following characteristics:

    a. 4 GB of memory (not dynamically allocated)

    b. An Internet connection via your PC's network card (preferably using an external virtual switch or bridged mode)

    c. Two 50 GB SATA/SAS/SCSI virtual hard disk drives (both dynamically allocated)

    d. The virtual machine DVD drive attached to the live media ISO image of Fedora Workstation Linux

Next, perform an installation of Fedora Linux that contains a / (root) filesystem that uses BTRFS RAID 1 fault tolerance for both data and metadata from space on both virtual hard disk files. In order to configure this during the Fedora installation program, you will need to choose the Advanced Custom (Blivet-GUI) option on the Installation Destination screen. Also note that the /boot filesystem cannot use BTRFS. Following the installation, verify your BTRFS configuration using the appropriate commands. When finished, remove your virtual machine and both virtual hard disk files.

Discovery Exercise 6-3

Estimated Time: 60 minutes
Objective: Configure software RAID during Linux installation.
Description: An alternative to BTRFS RAID 1 for operating system and application fault tolerance is software RAID 1. Perform Discovery Exercise 6-2 again, but instead of using a BTRFS RAID 1 volume for the / (root) filesystem, select the appropriate options to create a software RAID 1 volume formatted with ext4.

Discovery Exercise 6-4

Estimated Time: 40 minutes

Objective: Configure LVM RAID.

Description: The LVM can also be used to provide RAID for logical volumes, provided that the underlying volume group consists of multiple physical volumes. View the `lvmraid` manual page to learn how to implement LVM RAID 0, 1, and 5 using the `lvcreate` command. Next, add three 10 GB SATA/SCSI/SAS virtual hard disk files (dynamically expanding) to your Fedora Linux virtual machine, and configure them as a single LVM RAID 5 logical volume.

Discovery Exercise 6-5

Estimated Time: 30 minutes

Objective: Research Linux installation issues.

Description: Search the Internet for information about five Linux installation problems that are different from those described in this chapter. How have other people solved these problems? If you had similar difficulties during installation, how could you get help?

Discovery Exercise 6-6

Estimated Time: 10 minutes

Objective: Describe physical server security practices.

Description: Linux servers are typically stored in a locked server closet to prevent physical access by unauthorized persons. Given the steps that you performed in Project 6-6, describe why these physical restrictions are warranted.

Chapter 7

Working with the Shell

Chapter Objectives

1   Redirect the input and output of a command.

2   Identify and manipulate common shell environment variables.

3   Create and export new shell variables.

4   Edit environment files to create variables upon shell startup.

5   Describe the purpose and nature of shell scripts.

6   Create and execute basic shell scripts.

7   Effectively use constructs, special variables, and functions in shell scripts.

8   Use Git to perform version control for shell scripts and other files.

9   Compare and contrast BASH and Z shell features and configuration.

A solid understanding of shell features is vital to both administrators and users who must interact with the shell daily. The first part of this chapter describes how the shell can manipulate command input and output using redirection and pipe shell metacharacters. Next, you explore the different types of variables present in a shell after login, as well as their purpose and usage. Following this, you learn how to create and execute shell scripts, as well as use Git to provide version control for them. Finally, this chapter ends with an introduction to the Z shell.

Command Input and Output

Recall from Chapter 2 that the shell is responsible for providing a user interface and interpreting commands entered on the command line. In addition, the shell can manipulate command input and output, provided the user specifies certain shell metacharacters on the command line alongside the command. Command input and output are represented by labels known as **file descriptors**. For each command that can be manipulated by the shell, there are three file descriptors:

- Standard Input (stdin)
- Standard Output (stdout)
- Standard Error (stderr)

Standard Input (stdin) refers to the information processed by the command during execution; this often takes the form of user input typed on the keyboard. **Standard Output (stdout)** refers to the normal output of a command, whereas **Standard Error (stderr)** refers to any error messages generated by the command. Both stdin and stderr are displayed on the terminal screen by default. All three components are depicted in Figure 7-1.

Figure 7-1   The three common file descriptors

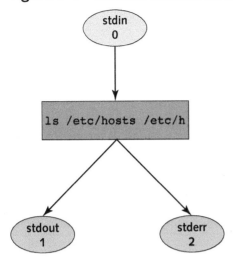

As shown in Figure 7-1, each file descriptor is represented by a number, with stdin represented by the number 0, stdout represented by the number 1, and stderr represented by the number 2.

Although all three descriptors are available to any command, not all commands use every descriptor. The ls /etc/hosts /etc/h command used in Figure 7-1 gives stdout (the listing of the /etc/hosts file) and stderr (an error message indicating that the /etc/h file does not exist) to the terminal screen, as shown in the following output:

```
[root@server1 ~]# ls /etc/hosts /etc/h
ls: cannot access '/etc/h': No such file or directory
/etc/hosts
[root@server1 ~]#_
```

Redirection

You can use the shell to redirect stdout and stderr from the terminal screen to a file on the filesystem. To do this, include the > shell metacharacter followed by the absolute or relative pathname of the file. For example, to redirect only the stdout to a file called goodoutput for the command used in Figure 7-1, you append the number of the file descriptor (1) followed by the redirection symbol > and the file to redirect the stdout to (goodoutput), as shown in the following output:

```
[root@server1 ~]#  ls /etc/hosts /etc/h  1>goodoutput
ls: cannot access '/etc/h': No such file or directory
[root@server1 ~]#_
```

Note 1

You can include a space character after the > metacharacter, but it is not necessary.

In the preceding output, the stderr is still displayed to the terminal screen because it was not redirected to a file. The listing of /etc/hosts was not displayed, however; instead, it was redirected to a file called goodoutput in the current directory. If the goodoutput file did not exist prior to running the command in the preceding output, Linux creates it automatically. However, if the goodoutput file did exist prior to the redirection, the shell clears its contents before executing the command. To see that the stdout was redirected to the goodoutput file, you can run the following commands:

```
[root@server1 ~]# ls -F
Desktop/   goodoutput
```

```
[root@server1 ~]# cat goodoutput
/etc/hosts
[root@server1 ~]#_
```

Similarly, you can redirect the stderr of a command to a file by specifying file descriptor number 2, as shown in the following output:

```
[root@server1 ~]# ls /etc/hosts /etc/h  2>badoutput
/etc/hosts
[root@server1 ~]# cat badoutput
ls: cannot access '/etc/h': No such file or directory
[root@server1 ~]#_
```

In the preceding output, only the stderr was redirected to a file called badoutput. The stdout (a listing of /etc/hosts) was displayed on the terminal screen.

Because redirecting the stdout to a file for later use is more common than redirecting the stderr to a file, the shell assumes stdout in the absence of a numeric file descriptor:

```
[root@server1 ~]# ls /etc/hosts /etc/h  >goodoutput
ls: cannot access '/etc/h': No such file or directory
[root@server1 ~]# cat goodoutput
/etc/hosts
[root@server1 ~]#_
```

In addition, you can redirect both stdout and stderr to separate files at the same time, as shown in the following output:

```
[root@server1 ~]# ls /etc/hosts /etc/h  >goodoutput  2>badoutput
[root@server1 ~]# cat goodoutput
/etc/hosts
[root@server1 ~]# cat badoutput
ls: cannot access '/etc/h': No such file or directory
[root@server1 ~]#_
```

Note 2

The order of redirection on the command line does not matter; the command ls /etc/hosts /etc/h >goodoutput 2>badoutput is the same as ls /etc/hosts /etc/h 2>badoutput >goodoutput.

It is important to use separate filenames to hold the contents of stdout and stderr. Using the same filename for both results in a loss of data because the system attempts to write both contents to the file at the same time:

```
[root@server1 ~]#ls /etc/hosts /etc/h  >goodoutput  2>goodoutput
[root@server1 ~]# cat goodoutput
/etc/hosts
access '/etc/h': No such file or directory
[root@server1 ~]#_
```

To redirect both stdout and stderr to the same file without any loss of data, you must use special notation. To send stdout to the file goodoutput and stderr to the same place as stdout, you can do the following:

```
[root@server1 ~]# ls /etc/hosts /etc/h  >goodoutput  2>&1
[root@server1 ~]# cat goodoutput
ls: cannot access '/etc/h': No such file or directory
```

```
/etc/hosts
[root@server1 ~]#_
```

Alternatively, you can send stderr to the file badoutput and stdout to the same place as stderr:

```
[root@server1 ~]# ls /etc/hosts /etc/h  2>badoutput   >&2
[root@server1 ~]# cat badoutput
ls: cannot access '/etc/h': No such file or directory
/etc/hosts
[root@server1 ~]#_
```

An easier alternative is to use the &> special notation. For example, to redirect both stdout and stderr to the alloutput file, you could use the following command:

```
[root@server1 ~]# ls /etc/hosts /etc/h  &>alloutput
[root@server1 ~]# cat alloutput
ls: cannot access '/etc/h': No such file or directory
/etc/hosts
[root@server1 ~]#_
```

> ## Note 3
>
> To remove errors from command output, you can redirect the stderr to /dev/null to discard them. For example, the command find / -name httpd.conf 2>/dev/null would only display the locations of the httpd.conf file; any errors resulting from attempting to search protected filesystems (such as /proc) would be omitted from the search results.

In all of the examples used earlier, the contents of the files used to store the output from commands were cleared prior to use by the shell. Another example of this is shown in the following output when redirecting the stdout of the date command to the file dateoutput:

```
[root@server1 ~]# date >dateoutput
[root@server1 ~]# cat dateoutput
Fri Aug 20 07:54:00 EDT 2023
[root@server1 ~]# date >dateoutput
[root@server1 ~]# cat dateoutput
Fri Aug 20 07:54:41 EDT 2023
[root@server1 ~]#_
```

To prevent the file from being cleared by the shell and append output to the existing output, you can specify two > metacharacters alongside the file descriptor, as shown in the following output:

```
[root@server1 ~]# date >dateoutput
[root@server1 ~]# cat dateoutput
Fri Aug 20 07:55:32 EDT 2023
[root@server1 ~]# date >>dateoutput
[root@server1 ~]# cat dateoutput
Fri Aug 20 07:55:32 EDT 2023
Fri Aug 20 07:55:48 EDT 2023
[root@server1 ~]#_
```

You can also redirect a file to the stdin of a command using the < metacharacter. Because input has only one file descriptor, you do not need to specify the number 0 before the < metacharacter to indicate stdin, as shown next:

```
[root@server1 ~]# cat </etc/issue
\S
```

```
Kernel \r on an \m (\l)
[root@server1 ~]#_
```

In the preceding output, the shell located and sent the /etc/issue file to the cat command as stdin. Because the cat command normally takes the filename to display as an argument on the command line (e.g., cat /etc/issue), you do not need to use stdin redirection with the cat command as in the previous example. However, some commands only accept files that the shell passes through stdin. The tr command is one such command that can be used to replace characters in a file sent via stdin. To replace all the lowercase r characters in the /etc/issue file with uppercase R characters, you can run the following command:

```
[root@server1 ~]# tr r R </etc/issue
\S
KeRnel \R on an \m (\l)
[root@server1 ~]#_
```

The preceding command does not modify the /etc/issue file; it simply takes a copy of the /etc/issue file, manipulates it, and then sends the stdout to the terminal screen. To save a copy of the stdout for later use, you can use both stdin and stdout redirection together:

```
[root@server1 ~]# tr r R </etc/issue >newissue
[root@server1 ~]# cat newissue
\S
KeRnel \R on an \m (\l)
[root@server1 ~]#_
```

As with redirecting stdout and stderr in the same command, you should use different filenames when redirecting stdin and stdout. In this case, the shell clears a file that already exists before performing the redirection. An example is shown in the following output:

```
[root@server1 ~]# sort <newissue >newissue
[root@server1 ~]# cat newissue
[root@server1 ~]#_
```

The newissue file has no contents when displayed in the preceding output. The shell saw that output redirection was indicated on the command line, cleared the contents of the file newissue, then sorted the blank file and saved the output (nothing in our example) into the file newissue. Because of this feature of shell redirection, Linux administrators commonly use the command >filename at the command prompt to clear the contents of a file.

Note 4

The contents of log files are typically cleared periodically using the command >/path/to/logfile.

You can also use two < metacharacters to redirect multiple lines of stdin from the keyboard into a command. This is often called a **here document** and requires a special delimiter that indicates the last line, such as the letters EOF (which is a common delimiter that stands for End Of File). For example, to redirect the three lines of input into the cat command, you can run the following command, supply the three lines when prompted (pressing Enter after each one), followed by a single line with the delimiter (in our example, EOF) to indicate the end of the input:

```
[root@server1 ~]# cat << EOF
>This is line one.
>This is line two.
>This is line three.
>EOF
```

```
This is line one.
This is line two.
This is line three.
[root@server1 ~]#_
```

The shell in the preceding output accepts each line of input, and when the line of input matches the delimiter, it sends the multiline stdin to the `cat` command, which displays the three lines on the screen.

Table 7-1 summarizes the different types of redirection discussed in this section.

Table 7-1   Common redirection examples

Command	Description
`command 1>file` `command >file`	The Standard Output of the command is sent to a file instead of to the terminal screen.
`command 2>file`	The Standard Error of the command is sent to a file instead of to the terminal screen.
`command 1>fileA 2>fileB` `command >fileA 2>fileB`	The Standard Output of the command is sent to fileA instead of to the terminal screen, and the Standard Error of the command is sent to fileB instead of to the terminal screen.

`command 1>file 2>&1`
`command >file 2>&1`
`command 1>&2 2>file`
`command >&2 2>file`
`command &>file`
	Both the Standard Output and the Standard Error are sent to the same file instead of to the terminal screen.

`command 1>>file` `command >>file`	The Standard Output of the command is appended to a file instead of being sent to the terminal screen.
`command 2>>file`	The Standard Error of the command is appended to a file instead of being sent to the terminal screen.
`command 0<file` `command <file`	The Standard Input of a command is taken from a file.
`command <<delimiter`	The Standard Input of a command is taken from multiple lines of input that end with a specified delimiter. Often called a here document.

Pipes

Note from Table 7-1 that redirection only occurs between a command and a file and vice versa. However, you can send the stdout of one command to another command as stdin. To do this, you use the | (pipe) metacharacter and specify commands on either side. The shell sends the stdout of the command on the left to the command on the right, which interprets the information as stdin. This process is shown in Figure 7-2.

Note 5

The pipe metacharacter can be created on most keyboards by pressing Shift+\.

Note 6

A series of commands that includes the pipe metacharacter is commonly referred to as a pipe.

Figure 7-2   Piping information from one command to another

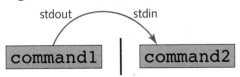

For example, the stdout of the `ls -l /etc` command is too large to fit on one terminal screen. To send the stdout of this command to the `less` command, which views stdin page by page, you can use the following command:

```
[root@server1 ~]# ls -l /etc | less
total 2196
drwxr-xr-x.  3 root root    4096 Apr 25 02:35 abrt
-rw-r--r--.  1 root root      16 Jul  8 20:13 adjtime
-rw-r--r--.  1 root root    1518 Feb 22 11:56 aliases
drwxr-xr-x.  3 root root    4096 Apr 25 02:36 alsa
drwxr-xr-x.  2 root root    4096 Jul 11 15:01 alternatives
-rw-r--r--.  1 root root     541 Feb  7 00:58 anacrontab
-rw-r--r--.  1 root root     769 Apr  4 11:53 appstream.conf
-rw-r--r--.  1 root root      55 Apr  4 05:05 asound.conf
-rw-r--r--.  1 root root       1 Feb 25 05:54 at.deny
-rw-r--r--.  1 root root     186 Feb  8 05:02 atmsigd.conf
drwxr-x---.  3 root root    4096 Apr 25 02:36 audisp
drwxr-x---.  3 root root    4096 Jul  8 20:15 audit
drwxr-xr-x.  3 root root    4096 Apr 25 02:38 authselect
drwxr-xr-x.  4 root root    4096 Apr 25 02:35 avahi
drwxr-xr-x.  2 root root    4096 Jul  9 13:59 bash_completion.d
-rw-r--r--.  1 root root    3001 Feb 22 11:56 bashrc
drwxr-xr-x.  2 root root    4096 Apr 18 18:00 binfmt.d
drwxr-xr-x.  2 root root    4096 Apr 25 02:34 bluetooth
-rw-r-----.  1 root brlapi    33 Apr 25 02:35 brlapi.key
drwxr-xr-x.  7 root root    4096 Apr 25 02:35 brltty
-rw-r--r--.  1 root root   25696 Mar  6 09:47 brltty.conf
-rw-r--r--.  1 root root     520 Feb  6 23:29 cagibid.conf
:
```

You do not need spaces around the | metacharacter. The commands `ls -l /etc|less` and `ls -l /etc | less` are equivalent.

A common use of piping is to reduce the amount of information displayed on the terminal screen from commands that display too much information. For example, by showing all mounted filesystems, including special filesystems, the `mount` command normally displays too much information for a Linux administrator. To view only those lines regarding ext4 or xfs filesystems, you could send the stdout of the `mount` command to the `egrep` command as stdin, which can then print only the results that match the appropriate extended regular expression as shown in the following output:

```
[root@server1 ~]# mount | egrep "(ext4|xfs)"
/dev/sda3 on / type ext4 (rw,relatime,seclabel,data=ordered)
selinuxfs on /sys/fs/selinux type selinuxfs (rw,relatime)
/dev/sda5 on /newmount type ext4 (rw,relatime,seclabel,data=ordered)
/dev/mapper/vg00-data1 on /data type ext4 (rw,relatime,data=ordered)
/dev/sda1 on /boot type ext4 (rw,relatime,seclabel,data=ordered)
/dev/sda8 on /data2 type xfs (rw,relatime,attr2,inode64,noquota)
[root@server1 ~]#_
```

The egrep command in the preceding output receives the full output from the mount command and then displays only those lines that have ext4 or xfs in them. The egrep command normally takes two arguments; the first specifies the text to search for and the second specifies the filename(s) to search within. The egrep command used in the preceding output requires no second argument because the material to search comes from stdin (the mount command) instead of from a file.

Furthermore, you can use more than one pipe | metacharacter on the command line to pipe information from one command to another command, like an assembly line in a factory. Typically, an assembly line goes through several departments, each of which performs a specialized task. For example, one department might assemble the product, another might paint the product, and another might package the product. Every product must pass through each department to be complete.

You can use Linux commands that manipulate data in the same way, connecting them into an assembly line via piping. One command manipulates information, and then that manipulated information is sent to another command, which manipulates it further. The process continues until the information attains the form required by the user.

Recall from the previous output that the special selinuxfs filesystem was also shown in the output because it contains the letters "xfs" and was matched by the egrep command as a result. To omit these results, you could send the stdout of the previous command to the grep -v selinuxfs command which can show all lines except those that contain selinuxfs as shown in the following output:

```
[root@server1 ~]# mount | egrep "(ext4|xfs)" | grep -v selinuxfs
/dev/sda3 on / type ext4 (rw,relatime,seclabel,data=ordered)
/dev/sda5 on /newmount type ext4 (rw,relatime,seclabel,data=ordered)
/dev/mapper/vg00-data1 on /data type ext4 (rw,relatime,data=ordered)
/dev/sda1 on /boot type ext4 (rw,relatime,seclabel,data=ordered)
/dev/sda8 on /data2 type xfs (rw,relatime,attr2,inode64,noquota)
[root@server1 ~]#_
```

The pipe in the preceding output uses three commands; the mount command sends its stdout to the egrep command, which then sends its stdout to the grep command. A piping process using multiple commands is depicted in Figure 7-3.

Figure 7-3 Piping several commands

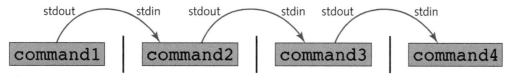

Any command that can take stdin and transform it into stdout is called a filter. However, commands such as ls and mount are not filter commands because they do not accept stdin from other commands, but instead find information from the system and display it to the user. As a result, these commands must be at the beginning of a pipe. Other commands, such as vi, are interactive and cannot appear between two pipe symbols because they cannot take from stdin and give to stdout.

Several hundred filter commands are available to Linux users. Table 7-2 lists some common ones that are useful within pipes.

Table 7-2 Common filter commands

Command	Description
`sort`	Sorts lines alphanumerically
`sort -r`	Reverse-sorts lines alphanumerically
`wc`	Counts the number of lines, words, and characters
`wc -l`	Counts the number of lines
`wc -w`	Counts the number of words
`wc -c`	Counts the number of characters
`pr`	Formats text for printing, with several options available; it places a date and page number at the top of each page
`pr -d`	Formats text to be double-spaced
`uniq`	Omits duplicate results
`cut`	Displays specific columns of delimited data
`paste`	Combines lines together from two separate sources
`tr`	Replaces text characters
`printf`	Formats text using a special backslash notation; for example, `printf "Hello \tWorld"` will print Hello followed by a tab (\t) followed by World
`tee `*`filename`*	Sends stdin to a specified filename as well as stdout; the contents of the file are overwritten unless the `-a` (append) option is specified
`xargs `*`command`*	Converts stdin to command line arguments that are executed by a specified command; for example, `find / -name "core*"	xargs rm` will search the system for filenames starting with "core" and convert those filenames to arguments of the `rm` command (to remove the associated files)
`split`	Splits a file or stdin into smaller sections for easier processing; for example, `split -n 400` would save the first 400 lines to xaa, the second 400 lines to xab, and so on
`grep`	Displays lines that match a regular expression
`nl`	Numbers lines
`awk`	Extracts, manipulates, and formats text using pattern-action statements
`sed`	Manipulates text using search-and-replace expressions

Take, for example, the prologue from Shakespeare's *Romeo and Juliet*:

```
[root@server1 ~]# cat prologue
Two households, both alike in dignity,
In fair Verona, where we lay our scene,
From ancient grudge break to new mutiny,
Where civil blood makes civil hands unclean.
From forth the fatal loins of these two foes
A pair of star-cross'd lovers take their life;
Whole misadventured piteous overthrows
Do with their death bury their parents' strife.
The fearful passage of their death-mark'd love,
And the continuance of their parents' rage,
Which, but their children's end, nought could remove,
Is now the two hours' traffic of our stage;
The which if you with patient ears attend,
What here shall miss, our toil shall strive to mend.
[root@server1 ~]#_
```

Now suppose you want to replace all lowercase "a" characters with uppercase "A" characters in the preceding file, sort the contents by the first character on each line, double-space the output, and view the results page-by-page. To accomplish these tasks, you can use the following pipe:

```
[root@server1 ~]# cat prologue | tr a A | sort | pr -d | less
```

```
2023-08-20 08:06                                          Page 1


And the continuAnce of their pArents' rAge,

A pAir of stAr-cross'd lovers tAke their life;

Do with their deAth bury their pArents' strife.

From Ancient grudge breAk to new mutiny,

From forth the fAtAl loins of these two foes

In fAir VeronA, where we lAy our scene,

Is now the two hours' trAffic of our stAge;

The feArful pAssAge of their deAth-mArk'd love,

The which if you with pAtient eArs Attend,

Two households, both Alike in dignity,

WhAt here shAll miss, our toil shAll strive to mend.

Where civil blood mAkes civil hAnds uncleAn.

Which, but their children's end, nought could remove,

Whole misAdventured piteous overthrows
:
```

The command used in the preceding example displays the final stdout to the terminal screen via the `less` command. In many cases, you might want to display the results of the pipe while saving a copy in a file on the filesystem using the `tee` command, which takes information from stdin and sends that information to a file, as well as to stdout.

To save a copy of the manipulated prologue before displaying it to the terminal screen with the `less` command, you can use the following command:

```
[root@server1 ~]# cat prologue|tr a A|sort|pr -d|tee newfile|less
```

```
2023-08-20 08:06                                          Page 1


And the continuAnce of their pArents' rAge,

A pAir of stAr-cross'd lovers tAke their life;

Do with their deAth bury their pArents' strife.

From Ancient grudge breAk to new mutiny,
```

```
From forth the fAtAl loins of these two foes

In fAir VeronA, where we lAy our scene,

Is now the two hours' trAffic of our stAge;

The feArful pAssAge of their deAth-mArk'd love,

The which if you with pAtient eArs Attend,

Two households, both Alike in dignity,

WhAt here shAll miss, our toil shAll strive to mend.

Where civil blood mAkes civil hAnds uncleAn.

Which, but their children's end, nought could remove,

Whole misAdventured piteous overthrows
:q
[root@server1 ~]#_
[root@server1 ~]# cat newfile

2023-08-20 08:06                                        Page 1

And the continuAnce of their pArents' rAge,

A pAir of stAr-cross'd lovers tAke their life;

Do with their deAth bury their pArents' strife.

From Ancient grudge breAk to new mutiny,

From forth the fAtAl loins of these two foes

In fAir VeronA, where we lAy our scene,

Is now the two hours' trAffic of our stAge;

The feArful pAssAge of their deAth-mArk'd love,

The which if you with pAtient eArs Attend,

Two households, both Alike in dignity,

WhAt here shAll miss, our toil shAll strive to mend.

Where civil blood mAkes civil hAnds uncleAn.

Which, but their children's end, nought could remove,

Whole misAdventured piteous overthrows
[root@server1 ~]#_
```

You can also combine redirection and piping, if input redirection occurs at the beginning of the pipe and output redirection occurs at the end of the pipe. An example of this is shown in the following output, which replaces all lowercase a characters with uppercase A characters in the prologue file used in the previous example, then sorts the file, numbers each line, and saves the output to a file called newprologue instead of sending the output to the terminal screen.

```
[root@server1 ~]# tr a A <prologue | sort | nl >newprologue
[root@server1 ~]# cat newprologue
     1  And the continuAnce of their pArents' rAge,
     2  A pAir of stAr-cross'd lovers tAke their life;
     3  Do with their deAth bury their pArents' strife.
     4  From Ancient grudge breAk to new mutiny,
     5  From forth the fAtAl loins of these two foes
     6  In fAir VeronA, where we lAy our scene,
     7  Is now the two hours' trAffic of our stAge;
     8  The feArful pAssAge of their deAth-mArk'd love,
     9  The which if you with pAtient eArs Attend,
    10  Two households, both Alike in dignity,
    11  WhAt here shAll miss, our toil shAll strive to mend.
    12  Where civil blood mAkes civil hAnds uncleAn.
    13  Which, but their children's end, nought could remove,
    14  Whole misAdventured piteous overthrows
[root@server1 ~]#_
```

Many Linux commands can provide large amounts of useful text information. As a result, Linux administrators often use the sed and awk filter commands with pipes to manipulate text information that these commands produce.

The sed command is typically used to search for a certain string of text and replaces that text string with another text string using the syntax s/search/replace/. For example, the following output demonstrates how to use sed to search for the string "the" and replace it with the string "THE" in the prologue file used earlier:

```
[root@server1 ~]# cat prologue | sed s/the/THE/
Two households, both alike in dignity,
In fair Verona, where we lay our scene,
From ancient grudge break to new mutiny,
Where civil blood makes civil hands unclean.
From forth THE fatal loins of these two foes
A pair of star-cross'd lovers take THEir life;
Whole misadventured piteous overthrows
Do with THEir death bury their parents' strife.
The fearful passage of THEir death-mark'd love,
And THE continuance of their parents' rage,
Which, but THEir children's end, nought could remove,
Is now THE two hours' traffic of our stage;
The which if you with patient ears attend,
What here shall miss, our toil shall strive to mend.
[root@server1 ~]#_
```

Notice from the preceding output that sed only searched for and replaced the first occurrence of the string "the" in each line. To have sed globally replace all occurrences of the string "the" in each line, append a g to the search-and-replace expression:

```
[root@server1 ~]# cat prologue | sed s/the/THE/g
Two households, both alike in dignity,
```

```
In fair Verona, where we lay our scene,
From ancient grudge break to new mutiny,
Where civil blood makes civil hands unclean.
From forth THE fatal loins of THESe two foes
A pair of star-cross'd lovers take THEir life;
Whole misadventured piteous overthrows
Do with THEir death bury THEir parents' strife.
The fearful passage of THEir death-mark'd love,
And THE continuance of THEir parents' rage,
Which, but THEir children's end, nought could remove,
Is now THE two hours' traffic of our stage;
The which if you with patient ears attend,
What here shall miss, our toil shall strive to mend.
[root@server1 ~]#_
```

You can also tell sed the specific lines to search by prefixing the search-and-replace expression. For example, to force sed to replace the string "the" with "THE" globally on lines that contain the string "love," you can use the following command:

```
[root@server1 ~]# cat prologue | sed /love/s/the/THE/g
Two households, both alike in dignity,
In fair Verona, where we lay our scene,
From ancient grudge break to new mutiny,
Where civil blood makes civil hands unclean.
From forth the fatal loins of these two foes
A pair of star-cross'd lovers take THEir life;
Whole misadventured piteous overthrows
Do with their death bury their parents' strife.
The fearful passage of THEir death-mark'd love,
And the continuance of their parents' rage,
Which, but their children's end, nought could remove,
Is now the two hours' traffic of our stage;
The which if you with patient ears attend,
What here shall miss, our toil shall strive to mend.
[root@server1 ~]#_
```

You can also force sed to perform a search-and-replace on certain lines only. To replace the string "the" with "THE" globally on lines 5 to 8 only, you can use the following command:

```
[root@server1 ~]# cat prologue | sed 5,8s/the/THE/g
Two households, both alike in dignity,
In fair Verona, where we lay our scene,
From ancient grudge break to new mutiny,
Where civil blood makes civil hands unclean.
From forth THE fatal loins of THESe two foes
A pair of star-cross'd lovers take THEir life;
Whole misadventured piteous overthrows
Do with THEir death bury THEir parents' strife.
The fearful passage of their death-mark'd love,
And the continuance of their parents' rage,
Which, but their children's end, nought could remove,
Is now the two hours' traffic of our stage;
The which if you with patient ears attend,
What here shall miss, our toil shall strive to mend.
[root@server1 ~]#_
```

You can also use sed to remove unwanted lines of text. To delete all the lines that contain the word "the," you can use the following command:

```
[root@server1 ~]# cat prologue | sed /the/d
Two households, both alike in dignity,
In fair Verona, where we lay our scene,
From ancient grudge break to new mutiny,
Where civil blood makes civil hands unclean.
Whole misadventured piteous overthrows
The which if you with patient ears attend,
What here shall miss, our toil shall strive to mend.
[root@server1 ~]#_
```

Like sed, the awk command searches for patterns of text and performs some action on the text it finds. However, the awk command treats each line of text as a record in a database, and each word in a line as a database field. For example, the line "Hello, how are you?" has four fields: "Hello,", "how", "are", and "you?". These fields can be referenced in the awk command using $1, $2, $3, and $4. For example, to display only the first and fourth words on lines of the prologue file that contain the word "the," you can use the following command:

```
[root@server1 ~]# cat prologue | awk '/the/ {print $1, $4}'
From fatal
A star-cross'd
Do death
The of
And of
Which, children's
Is two
[root@server1 ~]#_
```

By default, the awk command uses space or tab characters as delimiters for each field in a line. Most configuration files on Linux systems, however, are delimited using colon (:) characters. To change the delimiter that awk uses, you can specify the –F option to the command. For example, the following example lists the last 10 lines of the colon-delimited file /etc/passwd and views only the sixth and seventh fields for lines that contain the word "bob" in the last 10 lines of the file:

```
[root@server1 ~]# tail /etc/passwd
news:x:9:13:News server user:/etc/news:/sbin/nologin
smolt:x:490:474:Smolt:/usr/share/smolt:/sbin/nologin
backuppc:x:489:473::/var/lib/BackupPC:/sbin/nologin
pulse:x:488:472:PulseAudio System Daemon:/var/run/pulse:/sbin/nologin
gdm:x:42:468::/var/lib/gdm:/sbin/nologin
hsqldb:x:96:96::/var/lib/hsqldb:/sbin/nologin
jetty:x:487:467::/usr/share/jetty:/bin/sh
bozo:x:500:500:bozo the clown:/home/bozo:/bin/bash
bob:x:501:501:Bob Smith:/home/bob:/bin/bash
user1:x:502:502:sample user one:/home/user1:/bin/bash
[root@server1 ~]# tail /etc/passwd | awk -F : '/bob/ {print $6, $7}'
/home/bob /bin/bash
[root@server1 ~]#_
```

Note 7

Both awk and sed allow you to specify regular expressions in the search pattern.

Because Linux systems have a rich set of utilities that can be used within a pipe, you can often use more than one way to obtain the same results. For example, the following pipe would also display the sixth and seventh field from the colon-delimited /etc/passwd file for the user bob, using the `grep` and `cut` commands:

```
[root@server1 ~]# grep bob /etc/passwd | cut -d: -f6,7
/home/bob:/bin/bash
[root@server1 ~]#_
```

However, note from the preceding output that the : character was included by the `cut` command when multiple lines were cut. To remove this colon, you could extend the pipe to use the `tr` command to replace colon characters with space characters:

```
[root@server1 ~]# grep bob /etc/passwd | cut -d: -f6,7 | tr ":" " "
/home/bob /bin/bash
[root@server1 ~]#_
```

Alternatively, you could use a combination of piped and non-piped commands together. For example, you could use pipes to save the output of each column to a file and then combine those files afterwards using the `paste` command, which will separate the contents of the two files using a space delimiter:

```
[root@server1 ~]# grep bob /etc/passwd | cut -d: -f6 >file1
[root@server1 ~]# grep bob /etc/passwd | cut -d: -f7 >file2
[root@server1 ~]# paste -d " " file1 file2
/home/bob /bin/bash
[root@server1 ~]#_
```

Shell Variables

A shell has several **variables** in memory at any one time. Recall that a variable is simply a reserved portion of memory containing information that might be accessed. Most variables in the shell are referred to as **environment variables** because they are typically set by the system and contain information that the system and programs access regularly. Users can also create their own custom variables. These variables are called **user-defined variables**. In addition to these two types of variables, special variables are available that are useful when executing commands and creating new files and directories.

Environment Variables

Many environment variables are set by default in the shell. To see a list of these variables and their current values, you can use the `set command`, as shown in the following output:

```
[root@server1 ~]# set | less
BASH=/bin/bash
BASHOPTS=checkwinsize:cmdhist:complete_fullquote:expand_aliases:extglob:extquote:
force_fignore:histappend:interactive_comments:login_shell:progcomp:promptvars:
sourcepath
BASHRCSOURCED=Y
BASH_ALIASES=()
BASH_ARGC=()
BASH_ARGV=()
BASH_CMDS=()
BASH_COMPLETION_VERSINFO=([0]="2" [1]="7")
```

```
BASH_ENV=/usr/share/Modules/init/bash
BASH_LINENO=()
BASH_REMATCH=([0]=":/usr/share/man:")
BASH_SOURCE=()
BASH_VERSINFO=([0]="4" [1]="4" [2]="19" [3]="1" [4]="release"
[5]="x86_64-redhat-linux-gnu")
BASH_VERSION='4.4.19(1)-release'
COLUMNS=80
DBUS_SESSION_BUS_ADDRESS=unix:path=/run/user/0/bus
DIRSTACK=()
ENV=/usr/share/Modules/init/profile.sh
EUID=0
:
```

Some environment variables are used by programs that require information about the system; the OSTYPE (Operating System TYPE) and SHELL (Pathname to shell) variables are examples of these. Other variables are used to set the user's working environment; the most common of these include the following:

- PS1—The default shell prompt
- HOME—The absolute pathname to the user's home directory
- PWD—The present working directory in the directory tree
- PATH—A list of directories to search for executable programs
- HISTSIZE—The number of previously executed commands to store in memory
- HISTFILESIZE—The number of previously executed commands to save to a file upon shell exit
- HISTFILE—The file that contains previously executed commands

The PS1 variable represents the shell prompt. To view the contents of this variable only, you can use the echo command and specify the variable name prefixed by the $ shell metacharacter, as shown in the following output:

```
[root@server1 ~]# echo $PS1
[\u@\h \W]\$
[root@server1 ~]#_
```

Note that a special backslash notation is used to define the prompt in the preceding output: \u indicates the user name, \h indicates the host name, and \W indicates the name of the current directory. A list of notations can be found by navigating the manual page for the shell (e.g., man bash).

To change the value of a variable, you specify the variable name followed immediately by an equal sign (=) and the new value. The following output demonstrates how you can change the value of the PS1 variable. The new prompt takes effect immediately and allows the user to type commands.

```
[root@server1 ~]# PS1="This is the new prompt: #"
This is the new prompt: #_
This is the new prompt: # date
Fri Aug 20 08:16:59 EDT 2023
This is the new prompt: #_
This is the new prompt: # who
root     tty5          2023-08-07 13:31
root     tty6          2023-08-07 13:31
This is the new prompt: #_
This is the new prompt: # PS1="[\u@\h \W]#"
[root@server1 ~]#_
```

The HOME variable is used by programs that require the pathname to the current user's home directory to store or search for files; therefore, it should not be changed. If the root user logs in to the system, the HOME variable is set to /root; alternatively, the HOME variable is set to /home/user1 if the user named user1 logs in to the system. Recall that the tilde ~ metacharacter represents the current user's home directory; this metacharacter is a pointer to the HOME variable, as shown here:

```
[root@server1 ~]# echo $HOME
/root
[root@server1 ~]# echo ~
/root
[root@server1 ~]# HOME=/etc
[root@server1 root]# echo $HOME
/etc
[root@server1 root]# echo ~
/etc
[root@server1 root]#_
```

Like the HOME variable, the PWD (Print Working Directory) variable is vital to the user's environment and should not be changed. PWD stores the current user's location in the directory tree. It is affected by the cd command and used by other commands such as pwd when the current directory needs to be identified. The following output demonstrates how this variable works:

```
[root@server1 ~]# pwd
/root
[root@server1 ~]# echo $PWD
/root
[root@server1 ~]# cd /etc
[root@server1 etc]# pwd
/etc
[root@server1 ~]# echo $PWD
/etc
[root@server1 ~]#_
```

The PATH variable is one of the most important variables in the shell, as it allows users to execute commands by typing the command name alone. Recall that most commands are represented by an executable file on the hard drive. These executables are typically stored in directories named bin or sbin in various locations throughout the Linux directory tree. To execute the ls command, you could either type the absolute or relative pathname to the file (e.g., /usr/bin/ls or ../usr/bin/ls) or simply type the letters "ls" and allow the system to search the directories listed in the PATH variable for a command named ls. Sample contents of the PATH variable are shown in the following output:

```
[root@server1 ~]# echo $PATH
/usr/local/sbin:/usr/local/bin:/usr/sbin:/usr/bin:/root/bin
[root@server1 ~]#_
```

In this example, if the user had typed the command ls at the command prompt and pressed Enter, the shell would have noticed the lack of a / character in the pathname and proceeded to search for the file ls in the /usr/local/sbin directory, then the /usr/local/bin directory, the /usr/sbin directory, and then the /usr/bin directory before finding the ls executable file. If no ls file is found in any directory in the PATH variable, the shell returns an error message, as shown here with a misspelled command and any similar command suggestions:

```
[root@server1 ~]# lss
bash: lss: command not found...
Similar command is: 'ls'
[root@server1 ~]#_
```

Thus, if a command is located within a directory that is listed in the PATH variable, you can simply type the name of the command on the command line to execute it. The shell will then find the appropriate executable file on the filesystem. All of the commands used in this book so far have been located in directories listed in the PATH variable. However, if the executable file is not in a directory listed in the PATH variable, the user must specify either the absolute or relative pathname to the executable file. The following example uses the myprogram file in the /root directory (a directory that is not listed in the PATH variable):

```
[root@server1 ~]# pwd
/root
[root@server1 ~]# ls -F
Desktop/  myprogram*
[root@server1 ~]# myprogram
bash: myprogram: command not found...
[root@server1 ~]# /root/myprogram
This is a sample program.
[root@server1 ~]# ./myprogram
This is a sample program.
[root@server1 ~]# cp myprogram /usr/bin
[root@server1 ~]# myprogram
This is a sample program.
[root@server1 ~]#_
```

After the myprogram executable file was copied to the /usr/bin directory in the preceding output, the user was able to execute it by typing its name, because the /usr/bin directory is listed in the PATH variable.

Another important feature of your shell is the ability to recall and execute previous commands; you can cycle through previously executed commands using the up and down cursor keys on your keyboard. Alternatively, you can use the `history command` to view a list of previously executed commands; for example, to view the last five commands that you entered in the shell, you could run the following command:

```
[root@server1 ~]# history 5
 102  ls -l /etc
 103  cp /etc/hosts ~
 104  cat hosts
 105  ls -l hosts
 106  history 5
[root@server1 ~]#_
```

To recall and execute the command 105 from the previous output, you could enter !105 on the command line as shown below:

```
[root@server1 ~]# !105
ls -l hosts
-rw-r--r--. 1 root root 158 Aug  8 09:51 hosts.
[root@server1 ~]#_
```

Variables within your shell provide the functionality needed to recall previous commands, as well as use the `history` and `!` commands. The HISTSIZE variable determines the maximum number of commands that will be stored in shell memory before the oldest ones are removed. The HISTFILESIZE variable determines how many of these commands will be saved to the file listed within the HISTFILE variable when you exit your shell, such that they are available for recall when you start a new shell.

Table 7-3 provides a list of environment variables used in most BASH shells.

Table 7-3   Common BASH environment variables

Variable	Description
BASH	The full path to the BASH shell
BASH_VERSION	The version of the current BASH shell
DISPLAY	The variable used to redirect the output of X Windows to another computer or device
EDITOR	The default text editor used by commands on the system (usually vi or nano)
ENV	The location of the BASH run-time configuration file
EUID	The effective UID (User ID) of the current user
HISTFILE	The filename used to store previously entered commands in the BASH shell (usually ~/.bash_history)
HISTFILESIZE	The number of previously entered commands that can be stored in the HISTFILE upon logout for use during the next login; it is typically 1000 commands
HISTSIZE	The number of previously entered commands that will be stored in memory during the current login session; it is typically 1000 commands
HOME	The absolute pathname of the current user's home directory
HOSTNAME	The host name of the Linux system
LOGNAME	The user name of the current user used when logging in to the shell
MAIL	The location of the mailbox file (where e-mail is stored)
OSTYPE	The current operating system
PATH	The directories to search for executable program files in the absence of an absolute or relative pathname containing a / character
PS1	The current shell prompt
PWD	The current working directory
RANDOM	The variable that creates a random number when accessed
SHELL	The absolute pathname of the current shell
TERM	The variable used to determine the terminal settings; it is typically set to "linux" or "xterm" on newer Linux systems and "console" on older Linux systems
TERMCAP	The variable used to determine the terminal settings on Linux systems that use a TERMCAP database (/etc/termcap)

User-Defined Variables

You can set your own variables using the same method discussed earlier to change the contents of existing environment variables. To do so, you specify the name of the variable (known as the **variable identifier**) immediately followed by the equal sign (=) and the new contents. When creating new variables, it is important to note the following features of variable identifiers:

- They can contain alphanumeric characters (0–9, A–Z, a–z), the dash (-) character, or the underscore (_) character.
- They must not start with a number.
- They are typically capitalized to follow convention (e.g., HOME, PATH).

To create a variable called MYVAR with the contents "This is a sample variable" and display its contents, you can use the following commands:

```
[root@server1 ~]# MYVAR="This is a sample variable"
[root@server1 ~]# echo $MYVAR
This is a sample variable
[root@server1 ~]#_
```

The preceding command created a variable that is available to the current shell. Most commands that are run by the shell are run in a separate subshell, which is created by the current shell. Any variables created in the current shell are not available to those subshells and the commands running within them. Thus, if a user creates a variable to be used within a certain program such as a database editor, that variable should be exported to all subshells using the export command to ensure that all programs started by the current shell can access the variable.

As explained earlier in this chapter, all environment variables in the shell can be listed using the set command; user-defined variables are also indicated in this list. Similarly, to see a list of all exported environment and user-defined variables in the shell, you can use the env command. Because the outputs of set and env are typically large, you would commonly redirect the stdout of these commands to the grep command to display certain lines only.

To see the difference between the set and env commands as well as export the MYVAR variable created earlier, you can perform the following commands:

```
[root@server1 ~]# set | grep MYVAR
MYVAR='This is a sample variable'
[root@server1 ~]# env | grep MYVAR
[root@server1 ~]#_
[root@server1 ~]# export MYVAR
[root@server1 ~]# env | grep MYVAR
MYVAR=This is a sample variable
[root@server1 ~]#_
```

Note 8

You can also use the printenv command to view the exported variables in your shell.

Not all environment variables are exported; the PS1 variable is an example of a variable that does not need to be available to subshells and is not exported as a result. However, it is good form to export user-defined variables because they will likely be used by processes that run in subshells. This means, to create and export a user-defined variable called MYVAR2, you can use the export command alone, as shown in the following output:

```
[root@server1 ~]# export MYVAR2="This is another sample variable"
[root@server1 ~]# set | grep MYVAR2
MYVAR2='This is another sample variable'
_=MYVAR2
[root@server1 ~]# env | grep MYVAR2
MYVAR2=This is another sample variable
[root@server1 ~]#_
```

Note 9

You can also use the unset command to remove a variable from shell memory.

Other Variables

Other variables are not displayed by the set or env commands; these variables perform specialized functions in the shell.

The umask variable used earlier in this textbook is an example of a special variable that performs a special function in the shell and must be set by the umask command. Also recall that when you type the cp command, you are actually running an alias to the cp -i command. Aliases are shortcuts to commands stored in special variables that can be created and viewed using the alias command. To create an alias to the command mount /dev/cdrom /mnt called mdisc and view it, you can use the following commands:

```
[root@server1 ~]# alias mdisc="mount /dev/cdrom /mnt"
[root@server1 ~]# alias
alias cp='cp -i'
alias egrep='egrep --color=auto'
alias fgrep='fgrep --color=auto'
alias grep='grep --color=auto'
alias l.='ls -d .* --color=auto'
alias ll='ls -l --color=auto'
alias ls='ls --color=auto'
alias mdisc='mount /dev/cdrom /mnt'
alias mv='mv -i'
alias rm='rm -i'
alias which='(alias; declare -f) | /usr/bin/which --tty-only --read-
alias --read-functions --show-tilde --show-dot'
alias xzegrep='xzegrep --color=auto'
alias xzfgrep='xzfgrep --color=auto'
alias xzgrep='xzgrep --color=auto'
alias zegrep='zegrep --color=auto'
alias zfgrep='zfgrep --color=auto'
alias zgrep='zgrep --color=auto'
[root@server1 ~]#_
```

Now, you can run the mdisc command to mount a CD or DVD to the /mnt directory, as shown in the following output:

```
[root@server1 ~]# mdisc
[root@server1 ~]# mount | grep mnt
/dev/sr0 on /mnt type iso9660 (ro,relatime,nojoliet,blocksize=2048)
[root@server1 ~]#_
```

You can also create aliases to multiple commands, provided they are separated by the ; metacharacter introduced in Chapter 2. To create and test an alias called dw that runs the date command followed by the who command, you can do the following:

```
[root@server1 ~]# alias dw="date;who"
[root@server1 ~]# alias | grep dw
alias dw='date;who'
[root@server1 ~]# dw
Tue Aug  7 13:54:43 EDT 2023
root       tty5            2023-08-07 13:31
root       pts/0           2023-08-07 13:38
[root@server1 ~]#_
```

> **Note 10**
>
> Use unique alias names because the shell searches for them before it searches for executable files. For example, if you create an alias called who, that alias would be used instead of the who command on the filesystem.

> **Note 11**
>
> You can also use the `unalias command` to remove an alias from shell memory.

Environment Files

Recall that variables are stored in memory. When a user exits the shell, all variables stored in memory are destroyed along with the shell itself. To ensure that variables are always accessible to a shell, you must place variables in a file that is executed each time a user logs in and starts a shell. These files are called environment files. Common BASH shell environment files and the order in which they are typically executed are as follows:

/etc/profile
/etc/profile.d/*
/etc/bashrc
~/.bashrc
~/.bash_profile
~/.bash_login
~/.profile

The BASH runtime configuration files (/etc/bashrc and ~/.bashrc) are typically used to set aliases and variables that must be present in the shell. They are executed immediately after a new login as well as when a new shell is created after login. The /etc/bashrc file contains aliases and variables for all users on the system, whereas the ~/.bashrc file contains aliases and variables for a specific user.

The other environment files are only executed after a new login. The /etc/profile file and all files under the /etc/profile.d/ directory are executed after login for all users on the system; they set most aliases and environment variables. After they finish executing, the home directory of the user is searched for the hidden environment files .bash_profile, .bash_login, and .profile. If these files exist, the first one found is executed; as a result, only one of these files is typically used. These hidden environment files allow a user to set customized variables independent of shells used by other users on the system; any values assigned to variables in these files override those set in /etc/profile, /etc/profile.d/*, /etc/bashrc, and ~/.bashrc due to the order of execution.

To add a variable to any of these files, you add a line that has the same format as the command used on the command line. For example, to add the MYVAR2 variable used previously to the .bash_profile file, edit the file using a text editor such as vi and add the line `export MYVAR2="This is another sample variable"` to the file.

Variables are not the only type of information that can be entered into an environment file; any command that can be executed on the command line can also be placed inside any environment file. If you want to set the umask to 077, display the date after each login, and create an alias, you can add the following lines to one of the hidden environment files in your home directory:

```
umask 077
date
alias dw="date;who"
```

Also, you might want to execute cleanup tasks upon exiting the shell; to do this, add those cleanup commands to the .bash_logout file in your home directory.

Shell Scripts

> Talk is cheap. Show me the code.
> —*Linus Torvalds*

In the previous section, you learned that the shell can execute commands that exist within environment files. The shell can also execute text files containing commands and special constructs. These files are referred to as **shell scripts** and are typically used to create custom programs that perform administrative tasks on Linux systems. Throughout the remainder of this book, we'll introduce administrative commands that can be used within a shell script, as well as sample shell scripts that can be used to automate key system administration tasks. In this section, we'll examine the structure and methods used to write and execute shell scripts.

Any command that can be entered on the command line in Linux can be entered into a shell script because it is a shell that interprets the contents of the shell script itself. The most basic shell script is one that contains a list of commands, one per line, for the shell to execute in order, as shown here in the text file called myscript:

```
[root@server1 ~]# cat myscript
#!/bin/bash
#this is a comment
date
who
ls -F /
[root@server1 ~]#_
```

The first line in the preceding shell script (#!/bin/bash) is called the **hashpling** or **shebang** line; it specifies the pathname to the shell that interprets the contents of the shell script. Some shells can use different constructs in their shell scripts. Thus, it is important to identify which shell was used to create a particular shell script. The hashpling allows a Korn shell or C shell user to use a BASH shell when executing the myscript shell script shown previously. The second line of the shell script is referred to as a comment because it begins with a # character and is ignored by the shell; the only exception to this is the hashpling on the first line of a shell script. The remainder of the shell script shown in the preceding output consists of three commands that will be executed by the shell in order: date, who, and ls -F /.

Note 12

Like other Linux files, shell scripts don't need to have a file extension, but many Linux administrators add the .sh file extension (e.g., myscript.sh) for ease in identifying shell scripts.

If you have read permission to a shell script, you can execute the shell script by starting another shell and specifying the shell script as an argument. To execute the myscript shell script shown earlier in a new BASH shell, you can use the following command:

```
[root@server1 ~]# bash myscript
Fri Aug 20 11:36:18 EDT 2023
user1     tty1          2023-08-20 07:47
root      tty2          2023-08-20 11:36
bin/    dev/     home/         media/   proc/    sbin/       sys/   var/
boot/   etc/     lib/          mnt/     public/  selinux/    tmp/
data/   extras/  lost+found/   opt/     root/    srv/        usr/
[root@server1 ~]#_
```

Alternatively, if you have read and execute permission to a shell script, you can execute the shell script like any other executable program on the system, as shown here using the myscript shell script:

```
[root@server1 ~]# chmod a+x myscript
[root@server1 ~]# ./myscript
Fri Aug 20 11:36:58 EDT 2023
user1    tty1            2023-08-20 07:47
root     tty2            2023-08-20 11:36
bin/   dev/     home/          media/  proc/     sbin/      sys/  var/
boot/  etc/     lib/           mnt/    public/   selinux/   tmp/
data/  extras/  lost+found/    opt/    root/     srv/       usr/
[root@server1 ~]#_
```

The preceding output is difficult to read because the output from each command is not separated by blank lines or identified by a label. Using the echo command results in a more user-friendly myscript, as shown here:

```
[root@server1 ~]# cat myscript
#!/bin/bash
echo "Today's date is:"
date
echo ""
echo "The people logged into the system include:"
who
echo ""
echo "The contents of the / directory are:"
ls -F /
[root@server1 ~]# ./myscript
Today's date is:
Fri Aug 20 11:37:24 EDT 2023

The people logged into the system include:
user1    tty1            2023-08-20 07:47
root     tty2            2023-08-20 11:36

The contents of the / directory are:
bin/   dev/     home/          media/  proc/     sbin/      sys/  var/
boot/  etc/     lib/           mnt/    public/   selinux/   tmp/
data/  extras/  lost+found/    opt/    root/     srv/       usr/
[root@server1 ~]#_
```

Shell scripts are executed within subshells like most other commands on a Linux system. As a result, if your shell script needs to access environment or user variables in your current shell, those variables need to be exported. Alternatively, you could use the source command or dot (.) command to prevent your shell script from executing within a subshell; for example, the source ./myscript command (or . ./myscript command) would execute the myscript shell script in the previous example within the current shell.

Note 13

You can also use the -xv options with the bash command when executing a BASH shell script to display each command and argument executed within the shell script. This is often useful when troubleshooting shell scripts that do not function as expected. For example, you could use the bash -xv myscript command to troubleshoot myscript.

Escape Sequences

In the previous example, you used the echo command to manipulate data that appeared on the screen. The echo command also supports several special backslash notations called escape sequences. You can use escape sequences to further manipulate the way text is displayed to the terminal screen, provided the −e option is specified to the echo command. Table 7-4 provides a list of these echo escape sequences.

Table 7-4 Common echo escape sequences

Escape Sequence	Description
\0???	Inserts an ASCII character represented by a three-digit octal number (???)
\x??	Inserts an ASCII character represented by a two-digit hexadecimal number (??)
\\	Backslash
\a	ASCII beep
\b	Backspace
\c	Prevents a new line following the command
\f	Form feed
\n	Starts a new line
\r	Carriage return
\t	Horizontal tab
\v	Vertical tab

The escape sequences listed in Table 7-4 can be used to further manipulate the output of the myscript shell script used earlier, as shown in the following example:

```
[root@server1 ~]# cat myscript
#!/bin/bash
echo -e "Today's date is: \c"
date
echo -e "\nThe people logged into the system include:"
who
echo -e "\nThe contents of the / directory are:"
ls -F /
[root@server1 ~]# ./myscript
Today's date is: Fri Aug 20 11:44:24 EDT 2023

The people logged into the system include:
user1     tty1          2023-08-20 07:47
root      tty2          2023-08-20 11:36

The contents of the / directory are:
bin/     dev/      home/          media/    proc/      sbin/      sys/    var/
boot/    etc/      lib/           mnt/      public/    selinux/   tmp/
data/    extras/   lost+found/    opt/      root/      srv/       usr/
[root@server1 ~]#_
```

Notice from the preceding output that the \c escape sequence prevented the newline character at the end of the output "Today's date is:" when myscript was executed. Similarly, newline characters (\n) were inserted prior to displaying "The people logged into the system include:" and "The contents of the / directory are:" to create blank lines between command outputs. This eliminated the need for using the echo "" command shown earlier.

Reading Standard Input

At times, a shell script might need input from the user executing the program; this input can then be stored in a variable for later use. The read command takes user input from Standard Input and places it in a variable specified by an argument to the read command. After the input has been read into a variable, the contents of that variable can then be used, as shown in the following shell script:

```
[root@server1 ~]# cat newscript
#!/bin/bash
echo -e "What is your name? -->\c"
read USERNAME
echo "Hello $USERNAME"
[root@server1 ~]# chmod a+x newscript
[root@server1 ~]# ./newscript
What is your name? --> Fred
Hello Fred
[root@server1 ~]#_
```

Note from the preceding output that the echo command used to pose a question to the user ends with --> to simulate an arrow prompt on the screen and the \c escape sequence to place the cursor after the arrow prompt; this is common among Linux administrators when writing shell scripts that require user input.

Decision Constructs

Decision constructs are the most common type of construct used in shell scripts. They alter the flow of a program based on whether a command in the program completed successfully or based on a decision that the user makes in response to a question posed by the program. Figures 7-4 and 7-5 illustrate some decision constructs.

Figure 7-4   A two-question decision construct

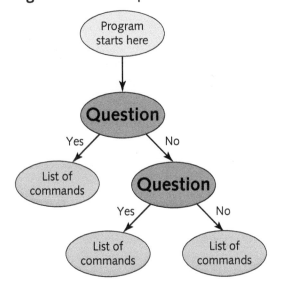

Figure 7-5 A command-based decision construct

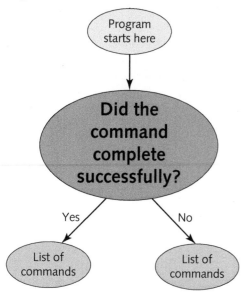

The `if` Construct

The most common type of decision construct, the `if` construct, has the following syntax:

```
if this is true
then
do these commands
elif this is true
then
do these commands
else
do these commands
fi
```

Some common rules govern `if` constructs:

1. elif (else if) and else statements are optional.
2. You can have an unlimited number of elif statements.
3. The *do these commands* section can consist of multiple commands, one per line.
4. The *do these commands* section is typically indented from the left side of the text file for readability but does not need to be.
5. The end of the statement must be a backward "if" (`fi`).
6. The *this is true* part of the if syntax shown earlier can be a command or a **test statement**:
   - Commands return true if they perform their function properly.
   - Test statements are enclosed within square brackets [ ] or prefixed by the word "test" and used to test certain conditions on the system.

In the following example, a basic `if` construct is used to ensure that the /etc/hosts file is only copied to the /etc/sample directory if that directory could be created successfully:

```
[root@server1 ~]# cat testmkdir
#!/bin/bash
if mkdir /etc/sample
then
cp /etc/hosts /etc/sample
echo "The hosts file was successfully copied to /etc/sample"
```

```
else
echo "The /etc/sample directory could not be created."
fi
[root@server1 ~]# chmod a+x testmkdir
[root@server1 ~]# ./testmkdir
The hosts file was successfully copied to /etc/sample
[root@server1 ~]#_
```

In the preceding output, the mkdir /etc/sample command is always run. If it runs success-fully, the shell script proceeds to the cp /etc/hosts /etc/sample and echo "The hosts file was successfully copied to /etc/sample" commands. If the mkdir /etc /sample command is unsuccessful, the shell script skips ahead and executes the echo "The /etc/sample directory could not be created." command. If there were more lines of text following the fi in the preceding shell script, they would be executed after the if construct, regardless of its outcome.

Note 14

For a decision construct to work, there must be a condition that returns true or false. True and false are represented by an **exit status** number within Linux systems; an exit status of 0 is true, whereas an exit status of 1-255 is false. When a command (such as mkdir /etc/sample in the previous example) finishes successfully, it returns a 0 exit status. If a command fails to execute successfully, it will return an exit status between 1 and 255, depending on how the program was written. Because all Linux commands return a true or false exit status, they can be easily used to provide the decision within a decision construct.

Often, it is useful to use the if construct to alter the flow of the program given input from the user. Recall the myscript shell script used earlier:

```
[root@server1 ~]# cat myscript
#!/bin/bash
echo -e "Today's date is: \c"
date
echo -e "\nThe people logged into the system include:"
who
echo -e "\nThe contents of the / directory are:"
ls -F /
[root@server1 ~]#_
```

To ask the user whether to display the contents of the / directory, you could use the following if construct in the myscript file:

```
[root@server1 ~]# cat myscript
#!/bin/bash
echo -e "Today's date is: \c"
date
echo -e "\nThe people logged into the system include:"
who
echo -e "\nWould you like to see the contents of /?(y/n)-->\c"
read ANSWER
if [ $ANSWER = "y" ]
then
echo -e "\nThe contents of the / directory are:"
ls -F /
fi
```

```
[root@server1 ~]# ./myscript
Today's date is: Fri Aug 20 11:47:14 EDT 2023

The people logged into the system include:
user1     tty1          2023-08-20 07:47
root      tty2          2023-08-20 11:36

Would you like to see the contents of /? (y/n)--> y

The contents of the / directory are:
bin/    dev/      home/         media/   proc/     sbin/       sys/   var/
boot/   etc/      lib/          mnt/     public/   selinux/    tmp/
data/   extras/   lost+found/   opt/     root/     srv/        usr/
[root@server1 ~]#_
```

In the preceding output, the test statement [$ANSWER = "y"] is used to test whether the contents of the ANSWER variable are equal to the letter "y." Any other character in this variable causes this test statement to return false, and the directory listing is then skipped altogether. The type of comparison used previously is called a string comparison because two values are compared for strings of characters; it is indicated by the operator of the test statement, which is the equal sign (=) in this example. Table 7-5 shows a list of common operators used in test statements and their definitions.

Note 15

The test statement [$ANSWER = "y"] is equivalent to the test statement test $ANSWER = "y".

Note 16

It is important to include a space character after the beginning square bracket and before the ending square bracket; otherwise, the test statement produces an error.

Table 7-5   Common test statements

Test Statement	Returns True If:
[A = B]	String A is equal to String B.
[A != B]	String A is not equal to String B.
[A -eq B]	A is numerically equal to B.
[A -ne B]	A is numerically not equal to B.
[A -lt B]	A is numerically less than B.
[A -gt B]	A is numerically greater than B.
[A -le B]	A is numerically less than or equal to B.
[A -ge B]	A is numerically greater than or equal to B.
[-r A]	A is a file/directory that exists and is readable (r permission).
[-w A]	A is a file/directory that exists and is writable (w permission).
[-x A]	A is a file/directory that exists and is executable (x permission).
[-f A]	A is a file that exists.
[-d A]	A is a directory that exists.

You can combine any test statement with another test statement using the comparison operators −o (OR) and −a (AND). To reverse the meaning of a test statement, you can use the ! (NOT) operator. Table 7-6 provides some examples of using these operators in test statements.

> **Note 17**
>
> One test statement can contain several −o, −a, and ! operators.

Table 7-6   Special operators in test statements

Test Statement	Returns True If:
[A = B −o C = D]	String A is equal to String B OR String C is equal to String D.
[A = B −a C = D]	String A is equal to String B AND String C is equal to String D.
[! A = B]	String A is NOT equal to String B.

By modifying the myscript shell script in the previous output, you can proceed with the directory listing if the user enters "y" or "Y," as shown in the following example:

```
[root@server1 ~]# cat myscript
#!/bin/bash
echo -e "Today's date is: \c"
date
echo -e "\nThe people logged into the system include:"
who
echo -e "\nWould you like to see the contents of /? (y/n)-->\c"
read ANSWER
if [ $ANSWER = "y" -o $ANSWER = "Y" ]
then
echo -e "\nThe contents of the / directory are:"
ls -F /
fi
[root@server1 ~]# ./myscript
Today's date is: Fri Aug 20 12:01:22 EDT 2023

The people logged into the system include:
user1    tty1          2023-08-20 07:47
root     tty2          2023-08-20 11:36

Would you like to see the contents of /? (y/n)--> Y

The contents of the / directory are:
bin/    dev/      home/        media/   proc/    sbin/      sys/  var/
boot/   etc/      lib/         mnt/     public/  selinux/   tmp/
data/   extras/   lost+found/  opt/     root/    srv/       usr/
[root@server1 ~]#_
```

The case Construct

The if construct used earlier is well suited for a limited number of choices. In the following example, which uses the myscript example presented earlier, several elif statements perform tasks based on user input:

```
[root@server1 ~]# cat myscript
#!/bin/bash
echo -e "What would you like to see?
Today's date (d)
Currently logged in users (u)
The contents of the / directory (r)

Enter your choice(d/u/r)-->\c"
read ANSWER
if [ $ANSWER = "d" -o $ANSWER = "D" ]
then
echo -e "Today's date is: \c"
date
elif [ $ANSWER = "u" -o $ANSWER = "U" ]
then
echo -e "\nThe people logged into the system include:"
who
elif [ $ANSWER = "r" -o $ANSWER = "R" ]
then
echo -e "\nThe contents of the / directory are:"
ls -F /
fi
[root@server1 ~]#_

[root@server1 ~]# ./myscript
What would you like to see?
Today's date (d)
Currently logged in users (u)
The contents of the / directory (r)

Enter your choice(d/u/r)--> d
Today's date is: Fri Aug 20 12:13:12 EDT 2023
[root@server1 ~]#_
```

The preceding shell script becomes increasingly difficult to read as the number of choices available increases. Thus, when presenting several choices, it is commonplace to use a case construct. The syntax of the case construct is as follows:

```
case variable in
pattern1  )   do these commands
              ;;
pattern2  )   do these commands
              ;;
pattern3  )   do these commands
              ;;
esac
```

The case statement compares the value of a variable with several patterns of text or numbers. When a match occurs, the commands to the right of the pattern are executed (*do these commands* in the preceding syntax). As with the `if` construct, the `case` construct must be ended by a backward "case" (esac).

An example that simplifies the previous myscript example by using the `case` construct is shown in the following output:

```
[root@server1 ~]# cat myscript
#!/bin/bash
echo -e "What would you like to see?
Today's date (d)
Currently logged in users (u)
The contents of the / directory (r)

Enter your choice(d/u/r)-->\c"
read ANSWER

case $ANSWER in
d | D ) echo -e "\nToday's date is: \c"
date
        ;;
u | U ) echo -e "\nThe people logged into the system include:"
who
        ;;
r | R ) echo -e "\nThe contents of the / directory are:"
ls -F /
        ;;
*)      echo -e "Invalid choice! \a"
        ;;
esac
[root@server1 ~]# ./myscript
What would you like to see?
Today's date (d)
Currently logged in users (u)
The contents of the / directory (r)

Enter your choice(d/u/r)--> d
Today's date is: Fri Aug 20 12:33:08 EDT 2023
[root@server1 ~]#_
```

The preceding example prompts the user with a menu and allows the user to select an item that is then placed into the ANSWER variable. If the ANSWER variable is equal to the letter "d" or "D," the `date` command is executed; however, if the ANSWER variable is equal to the letter "u" or "U," the `who` command is executed, and if the ANSWER variable is equal to the letter "r" or "R," the `ls -F /` command is executed. If the ANSWER variable contains something other than the aforementioned letters, the * wildcard metacharacter matches it and prints an error message to the screen. As with `if` constructs, any statements present in the shell script following the `case` construct are executed after the `case` construct.

The && and || Constructs

Although the `if` and `case` constructs are versatile, when only one decision needs to be made during the execution of a program, it's faster to use the && and || constructs. The syntax of these constructs is listed as follows:

```
command && command
command || command
```

For the preceding `&&` syntax, the command on the right of the `&&` construct is executed only if the command on the left of the `&&` construct completed successfully. The opposite is true for the `||` syntax; the command on the right of the `||` construct is executed only if the command on the left of the `||` construct did not complete successfully.

Consider the testmkdir example presented earlier in this chapter:

```
[root@server1 ~]# cat testmkdir
#!/bin/bash
if mkdir /etc/sample
then
cp /etc/hosts /etc/sample
echo "The hosts file was successfully copied to /etc/sample"
else
echo "The /etc/sample directory could not be created!"
fi
[root@server1 ~]#_
```

You can rewrite the preceding shell script using the `&&` construct as follows:

```
[root@server1 ~]# cat testmkdir
#!/bin/bash
mkdir /etc/sample && cp /etc/hosts /etc/sample
[root@server1 ~]#_
```

The preceding shell script creates the directory /etc/sample and only copies the /etc/hosts file to it if the `mkdir /etc/sample` command was successful. You can instead use the `||` construct to generate error messages if one of the commands fails to execute properly:

```
[root@server1 ~]# cat testmkdir
#!/bin/bash
mkdir /etc/sample || echo "Could not create /etc/sample"
cp /etc/hosts /etc/sample || echo "Could not copy /etc/hosts"
[root@server1 ~]#_
```

Loop Constructs

To execute commands repetitively, you can write shell scripts that contain loop constructs. Like decision constructs, loop constructs alter the flow of a program based on the result of a particular statement. But unlike decision constructs, which run different parts of a program depending on the results of the test statement, a loop construct simply repeats the entire program. Although several loop constructs are available within the shell, the most common are for, while, and until.

The for Construct

The for construct is the most useful looping construct for Linux administrators because it can be used to process a list of objects, such as files, directories, users, printers, and so on. The syntax of the for construct is as follows:

```
for var_name in string1   string2   string3 … …
do
these commands
done
```

When a for construct is executed, it creates a variable (var_name), sets its value equal to string1, and executes the commands between do and done, which can access the var_name variable. Next, the for construct sets the value of var_name to string2 and executes the commands between do and done again. Following this, the for construct sets the value of var_name to string3 and executes the commands between do and done again. This process repeats as long as there are strings to process. Thus, if there are three strings, the for construct will execute three times. If there are 20 strings, the for construct will execute 20 times.

The following example uses the for construct to email a list of users with a new schedule:

```
[root@server1 ~]# cat emailusers
#!/bin/bash
for NAME in bob sue mary jane frank lisa jason
do
mail -s "Your new project schedule" < newschedule $NAME
echo "$NAME was emailed successfully"
done
[root@server1 ~]#_
[root@server1 ~]# chmod a+x emailusers
[root@server1 ~]# ./emailusers
bob was emailed successfully
sue was emailed successfully
mary was emailed successfully
jane was emailed successfully
frank was emailed successfully
lisa was emailed successfully
jason was emailed successfully
[root@server1 ~]#_
```

When the for construct in the preceding example is executed, it creates a NAME variable and sets its value to bob. Then it executes the mail command to email bob the contents of the newschedule file with a subject line of Your new project schedule. Next, it sets the NAME variable to sue and executes the mail command to send sue the same email. This process is repeated until the last person receives the email.

A more common use of the for construct within shell scripts is to process several files. The following example renames each file within a specified directory to include a .txt extension.

```
[root@server1 ~]# ls stuff
file1   file2   file3   file4   file5   file6   file7   file8
[root@server1 ~]#_
[root@server1 ~]# cat multiplerename
#!/bin/bash
echo -e "What directory has the files that you would like to rename? -->\c"
read DIR
for NAME in $DIR/*
do
mv $NAME $NAME.txt
done
[root@server1 ~]#_
[root@server1 ~]# chmod a+x multiplerename
[root@server1 ~]# ./multiplerename
What directory has the files that you would like to rename? --> stuff
[root@server1 ~]# ls stuff
file1.txt   file2.txt   file3.txt   file4.txt   file5.txt   file6.txt   file7.txt
file8.txt
[root@server1 ~]#_
```

When the for construct in the previous example is executed, it sets the list of strings to stuff/* (which expands to file1 file2 file3 file4 file5 file6 file7 file8). It then creates a NAME variable, sets its value to file1, and executes the `mv` command to rename file1 to file1.txt. Next, the `for` construct sets the value of the NAME variable to file2 and executes the `mv` command to rename file2 to file2.txt. This is repeated until all the files have been processed.

You can also specify that the `for` construct should run a specific number of times by generating a list of strings using a command. The `seq command` is often used for this purpose; it generates a list of incremented integer numbers. For example, the shell script in the following output displays a message five times using a `for` loop:

```
[root@server1 ~]# seq 5
1
2
3
4
5
[root@server1 ~]#_
[root@server1 ~]# cat echorepeat
#!/bin/bash
for NUM in `seq 5`
do
      echo "All work and no play makes Jack a dull boy"
done
[root@server1 ~]# chmod a+x echorepeat
[root@server1 ~]# ./echorepeat
All work and no play makes Jack a dull boy
All work and no play makes Jack a dull boy
All work and no play makes Jack a dull boy
All work and no play makes Jack a dull boy
All work and no play makes Jack a dull boy
[root@server1 ~]#_
```

The `seq` command within the echorepeat shell script in the previous example is executed using backquotes (command substitution) and serves simply to generate a list of strings that the `for` construct will process. Also note that in the previous example, the NUM variable is not processed at all within the body of the loop.

The `while` Construct

The `while` construct is another common loop construct used within shell scripts. Unlike the `for` construct, the `while` construct begins with a test statement. As long as (or while) the test statement returns true, the commands within the loop construct are executed. When the test statement returns false, the commands within the `while` construct stop executing. A while construct typically contains a variable, called a counter variable, whose value changes each time through the loop. For the `while` construct to work properly, it must be set up so that when the counter variable reaches a certain value, the test statement returns false. This prevents the loop from executing indefinitely.

The syntax of the `while` construct is as follows:

```
while this returns true
do
these commands
done
```

The following example illustrates the general use of the `while` construct.

```
[root@server1 ~]# cat echorepeat
#!/bin/bash
COUNTER=0
```

```
while [ $COUNTER -lt 7 ]
do
        echo "All work and no play makes Jack a dull boy" >> /tmp/redrum
        COUNTER=`expr $COUNTER + 1`
done
[root@server1 ~]#_
[root@server1 ~]# ./echorepeat
[root@server1 ~]# cat /tmp/redrum
All work and no play makes Jack a dull boy
All work and no play makes Jack a dull boy
All work and no play makes Jack a dull boy
All work and no play makes Jack a dull boy
All work and no play makes Jack a dull boy
All work and no play makes Jack a dull boy
All work and no play makes Jack a dull boy
[root@server1 ~]#_
```

The preceding echorepeat shell script creates a counter variable called COUNTER and sets its value to 0. Next, the while construct uses a test statement to determine whether the value of the COUNTER variable is less than 7 before executing the commands within the loop. Because the initial value of COUNTER variable is 0, it appends the text "All work and no play makes Jack a dull boy" to the /tmp/redrum file and increments the value of the COUNTER variable to 1. Note the backquotes surrounding the expr command, which are required to numerically add 1 to the COUNTER variable $(0 + 1 = 1)$. Because the value of the COUNTER variable at this stage (1) is still less than 7, the while construct executes the commands again. This process repeats until the value of the COUNTER variable is equal to 8.

Note 18

You can use true or : in place of a test statement to create a while construct that executes indefinitely.

The until Construct

The until construct is simply the opposite of the while construct; it begins with a test statement, and the commands within the loop construct are executed until the test statement returns true. As a result, the until construct typically contains a counter variable and has nearly the same syntax as the while construct:

```
until this returns true
do
these commands
done
```

For example, the following until construct would be equivalent to the while construct in the previous example:

```
[root@server1 ~]# cat echorepeat
#!/bin/bash
COUNTER=0
until [ $COUNTER -eq 7 ]
do
        echo "All work and no play makes Jack a dull boy" >> /tmp/redrum
        COUNTER=`expr $COUNTER + 1`
done
[root@server1 ~]#_
```

Special Variables

As shown in previous examples, variables are often used within shell scripts to hold information for processing by commands and constructs. However, there are some special variables that are useful specifically for shell scripts, including shell expansion variables, array variables, positional parameters, and built-in variables.

Shell Expansion Variables

Normally, the $ metacharacter is used to expand the results of a user or environment variable in shell memory. However, you can also use the $ metacharacter alongside regular brackets to perform command substitution using the $(command) syntax. While this functionality is identical to using backquotes, it is more common to see shell expansion variable syntax for performing command substitution within a shell script as it is easier to read. Take, for example, the shell script used in the previous example:

```
[root@server1 ~]# cat echorepeat
#!/bin/bash
COUNTER=0
until [ $COUNTER -eq 7 ]
do
    echo "All work and no play makes Jack a dull boy" >> /tmp/redrum
    COUNTER=`expr $COUNTER + 1`
done
[root@server1 ~]#_
```

The expr $COUNTER + 1 command is performed using backquote command substitution. The following example is the same shell script written using a shell expansion variable:

```
[root@server1 ~]# cat echorepeat
#!/bin/bash
COUNTER=0
until [ $COUNTER -eq 7 ]
do
    echo "All work and no play makes Jack a dull boy" >> /tmp/redrum
    COUNTER=$(expr $COUNTER + 1)
done
[root@server1 ~]#_
```

You can also use shell expansion to perform variable substitution; simply use curly braces instead of regular brackets. For example, to return variable names in memory that match a certain pattern, you could use the ${!pattern} syntax. The following example returns any variable names that start with HOST:

```
[root@server1 ~]# echo ${!HOST*}
HOSTNAME HOSTTYPE
[root@server1 ~]#_
```

Alternatively, you could use the ${VAR:=value} syntax to create a variable as well as return its value as shown in the example below:

```
[root@server1 ~]# echo ${MYVAR:="This is a sample variable"}
This is a sample variable
[root@server1 ~]#_
```

Array Variables

The user-defined variables shown in previous shell script examples contained a single value, regardless of whether that value was a string or a number. However, you can create variables that contain multiple values at different numbered positions, starting from 0. These are called array variables and are an efficient way for storing information that must be referenced throughout a shell script. The following example illustrates the use of a MYVAR array variable that contains three different values:

```
[root@server1 ~]# cat arraytest
#!/bin/bash
MYVAR=("one" 2 "three")
echo The first value is: ${MYVAR[0]}
echo The second value is: ${MYVAR[1]}
echo The third value is: ${MYVAR[2]}
echo -e "\nChanging values\n"
MYVAR[0]=1
MYVAR[1]="two"
MYVAR[2]=3
echo The first value is: ${MYVAR[0]}
echo The second value is: ${MYVAR[1]}
echo The third value is: ${MYVAR[2]}
[root@server1 ~]# chmod a+x arraytest
[root@server1 ~]# ./arraytest
The first value is one
The second value is 2
The third value is three

Changing values

The first value is 1
The second value is two
The third value is 3
[root@server1 ~]#_
```

Positional Parameters

A shell script can take arguments when it is executed on the command line; these arguments are called positional parameters and may be referenced using special variables within the shell script itself. The special variable $1 refers to the contents of the first argument, $2 refers to the contents of the second argument, $3 refers to the contents of the third argument, and so on. If there are more than nine arguments, then you can use curly braces to indicate the appropriate positional parameter; for example, ${10} refers to the contents of the tenth argument. The special variable $0 refers to the command itself.

The following example illustrates the use of positional parameters:

```
[root@server1 ~]# cat pptest
#!/bin/bash
echo The command you typed was: $0
echo The first argument you typed was: $1
echo The second argument you typed was: $2
echo The third argument you typed was: $3
[root@server1 ~]# chmod a+x pptest
[root@server1 ~]# ./pptest
The command you typed was: ./pptest
```

```
The first argument you typed was:
The second argument you typed was:
The third argument you typed was:
[root@server1 ~]# ./pptest one two three
The command you typed was: ./pptest
The first argument you typed was: one
The second argument you typed was: two
The third argument you typed was: three
[root@server1 ~]#_
```

Using positional parameters is an efficient alternative to prompting the user for input. For example, you could modify the testmkdir shell script described earlier in this chapter to instead use two positional parameters that specify the source file and target directory. Each time the script is run, different arguments can be specified to perform different actions, as shown in the following output:

```
[root@server1 ~]# cat testmkdir
#!/bin/bash
#This script requires two arguments: <file> and <target directory>
if mkdir $2
then
cp $1 $2
echo "The $1 file was successfully copied to $2"
else
echo "The $2 directory could not be created."
fi
[root@server1 ~]#_
[root@server1 ~]# ./testmkdir /etc/hosts /etc/sample
The /etc/hosts file was successfully copied to /etc/sample
[root@server1 ~]# ./testmkdir /etc/issue /var
mkdir: cannot create directory '/var': File exists
The /var directory could not be created.
[root@server1 ~]# ./testmkdir /etc/issue /var/backup
The /etc/issue file was successfully copied to /var/backup
[root@server1 ~]#_
```

Built-in Variables

Many built-in special shell variables are useful within shell scripts; the most common are shown in Table 7-7. To demonstrate the use of some of these built-in variables, let's examine the following output of the addtxt shell script that accepts filename arguments, renames each filename to end with .txt, and displays the results:

Table 7-7 Special built-in shell variables

Variable	Return Value
$#	The number of positional parameters
$*	All positional parameter values
$@	
$?	Exit status of the last foreground process
$$	Process ID (PID) of the current shell
$!	Process ID (PID) of the last background process
$-	Flags set in the current shell

```
[root@server1 ~]# ls
addtxt file1  file2  file3  file4  file5
[root@server1 ~]#_
[root@server1 ~]# cat addtxt
#!/bin/bash
if [ $# -eq 0 ]
then
echo You must enter at least one filename to rename as an argument.
exit 255
fi

for NAME in $@
do
mv $NAME $NAME.txt
echo $NAME was successfully renamed $NAME.txt >>/tmp/$$.tmp
done

cat /tmp/$$
rm -f /tmp/$$
[root@server1 ~]#_
[root@server1 ~]# chmod a+x addtxt
[root@server1 ~]# ./addtxt
You must enter at least one filename to rename as an argument.
[root@server1 ~]# echo $?
255
[root@server1 ~]# ./addtxt file1 file2 file3
file1 was successfully renamed file1.txt
file2 was successfully renamed file2.txt
file3 was successfully renamed file3.txt
[root@server1 ~]# echo $?
0
[root@server1 ~]# ls
addtxt file1.txt  file2.txt  file3.txt  file4  file5
[root@server1 ~]#_
```

The if decision construct at the beginning of the shell script checks to see if the number of positional parameters ($#) is equal to 0; if it is, then a message is printed indicating the proper use of the shell script and the shell script stops executing, returning a false exit status (exit 255). If the decision construct evaluates as false, then a for loop construct processes the list of filenames specified as arguments ($@) and renames each filename to end with .txt. It also appends a line to a file in the /tmp directory named for the process ID of the current shell ($$), which is likely to be unique within the /tmp directory. Finally, the shell script displays the contents of the /tmp/$$ file to indicate which files were renamed, and then the shell script completes successfully, returning a true exit status.

Functions

Some shell scripts contain specific commands and constructs that are used in various places throughout the shell script. To save time typing these commands and constructs each time they are needed, you can create a shell function that contains the appropriate commands and constructs at the beginning of the shell script. Each time you need to perform these commands and constructs throughout the shell script, you can execute the shell function with a single command. Much like aliases, a shell function is simply a special variable that contains one or more commands that are executed when you execute (or call) the shell function. However, functions can also accept positional parameters that refer to the arguments specified when the function is executed (or called). The BASH shell has several shell functions built into it that you have used throughout the book, including cd, exit, and help.

The shell script in the following output uses a function called createdir that creates a directory after checking whether it exists:

```
[root@server1 ~]# ls -F
functionscript
[root@server1 ~]# cat functionscript
#!/bin/bash

function createdir(){
  if  [ ! -d $1 ]
  then
    mkdir $1
  else
    echo Directory $1 already exists. Exiting script.
    exit 255
  fi
}

createdir dir1
createdir dir2
createdir dir3
[root@server1 ~]# ls
Functionscript  dir1/  dir2/  dir3/
[root@server1 ~]#_
```

Note 19

You can omit the word `function` in the example above and the resulting function would still be created.

In the previous example, the `createdir` function was called three times, each with a different, single argument that was associated with the first positional parameter within the function ($1).

Functions are special variables that are stored in memory; to view the functions in your shell, you can use the `set` command. To make a function available to subshells you can use the `export -f functionname` command, and view exported functions using the `env` command. To remove a function from your shell, use the `unset -f functionname` command.

As you create more shell scripts, you may find yourself using the same functions again and again. To save time, add these functions to a single shell script that contains functions only; this shell script is commonly called a **function library**. You can then use the `source` or dot (.) command to execute this function library at the beginning of each shell script that you create in order to re-create all of the functions within the function library within the shell, executing your shell script as shown below:

```
[root@server1 ~]# cat /etc/functionlibrary
#!/bin/bash
function createdir(){
  if  [ ! -d $1 ]
  then
    mkdir $1
  else
```

```
      echo Directory $1 already exists. Exiting script.
      exit 255
   fi
}
function helloworld(){
   echo Hello World
}
[root@server1 ~]# cat newscript
#!/bin/bash
source /etc/functionlibrary

createdir lala
createdir music
createdir notes
helloworld
[root@server1 ~]#_
```

Version Control Using Git

Version control is a system that keeps track of the changes that you make to files that you create, such as shell scripts, by tracking changes made to the files over time. If you create changes that you later find undesirable, it allows you to revert a file to a previous state easily, and if you work collaboratively on files with others, it allows you to see who made changes at different times.

Git is the most common open source version control system used today; it was originally designed in 2005 by Linus Torvalds to aid in making changes to the Linux kernel source code, and is primarily used to provide version control for software development projects on Linux, UNIX, macOS, and Windows computers. Git performs version control by taking snapshots of what your files look like at different points in time. Each snapshot is called a commit, and includes the changes made to the files since the previous commit to allow you to undo or compare changes made to your files over time.

While Git can perform version control for files on your local computer, it also allows you to maintain version control for files that you work on collaboratively with others. Moreover, Git does not require constant Internet access for collaboration; each user downloads an original copy of the files (a process called cloning), and then creates commits periodically after making key changes to the files. These commits can then be pushed back to the original location, where they can be merged into the original copy or pulled to other cloned copies that others are working on.

The files and the associated commits that are managed by Git are stored in a directory called a Git repository (or Git repo). Any computer running Git can host Git repos that can be cloned to other computers running Git across the Internet. Many servers on the Internet provide free Git repo hosting, including GitHub.com.

Note 20

GitHub.com hosts the source code for most open source software projects today. Software developers that wish to contribute to an existing open source software project on GitHub.com can clone the associated repository, modify the cloned source code, and commit the changes. Following this, they can create a pull request on GitHub.com to request that their changes be reviewed for possible inclusion by the maintainers of the open source software project.

By default, any changes you make to an original or cloned Git repo are said to be made to the main branch (formerly called the master branch). To make collaboration easier, each user that clones a Git repo can create a separate branch to store just the changes that they are experimenting with; they would make all of their commits within this branch instead of the main branch. This branch (and the related commits) can then be pushed back to the original repo and merged into the main branch or pulled down to other computers that are also working on the same branch.

Nearly all Git management is performed using the `git command`. Before you use Git to provide version control for your files, you must first provide information about yourself that Git will use when tracking changes made to the files themselves. Additionally, you should choose the name of your main branch, since the default name may be different on different systems. All of this configuration will be stored in the ~/.gitconfig file. The following output configures a user name (Jason Eckert), user email address (jason@lala.com), and main branch name (main):

```
[root@server1 ~]# git config --global user.name "Jason Eckert"
[root@server1 ~]# git config --global user.email "jason@lala.com"
[root@server1 ~]# git config --global init.defaultBranch main
[root@server1 ~]# cat ~/.gitconfig
[user]
        email = jason@lala.com
        name = Jason Eckert
[init]
        defaultBranch = main
[root@server1 ~]#_
```

Next, you must ensure that the files you want Git to provide version control for are within a directory, and that the directory is labelled as a Git repo using the `git init` command. This creates a hidden .git subdirectory that stores all information about the Git repo, including future commits. In the following output, a Git repo is created from the /scripts directory, which contains three shell scripts:

```
[root@server1 ~]# ls -aF /scripts
./  ../  script1.sh*  script2.sh*  script3.sh*
[root@server1 ~]# cd /scripts
[root@server1 scripts]# git init
Initialized empty Git repository in /scripts/.git/
[root@server1 scripts]# ls -aF
./  ../  .git/  script1.sh*  script2.sh*  script3.sh*
[root@server1 scripts]# git status
On branch main

No commits yet

Untracked files:
  (use "git add <file>…" to include in what will be committed)
    script1.sh
    script2.sh
    script3.sh

nothing added to commit but untracked files present (use "git add"
to track)
[root@server1 scripts]#_
```

Note from the previous output that the `git status` command indicates that the three shell scripts are not currently being tracked by Git for version control; this is because Git does not assume that all files in the directory should be automatically added to the version control. Instead, you must specify which files should be version tracked by adding those files to a Git index using the `git add` command (this process is called staging). You can specify individual files by filename, specify multiple files using wildcard metacharacters, or specify all of the files in the current directory (.). After the necessary files have been staged, you can use the `git commit` command to create a snapshot of them with a suitable description (e.g., My first commit), as shown in the following output:

```
[root@server1 scripts]# git add .
[root@server1 scripts]# git status
On branch main

No commits yet

Changes to be committed:
   (use "git rm --cached <file>…" to unstage)
      new file:   script1.sh
      new file:   script2.sh
      new file:   script3.sh
[root@server1 scripts]# git commit -m "My first commit"
[main (root-commit) 07a2ada] My first commit
 3 files changed, 40 insertions(+)
 create mode 100755 script1.sh
 create mode 100755 script2.sh
 create mode 100755 script3.sh
[root@server1 scripts]#_
```

Note 21

To exclude files within your Git repo from being staged, add their filenames (or wildcard matches) to a .gitignore file; this allows you to safely use the `git add.` command shown in the previous output without inadvertently adding any unnecessary files.

Now, you can modify one or more of the scripts, stage the modified scripts, and create a snapshot of them. The following output demonstrates this process with script3.sh:

```
[root@server1 scripts]# vi script3.sh
[root@server1 scripts]# git status
On branch main
Changes not staged for commit:
   (use "git add <file>…" to update what will be committed)
   (use "git restore <file>…" to discard changes in working directory)
      modified:   script3.sh

no changes added to commit (use "git add" and/or "git commit -a")
[root@server1 scripts]# git add script3.sh
[root@server1 scripts]# git commit -m "Added comment to script3.sh"
[main d49d100] Added comment to script3.sh
 1 file changed, 1 insertion(+)
[root@server1 scripts]#_
```

To see a list of all modifications to files within your Git repo, you can use the `git log` command; the word HEAD is used to refer to the most recent commit in the output. To revert to a previous version of files within a commit, you can use the `git reset --hard` command alongside the first seven digits (or more) of the commit number as shown below:

```
[root@server1 scripts]# git log
commit d49d10096e7a6a1aff0cc4cfbbc6068f85d24210 (HEAD -> main)
Author: Jason Eckert <jason@lala.com>
Date:   Wed Sep 14 19:04:45 2023 -0400
```

```
    Added comment to script3.sh

commit 07a2ada8fa01559696b27bcdbc4d6ca34effcc80
Author: Jason Eckert <jason@lala.com>
Date:   Wed Sep 14 19:01:35 2023 -0400

    My first commit
[root@server1 scripts]# git reset --hard 07a2ada
HEAD is now at 07a2ada My first commit
[root@server1 scripts]# git log
commit 07a2ada8fa01559696b27bcdbc4d6ca34effcc80 (HEAD -> main)
Author: Jason Eckert <jason@lala.com>
Date:   Wed Sep 14 19:01:35 2023 -0400

    My first commit
[root@server1 scripts]#_
```

Instead of working with commit numbers, you can tag each commit you create with a friendlier label. For example, after creating a commit, you can use the `git tag v1.0` command to give the commit a label of v1.0. Following this, you can use `git reset --hard v1.0` to revert your repo to that commit.

You can also use Git to perform version control for other users that need to modify the scripts in the /scripts directory. Say, for example, that a user named Bob on the same system needs to modify the scripts within the /scripts directory. Bob can run the `git clone` command to download a copy of the /scripts repo to his current directory as shown in the following output:

```
[Bob@server1 ~]$ git clone /scripts
Cloning into 'scripts'…
done.
[Bob@server1 ~]$ cd scripts
[Bob@server1 scripts]$ pwd
/home/Bob/scripts
[Bob@server1 scripts]$ ls -aF
./  ../  .git/  script1.sh*  script2.sh*  script3.sh*
[Bob@server1 scripts]$_
```

Note 22

To download a Git repo from a remote computer, you must additionally supply the hostname of the remote computer, and a user name with access to the Git repo on that computer. For example, `git clone root@server1:/scripts` could be used to download the /scripts repo from server1 as the root user (you will be prompted for root's password).

Note 23

After a repo has been cloned, the location of the original repo is referred to as "origin" from that point onwards within Git commands.

Bob can then create a new branch to perform and test his modifications without affecting the original cloned scripts within the main branch. For example, to create and switch to a new branch called AddErrorChecks, and then view the results, Bob could run the following commands:

```
[Bob@server1 scripts]$ git checkout -b AddErrorChecks
Switched to a new branch 'AddErrorChecks'
```

```
[Bob@server1 scripts]$ git branch
* AddErrorChecks
  main
[Bob@server1 scripts]$_
```

The * character next to AddErrorChecks in the previous output of the git branch command indicates that it is the current branch being used. Next, Bob can modify script2.sh in the AddErrorChecks branch, and test the results. Once Bob is satisfied that the modifications work as expected, he could stage and commit script2.sh within the AddErrorChecks branch as shown below:

```
[Bob@server1 scripts]$ git add script2.sh
[Bob@server1 scripts]$ git status
On branch AddErrorChecks
Changes to be committed:
  (use "git restore --staged <file>…" to unstage)
      modified:   script2.sh
[Bob@server1 scripts]$ git commit -m "Added error checks to script2.sh"
[AddErrorChecks 0a04625] Added error checks to script2.sh
 1 file changed, 19 additions(-)
[Bob@server1 scripts]$_
```

If Bob switched to the main branch at this point using the git checkout main command and then viewed the contents of script2.sh, he would not see his modifications, as they were performed only within the AddErrorChecks branch. By creating and using a separate branch called AddErrorChecks, Bob separated his modifications from the main branch. The AddErrorChecks branch can then easily be pushed back to the original repo (/scripts) as shown below:

```
[Bob@server1 scripts]$ git push origin AddErrorChecks
Enumerating objects: 5, done.
Counting objects: 100% (5/5), done.
Delta compression using up to 4 threads
Compressing objects: 100% (3/3), done.
Writing objects: 100% (3/3), 344 bytes | 344.00 KiB/s, done.
Total 3 (delta 1), reused 0 (delta 0), pack-reused 0
To /scripts/
 * [new branch]      AddErrorChecks -> AddErrorChecks
[Bob@server1 scripts]$_
```

The user that manages the original /scripts repo (in our example, root) can then use git show to view the changes Bob made within the branch, as well as merge the branch into the original repo's main branch using the following commands:

```
[root@server1 scripts]# git branch
  AddErrorChecks
* main
[root@server1 scripts]# git show AddErrorChecks
<<<lengthy output omitted>>>
[root@server1 scripts]# git merge AddErrorChecks
Updating 07a2ada..0a04625
Fast-forward
 script2.sh | 1 -
 1 file changed, 1 deletion(-)
[root@server1 scripts]#_
```

At this point, other users with a cloned repo can pull the updated copy of the main branch from the original repo; for example, Bob can pull the updated copy of the main branch from the original repo using the following command:

```
[Bob@server1 scripts]$ git pull origin main
From /scripts
 * branch              main        -> FETCH_HEAD
   07a2ada..0a04625   main        -> origin/main
Already up to date.
[Bob@server1 scripts]$_
```

Following this, Bob can repeat this process by creating additional branches to experiment with script modifications, pushing them to the original repo where they can be merged into the main branch, and then pulling updated copies of the original main branch.

In practice, software developers often create several commits in a branch over a long period of time while other changes are being committed or merged into the main branch. In this case, periodically using git rebase to move the branch ahead of the most recent commit in the main branch will make git log output easier to read. For example, if Bob is working in the AddErrorChecks branch for a long period of time, he can run git rebase AddErrorChecks main to ensure that the AddErrorChecks branch is listed first in the output of the git log command.

Table 7-8 lists common commands for use in Git version control.

Table 7-8   Common Git commands

Command	Description
git config	Sets general Git parameters
git init	Creates a Git repo within the current directory
git clone *pathname*	Clones a local Git repo (specified by absolute or relative pathname) to the current directory
git clone *username@hostname:pathname*	Clones a remote Git repo to the current directory
git clone https://*website/username/repo*.git	Clones a remote Git repo hosted on a website (e.g., GitHub.com) to the current directory
git add *filenames*	Adds files to a Git index
git rm *filenames*	Removes files from a Git index
git commit -m *description*	Creates a commit with the specified description from the files listed in the Git index
git tag *label*	Adds a label to the most recent commit
git tag -a *label* -m *description*	Adds a label and description to the most recent commit
git show *commit*	Displays the changes within a commit (specified by either commit number or label)
git status	Views repo status
git log	Views commit history for the current branch
git checkout -b *branch*	Creates a new branch and switches to it
git checkout *branch*	Switches to a different branch
git branch	Views branches in the repo
git branch -d *branch*	Deletes a branch
git push origin *branch*	Pushes a branch to the original repo location
git pull origin *branch*	Pulls a branch from the original repo location
git reset --hard *commit*	Reverts files within a repo to a previous commit (specified by either commit number or label)
git rebase *branch* main	Relocates the commit history of a branch to the end of the main branch

The Z Shell

While BASH is the default shell on most Linux systems, there are other shells that you can install and use. Of these other shells, the Z shell is the most common, and a superset of the BASH shell. Thus, if you understand how to work within a BASH shell and create BASH shell scripts, you can easily work within a Z shell and create Z shell scripts. The redirection, piping, variable, and shell scripting concepts discussed in this chapter work identically in Z shell with only three exceptions:

- Z Shell scripts use a hashpling of #!/bin/zsh
- The values within Z shell array variables are numbered starting from 1 (instead of 0 as in the BASH shell)
- The Z shell uses different environment files compared to BASH

Most Z shell configuration is stored in the /etc/zshrc and ~/.zshrc environment files, which are functionally equivalent to the /etc/bashrc and ~/.bashrc environment files used by the BASH shell. Other environment files that can be used by the Z shell (if present) include /etc/zshenv, /etc/zprofile, /etc/zlogin, ~/.zshenv, ~/.zprofile, and ~/.zlogin.

Like the BASH shell, the Z shell provides a # prompt for the root user. However, regular users receive a % prompt within the Z shell. If your default shell is BASH, you can run the zsh command within an existing BASH shell to start a Z shell. To change the default shell for your user account to the Z shell, you can use the chsh command. For example, chsh -s /bin/zsh would modify your default shell to the Z shell.

In addition to the features provided by the BASH shell, the Z shell includes flexible redirection and piping, as well as special Z shell options, modules, function libraries, plugins, and themes.

> **Note 24**
>
> The Z shell is the default shell on some Linux distributions and UNIX flavors, including Kali Linux and macOS.

> **Note 25**
>
> The first time you start a Z shell, the zsh-newuser-install function is executed and prompts you to configure the contents of ~/.zshrc.

Flexible Redirection and Piping

Using the Z shell, you can redirect Standard Input from multiple files, as well as redirect Standard Output and Standard Error to multiple files. For example, to combine the sorted results of file1 and file2 into a new file called sortedresults, you can run the sort <file1 <file2 >sortedresults command. Similarly, you can run the df -hT >file1 >file2 command to save a report of mounted filesystems to both file1 and file2.

You can also use Standard Output and Standard Error redirection within a pipe, eliminating the need for the tee command. For example, to save a report of mounted filesystems to file1 and a report of mounted ext4 filesystems to file2, you can run the df -hT >file1 | grep ext4 >file2 command.

Standard Input redirection can also be used in the Z shell to view text files. For example, running the <file1 command within the Z shell will open file1 using the more command.

Z Shell Options

The Z shell provides many different shell options that you can set within your ~/.zshrc file to control shell features such as auto-completion, file globbing, command history, input/output processing, shell emulation, and function handling.

Two commonly used Z shell options are *autocd* and *correct*. You can set these two options by adding the setopt autocd correct line to your ~/.zshrc file. The *autocd* option allows you to switch to a subdirectory in your Z shell without using the cd command. For example, to switch to the Documents subdirectory under your current directory, you can type Documents at the Z shell prompt and press Enter. The *correct* option allows the Z shell to recommend replacements for misspelled commands, as shown in the following example:

```
[user1@server1]~% cla
zsh: correct 'cla' to 'cal' [nyae]? y
    November 2023
Su Mo Tu We Th Fr Sa
          1  2  3  4
 5  6  7  8  9 10 11
12 13 14 15 16 17 18
19 20 21 22 23 24 25
26 27 28 29 30
[user1@server1]~%_
```

Note 26

After editing the ~/.zshrc file, you must obtain a new Z shell, or run either the source ~/.zshrc or . ~/.zshrc command for the changes to take effect.

Z Shell Modules

The Z shell also includes several built-in commands that aren't available in the BASH shell. Moreover, you can choose which built-in commands are available in the Z shell by loading the appropriate modules. To view the modules currently loaded in your Z shell, you can use the zmodload command without arguments, as shown here:

```
[user1@server1]~% zmodload
zsh/complete
zsh/main
zsh/parameter
zsh/stat
zsh/zle
zsh/zutil
[user1@server1]~%_
```

You can also use the zmodload command to load additional Z shell modules. The following example loads the *zsh/datetime* module, which includes the strftime built-in Z shell command that displays formatted time and date information:

```
[user1@server1]~% zmodload zsh/datetime
[user1@server1]~% strftime "%a %d %b %y %T %z"
Sun 01 Nov 26 08:57:08 -0500
[user1@server1]~%_
```

To ensure that the *zsh/datetime* module is loaded alongside the default Z shell modules each time you start a Z shell, add the line `zmodload zsh/datetime` to your ~/.zshrc file.

Z Shell Function Libraries

The Z shell searches for function libraries under directories specified by the $fpath variable. If you add a function library file called mylibrary to one of these directories, you can add the line `autoload -U mylibrary && mylibrary` to your ~/.zshrc file to ensure that each new Z shell loads and executes the functions within the mylibrary file.

Additionally, there are many default function libraries located within the $fpath directories, such as the *compinit* function library that extends the built-in Tab-completion feature to also include command options and arguments. For example, if you press Tab after - following the `lsblk` command, you will be presented with the available options for the command:

```
[user1@server1]~% lsblk -
--all        -a  -- print all devices
--ascii      -i  -- output ascii characters only
--dedup      -E  -- de-duplicate output by specified column
--discard    -D  -- output discard capabilities
--exclude    -e  -- exclude devices by major number
--fs         -f  -- output info about filesystems
--help       -h  -- display help information
--include    -I  -- show only devices with specified major numbers
--inverse    -s  -- reverse dependency order
--json       -J  -- use JSON output format
```

If the available options are POSIX options (e.g.`--include`), you can also use the Tab key to autocomplete the option name after typing the first few letters. For complex commands that require specific option combinations, you'll be prompted to select required options before selecting secondary options. You can also use the Tab key to autocomplete arguments for commands that accept a predefined list of arguments.

To ensure that the *compinit* function library is loaded and executed each time you start a new Z shell, add the line `autoload -U compinit && compinit` to your ~/.zshrc file.

> **Note 27**
>
> For a full list of Z Shell options, modules, and function libraries available, visit zsh.sourceforge.io.

Z Shell Plugins and Themes

The Z shell provides the ability for developers to create custom plugins that provide for advanced functionality, such as integrating Git features, or displaying the current weather using symbols within the Z shell prompt. Developers can also create custom themes that modify the look and feel of the Z shell prompt and terminal window. To search for and install Z shell plugins and themes, follow the instructions online at github.com/ohmyzsh/ohmyzsh. At the time of this writing, there are over 250 plugins and 150 themes available for the Z shell. Once you install the appropriate plugins and themes on your system, you must list the plugins and themes you wish to use in your ~/.zshrc file.

Summary

- Three components are available to commands: Standard Input (stdin), Standard Output (stdout), and Standard Error (stderr). Not all commands use every component.
- Standard Input is typically user input taken from the keyboard, whereas Standard Output and Standard Error are sent to the terminal screen by default.
- You can redirect the Standard Output and Standard Error of a command to a file using redirection symbols. Similarly, you can use redirection symbols to redirect a file to the Standard Input of a command.
- To redirect the Standard Output from one command to the Standard Input of another, you must use the pipe symbol (|).
- Most variables available to the shell are environment variables that are loaded into memory after login from environment files.
- You can create your own variables in the shell and export them to programs started by the shell. These variables can also be placed in environment files, so that they are loaded into memory on every shell login.
- The umask variable and command aliases are special variables that must be set using a certain command.
- Shell scripts can be used to execute several Linux commands.
- Decision constructs can be used within shell scripts to execute certain Linux commands based on user input or the results of a certain command.
- Loop constructs can be used within shell scripts to execute a series of commands repetitively.
- Special variables can be used within shell scripts to access built-in shell information, access positional parameters, and to expand commands and variables.
- Functions can be created within a shell script to store commands and constructs for later execution. Function libraries are shell scripts that only contain functions; they can be run at the beginning of other shell scripts to provide a rich set of functions.
- Git can be used to provide version control for files on your system that are modified over time, including shell scripts. These files are stored as a main branch within a Git repository that can be cloned to other computers for collaboration. Git users can create additional branches to test file modifications before merging them into the main branch.
- After changes are made to files within a Git repo, they are normally staged and added to a commit that provides a snapshot of the files at that time. You can revert files to a previous state by referencing the associated commit.
- The Z shell is a superset of BASH with flexible redirection and piping. It provides additional shell features using specific options, modules, function libraries, plugins, and themes.

Key Terms

alias command
array variable
branch
chsh command
cloning
commit
counter variable
decision construct
dot (.) command
echo command
env command
environment file
environment variable

escape sequence
exit status
export command
expr command
file descriptors
filter
function
function library
Git
git command
Git repo
Git repository
hashpling

here document
history command
loop construct
main branch
master branch
pipe
positional parameter
printenv command
pull request
read command
redirection
seq command
set command

shebang	subshell	variable identifier
shell script	test statement	version control
`source` command	`tr` command	Z shell
staging	`unalias` command	`zmodload` command
Standard Error (stderr)	`unset` command	`zsh` command
Standard Input (stdin)	user-defined variables	
Standard Output (stdout)	variable	

Review Questions

1. Because stderr and stdout represent the results of a command and stdin represents the input required for a command, only stderr and stdout can be redirected to/from a file.

   a. True
   b. False

2. Before a user-defined variable can be used by processes that run in subshells, that variable must be _____.

   a. imported
   b. validated by running the `env` command
   c. exported
   d. redirected to the shell

3. Both aliases and functions can be used to store commands that can be executed, but functions can also accept positional parameters.

   a. True
   b. False

4. Which of the following files is always executed immediately after any user logs in to a Linux system and receives a BASH shell?

   a. /etc/profile
   b. ~/.bash_profile
   c. ~/.bash_login
   d. ~/.profile

5. Which command could you use to see a list of all environment and user-defined shell variables as well as their current values?

   a. `ls /var`
   b. `env`
   c. `set`
   d. `echo`

6. Every `if` construct begins with `if` and must be terminated with .

   a. `end`
   b. `endif`

   c. `stop`
   d. `fi`

7. Which of the following will display the message `welcome home` if the `cd /home/user1` command is successfully executed?

   a. `cd /home/user1 && echo "welcome home"`
   b. `cat "welcome home" || cd /home/user1`
   c. `cd /home/user1 || cat "welcome home"`
   d. `echo "welcome home" && cd /home/user1`

8. The current value for the HOME variable is displayed by which of the following commands? (Choose all that apply.)

   a. `echo HOME=`
   b. `echo ~`
   c. `echo $HOME`
   d. `echo ls HOME`

9. Which of the following variables could access the value "/etc" within the sample shell script, if the sample shell script was executed using the `bash sample /var /etc /bin` command?

   a. $0
   b. $1
   c. $2
   d. $3

10. Which of the following operators reverses the meaning of a test statement?

    a. `#!`
    b. `-o`
    c. `-a`
    d. `!`

11. What would be the effect of using the `alias` command to make an alias for the `date` command named `cat` in honor of your favorite pet?

a. It cannot be done because there already is an environment variable cat associated with the `cat` command.

b. It cannot be done because there already is a command `cat` on the system.

c. When you use the `cat` command at the command prompt with the intention of viewing a text file, the date appears instead.

d. There is no effect until the alias is imported because it is a user-declared variable.

12. How do you indicate a comment line in a shell script?

a. There are no comment lines in a shell script.

b. Begin the line with #!.

c. Begin the line with !.

d. Begin the line with #.

13. You have redirected stderr to a file called Errors. You view the contents of this file afterward and notice that there are six error messages. After repeating the procedure, you notice that there are only two error messages in this file. Why?

a. After you open the file and view the contents, the contents are lost.

b. The system generated different stdout.

c. You did not append the stderr to the Error file, and, as a result, it was overwritten when the command was run a second time.

d. You must specify a new file each time you redirect because the system creates the specified file by default.

14. The `sed` and `awk` commands are filter commands commonly used to format data within a pipe.

a. True

b. False

15. A user attempts to perform the `git commit -m "Added listdir function"` but the command fails. What are possible reasons for the failure? (Choose all that apply.)

a. The user performing the commit has not set their Git user information.

b. No files were added to the Git index beforehand.

c. The user performing the commit is not running the command from within the Git repo directory.

d. The main branch was not specified within the command itself.

16. Which of the following lines can be used to perform command substitution within a shell script? (Choose all that apply.)

a. `'command'`

b. `${command}`

c. `${!command}`

d. `$(command)`

17. Which construct can be used in a shell script to read stdin and place it in a variable?

a. `read`

b. `sum`

c. `verify`

d. `test`

18. A `for` construct is a loop construct that processes a specified list of objects. As a result, it is executed as long as there are remaining objects to process.

a. True

b. False

19. What does `&>` accomplish when entered on the command line after a command?

a. It redirects stderr and stdout to the same location.

b. It does not accomplish anything.

c. It redirects stderr and stdin to the same location.

d. It appends stdout to a file.

20. Consider the following shell script:

```
echo -e "What is your favorite
color?--> \c"
read REPLY
if [ "$REPLY" = "red"  -o  "$REPLY" =
"blue" ]
then
echo "The answer is red or blue."
else
echo "The answer is not red nor blue."
fi
```

What would be displayed if a user executes this shell script and answers Blue when prompted?

a. The answer is red or blue.

b. The answer is not red nor blue.

c. The code would cause an error.

d. The answer is red or blue. The answer is not red nor blue.

Hands-On Projects

These projects should be completed in the order given. The hands-on projects presented in this chapter should take a total of four hours to complete. The requirements for this lab include:

- A computer with Fedora Linux installed according to Hands-On Project 2-1.

Project 7-1

Estimated Time: 20 minutes
Objective: Perform shell redirection.
Description: In this hands-on project, you use the shell to redirect the stdout and stderr to a file and take stdin from a file.

1. Boot your Fedora Linux virtual machine. After your Linux system has been loaded, switch to a command-line terminal (tty5) by pressing **Ctrl+Alt+F5** and log in to the terminal using the user name of **root** and the password of **LINUXrocks!**.

2. At the command prompt, type `touch sample1 sample2` and press **Enter** to create two new files named sample1 and sample2 in your home directory. Verify their creation by typing `ls -F` at the command prompt, and press **Enter**.

3. At the command prompt, type `ls -l sample1 sample2 sample3` and press **Enter**. Is there any stdout displayed on the terminal screen? Is there any stderr displayed on the terminal screen? Why?

4. At the command prompt, type `ls -l sample1 sample2 sample3 > file` and press **Enter**. Is there any stdout displayed on the terminal screen? Is there any stderr displayed on the terminal screen? Why?

5. At the command prompt, type `cat file` and press **Enter**. What are the contents of the file and why?

6. At the command prompt, type `ls -l sample1 sample2 sample3 2> file` and press **Enter**. Is there any stdout displayed on the terminal screen? Is there any stderr displayed on the terminal screen? Why?

7. At the command prompt, type `cat file` and press **Enter**. What are the contents of the file and why? Were the previous contents retained? Why?

8. At the command prompt, type `ls -l sample1 sample2 sample3 > file 2>file2` and press **Enter**. Is there any stdout displayed on the terminal screen? Is there any stderr displayed on the terminal screen? Why?

9. At the command prompt, type `cat file` and press **Enter**. What are the contents of the file and why?

10. At the command prompt, type `cat file2` and press **Enter**. What are the contents of the file2 and why?

11. At the command prompt, type `ls -l sample1 sample2 sample3 > file 2>&1` and press **Enter**. Is there any stdout displayed on the terminal screen? Is there any stderr displayed on the terminal screen? Why?

12. At the command prompt, type `cat file` and press **Enter**. What are the contents of the file and why?

13. At the command prompt, type `ls -l sample1 sample2 sample3 >&2 2>file2` and press **Enter**. Is there any stdout displayed on the terminal screen? Is there any stderr displayed on the terminal screen? Why?

14. At the command prompt, type `cat file2` and press **Enter**. What are the contents of file2 and why?

15. At the command prompt, type `date > file` and press **Enter**.

16. At the command prompt, type `cat file` and press **Enter**. What are the contents of the file and why?

17. At the command prompt, type `date >> file` and press **Enter**.

18. At the command prompt, type `cat file` and press **Enter**. What are the contents of the file and why? Can you tell when each `date` command was run?

19. At the command prompt, type `tr o O /etc/hosts` and press **Enter**. What error message do you receive and why?

20. At the command prompt, type `tr o O </etc/hosts` and press **Enter**. What happened and why?

21. At the command prompt, type `tr o O <<EOF` and press **Enter**. At the secondary prompt, type `oranges` and press **Enter**. Next, type `Toronto` and press **Enter**, type `Donkey Kong` and press **Enter**, and then type `EOF` and press **Enter**. Note the output. What is this type of input redirection called?

22. Type `exit` and press **Enter** to log out of your shell.

Project 7-2

Estimated Time: 20 minutes
Objective: Perform shell piping.
Description: In this hands-on project, you redirect stdout and stdin using pipe metacharacters.

1. Switch to a command-line terminal (tty5) by pressing **Ctrl+Alt+F5** and log in to the terminal using the user name of **root** and the password of **LINUXrocks!**.

2. At the command prompt, type `cat /etc/services` and press **Enter** to view the **/etc/**services file. Next, type `cat /etc/services | less` at the command prompt and press **Enter** to perform the same task page-by-page. Explain what the | metacharacter does in the previous command. How is this different from the `less /etc/services` command?

3. At the command prompt, type `cat /etc/services | grep NFS` and press **Enter**. How many lines are displayed? Why did you not need to specify a filename with the `grep` command?

4. At the command prompt, type `cat /etc/services | grep NFS | tr F f` and press **Enter**. Explain the output on the terminal screen.

5. At the command prompt, type `cat /etc/services | grep NFS | tr F f | sort -r` and press **Enter**. Explain the output on the terminal screen.

6. At the command prompt, type `cat /etc/services | grep NFS | tr F f | sort -r | tee file` and press **Enter**. Explain the output on the terminal screen. Next, type `cat file` at the command prompt and press **Enter**. What are the contents? Why? What does the `tee` command do in the pipe above?

7. At the command prompt, type `cat /etc/services | grep NFS | tr F f | sort -r | tee file | wc -l` and press **Enter**. Explain the output on the terminal screen. Next, type `cat file` at the command prompt and press **Enter**. What are the contents and why?

8. At the command prompt, type `cat /etc/services | grep NFS | tr F f | sort -r | sed /udp/d | sed /tcp/s/mount/MOUNT/g` and press **Enter**. Explain the output on the terminal screen. Can this output be obtained with the `grep` and `tr` commands instead of `sed`?

9. At the command prompt, type `cat /etc/hosts`. Next, type `cat /etc/hosts | awk '/localhost/ {print $1, $3}'` and press **Enter**. Explain the output on the terminal screen.

10. Type `exit` and press **Enter** to log out of your shell.

Project 7-3

Estimated Time: 30 minutes
Objective: Create and manage variables.
Description: In this hands-on project, you create and use an alias, as well as view and change existing shell variables. In addition, you export user-defined variables and load variables automatically upon shell startup.

1. Switch to a command-line terminal (tty5) by pressing **Ctrl+Alt+F5** and log in to the terminal using the user name of **root** and the password of **LINUXrocks!**.

2. At the command prompt, type `set | less` and press **Enter** to view the BASH shell environment variables currently loaded into memory. Scroll through this list using the cursor keys on the keyboard. When finished, press q to quit the less utility.

3. At the command prompt, type `env | less` and press **Enter** to view the exported BASH shell environment variables currently loaded into memory. Scroll through this list using the cursor keys on the keyboard. Is this list larger or smaller than the list generated in Step 2? Why? When finished, press q to quit the less utility.

4. At the command prompt, type `PS1="Hello There: "` and press **Enter**. What happened and why? Next, type `echo $PS1` at the command prompt and press **Enter** to verify the new value of the PS1 variable.

5. At the command prompt, type `exit` and press **Enter** to log out of the shell. Next, log in to the terminal again using the user name of **root** and the password of **LINUXrocks!**. What prompt did you receive and why? How could you ensure that the "Hello There: " prompt occurs at every login?

6. At the command prompt, type `vi .bash_profile` and press **Enter**. At the bottom of the file, add the following lines. When finished, save and quit the vi editor.

```
echo -e "Would you like a hello prompt? (y/n) -->\c"
read ANSWER
if [ $ANSWER = "y" -o $ANSWER = "Y" ]
then
PS1="Hello There: "
fi
```

Explain what the preceding lines will perform after each login.

7. At the command prompt, type `exit` and press **Enter** to log out of the shell. Next, log in to the terminal using the user name of **root** and the password of **LINUXrocks!**. When prompted for a hello prompt, type y and press **Enter**. What prompt did you receive and why?

8. At the command prompt, type `exit` and press **Enter** to log out of the shell. Next, log in to the terminal using the user name of **root** and the password of **LINUXrocks!**. When prompted for a hello prompt, type n and press **Enter** to receive the default prompt.

9. At the command prompt, type `MYVAR="My sample variable"` and press **Enter** to create a variable called MYVAR. Verify its creation by typing `echo $MYVAR` at the command prompt, and press **Enter**.

10. At the command prompt, type `set | grep MYVAR` and press **Enter**. Is the MYVAR variable listed? Why?

11. At the command prompt, type `env | grep MYVAR` and press **Enter**. Is the MYVAR variable listed? Why?

12. At the command prompt, type `export MYVAR` and press **Enter**. Next, type `env | grep MYVAR` at the command prompt and press **Enter**. Is the MYVAR variable listed now? Why?

13. At the command prompt, type `exit` and press **Enter** to log out of the shell. Next, log in to the terminal using the user name of **root** and the password of **LINUXrocks!**.

14. At the command prompt, type `echo $MYVAR` and press **Enter** to view the contents of the MYVAR variable. What is listed and why?

15. At the command prompt, type `vi .bash_profile` and press **Enter**. At the bottom of the file, add the following line. When finished, save and quit the vi editor.

```
export MYVAR="My sample variable"
```

16. At the command prompt, type `exit` and press **Enter** to log out of the shell. Next, log in to the terminal using the user name of **root** and the password of **LINUXrocks!**.

17. At the command prompt, type `echo $MYVAR` and press **Enter** to list the contents of the MYVAR variable. What is listed and why?

18. At the command prompt, type `alias` and press **Enter**. Note the aliases that are present in your shell.

19. At the command prompt, type `alias asample="cd /etc ; cat hosts ; cd ~ ; ls -F"` and press **Enter**. What does this command do?

20. At the command prompt, type `asample` and press **Enter**. What happened and why? What environment file could you add this alias to such that it is executed each time a new BASH shell is created?

21. Type `exit` and press **Enter** to log out of your shell.

Project 7-4

Estimated Time: 20 minutes
Objective: Create a basic shell script.
Description: In this hands-on project, you create a basic shell script and execute it on the system.

1. Switch to a command-line terminal (tty5) by pressing **Ctrl+Alt+F5** and log in to the terminal using the user name of **root** and the password of **LINUXrocks!**.

2. At the command prompt, type `vi myscript` and press **Enter** to open a new file for editing called myscript in your home directory.

3. Enter the following text into the myscript file. When finished, save and quit the vi editor.

```
#!/bin/bash
echo -e "This is a sample shell script. \t It displays mounted
filesystems: \a"
df -hT
```

4. At the command prompt, type `ls -l myscript` and press **Enter**. What permissions does the myscript file have? Next, type `bash myscript` at the command prompt and press **Enter**. Did the shell script execute? What do the \t and \a escape sequences do?

5. Next, type `./myscript` at the command prompt and press **Enter**. What error message did you receive and why?

6. At the command prompt, type `chmod u+x myscript` and press **Enter**. Next, type `./myscript` at the command prompt and press **Enter**. Did the script execute? Why?

7. Type `exit` and press **Enter** to log out of your shell.

Project 7-5

Estimated Time: 90 minutes
Objective: Create system administration shell scripts.
Description: In this hands-on project, you create a shell script that uses decision and loop constructs to analyze user input.

1. Switch to a command-line terminal (tty5) by pressing **Ctrl+Alt+F5** and log in to the terminal using the user name of **root** and the password of **LINUXrocks!**.

2. At the command prompt, type `vi diskconfig.sh` and press **Enter** to open a new file for editing called diskconfig.sh in your home directory. Why is it good form to use a .sh extension for shell scripts?

3. Enter the following text into the diskconfig.sh file. As you are typing the contents, ensure that you understand the purpose of each line (reviewing the chapter contents and appropriate man pages as necessary). When finished, save and quit the vi editor.

```
#!/bin/bash
#This script creates a report of our disk configuration
```

```
FILENAME='hostname'
echo "Disk report saved to $FILENAME.report"

echo -e "\n LVM Configuration: \n\n" >>$FILENAME.report
lvscan >>$FILENAME.report

echo -e "\n\n Partition Configuration: \n\n" >>$FILENAME.report
fdisk -l | head -17 >>$FILENAME.report

echo -e "\n\n Mounted Filesystems: \n\n" >>$FILENAME.report
df -hT | grep -v tmp >>$FILENAME.report
```

4. At the command prompt, type chmod u+x diskconfig.sh and press **Enter**. Next, type ./diskconfig.sh at the command prompt and press **Enter**. Note the filename that your report was saved to.

5. At the command prompt, type less *filename* where filename is the *filename* you noted in the previous step, and press **Enter**. View the contents. Would this shell script work well to record storage configuration from different systems? Why?

6. At the command prompt, type vi dirbackup.sh and press **Enter** to open a new file for editing called dirbackup.sh in your home directory.

7. Enter the following text into the dirbackup.sh file. As you are typing the contents, ensure that you understand the purpose of each line (reviewing the chapter contents and appropriate man pages as necessary; the tar backup command will be discussed in Chapter 11 and does not require detailed interpretation here). When finished, save and quit the vi editor.

```
#!/bin/bash
#This script backs up a directory of your choice

if [ $# -ne 1 ]
then
echo "Usage is $0 <directory to back up>"
exit 255
fi

echo "Performing backup....."
sleep 3
tar -zcvf ~/backupfile.tar.gz $1

echo "Backup completed successfully to ~/backupfile.tar.gz"
```

8. At the command prompt, type chmod u+x dirbackup.sh and press **Enter**. Next, type ./dirbackup.sh at the command prompt and press **Enter**. Note the error that you receive because you did not specify a positional parameter. Type ./dirbackup.sh /etc/samba at the command prompt and press **Enter** to create a backup of the /etc/samba directory within the backupfile.tar.gz file in your home directory.

9. At the command prompt, type ls -F and press **Enter**. Was the backupfile.tar.gz file successfully created?

10. At the command prompt, type vi dirbackup.sh and press **Enter**. As you are modifying the contents, ensure that you understand the purpose of each change (reviewing the chapter contents and appropriate man pages as necessary). Edit the text inside the dirbackup.sh shell script such that it reads:

```
#!/bin/bash
#This script backs up a directory of your choice

echo -e "What directory do you want to back up?-->\c"
read ANS

echo "Performing backup....."
sleep 3
tar -zcvf ~/backupfile.tar.gz $ANS

echo "Backup completed successfully to ~/backupfile.tar.gz"
```

11. At the command prompt, type `./dirbackup.sh` and press **Enter**. Type `/etc/httpd` and press **Enter** when prompted to back up the /etc/httpd directory to backupfile.tar.gz in your home directory. Note that the backup file does not represent the directory or time the backup was performed.

12. At the command prompt, type `vi dirbackup.sh` and press **Enter**. As you are modifying the contents, ensure that you understand the purpose of each change (reviewing the chapter contents and appropriate man pages as necessary). Edit the text inside the dirbackup.sh shell script such that it reads:

```
#!/bin/bash
#This script backs up a directory of your choice

echo -e "What directory do you want to back up?-->\c"
read ANS

echo "Performing backup....."
sleep 3
FILE='echo $ANS | sed s#/#-#g'
DATE='date +%F'
tar -zcvf ~/backup-$FILE-$DATE.tar.gz $ANS

echo "Backup performed to ~/backup-$FILE-$DATE.tar.gz"
```

13. At the command prompt, type `./dirbackup.sh` and press **Enter**. Type `/etc/httpd` and press **Enter** when prompted to back up the /etc/httpd directory. Note that the filename of the backup now reflects the directory that was backed up as well as the date the backup was performed.

14. At the command prompt, type `vi familydatabase.sh` and press **Enter** to open a new file for editing called familydatabase.sh in your home directory.

15. Enter the following text into the familydatabase.sh file. As you are typing the contents, ensure that you understand the purpose of each line (reviewing the chapter contents and appropriate man pages as necessary). When finished, save and quit the vi editor.

```
#!/bin/bash
while true
do
clear
echo -e "What would you like to do?
Add an entry (a)
Search an entry (s)
Quit (q)
Enter your choice (a/s/q)-->\c"
```

```
    read ANSWER
    case $ANSWER in
    a|A ) echo -e "Name of the family member --> \c"
          read NAME
          echo -e "Family member's relation to you -->\c"
          read RELATION
          echo -e "Family member's telephone number --> \c"
          read PHONE
          echo "$NAME\t$RELATION\t$PHONE" >> database
          ;;
    s|S ) echo "What word would you like to look for? --> \c"
          read WORD
          grep "$WORD" database
          sleep 4
          ;;
    q|Q ) exit
          ;;
    *)    echo "You must enter either the letter a or s."
          sleep 4
          ;;
    esac
    done
```

16. At the command prompt, type `chmod u+x familydatabase.sh` and press **Enter**. Next, type `./familydatabase.sh` at the command prompt and press **Enter**. Type a, and press **Enter** when prompted and supply the appropriate values for a family member of your choice. Does the menu continue to appear when you have finished entering your record? Type a, and press **Enter** and supply the appropriate values for a different family member. Type s and press **Enter** and supply a piece of information you previously entered for a family member to see the results. Type x, and press **Enter** to view the usage error. Finally, type q, and press **Enter** to quit your shell script.

17. Type `exit`, and press **Enter** to log out of your shell.

Project 7-6

Estimated Time: 30 minutes
Objective: Practice using Git.
Description: In this hands-on project, you create a local Git repository for the shell scripts that you created in Project 7-5 and explore Git version control.

1. Switch to a command-line terminal (tty5) by pressing **Ctrl+Alt+F5** and log in to the terminal using the user name of **root** and the password of **LINUXrocks!**.

2. At the command prompt, type `mkdir /shellscripts` and press **Enter**. Next, type `mv diskconfig.sh dirbackup.sh familydatabase.sh /shellscripts` and press **Enter** to move your shell scripts from Project 7-5 to the /shellscripts directory.

3. At the command prompt, type `git config --global user.email "root@domain.com"` and press **Enter** to set your email address. Next, type `git config --global user.name "root user"` and press **Enter** to set your user name. Finally, type `git config --global init.defaultBranch main` and press **Enter** to set the default branch name.

4. At the command prompt, type `cd /shellscripts` and press **Enter**. Next, type `git init` and press **Enter** to create a Git repo in your current directory. Finally, type `ls -a` and press **Enter** to verify the creation of the .git subdirectory.

5. At the command prompt, type `git status` and press **Enter**. Note that your shell scripts are detected but not managed by Git yet. Next, type `git add .` and press **Enter** to add your shell scripts to the index. Finally, type `git status` and press **Enter** to verify that your shell scripts are ready for commit.

6. At the command prompt, type `git commit -m "First commit"` and press **Enter** to create your first commit.

7. At the command prompt, type `vi diskconfig.sh` and press **Enter**. Add the following lines to the bottom of the diskconfig.sh file. When finished, save and quit the vi editor.

```
echo -e "\n\n RAID Configuration: \n\n" >>$FILENAME.report
mdadm --detail /dev/md0 >>$FILENAME.report
```

8. At the command prompt, type `git status` and press **Enter**. Did Git detect the modification to disk-config.sh? Next, type `git add .` and press **Enter** to add your shell scripts to the index. Finally, type `git commit -m "Added RAID to diskconfig.sh"` and press **Enter** to create a second commit that represents your change.

9. At the command prompt, type `git log` and press **Enter**. Note the commit identifier next to your original commit (before the RAID section was added). Next, type `git reset --hard commit` and press **Enter**, where *commit* is the first 7 digits of the commit number for your original commit. Finally, type `cat diskconfig.sh` and press **Enter**. Was your RAID addition to the diskconfig.sh shell script removed?

10. At the command prompt, type `cd` and press **Enter** to return to your home directory. Next, type `git clone /shellscripts` and press **Enter** to clone your local /shellscripts repo to your home directory. Next, type `cd shellscripts` and press **Enter** to switch to your cloned repo. Finally, type `ls -a` and press **Enter** to verify that your cloned repo contains the same contents as the original repo.

11. At the command prompt, type `git branch` and press **Enter**. What is the default branch called? Next, type `git checkout -b AddRAID` and press **Enter** to create a branch called AddRAID to your cloned repo. Finally, type `git branch` and press **Enter** to verify that your AddRAID branch was added. How can you tell that your AddRAID branch is the active branch in the output?

12. At the command prompt, type `vi diskconfig.sh` and press **Enter**. Add the following lines to the bottom of the diskconfig.sh file. When finished, save and quit the vi editor.

```
echo -e "\n\n RAID Configuration: \n\n" >>$FILENAME.report
mdadm --detail /dev/md0 >>$FILENAME.report
```

13. At the command prompt, type `git add .` and press **Enter** to add your shell scripts to the index within your AddRAID branch. Finally, type `git commit -m "Added RAID to diskconfig.sh"` and press **Enter** to create a commit within your AddRAID branch that represents your change.

14. At the command prompt, type `cat diskconfig.sh` and press **Enter** and note that your RAID modification is shown. Next, type `git checkout main` and press **Enter** to switch back to the main branch of your cloned repo. Finally, type `cat diskconfig.sh` and press **Enter**. Is your RAID modification visible in the main branch?

15. At the command prompt, type `git push origin AddRAID` and press **Enter** to push your AddRAID branch to the original repo. Next, type `cd /shellscripts` and press **Enter** to switch your current directory to the original repo. Finally type `git branch` and press **Enter** to verify that the branch was pushed successfully to the original repo from the cloned repo. Also note that your current branch in the original repo is still set to main.

16. At the command prompt, type `git show AddRAID` and press **Enter** to view the changes made within the AddRAID branch.

17. At the command prompt, type `git merge AddRAID` and press **Enter** to merge the changes from the AddRAID branch to your main branch. Next, type `cat diskconfig.sh` and press **Enter**. Is your modification visible in the main branch?

18. At the command prompt, type `cd ~/shellscripts` and press **Enter** to switch your cloned repo in your home directory. Next, type `git pull origin main`, and press **Enter** to pull a new copy of the main branch from your original repo. Was the pull successful?

19. Type `exit` and press **Enter** to log out of your shell.

Project 7-7

Estimated Time: 30 minutes
Objective: Set up and use the Z shell.
Description: In this hands-on project, you install and explore the Z shell.

1. Switch to a command-line terminal (tty5) by pressing **Ctrl+Alt+F5** and log in to the terminal using the user name of **root** and the password of **LINUXrocks!**.

2. At the command prompt, type `dnf -y install zsh` and press **Enter** to install the Z shell. After the installation has finished, type `exit` and press **Enter** to log out of your shell.

3. Log in to the terminal using the user name of **user1** and the password of **LINUXrocks!**.

4. At the command prompt, type `zsh` and press **Enter** to open a new Z shell. At the initial Z shell configuration screen:

   a. Press 1 to configure your ~/.zshrc options.

   b. Press 1 to configure history variables, and then press 0 to use the default configuration.

   c. Press 2 to configure completion features, and then press 1 to use the default configuration.

   d. Press 4 to configure common shell options, and then press 1 to configure the autocd option. Press **s** to enable the option, and then press 0 to return to the main menu.

   e. Press 0 to save your configuration settings to ~/.zshrc. What prompt do you receive from the Z shell and why?

5. At the command prompt, type `vi .zshrc` and press **Enter**. Note the history variables, compinit function, and autocd option that you configured in Step 4. Edit the setopt line to read `setopt autocd correct` to add the autocorrect option. Save your changes and quit the vi editor when finished.

6. At the command prompt, type `source .zshrc` and press **Enter** to execute ~/.zshrc in your current shell. What other methods can be used to perform the same action?

7. At the command prompt, type `grep NFS /etc/services >file1 >file2` and press **Enter**. Type `cat file1` and press **Enter** to view the contents of file1. Next, type `cat file2` and press **Enter** to view the contents of file2. Are the contents identical? Why?

8. At the command prompt, type `grep NFS /etc/services >file1 | grep protocol >file2` and press **Enter**. Type `cat file1` and press **Enter** to view the contents of file1. Next, type `cat file2` and press **Enter** to view the contents of file2. Are the contents identical? Why?

9. At the command prompt, type `sort <file1 <file2 >file3` and press **Enter**. Type `cat file3` and press **Enter**. Are the contents of both file1 and file2 combined and sorted?

10. At the command prompt, type `grp NFS /etc/services` and press **Enter**. When prompted to correct the command to grep, press **y**.

11. At the command prompt, type `date -` and press **Tab**. View the available options and then complete the `date --universal` command to view the date and time in UTC format.

12. At the command prompt, type `pwd` and press **Enter**. What directory are you currently using? Type `Desktop` and press **Enter**. Next, type `pwd` and press **Enter**. What directory are you currently using?

13. Type `exit` and press **Enter** to log out of your shell.

Discovery Exercises

Discovery Exercise 7-1

Estimated Time: 20 minutes
Objective: Create commands that use shell features.
Description: Name the command that can be used to do each of the following:

a. Create an alias called mm that displays only those filesystems that are mounted and contain an ext4 filesystem.

b. Create and export a variable called NEWHOME that is equivalent to the value contained in the HOME variable.

c. Find all files that start with the word "host" starting from the /etc directory and save the Standard Output to a file called file1 and the Standard Error to the same file.

d. Display only the lines from the output of the set command that have the word "bash" in them. This output on the terminal screen should be sorted alphabetically.

e. Display only the user name (first field) in the colon-delimited /etc/passwd file and save the output to a file called users in the current directory.

Discovery Exercise 7-2

Estimated Time: 20 minutes
Objective: Explain shell piping and redirection.
Description: What would happen if the user executed the following commands?

```
cp /etc/hosts ~
cd
tr a A <hosts | sort -r | pr -d >hosts
```
Explain the output.

Discovery Exercise 7-3

Estimated Time: 10 minutes
Objective: Explain shell piping.
Description: Recall that only Standard Output can be sent across a pipe to another command. Using the information presented in this chapter, how could you send Standard Error across the pipe in the following command?

```
ls /etc/hosts /etc/h | tr h H
```

Discovery Exercise 7-4

Estimated Time: 20 minutes
Objective: Create test statements.
Description: Name the test statement that can be used to test the following scenarios:

a. The user has read permission to the /etc/hosts file.

b. The user has read and execute permission to the /etc directory.

c. The contents of the variable $TEST are equal to the string "success."

d. The contents of the variable $TEST are numerically equal to the contents of the variable $RESULT.

e. The contents of the variable $TEST are equal to the string "success" and the file /etc/hosts exists.

f. The contents of the variable $TEST are equal to the string "success," or the number 5, or the contents of the variable $RESULT.

Discovery Exercise 7-5

Estimated Time: 20 minutes
Objective: Explain shell script features.
Description: Examine the sample **/root/.bash_profile** file shown next. Using the information presented in this chapter, describe what each line of this file does.

```
# .bash_profile

# Get the aliases and functions
if [ -f ~/.bashrc ]; then
    . ~/.bashrc
fi

# User specific environment and startup programs

PATH=$PATH:$HOME/bin
BASH_ENV=$HOME/.bashrc
USERNAME="root"

export USERNAME BASH_ENV PATH
```

Discovery Exercise 7-6

Estimated Time: 20 minutes
Objective: Explain shell script features.
Description: Examine the following shell script and describe its function line-by-line:

```
#!/bin/bash
echo -e "This program copies a file to the /stuff directory.\n"
echo -e "Which file would you like to copy? --> \c"
read FILENAME
mkdir /stuff || echo "The /stuff directory could not be created."
cp -f $FILENAME /stuff && echo "$FILENAME was successfully copied to
/stuff"
```

Discovery Exercise 7-7

Estimated Time: 25 minutes
Objective: Explain shell script features.
Description: Examine the following shell script and describe its function line-by-line:

```
#!/bin/bash
#This script backs up the Oracle DB

rm -f /SAN/backup-oracle*

if tar -zcvf /SAN/backup-oracle-'date +%F'.tar.gz /oracledb/*
  then
  echo "Oracle backup completed on 'date'" >>/var/log/oraclelog

  else
  echo "Oracle backup failed on 'date'" >>/var/log/oraclelog
  mail -s ALERT jason.eckert@trios.com </var/log/oraclelog
fi
```

Discovery Exercise 7-8

Estimated Time: 30 minutes

Objective: Use GitHub repositories.

Description: Navigate to GitHub.com using a web browser and create a free account by navigating the appropriate options provided. Following this, create a public repository called shellscripts. Next, create a personal access token by navigating to user Settings, Developer settings, Personal access tokens.

On your Fedora Linux virtual machine, run the following commands as root (where *name* is your GitHub account name) to push the contents of the /shellscripts repo from Project 7-6 to GitHub and set GitHub as the original repo. Supply your GitHub user name and personal access token when prompted.

```
cd /shellscripts
git remote add origin https://github.com/name/shellscripts.git
git push -u origin main
```

Finally, log into another terminal as user1 on your Fedora Linux virtual machine and clone your public shellscripts repository from GitHub using the following command (where *name* is your GitHub account name):

```
git clone https://github.com/name/shellscripts.git
```

Verify the results when finished.

Discovery Exercise 7-9

Estimated Time: 30 minutes

Objective: Use Z shell themes.

Description: In addition to those available at github.com/ohmyzsh/ohmyzsh, there are many other Z shell plugins and themes available on other GitHub repositories. One of the most popular Z shell themes is Powerlevel10k. While logged into GNOME as user1, visit github.com/romkatv/powerlevel10k and follow the instructions to perform a manual installation of Powerlevel10k. Next, open a new Z shell as user1 and follow the setup wizard to configure the Powerlevel10k theme to your liking. Finally, explore the entries added to ~user1/.zshrc that configure the Powerlevel10k theme.

Chapter 8

System Initialization, X Windows, and Localization

Chapter Objectives

1 Summarize the major steps necessary to boot a Linux system.

2 Outline the configuration of the GRUB boot loader.

3 Detail the UNIX SysV and Systemd system initialization processes.

4 Start, stop, and restart daemons.

5 Configure the system to start and stop daemons upon entering certain runlevels and targets.

6 Explain the purpose of the major Linux GUI components: X Windows, window manager, and desktop environment.

7 Configure X Windows settings and accessibility options.

8 Configure time, time zone, and locale information on a Linux system.

In this chapter, you investigate the boot process in greater detail. You explore how to configure boot loaders and the process used to start daemons after the kernel has loaded. Additionally, you examine the procedures used to start and stop daemons and set them to start automatically at boot time. Next, you examine the various components that comprise the Linux GUI and how to configure them using common Linux utilities. Finally, you examine the Linux tools and processes used to configure localization options, including locale, date, and time zone information.

The Boot Process

When a computer first initializes, the system BIOS performs a Power On Self Test (POST). Following the POST, the BIOS checks its configuration for boot devices and operating systems to execute. Typically, computers first check for an operating system on removable media devices, such as DVDs and USB flash memory drives, because they can contain installation media for an operating system. If it fails to find an operating system on any of these options, the BIOS usually checks the MBR/GPT on the first hard disk drive inside the computer.

> **Note 1**
>
> Recall that you can alter the order in which boot devices are checked in the computer BIOS.

Note 2

A computer BIOS can also be configured to boot an operating system from an NFS, HTTP, or FTP server across the network, provided that the computer network interface supports the Preboot Execution Environment (PXE) standard. This process is called **netbooting** and is primarily used to boot Linux live install media on a computer from across a network in order to perform a new local Linux installation.

The MBR/GPT normally contains the first part of a **boot loader** that can then locate and execute the kernel of the operating system. Alternatively, the MBR/GPT might contain a pointer to a partition on the system that contains a boot loader on the first sector; this partition is referred to as the **active partition**. There can be only one active partition per hard disk drive.

Note 3

In addition to storing the list of all partitions on the hard disk drive, the MBR/GPT stores the location of the active partition.

If the system has a UEFI BIOS, then boot loader is not loaded from the MBR/GPT or first sector of the active partition; it is instead loaded from the UEFI System Partition by the UEFI BIOS. There can only be one UEFI System Partition per hard disk drive. If **secure boot** is enabled in the UEFI BIOS, the digital signature of the boot loader within the UEFI System Partition is first checked to ensure that it has not been modified by malware.

Regardless of whether the boot loader is loaded from the MBR/GPT, the first sector of the active partition, or the UEFI System Partition, the remainder of the boot process is the same. The boot loader then executes the Linux kernel from the partition that contains it.

Note 4

The Linux kernel is stored in the /boot directory and is named vmlinux-<kernel version> if it is not compressed, or vmlinuz-<kernel version> if it is compressed.

After the Linux kernel is loaded into memory, the boot loader is no longer active; instead, the Linux kernel continues to initialize the system by loading daemons into memory. Recall from Chapter 1 that a daemon is a system process that provides useful services, such as printing, scheduling, and operating system maintenance. The first daemon process on the system is called the **initialize (init) daemon**; it is responsible for loading all other daemons on the system required to bring the system to a usable state in which users can log in and interact with services. The whole process is depicted in Figure 8-1.

Figure 8-1   The boot process

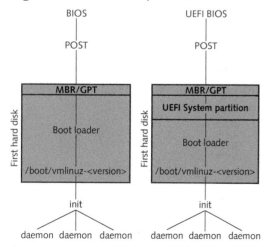

Boot Loaders

As discussed in the previous section, the primary function of boot loaders during the boot process is to load the Linux kernel into memory. However, boot loaders can perform other functions as well, including passing information to the kernel during system startup and booting other operating systems that are present on the hard disk drive. Using one boot loader to boot one of several operating systems is known as multi booting; the boot loader simply loads a different operating system kernel based on user input.

Note 5

Unless virtualization software is used, only one operating system can be active at any one time.

The two most common boot loaders used on Linux systems are GRUB and GRUB2.

GRUB Legacy

The original GRand Unified Bootloader (GRUB) boot loader was created in 1999 as a replacement boot loader for the original Linux boot loader for hard disk drives that have an MBR. It supports the booting of several different operating systems, including Linux, macOS, BSD UNIX, Solaris UNIX, and Windows.

Note 6

The original GRUB boot loader is called GRUB Legacy today as it is not used on modern Linux systems. However, because specialized Linux systems typically have a very long lifetime within production environments, it is not uncommon to see a Linux system that still uses GRUB legacy today.

The first major part of the GRUB Legacy boot loader (called Stage 1) typically resides on the MBR. The remaining parts of the boot loader are called Stage 1.5 and Stage 2. Stage 1.5 resides in the unused 30 KB of space following the MBR, and Stage 2 resides in the /boot/grub directory. Stage 1 simply points to Stage 1.5, which loads filesystem support and proceeds to load Stage 2. Stage 2 performs the actual boot loader functions and displays a graphical boot loader screen like that shown in Figure 8-2.

Note 7

Recall that the /boot directory is normally mounted to its own filesystem on most Linux systems; as a result, Stage 2 typically resides on the /boot filesystem alongside the Linux kernel.

Figure 8-2   The legacy GRUB boot screen for a Fedora system

Press any key to enter the menu

Booting Fedora (2.6.33.3-85.fc13.i686.PAE) in 1 seconds...

Source: GNU GRUB

You configure GRUB Legacy by editing a configuration file (/boot/grub/grub.conf) that is read directly by the Stage 2 boot loader. An example /boot/grub/grub.conf file for a legacy Fedora system is shown next:

```
[root@server1 ~]# cat /boot/grub/grub.conf
# NOTE: You do not have a /boot partition. This means that all
# kernel and initrd paths are relative to /, or root (hd0,0)

boot=/dev/sda
default=0
timeout=5
splashimage=(hd0,0)/boot/grub/splash.xpm.gz
hiddenmenu

title Fedora (2.6.33.3-85.fc13.i686.PAE)
  root (hd0,0)
  kernel /boot/vmlinuz-2.6.fc13.i686.PAE ro root=/dev/sda1 rhgb quiet
  initrd /boot/initramfs-2.6.fc13.i686.PAE.img
[root@server1 ~]#_
```

Note 8

Alternatively, you can view and edit the /etc/grub.conf file, which is simply a symbolic link to /boot/grub/grub.conf.

Note 9

As with shell scripts, lines can be commented out of /boot/grub/grub.conf by preceding those lines with a # symbol.

Note 10

Some other Linux distributions, such as Ubuntu Linux, use a /boot/grub/menu.lst file in place of /boot/grub/grub.conf to hold GRUB Legacy configuration.

To understand the entries in the /boot/grub/grub.conf file, you must first understand how GRUB refers to partitions on hard disk drives. Hard disk drives and partitions on those hard disk drives are identified by numbers in the following format: (hd<drive#>,<partition#>). Thus, the (hd0,0) notation in the preceding /boot/grub/grub.conf file refers to the first hard disk drive on the system (regardless of whether it is SCSI, SATA, or PATA) and the first partition on that hard disk drive, respectively. Similarly, the second partition on the first hard disk drive is referred to as (hd0,1), and the fourth partition on the third hard disk drive is referred to as (hd2,3).

In addition, GRUB calls the partition that contains Stage 2 the **GRUB root partition**. Normally, the GRUB root partition is the filesystem that contains the /boot directory and should not be confused with the Linux root filesystem. If your system has a separate partition mounted to /boot, GRUB refers to the file /boot/grub/grub.conf as /grub/grub.conf. If your system does not have a separate filesystem for the /boot directory, this file is simply referred to as /boot/grub/grub.conf in GRUB.

Thus, the example /boot/grub/grub.conf file shown earlier displays a graphical boot screen (splashimage=(hd0,0)/boot/grub/splash.xpm.gz) and boots the default operating system kernel on the first hard drive (default=0) in 5 seconds (timeout=5) without showing any additional menus (hiddenmenu). The default operating system kernel is located on the GRUB root filesystem (root (hd0,0)) and is called /boot/vmlinuz-2.6.fc13.i686.PAE.

The kernel then mounts the root filesystem on /dev/sda1 (root=/dev/sda1) initially as read-only (ro) to avoid problems with the fsck command and uses a special **initramfs** disk filesystem image to load modules into RAM that are needed by the Linux kernel at boot time (initrd /boot/initramfs-2.6.fc13.i686.PAE.img).

> ### Note 11
>
> Most Linux distributions use a UUID (e.g., root=UUID=42c0fce6-bb79-4218-af1a-0b89316bb7d1) in place of root=/dev/sda1 to identify the partition that holds the root filesystem at boot time.

All other keywords on the kernel line within /boot/grub/grub.conf are used to pass information to the kernel from Stage 2. For example, the keyword rhgb (Red Hat Graphical Boot) tells the Linux kernel to use a graphical boot screen as it is loading daemons, and the keyword quiet tells the Linux kernel to avoid printing errors to the screen during system startup. You can add your own keywords to the kernel line in /boot/grub/grub.conf to control how your Linux kernel is loaded. For example, appending the text nosmp to the kernel line disables Symmetric Multi-Processing (SMP) support within the Linux kernel. Alternatively, appending the text mem=16384M to the kernel line forces your Linux kernel to see 16384 MB of physical RAM in case your Linux kernel does not detect all the RAM in your computer properly.

Normally, GRUB Legacy allows users to manipulate the boot loader during system startup; to prevent this, you can optionally password protect GRUB modifications during boot time.

Recall from the /boot/grub/grub.conf file shown earlier that you have five seconds after the BIOS POST to interact with the boot screen shown in Figure 8-2. If you press any key within these five seconds, you will be presented with a graphical boot menu screen like the one shown in Figure 8-3 that you can use to manipulate the boot process. If you have several Linux kernels installed on your system (from updating your system software), you can select the kernel that you would like to boot, highlight your kernel and press a to append keywords to the kernel line, or press e to edit the entire boot configuration for the kernel listed in /boot/grub/grub.conf at boot time. You can also press c to obtain a grub> prompt where you can enter a variety of commands to view system hardware configuration, find and display files, alter the configuration of GRUB, or boot an operating system kernel. Typing help at this grub> prompt will display a list of available commands and their usage.

Figure 8-3   The legacy GRUB boot menu for a Fedora system

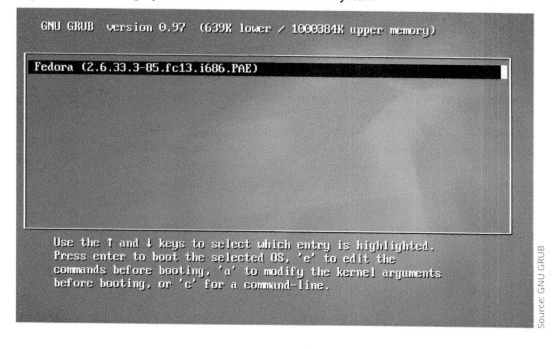

If the GRUB Legacy boot loader becomes damaged, you can reinstall it using the `grub-install` command that is available on the system or on a live Linux system used for system rescue. To install GRUB Legacy Stage 1 on the MBR of the first SATA hard disk drive, you can type the following command:

```
[root@server1 ~]# grub-install /dev/sda
Installation finished. No error reported.
Below are the contents of the device map /boot/grub/device.map.
If lines are incorrect, fix them and re-run the script 'grub-install'.
(hd0)    /dev/sda
[root@server1 ~]#_
```

Note 12

Alternatively, you can use the `grub-install /dev/sda1` command to install GRUB Legacy Stage 1 at the beginning of the first primary partition of the same hard disk drive.

GRUB2

GRand Unified Bootloader version 2 (GRUB2) is the boot loader commonly used on modern Linux systems; it supports storage devices that use either an MBR or GPT, as well as newer storage technologies such as NVMe.

Note 13

GRUB2 has additional support for modern systems that do not use the Intel x86_64 architecture (e.g., ARM64), as well as specialized hardware systems.

For a system that uses a standard BIOS, GRUB2 has a similar structure to GRUB Legacy. GRUB2 Stage 1 typically resides on the MBR or GPT. On MBR hard disk drives, Stage 1.5 resides in the unused 30 KB of space following the MBR, and on GPT hard disk drives, Stage 1.5 resides in a BIOS Boot partition that is created for this purpose by the Linux installation program. Stage 2 resides in the /boot/grub directory (or /boot/grub2 directory on some Linux distributions) and loads a terminal-friendly boot loader screen like that shown in Figure 8-4. As with GRUB Legacy, you can select the kernel that you would like to boot at the boot loader screen, as well as highlight your kernel and press e to edit the entire boot configuration for the kernel or press c to obtain a prompt where you can enter GRUB configuration commands.

For a system that uses a UEFI BIOS, all GRUB2 stages are stored entirely on the UEFI System Partition within a UEFI application called grubx64.efi on Intel x86_64-based systems. If it isn't already present, the UEFI System Partition is created during Linux installation, formatted using the FAT filesystem, and mounted to the /boot/efi directory during the Linux boot process. Because the UEFI System Partition can contain boot loaders for multiple different operating systems, grubx64.efi is stored underneath a subdirectory. For example, on Fedora systems, you can find grubx64.efi under the /boot/efi/EFI/fedora directory after the Linux system has booted. If the UEFI BIOS has secure boot enabled, you will also find UEFI applications within this subdirectory that store the digital signature information used to ensure that GRUB2 has not been modified by malware; for a Fedora system, these are called shim.efi and shimx64.efi.

Note 14

There is still a /boot/grub (or /boot/grub2) directory on systems that use GRUB2 alongside a UEFI BIOS, but it only contains files that are referenced by GRUB2 after it is fully loaded, such as the background image used for the GRUB boot screen.

Figure 8-4 The GRUB2 boot screen on a Fedora system

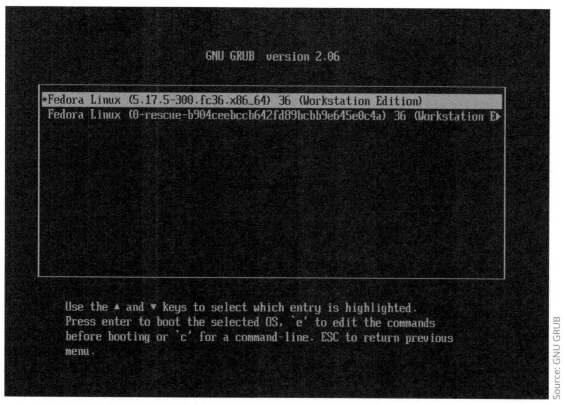

After grubx64.efi is executed by the UEFI BIOS, GRUB2 displays the same boot loader screen shown in Figure 8-4, where you can interact with GRUB or boot the Linux kernel but will include an additional menu option called UEFI Firmware Settings that allows you to configure UEFI BIOS settings.

The main configuration file for GRUB2 is called grub.cfg; it is stored within the /boot/grub (or /boot/grub2) directory on computers that have a standard BIOS, and within the UEFI System Partition on computers with a UEFI BIOS (e.g., in the /boot/efi/EFI/fedora directory on Fedora Linux).

The syntax of the grub.cfg file used by GRUB2 is different than the grub.conf file used by GRUB Legacy, as shown in the following excerpt:

```
set timeout=5

menuentry 'Fedora (5.17.5-300.fc36.x86_64) 36 (Workstation Edition)' --class fedora
--class gnu-linux --class gnu --class os --unrestricted $menuentry_id_option
'gnulinux-5.17.5-300.fc36.x86_64-advanced-9ff25add-035b-4d26-9129-a9da6d0a6fa3' {
     load_video
     set gfxpayload=keep
     insmod gzio
     insmod part_gpt
     insmod ext2
     set root='hd0,gpt2'

     linuxefi  /vmlinuz-5.17.5-300.fc36.x86_64  root=UUID=9ff25add-035b-4d26-9129-
     a9da6d0a6fa3  ro  resume=UUID=4837de7b-d96e-4edc-8d3d-56df0a17ca62  rhgb  quiet
     LANG=en_US.UTF-8

     initrdefi /initramfs-5.17.5-300.fc36.x86_64.img
}
```

Each menu entry at the graphical boot screen is identified by a `menuentry` paragraph that first loads required hardware support using `insmod` commands before accessing the GRUB root partition (mounted to /boot). The notation for identifying hard disk drives in GRUB2 is different from GRUB Legacy; partition numbers start at 1 and are prefixed by `msdos` for MBR partitions and `gpt` for GPT partitions. Thus, the `set root='hd0,gpt2'` notation in the preceding excerpt indicates that the GRUB root partition is the second GPT partition on the first hard disk drive. Next, the Linux kernel is loaded from the specified file on the GRUB root partition (`linuxefi /vmlinuz-5.17.5-300.fc36.x86_64` if the system has a UEFI BIOS, or `linux16 /vmlinuz-5.17.5-300.fc36.x86_64` if the system has a standard BIOS). The options following the Linux kernel are used to specify the UUID of the root filesystem that is initially loaded read-only (`ro`), as well as the use of a graphical boot screen (`rhgb`) that suppresses errors from being shown during the boot process (`quiet`). The `LANG=en_US.UTF-8` kernel option sets the default locale information that is discussed later in this chapter. As with GRUB Legacy, an initramfs image is used to load modules into RAM that are needed by the Linux kernel at boot time (`initrdefi /initramfs-5.17.5-300.fc36.x86_64.img` if the system has a UEFI BIOS, or `initrd16 /initramfs-5.17.5-300.fc36.x86_64.img` if the system has a standard BIOS). By default, GRUB2 stores the last menu entry chosen by the user at the graphical boot screen in the /boot/grub/grubenv (or /boot/grub2/grubenv) file and sets it as the default for the subsequent boot process if you do not select a menu entry within 5 seconds (`set timeout=5`).

Note 15

If you do not see `menuentry` paragraphs within grub.cfg, GRUB2 is configured to use the BootLoaderSpec (blscfg) module. In this case, the information for each kernel is stored within a *UUID-kernel*.conf file under the /boot/loader/entries directory, where *UUID* is the UUID of the root filesystem, and *kernel* is the version of the Linux kernel.

The grub.cfg file was not meant to be edited manually; instead, it is automatically built via entries within the /etc/default/grub file, and the output of any shell scripts stored within the /etc/grub.d directory. When you install a device driver that needs to be loaded by the boot loader (e.g., disk controller devices), the device driver package will often add a file to the /etc/grub.d directory that provides the necessary configuration. For any other settings, you should add or modify the existing lines within the /etc/default/grub file. A sample /etc/default/grub file on a Fedora system is shown here:

```
[root@server1 ~]# cat /etc/default/grub
GRUB_TIMEOUT=5
GRUB_DISTRIBUTOR="$(sed 's, release .*$,,g' /etc/system-release)"
GRUB_DEFAULT=saved
GRUB_DISABLE_SUBMENU=true
GRUB_TERMINAL_OUTPUT="console"
GRUB_CMDLINE_LINUX="rhgb quiet"
GRUB_DISABLE_RECOVERY="true"
GRUB_ENABLE_BLSCFG="true"
[root@server1 ~]#_
```

From the preceding output, you could change the GRUB_TIMEOUT line to modify the number of seconds that the GRUB2 boot loader screen appears before the default operating system is loaded or add parameters that are passed to the Linux kernel by modifying the GRUB_CMDLINE_LINUX line. Also note that the /etc/default/grub file does not list any operating system information. This is because GRUB2 uses the /etc/grub.d/30_os-prober script to automatically detect available operating system kernels on the system and configure them for use with GRUB2. If you would like to manually set the default operating system kernel listed at the GRUB2 boot loader screen, you can set the GRUB_DEFAULT line to the appropriate line number, starting from 0. For example, to set the second OS line shown in Figure 8-4 (Fedora (0-rescue-b904ceebccb642fd89bcbb9e645e0c4a)) as the default OS to boot, set GRUB_DEFAULT=1 in the /etc/default/grub file.

After modifying the /etc/default/grub file or adding scripts to the /etc/grub.d directory, you can run the `grub2-mkconfig command` to rebuild the grub.cfg file. For example, to rebuild the /boot/grub2/grub.cfg file on a Fedora system, you can use the following:

```
[root@server1 ~]# grub2-mkconfig -o /boot/grub2/grub.cfg
Generating grub configuration file …
done
[root@server1 ~]#_
```

On a system with a UEFI BIOS, you instead specify the location of the grub.cfg file within the UEFI System Partition (e.g., grub2-mkconfig -o /boot/efi/EFI/fedora/grub.cfg).

> **Note 16**
>
> On some Linux distributions, you can use the `update-grub2 command` without arguments to rebuild the grub.cfg file. The `update-grub2` command runs the appropriate `grub2-mkconfig` command to rebuild grub.cfg in the correct location on the system.

As with GRUB Legacy, if the GRUB2 boot loader becomes damaged, you can reinstall it. For systems with a standard BIOS, you can use the `grub2-install command`. To reinstall GRUB2 Stage 1 on the MBR/GPT of the first SATA hard disk drive on a Fedora system, you can type the following command:

```
[root@server1 ~]# grub2-install /dev/sda
Installation finished. No error reported.
[root@server1 ~]#_
```

For systems with a UEFI BIOS, you can reinstall GRUB2 by reinstalling the associated GRUB2 UEFI packages. To reinstall the GRUB2 UEFI packages, you can use the dnf reinstall grub2-efi grub2-efi-modules shim command on a Fedora system, or the apt-get install --reinstall grub-efi command on an Ubuntu system.

> **Note 17**
>
> If the system is unable to boot, you can boot a live Linux system used for system rescue, change to the root filesystem on the hard disk drive using the `chroot` command, and then run the appropriate command to reinstall GRUB2.

> **Note 18**
>
> For simplicity, some Linux distributions use `grub-mkconfig`, `grub-install` and `update-grub` in place of `grub2-mkconfig`, `grub2-install` and `update-grub2`, respectively.

Note 19

When you update your Linux operating system software, you may receive an updated version of your distribution kernel. In this case, the software update copies the new kernel to the /boot directory, creates a new initramfs to match the new kernel, and modifies the GRUB2 configuration to ensure that the new kernel is listed at the top of the graphical boot menu and set as the default for subsequent boot processes.

Note 20

Invalid entries in the GRUB2 configuration file or a damaged initramfs can prevent the kernel from loading successfully; this is called a **kernel panic** and will result in a system halt immediately after GRUB attempts to load the Linux kernel. In this case, you will need to edit the GRUB2 configuration file from a live Linux system used for system rescue or generate a new initramfs using either the `dracut` `command` or `mkinitrd` `command`.

Linux Initialization

Recall that after a boot loader loads the Linux operating system kernel into memory, the kernel resumes control and executes the init daemon, which then performs a system initialization process to execute other daemons and bring the system into a usable state.

Traditional Linux systems have used a system initialization process from the UNIX SysV standard. However, most modern Linux distributions have adopted the Systemd system initialization process. Systemd is completely compatible with the UNIX SysV standard yet implements new features for managing all system devices, including Linux kernel modules, daemons, processes, filesystems, and network sockets.

Note 21

Because Systemd is a recent technology, not all Linux daemons have been rewritten to use it. As a result, modern Linux distributions that have adopted Systemd may still use the UNIX SysV system initialization process to initialize some daemons.

Working with the UNIX SysV System Initialization Process

Linux systems that use the UNIX SysV system initialization process can choose from the traditional UNIX SysV system initialization process or the upstart system initialization process derived from UNIX SysV. In both systems, the init daemon runs a series of scripts to start other daemons on the system to provide system services and ultimately allow users to log in and use the system. Furthermore, the init daemon is responsible for starting and stopping daemons after system initialization, including stopping daemons before the system is halted or rebooted.

Runlevels

Because the init daemon must often manage several daemons at once, it categorizes the system into runlevels. A **runlevel** defines the number and type of daemons that are loaded into memory and executed by the kernel on a particular system. At any time, a Linux system might be in any of the seven standard runlevels defined in Table 8-1.

Table 8-1 Linux runlevels

Runlevel	Common Name	Description
0	Halt	A system that has no daemons active in memory and is ready to be powered off
1 s S single	Single User Mode	A system that has only enough daemons to allow one user (the root user) to log in and perform system maintenance tasks
2	Multiuser Mode	A system that has most daemons running and allows multiple users the ability to log in and use system services; most common network services other than specialized network services are available in this runlevel as well
3	Extended Multiuser Mode	A system that has the same abilities as Multiuser Mode, yet with all extra networking services started (e.g., FTP, Apache, NFS)
4	Not used	Not normally used, but can be customized to suit your needs
5	Graphical Mode	A system that has the same abilities as Extended Multiuser Mode, yet with a graphical login program; on systems that use the GNOME desktop, this program is called the GNOME Display Manager (GDM) and is typically started on tty1 to allow for graphical logins
6	Reboot	A special runlevel used to reboot the system

Note 22

Because the init daemon is responsible for starting and stopping daemons and, hence, changing runlevels, runlevels are often called initstates.

To see the current runlevel of the system and the previous runlevel (if runlevels have been changed since system startup), you can use the `runlevel` command, as shown in the following output:

```
[root@server1 ~]# runlevel
N 5
[root@server1 ~]#_
```

The preceding runlevel command indicates that the system is in runlevel 5 and that the most recent runlevel prior to entering this runlevel is nonexistent (N).

To change the runlevel on a running system, you can use the `init` command, as shown in the following output:

```
[root@server1 ~]# runlevel
N 5
[root@server1 ~]# init 1
*A list of daemons that are being stopped by the init
daemon while the system enters single user mode.*

Telling INIT to go to single user mode.
[root@server1 /]#_
[root@server1 /]# runlevel
5 1
[root@server1 /]#_
```

> ## Note 23
>
> The **telinit command** can be used in place of the `init` command when changing runlevels. Thus, the command `telinit 1` can instead be used to switch to Single User Mode.

> ## Note 24
>
> You can also pass options from the boot loader to the Linux kernel to force the system to boot to a particular runlevel. If you append the keyword `single` to the kernel line within the GRUB Legacy or GRUB2 configuration screen, you will boot to Single User Mode.

The /etc/inittab File

Unless you specify otherwise, the init daemon enters the default runlevel indicated in the /etc/inittab file. In the past, the /etc/inittab file contained the entire configuration for the init daemon. However, on systems that use the UNIX SysV system initialization process exclusively today, the /etc/inittab often contains a single uncommented line that configures the default runlevel, as shown here:

```
[root@server1 ~]# cat /etc/inittab
id:5:initdefault:
[root@server1 ~]#_
```

The line `id:5:initdefault:` in the /etc/inittab file tells the init daemon that runlevel 5 is the default runlevel to boot to when initializing the Linux system at system startup.

> ## Note 25
>
> Runlevel 5 is the default runlevel in most Linux distributions that have a desktop environment installed.

Runtime Configuration Scripts

During the boot process, the init daemon must execute several scripts that prepare the system, start daemons, and eventually bring the system to a usable state. These scripts are called **runtime configuration (rc) scripts**.

On Linux systems that use the traditional UNIX SysV system initialization process, the init daemon identifies the default runlevel in the /etc/inittab file and then proceeds to execute the files within the /etc/rc#.d directory that start with S or K, where # is the runlevel number. If the default runlevel is 5, then the init daemon would execute all files that start with S or K in the /etc/rc5.d directory in alphabetical order. The S or the K indicates whether to Start or Kill (stop) the daemon upon entering this runlevel, respectively. Some sample contents of the /etc/rc.d/rc5.d directory are shown in the following output:

```
[root@server1 ~]# ls /etc/rc5.d
README           S20screen-cleanup   S91apache2
S15bind9         S20zfs-mount        S92tomcat7
S19postgresql    S20zfs-share        S99grub-common
S20postfix       S70dns-clean        S99ondemand
S20rsync         S70pppd-dns         S99rc.local
[root@server1 ~]#_
```

From the preceding output, you can see that the init daemon will start the postfix daemon (S20postfix) upon entering this runlevel. To ensure that the files in the preceding directory are executed in a specific order, a sequence number is added following the S or K at the beginning of the filename. Thus, the file S19postgresql is always executed before the file S20postfix.

Recall that runlevel 1 (Single User Mode) contains only enough daemons for a single user to log in and perform system tasks. If a user tells the init daemon to change to this runlevel using the `init 1` command, the init daemon will execute every file that starts with S or K in the /etc/rc1.d directory. Because few daemons are started in Single User Mode, most files in this directory start with a K, as shown in the following output:

```
[root@server1 ~]# ls /etc/rc1.d
K08tomcat7   K20screen-cleanup   K80ebtables    S70dns-clean
K09apache2   K20zfs-mount        K85bind9       S70pppd-dns
K20postfix   K20zfs-share        README         S90single
K20rsync     K21postgresql       S30killprocs
[root@server1 ~]#_
```

Each file in an /etc/rc#.d directory is a symbolic link to an executable rc script in the /etc/init.d directory that can be used to start or stop a certain daemon, depending on whether the symbolic link filename started with an S (start) or K (kill/stop).

Figure 8-5 illustrates the traditional UNIX SysV system initialization process for a system that boots to runlevel 5.

Figure 8-5 A traditional UNIX SysV system initialization process

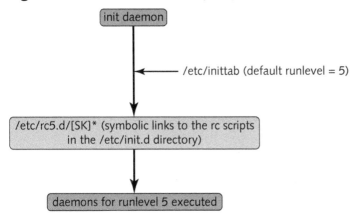

Note 26

After executing the runtime configuration scripts in the /etc/rc#.d directories, the init daemon executes the /etc/rc.local shell script, if present. As a result, Linux administrators often add commands to /etc/rc.local that must be run at the end of system initialization.

Note 27

Some Linux distributions use the /etc/rc.d/rc#.d directory in place of /etc/rc#.d and use the /etc/rc.d/init.d directory in place of /etc/init.d.

On Linux systems that use the upstart init system, the /etc/rc#.d directories are not used. Instead, the init daemon identifies the default runlevel in the /etc/inittab file and then directly executes the rc scripts within the /etc/init.d directory to start or stop the appropriate daemons based on the information specified in the configuration files within the /etc/init directory. Each daemon has a separate configuration file within the /etc/init directory that uses standard wildcard notation to identify the runlevels that it should be started or stopped in. For example, the /etc/init/cron.conf file shown next indicates that the cron daemon should be started in runlevels 2, 3, 4, and 5 ([2345]) and not be stopped in runlevels 2, 3, 4, and 5 ([!2345]):

```
[root@server1 ~]# cat /etc/init/cron.conf
# cron is a standard UNIX program that runs user-specified programs at
# periodic scheduled times
description     "regular background program processing daemon"
start on runlevel [2345]
stop on runlevel [!2345]
expect fork
respawn
exec cron
[root@server1 ~]#_
```

Figure 8-6 illustrates the upstart system initialization process for a system that boots to runlevel 5.

Figure 8-6   An upstart system initialization process

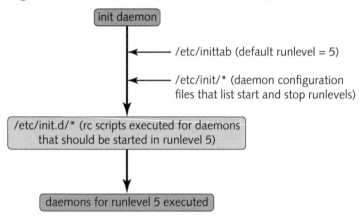

Note 28

Some daemons are not compatible with the upstart init system. As a result, Linux distributions that use the upstart init system often host several traditional UNIX SysV daemons that are started via entries in the /etc/rc#.d directories.

Starting and Stopping Daemons Manually

Recall from the preceding section that the init daemon starts daemons at system initialization as well as starts and stops daemons afterwards when the runlevel is changed by executing the rc scripts within the /etc/init.d directory. To manipulate daemons after system startup, you can execute them directly from the /etc/init.d directory with the appropriate argument (start, stop, or restart). For example, to restart the cron daemon, you could run the following command:

```
[root@server1 ~]# /etc/init.d/cron restart
cron stop/waiting
cron start/running, process 3371
[root@server1 ~]#_
```

You can also use the service command to start, stop, or restart any daemons listed within the /etc/init.d directory. For example, you can restart the cron daemon using the following command:

```
[root@server1 ~]# service cron restart
cron stop/waiting
cron start/running, process 3352
[root@server1 ~]#_
```

If you modify a daemon configuration file, you often have to restart a daemon to ensure that the configuration file is reloaded by the daemon. However, some daemons allow you to simply reload configuration files without restarting the daemon; for example, to force the cron daemon to reload its configuration files, you could run the `/etc/init.d/cron reload` or `service cron reload` command. You can also see the status of a daemon at any time by using the status argument to the service command or daemon script within the /etc/init.d directory; for example, to see the status of the cron daemon, you could run the `/etc/init.d/cron status` or `service cron status` command.

The upstart init system also provides the `stop command` to stop a daemon, the `start command` to start a daemon, the `restart command` to restart a daemon, the `reload command` to reload the configuration files for a daemon, and the `status command` to view the status of a daemon. Thus, you could also restart the cron daemon using the following command:

```
[root@server1 ~]# restart cron
cron start/running, process 3389
[root@server1 ~]#_
```

Configuring Daemons to Start in a Runlevel

If your Linux distribution uses the upstart init system, then configuring a daemon to start or stop in a particular runlevel is as easy as modifying the associated daemon configuration file in the /etc/init directory, as shown earlier.

However, for systems that use traditional UNIX SysV system initialization, you must create or modify the symbolic links within the /etc/rc#.d directories. To make this process easier, there are commands that you can use to do this for you. The `chkconfig command` is available on many Linux systems, and can be used to both list and modify the runlevels that a daemon is started in. For example, the following command indicates that the postfix daemon is not started in any runlevel:

```
[root@server1 ~]# chkconfig --list postfix
postfix           0:off 1:off 2:off 3:off 4:off 5:off 6:off
[root@server1 ~]#_
```

To configure the postfix daemon to start in runlevels 3 and 5 and to verify the results, you could run the following commands:

```
[root@server1 ~]# chkconfig --level 35 postfix on
[root@server1 ~]# chkconfig --list postfix
postfix           0:off 1:off 2:off 3:on  4:off 5:on  6:off
[root@server1 ~]#_
```

You can also customize `chkconfig` to manage only the daemons you specify. For example, to remove the ability for `chkconfig` to manage the postfix daemon, you could run the `chkconfig --del postfix` command. Alternatively, the `chkconfig --add postfix` command would allow `chkconfig` to manage the postfix daemon.

Ubuntu systems use the `update-rc.d command` instead of `chkconfig` to configure the files within the /etc/rc#.d directories. To configure the postfix daemon, for example, you should remove any existing symbolic links within the /etc/rc#.d directories for the postfix daemon using the following command:

```
[root@server1 ~]# update-rc.d -f postfix remove
Removing any system startup links for /etc/init.d/postfix …
   /etc/rc0.d/K20postfix
   /etc/rc1.d/K20postfix
   /etc/rc2.d/S20postfix
   /etc/rc3.d/S20postfix
   /etc/rc4.d/S20postfix
```

```
    /etc/rc5.d/S20postfix
    /etc/rc6.d/K20postfix
[root@server1 ~]#_
```

Next, you can use the update-rc.d command to configure the appropriate symbolic links within the /etc/rc#.d directories for the postfix daemon. Because most daemons are started in runlevels 2 through 5, you can specify the defaults keyword to create symbolic links that start the postfix daemon in runlevels 2 through 5, as shown in the following output:

```
[root@server1 ~]# update-rc.d postfix defaults
Adding system startup for /etc/init.d/postfix …
    /etc/rc0.d/K20postfix -> ../init.d/postfix
    /etc/rc1.d/K20postfix -> ../init.d/postfix
    /etc/rc6.d/K20postfix -> ../init.d/postfix
    /etc/rc2.d/S20postfix -> ../init.d/postfix
    /etc/rc3.d/S20postfix -> ../init.d/postfix
    /etc/rc4.d/S20postfix -> ../init.d/postfix
    /etc/rc5.d/S20postfix -> ../init.d/postfix
[root@server1 ~]#_
```

Alternatively, you can specify to start the postfix daemon only in runlevels 2 and 5 using the following command, which creates the rc scripts using a sequence number of 20:

```
[root@server1 ~]# update-rc.d postfix start 20 2 5 . stop 90 1 3 4 6 .
postfix Default-Start values (2 3 4 5)
postfix Default-Stop values (0 1 6)
 Adding system startup for /etc/init.d/postfix …
    /etc/rc1.d/K90postfix -> ../init.d/postfix
    /etc/rc3.d/K90postfix -> ../init.d/postfix
    /etc/rc4.d/K90postfix -> ../init.d/postfix
    /etc/rc6.d/K90postfix -> ../init.d/postfix
    /etc/rc2.d/S20postfix -> ../init.d/postfix
    /etc/rc5.d/S20postfix -> ../init.d/postfix
[root@server1 ~]#_
```

Working with the Systemd System Initialization Process

Like the UNIX SysV init daemon, the Systemd init daemon is used to start daemons during system initialization as well as start and stop daemons after system initialization. However, Systemd can also be used to start, stop, and configure many other operating system components. To Systemd, each operating system component is called a unit. Daemons are called service units because they provide a system service, and runlevels are called target units (or targets). By default, each target maps to a UNIX SysV runlevel:

- Poweroff.target is the same as Runlevel 0.
- Rescue.target is the same as Runlevel 1 (Single User Mode).
- Multi-user.target is the same as Runlevel 2, 3, and 4.
- Graphical.target is the same as Runlevel 5.
- Reboot.target is the same as Runlevel 6.

Note 29

The graphical.target first loads all daemons from the multi-user.target.

Note 30

For ease, many Linux distributions create shortcuts to targets named for the UNIX SysV runlevel; for example, runlevel5.target is often a shortcut to graphical.target, and runlevel1.target is often a shortcut to rescue.target.

The default target on a system that has a desktop environment installed is the graphical.target. To configure your system to instead boot to the multi-user.target, you can update the /etc/systemd/system/default.target symbolic link to point to the correct runlevel using the following command:

```
[root@server1 ~]# ln -s /lib/systemd/system/multi-user.target
/etc/systemd/system/default.target
[root@server1 ~]#_
```

Most of the service units that are used by Systemd to start and stop daemons are stored in the /lib/systemd/system directory and called *daemon*.service, where *daemon* is the name of the daemon. For example, the script for the cron daemon on a Fedora system is /lib/systemd/system/crond.service. To ensure that the cron daemon is started when entering the multi-user.target, you can create a symbolic link to /lib/systemd/system/crond.service called /etc/systemd/system/multi-user.target.wants/crond.service (i.e., the multi-user target wants the crond daemon).

Figure 8-7 illustrates the Systemd system initialization process for a system that boots to multi-user.target.

Figure 8-7   A Systemd system initialization process

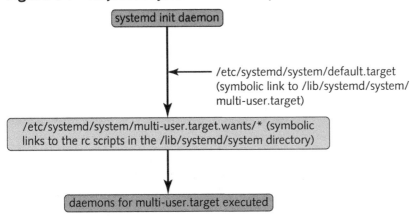

Note 31

The /lib/systemd/system directory stores the default configuration files for Systemd. These files are overridden by the same files in the /etc/systemd/system directory. Thus, to preserve default Systemd configuration settings, you should only create or modify files under /etc/systemd/system.

Note 32

On many Linux distributions, the /usr/lib/systemd and /lib/systemd directories are hard linked and contain identical contents as a result.

To start and stop daemons, as well as configure them to automatically start during system initialization, you can use the `systemctl command`. To start, stop, or restart a Systemd daemon, you can specify the appropriate action (start, stop, or restart) and name of the service unit as arguments. For example, to restart the cron daemon on Fedora Linux, you could use the following command:

```
[root@server1 ~]# systemctl restart crond.service
[root@server1 ~]#_
```

To reload the configuration files for the cron daemon on Fedora Linux, you could run the `systemctl reload crond.service` command, and to force Systemd to reload all units, you could run the `systemctl daemon-reload` command. You can also use the `systemctl` command to see detailed information about a particular Systemd daemon. For example, `systemctl status crond.service` would show detailed information about the cron daemon on Fedora Linux.

Without arguments, the `systemctl` command displays a list of all units that are currently executing in memory and their status. You can narrow this list to only services by piping the results to the `grep service` command. Moreover, to see all possible services regardless of whether they are loaded into memory or not, you can add the `-a` (or `--all`) option to the `systemctl` command. The following command displays all Systemd services and their state (dead indicates that it is currently not running):

```
[root@server1 ~]# systemctl -a | grep service | less
abrt-ccpp.service      loaded active exited    Install ABRT coredump
abrt-oops.service      loaded active running   ABRT kernel log watcher
abrt-vmcore.service    loaded active exited    Harvest vmcores for ABRT
abrtd.service          loaded active running   ABRT Automated Bug Repo
acpid.service          loaded active running   ACPI Event Daemon
alsa-store.service     loaded inactive dead    Store Sound Card State
arp-ethers.service     loaded inactive dead    Load static arp entries
atd.service            loaded active running   Job spooling tools
auditd.service         loaded active running   Security Auditing
avahi-daemon.service   loaded active running   Avahi mDNS/DNS-SD Stack
crond.service          loaded active running   Command Scheduler
cups.service           loaded active running   CUPS Printing Service
dbus-org.bluez.service error  inactive dead    dbus-org.bluez.service
dbus.service           loaded active running   D-Bus System Message Bus
:
```

You can also use the `systemd-analyze command` to view information about Systemd units; for example, to see a list of Systemd units sorted by the time they took to load, you could run the `systemd-analyze blame | less` command.

To configure a Systemd daemon to start in the default target (e.g., multi-user.target), you can use the `enable` argument to the `systemctl` command. For example, to ensure that the cron daemon is started at system initialization, you can run the `systemctl enable crond.service` command, which creates the appropriate symbolic link to /lib/systemd/system/crond.service within the /etc/systemd/system/multi-user.target.wants directory. Alternatively, the `systemctl disable crond.service` would prevent the cron daemon from starting when your system is booted by removing the symbolic link to /lib/systemd/system/crond.service within the /etc/systemd/system/multi-user.target.wants directory. However, another daemon started in the default target that depends on the cron daemon could potentially start the cron daemon. To fully ensure that the cron daemon cannot be started, you could run the `systemctl mask crond.service` command, which redirects the symbolic link for the cron daemon in /etc/systemd/system/multi-user.target.wants to /dev/null.

The `systemctl` command can also be used to change between targets. You can switch to multi-user.target (which is analogous to runlevel 3) by running either the `systemctl isolate multi-user.target` or `systemctl isolate runlevel3.target` command. Alternatively, you can switch to graphical.target (which is analogous to runlevel 5) by running the `systemctl isolate graphical.target` or `systemctl isolate runlevel5.target` command.

You can also create service-specific environment variables that Systemd will load into memory when it starts a particular service. To create a variable called MYVAR with the value SampleValue for use with the cron daemon on Fedora Linux, you could use the command `systemctl edit crond.service` and add the line `Environment="MYVAR=SampleValue"` into the nano editor and save your changes when finished. This line will be stored in the /etc/systemd/system/crond.service.d/override.conf file and executed each time Systemd starts the cron daemon.

Working with Systemd Unit Files

The text files under the /lib/systemd/system and /etc/systemd/system directories that provide the configuration used by Systemd are called unit files. You can modify unit files to alter the actions that Systemd performs or create unit files to configure additional Systemd functionality.

The following output examines sample contents of the graphical.target unit file:

```
[root@server1 ~]# cat /lib/systemd/system/graphical.target
[Unit]
Requires=multi-user.target
Wants=display-manager.service
Conflicts=rescue.target
After=multi-user.target display-manager.service
AllowIsolate=yes
[root@server1 ~]#_
```

The graphical.target unit file has a single [Unit] section that:

- `Requires` all services from the multi-user target be started; otherwise, the system will fail to switch to graphical.target.
- `Wants` the display-manager service to be started; if display-manager cannot be started, switching to the graphical target will still succeed.
- Cannot be run at the same time (`Conflicts`) as the rescue target.
- Instructs Systemd to start the multi-user target and display-manager service before entering (`After`) the graphical target (`Before` would start these services after entering the graphical target).
- Allow users to switch to the target (`AllowIsolate`) using the `systemctl` command following system initialization.

This configuration ensures that when Systemd switches to graphical.target, it will first execute the service unit files in the /lib/systemd/system/multi-user.target.wants and /etc/systemd/system/multi-user.target.wants directories. If any of these rc scripts unit files fail to execute, Systemd will not switch to graphical.target. Next, Systemd will execute the /etc/systemd/system/display-manager.service unit file. Regardless of whether the display-manager unit file executed successfully, Systemd will then execute the rc script unit files in the /lib/systemd/system/graphical.target.wants and /etc/systemd/system/graphical.target.wants directories to complete the switch to graphical.target.

Each service unit also has a service unit file that specifies the daemon it needs to start, the targets it should start and stop in, as well as any other necessary options. The following output examines sample contents of the crond.service unit file:

```
[root@server1 ~]# cat /lib/systemd/system/crond.service
[Unit]
Wants=network-online.target
After=network-online.target auditd.service systemd-user-
sessions.service

[Service]
Type=simple
User=root
EnvironmentFile=/etc/sysconfig/crond
```

```
ExecStart=/usr/sbin/crond
ExecStop=/bin/kill -INT $MAINPID
ExecReload=/bin/kill -HUP $MAINPID
KillMode=process
Restart=on-failure
RestartSec=30s

[Install]
WantedBy=multi-user.target
[root@server1 ~]#_
```

The crond.service unit file has a `[Unit]`, `[Service]`, and `[Install]` section that instructs Systemd to:

- Ensure that the network is fully started before starting the crond service (`Wants=network-online.target`).
- Start the network-online, auditd, and systemd-user-sessions services before starting (`After`) the crond service.
- Treat the crond service as a regular daemon process (`simple`) started as the `root` user.
- Load crond-specific environment settings from a file (`EnvironmentFile`).
- Use specific commands to start, stop, and restart the crond service (`ExecStart`, `ExecStop`, and `ExecReload`).
- Restart the crond service 30 seconds after a failure (`RestartSec=30s`).
- Start the crond service when entering the multi-user target (`WantedBy`).

Note 33

Service unit files are also used to start daemons that provide server services on the network. To ensure that a daemon is only started when the system receives an associated request from a computer on the network, you can instead configure a **socket unit** file. For example, a telnet.socket unit file would instruct Systemd to start a telnet server daemon only when the system receives a telnet request from a computer on the network.

In addition to controlling the system initialization process using target units and service units, you can configure **timer units** to run programs periodically or **mount units** to mount filesystems.

Timer units are an alternative to the cron daemon (discussed in Chapter 9) that Linux systems use for scheduling programs. They are often used to schedule low-level system maintenance tasks on modern Linux systems. For example, many Linux systems use a timer unit to periodically run the `fstrim command` on all physical SSDs in the system to reclaim unused blocks and improve performance. Following is an example fstrim.timer unit file that instructs Systemd to automatically run fstrim.service (which in turn runs the `fstrim` command) Monday through Friday at 11:30 pm and 3600 seconds after system boot, but only if the Linux system is not run within a virtual machine or container:

```
[root@server1 ~]# cat /etc/systemd/system/fstrim.timer
[Unit]
ConditionVirtualization=!container

[Timer]
Unit=fstrim.service
OnCalendar=Mon..Fri 23:30
OnBootSec=3600
```

```
[Install]
WantedBy=timers.target
[root@server1 ~]#_
```

Mount units are an alternative to /etc/fstab for mounting filesystems. Following is an example data.mount unit file that instructs Systemd to mount an ext4 filesystem (identified by UUID) to the /data directory when the system enters the graphical.target. After creating a new mount unit, you must ensure that it is configured to start in the desired target using the `systemctl enable` command.

```
[root@server1 ~]# cat /etc/systemd/system/data.mount
[Unit]
Description=Mount data filesystem in graphical target

[Mount]
What=/dev/disk/by-uuid/4f07cfa5-fb5b-4511-8688-3305759d9006
Where=/data
Type=ext4
Options=defaults

[Install]
WantedBy=graphical.target
[root@server1 ~]# systemctl enable data.mount
[root@server1 ~]#_
```

Note 34

To mount a filesystem using a mount unit, you must specify the filesystem to mount using the UUID device file.

If you instead name the same mount unit file data.automount, the filesystem will only be mounted by Systemd when the /data directory is accessed for the first time by a user.

You can also use the `systemd-mount command` and `systemd-umount command` to manually mount and unmount filesystems using Systemd, respectively. For example, the `systemd-mount -A /dev/sda5 /data` command will instruct Systemd to mount /dev/sda5 to the /data directory, but only when the /data directory is accessed for the first time by a user (-A).

The X Windows System

This chapter has so far focused on performing tasks using the command-line shell interface. Although most Linux administrators perform tasks exclusively within a shell, other Linux users use a GUI for running graphical programs. Thus, you need to understand the components that make up the Linux GUI. Additionally, you need to know how to start, stop, and configure them.

Linux GUI Components

The Linux GUI was designed to function consistently, no matter what video adapter card and monitor are installed on the computer system. It is composed of many components, each of which works separately from the video hardware.

A Linux installation usually includes all the GUI components listed in Figure 8-8. Together, these GUI components and related programs use over 4 GB of storage space on a typical Linux installation.

Figure 8-8   Components of the Linux GUI

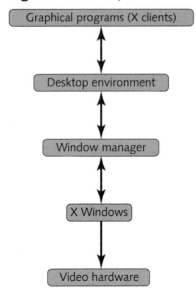

X Windows

Recall from Chapter 1 that the core component of a Linux GUI is called X Windows and provides the ability to draw graphical images in windows that are displayed on a terminal screen. The programs that tell X Windows how to draw the graphics and display the results are known as **X clients**. X clients need not run on the same computer as X Windows; you can use X Windows on one computer to send graphical images to an X client on an entirely different computer by changing the DISPLAY environment variable discussed in Chapter 7. Because of this, X Windows is sometimes referred to as the server component of X Windows, or simply the **X server**.

X Windows was jointly developed by Digital Equipment Corporation (DEC) and the Massachusetts Institute of Technology (MIT) in 1984. At that time, it was code-named Project Athena and was released in 1985 as X Windows in hopes that a new name would be found to replace the X. Shortly thereafter, X Windows was sought by many UNIX vendors; and by 1988, MIT released version 11 release 2 of X Windows (X11R2). Since 1988, X Windows has been maintained by The Open Group, which released version 11 release 6 of X Windows (X11R6) in 1995. Since 2004, X Windows has been maintained as Open Source Software by the **X.org** Foundation.

Wayland is a new version of X Windows designed to replace X.org; it has additional security features and an architecture that makes graphical application development easier. While it is still currently in development, many recent Linux distributions use Wayland as the default X server but have X.org installed to ensure that Wayland-incompatible applications can still be used.

Note 35

To find out more about X Windows, visit the X.org Foundation's website at x.org. To learn more about Wayland, visit wayland.freedesktop.org.

Note 36

When Linux was first released, X Windows was governed by a separate license than the GPL, which restricted the usage of X Windows and its source code. As a result, early Linux distributions used an open source version of X Windows called XFree86.

Window Managers and Desktop Environments

To modify the look and feel of X Windows, you can use a window manager. For example, the dimensions and color of windows that are drawn on a graphical screen, as well as the method used to move windows around on a graphical screen, are functions of a window manager.

Note 37

Window managers that are compatible with Wayland are called Wayland compositors.

Many window managers are available for Linux, including those listed in Table 8-2.

Table 8-2   Common window managers

Window Manager	Description
Compiz	A highly configurable and expandable window manager that uses 3D acceleration to produce 3D graphical effects, including 3D window behavior and desktop cube workspaces
Enlightenment (E)	A highly configurable window manager that allows for multiple desktops with different settings
F Virtual Window Manager (FVWM)	A window manager, based on Tab Window Manager, that uses less computer memory and gives the desktop a 3D look
KWin	The window manager used by the K Desktop Environment; it is also a Wayland compositor
Lightweight X11 Desktop Environment (LXDE)	A window manager specifically designed for use on underpowered, mobile, and legacy systems
Metacity	The default window manager used by GNOME version 1 and 2
Mutter	The default window manager used by GNOME version 3 and later; it is also a Wayland compositor
i3	A tiling window manager commonly used by software developers and systems administrators that require a heavily customized desktop for working with code and commands
Sway	A tiling window manager that is used exclusively as a Wayland compositor; it is an alternative to i3 for Wayland users
Tab Window Manager (twm)	One of the oldest and most basic of window managers that is supported today; it provides the same features as early UNIX graphical desktops
Window Maker	A window manager that imitates the NeXTSTEP UNIX interface on which macOS is based

You can use a window manager alone or in conjunction with a desktop environment.

Recall from Chapter 1 that a desktop environment provides a standard look and feel for the GUI; it contains a standard set of GUI tools designed to be packaged together, including web browsers, file managers, and drawing programs. Desktop environments also provide sets of development tools, known as toolkits, that speed up the process of creating new software. As discussed in Chapter 1, the two most common desktop environments used on Linux are the K Desktop Environment (KDE) and the GNU Network Object Model Environment (GNOME).

KDE is the traditional desktop environment used on Linux systems. First released by Matthias Ettrich in 1996, KDE uses the KWin window manager and the Qt toolkit for the C++ programming language. The graphical interface components of KDE are collectively called the Plasma Desktop; KDE Plasma Desktop 5 is the latest version at the time of this writing.

Note 38

To learn more about KDE, visit kde.org.

The Qt toolkit included in KDE was created by a company called Trolltech in Norway in the 1990s. However, it took a while to build a following because, at the time, most open source developers preferred to develop in the C programming language instead of C++. Also, the fact that Qt was not released as Open Source Software until 1998 was a drawback, because most developers preferred source code that was freely modifiable.

As a result of the general dissatisfaction with the Qt toolkit, GNOME was created in 1997, and has since become the default desktop environment on most Linux distributions. GNOME 42 is the latest version of GNOME at the time of this writing; it uses the Mutter window manager and the GTK+ toolkit for the C programming language. The GTK+ toolkit was originally developed for the GNU Image Manipulation Program (GIMP); like the GIMP, it is open source. The graphical interface components of GNOME 42 are collectively called the GNOME Shell. Alternatives to the GNOME Shell have been developed that provide different features, including the mobile-focused Unity. There are also many modern desktop environments that are based on GNOME, including the Cinnamon desktop environment derived from GNOME 3, and the MATE desktop environment derived from GNOME 2.

Note 39

To learn more about GNOME, visit gnome.org.

KDE, GNOME, and GNOME-based desktop environments use system resources, such as memory and CPU time, to provide their graphical interface. As a result, most Linux administrators do not install a desktop environment on a Linux server. For Linux servers that require a desktop environment, many Linux administrators choose to install a lightweight desktop environment that uses very few system resources. XFCE is a common lightweight desktop environment used today.

Note 40

To learn more about XFCE, visit xfce.org.

Note 41

Desktop environments are often used to run many different programs. As a result, they must provide a mechanism that allows programs to easily communicate with one another for functions such as copy-and-paste. While this functionality can be provided by Wayland compositors, most Wayland- and X.org-based systems use the Desktop Bus (D-Bus) software component to provide communication between graphical programs.

Starting and Stopping X Windows

As explained earlier in this chapter, when the init daemon boots to runlevel 5 or graphical.target, a program called the GNOME Display Manager (GDM) is started that displays a graphical login screen. If you click a user account within the GDM and choose the settings (cog wheel) icon, you will be able to choose from a list of installed desktop environments or window managers, as shown in Figure 8-9.

Figure 8-9 Selecting a graphical session within the GNOME Display Manager on a Fedora system

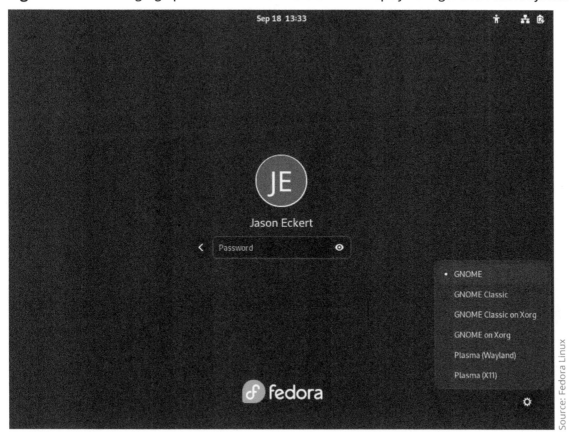

Source: Fedora Linux

Note 42

The GNOME Display Manager is a variant of the **X Display Manager (XDM)**, which displays a basic graphical login for users. Other common display managers used on Linux distributions include the **KDE Display Manager (KDM)**, the **Simple Desktop Display Manager (SDDM)**, and the **LightDM** display manager.

The default desktop environment started by the GNOME Display Manager on Fedora Linux is GNOME using Wayland. However, after you select a particular user, select Plasma using the Session menu, and the GNOME Display Manager will continue to use the KDE Plasma as the default desktop environment for the user account unless you choose otherwise.

The GNOME Display Manager is the easiest way to log in and access the desktop environments that are available on your system. If, however, you use runlevel 1 (or rescue.target) or runlevel 2 through 4 (multi-user.target), the GNOME Display Manager is not started by default. In this case, you can run the `startx command` from a shell to start X Windows and the default window manager or desktop environment (e.g., GNOME on Wayland).

Configuring X Windows

X Windows is the component of the GUI that interfaces with the video hardware in the computer. For X Windows to perform its function, it needs information regarding the mouse, monitor, and video adapter card. This information is normally detected from the associated kernel modules that are loaded at boot time but can also be specified within configuration files. The keyboard type (e.g., English, US layout) is normally specified manually during the installation process, as shown earlier in Figure 2-8, but can be changed afterwards by accessing the Settings utility within a desktop environment, or by modifying the appropriate localization options as discussed later in this chapter.

If you use X.org, X Windows stores its configuration in the file /etc/X11/xorg.conf as well as within files stored in the /etcX11/xorg.conf.d directory. Although there is no /etc/X11/xorg.conf file in Fedora by default, it will be used if present. Instead, the keyboard type and any user-configured settings are stored in files under the /etc/X11/xorg.conf.d directory, and common settings such as the display resolution can be modified using the Settings utility within a desktop environment. In GNOME, you can navigate to Activities, Show Applications, Settings to open the Settings utility, and then select Displays to view available settings, as shown in Figure 8-10.

Figure 8-10   Selecting display settings

Note 43

Wayland does not have an xorg.conf equivalent; instead, all manual configuration for Wayland must be performed by the Wayland compositor.

Note 44

If you choose incompatible X Windows settings, any errors generated will be written to the ~/.xsession-errors file.

Accessibility

Many desktop environments can be configured to suit the needs of users, thus increasing the accessibility of the desktop environment. The tools used to increase accessibility are collectively called **assistive technologies**. You can configure assistive technologies using the Settings utility within a desktop environment. In GNOME, you can navigate to Activities, Show Applications, Settings to open the Settings utility, and then select Accessibility to configure assistive technologies, as shown in Figure 8-11.

If you turn on the Always Show Accessibility Menu option shown in Figure 8-11, you can enable and disable each assistive technology using the Accessibility icon in the upper-right corner of the GNOME desktop. Following is a list of the assistive technologies that you can configure within GNOME:

- High Contrast, which modifies the color scheme to suit those with low vision
- Large Text, which increases the font size of text to suit those with low vision
- Enable Animations, which allows visual effects to appear on windows and icons for easy identification

Figure 8-11   Configuring assistive technologies

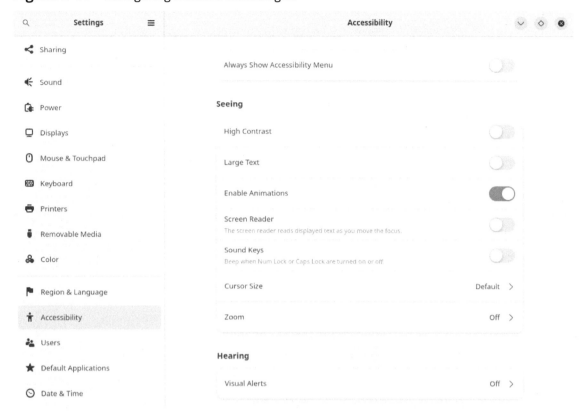

- Screen Reader, which narrates the text on the active window on the screen
- Sound Keys, which beep when the Num Lock or Caps Lock keys are pressed
- Cursor Size, which enlarges the mouse pointer size for easy visibility
- Zoom, which allows you to enable magnification for parts of the screen that your mouse follows, as well as modify the color and crosshair effects during magnification
- Visual Alerts, which displays a visual alert in place of beep sounds
- Screen Keyboard, which displays an on-screen keyboard that can be used with a mouse
- Repeat Keys, which simulates multiple key presses when a single key is continually pressed
- Cursor Blinking, which adds a blinking cursor to the current text field
- Typing Assist, which provides three keyboard assistive features:
  - Sticky keys, which simulate simultaneous key presses when two keys are pressed in sequence
  - Slow keys, which add a delay following each key press
  - Bounce keys, which ignore fast duplicate key presses
- Mouse Keys, which allow the user to control the mouse using the cursor keys on the keyboard
- Locate Pointer, which will increase the size of the mouse cursor (making it easier to locate on the screen) if you move your mouse rapidly
- Click Assist, which can be used to simulate a right-click by holding down a left-click for a period of time, or trigger a left-click by hovering the mouse pointer over an area of the desktop
- Double-Click Delay, which can be used to set the time delay between two clicks that the desktop will interpret as a double-click action (e.g., to open an app)

You can also provide many other assistive technologies if your computer has the appropriate software and hardware. For example, if your system has a braille interface device, you can install braille display software that will allow it to work with the desktop environment. Similarly, you can configure voice recognition software if your system has an audio microphone, or gesture recognition software if your system has a web camera or trackpad.

Localization

Localization refers to the collective settings on a system that are specific to a specific region within the world. For example, a Linux system within Toronto, Canada will have different settings compared to a Linux system in Paris, France, including time, time zone, language, character set, and keyboard type. Localization settings are normally chosen during the installation process of the Linux distribution (as shown earlier in Figures 2-7 and 2-8) but can be changed afterwards.

Time Localization

The Linux kernel does not store time information in a format that represents the year, month, day, hour, minute and second as in the output of the date command in Chapter 2. Instead, the Linux kernel stores time as the number of seconds since January 1, 1970 UTC (the birth of UNIX); this is called epoch time and can be shown by supplying arguments to the date command, as shown in the following output:

```
[root@server1 ~]# date +%s
1535823499
[root@server1 ~]#_
```

By default, the system obtains the current time from the BIOS on your system. You can view or modify the time within the BIOS using the hwclock command. Without arguments, hwclock simply prints the time from the BIOS, but you can specify options to modify the BIOS time as well. For example, the hwclock --set --date='2023-08-20 08:16:00' would set the BIOS time to 8:16 AM on August 20, 2023.

Alternatively, you can set the Linux time using the date command. For example, the command date -s "20 AUG 2023 08:16:00" would set the Linux time to 8:16 AM on August 20, 2023. You could then use the hwclock -w command to set the BIOS time to match the current Linux time to ensure that the correct time is loaded from the BIOS at boot time.

> **Note 45**
>
> Recall from Chapter 1 that you can also obtain time from a server across a network, such as the Internet, using the Network Time Protocol (NTP). The configuration of NTP will be discussed in Chapter 13.

Time information is dependent on the regional time zone. For example, 8:16 AM in Toronto, Canada is 2:16 PM in Paris, France. Time zone information is stored in the binary /etc/localtime file, which contains the rules for calculating the time based on your time zone relative to epoch time. This file is normally a copy of, or symbolic link to, the correct file under the /usr/share/zoneinfo directory, which stores all zone information files, as shown below:

```
[root@server1 ~]# ll /etc/localtime
lrwxrwxrwx. 1 root root 37 Jul  8 20:13 /etc/localtime ->
../usr/share/zoneinfo/America/Toronto
[root@server1 ~]#_
```

To change the system time zone, you can copy the appropriate time zone information file from the /usr/share/zoneinfo directory to /etc/localtime or modify the /etc/localtime symbolic link to point to the correct zone information file under the /usr/share/zoneinfo directory.

In addition to /etc/localtime, some distributions also have an /etc/timezone text file that contains a reference to the correct time zone file path underneath the /usr/share/zoneinfo directory for use by certain applications, as shown in the following output:

```
[root@server1 ~]# cat /etc/timezone
America/Toronto
[root@server1 ~]#_
```

You can also override the default system time zone within your current shell by modifying the contents of the TZ variable. For example, running the `export TZ='America/Toronto'` command would ensure that any commands that you run in your shell display time information using the Toronto, Canada time zone. To ensure that the commands within a particular shell script use a particular time zone, set the TZ variable at the beginning of the shell script under the hashpling line. If you are unsure which time zone file you should use with the TZ variable (e.g., America/Toronto), you can run the `tzselect command`, which will prompt you to answer a series of questions to determine the correct time zone file name.

The `timedatectl command` can also be used to view and set both the time and time zone information on your system. Without arguments, `timedatectl` displays system time information. However, you could run the `timedatectl set-time "2023-08-20 08:16:00"` command to set the system time to 8:16 AM on August 20, 2023, or the `timedatectl set-timezone 'America/Toronto'` command to set the time zone to Toronto, Canada. You can also use the `timedatectl set-ntp true` command to ensure that time and time zone information is obtained using NTP.

Format Localization

In addition to time localization, different regions may have different formats used to represent data. This primarily includes the language, but also includes conventions used by the region. For example, while North America often expresses money in the format $4.50 (four dollars and fifty cents), Europe would express the same format as 4,50$. Similarly, Asia typically represents dates in the form YYYYMMDD (Year, Month, Day), whereas the United States typically represents dates in the form MMDDYYYY (Month, Day, Year).

Different languages may also have different character sets that must be represented by software as well as mapped to keyboard keys for input. The American Standard Code for Information Interchange (ASCII) character set used on early computers of the 1960s was specific to English characters and thus had no international localization options. It was extended to include some other languages with the introduction of the ISO-8859 standard, but still lacked many of the extended characters used by these languages. A new standard called Unicode extends ASCII to allow for the representation of characters in nearly all languages used worldwide, and the UTF-8 character set allows software to use one to four 8-bit bytes to represent the characters defined by Unicode.

Note 46

You can convert data between different character sets using the `iconv command`.

Moreover, the same language may have slightly different character sets, keyboard layouts, and formats for different regions; for example, a Canadian French keyboard will differ from a European French keyboard, and Canadian French date and money formats differ from European French date and money formats. As a result, the format localization on most systems includes a language, region, and character set, and is referred to as a locale. For example, the en_US.UTF-8 locale represents US regional English, with a UTF-8 character set. If the character set is omitted from the locale, the ASCII character set is assumed; for example, en_US represents US regional English, with an ASCII character set.

Some Linux distributions pass the correct locale to the Linux kernel as it is loaded by the GRUB2 boot loader using the LANG option on the kernel line of the GRUB2 configuration file. This instructs Linux to set the LANG variable following system startup to the correct locale. You can also view the contents of /proc/cmdline to see if your Linux kernel was loaded with the LANG option:

```
[root@server1 ~]# cat /proc/cmdline
BOOT_IMAGE=(hd0,gpt2)/vmlinuz-5.17.5-300.fc36.x86_64
root=UUID=9ff25add-035b-4d26-9129-a9da6d0a6fa3 ro rhgb quiet
LANG=en_US.UTF-8
[root@server1 ~]#_
```

If the LANG variable was not created by the Linux kernel during boot, it is loaded from a file; on Ubuntu systems, the LANG variable is loaded from /etc/default/locale, and on Fedora systems it is loaded from /etc/locale.conf as shown below:

```
[root@server1 ~]# cat /etc/locale.conf
LANG="en_US.UTF-8"
[root@server1 ~]#_
```

You can display the values for locale variables using the `locale command` as shown below:

```
[root@server1 ~]# locale
LANG=en_US.UTF-8
LC_CTYPE="en_US.UTF-8"
LC_NUMERIC="en_US.UTF-8"
LC_TIME="en_US.UTF-8"
LC_COLLATE="en_US.UTF-8"
LC_MONETARY="en_US.UTF-8"
LC_MESSAGES="en_US.UTF-8"
LC_PAPER="en_US.UTF-8"
LC_NAME="en_US.UTF-8"
LC_ADDRESS="en_US.UTF-8"
LC_TELEPHONE="en_US.UTF-8"
LC_MEASUREMENT="en_US.UTF-8"
LC_IDENTIFICATION="en_US.UTF-8"
LC_ALL=
[root@server1 ~]#_
```

Note from the previous output that the value of the LANG variable is set to en_US.UTF-8. Also note that other format-specific locale variables exist and are set to use the value of LANG by default. This allows users to override the default locale for a particular format type, such as units of measurement. For example, to ensure that operating system components and applications use the Canadian metric system for measurement, you could add the line `export LC_MEASUREMENT="en_CA.UTF-8"` to a shell environment file; this will use Canadian regional English with a UTF-8 character set for measurement, and US regional English for all other formats. Alternatively, to ensure that the same locale is used for all format types, you can set the value of the LC_ALL variable, which overrides LANG and all other LC variables. To see a list of all locales that you can use, run the `locale -a` command.

Note 47

The C locale is a standard locale that all UNIX and Linux systems can use. Many Linux administrators add `export LANG=C` at the beginning of shell scripts (underneath the hashpling line) to ensure that the stdout of any commands within the shell script is not dependent on the locale of the system that executes it. Most shell scripts within a Linux distribution use the C locale to ensure that any stdout can be compared to standardized online documentation for troubleshooting and learning purposes.

You can also use the `localectl command` to view and change locale settings on your system. Without arguments, `localectl` displays the current locale. To see a list of available locales, you can run the `localectl list-locales` command, and to set the default locale to en_CA.UTF-8, you can run the `localectl set-locale LANG=en_CA.UTF-8` command.

Normally, the keyboard type on a system matches the language and region within the locale (e.g., en_US for US English keyboard, or en_CA for Canadian English keyboard). However, there may be times when you must choose a layout that varies from the regional standard. For example, to ensure that your Linux system can use a US English Apple Macintosh keyboard, you could use the `localectl set-keymap mac-us` command. To see a list of available keyboard types, you can use the `localectl list-keymaps` command.

Summary

- The GRUB boot loader is normally loaded from the MBR or GPT of a storage device by a standard BIOS, or from the UEFI System Partition by a UEFI BIOS. GRUB Legacy supports systems with a standard BIOS and MBR storage devices, whereas GRUB2 supports both standard and UEFI BIOS systems as well as MBR and GPT storage devices.

- After the boot loader loads the Linux kernel, a system initialization process proceeds to load daemons that bring the system to a usable state.

- There are two common system initialization processes: UNIX SysV and Systemd.

- UNIX SysV uses seven runlevels to categorize a Linux system based on the number and type of daemons loaded in memory. Systemd uses five standard targets that correspond to the seven UNIX SysV runlevels.

- The init daemon is responsible for loading and unloading daemons when switching between runlevels and targets, as well as at system startup and shutdown.

- Daemons are typically executed during system initialization via UNIX SysV rc scripts or Systemd unit files. The /etc/init.d directory contains most UNIX SysV rc scripts, and the /lib/systemd/system and /etc/systemd/system directories contain most Systemd unit files.

- In addition to managing the system initialization process using target units and service units, Systemd can use socket units to manage network daemons, timer units to schedule programs, and mount units to mount filesystems.

- You can use a variety of different commands to start, stop, and restart daemons following system initialization. The service command is commonly used to start, stop, and restart UNIX SysV daemons, and the systemctl command is commonly used to start, stop, and restart Systemd daemons.

- You can use the chkconfig or update-rc.d commands to configure UNIX SysV daemon startup at boot time, as well as the systemctl command to configure Systemd daemon startup at boot time.

- The Linux GUI has several interchangeable components, including the X server, X clients, window manager, and optional desktop environment. You can use assistive technologies to make desktop environments more accessible to users.

- X Windows is the core component of the Linux GUI that draws graphics to the terminal screen. It comes in one of two open source implementations today: X.org and Wayland. The hardware information required by X Windows is automatically detected but can be modified using several utilities.

- You can start the Linux GUI from runlevel 3 by typing startx at a command prompt, or from runlevel 5 via a display manager, such as GDM.

- Linux has many region-specific settings, including time, date, and locale. Locale settings provide region-specific formats, language, and character support; they can be set for an entire system, or for a specific shell or shell script.

Key Terms

active partition
American Standard Code for
  Information Interchange (ASCII)
assistive technologies
boot loader
chkconfig command
Cinnamon
Desktop Bus (D-Bus)
dracut command
epoch time
fstrim command
GNOME Display Manager (GDM)
GNOME Shell

GRand Unified Bootloader (GRUB)
GRand Unified Bootloader version
  2 (GRUB2)
GRUB Legacy
GRUB root partition
grub-install command
grub2-install command
grub2-mkconfig command
hwclock command
iconv command
init command
initialize (init) daemon
initramfs

initstate
ISO-8859
KDE Display Manager (KDM)
kernel panic
LightDM
locale
locale command
localectl command
localization
MATE
mkinitrd command
mount unit
multi boot

netbooting

Plasma Desktop

Power On Self Test (POST)

`reload` command

`restart` command

runlevel

`runlevel` command

runtime configuration (rc) scripts

secure boot

`service` command

service unit

Simple Desktop Display Manager
   (SDDM)

socket unit

`start` command

`startx` command

`status` command

`stop` command

system initialization process

`systemctl` command

Systemd

`systemd-analyze` command

`systemd-mount` command

`systemd-umount` command

target

target unit

`telinit` command.

`timedatectl` command

timer unit

`tzselect` command

Unicode

unit file

Unity

UNIX SysV

`update-grub2` command

`update-rc.d` command

upstart

UTF-8

Wayland

Wayland compositor

window manager

X client

X Display Manager (XDM)

X server

X.org

XFCE

Review Questions

1. Which command can be used to modify the default locale on the system?
   - **a.** `tzselect`
   - **b.** `cmdline`
   - **c.** `localectl`
   - **d.** `export LANG=C`

2. Which of the following statements is true?
   - **a.** GRUB Legacy can be loaded from a MBR or GPT.
   - **b.** After modifying /etc/default/grub, you must run the `grub2-mkconfig` command before the changes are made to GRUB2.
   - **c.** GRUB2 can only be loaded from a UEFI System Partition.
   - **d.** GRUB needs to be reinstalled after it has been modified.

3. Which runlevel starts a display manager, such as GDM?
   - **a.** 1
   - **b.** 6
   - **c.** 0
   - **d.** 5

4. Which of the following Systemd units is functionally equivalent to a runlevel?
   - **a.** service
   - **b.** target
   - **c.** timer
   - **d.** mount

5. Which command can be used to start X Windows, the window manager, and the default desktop environment?
   - **a.** `startgui`
   - **b.** `startgdm`
   - **c.** `startx`
   - **d.** `gstart`

6. Which of the following statements is true?
   - **a.** Unicode provides the least localization support for different languages.
   - **b.** ASCII is the most common character set used today.
   - **c.** UTF-8 is commonly used to provide Unicode character set support.
   - **d.** ASCII is an extension of the ISO-8859 standard.

7. Which of the following indicates the second MBR partition on the third hard disk drive to GRUB2?
   - **a.** hd2,msdos2
   - **b.** hd4,mbr3
   - **c.** hd3,mbr2
   - **d.** hd2,msdos1

8. Which two implementations of X Windows are commonly used in Linux? (Choose two answers.)
   - **a.** X.org
   - **b.** XFCE
   - **c.** winX
   - **d.** Wayland

9. What is the name of the directory that contains symbolic links to UNIX SysV rc scripts for runlevel 2?
   - **a.** /etc/rc2.d
   - **b.** /etc/init.d/rc2.d
   - **c.** /etc/runlevel/2
   - **d.** /etc/inittab/rc2/d

10. Under what directory is Stage 2 of the GRUB2 boot loader stored?
   - **a.** /boot
   - **b.** /root
   - **c.** /bin
   - **d.** /

11. Which command instructs the UNIX SysV init or Systemd daemon to reboot the system?
    a. `init 0`
    b. `telinit 1`
    c. `init 6`
    d. `telinit 5`

12. Which assistive technology will make a desktop environment more accessible to a person with low vision?
    a. High Contrast
    b. Visual Alerts
    c. Repeat Keys
    d. Click Assist

13. You have recently modified the system time using the `date` command. What command can you run to ensure that the same time is updated within the system BIOS?
    a. `timedatectl --update`
    b. `tzselect`
    c. `hwclock -w`
    d. `date --set`

14. You want to configure the runlevels that a particular upstart daemon is started in. What should you do?
    a. Run the appropriate `update-rc.d` command.
    b. Modify the contents of the /etc/rc#.d directories.
    c. Modify the daemon configuration file within the /etc/init directory.
    d. Run the appropriate `systemctl` command.

15. Which of the following Systemd commands can be used to stop a daemon called lala?
    a. `service stop lala`
    b. `systemctl stop lala.service`
    c. `chkconfig stop lala`
    d. `stop lala`

16. Which of the following commands can be used to start a UNIX SysV daemon called lala in runlevels 1, 2, and 3?

a. `chkconfig --level 123 lala on`
b. `update-rc.d lala defaults`
c. `systemctl enable lala 123`
d. `service enable lala 123`

17. You have created a Systemd mount unit file that mounts a filesystem upon entering the multi-user target. However, when you switch to the multi-user target, you notice that the filesystem is not mounted. Which of the following troubleshooting steps should you take? (Choose all that apply.)
    a. Verify that the filesystem was specified using a UUID in the mount unit file.
    b. Remove any entries for the filesystem from /etc/fstab.
    c. Ensure that the mount unit is activated using the `systemctl enable` command.
    d. Run the `update-rc.d` command to reindex all unit files.

18. What kernel option can be specified within a boot loader to force the system to boot to Single User Mode?
    a. `init`
    b. `rescue`
    c. `single`
    d. `telinit`

19. What variable is often set at the beginning of a shell script to set a specific locale?
    a. LC
    b. LANG
    c. LOCALE
    d. CMDLINE

20. What desktop environment is most likely to be installed on a Linux server system?
    a. XFCE
    b. XDM
    c. KDE
    d. GNOME

Hands-On Projects

These projects should be completed in the order given. The hands-on projects presented in this chapter should take a total of three hours to complete. The requirements for this lab include:
- A computer with Fedora Linux installed according to Hands-On Project 2-1.

Project 8-1

Estimated Time: 35 minutes
Objective: Use GRUB2.
Description: In this hands-on project, you use and configure the GRUB2 boot loader on Fedora Linux.

1. Boot your Fedora Linux virtual machine. After your Linux system has been loaded, switch to a command-line terminal (tty5) by pressing **Ctrl+Alt+F5** and log in to the terminal using the user name of **root** and the password of **LINUXrocks!**.

2. If your virtual machine emulates a UEFI BIOS, type `cat /boot/efi/EFI/fedora/grub.cfg` and press **Enter**. Note that the "set prefix" and "configfile" lines in this file refer to the contents of the /boot/grub2/grub.cfg file.

3. At the command prompt, type `less /boot/grub2/grub.cfg` and press **Enter**. Which line sets the default timeout for user interaction at the boot screen? Are there any menuentry paragraphs? Why? Press q when finished.

4. At the command prompt, type `ls -l /boot/loader/entries` and press **Enter**. What do these files represent? Next, type `cat /boot/loader/entries/*64.conf` and press **Enter**. Note the lines that load the Linux kernel and initramfs.

5. At the command prompt, type `vi /etc/default/grub` and press **Enter** to edit the GRUB2 configuration file. Change the value of GRUB_TIMEOUT to 30. Save your changes and quit the vi editor.

6. At the command prompt, type `grub2-mkconfig -o /boot/grub2/grub.cfg` and press **Enter** to rebuild the GRUB2 configuration file with your change.

7. Reboot your system by typing `reboot` and pressing **Enter**. At the GRUB2 boot screen, view the available options. How long do you have to interact with the GRUB2 boot loader after POST before the default operating system is booted? Next, press **c** to obtain a command prompt.

8. At the grub> prompt, type `help` and press **Enter** to see a list of available commands, pressing the **spacebar** to cycle through the entire list. Next, type `lsmod` and press **Enter** to see a list of modules loaded by GRUB2. Is the blscfg module loaded? Following this, type `list_env` and press **Enter** to view the variables present. By default, there should be a variable called saved_entry that lists the default OS that is booted by GRUB2 (the previously chosen OS stored within /boot/grub2/grubenv). Type `reboot` and press **Enter** to reboot your system.

9. At the GRUB2 boot screen, press **e** to edit your configuration. Where did you see these contents recently?

10. Locate the first line that starts with the word "linux" and navigate to the end of this line (the last two keywords on this line should be rhgb and quiet). Add the word `single` after the word quiet and press **F10** to boot your modified configuration. What does this option tell the boot loader to do?

11. Supply your root password of **LINUXrocks!** when prompted.

12. At the command prompt, type `runlevel` and press **Enter**. What is your current runlevel? What is the most recent runlevel?

13. At the command prompt, type `cat /proc/cmdline` and press **Enter**. Note the command used to start your current Linux kernel.

14. Reboot your system by typing `reboot` and pressing **Enter**. Allow your system to boot normally.

Project 8-2

Estimated Time: 35 minutes

Objective: Use SysV init and Systemd.

Description: In this hands-on project, you explore and configure the SysV and Systemd system initialization processes on Fedora Linux.

1. Switch to a command-line terminal (tty5) by pressing **Ctrl+Alt+F5** and log in to the terminal using the user name of **root** and the password of **LINUXrocks!**.

2. At the command prompt, type `runlevel` and press **Enter**. What is your current runlevel? What is the most recent runlevel?

3. At the command prompt, type `cat /etc/inittab` and press **Enter**. View the commented sections. Why is /etc/inittab not used on your Fedora system?

4. At the command prompt, type `ls /lib/systemd/system` and press **Enter**. What do the contents represent?

5. At the command prompt, type `ls /etc/rc.d` and press **Enter**. Do you see init.d and rc#.d subdirectories? Why?

6. At the command prompt, type `ls /etc/rc.d/init.d` and press **Enter**. Which UNIX SysV daemons are available on your Fedora system?

7. At the command prompt, type `chkconfig --list livesys` and press **Enter**. In which runlevels is the livesys daemon started by default?

8. At the command prompt, type `chkconfig --level 2345 livesys on` and press **Enter** to configure the livesys daemon to start in runlevels 2 through 5. Next, type `ls /etc/rc.d/rc[2-5].d` and press **Enter**. Does the symbolic link to the livesys rc script start with S? Why?

9. At the command prompt, type `init 3` and press **Enter** to switch to runlevel 3 (multi-user.target).

10. Switch to tty1 by pressing **Ctrl+Alt+F1** and note that the GDM is not loaded. Log in to the terminal using the user name of **root** and the password of **LINUXrocks!**.

11. Next, type `runlevel` and press **Enter**. What is your current and most recent runlevel?

12. At the command prompt, type `init 1` and press **Enter** to switch to single user mode (rescue.target). Supply the root password of **LINUXrocks!** when prompted.

13. Next, type `runlevel` and press **Enter**. What is your current and most recent runlevel?

14. At the command prompt, type `systemctl isolate graphical.target` and press **Enter** to switch to runlevel 5 (graphical.target). Note that the GDM is loaded. Press **Ctrl+Alt+F5** and log in to the terminal using the user name of **root** and the password of **LINUXrocks!**.

15. At the command prompt, type `systemctl status crond.service` and press **Enter**. Is the Systemd cron daemon running and enabled in your current runlevel/target?

16. At the command prompt, type `systemctl restart crond.service` and press **Enter** to restart the cron daemon.

17. At the command prompt, type `systemctl disable crond.service` and press **Enter** to prevent the system from starting the cron daemon in your current runlevel/target. Note that the existing symbolic link for the crond.service rc script was removed. Why was this link from the /etc/systemd/system/multi-user.target.wants directory instead of the /etc/systemd/system/graphical.target.wants directory?

18. At the command prompt, type `systemctl enable crond.service` and press **Enter** to start the cron daemon in your current runlevel/target. Was the symbolic link re-created?

19. At the command prompt, type `systemd-analyze blame | head -5` and press **Enter** to display the five service units that took the longest to start.

20. At the command prompt, type `service livesys restart` and press **Enter**. Note that Systemd restarted the UNIX SysV livesys daemon using the `systemctl` command because Systemd is backwards compatible with UNIX SysV.

21. At the command prompt, type `exit` and press **Enter** to log out of your shell.

Project 8-3

Estimated Time: 40 minutes
Objective: Configure service units.
Description: In this hands-on project, you configure a service unit file that is used to execute a shell script (/bootscript.sh) during the Systemd system initialization process on Fedora Linux.

1. Switch to a command-line terminal (tty5) by pressing **Ctrl+Alt+F5** and log in to the terminal using the user name of **root** and the password of **LINUXrocks!**.

2. At the command prompt, type `vi /bootscript.sh` and press **Enter**. Add the following lines. When finished, save and quit the vi editor.

```
#!/bin/bash
echo "Boot script started" >>/tmp/bootscript.txt
```

3. At the command prompt, type `chmod u+x /bootscript.sh` and press **Enter** to ensure that the newly created script can be executed by the system.

4. At the command prompt, type `vi /etc/systemd/system/bootscript.service` and press **Enter**. Add the following lines. When finished, save and quit the vi editor.

```
Unit]
Description=Sample boot script

[Service]
ExecStart=/bootscript.sh

[Install]
WantedBy=multi-user.target
```

5. At the command prompt, type `systemctl start bootscript.service` and press **Enter**. Next, type `cat /tmp/bootscript.txt` at the command prompt and press **Enter**. Did bootscript.sh execute?

6. At the command prompt, type `journalctl | grep bootscript` and press **Enter**. Note the line that indicates the successful starting of the bootscript service unit.

7. At the command prompt, type `systemctl enable bootscript.service` and press **Enter**. Why was a symbolic link created in the /etc/systemd/system/multi-user.target.wants directory?

8. At the command prompt, type `reboot` and press **Enter**. After the system has rebooted, press **Ctrl+Alt+F5** and log in to the terminal using the user name of **root** and the password of **LINUXrocks!**.

9. At the command prompt, type `journalctl | grep bootscript` and press **Enter**. Note the timestamps shown. Did your boot script execute successfully during the previous boot?

10. At the command prompt, type `exit` and press **Enter** to log out of your shell.

Project 8-4

Estimated Time: 40 minutes
Objective: Configure mount units.
Description: In this hands-on project, you configure a mount unit file that is used to mount a filesystem during the Systemd system initialization process on Fedora Linux.

1. Switch to a command-line terminal (tty5) by pressing **Ctrl+Alt+F5** and log in to the terminal using the user name of **root** and the password of **LINUXrocks!**.

2. At the command prompt, type `lsblk --fs` and press **Enter**. Note the UUID of the /newmount filesystem you created in Hands-on Project 5-3.

3. At the command prompt, type `vi /etc/systemd/system/newmount.mount` and press **Enter**. Add the following lines, replacing *UUID* with the UUID you noted from Step 2 (you can use `:r !lsblk --fs|grep newmount|awk '{print $3}'` within command mode to insert this UUID into the vi editor). When finished, save and quit the vi editor.

```
[Unit]
Description=Mount newmount filesystem in graphical target

[Mount]
What=/dev/disk/by-uuid/UUID
Where=/newmount
Type=ext4
Options=defaults

[Install]
WantedBy=graphical.target
```

4. At the command prompt, type `systemctl enable newmount.mount` and press **Enter** to enable your mount unit.

5. At the command prompt, type `vi /etc/fstab` and press **Enter**. Remove the line you added in Hands-on Project 5-3 to automatically mount the /newmount filesystem. When finished, save and quit the vi editor.

6. At the command prompt, type `telinit 6` and press **Enter** to reboot your system. Once your system has rebooted, log into tty5 using the user name of **root** and the password of **LINUXrocks!**.

7. At the command prompt, type `df -hT` and press **Enter**. Was your /newmount filesystem mounted by Systemd? Will /newmount be mounted if you boot your system to the rescue or multi-user target?

8. At the command prompt, type `exit` and press **Enter** to log out of your shell.

Project 8-5

Estimated Time: 30 minutes
Objective: Examine X Windows, accessibility, and localization options.
Description: In this hands-on project, you start X Windows without the GDM as well as examine X Windows configuration utilities, accessibility options, and localization.

1. Switch to a command-line terminal (tty5) by pressing **Ctrl+Alt+F5** and log in to the terminal using the user name of **root** and the password of **LINUXrocks!**.

2. At the command prompt, type `init 3` and press **Enter** to switch to runlevel 3 (multi-user.target).

3. At the command prompt, type `startx` and press **Enter**. What desktop environment was loaded by default and why? What warning appears?

4. Click the power icon in the upper-right corner of the GNOME desktop, click **Power Off / Log Out**, and then click **Log Out**. Click **Log Out** to log out of the GNOME desktop.

5. At the command prompt, type `who` and press **Enter**. Were you returned to your original BASH shell on tty5?

6. At the command prompt, type `init 5` and press **Enter** to switch to runlevel 5 (graphical.target). Note that the GDM is now loaded in tty1. Select your user account and click the settings (cog wheel) icon. Ensure that GNOME is selected using the default of Wayland and supply your password of **LINUXrocks!** to log in.

7. Click **Show Applications** and then click **Settings**. Highlight **Displays** in the left pane and note that you can configure the resolution for your current display, which is provided by your hypervisor. Next, highlight **Keyboard** in the left pane and note that you can optionally configure different keyboard localization settings, or add a second keyboard localization setting to choose from within GNOME. Next, highlight **Accessibility** in the left pane. Explore the different assistive technologies available and close the Settings window when finished.

8. Click the **Activities** menu and navigate to **Show Applications**, **Terminal** to open a command-line terminal. At the command prompt, type `su - root` and press **Enter** to switch to the root user. Supply the root user password of **LINUXrocks!** when prompted.

9. At the command prompt, type `cat /etc/X11/xorg.conf.d/00-keyboard.conf` and press **Enter**. Note the keyboard localization used by X.org.

10. At the command prompt, type `locale` and press **Enter**. Which locale is used by default for all format types? Next, type `locale -a | less` and press **Enter**. View the available locales on your system and press `q` to return to your command prompt when finished.

11. At the command prompt, type `cat /etc/locale.conf` and press **Enter**. Next, type `localectl` and press **Enter**. Does the default locale listed by both commands match the output of the previous step?

12. At the command prompt, type `timedatectl` and press **Enter**. Next, type `ll /etc/localtime` and press **Enter**. Does the target of the symbolic link indicate the correct time zone information for your system?

13. At the command prompt, type `poweroff` and press **Enter** to power off your Fedora Linux virtual machine.

Discovery Exercises

Discovery Exercise 8-1

Estimated Time: 10 minutes
Objective: Explain runlevels and targets.
Description: Describe what would happen if you changed the default runlevel/target on your system to runlevel 6 or reboot.target.

Discovery Exercise 8-2

Estimated Time: 40 minutes
Objective: Configure timer units.
Description: Create a timer unit on your Fedora Linux virtual machine that runs the bootscript.service that you created in Hands-on Project 8-3 every day at noon and 5 minutes following system initialization. Reboot your system and review the output of the `journalctl | grep bootscript` command 5 minutes following system initialization to verify that your timer unit is working successfully.

Discovery Exercise 8-3

Estimated Time: 50 minutes
Objective: Apply chapter concepts to Ubuntu Linux.
Description: On the Ubuntu Linux virtual machine that you installed in Hands-On Project 6-1:

  a. Perform the same steps that you performed in Project 8-1. To accomplish this, you'll need to remember that Ubuntu Server uses slightly different names for GRUB2 configuration files and commands.

  b. Use the appropriate commands to view, start, and stop daemons, as well as configure them to start within a particular runlevel/target.

  c. Use the appropriate commands to explore the localization files, commands, and options available.

Discovery Exercise 8-4

Estimated Time: 60 minutes
Objective: Use the upstart init system.
Description: Download the ISO image for the Ubuntu Server 14.04 LTS distribution from old-releases.ubuntu.com. Next, install a new virtual machine called Legacy Ubuntu Linux from this ISO image that uses 1 GB of memory (not dynamically allocated) and a 50 GB SATA/SAS/SCSI virtual hard disk drive (dynamically allocated). Following installation, set the root user password and then switch to the root user. Next, use the appropriate commands to explore the upstart system initialization system. At minimum, ensure that you perform the following actions:

  a. View and configure upstart configuration files.

  b. View, start, and stop upstart daemons.

  c. Configure upstart daemons to start and stop in a particular runlevel.

Discovery Exercise 8-5

Estimated Time: 180 minutes
Objective: Configure the i3 window manager.
Description: On your Fedora Linux virtual machine, run the `dnf -y install i3-gaps` command as the root user to install the i3 tiling window manager with window gap support. Once the installation has finished, reboot your system and log into the i3 tiling window manager from the GDM. Follow the prompts to generate an i3 configuration using the default selections. Next, follow the guide at i3wm.org/docs/userguide.html to learn how to use and configure it.

Chapter 9

Managing Linux Processes

Chapter Objectives

1 Categorize the different types of processes on a Linux system.

2 View processes using standard Linux utilities.

3 Explain the difference between common kill signals.

4 Describe how binary programs and shell scripts are executed.

5 Create and manipulate background processes.

6 Use standard Linux utilities to modify the priority of a process.

7 Schedule commands to execute in the future using the at daemon.

8 Schedule commands to execute repetitively using the cron daemon.

A typical Linux system can run thousands of processes simultaneously, including those that you have explored in previous chapters. In this chapter, you focus on viewing and managing processes. In the first part of the chapter, you examine the different types of processes on a Linux system and how to view them and terminate them. You then discover how processes are executed on a system, run in the background, and prioritized. Finally, you examine the various methods used to schedule commands to execute in the future.

Linux Processes

Throughout this book, the terms "program" and "process" are used interchangeably. The same is true in the workplace. However, a fine distinction exists between these two terms. Technically, a **program** is an executable file on the filesystem that can be run when you execute it. A **process**, on the other hand, is a program that is running in memory and on the CPU. In other words, a process is a program in action.

If you start a process while logged in to a terminal, that process runs in that terminal and is labeled a **user process**. Examples of user processes include ls, grep, and find, not to mention most of the other commands that you have executed throughout this book. Recall that a system process that is not associated with a terminal is called a **daemon process**; these processes are typically started on system startup, but you can also start them manually. Most daemon processes provide system services, such as printing, scheduling, and system maintenance, as well as network server services, such as web servers, database servers, file servers, and print servers.

Every process has a unique **process ID (PID)** that allows the kernel to identify it uniquely. In addition, each process can start an unlimited number of other processes called **child processes**. Conversely, each process must have been started by an existing process called a **parent process**. As a result, each process has a **parent process ID (PPID)**, which identifies the process that started it. An example of the relationship between parent and child processes is depicted in Figure 9-1.

Figure 9-1 Parent and child processes

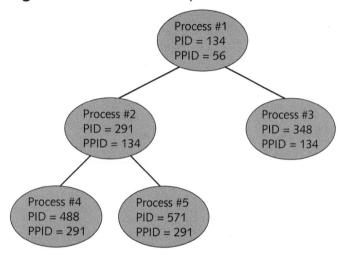

The first process started by the Linux kernel is the initialize (or init) daemon, which has a PID of 1 and a PPID of 0, the latter of which refers to the kernel itself. The init daemon then starts most other daemons during the system initialization process, including those that allow for user logins. After you log in to the system, the login program starts a shell. The shell then interprets user commands and starts all user processes. Thus, each process on the Linux system can be traced back to the init daemon by examining the series of PPIDs, as shown in Figure 9-2.

Figure 9-2 Process genealogy

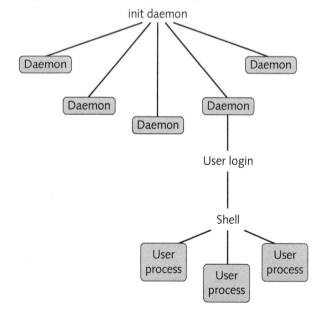

Note 3

The init daemon is often referred to as the "grandfather of all user processes."

Note 4

On Linux systems that use the UNIX SysV system initialization process, the init daemon will be listed as `init` within command output. On Linux systems that use the Systemd system initialization process, the init daemon will either be listed as `init` or `systemd` within command output.

Viewing Processes

Although several Linux utilities can view processes, the most versatile and common is the `ps` command. Without arguments, the `ps` command simply displays a list of processes that are running in the current shell. The following example shows the output of this command while the user is logged in to tty2:

```
[root@server1 ~]# ps
  PID TTY          TIME CMD
 2159 tty2     00:00:00 bash
 2233 tty2     00:00:00 ps
[root@server1 ~]#_
```

The preceding output shows that two processes were running in the terminal tty2 when the `ps` command executed. The command that started each process (CMD) is listed next to the time it has taken on the CPU (TIME), its PID, and terminal (TTY). In this case, the process took less than one second to run, and so the time elapsed reads nothing. To find out more about these processes, you could instead use the `-f`, or full, option to the `ps` command, as shown next:

```
[root@server1 ~]# ps -f
UID          PID   PPID  C STIME TTY          TIME CMD
root        2159   2156  0 16:18 tty2     00:00:00 -bash
root        2233   2159  3 16:28 tty2     00:00:00 ps -f
[root@server1 ~]#_
```

This listing provides more information about each process. It displays the user who started the process (UID), the PPID, the time it was started (STIME), as well as the CPU utilization (C), which starts at zero and is incremented with each processor cycle that the process runs on the CPU.

The most valuable information provided by the `ps -f` command is each process's PPID and lineage. The bash process (PID = 2159) displays a shell prompt and interprets user input; it started the `ps` process (PID = 2233) because the `ps` process had a PPID of 2159.

Because daemon processes are not associated with a terminal, they are not displayed by the `ps -f` command. To display an entire list of processes across all terminals and including daemons, you can add the `-e` option to any `ps` command, as shown in the following output:

```
[root@server1 ~]# ps -ef
UID         PID  PPID  C STIME TTY          TIME CMD
root          1     0  0 21:22 ?        00:00:00 /usr/lib/systemd/systemd
root          2     0  0 21:22 ?        00:00:00 [kthreadd]
root          3     2  0 21:22 ?        00:00:00 [ksoftirqd/0]
root          5     2  0 21:22 ?        00:00:00 [kworker/0:0H]
root          6     2  0 21:22 ?        00:00:00 [kworker/u128:0]
root          7     2  0 21:22 ?        00:00:00 [migration/0]
root          8     2  0 21:22 ?        00:00:00 [rcu_bh]
```

```
root         9       2    0 21:22 ?       00:00:00 [rcu_sched]
root        10       2    0 21:22 ?       00:00:00 [watchdog/0]
root        11       2    0 21:22 ?       00:00:00 [khelper]
root        12       2    0 21:22 ?       00:00:00 [kdevtmpfs]
root        13       2    0 21:22 ?       00:00:00 [netns]
root        14       2    0 21:22 ?       00:00:00 [writeback]
root       394       1    0 21:22 ?       00:00:00 /sbin/auditd -n
avahi      422       1    0 21:22 ?       00:00:00 avahi-daemon: running
dbus       424       1    0 21:22 ?       00:00:00 /bin/dbus-daemon --system
chrony     430       1    0 21:22 ?       00:00:00 /usr/sbin/chronyd -u
root       431       1    0 21:22 ?       00:00:00 /usr/sbin/crond -n
root       432       1    0 21:22 ?       00:00:00 /usr/sbin/atd -f
root       435       1    0 21:22 ?       00:00:00 /usr/sbin/abrtd -d -s
root       437       1    0 21:22 ?       00:00:00 /usr/bin/abrt-watch-log
root       441       1    0 21:22 ?       00:00:00 /usr/sbin/gdm
root       446       1    0 21:22 ?       00:00:00 /usr/sbin/mcelog
root       481     441    0 21:22 ?       00:00:00 /usr/libexec/gdm-simple
polkitd    482       1    0 21:22 ?       00:00:00 /usr/lib/polkit-1/polkitd
root       488     481    0 21:22 tty1    00:00:00 /usr/bin/Xorg :0
root       551     481    0 21:22 ?       00:00:00 gdm-session-worker
root       552       1    0 21:22 ?       00:00:00 /usr/sbin/NetworkManager
gdm        852     551    0 21:23 ?       00:00:00 /usr/bin/gnome-session
gdm        856       1    0 21:23 ?       00:00:00 /usr/bin/dbus-launch
gdm       1018       1    0 21:23 ?       00:00:00 /bin/dbus-daemon --fork
root      1020     552    0 21:23 ?       00:00:00 /sbin/dhclient -d -sf
gdm       1045    1018    0 21:23 ?       00:00:00 /bin/dbus-daemon
root      1072       1    0 21:23 ?       00:00:00 /usr/libexec/upowerd
gdm       1077     852    0 21:23 ?       00:00:03 gnome-shell --mode=gdm
gdm       1087       1    0 21:23 ?       00:00:00 /usr/bin/pulseaudio
gdm       1148       1    0 21:23 ?       00:00:00 /usr/libexec/goa-daemon
root      1164       1    0 21:23 ?       00:00:00 login -- root
root      1175    1164    0 21:23 tty2    00:00:00 -bash
root      1742    1175    0 21:33 tty2    00:00:00 ps -ef
[root@server1 ~]#_
```

As shown in the preceding output, the kernel thread daemon (kthreadd) has a PID of 2 and starts most subprocesses within the actual Linux kernel because those subprocesses have a PPID of 2, whereas the init daemon (/usr/lib/systemd/systemd, PID=1) starts most other daemons because those daemons have a PPID of 1. In addition, there is a ? in the TTY column for daemons and kernel subprocesses because they do not run on a terminal.

Because the output of the ps -ef command can be several hundred lines long on a Linux server, you usually pipe its output to the less command to send the output to the terminal screen page-by-page, or to the grep command, which can be used to display lines containing only certain information. For example, to display only the BASH shells on the system, you could use the following command:

```
[root@server1 ~]# ps -ef | grep bash
user1     2094    2008    0 14:29 pts/1   00:00:00 -bash
root      2159    2156    0 14:30 tty2    00:00:00 -bash
root      2294    2159    0 14:44 tty2    00:00:00 grep --color=auto bash
[root@server1 ~]#_
```

Notice that the grep bash command is also displayed alongside the BASH shells in the preceding output because it was running in memory at the time the ps command was executed. This might not always be the case because the Linux kernel schedules commands to run based on a variety of factors.

The −e and −f options are the most common options used with the ps command; however, many other options are available. The −l option to the ps command lists even more information about each process than the −f option. An example of using this option to view the processes in the terminal tty2 is shown in the following output:

```
[root@server1 ~]# ps -l
F S    UID    PID   PPID  C PRI   NI ADDR SZ WCHAN   TTY          TIME CMD
4 S      0   2159   2156  0  80    0 -  1238 wait    tty2     00:00:00 bash
4 R      0   2295   2159  2  80    0 -   744 -       tty2     00:00:00 ps
[root@server1 ~]#_
```

The process flag (F) indicates particular features of the process; the flag of 4 in the preceding output indicates that the root user ran the process. The **process state** (S) column is the most valuable to systems administrators because it indicates what the process is currently doing. If a process is not being run on the processor at the current time, you see an S (interruptible sleep) in the process state column; processes are in this state most of the time and are awoken (interrupted) by other processes when they are needed, as seen with bash in the preceding output. You will see an R in this column if the process is currently running on the processor, a D (uninterruptible sleep) if it is waiting for disk access, or a T if it has stopped or is being traced by another process. In addition to these, you might also see a Z in this column, indicating a **zombie process**. When a process finishes executing, the parent process must check to see if it executed successfully and then release the child process's PID so that it can be used again. While a process is waiting for its parent process to release the PID, the process is said to be in a zombie state, because it has finished but still retains a PID. On a busy Linux server, zombie processes can accumulate and prevent new processes from being created; if this occurs, you can kill the parent process of the zombies, as discussed in the next section.

Note 5

Zombie processes are also known as defunct processes.

Note 6

To view a list of zombie processes on your entire system, you could use the ps -el | grep Z command.

Process priority (PRI) is the priority used by the kernel for the process; it is measured between 0 (high priority) and 127 (low priority). The **nice value** (NI) can be used to affect the process priority indirectly; it is measured between –20 (a greater chance of a high priority) and 19 (a greater chance of a lower priority). The ADDR in the preceding output indicates the memory address of the process, whereas the WCHAN indicates what the process is waiting for while sleeping. In addition, the size of the process in memory (SZ) is listed and measured in kilobytes; often, it is roughly equivalent to the size of the executable file on the filesystem.

Some options to the ps command are not prefixed by a dash character; these are referred to as Berkeley style options. The two most common of these are the a option, which lists all processes across terminals, and the x option, which lists processes that do not run on a terminal, as shown in the following output for the first 10 processes on the system:

```
[root@server1 ~]# ps ax | head -11
  PID TTY      STAT   TIME COMMAND
    1 ?        S      0:01 /usr/lib/systemd/systemd
    2 ?        S      0:00 [kthreadd]
    3 ?        S      0:00 [migration/0]
    4 ?        S<     0:00 [ksoftirqd/0]
```

```
   5 ?           S          0:00  [watchdog/0]
   6 ?           S          0:00  [migration/1]
   7 ?           S          0:00  [ksoftirqd/1]
   8 ?           S          0:00  [watchdog/1]
   9 ?           S          0:00  [events/0]
  10 ?           S          0:00  [events/1]
[root@server1 ~]#_
```

The columns just listed are equivalent to those discussed earlier; however, the process state column is identified with STAT and might contain additional characters to indicate the full nature of the process state. For example, a W indicates that the process has no contents in memory, a < symbol indicates a high-priority process, and an N indicates a low-priority process.

Note 7

For a full list of symbols that may be displayed in the STAT or S columns shown in prior output, consult the manual page for the ps command.

Several dozen options to the ps command can be used to display processes and their attributes; the options listed in this section are the most common and are summarized in Table 9-1.

Table 9-1   Common options to the ps command

Option	Description
-e	Displays all processes running on terminals as well as processes that do not run on a terminal (daemons)
-f	Displays a full list of information about each process, including the UID, PID, PPID, CPU utilization, start time, terminal, processor time, and command name
-l	Displays a long list of information about each process, including the flag, state, UID, PID, PPID, CPU utilization, priority, nice value, address, size, WCHAN, terminal, and command name
-Z	Displays SELinux context information about each process (discussed further in Chapter 14)
a	Displays all processes running on terminals
x	Displays all processes that do not run on terminals

The ps command is not the only command that can view process information. The kernel exports all process information subdirectories under the /proc directory. Each subdirectory is named for the PID of the process that it contains information for, as shown in the following output:

```
[root@server1 ~]# ls /proc
1      1174  1746  28   407  473  852        irq           slabinfo
10     1175  175   292  409  48   856        kallsyms      softirqs
1018   12    1754  3    411  481  9          kcore         stat
1020   1213  176   307  412  482  acpi       keys          swaps
1025   1216  1760  328  414  488  buddyinfo  key-users     sys
1045   1220  177   350  415  49   bus        kmsg          sysrq
1052   13    178   351  418  5    cgroups    kpagecount    sysvipc
1065   14    179   353  420  551  cmdline    kpageflags    timer_list
1072   15    18    354  421  552  consoles   loadavg       timer_stats
1077   16    180   357  422  58   cpuinfo    locks         tty
1080   164   181   358  424  59   crypto     mdstat        uptime
```

```
1087    165    1810   359   430   6      devices        meminfo        version
1097    167    188    370   431   60     diskstats      misc           vmallocinfo
11      168    189    371   432   62     dma            modules        vmstat
1111    169    19     372   435   64     driver         mounts         zoneinfo
1114    17     191    383   437   7      execdomains    mtrr
1117    170    2      384   440   72     fb             net
1122    171    20     385   441   748    filesystems    pagetypeinfo
1144    172    204    386   446   8      fs             partitions
1148    173    205    387   45    814    interrupts     sched_debug
1164    174    206    388   46    823    iomem          scsi
1171    1745   276    394   47    842    ioports        self
[root@server1 ~]#_
```

Thus, any program that can read from the /proc directory can display process information. For example, the `pstree command` displays the lineage of a process by tracing its PPIDs until the init daemon. The first 26 lines of this command are shown in the following output:

```
[root@server1 ~]# pstree | head -26
systemd─┬─ModemManager───2*[{ModemManager}]
        ├─NetworkManager─┬─dhclient
        │                └─3*[{NetworkManager}]
        ├─2*[abrt-watch-log]
        ├─abrtd
        ├─accounts-daemon───2*[{accounts-daemon}]
        ├─alsactl
        ├─at-spi-bus-laun─┬─dbus-daemon───{dbus-daemon}
        │                 └─3*[{at-spi-bus-laun}]
        ├─at-spi2-registr───{at-spi2-registr}
        ├─atd
        ├─auditd─┬─audispd─┬─sedispatch
        │        │         └─{audispd}
        │        └─{auditd}
        ├─avahi-daemon───avahi-daemon
        ├─bluetoothd
        ├─chronyd
        ├─colord───2*[{colord}]
        ├─crond
        ├─2*[dbus-daemon───{dbus-daemon}]
        ├─dbus-launch
        ├─dconf-service───2*[{dconf-service}]
        ├─firewalld───{firewalld}
        ├─gdm─┬─gdm-simple-slav─┬─Xorg
        │     │                 └─gdm-session─┬─gnome-session─┬─gnome-settings
        │     │                               │               └─gnome-shell
[root@server1 ~]# _
```

The most common program used to display processes, aside from ps, is the `top` command. The `top` command displays an interactive screen listing processes organized by processor time. Processes that use the most processor time are listed at the top of the screen. An example of the screen that appears when you type the `top` command is shown next:

```
top - 21:55:15 up 32 min,  3 users,  load average: 0.15, 0.06, 0.02
Tasks: 134 total,  1 running, 133 sleeping,  0 stopped,  0 zombie
%Cpu(s):  0.4 us,  0.4 sy,  0.0 ni, 95.9 id,  2.0 wa,  1.1 hi,  0.1 si,  0.0 st
MiB Mem:   7944.0 total,  7067.5 free,  467.3 used,   409.2 buff/cache
MiB Swap:  7944.0 total,  7944.0 free,    0.0 used,  7226.7 avail Mem

  PID USER     PR  NI    VIRT    RES    SHR S %CPU %MEM     TIME+ COMMAND
 1077 gdm      20   0 1518192 150684  36660 R 19.4  7.4   0:33.93 gnome-shell
 2130 root     20   0  123636   1644   1180 R  0.7  0.1   0:00.05 top
    1 root     20   0   51544   7348   2476 S  0.0  0.4   0:00.98 systemd
```

2	root	20	0	0	0	0	S	0.0	0.0	0:00.00	kthreadd
3	root	20	0	0	0	0	S	0.0	0.0	0:00.01	ksoftirqd/0
5	root	0	-20	0	0	0	S	0.0	0.0	0:00.00	kworker/0:0H
6	root	20	0	0	0	0	S	0.0	0.0	0:00.02	kworker/u12+
7	root	rt	0	0	0	0	S	0.0	0.0	0:00.00	migration/0
8	root	20	0	0	0	0	S	0.0	0.0	0:00.00	rcu_bh
9	root	20	0	0	0	0	S	0.0	0.0	0:00.34	rcu_sched
10	root	rt	0	0	0	0	S	0.0	0.0	0:00.00	watchdog/0
11	root	0	-20	0	0	0	S	0.0	0.0	0:00.00	khelper
12	root	20	0	0	0	0	S	0.0	0.0	0:00.00	kdevtmpfs
13	root	0	-20	0	0	0	S	0.0	0.0	0:00.00	netns
14	root	0	-20	0	0	0	S	0.0	0.0	0:00.00	writeback
15	root	0	-20	0	0	0	S	0.0	0.0	0:00.00	kintegrityd
16	root	0	-20	0	0	0	S	0.0	0.0	0:00.00	bioset

Note that the top command displays many of the same columns that the ps command does, yet it contains a summary paragraph at the top of the screen and a cursor between the summary paragraph and the process list. From the preceding output, you can see that the gnome-shell uses the most processor time, followed by the top command itself (top) and the init daemon (systemd).

You might come across a process that has encountered an error during execution and continuously uses up system resources. These processes are referred to as **rogue processes** and appear at the top of the listing produced by the top command. The top command can also be used to change the priority of processes or kill them. Thus, you can stop rogue processes from the top command immediately after they are identified. Process priority and killing processes are discussed later in this chapter. To get a full listing of the different commands that you can use while in the top utility, press h to get a help screen.

Note 8

Rogue processes are also known as runaway processes.

Note 9

Many Linux administrators choose to install and use the htop command instead of top. The htop command provides the same functionality as top but displays results in color and includes a resource utilization graph at the top of the screen, as well as a usage legend at the bottom of the screen.

Killing Processes

As indicated earlier, a large number of rogue and zombie processes use up system resources. When system performance suffers due to these processes, you should send them a **kill signal**, which terminates a process. The most common command used to send kill signals is the kill command. All told, the kill command can send many different kill signals to a process. Each of these kill signals operates in a different manner. To view the kill signal names and associated numbers, you can use the -l option to the kill command, as shown in the following output:

```
[root@server1 ~]# kill -l
 1) SIGHUP        2) SIGINT       3) SIGQUIT      4) SIGILL
 5) SIGTRAP       6) SIGABRT      7) SIGBUS       8) SIGFPE
 9) SIGKILL      10) SIGUSR1     11) SIGSEGV     12) SIGUSR2
13) SIGPIPE      14) SIGALRM     15) SIGTERM     17) SIGCHLD
18) SIGCONT      19) SIGSTOP     20) SIGTSTP     21) SIGTTIN
```

```
22) SIGTTOU      23) SIGURG       24) SIGXCPU      25) SIGXFSZ
26) SIGVTALRM    27) SIGPROF      28) SIGWINCH     29) SIGIO
30) SIGPWR       31) SIGSYS       33) SIGRTMIN     34) SIGRTMIN+1
35) SIGRTMIN+2   36) SIGRTMIN+3   37) SIGRTMIN+4   38) SIGRTMIN+5
39) SIGRTMIN+6   40) SIGRTMIN+7   41) SIGRTMIN+8   42) SIGRTMIN+9
43) SIGRTMIN+10 44) SIGRTMIN+11 45) SIGRTMIN+12 46) SIGRTMIN+13
47) SIGRTMIN+14 48) SIGRTMIN+15 49) SIGRTMAX-15 50) SIGRTMAX-14
51) SIGRTMAX-13 52) SIGRTMAX-12 53) SIGRTMAX-11 54) SIGRTMAX-10
55) SIGRTMAX-9  56) SIGRTMAX-8   57) SIGRTMAX-7  58) SIGRTMAX-6
59) SIGRTMAX-5  60) SIGRTMAX-4   61) SIGRTMAX-3  62) SIGRTMAX-2
63) SIGRTMAX-1  64) SIGRTMAX
[root@server1 ~]#_
```

Most of the kill signals listed in the preceding output are not useful for systems administrators. The five most common kill signals used for administration are listed in Table 9-2.

Table 9-2   Common administrative kill signals

Name	Number	Description
SIGHUP	1	Also known as the hang-up signal, it stops a process, then restarts it with the same PID. If you edit the configuration file used by a running daemon, that daemon might be sent a SIGHUP to restart the process; when the daemon starts again, it reads the new configuration file.
SIGINT	2	This signal sends an interrupt signal to a process. Although this signal is one of the weakest kill signals, it works most of the time. When you use the Ctrl+c key combination to kill a currently running process, a SIGINT is actually being sent to the process.
SIGQUIT	3	Also known as a core dump, the quit signal terminates a process by taking the process information in memory and saving it to a file called core on the filesystem in the current working directory. You can use the Ctrl+\ key combination to send a SIGQUIT to a process that is currently running.
SIGTERM	15	The software termination signal is the most common kill signal used by programs to kill other processes. It is the default kill signal used by the `kill` command.
SIGKILL	9	Also known as the absolute kill signal, it forces the Linux kernel to stop executing the process by sending the process's resources to a special device file called /dev/null.

To send a kill signal to a process, you specify the kill signal to send as an option to the `kill` command, followed by the appropriate PID of the process. For example, to send a SIGQUIT to a process called `sample`, you could use the following commands to locate and terminate the process:

```
[root@server1 ~]# ps -ef | grep sample
root       1199      1   0 Jun30 tty3      00:00:00 /sbin/sample
[root@server1 ~]# kill -3 1199
[root@server1 ~]#_
[root@server1 ~]# ps -ef | grep sample
[root@server1 ~]#_
```

Note 10

The `kill -SIGQUIT 1199` command does the same thing as the `kill -3 1199` command shown in the preceding output.

Note 11

If you do not specify the kill signal when using the `kill` command, the `kill` command uses the default kill signal, the SIGTERM signal.

Note 12

You can also use the `pidof command` to find the PID of a process to use as an argument to the `kill` command. For example, `pidof sample` will return the PID of the sample process.

When sending a kill signal to several processes, it is often easier to locate the process PIDs using the `pgrep command`. The `pgrep` command returns a list of PIDs for processes that match a regular expression, or other criteria. For example, to send a SIGQUIT to all processes started by the user bini whose process name starts with the letters `psql`, you could use the following commands to locate and terminate the process:

```
[root@server1 ~]# pgrep -u bini "^psql"
1344
1501
1522
[root@server1 ~]# kill -3 1344 1501 1522
[root@server1 ~]#_
[root@server1 ~]# pgrep -u bini "^psql"
[root@server1 ~]#_
```

Some processes have the ability to ignore, or trap, certain kill signals that are sent to them. The only kill signal that cannot be trapped by any process is the SIGKILL. Thus, if a SIGINT, SIGQUIT, and SIGTERM do not terminate a stubborn process, you can use a SIGKILL to terminate it. However, you should only use SIGKILL as a last resort because it prevents a process from closing open files and other resources properly.

Note 13

You can use the `lsof (list open files) command` to view the files that a process has open before sending a SIGKILL. For example, to see the files that are used by the process with PID 1399, you can use the `lsof -p 1399` command.

If you send a kill signal to a process that has children, the parent process terminates all of its child processes before terminating itself. Thus, to kill several related processes, you can simply send a kill signal to their parent process. In addition, to kill a zombie process, it is often necessary to send a kill signal to its parent process.

Note 14

To prevent a child process from being terminated when the parent process is terminated, you can start the child process with the `nohup command`. For example, executing the `nohup cathena` command within your shell would execute the cathena child process without any association to the parent shell process that started it.

Another command that can be used to send kill signals to processes is the `killall command`. The `killall` command works similarly to the `kill` command in that it takes the kill signal as an option; however, it uses the process name to kill instead of the PID. This allows multiple processes of the same name to be killed in one command. An example of using the `killall` command to send a SIGQUIT to multiple `sample` processes is shown in the following output:

```
[root@server1 ~]# ps -ef | grep sample
root      1729     1  0 Jun30 tty3      00:00:00 /sbin/sample
root     20198     1  0 Jun30 tty4      00:00:00 /sbin/sample
[root@server1 ~]# killall -3 sample
[root@server1 ~]#_
[root@server1 ~]# ps -ef | grep sample
[root@server1 ~]#_
```

Note 15

Alternatively, you could use the command `killall -SIGQUIT sample` to do the same as the `killall -3 sample` command used in the preceding output.

Note 16

As with the `kill` command, if you do not specify the kill signal when using the `killall` command, it sends a SIGTERM signal by default.

You can also use the `pkill command` to kill processes by process name. However, the `pkill` command allows you to identify process names using regular expressions as well as specify other criteria. For example, the `pkill -u bini -3 "^psql"` command will send a SIGQUIT signal to processes started by the bini user that begin with the letters `psql`.

In addition to the `kill`, `killall`, and `pkill` commands, the `top` command can be used to kill processes. While in the top utility, press the k key and supply the appropriate PID and kill signal when prompted.

Process Execution

You can execute three main types of Linux commands:

- Binary programs
- Shell scripts
- Shell functions

Most commands, such as `ls`, `find`, and `grep`, are binary programs that exist on the filesystem until executed. They were written in a certain programming language and compiled into a binary format that only the computer can understand. Other commands, such as `cd` and `exit`, are built into the shell running in memory, and they are called shell functions. Shell scripts can also contain a list of binary programs, shell functions, and special constructs for the shell to execute in order.

When executing compiled programs or shell scripts, the shell that interprets the command you typed creates a new shell. This creation of a new subshell is known as **forking** and is carried out by the fork function in the shell. The new subshell then executes the binary program or shell script using its exec function. After the binary program or shell script has completed, the new shell uses its exit function to kill itself and return control to the original shell. The original shell uses its wait function to wait for the new shell to carry out the aforementioned tasks before returning a prompt to the user. Figure 9-3 depicts this process when a user types the `ls` command at the command line.

Figure 9-3   Process forking

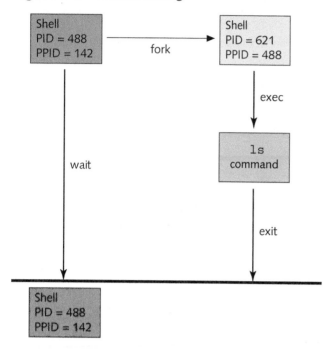

Running Processes in the Background

As discussed in the previous section, the shell creates, or forks, a subshell to execute most commands on the Linux system. Unfortunately, the original shell must wait for the command in the subshell to finish before displaying a shell prompt to accept new commands. Commands run in this fashion are known as foreground processes.

Alternatively, you can omit the wait function shown in Figure 9-3 by appending an ampersand (&) character to the command. Commands run in this fashion are known as background processes. When a command is run in the background, the shell immediately returns the shell prompt for the user to enter another command. To run the sample command in the background, you can enter the following command:

```
[root@server1 ~]# sample &
[1] 2583
[root@server1 ~]#_
```

Note 17

Space characters between the command and the ampersand (&) are optional. In other words, the command sample& is equivalent to the command sample & used in the preceding output.

The shell returns the PID (2583 in the preceding example) and the background job ID (1 in the preceding example) so that you can manipulate the background job after it has been run. After the process has been started, you can use the ps command to view the PID or the jobs command to view the background job ID, as shown in the following output:

```
[root@server1 ~]# jobs
[1]+  Running                 sample &
[root@server1 ~]# ps | grep sample
2583 tty2    00:00:00 sample
[root@server1 ~]#_
```

To terminate the background process, you can send a kill signal to the PID (as shown earlier in this chapter), or you can send a kill signal to the background job ID. Background job IDs must be prefixed with a % character. To send the sample background process created earlier a SIGINT signal, you could use the following `kill` command:

```
[root@server1 ~]# jobs
[1]+  Running                   sample &
[root@server1 ~]# kill -2 %1
[1]+  Interrupt                 sample
[root@server1 ~]# jobs
[root@server1 ~]#_
```

Note 18

You can also use the `killall -2 sample` command or the `top` utility to terminate the sample background process used in the preceding example.

After a background process has been started, you can move it to the foreground by using the `fg` (foreground) command followed by the background job ID. Similarly, you can pause a foreground process by using the Ctrl+z key combination. You can then send the process to the background with the `bg` (background) command. The Ctrl+z key combination assigns the foreground process a background job ID that is then used as an argument to the `bg` command. To start a sample process in the background and move it to the foreground, then pause it and move it to the background again, you can use the following commands:

```
[root@server1 ~]# sample &
[1] 7519
[root@server1 ~]# fg %1
sample

Ctrl+z

[1]+  Stopped                   sample
[root@server1 ~]# bg %1
[1]+ sample &
[root@server1 ~]# jobs
[1]+  Running                   sample &
[root@server1 ~]#_
```

When there are multiple background processes executing in the shell, the `jobs` command indicates the most recent one with a + symbol, and the second most recent one with a – symbol. If you place the % notation in a command without specifying the background job ID, the command operates on the most recent background process. An example of this is shown in the following output, in which four sample processes are started and sent SIGQUIT kill signals using the % notation:

```
[root@server1 ~]# sample &
[1] 7605
[root@server1 ~]# sample2 &
[2] 7613
[root@server1 ~]# sample3 &
[3] 7621
[root@server1 ~]# sample4 &
[4] 7629
[root@server1 ~]# jobs
```

```
[1]    Running                     sample &
[2]    Running                     sample2 &
[3]-   Running                     sample3 &
[4]+   Running                     sample4 &
[root@server1 ~]# kill -3 %
[root@server1 ~]# jobs
[1]    Running                     sample &
[2]-   Running                     sample2 &
[3]+   Running                     sample3 &
[root@server1 ~]# kill -3 %
[root@server1 ~]# jobs
[1]-   Running                     sample &
[2]+   Running                     sample2 &
[root@server1 ~]# kill -3 %
[root@server1 ~]# jobs
[1]+   Running                     sample &
[root@server1 ~]# kill -3 %
[root@server1 ~]# jobs
[root@server1 ~]#_
```

Process Priorities

Recall that Linux is a multitasking operating system. That is, it can perform several tasks at the same time. Because most computers contain only a single CPU, Linux executes small amounts of each process on the processor in series. This makes it seem to the user as if processes are executing simultaneously. The amount of time a process has to use the CPU is called a **time slice**; the more time slices a process has, the more time it has to execute on the CPU and the faster it executes. Time slices are typically measured in milliseconds. Thus, several hundred processes can be executing on the processor in a single second.

The ps -l command lists the Linux kernel priority (PRI) of a process. This value is directly related to the amount of time slices a process has on the CPU. A PRI of 0 is the most likely to get time slices on the CPU, and a PRI of 127 is the least likely to receive time slices on the CPU. An example of this command is shown next:

```
[root@server1 ~]# ps -l
F S   UID   PID  PPID  C PRI  NI ADDR SZ WCHAN  TTY       TIME CMD
4 S     0  3194  3192  0  75   0 -  1238 wait4  pts/1  00:00:00 bash
4 S     0  3896  3194  0  76   0 -   953 -      pts/1  00:00:00 sleep
4 S     0  3939  3194 13  75   0 -  7015 -      pts/1  00:00:01 gedit
4 R     0  3940  3194  0  77   0 -   632 -      pts/1  00:00:00 ps
[root@server1 ~]#_
```

The bash, sleep, gedit, and ps processes all have different PRI values because the kernel automatically assigns time slices based on several factors. You cannot change the PRI directly, but you can influence it indirectly by assigning a certain nice value to a process. A negative nice value increases the likelihood that the process will receive more time slices, whereas a positive nice value does the opposite. The range of nice values is depicted in Figure 9-4.

Figure 9-4 The nice value scale

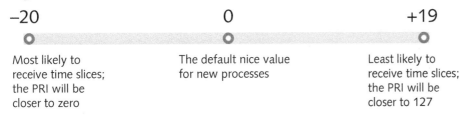

−20   0   +19

Most likely to
receive time slices;
the PRI will be
closer to zero

The default nice value
for new processes

Least likely to
receive time slices;
the PRI will be
closer to 127

All users can be "nice" to other users of the same computer by lowering the priority of their own processes by increasing their nice value. However, only the root user has the ability to increase the priority of a process by lowering its nice value.

Processes are started with a nice value of 0 by default, as shown in the NI column of the previous ps -l output. To start a process with a nice value of +19 (low priority), you can use the nice command and specify the nice value using the −n option and the command to start. If the -n option is omitted, a nice value of +10 is assumed. To start the ps -l command with a nice value of +19, you can issue the following command:

```
[root@server1 ~]# nice -n 19 ps -l
F S   UID   PID  PPID  C PRI  NI ADDR SZ WCHAN   TTY        TIME CMD
4 S     0  3194  3192  0  75   0 -  1238 wait4   pts/1   00:00:00 bash
4 S     0  3896  3194  0  76   0 -   953 -       pts/1   00:00:00 sleep
4 S     0  3939  3194  0  76   0 -  7015 -       pts/1   00:00:02 gedit
4 R     0  3946  3194  0  99  19 -   703 -       pts/1   00:00:00 ps
[root@server1 ~]#_
```

Notice from the preceding output that NI is 19 for the ps command, as compared to 0 for the bash, sleep, and bash commands. Furthermore, the PRI of 99 for the ps command results in fewer time slices than the PRI of 76 for the sleep and gedit commands and the PRI of 75 for the bash shell.

Conversely, to increase the priority of the ps -l command, you can use the following command:

```
[root@server1 ~]# nice -n -20 ps -l
F S   UID   PID  PPID  C PRI  NI ADDR SZ WCHAN   TTY        TIME CMD
4 S     0  3194  3192  0  75   0 -  1238 wait4   pts/1   00:00:00 bash
4 S     0  3896  3194  0  76   0 -   953 -       pts/1   00:00:00 sleep
4 S     0  3939  3194  0  76   0 -  7015 -       pts/1   00:00:02 gedit
4 R     0  3947  3194  0  60 -20 -   687 -       pts/1   00:00:00 ps
[root@server1 ~]#_
```

Note from the preceding output that the nice value of -20 for the ps command resulted in a PRI of 60, which is more likely to receive time slices than the PRI of 76 for the sleep and gedit commands and the PRI of 75 for the bash shell.

Note 19

On some Linux systems, background processes are given a nice value of 4 by default to lower the chance they will receive time slices.

After a process has been started, you can change its priority by using the renice command and specifying the change to the nice value, as well as the PID of the processes to change. Suppose, for example, three sample processes are currently executing on a terminal:

```
[root@server1 ~]# ps -l
F S   UID   PID  PPID  C PRI  NI ADDR   SZ WCHAN   TTY       TIME CMD
4 S     0  1229  1228  0  71   0  -     617 wait4   pts/0  00:00:00 bash
```

```
4 S    0  1990  1229  0  69  0   -   483 nanosl pts/0  00:00:00 sample
4 S    0  2180  1229  0  70  0   -   483 nanosl pts/0  00:00:00 sample
4 S    0  2181  1229  0  71  0   -   483 nanosl pts/0  00:00:00 sample
4 R    0  2196  1229  0  75  0   -   768 -      pts/0  00:00:00 ps
[root@server1 ~]#_
```

To lower priority of the first two sample processes by changing the nice value from 0 to +15 and view the new values, you can execute the following commands:

```
[root@server1 ~]# renice +15 1990 2180
1990 (process ID) old priority 0, new priority 15
2180 (process ID) old priority 0, new priority 15
[root@server1 ~]# ps -l
F S  UID   PID  PPID  C PRI  NI ADDR   SZ WCHAN  TTY       TIME CMD
4 S    0  1229  1228  0  71   0   -  617 wait4  pts/0  00:00:00 bash
4 S    0  1990  1229  0  93  15   -  483 nanosl pts/0  00:00:00 sample
4 S    0  2180  1229  0  96  15   -  483 nanosl pts/0  00:00:00 sample
4 S    0  2181  1229  0  71   0   -  483 nanosl pts/0  00:00:00 sample
4 R    0  2196  1229  0  75   0   -  768 -      pts/0  00:00:00 ps
[root@server1 ~]#_
```

Note 20

You can also use the `top` utility to change the nice value of a running process. Press the `r` key, then supply the PID and the nice value when prompted.

Note 21

As with the `nice` command, only the root user can change the nice value to a negative value using the `renice` command.

The root user can use the `renice` command to change the priority of all processes that are owned by a certain user or group. To change the nice value to +15 for all processes owned by the users mary and bini, you could execute the command `renice +15 -u mary bini` at the command prompt. Similarly, to change the nice value to +15 for all processes started by members of the group sys, you could execute the command `renice +15 -g sys` at the command prompt.

Scheduling Commands

Although most processes are begun by users executing commands while logged in to a terminal, at times you might want to schedule a command to execute at some point in the future. For example, scheduling system maintenance commands to run during nonworking hours is good practice, as it does not disrupt normal business activities.

You can use two different daemons to schedule commands: the **at daemon (atd)** and the **cron daemon (crond)**. The at daemon can be used to schedule a command to execute once in the future, whereas the cron daemon is used to schedule a command to execute repeatedly in the future.

Scheduling Commands with atd

To schedule a command or set of commands for execution at a later time by the at daemon, you can specify the time as an argument to the **at command**; some common time formats used with the at command are listed in Table 9-3.

Table 9-3   Common `at` commands

Command	Description
`at 10:15pm`	Schedules commands to run at 10:15 PM on the current date
`at 10:15pm July 15`	Schedules commands to run at 10:15 PM on July 15
`at midnight`	Schedules commands to run at midnight on the current date
`at noon July 15`	Schedules commands to run at noon on July 15
`at teatime`	Schedules commands to run at 4:00 PM on the current date
`at tomorrow`	Schedules commands to run the next day
`at now + 5 minutes`	Schedules commands to run in five minutes
`at now + 10 hours`	Schedules commands to run in 10 hours
`at now + 4 days`	Schedules commands to run in four days
`at now + 2 weeks`	Schedules commands to run in two weeks
`at now` `at batch`	Schedules commands to run immediately

`at 9:00am 01/03/2023`
`at 9:00am 01032023`
`at 9:00am 03.01.2023`
	Schedules commands to run at 9:00 AM on January 3, 2023

After being invoked, the `at` command displays an `at>` prompt allowing you to type commands to be executed, one per line. After the commands have been entered, use the Ctrl+d key combination to schedule the commands using atd.

Note 22

The at daemon uses the current shell's environment when executing scheduled commands. The shell environment and scheduled commands are stored in the /var/spool/at directory on Fedora systems and the /var/spool/cron/atjobs directory on Ubuntu systems.

Note 23

If the standard output of any command scheduled using atd has not been redirected to a file, it is normally mailed to the user. You can check your local mail by typing `mail` at a command prompt. Because most modern Linux distributions do not install a mail daemon by default, it is important to ensure that the output of any commands scheduled using atd are redirected to a file.

To schedule the commands `date` and `who` to run at 10:15 PM on July 15, you can use the following commands:

```
[root@server1 ~]# at 10:15pm July 15
at> date > /root/atfile
at> who >> /root/atfile
at> Ctrl+d
job 1 at Wed Jul 15 22:15:00 2023
[root@server1 ~]#_
```

As shown in the preceding output, the at command returns an at job ID. You can use this ID to query or remove the scheduled command. To display a list of at job IDs, you can specify the -1 option to the at command:

```
[root@server1 ~]# at -l
1          Wed Jul 15 22:15:00 2023 a root
[root@server1 ~]#_
```

> **Note 24**
>
> Alternatively, you can use the **atq command** to see scheduled at jobs. The atq command is simply a shortcut to the at -1 command.

> **Note 25**
>
> When running the at -1 command, a regular user only sees their own scheduled at jobs; however, the root user sees all scheduled at jobs.

To see the contents of the at job listed in the previous output alongside the shell environment at the time the at job was scheduled, you can use the -c option to the at command and specify the appropriate at job ID:

```
[root@server1 ~]# at -c 1
#!/bin/sh
# atrun uid=0 gid=0
# mail root 0
umask 22
XDG_VTNR=2; export XDG_VTNR
XDG_SESSION_ID=1; export XDG_SESSION_ID
HOSTNAME=server1; export HOSTNAME
SHELL=/bin/bash; export SHELL
HISTSIZE=1000; export HISTSIZE
QT_GRAPHICSSYSTEM_CHECKED=1; export QT_GRAPHICSSYSTEM_CHECKED
USER=root; export USER
MAIL=/var/spool/mail/root; export MAIL
PATH=/usr/local/sbin:/usr/local/bin:/sbin:/bin:/usr/sbin:/usr/bin:/root
/bin; export PATH
PWD=/root; export PWD
LANG=en_US.UTF-8; export LANG
KDEDIRS=/usr; export KDEDIRS
HISTCONTROL=ignoredups; export HISTCONTROL
SHLVL=1; export SHLVL
XDG_SEAT=seat0; export XDG_SEAT
HOME=/root; export HOME
LOGNAME=root; export LOGNAME
LESSOPEN=\|\|/usr/bin/lesspipe.sh\ %s; export LESSOPEN
XDG_RUNTIME_DIR=/run/user/0; export XDG_RUNTIME_DIR
cd /root || {
        echo 'Execution directory inaccessible' >&2
        exit 1
}
${SHELL:-/bin/sh} << 'marcinDELIMITER2b2a920e'
date >/root/atfile
who >>/root/atfile
```

```
marcinDELIMITER2b2a920e
[root@server1 ~]#_
```

To remove the at job used in the preceding example, specify the −d option to the at command, followed by the appropriate at job ID, as shown in the following output:

```
[root@server1 ~]# at -d 1
[root@server1 ~]# at -l
[root@server1 ~]#_
```

Note 26

Alternatively, you can use the atrm 1 command to remove the first at job. The **atrm command** is simply a shortcut to the at −d command.

If there are many commands to be scheduled using the at daemon, you can place these commands in a shell script and then schedule the shell script to execute at a later time using the −f option to the at command. An example of scheduling a shell script called myscript using the at command is shown next:

```
[root@server1 ~]# cat myscript
#this is a sample shell script
date > /root/atfile
who >> /root/atfile
[root@server1 ~]# at 10:15pm July 16 -f myscript
job 2 at Wed Jul 15 22:15:00 2023
[root@server1 ~]#_
```

If the /etc/at.allow and /etc/at.deny files do not exist, only the root user is allowed to schedule tasks using the at daemon. To give this ability to other users, create an /etc/at.allow file and add the names of users allowed to use the at daemon, one per line. Conversely, you can use the /etc/at.deny file to deny certain users access to the at daemon; any user not listed in this file is then allowed to use the at daemon. If both files exist, the system checks the /etc/at.allow file and does not process the entries in the /etc/at.deny file.

Note 27

On Fedora systems, only an /etc/at.deny file exists by default. Because this file is initially left blank, all users are allowed to use the at daemon. On Ubuntu systems, only an /etc/at.deny file exists by default, and lists daemon user accounts. As a result, the root user and other regular user accounts are allowed to use the at daemon.

Scheduling Commands with cron

The at daemon is useful for scheduling tasks that occur on a certain date in the future but is ill suited for scheduling repetitive tasks, because each task requires its own at job ID. The cron daemon is better suited for repetitive tasks because it uses configuration files called cron tables to specify when a command should be executed.

A cron table includes six fields separated by space or tab characters. The first five fields specify the times to run the command, and the sixth field is the absolute pathname to the command to be executed. As with the at command, you can place commands in a shell script and schedule the shell script to run repetitively; in this case, the sixth field is the absolute pathname to the shell script. Each of the fields in a cron table is depicted in Figure 9-5.

Figure 9-5   User cron table format

1   2   3   4   5   command

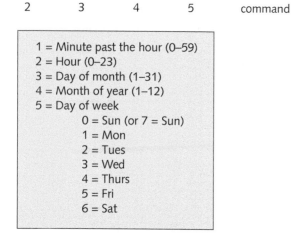

1 = Minute past the hour (0–59)
2 = Hour (0–23)
3 = Day of month (1–31)
4 = Month of year (1–12)
5 = Day of week
        0 = Sun (or 7 = Sun)
        1 = Mon
        2 = Tues
        3 = Wed
        4 = Thurs
        5 = Fri
        6 = Sat

Thus, to execute the /root/myscript shell script at 5:20 PM and 5:40 PM Monday to Friday regardless of the day of the month or month of the year, you could use the cron table depicted in Figure 9-6.

Figure 9-6   Sample user cron table entry

1	2	3	4	5	command
20,40	17	*	*	1–5	/root/myscript

The first field in Figure 9-6 specifies the minute past the hour. Because the command must be run at 20 minutes and 40 minutes past the hour, this field has two values, separated by a comma. The second field specifies the time in 24-hour format, with 5 PM being the 17th hour. The third and fourth fields specify the day of month and month of year, respectively, to run the command. Because the command might run during any month regardless of the day of month, both fields use the * wildcard shell metacharacter to match all values. The final field indicates the day of the week to run the command; as with the first field, the command must be run on multiple days, but a range of days was specified (day 1 to day 5).

Two types of cron tables are used by the cron daemon: user cron tables and system cron tables. User cron tables represent tasks that individual users schedule and exist in the /var/spool/cron directory on Fedora systems and the /var/spool/cron/crontabs directory on Ubuntu systems. System cron tables contain system tasks and exist in the /etc/crontab file as well as the /etc/cron.d directory.

User Cron Tables

On a newly installed Fedora system, all users have the ability to schedule tasks using the cron daemon because the /etc/cron.deny file has no contents. However, if you create an /etc/cron.allow file and add a list of users to it, only those users will be able to schedule tasks using the cron daemon. All other users are denied. Conversely, you can modify the /etc/cron.deny file to list those users who are denied the ability to schedule tasks. Thus, any users not listed in this file are allowed to schedule tasks. If both files exist, only the /etc/cron.allow file is processed. If neither file exists, all users are allowed to schedule tasks, which is the case on a newly installed Ubuntu system.

To create or edit a user cron table, you can use the -e option to the `crontab command`, which opens the nano editor by default on Fedora systems. You can then enter the appropriate cron table entries. Suppose, for example, that the root user executed the `crontab -e` command on a Fedora system. To schedule /bin/command1 to run at 4:30 AM every Friday and /bin/command2 to run at 2:00 PM on the first day of every month, you can add the following lines while in the nano editor:

```
30 4 * * 5 /bin/command1
0 14 1 * * /bin/command2
```

Note 28

When you run the `crontab -e` command on an Ubuntu system, you are prompted for the editor to use.

When the user saves the changes and quits the nano editor, the information is stored in the file /var/spool/cron/*username*, where *username* is the name of the user who executed the `crontab -e` command. In the preceding example, the file would be named /var/spool/cron/root.

To list your user cron table, you can use the `-l` option to the `crontab` command. The following output lists the cron table created earlier:

```
[root@server1 ~]# crontab -l
30 4 * * 5 /bin/command1
0 14 1 * * /bin/command2
[root@server1 ~]#_
```

Furthermore, to remove a cron table and all scheduled jobs, you can use the `-r` option to the `crontab` command, as illustrated next:

```
[root@server1 ~]# crontab -r
[root@server1 ~]# crontab -l
no crontab for root
[root@server1 ~]#_
```

The root user can edit, list, or remove any other user's cron table by using the `-u` option to the `crontab` command followed by the user name. For example, to edit the cron table for the user mary, the root user could use the command `crontab -e -u mary` at the command prompt. Similarly, to list and remove mary's cron table, the root user could execute the commands `crontab -l -u mary` and `crontab -r -u mary`, respectively.

System Cron Tables

Linux systems are typically scheduled to run many commands during nonbusiness hours. These commands might perform system maintenance, back up data, or run CPU-intensive programs. While Systemd timer units can be configured to run these commands, they are often scheduled by the cron daemon from entries in the system cron table /etc/crontab, which can only be edited by the root user. The default /etc/crontab file on a Fedora system is shown in the following output:

```
[root@server1 ~]# cat /etc/crontab
SHELL=/bin/bash
PATH=/sbin:/bin:/usr/sbin:/usr/bin
MAILTO=root

# For details see man 4 crontabs

# Example of job definition:
# .---------------- minute (0 - 59)
# |  .------------- hour (0 - 23)
# |  |  .---------- day of month (1 - 31)
# |  |  |  .------- month (1 - 12) OR jan,feb,mar,apr ...
# |  |  |  |  .---- day of week (0 - 6) (Sunday=0 or 7) OR
# |  |  |  |  |          sun,mon,tue,wed,thu,fri,sat
# |  |  |  |  |
# *  *  *  *  * user-name command to be executed

[root@server1 ~]#_
```

The initial section of the cron table specifies the environment used while executing commands. The remainder of the file contains comments that identify the format of a cron table entry. If you add your own cron table entries to the bottom of this file, they will be executed as the root user. Alternatively, you may prefix the command within a system cron table entry with the user account that it should be executed as. For example, the /bin/cleanup command shown in the following output will be executed as the apache user every Friday at 11:30 PM:

```
[root@server1 ~]# cat /etc/crontab
SHELL=/bin/bash
PATH=/sbin:/bin:/usr/sbin:/usr/bin
MAILTO=root


# For details see man 4 crontabs

# Example of job definition:
# .---------------- minute (0 - 59)
# |  .------------- hour (0 - 23)
# |  |  .---------- day of month (1 - 31)
# |  |  |  .------- month (1 - 12) OR jan,feb,mar,apr ...
# |  |  |  |  .---- day of week (0 - 6) (Sunday=0 or 7) OR
# |  |  |  |  |           sun,mon,tue,wed,thu,fri,sat
# |  |  |  |  |
# *  *  *  *  * user-name command to be executed

  30 23  *  *  5    apache  /bin/cleanup

[root@server1 ~]#_
```

You can also place a cron table with the same information in the /etc/cron.d directory. Any cron tables found in this directory can have the same format as /etc/crontab and are run by the system. In the following example, the cron daemon is configured to run the sa1 command every 10 minutes as the root user, and the sa2 command at 11:53 PM as the root user each day:

```
[root@server1 ~]# cat /etc/cron.d/sysstat
# Run system activity accounting tool every 10 minutes
*/10 * * * * root /usr/lib/sa/sa1 -S DISK 1 1
# Generate a daily summary of process accounting at 23:53
53 23 * * * root /usr/lib/sa/sa2 -A
[root@server1 ~]#_
```

> **Note 29**
>
> The watch command can be used instead of the cron daemon for scheduling very frequent tasks. For example, to run the sa1 command shown in the previous output every 1 minute (60 seconds), you could run the watch -n 60 /usr/lib/sa/sa1 -S DISK 1 1 command.

Many administrative tasks are performed on an hourly, daily, weekly, or monthly basis. If you have a task of this type, you don't need to create a system cron table. Instead, you can place a shell script that runs the appropriate commands in one of the following directories:

- Scripts that should be executed hourly in the /etc/cron.hourly directory
- Scripts that should be executed daily in the /etc/cron.daily directory
- Scripts that should be executed weekly in the /etc/cron.weekly directory
- Scripts that should be executed monthly in the /etc/cron.monthly directory

On Fedora systems, the cron daemon runs the /etc/cron.d/0hourly script, which executes the contents of the /etc/cron.hourly directory 1 minute past the hour, every hour on the hour. The /etc/cron.hourly/0anacron file starts the anacron daemon, which then executes the contents of the /etc/cron.daily, /etc/cron.weekly, and /etc/cron.monthly directories at the times specified in /etc/anacrontab.

On Ubuntu systems, cron table entries within the /etc/crontab file are used to execute the contents of the /etc/cron.hourly, as well as the contents of the /etc/cron.daily, /etc/cron.weekly, and /etc/cron.monthly directories using the anacron daemon.

> **Note 30**
>
> If the computer is powered off during the time of a scheduled task, the cron daemon will simply not execute the task. This is why cron tables within the /etc/cron.daily, /etc/cron.weekly, and /etc/cron.monthly directories are often executed by the anacron daemon, which will resume task execution at the next available time if the computer is powered off during the time of a scheduled task.

Summary

- Processes are programs that are executing on the system.
- User processes are run in the same terminal as the user who executed them, whereas daemon processes are system processes that do not run on a terminal.
- Every process has a parent process associated with it and, optionally, several child processes.
- Process information is stored in the /proc filesystem. You can use the ps, pstree, pgrep, and top commands to view this information.
- Zombie and rogue processes that exist for long periods of time use up system resources and should be killed to improve system performance.
- You can send kill signals to a process using the kill, killall, pkill, and top commands.
- The shell creates, or forks, a subshell to execute most commands.
- Processes can be run in the background by appending an & to the command name. The shell assigns each background process a background job ID such that it can be manipulated afterward.
- The priority of a process can be affected indirectly by altering its nice value; nice values range from –20 (high priority) to +19 (low priority). Only the root user can increase the priority of a process.
- You can use the at and cron daemons to schedule commands to run at a later time. The at daemon schedules tasks to occur once at a later time, whereas the cron daemon uses cron tables to schedule tasks to occur repetitively in the future.

Key Terms

anacron daemon
at command
at daemon (atd)
atq command
atrm command
background process
bg (background) command
child process
cron daemon (crond)
cron table
crontab command
daemon process
fg (foreground) command
foreground process
forking

htop command
jobs command
kill command
kill signal
killall command
lsof (list open files) command
nice command
nice value
nohup command
parent process
parent process ID (PPID)
pgrep command
pidof command
pkill command
process

process ID (PID)
process priority
process state
program
ps command
pstree command
renice command
rogue process
time slice
top command
trap
user process
watch command
zombie process

Review Questions

1. Which command entered without arguments is used to display a list of processes running in the current shell?
   a. pgrep
   b. list
   c. pid
   d. ps

2. Which of the following statements is true? (Choose all that apply.)
   a. If /etc/at.allow exists, only users listed in it can use the at command.
   b. If /etc/cron.allow exists, only users listed in it can use the crontab command.
   c. If /etc/cron.deny exists and /etc/cron.allow does not exist, any user not listed in /etc/cron.deny can use the crontab command.
   d. If /etc/cron.allow and /etc/cron.deny exist, only users listed in the former can use the crontab command, and any users listed in the latter are denied access to the crontab command.
   e. If a user is listed in both /etc/cron.allow and /etc/cron.deny, then /etc/cron.deny takes precedence and the user cannot access the crontab command.

3. Where are individual user tasks scheduled to run with the cron daemon stored on a Fedora system?
   a. /etc/crontab
   b. /etc/cron/*username*
   c. /var/spool/cron
   d. /var/spool/cron/*username*

4. Which process has a PID of 1 and a PPID of 0?
   a. the kernel itself
   b. ps
   c. init/systemd
   d. top

5. A process spawning or initiating another process is referred to as _____.
   a. a child process
   b. forking
   c. branching
   d. parenting

6. As daemon processes are not associated with terminals, you must use an option such as -e alongside the ps command to view them.
   a. True
   b. False

7. Which of the following commands will most likely increase the chance of a process receiving more time slices?
   a. renice 0
   b. renice 15
   c. renice -12
   d. renice 19

8. How can you bypass the wait function and send a user process to the background?
   a. This cannot happen once a process is executing; it can be done only when the command is started by placing an ampersand (&) after it.
   b. This cannot happen; only daemon processes can run in the background.
   c. You can use the ps command.
   d. You can use the Ctrl+z key combination and the bg command.

9. The at command is used to _____.
   a. schedule processes to run periodically in the background
   b. schedule processes to run periodically on a recurring basis in the future
   c. schedule processes to run at a single instance in the future
   d. schedule processes to run in the foreground

10. What command is used to view and modify user jobs scheduled to run with cron?
    a. crontab
    b. cron
    c. ps
    d. sched

11. Every process has a process ID and a _____.
    a. fork process
    b. daemon
    c. child process
    d. parent process ID

12. The pkill command terminates _____.
    a. all instances of a process with the same PPID
    b. all instances of a process with the same PID
    c. all instances of a process with the same priority
    d. all instances of a process with the same name matched by a regular expression

13. Nice values are used to affect process priorities using a range between _____.
    a. 0 and 20
    b. 0 and -19
    c. -19 and 20
    d. -20 and 19

14. What is the name given to a process not associated with a terminal?

 a. child process

 b. parent process

 c. user process

 d. daemon process

15. To kill a process running in the background, you must place a % character before its process ID.

 a. True

 b. False

16. What kill level signal cannot be trapped?

 a. 1

 b. 9

 c. 3

 d. 15

17. A runaway process that is faulty and consuming mass amounts of system resources _____.

 a. is a zombie process

 b. is an orphaned process

 c. has a PPID of Z

 d. is a rogue process

18. When you run the ps command, how are daemon processes recognized?

 a. The terminal is listed as tty0.

 b. There is a question mark in the TTY column.

 c. There is an asterisk in the STIME column.

 d. There is a "d" for daemon in the terminal identification column.

19. Which command is used to gain real-time information about processes running on the system, with the most processor-intensive processes appearing at the beginning of the list?

 a. ps

 b. ps -elf

 c. top

 d. pstree

20. Which command can be used to see processes running in the background?

 a. bg

 b. jobs

 c. ps -%

 d. fg

Hands-On Projects

These projects should be completed in the order given. The hands-on projects presented in this chapter should take a total of three hours to complete. The requirements for this lab include:

- A computer with Fedora Linux installed according to Hands-On Project 2-1

Project 9-1

Estimated Time: 30 minutes

Objective: View processes.

Description: In this hands-on project, you view characteristics of processes using the ps command.

1. Boot your Fedora Linux virtual machine. After your Linux system has been loaded, switch to a command-line terminal (tty5) by pressing **Ctrl+Alt+F5** and log in to the terminal using the user name of **root** and the password of **LINUXrocks!**.

2. At the command prompt, type ps -ef | less and press **Enter** to view the first processes started on the entire Linux system.

3. Fill in the following information from the data displayed on the terminal screen after typing the command:

 a. Which process has a Process ID of 1? (PID=1) _____

 b. What character do most processes have in the terminal column (tty)? _____

 c. What does this character in the terminal column indicate? _____

 d. Which user started most of these processes? _____

e. Most processes that are displayed on the screen are started by a certain parent process indicated in the Parent Process ID column (PPID). Which process is the parent to most processes? _____

Type q at the MORE prompt to quit.

4. At the command prompt, type `ps -el | less` and press **Enter** to view the process states for the first processes started on the entire Linux system.

5. Fill in the following information from the data displayed on the terminal screen after typing the command:

   a. What character exists in the State (S) column for most processes, and what does this character indicate? _____

   b. What range of numbers is it possible to have in the Nice (NI) column? _____

   c. Which processes have the number 4 in the Flag (F) column, and what does this number indicate? _____

Type q at the MORE prompt to quit.

6. At the command prompt, type `ps -el | grep Z` and press **Enter** to display zombie processes on your Linux system. Are there any zombie processes indicated in the State (S) column?

7. Type `exit` and press **Enter** to log out of your shell.

Project 9-2

Estimated Time: 20 minutes
Objective: Kill processes.
Description: In this hands-on project, you use kill signals to terminate processes on your system.

1. On your Fedora Linux virtual machine, switch to a command-line terminal (tty5) by pressing **Ctrl+Alt+F5** and log in to the terminal using the user name of **root** and the password of **LINUXrocks!**.

2. At the command prompt, type `ps -ef | grep bash` and press **Enter** to view the BASH shells that are running in memory on your computer. Record the PID of the BASH shell running in your terminal (tty5): _____.

3. At the command prompt, type `pgrep -t tty5 bash` and press **Enter** to view the PID of BASH shells that are running in memory within your terminal (tty5). Does the PID shown match the one from Step 2?

4. At the command prompt, type `kill -l` and press **Enter** to list the available kill signals that you can send to a process.

5. At the command prompt, type `kill -2 PID` (where PID is the PID that you recorded in Question 2) and press **Enter**. Did your shell terminate?

6. At the command prompt, type `kill -3 PID` (where PID is the PID that you recorded in Question 2) and press **Enter**. Did your shell terminate?

7. At the command prompt, type `kill -15 PID` (where PID is the PID that you recorded in Question 2) and press **Enter**. Did your shell terminate?

8. At the command prompt, type `kill -9 PID` (where PID is the PID that you recorded in Question 2) and press **Enter**. Did your shell terminate? Why did this command work when the others did not?

Project 9-3

Estimated Time: 30 minutes
Objective: Create, modify, and kill background processes.
Description: In this hands-on project, you run processes in the background, kill them using the `kill`, `killall`, and `pgrep` commands, and change their priorities using the `nice` and `renice` commands.

1. On your Fedora Linux virtual machine, switch to a command-line terminal (tty5) by pressing **Ctrl+Alt+F5** and log in to the terminal using the user name of **root** and the password of **LINUXrocks!**.

2. At the command prompt, type `sleep 6000` and press **Enter** to start the `sleep` command, which waits 6000 seconds in the foreground. Do you get your prompt back after you enter this command? Why? Send the process a SIGINT signal by typing the **Ctrl+c** key combination.

3. At the command prompt, type `sleep 6000&` and press **Enter** to start the `sleep` command, which waits 6000 seconds in the background. Observe the background Job ID and PID that is returned.

4. Bring the background sleep process to the foreground by typing `fg %1` at the command prompt, then press **Enter**. Send the process a SIGINT signal by typing the **Ctrl+c** key combination.

5. Place another `sleep` command in memory by typing the `sleep 6000&` command and pressing **Enter**. Repeat this command three more times to place a total of four `sleep` commands in memory.

6. At the command prompt, type `jobs` and press **Enter** to view the jobs running in the background. What does the + symbol indicate?

7. At the command prompt, type `kill %` and press **Enter** to terminate the most recent process. Next, type `jobs` and press **Enter** to view the results.

8. At the command prompt, type `kill %1` and press **Enter** to terminate background job #1. Next, type `jobs` and press **Enter** to view the results.

9. At the command prompt, type `killall sleep` and press **Enter** to terminate the remaining sleep processes in memory. Verify that there are no more sleep processes in memory by typing the `jobs` command, then press **Enter**.

10. Place a `sleep` command in memory by typing `sleep 6000&` at a command prompt and pressing **Enter**.

11. Place a `sleep` command in memory with a lower priority by typing `nice -n 19 sleep 6000&` at a command prompt and pressing **Enter**.

12. Verify that these two processes have different nice values by typing the command `ps -el | grep sleep` at the command prompt and pressing **Enter**. Record the PID of the process with a nice value of 0: _____.

13. At the command prompt, type `renice +10 PID` (where PID is the PID you recorded in the previous question) to change the priority of the process. Type the command `ps -el | grep sleep` and press **Enter** to verify the new priority.

14. At the command prompt, type `pkill -t tty5 sleep` to kill all sleep processes running within your terminal (tty5).

15. Type `exit` and press **Enter** to log out of your shell.

Project 9-4

Estimated Time: 40 minutes
Objective: Use the top utility.
Description: In this hands-on project, you view and manage processes using the top command-line utility.

1. On your Fedora Linux virtual machine, switch to a command-line terminal (tty5) by pressing **Ctrl+Alt+F5** and log in to the terminal using the user name of **root** and the password of **LINUXrocks!**.

2. At the command prompt, type `top` and press **Enter**.

3. From the output on the terminal screen, record the following information:

   a. Number of processes: _____

   b. Number of sleeping processes: _____

   c. Amount of total memory: _____

   d. Amount of total swap memory: _____

4. While in the top utility, press the **h** key and observe the output. When finished, press any key to return to the previous top output.

5. By observing the output under the COMMAND column on your terminal screen, identify the PID of the top command in the output and record it here: _____

6. Type **r** in the top utility to change the priority of a running process. When asked which process to change (renice), type the **PID** from the previous question. When asked which value to use, type 10 to lower the priority of the top process to 10. Does this new priority take effect immediately?

7. Type **k** in the top utility to send a kill signal to a process. When asked which process, type the **PID** used in the previous question. When asked which signal to send, type 2 to send a SIGINT signal. Did the top utility terminate?

8. At the command prompt, type `top` and press **Enter**.

9. By observing the output under the COMMAND column on your terminal screen, identify the PID of the top command in the output and record it here: _____

10. Type **k** in the top utility to send a kill signal to a process. When asked which process, type the **PID** from the previous question. When asked which signal to send, type 15 to send a SIGTERM signal. Did the SIGTERM signal allow top to exit cleanly?

11. At the command prompt, type `clear` and press **Enter** to clear the screen.

12. At the command prompt, type `dnf -y install htop` and press **Enter** to install the htop utility.

13. At the command prompt, type `htop` and press **Enter**. View the information displayed for each process as well as the resource utilization shown. Note the different function key actions listed at the bottom of the screen that can be used to search, sort, renice, and kill processes. When finished, press **F10** to quit the htop utility.

14. Type `exit` and press **Enter** to log out of your shell.

Project 9-5

Estimated Time: 40 minutes
Objective: Schedule processes.
Description: In this hands-on project, you schedule processes using the at and cron daemons.

1. On your Fedora Linux virtual machine, switch to a command-line terminal (tty5) by pressing **Ctrl+Alt+F5** and log in to the terminal using the user name of **root** and the password of **LINUXrocks!**.

2. Schedule processes to run 1 minute in the future by typing the command `at now + 1 minute` at a command prompt, then press **Enter**.

3. When the at> prompt appears, type `date > /root/datefile` and press **Enter**.

4. When the second at> prompt appears, type `who >> /root/datefile` and press **Enter**.

5. When the third at> prompt appears, press the **Ctrl+d** key combination to finish the scheduling and observe the output. When will your job run? Where will the output of the `date` and `who` commands be sent?

6. In approximately one minute, type `cat datefile` and press **Enter**. View the output from your scheduled at job.

7. At the command prompt, type `crontab -l` and press **Enter** to list your cron table. Do you have one?

8. At the command prompt, type `crontab -e` and press **Enter** to edit a new cron table for the root user. When the vi editor appears, add the line: `30 20 * * 5 /bin/false`

9. When you finish typing, save and quit the vi editor and observe the output on the terminal screen.

10. At the command prompt, type `crontab -l` and press **Enter** to list your cron table. When will the `/bin/false` command run?

11. At the command prompt, type `cat /var/spool/cron/root` and press **Enter** to list your cron table from the cron directory. Is it the same as the output from the previous command?

12. At the command prompt, type `crontab -r` and press **Enter** to remove your cron table.

13. At the command prompt, type `ls /etc/cron.daily` and press **Enter**. Are there any scripts that will be run daily on your system?

14. At the command prompt, type `ls /etc/cron.d` and press **Enter**. Are there any custom system cron tables on your system?

15. At the command prompt, type `cat /etc/cron.d/0hourly` and press **Enter**. When are the contents of the /etc/cron.hourly directory run by the cron daemon?

16. Type `exit` and press **Enter** to log out of your shell.

Project 9-6

Estimated Time: 20 minutes
Objective: Examine /proc.
Description: In this hands-on project, you view information that is exported by the Linux kernel to the /proc directory.

1. On your Fedora Linux virtual machine, switch to a command-line terminal (tty5) by pressing **Ctrl+Alt+F5** and log in to the terminal using the user name of **root** and the password of **LINUXrocks!**.

2. At the command prompt, type `cd /proc` and press **Enter** to change your current directory to /proc. Then type `ls` to list the directory contents and examine the output on the terminal screen. Why are the subdirectories named using numbers?

3. At the command prompt, type `cat meminfo | less` and press **Enter** to list information about total and available memory. How does the value for total memory (MemTotal) compare to the information from Step 3 in Project 9-4?

4. At the command prompt, type `cat swaps` and press **Enter** to list information about total and available swap memory. How does the value for total swap memory (Size) compare with the information from Step 3 in Project 9-4?

5. At the command prompt, type `cd 1` and press **Enter** to enter the subdirectory that contains information about the init daemon (PID = 1).

6. At the command prompt, type `ls` and press **Enter** to list the files in the /proc/1 directory. Next, type `cat status | less` and press **Enter**. What is the state of the init (systemd) daemon? Does it list the correct PID and PPID?

7. Type `exit` and press **Enter** to log out of your shell.

Discovery Exercises

Discovery Exercise 9-1

Estimated Time: 15 minutes
Objective: Explain background process execution.
Description: Type the command `sleep 5` at a command prompt and press **Enter**. When did you receive your shell prompt? Explain the events that occurred by referencing Figure 9-3. Next, type `exec sleep 5` at a command prompt and press **Enter**. What happened? Can you explain the results using Figure 9-3? Redraw Figure 9-3 to indicate what happens when a command is directly executed.

Discovery Exercise 9-2

Estimated Time: 20 minutes

Objective: Research `ps` options.

Description: Using the man or info pages, research four more options to the `ps` command. What processes does each option display? What information is given about each process?

Discovery Exercise 9-3

Estimated Time: 20 minutes

Objective: Investigate graphical background processes.

Description: Log in to the GNOME desktop on your Fedora system as user1, open a command-line terminal and switch to the root user. At the shell prompt, run `dnf -y install xeyes` to install the xeyes program, and then run `xeyes` to execute it. Does the terminal window stay open? Click the terminal window to bring it to the foreground. Do you see your shell prompt? Why? Close your terminal window. What happened to the xeyes program and why? Next, open another command-line terminal and type `xeyes&` at the command prompt to execute the xeyes program in the background. Click the terminal window to bring it to the foreground. Do you see your shell prompt? Why? Close your terminal window. What happened to the xeyes program and why?

Finally, open another command-line terminal and type `nohup  xeyes&` at the command prompt to execute the xeyes program in the background from the nohup command. Click the terminal window to bring it to the foreground and press **Enter**. Close your terminal. Visit the nohup manual page to explain why the xeyes program is still available.

Discovery Exercise 9-4

Estimated Time: 15 minutes

Objective: Explain kill signals.

Description: You are the systems administrator for a large trust company. Most of the Linux servers in the company host databases that are accessed frequently by company employees. One particular Linux server has been reported as being very slow today. Upon further investigation using the top utility, you have found a rogue process that is wasting a great deal of system resources. Unfortunately, the rogue process is a database maintenance program and should be killed with caution. Which kill signal would you send this process and why? If the rogue process traps this signal, which other kill signals would you try? Which command could you use as a last resort to kill the rogue process? What command can list the files that could be impacted if you terminate the rogue process?

Discovery Exercise 9-5

Estimated Time: 20 minutes

Objective: Create cron tables entries.

Description: Write the lines that you could use in your user cron table to schedule the `/bin/myscript` command to run:

a. every Wednesday afternoon at 2:15 PM

b. every hour on the hour every day of the week

c. every 15 minutes on the first of every month

d. only on February 25th at 6:00 PM

e. on the first Monday of every month at 12:10 PM

Discovery Exercise 9-6

Estimated Time: 180 minutes

Objective: Apply chapter concepts to Ubuntu Linux.

Description: Time-permitting, perform Project 9-1 through 9-6 on your Ubuntu Linux virtual machine. You will need to run the `apt install at` command as the root user to install the at daemon and related commands. Note any differences between the Fedora and Ubuntu distributions with regards to process management.

## Chapter 10

Common Administrative Tasks

Chapter Objectives

1 Set up, manage, and print to printers on a Linux system.

2 Outline the purpose of log files and how they are administered.

3 Create and manage user and group accounts.

In previous chapters, you learned how to administer filesystems, X Windows, system startup, and processes. In this chapter, you examine other essential areas of Linux administration. First, you learn about the print process and how to administer and set up printers, followed by a discussion on viewing and managing log files. Finally, you examine system databases that store user and group information, and the utilities that can be used to create, modify, and delete user and group accounts on a Linux system.

Printer Administration

Many Linux users need to print files, as do users of other systems on the network that need to print to a shared printer via a Linux print server. Moreover, printing log files and system configuration information is good procedure in case of a system failure. Thus, a firm understanding of how to set up, manage, and print to printers is vital for those who set up and administer Linux servers.

The Common UNIX Printing System

The most common printing system used on Linux computers is the Common Unix Printing System (CUPS), which is currently maintained by the OpenPrinting project of The Linux Foundation. Fundamental to using CUPS on a Linux system is an understanding of how information is sent to a printer. A set of information sent to a printer at the same time is called a print job. Print jobs can consist of a file, several files, or the output of a command. To send a print job to a printer, you must first use the lp command and specify what to print.

Next, the CUPS daemon (cupsd) assigns the print job a unique print job ID and places a copy of the print job into a temporary directory on the filesystem called the print queue, provided the printer is accepting requests. If the printer is rejecting requests, the CUPS daemon displays an error message stating that the printer is not accepting print jobs.

> **Note 1**
>
> Accepting print jobs into a print queue is called spooling or queuing.

Note 2

The print queue for a printer is typically /var/spool/cups. Regardless of how many printers you have on your Linux system, all print jobs are sent to the same directory.

When a print job is in the print queue, it is ready to be printed. If the printer is enabled and ready to accept the print job, the CUPS daemon sends the print job from the print queue to the printer and removes the copy of the print job in the print queue. Conversely, if the printer is disabled, the print job remains in the print queue.

Note 3

Sending print jobs from a print queue to a printer is commonly called printing.

An example of this process for a printer called printer1 is illustrated in Figure 10-1.

Figure 10-1   The print process

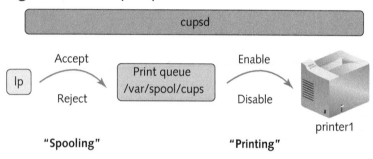

To see a list of all printers on the system and their status, you can use the -t (total) option to the `lpstat` command, as shown in the following output:

```
[root@server1 ~]# lpstat -t
scheduler is running
system default destination: printer1
device for printer1: parallel:/dev/lp0
device for printer2: usb:///Brother/HL2040series
device for printer3: smb://server5/HPLaserJet6MP
printer1 accepting requests since Thu 26 Aug 2023 08:34:30 AM EDT
printer2 accepting requests since Thu 26 Aug 2023 08:36:22 AM EDT
printer3 accepting requests since Thu 26 Aug 2023 08:37:05 AM EDT
printer printer1 is idle. enabled since Thu 26 Aug 2023 08:34:30 AM EDT
printer printer2 is idle. enabled since Thu 26 Aug 2023 08:36:22 AM EDT
printer printer3 is idle. enabled since Thu 26 Aug 2023 08:37:05 AM EDT
[root@server1 ~]#_
```

This output indicates the system has three printers: printer1 prints to a standard printer connected to the first parallel port on the computer (/dev/lp0), printer2 prints to a Brother HL2040-series printer connected to a USB port on the computer, and printer3 prints across the network to an HP LaserJet 6MP printer that is shared by server5 using the SMB protocol. In addition, the CUPS daemon (scheduler) is running and accepting jobs into the print queue for all three printers. The CUPS daemon sends print jobs from the print queue to the three printers because each printer is enabled, and there are no print jobs currently waiting in its print queue.

You can manipulate the status of a printer using the `cupsaccept`, `cupsreject`, `cupsenable`, or `cupsdisable` command followed by the printer name. To enable spooling and disable printing for the printer *printer1*, you can use the following commands:

```
[root@server1 ~]# cupsaccept printer1
[root@server1 ~]# cupsdisable printer1
[root@server1 ~]# lpstat -t
scheduler is running
system default destination: printer1
device for printer1: parallel:/dev/lp0
device for printer2: usb:///Brother/HL2040series
device for printer3: smb://server5/HPLaserJet6MP
printer1 accepting requests since Thu 26 Aug 2023 08:34:30 AM EDT
printer2 accepting requests since Thu 26 Aug 2023 08:36:22 AM EDT
printer3 accepting requests since Thu 26 Aug 2023 08:37:05 AM EDT
printer printer1 disabled since Thu 26 Aug 2023 08:51:21 AM EDT -
        Paused
printer printer2 is idle. enabled since Thu 26 Aug 2023 08:36:22 AM EDT
printer printer3 is idle. enabled since Thu 26 Aug 2023 08:37:05 AM EDT
[root@server1 ~]#_
```

Any print jobs now sent to the printer *printer1* are sent to the print queue but remain in the print queue until the printer is started again.

You can also use the `-r` option to the `cupsdisable` and `cupsreject` commands to specify a reason for the action, as shown in the following output:

```
[root@server1 ~]# cupsdisable -r "Changing toner cartridge" printer1
[root@server1 ~]# lpstat -t
scheduler is running
system default destination: printer1
device for printer1: parallel:/dev/lp0
device for printer2: usb:///Brother/HL2040series
device for printer3: smb://server5/HPLaserJet6MP
printer1 accepting requests since Thu 26 Aug 2023 08:34:30 AM EDT
printer2 accepting requests since Thu 26 Aug 2023 08:36:22 AM EDT
printer3 accepting requests since Thu 26 Aug 2023 08:37:05 AM EDT
printer printer1 disabled since Thu 26 Aug 2023 08:52:44 AM EDT -
        Changing toner cartridge
printer printer2 is idle. enabled since Thu 26 Aug 2023 08:36:22 AM EDT
printer printer3 is idle. enabled since Thu 26 Aug 2023 08:37:05 AM EDT
[root@server1 ~]#_
```

Managing Print Jobs

Recall that you create a print job by using the `lp` command. To print a copy of the /etc/inittab file to the printer *printer1* shown in earlier examples, you can use the following command, which returns a print job ID that you can use to manipulate the print job afterward:

```
[root@server1 ~]# lp -d printer1 /etc/inittab
request id is printer1-1 (1 file(s))
[root@server1 ~]#_
```

The `lp` command uses the `-d` option to specify the destination printer name. If you omit this option, the `lp` command assumes the default printer on the system. Because *printer1* is the only printer on the system making it the default printer, the command `lp /etc/inittab` is equivalent to the one used in the preceding output.

> **Note 4**
>
> You can set the default printer for all users on your system by using the `lpoptions -d printername` command, where `printername` is the name of the default printer. This information is stored in the /etc/cups/lpoptions file.

> **Note 5**
>
> You can specify your own default printer by adding the line `default printername` to the .lpoptions file in your home directory, where `printername` is the name of the default printer. Alternatively, you can use the PRINTER or LPDEST variables to set the default printer. For example, to specify *printer2* as the default printer, you can add either the line `export PRINTER=printer2` or the line `export LPDEST=printer2` to an environment file in your home directory, such as .bash_profile.

Table 10-1 lists some common options to the `lp` command.

Table 10-1   Common options to the `lp` command

Option	Description
`-d name`	Specifies the name of the destination printer
`-i job`	Specifies a certain print job to modify (by job ID)
`-n number`	Prints a specified number of copies
`-m`	Mails you confirmation of print job completion
`-o option`	Specifies certain printing options; common printing options include the following:
	`cpi=`*number*—Sets the characters per inch to *number*
	`landscape`—Prints in landscape orientation
	`number-up=`*number*—Prints a specified *number* of pages on a single piece of paper, where *number* is 2, 4, 6, 9, or 16
	`sides=`*string*—Sets double-sided printing, where *string* is either "two-sided-short-edge" or "two-sided-long-edge"
`-q priority`	Specifies a print job priority from 1 (low priority) to 100 (high priority); by default, all print jobs have a priority of 50

You can also specify several files to print using a single `lp` command by including the files as arguments. In this case, the system creates only one print job to print all of the files. To print the files /etc/hosts and /etc/issue to the printer *printer1*, you can execute the following command:

```
[root@server1 ~]# lp -d printer1 /etc/hosts /etc/issue
request id is printer1-2 (2 file(s))
[root@server1 ~]#_
```

The `lp` command accepts information from Standard Input, so you can place the `lp` command at the end of a pipe to print information. To print a list of logged-in users, you can use the following pipe:

```
[root@server1 ~]# who | lp -d printer1
request id is printer1-3 (1 file(s))
[root@server1 ~]#_
```

To see a list of print jobs in the queue for *printer1*, you can use the `lpstat` command. Without arguments, this command displays all jobs in the print queue that you have printed:

```
[root@server1 ~]# lpstat
printer1-1          root         2048    Thu 26 Aug 2023 08:54:18 AM EDT
printer1-2          root         3072    Thu 26 Aug 2023 08:54:33 AM EDT
printer1-3          root         1024    Thu 26 Aug 2023 08:54:49 AM EDT
[root@server1 ~]#_
```

Table 10-2 lists other options that you can use with the `lpstat` command.

Table 10-2   Common options to the `lpstat` command

Option	Description
-a	Displays a list of printers that are accepting print jobs
-d	Displays the default destination printer
-o name	Displays the print jobs in the print queue for a specific printer name
-p	Displays a list of printers that are enabled
-r	Shows whether the CUPS daemon (scheduler) is running
-t	Shows all information about printers and their print jobs

To remove a print job from the print queue, you can use the `cancel command` followed by the IDs of the print jobs to remove. To remove the print job IDs printer1-1 and printer1-2 created earlier, you can use the following command:

```
[root@server1 ~]# cancel printer1-1 printer1-2
[root@server1 ~]# lpstat
printer1-3          root         3072    Thu 26 Aug 2023 08:54:49 AM EDT
[root@server1 ~]#_
```

You can also remove all jobs started by a certain user by specifying the –u option to the `cancel` command followed by the user name. To remove all jobs in a print queue, you can use the –a option to the `cancel` command, as shown in the following example, which removes all jobs destined for printer1:

```
[root@server1 ~]# cancel -a printer1
[root@server1 ~]# lpstat
[root@server1 ~]#_
```

Not all users might be allowed access to a certain printer. As a result, you can restrict access to certain printers by using the `lpadmin command`. For example, to deny all users other than root and user1 from printing to the *printer1* printer created earlier, you can use the following command:

```
[root@server1 ~]# lpadmin -u allow:root,user1 -u deny:all -d printer1
[root@server1 ~]#_
```

The LPD Printing System

Although CUPS is the preferred printing system for Linux computers today, some Linux systems use the traditional **Line Printer Daemon (LPD)** printing system. In this printing system, you use the `lpr command` to print documents to the print queue much like the `lp` command. You can use the `lpc command` to view the status of printers, the `lpq command` to view print jobs in the print queue, much like the `lpstat` command, and the `lprm command` to remove print jobs, much like the `cancel` command.

For those who are accustomed to using the LPD printing system, CUPS contains versions of the `lpr`, `lpc`, `lpq`, and `lprm` commands. The following output displays the status of all printers on the system, prints two copies of /etc/inittab to *printer1*, views the print job in the queue, and removes the print job:

```
[root@server1 ~]# lpc status
printer1:
        queuing is enabled
        printing is enabled
        no entries
        daemon present
printer2:
        printer is on device 'usb'
        queuing is enabled
        printing is enabled
        no entries
        daemon present
printer2:
        printer is on device 'smb' speed -1
        queuing is enabled
        printing is enabled
        no entries
        daemon present
[root@server1 ~]# lpr -#2 -P printer1 /etc/inittab
[root@server1 ~]# lpq
printer1 is ready and printing
Rank    Owner   Job     File(s)                 Total Size
1st     root    1       inittab                 2048 bytes
[root@server1 ~]# lprm 1
[root@server1 ~]# lpq
printer1 is ready
no entries
[root@server1 ~]#_
```

Configuring Printers

Recall that the core component of printing is the CUPS daemon, which accepts print jobs into a queue and sends them to the printer. The file that contains settings for the CUPS daemon is /etc/cups/cupsd.conf, and the file that contains the configuration information for each printer installed on the system is /etc/cups/printers.conf. By default, the CUPS daemon detects locally connected and network-shared printers and automatically adds an entry for them in the /etc/cups/printers.conf file using a name based on the printer model number (e.g., HP Laserjet 6M). For any printers that the CUPS daemon does not detect and configure, you must provide the necessary information.

Because the format of the /etc/cups/printers.conf file is rigid, it is safer to use a program to create or modify its entries. You can provide a series of options to the `lpadmin` command discussed earlier to configure a printer on the system, or you can use one of several graphical utilities within a desktop environment that can do the same. In GNOME, you can navigate to Activities, Show Applications, Settings to open the Settings utility, and then select Printers, as shown in Figure 10-2. When you access the Printers section of Settings, you will be presented with an Unlock button; you must click this button and supply your password to manage print jobs and printer settings. For example, you can click the 1 Job button in Figure 10-2 to modify or remove the single print job in the queue for printer1 or click the settings (cog wheel) button to manage the device configuration and printing options for printer1. To manually add a printer, you can click the Add Printer button and select your device from a list of detected printers or specify the name or IP address of a printer on the network.

Figure 10-2   The Printers section of GNOME Settings

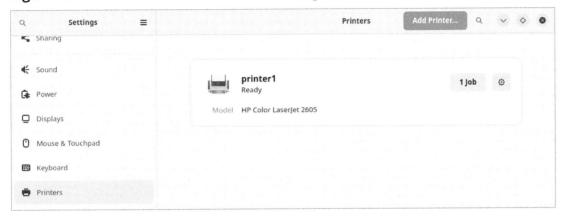

> **Note 6**
>
> The Printers section within GNOME Settings provides for a quick and easy method of configuring and managing printers on a system. It does not allow you to specify detailed printer configuration when adding a printer.

The most comprehensive way to create and manage CUPS printers is by using the **CUPS web administration tool**, which allows Linux administrators to create and manage all printer settings. You can access the CUPS web administration tool using a web browser on TCP port 631 by navigating to http://*servername*:631, as shown in Figure 10-3.

Figure 10-3   The CUPS web administration tool

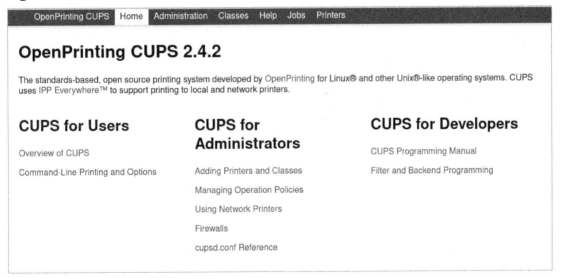

To create a new printer using this tool, select the Administration tab, click Add Printer, and log in using the root user name and password. You are then prompted to choose the type of printer, as shown in Figure 10-4. You can choose to print to a printer connected to a local serial, parallel, or USB port, to a printer connected to the network using Hewlett-Packard JetDirect technology, or to a printer that is shared on a remote computer across a network with the **Internet Printing Protocol (IPP)**, the Line Printer Daemon (LPD), or the Windows Server Message Blocks (SMB/SAMBA) printing service.

Figure 10-4 Selecting the printer type for a new printer

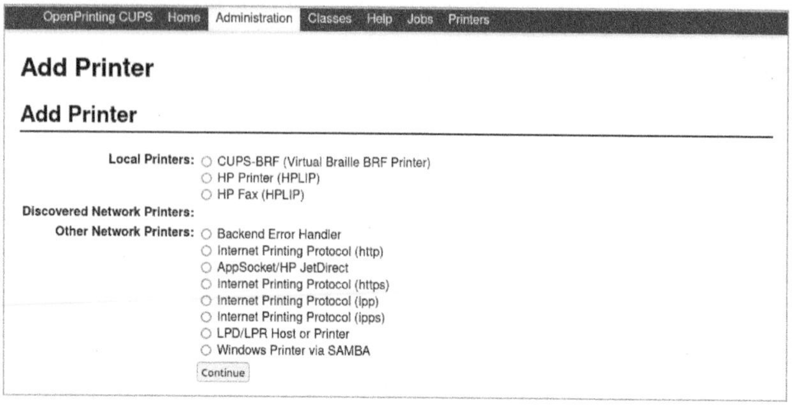

Note 7

The local HP Printer selections shown in Figure 10-4 can be used to configure other brands of locally connected printers as well.

After selecting a printer type, you specify information related to the printer type (e.g., the network address for a network printer), as well as a printer name, description, manufacturer and model, default printer options, and whether to share the printer using IPP to other systems on the network.

After creating a printer, you can use the other options available on the Administration tab of the CUPS web administration tool to configure and manage the CUPS printing service, as shown in Figure 10-5.

Figure 10-5 CUPS administration options

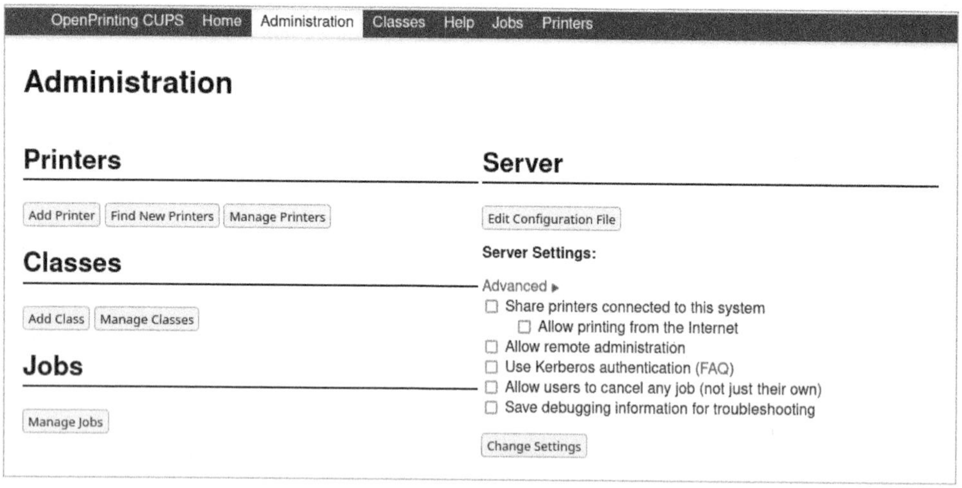

The Find New Printers button shown in Figure 10-5 performs a detailed local and network search for new printer devices. The Manage Printers button (which switches to the Printers tab) allows you to configure individual printer settings.

CUPS also allows you to configure collections of printers to use as a single unit. These collections are called **printer classes**. When you print to a printer class, the print job is sent to the first available printer in the printer class. Printer classes are often used in larger organizations, where multiple printers are stored in a print room. To create a printer class, select the Add Class button shown in Figure 10-5, supply a name and description for the new class, and then choose the printers to include in the class. Next, you can click the Manage Classes button (which switches to the Classes tab) to configure settings for your new printer class.

Clicking Manage Jobs shown in Figure 10-5 (which switches to the Jobs tab) allows you to view, modify, and delete print jobs in the queue. Regular users can also access the CUPS web administration tool and select the Jobs tab to manage their own jobs after logging in with their user name and password.

The Server section shown in Figure 10-5 allows you to edit the CUPS configuration file, access log files, and perform advanced functions. Select the Allow remote administration option to access the CUPS web administration tool from other computers on the network. By selecting the Share printers connected to this system and Allow printing from the Internet options, IPP printer sharing will be enabled for all printers that allow IPP printer sharing in their settings. To configure a shared printer on a remote system using IPP, you can specify the URL http://*servername*:631/printers/*printername* when adding the printer.

Note 8

To allow for IPP printer sharing, any firewalls must allow TCP port 80, 443, and 631. Firewall configuration is discussed in Chapter 14.

Log File Administration

To identify and troubleshoot problems on a Linux system, you must view the events that occur over time. Because administrators cannot observe all events that take place on a Linux system, most daemons record information and error messages to files stored on the filesystem. As discussed in Chapter 3, these files are referred to as log files and are typically stored in the /var/log directory.

Many programs store their log files in subdirectories of the /var/log directory. For example, the /var/log/samba directory contains the log files created by the SAMBA file-sharing daemons. Table 10-3 lists some common log files that you may find in the /var/log directory, depending on your Linux distribution.

Table 10-3   Common Linux log files found in /var/log

Log File	Description
auth.log	Contains a history of all authentication requests on the system by users and daemons
btmp	Contains a history of failed login sessions; can be viewed using the `lastb` command
boot.log bootstrap.log	Contains basic information regarding daemon startup obtained during system initialization
cron cron.log	Contains information and error messages generated by the cron and at daemons
dmesg	Contains detected hardware information obtained during system startup
faillog	Contains failed login history for users; can be viewed using the `faillog -u` *username* command
kern.log	Contains information and error messages generated by the kernel
mail.log	Contains information and error messages generated by the sendmail or postfix daemon
secure	Contains information and error messages regarding network access generated by daemons such as sshd and xinetd
wtmp	Contains a history of all login sessions; can be viewed using either the `who /var/log/wtmp` or `last` command
rpmpkgs yum.log dnf.log	Contains messages for actions taken and packages installed by the Red Hat Package Manager
dpkg.log	Contains messages for actions taken and packages installed by the Debian Package Manager
Xorg.0.log	Contains information and error messages generated by X Windows
lastlog	Contains a list of users and their last login time; can be viewed using the `lastlog` command
messages syslog daemon.log	Contains detailed information regarding daemon startup obtained at system initialization as well as important system messages produced after system initialization

Daemons that provide a service to other computers on the network typically manage their own log files within the /var/log directory. The logging for other daemons and operating system components is performed by a logging daemon. The two most common logging daemons used on Linux systems today are the System Log Daemon (rsyslogd) and the Systemd Journal Daemon (journald).

> **Note 9**
>
> Many third-party software suites can monitor different systems on the network; these software suites provide a small program that is installed on each Linux server (called an agent) that collects the events logged by rsyslogd or journald and sends them to a central monitoring server on the network.

Working with the System Log Daemon

The System Log Daemon (rsyslogd) is the traditional logging daemon used on Linux systems. When this daemon is loaded upon system startup, it creates a socket (/dev/log) for other system processes to write to. It then reads any event information written to this socket and saves the information in the appropriate log file according to entries in the /etc/rsyslog.conf file and any *.conf files within the /etc/rsyslog.d directory. A sample /etc/rsyslog.conf file is shown in the following output:

```
[root@server1 ~]# cat /etc/rsyslog.conf
# /etc/rsyslog.conf configuration file for rsyslog
# For more information install rsyslog-doc and see
# /usr/share/doc/rsyslog-doc/html/configuration/index.html
# Additional default rules are in /etc/rsyslog.d/50-default.conf


#################
#### MODULES ####
#################


module(load="imuxsock") # provides support for local system logging
#module(load="immark")   # provides --MARK-- message capability

# provides UDP syslog reception
#module(load="imudp")
#input(type="imudp" port="514")

# provides TCP syslog reception
#module(load="imtcp")
#input(type="imtcp" port="514")

# provides kernel logging support and enable non-kernel klog messages
module(load="imklog" permitnonkernelfacility="on")


###########################
#### GLOBAL DIRECTIVES ####
###########################


# Use traditional timestamp format.
# To enable high precision timestamps, comment out the following line.
$ActionFileDefaultTemplate RSYSLOG_TraditionalFileFormat
```

```
# Filter duplicated messages
$RepeatedMsgReduction on

# Set the default permissions for all log files.
$FileOwner syslog
$FileGroup adm
$FileCreateMode 0640
$DirCreateMode 0755
$Umask 0022
$PrivDropToUser syslog
$PrivDropToGroup syslog

# Where to place spool and state files
$WorkDirectory /var/spool/rsyslog


###############
#### RULES ####
##############

*.info;authpriv.none;cron.none          /var/log/messages
authpriv.*                              /var/log/secure
mail.warn                              -/var/log/mail.log
cron.*                                  /var/log/cron

# Emergencies are sent to everybody logged in.
*.emerg                                 :omusrmsg:*

# Save boot messages also to boot.log
local7.*                                /var/log/boot.log

# Include all config files in /etc/rsyslog.d/
$IncludeConfig /etc/rsyslog.d/*.conf
[root@server1 ~]#_
```

> **Note 10**
>
> On legacy Linux systems, the System Log Daemon is represented by syslogd and configured using the /etc/syslog.conf file.

Lines in the /etc/rsyslog.conf file or in files within the /etc/rsyslog.d directory that start with a # character are comments. All other entries are used to load rsyslogd modules, configure global rsyslogd settings, or create logging rules. Logging rules have the following format:

```
facility.priority      /var/log/logfile
```

The **facility** is the area of the system to listen to, whereas the **priority** refers to the importance of the information. For example, a facility of kern and priority of warning indicates that the System Log Daemon should listen for kernel events of priority warning and more serious. When found, the System Log Daemon places the associated event information in the /var/log/logfile file. This entry would read:

```
kern.warning      /var/log/logfile
```

To only log warning events from the kernel to /var/log/logfile, you can use the following entry instead:

```
kern.=warning     /var/log/logfile
```

Alternatively, you can log all error events from the kernel to /var/log/logfile by using the * wildcard, as shown in the following entry:

```
kern.*     /var/log/logfile
```

In addition, you can specify multiple facilities and priorities. To log all error events except warnings from the kernel to /var/log/logfile, you can use the following entry:

```
kern.!=warn     /var/log/logfile
```

To log all error events from the kernel and user processes, you can use the following entry:

```
kern,user.*     /var/log/logfile
```

To log all warning events from all facilities except for the kernel, you can use the "none" keyword, as shown in following entry:

```
*.=warn;kern.none     /var/log/logfile
```

You can also prefix the pathname to the log file in any entry to ensure that the system synchronizes changes to the disk immediately after a new event occurs, as shown in the following entry:

```
*.=warn;kern.none     -/var/log/logfile
```

Table 10-4 describes the different facilities available and their descriptions.

Table 10-4   Facilities used by the System Log Daemon

Facility	Description
auth or security	Specifies events from the login system, such as the login program and the su command
authpriv	Specifies events from the login system when authenticating users across the network or to system databases
cron	Specifies events from the cron and at daemons
daemon	Specifies events from all daemons
kern	Specifies events from the Linux kernel
lpr	Specifies events from the printing system (lpd)
mail	Specifies events from the email system (sendmail)
mark	Specifies time stamps used by syslogd; used internally only
news	Specifies events from the Inter Network News daemon and other USENET daemons
syslog	Specifies events from the syslog daemon
user	Specifies events from user processes
uucp	Specifies events from the uucp (UNIX to UNIX copy) daemon
local0-7	Specifies local events; these are not used by default but can be defined for custom use

Table 10-5 displays the different priorities available listed in ascending order.

Table 10-5   Priorities used by the System Log Daemon

Priority	Description
none	Indicates that no information from a certain facility be logged
debug	Indicates all information from a certain facility
info	Indicates information that results from normal system operations
notice	Indicates information that should be noted for future reference, yet does not indicate a problem
warning warn	Indicates information that might be the result of an error but are not critical to system operations
error err	Indicates all other error information not described by other priorities
crit	Indicates critical state information, such as hard disk drive failure
alert	Indicates system conditions that should be rectified immediately, such as a corrupt system database
emerg panic	Indicates serious conditions that cause system instability; these are normally broadcast to all users on the system

The /etc/rsyslog.conf file may also send event information to another computer using the format `facility.priority @hostname:portnumber`; however, the remote computer must have the modules that listen on either the TCP or UDP protocol uncommented in the /etc/rsyslog.conf file. For example, by uncommenting the same lines shown next in the /etc/rsyslog.conf file, you allow your system to accept incoming requests from another System Log Daemon on TCP and UDP port 514 (the default System Log Daemon port):

```
# provides UDP syslog reception
module(load="imudp")
input(type="imudp" port="514")

# provides TCP syslog reception
module(load="imtcp")
input(type="imtcp" port="514")
```

Working with the Systemd Journal Daemon

The Systemd Journal Daemon (journald) replaces the System Log Daemon on Linux distributions that use Systemd. As with the System Log Daemon, journald creates a socket (/run/systemd/journal/dev-log) for other system processes to write to and reads any information that is written to this socket. However, the events logged are not controlled by specific rules. Instead, journald logs all information to a database under the /var/log/journal directory, and events are tagged with labels that identify the same facility and priority information that you examined earlier with the rsyslogd daemon. To configure journald settings, you can edit the appropriate settings in the /etc/systemd/journald.conf file and then restart journald using the `systemctl restart systemd-journald.service` command.

> **Note 11**
>
> While journald stores the events it collects within a database, it copies the appropriate events to the common log files shown in Table 10-3.

> **Note 12**
>
> If you install rsyslogd on a system that already uses journald, rsyslogd will obtain events directly from journald by default.

To view events within the journald database, you can use the same `journalctl` command introduced in Chapter 6 to view boot-related messages. By default, `journalctl` displays all events and you can send those events to the `grep` command to narrow the results by keyword. For example, you could run `journalctl | grep -i cron | less` to do a case-insensitive search for events with the word cron in them and display the results page-by-page. However, the output may be very long and difficult to parse. Consequently, it is much better to use options and arguments alongside `journalctl` to specify search criteria. If you type `journalctl` at a command prompt and press the Tab key, you will see a multipage list of criteria that can be queried, as shown in the following sample excerpt:

```
_AUDIT_ID=                        PRIORITY=
_AUDIT_LOGINUID=                  QT_CATEGORY=
_AUDIT_SESSION=                   REALMD_OPERATION=
_AUDIT_TYPE=                      REF=
_AUDIT_TYPE_NAME=                 REMOTE=
AVAILABLE=                        SEAT_ID=
AVAILABLE_PRETTY=                 _SELINUX_CONTEXT=
_BOOT_ID=                         SESSION_ID=
_CAP_EFFECTIVE=                   SHUTDOWN=
_CMDLINE=                         _SOURCE_MONOTONIC_TIMESTAMP=
CODE_FILE=                        _SOURCE_REALTIME_TIMESTAMP=
CODE_FUNC=                        SSSD_DOMAIN=
CODE_LINE=                        SSSD_PRG_NAME=
_COMM=                            _STREAM_ID=
COMMAND=                          SYSLOG_FACILITY=
COMMIT=                           SYSLOG_IDENTIFIER=
CPU_USAGE_NSEC=                   SYSLOG_PID=
CURRENT_USE=                      SYSLOG_RAW=
--More--
```

Say, for example, that you want to search for information in the logs from a particular process (command) on the system. You can type `journalctl _COMM=` and press the Tab key to see a multipage list of the available commands that perform logging via journald on the system, as shown in the following sample excerpt:

```
akonadi_maildir    gdm-x-session      korgac             sshd
akonadi_mailfil    gnome-clocks       kscreen_backend    start-pulseaudi
akonadi_migrati    gnome-contacts-    ksmserver          su
akonadi_newmail    gnome-control-c    ksmserver-logou    sudo
akonadiserver      gnome-documents    kwin_x11           (systemd)
alsactl            gnome-initial-s    logger             systemd
anacron            gnome-keyring-d    login              systemd-coredum
atd                gnome-session-b    lvm                systemd-fsck
at-spi2-registr    gnome-session-f    mcelog             systemd-hiberna
at-spi-bus-laun    gnome-shell        ModemManager       systemd-hostnam
```

audispd	gnome-shell-cal	mount	systemd-journal
auditd	gnome-software	mtp-probe	systemd-logind
augenrules	gnome-terminal-	netconsole	systemd-tty-ask
avahi-daemon	gnome-welcome-t	NetworkManager	systemd-udevd
backlighthelper	goa-daemon	nm-dispatcher	systemd-vconsol
baloo_file	goa-identity-se	obexd	tracker-extract
bash	groupadd	org_kde_powerde	tracker-miner-a
boltd	gsd-color	packagekitd	tracker-miner-f
bootscript.sh	gsd-media-keys	passwd	tracker-store
canberra-gtk-pl	gsd-print-notif	PK-Backend	udisksd
chronyd	gsd-rfkill	plasmashell	umount
colord	gsd-sharing	plymouthd	unbound-anchor
crond	gsd-smartcard	polkitd	unix_chkpwd

--More--

To see the events from the cron daemon (crond), you can run the command `journalctl _COMM=crond | less` because the output will likely have many lines. However, when troubleshooting an issue regarding the cron daemon, it is more useful to narrow the time period. The following command displays crond events from 1:00 pm (13:00) until 2:00 pm (14:00) from the current day:

```
[root@server1 ~]# journalctl _COMM=crond --since "13:00" --until "14:00"
Sep 24 13:40:58 server1 crond[884]: (CRON) STARTUP (1.5.7)
Sep 24 13:40:58 server1 crond[884]: (CRON) INFO (Syslog will be used >
Sep 24 13:40:58 server1 crond[884]: (CRON) INFO (RANDOM_DELAY will be>
Sep 24 13:40:58 server1 crond[884]: (CRON) INFO (running with inotify>
Sep 24 13:57:01 server1 crond[884]: (CRON) INFO (Shutting down)
[root@server1 ~]#_
```

Note 13

Lines that end with a > symbol in the output of `journalctl` are truncated; you can use the right cursor key on your keyboard to scroll to the right to read the remainder of the event information, as well as use the left cursor key to return to the beginning of the event.

The time format used within the `journalctl` command follows the standard YYYY-MM-DD HH-MM-SS. Thus, to display crond events since 5:30 pm (17:30) on August 22, 2023, you could instead run the `journalctl _COMM=crond --since "2023-08-22 17:30:00"` command.

The `journalctl` command also accepts criteria options. For example, the `journalctl --unit=crond.service` command will display events generated by the crond service unit.

You can also query events related to a specific process or daemon if you specify the path name to the executable file or PID. For example, because the Systemd init daemon has a path of /usr/lib/systemd/systemd and a PID of 1, you could run the `journalctl /usr/lib/systemd/systemd` command or the `journalctl _PID=1` command to view events related to the Systemd init daemon.

Note 14

You can use the `systemd-cat` command or `logger` command to add custom log file entries to the journald database; for example, you could use the `echo "Backup of $DIR completed successfully at $(date)" | systemd-cat` command or the `logger "Backup of $DIR completed successfully at $(date)"` command within a shell script to log a message to the journald database indicating that a backup of a directory within the $DIR variable was completed at a particular time. The `logger` command can also be used to add custom log file entries on a system that uses the System Log Daemon; simply specify the `-p facility.priority` option alongside the `logger` command to control how the events are logged.

Managing Log Files and the journald Database

Although log files and the journald database contain important system information, they might take up unnecessary space on the filesystem over time because journald is configured to use persistent storage by default. However, you can uncomment and configure the line `Storage=volatile` within /etc/systemd/journald.conf to ensure that events are only stored in memory and not on the filesystem. Alternatively, you could limit the amount of space on the filesystem that journald will use to store events by uncommenting and configuring the SystemMaxUse line in /etc/systemd/journald.conf. For example, `SystemMaxUse=75M` would limit the database to 75 MB, and the oldest events would be deleted as new events are logged. To prevent key older events from being overwritten, you can create a shell script that executes the appropriate `journalctl` commands and either prints the results or saves them to a text file. You can then configure the cron daemon or a System timer unit to execute this shell script periodically.

For log files within the /var/log directory, you can periodically clear their contents to reclaim space on the filesystem.

Note 15

Do not remove log files, because the permissions and ownership will be removed as well.

Note 16

Before clearing important log files, it is good form to save them to a different location or print their contents for future reference.

To clear a log file, you can use output redirection without specifying a command. The following commands display the size of the /var/log/boot.log file before and after it has been printed and cleared:

```
[root@server1 ~]# ls -l /var/log/boot.log
-rw-------    1 root      root      21705 Aug 27 10:52 /var/log/boot.log
[root@server1 ~]# lp -d printer1 /var/log/boot.log
[root@server1 ~]# >/var/log/boot.log
[root@server1 ~]# ls -l /var/log/boot.log
-rw-------    1 root      root          0 Aug 27 10:52 /var/log/boot.log
[root@server1 ~]#_
```

Alternatively, you can schedule the `logrotate command` to back up and clear log files from entries stored in the /etc/logrotate.conf file and files stored in the /etc/logrotate.d directory. The `logrotate` command typically renames (or rotates) log files on a cyclic basis; the log file will be renamed to contain a numeric or date extension, and a new log file will be created to accept system information. You can specify the type of extension as well as the number of log files that are kept. If configured to keep only two copies of old log files, then after two log rotations, the oldest log file will automatically be removed.

An example of the /etc/logrotate.conf file is shown in the following output:

```
[root@server1 ~]# cat /etc/logrotate.conf
# see "man logrotate" for details
# rotate log files weekly
weekly

# keep 4 weeks worth of backlogs
rotate 4
```

```
# create new (empty) log files after rotating old ones
create

# use date as a suffix of the rotated file
dateext

# uncomment this if you want your log files compressed
#compress

# RPM packages drop log rotation information into this directory
include /etc/logrotate.d

# no packages own wtmp and btmp -- we'll rotate them here
/var/log/wtmp {
    monthly
    create 0664 root utmp
    minsize 1M
    rotate 1
}

/var/log/btmp {
    missingok
    monthly
    create 0600 root utmp
    rotate 1
}
[root@server1 ~]#_
```

In the preceding output, any # characters indicate a comment and are ignored. The other lines indicate that log files contained in this file and all other files in the /etc/logrotate.d directory (include /etc/logrotate.d) are rotated on a weekly basis unless otherwise specified (weekly) using a date extension (dateext), and up to 4 weeks of log files will be kept (rotate 4).

The bottom of the /etc/logrotate.conf file has two entries that override these values. For the file /var/log/wtmp, this rotation occurs monthly instead of weekly, only if the size of the log file is greater than 1 MB. Only one old log file is kept, and the new log file created has the permissions 0664 (rw-rw-r--), the owner root, and the group utmp. For the file /var/log/btmp, this rotation occurs monthly instead of weekly, and no errors are reported if the log file is missing. Only one old log file is kept, and the new log file created has the permissions 0600 (rw-------), the owner root, and the group utmp.

Most rotation information within /etc/logrotate.conf is overridden from files stored in the /etc/logrotate.d directory. Take the file /etc/logrotate.d/psacct as an example:

```
[root@server1 ~]# cat /etc/logrotate.d/psacct
# Logrotate file for psacct RPM

/var/account/pacct {
    compress
    delaycompress
    notifempty
    daily
    rotate 31
    create 0600 root root
    postrotate
```

```
    if /usr/bin/systemctl --quiet is-active psacct.service ; then
        /usr/sbin/accton /var/account/pacct
  fi
 endscript
}
[root@server1 ~]#_
```

This file indicates that the /var/account/pacct file should be rotated daily if it is not empty, and that new log files will be owned by the root user/group and have the permissions 0600 (rw----). Up to 31 old log files will be kept and compressed, but only on the next rotation (delaycompress). In addition, the /usr/sbin/accton /var/account/pacct command is run after each rotation if the /usr/bin/systemctl --quiet is-active psacct.service command returns true.

On most Linux systems, the logrotate command is automatically scheduled to run daily via cron or a Systemd timer unit; however, you might choose to run it manually by typing logrotate /etc/logrotate.conf at a command prompt.

Over time, the logrotate command generates several copies of each log file, as shown in the following listing of the /var/log directory:

```
[root@server1 ~]# ls /var/log
anaconda            dnf.rpm.log         private
audit               firewalld           qemu-ga
blivet-gui          gdm                 README
boot.log            glusterfs           samba
boot.log-20230917   hawkey.log          secure
boot.log-20230918   hawkey.log-20230911 secure-20230911
boot.log-20230919   hawkey.log-20230918 secure-20230918
boot.log-20230920   httpd               speech-dispatcher
boot.log-20230922   journal             spooler
boot.log-20230923   lastlog             spooler-20230911
boot.log-20230924   libvirt             spooler-20230918
btmp                maillog             sssd
chrony              maillog-20230911    swtpm
cron                maillog-20230918    tallylog
cron-20230912       mariadb             wtmp
cron-20230918       messages            Xorg.0.log
cups                messages-20230911   Xorg.0.log.old
dnf.librepo.log     messages-20230918
dnf.log             ppp [root@server1 ~]#_
```

Given the preceding output, the most recent events for the cron daemon are recorded in the cron file, followed by the cron-20230918 file, and the cron-20230912 file.

Administering Users and Groups

Recall from Chapter 1 that you must log in (or authenticate) to a Linux system with a valid user name and password before a shell is granted. This process verifies the user name and password against a system database that contains all **user account** information. Authenticated users are then granted access to files, directories, and other resources on the system based on their user account.

The system database that contains user account information typically consists of two files: /etc/passwd and /etc/shadow. Every user has a line that describes the user account in /etc/passwd and a line that contains the encrypted password and expiration information in /etc/shadow.

Legacy Linux systems stored the encrypted password in the /etc/passwd file and did not use an /etc/shadow file at all. This is considered poor security today because processes often require access to the user information in /etc/passwd. Storing the encrypted password in a separate file that cannot be accessed by processes prevents a process from obtaining all user account information. By default, Linux configures passwords using an /etc/shadow file. However, you can use the `pwunconv` `command` to revert to using an /etc/passwd file only, or the `pwconv` `command` to configure the system again using an /etc/shadow file for password storage.

Each line of the /etc/passwd file has the following colon-delimited format:

```
name:password:UID:GID:GECOS:homedirectory:shell
```

The name in the preceding output refers to the name of the user. If an /etc/shadow is not used, the password field contains the encrypted password for the user; otherwise, it just contains an x character as a placeholder for the password stored in /etc/shadow.

The **User Identifier (UID)** specifies the unique User ID that is assigned to each user. Typically, UIDs that are less than 1000 refer to user accounts that are used by daemons when logging in to the system. The root user always has a UID of zero.

The **Group Identifier (GID)** is the primary Group ID for the user. Each user can be a member of several groups, but only one of those groups can be the primary group. Recall from Chapter 4 that the primary group of a user is the group that is made the group owner of any file or directory that the user creates. Similarly, when a user creates a file or directory, that user becomes the owner of that file or directory.

GECOS represents an optional text description of the user; this information was originally used in the **General Electric Comprehensive Operating System (GECOS)**. The last two fields represent the absolute pathname to the user's home directory and the shell, respectively.

An example of an /etc/passwd file is shown next:

```
[root@server1 ~]# cat /etc/passwd
root:x:0:0:root:/root:/bin/bash
bin:x:1:1:bin:/bin:/sbin/nologin
daemon:x:2:2:daemon:/sbin:/sbin/nologin
adm:x:3:4:adm:/var/adm:/sbin/nologin
lp:x:4:7:lp:/var/spool/lpd:/sbin/nologin
sync:x:5:0:sync:/sbin:/bin/sync
shutdown:x:6:0:shutdown:/sbin:/sbin/shutdown
halt:x:7:0:halt:/sbin:/sbin/halt
mail:x:8:12:mail:/var/spool/mail:/sbin/nologin
operator:x:11:0:operator:/root:/sbin/nologin
games:x:12:100:games:/usr/games:/sbin/nologin
ftp:x:14:50:FTP User:/var/ftp:/sbin/nologin
nobody:x:65534:65534:Kernel Overflow User:/:/sbin/nologin
apache:x:48:48:Apache:/usr/share/httpd:/sbin/nologin
dbus:x:81:81:System message bus:/:/sbin/nologin
pulse:x:171:171:PulseAudio System Daemon:/var/run/pulse:/sbin/nologin
chrony:x:994:988::/var/lib/chrony:/sbin/nologin
dnsmasq:x:987:987:Dnsmasq DHCP and DNS server:/var/lib/dnsmasq:/sbin/nologin
rpc:x:32:32:Rpcbind Daemon:/var/lib/rpcbind:/sbin/nologin
usbmuxd:x:113:113:usbmuxd user:/:/sbin/nologin
openvpn:x:986:986:OpenVPN:/etc/openvpn:/sbin/nologin
radvd:x:75:75:radvd user:/:/sbin/nologin
saslauth:x:985:76:Saslauthd user:/run/saslauthd:/sbin/nologin
abrt:x:173:173::/etc/abrt:/sbin/nologin
pipewire:x:982:980:PipeWire System Daemon:/var/run/pipewire:/sbin/nologin
gdm:x:42:42::/var/lib/gdm:/sbin/nologin
rpcuser:x:29:29:RPC Service User:/var/lib/nfs:/sbin/nologin
user1:x:1000:1000:Jason Eckert:/home/user1:/bin/zsh
[root@server1 ~]#_
```

The root user is usually listed at the top of the /etc/passwd file, as just shown, followed by user accounts used by daemons when logging in to the system, followed by regular user accounts. The final line of the preceding output indicates that the user user1 has a UID of 1000, a primary GID of 1000, a GECOS of "Jason Eckert", the home directory /home/user1, and it uses the Z shell.

Like /etc/passwd, the /etc/shadow file is colon-delimited yet has the following format:

```
name:password:lastchange:min:max:warn:disable1:disable2:
```

Although the first two fields in the /etc/shadow file are the same as those in /etc/passwd, the contents of the password field are different. The password field in the /etc/shadow file contains the encrypted password, whereas the password field in /etc/passwd contains an x character, because it is not used.

The lastchange field represents the date of the most recent password change; it is measured in the number of days since January 1, 1970. For example, the number 10957 represents January 1, 2000, because January 1, 2000, is 10957 days after January 1, 1970.

Note 17

Traditionally, a calendar date was represented by a number indicating the number of days since January 1, 1970. Many calendar dates found in configuration files follow the same convention.

To prevent unauthorized access to a Linux system, it is good form to change passwords for user accounts regularly. To ensure that passwords are changed, you can set them to expire at certain intervals. The next three fields of the /etc/shadow file indicate information about password expiration: min represents the number of days a user must wait before they change their password after receiving a new one, max represents the number of days a user can use the same password without changing it, and warn represents the number of days a user has to change their password before it expires.

By default, on most Linux systems, min is equal to zero days, max is equal to 99999 days, and warn is equal to seven days. This means you can change your password immediately after receiving a new one, your password expires in 99999 days, and you are warned seven days before your password needs to be changed.

When a password has expired, the user is still allowed to log in to the system for a certain period of time, after which point the user is disabled from logging in. The number of days before a user account is disabled after a password expires is represented by the disable1 field in /etc/shadow. In addition, you can choose to disable a user from logging in at a certain date, such as the end of an employment contract. The disable2 field in /etc/shadow represents the number of days since January 1, 1970 after which a user account will be disabled.

An example /etc/shadow file is shown next:

```
[root@server1 ~]# cat /etc/shadow
root:$6$PpnHJ3rl/6OouP9G$cKhZbi96b9UxfkHOt4ahHvrW9V73vg9BLqiEHKFOfcIAvktJ.
fP2V9RoFkxgz6tcW9LlEspV2FN1j4g5vy90M1:17745:0:99999:7:::
bin:*:17589:0:99999:7:::
daemon:*:17589:0:99999:7:::
adm:*:17589:0:99999:7:::
lp:*:17589:0:99999:7:::
sync:*:17589:0:99999:7:::
shutdown:*:17589:0:99999:7:::
halt:*:17589:0:99999:7:::
mail:*:17589:0:99999:7:::
operator:*:17589:0:99999:7:::
games:*:17589:0:99999:7:::
ftp:*:17589:0:99999:7:::
nobody:*:17589:0:99999:7:::
apache:!!:17646::::::
```

```
dbus:!!:17646::::::
pulse:!!:17646::::::
chrony:!!:17646::::::
dnsmasq:!!:17646::::::
rpc:!!:17646:0:99999:7:::
usbmuxd:!!:17646::::::
openvpn:!!:17646::::::
radvd:!!:17646::::::
saslauth:!!:17646::::::
abrt:!!:17646::::::
pipewire:!!:17646::::::
gdm:!!:17646::::::
rpcuser:!!:17646::::::
user1:$6$YQ.IzyVU9.QVZgxK$hQbMxA0TNdWNF5Aeefa9.2WBKnbm2pofKZSeARUWXuzZTj.
UyYcwRVqVBVikYz8/HauSBLgy2ar2Yw7X8UplM.:17721:0:99999:7:::
[root@server1 ~]#_
```

Note from the preceding output that most user accounts used by daemons do not receive an encrypted password.

Although every user must have a primary group listed in the /etc/passwd file, each user can be a member of multiple groups. All groups and their members are listed in the /etc/group file. The /etc/group file has the following colon-delimited fields:

```
name:password:GID:members
```

The first field is the name of the group, followed by a group password.

Note 18

The password field in /etc/group usually contains an x, because group passwords are rarely used. If group passwords are used on your system, you need to specify a password to change your primary group membership using the newgrp command discussed later in this chapter. These passwords are set using the gpasswd command and can be stored in the /etc/gshadow file for added security. Refer to the gpasswd manual or info page for more information.

The GID represents the unique Group ID for the group, and the members field indicates the list of group members. An example /etc/group file is shown next:

```
[root@server1 ~]# cat /etc/group
root:x:0:
bin:x:1:root,bin,daemon
daemon:x:2:
sys:x:3:
adm:x:4:
tty:x:5:
disk:x:6:
lp:x:7:
mem:x:8:
kmem:x:9:
wheel:x:10:user1
cdrom:x:11:
mail:x:12:
man:x:15:
dialout:x:18:
```

```
floppy:x:19:
games:x:20:
tape:x:33:
video:x:39:
ftp:x:50:
lock:x:54:
audio:x:63:
users:x:100:
nobody:x:65534:
utmp:x:22:
apache:x:48:
ssh_keys:x:999:
input:x:998:
kvm:x:36:qemu
render:x:997:
dbus:x:81:
dip:x:40:
pulse:x:171:
avahi:x:70:
chrony:x:988:
saslauth:x:76:
abrt:x:173:
pipewire:x:980:
gdm:x:42:
rpcuser:x:29:
sshd:x:74:
slocate:x:21:
user1:x:1000:
[root@server1 ~]#_
```

From the preceding output, the "bin" group has a GID of 1 and three users as members: root, bin, and daemon. Similarly, the wheel group has a GID of 10 and user1 as a member.

Note 19

The wheel group is a special group that provides its members with the ability to run the su and sudo commands; as a result, the first user that you create during a Linux installation is added to the wheel group to allow them to set the root password using the sudo command. Some Linux distributions, including Ubuntu, use the sudo group in place of the wheel group.

Note 20

You can also use the getent command to view the entries within system databases such as /etc/passwd, /etc/shadow, /etc/group, and /etc/gshadow; for example, getent shadow will display the entries within the shadow database (/etc/shadow).

Creating User Accounts

You can create user accounts on the Linux system by using the useradd command, specifying the user name as an argument, as shown next:

```
[root@server1 ~]# useradd binigr
[root@server1 ~]#_
```

In this case, all other information, such as the UID, shell, and home directory location, is taken from two files that contain user account creation default values.

The first file, /etc/login.defs, contains parameters that set the default location for email, password expiration information, minimum password length, and the range of UIDs and GIDs available for use. In addition, it determines whether home directories will be automatically made during user creation, as well as the password hash algorithm used to store passwords within /etc/shadow.

A sample /etc/login.defs file is depicted in the following example:

```
[root@server1 ~]# cat /etc/login.defs
# Directory where mailboxes reside, _or_ name of file, relative to the
# home directory.  If you _do_ define both, MAIL_DIR takes precedence.
MAIL_DIR   /var/spool/mail
#MAIL_FILE   .mail


# Password aging controls:
# PASS_MAX_DAYS     Maximum days a password may be used.
# PASS_MIN_DAYS     Minimum days allowed between password changes.
# PASS_MIN_LEN      Minimum acceptable password length.
# PASS_WARN_AGE     Number of days warning before a password expires.
PASS_MAX_DAYS       99999
PASS_MIN_DAYS       0
PASS_MIN_LEN        5
PASS_WARN_AGE       7


# Min/max values for automatic uid selection in useradd
UID_MIN                 1000
UID_MAX                 60000
# System accounts
SYS_UID_MIN             201
SYS_UID_MAX             999


# Min/max values for automatic gid selection in groupadd
GID_MIN                 1000
GID_MAX                 60000
# System accounts
SYS_GID_MIN             201
SYS_GID_MAX             999


# Max number of login(1) retries if password is bad
#LOGIN_RETRIES          3


# Max time in seconds for login(1)
#LOGIN_TIMEOUT          60


# If defined, this command is run when removing a user.
# It should remove any at/cron/print jobs etc. owned by
# the user to be removed (passed as the first argument).
#USERDEL_CMD   /usr/sbin/userdel_local


# If useradd(8) should create home directories for users by default
# (non system users only). This option is overridden with the -M or
# -m flags on the useradd(8) command-line.
CREATE_HOME   yes
```

```
# HOME_MODE is used by useradd(8) and newusers(8) to set the mode for
# new home directories. If HOME_MODE is not set, the value of UMASK
# is used to create the mode.
HOME_MODE        0700

# The permission mask is initialized to this value. If not specified,
# the permission mask will be initialized to 022.
UMASK            077

# This enables userdel to remove user groups if no members exist.
USERGROUPS_ENAB yes

# If set to MD5, MD5 will be used for encrypting password
# If set to SHA256, SHA256 will be used for encrypting password
# If set to SHA512, SHA512 will be used for encrypting password
# If set to BCRYPT, BCRYPT will be used for encrypting password
# If set to YESCRYPT, YESCRYPT will be used for encrypting password
# If set to DES, DES will be used for encrypting password (default)
ENCRYPT_METHOD YESCRYPT
[root@server1 ~]#_
```

The second file, /etc/default/useradd, contains information regarding the default primary group, the location of home directories, the default number of days to disable accounts with expired passwords, the date to disable user accounts, the shell used, and the skeleton directory used. The skeleton directory, which is /etc/skel on most Linux systems, contains files that are copied to all new users' home directories when the home directory is created. Most of these files are environment files, such as .bashrc and .zshrc.

A sample /etc/default/useradd file is shown in the following output:

```
[root@server1 ~]# cat /etc/default/useradd
# useradd defaults file
GROUP=100
HOME=/home
INACTIVE=-1
EXPIRE=
SHELL=/bin/bash
SKEL=/etc/skel
CREATE_MAIL_SPOOL=yes
[root@server1 ~]#_
```

To override any of the default parameters for a user in the /etc/login.defs and /etc/default/useradd files, you can specify options to the useradd command when creating user accounts. For example, to create a user named maryj with a UID of 762, you can use the –u option to the useradd command, as shown in the following example:

```
[root@server1 ~]# useradd -u 762 maryj
[root@server1 ~]#_
```

Table 10-6 lists some common options available to the useradd command and their descriptions.

Table 10-6   Common options to the `useradd` command

Option	Description
`-c "description"`	Adds a description for the user to the GECOS field of /etc/passwd
`-d directory`	Specifies the absolute pathname to the user's home directory
`-e expirydate`	Specifies a date to disable the account from logging in
`-f days`	Specifies the number of days until a user account with an expired password is disabled
`-g group`	Specifies the primary group for the user account; on most Linux distributions, a group is created with the same name as the user and made the primary group for that user via the USERGROUPS_ENAB entry in the /etc/login.defs file
`-G group1,group2,etc.`	Specifies all other group memberships for the user account
`-m`	Specifies that a home directory should be created for the user account; on most Linux distributions, home directories are created for all users by default via the CREATE_HOME entry in the /etc/login.defs file
`-k directory`	Specifies the skeleton directory used when copying files to a new home directory
`-s shell`	Specifies the absolute pathname to the shell used for the user account
`-u UID`	Specifies the UID of the user account

After a user account has been added, the password field in the /etc/shadow file contains either two ! characters or a single * character, indicating that no password has been set for the user account. To set the password, you can use the `passwd` command introduced in Chapter 4. Following is an example of setting the password for the binigr user:

```
[root@server1 ~]# passwd binigr
Changing password for user binigr.
New UNIX password:
Retype new UNIX password:
passwd: all authentication tokens updated successfully.
[root@server1 ~]#_
```

Note 21

Without arguments, the `passwd` command changes the password for the current user.

Note 22

All user accounts must have a password set before they are used to log in to the system.

Note 23

The root user can set the password on any user account using the `passwd` command; however, regular users can change their password only using this command.

Note 24

Passwords should be difficult to guess and contain a combination of uppercase, lowercase, and special characters to increase system security. An example of a good password is C2Jr1;Pwr.

Modifying User Accounts

To modify the information regarding a user account after creation, you can edit the /etc/passwd or /etc/shadow file. This is not recommended, however, because typographical errors in these files might prevent the system from functioning. Instead, it's better to use the `usermod command`, which you can use to modify most information regarding user accounts. For example, to change the login name of the user binigr to barbgr, you can use the -l option to the `usermod` command:

```
[root@server1 ~]# usermod -l barbgr binigr
[root@server1 ~]#_
```

Table 10-7 displays a complete list of options used with the `usermod` command to modify user accounts.

Table 10-7 Common options to the `usermod` command

Option	Description
-a	Used alongside the -G option to add another group membership to the existing list of groups that a user already belongs to
-c "description"	Specifies a new description for the user in the GECOS field of /etc/passwd
-d directory	Specifies the absolute pathname to a new home directory
-e expirydate	Specifies a date to disable the account from logging in
-f days	Specifies the number of days until a user account with an expired password is disabled
-g group	Specifies a new primary group for the user account
-G group1,group2,etc.	Specifies all group memberships for the user account other than the primary group
-l name	Specifies a new login name
-s shell	Specifies the absolute pathname to a new shell used for the user account
-u UID	Specifies a new UID for the user account

Note 25

If installed, the `finger` command can be used to view information about users. This information is stored in the GECOS field of /etc/passwd. As a result, instead of using the -c option to the `usermod` command, users can change their own GECOS, or finger information, using the `chfn command`.

The only user account information that the `usermod` command cannot modify is the password expiration information stored in /etc/shadow (min, max, warn), discussed earlier. To change this information, you can use the `chage command` with the appropriate option. For example, to specify that Bini—that is, the user binigr—must wait 2 days before changing his password after receiving a new password, as well as to specify that his password expires every 50 days with 7 days of warning prior to expiration, you can use the following options to the `chage` command:

```
[root@server1 ~]# chage -m 2 -M 50 -W 7 binigr
[root@server1 ~]#_
```

Note 26

You can also use the `chage` command to view password expiration information. For example, the `chage -l binigr` command displays the password expiration information for the user binigr.

Sometimes it's necessary to temporarily prevent a user from logging in by locking their user account. To lock an account, you can use the command usermod -L *username* at the command prompt. This places a ! character at the beginning of the encrypted password field in the /etc/shadow file. To unlock the account, type usermod -U *username* at the command prompt, which removes the ! character from the password field in the /etc/shadow file.

Alternatively, you can use the passwd -l *username* command to lock a user account, and the passwd -u *username* command to unlock a user account. These commands place and remove two ! characters at the beginning of the encrypted password field in the /etc/shadow file, respectively.

Yet another method commonly used to lock a user account is to change the shell specified in /etc/passwd for a user account from /bin/bash to an invalid shell such as /bin/false or /sbin/nologin. Without a valid shell, a user cannot use the system. To lock a user account this way, you can edit the /etc/passwd file and make the appropriate change, use the -s option to the usermod command, or use the chsh command (discussed in Chapter 7) to change the default shell to a non-interactive program. The following example uses the chsh command to change the shell to /bin/false for the user binigr:

```
[root@server1 ~]# chsh -s /bin/false binigr
Changing shell for binigr.
chsh: Warning: "/bin/false" is not listed in /etc/shells
Shell changed.
[root@server1 ~]#_
```

Deleting User Accounts

To delete a user account, you can use the userdel command and specify the user name as an argument. This removes entries from the /etc/passwd and /etc/shadow files corresponding to the user account. Furthermore, you can specify the -r option to the userdel command to remove the home directory for the user and all of its contents.

When a user account is deleted, any files that were previously owned by the user become owned by a number that represents the UID of the deleted user. Any future user account that is given the same UID then becomes the owner of those files.

Suppose, for example, that the user binigr leaves the company. To delete binigr's user account and display the ownership of his old files, you can use the following commands:

```
[root@server1 ~]# userdel binigr
[root@server1 ~]# ls -la /home/binigr
total 52
drwx------    4 1002    1002      4096 Jul 17 15:37 .
drwxr-xr-x    5 root    root      4096 Jul 17 15:37 ..
-rw-r--r--    1 1002    1002        24 Jul 17 15:37 .bash_logout
-rw-r--r--    1 1002    1002       191 Jul 17 15:37 .bash_profile
-rw-r--r--    1 1002    1002       124 Jul 17 15:37 .bashrc
-rw-r--r--    1 1002    1002      5542 Jul 17 15:37 .canna
-rw-r--r--    1 1002    1002       820 Jul 17 15:37 .emacs
-rw-r--r--    1 1002    1002       118 Jul 17 15:37 .gtkrc
-rw-r--r--    3 1002    1002      4096 Jul 17 15:37 .kde
drwxr-xr-x    2 1002    1002      4096 Jul 17 15:37 .xemacs
-rw-r--r--    1 1002    1002      3511 Jul 17 15:37 .zshrc
[root@server1 ~]#_
```

From the preceding output, you can see that the UID of the binigr user was 1002. Now suppose the company hires Sahar—that is, the user saharjo—to replace binigr. You can then assign the UID of 1002 to Sahar's user account. Although she will have her own home directory (/home/saharjo), she will also own all of binigr's old files within /home/binigr and otherwise. She can then copy the files that she needs to her own home directory and remove any files that she doesn't need as part of her job function.

To create the user saharjo with a UID of 1002 and list the ownership of the files in binigr's home directory, you can use the following commands:

```
[root@server1 ~]# useradd -u 1002 saharjo
[root@server1 ~]# ls -la /home/binigr
total 52
drwx------     4 saharjo   saharjo       4096 Jul 17 15:37 .
drwxr-xr-x     5 root      root          4096 Jul 17 18:56 ..
-rw-r--r--     1 saharjo   saharjo         24 Jul 17 15:37 .bash_logout
-rw-r--r--     1 saharjo   saharjo        191 Jul 17 15:37 .bash_profile
-rw-r--r--     1 saharjo   saharjo        124 Jul 17 15:37 .bashrc
-rw-r--r--     1 saharjo   saharjo       5542 Jul 17 15:37 .canna
-rw-r--r--     1 saharjo   saharjo        820 Jul 17 15:37 .emacs
-rw-r--r--     1 saharjo   saharjo        118 Jul 17 15:37 .gtkrc
-rw-r--r--     3 saharjo   saharjo       4096 Jul 17 15:37 .kde
drwxr-xr-x     2 saharjo   saharjo       4096 Jul 17 15:37 .xemacs
-rw-r--r--     1 saharjo   saharjo       3511 Jul 17 15:37 .zshrc
[root@server1 ~]#_
```

Managing Groups

By far, the easiest way to add groups to a system is to edit the /etc/group file using a text editor. Another method is to use the groupadd command. To add a group called group1 to the system and assign it a GID of 492, you can use the following command:

```
[root@server1 ~]# groupadd -g 492 group1
[root@server1 ~]#_
```

Then, you can use the -a and -G options to the usermod command to add members to the group while preserving those members' existing group memberships. To add the user maryj to this group and view the addition, you can use the following usermod command:

```
[root@server1 ~]# usermod -aG group1 maryj
[root@server1 ~]# tail -1 /etc/group
group1:x:492:maryj
[root@server1 ~]#_
```

You can use the groupmod command to modify the group name and GID, and use the groupdel command to remove groups from the system.

To see a list of groups of which you are a member, run the groups command; to see the GIDs for each group, run the id command. Each command always lists the primary group first. The following output shows sample output of these commands when executed by the root user:

```
[root@server1 ~]# groups
root bin daemon sys adm disk wheel
[root@server1 ~]# id
uid=0(root) gid=0(root) groups=0(root),1(bin),2(daemon),3(sys),
4(adm),6(disk),10(wheel)
[root@server1 ~]#_
```

In the preceding output the primary group for the root user is the root group. This group is attached as the group owner for all files that are created by the root user, as shown in the following output:

```
[root@server1 ~]# touch samplefile1
[root@server1 ~]# ls -l samplefile1
-rw-r--r--     1 root      root             0 Aug 27 19:22 samplefile1
[root@server1 ~]#_
```

To change the primary group temporarily to another group that is listed in the output of the `groups` and `id` commands, you can use the `newgrp` command. Any new files created afterward will then have the new group owner. The following output demonstrates how changing the primary group for the root user affects file ownership:

```
[root@server1 ~]# newgrp sys
[root@server1 root]# id
uid=0(root) gid=3(sys)
groups=0(root),1(bin),2(daemon),3(sys),4(adm),6(disk),10(wheel)
[root@server1 ~]# touch samplefile2
[root@server1 ~]# ls -l samplefile2
-rw-r--r--    1 root      sys              0 Aug 27 19:28 samplefile2
[root@server1 ~]#_
```

Note 27

If you use group passwords as described earlier in this section, you can use the `newgrp` command to change your primary group to a group of which you are not a member, provided you supply the appropriate group password when prompted.

Note 28

The root user can use the `newgrp` command to change their primary group to any other group.

Summary

- Print jobs are spooled to a print queue before being printed to a printer.

- You can configure spooling or printing for a printer by using the `cupsaccept`, `cupsreject`, `cupsenable`, and `cupsdisable` commands.

- Print jobs are created using the `lp` command, can be viewed in the print queue using the `lpstat` command, and are removed from the print queue using the `cancel` command.

- You can configure printers using the `lpadmin` command, the CUPS web administration tool, or by modifying the /etc/cups/printers.conf file.

- Most log files on a Linux system are stored in the /var/log directory.

- System events are typically logged to files by the System Log Daemon (rsyslogd) or to a database by the Systemd Journal Daemon (journald).

- You can use the `journalctl` command to view the contents of the journald database.

- Log files should be cleared or rotated over time to save disk space; the `logrotate` command can be used to rotate log files.

- User and group account information is typically stored in the /etc/passwd, /etc/shadow, and /etc/group files.

- You can use the `useradd` command to create users and the `groupadd` command to create groups.

- All users must have a valid password before logging in to a Linux system.

- Users can be modified with the `usermod`, `chage`, `chfn`, `chsh`, and `passwd` commands, and groups can be modified using the `groupmod` command.

- The `userdel` and `groupdel` commands can be used to remove users and groups from the system, respectively.

Key Terms

agent	groupdel command	print queue
cancel command	groupmod command	printer class
chage command	groups command	priority
chfn command	id command	pwconv command
Common Unix Printing System (CUPS)	Internet Printing Protocol (IPP)	pwunconv command
CUPS daemon (cupsd)	Line Printer Daemon (LPD)	queuing
CUPS web administration tool	logger command	skeleton directory
cupsaccept command	logrotate command	spooling
cupsdisable command	lp command	System Log Daemon (rsyslogd)
cupsenable command	lpadmin command	Systemd Journal Daemon (journald)
cupsreject command	lpc command	systemd-cat command
facility	lpq command	user account
General Electric Comprehensive Operating System (GECOS)	lpr command	User Identifier (UID)
getent command	lprm command	useradd command
Group Identifier (GID)	lpstat command	userdel command
groupadd command	newgrp command	usermod command
	print job	
	print job ID	

Review Questions

1. The process of sending print jobs from the print queue to the printer is called _____.
   a. spooling
   b. queuing
   c. redirecting
   d. printing

2. You can clear a log file simply by redirecting nothing into it.
   a. True
   b. False

3. When a printer is disabled, _____.
   a. the print queue does not accept jobs and sends a message to the user noting that the printer is unavailable
   b. the print queue accepts jobs into the print queue and holds them there until the printer is enabled again
   c. the printer appears as offline when an lp request is sent
   d. the print queue redirects all print jobs sent to it to /dev/null

4. What is the term used to describe a user providing a user name and password to log in to a system?
   a. validation
   b. authorization
   c. login
   d. authentication

5. Which command can you use to lock a user account?
   a. lock username
   b. secure username
   c. usermod -L username
   d. useradd -L username

6. Which command can be used to temporarily alter the primary group associated with a given user?
   a. usermod
   b. chggrp
   c. gpasswd
   d. newgrp

7. Which command can be used to send a print job to the default printer named Printer1? (Choose all that apply.)
   a. lp -d Printer1 file
   b. lp Printer1 file
   c. lp file
   d. lp -m Printer1 file

8. What is the name of the file that contains a listing of all users on the system and their home directories?
   a. /etc/passwd
   b. /etc/users
   c. /etc/shadow
   d. /etc/password

9. UIDs and GIDs are unique to the system and, once used, can never be reused.
   a. True
   b. False

10. What is the name of the utility used to rotate log files?
    a. syslog
    b. jetpack
    c. logrotate
    d. logbackup

11. You can lock a user account by changing the default login shell to an invalid shell in /etc/passwd.
    a. True
    b. False

12. When a printer is rejecting requests, _____.
    a. the print queue does not accept jobs and sends a message to the user noting that the printer is unavailable
    b. the print queue accepts jobs into the print queue and holds them there until the printer is accepting requests again
    c. the printer appears as offline when an lp request is sent
    d. the print queue redirects all print jobs sent to it to /dev/null

13. When referring to the /etc/rsyslog.conf file, _____ specifies information from a certain area of the system, whereas _____ is the level of importance of that information.
    a. section, priority
    b. service, precedents
    c. process, degree
    d. facility, priority

14. Most log files on the system are found in which directory?
    a. /etc/logfiles
    b. /etc/log
    c. /var/log
    d. /dev/log

15. Which file contains default information such as UID and GID ranges and minimum password length to be used at user creation?
    a. /etc/skel
    b. /etc/passwd
    c. /etc/login.defs
    d. /etc/default/useradd

16. What command can you use to view journald log entries on a system that uses Systemd?
    a. `less`
    b. `journalctl`
    c. `syslog`
    d. `catlog`

17. Which command would you use to unlock a user account?
    a. `unlock username`
    b. `open username`
    c. `passwd -u username`
    d. `useradd -U username`

18. Along with a listing of user accounts, the /etc/passwd file contains information on account expiry.
    a. True
    b. False

19. You use `lpstat` and determine that a user named User1 has placed two large print jobs in the queue for Printer1 that have yet to start printing. They have print job IDs of Printer1-17 and Printer1-21, respectively. Which command would you use to remove these two jobs from the print queue?
    a. `cancel Printer1-17 Printer1-21`
    b. `cancel -u Printer1-17 Printer1-21`
    c. `cancel -a Printer1-17 Printer1-21`
    d. `cancel 17 21`

20. Which command is used to delete a user account?
    a. `usermod -d username`
    b. `del username`
    c. `userdel username`
    d. `rm username`

Hands-On Projects

These projects should be completed in the order given. The hands-on projects presented in this chapter should take a total of three hours to complete. The requirements for this lab include:
- A computer with Fedora Linux installed according to Hands-On Project 2-1 and Ubuntu Linux installed according to Hands-on Project 6-1.

Project 10-1

Estimated Time: 20 minutes

Objective: Use printers on the command line.

Description: In this hands-on project, you use commands to create and configure a printer as well as submit and manage print jobs.

1. Boot your Fedora Linux virtual machine. After your Linux system has been loaded, switch to a command-line terminal (tty5) by pressing **Ctrl+Alt+F5** and log in to the terminal using the user name of **root** and the password of **LINUXrocks!**.

2. At the command prompt, type `lpadmin -p printer1 -E -v /dev/null` and press **Enter** to create a sample printer called printer1 that prints to /dev/null.

3. At the command prompt, type `lpoptions -d printer1` and press **Enter** to ensure that printer1 is the default printer on the system.

4. At the terminal screen prompt, type `cat /etc/cups/printers.conf` and press **Enter**. Do you see an entry for printer1 that prints to /dev/null?

5. At the command prompt, type `lpstat -t` and press **Enter**. Is the CUPS daemon running? Is printer1 enabled and accepting requests? Is printer1 the default printer on the system?

6. At the command prompt, type `cupsdisable -r "To keep print jobs in the queue" printer1` and press **Enter** to disable printer1 with an appropriate reason. Next, type `lpstat -t` at the command prompt and press **Enter**. Is printer1 disabled with a reason?

7. At the command prompt, type `lp -n 2 /etc/issue` and press **Enter** to print two copies of /etc/issue to printer1. What is the print job ID? Why did you not need to specify the printer name when running the `lp` command?

8. At the command prompt, type `lp /etc/hosts /etc/nsswitch.conf` and press **Enter** to print the /etc/hosts and /etc/nsswitch.conf files. What is the print job ID?

9. At the command prompt, type `df -hT | lp` and press **Enter** to print the output of the `df -hT` command to printer1. What is the print job ID?

10. At the command prompt, type `lpstat` and press **Enter**. Are your print jobs shown in the queue? How long will they remain in the queue and why?

11. At the command prompt, type `ls /var/spool/cups` and press **Enter**. You should notice contents within this directory for your three print jobs. The data for your print jobs should have file names that start with d, and the settings for your print jobs should have file names that start with c. Type `cat /var/spool/cups/d00001-001` at the command prompt and press **Enter** to view the data for the first print job on the system. What is shown and why?

12. At the command prompt, type `cancel printer1-1` and press **Enter** to remove the first print job from the queue. Next, type `lpstat printer1` at the command prompt and press **Enter**. Has the printer1-1 job been removed?

13. At the command prompt, type `lpc status` and press **Enter** to view the status of CUPS using the traditional BSD `lpc` command. Is the CUPS daemon running? Is the status of printing and spooling correct? Next, type `lpq` at the command prompt and press **Enter**. Do you see the two remaining jobs in the print queue for printer1? Do the job numbers displayed correspond with the job numbers in the `lpstat` output from the previous step?

14. At the command prompt, type `lpr -#2 /etc/issue` and press **Enter** to print two copies of /etc/issue to the default printer using the traditional BSD `lpr` command. Next, type `lpq` at the command prompt and press **Enter**. Do you see an additional job in the print queue? What is the job ID?

15. At the command prompt, type `lprm 4` and press **Enter** to remove the most recent print job that you submitted. Next, type `lpq` at the command prompt and press **Enter**. Was print job 4 removed successfully?

16. Type `exit` and press **Enter** to log out of your shell.

Project 10-2

Estimated Time: 20 minutes

Objective: Manage printers in a desktop environment.

Description: In this hands-on project, you submit a print job from a graphical program as well as explore the Printers tool and the CUPS web administration tool.

1. On your Fedora Linux virtual machine, switch to tty1 by pressing **Ctrl+Alt+F1** and log in to the GNOME desktop using your user name and the password of **LINUXrocks!**.

2. In the GNOME desktop, click the **Activities** menu, select the **Show Applications** icon, and click **LibreOffice Writer**. Type a line of your choice within the document, select the **File** menu, and choose **Print**. Is printer1 listed as the default printer? Click **Print** to print one copy of your document. Close the LibreOffice Writer window and click **Don't Save** when prompted.

3. In the GNOME desktop, click the **Activities** menu, select the **Show Applications** icon, and click **Settings** to open the Settings window. Navigate to **Printers** and note that printer1 is displayed, and that a button indicating the number of jobs within the queue is shown.

4. In the Printers section, click the **1 Job** button and note that your recently submitted print job is shown. Why aren't the two other print jobs in the printer1 queue shown? Close the printer1 - Active Jobs window when finished.

5. In the Printers tool, click the settings (cog wheel) icon and select **Printing Options**. Next, click **Test Page** to submit a test page print job and close the printer1 window when finished. Note that the button indicating the number of jobs displays 2 jobs. Click the **2 Jobs** button, click the **Delete** (trash bin) icon to remove the Test Page job from the queue, and then close the printer1 – Active Jobs window. Close the Printers tool when finished.

6. In the GNOME desktop, click the **Activities** menu and select the **Firefox** icon. Enter the address **localhost:631** in the navigation dialog box and press **Enter** to access the CUPS web administration tool.

7. In the CUPS web administration tool, highlight the **Administration** tab and select the **Allow remote administration**, **Share printers connected to this system**, and **Allow printing from the Internet** options. Click the **Change Settings** button to activate your changes. Supply the user name **root** and password **LINUXrocks!** when prompted and click **OK**.

> ## Note 29
>
> Note that if your configuration is not applied, you will not be able to access the CUPS web administration tool; in this case, you will need to log into a BASH shell as the root user and restart the CUPS daemon using the `systemctl restart cups.service` command.

8. On the Administration tab of the CUPS web administration tool, click **Add Class**, supply a name of **SampleClass**, select **printer1**, and click **Add Class**.

9. Highlight the **Printers** tab of the CUPS web administration tool and click **printer1**. Select the **Maintenance** drop-down menu and note the maintenance tasks that you can perform for printer1. Next, select the **Administration** drop-down menu and note the administrative tasks that you can perform for printer1. View the print jobs at the bottom of the page and note the management functions that you can perform for each one.

10. Highlight the **Jobs** tab of the CUPS web administration tool. Are the jobs shown the same as those shown on the Printers tab for printer1? Can you perform the same management functions for each job?

11. Highlight the **Classes** tab of the CUPS web administration tool and click **SampleClass**. Select the **Maintenance** drop-down menu and note the maintenance tasks that you can perform for printer1. Next, select the **Administration** drop-down menu and note the administrative tasks that you can perform for printer1. Do these options match those shown on the Printers tab for printer1?

12. Close the Firefox web browser window and switch to a command-line terminal (tty5) by pressing **Ctrl+Alt+F5** and log in to the terminal using the user name of **root** and the password of **LINUXrocks!**.

13. At the command prompt, type `lpstat -t` and press **Enter**. Is your SampleClass shown in the output? Why is user1 listed as the user for the most recent print job?

14. At the command prompt, type `lp -d SampleClass /etc/hosts` and press **Enter** to print a copy of /etc/hosts to the SampleClass printer class. Why does the print job ID reflect the printer class name and not printer1?

15. At the command prompt, type `lpstat -t` and press **Enter**. Is the print job submitted to your printer class shown?

16. At the command prompt, type `cancel -a printer1 SampleClass` and press **Enter** to remove all print jobs in the queue for printer1 and SampleClass. Next, type `lpstat -t` and press **Enter** to verify that no print jobs exist within the print queue.

17. Type `exit` and press **Enter** to log out of your shell.

Project 10-3

Estimated Time: 30 minutes
Objective: Configure rsyslog and logrotate.
Description: In this hands-on project, you install and explore the configuration of the System Log Daemon and the logrotate utility on Ubuntu Linux.

1. Boot your Ubuntu Linux virtual machine. After your Linux system has been loaded, log into tty1 using the user name of **root** and the password of **LINUXrocks!**.

2. At the command prompt, type `apt install rsyslog` and press **Enter** to install the System Log Daemon.

3. At the command prompt, type `ls -l /dev/log` and press **Enter** to view the target of the symbolic link. Where is the System Log Daemon obtaining logging events from by default? Next, type `ls -l /run/systemd/journal/dev-log` and press **Enter**. What is the file type?

4. At the command prompt, type `less /etc/rsyslog.conf` and press **Enter** to view the configuration file for the System Log Daemon. Are there any entries that specify facilities, priorities, or log file locations? What does the last line of the file specify? Press **q** when finished to quit the less utility.

5. At the command prompt, type `less /etc/rsyslog.d/50-default.conf` and press **Enter**. Where do kernel messages of any priority get logged to by default? What does the – character next to the filename indicate? Press **q** when finished to quit the less utility.

6. At the command prompt, type `tail /var/log/kern.log` and press **Enter**. Observe the entries.

7. At the command prompt, type `vi /etc/rsyslog.d/50-default.conf` and press **Enter**. Uncomment the `user.* -/var/log/user.log` line, save your changes and quit the vi editor. Next, type `systemctl restart rsyslog.service` and press **Enter** to restart the System Log Daemon.

8. At the command prompt, type `logger -p user.warn "Sample user program event message"` and press **Enter** to log a warning event using the user facility. Next, type `cat /var/log/user.log` and press **Enter**. Was your event logged successfully using the System Log Daemon? Next, type `journalctl | grep -i "sample user"` and press **Enter**. Was your event logged successfully by the Systemd Journal Daemon? Why?

9. At the command prompt, type `apt install cups` and press **Enter**. Next, type `ls /var/log/cups` and press **Enter**. What daemon creates the log files within the /var/log/cups directory?

10. At the command prompt, type `cat /etc/cron.daily/logrotate` and press **Enter**. Note that if a Systemd timer is configured to run logrotate, this script will not be executed by the cron daemon. Next, type `cat /lib/systemd/system/logrotate.timer` and press **Enter** to view the Systemd timer that runs the logrotate service unit daily. Finally, type `cat /lib/systemd/system/logrotate.service` and press **Enter** to view the logrotate service unit that executes the `logrotate` command.

11. At the command prompt, type `less /etc/logrotate.conf` and press **Enter** to view the configuration file for the `logrotate` command. How many copies of old log files are kept by default? When finished, press **q** to quit the less utility.

12. At the command prompt, type `ls /etc/logrotate.d` and press **Enter**. Note the number of files in the directory. Will entries in these files override the same entries in /etc/logrotate.conf?

13. At the command prompt, type `cat /etc/logrotate.d/cups-daemon` and press **Enter**. How many copies of old log files are kept for the log files in the /var/log/cups directory? Will the log files be rotated if they contain no contents?

14. Type `exit` and press **Enter** to log out of your shell.

Project 10-4

Estimated Time: 30 minutes

Objective: Configure journald and logrotate.

Description: In this hands-on project, you explore the configuration and log entries created by the Systemd Journal Daemon as well as the configuration of the logrotate utility on Fedora Linux.

1. On your Fedora Linux virtual machine, switch to a command-line terminal (tty5) by pressing **Ctrl+Alt+F5** and log in to the terminal using the user name of **root** and the password of **LINUXrocks!**.

2. At the command prompt, type `ls -l /dev/log` and press **Enter**. Is the target of this symbolic link the same as on Ubuntu Linux?

3. At the command prompt, type `cat /etc/systemd/journald.conf` and press **Enter** to view the configuration file for the Systemd Journal Daemon. What line could you uncomment and configure to set a maximum size for the journald database?

4. At the command prompt, type `journalctl _COMM=` and press the **Tab** key twice. Which keyword could you use to view log entries from the GNOME display manager? Press **Ctrl+c** to return to your command prompt. Next, type `journalctl _COMM=gdm` and press **Enter** to view log entries from the GNOME display manager. Are entries shown for multiple days? Use the right cursor key to view the end of long lines as necessary. When finished, press q to quit.

5. At the command prompt, type `journalctl _COMM=gdm --since "5:00"` and press **Enter** to view log entries from the GNOME display manager since 5:00am. When finished, press q to quit.

6. At the command prompt, type `journalctl --unit=gdm` and press **Enter** to view log entries produced by the GNOME display manager Systemd service unit. When finished, press q to quit.

7. At the command prompt, type `which crond` and press **Enter**. What is the path to the cron daemon executable file? Next, type `journalctl /usr/sbin/crond --since "5:00"` and press **Enter** to view the log entries produced by the cron daemon executable since 5:00am.

8. At the command prompt, type `echo "Sample event message" | systemd-cat` and press **Enter**. Next, type `journalctl | grep -i "Sample event"` and press **Enter**. Was your event logged successfully?

9. At the command prompt, type `ls /var/log` and press **Enter**. Observe the default log files generated, as well as the subdirectories available. Next, type `ls /var/log/cups` and press **Enter**. Are there any contents? Finally, type `cat /var/log/README` and press **Enter**. Why are subdirectories made available under /var/log and some standard log files generated?

10. At the command prompt, type `ls /lib/systemd/system/logrotate*` and press **Enter**. Is a Systemd timer and service unit created for running the `logrotate` command as on Ubuntu Linux?

11. At the command prompt, type `less /etc/logrotate.conf` and press **Enter** to view the configuration file for the `logrotate` command. How often are log files rotated, and how many copies of old log files are kept by default? When finished, press **q** to quit the less utility.

12. At the command prompt, type `ls /etc/logrotate.d` and press **Enter**. Note the number of files in the directory. Will entries in these files override the same entries in /etc/logrotate.conf?

13. At the command prompt, type `cat /etc/logrotate.d/wtmp` and press **Enter**. How many copies of old log files are kept for the /var/log/wtmp log file, and how often will it be rotated?

14. Type `exit` and press **Enter** to log out of your shell.

Project 10-5

Estimated Time: 20 minutes
Objective: Create user accounts.
Description: In this hands-on project, you observe user account databases on Fedora Linux and create a user account using command-line utilities.

1. On your Fedora Linux virtual machine, switch to a command-line terminal (tty5) by pressing **Ctrl+Alt+F5** and log in to the terminal using the user name of **root** and the password of **LINUXrocks!**.

2. At the command prompt, type `less /etc/passwd` and press **Enter**. Where is the line that describes the root user located in this file? Where is the line that describes the user1 user in this file? Do you notice user accounts that are used by daemons? What is in the password field for all accounts? When finished, press the **q** key to quit the less utility.

3. At the command prompt, type `ls -l /etc/passwd` and press **Enter**. Who is the owner and group owner of this file? Who has permission to read this file?

4. At the command prompt, type `less /etc/shadow` and press **Enter**. What is in the password field for the root user and user1 user accounts? What is in the password field for most daemon accounts? Press the **q** key to quit the less utility.

5. At the command prompt, type `ls -l /etc/shadow` and press **Enter**. Who is the owner and group owner of this file? Who has permission to read this file? Compare the permissions for /etc/shadow to those of /etc/passwd obtained in Step 3 and explain the difference.

6. At the command prompt, type `pwunconv` and press **Enter**. Next, type `less /etc/shadow` at the command prompt and press **Enter**. What error message do you receive? Why?

7. At the command prompt, type `less /etc/passwd` and press **Enter**. What is in the password field for the root and user1 accounts? Why? When finished, press the **q** key to quit the less utility.

8. At the command prompt, type `pwconv` and press **Enter**. What does the `pwconv` command do?

9. Next, type `less /etc/shadow` at the command prompt and press **Enter**. Verify that the file has contents and press **q** when finished. Next, type `less /etc/passwd` at the command prompt and press **Enter**. Verify that the file has no password contents and press **q** when finished.

10. At the command prompt, type `cat /etc/default/useradd` and press **Enter**. What is the default shell used when creating users? What is the default location of the skel directory used when creating users? Where are user home directories created by default?

11. At the command prompt, type `ls -a /etc/skel` and press **Enter**. Note the files stored in this directory. What is the purpose of this directory when creating users?

12. At the command prompt, type `cp /etc/issue /etc/skel` and press **Enter** to create a copy of the issue file in the /etc/skel directory.

13. At the command prompt, type `useradd -m bozo` and press **Enter**. What does the -m option specify? From where is the default shell, home directory information taken?

14. At the command prompt, type `less /etc/login.defs` and press **Enter**. Observe the entries and descriptive comments. Did you need to specify the -m option to the `useradd` command in Step 13? Explain. Press the **q** key to quit the less utility.

15. At the command prompt, type `cat /etc/passwd` and press **Enter**. What shell and home directory does bozo have? What is bozo's UID?

16. At the command prompt, type `cat /etc/shadow` and press **Enter**. Does bozo have a password? Can bozo log in to the system?

17. At the command prompt, type `passwd bozo` and press **Enter**. Enter the password of **LINUXrocks!** and press **Enter**. Enter the password of **LINUXrocks!** again to confirm and press **Enter**.

18. At the command prompt, type `ls -a /home/bozo` and press **Enter**. How many files are in this directory? Compare this list to the one obtained in Step 11. Is the issue file present?

19. Type `exit` and press **Enter** to log out of your shell.

Project 10-6

Estimated Time: 20 minutes

Objective: Modify user accounts.

Description: In this hands-on project, you modify user accounts on Fedora Linux using command-line utilities.

1. On your Fedora Linux virtual machine, switch to a command-line terminal (tty5) by pressing **Ctrl+Alt+F5** and log in to the terminal using the user name of **root** and the password of **LINUXrocks!**.

2. At the command prompt, type `grep bozo /etc/passwd` and press **Enter**. Note the line used to describe the user bozo.

3. At the command prompt, type `grep bozo /etc/shadow` and press **Enter**. Note the line used to describe the user bozo.

4. At the command prompt, type `usermod -l bozo2 bozo` and press **Enter** to change the login name for the user bozo to bozo2. Next, type `grep bozo /etc/passwd` at the command prompt and press **Enter**. Was the login name changed from bozo to bozo2? Was the UID changed? Was the home directory changed?

5. At the command prompt, type `usermod -l bozo bozo2` and press **Enter** to change the login name for the user bozo2 back to bozo.

6. At the command prompt, type `usermod -u 666 bozo` and press **Enter** to change the UID of the user bozo to 666. Next, type `grep bozo /etc/passwd` at the command prompt and press **Enter**. Was the UID changed?

7. At the command prompt, type `usermod -f 14 bozo` and press **Enter** to disable bozo's user account 14 days after the password expires. Next, type `grep bozo /etc/shadow` at the command prompt and press **Enter**. Which field was changed?

8. At the command prompt, type `usermod -e "01/01/2032" bozo` and press **Enter** to expire bozo's user account on January 1, 2032. Next, type `grep bozo /etc/shadow` at the command prompt and press **Enter**. Which field was changed? What does the number represent in this field?

9. At the command prompt, type `chage -m 2 bozo` and press **Enter** to require that the user bozo wait at least two days before making password changes. Next, type `grep bozo /etc/shadow` at the command prompt and press **Enter**. Which field was changed?

10. At the command prompt, type `chage -M 40 bozo` and press **Enter** to require that the user bozo change passwords every 40 days. Next, type `grep bozo /etc/shadow` at the command prompt and press **Enter**. Which field was changed?

11. At the command prompt, type `chage -W 5 bozo` and press **Enter** to warn the user bozo five days before a password change is required. Next, type `grep bozo /etc/shadow` at the command prompt and press **Enter**. Which field was changed?

12. Type `exit` and press **Enter** to log out of your shell.

Project 10-7

Estimated Time: 15 minutes

Objective: Lock user accounts.

Description: In this hands-on project, you lock and unlock user accounts on Fedora Linux using command-line utilities.

1. On your Fedora Linux virtual machine, switch to a command-line terminal (tty5) by pressing **Ctrl+Alt+F5** and log in to the terminal using the user name of **root** and the password of **LINUXrocks!**.

2. At the command prompt, type `grep bozo /etc/shadow` and press **Enter**. Note the encrypted password for bozo's user account.

3. At the command prompt, type `passwd -l bozo` and press **Enter** to lock bozo's user account.

4. At the command prompt, type `grep bozo /etc/shadow` and press **Enter**. What has been changed regarding the original encrypted password noted in Step 2?

5. Switch to a different command-line terminal (tty6) by pressing **Ctrl+Alt+F6** and attempt to log in to the terminal using the user name of **bozo** and the password of **LINUXrocks!**. Were you successful?

6. Switch back to tty5 by pressing **Ctrl+Alt+F5**.

7. At the command prompt, type `passwd -u bozo` and press **Enter** to unlock bozo's user account.

8. At the command prompt, type `grep bozo /etc/shadow` and press **Enter**. Compare the encrypted password for bozo's user account to the one noted in Step 2.

9. Switch to tty6 by pressing **Ctrl+Alt+F6** and attempt to log in to the terminal using the user name of **bozo** and the password of **LINUXrocks!**. Were you successful?

10. Type `exit` and press **Enter** to log out of your shell.

11. Switch back to tty5 by pressing **Ctrl+Alt+F5**.

12. At the command prompt, type `chsh -s /bin/false bozo` and press **Enter** to change bozo's shell to /bin/false. What message did you receive? Was the shell changed? Type `grep bozo /etc/passwd` at a command prompt to verify that the shell was changed to /bin/false for bozo's user account.

13. Switch to tty6 by pressing **Ctrl+Alt+F6** and attempt to log in to the terminal using the user name of **bozo** and the password of **LINUXrocks!**. Were you successful?

14. Switch back to tty5 by pressing **Ctrl+Alt+F5**.

15. At the command prompt, type `chsh -s /bin/bash bozo` and press **Enter** to change bozo's shell to /bin/bash.

16. Switch to tty6 by pressing **Ctrl+Alt+F6** and attempt to log in to the terminal using the user name of **bozo** and the password of **LINUXrocks!**. Were you successful?

17. Type `exit` and press **Enter** to log out of your shell.

18. Switch back to tty5 by pressing **Ctrl+Alt+F5**.

19. Type `exit` and press **Enter** to log out of your shell.

Project 10-8

Estimated Time: 10 minutes

Objective: Remove user accounts.

Description: In this hands-on project, you remove a user account on Fedora Linux and create a new user account in its place using command-line utilities.

1. On your Fedora Linux virtual machine, switch to a command-line terminal (tty5) by pressing **Ctrl+Alt+F5** and log in to the terminal using the user name of **root** and the password of **LINUXrocks!**.

2. At the command prompt, type `ls -la /home/bozo` and press **Enter**. Who owns most files in this directory? Why?

3. At the command prompt, type `userdel bozo` and press **Enter**. Was the home directory removed for bozo as well?

4. At the command prompt, type `ls -la /home/bozo` and press **Enter**. Who owns most files in this directory? Why?

5. At the command prompt, type `useradd -m -u 666 bozoette` and press **Enter**. What do the `-m` and the `-u` options do in this command?

6. At the command prompt, type `passwd bozoette` and press **Enter**. Enter the password of **LINUXrocks!** and press **Enter**. Enter the password of **LINUXrocks!** again to confirm and press **Enter**.

7. At the command prompt, type `grep bozoette /etc/passwd` and press **Enter**. What is bozoette's home directory? What is bozoette's UID?

8. At the command prompt, type `ls -la /home/bozo` and press **Enter**. Who owns most files in this directory? Why? Can bozoette manage these files?

9. Type `exit` and press **Enter** to log out of your shell.

Project 10-9

Estimated Time: 15 minutes

Objective: Create and manage groups.

Description: In this hands-on project, you create, use, and delete groups on Fedora Linux using command-line utilities.

1. On your Fedora Linux virtual machine, switch to a command-line terminal (tty5) by pressing **Ctrl+Alt+F5**, and log in to the terminal using the user name of **root** and the password of **LINUXrocks!**.

2. At the command prompt, type `vi /etc/group` and press **Enter** to open the /etc/group file in the vi editor. Add a line to the bottom of this file that reads:

   `groupies:x:1234:root,bozoette`

   This adds a group to the system with a GID of 1234, the members root, and bozoette. When finished, save and quit the vi editor.

3. Switch to a different command-line terminal (tty6) by pressing **Ctrl+Alt+F6** and log in to the terminal using the user name of **bozoette** and the password of **LINUXrocks!**.

4. At the command prompt, type `groups` and press **Enter**. Of which groups is bozoette a member?

5. At the command prompt, type `id` and press **Enter**. Which group is the primary group for the user bozoette?

6. At the command prompt, type `touch file1` and press **Enter** to create a new file called file1 in the current directory.

7. At the command prompt, type `ls -l` and press **Enter**. Who is the owner and group owner of the file file1? Why?

8. At the command prompt, type `newgrp groupies` and press **Enter** to temporarily change bozoette's primary group to groupies.

9. At the command prompt, type `touch file2` and press **Enter** to create a new file called file2 in the current directory.

10. At the command prompt, type `ls -l` and press **Enter**. Who is the owner and group owner of the file file2? Why?

11. Type `exit` and press **Enter** to log out of the new shell created when you used the `newgrp` command. Next, type `exit` and press **Enter** to log out of your shell.

12. Switch back to tty5 by pressing **Ctrl+Alt+F5**.

13. At the command prompt, type `groupdel groupies` and press **Enter** to remove the group groupies from the system. Which file is edited by the `groupdel` command?

14. Type `exit` and press **Enter** to log out of your shell.

Discovery Exercises

Discovery Exercise 10-1

Estimated Time: 20 minutes

Objective: Configure rsyslogd.

Description: Write the entry you could add to /etc/rsyslog.conf to:

    a. Log all critical messages from the kernel to /var/log/alert

    b. Log all messages from the user processes to /var/log/userlog

    c. Log all debug messages and more serious from the printing daemon to /var/log/printer

    d. Log all messages except notices from the mail daemon to /var/log/mailman

    e. Log all alerts and critical error messages to /var/log/serious

    f. Log all warnings and errors from the kernel and the printing daemon to /var/log/shared

Discovery Exercise 10-2

Estimated Time: 15 minutes

Objective: Research useradd options.

Description: Use the man or info pages to find a description of the -D option to the useradd command. What does this option do? What file does it edit? Use this option with the useradd command to set the date that all new user accounts will be disabled to March 5, 2055. What command did you use?

Discovery Exercise 10-3

Estimated Time: 40 minutes

Objective: Configure CUPS printer sharing.

Description: In Project 10-2, you enabled the remote administration and IPP print sharing options within the CUPS remote administration tool on your Fedora Linux virtual machine. However, in order to access CUPS remotely or print to your shared IPP printers, you must allow the ports for the HTTP (TCP port 80), HTTPS (TCP port 443), and IPP (TCP port 631) protocols in the firewall that is enabled by default in Fedora. Run the following commands to enable those ports:

```
firewall-cmd --add-service http
firewall-cmd --add-service https
firewall-cmd --add-service ipp
```

Next, use the ip addr show command to determine the IP address of your Fedora Linux virtual machine. Following this, access the CUPS administration website using the web browser on your Windows or macOS host computer by navigating to http://*IPaddress*:631 where *IPaddress* is the IP address of your Fedora virtual machine. Finally, add a new printer within the Settings app on Windows or the System Preferences app on macOS that prints to the URL http://*IPaddress*:631/printers/printer1. Print to this new printer from a Windows or macOS program of your choice and verify that the job was submitted to the printer1 print queue using the lpstat -t command on your Fedora Linux virtual machine.

Discovery Exercise 10-4

Estimated Time: 40 minutes

Objective: Configure CUPS remote management.

Description: The CUPS commands introduced in this chapter work identically on both Fedora and Ubuntu systems. Because remote administration of the CUPS web administration tool is disabled by default and Ubuntu Server does not contain a desktop environment that allows you to access a web browser and the CUPS web administration tool, you must manually enable remote administration within the /etc/cups/cupsd.conf file.

On your Ubuntu Server Linux virtual machine, edit the /etc/cups/cupsd.conf file and change the line that reads Listen localhost:631 to Port 631 as well as add three Allow from all lines within the access sections, as shown here:

```
# Restrict access to the server...
<Location />
```

```
    Order allow,deny
    Allow from all
</Location>

# Restrict access to the admin pages...
<Location /admin>
    Order allow,deny
    Allow from all
</Location>

# Restrict access to configuration files...
<Location /admin/conf>
    AuthType Default
    Require user @SYSTEM
    Order allow,deny
    Allow from all
</Location>
```

Next, save your changes, run the `systemctl restart cups.service` command to restart the CUPS daemon, and run the `ip addr show` command to determine the IP address of your Ubuntu Linux virtual machine. Since Ubuntu Server does not enable a firewall by default, there is no need to open ports to allow CUPS access. Finally, access the CUPS administration website using the web browser on your Windows or macOS host computer by navigating to http://*IPaddress*:631 where *IPaddress* is the IP address of your Ubuntu virtual machine.

Discovery Exercise 10-5

Estimated Time: 15 minutes
Objective: Use `newusers` to create user accounts.
Description: When adding several user accounts, you might want to use the `newusers` utility, which can process a text file full of entries to add user accounts. Use the man or info page to find out how to use this utility and use it to add three users. When finished, view the /etc/passwd, /etc/shadow, and /etc/group files to verify that the users were added successfully.

Discovery Exercise 10-6

Estimated Time: 30 minutes
Objective: Create and manage user accounts.
Description: Write commands to accomplish the following (use the manual or info pages if necessary):

a. Create a user with a login name of bsmith, a UID of 733, a GECOS field entry of "accounting manager," and a password of Gxj234.

b. Delete the user jdoe but leave the home directory intact.

c. Change the properties of the existing user wjones such that the user has a new comment field of "shipping" and an account expiry of March 23, 2032.

d. Lock the account of wjenkins.

e. Change the password of bsmith to We34Rt.

f. Change the properties of the existing user tbanks such that the user is a member of the managers group and has a login name of artbanks.

g. Create a user with the same UID and primary group as root and a login name of wjones.

h. Change the primary group of the user wsmith to root.

i. Add the users tbanks and jdoe to the group acctg while preserving existing group memberships.

Chapter 11

Compression, System Backup, and Software Installation

Chapter Objectives

1   Outline the features of common compression utilities.

2   Compress and decompress files using common compression utilities.

3   Perform system backups using the `tar`, `cpio`, `dump`, and `dd` commands.

4   View and extract archives using the `tar`, `cpio`, `restore`, and `dd` commands.

5   Use burning software to back up files to CD and DVD.

6   Describe common types of Linux software.

7   Compile and install software packages from source code.

8   Install and manage software packages using the Red Hat Package Manager (RPM) and Debian Package Manager (DPM).

9   Identify and support shared libraries used by software.

10 Install and manage Snap, Flatpak, and AppImage applications.

In the preceding chapter, you examined common administrative tasks that are performed on a regular basis. In this chapter, you learn common data- and software-related tasks that are performed frequently. You begin this chapter by learning about utilities commonly used to compress files on filesystems, followed by a discussion of system backup and archiving utilities. Finally, you learn about the different forms of software available for Linux systems, how to compile source code into functional programs, the usage of the Red Hat and Debian package managers, and how to work with sandboxed applications.

Compression

At times, you might want to reduce the size of a file or set of files due to limited disk space. You might also want to compress files that are sent across the Internet to decrease transfer time. In either case, you can choose from several utilities that reduce a file's size by stripping out certain patterns of data via a process known as **compression**. The standard set of instructions used to compress a file is known as a **compression algorithm**. To decompress a file, you run the compression algorithm in reverse.

Because compression utilities use compression algorithms in different ways, they achieve different rates of compression, or **compression ratios**, for similar file types. To calculate the compression ratio for a utility, you subtract the compressed percentage from 100. For example, if a compression utility compresses a file to 52 percent of its original size, it has a compression ratio of 48 percent.

Many compression utilities are available to Linux users; this section examines the five most common utilities:

- compress
- GNU zip
- xz
- zip
- bzip2

Using compress

The `compress command` is one of the oldest compression utilities on UNIX and Linux systems. Its compression algorithm, which is called Adaptive Lempel-Ziv coding (LZW), has an average compression ratio of 40–50 percent.

To compress a file using `compress`, you specify the files to compress as arguments. Each file is renamed with a `.Z` filename extension to indicate that it is compressed. In addition, you can use the `-v` (verbose) option to the `compress` command to display the compression ratio. The following output displays the filenames and size of the samplefile and samplefile2 files before and after compression:

```
[root@server1 ~]# ls -l
total 28
drwx------    3 root      root          4096 Jul 21 08:15 Desktop
-rw-r--r--    1 root      root         27298 Jul 21 08:15 samplefile
-rw-rw-r--    1 root      root           540 Jul 21 08:18 samplefile2
[root@server1 ~]# compress -v samplefile samplefile2
samplefile:   -- replaced with samplefile.Z Compression: 59.65%
samplefile2:  -- replaced with samplefile2.Z Compression: 37.22%
[root@server1 root]# ls -l
total 20
drwx------    3 root      root          4096 Jul 21 08:15 Desktop
-rw-rw-r--    1 root      root           339 Jul 21 08:18 samplefile2.Z
-rw-r--r--    1 root      root         11013 Jul 21 08:15 samplefile.Z
[root@server1 ~]#_
```

Note 1

The `compress` command is not installed on most Linux distributions by default. To install it from a software repository on the Internet, you can run the `dnf install ncompress` command as the root user on Fedora Linux, or the `apt install ncompress` command as the root user on Ubuntu Linux.

Note 2

The `compress` command preserves the original ownership, modification, and access time for each file that it compresses.

Note 3

By default, `compress` does not compress symbolic links, hard links, or very small files unless you use the `-f` option.

> **Note 4**
>
> You can compress all of the files in a certain directory by using the −r option and specifying the direc-
> tory name as an argument to the compress command.

After compression, the zcat command can be used to display the contents of a compressed
file, as shown in the following output:

```
[root@server1 ~]# zcat samplefile2.Z
Hi there, I hope this day finds you well.

Unfortunately, we were not able to make it to your dining
room this year while vacationing in Algonquin Park - I
especially wished to see the model of the Highland Inn
and the train station in the dining room.

I have been reading on the history of Algonquin Park but
nowhere could I find a description of where the Highland
Inn was originally located on Cache Lake.

If it is no trouble, could you kindly let me know such that
I need not wait until next year when I visit your lodge?

Regards,
Mackenzie Elizabeth


[root@server1 ~]#_
```

> **Note 5**
>
> You can also use the zmore command and zless command to view the contents of a compressed
> file page by page, or the zgrep command to search the contents of a compressed file.

To decompress files that have been compressed with the compress command, use the
uncompress command followed by the names of the files to be decompressed. This restores the
original filename. The following output decompresses and displays the filenames for the samplefile.Z
and samplefile2.Z files created earlier:

```
[root@server1 ~]# uncompress -v samplefile.Z samplefile2.Z
samplefile.Z:        -- replaced with samplefile
samplefile2.Z:         -- replaced with samplefile2
[root@server1 ~]# ls -l
total 28
drwx------    3 root     root          4096 Jul 21 08:15 Desktop
-rw-r--r--    1 root     root         27298 Jul 21 08:15 samplefile
-rw-rw-r--    1 root     root           540 Jul 21 08:18 samplefile2
[root@server1 ~]#_
```

> **Note 6**
>
> The uncompress command prompts you for confirmation if any existing files will be overwritten during
> decompression. To prevent this confirmation, you can use the −f option to the uncompress command.

> ## Note 7
>
> You can omit the .z extension when using the uncompress command. The command uncompress -v samplefile samplefile2 would achieve the same results as the command shown in the preceding output.

Furthermore, the compress utility is a filter command that can take information from Standard Input and send it to Standard Output. For example, to send the output of the who command to the compress utility and save the compressed information to a file called file.Z, you can execute the following command:

```
[root@server1 ~]# who | compress -v >file.Z
Compression: 17.0%
[root@server1 ~]#_
```

Following this, you can display the contents of file.Z using the zcat command, or decompress it using the uncompress command, as shown in the following output:

```
[root@server1 ~]# zcat file.Z
root      pts/1     Jul 20 19:22 (3.0.0.2)
root      tty5      Jul 15 19:03
root      pts/2     Jul 17 19:58
[root@server1 root]# uncompress -v file.Z
file.Z:       -- replaced with file
[root@server1 ~]#_
```

Table 11-1 provides a summary of options commonly used with the compress utility.

Table 11-1   Common options used with the compress utility

Option	Description
-c	When used with the uncompress command, it displays the contents of the compressed file to Standard Output (same function as the zcat command).
-f	When used with the compress command, it can be used to compress linked files. When used with the uncompress command, it overwrites any existing files without prompting the user.
-r	Specifies to compress or decompress all files recursively within a specified directory.
-v	Displays verbose output (compression ratio and filenames) during compression and decompression.

Using GNU zip

GNU zip uses a Lempel-Ziv compression algorithm (LZ77) that varies slightly from the one used by the compress command. Typically, this algorithm yields better compression than the one used by compress. The average compression ratio for GNU zip is 60–70 percent. To compress files using GNU zip, you can use the gzip command.

Like compress, linked files are not compressed by the gzip command unless the -f option is given, and the -r option can be used to compress all files in a certain directory. In addition, the ownership, modification, and access times of compressed files are preserved by default, and the -v option to the gzip command can be used to display the compression ratio and filename. However, gzip uses the .gz filename extension by default.

To compress the samplefile and samplefile2 files shown earlier and view the compression ratio, you can use the following command:

```
[root@server1 ~]# gzip -v samplefile samplefile2
samplefile:          82.2% -- replaced with samplefile.gz
samplefile2:         65.0% -- replaced with samplefile2.gz
[root@server1 ~]#_
```

Because GNU zip uses the same fundamental compression algorithm as compress, you can use the zcat, zmore, zless, and zgrep commands to send the contents of a gzip-compressed file to Standard Output. Similarly, the gzip command can accept information via Standard Input. Thus, to compress the output of the date command to a file called file.gz and view its contents afterward, you can use the following commands:

```
[root@server1 ~]# date | gzip -v >file.gz
6.9%
[root@server1 ~]# zcat file.gz
Sun Jul 25 19:24:56 EDT 2023
[root@server1 ~]#_
```

To decompress the file.gz file in the preceding output, you can use the -d option to the gzip command, or the gunzip command, as shown in the following output:

```
[root@server1 ~]# gunzip -v file.gz
file.gz:         6.9% -- replaced with file
[root@server1 ~]#_
```

Like the uncompress command, the gunzip command prompts you to overwrite existing files unless the -f option is specified. Furthermore, you can omit the .gz extension when decompressing files, as shown in the following example:

```
[root@server1 ~]# ls -l
total 20
drwx------   3 root     root           4096 Jul 21 08:15 Desktop
-rw-rw-r--   1 root     root            219 Jul 21 08:18 samplefile2.gz
-rw-r--r--   1 root     root           4898 Jul 21 08:15 samplefile.gz
[root@server1 ~]# gunzip -v samplefile samplefile2
samplefile.gz:       82.2% -- replaced with samplefile
samplefile2.gz:      65.0% -- replaced with samplefile2
[root@server1 ~]# ls -l
total 28
drwx------   3 root     root           4096 Jul 21 08:15 Desktop
-rw-r--r--   1 root     root          27298 Jul 21 08:15 samplefile
-rw-rw-r--   1 root     root            540 Jul 21 08:18 samplefile2
[root@server1 ~]#_
```

One of the largest advantages that gzip has over compress is its ability to control the level of compression via a numeric option. The -1 option is also known as fast compression and results in a lower compression ratio. Alternatively, the -9 option is known as best compression and results in the highest compression ratio at the expense of time. If no level of compression is specified, the gzip command assumes the -6 option.

The following command compresses the samplefile file shown earlier using fast compression and displays the compression ratio:

```
[root@server1 ~]# gzip -v -1 samplefile
samplefile:          78.8% -- replaced with samplefile.gz
[root@server1 ~]#_
```

Notice from the preceding output that samplefile was compressed with a compression ratio of 78.8 percent, which is lower than the compression ratio of 82.2 percent obtained earlier when samplefile was compressed with the default level of 6.

> ## Note 8
>
> You need not specify the level of compression when decompressing files, as it is built into the compressed file itself.

Many more options are available to gzip than to compress, and many of these options have a POSIX option equivalent. Table 11-2 shows a list of these options.

Table 11-2   Common GNU zip options

Option	Description
-#	When used with the gzip command, it specifies how thorough the compression will be, where # can be the number 1–9. The option -1 represents fast compression, which takes less time to compress but results in a lower compression ratio. The option -9 represents thorough compression, which takes more time but results in a higher compression ratio.
--best	When used with the gzip command, it results in a higher compression ratio; same as the -9 option.
-c --stdout --to-stdout	Displays the contents of the compressed file to Standard Output (same function as the zcat command) when used with the gunzip command.
-d --decompress --uncompress	Decompresses the files specified (same as the gunzip command) when used with the gzip command.
-f --force	Compresses linked files and files with special permissions set when used with the gzip command. When used with the gunzip command, it overwrites any existing files without prompting the user.
--fast	When used with the gzip command, it results in a lower compression ratio; same as the -1 option.
-h --help	Displays the syntax and available options for the gzip and gunzip commands.
-l --list	Lists the compression ratio for files that have been compressed with gzip.
-n --no-name	Does not allow gzip and gunzip to preserve the original modification and access time for files.
-q --quiet	Suppresses all warning messages.
-r --recursive	Specifies to compress or decompress all files recursively within a specified directory.
-S .suffix --suffix .suffix	Specifies a file suffix other than .gz when compressing or decompressing files.
-t --test	Performs a test decompression such that a user can view any error messages before decompression, when used with the gunzip command; it does not decompress files.
-v --verbose	Displays verbose output (compression ratio and filenames) during compression and decompression.

Using xz

Like `compress` and `gzip`, the `xz command` can be used to compress files and Standard Input using a Lempel-Ziv compression algorithm (LZMA); however, it uses a different implementation that typically yields a higher compression ratio compared to `compress` and `gzip` for most files (60–80 percent, on average). Additionally, `xz` uses the .xz extension for compressed files by default, and implements the same `gzip` options shown in Table 11-2 with the exception of `-n` and `-r`. To decompress xz-compressed files, you can use the `-d` option to the `xz` command, or the `unxz command`.

The following example compresses the samplefile and samplefile2 files shown earlier with the highest possible compression ratio using `xz`, as well as decompresses the same files using `unxz`.

```
[root@server1 ~]# ls -l
total 20
drwx------     3 root      root          4096 Jul 21 08:15 Desktop
-rw-r--r--     1 root      root         27298 Jul 21 08:15 samplefile
-rw-rw-r--     1 root      root           540 Jul 21 08:18 samplefile2
[root@server1 ~]# xz -v -9 samplefile samplefile2
samplefile (1/2)
  100 %          4,632 B / 26.7 KiB = 0.170

samplefile2 (2/2)
  100 %             264 B / 540 B = 0.489
[root@server1 ~]# ls -l
total 28
drwx------     3 root      root          4096 Jul 21 08:15 Desktop
-rw-r--r--     1 root      root          4632 Jul 21 08:15 samplefile.xz
-rw-rw-r--     1 root      root           264 Jul 21 08:18 samplefile2.xz
[root@server1 ~]# unxz -v samplefile.xz samplefile2.xz
samplefile.xz (1/2)
  100 %          4,632 B / 26.7 KiB = 0.170

samplefile2.xz (2/2)
  100 %             264 B / 540 B = 0.489
[root@server1 ~]# ls -l
total 20
drwx------     3 root      root          4096 Jul 21 08:15 Desktop
-rw-r--r--     1 root      root         27298 Jul 21 08:15 samplefile
-rw-rw-r--     1 root      root           540 Jul 21 08:18 samplefile2
[root@server1 ~]#_
```

Note 9

Unlike `uncompress` and `gunzip`, you must include the filename extension when decompressing files using the `unxz` command.

Note 10

You can use the `xzcat`, `xzmore`, `xzless`, or `xzgrep command` to send the contents of an xz-compressed file to Standard Output.

Using zip

The `zip command` is a Linux implementation of the cross-platform PKZIP utility, which was originally designed to compress multiple files into a single compressed file. Because it compresses files and Standard Input using the same implementation of the Lempel-Ziv compression algorithm that `gzip` uses, it often yields a similar compression ratio on average. The `zip` command compresses linked files, as well as preserves file ownership, modification, and access time during compression. While there is no default file extension used for zip-compressed archives, `.zip` is often used by convention.

> ## Note 11
>
> The zip command is not installed on Ubuntu by default. To install it from a software repository on the Internet, you can run the `apt install zip` command as the root user.

The following example compresses the samplefile and samplefile2 files shown earlier into a single samplefile.zip file and displays the compression ratio (`-v`) during the process:

```
[root@server1 ~]# ls -l
total 20
drwx------    3 root     root         4096 Jul 21 08:15 Desktop
-rw-r--r--    1 root     root        27298 Jul 21 08:15 samplefile
-rw-rw-r--    1 root     root          540 Jul 21 08:18 samplefile2
[root@server1 ~]# zip -v samplefile.zip samplefile samplefile2
 adding: samplefile  (in=27298) (out=4869) (deflated 82%)
 adding: samplefile2  (in=540) (out=189) (deflated 65%)
total bytes=27838, compressed=5058 -> 82% savings
[root@server1 ~]# ls -l
total 22
drwx------    3 root     root         4096 Jul 21 08:15 Desktop
-rw-r--r--    1 root     root        27298 Jul 21 08:15 samplefile
-rw-rw-r--    1 root     root          540 Jul 21 08:18 samplefile2
-rw-r--r--    1 root     root         5378 Jul 22 07:28 samplefile.zip
[root@server1 ~]#_
```

> ## Note 12
>
> You can use the `zcat`, `zmore`, `zless`, or `zgrep` commands to send the contents of a zip-compressed file to Standard Output.

To view the contents of, or extract a zip-compressed file, you can use the `unzip command`. The following example views the contents of the samplefile.zip archive, and then extracts those contents to the current folder:

```
[root@server1 ~]# unzip -v samplefile.zip
Archive:  samplefile.zip
 Length   Method    Size  Cmpr     Date     Time   CRC-32    Name
--------  -------  ------- ----  ---------- ----- --------   ----
   27298  Defl:N     4869  82%  2023-06-21 08:15 a57ea058   samplefile
     540  Defl:N      189  65%  2023-06-21 08:18 b6509945   samplefile2
--------           ------- ---                   --------   -------
   27838              5058  82%                             2 files
```

```
[root@server1 ~]# unzip samplefile.zip
Archive:  samplefile.zip
  inflating: samplefile
  inflating: samplefile2
[root@server1 ~]# ls -l
total 22
drwx------    3 root      root          4096 Jul 21 08:15  Desktop
-rw-r--r--    1 root      root         27298 Jul 21 08:15  samplefile
-rw-rw-r--    1 root      root           540 Jul 21 08:18  samplefile2
-rw-r--r--    1 root      root          5378 Jul 22 07:28  samplefile.zip
[root@server1 ~]#_
```

Table 11-3 provides a summary of options commonly used with the zip utility.

Table 11-3   Common options used with the zip utility

Option	Description
-#	When used with the zip command, it specifies how thorough the compression will be, where # can be the number 1–9. The option -1 represents fast compression, which takes less time to compress but results in a lower compression ratio. The option -9 represents thorough compression, which takes more time but results in a higher compression ratio.
-c	Displays the contents of the compressed file to Standard Output (same function as the zcat command) when used with the unzip command.
-d directory	When used with the unzip command, it extracts the contents of the zip-compressed file to the specified directory.
-e	When used with the zip command, it encrypts the contents of the zip-compressed file using a password that the user is prompted to enter following the command. The user will be prompted for this password when using the unzip command.
-h --help	Displays the syntax and available options for the zip and unzip commands.
-m --move	When used with the zip command, it moves the specified files into the zip-compressed file.
-q --quiet	Suppresses all warning messages.
-r --recurse-path	When used with the zip command, it compresses all files recursively within a specified directory.
-v --verbose	When used with the zip command, it displays the compression ratio and filenames. When used with the unzip command, it displays the contents and compression ratios of the files within the zip-compressed file.

Using bzip2

The bzip2 command differs from the compress, gzip, zip, and xz commands previously discussed in that it uses the Burrows-Wheeler Block Sorting Huffman Coding algorithm when compressing files, which is better suited to compressing already compressed files as well as files with binary data contents. It provides a compression ratio of 60–80 percent on average.

As with compress and gzip, symbolic links are only compressed if the −f option is used, and the −v option can be used to display compression ratios. Also, file ownership, modification, and access time are preserved during compression.

The filename extension given to files compressed with bzip2 is .bz2. To compress the sample-file and samplefile2 files and view their compression ratios and filenames, you can use the following commands:

```
[root@server1 ~]# bzip2 -v samplefile samplefile2
samplefile: 5.044:1, 1.586 bits/byte, 80.17% saved, 27298 in, 5412 out.
samplefile2: 2.101:1, 3.807 bits/byte, 52.41% saved, 540 in, 257 out.
[root@server1 ~]# ls -l
total 16
drwx------    3 root      root         4096 Jul 21 08:15 Desktop
-rw-rw-r--    1 root      root          257 Jul 21 08:18 samplefile2.bz2
-rw-r--r--    1 root      root         5412 Jul 21 08:15 samplefile.bz2
[root@server1 ~]#_
```

Because the compression algorithm is different from the one used by compress, gzip, zip, and xz, you must use the bzcat command to display the contents of bzip2-compressed files to Standard Output, as shown in the following example:

```
[root@server1 ~]# bzcat samplefile2.bz2
Hi there, I hope this day finds you well.

Unfortunately, we were not able to make it to your dining
room this year while vacationing in Algonquin Park - I
especially wished to see the model of the Highland Inn
and the train station in the dining room.

I have been reading on the history of Algonquin Park but
nowhere could I find a description of where the Highland
Inn was originally located on Cache Lake.

If it is no trouble, could you kindly let me know such that
I need not wait until next year when I visit your lodge?

Regards,
Mackenzie Elizabeth

[root@server1 ~]#_
```

> **Note 13**
>
> You can also use the bzmore and bzless commands to view the contents of a bzip2-compressed file page by page, or the bzgrep command to search the contents of a bzip2-compressed file.

To decompress files, you can use the bunzip2 command followed by the filename(s) to decompress; the following command decompresses the samplefile.bz2 and samplefile2.bz2 files created earlier and displays the results:

```
[root@server1 ~]# bunzip2 -v samplefile.bz2 samplefile2.bz2
  samplefile.bz2:  done
  samplefile2.bz2: done
[root@server1 ~]#_
```

If any files are about to be overwritten, the bunzip2 command prompts the user for confirmation. To skip this confirmation, you can include the -f option. Table 11-4 lists other common options used with the bzip2 utility.

Table 11-4   Common options used with the bzip2 utility

Option	Description
-#	When used with the bzip2 command, # specifies the block size used during compression; 1 indicates a block size of 100 KB, whereas 9 indicates a block size of 900 KB.
-c --stdout	Displays the contents of the compressed file to Standard Output when used with the bunzip2 command.
-d --decompress	Decompresses the files specified (same as the bunzip2 command) when used with the bzip2 command.
-f --force	Compresses symbolic links when used with the bzip2 command. When used with the bunzip2 command, it overwrites any existing files without prompting the user.
-k --keep	Keeps the original file during compression; a new file is created with the extension .bz2.
-q --quiet	Suppresses all warning messages.
-s --small	Minimizes memory usage during compression.
-t --test	Performs a test decompression when used with the bunzip2 command, such that a user can view any error messages before decompression; it does not decompress files.
-v --verbose	Displays verbose output (compression ratio) during compression and decompression.

System Backup

It's a good idea to create backup copies of files and directories regularly and store them at an alternate location. You can then distribute these backup copies to other computers or use them to restore files lost because of a system failure or user error. This entire process is known as **system backup**, and the backup copies of files and directories are called **archives**.

You can create an archive on many types of media, such as tapes, CDs, and DVDs. Alternatively, you can create an archive within a single file stored in an existing filesystem on a USB flash drive, hard disk drive, or SSD. Traditionally, tapes were used to back up data, and while some organizations still use tapes to store archives, most archives are stored within files on a filesystem today. Larger backups are typically performed to files stored on hard disk drives, while smaller backups are typically performed to files stored on USB flash drives. Some organizations perform smaller backups to DVDs, which require special disc burning software described later in this chapter.

After creating an archive within a file on a filesystem, it is good practice to copy that file to another server across the Internet; this is called an **offsite backup** and ensures that data can be recovered following a catastrophic event, such as a building fire. We will examine many commands in Chapters 12 and 13 that can be used to copy an archive file to a remote server across the Internet.

A typical Linux system can include hundreds of thousands of files, but you don't have to include all of them in an archive. For example, you don't have to include temporary files in the /tmp and /var/tmp directories.

As a rule of thumb, you should back up files used by system services. For example, you should back up website content files if the Linux computer is used as a web server, and database files if the Linux computer hosts a database server. In addition, you should back up user files from home directories and any important system configuration files such as /etc/passwd. Operating system components and programs such as grep and vi need not be backed up because they can be reinstalled in the event of a system failure.

After files have been selected for system backup, you can use a backup utility to copy the files to the appropriate media or archive file on a filesystem. Several backup utilities are available to Linux administrators. The most common are the following:

- tape archive (tar)
- copy in/out (cpio)
- dump/restore
- dd
- disc burning software

Note 14

In addition to the utilities mentioned here, many third-party commercial backup software suites can be used to back up data on multiple computers across the network; common examples include Arcserve Backup, Veritas NetBackup, NetApp, and Acronis Backup.

Note 15

While software RAID, ZFS, and BTRFS can be configured to perform fault tolerance for data, you should still regularly back up the data stored on these volumes to ensure that data can be recovered if an entire software RAID, ZFS, or BTRFS volume fails.

Note 16

Some storage technologies provide features that can provide duplicate copies of data for backup purposes. For example, ZFS supports snapshot clones, which can be used to create backup copies of ZFS filesystems, and the LVM supports automatic mirroring of logical volumes, which can be used to store backup copies of logical volumes on different physical volumes.

Using tape archive (tar)

The tape archive (tar) utility is one of the oldest, most widely used backup utilities and is executed via the tar command. It can create an archive in a file on a filesystem or directly on a device using the appropriate device file (e.g., /dev/st0 for the first SCSI tape device).

Like the compression utilities discussed earlier, the tar command accepts options to determine the location of the archive and the action to perform on the archive. Any arguments specified to the tar command list the file(s) to place in the archive. Table 11-5 lists common options used with the tar command.

Table 11-5   Common options used with the `tar` command

Option	Description

`-A`
`--catenate`
`--concatenate`
	Appends whole archives to another archive.

`-c` `--create`	Creates a new archive.
`--exclude pattern`	Excludes files that have a matching pattern in their filename when creating an archive.
`-f filename` `--file filename`	Specifies the location of the archive file; it can be a file on a filesystem or a device file.
`-h` `--dereference`	Prevents tar from backing up symbolic links; instead, tar backs up the target files of symbolic links.
`-j` `--bzip`	Compresses/decompresses the archive using the `bzip2` utility.
`-J` `--xz`	Compresses/decompresses the archive using the `xz` utility.
`-P` `--absolute-paths`	Stores filenames in an archive using absolute pathnames.
`-r` `--append`	Appends files to an existing archive.
`--remove-files`	Removes files after adding them to an archive.
`-t` `--list`	Lists the filename contents (table of contents) of an existing archive.
`-u` `--update`	Appends files to an existing archive only if they are newer than the same filename inside the archive.
`-v` `--verbose`	Displays verbose output (file and directory information) when manipulating archives.

`-w`
`--interactive`
`--confirmation`
	Prompts the user for confirmation of each action.

`-W` `--verify`	Verifies the contents of each archive after creation.

`-x`
`--extract`
`--get`
	Extracts the contents of an archive.

`-z`
`--gzip`
`--ungzip`
	Compresses/decompresses the archive using the `gzip` utility.

`-Z`
`--compress`
`--uncompress`
	Compresses/decompresses the archive using the `compress` utility.

To create an archive file called /backup.tar that contains the contents of the current directory and view the results, you can use the following commands:

```
[root@server1 ~]# tar -cvf /backup.tar *
Desktop/
Desktop/Home.desktop
Desktop/trash.desktop
samplefile
samplefile2
[root@server1 ~]# ls -l /backup.tar
-rw-r--r--   1 root      root          40960 Jul 27 10:49 /backup.tar
[root@server1 ~]#_
```

Note from the preceding command that the -f option is followed by the pathname of the archive file and that the * metacharacter indicates that all files in the current directory will be added to this archive. Also note that files are backed up recursively by default and stored using relative pathnames; to force the use of absolute pathnames when creating archives, use the -P option to the tar command.

Note 17

The filename used for an archive need not have an extension. However, it is good practice to name archive files with an extension to identify their contents, as with /backup.tar in the preceding example.

Note 18

The tar utility cannot back up device files or files with filenames longer than 255 characters.

After creating an archive, you can view its detailed contents by specifying the -t (table of contents) option to the tar command and the archive to view. For example, to view the detailed contents of the /backup.tar archive created earlier, you can issue the following command:

```
[root@server1 ~]# tar -tvf /backup.tar
drwx------ root/root         0 2023-07-21 08:15 Desktop/
-rw-r--r-- root/root      3595 2023-06-21 20:32 Desktop/Home.desktop
-rw-r--r-- root/root      3595 2023-06-21 20:32 Desktop/trash.desktop
-rw-r--r-- root/root     20239 2023-07-21 08:15 samplefile
-rw-rw-r-- root/root       574 2023-07-21 08:18 samplefile2
[root@server1 ~]#_
```

You can use the -x option with the tar command to extract a specified archive. To extract the contents of the /backup.tar file to a new directory called /tartest and view the results, you can issue the following commands:

```
[root@server1 ~]# mkdir /tartest
[root@server1 ~]# cd /tartest
[root@server1 tartest]# tar -xvf /backup.tar
Desktop/
Desktop/Home.desktop
Desktop/trash.desktop
samplefile
samplefile2
[root@server1 tartest]# ls -F
Desktop/  samplefile  samplefile2
[root@server1 tartest]#_
```

After an archive has been created in a file on a filesystem, that file can be sent to other computers across a network or the Internet. This is the most common form of backup today and a common method used to distribute software across the Internet. Unfortunately, the tar utility does not compress files inside the archive. Thus, the time needed to transfer the archive across a network is high. To reduce transfer times, you can compress the archive using a compression utility before transmission. Because this is a common task, the tar command accepts options that allow you to compress an archive immediately after creation using the compress, gzip, xz, or bzip2 command.

To create a gzip-compressed archive called /backup.tar.gz that contains the contents of the current directory and view the results, you can use the following commands:

```
[root@server1 ~]# tar -zcvf /backup.tar.gz *
Desktop/
Desktop/Home.desktop
Desktop/trash.desktop
samplefile
samplefile2
[root@server1 ~]# ls -l /backup.tar*
-rw-r--r--    1 root       root         40960 Jul 27 10:49 /backup.tar
-rw-r--r--    1 root       root         12207 Jul 27 11:18 /backup.tar.gz
[root@server1 ~]#_
```

Note in the preceding output that the -z option indicated compression using the gzip utility, and that we chose to end the filename with the .tar.gz extension. In addition, the size of the /backup.tar.gz file is much less than the /backup.tar file created earlier.

> **Note 19**
>
> Recall from Chapter 1 that a compressed tar archive is commonly called a tarball.

To view the contents of a gzip-compressed archive, you must use the -z option in addition to the -t option followed by the archive to view. The detailed contents of the /backup.tar.gz file can be viewed using the following command:

```
[root@server1 ~]# tar -ztvf /backup.tar.gz
drwx------ root/root        0 2023-07-21 08:15 Desktop/
-rw-r--r-- root/root     3595 2023-06-21 20:32 Desktop/Home.desktop
-rw-r--r-- root/root     3595 2023-06-21 20:32 Desktop/trash.desktop
-rw-r--r-- root/root    20239 2023-07-21 08:15 samplefile
-rw-rw-r-- root/root      574 2023-07-21 08:18 samplefile2
[root@server1 ~]#_
```

Similarly, when extracting a gzip-compressed archive, you must supply the -z option to the tar command. To extract the contents of the /backup.tar.gz file to a new directory called /tartest2 and view the results, you can issue the following commands:

```
[root@server1 ~]# mkdir /tartest2
[root@server1 ~]# cd /tartest2
[root@server1 tartest2]# tar -zxvf /backup.tar.gz
Desktop/
Desktop/Home.desktop
Desktop/trash.desktop
samplefile
samplefile2
```

```
[root@server1 tartest2]# ls -F
Desktop/  samplefile  samplefile2
[root@server1 tartest2]#_
```

Backing up files to a compressed archive on a filesystem is useful when you plan to transfer the archived data across a network. However, you can use `tar` to back up data directly to a device such as a tape. To back up files to a device, you can use the `-f` option to the `tar` command to specify the pathname to the appropriate device file. Files are then transferred directly to the device, overwriting any other data or filesystems that might be present.

For example, to create an archive on the first SCSI tape device containing the contents of the current directory, you can use the following command:

```
[root@server1 ~]# tar -cvf /dev/st0 *
Desktop/
Desktop/Home.desktop
Desktop/trash.desktop
samplefile
samplefile2
[root@server1 ~]#_
```

You can then view the contents of the archive on the tape device used in the preceding example using the command `tar -tvf /dev/st0` or extract the contents of the archive on the tape device using the command `tar -xvf /dev/st0` in a similar fashion to the examples shown earlier.

Because tape devices can hold large amounts of information, you might want to add to a `tar` archive that already exists on the tape device. To do this, replace the `-c` option with the `-r` option when using the tar utility. For example, to append a file called samplefile3 to the archive created in the previous output and view the results, you can use the following commands:

```
[root@server1 ~]# tar -rvf /dev/st0 samplefile3
samplefile3
[root@server1 ~]# tar -tvf /dev/st0
drwx------ root/root         0 2023-07-21 08:15 Desktop/
-rw-r--r-- root/root      3595 2023-06-21 20:32 Desktop/Home.desktop
-rw-r--r-- root/root      3595 2023-06-21 20:32 Desktop/trash.desktop
-rw-r--r-- root/root     20239 2023-07-21 08:15 samplefile
-rw-rw-r-- root/root       574 2023-07-21 08:18 samplefile2
-rw-r--r-- root/root       147 2023-07-27 16:15 samplefile3
[root@server1 ~]#_
```

Using copy in/out (cpio)

Another common backup utility is **copy in/out (cpio)**, which can be executed via the `cpio` command. Although `cpio` uses options similar to `tar`, it has some added features, including long filenames and the ability to back up special files, such as device files.

Because its primary use is to back up files in case of system failure, `cpio` uses absolute pathnames by default when archiving. In addition, `cpio` normally takes a list of files to archive from Standard Input and sends the files "out" to the archive specified by the `-o` option. Conversely, when extracting an archive, you must include the `-I` option to indicate the archive from which to read "in" files.

Table 11-6 provides a list of commonly used options to the `cpio` command and their descriptions.

Table 11-6 Common options used with the cpio utility

Option	Description
`-A` `--append`	Appends files to an existing archive.
`-B`	Changes the default block size from 512 bytes to 5 KB, thus speeding up the transfer of information.
`-c`	Uses a storage format (SVR4) that is widely recognized by different versions of `cpio` for UNIX and Linux.
`-d` `--make-directories`	Creates directories as needed during extraction.
`-i` `--extract`	Reads files from an archive.
`-I filename`	Specifies the input archive file or device file used when viewing or extracting files.
`-L` `--dereference`	Prevents `cpio` from backing up symbolic links; instead, `cpio` backs up the target files of symbolic links.
`--no-absolute-filenames`	Stores filenames in an archive using relative pathnames.
`-o` `--create`	Creates a new archive.
`-O filename`	Specifies the output archive file or device file when backing up files.
`-t` `--list`	Lists the filename contents (table of contents) of an existing archive.
`-u` `--unconditional`	Overwrites existing files during extraction without prompting for user confirmation.
`-v` `--verbose`	Displays verbose output (file and directory information) when manipulating archives.

To create an archive using `cpio`, you must first generate a list of filenames. You can do this using the `find` command. To list all filenames under the /root/sample directory, you can use the following command:

```
[root@server1 ~]# find /root/sample
/root/sample
/root/sample/samplefile
/root/sample/samplefile2
[root@server1 ~]#_
```

Next, you can send this list via Standard Input to the `cpio` command. For example, to verbosely back up all files in /root/sample to the sample.cpio file using a block size of 5 KB and a common format, you can use the following command:

```
[root@server1 ~]# find /root/sample | cpio -vocB -O sample.cpio
/root/sample
/root/sample/samplefile
/root/sample/samplefile2
5 blocks
[root@server1 ~]#_
```

As with the tar utility, `cpio` archive filenames need not have an extension to identify their contents. However, it is good practice to use extensions, as shown with sample.cpio in the preceding example. To view the verbose table of contents of the sample.cpio archive, you can use the following command:

```
[root@server1 ~]# cpio -vitB -I sample.cpio
drwxr-xr-x   2 root   root       0 Jul 27 13:40 /root/sample
-rw-r--r--   1 root   root   20239 Jul 21 08:15 /root/sample/samplefile
-rw-rw-r--   1 root   root     574 Jul 21 08:18 /root/sample/samplefile2
5 blocks
[root@server1 ~]#_
```

Following this, you can extract the contents of the sample.cpio archive, creating directories and overwriting files as needed by using the following command:

```
[root@server1 ~]# cpio -vicduB -I sample.cpio
/root/sample
/root/sample/samplefile
/root/sample/samplefile2
5 blocks
[root@server1 ~]#_
```

Like tar, the cpio command can be used to create an archive on a device by specifying the appropriate device file in place of the archive file. For example, to create an archive on the first SCSI tape device that contains the files from the directory /root/sample, using a block size of 5 KB as well as a common header, you can issue the following command:

```
[root@server1 ~]# find /root/sample | cpio -vocB -O /dev/st0
/root/sample
/root/sample/samplefile
/root/sample/samplefile2
5 blocks
[root@server1 ~]#_
```

Using dump/restore

Like tar and cpio, the dump command can be used to back up files and directories to a device or to a file on the filesystem, and the restore command can be used to restore those files and directories. However, dump and restore can only work with files on ext2, ext3, and ext4 filesystems.

> **Note 20**
>
> The dump and restore commands are not installed on Fedora or Ubuntu Linux by default. To install them from a software repository on the Internet, you can run the dnf install dump command as the root user on Fedora Linux, or the apt install dump command as the root user on Ubuntu Linux.

Although dump can be used to back up only certain files and directories, it was designed to back up entire filesystems to an archive and keep track of these filesystems in a file called /etc/dumpdates. Because archiving all data on a filesystem (known as a full backup) might take a long time, you can choose to perform a full backup only on weekends and incremental backups each evening during the week. An incremental backup backs up only the data that has been changed since the last backup. In the case of a system failure, you can restore the information from the full backup and then restore the information from all subsequent incremental backups in sequential order. You can perform up to nine different incremental backups using dump; number 0 represents a full backup, whereas numbers 1 through 9 represent incremental backups.

Suppose, for example, that you perform a full backup of the /dev/sda3 filesystem on Sunday, perform incremental backups from Monday to Wednesday, and on Thursday the /dev/sda3 filesystem becomes corrupted, as depicted in Figure 11-1.

Figure 11-1   A sample backup strategy

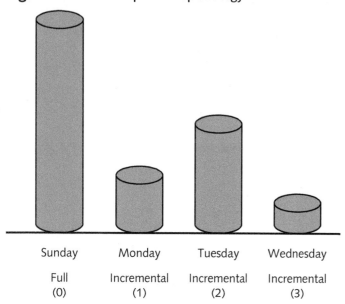

Sunday	Monday	Tuesday	Wednesday
Full	Incremental	Incremental	Incremental
(0)	(1)	(2)	(3)

After the filesystem has been re-created, you should restore the full backup (0) followed by the first incremental backup (1), the second incremental backup (2), and the third incremental backup (3) to ensure that data has been properly recovered.

> **Note 21**
>
> **Differential backups** are an alternative to incremental backups; they back up only the data that has been changed since the last full backup. This allows you to recover data by restoring a full backup followed by the most recent differential backup only. While dump/restore cannot perform differential backups, many third-party software suites can.

The dump and restore commands have many options available; Table 11-7 provides a list of these options.

Table 11-7   Common options used with dump/restore

Option	Description
-#	Specifies the type of backup when used with the dump command; if 0, a full backup is performed. If 1 through 9, the appropriate incremental backup is performed.
-b size	When used with the dump command, it specifies a certain block size to use in kilobytes; the default block size is 10 KB.
-f filename	Specifies the pathname to the archive file or device file.
-u	Specifies to update the /etc/dumpdates file after a successful backup.
-n	When used with the dump command, it notifies the user if any errors occur and when the backup has completed.
-r	Extracts an entire archive when used with the restore command.
-x filename	Specifies the archive file or device file when used with the restore command.
-i	Restores files interactively, prompting the user for confirmation for all actions, when used with the restore command.
-t	Lists the filename contents (table of contents) of an existing archive when used with the restore command.
-v	Displays verbose output (file and directory information) when manipulating archives.

Take, for example, the output from the following df command:

```
[root@server1 ~]# df | grep sda3
/dev/sda3                15481840      169484   14525924    2% /data
[root@server1 ~]#_
```

To perform a full backup of the /data partition (/dev/sda3) to the data0.dump file and update the /etc/dumpdates file when completed, you can issue the following command:

```
[root@server1 ~]# dump -0uf data0.dump /dev/sda3
  DUMP: Date of this level 0 dump: Sat Aug 28 10:39:12 2023
  DUMP: Dumping /dev/sda3 (/data) to data0.dump
  DUMP: Label: none
  DUMP: Writing 10 Kilobyte records
  DUMP: mapping (Pass I) [regular files]
  DUMP: mapping (Pass II) [directories]
  DUMP: estimated 300 blocks.
  DUMP: Volume 1 started with block 1 at: Sat Aug 28 10:39:12 2023
  DUMP: dumping (Pass III) [directories]
  DUMP: dumping (Pass IV) [regular files]
  DUMP: Closing data0.dump
  DUMP: Volume 1 completed at: Sat Aug 28 10:39:12 2023
  DUMP: Volume 1 290 blocks (0.28MB)
  DUMP: 290 blocks (0.28MB) on 1 volume(s)
  DUMP: finished in less than a second
  DUMP: Date of this level 0 dump: Sat Aug 28 10:39:12 2023
  DUMP: Date this dump completed:  Sat Aug 28 10:39:12 2023
  DUMP: Average transfer rate: 340 kB/s
  DUMP: DUMP IS DONE
[root@server1 ~]#_
```

Note 22

Alternatively, you can specify the filesystem mount point when using the dump command. The command dump -0uf data0.dump /data is equivalent to the one used in the preceding example.

Note 23

To create a dump archive on a specific device, you can specify a device file in place of an archive file. For example, the dump -0uf /dev/st0 /data would create the same archive used in the preceding example on the first SCSI tape device.

The contents of the /etc/dumpdates file now indicate that a full backup has taken place:

```
[root@server1 ~]# cat /etc/dumpdates
/dev/sda3 0 Sat Aug 28 10:39:12 2023 -0400
[root@server1 ~]#_
```

To perform the first incremental backup to a file called data1.dump and view the contents of the /etc/dumpdates file, you can issue the following commands:

```
[root@server1 ~]# dump -1uf data1.dump /dev/sda3
  DUMP: Date of this level 1 dump: Sat Aug 28 10:41:09 2023
  DUMP: Date of last level 0 dump: Sat Aug 28 10:39:12 2023
  DUMP: Dumping /dev/sda3 (/data) to data1.dump
```

```
DUMP: Label: none
DUMP: Writing 10 Kilobyte records
DUMP: mapping (Pass I) [regular files]
DUMP: mapping (Pass II) [directories]
DUMP: estimated 255 blocks.
DUMP: Volume 1 started with block 1 at: Sat Aug 28 10:41:10 2023
DUMP: dumping (Pass III) [directories]
DUMP: dumping (Pass IV) [regular files]
DUMP: Closing data1.dump
DUMP: Volume 1 completed at: Sat Aug 28 10:41:10 2023
DUMP: Volume 1 250 blocks (0.24MB)
DUMP: 250 blocks (0.24MB) on 1 volume(s)
DUMP: finished in less than a second
DUMP: Date of this level 1 dump: Sat Aug 28 10:41:09 2023
DUMP: Date this dump completed:  Sat Aug 28 10:41:10 2023
DUMP: Average transfer rate: 299 kB/s
DUMP: DUMP IS DONE
[root@server1 ~]# cat /etc/dumpdates
/dev/sda3 0 Sat Aug 28 10:39:12 2023 -0400
/dev/sda3 1 Sat Aug 28 10:41:09 2023 -0400
[root@server1 ~]#_
```

To view the contents of an archive, you can specify the -t option to the restore command followed by the archive information. To view the contents of the full backup performed earlier, you can execute the following command:

```
[root@server1 ~]# restore -tf data0.dump
Dump   date: Sat Aug 28 10:39:12 2023
Dumped from: the epoch
Level 0 dump of /data on server1:/dev/sda3
Label: none
        2  .
       11  ./lost+found
       12  ./inittab
       13  ./hosts
       14  ./issue
       17  ./aquota.user
       15  ./aquota.group
[root@server1 ~]#_
```

To extract the full backup shown in the preceding output, you can specify the -r option to the restore command followed by the archive information. In addition, you can specify the -v option to list the filenames restored, as shown in the following example:

```
[root@server1 ~]# restore -vrf data0.dump
Verify tape and initialize maps
Input is from a local file/pipe
Input block size is 32
Dump   date: Sat Aug 28 10:39:12 2023
Dumped from: the epoch
Level 0 dump of /data on server1:/dev/sda3
Label: none
Begin level 0 restore
Initialize symbol table.
```

```
Extract directories from data0.dump
Calculate extraction list.
Make node ./lost+found
Extract new leaves.
Check pointing the restore
extract file ./inittab
extract file ./hosts
extract file ./issue
extract file ./aquota.group
extract file ./aquota.user
Add links
Set directory mode, owner, and times.
Check the symbol table.
Check pointing the restore
[root@server1 ~]#_
```

Using dd

Unlike the tar, cpio, and dump commands, which back up data in a file-based format, the dd command backs up data block by block to an archive device or file, without keeping track of the files that the blocks comprise. This type of backup is called an image backup and is often used to create archives of entire filesystems or disk structures (e.g., MBR).

At minimum, the dd command requires an input file (if) and an output file (of) option to be specified. For example, to create an image backup of the filesystem on /dev/sda2 within the archive file /sda2.img, you could use the following command:

```
[root@server1 ~]# dd if=/dev/sda2 of=/sda2.img
2097152+0 records in
2097152+0 records out
1073741824 bytes (1.1 GB, 1.0 GiB) copied, 9.29465 s, 116 MB/s
[root@server1 ~]#_
```

Note 24

By default, the dd command copies information 512 bytes at a time, but you can modify this behavior using the bs (block size) option. For example, dd if=/dev/sda2 of=/sda2.img bs=1M would transfer information 1 MB at a time, which would result in a faster transfer rate compared to the default.

To restore the filesystem on /dev/sda2 from the /sda2.img archive file, you could unmount the existing filesystem from /dev/sda2 and run the dd command with the input and output files reversed:

```
[root@server1 ~]# umount /dev/sda2
[root@server1 ~]# dd if=/sda2.img of=/dev/sda2
2097152+0 records in
2097152+0 records out
1073741824 bytes (1.1 GB, 1.0 GiB) copied, 44.7753 s, 24.0 MB/s
[root@server1 ~]#_
```

Following this, you can remount the filesystem normally and access the data within.

Note 25

The dd command can also be used to back up specific storage locations, such as the MBR, which uses the first 512 bytes of a disk device. For example, to back up the MBR on /dev/sda to the /MBRarchive.img file, you could use the dd if=/dev/sda of=/MBRarchive.img bs=512 count=1 command.

Using Disc Burning Software

The backup utilities you've examined thus far are primarily used to create archive files on filesystems or tape devices. To create an archive on CD or DVD media, you must use a program that allows you to select the data to copy, organize that data, build a CD or DVD filesystem, and write the entire filesystem (including the data) to the CD or DVD. Recall from Chapter 2 that the programs that can be used to do this are called disc burning software. Figure 11-2 shows the Brasero disc burning software. You can install Brasero on a Fedora system using the `dnf install brasero` command as the root user, and launch it from the GNOME desktop by navigating to Activities, Show Applications, Brasero. You can then click the Data project button shown in Figure 11-2, select the data that you wish to back up, and click Burn to write it to your CD or DVD drive.

Figure 11-2   The Brasero disc burning software

Source: Brasero

Software Installation

Primary responsibilities of most Linux administrators typically include installing and maintaining software packages. Software for Linux can consist of binary files that have been precompiled to run on certain hardware architectures such as 64-bit Intel (x86_64), or as source code, which must be compiled on the local architecture before use. The largest advantage to obtaining and compiling source code is that the source code is not created for a particular hardware architecture. After being compiled, the program executes natively on the architecture from which it was compiled.

> **Note 26**
>
> The most common method for obtaining software for Linux is via the Internet. Appendix B lists some common websites that host Linux Open Source Software for download.

> **Note 27**
>
> When downloading software files from the Internet, you may notice that the Internet site lists a **checksum** value for the file, which was calculated from the exact file contents. To ensure that the file was received in its entirety after you download it, you should verify that the checksum value is still the same. You can use one of several ***sum commands**, depending on the algorithm used to create the checksum. For example, you can use the `md5sum programfile` command to check an MD5 checksum, the `sha1sum programfile` command to check an SHA-1 checksum, the `sha256sum programfile` command to check an SHA-256 checksum, or the `sha512sum programfile` command to check an SHA-512 checksum.

Precompiled binary programs are typically distributed in a format for use with a package manager. Recall from Chapter 1 that a package manager provides a standard format for distributing programs as well as a central database to store information about software packages installed on the system; this allows software packages to be queried and easily uninstalled. Many Linux distributions today, including Fedora, use the Red Hat Package Manager (RPM). However, Debian and Debian-based Linux distributions, such as Ubuntu Linux, use the Debian Package Manager (DPM). Also recall from Chapter 1 that you can also choose to install software in a sandbox that contains all the supporting files that the software requires. Snap, Flatpak, and AppImage are common sandbox formats for Linux software.

Note 28

While RPM and DPM are supported by nearly all mainstream Linux distributions, they are not the only package managers available. For example, Arch Linux uses the Pacman package manager, and Gentoo Linux uses the Portage package manager.

Compiling Source Code into Programs

Program source code is typically obtained by cloning an online git repository as described in Chapter 7, or by downloading a tarball that contains the source code and extracting its contents. If your system has a desktop environment installed, you can download a source code tarball from the Internet using a web browser. Alternatively, if your system does not have a desktop environment installed, you can use the wget (web get) command or curl (client for URLs) command to download a source code tarball. For example, to download a sample source code tarball called sample.tar.gz from https://sample.com to your current directory, you could use the get https://sample.com/sample.tar.gz or curl https://sample.com/sample.tar.gz --output sample.tar.gz command.

After you clone a git repository of source code or download and extract the contents of a source code tarball, there will be a subdirectory under the current directory containing the source code. This directory typically contains a text file that starts with README or INSTALL with information about the program and instructions for installation.

While inside the source code directory, the first step to installation is to run the configure program. This performs a preliminary check for system requirements and creates a list of what to compile inside a file called Makefile in the current directory.

Next, you can type the make command, which looks for the Makefile file and uses the information in it to compile the source code into binary programs using the appropriate compiler program for the local hardware architecture. For example, software written in the C programming language is compiled using the GNU C Compiler (gcc). After compilation, the binary files the program comprises remain in the source code directory. To install the compiled program on your system, you must type make install to copy the newly compiled executable files to a directory listed in your PATH variable, as well as copy supporting files, such as man pages, to the correct location on the filesystem.

Note 29

Most Linux programs compiled from source code are installed to a subdirectory of the /usr/local directory after compilation.

After the program has been compiled and copied to the correct location on the filesystem, you can remove the source code directory and its contents from the system.

Suppose, for example, that you download the source code tarball for conky (a desktop system monitor) version 1.9.0 from the Internet at sourceforge.net:

```
[root@server1 ~]# ls -F
Desktop/    conky-1.9.0.tar.bz2
[root@server1 ~]#_
```

The first step to installing this program is to extract the contents of the tarball, which will create a directory containing the source code and supporting files. Next, you can move to this directory and view the file contents, as shown in the following output:

```
[root@server1 ~]# tar -jxf conky-1.9.0.tar.bz2
[root@server1 ~]# ls -F
Desktop/    conky-1.9.0/    conky-1.9.0.tar.bz2
[root@server1 ~]# cd conky-1.9.0
[root@server1 conky-1.9.0]# ls -F
aclocal.m4      config.rpath*    data/          ltmain.sh      NEWS
AUTHORS         config.sub*      depcomp*       lua/           README
autogen.sh*     configure*       doc/           m4/            src/
ChangeLog       configure.ac     extras/        Makefile.am    text2c.sh
compile*        configure.ac.in  INSTALL        Makefile.in    TODO
config.guess*   COPYING          install-sh*    missing*
[root@server1 conky-1.9.0]#_
```

In the preceding output, you can see that a README, INSTALL, and configure file exist and that the configure file is executable. To execute the configure shell script without using the PATH variable, you can enter the following command:

```
[root@server1 conky-1.9.0]# ./configure
checking for a BSD-compatible install... /usr/bin/install -c
checking whether build environment is sane... yes
checking for a thread-safe mkdir -p... /usr/bin/mkdir -p
checking for gawk... gawk
checking whether make sets $(MAKE)... yes
checking for gcc... gcc
checking whether the C compiler works... yes
checking for C compiler default output file name... a.out
checking for suffix of executables...
checking whether we are cross compiling... no
checking for suffix of object files... o
checking whether we are using the GNU C compiler... yes
checking whether gcc accepts -g... yes
checking for gcc option to accept ISO C89... none needed
checking for style of include used by make... GNU
checking dependency style of gcc... gcc3
checking build system type... x86_64-unknown-linux-gnu

<Additional contents omitted here>

[root@server1 conky-1.9.0]#_
```

If the configure shell script produces errors instead of running successfully, you will likely need to install the specified **shared library** necessary to support the program, often using a package manager as described later in this chapter. Shared libraries are files that contain executable code that can be used by multiple, different programs; rather than implementing that code within a program, most program developers reuse the code from a shared library to save time. If the required shared library is for an optional program feature you can instead choose to disable the optional program feature by specifying an option to the configure script. To see a list of available options for your configure script, you can run the `./configure --help` command.

After the configure script has run successfully, a Makefile exists in the current directory, as shown in the following output:

```
[root@server1 conky-1.9.0]# head -2 Makefile
# Makefile.in generated by automake 1.11.5 from Makefile.am.
# Makefile.  Generated from Makefile.in by configure.
[root@server1 conky-1.9.0]#_
```

This Makefile contains most of the information and commands necessary to compile the program. Some program source code that you download might contain commented lines that you need to uncomment to enable certain features of the program or to allow the program to compile on your computer architecture. Instructions for these commented areas are documented in the Makefile itself; thus, it is good form to read the Makefile after you run the configure script. You can also edit the Makefile if you want to change the location to which the program is installed. For example, the line `prefix=/usr/local` within the Makefile installs the program to subdirectories under /usr/local.

Next, you must compile the program according to the settings stored in the Makefile by typing the `make` command while in the source code directory. This typically uses the `gcc` program to compile the source code files, as shown in the following output:

```
[root@server1 conky-1.9.0]# make
Making all in src
make[1]: Entering directory '/root/conky-1.9.0/src'
make  all-am
make[2]: Entering directory '/root/conky-1.9.0/src'
gcc -DHAVE_CONFIG_H -I. -DSYSTEM_CONFIG_FILE=\"/usr/local/etc/conky/
conky.conf\" -DPACKAGE_LIBDIR=\"/usr/local/lib/conky\"   -I/usr/include/
freetype2 -I/usr/include/libpng16 -I/usr/include/uuid  -I/usr/include/
glib-2.0 -I/usr/lib64/glib-2.0/include  -Wall -W  -MT conky-conf_
cookie.o -MD -MP -MF .deps/conky-conf_cookie.Tpo -c -o conky-conf_
cookie.o `test -f 'conf_cookie.c' || echo './'`conf_cookie.c
mv -f .deps/conky-conf_cookie.Tpo .deps/conky-conf_cookie.Po
gcc -DHAVE_CONFIG_H -I.
-DSYSTEM_CONFIG_FILE=\"/usr/local/etc/conky
/conky.conf\" -DPACKAGE_LIBDIR=\"/usr/local/lib/conky\"   -I/usr/include
/freetype2 -I/usr/include/libpng16 -I/usr/include/uuid  -I/usr/include
/glib-2.0 -I/usr/lib64/glib-2.0/include  -Wall -W  -MT conky-mpd.o -MD
-MP -MF .deps/conky-mpd.Tpo -c -o conky-mpd.o `test -f 'mpd.c' || echo
'./'`mpd.c
mv -f .deps/conky-mpd.Tpo .deps/conky-mpd.Po
gcc -DHAVE_CONFIG_H -I.
-DSYSTEM_CONFIG_FILE=\"/usr/local/etc/conky/
conky.conf\" -DPACKAGE_LIBDIR=\"/usr/local/lib/conky\"   -I/usr/include/
freetype2 -I/usr/include/libpng16 -I/usr/include/uuid  -I/usr/include/
glib-2.0 -I/usr/lib64/glib-2.0/include  -Wall -W  -MT conky-libmpdclient
.o -MD -MP -MF .deps/conky-libmpdclient.Tpo -c -o conky-libmpdclient.o
`test -f 'libmpdclient.c' || echo './'`libmpdclient.c
mv -f .deps/conky-libmpdclient.Tpo .deps/conky-libmpdclient.Po
```

```
gcc -DHAVE_CONFIG_H -I. -DSYSTEM_CONFIG_FILE=\"/usr/local/etc/conky/
conky.conf\" -DPACKAGE_LIBDIR=\"/usr/local/lib/conky\"   -I/usr/include/
freetype2 -I/usr/include/libpng16 -I/usr/include/uuid  -I/usr/include/
glib-2.0 -I/usr/lib64/glib-2.0/include  -Wall -W  -MT conky-moc.o -MD
-MP -MF .deps/conky-moc.Tpo -c -o conky-moc.o `test -f 'moc.c' || echo
'./'`moc.c
mv -f .deps/conky-moc.Tpo .deps/conky-moc.Po

<Additional gcc commands omitted here>

[root@server1 conky-1.9.0]#_
```

After you compile the source code files, you can copy the program files to the correct location on the filesystem by typing the following command:

```
[root@server1 conky-1.9.0]# make install
Making install in src
make[1]: Entering directory '/root/conky-1.9.0/src'
make  install-am
make[2]: Entering directory '/root/conky-1.9.0/src'
make[3]: Entering directory '/root/conky-1.9.0/src'
 /usr/bin/mkdir -p '/usr/local/bin'
  /bin/sh ../libtool   --mode=install /usr/bin/install -c conky '/usr/local/bin'
libtool: install: /usr/bin/install -c conky /usr/local/bin/conky
make[3]: Nothing to be done for 'install-data-am'.
make[3]: Leaving directory '/root/conky-1.9.0/src'
make[2]: Leaving directory '/root/conky-1.9.0/src'
make[1]: Leaving directory '/root/conky-1.9.0/src'
Making install in doc
make[1]: Entering directory '/root/conky-1.9.0/doc'
make[2]: Entering directory '/root/conky-1.9.0/doc'
make[2]: Nothing to be done for 'install-exec-am'.
 /usr/bin/mkdir -p '/usr/local/share/man/man1'
 /usr/bin/install -c -m 644 conky.1 '/usr/local/share/man/man1'
make[2]: Leaving directory '/root/conky-1.9.0/doc'
make[1]: Leaving directory '/root/conky-1.9.0/doc'

<Additional contents omitted here>

[root@server1 conky-1.9.0]#_
```

After the program files are copied to the appropriate directories, you can remove the source code directory and tarball and locate the main binary file for the program, as shown in the following example:

```
[root@server1 conky-1.9.0]# cd ..
[root@server1 ~]# rm -Rf conky-1.9.0
[root@server1 ~]# rm -f conky-1.9.0.tar.bz2
[root@server1 ~]# which conky
/usr/local/bin/conky
[root@server1 ~]#_
```

Finally, you can view the conky manual page, and then switch to a desktop environment and run the command conky& within a graphical terminal to execute the conky program, as shown in Figure 11-3.

Figure 11-3   The conky program

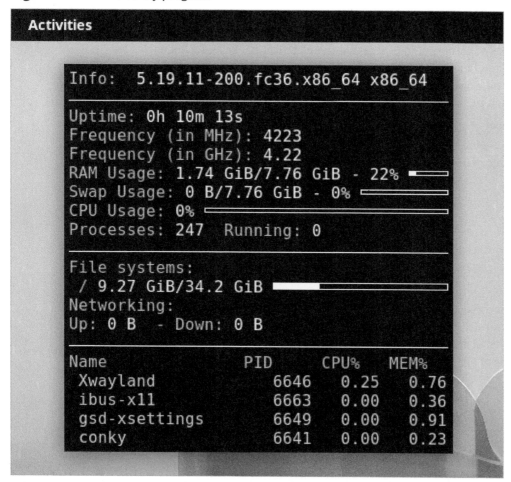

Working with the Red Hat Package Manager (RPM)

RPM is the most widely used format for Linux software distributed via the Internet on distributions derived from Red Hat Linux. RPM packages have filenames that indicate the hardware architecture for which the software was compiled and end with the .rpm extension. The following output indicates that the bluefish RPM package (a web page editor) version 2.2.12-6 was compiled for Fedora 36 (fc36) on the Intel x86_64 platform:

```
[root@server1 ~]# ls -F
Desktop/        bluefish-2.2.12-6.fc36.x86_64.rpm
[root@server1 ~]#_
```

To install an RPM package, you can use the -i option to the rpm command. In addition, you can use the -v and -h options to print the verbose information and hash marks, respectively, during installation.

Some RPM packages require that other RPM packages or shared libraries be installed on your system first. This type of relationship is known as a package dependency. If you attempt to install an RPM package that has package dependencies, you receive an error message that indicates the packages and shared libraries that need to be installed first. After installing these prerequisites, you can successfully install your desired RPM package. Say, for example, that you download the RPM package for the Bluefish web page editor and run the following command to install it:

```
[root@server1 ~]# rpm -ivh bluefish-2.2.12-6.fc36.x86_64.rpm
error: Failed dependencies:
bluefish-shared-data = 2.2.12-6.fc36 is needed by
        bluefish-2.2.12-6.fc36.x86_64
```

```
libgucharmap_2_90.so.7()(64bit) is needed by
      bluefish-2.2.12-6.fc36.x86_64
[root@server1 ~]#_
```

The error shown in the preceding output indicates that there are two package dependencies for the Bluefish RPM package called bluefish-shared-data and libgucharmap. Consequently, you must download the bluefish-shared-data package and libgucharmap shared library (part of the gucharmap-libs package) for your architecture. Following this, you can run the following command to install all three packages:

```
[root@server1 ~]# rpm -ivh bluefish-2.2.12-6.fc36.x86_64.rpm bluefish-shared-
data-2.2.12-6.fc36.noarch.rpm gucharmap-libs-14.0.3-1.fc36.x86_64.rpm
Verifying...                     ###################### [100%]
Preparing...                     ###################### [100%]
Updating / installing...
   1:gucharmap-libs-14.0.3-1.fc36    ###################### [ 33%]
   2:bluefish-shared-data-2.2.12-6.fc3######################[ 67%]
   3:bluefish-2.2.12-6.fc36          ###################### [100%]
[root@server1 ~]#_
```

After you install an RPM package, the RPM database (stored within files in the /var/lib/rpm directory) is updated to contain information about the package and the files contained within. To query the full package name after installation, you can use the −q (query) option to the rpm command followed by the common name of the package:

```
[root@server1 ~]# rpm -q bluefish
bluefish-2.2.12-6.fc36.x86_64
[root@server1 ~]#_
```

In addition, you can add the −i (info) option to the preceding command to display the detailed package information for the bluefish package:

```
[root@server1 ~]# rpm -qi bluefish
Name        : bluefish
Version     : 2.2.12
Release     : 6.fc36
Architecture: x86_64
Install Date: Mon 26 Sep 2023 01:14:29 PM EDT
Group       : Unspecified
Size        : 1739019
License     : GPLv3+
Signature   : RSA/SHA256, Wed 02 Feb 2023 10:23:18 AM EST, Key ID 999f7cbf38ab71f4
Source RPM  : bluefish-2.2.12-6.fc36.src.rpm
Build Date  : Wed 02 Feb 2022 10:19:27 AM EST
Build Host  : buildhw-x86-15.iad2.fedoraproject.org
Packager    : Fedora Project
Vendor      : Fedora Project
URL         : http://bluefish.openoffice.nl/
Bug URL     : https://bugz.fedoraproject.org/bluefish
Summary     : web development application for experienced users
Description :
Bluefish is a powerful editor for experienced web designers and
programmers. Bluefish supports many programming and markup languages,
but it focuses on editing dynamic and interactive websites.
[root@server1 ~]#_
```

Because the Red Hat Package Manager keeps track of all installed files, you can find the executable file for the Bluefish program by using the -q and -l (list) options followed by the RPM package name to list all files contained within the package. The following command lists the first 10 files in the bluefish package:

```
[root@server1 ~]# rpm -ql bluefish
/usr/bin/bluefish
/usr/lib64/bluefish
/usr/lib64/bluefish/about.so
/usr/lib64/bluefish/charmap.so
/usr/lib64/bluefish/entities.so
/usr/lib64/bluefish/htmlbar.so
/usr/lib64/bluefish/infbrowser.so
/usr/lib64/bluefish/snippets.so
/usr/lib64/bluefish/zencoding.so
/usr/share/licenses/bluefish
/usr/share/licenses/bluefish/COPYING
[root@server1 ~]#_
```

From the preceding output, you can see that the pathname to the executable file is /usr/bin/bluefish, which resides in a directory in the PATH variable. Upon execution in a desktop environment, you see the screen depicted in Figure 11-4.

Figure 11-4 The Bluefish program

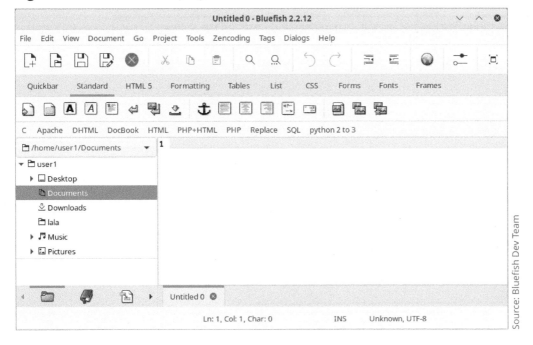

Source: Bluefish Dev Team

Conversely, you can find out to which RPM package a certain file belongs by using the -q and -f (file) options with the rpm command, followed by the filename:

```
[root@server1 ~]# rpm -qf /usr/bin/bluefish
bluefish-2.2.12-6.fc36.x86_64
[root@server1 ~]#_
```

To remove an RPM package from the system, you can use the −e option to the rpm command; all files that belong to the package will be removed as well. To remove the bluefish and bluefish-shared-data RPM packages and verify the deletion, you can use the following commands:

```
[root@server1 ~]# rpm -e bluefish bluefish-shared-data
[root@server1 ~]# rpm -q bluefish bluefish-shared-data
package bluefish is not installed
package bluefish-shared-data is not installed
[root@server1 ~]#_
```

Table 11-8 displays a list of common options used with the rpm command.

Table 11-8   Common options used with the rpm command

Option	Description
-a --all	Displays all package names installed on the system (when used with the −q option).
-c --configfiles	Displays the locations of the configuration files for a package installed on the system (when used with the −q option).
--dump	Displays detailed information regarding configuration files for a package installed on the system (when used following the −q and −c options).
-e --erase	Removes a specified package from the system.
-F --freshen	Upgrades a specified package only if an older version exists on the system.
-f --file	Displays the package to which the specified file belongs (when used with the −q option).
-h --hash	Prints hash marks on the screen to indicate installation progress (when used with the −i option).
-i --install	Installs a specified package (provided the −q option is not used).
-i --info	Displays full information about the specified package (when used with the −q option).
-K	When used before a filename argument, validates the checksum listed within the RPM file.
-l --list	Lists the filenames the specified package comprises (when used with the −q option).
--nodeps	Forces the RPM to avoid checking for dependencies before installing packages (when used following the −i option).
-q --query	Queries information about packages on the system.
--test	Performs a test installation only (when used with the −i option).
-U --upgrade	Upgrades a specified package; the package is installed even if no older version exists on the system.
-V --verify	Verifies the location of all files that belong to the specified package.
-v	Prints verbose information when installing or manipulating packages.

Note 30

RPM packages can also be converted to cpio archives using the `rpm2cpio` command. This allows you to easily inspect or extract file contents from an RPM package without installing the package on the system.

There are thousands of different RPM packages available for free download on Internet servers called **software repositories**. Moreover, each RPM on a software repository may have several package dependencies. Luckily, you can use the `yum` **(Yellowdog Updater Modified) command** to search Internet software repositories for RPM packages that map to your architecture, and automatically install or upgrade those packages on your system. Prior to installing the desired RPM package, the `yum` command also downloads and installs any package dependencies. The /etc/yum.conf and /etc/yum.repos.d/* files are used to specify the locations of Internet software repositories.

While many current Linux distributions still use the `yum` command, Fedora and many other modern Linux distributions use the `dnf` **(Dandified YUM) command** alongside the repository information stored in the /etc/dnf/dnf.conf and /etc/yum.repos.d/* files.

Note 31

The `dnf` command is simply a faster version of the `yum` command that provides the same core options and functionality.

Note 32

The SUSE and openSUSE Linux distributions use the `zypper` **command** to provide the same functionality as the `yum` command.

To install a particular RPM package and its dependencies following a Fedora Linux installation, you can use the `dnf install packagename` command. Multiple software packages can be installed using a single `dnf` command. For example, the `dnf install package1name package2name package3name` command will install three packages, including any package dependencies.

Note 33

You have used the `dnf` command in previous chapters to install several programs on your Fedora Linux virtual machine from software repositories on the Internet.

Because newer versions of RPM packages are frequently added to software repositories, you can also upgrade an installed package to the latest version using the `dnf upgrade packagename` command. For example, to upgrade your Linux kernel to the latest version, you could use the following command and press y when prompted to download and install the latest packages:

```
[root@server1 ~]# dnf upgrade kernel
Last metadata expiration check: 1:17:22 ago on Mon 26
Sep 2023 12:19:19 PM EDT.
Dependencies resolved.
========================================================================
 Package           Architecture Version           Repository     Size
========================================================================
Installing:
 kernel            x86_64       5.19.11-200.fc36   updates       262 k
 kernel-modules    x86_64       5.19.11-200.fc36   updates        58 M
Installing dependencies:
 kernel-core       x86_64       5.19.11-200.fc36   updates        50 M
```

```
Transaction Summary
========================================================================
Install  3 Packages

Total download size: 108 M
Installed size: 150 M
Is this ok [y/N]: y
Downloading Packages:
(1/3): kernel-5.19.11-200.fc36.x86_64          106 kB/s | 262 kB 00:02
(2/3): kernel-core-5.19.11-200.fc36.x86_64     378 kB/s |  50 MB 02:14
(3/3): kernel-modules-5.19.11-200.fc36.x86_64 404 kB/s |  58 MB 02:27
------------------------------------------------------------------------
Total                                          749 kB/s | 108 MB
02:27
Running transaction check
Transaction check succeeded.
Running transaction test
Transaction test succeeded.
Running transaction
  Preparing          :                                          1/1
  Installing         : kernel-core-5.19.11-200.fc36.x86_64      1/3
  Running scriptlet: kernel-core-5.19.11-200.fc36.x86_64        1/3
  Installing         : kernel-modules-5.19.11-200.fc36.x86_64   2/3
  Running scriptlet: kernel-modules-5.19.11-200.fc36.x86_64     2/3
  Installing         : kernel-5.19.11-200.fc36.x86_64           3/3
  Running scriptlet: kernel-core-5.19.11-200.fc36.x86_64        3/3
  Running scriptlet: kernel-modules-5.19.11-200.fc36.x86_64     3/3
  Running scriptlet: kernel-5.19.11-200.fc36.x86_64             3/3
  Verifying: kernel-5.19.11-200.fc36.x86_64                     1/3
  Verifying: kernel-core-5.19.11-200.fc36.x86_64                2/3
  Verifying: kernel-modules-5.19.11-200.fc36.x86_64             3/3

Installed:
  kernel-5.19.11-200.fc36.x86_64 kernel-core-5.19.11-200.fc36.x86_64
  kernel-modules-5.19.11-200.fc36.x86_64

Complete!
[root@server1 ~]#_
```

Note 34

If you add the `-y` option to the `dnf` command, you will not be prompted to press y to continue with the package installation.

Note 35

Without a package name argument, the `dnf upgrade` command will attempt to upgrade all installed packages. You can also use the `dnf check-update` command to check for installed software updates.

Note 36

If a package upgrade includes a new version of a configuration file, the update will either overwrite the original configuration file, after saving it to *filename*.rpmsave, or preserve the original configuration file and create a new one called *filename*.rpmnew with the new settings. To ensure that packages contain the settings you want following a package upgrade, run `find / | egrep "(rpmsave$|rpmnew$)"` to locate these files. You can then view their contents to determine if you need to modify the configuration file settings for the package.

Note from the previous output that the `dnf` command also upgraded the associated kernel-modules package (since kernel modules are specific to the version of the kernel) as well as the kernel-core package dependency. You may also find that the `dnf` command tries several different software repositories that contain the necessary software (called **software mirrors**) before finding one that accepts a connection. This is common because software repositories limit their concurrent download connections to allow for fast download. When a software repository reaches its concurrent connection limit, it returns a negative response to the `dnf` command and the `dnf` command searches for the RPM package on the next software mirror listed in the repository configuration files.

In some cases, you may not know the exact RPM package name to use alongside the `dnf` command. Luckily, you can use the `dnf search keyword` command to search a software repository by keyword, or the `dnf list available` command to list available RPM packages. The `dnf grouplist available` command will display a list of package group names that are available for installation. A **package group** is a group of related RPM packages that are often installed together to provide a key function. For example, to install the Development Tools package group on Fedora Linux (which contains a core set of development libraries and commands), you can use the `dnf groupinstall "Development Tools"` command.

You can use the `dnf repolist` command to view the software repositories that are configured within the /etc/dnf/dnf.conf and /etc/yum.repos.d/* files on your system. Many software authors host their RPM packages on private software repositories and include instructions on their website that guide you through the process of adding the private software repository to your repository configuration files (usually by installing a special RPM package). For example, a website for a particular software package may instruct you to run the `dnf install https://`*website*`/fedora.noarch.rpm` command to install the appropriate files to the /etc/yum.repos.d directory that list the locations of the repositories that contain the packages for Fedora Linux. Next, you can run the `dnf install packagename` command to install the package.

Note 37

The `dnf` command caches repository information and packages. You can run the `dnf clean all` command to clear these caches, which is often used to fix `dnf`-related problems.

The `dnf` command can also be used to view and manage installed RPM packages. The `dnf list installed` command will list installed RPM packages, the `dnf grouplist installed` command will list installed package groups, the `dnf info packagename` command will display detailed information for an installed RPM package, and the `dnf groupinfo packagegroupname` command will display the contents of a package group. You can also use the `dnf remove packagename` command to remove an installed RPM package, or the `dnf groupremove packagegroupname` command to remove all of the RPM packages within a particular package group.

Each Linux distribution includes a graphical application that provides desktop users with an easy method for managing the software on the system as well as installing or updating packages from available software repositories on the Internet. Similarly, any packages downloaded within a desktop environment are opened by this graphical application by default, which automatically downloads and installs any dependencies before installing the package. On Fedora Linux, the graphical Software utility shown in Figure 11-5 is used to view, manage, and install software within a desktop environment. To start the Software utility within GNOME, navigate to Activities, Show Applications, Software.

Figure 11-5   The Software utility

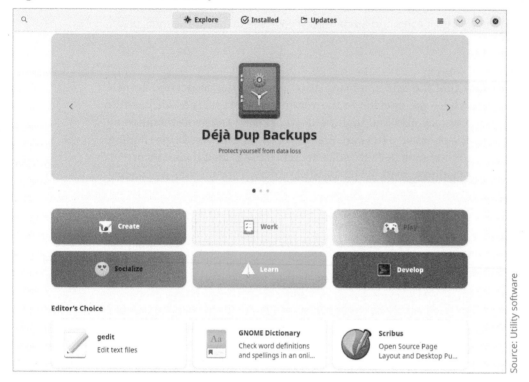

Source: Utility software

Working with the Debian Package Manager (DPM)

The Debian Package Manager (DPM) is used by default on Linux distributions based on the Debian Linux distribution, such as Ubuntu Linux. Like RPM packages, DPM packages contain software that has been precompiled for a specific platform, and they may have package dependencies. However, DPM packages use the .deb extension and are installed and maintained by the dpkg command. For example, to install the bluefish web page editor on an Ubuntu Linux system from the downloaded DPM file bluefish_2.2.12-6_amd64.deb, you can use the dpkg -i bluefish_2.2.12-6_amd64.deb command. Table 11-9 displays a list of common options used with the dpkg command.

> **Note 38**
>
> The amd64 architecture is identical to the x86_64 architecture; you will often find amd64 used in place of x86_64 within DPM package names.

> **Note 39**
>
> Some DPM packages prompt you to supply configuration options during installation. You can use dpkg-reconfigure command after package installation to modify these configuration options.

Table 11-9   Common options used with the `dpkg` command

Option	Description
`-i` `--install`	Installs a specified package.
`--ignore-depends`	Ignores any dependency checking for a specified package.
`-l` `--list`	Displays information for a specified package by name or wildcard pattern (or all packages if no argument is given); it may also be used with the `dpkg-query` command.
`-L` `--listfiles`	Displays the files that comprise a specified package; it may also be used with the `dpkg-query` command.
`-p` `--print-avail`	Displays detailed package information for a specified package; it may also be used with the `dpkg-query` command.
`-P` `--purge`	Removes a specified package from the system, including any configuration files used by the package.
`-r` `--remove`	Removes a specified package from the system, excluding any configuration files used by the package.
`-S` `--search`	Displays the package to which the specified file belongs; it may also be used with the `dpkg-query` command.
`-s` `--status`	Displays the status for a specified package; it may also be used with the `dpkg-query` command.
`--test`	Performs a test installation only (when used with the `-i` option).
`-V` `--verify`	Verifies the location of all files that belong to the specified package.

After you install a DPM package, the DPM database (stored within files in the /var/lib/dpkg directory) is updated to contain information about the package and the files contained within. As with the RPM, you can query package information for installed packages. For example, to list information about the BASH shell package, you can use the following command:

```
[root@server1 ~]# dpkg -l bash
Desired=Unknown/Install/Remove/Purge/Hold
| Status=Not/Inst/Conf-files/Unpacked/halF-conf/Half-inst/trig-aWait/
Trig-pend
|/ Err?=(none)/Reinst-required (Status,Err: uppercase=bad)
||/ Name           Version        Architecture Description
+++-==============-============-============-==================================
ii  bash           5.1-6ubuntu1 amd64         GNU Bourne Again SHell
[root@server1 ~]#_
```

Note 40

You can instead use the `dpkg-query` command when searching for DPM package information. The `dpkg-query` command takes the same search arguments as the `dpkg` command.

Alternatively, you could use the following command to list detailed information about the BASH shell package:

```
[root@server1 ~]# dpkg -p bash
Package: bash
Essential: yes
Priority: required
Section: shells
Installed-Size: 1864
Origin: Ubuntu
Maintainer: Ubuntu Developers <ubuntu-devel-discuss@lists.ubuntu.com>
Bugs: https://bugs.launchpad.net/ubuntu/+filebug
Architecture: amd64
Multi-Arch: foreign
Version: 5.1-6ubuntu1
Replaces: bash-completion (<< 20060301-0), bash-doc (<= 2.05-1)
Depends: base-files (>= 2.1.12), debianutils (>= 2.15)
Pre-Depends: libc6 (>= 2.34), libtinfo6 (>= 6)
Recommends: bash-completion (>= 20060301-0)
Suggests: bash-doc
Conflicts: bash-completion (<< 20060301-0)
Filename: pool/main/b/bash/bash_5.1-6ubuntu1_amd64.deb
Size: 768660
MD5sum: 11adc5970b295d29ff2a206bcef6224f
Description: GNU Bourne Again SHell
Original-Maintainer: Matthias Klose <doko@debian.org>
SHA1: 69b0696ad1f101d2ec4c599c279e9524c4b744c9
SHA256: 543fc0be88d2cf33ada88fe0cf82e1ec3fdcdd56e411dd2958eb3ef6e1a3d2fa
SHA512: 89af38fe631eb29e89b8659aca7fa2b26e4a88c907ee1b759f336c-
c8e0a6d56562380651f210b1ed480bd727d21dfb9b9de9e839310cecdc619d7362cac607b4
Homepage: http://tiswww.case.edu/php/chet/bash/bashtop.html
Task: minimal
Description-md5: 3522aa7b4374048d6450e348a5bb45d9
[root@server1 ~]#_
```

Because the Debian Package Manager keeps track of all installed files, you can also list the files that belong to a DPM package, verify DPM package contents, or search for the DPM package name for a specified file using the appropriate options from Table 11-9. For example, the following command lists the first 10 files in the BASH shell DPM package:

```
[root@server1 ~]# dpkg -L bash | head
/.
/bin
/bin/bash
/etc
/etc/bash.bashrc
/etc/skel
/etc/skel/.bash_logout
/etc/skel/.bashrc
/etc/skel/.profile
/usr
[root@server1 ~]#_
```

As with RPM, most DPM packages are hosted on Internet software repositories for free download. To download and install DPM packages, including any package dependencies, you can use the `apt` (**Advanced Package Tool**) **command** or `apt-get` **command**. You can search available repository information using the `apt` command or the `apt-cache` **command**.

Note 41

The `apt` command is a newer alternative to the `apt-get` and `apt-cache` commands. It uses the same core options but provides more detailed and useful output on the terminal screen. As a result, this section focuses primarily on the `apt` command.

Note 42

In Chapter 6, you used the `apt` command to install the DPM packages required for ZFS and the `lsdev`, `lsscsi`, and `hwinfo` commands on your Ubuntu Linux virtual machine.

The `apt` command is as easy to use as the `dnf` command and accepts many of the same options and arguments. For example, to install the nmap DPM package (a network port scanner) from an Internet software repository, you could run the following command:

```
[root@server1 ~]# apt install nmap -y
Reading package lists... Done
Building dependency tree... Done
Reading state information... Done
Suggested packages:
  ncat ndiff zenmap
The following NEW packages will be installed:
  nmap
0 upgraded, 1 newly installed, 0 to remove and 41 not upgraded.
Need to get 1,731 kB of archives.
After this operation, 4,341 kB of additional disk space will be used.
Get:1 http://ca.archive.ubuntu.com/ubuntu jammy/universe amd64 nmap amd64
7.91+dfsg1+really7.80+dfsg1-2build1 [1,731 kB]
Fetched 1,731 kB in 2s (816 kB/s)
Selecting previously unselected package nmap.
(Reading database ... 114335 files and directories currently installed.)
Preparing to unpack .../nmap_7.91+dfsg1+really7.80+dfsg1-2build1_amd64.deb ...
Unpacking nmap (7.91+dfsg1+really7.80+dfsg1-2build1) ...
Setting up nmap (7.91+dfsg1+really7.80+dfsg1-2build1) ...
Processing triggers for man-db (2.10.2-1) ...
Scanning processes...
Scanning linux images...

Running kernel seems to be up-to-date.
No services need to be restarted.
No containers need to be restarted.
No user sessions are running outdated binaries.
No VM guests are running outdated hypervisor (qemu) binaries on this host.
[root@server1 ~]#_
```

To remove the nmap DPM package, excluding any nmap configuration files, you could use the `apt remove nmap` command. Alternatively, you could use the `apt purge nmap` command to remove the nmap DPM package, including all nmap configuration files. If you remove a package, the package dependencies are not removed; however, you can use the `apt autoremove` command to remove package dependencies that are no longer required by programs on the system.

You can also use the `apt update` command to update the list of available DPM packages from Internet software repositories, as well as the `apt upgrade` command to upgrade the DPM packages on your system to the latest versions based on the updated package list.

> **Note 43**
>
> All of the `apt` commands discussed thus far have an `apt-get` equivalent. For example, the `apt install nmap` command is equivalent to the `apt-get install nmap` command, and the `apt purge nmap` command is equivalent to the `apt-get purge nmap` command.

DPM configuration is stored in files under the /etc/apt/apt.conf.d directory and DPM repository information is stored in the /etc/apt/sources.list file as well as in files under the /etc/apt/sources.list.d directory. You can add new repositories using the `add-apt-repository` command and search available repository and package information using either the `apt` or `apt-cache` command. For example, to search software repositories for DPM packages that contain the word nmap, you could use the `apt search nmap` or `apt-cache search nmap` command. To list all DPM packages available on software repositories, you could use the `apt search .` or `apt-cache search .` command. To view detailed information regarding the nmap package, use the `apt show nmap` or `apt-cache show nmap` command.

You can also use the **Aptitude** utility (shown in Figure 11-6) to install, query, and remove DPM packages. You can start this utility by executing the `aptitude` command in a command-line or graphical terminal. In a command-line terminal, you can access the different Aptitude menus by pressing the Ctrl+t key combination. The `aptitude` command also accepts many of the same arguments as `apt` and `apt-get`. For example, `aptitude install nmap` will install the nmap DPM package from an Internet repository, `aptitude remove nmap` will remove the installed nmap DPM package (excluding nmap configuration files), and `aptitude purge nmap` will remove the installed nmap DPM package (including nmap configuration files).

Figure 11-6   The Aptitude utility

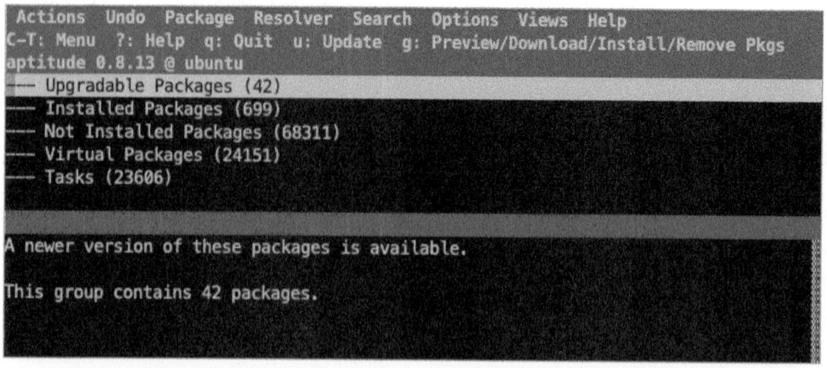

```
Actions  Undo  Package  Resolver  Search  Options  Views  Help
C-T: Menu  ?: Help  q: Quit  u: Update  g: Preview/Download/Install/Remove Pkgs
aptitude 0.8.13 @ ubuntu
--- Upgradable Packages (42)
--- Installed Packages (699)
--- Not Installed Packages (68311)
--- Virtual Packages (24151)
--- Tasks (23606)


A newer version of these packages is available.

This group contains 42 packages.
```

> **Note 44**
>
> The Aptitude utility is not installed in Ubuntu Linux by default. It can be installed using the `apt install aptitude` command.

Understanding Shared Libraries

Recall that when you install an RPM or DPM package, the package manager does a preliminary check to ensure that all shared libraries and prerequisite packages (package dependencies) required for the program to work properly have been installed. If you are using yum, dnf zypper, apt-get, or apt to install the package, then the package dependencies are automatically downloaded and installed; however, if you are using the rpm or dpkg command to install the package, then the installation will fail if the package dependencies are not installed. Similarly, when you compile a program from source code, the configure script checks for shared library dependencies; if those shared libraries are not present, the configure script will fail to create the Makefile necessary to compile the program.

If you uninstall an RPM or DPM package, including packages that contain shared libraries, the removal process normally stops if that package is a dependency for another package. However, this dependency check sometimes fails, the package dependency is removed from the system, and any programs that require the package dependency will fail to execute properly. Furthermore, if you remove an RPM or DPM package containing a shared library that is a dependency for other programs that were compiled from source code on the system, the removal process will be unaware that the package is a dependency. In this case, the package will be removed from the system and the programs that were compiled from source code that require the shared library will fail to execute.

Shared libraries are typically installed under the /lib, /lib64, /usr/lib, or /usr/lib64 directories. To identify which shared libraries are required by a certain program, you can use the ldd command. For example, the following output displays the shared libraries required by the /bin/bash program:

```
[root@server1 ~]# ldd /bin/bash
linux-vdso.so.1 (0x00007ffd595fa000)
libtinfo.so.6 => /lib64/libtinfo.so.6 (0x00007f109d7a3000)
libc.so.6 => /lib64/libc.so.6 (0x00007f109d400000)
/lib64/ld-linux-x86-64.so.2 (0x00007f109d944000)
[root@server1 ~]#_
```

If any shared libraries listed by the ldd command are missing, the ldd command will identify them as "not found" in the output. In this case, you can locate the appropriate RPM or DPM package that contains the library and install it on your system. After downloading and installing any shared libraries, it is good practice to run the ldconfig command to ensure that the list of shared library directories (/etc/ld.so.conf) and the list of shared libraries (/etc/ld.so.cache) are updated. Alternatively, you can create a variable in your BASH shell called LD_LIBRARY_PATH that lists the directories that contain the shared libraries.

Sometimes, the files that comprise a shared library can become corrupted. If this is the case, output of the ldd command will not report any problems, but the programs that depend on the shared library will produce errors that identify the shared library that is not functioning properly. In this case, you should reinstall the RPM or DPM package that contains the shared library to remedy these errors. For example, to reinstall the samplelibrary RPM package, you could use the dnf reinstall samplelibrary command, and to reinstall the samplelibrary DPM package, you could use the apt install --reinstall samplelibrary command.

Working with Sandboxed Applications

While the RPM and DPM package managers are the most common way to install software on Linux systems today, their packages often have several dependencies, including shared libraries. As mentioned in the previous section, if one of these dependent packages or shared libraries were removed, the associated software would become unstable or fail to execute.

Sandboxed applications solve this issue by ensuring that each software package include a unique copy of each required dependency. While this approach consumes additional storage for each application, it ensures that dependency issues cannot cause application problems.

Flatpak and Snap are two package managers designed to obtain and manage sandboxed applications in their respective format from online software repositories. Flatpak is installed by default on Fedora systems, while Snap is installed by default on Ubuntu systems.

To install and manage sandboxed applications using Flatpak, you can use the `flatpak command`. While some distributions ship with a default Flatpak software repository configured, others require that you manually add one. For example, `flatpak remote-add flathub https://flathub .org/repo/flathub.flatpakrepo` ; `flatpak remote-modify --enable flathub` will add the popular flathub repository and enable it for use. Following this, you can run the `flatpak remote-ls` command to list the sandboxed applications available on the repository and the `flatpak install` *application* command to install a sandboxed application. Once installed, you can run the `flatpak run` *application* command to execute it or click on the application icon that Flatpak adds to the list of available applications within your desktop environment. You can also use the `flatpak list` command to view installed Flatpak applications, the `flatpak info` *application* command to view detailed information for a Flatpak application, or the `flatpak uninstall` *application* command to remove a Flatpak application.

Note 45

By default, Flatpak applications are available to all users on the system. However, you can add the `--user` option to the `flatpak install` command to ensure that an application is only available for the current user.

To install and manage sandboxed applications using Snap, you can use the `snap command`. Snap comes preconfigured with a software repository maintained by its creators. You can use `snap search` *keyword* command to search this repository by keyword and the `snap install` *application* command to install a Snap application from it. Once installed, you can execute a Snap application by name as you would any other Linux program. You can also use `snap list` command to view installed Snap applications, the `snap info` *application* command to view detailed information for a Snap application, or the `snap remove` *application* command to remove a Snap application.

Note 46

By default, Snap only allows applications to access resources that the user has access to. To ensure that a Snap application can access other resources on the system, add the `--classic` option to the `snap install` command.

You don't need a package manager such as Flatpak or Snap to run sandboxed Linux applications. AppImage applications contain all dependencies but can be executed directly and do not require any additional management software. You download an AppImage application file, grant it execute permission and execute it as you would any Linux program. AppImage files have an `.AppImage` extension and can be downloaded from many different websites, including appimagehub.com. To remove an AppImage application, you can simply delete the AppImage application file.

Note 47

When AppImage files are executed, a sandboxed filesystem is created to execute the application within. This feature is called **Filesystem in Userspace (FUSE)** and is used by software and operating system components that need to create filesystems without relying on support from the Linux kernel.

Summary

- Many compression utilities are available for Linux systems; each of them uses a different compression algorithm and produces a different compression ratio.

- Files can be backed up to an archive using a backup utility. To back up files to CD or DVD, you must use burning software instead of a backup utility.

- The tar command is the most common backup utility used today; it is typically used to create compressed archives called tarballs.

- The source code for Linux software can be obtained and compiled afterward; most source code is available from GitHub repositories or in tarball format via the Internet.

- Package managers install and manage compiled software of the same format. The Red Hat Package Manager (RPM) and Debian Package Manager (DPM) are the most common package managers available for Linux systems today.

- In addition to managing and removing installed RPM packages, you can install and upgrade RPM packages from software repositories on the Internet using the dnf, yum, or zypper commands, depending on your Linux distribution. You can also use the rpm command to query installed RPM packages as well as perform RPM package management.

- In addition to managing and removing installed DPM packages, you can install or upgrade DPM packages from software repositories on the Internet using the apt and apt-get commands. You can also use the dpkg command to view installed DPM packages or perform DPM package management.

- Most programs depend on shared libraries for functionality. If a shared library is removed from the system, programs that depend on it will encounter errors.

- Sandboxed applications contain a unique copy of all required software components and are immune to dependency-related problems. You can use the flatpak and snap commands to install and manage Flatpak and Snap sandboxed applications, respectively. AppImage sandboxed applications are files that you can download and execute directly.

Key Terms

*sum commands
add-apt-repository command
AppImage
apt (Advanced Package Tool) command
apt-cache command
apt-get command
Aptitude
aptitude command
archive
Brasero
bunzip2 command
bzcat command
bzgrep command
bzip2 command
bzless command
bzmore command
checksum
compress command
compression

compression algorithm
compression ratio
cpio (copy in/out) command
curl (client for URLs) command
dd command
Debian Package Manager (DPM)
differential backup
dnf (Dandified YUM) command
dpkg command
dpkg-query command
dpkg-reconfigure command
dump command
Filesystem in Userspace (FUSE)
Flatpak
flatpak command
full backup
gcc (GNU C Compiler) command
gzip (GNU zip) command
gunzip command
image backup

incremental backup
ldconfig command
ldd command
offsite backup
package dependency
package group
Red Hat Package Manager (RPM)
restore command
rpm command
rpm2cpio command
shared library
Snap
snap command
software mirror
software repository
Software utility
system backup
tar (tape archive) command
uncompress command
unxz command

`unzip` command	`xzless` command	`zgrep` command
`wget` (web get) command	`xzmore` command	`zip` command
`xz` command	`yum` (Yellowdog Updater Modified)	`zless` command
`xzcat` command	command	`zmore` command
`xzgrep` command	`zcat` command	`zypper` command

Review Questions

1. Most source code is typically available on the Internet in tarball format or as a git repository.
   a. True
   b. False

2. Which of the following are package managers that can be used to install sandboxed applications? (Choose all that apply.)
   a. Snap
   b. RPM
   c. Flatpak
   d. DPM

3. Which filename extension indicates a tarball?
   a. .tar.xz
   b. .cpio
   c. .dump
   d. .tar

4. Files that have been compressed using the xz utility typically have the _____ extension.
   a. .zip
   b. .gz
   c. .xz
   d. .bz2

5. AppImage applications have a .app extension and can be executed directly on a system.
   a. True
   b. False

6. When compiling source code into a binary program, which command does the compiling of the program itself?
   a. `tar`
   b. `./configure`
   c. `make`
   d. `make install`

7. The `-9` option to the gzip command results in a higher compression ratio.
   a. True
   b. False

8. You have created a full backup and four incremental backups using `dump`. In which order must you restore these backups based on their dump level?
   a. 0,1,2,3,4
   b. 0,4,3,2,1
   c. 4,3,2,1,0
   d. 1,2,3,4,0

9. Which of the following commands extracts an archive?
   a. `cpio -vocBL archive.cpio`
   b. `cpio -vicdu -I archive.cpio`
   c. `cpio -vicdu -O archive.cpio`
   d. `cpio -vti -I archive.cpio`

10. The Debian Package Manager (DPM) is the default package manager used by Ubuntu Linux.
    a. True
    b. False

11. Which of the following commands can be used to list the files contained within an installed RPM package?
    a. `rpm -qa packagename`
    b. `rpm -qi packagename`
    c. `rpm -ql packagename`
    d. `rpm -q packagename`

12. Which of the following commands can be used to remove the test DPM package, including any test configuration files?
    a. `dpkg remove test`
    b. `apt remove test`
    c. `dpkg purge test`
    d. `apt purge test`

13. To install a new program from RPM software repositories on the Internet, you can use the `dnf get programname` command.
    a. True
    b. False

14. Which command can be used to create an image backup of a partition?
    a. `tar`
    b. `dd`
    c. `dump`
    d. `cpio`

15. Which of the following commands should be run following the installation of a shared library to update the /etc/ld.so.conf and /etc/ld.so.cache files?
    a. `ldd`
    b. `updatedb`
    c. `ldconfig`
    d. `dpkg-reconfigure`

16. Which option to the `dpkg` command can be used to list the files that comprise a package?
    a. `-l`
    b. `-L`
    c. `-s`
    d. `-i`

17. Which option to the `rpm` command can be used to remove a package from the system?
    a. `-r`
    b. `-e`
    c. `-u`
    d. `-U`

18. Which of the following commands creates an archive?
    a. `tar -cvf /dev/st0`
    b. `tar -xvf /dev/st0`
    c. `tar -tvf /dev/st0`
    d. `tar -zcvf /dev/st0 *`

19. Which command will list the Flatpak applications available on a remote Flatpak repository?
    a. `flatpak remote-ls`
    b. `flatpak info`
    c. `flatpak list`
    d. `flatpak query`

20. Which of the following commands can be used to search for packages that contain the word "oobla" on RPM software repositories?
    a. `dnf search oobla`
    b. `rpm -qS oobla`
    c. `dnf list oobla`
    d. `rpm -ql oobla`

Hands-On Projects

These projects should be completed in the order given. The hands-on projects presented in this chapter should take a total of three hours to complete. The requirements for this lab include:

- A computer with Fedora Linux installed according to Hands-On Project 2-1 and Ubuntu Linux installed according to Hands-On Project 6-1.

Project 11-1

Estimated Time: 25 minutes
Objective: Use compression utilities.
Description: In this hands-on project, you use common compression utilities to compress and uncompress information on Fedora Linux.

1. Boot your Fedora Linux virtual machine. After your Linux system has been loaded, switch to a command-line terminal (tty5) by pressing **Ctrl+Alt+F5** and log in to the terminal using the user name of **root** and the password of **LINUXrocks!**.

2. At the command prompt, type `dnf install ncompress` and press **Enter**. Press y when prompted to complete the installation of the ncompress RPM package (and any package dependencies).

3. At the command prompt, type `cp /etc/services ~` and press **Enter** to make a copy of the /etc/ services file in your home directory. Next, type `ls -l services` at the command prompt and press **Enter**. Note the size of the services file.

4. At the command prompt, type `compress -v services` and press **Enter** to compress the services file. Note the compression ratio. Next, type `ls -l services.Z` at the command prompt and press **Enter**. Note the size of the services.Z file. Is it smaller than the original services file from Step 3?

5. At the command prompt, type `uncompress -v services.Z` and press **Enter** to decompress the services file.

6. At the command prompt, type `mkdir compresstest; cp /etc/hosts /etc/services compresstest` and press **Enter** to create a subdirectory called compresstest and copy the /etc/hosts and /etc/services files to it.

7. At the command prompt, type `compress -vr compresstest` and press **Enter** to compress the contents of the compresstest subdirectory. Next, type `ls -l compresstest` at the command prompt and press **Enter** to view the contents of the compresstest directory. Which files were compressed? If there were symbolic links in this directory, how could you force the compress utility to compress these files as well?

8. At the command prompt, type `uncompress -vr compresstest` and press **Enter** to decompress the contents of the compresstest subdirectory.

9. At the command prompt, type `ps -ef | compress -v >psfile.Z` and press **Enter** to compress the output of the `ps -ef` command to a file called psfile.Z. Note the compression ratio.

10. At the command prompt, type `zless psfile.Z` and press **Enter** to view the compressed contents of the psfile.Z file. When finished, press **q** to quit the more utility.

11. At the command prompt, type `zip -v compresstest.zip compresstest/*` and press **Enter** to compress the contents of the compresstest subdirectory into a single compresstest.zip file. Note the overall compression ratio.

12. At the command prompt, type `unzip -v compresstest.zip` and press **Enter** to view the contents of compresstest.zip. Next, type `unzip compresstest.zip` and press **Enter** to extract the contents of compresstest.zip. Press **A** when prompted to overwrite all existing files during decompression.

13. At the command prompt, type `gzip -v services` and press **Enter** to compress the services file. Note the compression ratio. How does this ratio compare to the one obtained in Step 4? Why? Next, type `ls -l services.gz` at the command prompt and press **Enter**. Note the file size.

14. At the command prompt, type `gunzip -v services.gz` and press **Enter** to decompress the services file.

15. At the command prompt, type `gzip -v -9 services` and press **Enter** to compress the services file. Was the compression ratio better than Step 13?

16. At the command prompt, type `gunzip -v services.gz` and press **Enter** to decompress the services file.

17. At the command prompt, type `gzip -v -1 services` and press **Enter** to compress the services file. Was the compression ratio worse than Step 13?

18. At the command prompt, type `gunzip -v services.gz` and press **Enter** to decompress the services file.

19. At the command prompt, type `xz -v -9 services` and press **Enter** to compress the services file. Was the compression ratio better than in Step 15? Why?

20. At the command prompt, type `unxz -v services.xz` and press **Enter** to decompress the services file.

21. At the command prompt, type `bzip2 -v services` and press **Enter** to compress the services file. Note the compression ratio. How does this compare to the ratios from Step 4, Step 13, and Step 19? Next, type `ls -l services.bz2` at the command prompt and press **Enter**. Note the file size.

22. At the command prompt, type `bunzip2 -v services.bz2` and press **Enter** to decompress the services file.

23. Type `exit` and press **Enter** to log out of your shell.

Project 11-2

Estimated Time: 20 minutes

Objective: Use `tar` archives.

Description: In this hands-on project, you create, view, and extract archives using the `tar` utility.

1. On your Fedora Linux virtual machine, switch to a command-line terminal (tty5) by pressing **Ctrl+Alt+F5** and log in to the terminal using the user name of **root** and the password of **LINUXrocks!**.

2. At the command prompt, type `tar -cvf test1.tar /etc/samba` and press **Enter** to create an archive called test1.tar in the current directory that contains the /etc/samba directory and its contents. Next, type `ls -l test1.tar` at the command prompt and press **Enter**. Note the size of the test1.tar file.

3. At the command prompt, type `tar -tvf test1.tar` and press **Enter**. What is displayed?

4. At the command prompt, type `mkdir /new1` and press **Enter**. Next, type `cd /new1` at the command prompt and press **Enter** to change the current directory to the /new1 directory.

5. At the command prompt, type `tar -xvf /root/test1.tar` and press **Enter** to extract the contents of the test1.tar archive. Next, type `ls -RF` at the command prompt and press **Enter** to view the contents of the /new1 directory. Was the extraction successful?

6. At the command prompt, type `cd` and press **Enter** to return to your home directory.

7. At the command prompt, type `tar -zcvf test2.tar.gz /etc/samba` and press **Enter** to create a `gzip`-compressed archive called test2.tar.gz in the current directory that contains the /etc/samba directory and its contents. Next, type `ls -l test2.tar.gz` at the command prompt and press **Enter**. Is the file size smaller than for test1.tar in Step 2? Why?

8. At the command prompt, type `tar -ztvf test2.tar.gz` and press **Enter**. What is displayed?

9. At the command prompt, type `mkdir /new2` and press **Enter**. Next, type `cd /new2` at the command prompt and press **Enter** to change the current directory to the /new2 directory.

10. At the command prompt, type `tar -zxvf /root/test2.tar.gz` and press **Enter** to uncompress and extract the contents of the test2.tar.gz archive. Next, type `ls -RF` at the command prompt and press **Enter** to view the contents of the /new2 directory. Was the extraction successful?

11. At the command prompt, type `cd` and press **Enter** to return to your home directory.

12. At the command prompt, type `rm -Rf /new[12]` and press **Enter** to remove the directories created in this hands-on project.

13. At the command prompt, type `rm -f test*` and press **Enter** to remove the tar archives created in this hands-on project.

14. Type `exit` and press **Enter** to log out of your shell.

Project 11-3

Estimated Time: 25 minutes
Objective: Manage `cpio`, `dump`, and `dd` archives.
Description: In this hands-on project, you create, view, and extract archives using the `cpio`, `dump`, and `dd` utilities.

1. On your Fedora Linux virtual machine, switch to a command-line terminal (tty5) by pressing **Ctrl+Alt+F5** and log in to the terminal using the user name of **root** and the password of **LINUXrocks!**.

2. At the command prompt, type `find /etc/samba | cpio -ovcBL -O test.cpio` and press **Enter** to create an archive in the file test.cpio that contains the /etc/samba directory and its contents. What does each option indicate in the aforementioned command?

3. At the command prompt, type `cpio -ivtB -I test.cpio` and press **Enter**. What is displayed? What does each option indicate in the aforementioned command?

4. At the command prompt, type `cpio -ivcdumB -I test.cpio` and press **Enter** to extract the contents of the archive in the test.cpio file. To what location were the files extracted? Were any files overwritten? What does each option indicate in the aforementioned command?

5. At the command prompt, type `dnf install dump` and press **Enter**. Press **y** when prompted to complete the installation of the dump RPM package (and any package dependencies).

6. At the command prompt, type `df -hT` and press **Enter**. Note the device file for the /boot filesystem. Next, type `dump -0uf test.dump file` and press **Enter**, where *file* is the device file for the /boot filesystem to create an archive of the /boot filesystem in the archive file test.dump. What type of backup was performed? Will the /etc/dumpdates file be updated?

7. At the command prompt, type `cat /etc/dumpdates` and press **Enter**. Does the file indicate your full backup and time?

8. At the command prompt, type `mkdir /new` and press **Enter**. Next, type `cd /new` at the command prompt and press **Enter** to change the current directory to the /new directory.

9. At the command prompt, type `restore -rf /root/test.dump` and press **Enter**.

10. Type `ls -F` at the command prompt and press **Enter** to view the contents of the /new directory. Was your backup restored successfully to this alternate location? Were absolute or relative pathnames used during the restore operation?

11. At the command prompt, type `cd` and press **Enter** to return to your home directory.

12. At the command prompt, type `dd if=file of=test.img` and press **Enter**, where *file* is the device file for the /boot filesystem to create an image backup of your /boot filesystem.

13. At the command prompt, type `ls -l test.img test.dump` and press **Enter**. Why is the test.img file much larger than the test.dump file, even though both were used to back up the /boot filesystem?

14. At the command prompt, type `rm -Rf /new` and press **Enter** to remove the directory created in this hands-on project.

15. At the command prompt, type `rm -f test*` and press **Enter** to remove the archives created in this hands-on project.

16. Type **exit** and press **Enter** to log out of your shell.

Project 11-4

Estimated Time: 20 minutes

Objective: Compile software from source code.

Description: In this hands-on project, you compile and install the `nms` (no-more-secrets) and `sneakers` programs depicted in the 1992 movie Sneakers.

1. On your Fedora Linux virtual machine, switch to a command-line terminal (tty5) by pressing **Ctrl+Alt+F5** and log in to the terminal using the user name of **root** and the password of **LINUXrocks!**.

2. At the command prompt, type `dnf groupinstall "Development Tools" -y` and press **Enter** to install the compiler tools from a software repository.

3. At the command prompt, type `git clone https://github.com/bartobri/no-more-secrets.git` and press **Enter** to clone the source code repository for the `sneakers` and `nms` (no-more-secrets) programs from GitHub.

4. At the command prompt, type `cd no-more-secrets` and press **Enter**. Next, type `ls -F` at the command prompt and press **Enter**. Why is no configure script present? Are there README and INSTALL files present?

5. At the command prompt, type `less README.md` and press **Enter**. Read the Install section, noting the commands needed to install the programs.

6. At the command prompt, type `make nms` and press **Enter**. Next, type `make sneakers` and press **Enter**. Note that the `make` command compiles the program using the GNU C compiler (/usr/bin/cc is a symbolic link to /usr/bin/gcc).

7. At the command prompt, type `make install` and press **Enter**. What does this command do?

8. At the command prompt, type **cd** and press **Enter** to return to your home directory. Next, type `rm -Rf no-more-secrets` to remove the cloned GitHub repository as it is no longer needed.

9. At the command prompt, type **which nms sneakers** and press **Enter**. Which directory contains the nms and sneakers executable programs? Is a central database updated with this information?

10. At the command prompt, type **man nms** and press **Enter**. View the available options for the nms command and press **q** to quit when finished.

11. At the command prompt, type **man sneakers** and press **Enter**. View the description for the sneakers command and press **q** to quit when finished.

12. At the command prompt, type **sneakers** and press **Enter**. Press any key to decrypt the screen contents and then press **q** to quit.

13. At the command prompt, type **ls -l | nms** and press **Enter**. Press any key to decrypt the screen contents.

14. Type **exit** and press **Enter** to log out of your shell.

Project 11-5

Estimated Time: 20 minutes
Objective: Use the RPM.
Description: In this hands-on project, you query, remove, and install the ncompress and sl RPM packages.

1. On your Fedora Linux virtual machine, switch to a command-line terminal (tty5) by pressing **Ctrl+Alt+F5** and log in to the terminal using the user name of **root** and the password of **LINUXrocks!**.

2. At the command prompt, type **rpm -qa | less** and press **Enter** to view the RPM packages installed on your computer. Are there many of them? Briefly scroll through the list and press **q** when finished to exit the less utility.

3. At the command prompt, type **rpm -q ncompress** and press **Enter**. Is the ncompress RPM package installed on your computer? When did you install it?

4. At the command prompt, type **rpm -qi ncompress** and press **Enter** to view the information about the ncompress RPM package. What license does this package use?

5. At the command prompt, type **rpm -ql ncompress** and press **Enter** to view the locations of all files that belong to the ncompress package. What directory holds the compress and uncompress executables?

6. At the command prompt, type **ldd /usr/bin/compress** and press **Enter** to view the shared libraries needed by /usr/bin/compress. Were any libraries marked as not found?

7. At the command prompt, type **rpm -e ncompress** and press **Enter**. What does this option to the rpm command do?

8. At the command prompt, type **rpm -q ncompress** and press **Enter**. Is the ncompress RPM package installed?

9. At the command prompt, type **dnf search ncompress** and press **Enter**. Is the ncompress RPM package listed?

10. At the command prompt, type **dnf list available | grep ncompress** and press **Enter**. Is the ncompress RPM package available for installation from a software repository?

11. At the command prompt, type **dnf install ncompress -y** and press **Enter**. Next, type **rpm -q ncompress** and press **Enter** to verify that the installation completed successfully.

12. At the command prompt, type **dnf install sl -y** and press **Enter**.

13. At the command prompt, type **rpm -qi sl** and press **Enter** to learn about the sl package. Next, type **rpm -ql sl** and press **Enter** to view the files within the package. Where is the single executable program located?

14. At the command prompt, type **sl** and press **Enter** to run the sl command. Next, type **rpm -e sl** and press **Enter** to remove the sl package.

15. Type **exit** and press **Enter** to log out of your shell.

Project 11-6

Estimated Time: 20 minutes

Objective: Use the DPM.

Description: In this hands-on project, you install, query, and remove the ncompress and hollywood DPM packages.

1. Boot your Ubuntu Linux virtual machine, and log into tty1 using the user name of **root** and the password of **LINUXrocks!**.

2. At the command prompt, type `dpkg -l | less` and press **Enter** to view the DPM packages installed on your computer. Are there many of them? Briefly scroll through the list and press q when finished to exit the less utility.

3. At the command prompt, type `dpkg -l ncompress` and press **Enter**. Is the ncompress DPM package installed on your computer?

4. At the command prompt, type `apt-cache search compress | grep ncompress` and press **Enter**. Is ncompress listed? What other command can be used instead of apt-cache to search for programs within online repositories?

5. At the command prompt, type `apt install ncompress -y` and press **Enter** to install the ncompress DPM package from a software repository. What other command could you have used to perform the same action?

6. At the command prompt, type `dpkg -L ncompress` and press **Enter** to list the files that comprise the ncompress package. Next, type `dpkg -l ncompress` at the command prompt and press **Enter** to view the detailed information about the ncompress package.

7. At the command prompt, type `apt purge ncompress -y` and press **Enter**. What does the purge option do? What other command could you have used to perform the same action?

8. At the command prompt, type `apt install hollywood -y` and press **Enter** to install the hollywood package and its dependencies.

9. At the command prompt, type `dpkg -L hollywood` and press **Enter** to list the files that comprise the hollywood package. Next, type `dpkg -l hollywood` at the command prompt and press **Enter** to view the detailed information about the hollywood package.

10. At the command prompt, type `hollywood` and press **Enter** to run the hollywood program. After a few minutes, press **Ctrl+c** twice to quit the program.

11. At the command prompt, type `apt purge hollywood -y` and press **Enter**.

12. Type `exit` and press **Enter** to log out of your shell.

Project 11-7

Estimated Time: 15 minutes

Objective: Configure Snap packages.

Description: In this hands-on project, you install and explore the Snap application for Microsoft PowerShell.

1. On your Ubuntu Linux virtual machine, log into tty1 using the user name of **root** and the password of **LINUXrocks!**.

2. At the command prompt, type `snap search powershell` and press **Enter**. Is Microsoft PowerShell available for Linux systems?

3. At the command prompt, type `snap install powershell --classic` and press **Enter** to install the Microsoft PowerShell application from the Snap repository.

4. At the command prompt, type `snap list` and press **Enter**. What Snap applications are currently installed on your system?

5. At the command prompt, type `snap info powershell` and press **Enter**. What command represents the Microsoft PowerShell application?

6. At the command prompt, type `powershell` and press **Enter** to start Microsoft PowerShell. At the PS prompt, type `Get-Host` and press **Enter** to view your PowerShell version information. Next, type `exit` and press **Enter** to exit Microsoft PowerShell.

7. Type `exit` and press **Enter** to log out of your shell.

Project 11-8

Estimated Time: 20 minutes
Objective: Configure Flatpak packages.
Description: In this hands-on project, you install and explore the Flatpak application for the Microsoft Teams application.

1. On your Fedora Linux virtual machine, switch to a command-line terminal (tty5) by pressing **Ctrl+Alt+F5** and log in to the terminal using the user name of **root** and the password of **LINUXrocks!**.

2. At the command prompt, type `flatpak remote-add flathub https://flathub.org/repo/flathub.flatpakrepo` and press **Enter** to add the flathub Flatpak repository. Next, type `flatpak remote-modify --enable flathub` and press **Enter** to enable the repository.

3. At the command prompt, type `flatpak remote-ls | grep Teams` and press **Enter** to search the remote flathub repository using the Teams keyword. Is a Microsoft Teams application available in flathub?

4. At the command prompt, type `flatpak install flathub com.microsoft.Teams` and press **Enter** to install the Teams application maintained by microsoft.com.

5. At the command prompt, type `flatpak info com.microsoft.Teams` and press **Enter** to view the description and version information for the Microsoft Teams application. Next, type `flatpak list` and press **Enter** to view the Flatpak applications installed on the system.

6. Type `exit` and press **Enter** to log out of your shell. Next, switch to tty1 by pressing **Ctrl+Alt+F1** and log in to the GNOME desktop using your user name and the password of **LINUXrocks!**.

7. In the GNOME desktop, click the **Activities** menu, select the **Show Applications** icon, and click **Microsoft Teams**. If you have a Microsoft account, optionally log into Microsoft Teams and explore the features available. When finished, close the Microsoft Teams application and log out of the GNOME desktop.

Project 11-9

Estimated Time: 15 minutes
Objective: Configure AppImage packages.
Description: In this hands-on project, you install and explore the AppImage application for the Conky system monitoring tool.

1. On your Fedora Linux virtual machine, switch to tty1 by pressing **Ctrl+Alt+F1** and log in to the GNOME desktop using your user name and the password of **LINUXrocks!**.

2. In the GNOME desktop, click the **Activities** menu, select the **Show Applications** icon, and click **Firefox**. In the Firefox web browser, navigate to **appimagehub.com** and search for **conky**. Select the Conky system monitoring tool and click the download icon in the Files section to download the Conky AppImage application to your Downloads folder. Close Firefox when finished.

3. In the GNOME desktop, click the **Activities** menu, select the **Show Applications** icon, and click **Terminal** to open a shell in your GNOME desktop.

4. At the command prompt, type `chmod +x Downloads/conky*.AppImage` to add execute permission to the Conky sandbox file.

5. At the command prompt, type `Downloads/conky*.AppImage &` to run the Conky application in the background. Did it run successfully?

6. At the command prompt, type `kill %1` to stop the Conky application running as the first background job.

7. Type `exit` and press **Enter** to log out of your shell.

Discovery Exercises

Discovery Exercise 11-1

Estimated Time: 20 minutes
Objective: Use compression utilities.
Description: Write the command that can be used to perform the following:

    a. Compress the symbolic link /root/sfile using the compress utility and display the compression ratio.

    b. Compress the contents of the directory /root/dir1 using the gzip utility and display the compression ratio.

    c. View the contents of the file /root/letter.zip.

    d. Compress the file /root/letter using xz fast compression.

    e. Find the compression ratio of the file /root/letter.gz.

    f. Perform a test compression of the file /root/sample using the bzip2 utility.

    g. Compress the file /root/sample using the bzip2 utility while minimizing memory usage during the compression.

Discovery Exercise 11-2

Estimated Time: 30 minutes
Objective: Use archives.
Description: Write the command that can be used to perform the following:

    a. Back up the contents of the /var directory (which contains symbolically linked files) to the second nonrewinding SCSI tape device on the system using the tar utility.

    b. Append the file /etc/inittab to the archive created in Exercise 2a.

    c. Create a tarball called /stuff.tar.gz that contains all files in the /root/stuff directory.

    d. Use the cpio utility to back up all files in the /var directory (which contains symbolically linked files) to the first rewinding IDE tape device that has a block size of 5 KB.

    e. Perform a full filesystem backup of the /var filesystem using the dump utility and record the event in the /etc/dumpdates file.

    f. Create an image of the /dev/sdb4 filesystem to the /sdb4.img file.

    g. View the contents of the archives created in Exercises 2a, 2c, 2d, and 2e.

    h. Extract the contents of the archives created in Exercises 2a and 2c to the /root directory.

    i. Extract the contents of the archives created in Exercises 2d and 2e to their original locations.

    j. Restore the image of the /dev/sdb4 filesystem created in Exercise 2f.

Discovery Exercise 11-3

Estimated Time: 40 minutes
Objective: Use the DPM.
Description: Install and explore the graphical Aptitude tool on your Ubuntu Linux virtual machine. Next, use Aptitude to search for and install Cockpit (a remote web admin tool that is commonly installed on Linux servers). After Cockpit has been installed, run the **ip addr show** command to determine the IP address of your Ubuntu system. Next, navigate to **http://IP:9090** within a web browser on your Windows or macOS system, where *IP* is the IP address of your Ubuntu system. Log in as the root user and explore the functionality provided by Cockpit.

Discovery Exercise 11-4

Estimated Time: 30 minutes

Objective: Use the RPM.

Description: On your Fedora Linux virtual machine, log into a GNOME desktop and use your Firefox web browser to download the xbill (a graphical game) RPM package for your version of Fedora from fedora.pkgs.org. Use the Files application to open and install your RPM package using the Software utility, which will download any dependencies necessary for the xbill package. Finally, use the appropriate rpm and dnf commands to explore the installed program and execute the xbill program within a graphical terminal, as well as using the application icon within the GNOME desktop.

Discovery Exercise 11-5

Estimated Time: 90 minutes

Objective: Use the RPM on openSUSE.

Description: Download the installation ISO image for the latest openSUSE Leap Linux distribution for your architecture from opensuse.org. Next, create and install a new virtual machine called openSUSE Linux from this ISO image that uses 4 GB of memory (not dynamically allocated), an Internet connection via your PC's network card (preferably using an external virtual switch or bridged mode), and a 50 GB SATA/SAS/SCSI virtual hard disk drive (dynamically allocated). Following installation, explore the man page for the zypper command. Are the options similar to yum and dnf? Search for and install a software package of your choice using the zypper command from an Internet software repository. Next, use the appropriate zypper and rpm commands to view package information. Finally use the zypper command to remove your package.

Chapter 12

Network Configuration

Chapter Objectives

1 Describe the purpose and types of networks, protocols, and media access methods.

2 Explain the basic configuration of IP.

3 Configure a network interface to use IP.

4 Configure a PPP interface.

5 Describe the purpose of host names and how they are resolved to IP addresses.

6 Configure IP routing.

7 Identify common network services.

8 Use command-line and graphical utilities to perform remote administration.

Throughout this book, you have examined the installation and administration of local Linux services. This chapter focuses on configuring Linux to participate on a network. First, you become acquainted with some common network terminology, then you learn about IP and the procedure for configuring a network interface. Next, you learn about the Domain Name Space and the processes by which host names are resolved to IP addresses. Finally, you learn how to configure IP routing as well as how to set up and use various utilities to perform remote administration of a Linux system.

Networks

Most functions that computers perform today involve the sharing of information between computers. Information is usually transmitted from computer to computer via media such as fiber optic, telephone, coaxial, or unshielded twisted pair (UTP) cable, but it can also be transmitted via wireless media such as radio, micro, or infrared waves. These media typically interact directly with a peripheral device on the computer, such as a network interface or modem.

Two or more computers connected via media that can exchange information are called a **network**. Networks that connect computers within close proximity are called **local area networks (LANs)**, whereas networks that connect computers separated by large distances are called **wide area networks (WANs)**.

Many companies use LANs to allow employees to connect to databases and other shared resources such as shared files and printers. Home users can also use LANs to connect several home computers together. Alternatively, home users can use a WAN to connect home computers to an Internet service provider (ISP) to gain access to resources such as websites on the worldwide public network called the Internet.

Note 1

The Internet (the name is short for "internetwork") is merely several interconnected public networks. Both home and company networks can be part of the Internet. Recall from Chapter 1 that special computers called routers transfer information from one network to another.

Network media serve as the conduit for information as it travels across a network. But sending information through this conduit is not enough. For devices on the network to make sense of this information, it must be organized according to a set of rules, or protocols. A network **protocol** breaks information down into **packets** that can be recognized by workstations, routers, and other devices on a network.

While you can configure many network protocols in Linux, nearly all Linux computers use the following three protocols by default:

- **Transmission Control Protocol/Internet Protocol (TCP/IP)**, which provides reliable communication of packets across the Internet.
- **User Datagram Protocol/Internet Protocol (UDP/IP)**, which provides fast, yet unreliable communication of packets across the Internet.
- **Internet Control Message Protocol (ICMP)**, which is used to send network-related information and error messages across the Internet.

Note 2

While both TCP/IP and UDP/IP can send information packets across the Internet, TCP/IP is the most common network protocol used today, and the one that we'll focus on within this chapter.

Note 3

When transmitting information across a WAN, you might use a WAN protocol in addition to a specific LAN protocol to format packets for safer transmission. The most common WAN protocol is **Point-to-Point Protocol (PPP)**.

Another important part of the puzzle, the **media access method**, is a set of rules that govern how the various devices on the network share the network media. The media access method is usually contained within the hardware on the network interface or modem. Although many media access methods are available, the one most used to send packets onto network media is called **Ethernet**. It ensures that any packets are retransmitted onto the network if a network error occurs.

Note 4

Wireless-Fidelity (Wi-Fi) LANs also use Ethernet to place packets onto the network medium (in this case, the air).

The IP Protocol

TCP/IP is actually a set, or suite, of protocols with two core components: TCP and IP. Together, these two protocols ensure that information packets travel across a network as quickly as possible, without getting lost or mislabeled.

When you transfer information across a network such as the Internet, that information is often divided into many thousands of small IP packets. Each of these packets may take a different physical route when reaching its destination as routers can transfer information to multiple interconnected networks. TCP ensures that packets can be assembled in the correct order at their destination regardless of the order in which they arrive. Additionally, TCP ensures that any lost packets are retransmitted.

> ## Note 5
>
> UDP is an alternative to TCP that does not provide packet ordering or retransmission.

IP is responsible for labeling each packet with the destination address. Recall from Chapter 1 that each computer that participates on an IP network must have a valid Internet Protocol (IP) address that identifies itself to the IP protocol. Many computers on the Internet use a version of the IP protocol called IP version 4 (IPv4). However, nearly all IoT devices and an increasing number of computers now use a next-generation IP protocol called IP version 6 (IPv6). We will examine the structure and configuration of IPv4 and IPv6 in this chapter.

The IPv4 Protocol

To participate on an IPv4 network, your computer must have a valid IP address as well as a subnet mask. Optionally, you can configure a default gateway to participate on larger networks such as the Internet.

IPv4 Addresses

An IP address is a unique number assigned to the computer that identifies itself on the network, similar to a unique postal address that identifies your location in the world. If any two computers on the same network have the same IP address, it is impossible for information to be correctly delivered to them. Directed communication from one computer to another single computer using IP is referred to as a unicast.

The most common format for IPv4 addresses is four numbers called octets that are separated by periods. Each octet represents an 8-bit binary number (0–255). An example of an IP address in this notation is 192.168.5.69.

You can convert between decimal and binary by recognizing that an 8-bit binary number represents the decimal binary powers of two in the following order:

```
128 64 32 16 8 4 2 1
```

Thus, the number 255 is 11111111 (128+64+32+16+8+4+2+1) in binary, and the number 69 is 01000101 (64+4+1) in binary. When the computer looks at an IP address, the numbers are converted to binary. To learn more about binary/decimal number conversion, visit wikihow.com/Convert-from-Decimal-to-Binary.

All IPv4 addresses are composed of two parts: the network ID and the host ID. The network ID represents the network on which the computer is located, whereas the host ID represents a single computer on that network. No two computers on the same network can have the same host ID; however, two computers on different networks can have the same host ID.

The network ID and the host ID are similar to postal mailing addresses, which are made up of a street name and a house number. The street name is like a network ID. No two streets in the same city can have the same name, just as no two networks can have the same network ID. The host ID is like the house number. Two houses can have the same house number as long as they are on different streets, just as two computers can have the same host ID as long as they are on different networks.

Only computers with the same network ID can communicate with each other without the use of a router. This allows administrators to logically separate computers on a network; computers in the Accounting Department could use one network ID, whereas computers in the Sales Department could use a different network number. If the two departments are connected by a router, computers in the Accounting Department can communicate with computers in the Sales Department and vice versa.

Note 6

If your IP network is not connected to the Internet, the choice of IP address is entirely up to you. However, if your network is connected to the Internet, you might need to use preselected IP addresses for the computers on your network. IP addresses that can be used on the public Internet are assigned by your Internet service provider.

Note 7

The IP address 127.0.0.1 is called the loopback IP address. It always refers to the local computer. In other words, on your computer, 127.0.0.1 refers to your computer. On your coworker's computer, 127.0.0.1 refers to your coworker's computer.

Subnet Masks

Each computer with an IPv4 address must also be configured with a subnet mask to define which part of its IP address is the network ID and which part is the host ID. Subnet masks are composed of four octets, just like an IP address. The simplest subnet masks use only the values 0 and 255. An octet in a subnet mask containing 255 is part of the network ID. An octet in a subnet mask containing 0 is part of the host ID. Your computer uses the binary process called ANDing to find the network ID. ANDing is a mathematical operation that compares two binary digits and gives a result of 1 or 0. If both binary digits being compared have a value of 1, the result is 1. If one digit is 0 and the other is 1, or if both digits are 0, the result is 0.

When an IP address is ANDed with a subnet mask, the result is the network ID. Figure 12-1 shows an example of how the network ID and host ID of an IP address can be calculated using the subnet mask.

Thus, the IP address shown in Figure 12-1 identifies the first computer (host portion 0.1) on the 144.58 network (network portion 144.58).

Figure 12-1   A sample IP address and subnet mask

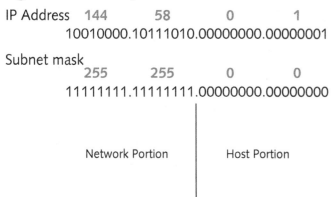

IP Address   144   58   0   1
              10010000.10111010.00000000.00000001

Subnet mask
        255   255   0   0
          11111111.11111111.00000000.00000000

Network Portion   Host Portion

Note 8

IP addresses and their subnet masks are often written using the classless interdomain routing (CIDR) notation. For example, the notation 144.58.0.1/16 refers to the IP address 144.58.0.1 with a 16-bit subnet mask (255.255.0.0).

The IP addresses 0.0.0.0 and 255.255.255.255 cannot be assigned to a host computer because they refer to all networks and all computers on all networks, respectively. Similarly, using the number 255 (all 1s in binary format) in an IP address can specify many hosts. For example, the IP address 192.168.131.255 refers to all hosts on the 192.168.131 network; this IP address is also called the broadcast address for the 192.168.131 network.

Note 9

A computer uses its IP address and subnet mask to determine what network it is on. If two computers are on the same network, they can deliver packets directly to each other. If two computers are on different networks, they must use a router to communicate.

Default Gateway

Typically, all computers on a LAN are configured with the same network ID and different host IDs. A LAN can connect to another LAN by means of a router, which has IP addresses for both LANs and can forward packets to and from each network. Each computer on a LAN can contain the IP address of a router in its IP configuration; any packets that are not destined for the local LAN are then sent to the router, which can forward the packet to the appropriate network or to another router. The IP address of the network interface on the router to which you send packets is called the default gateway.

A router is often a dedicated hardware device from a vendor such as Cisco, D-Link, or HP. Other times, a router is a computer with multiple network cards. The one consistent feature of routers, regardless of the manufacturer, is that they can distinguish between different networks and move (or route) packets between them. A router has an IP address on every network to which it is attached. When a computer sends a packet to the default gateway for further delivery, the address of the router must be on the same network as the computer, as computers can send packets directly to devices only on their own network.

IPv4 Classes and Subnetting

IPv4 addresses are divided into classes to make them easier to manage. The class of an IP address defines the default subnet mask of the device using that address. All the IP address classes can be identified by the first octet of the address, as shown in Table 12-1.

Table 12-1 IP address classes

Class	Subnet Mask	First Octet	Maximum Number of Networks	Maximum Number of Hosts	Example IP Address
A	255.0.0.0	1–127	127	16,777,214	3.4.1.99
B	255.255.0.0	128–191	16,384	65,534	144.129.188.1
C	255.255.255.0	192–223	2,097,152	254	192.168.1.1
D	N/A	224–239	N/A	N/A	224.0.2.1
E	N/A	240–254	N/A	N/A	N/A

Class A addresses use 8 bits for the network ID and 24 bits for the host ID. You can see this is true by looking at the subnet mask, 255.0.0.0. The value of the first octet will always be somewhere in the range 1 to 127. This means there are only 127 potential Class A networks available for the entire Internet. Class A networks are only assigned to very large companies and Internet providers.

Class B addresses, which are identified by the subnet mask 255.255.0.0, use 16 bits for the network ID and 16 bits for the host ID. The value of the first octet ranges from 128 to 191. There are 16,384 Class B networks, with 65,534 hosts on each network. Class B networks are assigned to many larger organizations, such as governments, universities, and companies with several thousand users.

Class C addresses, which are identified by the subnet mask 255.255.255.0, use 24 bits for the network ID and 8 bits for the host ID. The value of the first octet ranges from 192 to 223. There are 2,097,152 Class C networks, with 254 hosts on each network. Although there are very many Class C networks, they have a relatively small number of hosts; thus, they are suited only to smaller organizations.

Class D addresses are not divided into networks, and they cannot be assigned to computers as IP addresses; instead, Class D addresses are used for multicasting. Multicast addresses are used by groups of computers. A packet addressed to a multicast address is delivered to each computer in the multicast group. This is better than a broadcast message because routers can be configured to allow multicast traffic to move from one network to another. In addition, all computers on the network process broadcasts, while only computers that are part of that multicast group process multicasts. Streaming media and network conferencing software often use multicasting to communicate to several computers at once.

Like Class D addresses, Class E addresses are not typically assigned to a computer. Class E addresses are considered experimental and are reserved for future use.

Notice from Table 12-1 that Class A and B networks can have many thousands or millions of hosts on a single network. Because this is not practically manageable, Class A and B networks are typically subnetted. Subnetting is the process in which a single large network is subdivided into several smaller networks to control traffic flow and improve manageability. After a network has been subnetted, a router is required to move packets from one subnet to another.

Note 10

You can subnet any Class A, B, or C network.

To subnet a network, you take some bits from the host ID and give them to the network ID. Suppose, for example, that you want to divide the 3.0.0.0/8 network into 17 subnets. The binary representation of this network is:

```
3.0.0.0 = 00000011.00000000.00000000.00000000
255.0.0.0 = 11111111.00000000.00000000.00000000
```

You then borrow some bits from the host portion of the subnet mask. Because the number of combinations of binary numbers can be represented in binary powers of two, and because valid subnet masks do not contain all 0s or 1s, you can use the equation 2^n to represent the minimum number of subnets required, where n is the number of binary bits that are borrowed from the host portion of the subnet mask. For our example, this is represented as:

```
2ⁿ ≥ 15
```

Thus, $n = 4$ (because $2^3 = 8$ is less than 15, but $2^4 = 16$ is greater than 15). Following this, our subnet mask borrows four bits from the default Class A subnet mask:

```
255.240.0.0 = 11111111.11110000.00000000.00000000
```

Similarly, because there are 20 zeros in the preceding subnet mask, you can use the $2^n - 2$ equation to identify the number of hosts per subnet (the –2 accounts for the broadcast and network address for the subnet):

```
2²⁰ - 2 = number of hosts per subnet
        = 1,048,574 hosts per subnet
```

You can then work out the IP address ranges for each of the network ranges. Because four bits in the second octet were not borrowed during subnetting, the ranges of IP addresses that can be given to each subnet must be in ranges of $2^4 = 16$. Thus, the first five ranges that can be given to different subnets on the 3.0.0.0/8 network that use the subnet mask 255.240.0.0 are as follows:

```
3.0.0.1-3.15.255.254
3.16.0.1-3.31.255.254
3.32.0.1-3.47.255.254
3.48.0.1-3.63.255.254
3.64.0.1-3.79.255.254
```

From the preceding ranges, a computer with the IP address 3.34.0.6/12 cannot communicate directly with the computer 3.31.0.99/12 because they are on different subnets. To communicate, there must be a router between them.

Note 11

When subnetting a Class C network, ensure that you discard the first and last IP address in each range to account for the broadcast and network address for the subnet.

The IPv6 Protocol

As the Internet grew in the 1990s, ISPs realized that the number of IP addresses available using IPv4 was inadequate to accommodate future growth. As a result, the IPv6 protocol was designed in 1998 to accommodate far more IP addresses. IPv6 uses 128 bits to identify computers, whereas IPv4 only uses 32 bits (4 octets). This allows IPv6 to address up to 340,282,366,920,938,463,463,374,607,431, 768,211,456 (or 340 trillion trillion trillion) unique computers.

IPv6 IP addresses are written using 8 colon-delimited 16-bit hexadecimal numbers—for example, 2001:0db8:3c4d:0015:0000:0000:adb6:ef12. If an IPv6 IP address contains 0000 segments, they are often omitted in most notation, thus 2001:0db8:3c4d:0015:::adb6:ef12 is equivalent to 2001:0db8:3c4d: 0015:0000:0000:adb6:ef12. The IPv6 loopback address is 0000:0000:0000:0000:0000:0000:0000:0001, but it is often referred to as ::1 for simplicity.

Note 12

Unlike our traditional decimal numbering scheme, hexadecimal uses an expanded numbering system that includes the letters A through F in addition to the numbers 0–9. Thus, the number 10 is called A in hexadecimal, the number 11 is called B in hexadecimal, the number 12 is called C in hexadecimal, the number 13 is called D in hexadecimal, the number 14 is called E in hexadecimal, and the number 15 is called F in hexadecimal.

Although IPv6 addresses can be expressed several ways, the first half (64 bits) of an IPv6 address identifies your network (the network ID); the first 46 bits are typically assigned by your ISP and identify your organization uniquely on the public Internet, and the following 16 bits can be used to identify unique subnets within your organization. The last 64 bits of an IPv6 address is used to uniquely identify a computer in your LAN (the host ID) and is often generated from the unique hardware address on each computer's network interface.

Note 13

The hardware address on a network interface is a 48-bit hexadecimal number called the Media Access Control (MAC) address that is unique for each network interface manufactured. Ethernet translates IPv4- and IPv6-addressed packets into MAC-addressed frames before sending it to the nearest host or router.

Although all operating systems today support IPv6, it has not replaced IPv4 on most server and client computers because the addressing is more difficult to work with compared to IPv4. Instead, IPv6 has primarily allowed the plethora of IoT devices available today to participate on the Internet without affecting the available IPv4 address space. Some example IoT devices include the NEST smart thermostat and the Google Home personal assistant; both of which run the Linux operating system. IoT devices often use an automatically configured IPv6 address that can be accessed by an online app, and the IPv6 traffic they send is often encapsulated in IPv4 traffic using a protocol such as Teredo to allow it to work within IPv4-only networks.

This slow adoption of IPv6 among server and client computers is primarily the result of two technologies introduced in Chapter 1 that allow IPv4 to address many more computers than was previously possible: proxy servers and Network Address Translation (NAT) routers.

Proxy servers and NAT routers are computers or hardware devices that have an IP address and access to a network such as the Internet. Other computers on the network can use a proxy server or NAT router to obtain network or Internet resources on their behalf. Moreover, there are three reserved ranges of IPv4 addresses that are not distributed to computers on the Internet and are intended only for use behind a proxy server or NAT router:

- The entire 10.0.0.0 Class A network (10.0.0.0/8)
- The 172.16 through 172.31 Class B networks (172.16–31.0.0/16)
- The 192.168 Class C networks (192.168.0–255.0/24)

Thus, a computer behind a proxy server in Iceland and a computer behind a NAT router in Seattle could use the same IPv4 address—say, 10.0.5.4—without problems because each of these computers only requests Internet resources using its own proxy server or NAT router. A company may use a Cisco NAT router, for example, to allow other networks and computers in the company to gain access to the Internet. Similarly, a high-speed home Internet modem typically functions as a NAT router to allow multiple computers in your home to access the Internet.

Most computers in the world today obtain Internet access via a proxy server or NAT router. Because these computers share IPv4 addresses on a reserved network range, rather than using a unique IP address, the number of available IPv4 addresses has remained high and slowed the adoption of IPv6.

Configuring a Network Interface

Linux computers in a business environment typically connect to the company network via a wired or wireless network interface. At home, people typically connect to the Internet by means of a network interface, using technologies such as Fiber optic, cellular wireless, Wi-Fi, Digital Subscriber Line (DSL), and Broadband Cable Networks (BCNs).

Recall from Chapter 6 that network interface drivers are provided by modules that are inserted into the Linux kernel at boot time and given an alias that can be used to refer to the network interface afterwards. To view the driver modules and associated aliases for network interfaces in your system, you can use the `lshw -class network` command. On legacy Linux systems, the first wired Ethernet network interface is called eth0, the second wired Ethernet network interface is called eth1, and so on. Similarly, the first wireless Ethernet network interface on a legacy Linux system is called wlan0, the second wireless Ethernet network interface in your system is called wlan1, and so on. While this naming convention can also be used on modern Linux systems, some modern Linux distributions that use Systemd instead provide a more descriptive name that reflects the location of the hardware in the system. For example, enp0s3 refers to the wired Ethernet network interface on PCI bus 00 slot 03, and wlp8s0 refers to the wireless Ethernet network interface on PCI bus 08 slot 00. The information reflected by these names will match the PCI information displayed by the `lspci` command for the network interface hardware.

Note 14

You can also use the `ethtool` command to display detailed information for network hardware. For example, `ethtool -i enp0s3` will display driver information for the enp0s3 network interface.

After a driver module for a network interface has been loaded into the Linux kernel and given an alias, you can configure it to use IP. Legacy Linux systems use the UNIX `ifconfig (interface configuration)` command to assign an IP configuration to a network interface. For example, to assign eth0 the IPv4 address of 3.4.5.6 with a subnet mask of 255.0.0.0 and broadcast address of 3.255.255.255, you can use the `ifconfig eth0 3.4.5.6 netmask 255.0.0.0 broadcast 3.255.255.255` command. Modern Linux systems use the **ip command** to configure IP. For example, you can use the `ip addr add 3.4.5.6/8 dev eth0` command to configure eth0 with the IPv4 address 3.4.5.6 and an 8-bit subnet mask (255.0.0.0).

Note 15

You can install the net-tools package on a modern Linux distribution to obtain the `ipconfig` command or install the iproute or iproute2 package on a legacy Linux distribution to obtain the `ip` command.

Alternatively, you can receive IP configuration from a Dynamic Host Configuration Protocol (DHCP) or Boot Protocol (BOOTP) server on the network. To obtain and configure IP information from a server on the network, you can use the **dhclient command**; for example, `dhclient eth0` would attempt to obtain IP configuration from the network connected to eth0.

The process of obtaining an IP address for your network interface varies, depending on whether your computer is on an IPv4 or IPv6 network. If you attempt to obtain IPv4 configuration for your network interface from a DHCP or BOOTP server and no DHCP or BOOTP server exists on your network, your system will assign an IPv4 address of 169.254.*x.x* where *.x.x* is a randomly generated host ID. This automatic assignment feature is called **Automatic Private IP Addressing (APIPA)**. If your network has IPv6-configured routers, an IPv6 address is automatically assigned to each network interface. This is because network interfaces use **Internet Control Message Protocol version 6 (ICMPv6)** router discovery messages to probe their network for IPv6 configuration information. Alternatively, you can obtain your IPv6 configuration from a DHCP server on the network. If there are no IPv6-configured routers or DHCP servers on your network from which you can obtain an IPv6 configuration for your network interface, your system will assign an IPv6 APIPA address that begins with fe80.

Note 16

A single network interface can have both an IPv4 and an IPv6 address. Each address can be used to access the Internet using the IPv4 and IPv6 protocols, respectively.

To view the configuration of all interfaces, you can use the `ifconfig` command without arguments, or the `ip addr` command (a shortcut to `ip addr show`), as shown in the following output:

```
[root@server1 ~]# ifconfig
eth0: flags=4163<UP,BROADCAST,RUNNING,MULTICAST>  mtu 1500
        inet 3.4.5.6 netmask 255.0.0.0 broadcast 3.255.255.255
        inet6 fe80::bbc3:3b03:591:801b prefixlen 64 scopeid 0x20<link>
        ether 00:15:5d:01:6e:d6  txqueuelen 1000  (Ethernet)
        RX packets 955  bytes 111767 (109.1 KiB)
        RX errors 0  dropped 0  overruns 0  frame 0
        TX packets 272  bytes 61744 (60.2 KiB)
        TX errors 0  dropped 0 overruns 0  carrier 0  collisions 0

lo: flags=73<UP,LOOPBACK,RUNNING>  mtu 65536
        inet 127.0.0.1  netmask 255.0.0.0
        inet6 ::1  prefixlen 128  scopeid 0x10<host>
        loop  txqueuelen 1000  (Local Loopback)
        RX packets 74  bytes 26434 (25.8 KiB)
        RX errors 0  dropped 0  overruns 0  frame 0
        TX packets 74  bytes 26434 (25.8 KiB)
        TX errors 0  dropped 0 overruns 0  carrier 0  collisions 0
```

```
[root@server1 ~]# ip addr
1: lo: <LOOPBACK,UP,LOWER_UP> mtu 65536 qdisc noqueue
    link/loopback 00:00:00:00:00:00 brd 00:00:00:00:00:00
    inet 127.0.0.1/8 scope host lo
       valid_lft forever preferred_lft forever
    inet6 ::1/128 scope host
       valid_lft forever preferred_lft forever
2: eth0: <BROADCAST,MULTICAST,UP,LOWER_UP> mtu 1500 qdisc mq state UP
    link/ether 00:15:5d:01:6e:d6 brd ff:ff:ff:ff:ff:ff
    inet 3.4.5.6/8 brd 3.255.255.255 scope global dynamic eth0
       valid_lft 258581sec preferred_lft 258581sec
    inet6 fe80::bbc3:3b03:591:801b/64 scope link noprefixroute
       valid_lft forever preferred_lft forever
[root@server1 ~]#_
```

The previous output shows that the eth0 network interface has an IPv4 address of 3.4.5.6 and an IPv6 address of fe80::bbc3:3b03:591:801b that you can tell was automatically configured by the system because it starts with fe80. The special loopback adapter (lo) is configured automatically using the IPv4 address 127.0.0.1 and IPv6 address ::1; these IP addresses represent the local computer and are required on all computers that use IP. The ifconfig command also displays receive (RX) and transmit (TX) statistics for each network interface.

Note 17

You can also use the -i option to the netstat command to show interface statistics.

If you restart the computer, the IP information configured for eth0 will be lost. To allow the system to activate and configure the IP information for an interface at each boot time, you can place entries in a configuration file that is read at boot time by your Linux distribution when activating the network. On legacy Ubuntu systems you could add entries for eth0 to a file called /etc/network/interfaces, and on legacy Fedora systems you could add entries to a /etc/sysconfig/network-scripts/ifcfg-eth0 file. Following this, you could run ifconfig eth0 down ; ifconfig eth0 up or ifdown eth0 ; ifup eth0 or ip link set eth1 down ; ip link set eth0 up to deactivate and then reactivate your IP configuration based on the lines within these files. However, on modern Linux systems, the configuration of IP is typically performed at system initialization by a network renderer service, such as NetworkManager or Systemd-networkd.

On modern Fedora Workstation systems, NetworkManager configures network interfaces at system initialization using IP configuration information stored within *.nmconnection files under the /etc/NetworkManager/system-connections directory. If no files exist under this directory, NetworkManager obtains IP configuration for each network interface using DHCP. A sample /etc/NetworkManager/system-connections/Wired1.nmconnection file that configures IP on the eth0 network interface is shown in the following output:

```
[root@server1 ~]# cd /etc/NetworkManager/system-connections
[root@localhost system-connections]# cat Wired1.nmconnection
[connection]
id=Wired1
uuid=e4006c02-9479-340a-b065-01a328727a75
type=ethernet
interface-name=eth0

[ipv4]
address1=3.4.5.6/8,3.0.0.1
dns=8.8.8.8;1.1.1.1;
```

```
method=manual

[ipv6]
addr-gen-mode=stable-privacy
method=auto
[root@server1 ~]#_
```

The entries in the preceding output indicate that IPv6 configuration will be obtained automatically using DHCP (`method=auto`) if it has not already been obtained via ICMPv6. IPv4 is configured manually (`method=manual`) using the IP address 3.4.5.6, an 8-bit subnet mask, and a default gateway of 3.0.0.1 (`address1=3.4.5.6/8,3.0.0.1`). To resolve Internet names, the first DNS server queried will be 8.8.8.8 followed by 1.1.1.1 if the first DNS server is unavailable (`dns=8.8.8.8;1.1.1.1;`). After making changes to a *.nmconnection file, you must instruct NetworkManager to activate your changes using the `nmcli` command. For example, after making changes to the Wired1.nmconnection file shown in the preceding output, you can run the `nmcli connection down Wired1` to deactivate eth0, and then run the `nmcli connection up Wired1` command to activate eth0 again using the new IP configuration information in the /etc/NetworkManager/system-connections/Wired1.nmconnection file.

On modern Ubuntu Server systems, the `netplan command` configures network interfaces at system initialization using either the NetworkManager or Systemd-networkd renderer from IP configuration information stored within *.yaml files under the /etc/netplan directory. A sample /etc/netplan/00-installer-config.yaml file that instructs Systemd-networkd to configure IP on eth0 is shown in the following output:

```
[root@server1 ~]# cat /etc/netplan/00-installer-config.yaml
network:
 version: 2
 renderer: networkd
 ethernets:
   eth0:
     dhcp4: no
     dhcp6: yes
     addresses: [3.4.5.6/8]
     gateway4: 3.0.0.1
     nameservers:
       addresses: [8.8.8.8,1.1.1.1]
[root@server1 ~]#_
```

The entries in the preceding output indicate that IPv6 configuration will be obtained automatically using DHCP (`dhcp6: yes`) if it has not already been obtained via ICMPv6. IPv4 is configured manually (`dhcp6: no`) using the IP address 3.4.5.6 alongside an 8-bit subnet mask (`addresses: [3.4.5.6/8]`) and a default gateway of 3.0.0.1 (`gateway4: 3.0.0.1`). The DNS servers (`nameservers:`) used to resolve Internet names will be 8.8.8.8 followed by 1.1.1.1 if 8.8.8.8 is unavailable (`addresses: [8.8.8.8,1.1.1.1]`). After modifying the /etc/netplan/00-installer-config.yaml file, you can activate your new configuration by using the `netplan apply` command.

Note 18

YAML (YAML Ain't Markup Language) is a file format that uses the `attribute: value` syntax defined by JSON (JavaScript Object Notation), but with additional support for comments. Due to its simplicity, YAML is increasingly being used to provide configuration information for modern Linux systems and cloud-related services.

To make the configuration of a network interface easier, you may access your configuration from the Settings utility within a desktop environment. In GNOME, you can navigate to Activities, Show Applications, Settings to open the Settings utility, navigate to Network, and click the settings (cog wheel) button next to your wired or wireless network interface, as shown in Figure 12-2.

Figure 12-2   Network interface configuration within GNOME Settings

Most workstation-focused Linux distributions use NetworkManager as the network renderer. NetworkManager was designed to keep track of the many different wired and wireless networks that a portable workstation may connect to over time and is supported by all desktop environments that allow you to switch between different networks using graphical tools. If your system is running NetworkManager, you can use the nmcli command without arguments to display information about each network interface, including the active connection as shown in the following output:

```
[root@server1 ~]# nmcli
wlan0: connected to CLASSWIFI
        "Qualcomm Atheros AR93xx Wireless Network Adapter (Killer
            Wireless-N 1103 Half-size Mini PCIe Card [AR9380])"
        wifi (ath9k), B8:76:3F:16:F9:F4, hw, mtu 1500
        ip4 default
        inet4 192.168.1.101/24
        route4 0.0.0.0/0
        route4 192.168.1.0/24
        inet6 fe80::3157:d86d:5da1:2292/64
        route6 ff00::/8
        route6 fe80::/64
        route6 fe80::/64

eth0: unavailable
        "Qualcomm Atheros AR8151 v2.0 Gigabit Ethernet"
        ethernet (atl1c), B8:CA:3A:D5:61:A9, hw, mtu 1500

lo: unmanaged
        "lo"
        loopback (unknown), 00:00:00:00:00:00, sw, mtu 65536

DNS configuration:
        servers: 192.168.1.1
        interface: wlan0

Use "nmcli device show" to get complete information about known devices
and "nmcli connection show" to get an overview on active connection profiles.

Consult nmcli(1) and nmcli-examples(5) manual pages for complete usage details.
[root@server1 ~]#_
```

In the previous output, the wireless Ethernet network interface wlan0 is connected to a wireless network called CLASSWIFI. On a Fedora system, NetworkManager will store the network configuration and Wi-Fi password for this connection in a separate file called /etc/NetworkManager/system-connections/CLASSWIFI.nmconnection, such that it can be reused if the system connects to the network in the future. This is especially useful if you manually configure IP addresses for a wireless network, such as a home or work network; each time you connect to the wireless network, the

IP address information you configured previously will automatically be applied from the associated configuration file. To see a list of all wired and wireless networks that NetworkManager has connected to in the past, you can run the `nmcli conn show` command as shown in the following output:

```
[root@server1 ~]# nmcli conn show
NAME          UUID                                   TYPE      DEVICE
CLASSWIFI     562a0a70-7944-4621-ac4d-35572f08b1ed   wifi      wlan0
Starbucks     59683e0b-5e1d-405c-b88f-8289899b60bd   wifi      --
McDonalds     0dc84378-4e04-4b43-a7fc-2ce25cff9401   wifi      --
HomeWifi      1966c022-8cc5-422c-9fcf-1fdfd8cdef4e   wifi      --
Wired1        f1b34bb3-b621-36d0-bdd0-c23e646c9a51   ethernet  --
[root@server1 ~]#_
```

While Systemd-networkd can also be used to provide the same functionality as NetworkManager, it is more commonly used by Linux server distributions that do not use a desktop environment. You can use the `networkctl command` to view and modify connection information for Systemd-networkd; without arguments, it displays information about each network interface, including the active connection. The following output indicates that eth0 is actively connected and managed by Systemd-networkd:

```
[root@server1 ~]# networkctl
IDX LINK            TYPE            OPERATIONAL SETUP
  1 lo              loopback        carrier     unmanaged
  2 eth0            ether           routable    configured
  3 wlan0           ether           no-carrier  unmanaged

3 links listed.
[root@server1 ~]#_
```

Note 19

Both NetworkManager and Systemd-networkd are optional. If used, only one can be active at any time.

After a network interface has been configured to use IP, you should test the configuration by using the `ping (Packet Internet Groper) command`. The `ping` command sends an ICMP packet to another IP address and awaits a response. By default, the `ping` command sends packets continuously every second until the Ctrl+c key combination is pressed; to send only five ping requests to the loopback interface, you can use the `-c` option to the `ping` command, as shown in the following example:

```
[root@server1 ~]# ping -c 5 127.0.0.1
PING 127.0.0.1 (127.0.0.1) 56(84) bytes of data.
64 bytes from 127.0.0.1: icmp_seq=0 ttl=64 time=0.154 ms
64 bytes from 127.0.0.1: icmp_seq=1 ttl=64 time=0.109 ms
64 bytes from 127.0.0.1: icmp_seq=2 ttl=64 time=0.110 ms
64 bytes from 127.0.0.1: icmp_seq=3 ttl=64 time=0.119 ms
64 bytes from 127.0.0.1: icmp_seq=4 ttl=64 time=0.111 ms

--- 127.0.0.1 ping statistics ---
5 packets transmitted, 5 received, 0% packet loss, time 3999ms
rtt min/avg/max/mdev = 0.109/0.120/0.154/0.020 ms
[root@server1 ~]#_
```

Note 20

If the `ping` command fails to receive any responses from the loopback interface, there is a problem with IP itself.

Next, you need to test whether the Linux computer can ping other computers on the same network; the following command can be used to send five ping requests to the computer that has the IP address 3.0.0.2 configured:

```
[root@server1 ~]# ping -c 5 3.0.0.2
PING 3.0.0.2 (3.0.0.2) 56(84) bytes of data.
64 bytes from 3.0.0.2: icmp_seq=0 ttl=128 time=0.448 ms
64 bytes from 3.0.0.2: icmp_seq=1 ttl=128 time=0.401 ms
64 bytes from 3.0.0.2: icmp_seq=2 ttl=128 time=0.403 ms
64 bytes from 3.0.0.2: icmp_seq=3 ttl=128 time=0.419 ms
64 bytes from 3.0.0.2: icmp_seq=4 ttl=128 time=0.439 ms

--- 3.0.0.2 ping statistics ---
5 packets transmitted, 5 received, 0% packet loss, time 4001ms
rtt min/avg/max/mdev = 0.401/0.422/0.448/0.018 ms
[root@server1 ~]#_
```

Note 21

If the `ping` command fails to receive any responses from other computers on the network, there is a problem with the network media.

You can use the `ping6 command` to send an ICMP6 message to an IPv6 address.

Configuring a PPP Interface

Instead of configuring IP to run on a network interface to gain network access, you can run IP over serial lines (such as telephone lines) using the PPP WAN protocol. Three common technologies use PPP to connect computers to the Internet or other networks:

- Modems
- ISDN
- DSL

Modem (modulator-demodulator) devices use PPP to send IP information across normal telephone lines; they were the most common method for home users to gain Internet access in the 1990s. Modem connections are considered slow today compared to most other technologies; most modems can only transmit data at 56 Kb/s. Because modems transmit information on a serial port, the system typically makes a symbolic link called /dev/modem that points to the correct serial port device, such as /dev/ttyS0 for COM1.

Integrated Services Digital Network (ISDN) is a set of standards designed for transmitting voice, video, and data over normal copper telephone lines. It allows data to be transferred at 128 Kb/s. ISDN uses an ISDN modem device to connect to a different type of media than regular phone lines.

While modems and ISDN are rare today, many home and rural networks connect to the Internet using DSL. DSL has many variants, such as Asynchronous DSL (ADSL), which is the most common DSL used in homes across North America, and High-bit-rate DSL (HDSL), which is common in business environments; for simplification, all variants of DSL are referred to as xDSL. You use an Ethernet network interface to connect to a DSL modem using IP and PPP; as a result, DSL connections are said to use PPP over Ethernet (PPPoE). The DSL modem then transmits information across normal telephone lines at speeds that can exceed 100 Mb/s.

Because modem, ISDN, and DSL connections require additional configuration information that is specific to the ISP, they are not normally configured during the Linux installation and must be configured manually.

Configuring a PPP connection requires support for PPP compiled into the kernel or available as a module, the PPP daemon (pppd), and a series of supporting utilities such as the chat program, which is used to communicate with a modem. PPP configuration in the past was tedious at best; you needed to create a chat script that contained the necessary information to establish a PPP connection (user name, password, and so on), a connection script that contained device parameters used by the PPP daemon, as well as use a program such as minicom to initiate network communication. Because the IP configuration is typically assigned by the ISP to which you connect, it rarely needs to be configured during the process.

Because modems and ISDN modems are relatively rare today, modern Linux distributions typically don't ship with a graphical configuration tool by default. However, you can download and install the **Modem Manager utility** to configure modems and ISDN modems. On a Fedora system, you can run the `dnf install modem-manager-gui` command as the root user to install this package, and then navigate to Activities, Show Applications, Modem Manager GUI to start the Modem Manager shown in Figure 12-3. The Modem Manager automatically detects any modem or ISDN hardware in your computer and allows you to configure the associated ISP configuration, including the ISP account user name and password.

Figure 12-3   The Modem Manager utility

DSL connections are very common today. As a result, nearly all modern Linux workstation distributions contain a utility that can configure your network interface to work with a DSL modem. On Fedora Workstation, you can configure a DSL connection by running the `nm-connection-editor` command within a terminal in a desktop environment. This command starts the graphical **Network Connections utility** shown in Figure 12-4, which is a component of NetworkManager. If you click the + button shown in Figure 12-4 and choose your device type (DSL/PPPoE), the Network Connections tool will attempt to detect your DSL modem and prompt you to supply the ISP account user name and password.

Figure 12-4   The Network Connections utility

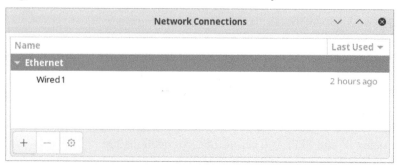

Note 22

In addition to DSL, the Network Connections tool can also be used to configure many other network technologies, including:
- Overlay networks, including Virtual Private Network (VPN) connections that provide an encrypted virtual IP network on top of the existing unencrypted IP network.
- Specialized technologies, such as Infiniband, that allow network interfaces to communicate directly to each other using Remote Direct Memory Access (RDMA).
- Bonding (also called aggregation), in which two separate network interfaces connected to the same network can be combined to provide fault tolerance (in an active/passive configuration) or load balancing of network traffic to achieve higher transmission rates.
- Bridging, in which two network interfaces connected to separate networks provide for seamless connectivity between the networks.

To configure a DSL connection on a system without a desktop environment that contains NetworkManager, you can run the nmcli command with the appropriate options. If NetworkManager is not installed (the default on Ubuntu Server), you can instead execute the pppoeconf **command**, which will open a basic graphical screen within your terminal and scan for DSL devices, as shown in Figure 12-5. If a DSL device is found, you will be prompted to supply the ISP account user name and password to complete the configuration.

Figure 12-5   Scanning for DSL devices using pppoeconf

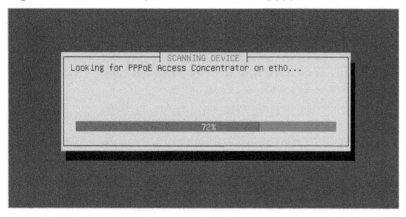

After a PPP modem, ISDN, or DSL connection has been configured, it will normally be activated automatically at boot time like other network interfaces on the system. On a Fedora Workstation system, you will notice a new *.nmconnection file for the connection under the /etc/NetworkManager/system-connections directory. On an Ubuntu Server system, there will be an additional YAML configuration file within the /etc/netplan directory. Other configuration used by the PPP daemon is stored within the /etc/ppp and /etc/isdn directories. It is good form to double-check the passwords used to connect to the ISP because incorrect passwords represent the most common problem with PPP connections. These passwords are stored in two files: /etc/ppp/pap-secrets (Password Authentication Protocol secrets) and /etc/ppp/chap-secrets (Challenge Handshake Authentication Protocol secrets). If the ISP accepts passwords sent across the network in text form, the /etc/ppp/pap-secrets file is consulted for the correct password; however, if the ISP requires a more secure method for validating the identity of a user, the passwords in the /etc/ppp/chap-secrets file are used. When you configure a PPP connection, this information is automatically added to both files, as shown in the following output:

```
[root@server1 ~]# cat /etc/ppp/pap-secrets
# Secrets for authentication using PAP
# client          server     secret                    IP addresses
```

```
####### system-config-network will overwrite this part!!! (begin) ####
"user1"          "isp"    "secret"
####### system-config-network will overwrite this part!!! (end) ######
[root@server1 ~]# cat /etc/ppp/chap-secrets
# Secrets for authentication using CHAP
# client          server   secret                  IP addresses
####### system-config-network will overwrite this part!!! (begin) ####
"user1"          "isp"    "secret"
####### system-config-network will overwrite this part!!! (end) ######
[root@server1 ~]#_
```

After a PPP device has been configured, the output of the ifconfig and ip addr commands indicate the PPP interface using the appropriate name; ppp0 is typically used for the first modem or xDSL device, and ippp0 is typically used for the first ISDN device.

Name Resolution

Computers that communicate on an IP network identify themselves using unique IP addresses; however, this identification scheme is impractical for human use because it is difficult to remember IP addresses. As a result, every computer on a network is identified by a name that makes sense to humans, such as "Accounting1" or "ReceptionKiosk." Because each computer on a network is called a host, the name assigned to an individual computer is its host name.

For computers that require a presence on the Internet, simple host names are rarely used. Instead, they are given a host name called a fully qualified domain name (FQDN) according to a hierarchical naming scheme called Domain Name Space (DNS), as discussed in Chapter 1. At the top of the Domain Name Space is the root domain, which is just a theoretical starting point for the branching, tree-like structure. Below the root domain are the top-level domain names, which identify the type of organization in which a network is located. For example, the com domain is primarily used for business, or commercial, networks. Several second-level domains exist under each top-level domain name to identify the name of the organization, and simple host names are listed under the second-level domains. Figure 12-6 shows a portion of the Domain Name Space.

Note 23

For simplicity, FQDNs are often referred to as host names.

Thus, the host computer shown in Figure 12-6 has an FQDN of www.linux.org.

Figure 12-6   The Domain Name Space

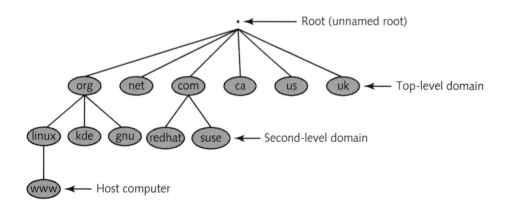

> ### Note 24
>
> The host name www (World Wide Web) has traditionally been used by servers that host webpages.

Second-level domains must be purchased and registered with an ISP in order to be recognized by other computers on the Internet. You can use the `whois` command to obtain registration information about any domain within the Domain Name Space. For example, to obtain information about the organization responsible for maintaining the linux.org domain, you can use the following command:

```
[root@server1 ~]# whois linux.org | head -22
[Querying whois.pir.org]
[whois.pir.org]
Domain Name: linux.org
Registry Domain ID: eac371bee0f24a089943a58c8b182080-LROR
Registrar WHOIS Server: http://whois.networksolutions.com
Registrar URL: http://www.networksolutions.com
Updated Date: 2019-01-08T09:43:32Z
Creation Date: 1994-05-10T04:00:00Z
Registry Expiry Date: 2027-05-11T04:00:00Z
Registrar: Network Solutions, LLC
Registrar IANA ID: 2
Registrar Abuse Contact Email: domain.operations@web.com
Registrar Abuse Contact Phone: +1.8777228662
Domain Status: clientTransferProhibited https://icann.org/epp#clientTransferProhibited
Registry Registrant ID: REDACTED FOR PRIVACY
Registrant Name: REDACTED FOR PRIVACY
Registrant Organization: Linux Online, Inc
Registrant Street: REDACTED FOR PRIVACY
Registrant City: REDACTED FOR PRIVACY
Registrant State/Province: NY
Registrant Postal Code: REDACTED FOR PRIVACY
Registrant Country: US
[root@server1 ~]#_
```

You can view or set the host name for a Linux computer using the `hostname` command, as shown in the following output:

```
[root@server1 ~]# hostname
server1.class.com
[root@server1 ~]# hostname computer1.sampledomain.com
[root@server1 ~]# hostname
computer1.sampledomain.com
[root@server1 ~]# bash
[root@computer1 ~]#_
```

Note that the new hostname isn't shown in your shell prompt until a new shell is started. To configure the host name shown in the preceding output at system startup, add the desired hostname to the /etc/hostname file, or run the `hostnamectl` command. For example, the commands in the following output set the host name to computer1.sampledomain.com and verify the configuration within /etc/hostname:

```
[root@computer1 ~]# hostnamectl set-hostname computer1.sampledomain.com
[root@computer1 ~]# cat /etc/hostname
computer1.sampledomain.com
[root@computer1 ~]#_
```

Note 25

Many network services record the system host name in their configuration files during installation. As a result, most Linux server distributions prompt you for the host name during the Linux installation to ensure that you don't need to modify network service configuration files afterwards.

Although host names are easier to use when specifying computers on the network, IP cannot use them to identify computers. Thus, you must map host names to their associated IP addresses so that applications that contact other computers across the network can find the appropriate IP address for a host name.

The simplest method for mapping host names to IP addresses is by placing entries into the /etc/hosts file, as shown in the following example:

```
[root@server1 ~]# cat /etc/hosts
127.0.0.1   server1 server1.class.com localhost localhost.localdomain
::1         server1 server1.class.com localhost6 localhost6.localdomain6
3.0.0.2     ftp.sampledomain.com fileserver
10.3.0.1    alpha
[root@server1 ~]#_
```

Note 26

You can also use the `getent hosts` command to view the contents of the /etc/hosts file.

The entries in the preceding output identify the local computer, 127.0.0.1, by the host names server1, server1.class.com, localhost, and localhost.localdomain. Similarly, you can use the host name ftp.sampledomain.com or fileserver to refer to the computer with the IP address of 3.0.0.2. Also, the computer with the IP address of 10.3.0.1 can be referred to using the name alpha.

Because it would be cumbersome to list names for all hosts on the Internet in the /etc/hosts file, ISPs can list FQDNs in DNS servers on the Internet. Applications can then ask DNS servers for the IP address associated with a certain FQDN. To configure your system to resolve names to IP addresses by contacting a DNS server, you can specify the IP address of the DNS server in the /etc/resolv.conf file. This file can contain up to three DNS servers; if the first DNS server is unavailable, the system attempts to contact the second DNS server, followed by the third DNS server listed in the file. An example /etc/resolv.conf file is shown in the following output:

```
[root@server1 ~]# cat /etc/resolv.conf
nameserver 209.121.197.2
nameserver 192.139.188.144
nameserver 6.0.4.211
[root@server1 ~]#_
```

On Linux distributions that use Systemd, the Systemd-resolved service handles name resolution requests. In this case, /etc/resolv.conf is merely a symlink to /run/systemd/resolve/stub-resolv .conf, which contains a single entry that redirects name resolution requests to the special 127.0.0.53 loopback address as shown below:

```
[root@server1 ~]# ls -l /etc/resolv.conf
lrwxrwxrwx. 1 root root 39 Sep 20 11:33 /etc/resolv.conf ->
../run/systemd/resolve/stub-resolv.conf
[root@server1 ~]# cat /run/systemd/resolve/stub-resolv.conf
nameserver 127.0.0.53
[root@server1 ~]#_
```

The Systemd-resolved service listens to name resolution requests sent to 127.0.0.53. It then queries the DNS servers configured by the network renderer (NetworkManager or Systemd-networkd) to resolve the name and responds to the original request with the answer. Systemd-networkd caches the results of names resolved by DNS servers to speed future queries. You can manage Systemd-resolved using the `resolvectl command`. For example, `resolvectl dns eth0 8.8.8.8` will configure eth0 to use a DNS server of 8.8.8.8, overriding the configuration provided by the network renderer. You can also use `resolvectl status` to display the current Systemd-resolved configuration, as well as `resolvectl flush-caches` to clear cached results.

Note 27

> To test the DNS configuration by resolving a host name or FQDN to an IP address, you can supply the host name or FQDN as an argument to the `resolvectl query`, `nslookup`, `dig`, or `host command` at a command prompt.

When you specify a host name while using a certain application, that application must then resolve that host name to the appropriate IP address by searching either the local /etc/hosts file or a DNS server. The method that applications use to resolve host names is determined by the "hosts:" line in the /etc/nsswitch.conf file; an example of this file is shown in the following output:

```
[root@server1 ~]# grep hosts /etc/nsswitch.conf
hosts:       files dns
[root@server1 ~]#_
```

The preceding output indicates that applications first try to resolve host names using the /etc/hosts file (`files`). If unsuccessful, applications contact the DNS servers listed in the /etc/resolv .conf file (`dns`).

Legacy Linux systems used the /etc/host.conf file instead of /etc/nsswitch.conf. The /etc/host .conf file still exists on modern Linux systems to support older programs and should contain the same name resolution order as /etc/nsswitch.conf if older programs are installed. An example /etc/host .conf file that tells applications to search the /etc/hosts file (`hosts`) followed by DNS servers (`bind`) is shown in the following output:

```
[root@server1 ~]# cat /etc/host.conf
multi on
order hosts,bind
[root@server1 ~]#_
```

Routing

Every computer on a network maintains a list of IP networks so that packets are sent to the appropriate location; this list is called a route table and is stored in system memory. To see the route table, you can use the `route command` if the net-tools package is installed on your system, or the `ip route` command (a shortcut to `ip route show`) if your system has the iproute or iproute2 package. The following illustrates sample output from these commands:

```
[root@server1 ~]# route
Kernel IP routing table
Destination    Gateway       Genmask         Flags Metric Ref  Use Iface
default        192.168.1.1   0.0.0.0         UG    100    0      0 eth0
192.168.1.0    0.0.0.0       255.255.255.0   U     100    0      0 eth0
10.0.0.0       0.0.0.0       255.255.255.0   U     101    0      0 wlan0
[root@server1 ~]# ip route
```

```
default via 192.168.1.1 dev eth0 proto src 192.168.1.105 metric 100
192.168.1.0/24 dev eth0 proto kernel src 192.168.1.105 metric 100
10.0.0.0/8 dev wlan0 proto kernel src 10.0.0.5 metric 101
[root@server1 ~]#_
```

Note 28

The netstat -r command is equivalent to the route command.

Note 29

The /etc/networks file contains aliases for IP networks. The "default" line in the previous output refers to the 0.0.0.0 network because the /etc/networks file provides an alias for the 0.0.0.0 network called "default." To view the route table without aliases, supply the -n option to the route or netstat -r command, or the -N option to the ip route command.

The route tables shown in the preceding output indicates that all packets destined for the 10.0.0.0 network will be sent to the wlan0 network interface (which has an IPv4 address of 10.0.0.5). Similarly, all packets destined for the 192.168.1.0 network will be sent to the eth0 network interface (which has an IPv4 address of 192.168.1.105). Packets that must be sent to any other network will be sent to the default gateway (which has an IPv4 address of 192.168.1.1) via the eth0 network interface.

Note 30

The default gateway is normally specified within the IP configuration file for the network interface as shown earlier in this chapter and loaded when the network interface is activated.

If your computer has more than one network interface configured, the route table will have more entries that define the available IP networks; computers that have more than one network interface are called **multihomed hosts**. Multihomed hosts can be configured to forward packets from one interface to another to aid a packet in reaching its destination; this process is commonly called **routing** or **IP forwarding**. To enable routing on your Linux computer, place the number 1 in the file /proc/sys/net/ipv4/ip_forward for IPv4 or /proc/sys/net/ipv6/conf/all/forwarding for IPv6, as shown in the following output:

```
[root@server1 ~]# cat /proc/sys/net/ipv4/ip_forward
0
[root@server1 ~]# cat /proc/sys/net/ipv6/conf/all/forwarding
0
[root@server1 ~]# echo 1 > /proc/sys/net/ipv4/ip_forward
[root@server1 ~]# echo 1 > /proc/sys/net/ipv6/conf/all/forwarding
[root@server1 ~]# cat /proc/sys/net/ipv4/ip_forward
1
[root@server1 ~]# cat /proc/sys/net/ipv6/conf/all/forwarding
1
[root@server1 ~]#_
```

Note 31

The **sysctl command** can also be used to modify the contents of files under the /proc/sys directory. For example, sysctl net.ipv4.ip_forward=1 would be equivalent to the echo 1 > /proc/sys/net/ipv4/ip_forward command.

To enable IPv4 routing at every boot, ensure that the line `net.ipv4.ip_forward = 1` exists in the /etc/sysctl.conf file or within a file under the /etc/sysctl.d directory. To enable IPv6 routing at every boot, ensure that the line `net.ipv6.conf.default.forwarding = 1` exists in the /etc/sysctl.conf file or within a file under the /etc/sysctl.d directory.

If your computer has more than one network interface and routing is enabled, your computer will route packets only to networks for which it has a network interface. On larger networks, however, you might have several routers, in which case packets might have to travel through several routers to reach their destination. Because routers only know the networks to which they are directly connected, you might need to add entries to the route table on a router so that it knows where to send packets that are destined for a remote network. Suppose, for example, your organization has three IPv4 networks (1.0.0.0/8, 2.0.0.0/8, and 3.0.0.0/8) divided by two routers, as shown in Figure 12-7.

Figure 12-7 A sample routed network

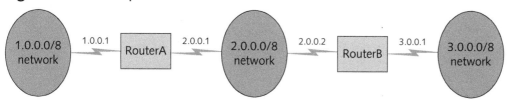

By default, RouterA will have two entries in its route table that are established when IP is configured. The first entry will identify that it is connected to the 1.0.0.0/8 network via the network interface that has the IP address 1.0.0.1, and the second entry will identify that it is connected to the 2.0.0.0/8 network via the network interface that has the IP address 2.0.0.1. If RouterA receives a packet that is destined for the 3.0.0.0/8 network, it does not know where to forward it because it does not have a route for the 3.0.0.0/8 network in its routing table. Thus, you must add a route to the route table on RouterA that allows it to forward packets destined for the 3.0.0.0/8 network to Router2 (2.0.0.2). To add this route on RouterA, you can run either the `route add -net 3.0.0.0 netmask 255.0.0.0 gw 2.0.0.2` command or the `ip route add 3.0.0.0/8 via 2.0.0.2` command.

Similarly, for RouterB to forward packets it receives destined for the 1.0.0.0/8 network, it must have a route that sends those packets to RouterA via the interface 2.0.0.1. To add this route on RouterB, you can run either the `route add -net 1.0.0.0 netmask 255.0.0.0 gw 2.0.0.1` command or the `ip route add 1.0.0.0/8 via 2.0.0.1` command.

> **Note 32**
>
> You can use the `route del <route>` or `ip route del <route>` command to remove entries from the route table.

> **Note 33**
>
> The contents of the route table are lost when the computer is powered off; to load the additional routes to the route table at every boot time, you must add the appropriate lines to the IP configuration file for the network interface as shown earlier in this chapter. For example, to add a single additional route to the 1.0.0.0/8 network via the 2.0.0.1 router on a Fedora system, you could add the line `route1=1.0.0.0/8,2.0.0.1` to the `[ipv4]` section of the /etc/NetworkManager/system-connections/Wired1.nmconnection file. For an Ubuntu system, you can instead add the following lines under the network interface section of the YAML file under the /etc/netplan directory:
>
> ```
> routes:
>   - to: 1.0.0.0/8
>     via: 2.0.0.1
> ```

> ## Note 34
>
> You can also use a routing protocol on routers within your network to automate the addition of routes to the routing table. Two common routing protocols are Routing Information Protocol (RIP) and Open Shortest Path First (OSPF). If you install the FRRouting (frr) package, you can configure the RIP and OSPF routing protocols using the `vtysh` command.

Because the list of all routes on large networks such as the Internet is too large to be stored in a route table on a router, most routers are configured with a default gateway. Any packets that are addressed to a destination that is not listed in the route table are sent to the default gateway, which is a router that can forward the packet to the appropriate network or to the router's own default gateway and so on until the packets reach their destination.

If computers on your network are unable to connect to other computers on a remote network, the problem is likely routing related. A common utility used to troubleshoot routing is the `traceroute` command; it displays all routers between the current computer and a remote computer. To trace the path from the local computer to the computer with the IP address 3.4.5.6, you can use the following command:

```
[root@server1 ~]# traceroute 3.4.5.6
traceroute to 3.4.5.6 (3.4.5.6), 30 hops max, 38 byte packets
1   linksys (192.168.0.1)   2.048 ms   0.560 ms   0.489 ms
2   apban.pso.com (7.43.111.2)   2.560 ms   0.660 ms   0.429 ms
3   tfs.ihtfcid.net (3.0.0.1)   3.521 ms   0.513 ms   0.499 ms
4   srl.lala.com (3.4.5.6)   5.028 ms   0.710 ms   0.554 ms
[root@server1 ~]#_
```

> ## Note 35
>
> Two common alternatives to the `traceroute` command include the `tracepath` command and the `mtr` command.

> ## Note 36
>
> To trace an IPv6 route, you can use the `mtr`, `traceroute6`, or `tracepath6` command.

Network Services

Recall from Chapter 1 that Linux provides a wide variety of services that are available to users across a network. Before you can configure the appropriate network services to meet your organization's needs, you must first identify the types and features of network services.

Network services are processes that provide some type of valuable service for other computers on the network. They are often represented by a series of daemon processes that listen for certain requests on the network. Daemons identify the packets to which they should respond using a port number that uniquely identifies each network service. Different daemons listen for different port numbers. A port number is like an apartment number for the delivery of mail. The network ID of the IP address ensures that the packet is delivered to the correct street (network); the host ID ensures that the packet is delivered to the correct building (host); and the port number ensures that the packet is delivered to the proper apartment in the building (service).

Ports and their associated protocols are defined in the /etc/services file. To see to which port the telnet daemon listens, you can use the following command:

```
[root@server1 ~]# grep telnet /etc/services
telnet          23/tcp
telnet          23/udp
rtelnet         107/tcp               # Remote Telnet
rtelnet         107/udp
telnets         992/tcp
telnets         992/udp
skytelnet       1618/tcp              # skytelnet
skytelnet       1618/udp              # skytelnet
hp-3000-telnet  2564/tcp             # HP 3000 NS/VT block mode telnet
hp-3000-telnet  2564/udp             # HP 3000 NS/VT block mode telnet
tl1-telnet      3083/tcp              # TL1-TELNET
tl1-telnet      3083/udp              # TL1-TELNET
telnetcpcd      3696/tcp              # Telnet Com Port Control
telnetcpcd      3696/udp              # Telnet Com Port Control
scpi-telnet     5024/tcp             # SCPI-TELNET
scpi-telnet     5024/udp             # SCPI-TELNET
ktelnet         6623/tcp             # Kerberos V5 Telnet
ktelnet         6623/udp             # Kerberos V5 Telnet
[root@server1 ~]#_
```

The preceding output indicates that the telnet daemon listens on port 23 using both TCP/IP and UDP/IP.

Ports range in number from 0 to 65534. The ports 0–1023 are called well-known ports because they represent commonly used services. Table 12-2 provides a list of common well-known ports.

Table 12-2   Common well-known ports

Service	Port
FTP	TCP 20, 21
Secure Shell (SSH)	TCP 22
Telnet	TCP 23
SMTP	TCP 25
HTTP/HTTPS	TCP 80/TCP 443
rlogin	TCP 513
DNS	TCP 53, UDP 53
Trivial FTP (TFTP)	UDP 69
NNTP/NNTPS	TCP 119/TCP 563
POP3/POP3S	TCP 110/TCP 995
IMAP4/IMAP4S	TCP 143/TCP 993
NTP	TCP 123, UDP 123
SNMP	TCP 161, TCP 162, UDP 161, UDP 162
NetBIOS	TCP 139, UDP 139
SMB/CIFS	TCP 445, UDP 445
Syslog	TCP 514, UDP 514
LDAP/LDAPS	TCP 389, UDP 389/TCP 636, UDP 636

Note 37

Many protocols have a secure version that uses encrypted communication. For example, secure HTTP is called HTTPS and uses a different port number as a result.

Note 38

You can use the `netstat` or `ss` **(socket statistics) command** to display active TCP/IP and UDP/IP connections on your system; the `netstat -t` or `ss -t` command will display active TCP/IP connections, whereas the `netstat -u` or `ss -u` command will display active UDP/IP connections.

Network utilities can connect to daemons that provide network services directly; these daemons are called **stand-alone daemons**. Alternatively, network utilities can connect to network services via the **Internet Super Daemon (inetd)** or the **Extended Internet Super Daemon (xinetd)**, which starts the appropriate daemon to provide the network service as needed. Because inetd and xinetd only start daemons on demand to conserve memory and processor cycles, they were more common on legacy Linux systems with few system resources. However, you may still find inetd or xinetd on smaller Linux systems today, such as IoT devices. Modern Linux systems with Systemd use **socket units** to provide the same functionality. Socket units are similar to service units but start daemons only when packets are received from other computers that request the associated port number. This structure is shown in Figure 12-8.

Figure 12-8 Interacting with network services

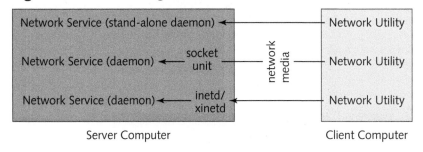

The inetd daemon is configured via entries within the /etc/inetd.conf file. For example, if you install the telnet daemon on a system that uses inetd, you can configure the following line in /etc/inetd.conf to start it:

```
[root@server1 ~]# grep telnet /etc/inetd.conf
telnet stream tcp nowait telnetd /usr/sbin/in.telnetd
[root@server1 ~]#_
```

The xinetd daemon is configured via entries within the /etc/xinetd.conf file. Normally, this file incorporates all of the files in the /etc/xinetd.d directory as well. Most daemons that are managed by xinetd are configured by files in the /etc/xinetd.d directory named after the daemons. For example, if you install the telnet daemon on a system that uses xinetd, you can configure it to be started via the /etc/xinetd.d/telnet file, as shown in the following output:

```
[root@server1 ~]# cat /etc/xinetd.d/telnet
service telnet
{
    flags           = REUSE
    socket_type     = stream
    wait            = no
    user            = root
    server          = /usr/sbin/in.telnetd
```

```
    log_on_failure    += USERID
    disable           = no
}
[root@server1 ~]#_
```

Many network daemons also have one or more configuration files that control how they operate. Most of these configuration files contain many commented lines that indicate the usage of certain configuration parameters. As a result, these configuration files can be very large; the main configuration file used by the Apache Web Server is often several hundred lines long. In addition to this, most stand-alone network daemons do not use the system log daemon (rsyslogd) or Systemd journal daemon (journald) to log information related to their operation. Instead, they log this information themselves to subdirectories of the same name under the /var/log directory. For example, log files for the Samba daemon are located under the /var/log/samba directory.

Table 12-3 lists the names and features of network services that are commonly found on Linux computers that participate in a network environment. You'll learn how to configure many of these network services in this chapter as well as within Chapter 13.

Table 12-3   Common network services

Network Service	Type	Port	Description
Apache Web Server (httpd)	stand-alone	TCP 80 TCP 443	Serves webpages using HTTP/HTTPS to other computers on the network that have a web browser Configuration file: /etc/httpd/conf/httpd.conf or /etc/apache2/apache2.conf
BIND/DNS Server (named)	stand-alone	TCP 53 UDP 53	Resolves fully qualified domain names to IP addresses for a certain namespace on the Internet Configuration file: /etc/named.conf
DHCP Server (dhcpd)	stand-alone	UDP 67 UDP 68	Provides IP configuration for computers on a network Configuration file: /etc/dhcp/dhcpd.conf
Washington University FTP Server (in.ftpd)	inetd/xinetd or socket unit	TCP 20 TCP 21 UDP 69	Transfers files to and accepts files from other computers on the network with an FTP utility Configuration file: /etc/ftpaccess Hosts denied FTP access: /etc/ftphosts Users denied FTP access: /etc/ftpusers FTP data compression: /etc/ftpconversions
Very Secure FTP Server (vsftpd)	stand-alone	TCP 20 TCP 21 UDP 69	Transfers files to and accepts files from other computers on the network with an FTP utility Configuration file: /etc/vsftpd/vsftpd.conf or /etc/vsftpd.conf Users denied FTP access: /etc/vsftpd/ftpusers or /etc/ftpusers
Internetwork News Server (innd)	stand-alone	TCP 119 TCP 563	Accepts and manages newsgroup postings and transfers them to other news servers Configuration file: /etc/news/inn.conf
NFS Server (rpc.nfsd)	stand-alone	TCP 2049	Shares files to other computers on the network that have an NFS client utility Configuration file: /etc/exports
POP3 Server (ipop3d)	stand-alone	TCP 110 TCP 995	Allows users with an email reader to obtain email from the server using the Post Office Protocol version 3

(continues)

Table 12-3 Common network services (*continued*)

Network Service	Type	Port	Description
IMAP4 Server (imapd)	stand-alone	TCP 143 TCP 993	Allows users with an email reader to obtain email from the server using the Internet Message Access Protocol
Sendmail Email Server (sendmail)	stand-alone	TCP 25	Accepts and sends email to users or other email servers on the Internet using the Simple Mail Transfer Protocol (SMTP) Configuration file: /etc/sendmail.cf
Postfix Email Server (postfix)	stand-alone	TCP 25	Accepts and sends email to users or other email servers on the Internet using the Simple Mail Transfer Protocol (SMTP) Configuration file: /etc/postfix/main.cf
rlogin Daemon (in.rlogind)	inetd/xinetd or socket unit	TCP 513	Allows users who use the `rlogin` and `rcp` utilities the ability to copy files and obtain shells on other computers on the network
rsh Daemon (in.rshd)	inetd/xinetd or socket unit	TCP 514	Allows users who use the `rsh` utility the ability to run commands on other computers on the network
Samba Server (smbd & nmbd)	stand-alone	TCP 137 TCP 138 TCP 139 TCP 445	Allows Windows users to view shared files and printers on a Linux server Configuration file: /etc/samba/smb.conf
Secure Shell Daemon (sshd)	stand-alone	TCP 22	Provides a secure alternative to the `telnet`, `rlogin`, and `rsh` utilities by using encrypted communication Configuration file: /etc/ssh/sshd_config
Squid Proxy Server (squid)	stand-alone	TCP 3128	Allows computers on a network to share one connection to the Internet. It is also known as a proxy server Configuration file: /etc/squid/squid.conf
telnet Daemon (in.telnetd)	inetd/xinetd or socket unit	TCP 23	Allows users who have a telnet utility the ability to log in to the system from across the network and obtain a shell
X.org (X11)	stand-alone	TCP 6000	Allows users who use X.org to obtain graphics from another X.org computer across the network using the XDMCP protocol. You can specify the hosts that can connect to X.org using the `xhost` command. Alternatively, you can use the `xauth` command to generate credentials (stored in ~/.Xauthority) that are used to connect to a remote X.org server.

To ensure that a service is responding to client requests, you can use the `ncat (net cat)` **command** to interact with it. For example, to interact with the sshd service running on port 22 on the local computer (127.0.0.1), you could run the `ncat 127.0.0.1 22` command and view the output. If the service doesn't display any output, you can often restart the daemon (sshd) to fix the problem. The ncat command can be used on two separate computers to communicate across a network on any port. For example, if you run `ncat -l -p 1234 > destination` on server1 and then run `ncat -w 3 server1 1234 < source` on server2, the source file on server2 will be copied to a new file called destination on server1 using port 1234.

Note 39

Different distributions often have different names for the `ncat` command. As a result, most Linux distributions create a symlink to their version of the `ncat` command called `nc`.

Remote Administration

As we discussed in Chapter 6, Linux servers are typically installed on a rackmount server system that is located on a rack in a server room and administered remotely. There are several ways to perform command-line and graphical administration of remote Linux servers, including telnet, remote commands, Secure Shell (SSH), and Virtual Network Computing (VNC).

Telnet

The easiest way to perform administration on a remote Linux computer is via a command-line interface. The `telnet` command has traditionally been used on Linux, macOS, and UNIX systems to obtain a command-line shell on remote servers across the network that run a telnet server daemon. For Windows systems, you can download the free **Putty** program at www.chiark.greenend.org.uk/~sgtatham/putty/ to start a telnet session to another computer.

The `telnet` command and telnet server daemon are not installed by default on most modern Linux distributions but can easily be installed from a software repository. On Linux systems that use Systemd, the telnet server daemon is usually managed using a socket unit (telnet.socket). On Linux systems that use SysV init, the telnet server daemon is managed by inetd or xinetd.

After the telnet daemon has been configured, you can connect to it from a remote computer. To do this, specify the host name or IP address of the target computer to the `telnet` command and log in with the appropriate user name and password. A shell obtained during a telnet session runs on a pseudo terminal (a terminal that does not obtain input directly from the computer keyboard) rather than a local terminal, and it works much the same way a normal shell does; you can execute commands and use the `exit` command to kill the shell and end the session. A sample telnet session is shown in the following output using a computer with a host name of server1:

```
[root@server1 ~]# telnet server1
Trying 192.168.1.105...
Connected to server1.
Escape character is '^]'.

Kernel 5.19.11-200.fc36.x86_64 on an x86_64 (1)
server1 login: root
Password: LINUXrocks!
Last login: Fri Oct 4 16:55:33 from 192.168.1.113
[root@server1 ~]# who
root       tty5            2023-10-09 14:23
root       pts/0           2023-10-09 18:49 (192.168.1.113)
[root@server1 ~]# exit
logout
Connection closed by foreign host.
[root@server1 ~]#_
```

Secure Shell (SSH)

Although the `telnet` command can be quickly used to perform remote administration, it doesn't encrypt the information that passes between computers. **Secure Shell (SSH)** was designed as a secure replacement for telnet (and other legacy commands, such as `rsh`, `rlogin`, and `rcp`) that encrypts information that passes across the network. As a result, the SSH daemon (sshd) is installed by default on most Linux distributions.

> **Note 40**
>
> On Linux workstation distributions, sshd is often installed by default but not set to start automatically at system initialization.

To connect to a remote Linux computer running sshd, you can use the `ssh` command followed by the host name or IP address of the target computer. For example, you can connect to a computer with the host name of appserver using the `ssh appserver` command. Your local user name will be passed to the server automatically during the SSH request, and you will be prompted to supply the password for the same user on the target computer. If you need to log in using a different user name on the remote appserver computer, you can instead use the `ssh -l username appserver` command or the `ssh username@appserver` command. A sample `ssh` session is shown in the following output:

```
[root@server1 ~]# ssh root@appserver
root@appserver's password: LINUXrocks!
Last login: Sun Oct  9 19:36:42 2023 from 192.168.1.113
[root@appserver ~]# who
root        tty5            2023-10-09 14:23
root        pts/0           2023-10-09 19:36 (192.168.1.113)
[root@appserver root]# exit
logout
Connection to appserver closed.
[root@appserver ~]#_
```

Note 41

You can also use the Putty program on a Windows computer to connect to sshd running on a Linux, macOS, or UNIX computer.

SSH can also be used to transfer files between computers. For example, to transfer the /root/sample file on a remote computer called appserver to the /var directory on the local computer, you could run the following command:

```
[root@server1 ~]# ssh root@appserver cat /root/sample > /var/sample
root@appserver's password: LINUXrocks!
[root@server1 ~]#_
```

Similarly, to transfer the /root/sample file on the local computer to the /var directory on a remote computer called appserver, you could run the following command:

```
[root@server1 ~]# ssh root@appserver cat </root/sample ">" /var/sample
root@appserver's password: LINUXrocks!
[root@server1 ~]#_
```

Alternatively, you can use the `scp` command to copy files using SSH. For example, to transfer the /root/sample file on a remote computer called appserver to the /var directory on the local computer, you could run the following `scp` command:

```
[root@server1 ~]# scp root@appserver:/root/sample /var
root@appserver's password: LINUXrocks!
[root@server1 ~]#_
```

Similarly, to copy the /root/sample file to the /var directory on appserver, you could use the following `scp` command:

```
[root@server1 ~]# scp /root/sample root@appserver:/var
root@appserver's password: LINUXrocks!
[root@server1 ~]#_
```

Many Linux utilities have built-in support for SSH, including the `rsync` command, which can also be used to copy files to other computers. For example, to copy the /root/sample file using `rsync` with SSH encryption to the /var directory on appserver, you could run the following `rsync` command:

```
[root@server1 ~]# rsync -e ssh /root/sample root@appserver:/var
root@appserver's password: LINUXrocks!
[root@server1 ~]#_
```

Alternatively, you could use SSH encryption to synchronize the contents of the /data directory with the /data directory on appserver using the following `rsync` command:

```
[root@server1 ~]# rsync -a -e ssh /data root@appserver:/data
root@appserver's password: LINUXrocks!
[root@server1 ~]#_
```

Although SSH is primarily used to perform command-line administration of remote systems, the -X option to the `ssh` command can be used to tunnel X Windows information through the SSH connection if you are using the `ssh` command within a desktop environment. For example, if you start a command-line terminal within a GNOME desktop and run the command `ssh -X root@appserver`, you will receive a command prompt where you can type commands as you would in any command-line SSH session. However, if you type a graphical command (e.g., `firefox`), you will execute the Firefox web browser on appserver across the SSH tunnel. All graphics, keystrokes, and mouse movement will be passed between X Windows on appserver and X Windows on the local system.

Understanding SSH Host and User Keys

SSH uses symmetric encryption to encrypt the data that is sent over the network but requires asymmetric encryption to securely communicate the symmetric encryption key between the two computers at the beginning of the SSH connection. This asymmetric encryption requires that each computer running sshd have a public key and private key for the various asymmetric encryption algorithms supported by SSH (DSA, RSA, ECDSA, and ED25519); these keys are called the SSH host keys and are stored in the /etc/ssh directory as shown in the following output:

```
[root@server1 ~]# ls /etc/ssh | grep key
ssh_host_dsa_key
ssh_host_dsa_key.pub
ssh_host_ecdsa_key
ssh_host_ecdsa_key.pub
ssh_host_ed25519_key
ssh_host_ed25519_key.pub
ssh_host_rsa_key
ssh_host_rsa_key.pub
[root@server1 ~]#_
```

In the previous output, the ssh_host_ecdsa_key file contains the ECDSA private key for the host, whereas the ssh_host_ecdsa_key.pub file contains the ECDSA public key for the host. At the beginning of the SSH connection, the two computers negotiate the strongest asymmetric encryption algorithm that is supported by both computers.

When you connect to a new computer for the first time using SSH, you will be prompted to accept the SSH public key for the target computer, which is stored in ~/.ssh/known_hosts for subsequent connections. If the target computer's encryption keys are regenerated, you will need to remove the old key from the ~/.ssh/known_hosts file before you connect again.

Note 42

You can regenerate the host keys used by sshd using the `ssh-keygen command`. For example, the `ssh-keygen -f /etc/ssh/ssh_host_ecdsa_key -t ecdsa` command regenerates the private and public keys stored in /etc/ssh/ssh_host_ecdsa_key and /etc/ssh/ssh_host_ecdsa_key.pub, respectively.

To make authenticating to remote SSH hosts easier, you can generate a public key and private key for your user account for use with SSH using the `ssh-keygen` command; these keys are called SSH user keys and are stored in the ~/.ssh directory. For example, the ~/.ssh/id_rsa file contains the RSA private key for your user, and the ~/.ssh/id_rsa.pub file contains the RSA public key for your user. SSH user keys can be used in place of a password when connecting to trusted computers. To do this, you use the `ssh-copy-id command` to copy your public key to the user account on each computer that you would like to connect to without supplying a password. The target computer will store your public key in the ~/.ssh/authorized_keys file for each user account you specified with the `ssh-copy-id` command. The following example generates SSH user keys for the root user on server1, copies them to the root user account on server2, and then connects to server2 as the root user without specifying a password:

```
[root@server1 ~]# ssh-keygen
Generating public/private rsa key pair.
Enter file in which to save the key (/root/.ssh/id_rsa):
Enter passphrase (empty for no passphrase):
Enter same passphrase again:
Your identification has been saved in /root/.ssh/id_rsa.
Your public key has been saved in /root/.ssh/id_rsa.pub.
The key fingerprint is:
SHA256:1Zu0U5EsQWcM1dFWNHvYK07YB5D8uQhgp/XuRACP5PQ root@server1
The key's randomart image is:
+---[RSA 2048]----+
|        +..=B*o.=+|
|       +o++.*=..o=|
|       .o=E*.o.ooo|
|        . + Boo. o|
|         S O..+.o |
|            =o.o  |
|           o  .   |
|          .       |
|                  |
+----[SHA256]-----+
[root@server1 ~]# ls .ssh
id_rsa   id_rsa.pub  known_hosts
[root@server1 ~]# ssh-copy-id root@server2
/usr/bin/ssh-copy-id: INFO: Source of key(s) to be installed:
"/root/.ssh/id_rsa.pub"
/usr/bin/ssh-copy-id: INFO: attempting to log in with the new key(s), to filter out
any that are already installed
/usr/bin/ssh-copy-id: INFO: 1 key(s) remain to be installed -- if you are prompted now
it is to install the new keys
root@server2's password: *********

Number of key(s) added: 1

Now try logging into the machine, with:  "ssh 'root@server2'"
and check to make sure that only the key(s) you wanted were added.

[root@server1 ~]# ssh root@server2
Last login: Sun Oct 14 20:17:41 2023 from server1
[root@server2 ~]# ls .ssh
authorized_keys
[root@server2 ~]#_
```

Note from the `ssh-keygen` command in the previous output that no passphrase was supplied to protect the private key. If you supply a passphrase, then you will need to supply that passphrase each time you use the private key, including each time you connect to another computer using your SSH user keys. To prevent this, you can use the `ssh-agent` command to start the SSH agent process on your computer and run the `ssh-add` command to add your private key to this process (supplying your passphrase when prompted). The SSH agent process will then automatically supply your passphrase when your SSH user keys are used to connect to other computers.

Configuring SSH

You can configure the functionality of sshd by editing the /etc/ssh/sshd_config file. Most of this file is commented and should only be edited to change the default settings that sshd uses when servicing SSH clients. The most commonly changed options in this file are those that deal with authentication and encryption. For example, to allow the root user to log into SSH, you can modify the value of the `PermitRootLogin` line to `yes` within /etc/ssh/sshd_config and restart sshd.

> ### Note 43
>
> On most Linux distributions, root access via SSH is denied by default. This is considered good security practice because malicious software on the Internet often attempts to log in as the root user. In this case, you can access SSH as a regular user and then use the `su` command to switch to the root user to perform administrative tasks.

Recall that the data communicated across the network with SSH is encrypted using a symmetric encryption algorithm that is negotiated at the beginning of the SSH connection, after the SSH host keys have been exchanged. Each symmetric encryption algorithm differs in its method of encryption and the cryptography key lengths used to encrypt data; the longer the key length, the more difficult it is for malicious users to decode the data. The main types of symmetric encryption supported by sshd are as follows:

- Triple Data Encryption Standard (3DES), which encrypts blocks of data in three stages using a 168-bit key length
- Advanced Encryption Standard (AES), an improvement on 3DES encryption and is available in 128-, 192-, and 256-bit key lengths
- Blowfish, an encryption algorithm that is much faster than 3DES and can use keys up to 448 bits in length
- Carlisle Adams Stafford Tavares (CAST), a general-purpose encryption similar to 3DES that is commonly available using a 128-bit key length
- ARCfour, a fast encryption algorithm that operates on streams of data instead of blocks of data and uses variable-length keys up to 2048 bits in length

In addition, all of the aforementioned types of encryption except ARCfour typically use Cipher Block Chaining (CBC), which can be used to encrypt larger amounts of data.

Client computers can use a /etc/ssh/ssh_config or ~/ssh/ssh_config file to set SSH options for use with the `ssh` command, including the symmetric encryption types that can be used, because the SSH client is responsible for randomly generating the symmetric encryption key at the beginning of the SSH connection. However, the encryption types on the client computer must match those supported by the SSH server for a connection to be successful.

Virtual Network Computing (VNC)

Like the -X option of `ssh`, **Virtual Network Computing (VNC)** is another graphical option for administrating a Linux system remotely. After installing a VNC server daemon on a computer, other computers that run a VNC client can connect to the VNC server daemon across a network to obtain a full desktop environment. VNC uses a special platform-independent protocol called Remote FrameBuffer (RFB) to transfer graphics, mouse movements, and keystrokes across the network.

Note 44

VNC server software and client software exist for Linux, macOS, UNIX, and Windows systems. This allows you to use a single technology to obtain the desktop of all of the Linux, macOS, UNIX, and Windows systems on your network.

Note 45

Because X Windows is not installed on Ubuntu Server by default, we'll focus on the configuration of VNC on Fedora in this section. However, the steps are similar on other Linux distributions.

On Fedora, you can install a VNC server by running the `dnf install tigervnc-server` command. Next, you can set a VNC connection password for a user using the `vncpasswd` command. The VNC password is stored in the ~/.vnc/passwd file; for user1, the VNC password will be stored in the /home/user1/.vnc/passwd file. Finally, you can run the `vncserver` command as the user you specified the VNC password for; this will start a VNC server process with the next available display number, starting from 1.

Note 46

By default, the VNC server process listens on port 5900 + display number. For display number 1, the VNC server will listen on port 5901, for display number 2, the VNC server will listen on port 5902, and so on.

Other computers can then connect to the VNC server using a **VNC viewer** program, such as RealVNC. When using a VNC viewer program to connect to a remote VNC server, you can specify the server name or IP address, port, and display number using the syntax *server:port:display*. For example, to connect to the VNC server that uses display number 1 on the computer server1 .class.com, you could use the syntax `server1.class.com:5901:1`. You will then obtain a desktop session on the remote computer, as shown in Figure 12-9.

Figure 12-9   A remote VNC session

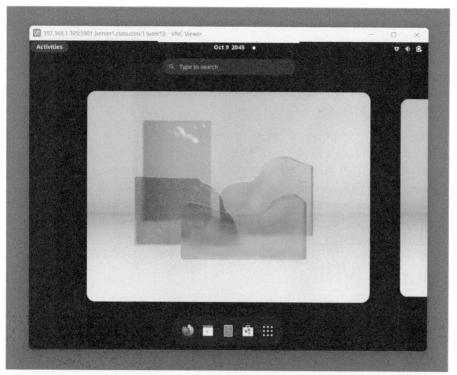

Note 47

Many VNC viewers allow you to specify the server name or IP address and either the port or display number. For example, you could specify `server1.class.com:5901` or `server1.class.com:1` within a VNC viewer to connect to the server shown in Figure 12-9.

Note 48

You can use the remote or local port forwarding feature of SSH to encrypt the traffic sent by other services, such as VNC. For example, if you run the command `ssh -R 5901:server1.class.com:5901 bob@client1.class.com`, bob on the client1.class.com computer can start a VNC viewer and connect to client1.class.com:5901 in order to access the VNC server running on port 5901 on server1.class.com via SSH. Alternatively, you can run the `ssh -L 5901:localhost:5901 bob@server1.class.com` command on your computer to start an SSH session that forwards any local traffic on port 5901 to server1.class.com on port 5901 as bob. Following this, you can start a VNC viewer and connect to localhost:5901 to access the VNC server running on port 5901 on server1.class.com via SSH.

To configure a VNC server process to run persistently, you must edit the /etc/tigervnc/vncserver.users file and add a line to associate a user account to each X Windows display you created a service unit for. For example, the line `:1=bob` would associate the user bob to the first X windows display. Next, you must ensure that the user specified within the /etc/tigervnc/vncserver.users file has a VNC connection password set using the `vncpasswd` command. Finally, you must create and start a VNC Systemd service unit that specifies the display number. To create and start a VNC Systemd service unit that listens on the first X Windows display, you can use the following command:

```
[root@server1 ~]# systemctl enable vncserver@:1.service
Create symlink /etc/systemd/system/multi-user.target.wants/vncserver@:
1.service -> /usr/lib/systemd/system/vncserver@.service
[root@server1 ~]# systemctl start vncserver@:1.service
[root@server1 ~]#_
```

Note 49

You can also specify user-specific VNC configuration by uncommenting and modifying the appropriate lines within the ~/.vnc/config file.

Note 50

On systems that do not use the Systemd system initialization system, the /etc/sysconfig/vncservers configuration file is used in place of /lib/systemd/system/vncserver@:1.service.

Note 51

There are many alternatives to VNC that provide for remote access to Linux desktops, including Xrdp, which uses the Microsoft Remote Desktop Protocol, and NoMachine, which uses the proprietary NX protocol.

Summary

- A network is a collection of connected computers that share information.
- A protocol is a set of rules that define the format of information that is transmitted across a network. TCP/IP is the standard protocol used by the Internet and most networks.
- Each computer on an IP network must have a valid IPv4 or IPv6 address.
- The IPv4 configuration of a network interface can be specified manually, obtained automatically from a DHCP or BOOTP server, or autoconfigured by the system.
- The IPv6 configuration of a network interface can be specified manually, obtained automatically from a DHCP server or router using ICMPv6, or autoconfigured by the system.
- The /etc/NetworkManager/system-connections directory on a Fedora Workstation system and the /etc/netplan directory on an Ubuntu Server system contain the configuration files for network interfaces.

- Host names are computer names that, unlike IP addresses, are easy for humans to remember. Host names that are generated by the hierarchical Domain Name Space are called FQDNs.
- Host names must be resolved to an IP address before network communication can take place.
- Routers are devices that forward IP packets from one network to another. Each computer and router has a route table that it uses to determine how IP packets are forwarded.
- Network services listen for requests on a certain port number. They are normally started by a stand-alone daemon, or on demand using inetd, xinetd, or a Systemd socket unit.
- There are many ways to remotely administer a Linux system. You can perform command-line administration remotely via the `telnet` and `ssh` commands. For graphical remote administration, you can use the `ssh -X` command or VNC.

Key Terms

aggregation
ANDing
Automatic Private IP Addressing (APIPA)
bonding
bridging
broadcast
classless interdomain routing (CIDR) notation
default gateway
`dhclient` command
`dig` command
Ethernet
`ethtool` command
Extended Internet Super Daemon (xinetd)
`host` command
host ID
host name
`hostname` command
`hostnamectl` command
`ifconfig` (interface configuration) command

Internet Control Message Protocol (ICMP)
Internet Control Message Protocol version 6 (ICMPv6)
Internet Super Daemon (inetd)
`ip` command
IP forwarding
IP version 4 (IPv4)
IP version 6 (IPv6)
local area network (LAN)
Media Access Control (MAC) address
media access method
Modem Manager utility
`mtr` command
multicast
multihomed hosts
`ncat` (net cat) command
`netplan` command
`netstat` command
network
Network Connections utility
network ID
network renderer

network service
`networkctl` command
NetworkManager
`nm-connection-editor` command
`nmcli` command
`nslookup` command
octet
packet
`ping` (Packet Internet Groper) command
`ping6` command
Point-to-Point Protocol (PPP)
port
PPP over Ethernet (PPPoE)
`pppoeconf` command
protocol
Putty
Remote Direct Memory Access (RDMA)
`resolvectl` command
`route` command
route table
routing

`rsync` command
`scp` command
Secure Shell (SSH)
socket unit
`ss` (socket statistics) command
`ssh` command
SSH host keys
`ssh-add` command
`ssh-agent` command
`ssh-copy-id` command
`ssh-keygen` command
stand-alone daemon
subnet mask

subnetting
`sysctl` command
Systemd-networkd
Systemd-resolved
`telnet` command
Teredo
`tracepath` command
`tracepath6` command
`traceroute` command
`traceroute6` command
Transmission Control Protocol/
   Internet Protocol (TCP/IP)
unicast

User Datagram Protocol/Internet
   Protocol (UDP/IP)
Virtual Network Computing (VNC)
Virtual Private Network (VPN)
VNC viewer
`vncpasswd` command
`vncserver` command
`vtysh` command
well-known ports
`whois` command
wide area network (WAN)
Wireless-Fidelity (Wi-Fi)
YAML (YAML Ain't Markup Language)

Review Questions

1. The NetworkManager or Systemd-networkd components must be installed on a Linux system in order to configure an IP address on a network interface.

   a. True
   b. False

2. Which Windows program is often used to connect to a Linux server via SSH?

   a. SSHD
   b. Putty
   c. Rdesktop
   d. mstsc

3. Network daemons are started on demand using inetd, xinetd, or Systemd socket units.

   a. True
   b. False

4. Which file stores the IP addresses of the DNS servers used to resolve host names if no DNS servers are specified within the network configuration file for the network interface?

   a. /etc/hosts
   b. /etc/host.conf
   c. /etc/resolve
   d. /etc/resolv.conf

5. To test DNS configuration by resolving a host name to an IP address, which command or commands can you use? (Choose all that apply.)

   a. `nslookup` *hostname*
   b. `dig` *hostname*
   c. `host` *hostname*
   d. `resolvectl query` *hostname*

6. Which two commands can be used to modify the route table on a Linux computer? (Choose two answers.)

   a. `route`
   b. `ipconfig`
   c. `ip`
   d. `traceroute`

7. Which file holds the methods to be used and the order in which they will be applied for host name resolution?

   a. /etc/nsswitch.conf
   b. /etc/resolve.conf
   c. /etc/hosts
   d. /etc/dns.conf

8. What are two means available to resolve a host name to the appropriate IP address? (Choose two answers.)

   a. DHCP
   b. DNS
   c. /etc/hosts
   d. /etc/resolve.conf

9. SSH encrypts all traffic that passes across the network, whereas telnet does not.

   a. True
   b. False

10. You want to generate SSH keys for your user account and copy them to a remote computer to simplify future SSH authentication. What two commands can you use to perform these actions? (Choose two answers.)

    a. `ssh-keygen`
    b. `ssh-add`
    c. `ssh-copy-id`
    d. `ssh-agent`

11. Which of the following can be used to provide graphical remote administration? (Choose all that apply.)

    a. `telnet`
    b. `ssh -X`
    c. `ssh`
    d. VNC

12. The daemons associated with network services listen for network traffic associated with a particular _____.

    a. station
    b. port
    c. IP address
    d. allocation number

13. The IP address of 127.0.0.1 is also referred to as the _____.

    a. local address
    b. lookup address
    c. local host
    d. loopback address

14. The line that configures the host name for the computer at boot time can be found in /etc/hostname.

    a. True
    b. False

15. Which commands can be used to display TCP/IP connections on your Linux system? (Choose all that apply.)

    a. `netstat -t`
    b. `mtr`
    c. `traceroute show`
    d. `ss -t`

16. Which of the following port numbers is associated with SSH?

    a. 22
    b. 137
    c. 49
    d. 23

17. Which file would you modify to permanently change the IP configuration of a network interface on a modern Fedora Workstation system?

    a. /etc/NetworkManager/system-connections/*name*.nmconnection
    b. /etc/sysconfig/network
    c. /etc/netplan/00-installer-config.yaml
    d. /etc/network/interfaces

18. Before a computer can use a router, with what configuration information must it be provided?

    a. routing table
    b. subnet mask
    c. default gateway
    d. default router

19. Which of the following are stand-alone daemons? (Choose all that apply.)

    a. Apache (httpd)
    b. Washington University FTP (in.ftpd)
    c. telnet (in.telnetd)
    d. DNS (named)

20. Which of the following utilities can be used to view and configure a network renderer? (Choose all that apply.)

    a. `ifconfig`
    b. `ip`
    c. `networkctl`
    d. `nmcli`

Hands-On Projects

These projects should be completed in the order given. The hands-on projects presented in this chapter should take a total of three hours to complete. The requirements for this lab include:

- A computer with Fedora Linux installed according to Hands-On Project 2-1 and Ubuntu Linux installed according to Hands-On Project 6-1.

Project 12-1

Estimated Time: 30 minutes
Objective: Configure IP.
Description: In this hands-on project, you explore the IP configuration of the network interface on your Fedora Linux and Ubuntu Linux virtual machines.

1. Boot your Fedora Linux virtual machine. After your Linux system has been loaded, switch to a command-line terminal (tty5) by pressing **Ctrl+Alt+F5** and log in to the terminal using the user name of **root** and the password of **LINUXrocks!**.

2. At the command prompt, type `nmcli connection show` and press **Enter**. Note the name of your wired network interface.

3. At the command prompt, type `ifconfig` and press **Enter**. Does your system have the net-tools package installed? Next, type `ip addr` and press **Enter**. Note your IP configuration. From where was this configuration obtained?

4. At the command prompt, type `ls /etc/NetworkManager/system-connections` and press **Enter**. Why are there no contents?

5. Switch to tty1 by pressing **Ctrl+Alt+F1** and log into the GNOME desktop using your user account and the password of **LINUXrocks!**.

6. Navigate to the **Activities** menu, **Show Applications**, **Settings** and click **Network**. Next to your Ethernet network interface, click the settings (cog wheel) icon. Note the IPv4 and IPv6 configuration for your Wired network interface.

7. Next, highlight the **IPv4** tab and select **Manual**. Supply an appropriate IP address, netmask (subnet mask), gateway (default gateway), and DNS server information for your LAN and click **Apply**. Log out of the GNOME desktop when finished.

8. Switch back to tty5 by pressing **Ctrl+Alt+F5**. At the command prompt, type `ls /etc/NetworkManager/system-connections` and press **Enter**. Note the name of your wired network connection.

9. At the command prompt, type `cat /etc/NetworkManager/system-connections/name.nmconnection` and press **Enter**, where *name* is the name of your wired network connection (if this name contains spaces, use the Tab key to perform autocompletion). Note the contents that reflect your manual IP configuration from Step 7.

10. At the command prompt, type `nmcli connection down name` and press **Enter**, where *name* is the name of your wired network connection (if this name contains spaces, use the Tab key to perform autocompletion). Next, type `ip addr` and press **Enter**. Does your network interface have an IP configuration?

11. At the command prompt, type `nmcli connection up name` and press **Enter**, where *name* is the name of your wired network connection (if this name contains spaces, use the Tab key to perform autocompletion). Next, type `ip addr` and press **Enter**. Does your network interface have the new manual configuration you specified in Step 7?

12. At the command prompt, type `nmcli` and press **Enter**. Does NetworkManager indicate that your network interface is actively connected?

13. At the command prompt, type `ping IP` and press **Enter**, where *IP* is the IPv4 address of your network interface. Do you receive ping responses from your network interface? Press **Ctrl+c** when finished to quit the `ping` command.

14. At the command prompt, type `netstat -i` and press **Enter**. View the statistics for your network interfaces. If necessary, consult the `netstat` manual page to determine the meaning of each column displayed.

15. Type `exit` and press **Enter** to log out of your shell.

16. Boot your Ubuntu Linux virtual machine. After your Linux system has been loaded, log into tty1 using the user name of **root** and the password of **LINUXrocks!**.

17. At the command prompt, type `lshw -C network` and press **Enter**. Note the logical name of your wired network interface.

18. At the command prompt, type `networkctl` and press **Enter**. Is your network interface currently managed by Systemd-networkd?

19. At the command prompt, type `ifconfig` and press **Enter**. Does your system have the net-tools package installed? Next, type `ip addr` and press **Enter**. Note your IP configuration. From where was this configuration obtained?

20. At the command prompt, type `cat /etc/netplan/00-installer-config.yaml` and press **Enter**. Is IP information obtained automatically for your network interface? What lines could you modify and add to this file to manually set the IP configuration?

21. At the command prompt, type `netplan apply` and press **Enter**. When would you normally run this command?

22. Type `exit` and press **Enter** to log out of your shell.

Project 12-2

Estimated Time: 20 minutes
Objective: Configure name resolution.
Description: In this hands-on project, you examine the host name configuration on your Fedora Linux virtual machine, as well as resolve host names.

1. On your Fedora Linux virtual machine, switch to a command-line terminal (tty5) by pressing **Ctrl+Alt+F5** and log in to the terminal using the user name of **root** and the password of **LINUXrocks!**.

2. At the command prompt, type `hostname` and press **Enter**. Note your host name. Next, type `cat /etc/hostname` at the command prompt and press **Enter**. Why are there no contents?

3. At the command prompt, type `hostnamectl set-hostname fedora.class.com` and press **Enter**. Next, type `bash` at the command prompt and press **Enter** to open a new BASH shell. Is your new host name reflected by the shell prompt? Next, type `cat /etc/hostname` at the command prompt and press **Enter**. Note that your new host name is listed and will be configured at system initialization.

4. At the command prompt, type `cat /etc/resolv.conf` and press **Enter**. What Linux component added the DNS server information to this file?

5. At the command prompt, type `cat /etc/nsswitch.conf` and press **Enter**. Will files such as /etc/hosts be used for name resolution before DNS?

6. At the command prompt, type `vi /etc/hosts` and press **Enter**. Note the existing lines in this file. Add a line to the bottom of the file that reads:

        1.2.3.4   fakehost.fakedomain.com sample

   When finished, save your changes and quit the `vi` editor.

7. At the command prompt, type `host localhost` and press **Enter**. Was the name resolved correctly? Next, type `host fakehost.fakedomain.com` and press **Enter**. Was the name resolved correctly?

8. At the command prompt, type `host www.kernel.org` and press **Enter**. Note the IPv4 and IPv6 address returned for www.kernel.org. Is there another name for www.kernel.org?

9. At the command prompt, type `resolvectl query www.kernel.org` and press **Enter**. Do the IPv4 and IPv6 results match those in Step 8?

10. At the command prompt, type `nslookup www.kernel.org` and press **Enter**. How do you know that this information was provided by Systemd-resolved?

11. At the command prompt, type the command `dig www.kernel.org` and press **Enter**. What additional information does dig provide compared to the nslookup and host utilities?

12. Type `exit` and press **Enter** to log out of your shell.

Project 12-3

Estimated Time: 20 minutes
Objective: Configure IP routing.
Description: In this hands-on project, you view and configure the route table on your Fedora Linux virtual machine as well as view and test your routing configuration.

1. On your Fedora Linux virtual machine, switch to a command-line terminal (tty5) by pressing **Ctrl+Alt+F5** and log in to the terminal using the user name of **root** and the password of **LINUXrocks!**.

2. At the command prompt, type `route -n` and press **Enter**. Next, type `ip route` and press **Enter**. Note the entries present and the difference between the output shown by each command. Note the IPv4 address listed as your default gateway. What other command can be used to list the route table?

3. At the command prompt, type `ip route add 1.0.0.0/8 via gwIP` and press **Enter**, where *gwIP* is the IPv4 address of your default gateway.

4. At the command prompt, type `route -n` and press **Enter**. Next, type `ip route` and press **Enter**. Is the route added in Step 3 visible? Will this route interfere with traffic that is sent to the 1.0.0.0 network? Explain.

5. At the command prompt, type `traceroute www.kernel.org` and press **Enter**. How many routers are used to pass your packet to the ftp.kernel.org computer?

6. At the command prompt, type `tracepath www.kernel.org` and press **Enter**. Is the same path taken? If not, explain why.

7. At the command prompt, type `mtr www.kernel.org` and press **Enter**. What information does mtr provide in addition to traceroute and tracepath? Press **q** to quit the mtr utility.

8. At the command prompt, type the command `cat /proc/sys/net/ipv4/ip_forward` and press **Enter**. Is your system configured as an IPv4 router? Next, type the command `cat /proc/sys/net/ipv6/conf/all/forwarding` and press **Enter**. Is your system configured as an IPv6 router? What file could you modify to set IP forwarding at boot time?

9. Type `exit` and press **Enter** to log out of your shell.

Project 12-4

Estimated Time: 40 minutes
Objective: Configure telnet.
Description: In this hands-on project, you install and configure the telnet server daemon on your Fedora Linux virtual machine. Next, you test remote administration of your Fedora Linux system from your Ubuntu Linux virtual machine, as well as your Windows or macOS host.

1. On your Fedora Linux virtual machine, switch to a command-line terminal (tty5) by pressing **Ctrl+Alt+F5** and log in to the terminal using the user name of **root** and the password of **LINUXrocks!**.

2. At the command prompt, type `dnf install telnet-server` and press **Enter** to install the telnet daemon on your Fedora Linux virtual machine. Press **y** when prompted to complete the installation.

3. At the command prompt, type `systemctl start telnet.socket` and press **Enter** to start the telnet daemon. Next, type `systemctl enable telnet.socket` and press **Enter** to start the telnet daemon at boot time.

4. At the command prompt, type `telnet localhost` and press **Enter**. Supply the user name of **root** and password of **LINUXrocks!** when prompted. Next, type `who` at the command prompt and press **Enter**. Are you using a pseudo terminal through a local connection? Type `exit` and press **Enter** to log out of your remote shell.

5. At the command prompt, type `firewall-cmd --add-service telnet` and press **Enter** to add an exception to the firewall on your Fedora Linux virtual machine for telnet. Next, type `firewall-cmd --add-service telnet --permanent` and press **Enter** to provide the same exception at system initialization. We discuss firewalls in Chapter 14.

6. Type `exit` and press **Enter** to log out of your shell.

7. On your Ubuntu Linux virtual machine, log into tty1 using the user name of **root** and the password of **LINUXrocks!**.

8. At the command prompt, type `apt install telnet` and press **Enter** to ensure that the `telnet` command is installed.

9. At the command prompt, type `telnet IP`, where `IP` is the IP address of your Fedora Linux virtual machine, and press **Enter**. Supply the user name of **root** and password of **LINUXrocks!** when prompted.

10. At the command prompt, type `uname -a` and press **Enter**. Are you remotely connected to your Fedora system? Next, type `who` at the command prompt and press **Enter**. What is listed in brackets next to your pseudo terminal session? Type `exit` and press **Enter** to log out of your remote shell.

11. Type `exit` and press **Enter** to log out of your shell.

12. If your host is running Windows, use a web browser on your Windows host to download the putty.exe program from **www.chiark.greenend.org.uk/~sgtatham/putty/download.html**.

13. Double-click the putty.exe file in your Downloads folder within the File Explorer app. What is the default connection type? Select **Other: Telnet** as the connection type, enter the IP address of your Fedora Linux virtual machine in the Host Name (or IP address) box, and click **Open**. Log into your Fedora Linux virtual machine using the user name of **root** and password of **LINUXrocks!**. Next, type `who` at the command prompt and press **Enter**. What is listed in brackets next to your pseudo terminal session?

14. Type `exit` and press **Enter** to log out of your remote shell (this closes the Putty program).

15. If your host is running macOS, use a web browser on your macOS host and navigate to **brew.sh**. Follow the instructions to install the Homebrew package manager. This will require that you paste a command into your Terminal app. You can open this app by navigating to Applications, Utilities, Terminal in the Finder.

16. Once Homebrew has been installed, type `brew install telnet` at the command prompt and press **Enter** to install the `telnet` command. Next, type `telnet IP`, where `IP` is the IP address of your Fedora Linux virtual machine, and press **Enter**. Supply the user name of **root** and password of **LINUXrocks!** when prompted.

17. At the command prompt, type `uname -a` and press **Enter**. Are you remotely connected to your Fedora system? Next, type `who` at the command prompt and press **Enter**. What is listed in brackets next to your pseudo terminal session? Type `exit` and press **Enter** to log out of your remote shell.

18. Close the macOS Terminal app.

Project 12-5

Estimated Time: 40 minutes
Objective: Configure SSH.
Description: In this hands-on project, you configure SSH on your Ubuntu Linux and Fedora Linux virtual machines. Additionally, you connect remotely to your Ubuntu Linux and Fedora Linux virtual machines using SSH from your Linux virtual machines, as well as your Windows or macOS host.

1. On your Fedora Linux virtual machine, switch to a command-line terminal (tty5) by pressing **Ctrl+Alt+F5** and log in to the terminal using the user name of **root** and the password of **LINUXrocks!**.

2. At the command prompt, type `ps -ef | grep sshd` and press **Enter**. Is the SSH daemon started by default?

3. At the command prompt, type `systemctl start sshd.service ; systemctl enable sshd.service` and press **Enter** to start the SSH daemon and ensure that it is started at system initialization.

4. At the command prompt, type `nc localhost 22` and press **Enter** to interact with the SSH daemon listening on port 22. What is displayed on the screen, and what does this indicate? Press **Ctrl+c** to return to your command prompt.

5. At the command prompt, type `vi /etc/ssh/sshd_config` and press **Enter**. Uncomment and modify the **PermitRootLogin** line such that it reads **PermitRootLogin yes**, save your changes, and quit the vi editor.

6. At the command prompt, type `systemctl reload sshd.service` and press **Enter** to force the SSH daemon to reload its configuration file.

7. At the command prompt, type `ssh root@localhost` and press **Enter**. When prompted to accept the negotiated SSH host keys of the target system, type `yes` and press **Enter**. Next supply the root user's password of **LINUXrocks!** and press **Enter**.

8. At the command prompt, type `who` and press **Enter**. Are you on a pseudo terminal? Next, type `ss -t` and press **Enter** to view your TCP connections. Is your SSH connection listed? Is IPv4 or IPv6 used to connect to the loopback adapter on the local host by default?

9. At the command prompt, type `exit` and press **Enter** to log out of your remote shell. Next, type `ss -t` and press **Enter**. Is your SSH connection listed?

10. At the command prompt, type `cat .ssh/known_hosts` and press **Enter**. Note the cached SSH host keys from the target computer (localhost).

11. Switch to a graphical terminal by pressing **Ctrl+Alt+F1** and log in to the GNOME desktop using your user account and the password of **LINUXrocks!**. Next, open a command-line terminal (Activities, Show Applications, Terminal).

12. At the command prompt, type `ssh -X root@localhost` and press **Enter**. When prompted to accept the negotiated SSH host keys of the target system, type `yes` and press **Enter**. Supply the root user's password of **LINUXrocks!** and press **Enter** when prompted.

13. At the command prompt, type `system-config-abrt` and press **Enter**. Note that this command starts the remote Problem Reporting Configuration utility (used to configure the abrtd daemon) in a graphical window through your SSH session. Close the Problem Reporting Configuration utility, type `exit`, and press **Enter** to close your remote shell. Log out of the GNOME desktop when finished.

14. Switch back to tty5 by pressing **Ctrl+Alt+F5** and type `ssh user1@IP`, where *IP* is the IP address of your Ubuntu Linux virtual machine. When prompted to accept the negotiated SSH host keys of the target system, type `yes` and press **Enter**. Supply the password of **LINUXrocks!** when prompted. Why is the SSH daemon started by default in Ubuntu Server?

15. At the command prompt, type `su - root` and press **Enter**. Supply the password of **LINUXrocks!** when prompted to obtain a root shell.

16. At the command prompt, type `vi /etc/ssh/sshd_config` and press **Enter**. Uncomment and modify the **PermitRootLogin** line such that it reads **PermitRootLogin yes**, save your changes, and quit the vi editor.

17. At the command prompt, type `systemctl reload ssh.service` and press **Enter** to force the SSH daemon to reload its configuration file.

18. At the command prompt, type `exit` and press **Enter** to switch back to the user1 shell. Next, type `exit` and press **Enter** to log out of your remote shell.

19. At the command prompt, type `ssh-keygen` and press **Enter** to generate SSH user keys for the root user account on your Fedora Linux virtual machine. Press **Enter** to accept the default location of your SSH user private key (/root/.ssh/id_rsa). Press **Enter**, and then press **Enter** again to prevent the use of a passphrase.

20. At the command prompt, type `ssh-copy-id root@IP`, where *IP* is the IP address of your Ubuntu Linux virtual machine and supply the root user password of **LINUXrocks!** when prompted. What does this command do?

21. At the command prompt, type `ssh root@IP`, where *IP* is the IP address of your Ubuntu Linux virtual machine. Were you prompted for a password? Why? Next, type `cat .ssh/authorized_keys` and

press **Enter** to view the root user's SSH user keys from your Fedora Linux virtual machine. Finally, type `exit` and press **Enter** to log out of your remote shell.

22. At the command prompt, type `ssh root@IP cat /etc/issue > /root/downloaded_issue` and press **Enter**, where *IP* is the IP address of your Ubuntu Linux virtual machine. Next, type `cat downloaded_issue` and press **Enter**. Was the /etc/issue file on your Ubuntu Server transferred successfully to your Fedora Workstation system via SSH?

23. At the command prompt, type `less /etc/ssh/ssh_config` and press **Enter**. Examine the SSH client options available and press **q** when finished.

24. At the command prompt, type `exit` and press **Enter** to log out of your shell.

25. If your host is running Windows, double-click the putty.exe file in your Downloads folder within the File Explorer app. Note that the default connection type is SSH, enter the IP address of your Fedora Linux virtual machine in the Host Name (or IP address) box, and click **Open**. Click **Accept** to accept the Fedora Linux host keys. Log into your Fedora Linux virtual machine using the user name of **root** and password of **LINUXrocks!**. When finished, type `exit` and press **Enter** to log out of your remote shell.

26. Repeat Step 25 using the IP address of your Ubuntu Server Linux virtual machine.

27. If your host is running macOS, open a Terminal app by navigating to Applications, Utilities, Terminal in the Finder. At the command prompt, type `ssh root@IP`, where *IP* is the IP address of your Fedora Linux virtual machine. When prompted to accept the negotiated SSH host keys of the target system, type `yes` and press **Enter**. Supply the root user password of **LINUXrocks!** when prompted. Type `exit` and press **Enter** to log out of your remote shell.

28. Repeat Step 27 using the IP address of your Ubuntu Server Linux virtual machine. Close the macOS Terminal app when finished.

Project 12-6

Estimated Time: 30 minutes
Objective: Configure VNC.
Description: In this hands-on project, you configure a VNC server on your Fedora Linux virtual machine and connect to it remotely from your Windows or macOS host.

1. On your Fedora Linux virtual machine, switch to a command-line terminal (tty5) by pressing **Ctrl+Alt+F5** and log in to the terminal using the user name of **root** and the password of **LINUXrocks!**.

2. At the command prompt, type `dnf install tigervnc-server` and press **Enter**. Press **y** when prompted to complete the installation of the tiger VNC server.

3. At the command prompt, type `vi /etc/tigervnc/vncserver.users` and press **Enter**. Add a line to the bottom of the file that reads:

       :2=user1

   When finished, save your changes and quit the **vi** editor.

4. At the command prompt, type `su -c "vncpasswd" user1` and press **Enter** to set a VNC password for user1. Supply a password of **LINUXrocks!** when prompted (twice) and press **n** when prompted to set a view-only password.

5. At the command prompt, type `systemctl enable vncserver@:2.service` and press **Enter** to allow the VNC server on the second display at system initialization. Note the symlink created to the VNC server service unit file.

6. At the command prompt, type `firewall-cmd --add-service=vnc-server --permanent` and press **Enter** to add a firewall exception for the VNC server at system initialization. Next, type `reboot` to reboot your system.

7. Use a web browser on your Windows or macOS host to download and install the RealVNC Viewer for your Windows or macOS operating system from **www.realvnc.com/en/connect/download/viewer/**. Open the VNC Viewer program following installation.

8. In the VNC Viewer program, enter *IP*:5902 in the VNC Server dialog box, where *IP* is the IP address of your Fedora Linux virtual machine and press **Enter**. When warned that you are about to connect using an unencrypted session, click **Continue**, supply the VNC password of **LINUXrocks!** and click **OK**. Explore your user1 desktop and close the VNC Viewer window when finished.

9. On your Fedora Linux virtual machine, switch to a command-line terminal (tty5) by pressing **Ctrl+Alt+F5** and log in to the terminal using the user name of **root** and the password of **LINUXrocks!**.

10. At the command prompt, type `systemctl disable vncserver@:2.service` and press **Enter** to prevent the VNC server on the second display from starting at system initialization.

11. At the command prompt, type `exit` and press **Enter** to log out of your shell.

Discovery Exercises

Discovery Exercise 12-1

Estimated Time: 20 minutes
Objective: Calculate IP subnets.
Description: Assuming that your company uses the Class A network 100.0.0.0/8, with what subnet mask would you need to configure all computers on the network to divide this network 11 times to match the company's 11 departments? How many hosts can you have per network? What are the first five ranges of addresses that you can assign to different departments?

Discovery Exercise 12-2

Estimated Time: 30 minutes
Objective: Configure IP.
Description: In Project 12-1, you manually configured the IPv4 settings for the network interface on your Fedora Linux virtual machine, as well as viewed the IPv4 configuration for the network interfaces on your Ubuntu Linux virtual machine. On your Ubuntu Linux virtual machine, perform a manual IPv4 configuration of the network interface using values appropriate for your classroom network, and test your configuration when finished.

Discovery Exercise 12-3

Estimated Time: 15 minutes
Objective: Explain SSH file transfer.
Description: In Project 12-5, you used the following method to transfer a file from a remote system to your local computer:

```
ssh remotecomputer cat remotefile > localfile
```

Using your knowledge of redirection, briefly describe how this command achieves this transfer. Can this command be used to transfer a binary file? Explain. What `scp` command would be an alternative to this command?

Discovery Exercise 12-4

Estimated Time: 50 minutes
Objective: Configure WSL.
Description: If your host computer runs Windows, you used the Putty SSH client in Project 12-5 to perform remote administration of two Linux systems. Windows 10 and 11 (Professional, Education, and Enterprise editions) also include the Windows Subsystem for Linux (WSL) feature that allows you to install a full Linux system and kernel that runs concurrently with your Windows kernel for development use (not virtualized). IT administrators often take advantage of this feature to perform remote administration of Linux systems from their Windows desktop.

If your host is running Windows, open a Windows PowerShell (Run as Administrator) app and run the `wsl --install` command. This will install the WSL feature as well as download and integrate an Ubuntu Linux system into Windows. When finished, select Ubuntu on Windows from the Windows Start menu and follow the prompts to create a local user account of your choice.

Take a few moments to explore the system. Next, connect to your Linux virtual machines using SSH from your WSL Ubuntu Linux system. Finally, generate SSH user keys within your WSL Ubuntu Linux system and add them to your Fedora and Ubuntu Linux virtual machines to allow for easy authentication from Windows. Note that you can access your WSL Ubuntu Linux system by choosing Ubuntu on Windows from the Start menu or by running the Terminal app and choosing Ubuntu from the drop-down menu.

Discovery Exercise 12-5

Estimated Time: 50 minutes
Objective: Configure RDP.
Description: In Project 12-6, you configured a VNC server on your Fedora Linux virtual machine for graphical remote management. The GNOME desktop also includes the gnome-remote-desktop-daemon that provides graphical remote access using the Microsoft Remote Desktop Protocol (RDP).

In the GNOME desktop, navigate to Activities, All Applications, Settings, click Sharing and then turn on sharing using the slider button. Next, click Remote Desktop and ensure that both Remote Desktop and Remote Control are enabled. Finally, specify **user1** and the password **LINUXrocks!** in the Authentication section and close Settings when finished.

If your host is running Windows, open the Remote Desktop Connection app from your Start menu. Enter the IP address of your Fedora Linux virtual machine in the Computer dialog box and click Connect. Click Yes when prompted to allow an unencrypted connection. Explore your GNOME desktop and close the Remote Desktop Connection app when finished.

If your host is running macOS, download and install the Microsoft Remote Desktop app from the App Store. Open the Microsoft Remote Desktop app, select PC Quick Connect from the Connections menu, enter the IP address of your Fedora Linux virtual machine in the PC Name dialog box and click Connect. Click Continue when prompted that the connection will be unencrypted. Explore your GNOME desktop and close the Microsoft Remote Desktop app when finished.

Chapter 13

Configuring Network Services and Cloud Technologies

Chapter Objectives

1 Configure infrastructure network services, including DHCP, DNS, and NTP.

2 Configure web services using the Apache web server.

3 Configure file-sharing services, including Samba, NFS, and FTP.

4 Configure email services using Postfix.

5 Configure database services using PostgreSQL.

6 Describe how virtual machines and containers are created and used within cloud environments.

7 Create and run containers using Docker.

8 Configure Kubernetes to run containers.

In the previous chapter, you examined the concepts and procedures that allow Linux to participate on a network. You also learned about the network services that are commonly used on Linux systems, including those that are used for remote administration. In this chapter, you examine the configuration of network services that provide infrastructure, web, file sharing, email, and database services to users across a network. Additionally, you explore the technologies and tools used to host web apps within cloud environments.

Infrastructure Services

Some networking services provide network configuration and support for other computers on a network in the form of TCP/IP configuration, name resolution, and time management. These services, which are collectively called infrastructure services, include DHCP, DNS, and NTP.

DHCP

Recall from the previous chapter that your network interface can be configured manually, or automatically using Dynamic Host Configuration Protocol (DHCP). If your network interface is configured using DHCP, it sends a DHCP broadcast on the network requesting IP configuration information. If a DHCP server on the network has a range of IP addresses, it leases an IP address to the client computer for a certain period of time; after this lease has expired, the client computer must send another DHCP request. Because DHCP servers keep track of the IP addresses they lease to client computers, they can ensure that no two computers receive the same IP address. If two computers are accidentally configured manually with the same IP address, neither would be able to communicate using the IP protocol.

DHCP servers can also send client computers other IP configuration information, such as the default gateway and the DNS server they should use.

DHCP Lease Process

The process by which a DHCP client requests IP configuration from a DHCP server involves several stages. First, the client sends a request (DHCPDISCOVER packet) to all hosts on the network. In reply, a DHCP server sends an offer (DHCPOFFER packet) that contains a potential IP configuration. The DHCP client then selects (accepts) the offer by sending a DHCPREQUEST packet to the associated DHCP server. Next, the DHCP server sends to the client an acknowledgment indicating the amount of time the client can use the IP configuration (DHCPACK packet). Finally, the client configures itself with the IP configuration. This process is illustrated in Figure 13-1.

Figure 13-1 The DHCP lease process

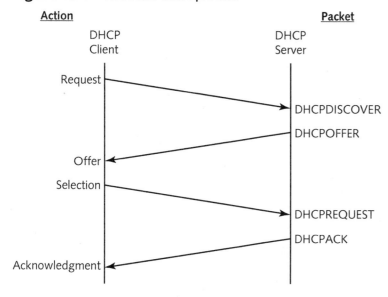

Note 1

If your network has multiple DHCP servers, DHCP clients will accept the first offer that they receive and decline all other offers by sending a DHCPDECLINE packet to the other DHCP servers.

Halfway through the time period specified by its lease (i.e., at 50 percent of its lease), the DHCP client will send another DHCPREQUEST packet to its DHCP server to renew its IP configuration. If its DHCP server is unreachable, it will try to renew its IP configuration again at 87.5 percent of its lease by sending a DHCPDISCOVER packet to all hosts on the network to allow any DHCP server on the network to respond with an offer. After the lease is up, the DHCP client discards its IP configuration obtained from the DHCP server and automatically configures the network interface using APIPA (the IPv4 169.254.0.0 network, or IPv6 FE80 network).

Note 2

IPv6 labels DHCP packets with different names. DHCPDISCOVER, DHCPOFFER, DHCPREQUEST, and DHCPACK packets are labeled as Solicit, Advertise, Request, and Reply, respectively.

Configuring a DHCP Server

To configure your Linux system as a DHCP server, you must first install the DHCP daemon (dhcpd), which is available from online software repositories. Next, you must add lines to the appropriate configuration files to list the appropriate IP address range for your network, as well as lease information and other IP configuration options. The dhcpd configuration files for IPv4 and IPv6 are as follows:

- /etc/dhcp/dhcpd.conf stores IPv4 configuration
- /etc/dhcp/dhcpd6.conf stores IPv6 configuration

> **Note 3**
>
> You don't need to configure the /etc/dhcp/dhcpd.conf file unless you want to configure IPv4 clients. Similarly, you don't need to configure the /etc/dhcp/dhcpd6.conf file unless you want to configure IPv6 clients.

> **Note 4**
>
> You can refer to the manual page for the dhcpd.conf file to obtain a complete list of parameters that can be configured within the /etc/dhcp/dhcpd.conf and /etc/dhcp/dhcpd6.conf files.

An example /etc/dhcp/dhcpd.conf file that leases IPv4 addresses on the 192.168.1.0/24 network is shown in the following output:

```
[root@server1 ~]# cat /etc/dhcp/dhcpd.conf
default-lease-time 36000;
option routers 192.168.1.254;
option domain-name-servers 192.168.1.200;
subnet 192.168.1.0 netmask 255.255.255.0 {
    range 192.168.1.1 192.168.1.100;
}
[root@server1 ~]#_
```

Note from the preceding output that the DHCP server leases clients an IP address between 192.168.1.1 and 192.168.1.100 for 36,000 seconds. In addition, the DHCP server configures the client with a default gateway of 192.168.1.254 and a DNS server of 192.168.1.200.

After the /etc/dhcp/dhcpd.conf file has been configured with the appropriate information, you can start dhcpd as well as configure it to start at system initialization. To view current DHCP leases, you can examine the /var/lib/dhcpd/dhcpd.leases file for IPv4 leases and the /var/lib/dhcpd/dhcpd6.leases file for IPv6 leases.

> **Note 5**
>
> After changing the /etc/dhcp/dhcpd.conf or /etc/dhcp/dhcpd6.conf configuration files, you must restart the DHCP daemon for the changes to take effect.

DNS

Recall that DNS is a hierarchical namespace used to identify computers on large TCP/IP networks such as the Internet. Each part of this namespace is called a zone, and DNS servers contain all host name information for a zone. DNS servers typically resolve FQDNs to IP addresses (called a forward lookup), but they can also resolve IP addresses to FQDNs (called a reverse lookup).

The DNS Lookup Process

When you contact a web server on the Internet using a web browser, the web browser performs a forward lookup of the FQDN such that it can contact the IP address of the web server. This forward lookup can be performed by a DNS server or a series of DNS servers. The whole process used to resolve the FQDN www.linux.org is illustrated in Figure 13-2.

Figure 13-2   The DNS lookup process

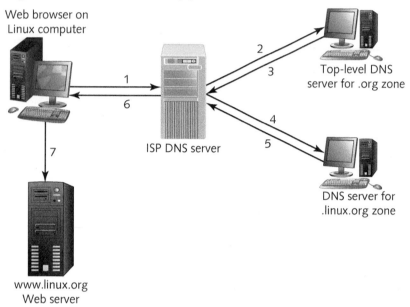

In the first step from Figure 13-2, the Linux computer sends a forward lookup request for www.linux.org to the first DNS server that is listed in /etc/resolv.conf or used by Systemd-resolved; this is typically the DNS server at your ISP. If the ISP DNS server has recently resolved the FQDN and placed the result in its local DNS cache, you receive the response immediately (a DNS lookup query that generates a reply from a DNS cache is called an **iterative query**). If it has not, the ISP DNS server normally contacts the DNS server for the .org top-level zone (Step 2) and repeats the forward lookup request for www.linux.org (called a **recursive query**). The .org DNS server will not contain the IP address for the www.linux.org computer in its zone but will reply with the IP address of the DNS server for the linux.org zone (Step 3).

> **Note 6**
>
> All DNS servers contain a **DNS cache file** that contains the IP addresses of DNS servers that hold top-level DNS zones.

Your ISP DNS server then contacts the DNS server for the linux.org zone (Step 4) and repeats the forward lookup request for www.linux.org (another recursive query). The DNS server for the linux.org domain contains a record that lists the IP address for the www.linux.org computer and returns this IP address to the ISP DNS server (Step 5). The ISP DNS server then caches and returns the result to the client web browser (Step 6), which then uses the IP address to connect to the web server (Step 7).

> **Note 7**
>
> Each zone typically has more than one DNS server to ensure that names can be resolved if one server is unavailable. The first DNS server in a zone is called the **master DNS server** or **primary DNS server**, and all additional DNS servers are called **slave DNS servers** or **secondary DNS servers**. New zone information is added to the master DNS server; slave DNS servers periodically copy the new records from the master DNS server in a process known as a **zone transfer**.

Configuring a DNS Server

To configure your Linux computer as a DNS server, you must install and configure the DNS name daemon (named) for a specific zone and add resource records that list FQDNs for computers in that zone as well as their associated IP addresses. Table 13-1 lists the files that can be used to configure this zone information.

Table 13-1 Common zone configuration files

File	Description
/etc/named.conf	Contains the list of DNS zones that the name daemon will manage and their type.
/var/named/*name* or /var/named/*name*.dns	Contains **resource records** used to perform forward lookups for a particular zone *name*. Lines in this file have a type that determines the kind of resource record: • A (add host) records map FQDNs to IPv4 addresses. • AAAA (add host) records map FQDNs to IPv6 addresses. • CNAME (canonical name) records provide additional aliases for A records. • NS (name server) records provide the names of DNS servers for the zone. • MX (mail exchange) records provide the IP address for the email server for a zone. • SOA (start of authority) determines the parameters used for zone transfers as well as how long information can be cached by the computer performing the forward or reverse lookup (called the **Time-To-Live (TTL)**).
/var/named/*reverse_networkID*.in-addr.arpa or /var/named/db.*networkID*	Contains resource records of type PTR (pointer), which list names used for reverse lookups for a particular network. The network is incorporated into the filename itself; for example, the filename that contains PTR records for the 192.168.1.0 IPv4 network is normally called 1.168.192.in-addr.arpa or db.192.168.1.
/var/named/named.local or /var/named/named.localhost or /var/named/named.loopback	Contains PTR records used to identify the loopback adapter (127.0.0.1 for IPv4, ::1 for IPv6).
/var/named/named.ca or /var/named/root.hints	Contains the IP addresses of top-level DNS servers; it is commonly called the DNS cache file.

Note 8

The name and location of zone configuration files can differ between Linux distributions. For example, on Ubuntu Server Linux, the zone configuration files listed in Table 13-1 are stored within the /etc/bind directory by default.

The files listed in Table 13-1 have a standard format called **Berkeley Internet Name Domain (BIND)**. As a result, it is best to copy and modify sample zone configuration files. After the files that contain the zone information have been created, you can start the DNS name daemon to provide DNS services on the network, as well as configure the DNS name daemon to start at boot time.

Note 9

If you modify any zone files (e.g., to add resource records), you must restart the DNS name daemon for those changes to take effect.

Note 10

The name of the DNS name daemon can differ between Linux distributions. For example, to restart the DNS name daemon on a Fedora system, you can use the `systemctl restart named.service` command. However, to restart the DNS name daemon on Ubuntu Server, you use the `systemctl restart bind9.service` command.

Recall from Chapter 12 that you can use the `dig` command to test name resolution. The `dig` command can also query the records that exist on a specific DNS server using the format `dig @server record type`, where `server` is the name or IP address of the DNS server, `record` is the name of the resource record or domain, and `type` is the type of record (A, CNAME, PTR, MX, NS, SOA, ANY, etc.). This is especially useful if you want to see whether a zone transfer from a primary (master) DNS server to a secondary (slave) DNS server was successful. You can query the secondary DNS server to find out whether the new records have been added.

NTP

Most system components and network services require the correct date and time to function properly, as well as log events at the correct time. Recall from Chapter 8 that the BIOS on each computer contains a system clock that stores the date and time used to generate the time localization needed by the Linux system during the boot process. After the boot process has completed, many Linux systems obtain their time information from other servers on the network using the Network Time Protocol (NTP). This ensures that the time used by system components and network services remains correct if the system clock is modified or contains inaccurate time information.

Note 11

NTP is an optional time service. Some Linux distributions, such as Ubuntu Server, do not install an NTP daemon during the installation process. In this case, all time information is obtained from the system clock at boot time.

NTP is one of the oldest Internet protocols still commonly used on the Internet. It is designed to simplify the setting of time and date information on computers across the Internet using TCP or UDP port 123. The two NTP daemons that are commonly used on Linux systems are the **NTP daemon (ntpd)** and **Chrony NTP daemon (chronyd)**.

Understanding NTP Strata

NTP uses a hierarchical series of time sources called **strata**. Stratum 0 is at the top of this hierarchy and consists of atomic devices or GPS clocks. Stratum 1 devices obtain their time directly from Stratum 0 devices. Stratum 2 devices obtain their time from Stratum 1 servers, and so on. This organization is shown in Figure 13-3.

Figure 13-3   A sample strata structure

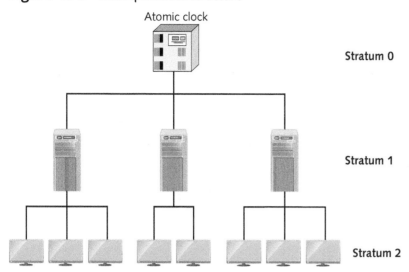

The stratum is not an indication of quality or reliability because NTP servers typically obtain time information from multiple time sources (NTP servers) and use an algorithm to determine the most reliable time information. As a result, it is common to find a Stratum 3 device that is more accurate than a Stratum 2 device.

Note 12

NTP supports up to 256 strata.

Note 13

Most Internet time servers, such as time.apple.com, are Stratum 1 devices.

Working with ntpd

Traditionally, most Linux systems used ntpd to provide for NTP functionality. It can act as both an NTP client to obtain time from an Internet time server or an NTP server that other computers can query for time information. Although Linux distributions typically install ntpd during the Linux installation process, it can be installed from a software repository if it is not available.

To configure a Linux system as an NTP client using ntpd, you can modify the /etc/ntp.conf file and add lines for different NTP servers the client can query. These servers could be any strata or combinations of different strata.

For example, the following lines in /etc/ntp.conf query three time servers using fast clock synchronization (iburst): ntp.research.gov, ntp.redhat.com, and 0.fedora.pool.ntp.org.

```
pool ntp.research.gov iburst
pool ntp.redhat.com iburst
pool 0.fedora.pool.ntp.org iburst
```

Note 14

Each of the FQDNs listed in the preceding output may point to multiple servers as NTP servers typically have several A (host) records in DNS that list the name FQDN for different IP addresses. This allows NTP requests to be spread across all servers to reduce server load.

If your time differs significantly from the time on these time servers, you must first stop ntpd and then run the `ntpdate command` to manually synchronize the time. You might need to run the `ntpdate` command several times until the time difference (or offset) is far less than 1 second. After manually synchronizing the time in this way, you can start the ntpd daemon again. This process is shown in the following output:

```
[root@server1 ~]# systemctl stop ntpd.service
[root@server1 ~]# ntpdate -u 0.fedora.pool.ntp.org
4 Sep 15:03:43 ntpdate[2908]: adjust time server 206.248.190.142 offset
0.977783 sec
[root@server1 ~]# ntpdate -u 0.fedora.pool.ntp.org
4 Sep 15:03:53 ntpdate[2909]: adjust time server 206.248.190.142 offset
0.001751 sec
[root@server1 ~]# ntpdate -u 0.fedora.pool.ntp.org
4 Sep 15:04:01 ntpdate[2910]: adjust time server 206.248.190.142 offset
0.001291 sec
[root@server1 ~]# systemctl start ntpd.service
[root@server1 ~]#_
```

After restarting the ntpd daemon, you can use the `ntpq command` to see what actual time servers you are synchronizing with. Because time varies greatly by location, NTP uses a jitter buffer to store the difference between the same time measurements from different NTP servers. The jitter information is used by NTP when determining the most reliable time when several NTP servers are queried for time information. The `ntpq -p` command shows the offset and jitter in milliseconds, as shown here:

```
[root@server1 ~]# ntpq -p
remote       refid          st t when poll reach  delay  offset jitter
==============================================================================
ox.eicat.ca 139.78.135.14  2  u    6   64    3  28.662  11.138  0.046
adelaide.ph 142.3.100.15   3  u    2   64    3  62.211  30.870  0.574
one.trx.com 209.51.161.238 2  u    3   64    3  43.329  22.867  0.190
[root@server1 ~]#_
```

By default, the NTP daemon is not configured as an NTP server because the /etc/ntp.conf file only contains two `restrict` lines that only allow the local host to query the NTP daemon with no restrictions via IPv4 or IPv6:

```
restrict 127.0.0.1
restrict ::1
```

If you want to allow other computers to query your NTP daemon (ntpd) for time information, edit the /etc/ntp.conf file again and add a line that identifies the specific computers or networks that are allowed to query your NTP daemon. For example, the following line within /etc/ntp.conf allows all computers on the 192.168.1.0 network to query your NTP daemon for time information but prevents other computers from modifying your NTP server configuration (`nomodify notrap`).

```
restrict 192.168.1.0 mask 255.255.255.0 nomodify notrap
```

Note 15

If you modify the /etc/ntp.conf file, you must restart ntpd for those changes to take effect.

Working with chronyd

Many modern Linux distributions use the newer chronyd NTP daemon in place of ntpd. It uses the /etc/chrony.conf configuration file. You can add the location of NTP servers to query for time information, as well as add lines that allow other NTP servers to query you on a particular subnet. As with ntpd, the line `pool 0.fedora.pool.ntp.org iburst` would configure chronyd to obtain time information from the pool of servers identified by the host name 0.fedora.pool.ntp.org using fast clock synchronization. However, to allow other NTP clients to query your time, you must add the line `allow` *subnet* to /etc/chrony.conf. For example, the line `allow 192.168.1/24` would allow NTP clients to connect from the 192.168.1.0 network (with a 24-bit subnet mask of 255.255.255.0).

For management, chronyd uses the `chronyc command` to provide the functionality that the `ntpdate` and `ntpq` commands do with ntpd. For example, to view the servers that you are currently polling for time, run the `chronyc sources` command, as shown here:

```
[root@server1 ~]# chronyc sources
MS Name/IP address       Stratum Poll LastRx Last sample
===============================================================
^+ 209.167.68.100            2     6    22    +11ms [  +11ms] +/-    87ms
^+ 66.102.79.92              2     6    32    +3556us [+3669us] +/-   62ms
^+ ox.eicat.ca               2     6    42    -4311us [-4198us] +/-   75ms
^* 216.234.161.11            2     6    50     -41us [  +72us] +/-    81ms
[root@server1 ~]#_
```

When run without arguments, the `chronyc` command provides an interactive chronyc> prompt that you can use to type additional commands. Typing `help` at the chronyc> prompt will display a list of common commands, including `polltarget` (which can be used to poll a specified NTP server) and `settime` (which can be used to manually set the date and time to a specified value).

Nearly all Linux workstation distributions are configured to obtain time from an Internet time server using NTP and allow you to configure NTP settings using a graphical application. For example, to obtain time from an Internet time server using chronyd on a Fedora Workstation system, you can navigate to Activities, Show Applications, Settings within the GNOME desktop, highlight Date & Time, and ensure that Automatic Date & Time is enabled, as shown in Figure 13-4.

Figure 13-4   Configuring NTP in GNOME Settings

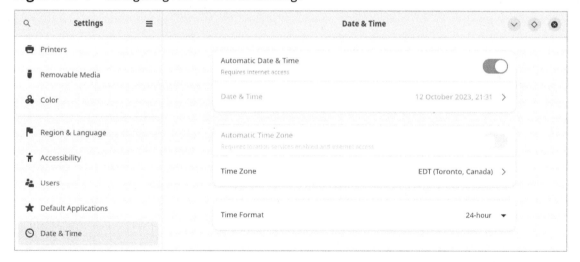

Web Services

Apache is the world's most common web server. It started as the HTTP Daemon (httpd) developed by Rob McCool for the NCSA (National Center for Supercomputing Applications) at the University of Illinois. In the early 1990s, Rob McCool became too busy to continue the project single-handedly, so he released the source code for httpd under the GPL. Open Source Software developers then made patches to this code, with each patch improving one component of the system. These patches gave rise to the name Apache server (a patchy server). After these early days, the Apache Group of Open Source Developers took over development of Apache. To learn more about this group, go to apache.org.

Recall that web servers hand out HTML files and other web content using the HyperText Transfer Protocol (HTTP) from a specific directory in the directory tree. This directory is called the **document root** directory and contains the default website that is used on the server. On most systems, the default document root directory is /var/www/html, and the default document that is handed out from this directory is index.html. The main configuration file for Apache differs based on your Linux distribution. On Fedora, the main Apache configuration file is /etc/httpd/conf/httpd.conf, and for Ubuntu Server, the main Apache configuration file is /etc/apache2/apache2.conf. Each line in the httpd.conf file is called a **directive**. Table 13-2 lists some common directives.

> **Note 16**
>
> The main Apache configuration file often references several other configuration files that contain directives used by Apache.

> **Note 17**
>
> The name of the Apache package and service differs in each Linux distribution. For example, to install Apache on Fedora systems, you can install the httpd package and use the command `systemctl start httpd.service` to start Apache. However, to install Apache on Ubuntu systems, you install the apache2 package and use the `systemctl start apache2.service` command to start Apache.

Table 13-2   Common Apache configuration file directives

Directive	What It Specifies
`Listen 80`	Apache daemon will listen for HTTP requests on port 80.
`ServerName server1.class.com`	Name of the local server is server1.class.com.
`DocumentRoot /var/www/html`	Document root directory is /var/www/html on the local computer.
`DirectoryIndex index.html`	The index.html file in the document root directory will be sent to clients who request an HTML document.
`ServerRoot /etc/httpd`	All paths listed within Apache configuration files are relative to the /etc/httpd directory.
`ErrorLog logs/error_log`	All Apache daemon messages will be written to the logs/error_log file under the ServerRoot.
`CustomLog logs/access_log combined`	All web requests will be written to the logs/access_log file under the ServerRoot using a combined log format.
`MaxClients 150`	Maximum number of simultaneous requests cannot exceed 150.
`User apache`	Apache daemon will run as the apache local user account.
`Group apache`	Apache daemon will run as the apache local group account.
`Include configurationfile`	Include directives that are listed in the specified configuration file.
`IncludeOptional configurationfile`	Include directives that are listed in the specified configuration file, if it exists.
`<Directory /var/www/html>` `Order allow,deny` `Allow from all` `Deny from 192.168.1.51` `</Directory>`	All hosts are allowed to access HTML files and other web content via Apache from the /var/www/html directory except for the computer with the IP address 192.168.1.51.

The default settings in the Apache configuration file are sufficient for most simple web servers; thus, you only need to copy the appropriate HTML files to the /var/www/html directory, including the index.html file, start Apache to host web content on your network, and ensure that Apache is started automatically at boot time. Client computers can then enter the location http://servername or http://IPaddress in their web browser to obtain the default webpage. Each time a client request is received by the Apache web server (called a webpage hit), a separate Apache daemon is started to service the request.

> ### Note 18
>
> You can also use the `curl` command at a shell prompt to obtain a webpage. For example, the `curl http://127.0.0.1/` command can be used to test your local Apache web server to ensure that your Apache web server is sending the correct webpage to clients.

On a busy web server, there may be several hundred Apache daemons running on the system responding to client requests. The first Apache daemon is started as the root user and is used to start all other Apache daemons. These non-root Apache daemons are started as a regular user account to prevent privileged access to the system. For example, the `User apache` directive shown in Table 13-2 will ensure that non-root Apache daemons are started as the apache user. In this case, any web content must have Linux permissions that allow it to be readable by the apache user. When you restart Apache, the root Apache daemon is restarted, which in turn restarts all other Apache daemons. If you change the HTML content inside the document root directory, you do not need to restart Apache. However, if you change the contents of an Apache configuration file, you need to restart Apache to activate those changes.

> ### Note 19
>
> The `apachectl command` is useful when managing Apache. The `apachectl graceful` command can be used to restart Apache without dropping any client connections, whereas the `apachectl configtest` command checks the syntax of lines within Apache configuration files and notes any errors.

> ### Note 20
>
> The `ab (Apache benchmark) command` can be used to monitor the performance of the Apache web server by sending null requests to it. To send 1000 requests to the local Apache web server (100 at a time), you could use `the ab -n1000 -c100 http://127.0.0.1/` command.

> ### Note 21
>
> Another popular web server used on Linux systems is Nginx. You can learn more about Nginx at nginx.com.

File Sharing Services

Many file sharing services are available on Linux systems. Each is tailored for a specific purpose and has a different configuration method. The most common include Samba, NFS, and FTP.

Samba

Microsoft Windows is the most used client computer operating system, so you need to know how to configure your Linux system to communicate with Windows computers. Windows computers format TCP/IP data using the Server Message Blocks (SMB) protocol. To share information with Windows client computers, you can use the Samba daemon (smbd), which emulates the SMB protocol. In addition, Windows computers advertise their computer names using the **NetBIOS** protocol. To create and advertise a NetBIOS name that Windows computers can use to connect to your Linux server, you can use the NetBIOS name daemon (nmbd).

Note 22

NetBIOS names can be up to 15 characters long and are normally resolved on the network using a WINS (Windows Internet Name Service) server or NetBIOS broadcasts. All NetBIOS names that are successfully resolved are placed in a NetBIOS name cache to speed future access to the same servers. The `nmblookup` command can be used to test NetBIOS name resolution in Linux.

Note 23

Because of the widespread popularity of SMB, nearly all operating systems, including Linux, macOS, UNIX, and Microsoft Windows, can connect to directories that are shared using the SMB protocol.

Note 24

SMB is sometimes referred to as the Common Internet File System (CIFS).

Configuring a Samba Server

When a Windows client computer accesses a shared directory using SMB, the Windows user name and password checksum are transmitted alongside the request in case the shared directory allows access to certain users only. As a result, you should first create local Linux user accounts for each Windows user and create a Samba password for them using the `smbpasswd` command that matches the password that they use on their Windows computer, as shown in the following output:

```
[root@server1 ~]# useradd mary
[root@server1 ~]# passwd mary
Changing password for user mary.
New UNIX password:
Retype new UNIX password:
passwd: all authentication tokens updated successfully.
[root@server1 ~]# smbpasswd -a mary
New SMB password:
Retype new SMB password:
Added user mary.
[root@server1 ~]#_
```

Following this, you can edit the main configuration file for Samba, /etc/samba/smb.conf. The smb .conf contains directives that can be used to set your NetBIOS name, server settings, shared directories, and shared printers. On most Linux systems, the default settings within the smb.conf file shares all CUPS printers and home directories (for recognized Windows users). However, you need to add a line under the [global] section of this file to set your NetBIOS name. For example, to set your NetBIOS name to server1, you could add the directive `netbios name = server1` to the smb.conf file. As with Apache, if you change the smb.conf file, you must restart the Samba and NetBIOS name daemons.

Note 25

You can use the `testparm` command to ensure that the /etc/samba/smb.conf file has no syntax errors. As a result, it is good practice to run this command after you edit the /etc/samba/smb.conf file.

Connecting to a Samba Server

After configuring Samba, you should test its functionality to ensure that it is functioning normally. To do this on a Windows client, you can browse to the name of your Samba server within the File Explorer app, or enter *server* within a Windows search dialog box, where *server* is the NetBIOS name or IP address of your Samba server. If successful, the Windows operating system will open a new window that displays your home directory, shared printers, and other shared directories that you have permission to access, as shown in Figure 13-5.

Figure 13-5   Accessing a Samba server from a Windows client

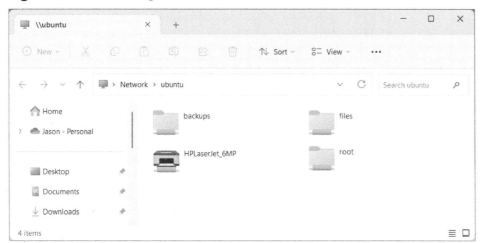

You can also connect to your Samba server from a macOS, UNIX, or Linux system by entering smb://*server* or cifs://*server* within the appropriate part of a graphical file browser app, where *server* is the NetBIOS name or IP address of your Samba server. Alternatively, you can use the smbclient command on your Linux computer to connect to a Samba server from a shell. For example, the following command connects to server1 as the current user (root) to list the shared directories and available printers:

```
[root@server1 ~]# smbclient -L server1
Enter root's password:
Domain=[WORKGROUP] OS=[Unix] Server=[Samba 4.15.9-Ubuntu]

    Sharename       Type        Comment
    ---------       ----        -------
    backups         Disk        Backup share
    files           Disk        Common file share
    root            Disk        root user home directory share
    print$          Disk        Printer Drivers
    IPC$            IPC         Service(server1 server (Samba,Ubuntu))
    HPLaserJet_6MP  Printer     HP LaserJet 6MP in the Accounting office
[root@server1 ~]#_
```

Note 26

You can use the smbclient command to connect to both Samba and Windows servers.

You can also use the `smbclient` command to display an FTP-like interface for transferring files to and from shared directories on Samba or Windows servers. The following output demonstrates how to connect to the shared directory called files on server1 using an FTP-like interface:

```
[root@server1 root]# smbclient //server1/files
Enter root's password:
Domain=[WORKGROUP] OS=[Unix] Server=[Samba 4.15.9-Ubuntu]
smb: \> dir
  .                          D        0  Mon Sep  6 22:28:12 2023
  ..                         D        0  Mon Sep  6 22:28:12 2023
  Final Exam.doc             A    26624  Mon Sep  6 23:17:30 2023
  homework questions.doc     A    46080  Mon Sep  6 23:33:03 2023
  Part 0.DOC                 A    13312  Mon Sep  6 23:27:51 2023
  Part 1.DOC                 A    35328  Mon Sep  6 23:24:44 2023
  Part 2.doc                 A    70656  Mon Sep  6 23:25:28 2023
  Part 3.DOC                 A    38912  Mon Sep  6 23:26:07 2023
  Part 4.doc                 A    75776  Mon Sep  6 23:26:57 2023
  Part 5.DOC                 A    26624  Mon Sep  6 23:27:23 2023
  Part 6.doc                 A    59904  Mon Sep  6 23:05:32 2023
  TOC.doc                    A    58880  Mon Sep  6 23:09:16 2023
39032 blocks of size 262144. 14180 blocks available

smb: \> help
?               allinfo         altname         archive         backup
blocksize       cancel          case_sensitive  cd              chmod
chown           close           del             dir             du
echo            exit            get             getfacl         geteas
hardlink        help            history         iosize          lcd
link            lock            lowercase       ls              l
mask            md              mget            mkdir           more
mput            newer           notify          open            posix
posix_encrypt   posix_open      posix_mkdir     posix_rmdir     posix_unlink
print           prompt          put             pwd             q
queue           quit            readlink        rd              recurse
reget           rename          reput           rm              rmdir
showacls        setea           setmode         stat            symlink
tar             tarmode         timeout         translate       unlock
volume          vuid            wdel            logon           listconnect
showconnect     tcon            tdis            tid             logoff
..              !
smb: \> get TOC.doc
getting file \TOC.doc of size 58880 as TOC.doc (16.0 KiloBytes/sec)
(average 16.0 KiloBytes/sec)
smb: \> exit
[root@server1 root]#_
```

NFS

Network File System (NFS) allows UNIX, Linux, macOS, and Windows computers to share files transparently. In NFS, one computer shares a directory in the directory tree by placing the name of that directory in the /etc/exports file. The other computer can then access that directory across the network by using the `mount` command to mount the remote directory on the local computer. Permissions to files and directories in the NFS share are processed by UID and GID. For example, a user with UID=1001 on an NFS client will be seen as the user with UID=1001 on the NFS server. Thus, it is important to coordinate the creation of users and their associated UIDs and GIDs across systems that share directories with NFS.

Configuring a Linux NFS Server

To configure an NFS server, you can edit the /etc/exports file and add a line that lists the directory to share and the appropriate options. For example, the following lines in the /etc/exports file share the /source directory to the computer server1, allowing users to read and write data while ensuring that the root user is treated as an anonymous user on the NFS server, as well as share the /admin directory to all users, allowing users to read and write data:

```
/source   server1(rw,root_squash)
/admin    *(rw)
```

After editing the /etc/exports file, you must run the command `exportfs -a` to update the list of exported filesystems in memory and restart the NFS daemon.

Note 27

The name of the NFS server package differs based on Linux distribution. On Fedora, you can install the nfs-utils package, and on Ubuntu you can install the nfs-kernel-server package.

Note 28

The name of the NFS daemon is nfsd. To restart this daemon on a Fedora system, you can use the `systemctl restart nfs-server.service` command. Alternatively, you can use the `systemctl restart nfs-kernel-server.service` command on an Ubuntu system to restart nfsd.

Connecting to a Linux NFS Server

You can see a list of available NFS shared directories on a remote server using the `showmount` command. For example, to see a list of the shared directories on the server nfs.sampledomain.com, you could use the following command:

```
[root@server1 ~]# showmount -e nfs.sampledomain.com
Export list for 192.168.1.104:
/var *
[root@server1 ~]#_
```

From the preceding output, the /var directory on the nfs.sampledomain.com server is shared to all hosts (*).

To access files using NFS, you mount a directory from a remote NFS server on the network to a directory on your local computer. That is, you specify the nfs filesystem type, server name or IP address, remote directory, and local directory as arguments to the `mount` command. For example, to mount the /var directory on the remote computer named nfs.sampledomain.com (IP address 192.168.0.1) to the /mnt directory on the local computer using NFS and view the results, you can use the following commands:

```
[root@server1 ~]# mount -t nfs nfs.sampledomain.com:/var /mnt
[root@server1 ~]# mount | grep nfs
192.168.0.1:/var on /mnt type nfs (rw,vers=4,clientaddr=192.168.1.105)
[root@server1 ~]# ls /mnt
arpwatch   ftpkerberos   lock   mailman   nis        run     tux
cachegdm   lib           log    mars_nwe  opt        spool   www
dbiptraf   local         mail   named     preserve   tmpyp
[root@server1 ~]#_
```

After running these commands, you can use the /mnt directory as any other local directory, with all file operations performed in the /var directory on the remote computer. You can then dismount the NFS filesystem using the umount command.

Note 29

UNIX and macOS users can access NFS shares on Linux systems using the same mount command syntax shown in the previous example. Windows users can also access NFS shares provided that their Windows system has the Client for NFS feature installed. In this case, Windows users can enter *server**directory* within a Windows search dialog box or the File Explorer app, where *server* is the name or IP address of the NFS server, and *directory* is the exported directory on the NFS server.

FTP

Recall from Chapter 1 that the protocol most used to transfer files on public networks is the File Transfer Protocol (FTP). FTP hosts files differently than NFS. In anonymous access, a special directory is available to any user who wants to connect to the FTP server. Alternatively, users can log in, via an FTP client program, to a home directory on the FTP server.

Configuring a Linux FTP Server

The traditional FTP server program is the Washington University FTP daemon (wu-ftpd). However, most Linux systems today use the **Very Secure FTP daemon (vsftpd)**, which provides additional security features, including support for SSH using **Secure FTP (SFTP)**. To configure vsftpd, you can edit the /etc/vsftpd.conf file and modify the appropriate commented options to control what actions the vsftpd daemon will allow from FTP clients. This includes:

- Whether to allow anonymous connections
- Whether to allow local user connections
- Whether to allow users to upload files
- Whether to prevent users from accessing files outside their home directory (called a "chroot jail")

After modifying the /etc/vsftpd.conf file, you must restart the vsftpd daemon.

When you connect to the vsftpd daemon using an FTP client utility, you are prompted to log in. If you log in as the user "anonymous," you will be placed in the /var/ftp or /srv/ftp directory, depending on your Linux distribution. Alternatively, if you log in as a valid user account on the system, you will be placed in that user's home directory.

Note 30

The root user is not allowed to connect to vsftpd by default. To log in as the root user to vsftpd, you must remove the line root from the /etc/ftpusers and /etc/user_list files, if they exist.

Note 31

On Fedora Linux, the configuration files for vsftpd are stored within the /etc/vsftpd directory. For example, the configuration file for vsftpd on Fedora would be /etc/vsftpd/vsftpd.conf.

Connecting to a Linux FTP Server

Most operating systems contain a command-line FTP utility that can connect to an FTP server. To use such a utility, you specify the host name or IP address of an FTP server as an argument to the ftp command for standard FTP, or the sftp command for Secure FTP (SFTP). This opens a connection that allows the transfer of files to and from that computer. You can then log in as a valid user on that computer, in which case you are automatically placed in your home directory. Alternatively, you can log in as the user "anonymous" and be placed in the /var/ftp or /srv/ftp directory, depending on your Linux distribution. After you are logged in, you receive an interactive prompt that accepts FTP commands. A list of common FTP commands is shown in Table 13-3.

Note 32

Most FTP servers require you enter a password when logging in as the anonymous user via a command-line FTP utility; this value you specify for this password is irrelevant.

Note 33

The `ftp` command will prompt you for a user name and password when connecting to an FTP server, whereas the `sftp` command assumes the current user name and prompts only for a password. To connect as a different user using SFTP, you can use the `sftp username@server` command, where *server* is the name or IP address of the FTP server.

Note 34

If the FTP server does not allow SSH logins as the root user, you will not be able to connect using SFTP as the root user, because SFTP negotiates SSH encryption prior to starting the FTP session.

Table 13-3   Common FTP commands

Command	Description
`help`	Displays a list of commands
`pwd`	Displays the current directory on the remote computer
`dir` `ls`	Displays a directory listing from the remote computer
`cd directory`	Changes the current directory to *directory* on the remote computer
`lcd directory`	Changes the current directory to *directory* on the local computer
`get filename`	Downloads the *filename* to the current directory on the local computer
`ascii`	Specifies text file downloads for standard FTP connections (default)
`binary`	Specifies binary file downloads for standard FTP connections
`mget filename`	Downloads the file named *filename* to the current directory on the local computer; it also allows the use of wildcard metacharacters to specify the *filename*
`put filename`	Uploads the *filename* from the current directory on the local computer to the current directory on the remote computer
`mput filename`	Uploads the *filename* from the current directory on the local computer to the current directory on the remote computer; it also allows the use of wildcard metacharacters to specify the *filename*
`!`	Runs a shell on the local computer
`close`	Closes the standard FTP connection to the remote computer
`open server`	Opens a standard FTP connection to the name or IP address of the *server* specified
`bye` `quit`	Quits the FTP utility

The exact output displayed during an FTP session varies slightly depending on the version of the FTP software used on the FTP server. The following output is an example of using the `ftp` command to connect to an FTP server named ftp.sampledomain.com as the root user:

```
[root@server1 ~]# ftp ftp.sampledomain.com
Connected to ftp.sampledomain.com.
220 (vsFTPd 3.0.5)
Name (ftp.sampledomain.com:root): root
331 Please specify the password.
Password:
230 Login successful.
Remote system type is UNIX.
Using binary mode to transfer files.
ftp>
```

The current directory on the remote computer is the home directory for the root user in the preceding output. To verify this and see a list of files to download, you can use the following commands at the `ftp>` prompt:

```
ftp> pwd
257 "/root"
ftp> ls
227 Entering Passive Mode (192,168,0,1,56,88).
150 Here comes the directory listing.
total 2064
-rw-r--r--    1 root      root          1756 Aug 14 08:48 file1
-rw-r--r--    1 root      root           160 Aug 14 08:48 file2
-rw-r--r--    1 root      root       1039996 Aug 14 08:39 file3
drwxr-xr-x    2 root      root          4096 Aug 14 08:50 stuff
226 Directory send OK.
ftp>
```

The preceding output shows three files and one subdirectory. To download file3 to the current directory on the local computer, you can use the following command:

```
ftp> get file3
local: file3 remote: file3
227 Entering Passive Mode (192,168,0,1,137,37)
150 Opening BINARY mode data connection for file3 (1039996 bytes).
226 Transfer complete.
ftp>
```

Similarly, to change the current directory on the remote computer to /root/stuff and upload a copy of file4 from the current directory on the local computer to it, as well as view the results and then exit the ftp utility, you can use the following commands at the `ftp>` prompt:

```
ftp> cd stuff
250 Directory successfully changed.
ftp> pwd
257 "/root/stuff"
ftp> mput file4
mput file4? y
227 Entering Passive Mode (192,168,0,1,70,109)
150 Opening BINARY mode data connection for file4.
226 Transfer complete.
929 bytes sent in 0.00019 seconds (4.8e+03 Kbytes/s)
```

```
ftp> ls
227 Entering Passive Mode (192,168,0,1,235,35)
150 Opening ASCII mode data connection for directory listing.
total 8
-rw-r--r--    1 root      root          929 Aug 14 09:26 file4
226 Transfer complete.
ftp> bye
221 Goodbye.
[root@server1 ~]#_
```

Note 35

In addition to the command-line FTP/SFTP client included with your computer's operating system, you can choose from many third-party graphical FTP/SFTP client programs, such as Filezilla.

Email Services

As mentioned in Chapter 1, email servers are often called Mail Transfer Agents (MTAs). They typically accept email and route it over the Internet using Simple Mail Transfer Protocol (SMTP) or Enhanced Simple Mail Transfer Protocol (ESMTP) on TCP port 25. Additionally, client computers can retrieve email from email servers using a variety of protocols such as Post Office Protocol (POP) or Internet Message Access Protocol (IMAP). Client computers can also send email to email servers using SMTP/ESMTP for later relay on the Internet.

To relay email to other servers on the Internet, an email server must look up the name of the target email server in the domain's MX (Mail Exchanger) records, which are stored on a public DNS server. For example, if your local email server needs to send email to jason.eckert@trios.com, the email server locates the name of the target email server by looking up the MX record for the trios .com domain. It then resolves the target email server name to the appropriate IP address using the A (host) record for the server on the public DNS server.

Daemons and other system components on Linux systems traditionally relied on email to send important information to the root user. Because Systemd can be used to log detailed daemon information intended for the root user, many modern Linux distributions that use Systemd do not install an email daemon by default, but an email daemon can easily be added afterwards from a software repository. The most common email daemon used on modern Linux systems is **Postfix**.

The Postfix daemon is configured by default to accept email on TCP port 25 and route it to the appropriate user on the Linux system. To test this, you can use the `telnet` command with port 25 as an argument. This displays a Welcome banner that identifies the email server, as shown in the following output. Additionally, you can use the EHLO command to test ESMTP support and the HELO command to test SMTP support, as shown in the following output:

```
[root@server1 ~]# telnet localhost 25
Connected to localhost.
Escape character is '^]'.
220 server1.class.com ESMTP Postfix
EHLO sample.com
250-server1.class.com
250-PIPELINING
250-SIZE 10240000
250-VRFY
250-ETRN
250-ENHANCEDSTATUSCODES
```

```
250-8BITMIME
250 DSN
HELO sample.com
250 server1.class.com
quit
221 2.0.0 Bye
Connection closed by foreign host.
[root@server1 ~]#_
```

To check your email on your local Linux system, you can use the `mail command`, as shown here:

```
[root@server1 ~]# mail
Mail version 8.1.2 01/15/2023.  Type ? for help.
"/var/spool/mail/root": 13 messages 6 new 10 unread
U  1 Cron Daemon              Sat Jul 11 07:01   26/981    "Cron"
U  2 logwatch@localhost.l     Mon Jul 20 11:43   42/1528   "Logwatch"
U  3 logwatch@localhost.l     Tue Jul 21 12:32  151/4669
N  4 jason.eckert@trios.c        Wed Sep 29 15:53   11/430
& 4
Message 4:
From jason.eckert@trios.com  Wed Sep 29 15:53:25 2023
Return-Path: <jason.eckert@trios.com>
Date: Wed, 29 Sep 2023 15:52:36 -0400
From: jason.eckert@trios.com
Status: R

Hey dude

& q
[root@server1 ~]#_
```

Note 36

Email for each user is stored within a file named for the user in the /var/spool/mail directory. For example, the email for the bob user will be stored within the /var/spool/mail/bob file.

Note 37

To forward email, users can create a ~/.forward file that lists a target email address. Any email sent to the user will automatically be forwarded to the target email address.

Note 38

The `mailq command` can be used to troubleshoot email delivery. By default, `mailq` displays any email messages awaiting delivery alongside the reason that they were not delivered.

The /etc/aliases file contains other email names that are used to identify the different users on the system. From the entries in the /etc/aliases file shown next, you can use the names postmaster, bin, daemon, or adm to refer to the root user:

```
[root@server1 ~]# head -17 /etc/aliases
# See man 5 aliases for format
postmaster: root
bin:        root
daemon:     root
adm:        root
[root@server1 ~]#_
```

If you modify the /etc/aliases file, you must run the `newaliases` command to rebuild the aliases database (/etc/aliases.db) based on the entries in the /etc/aliases file. Only the aliases database is used by the Postfix daemon.

While Postfix is normally configured to accept and route local email only, you can also configure it to relay email to other servers on the Internet as well as accept connections from email clients on your network using the POP and IMAP protocols. To do this, you must edit the /etc/postfix/main.cf file and restart the Postfix daemon afterwards. A common set of lines that you should modify or add at minimum is listed in Table 13-4.

Table 13-4   Sample lines in /etc/postfix/main.cf to modify or add when configuring Postfix

Line	Change
`mydomain = sample.com`	Sets the email domain name; changes to desired name
`myorigin = $mydomain`	Sets local access to the domain name
`inet_interfaces = all`	Configures Postfix to listen for email on all interfaces
`mydestination = $myhostname, localhost.$mydomain, localhost, $mydomain`	Configures destination domain for email
`mynetworks_style = class`	Trusts email from computers on the local network

Database Services

Recall from Chapter 1 that databases are large files that store important information in the form of tables. A **table** organizes information into a list. Within the list, the set of information about a particular item is called a **record**. For example, in a list of customer mailing addresses, a single record would contain a customer's first name, last name, street address, city, state, and Zip code. The various categories of information within a record are called **fields**. For example, in our customer mailing address example, one field contains the city information, one contains the state information, and so on.

Most databases consist of dozens or hundreds of tables that store information used by applications. For example, accounting software typically stores financial data within a database. In large databases, information within certain tables can be related to information within other tables in the same database. These databases are called **relational databases**, and the tables within are usually linked by a common field. Figure 13-6 shows a simple relational database that consists of two tables with a related EmployeeID field.

Figure 13-6   A simple relational database structure

EmployeeID	FirstName	LastName	Address	ZIP	Home Phone	Mobile Phone
A518	Bob	Smith	14 Wallington St.	49288	555-123-1399	555-144-2039
A827	Jill	Sagan	51 York Ave. N.	49282	555-132-1039	
A988	Frank	Kertz	623 Queen St.	44922	555-209-1039	555-199-2938
A472	Bethany	Weber	82 Shepherd Ave.	49100	555-299-0199	555-203-1000
A381	John	Lauer	55 Rooshill Ave.	49288	555-123-2883	555-203-2811

Common field

EmployeeID	Week	Hours	MgrOK	← Field names
A518	08/20/24	37	Yes	
A827	08/20/24	40	Yes	
A988	08/20/24	40	Yes	
A472	08/20/24	40	Yes	← Record
A381	08/20/24	22	Yes	
A518	08/27/24	40	Yes	
A827	08/27/24	35	Yes	
A988	08/27/24	0	Yes	
A472	08/27/24	40	Yes	
A381	08/27/24	22	Yes	

Structured Query Language (SQL) is a special programming language used to store and access the data in databases. The database server programs that allow users to access and update the data stored within a database are called **SQL servers**. Table 13-5 lists common SQL statements that are used to manipulate data on SQL servers.

Table 13-5   Common SQL statements

Command	Description
CREATE DATABASE *database_name*	Creates a database
DROP DATABASE *database_name*	Deletes a database
CREATE TABLE *table_name* *field_definitions*	Creates a table within a database
DROP TABLE *table_name*	Deletes a table within a database
INSERT INTO *table_name* VALUES *record*	Inserts a new record within a table
UPDATE *table_name* SET *record_modifications*	Modifies records within a table
DELETE FROM *table_name* *record*	Deletes a record within a table
SELECT * FROM *table_name*	Displays all records within a table
SELECT *fields* FROM *table_name* WHERE *criteria*	Displays one or more fields for records within a table that meet specific criteria
SELECT *fields* FROM *table_name* GROUP BY *field*	Displays one or more fields for records within a table and groups the results according to the values within a common field

Table 13-5   Common SQL statements (*continued*)

Command	Description
`SELECT fields FROM table_name ORDER BY field [ASC/DESC]`	Displays one or more fields for records within a table and sorts the results in ascending or descending order according to the values within a common field
`SELECT fields FROM table1 INNER JOIN table2 ON table1.common_field = table2.common_field`	Displays one or more fields for records within two related tables (`table1` and `table2`) that have a common field; only records that have matching information within the common field in both tables are displayed
`SELECT fields FROM table1 LEFT OUTER JOIN table2 ON table1.common_field = table2.common_field`	Displays one or more fields for all records within `table1` and any records within `table2` that have matching information within a common field
`SELECT fields FROM table1 RIGHT OUTER JOIN table2 ON table1.common_field = table2.common_field`	Displays one or more fields for all records within `table2` and any records within `table1` that have matching information within a common field
`CREATE USER user_name WITH PASSWORD`	Creates a user that can access the SQL server
`GRANT permissions ON table1 TO user_name`	Assigns permissions to a user that give the user the ability to work with `table1`, where `permissions` can include INSERT, UPDATE, SELECT, or DELETE

SQL servers usually offer advanced backup, repair, replication, and recovery utilities for the data within the database. In addition, SQL servers can store multiple databases, and they allow programs to access these databases from across the network. Thus, a single SQL server can store the data needed by all programs that exist on servers and client computers within the network. Although several SQL servers are available for Linux, PostgreSQL is one of the most widely used.

Configuring PostgreSQL

PostgreSQL is a powerful SQL server that provides a large number of features. Although some Linux server distributions allow you to install PostgreSQL during the Linux installation process, you can easily install it from a software repository afterwards. During installation, the PostgreSQL installation creates a postgres user within the /etc/passwd and /etc/shadow files that has a home directory of /var/lib/postgresql and a shell of /bin/bash. To manage PostgreSQL, you must assign this user a password using the `passwd postgres` command. To modify the default PostgreSQL configuration, you can modify the PostgreSQL configuration file, postgresql.conf. The location of this file differs depending on your Linux distribution, but it is often stored under the /var/lib/postgresql or /etc/postgresql directory.

Configuring PostgreSQL databases

To configure PostgreSQL databases, you must first log in as the postgres user. Next, you can execute one of several PostgreSQL command-line utilities to create and manage databases. These commands are summarized in Table 13-6.

Table 13-6 PostgreSQL command-line utilities

Command	Description
clusterdb	Associates a PostgreSQL database to another database on a different server
createdb	Creates a PostgreSQL database
createlang	Allows a new programming language to be used with PostgreSQL
createuser	Creates a PostgreSQL user
dropdb	Deletes a PostgreSQL database
droplang	Removes support for a programming language within PostgreSQL
dropuser	Deletes a PostgreSQL user
pg_dump	Backs up PostgreSQL database settings
pg_dumpall	Backs up PostgreSQL database cluster settings
pg_restore	Restores PostgreSQL database settings
psql	The PostgreSQL utility
reindexdb	Reindexes a PostgreSQL database
vacuumdb	Analyzes and regenerates internal PostgreSQL database statistics

For example, to create a database called sampledb after logging in as the postgres user, you could use the following command:

```
[postgres@server1 ~]$ createdb sampledb
[postgres@server1 ~]$ _
```

Next, you can run the `psql command` to connect to the employee database using the interactive **PostgreSQL utility**, where you can obtain information about the SQL statements and `psql` commands that can perform most database administration.

```
[postgres@server1 ~]$ psql sampledb
psql (14.5 (Ubuntu 14.5-0ubuntu-.22.04))
Type "help" for help.

sampledb=# help
You are using psql, the command-line interface to PostgreSQL.
Type:  \copyright for distribution terms
       \h for help with SQL commands
       \? for help with psql commands
       \g or terminate with semicolon to execute query
       \q to quit
sampledb=# _
```

You can create tables and add records within the PostgreSQL utility using the appropriate SQL statements. The following output shows how to create a table called "employee" with three fields (Name, Dept, Title) that each allow 20 characters of information, add three employee records, and display the results.

```
sampledb=# CREATE TABLE employee (Name char(20), Dept char(20), Title char(20));
CREATE TABLE
sampledb=# INSERT INTO employee VALUES ('Jeff Smith','Research','Analyst');
INSERT 0 1
sampledb=# INSERT INTO employee VALUES ('Mary Wong','Accounting','Manager');
```

```
INSERT 0 1
sampledb=# INSERT INTO employee VALUES ('Pat Clarke','Marketing','Coordinator');
INSERT 0 1
sampledb=# SELECT * from employee;
        name          |        dept          |        title
----------------------+----------------------+----------------------
 Jeff Smith           | Research             | Analyst
 Mary Wong            | Accounting           | Manager
 Pat Clarke           | Marketing            | Coordinator
(3 rows)

sampledb=#_
```

Note 39

Each SQL statement that is entered within the PostgreSQL utility must end with a ; metacharacter.

In addition to SQL statements, the PostgreSQL utility has many built-in commands. These commands, which are prefixed with a \ character, can be used to obtain database information or perform functions within the PostgreSQL utility. The most common of these built-in commands are listed in Table 13-7.

Table 13-7   Common built-in PostgreSQL utility commands

Command	Description
\l	Lists available databases
\c *database_name*	Connects to a different database
\d	Lists the tables within the current database
\d *table_name*	Lists the fields within a table
\q	Exits the PostgreSQL utility

Working with Cloud Technologies

Recall from Chapter 1 that complex web apps (and the data they access) are the most common Internet-accessible resource, and that the servers that host them are collectively referred to as the cloud. Organizations that provide access to web apps running in their data center are called cloud providers, and may provide public access to their data center, or may keep the access to their data center private to their own organization. Moreover, web apps may be hosted on a cloud server one of three ways:

- Within virtual machines on a cloud provider's hardware infrastructure. This is called the Infrastructure as a Service (IaaS) delivery model and illustrated in Figure 1-9.
- Within containers running on an underlying operating system platform via a container runtime. This is called the Platform as a Service (PaaS) delivery model and illustrated in Figure 1-10.
- Directly on an operating system maintained by the cloud provider. This is called the Software as a Service (SaaS) delivery model and illustrated in Figure 1-11.

PaaS is the most common delivery model used to host web apps today. By running web apps within containers, software developers can test them on their workstation using the same environment that will be used to run them in the cloud. In other words, the container running on a software developer's workstation will work the same way when it is run on a cloud provider. Moreover, containers use far less underlying system resources compared to virtual machines and can be easily scaled to match the needs of users. Say, for example, that you create an IoT device that can be controlled remotely from a web app running on a cloud provider, and that you plan on selling thousands of these devices to customers. In this case, you don't need to create a large, complex web app that is designed to connect to thousands of devices simultaneously and hosted using IaaS or SaaS on a cloud provider. Instead, you can create a small, simple web app that can connect to a single device and host that web app within a container that can be run thousands of times on a cloud provider. When a customer connects to their device, a new container is run on the cloud provider to start a unique copy of the web app for that customer's device. Similarly, when a customer disconnects from their device, the cloud provider stops running the customer's container to free up system resources.

> **Note 40**
>
> Because public cloud providers have ample hardware in their datacenters to scale containers thousands of times, they are often called **hyperscalers**.

Regardless of delivery model, storage is a key consideration in the design and hosting of a web app. This is because web apps often need to store large amounts of data on a cloud provider. One option is to store this data on a filesystem that is provided by the cloud provider; this type of storage is called **block storage**, and the cloud provider charges you based on the total amount of storage that you select for your filesystem. Because block storage is fast, it is often used for storing database files, but is normally associated with a single virtual machine or container only. Another storage option that most cloud providers offer is called **object storage**. Object storage allows web apps to directly store objects, such as pictures, files, and video using an HTTP request that is sent to the cloud provider's object storage service. While object storage is slower than block storage, it is often less expensive as you are charged only for the space that is used by the objects you've stored. In addition, object storage can easily be shared by several virtual machines or containers. Web apps that need to store and share thousands of pictures, files, and video typically use object storage.

> **Note 41**
>
> Block storage is often referred to as a **persistent volume**, and object storage is often called **Binary Large Object (BLOB)** storage.

A continuous deployment (CD) workflow is used to develop new versions of web apps and host them in the cloud. As illustrated in Figure 1-13 and described in Chapter 7, this workflow typically begins when a developer commits code changes within a Git branch to a code repository (e.g., GitHub), where the code can be reviewed, approved, and merged into the main branch. This part of the workflow is called continuous integration (CI) and often involves additional code security and compliance checks. Next, orchestration software will obtain a copy of the web app and deploy the appropriate environment (virtual machine or container) using build automation software. If the web app is tested successfully in this environment, it is placed into production and made available to users.

If you work as a Linux administrator supporting the CD workflow (i.e., a DevOp), you will need a solid understanding of how containers and microservices work, as well as the process used to create and deploy containers and virtual machines within the cloud.

Working with Containers

Recall from Chapter 1 that operating systems must use container runtime software to run containers. The most common container runtime software used today is **Docker**, which consists of a Docker daemon and a series of operating system frameworks that support it. Nearly all Docker configuration is performed using the `docker` command, which is often referred to as the **Docker client** program.

Note 42

Docker is available for most operating systems, including Linux, UNIX, macOS, and Windows.

Docker provides an online container registry of preconfigured container images that you can download and run on your system. This container registry is called Docker Hub and can be used to host public container images available to anyone, or private container images that are only available to your user account on Docker Hub.

Note 43

You can create a free Docker Hub user account at hub.docker.com.

Note 44

Some organizations choose to create their own container registries instead of using Docker Hub.

To search Docker Hub for public container images, you can use the `docker search` command. For example, to search for a container image for Alpine Linux, you could use the following command:

```
[root@server1 ~]# docker search alpine | less
NAME                    DESCRIPTION
alpine                  A minimal Docker image based on Alpine Linux…
mhart/alpine-node       Minimal Node.js built on Alpine Linux
anapsix/alpine-java     Oracle Java 8 (and 7) with GLIBC 2.28 over A…
gliderlabs/alpine       Image based on Alpine Linux will help you wi…
frolvlad/alpine-glibc   Alpine Docker image with glibc (~12MB)
alpine/git              A simple git container running in alpine li…
kiasaki/alpine-postgres PostgreSQL docker image based on Alpine Linux
zzrot/alpine-caddy       Caddy Server Docker Container running on Alp…
easypi/alpine-arm       AlpineLinux for RaspberryPi
davidcaste/alpine-tomcat Apache Tomcat 7/8 using Oracle Java 7/8 with…
byrnedo/alpine-curl     Alpine linux with curl installed and set :
[root@server1 ~]#_
```

The first result listed (`alpine`) is an official public Docker container image because it has a single name under the root of Docker Hub. Alternatively, the second result listed (`mhart/alpine-node`) is a container image called alpine-node hosted publicly by the user mhart. To download the latest version of the official Alpine Linux container image from Docker Hub, you can run the following command:

```
[root@server1 ~]# docker pull alpine
Using default tag: latest
latest: Pulling from library/alpine
4fe2ade4980c: Pull complete
Digest: sha256:621c2f39f8133acb8e64023a94dbdf0d5ca81896102b9e57c0dc184cadaf5528
Status: Downloaded newer image for alpine:latest
[root@server1 ~]#_
```

Container images on Docker Hub can have different version tags, much like files within a Git repository. The `docker pull alpine` command is essentially the same as `docker pull alpine:latest` (latest version of the alpine container). However, you can instead pull older versions of a container; for example, `docker pull alpine:3.6` would pull an older version (3.6) of the official Alpine Linux container. Downloaded container images are normally stored under the /var/lib/docker directory.

To view downloaded container images, you can use the `docker images` command. The following command indicates that the latest version of the Alpine Linux container image has been downloaded and is 4.41 MB in size:

```
[root@server1 ~]# docker images
REPOSITORY      TAG          IMAGE ID        CREATED        SIZE
alpine          latest       196d12cf6ab1    6 weeks ago    4.41MB
[root@server1 ~]#_
```

After you have a container image downloaded on your system, you can run copies of it as many times as you wish. To run a copy of the Alpine Linux container image on your Linux operating system and have it execute the `echo Hi` command, you could run the following `docker` command:

```
[root@server1 ~]# docker run alpine echo Hi
Hi
[root@server1 ~]#_
```

After the `echo Hi` command has completed executing, Docker stops running the container, releasing any resources it used back to the operating system. You can view currently running containers using the `docker ps` command, as well as see any previously run containers using the `docker ps -a` command. The following output demonstrates that the Alpine Linux container we ran in the previous output is no longer running, executed the `echo Hi` command 5 seconds ago, and exited successfully (exit status = 0) 4 seconds ago:

```
[root@server1 ~]# docker ps
CONTAINER ID   IMAGE   COMMAND     CREATED    STATUS              PORTS NAMES
[root@server1 ~]# docker ps -a
CONTAINER ID   IMAGE   COMMAND     CREATED    STATUS              PORTS NAMES
18280cdaf3bb   alpine  "echo Hi"   5s ago     Exited(0)4s ago           nice_cray
[root@server1 ~]#_
```

Note from the previous output that a random name was generated for the container during execution (`nice_cray`) because a name was not specified with the `docker run` command. This name is not mandatory, because all containers automatically receive a unique container ID when they are run that can be used to identify them afterwards.

Recall that containers can be identified uniquely on the network, as well as provide a sandboxed Linux environment to the web apps that they contain. To demonstrate this, the following commands run another copy of the Alpine Linux container image that interactively (`-it`) executes a shell (`sh`) to allow us to explore the filesystem, processes, host name, and IP configuration until we close the shell using the `exit` command:

```
[root@server1 ~]# docker run -it alpine sh
/ # ls
bin     etc     lib     mnt     root    sbin    sys     usr
dev     home    media   proc    run     srv     tmp     var
/ # ls /etc
TZ                 init.d           mtab            resolv.conf
alpine-release     inittab          network         securetty
apk                issue            opt             services
conf.d             localtime        os-release      shadow
crontabs           logrotate.d      passwd          shells
fstab              modprobe.d       periodic        ssl
group              modules          profile         sysctl.conf
hostname           modules-load.d   profile.d       sysctl.d
hosts              motd             protocols       udhcpd.conf
```

```
/ # ps -ef
PID   USER       TIME  COMMAND
    1 root       0:00  sh
    8 root       0:00  ps -ef
/ # hostname
260d4f5b3308
/ # ifconfig
eth0      Link encap:Ethernet  HWaddr 02:42:AC:11:00:02
          inet addr:172.17.0.2  Bcast:172.17.255.255  Mask:255.255.0.0
          UP BROADCAST RUNNING MULTICAST  MTU:1500  Metric:1
          RX packets:10 errors:0 dropped:0 overruns:0 frame:0
          TX packets:0 errors:0 dropped:0 overruns:0 carrier:0
          collisions:0 txqueuelen:0
          RX bytes:836 (836.0 B)  TX bytes:0 (0.0 B)

lo        Link encap:Local Loopback
          inet addr:127.0.0.1  Mask:255.0.0.0
          UP LOOPBACK RUNNING  MTU:65536  Metric:1
          RX packets:0 errors:0 dropped:0 overruns:0 frame:0
          TX packets:0 errors:0 dropped:0 overruns:0 carrier:0
          collisions:0 txqueuelen:1000
          RX bytes:0 (0.0 B)  TX bytes:0 (0.0 B)

/ # exit
[root@server1 ~]# docker ps
CONTAINER ID  IMAGE  COMMAND    CREATED   STATUS           PORTS NAMES
[root@server1 ~]# docker ps -a
CONTAINER ID  IMAGE  COMMAND    CREATED   STATUS           PORTS NAMES
260d4f5b3308  alpine "sh"       20s ago   Exited(0)1s ago        misty_tom
18280cdaf3bb  alpine "echo Hi"  3m ago    Exited(0)3m ago        nice_cray
[root@server1 ~]#_
```

The docker ps -a command shown in the previous output lists both Alpine Linux containers that we have run previously, and the container ID is used as the host name for the container by default. Because the list of previously run containers may grow large over time, you can run the docker container prune command to automatically remove any stopped containers that you don't plan to rerun in the future.

Although each container maintains a unique IP address and host name, any web apps that run within a container can be made available to the underlying operating system running the container on a unique port number. This simplifies the process of connecting to a web app running on a cloud provider, because you only need to know the host name of the underlying operating system running the container, and the port number it is using for your particular copy of the web app.

Say, for example, that you downloaded a private container image from Docker Hub called ex/webapp that is a copy of the Alpine Linux container with the Apache web server and JavaScript framework installed, as well as a JavaScript web app (app.js) that is designed to manage a customer's IoT device across the Internet on port 80. You could then configure a user-accessible website to automatically run a copy of this container image for each customer that wishes to manage their IoT device, and map port 80 for the associated web app to a unique port on the underlying operating system for each customer. In the following output, three copies of the ex/webapp container are run; each one is named for the customer (cust1, cust2, and cust3), and port 80 is mapped to a unique port number on the underlying operating system for each customer (36001, 36002, and 36003):

```
[root@server1 ~]# docker run -d -p 36001:80 --name cust1 ex/webapp
436be848fefd0da097eb711375a8dbded01d05c979ca944f14dd8ac9ab3fc585
```

```
[root@server1 ~]# docker run -d -p 36002:80 --name cust2 ex/webapp
cfcb44e2d4ce2d1fefd6ba63e051d0a4691b22cae3eb96a01ef9e532fe5fb96e
[root@server1 ~]# docker run -d -p 36003:80 --name cust3 ex/webapp
55a8677432743667a43d78ac477b654cee0a823a2c1084d85c0e8d20a827c851
[root@server1 ~]#_
[root@server1 ~]# docker ps
CONTAINER ID   IMAGE        COMMAND       CREATED    STATUS    PORTS          NAMES
55a867743274   ex/webapp    "app.js"      37s ago    Up 36s    36003->80/tcp  cust3
cfcb44e2d4ce   ex/webapp    "app.js"      44s ago    Up 43s    36002->80/tcp  cust2
436be848fefd   ex/webapp    "app.js"      51s ago    Up 50s    36001->80/tcp  cust1
[root@server1 ~]#_
```

The -d option of the docker run command shown in the previous output detaches the container from your terminal and keeps the container running until you stop it using the docker stop command. For example, the docker stop cust2 command would stop executing the cust2 container and release the resources it used to the underlying operating system; this could be triggered automatically when the cust2 logs out of the website used to manage their IoT device. Similarly, when cust2 logs into the website at a later time to manage their IoT device, the website could trigger the docker start cust2 command to run the container again.

You can also access a shell within a running container using the docker exec command. For example, docker exec -it cust2 sh would connect to the cust2 container and run a shell interactively for you to make configuration changes.

> **Note 45**
>
> You can use the --help option with any docker command to obtain available options and usage information. For example, docker --help will display general options and usage for the docker command, and docker run --help will display options and usage for the docker run command.

Understanding Microservices

Software developers can also design web apps to be comprised of several different smaller apps (called microservices) that each perform a unique function within the web app and run in their own container. For example, a software developer could create a JavaScript microservice in one container that collects data and works alongside a Python microservice in another container that analyzes the data from the JavaScript microservice using machine learning (artificial intelligence). The data collected and analyzed by these two microservices can be stored and retrieved by another container running a PostgreSQL microservice that has access to a persistent volume available on the network (e.g., NFS shared directory) or offered directly by the cloud provider. Figure 13-7 illustrates this structure.

Figure 13-7 A sample web app comprised of three microservices

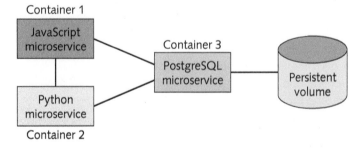

Note 46

Microservices running in different containers can be created to communicate directly with each other, or via a special proxy service called a **service mesh** that provides additional security and monitoring capabilities.

Web apps that are comprised of microservices are easier to develop, fix, and evolve. For example, to enhance the machine learning features in our previous example, software developers only need to modify the Python microservice and redeploy the associated container.

Creating Containers

During the development process, software developers create and run containers on their workstation to test their web app. To create a container, you must create a file called Dockerfile that contains the instructions used to generate the container. The following example Dockerfile specifies that the new container should be based on the latest official Ubuntu container image from Docker Hub, but with the postgresql, ruby-3.1.0 and libcap-dev packages installed. Additionally, all files in the current directory (.) will be copied to the /app directory in the container; normally, these are files that comprise the web app or microservice. When the container is run, the ruby command in the container will run with the argument /app/main.rb to execute the web app or microservice, and the associated port number (5009) will be made available to clients outside of the container.

```
[root@server1 ~]# cat Dockerfile
FROM ubuntu:latest
RUN apt install -y postgresql ruby-3.1.0 libcap-dev
COPY . /app
CMD ["ruby", "/app/main.rb "]
EXPOSE 5009
[root@server1 ~]#_
```

To create a container called webapp from a Dockerfile in the current directory, you can run the command docker build -t webapp *directory*, where *directory* is the directory on your system that contains the files referenced by the first argument of the COPY line in the Dockerfile. If these files and the Dockerfile are in the current directory, you can use the docker build -t webapp . command to build the container. After the container is built, you can execute the docker images command to view your container image and the docker run command to run it on your system. To troubleshoot issues with the web app or microservice while the container is running, you can view the log events generated by the container using the docker logs -f *container* command, where *container* is the name or container ID of your running container.

If the web app or microservice does not run as intended, you can remove the webapp container image from your system using the docker rmi webapp command. Alternatively, if the web app or microservice runs successfully, you can upload the webapp container image to Docker Hub using the docker push *username*/webapp command, where *username* is your Docker Hub user name.

Software developers that create web apps comprised of multiple microservices can choose to create each microservice container using the docker build command and then run them together on their workstation using the **docker-compose command** for testing. To run multiple containers using docker-compose, you must first create a YAML file called docker-compose.yml that lists the container images that should run, as well as the resources and network settings each container should use. Next, you can run the docker-compose up command in the same directory as the docker-compose.yml file to run the containers.

Note 47

For detailed syntax and options that can be used within a Dockerfile or docker-compose.yml file, visit docs.docker.com.

Running Containers within the Cloud

Once code changes for an existing or new web app have been approved as part of the CI process, the associated container images can be added to a container registry (e.g., Docker Hub) and pulled into a cloud environment by orchestration software. In most cloud environments, a **Kubernetes** cluster provides both orchestration and build automation for containers within a CD workflow but can also be configured to work alongside existing build automation software. This cluster can be used to test, deploy, and manage containers, as well as scale containers to run on many different servers as needed.

Note 48

Kubernetes is often shortened to K8s, which is the letter "K" followed by "8" characters and the letter "s".

Note 49

A popular version of Kubernetes that can be installed in a private cloud, workstation, or IoT environment is called K3s. K3s is Kubernetes without any public cloud provider-specific additions.

A Kubernetes cluster includes a series of virtual machines called **nodes**. One or more **master nodes** provide services for managing the cluster. All other nodes in the cluster are controlled by the master nodes and have a container runtime for running containers. The web apps that you run on each node are called **pods** and may consist of one or more related containers and optional persistent volumes. Figure 13-8 illustrates a sample Kubernetes node running four pods that are identified using a unique IP address.

Figure 13-8   A sample Kubernetes node

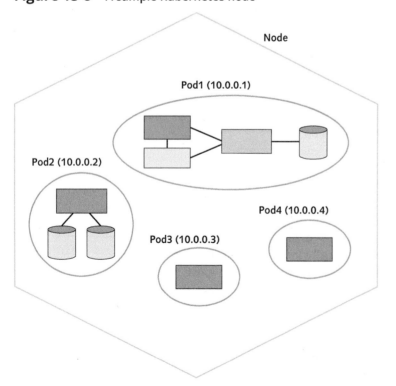

Note 50

Software developers often create a single node Kubernetes cluster on their workstation for testing web apps. In this case, there is a single master node that also has a container runtime for running containers.

Note 51

Not all containers in a pod may be involved in providing web app functionality. For example, you may have a container in a pod that functions to monitor the pod or provide service mesh capabilities; these containers are called **sidecar containers**. Another example are **ambassador containers**, which send requests from other containers in the pod to services outside of the pod, such as object storage.

To deploy a web app to a Kubernetes cluster, you must configure a **deployment** that determines how to start, manage, and scale the containers in a pod on each node, as well as a **service** that allows pods to be accessed from outside of their nodes. To provide access to a service from outside of the cluster, you need to set up either a **load balancer** or **ingress controller**. Public cloud providers often provide their own load balancer services that route a public IP address to your service for a fee. Alternatively, you can use an ingress controller within your cluster to route a public IP address from your cloud provider to a service. Figure 13-9 depicts a sample Kubernetes cluster that allows external access to a web app that has been scaled to run on three different nodes. In this case, the service will balance external requests for the web app evenly across the three nodes.

Figure 13-9   A sample Kubernetes cluster

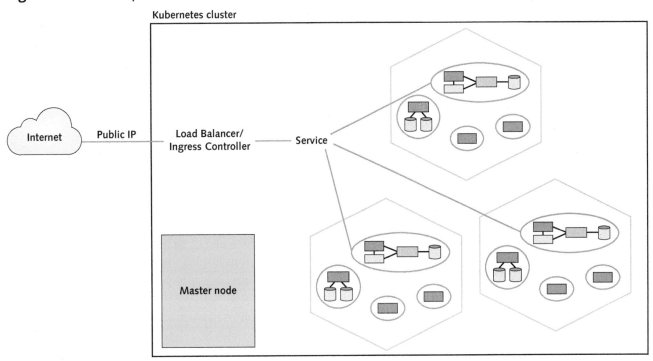

While there are many graphical Kubernetes management tools available, the most common tool for managing a Kubernetes cluster and the web apps it hosts is the `kubectl command`. Because Kubernetes stores nearly all of its configuration in YAML format, you can add append `-o yaml` to most `kubectl` commands to obtain Kubernetes configuration settings in YAML format. You can also use the `kubectl apply -f filename.yaml` command to configure Kubernetes components from the information stored within a filename.yaml file.

Running Virtual Machines within the Cloud

Some web apps require a large amount of dedicated processor resources or block storage, or an isolated operating system for security reasons. For these web apps, it is usually more cost-effective to deploy them within a virtual machine on a cloud provider. Most cloud providers supply several preconfigured virtual machine templates for you to choose from when creating virtual machines, but you can modify them or replace them with ones that you have created. Each virtual machine template is comprised of a virtual hard disk file (containing a preinstalled operating system) alongside one or more files that define the virtual machine settings, such as memory and virtual hardware required. Most virtual machine settings for cloud hosts are stored in Open Virtualization Format (OVF) files that use a `.ovf` extension.

> **Note 52**
>
> You can combine virtual hard disk and virtual machine settings files into a single file called a **virtual appliance** that can be easily imported within a cloud provider. A common virtual appliance format is **Open Virtualization Archive (OVA)**, which combines a virtual hard disk file and `.ovf` file into a single tar archive file that uses a `.ova` extension.

> **Note 53**
>
> Rather than copying a virtual machine template, you instead can choose to manually install an operating system to a virtual hard disk file from installation source files on a cloud provider.

To customize a copy of a virtual machine template that is running on a cloud provider, you can use **configuration management (CM)** software. CM software allows you to add apps (including new versions of web apps), modify existing configuration settings, or perform administrative tasks required for a specific system, or group of systems on a network. The systems managed by CM software are collectively called the **inventory**, and each individual system is called an **inventory member**. Many CM software packages are available that you can install on a server to manage your inventory; each one provides different methods for configuring inventory members. Most CM software packages require that software agents are installed on each inventory member. However, some CM software packages are **agentless**; they connect to inventory members using SSH to perform all configuration management. Moreover, some CM software requires that you define the individual procedures that must be executed on inventory members within a script file (called **imperative configuration**), whereas other CM software only requires that you specify the attributes (e.g., apps and settings) that the inventory members must have within a configuration file (called **declarative configuration**).

Following is an example YAML file that provides a declarative configuration for three inventory members (server1, server2, and server3) that can be used by CM software to install Apache (httpd) using `dnf`, add a home page (index.html), start Apache, create a new file (/tmp/httplog) using `touch`, and add a new user named fred that receives a BASH shell upon login:

```
---
- name: Sample Declarative Configuration
  hosts: server1,server2,server3
  become: true

  tasks:
  - name: Install Apache
    dnf:
      name: httpd
      state: present
```

```
- name: Add Home Page
  template:
    src: https://sample.com/source/index.html
    dest: /var/www/html/index.html

- name: Start Apache
  service:
    name: httpd
    state: started

- name: Create file
  file:
    path: /tmp/httplog
    state: touch

- name: Create user
  user:
    name: fred
    shell: /bin/bash
```

Note 54

Most build automation software also provide CM. Some common CM software are Puppet, Chef, SaltStack, Ansible, and Terraform. Puppet provides agent-based declarative configuration. Chef provides agent-based imperative configuration. SaltStack provides both agentless and agent-based declarative configuration. Terraform and Ansible provide agentless declarative configuration.

Note 55

The term **Infrastructure as Code (IaC)** is often used to describe the practice of using build automation and CM to provide a functional cloud infrastructure.

Some alternatives to CM are supported by many cloud providers for virtual machines. One alternative used on modern Linux distributions is cloud-init, which reads YAML configuration files to add apps, modify existing configuration settings, or perform administrative tasks at boot time. Many cloud providers, such as Amazon Web Services, allow you to customize a virtual machine template for a Linux distribution that uses cloud-init by providing a custom cloud-init configuration file; when the virtual machine is started, the cloud-init configuration file is automatically applied.

Another alternative to CM is Kickstart, which is a component of the Anaconda installation program used by many Linux distributions. Kickstart is only run during the installation of the operating system and reads the entries within a Kickstart configuration file to set system configuration. Many cloud providers allow you to supply a Kickstart configuration file when creating a new virtual machine of a distribution that uses Anaconda. In this case, the virtual machine is not copied from a template; instead, it is installed from an installation ISO image using the system configuration specified within the Kickstart configuration file.

Note 56

Ubuntu Server uses cloud-init and stores cloud-init configuration files under the /etc/cloud directory.

> **Note 57**
>
> Fedora Linux uses the Anaconda installation program. Following a Fedora installation, a sample Kickstart configuration file is written to /root/anaconda-ks.cfg that contains the configuration settings chosen during the installation program.

The CD components used to deploy new web apps or new versions of existing web apps to virtual machines in the cloud varies from organization to organization. There are many different orchestration software products on the market that can be used to copy web apps from a code repository, developer workstation, or test virtual machine within an organization to a virtual machine in the cloud. Most of these products leverage build automation or CM software to deploy web apps. Other organizations purchase custom tools offered by their cloud provider to automate web app deployment to virtual machines or install KubeVirt software to manage virtual machines and their web apps using Kubernetes.

Summary

- DHCP, DNS, and NTP are called infrastructure services as they provide network-related services to other computers on the network.
- DHCP servers lease other computers an IPv4 or IPv6 configuration.
- DNS servers provide name resolution services for other computers on the network. Each DNS server can contain several zones that store resource records for names that can be resolved.
- Linux computers can use the system time stored within the computer BIOS or obtain their time from an NTP server across the network. NTP servers obtain their time from other NTP servers in a hierarchical organization that consists of several strata. The two most common NTP servers are ntpd and chronyd.
- The Apache server shares webpages from its document root directory to computers on the network using the HTTP protocol.
- Samba can be used to share files to Linux, UNIX, macOS, and Windows computers using the SMB protocol.
- NFS can be used to share files between Linux, UNIX, macOS, and Windows systems that have NFS server or client software installed. NFS clients access files on NFS servers by mounting shared directories.
- FTP can be used to share files to any computer that has an FTP client utility and is the most common method for file sharing on the Internet.

- Email servers deliver email messages from one user to another on your system. They also accept new email messages from users and relay it to other email servers on the Internet for delivery. The most common email server used on Linux systems is Postfix.
- Many large applications store their data within databases on a database server. These applications use SQL statements to add, manipulate, and retrieve information within a database across the network. PostgreSQL is a common database server that provides advanced configuration and utilities.
- Web apps are often comprised of multiple, related microservices. Each microservice runs within its own container.
- Software developers can use the docker command to create and test containers that host their web apps and microservices before uploading those containers to a container registry, such as Docker Hub.
- Kubernetes is the most common orchestration and build software used to manage and scale containers on cloud providers. It can be managed using the kubectl command.
- Build automation and CM software are typically used to create virtual machines within cloud environments for hosting web apps.

Key Terms

`ab` (Apache benchmark) command	inventory	record
agentless	inventory member	recursive query
ambassador container	iterative query	relational database
`apachectl` command	jitter	resource records
Berkeley Internet Name Domain (BIND)	Kickstart	reverse lookup
	`kubectl` command	secondary DNS server
Binary Large Object (BLOB) storage	Kubernetes	Secure FTP (SFTP)
block storage	load balancer	Server Message Blocks (SMB)
Chrony NTP daemon (chronyd)	`mail` command	service
`chronyc` command	`mailq` command	service mesh
cloud-init	master DNS server	`sftp` command
configuration management (CM)	master node	`showmount` command
container registry	microservice	sidecar container
declarative configuration	NetBIOS	slave DNS server
deployment	Network File System (NFS)	`smbclient` command
DHCP daemon (dhcpd)	`newaliases` command	`smbpasswd` command
directive	`nmblookup` command	SQL server
DNS cache file	node	strata
Docker	NTP daemon (ntpd)	Structured Query Language (SQL)
Docker client	`ntpdate` command	table
`docker` command	`ntpq` command	`testparm` command
`docker-compose` command	object storage	Time-To-Live (TTL)
Docker Hub	offset	Very Secure FTP daemon (vsftpd)
document root	Open Virtualization Archive (OVA)	virtual appliance
field	Open Virtualization Format (OVF)	webpage hit
forward lookup	persistent volume	zone
`ftp` command	pod	zone transfer
hyperscaler	Postfix	
imperative configuration	PostgreSQL	
Infrastructure as Code (IaC)	PostgreSQL utility	
infrastructure services	primary DNS server	
ingress controller	`psql` command	

Review Questions

1. Cloud providers use the PaaS delivery model to host web apps using containers for scalability.

   a. True

   b. False

2. Which file stores the Apache configuration in Fedora?

   a. /etc/apache2/httpd.conf

   b. /etc/apache2.conf

   c. /etc/httpd.conf

   d. /etc/httpd/conf/httpd.conf

3. Which DNS resource record is an alias to other records?

   a. A

   b. AAAA

   c. CNAME

   d. NS

4. You can purchase object storage from a cloud provider to provide persistent filesystem-based storage.

   a. True

   b. False

5. Which command can be used to connect to check the /etc/samba/smb.conf file for syntax errors?

   a. `apachectl`
   b. `sambactl`
   c. `testparm`
   d. `psql`

6. You have modified the /etc/aliases file to include a new email alias. However, when you send email to the alias, it cannot be delivered. What should you do?

   a. Add the line to the /etc/aliases.db file instead.
   b. Run the `newaliases` command.
   c. Restart the Postfix daemon.
   d. Log out of the system and then log back into the system and resend the email.

7. Which command within the command-line FTP utility can be used to change the current directory on the local computer?

   a. `cd`
   b. `dir`
   c. `lcd`
   d. `get`

8. Which command can be used to list containers that are currently running on the operating system only?

   a. `docker ps`
   b. `docker ps -a`
   c. `docker run`
   d. `docker exec`

9. Which of the following must you perform to share a directory using NFS? (Choose all that apply.)

   a. Edit the /etc/exports file.
   b. Mount the directory to the /etc/exports directory using the `mount` command.
   c. Run the `exportfs -a` command.
   d. Start or restart the NFS daemons.

10. DHCP clients send a DHCPREQUEST packet when they require a new IP configuration.

    a. True
    b. False

11. Which command can be used to connect to a remote Windows share called data on the server called fileserver?

    a. `smbclient -L fileserver:data`
    b. `smbclient -L //fileserver/data`
    c. `smbclient //fileserver/data`
    d. `smbclient \\fileserver\data`

12. To create a container using the `docker build` command, you must first create a Dockerfile.

    a. True
    b. False

13. Which of the following can be used to create a database within PostgreSQL? (Choose all that apply.)

    a. The CREATE DATABASE statement within the PostgreSQL utility.
    b. The ADD DATABASE statement within the PostgreSQL utility.
    c. The `adddb` command.
    d. The `createdb` command.

14. Stratum 1 NTP servers do not obtain time information from other NTP servers.

    a. True
    b. False

15. What must you do to transform your computer into a DNS server? (Choose all that apply.)

    a. Create zone files.
    b. Create resource records for DNS lookups.
    c. Create NIS maps.
    d. Run the name daemon (named).

16. What directory are you placed in when you log in as the anonymous user to an Ubuntu FTP server?

    a. /srv/ftp
    b. /var/www/ftp
    c. /home/anonymous
    d. /var/ftp/pub

17. Docker Hub is an example of a container registry.

    a. True
    b. False

18. Which of the following terms refers to a single copy of a web app that is run within a Kubernetes cluster?

    a. service
    b. pod
    c. node
    d. ingress

19. Which command can you use to synchronize ntpd with an NTP time source?

    a. `ntp`
    b. `ntpquery`
    c. `ntpq`
    d. `hwclock`

20. Mary is a system administrator in your organization. She has recently made changes to the DHCP configuration file, but the DHCP daemon does not seem to recognize the new changes. What should she do?

    a. Log in as the root user and edit the configuration file.
    b. Run the `dhcpconf` command to reload the configuration file.
    c. Restart the DHCP daemon.
    d. Disable and enable the network interface.

Hands-On Projects

These projects should be completed in the order given. The hands-on projects presented in this chapter should take a total of three hours to complete. The requirements for this lab include:

- A computer with Fedora Linux installed according to Hands-On Project 2-1 and Ubuntu Linux installed according to Hands-on Project 6-1.

Project 13-1

Estimated Time: 40 minutes
Objective: Configure DHCP services.
Description: In this hands-on project, you configure the DHCP daemon on your Fedora Linux virtual machine and test your configuration by obtaining an IPv4 address from your Ubuntu Linux virtual machine.

1. Boot your Fedora Linux virtual machine. After your Linux system has been loaded, switch to a command-line terminal (tty5) by pressing **Ctrl+Alt+F5** and log in to the terminal using the user name of **root** and the password of **LINUXrocks!**.

2. At the command prompt, type `dnf install dhcp-server` and press **Enter** to install the DHCP server daemon. Type `y` and press **Enter** when prompted to continue the installation.

3. At the command prompt, type `vi /etc/dhcp/dhcpd.conf` and press **Enter**. Next, add the following lines:

```
default-lease-time 72000;
option routers IP_address_of_your_LAN_default_gateway;
option domain-name-servers IP_address_of_your_LAN_DNS_server;
subnet LAN_network netmask subnet_mask {
    range LAN_network.150 LAN_network.200;
}
```

For example, if your LAN uses the 192.168.1 network (subnet mask 255.255.255.0) and a default gateway and DNS server of 192.168.1.254, you would add the following lines:

```
default-lease-time 72000;
option routers 192.168.1.254;
option domain-name-servers 192.168.1.254;
subnet 192.168.1.0 netmask 255.255.255.0 {
    range 192.168.1.150 192.168.1.200;
}
```

When finished, save your changes and quit the vi editor.

4. At the command prompt, type `systemctl start dhcpd.service` and press **Enter** to start the DHCP daemon.

5. At the command prompt, type `ps -ef | grep dhcpd` and press **Enter** to ensure that the DHCP daemon has loaded successfully. If the DHCP daemon is not listed, check for errors in your /etc/dhcp/dhcpd.conf file and repeat the previous step.

6. At the command prompt, type `firewall-cmd --add-service dhcp` and press **Enter** to allow DHCP traffic through the firewall on your Fedora Linux virtual machine. Firewalls will be discussed in Chapter 14.

7. Next, boot your Ubuntu Linux virtual machine and log into tty1 using the user name of **root** and the password of **LINUXrocks!**.

8. At the command prompt, type `dhclient -r` and press **Enter** to release the existing DHCP leases on the system. Next, type `dhclient eth0` and press **Enter** to obtain a new DHCP lease. While this should obtain a DHCP lease from the nearest DHCP server (i.e., your Fedora Linux virtual machine), this

is not guaranteed, and your Ubuntu Linux virtual machine may obtain a DHCP lease from another DHCP server in your LAN.

9. Return to your Fedora Linux virtual machine. At the command prompt, type `cat /var/lib/dhcpd/dhcpd.leases` and press **Enter**. Did your DHCP server provide a DHCP lease to your Ubuntu Linux virtual machine? Next, type `journalctl --unit dhcpd.service` and press **Enter**. Even if your DHCP server did not provide a DHCP lease to your Ubuntu Linux virtual machine, you should see events from your DHCP daemon that provided DHCPOFFER responses to your Ubuntu Linux virtual machine for the first IP address in the range you configured in Step 3.

10. At the command prompt, type `systemctl stop dhcpd.service` and press **Enter** to stop the DHCP daemon. Next, type `exit` and press **Enter** to log out of your shell.

11. Return to your Ubuntu Linux virtual machine. At the command prompt, type `poweroff` and press **Enter** to shut down the system. What IP configuration will be configured on your Ubuntu Linux virtual machine when it is powered on again and why?

Project 13-2

Estimated Time: 40 minutes

Objective: Configure DNS services.

Description: In this hands-on project, you configure and test the DNS daemon on your Fedora Linux virtual machine.

1. On your Fedora Linux virtual machine, switch to a command-line terminal (tty5) by pressing **Ctrl+Alt+F5** and log in to the terminal using the user name of **root** and the password of **LINUXrocks!**.

2. At the command prompt, type `dnf install bind` and press **Enter** to install BIND (the named daemon). Type `y` and press **Enter** when prompted to continue the installation.

3. At the command prompt, type `vi /var/named/example.com.dns` and press **Enter**. Next, add the following lines:

```
$ORIGIN example.com.
$TTL 86400
@   SOA dns1.example.com.  hostmaster.example.com. (
        1            ; serial
        21600        ; refresh after 6 hours
        3600         ; retry after 1 hour
        604800       ; expire after 1 week
        86400 )      ; minimum TTL of 1 day
;
;
NS      dns1.example.com.
dns1    A       192.168.1.1
;
;
@       MX      10      mail.example.com.
mail    A       192.168.1.2
;
;
server1     A       192.168.1.3
server2     A       192.168.1.4
ftp     CNAME       server1.example.com.
www     CNAME       server2.example.com.
;
;
```

When finished, save your changes and quit the vi editor.

4. At the command prompt, type `chgrp named /var/named/example.com.dns` and press **Enter** to change the group ownership of the example.com.dns zone file. Next, type `chmod 640 /var/named/example.com.dns` and press **Enter** to allow named to read the contents of the example.com.dns zone file.

5. At the command prompt, type `vi /etc/named.conf` and press **Enter**. Under the line that reads:

   `allow-query { localhost; };`

   add the following line:

   `forwarders { IP_address_of_your_LAN_DNS_server; };`

6. At the bottom of the file, add the following lines that identify your example.com.dns zone file:

   ```
   zone "example.com" IN {
       type master;
       file "example.com.dns";
       allow-update { none; };
   };
   ```

   When finished, save your changes and quit the vi editor.

7. At the command prompt, type `systemctl start named.service` and press **Enter** to start the DNS name daemon.

8. At the command prompt, type `vi /etc/resolv.conf` and press **Enter**. Modify the nameserver line to read `nameserver 127.0.0.1` to ensure that your Linux computer uses the local DNS server daemon for name resolution. Save your changes and quit the editor when finished.

9. At the command prompt, type `host server1.example.com` and press **Enter**. Was the name resolved successfully?

10. At the command prompt, type `host ftp.example.com` and press **Enter**. Was the name resolved successfully?

11. At the command prompt, type `nslookup server2.example.com` and press **Enter**. Was the name resolved successfully?

12. At the command prompt, type `nslookup www.example.com` and press **Enter**. Was the name resolved successfully?

13. At the command prompt, type `dig @localhost example.com ANY` and press **Enter**. Are your resources records returned successfully?

14. At the command prompt, type `host www.linux.org` and press **Enter**. Explain why the name was resolved successfully.

15. At the command prompt, type `less /var/named/named.ca` and press **Enter**. View the entries. What do these entries represent?

16. Type `exit` and press **Enter** to log out of your shell.

Project 13-3

Estimated Time: 20 minutes

Objective: Configure time services.

Description: In this hands-on project, you install and explore the NTP daemon on your Ubuntu Linux virtual machine as well as explore the Chrony NTP daemon on your Fedora Linux virtual machine.

1. Boot your Ubuntu Linux virtual machine and log into tty1 using the user name of **root** and the password of **LINUXrocks!**.

2. At the command prompt, type `apt install ntp ntpdate` and press **Enter**. Press **y** when prompted to install the NTP daemon and `ntpdate` command. Next, type `ps -ef | grep ntpd` and press **Enter** to verify that the NTP daemon is running.

3. At the command prompt, type the `less /etc/ntp.conf` command. What lines indicate that your system is configured as an NTP client? Is your system configured as an NTP server? If not, what line could you modify to allow computers on your network to query your NTP server?

4. At the command prompt, type `systemctl stop ntp.service` and press **Enter** to stop the NTP daemon.

5. At the command prompt, type `ntpdate -u 0.ubuntu.pool.ntp.org` and press **Enter** to synchronize your clock with the first time server listed in /etc/ntp.conf. Repeat this command several times until the offset is very low.

6. At the command prompt, type `systemctl start ntp.service` and press **Enter** to start the NTP daemon.

7. At the command prompt, type `ntpq -p` and press **Enter** to view information about the time servers that you are synchronizing with (peers).

8. Type `exit` and press **Enter** to log out of your shell.

9. On your Fedora Linux virtual machine, switch to tty1 by pressing **Ctrl+Alt+F1** and log into the GNOME desktop using your user account and the password of **LINUXrocks!**.

10. Navigate to **Activities**, **Show Applications**, **Settings** to open the Settings window and then highlight **Date & Time**. Is time information obtained automatically from the Internet using NTP by default? Close the Settings window when finished.

11. Navigate to **Activities**, **Show Applications**, **Terminal** to open the Terminal app.

12. At the command prompt, type `su - root` and press **Enter**. Supply the password of `LINUXrocks!` and press **Enter** when prompted to switch to the root user.

13. At the command prompt, type `less /etc/chrony.conf` and press **Enter**. What lines indicate that your system is configured as an NTP client? Is your system configured as an NTP server? If not, what line could you modify to allow computers on your network to query your NTP server? When finished, press **q** to quit the less command.

14. At the command prompt, type `chronyc sources -v` and press **Enter** to view information about the time servers that you are synchronizing with (peers).

15. Close the Terminal app and log out of the GNOME desktop when finished.

Project 13-4

Estimated Time: 30 minutes
Objective: Configure web services.
Description: In this hands-on project, you configure the Apache web server on your Fedora Linux virtual machine and test daemon permissions to files on the system.

1. On your Fedora Linux virtual machine, switch to a command-line terminal (tty5) by pressing **Ctrl+Alt+F5** and log in to the terminal using the user name of **root** and the password of **LINUXrocks!**.

2. At the command prompt, type `dnf install httpd` and press **Enter**. Press **y** when prompted to complete the installation of the Apache web server.

3. At the command prompt, type `grep DocumentRoot /etc/httpd/conf/httpd.conf` and press **Enter**. What is the document root directory?

4. At the command prompt, type `grep DirectoryIndex /etc/httpd/conf/httpd.conf` and press **Enter**. What file(s) will automatically be handed out by the Apache daemon from the document root directory?

5. At the command prompt, type `grep "User " /etc/httpd/conf/httpd.conf` and press **Enter**. What user does the Apache daemon run as locally?

6. At the command prompt, type `grep "Group " /etc/httpd/conf/httpd.conf` and press **Enter**. What group does the Apache daemon run as locally?

7. At the command prompt, type `apachectl configtest` and press **Enter**. Are there any syntax errors within your /etc/httpd/conf/httpd.conf file?

8. At the command prompt, type `vi /var/www/html/index.html` and press **Enter**. Are there any entries? Add the following lines (vi will automatically indent these lines for readability as they are added):

   ```
   <html>
   <body>
   <h1>My sample website</h1>
   </body>
   </html>
   ```

   When finished, save your changes and quit the vi editor.

9. At the command prompt, type `systemctl start httpd.service ; systemctl enable httpd.service` and press **Enter** to start the Apache web server and ensure that it is started at system initialization.

10. At the command prompt, type `curl http://127.0.0.1/` and press **Enter**. Was your webpage successfully returned by Apache?

11. At the command prompt, type `ab -n 1000 http://127.0.0.1/` and press **Enter**. How long did Apache take to respond to 1000 requests?

12. At the command prompt, type `less /etc/httpd/logs/access_log` and press **Enter**. Why are there many webpage hits shown?

13. At the command prompt, type `firewall-cmd --add-service http ; firewall-cmd --add-service http --permanent` and press **Enter** to allow inbound HTTP connections in your firewall, as well as during system initialization.

14. On your Windows or macOS host, open a web browser and navigate to the location **http://IPaddress** (where *IPaddress* is the IP address of your Fedora Linux virtual machine). Is your webpage displayed?

15. Return to tty5 on your Fedora Linux virtual machine. At the command prompt, type `ls -l /var/www/html/index.html` and press **Enter**. Who owns the file? What is the group owner? What category do the Apache daemons use when they run as the user apache and group apache?

16. At the command prompt, type `chmod 640 /var/www/html/index.html` and press **Enter**.

17. In the web browser on your Windows or macOS host, refresh the webpage for **http://IPaddress** (where *IPaddress* is the IP address of your Fedora Linux virtual machine). What error do you receive and why?

18. Return to tty5 on your Fedora Linux virtual machine. At the command prompt, type `chgrp apache /var/www/html/index.html` and press **Enter**.

19. In the web browser on your Windows host, refresh the webpage for **http://IPaddress** (where *IPaddress* is the IP address of your Fedora Linux virtual machine). Does your page display properly now? Close the web browser on your Windows host.

20. Return to tty5 on your Fedora Linux virtual machine, type `poweroff`, and press **Enter** to shut down your virtual machine.

Project 13-5

Estimated Time: 30 minutes
Objective: Configure SMB file sharing services.
Description: In this hands-on project, you configure and test Samba file sharing on your Ubuntu Linux virtual machine.

1. Boot your Ubuntu Linux virtual machine, log into tty1 using the user name of **root** and the password of **LINUXrocks!**.

2. At the command prompt, type `apt install samba smbclient` and press **Enter**. Press **Enter** again to confirm the installation of the Samba file sharing daemons and `smbclient` command.

3. At the command prompt, type `vi /etc/samba/smb.conf` and press **Enter**. Spend a few minutes examining the comments within this file to understand the available Samba configuration options. Under the Share Definitions section, notice that the only two shares configured by default are the [printers] share (which shares all printers on the system using SMB) and the hidden [print$] share (which shares print drivers for each printer, as necessary).

4. Add the following line underneath the [global] line in this file:

   ```
   netbios name = ubuntu
   ```

5. Uncomment/modify the following section that shares out all home directories to users who authenticate successfully:

   ```
   [homes]
      comment = Home Directories
      browseable = yes
      read only = no
   ```

6. Next, add the following share definition to the bottom of the file to share out the /etc directory to all users as read-only:

   ```
   [etc]
      comment = The etc directory
      path = /etc
      browseable = yes
      guest ok = yes
      read only = yes
   ```

7. When finished, save your changes and quit the vi editor.

8. At the command prompt, type `testparm` and press **Enter**. If errors are found, repeat Steps 3 through 7 to remedy them. Otherwise, press **Enter** to view your Samba configuration.

9. At the command prompt, type `systemctl restart smbd.service` and press **Enter** to restart the Samba daemons.

10. At the command prompt, type `smbpasswd -a root` and press **Enter**. When prompted, supply the password **LINUXrocks!**. Repeat the same password when prompted a second time.

11. At the command prompt, type `smbclient -L 127.0.0.1` and press **Enter**. Supply your Samba password of **LINUXrocks!** when prompted. Do you see your shared home directory? Do you see any printer shares?

12. At the command prompt, type `smbclient //127.0.0.1/root` and press **Enter**. Supply your Samba password of **LINUXrocks!** when prompted.

13. At the smb:\> prompt, type `dir` and press **Enter**. Are you in your home directory?

14. At the smb:\> prompt, type `exit` and press **Enter** to disconnect from the SMB share.

15. At the command prompt type `exit` and press **Enter** to log out of your shell.

16. If your host is running Windows, open a Windows PowerShell (Run as Administrator) app. At the PowerShell command prompt, type `net use z: \\IPaddress\root /user:root` and press **Enter**, where *IPaddress* is the IP address of your Ubuntu Linux virtual machine. Supply the root user password of **LINUXrocks!** when prompted. Next, type `z:` and press **Enter** to switch to the drive letter that is associated with your home directory share. Type `dir` and press **Enter**. Are you in your home directory? Close the Windows PowerShell app when finished.

17. If your host is running macOS, open a Finder app, click the **Go** menu and then click **Connect to Server**. In the Connect to Server dialog box, type `smb://IPaddress/root` and click **Connect**, where

IPaddress is the IP address of your Ubuntu Linux virtual machine. Click **Connect** again and choose **Registered User**. Supply the user name **root**, password of **LINUXrocks!**, and click **Connect**. Is your Finder connected to your home directory? Close the Finder app when finished.

Project 13-6

Estimated Time: 20 minutes

Objective: Configure NFS file sharing services.

Description: In this hands-on project, you export the /etc directory using NFS on your Ubuntu Linux virtual machine and access it from your Fedora Linux virtual machine.

1. On your Ubuntu Linux virtual machine, log into tty1 using the user name of **root** and the password of **LINUXrocks!**.

2. At the command prompt, type `apt install nfs-kernel-server` and press **Enter**. Press **Enter** again to install NFS.

3. At the command prompt, type `vi /etc/exports` and press **Enter**. Add a line that reads:

   `/etc    *(rw)`

   When finished, save your changes and quit the vi editor.

4. At the command prompt, type `exportfs -a` and press **Enter**. Next, type `systemctl restart nfs-kernel-server.service` and press **Enter** to restart NFS.

5. Type `exit` and press **Enter** to log out of your shell.

6. Boot your Fedora Linux virtual machine. After your Linux system has been loaded, switch to a command-line terminal (tty5) by pressing **Ctrl+Alt+F5** and log in to the terminal using the user name of **root** and the password of **LINUXrocks!**.

7. At the command prompt, type `mount -t nfs IPaddress:/etc /mnt` (where *IPaddress* is the IP address of your Ubuntu Server Linux virtual machine) and press **Enter**.

8. At the command prompt, type `df -hT` and press **Enter**. What is mounted to the /mnt directory?

9. At the command prompt, type `ls -F /mnt` and press **Enter**. What directory are you observing? Type `cat /mnt/issue` at the command prompt and press **Enter**. Is the issue file from your Ubuntu Server Linux virtual machine?

10. At the command prompt, type `umount /mnt` and press **Enter** to unmount the NFS filesystem.

11. Type `exit` and press **Enter** to log out of your shell.

Project 13-7

Estimated Time: 40 minutes

Objective: Configure FTP file sharing services.

Description: In this hands-on project, you install and configure the Very Secure FTP daemon on your Ubuntu Linux virtual machine, as well as transfer files using FTP and SFTP.

1. On your Ubuntu Linux virtual machine, log into tty1 using the user name of **root** and the password of **LINUXrocks!**.

2. At the command prompt, type `apt install vsftpd` and press **Enter** to install vsftpd.

3. At the command prompt, type `cp /etc/hosts ~user1/file1 ; cp /etc/hosts ~user1/file2 ; cp /etc/hosts /srv/ftp/file3` and press **Enter** to create two copies of the file /etc/hosts within user1's home directory called file1 and file2 as well as a copy of the file /etc/hosts within the /srv/ftp directory called file3.

4. At the command prompt, type `vi /etc/vsftpd.conf` and press **Enter**. Take a few moments to read the options in this file and the comments that describe each option. Next, uncomment the

`write_enable=YES` line, modify the anonymous_enable line to read `anonymous_enable=YES`, save your changes, and quit the vi editor.

5. At the command prompt, type `systemctl restart vsftpd.service` and press **Enter** to restart vsftpd.

6. At the command prompt, type `ftp localhost` and press **Enter**. Log in as **user1** using the password **LINUXrocks!** when prompted.

7. At the ftp> prompt, type `dir` and press **Enter** to list the contents of the /home/user1 directory.

8. At the ftp> prompt, type `lcd /etc` and press **Enter** to change the current working directory on the FTP client to /etc.

9. At the ftp> prompt, type `put issue` and press **Enter** to upload the issue file to the remote FTP server.

10. At the ftp> prompt, type `dir` and press **Enter** to list the contents of the /home/user1 directory. Was the issue file uploaded successfully?

11. At the ftp> prompt, type `lcd /` and press **Enter** to change the current working directory on the FTP client to /.

12. At the ftp> prompt, type `get issue` and press **Enter** to download the issue file to the / directory on the local computer.

13. At the ftp> prompt, type `mget file*` and press **Enter**. Press **a** to download all files that match file* to the local computer.

14. At the ftp> prompt, type `help` and press **Enter** to list the commands available within the FTP client program.

15. At the ftp> prompt, type `bye` and press **Enter** to exit the FTP client program.

16. At the command prompt, type `ls /` and press **Enter**. Were the issue, file1, and file2 files downloaded to the / directory successfully?

17. At the command prompt, type `ftp localhost` and press **Enter**. Log in as **anonymous** using the password **nothing** when prompted (the actual password is not relevant for the anonymous user; you could use any password).

18. At the ftp> prompt, type `dir` and press **Enter** to list the contents of the /srv/ftp directory.

19. At the ftp> prompt, type `lcd /` and press **Enter** to change the current working directory on the FTP client to /.

20. At the ftp> prompt, type `get file3` and press **Enter** to download the hosts file to the / directory on the local computer.

21. At the ftp> prompt, type `bye` and press **Enter** to exit the FTP client program.

22. At the command prompt, type `ls /` and press **Enter**. Was file3 downloaded to the / directory successfully?

23. At the command prompt, type `ftp localhost` and press **Enter**. Log in as the **root** user and the password **LINUXrocks!** when prompted. Were you able to log in? At the ftp> prompt, type `bye` and press **Enter** to exit the FTP client program.

24. At the command prompt, type `vi /etc/ftpusers` and press **Enter**. Next, remove the following line:

    `root`

    When finished, save your changes and quit the vi editor.

25. At the command prompt, type `ftp localhost` and press **Enter**. Log in as the **root** user with the password **LINUXrocks!** when prompted.

26. At the ftp> prompt, type `dir` and press **Enter** to list the contents of the /root directory.

27. At the ftp> prompt, type `bye` and press **Enter** to exit the FTP client program.

28. At the command prompt, type `sftp user1@localhost` and press **Enter**. Type `yes` when prompted to accept the SSH user keys and then supply the password **LINUXrocks!** when prompted.

29. At the sftp> prompt, type `dir` and press **Enter** to list the contents of the /home/user1 directory.

30. At the sftp> prompt, type `lcd /etc` and press **Enter** to change the current working directory on the SFTP client to /etc.

31. At the sftp> prompt, type `put fstab` and press **Enter** to upload the fstab file to the remote SFTP server.

32. At the sftp> prompt, type `dir` and press **Enter** to list the contents of the /home/user1 directory. Was the fstab file uploaded successfully?

33. At the sftp> prompt, type `help` and press **Enter** to list the commands available within the SFTP client program.

34. At the sftp> prompt, type `bye` and press **Enter** to exit the SFTP client program.

35. At the command prompt, type `ls ~user1` and press **Enter**. Is the fstab file present?

36. Type `exit` and press **Enter** to log out of your shell.

37. On your Windows or macOS host, download and install the free Filezilla FTP client program from filezilla-project.org. Next, open the Filezilla program and enter **sftp://IPaddress** in the Host dialog box (where *IPaddress* is the IP address of your Ubuntu Linux virtual machine). Next, enter **user1** in the Username dialog box and **LINUXrocks!** in the Password dialog box and click **Quickconnect**. Explore copying files between your Windows or macOS host and Ubuntu Linux virtual machine. Close Filezilla when finished.

Project 13-8

Estimated Time: 20 minutes
Objective: Configure email services.
Description: In this hands-on project, you explore the Postfix email daemon on your Ubuntu Linux virtual machine.

1. On your Ubuntu Linux virtual machine, log in to tty1 using the user name of **root** and the password of **LINUXrocks!**.

2. At the command prompt, type `apt install postfix` and press **Enter**. When prompted for the general type of mail configuration, ensure that **Internet Site** is selected and select **OK**. At the Postfix Configuration screen, select **OK** to accept the default system mail name.

3. At the command prompt, type `vi /etc/aliases` and press **Enter**. Next, add the following line:

   ```
   webmaster: user1
   ```

   When finished, save your changes and quit the vi editor.

4. At the command prompt, type `newaliases` and press **Enter** to update the aliases database using the information within the /etc/aliases file.

5. At the command prompt, type `apt install mailutils` and press **Enter**. Press **Enter** to install the mail utilities package.

6. At the command prompt, type `mail webmaster` and press **Enter** to compose a new email message to user1. Press **Enter** at the Cc: prompt. At the Subject: prompt, type `Test email` and press **Enter**. Next, type `This is a test email that will be delivered using the Postfix daemon` and press **Enter**. Next, press **Ctrl+d** to complete and send the email message.

7. At the command prompt, type `su - user1` to switch to a new shell as user1.

8. At the command prompt, type `mail` to check your mailbox for email messages. Type `1` and press **Enter** to read the first message. Type `q` and press **Enter** when finished to exit the mail program.

9. At the command prompt, type `exit` and press **Enter** to return to your root shell.

10. At the command prompt, type `telnet localhost 25` and press **Enter**. Can you tell that you are interacting with the Postfix daemon?

11. Type `EHLO localhost` and press **Enter**. Does your Postfix daemon support 8-bit MIME? Type `quit` and press **Enter** to quit the telnet session.

12. Type `exit` and press **Enter** to log out of your shell.

Project 13-9

Estimated Time: 40 minutes
Objective: Configure database services.
Description: In this hands-on project, you create, query, and manage a database using PostgreSQL on your Ubuntu Linux virtual machine.

1. On your Ubuntu Linux virtual machine, log into tty1 using the user name of **root** and the password of **LINUXrocks!**.

2. At the command prompt, type `apt install postgresql` and press **Enter**. Press **Enter** to install PostgreSQL.

3. At the command prompt, type `passwd postgres` and press **Enter**. Type a password of **LINUXrocks!** and press **Enter** at both prompts to set a password of LINUXrocks! for the postgres user account.

4. At the command prompt, type `su - postgres` and press **Enter** to start a new shell as the postgres user.

5. At the command prompt, type `createdb sales` and press **Enter**.

6. At the command prompt, type `psql sales` and press **Enter** to start the PostgreSQL utility.

7. At the sales=# prompt, type `\l` and press **Enter** to view the databases on your PostgreSQL server. The postgres database stores all information used internally by the PostgreSQL server, and the template databases are used when creating new databases. Note that your sales database is listed and uses the UTF-8 character set for information.

8. At the sales=# prompt, type `CREATE TABLE customer (Name char(20),Address char(40),Balance char(10));` and press **Enter** to create a customer table that has three fields (Name, Address, Balance).

9. At the sales=# prompt, type `\d` and press **Enter** to view the tables within your database. Is the customer database listed?

10. At the sales=# prompt, type `\d customer` and press **Enter** to view the fields within the customer table. How many characters are allowed in each of the three fields?

11. At the sales=# prompt, type `INSERT INTO customer VALUES ('Lily Bopeep','123 Rutherford Lane','526.80');` and press **Enter** to add a record to your table.

12. At the sales=# prompt, type `INSERT INTO customer VALUES ('Harvey Lipshitz','51 King Street','122.19');` and press **Enter** to add a record to your table.

13. At the sales=# prompt, type `INSERT INTO customer VALUES ('John Escobar','14-6919 Franklin Drive','709.66');` and press **Enter** to add a record to your table.

14. At the sales=# prompt, type `SELECT * FROM customer;` and press **Enter** to view all records within your table.

15. At the sales=# prompt, type `SELECT * FROM customer ORDER BY Balance DESC;` and press **Enter** to view all records within your table in descending order by balance.

16. At the sales=# prompt, type `SELECT * FROM customer WHERE Name = 'Harvey Lipshitz';` and press **Enter** to view the record for Harvey Lipshitz.

17. At the sales=# prompt, type `CREATE USER bob WITH PASSWORD 'supersecret';` and press **Enter** to create a user account within PostgreSQL that can access the customer database.

18. At the sales=# prompt, type `GRANT ALL PRIVILEGES ON customer TO bob;` and press **Enter** to grant SELECT, UPDATE, DELETE, and INSERT permission on the customer table to the bob user.

19. At the sales=# prompt, type `\q` and press **Enter** to quit the PostgreSQL utility.

20. At the command prompt, type `exit` and press **Enter** to log out of your postgres user shell. Next, type `exit` and press **Enter** to log out of your shell.

Project 13-10

Estimated Time: 40 minutes
Objective: Run containers.
Description: In this hands-on project, you install Docker on your Ubuntu Linux virtual machine and use it to run the Busybox and Apache container images from Docker Hub.

1. On your Ubuntu Linux virtual machine, log into tty1 using the user name of **root** and the password of **LINUXrocks!**.

2. At the command prompt, type `apt install docker.io` and press **Enter**. Press **Enter** to install Docker.

3. At the command prompt, type `docker search busybox | less` and press **Enter**. Note that the Busybox Linux official Docker image is called busybox and press q to return to your command prompt.

4. At the command prompt, type `docker pull busybox` and press **Enter** to download the latest version of the official Busybox container image from Docker Hub.

5. At the command prompt, type `docker images` and press **Enter**. Is your Busybox container image listed?

6. At the command prompt, type `docker run busybox echo Hello World` and press **Enter** to run a Busybox container that runs the `echo Hello World` command and exits when finished.

7. At the command prompt, type `docker ps` and press **Enter**. Are there any running containers? Next, type `docker ps -a` and press **Enter**. Note the container run in the past based on the Busybox image (it should have a randomly generated name).

8. At the command prompt, type `docker run -it busybox sh` and press **Enter** to run another Busybox container that executes a shell. In the Busybox shell, run the following commands to explore the contents of the Busybox container at minimum. When finished type `exit` and press Enter:

   ```
   ls
   ls /etc
   ls /bin
   ps -ef
   ifconfig
   ```

9. At the command prompt, type `docker ps` and press **Enter**. Note that your Busybox container is no longer running after exiting the Busybox shell. Next, type `docker ps -a` and press **Enter**. Note the two containers run in the past based on the Busybox image.

10. At the command prompt, type `docker container prune` and press **Enter**. Press y when prompted to remove all stopped containers. How much space was freed on the filesystem? Next, type `docker ps -a` and press **Enter**. Are there any past containers listed?

11. At the command prompt, type `docker search apache | less` and press **Enter**. Note that the Apache HTTP Server Project official Docker image is called httpd and press q to return to your command prompt.

12. At the command prompt, type `docker pull httpd` and press **Enter** to download the latest version of the official httpd container image from Docker Hub.

13. At the command prompt, type `docker images` and press **Enter**. Is your httpd container image listed?

14. At the command prompt, type `docker run -d -p 50001:80 --name site1 httpd` and press **Enter** to run a detached copy of your httpd container image called site1 and map port 80 for the Apache web server to port 50001 within the underlying Ubuntu Linux operating system.

15. At the command prompt, type `docker run -d -p 50002:80 --name site2 httpd` and press **Enter** to run a detached copy of your httpd container image called site2 and map port 80 for the Apache web server to port 50002 within the underlying Ubuntu Linux operating system.

16. At the command prompt, type `docker ps` and press **Enter**. Note that both containers are running. Is port 80 mapped to the correct port in the underlying operating system for each container? What IP address in the output identifies the underlying operating system?

17. At the command prompt, type `docker exec -it site1 sh` and press **Enter** to start a shell within your site1 container.

18. At the site1 container shell prompt, type `pwd` and press **Enter**. Note that you are in the /usr/local/ apache2 directory by default. Next, type `ls -F` and press **Enter** to list the contents of this directory.

19. At the site1 container shell prompt, type `cd htdocs` and press **Enter** to enter the Apache document root directory in the site1 container. Next, type `cat index.html` and press **Enter** to view the contents of the default webpage.

20. At the site1 container shell prompt, type `echo "<html><body><h1>Site 1 works!</h1></body></html>" > index.html` and press **Enter** to write a simple webpage to the index.html file within the Apache document root directory. Next, type `exit` and press **Enter** to log out of your shell within the site1 container.

21. At the command prompt, type `docker exec -it site2 sh` and press **Enter** to start a shell within your site2 container.

22. At the site2 container shell prompt, type `cd htdocs` and press **Enter** to enter the Apache document root directory in the site2 container. Next, type `echo "<html><body><h1>Site 2 works!</h1></body></html>" > index.html` and press **Enter** to write a simple webpage to the index. html file within the Apache document root directory. Finally, type `exit` and press **Enter** to log out of your shell within the site2 container.

23. On your Windows or macOS host, open a web browser and connect to the URL **http://IPaddress:50001**, where *IPaddress* is the IP address of your Ubuntu Linux virtual machine. Is the webpage from your site1 container shown? Next, connect to the URL **http://IPaddress:50002**, where *IPaddress* is the IP address of your Ubuntu Linux virtual machine. Is the webpage from your site2 container shown? Leave your web browser open.

24. Return to tty1 on your Ubuntu Linux virtual machine. Type `docker stop site2` and press **Enter** to stop running the site2 container. Next, type `docker ps` and press **Enter** to verify that the site2 container is no longer running.

25. On your Windows or macOS host, refresh the webpage from your site2 container (**http://IPaddress:50002**, where *IPaddress* is the IP address of your Ubuntu Linux virtual machine). Is the webpage from your site2 container available? Leave your web browser open.

26. Return to tty1 on your Ubuntu Linux virtual machine. Type `docker start site2` and press **Enter** to re-run the site2 container. Next, type `docker ps` and press **Enter** to verify that the site2 container is running.

27. On your Windows or macOS host, refresh the webpage from your site2 container (**http://IPaddress:50002**, where *IPaddress* is the IP address of your Ubuntu Linux virtual machine). Is the webpage from your site2 container available? Close your web browser when finished.

28. Return to tty1 on your Ubuntu Linux virtual machine. Type `docker stop site1 site2` and press **Enter** to stop the site1 and site2 containers. Next, type `docker ps` and press **Enter** to verify that no containers are running.

29. At the command prompt, type `docker ps -a` and press **Enter** and note the status of your two containers. Type `docker container prune` and press **Enter** to remove any stopped containers.

Finally type `docker ps -a` and press **Enter** to verify that the site1 and site2 containers have been removed from the list.

30. At the command prompt, type `exit` and press **Enter** to log out of your shell.

Project 13-11

Estimated Time: 40 minutes
Objective: Create containers.
Description: In this hands-on project, you create a custom Docker image based on the Apache Docker image and upload it to Docker Hub.

1. On your Windows or macOS host, open a web browser and create a free Docker Hub account at **https://hub.docker.com**. Next, log into **https://hub.docker.com** using your new account and follow the instructions to create a free public repository called **webapp**. Following this, navigate to **Account Settings**, **Security**, **New Access Token** and follow the instructions to create an access token. This access token is the password you can use to upload container images to your Docker Hub repository.

2. On your Ubuntu Linux virtual machine, log into tty1 using the user name of **root** and the password of **LINUXrocks!**.

3. At the command prompt, type `mkdir webappcontainer && cd webappcontainer` and press **Enter** to create and change to a new directory that will store the files for container image creation.

4. At the command prompt, type `vi index.html` and press **Enter**. Next, add the following line:

   `<html><body><h1>This is a custom app!</h1></body></html>`

   When finished, save your changes and quit the vi editor.

5. At the command prompt, type `vi Dockerfile` and press **Enter**. Next, add the following lines:

   ```
   FROM httpd
   COPY ./index.html htdocs/index.html
   ```

   When finished, save your changes and quit the vi editor.

6. At the command prompt, type `docker build -t username/webapp .` and press **Enter**, where *username* is your Docker Hub user name. This will build a new container image called webapp that is based on the existing httpd container image but that incorporates the index.html file you created in Step 4.

7. At the command prompt, type `docker images` and press **Enter**. Is your Docker image available locally?

8. At the command prompt, type `docker run -d -p 80:80 --name testwebapp username/webapp` and press **Enter** to run a new container called testwebapp based on your webapp container image.

9. On your Windows or macOS host, open a web browser and connect to the URL **http://IPaddress**, where *IPaddress* is the IP address of your Ubuntu Linux virtual machine. Is the webpage from your testwebapp container shown? Close your web browser when finished.

10. Return to tty1 on your Ubuntu Linux virtual machine. Type `docker stop testwebapp` and press **Enter** to stop the testwebapp container.

11. At the command prompt, type `docker login -u username` press **Enter**, where *username* is your Docker Hub user name. Enter (or paste) your Docker Hub access token when prompted for a password. Next, type `docker push username/webapp:latest` and press **Enter**, where *username* is your Docker Hub user name. This will upload your webapp container image to your account on Docker Hub.

12. At the command prompt, type `exit` and press **Enter** to log out of your shell.

Project 13-12

Estimated Time: 60 minutes

Objective: Configure Kubernetes.

Description: In this hands-on project, you install a single-node Kubernetes cluster and configure it to host and auto-scale the webapp container you created in Project 13-11.

1. On your Ubuntu Linux virtual machine, log into tty1 using the user name of **root** and the password of **LINUXrocks!**.

2. At the command prompt, type `curl -sfL https://get.k3s.io | sh -` and press **Enter** to download and install K3s.

3. At the command prompt, type `kubectl get nodes` and press **Enter**. Do you have a single node Kubernetes cluster available?

4. At the command prompt, type `kubectl create deployment webapp --image=`*username*`/webapp:latest` and press **Enter**, where *username* is your Docker Hub user name. This will create a deployment configuration called webapp that pulls your webapp container image from Docker Hub.

5. At the command prompt, type `kubectl get deployment` and press **Enter**. Repeat this command every few minutes until you see READY 1/1 (i.e., your webapp container has been downloaded from Docker Hub and started in the Kubernetes cluster).

6. At the command prompt, type `kubectl expose deployment webapp --type=NodePort --port=80` and press **Enter** to create a service to expose your webapp deployment on your cluster node. NodePort ensures that this service uses the same port on each node in the cluster to access your webapp deployment.

7. At the command prompt, type `kubectl get service` and press **Enter**. Note that the service is exposed within the internal Kubernetes network (10.0.0.0).

8. At the command prompt, type `kubectl get pod` and press **Enter**. Note that one pod was created for the deployment.

9. At the command prompt, type `kubectl edit deployment webapp` and press **Enter**. Locate the `replicas: 1` line and modify it to read `replicas: 3`. When finished, save your changes and quit the vi editor.

10. At the command prompt, type `kubectl get deployment webapp` and press **Enter**. Note that three containers are now running based on the same container image. Requests sent to the service are load balanced across these containers.

11. At the command prompt, type `kubectl get pods -l app=webapp` and press **Enter**. Note the three pods created.

12. At the command prompt, type `kubectl logs -f -l app=webapp --prefix=true` and press **Enter**. Note the events related to webapp. This output is useful when troubleshooting deployment-related issues.

13. At the command prompt, type `kubectl get service webapp -o yaml` and press **Enter**. Note the port number listed in the `nodePort:` line. This is the port exposed outside of the Kubernetes cluster by the Traefik ingress controller that is configured by default in K3s.

14. On your Windows or macOS host, open a web browser and connect to the URL **http://*IPaddress:port***, where *IPaddress* is the IP address of your Ubuntu Linux virtual machine and *port* is the port number from Step 13. Are you able to access your webapp service from outside of your Kubernetes cluster?

15. Return to tty1 on your Ubuntu Linux virtual machine. Type `kubectl top nodes` and press **Enter**. Is system resource usage being monitored by Kubernetes? Next, type `kubectl get pods -A` and press **Enter**. Note that K3s starts a metrics-server sidecar container by default to monitor resource usage.

16. At the command prompt, type `kubectl autoscale deployment webapp --min=3 --max=8 --cpu-percent=50` and press **Enter** to create a horizontal pod autoscaler (HPA) configuration for webapp that automatically scales from 3 to 8 pods when a consistent trend of more than 50% of the CPU is consumed. Next, type `kubectl get hpa webapp` and press **Enter** to verify your HPA configuration.

17. At the command prompt, type `/usr/local/bin/k3s-uninstall.sh` and press **Enter** to remove your K3s cluster. After the removal has completed, type `exit` and press **Enter** to log out of your shell.

Discovery Exercises

Discovery Exercise 13-1

Estimated Time: 20 minutes
Objective: Configure time services.
Description: In Project 13-3, you examined the NTP configuration on your Ubuntu and Fedora Linux virtual machines. Configure the Chrony NTP daemon on your Fedora Linux virtual machine to share time information to other computers on your LAN. Next, edit the NTP daemon configuration file on your Ubuntu Linux virtual machine to obtain time information from your Fedora Linux virtual machine and test the results using the appropriate commands. Finally, restore your original configuration.

Discovery Exercise 13-2

Estimated Time: 30 minutes
Objective: Configure web services.
Description: In Project 13-4, you installed and configured the Apache web server on your Fedora Linux virtual machine. Install the Apache web server on your Ubuntu Linux virtual machine and perform the same configuration tasks. Note any pathname and configuration file differences.

Discovery Exercise 13-3

Estimated Time: 90 minutes
Objective: Configure file sharing services.
Description: The file sharing servers discussed in this chapter (vsftpd, NFS, and Samba) were installed and configured on your Ubuntu Linux virtual machine during Projects 13-5, 13-6, and 13-7. Install the same file-sharing servers on your Fedora Linux virtual machine and perform the same configuration tasks. Note any pathname and configuration file differences.

Discovery Exercise 13-4

Estimated Time: 20 minutes
Objective: Configure sshfs.
Description: You can use the SSH filesystem (sshfs) to provide NFS-like file sharing functionality using SSH. Like AppImage packages, sshfs uses Filesystem in Userspace (FUSE) and creates a virtual filesystem that represents a remote directory without relying on support from the Linux kernel. On your Fedora Linux virtual machine, run the `dnf install sshfs` command to install SSH filesystem support and then run the command `sshfs user1@`

`IPaddress:/etc  /mnt` (where *IPaddress* is the IP address of your Ubuntu Linux virtual machine) to access the /etc directory on your Ubuntu system as user1 via the /mnt directory on your Fedora system. View the mounted SSH filesystem using the `df  -hT` command, explore its contents, and unmount it when finished.

Discovery Exercise 13-5

Estimated Time: 60 minutes
Objective: Use Ansible to provide CM.
Description: Ansible is one of the most common CM software tools used today for agentless configuration of systems; it stores the configuration that needs to be applied to each inventory member using YAML files called Ansible Playbooks. Use the Internet to research the installation, configuration, and usage of Ansible. Next, install Ansible on your Fedora Linux virtual machine and create an Ansible Playbook that can be used to create a new user called AnsibleTest on your Ubuntu Linux virtual machine. Test your configuration when finished.

Discovery Exercise 13-6

Estimated Time: 15 minutes
Objective: Explain microservice architecture.
Description: Visit the Wikipedia webpage for the UNIX philosophy (en.wikipedia.org/wiki/Unix_philosophy). Next, describe how containerized microservices are an example of the UNIX philosophy in practice.

Discovery Exercise 13-7

Estimated Time: 30 minutes
Objective: Describe cloud terminology.
Description: There are many different cloud roles, technologies, and processes beyond those introduced in this chapter. Search the Internet to answer the following questions:

  a. How does the Site Reliability Engineer (SRE) role differ from the DevOp role?

  b. What is GitOps and how does it simplify the CD workflow? Give two examples of technologies that provide GitOps.

  c. What is DevSecOps? Give two examples of technologies that provide for DevSecOps.

  d. What does the phrase "shifting left" mean when it comes to the development of web apps in the cloud?

Chapter 14

Security, Troubleshooting, and Performance

Chapter Objectives

1   Describe the different facets of Linux security.

2   Increase the security of a Linux computer.

3   Describe and outline good troubleshooting practices.

4   Effectively troubleshoot common hardware, application, filesystem, and network problems.

5   Monitor system performance.

6   Identify and fix common performance problems.

Throughout this textbook, you have examined the various components that comprise a Linux system. In this chapter, you learn how to secure, troubleshoot, and monitor the performance of these components. First, you learn security concepts, good security practices, as well as the utilities that you can use to prevent both local and network-related security breaches. Next, you explore trouble-shooting procedures, common system problems, and performance monitoring utilities.

Security

In the past decade, hundreds of new services have been made available to Linux systems, and the number of Linux users has risen dramatically. In addition, Linux systems hosted by organizations and cloud providers are typically made available across networks such as the Internet. As a result, Linux is more prone today to security loopholes and attacks both locally and from across networks. To protect your Linux computer from unauthorized access and network attacks, you should take steps to improve local and network security.

Securing the Local Computer

A key component to providing security within an organization involves securing local access to each computer on the network. This involves limiting physical and operating system access, providing secure root user access, using encryption to protect data, and using secure system administration practices.

Limiting Physical Access

One of the most important security-related practices is to limit access to the physical Linux computer itself. If a malicious user has access to the Linux computer, that user could boot the computer using a USB flash drive, CD, or DVD that contains a small operating system and use it to access files within the filesystems on the hard disk drive of the Linux computer without having to log in to the operating system installed on that hard disk drive. To prevent this, you should lock important computers, such as Linux servers, in a specific room to which only Linux administrators or trusted users have key access. This room is commonly called a server closet. Unfortunately, some Linux computers, such as Linux workstations, must be in public areas. For these computers, you should remove the CD and DVD drives from the computer. In addition, you should configure the computer BIOS to prevent booting from the USB ports, as well as ensure that a system BIOS password is set to prevent other users from changing the boot order.

Note 1

To prevent users from spreading viruses and malware stored on personal USB flash drivers inadvertently, some organizations disable all access to USB ports on workstations. Other organizations discourage the use of USB flash drives for the same reason.

Some organizations use publicly accessible Linux computers running secure kiosk software to provide information to visitors. Normally, the Linux computer running the kiosk software is locked within a cabinet or display enclosure to prevent users from accessing the system. However, malicious users will often attempt to reboot the computer using the Ctrl+Alt+Del key combination and interact with the operating system before the kiosk software is loaded. As a result, it is good security to prevent publicly accessible Linux systems from rebooting when the Ctrl+Alt+Del key combination is used. To do this on a system that uses SysV init, you can comment the line that contains the `ctrlaltdel` action within the /etc/inittab file and restart the init daemon. For systems that use Systemd, you can run the `systemctl mask ctrl-alt-del.target` command to prevent the Ctrl+Alt+Del key combination from rebooting the system.

Limiting Access to the Operating System

In addition to limiting physical access to the physical Linux computer, it is important to provide mechanisms that limit unauthorized access to the Linux operating system. Enforcing complex passwords when users change their password and locking user accounts after multiple invalid password attempts are the most common ways used to limit unauthorized access to systems. To enable password enforcement or user account lockout, you can configure the appropriate Pluggable Authentication Module (PAM) on your Linux system by editing the appropriate file within the /etc/pam.d directory. On Fedora systems, you can modify the /etc/pam.d/password-auth or /etc/pam.d/system-auth file, and on Ubuntu systems, you can modify the /etc/pam.d/common-password or /etc/pam.d/common-auth file. For example, to ensure that users create passwords that are a minimum of 10 characters (`minlen=10`) and contain at least one number (`dcredit=1`), one uppercase character (`ucredit=1`), one lowercase character (`lcredit=1`), and four characters that are different from their previous password (`difok=4`), you could add the following line to the appropriate file within the /etc/pam.d directory:

```
password requisite pam_cracklib.so minlen=10 dcredit=1 ucredit=1
lcredit=1 difok=4
```

Note that the PAM used to enforce password complexity is called pam_cracklib.so. To lock user accounts after multiple invalid logins, you can use either pam_tally2.so or pam_faillock.so. For example, to use pam_tally2.so to lock users after they attempt to log in unsuccessfully three times (`deny=3`) within 300 seconds (`unlock_time=300`), you could add the following line to the appropriate file within the /etc/pam.d directory:

```
auth required pam_tally2.so deny=3 unlock_time=300
```

To enforce the same account lockout settings using pam_faillock.so, you could instead add the following line to the appropriate file within the /etc/pam.d directory:

```
auth required pam_faillock.so authfail deny=3 unlock_time=300
```

If a user supplies an incorrect password three times within 300 seconds, they will be unable to log into the system until their user account is unlocked. You can use the `pam_tally2` command to list users who have been locked out by pam_tally2.so, and the `faillock` command to list users who have been locked out by pam_faillock.so. To unlock a user named bob that was locked with pam_tally2.so, you can use the `pam_tally2 --reset --user bob` command, and to unlock a user named mary that was locked out using pam_faillock.so, you can use the `faillock --reset --user mary` command.

Authentication services can also be used to limit unauthorized access to the operating system. Most authentication services use a secure protocol, such as Kerberos, to authenticate users, as well as store user information and authentication requirements within a **Lightweight Directory Access Protocol (LDAP)** database. For example, the information within an LDAP database could be used to ensure that only users that are part of the Accounting group are allowed to log into computers within the Accounting Department.

Microsoft Active Directory is the most common authentication service used within organizations today. It stores user configuration within an LDAP database that represents the organization by DNS domain name and uses Kerberos to authenticate users. After a user authenticates to Active Directory, they receive a **Kerberos ticket** that automatically authenticates them to all other systems in the organization that they contact; a feature called **single sign-on (SSO)**. Thus, if Bob Burtt logs into Active Directory as the user bob.burtt@example.com, each system that is part of the Active Directory domain called example.com will automatically identify him as the user bob.burtt and grant him access to resources that he has been given permission to, such as SMB shared folders and printers.

If you join your Linux system to an Active Directory domain, you will be able to log into a graphical display manager or command-line terminal using an Active Directory user name and password to access domain resources using SSO. Additionally, domain users that access your Linux system across the network will be authenticated based on the Kerberos ticket they were issued, and a home directory will be created for them under /home. The **System Security Services Daemon (sssd)** on the Linux system provides for LDAP and Kerberos connectivity, and the **Realm Daemon (realmd)** is used to discover and join an Active Directory domain. On Fedora Workstation, sssd and realmd are installed by default, and you can join your system to an Active Directory domain by clicking the Enterprise Login button during the graphical Setup wizard following installation to access the Enterprise Login screen shown in Figure 14-1. At this screen, you must supply the name of the domain, as well as a valid user name and password in the domain.

Figure 14-1   Joining an Active Directory domain during Fedora installation

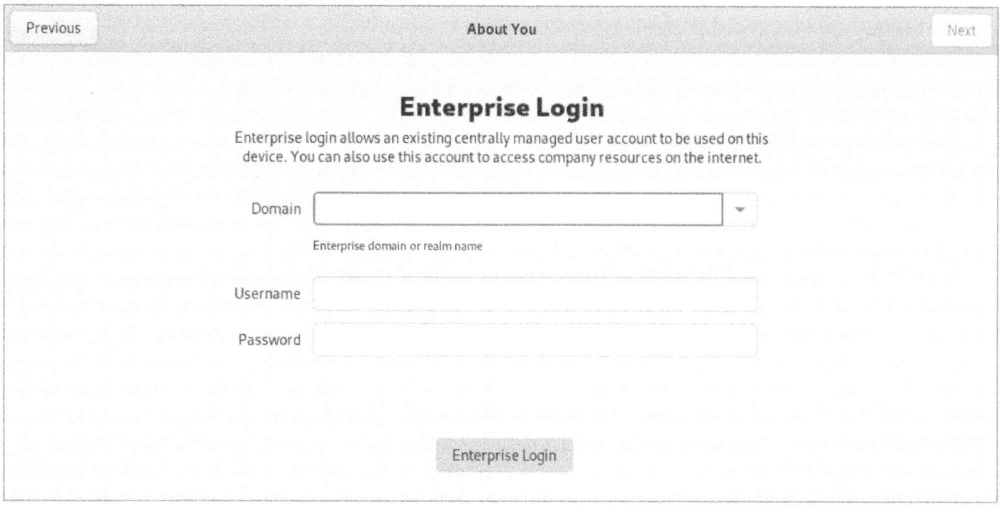

Alternatively, you can run the `realm` command following installation as the root user. For example, `realm join example.com -v` will join your system to the Active Directory domain called example. com after prompting you for a valid user name and password in the domain. Alternatively, you can use the `realm leave example.com` command to remove your system from the domain. Active Directory domain configuration settings are stored in files under the /etc/sssd directory.

> ### Note 2
>
> After logging into an Active Directory domain, you can use the `klist` command to view your Kerberos ticket information.

Some organizations use other software- and hardware-based authentication methods in addition to a user name and password to further limit access to the operating system; this practice is called **multi-factor authentication (MFA)**. For example, a Linux system with a biometric thumbprint reader and the associated software installed will prompt you to scan your thumbprint to further prove your identity after supplying your user name and password. Alternatively, a Linux system with the Yubico PAM installed will prompt you to insert your YubiKey token device into a USB port on your system after supplying your user name and password. The Yubico PAM uses the information you register on yubico.com to verify that you have inserted a YubiKey token device associated with your user account. Other MFA technologies prompt you to provide a certificate that matches a private key stored within your user account or require that you enter a number that is sent to an email address or mobile phone associated with your user account.

Another important security consideration is to limit access to graphical desktops and shells. If you walk away from your workstation for a few minutes and leave yourself logged in to the system, another person can use your operating system while you are away. To avoid this, you should exit your command-line shell, or lock your desktop environment screen before leaving the computer. To lock your screen within the GNOME desktop, you can access the drop-down menu in the upper-right corner of the desktop and choose the lock icon. To use your desktop again, you need to enter your password.

Providing Secure Root User Access

If you have root access to a Linux system, it is important to minimize the time that you are logged in as the root user to reduce the chance that another user can access your terminal if you accidentally leave your system without locking your desktop or exiting your shell. It is best practice to create a regular user account that you can use to check emails and perform other day-to-day tasks. Recall from Chapter 2 that you can then use the `su` command to obtain root access only when you need to perform an administrative task. When you are finished, you can use the `exit` command to return to your previous shell, where you are logged in as a regular user account.

> ### Note 3
>
> The root user can use the `su` command to switch to any other user account without specifying the user account password.

Still, some regular users, such as software developers, need to run certain commands as the root user in certain situations. Instead of giving them the root password, it is best to give them the ability to run certain commands as the root user via the `sudo` command. The `sudo` command checks the /etc/sudoers file to see if you have rights to run a certain command as a different user. The following /etc/sudoers configuration gives the software developers, mary and bob, the ability to run the `kill` and `killall` commands as the root user on the computers server1 and server2:

```
[root@server1 ~]# tail -5 /etc/sudoers
User_Alias SD = mary, bob
```

```
Cmnd_Alias KILL = /usr/bin/kill, /usr/bin/killall
Host_Alias SERVERS = server1, server2

SD      SERVERS = (root) KILL
[root@server1 ~]#_
```

Now, if mary needs to kill the cron daemon on server1 (which was started as the root user) to test a program that she wrote, she needs to use the sudo command, as shown in the following output, and supply her own password:

```
[mary@server1 ~]$ ps -ef |grep crond
root      2281      1  0 21:20 ?          00:00:00 /usr/sbin/crond -n
[mary@server1 ~]$ kill -9 2281
-bash: kill: (2281) - Operation not permitted
[mary@server1 ~]$ sudo kill -9 2281
[sudo] password for mary: ********
[mary@server1 ~]$_
```

Recall from Chapter 10 that the first regular user created on most modern Linux distributions is automatically assigned to the wheel group. Members of the wheel group are granted permission to perform all system administration tasks using the %wheel ALL = (ALL) ALL line within the /etc/sudoers file, including setting the root user password following installation. As a Linux administrator, you can choose to log into a regular user account that is a member of the wheel group to perform all administrative tasks; in this case, each system administration command you run must be prefixed with the sudo command. Additionally, you can use the sudoedit command while logged into a regular user account that is a member of the wheel group to edit text files, such as configuration files, as the root user. The sudoedit command opens text files using the default text editor on the system, which can be modified using the EDITOR environment variable.

Note 4

On Ubuntu systems, the sudo group is used in place of the wheel group.

Note 5

The root user does not have write permission to the /etc/sudoers file by default but has the ability to supersede all file permissions. As a result, when editing the /etc/sudoers file as the root user within the vi editor, you must use :w! when saving your changes to ensure that the vi editor allows you to supersede the underlying file permissions. Alternatively, you can use the visudo command to edit the /etc/sudoers file as the root user; this command edits a copy of /etc/sudoers using the default text editor on the system, and then replaces /etc/sudoers with this copy when you exit the text editor.

The **Polkit** framework (formerly PolicyKit) is an alternative to sudo that can be used to run commands as the root user. By default, Polkit allows members of the wheel group to execute commands as the root user by prefixing them with the pkexec command. Like the lines within /etc/sudoers, you can configure Polkit rules and policies that provide granular access to specific users and groups for certain system tasks. To do this, you must create *.rules, *.conf, or *.pkla files with the appropriate contents under the /etc/polkit-1 directory. To learn more about the syntax of these files, view the polkit manual page.

Using Encryption to Protect Data

Encryption can be used to prevent someone with physical access to your files from reading them. This is especially important on computers that can be easily stolen, such as laptop computers and computers that are in publicly accessible areas. For these systems, it's often best to use **Linux Unified Key Setup (LUKS)** to encrypt entire filesystems using AES symmetric encryption. It is best to configure LUKS on each filesystem during Linux installation; for example, you can select the Encrypt check box within Figure 2-10 to encrypt the contents of the root filesystem using LUKS and supply a passphrase of your choice when prompted. The passphrase serves as the symmetric encryption key used to decrypt the contents of the filesystem and must be specified each time the filesystem is mounted.

To set up LUKS after installation, you can run the `cryptsetup` command. For example, to configure LUKS encryption on the empty /dev/sdb1 partition, you could run the following command and supply a passphrase when prompted:

```
[root@server1 ~]# cryptsetup luksFormat /dev/sdb1
WARNING!
========
This will overwrite data on /dev/sdb1 irrevocably.

Are you sure? (Type 'yes' in capital letters): YES
Enter passphrase for /dev/sdb1: ********
Verify passphrase: ********
[root@server1 ~]#_
```

Next, you can make the encrypted /dev/sdb1 partition available to the Linux device mapper as a volume and create a filesystem on the mapped volume. To make /dev/sdb1 available as a volume called securedata and create an ext4 filesystem on the mapped volume (/dev/mapper/securedata), you could run the following commands:

```
[root@server1 ~]# cryptsetup luksOpen /dev/sdb1 securedata
Enter passphrase for /dev/sdb1: ********
[root@server1 ~]# mkfs -t ext4 /dev/mapper/securedata
mke2fs 1.46.5 (30-Dec-2021)
Creating filesystem with 2617088 4k blocks and 655360 inodes
Filesystem UUID: 24c81f14-5b16-43e2-95af-fef90d1cd85d
Superblock backups stored on blocks:
      32768, 98304, 163840, 229376, 294912, 819200, 884736, 1605632

Allocating group tables: done
Writing inode tables: done
Creating journal (16384 blocks): done
Writing superblocks and filesystem accounting information: done
[root@server1 ~]#_
```

After the filesystem has been created, you can create a mount point directory and mount the mapped volume to it as you would any other filesystem. The following commands create a /securedata mount point directory, mount the securedata volume to it, and examine the contents:

```
[root@server1 ~]# mkdir /securedata
[root@server1 ~]# mount /dev/mapper/securedata /securedata
[root@server1 ~]# ls /securedata
lost+found
[root@server1 ~]#_
```

To ensure that the encrypted volume in the previous example is mounted at system initialization, you must add the line securedata /dev/sdb1 to the /etc/crypttab file, as well as add the line /dev/mapper/securedata /securedata ext4 defaults 0 0 to the /etc/fstab file. Each time you boot your computer, you will be prompted to supply the passphrase needed to unlock the encrypted securedata volume, as shown in Figure 14-2.

Figure 14-2   Providing a LUKS passphrase at system initialization

Please enter passphrase for disk securedata on /securedata:

⌨ us

𝒹 fedora

Source: Fedora Linux

You can instead choose to encrypt only specific files that contain sensitive information using **GNU Privacy Guard (GPG)**. Because GPG uses asymmetric encryption, you must create a GPG public/private key pair using the gpg command as shown in the following output:

```
[root@server1 ~]# gpg --gen-key
gpg (GnuPG) 2.3.4; Copyright (C) 2021 Free Software Foundation, Inc.
This is free software: you are free to change and redistribute it.
There is NO WARRANTY, to the extent permitted by law.

Note: Use "gpg --full-generate-key" for a full featured key generation dialog.

GnuPG needs to construct a user ID to identify your key.

Real name: Jason Eckert
Email address: jason.eckert@trios.com
You selected this USER-ID:
    "Jason Eckert <jason.eckert@trios.com>"

Change (N)ame, (E)mail, or (O)kay/(Q)uit? O

<Interactive screen prompts you to choose passphrase>

We need to generate a lot of random bytes. It is a good idea to perform
some other action (type on the keyboard, move the mouse, utilize the
disks) during the prime generation; this gives the random number
generator a better chance to gain enough entropy.
We need to generate a lot of random bytes. It is a good idea to perform
some other action (type on the keyboard, move the mouse, utilize the
disks) during the prime generation; this gives the random number
generator a better chance to gain enough entropy.
gpg: directory '/root/.gnupg/openpgp-revocs.d' created
gpg: revocation certificate stored as '/root/.gnupg/
openpgp-revocs.d/B7CAC7BBA2AA7FAABB8B7CFE3D709D5ACB910B61.rev'
public and secret key created and signed.
```

```
pub    ed25519 2023-10-17 [SC] [expires: 2025-10-16]
       B7CAC7BBA2AA7FAABB8B7CFE3D709D5ACB910B61
uid                           Jason Eckert <jason.eckert@trios.com>
sub    cv25519 2023-10-17 [E] [expires: 2025-10-16]
[root@server1 ~]#_
```

The private key generated by the gpg --gen-key command is protected by a passphrase that you supply; this passphrase must be supplied each time the private key is used to digitally sign or decrypt files. Moreover, the GPG public/private key pair is stored in the ~/.gnupg directory alongside any other GPG configuration options.

After creating a GPG public/private key pair, you can use the gpg command to encrypt, decrypt, and digitally sign files on the filesystem. The following output demonstrates how to encrypt and digitally sign the topsecretdata text file, creating a topsecretdata.gpg file that can be decrypted by jason.eckert@trios.com:

```
[root@server1 ~]# file topsecretdata
topsecretdata: ASCII text
[root@server1 ~]# gpg --encrypt --sign -r
jason.eckert@trios.com topsecretdata

<Interactive screen prompts you to enter passphrase>

gpg: checking the trustdb
gpg: marginals needed: 3  completes needed: 1  trust model: pgp
gpg: depth: 0  valid:   1  signed:   0  trust: 0-, 0q, 0n, 0m, 0f, 1u
gpg: next trustdb check due at 2025-10-16
[root@server1 ~]# file topsecretdata.gpg
topsecretdata.gpg: data
[root@server1 ~]#_
```

To verify the digital signature and decrypt a file that was digitally signed and encrypted with GPG, you can supply the file name as an argument to the gpg command. For example, the following commands verify the digital signature and decrypt the topsecretdata.gpg file created earlier, as well as validate the results:

```
[root@server1 ~]# gpg topsecretdata.gpg

<Interactive screen prompts you to enter passphrase>

gpg: encrypted with cv25519, ID B4ABB8EBF5EC924F, created 2023-10-17
      "Jason Eckert <jason.eckert@trios.com>"
gpg: Signature made Mon 17 Oct 2023 11:03:48 AM EDT
gpg: using EDDSA key B7CAC7BBA2AA7FAABB8B7CFE3D709D5ACB910B61
gpg: Good signature from "Jason Eckert <jason.eckert@trios.com>"
[root@server1 ~]# file topsecretdata
topsecretdata: ASCII text
[root@server1 ~]#_
```

Note 6

To prevent having to enter your GPG passphrase each time you digitally sign or decrypt a file, you can start the **GPG agent** daemon, which prompts you for your passphrase once and supplies it automatically within GPG commands during the remainder of your login session. To learn how to start the GPG agent daemon for your user account, view the gpg-agent manual page.

Practicing Secure Linux Administration

Other considerations for securing the local computer involve using secure Linux administration practices. For example, ensuring that users do not have unnecessary file and directory permissions will minimize the chance that they could gain access to sensitive documents on the local system. Similarly, restricting the users who are allowed to schedule commands using the /etc/cron.allow, /etc/cron.deny, /etc/at.allow, and /etc/at.deny files would prevent a malicious user from scheduling tasks that could detract from system performance. Moreover, viewing the history of successful and failed login attempts using the who /var/log/wtmp, last and lastb commands may allow you to identify whether a malicious user has been using the system.

To remind users of secure computer etiquette techniques, or the acceptable computer use policy used by your organization, you can add a login banner. Login banners are messages that are displayed on the screen after a user logs into the system. To create a login banner, you can place the appropriate text within the /etc/motd (message of the day) file.

Many organizations donate or repurpose Linux servers or workstations when they reach the end of their warranty period or become obsolete. In this case, it is important that you securely remove all sensitive data from local storage devices. While deleting files removes them from the system, specialized utilities can still recover the data from hard disk drives and SSDs. To ensure that the data cannot be recovered, you can use the shred command to overwrite the data repeatedly to prevent it from being recovered. For example, you can use the shred file1 file2 command to securely remove file1 and file2, or the shred /dev/sdb1 command to securely remove all filesystem contents on the /dev/sdb1 partition.

Protecting against Network Attacks

Recall from Chapter 12 that network services listen for network traffic on a certain port number and interact with that traffic. If network services exist on a computer, there is always the possibility that hackers with network access can manipulate the network service by interacting with it in unusual ways. Network attacks may exploit a weakness with a particular service, compromise an authentication mechanism to gain access to the system, or even replace data used by the network service in memory with malicious data. There are many ways to minimize the chance of a network attack, including reducing the number of network services, using encryption, limiting system and client access, using secure file permissions, changing default ports, updating software, running vulnerability scanners, as well as using firewalls, SELinux, and AppArmor.

Reducing the Number of Network Services

The first step to securing your computer against network attacks is to minimize the number of network services running. If you run only the minimum number of network services necessary for your organization, you minimize the avenues that a hacker can use to gain access to systems. To see what network services are running on your network, you can run the nmap (network mapper) command. The following output demonstrates how nmap can be used to determine the number of services running on the server1 computer:

```
[root@server1 ~]# nmap -sT server1.class.com
Starting Nmap 7.93 ( https://nmap.org ) at 2023-10-17 11:08 EDT
Nmap scan report for server1.class.com (192.168.1.105)
Host is up (0.0019s latency).
rDNS record for 192.168.1.105: server1.class.com
Not shown: 995 closed ports
PORT      STATE  SERVICE
22/tcp    open   ssh
23/tcp    open   telnet
111/tcp   open   rpcbind
631/tcp   open   ipp
5903/tcp  open   vnc-3
```

```
Nmap done: 1 IP address (1 host up) scanned in 0.13 seconds
[root@server1 ~]#_
```

> **Note 7**
>
> The nmap command is not normally installed on a Linux distribution by default but can be added from a software repository.

From the preceding output, you can determine which services are running on your computer by viewing the service name or by searching the descriptions for the port numbers in the /etc/services file or on the Internet. For services that are not needed, ensure that they are not started automatically during system initialization. It is also important to ensure that services that do not provide encryption are minimized on your systems, as these services are more prone to network attacks. For example, the telnet service shown in the preceding output is unnecessary because the ssh service provides the same functionality, but with encryption. As a result, it is good form to stop the telnet service on this system and ensure that it isn't started at system initialization. For services that must be used because they are essential to your organization, you can take certain steps to ensure that they are as secure as possible, as described in the following sections.

> **Note 8**
>
> Some common network services that should be stopped or removed on a system if they are not used include printing (IPP, LPD, Samba), file sharing (FTP, NFS, Samba), email (Sendmail, Postfix), and legacy services that do not use encryption (telnet, rsh, finger).

Using Encryption

When possible, you should use network services that support encryption using SSH tunneling or SSL/TLS and configure those services to reject unencrypted connections. For example, the vsftpd daemon discussed in Chapter 13 supports both SFTP (FTP + SSH) as well as FTPS (FTP + SSL/TLS) encrypted connections. However, SFTP and unencrypted FTP are allowed by default. To prevent unencrypted FTP connections, you could force any connections that do not use SFTP to use FTPS by adding the following two lines to the vsftpd.conf file, and restarting the vsftpd daemon afterwards:

```
ssl_enable=YES
force_local_logins_ssl=YES
```

Recall from Chapter 1 that SSL/TLS uses a certificate to protect the integrity of the public key stored on the server. This server certificate contains a checksum of the public key that is digitally signed by a trusted CA. Before using the server's public key to encrypt data, each client decrypts the digital signature within the certificate and compares the checksum within to a checksum of the server's public key to ensure that it has not been modified by a hacker.

> **Note 9**
>
> When discussing certificates, checksums are often called **hashes**.

By default, most services generate a self-signed certificate for SSL/TLS, which includes a public key that is digitally signed by the server computer, and not a trusted CA. Because self-signed certificates can easily be impersonated by hackers, it is important that you replace this self-signed certificate with one that is obtained from a public CA, or a CA within your organization. There are many public CAs available on the Internet that will issue HTTPS certificates for web servers and other technologies that use SSL/TLS. The most popular free public CA is called Let's Encrypt.

To configure an Apache web server with a free Let's Encrypt HTTPS certificate, you must first ensure that you have a public IP address and DNS record registered for your FQDN (e.g., www.example .com), and that the ServerName directive in your Apache configuration specifies the FQDN. Next, you can install the `certbot command` and Apache web server plugin from a software repository. To do this on Ubuntu Server, you can run the `apt install certbot python3-certbot-apache` command. Finally, you can run the `certbot --apache` command and restart the Apache web server. This command generates a new public/private key, uploads the public key to Let's Encrypt for digital signing, downloads the associated certificate, and configures Apache to use it. Following this, users can access the web server using HTTPS within their web browser (e.g., https://www.example.com).

Note 10

Let's Encrypt uses a 3-month expiry for certificates. As a result, you will need to run the `certbot --renew` command periodically to ensure that your certificate does not expire.

Note 11

If your Apache web server hosts websites for several FQDNs (e.g., www.example.com, sales.example .com, support.example.com, and so on), you can create a public DNS record for *.example.com that resolves to the public IP address of your web server. When you run `certbot`, it will allow you to choose a wildcard certificate that can be used to provide HTTPS for all the FQDNs.

Note 12

You can also use the `openssl command` to view and troubleshoot certificates. For example, `openssl s_client -connect www.example.com:443` will connect to www.example.com using the HTTPS port (443) and display detailed information about the certificate used.

If you must run network services that do not provide encryption, you can use a VPN overlay network that adds encryption to existing network traffic. There are many types of VPN technologies available, including IP Security (IPSec), Layer 2 Tunneling Protocol (L2TP), Point-to-Point Tunneling Protocol (PPTP), OpenVPN, Cisco AnyConnect, SSL/TLS, SSH, and WireGuard. After you configure VPN software on a server or router, clients can connect to the VPN prior to accessing network services to ensure that their traffic is encrypted across the network. To configure a Fedora Workstation to connect to a VPN, you can click the + symbol within the Network Connections utility shown in Figure 12-4, choose a VPN type, and enter the VPN server and account information.

Limiting System Access for Network Services

Regardless of whether encryption is used with a network service, you should also take steps to limit the access that network services have to the underlying operating system. Firstly, you should ensure that network service daemons are not run as the root user on the system when possible. If a hacker gains access to your system via a network service daemon run as the root user, the hacker has root access as well. Many network daemons, such as Apache, set the user account by which they execute in their configuration files.

Similarly, for daemons such as Apache that run as a non-root user, you should ensure that the shell listed in /etc/passwd for the daemon is set to an invalid shell, such as /sbin/nologin. If a hacker attempted to remotely log into the system using a well-known daemon account, she would not be able to get a BASH shell. Instead, the /sbin/nologin merely prints the warning listed in the /etc/nologin.txt file to the screen and exits. If the /etc/nologin.txt file doesn't exist, the /sbin/nologin program prints a standard warning.

Limiting Client Access

By default, network services allow any client to connect. If you use network services that are started by inetd or xinetd, you can use TCP wrappers to specify the computers that are allowed to connect to the network service. A **TCP wrapper** is a program (/usr/sbin/tcpd) that can start a network daemon. To enable TCP wrappers, you must specify to start the network daemon as an argument to the TCP wrapper. For the telnet daemon started by inetd, you modify the telnet line in the /etc/inetd.conf file as shown in the following example:

```
[root@server1 ~]# grep telnet /etc/inetd.conf
telnet stream tcp nowait telnetd /usr/sbin/tcpd /usr/sbin/in.telnetd
[root@server1 ~]#_
```

For the telnet daemon started by xinetd, you modify the /etc/xinetd.d/telnet file, as shown in the following example:

```
[root@server1 ~]# cat /etc/xinetd.d/telnet
service telnet
{
        flags           = REUSE
        socket_type     = stream
        wait            = no
        user            = root
        server          = /usr/sbin/tcpd
        server_args     = /usr/sbin/in.telnetd
        log_on_failure  += USERID
        disable         = no
}
[root@server1 ~]#_
```

Now, the telnet daemon (/usr/sbin/in.telnetd) will be started by the TCP wrapper (/usr/sbin/tcpd). Before a TCP wrapper starts a network daemon, it first checks the /etc/hosts.allow and /etc/hosts.deny files. The following /etc/hosts.allow and /etc/hosts.deny files only give the computers client1 and client2 the ability to connect to your telnet server.

```
[root@server1 ~]# cat /etc/hosts.deny
in.telnetd:  ALL
[root@server1 ~]#_
[root@server1 ~]# cat /etc/hosts.allow
in.telnetd:  client1, client2
[root@server1 ~]#_
```

TCP wrapper functionality is not only limited to daemons started by inetd and xinetd. Some standalone daemons that provide network services can be configured to check the /etc/hosts.deny and /etc/hosts.allow file before granting access.

Using Secure File Permissions

Another important component of network security involves local file permissions. If everyone had read permission on the /etc/shadow file, any user could read the encrypted passwords for all user accounts, including the root user, and possibly decrypt the password using a decryption program. Fortunately, the default permissions on the /etc/shadow file allow read permission for the root user only to minimize this possibility. However, similar permission problems exist with many other important files, including those used by network services.

Take, for example, the Apache web server discussed in Chapter 13. Apache daemons on Fedora are run as the user apache and the group apache by default. These daemons read HTML files from the document root directory such that they can give the information to client web browsers. The following directory listing from a sample document root directory shows that the Apache daemons also have write permission because they own the index.html file:

```
[root@server1 ~]# ls -l /var/www/html
total 64
-rw-r-----  1 apache apache  61156  Sep  5 08:36 index.html
[root@server1 ~]#_
```

Thus, if a hacker was able to manipulate an Apache daemon, the hacker would have write access to the index.html file and would be able to modify it. It is secure practice to ensure that the index.html is owned by the web developer (who needs to modify the file) and that the Apache daemons are given read access only through membership in the group category. If your web developer logs into the system as the user account webdev, you could perform the following commands to change the permissions on the web content and verify the results:

```
[root@server1 ~]# chown webdev /var/www/html/index.html
[root@server1 ~]# ls -l /var/www/html
total 64
-rw-r-----  1 webdev apache   61156  Sep  5 08:36 index.html
[root@server1 ~]#_
```

In addition to examining regular permissions, you should minimize the number of files that have the SUID and SGID special permissions set, as these files can be executed by a hacker that gains access to the system to perform tasks as a privileged user. To find all files on the system that have the SUID permission set, you can use the `find / -perm /u=s` command, and to find all files that have the SGID permission set, you can use the `find / -perm /g=s` command.

Changing Default Ports

Recall from Chapter 12 that most network services use well-known ports; these ports are commonly searched by hackers when they are looking for systems to attack. Many daemons that provide network services allow you to specify a non-default port number in their configuration file to thwart hackers. For instance, if you change the port number within your Apache web server configuration file to TCP port 8019, then a hacker who is scanning for web services running on the default TCP port 80 for HTTP will not locate the web service running on your computer unless they examine other ports. However, any users that wish to connect to your web server must specify TCP port 8019 within their web browser, because web browsers connect to TCP port 80 by default. For example, if your web server uses a FQDN of webserver.example.com, you will need to ensure that clients connect to http://webserver.example.com:8019 within their web browser.

Updating Network Service Software

Because network attacks are regularly reported in the security and open source communities, new versions of network services usually include security-related fixes. As such, these new versions are more resilient to network attacks. Because of this, it is good form to periodically check for new versions of network services, install them, and check the associated documentation for new security-related parameters that can be set in the configuration file.

Running Vulnerability Scanners

Many organizations maintain databases of known vulnerabilities for operating systems and network services, as well as the associated fixes. Most vulnerabilities are given a unique **Common Vulnerabilities and Exposures (CVE)** number for identification. Other vulnerabilities may not use CVE numbers for identification. For example, the Open Web Application Security Project (OWASP) maintains a database of known web app vulnerabilities by category, with many of these vulnerabilities identified by a **Common Weakness Enumeration (CWE)** number.

There are many **vulnerability scanner** software packages that you can install and run to scan the systems on your network for the vulnerabilities listed within multiple online vulnerability databases. If vulnerabilities are found, the vulnerability scanner software will identify the steps needed to fix the vulnerability, which could include a configuration change, software update, or firewall rule change. By scanning the systems on your network periodically using a vulnerability scanner, and taking the recommended actions to fix detected vulnerabilities, you dramatically reduce the chance that a hacker could exploit a software vulnerability on the computers within your network environment.

Note 13

Open Vulnerability Assessment System (OpenVAS) is a popular vulnerability scanner available for Linux systems. It can be used to scan Windows, Linux, macOS, and UNIX systems for known vulnerabilities.

Vulnerability scanners are often incorporated into **Security Information and Event Management (SIEM)** software suites. SIEM can be used to continually monitor the systems on your network for vulnerabilities or attacks and alert you when one is discovered.

Note 14

Alienvault Open Source SIEM (OSSIM) is a popular SIEM software suite that can be used to monitor the security of a wide variety of systems on a network.

Configuring a Firewall

Another method that you can use to ensure that network services are as secure as possible is to configure a firewall on your Linux computer using a component of the Linux kernel called **netfilter**. Recall from Chapter 1 that firewalls can be used in your organization to block unwanted network traffic; as a result, firewalls are typically enabled on router interfaces.

Netfilter discards certain network packets according to **chains** of **rules** that are stored in your computer's memory. By default, you can specify firewall rules for three types of chains:

- INPUT chain, for network packets destined for your computer
- FORWARD chain, for network packets that must pass through your computer (if the computer is a router)
- OUTPUT chain, for network packets that originate from your computer

Note 15

Netfilter can also be used to configure a Linux computer with two or more network interfaces as a NAT router. To do this, you would use the PREROUTING, OUTPUT, and POSTROUTING chains. Consult the `iptables` manual page for more information.

In most cases, no rules exist for the INPUT, FORWARD, or OUTPUT chains after a Linux installation. To create rules that are used for each chain, you can use the `iptables command`. Rules can be based on the source IP address, destination IP address, protocol used (TCP, UDP, ICMP), or packet status. For example, to flush all previous rules from memory, specify that forwarded packets are dropped by default, and that packets are only to be forwarded if they originate from the 192.168.1.0 network, you can use the following commands:

```
[root@server1 ~]# iptables -F
[root@server1 ~]# iptables -P FORWARD DROP
[root@server1 ~]# iptables -A FORWARD -s 192.168.1.0/24 -j ACCEPT
[root@server1 ~]#_
```

You can then verify the list of rules for each chain in memory by using the following command:

```
[root@server1 ~]# iptables -L
Chain INPUT (policy ACCEPT)
target      prot opt source            destination

Chain FORWARD (policy DROP)
target      prot opt source            destination
ACCEPT      all  --  192.168.1.0/24    anywhere

Chain OUTPUT (policy ACCEPT)
target      prot opt source            destination
[root@server1 ~]#_
```

The previous firewall example uses static packet filtering rules. Most technologies today start by using a specific port and then switch to a random port above 32768. A good example of this is SSH. The first SSH packet is addressed to port 22, but the port number is changed in the return packet to a random port above 32768 for subsequent traffic. In a static filter, you would need to allow traffic for all ports above 32768 to use SSH.

Instead of doing this, you can use a dynamic (or stateful) packet filter rule by specifying the $-m$ state option to the `iptables` command. **Stateful packet filters** remember traffic that was originally allowed in an existing session and adjust their rules appropriately. For example, to forward all packets from your internal interface eth1 to your external interface eth0 on your Linux router that are addressed to port 22, you could use the following command:

```
[root@server1 ~]# iptables -A FORWARD -i eth1 -o eth0 -m state
--state NEW -dport 22 -j ACCEPT
[root@server1 ~]#_
```

Next, you can allow all subsequent packets that are part of an allowed existing session, as shown in the following output (remember that only SSH is allowed):

```
[root@server1 ~]# iptables -A FORWARD -i eth1 -o eth0 -m state
--state ESTABLISHED,RELATED -j ACCEPT
[root@server1 ~]#_
```

Table 14-1 provides a list of common options to the `iptables` command.

Table 14-1   Common iptables options

Option	Description
`-s address`	Specifies the source address of packets for a rule
`-d address`	Specifies the destination address of packets for a rule
`-sport port#`	Specifies the source port number for a rule
`-dport port#`	Specifies the destination port number for a rule
`-p protocol`	Specifies the protocol type for a rule
`-i interface`	Specifies the input network interface
`-o interface`	Specifies the output network interface
`-j action`	Specifies the action that is taken for a rule; common actions include ACCEPT (allow), DROP (disallow), REJECT (disallow and return ICMP error to the source computer), and LOG (allow and log event information)
`-m match`	Specifies a match parameter that should be used within the rule; the most common match used is `state`, which creates a stateful packet filtering firewall
`-A chain`	Specifies the chain used
`-L chain`	Lists rules for a certain chain; if no chain is given, all chains are listed
`-P policy`	Specifies the default policy for a certain chain type
`-D number`	Deletes a rule for a chain specified by additional arguments; rules start at number 1
`-R number`	Replaces a rule for a chain specified by additional arguments; rules start at number 1
`-F chain`	Removes all rules for a certain chain; if no chain is specified, it removes all rules for all chains

Note 16

The order in which firewall rules are defined is the order in which they are applied. Normally, firewall rules are defined to first DROP all traffic destined for the computer (the INPUT chain) and allow only specific traffic by port number.

Note 17

To configure firewall rules for IPv6, you can use the `ip6tables` command.

Note 18

Because firewall rules are stored in memory, they are lost when your computer is shut down. To ensure that they are loaded at system initialization, you can redirect the output of the `iptables-save` command (for IPv4 rules) or `ip6tables-save` command (for IPv6 rules) a filename that is used to load iptables rules at system initialization on your Linux distribution. On a Fedora system, you can run `iptables-save > /etc/sysconfig/iptables` to save IPv4 firewall rules and run `ip6tables-save > /etc/sysconfig/ip6tables` to save IPv6 firewall rules.

You can also use the `nft command` to configure netfilter chains and rules using a more straight-forward syntax that is processed by the **nftables** framework. For example, to add an nftable that matches IPv4 traffic, add an input chain that drops all traffic except for stateful traffic on port 80 (HTTP) and 443 (HTTPS), and view the results, you could run the following commands:

```
[root@server1 ~]# nft add table ip filter
[root@server1 ~]# nft add chain ip filter input
[root@server1 ~]# nft add rule ip filter input drop
[root@server1 ~]# nft add rule ip filter input tcp dport {80, 443} ct
state new,established accept
[root@server1 ~]# nft list table ip filter
table ip filter {
   chain input {
     drop
     tcp dport { 80, 443 } ct state established,new accept
   }
}
[root@server1 ~]#_
```

You can replace ip with ip6 within the commands in the previous example to create firewall rules for IPv6 traffic or replace ip with inet to match both IPv4 and IPv6 traffic. You can also use the iptables-translate command and ip6tables-translate command to convert existing iptables rules for IPv4 and IPv6 into the equivalent ones for nftables, respectively.

Note 19

To ensure that nftables firewall rules are loaded at system initialization, you can redirect the output of the nft list ruleset command to the filename that is used to load nftables firewall rules at system initialization on your Linux distribution. For example, on Ubuntu, you can run the nft list ruleset > /etc/nftables.conf command.

Ubuntu Linux systems can optionally use the Uncomplicated Firewall (UFW) system to provide easy configuration of stateful netfilter firewall rules via the ufw (Uncomplicated Firewall) command. By default, there are no firewall rules configured on Ubuntu Server distributions; to enable default firewall rules at system initialization that deny incoming traffic, but allow outgoing traffic, you can run the following commands:

```
[root@server1 ~]# ufw enable
Firewall is active and enabled on system startup
[root@server1 ~]# ufw default deny incoming
Default incoming policy changed to 'deny'
(be sure to update your rules accordingly)
[root@server1 ~]# ufw default allow outgoing
Default outgoing policy changed to 'allow'
(be sure to update your rules accordingly)
[root@server1 ~]#_
```

Next, you can provide firewall exceptions for other services running on Ubuntu Server. For example, to allow ssh and telnet connections for both IPv4 and IPv6, you could use the following command:

```
[root@server1 ~]# ufw allow ssh
Rule updated
Rule updated (v6)
[root@server1 ~]# ufw allow telnet
Rule updated
Rule updated (v6)
[root@server1 ~]#_
```

Alternatively, you could provide firewall exceptions by protocol and port number, as well as source and destination. For example, to allow TCP port 80 and 443 traffic from any host to any host using either IPv4 or IPv6, you could use the following command:

```
[root@server1 ~]# ufw allow proto tcp from any to any port 80,443
Rule updated
Rule updated (v6)
[root@server1 ~]#_
```

You can also enable UFW logging using the `ufw logging on` command; this will write all firewall access to the system log and could be used by other programs to locate malicious network traffic.

To view your current Ubuntu Firewall rules, you can use the following command:

```
[root@server1 ~]# ufw status verbose
Status: active
Logging: on (low)
Default: deny (incoming), allow (outgoing), deny (routed)
New profiles: skip

To                      Action        From
--                      ------        ----
22/tcp                  ALLOW IN      Anywhere
23/tcp                  ALLOW IN      Anywhere
80,443/tcp              ALLOW IN      Anywhere
22/tcp (v6)             ALLOW IN      Anywhere (v6)
23/tcp (v6)             ALLOW IN      Anywhere (v6)
80,443/tcp (v6)         ALLOW IN      Anywhere (v6)
[root@server1 ~]#_
```

> **Note 20**
>
> To view a list of common `ufw` arguments, you can run the `ufw help` command or view the `ufw` manual page.

> **Note 21**
>
> Ubuntu Firewall loads default firewall rules from files under the /etc/ufw directory. The `ufw` command automatically updates these files to ensure that any firewall configuration you perform is also performed at system initialization.

Because firewall rules can quickly become complex, many Linux distributions, including Fedora, implement a **firewall daemon (firewalld)** that can configure netfilter firewall rules with more flexibility using network zones and service names. A **network zone** defines the level of trust for network connections and can be mutable (modification to its definition is allowed) or immutable (its definition cannot be changed). Table 14-2 lists common network zones used by firewalld.

Network zones allow you to maintain different sets of firewall rules for different environments. When you connect to a new network using a laptop computer, NetworkManager will prompt you to choose the network zone that you wish to use with firewalld for your environment. If you choose the work network zone, firewalld will allow file sharing traffic by default. Alternatively, if you choose the public network zone, firewalld will prevent file sharing traffic by default.

Table 14-2   Common network zones

Network zone	Type	Description
drop	Immutable	Deny all incoming connections; outgoing ones are accepted
block	Immutable	Deny all incoming connections, with ICMP host-prohibited messages issued to the sender
trusted	Immutable	Allow all network connections
public	Mutable	Public areas, do not trust other computers
external	Mutable	For computers with masquerading enabled, protecting a local network
dmz	Mutable	For computers publicly accessible with restricted access
work	Mutable	For trusted work areas
home	Mutable	For trusted home network connections
internal	Mutable	For internal network, restrict incoming connections

The default network zone used on your system is defined in the /etc/firewalld/firewalld.conf file, and custom network zone configuration is stored in the /etc/firewalld/zones directory. You can manage network zones and firewall rules that allow or deny traffic by service or port using the `firewall-cmd command`. Some common options to the `firewall-cmd` command are listed in Table 14-3.

Table 14-3   Common firewall-cmd options

Option	Description
`--get-zones`	Displays all available network zones
`--get-services`	Displays a list of names used by firewalld to identify network services
`--get-default-zone`	Specifies the source port number for a rule
`--set-default-zone=zone`	Specifies the destination port number for a rule
`--get-active-zones`	Displays the network interfaces that are active for each network zone
`--list-all-zones`	Displays the services that are enabled (allowed) for each network zone
`--list-all`	Displays the services that are enabled (allowed) for the current network zone
`--zone=zone --list-all`	Displays the services that are enabled (allowed) for the specified network zone (*zone*)
`--add-service=service`	Enable (allow) the specified *service* within the current network zone
`--add-service=service --permanent`	Ensure that the specified *service* is enabled (allowed) within the current network zone at system initialization
`--add-port=port`	Enable (allow) the specified *port* within the current network zone
`--add-port=port --permanent`	Ensure that the specified *port* is enabled (allowed) within the current network zone at system initialization
`--remove-service=service`	Disable (disallow) the specified *service* within the current network zone
`--remove-service=service --permanent`	Ensure that the specified *service* is disabled (disallowed) within the current network zone at system initialization
`--remove-port=port`	Disable (disallow) the specified *port* within the current network zone
`--remove-port=port --permanent`	Ensure that the specified *port* is disabled (disallowed) within the current network zone at system initialization
`--query-service=service`	Returns yes if the specified *service* is enabled (allowed) within the current network zone, and no if it is not
`--query-port=port`	Returns yes if the specified *port* is enabled (allowed) within the current network zone, and no if it is not

To define a stateful firewall exception for postgresql in your default (current) network zone and also ensure that this exception is loaded at system initialization, you could use the following commands:

```
[root@server1 ~]# firewall-cmd --add-service=postgresql
success
[root@server1 ~]# firewall-cmd --add-service=postgresql --permanent
success
[root@server1 ~]#_
```

You can instead define a stateful firewall exception for traffic by port number. For example, to define a firewall exception for SSH (TCP port 22) in your default (current) network zone and also ensure that this exception is loaded at system initialization, you could use the following commands:

```
[root@server1 ~]# firewall-cmd --add-port=22/tcp
success
[root@server1 ~]# firewall-cmd --add-port=22/tcp --permanent
success
[root@server1 ~]#_
```

Note 22

You used the `firewall-cmd` command during the hands-on projects in Chapter 13 to allow traffic destined to your Fedora Linux virtual machine by service name.

Note 23

You can also use the `firewall-cmd --runtime-to-permanent` command to ensure that all currently set firewall rules are configured to load at system initialization.

Many Linux distributions also provide a graphical firewall configuration utility that can be used to configure netfilter by service name or port. On Fedora Workstation, the **Firewall Configuration utility** shown in Figure 14-3 automatically creates netfilter rules based on your selections via firewalld. These rules are activated immediately because the Configuration drop-down dialog box shown in Figure 14-3 is set to Runtime by default; to set rules that are loaded at system initialization, you must select Permanent from the Configuration drop-down dialog box. You can start the Firewall Configuration utility within the GNOME desktop by opening the Activities menu and navigating to Show Applications, Firewall.

Configuring SELinux

Security Enhanced Linux (SELinux) is a series of kernel patches and utilities created by the National Security Agency (NSA) that enforce security on your system using policies that prevent applications from being used to access resources and system components in insecure ways. SELinux adds a label to each file, directory, and process. Preconfigured SELinux policies contain rules that identify the process labels that should be allowed to access certain file and directory labels. When SELinux is enabled, the Linux kernel enforces the rules within the SELinux security policies to prevent processes from accessing areas of the system that could pose a security concern.

Figure 14-3   The Firewall Configuration utility

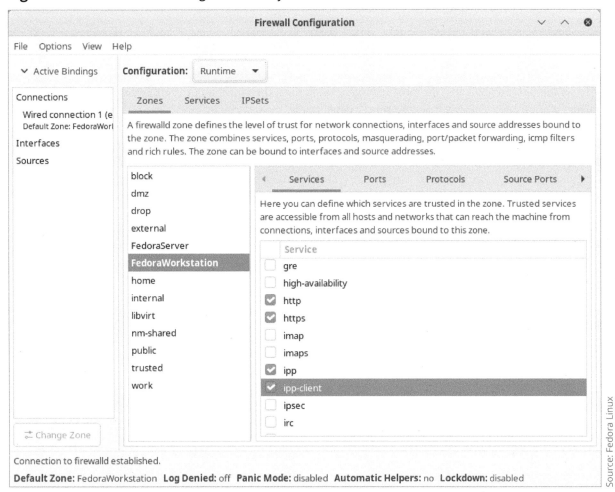

> **Note 24**
>
> SELinux is enabled by default in Fedora Linux.

Recall from Chapter 3 that a period (.) immediately following the mode of a file or directory within output of the `ls -l` command indicates that the file or directory has an SELinux label. To view the SELinux labels for files and directories, you can add the `-Z` option to the `ls` command. This is shown in the following output for the index.html file within the Apache document root directory on a Fedora system (/var/www/html):

```
[root@server1 html]# pwd
/var/www/html
[root@server1 html]# ls -l
total 4
-rw-r-----. 1 apache root 46 Nov 16 17:32 index.html
[root@server1 html]# ls -Z
unconfined_u:object_r:httpd_sys_content_t:s0 index.html
[root@server1 html]#_
```

The previous output indicates that the index.html file has an SELinux label of `unconfined_u:` `object_r:httpd_sys_content_t:s0`. SELinux labels consist of the following four colon (`:`) delimited sections:

`user:role:type:level`

The `user` section identifies the Linux user type, and the `role` section identifies the category the user belongs to within SELinux policies; for most user-generated files, these will be `unconfined_u` (unconfined user) and `object_r` (object access role), respectively.

The `type` section is the most important part of an SELinux label; it defines the classification of the file or directory. Only processes that contain the same classification prefix will normally be allowed to access the file or directory within SELinux policy rules. In the previous output, the index.html has a classification of `httpd_sys_content_t` (Apache system content type); thus, only processes that have a classification of `httpd_t` (Apache type) will be permitted to access the index.html file. To view the SELinux labels for processes, you can add the `-Z` option to the `ps` command. The following output indicates that the currently running Apache processes contain a `httpd_t` classification and will be able to access the index.html shown earlier as a result:

```
[root@server1 html]# ps -eZ | grep httpd
system_u:system_r:httpd_t:s0      1625 ?          00:00:00 httpd
system_u:system_r:httpd_t:s0      1626 ?          00:00:00 httpd
system_u:system_r:httpd_t:s0      1628 ?          00:00:00 httpd
system_u:system_r:httpd_t:s0      1629 ?          00:00:00 httpd
system_u:system_r:httpd_t:s0      1630 ?          00:00:00 httpd
[root@server1 html]#_
```

The `level` section is an optional attribute; it is only used if you extend SELinux functionality to use **Multi-Level Security (MLS)** or **Multi-Category Security (MCS)**. MLS can be used to restrict access to files, based on additional attributes provided by the organization (e.g., Top-Secret, Confidential, Public), whereas MCS can be used to restrict similar process types from accessing one another.

Note 25

You can use the `seinfo command` to view the values available on your system for SELinux label sections. For example, `seinfo -u` displays user values, `seinfo -r` displays role values, and `seinfo -t` displays type values.

To enable SELinux, you can edit the /etc/selinux/config file and set one of the following SELINUX options:

- `SELINUX = enforcing` (policy settings are enforced by SELinux)
- `SELINUX = permissive` (SELinux generates warnings only and logs events)
- `SELINUX = disabled` (SELinux is disabled)

Next, you can select an SELINUX policy by configuring one of the following SELINUXTYPE options within the /etc/selinux/config file:

- `SELINUXTYPE = targeted` (all network daemons are protected)
- `SELINUXTYPE = minimum` (only critical network daemons are protected)
- `SELINUXTYPE = mls` (use MLS attributes instead of type classifications)

Most Linux systems that use SELinux have definitions for the targeted policy that protect the system from malicious applications that can damage system files or compromise security. After modifying the /etc/selinux/config file to enable SELinux, you must reboot to relabel the existing files on the system. Following this, you can use the `sestatus` command to view your current SELinux status:

```
[root@server1 ~]# sestatus -v
SELinux status:              enabled
SELinuxfs mount:             /sys/fs/selinux
SELinux root directory:      /etc/selinux
Loaded policy name:          targeted
Current mode:                enforcing
Mode from config file:       enforcing
Policy MLS status:           enabled
Policy deny_unknown status:  allowed
Memory protection checking:  actual (secure)
Max kernel policy version:   33

Process contexts:
Current context: unconfined_u:unconfined_r:unconfined_t:s0-s0:c0.c1023
Init context:                system_u:system_r:init_t:s0
/usr/sbin/sshd               system_u:system_r:sshd_t:s0-s0:c0.c1023

File contexts:
Controlling terminal:        unconfined_u:object_r:user_devpts_t:s0
/etc/passwd                  system_u:object_r:passwd_file_t:s0
/etc/shadow                  system_u:object_r:shadow_t:s0
/bin/bash                    system_u:object_r:shell_exec_t:s0
/bin/login                   system_u:object_r:login_exec_t:s0
/bin/sh                      system_u:object_r:bin_t:s0 ->
system_u:object_r:shell_exec_t:s0
/sbin/agetty                 system_u:object_r:getty_exec_t:s0
/sbin/init                   system_u:object_r:bin_t:s0 ->
system_u:object_r:init_exec_t:s0
/usr/sbin/sshd               system_u:object_r:sshd_exec_t:s0
[root@server1 ~]#_
```

Note from the previous output that the system is enforcing the targeted SELinux policy. Sometimes, SELinux blocks network services from accessing files and directories that you would like the services to access. To determine whether a network service problem is the result of SELinux enforcement, you can temporarily change the SELinux mode from enforcing to permissive. If the problem is no longer present in permissive mode, then SELinux enforcement is the cause. You can use the `setenforce` command to easily switch between enforcing and permissive mode, as well as use the `getenforce` command to view your current mode. This is demonstrated in the following output:

```
[root@server1 ~]# getenforce
Enforcing
[root@server1 ~]# setenforce permissive
[root@server1 ~]# getenforce
Permissive
[root@server1 ~]# setenforce enforcing
[root@server1 ~]# getenforce
Enforcing
[root@server1 ~]#_
```

In most cases, SELinux enforcement problems are the result of an incorrect label applied to files and directories. SELinux automatically labels files and directories on the first system initialization after SELinux is enabled, as well as when new files and directories are created. If you copy a file that has an SELinux label to another directory, SELinux will set the correct label on the newly-created copy in the target directory. However, if you move a file that has an SELinux label to a new directory, the file will retain its original SELinux label because a new file was not created in the process. This is illustrated in the following output, in which an index.html is moved from the root user's home directory to the /var/www/html directory:

```
[root@server1 ~]# ls -Z index.html
unconfined_u:object_r:admin_home_t:s0 index.html
[root@server1 ~]# mv index.html /var/www/html
[root@server1 ~]# ls -Z /var/www/html/index.html
unconfined_u:object_r:admin_home_t:s0 /var/www/html/index.html
[root@server1 ~]#_
```

Because the index.html in the previous output retains its original classification following the move operation, it cannot be read by the Apache daemon, as SELinux prevents Apache from reading files that do not have a httpd_ classification. Consequently, clients will receive an HTTP 403 Forbidden error when attempting to access the webpage in their web browser. To remedy the issue, you can manually change the classification of the /var/www/html/index.html file to the correct classification (httpd_sys_content_t) using the chcon command as shown in the following output:

```
[root@server1 ~]# chcon -t httpd_sys_content_t /var/www/html/index.html
[root@server1 ~]# ls -Z /var/www/html/index.html
unconfined_u:object_r:httpd_sys_content_t:s0 /var/www/html/index.html
[root@server1 ~]#_
```

You can also use the restorecon command to force SELinux to relabel a file using the correct classification. For example, the restorecon /var/www/html/index.html command could have been used in place of the chcon command in the previous output to set the correct classification on the /var/www/html/index.html file.

> **Note 26**
>
> To force SELinux to relabel all files on the system during the next system initialization, you can create a /.autorelabel file using the touch /.autorelabel command.

Not all SELinux problems that you may encounter are related to incorrect labeling. For example, the default SELinux targeted policy does not allow the Apache daemon to read web content within user home directories. As a result, if you enable home directory hosting within Apache, SELinux will prevent the feature from working. To remedy the issue, you can change the targeted policy settings by modifying the appropriate files within the /etc/selinux/targeted directory. Alternatively, you can locate the policy setting that allows Apache to read web content within user home directories using the getsebool command and modify that setting using the setsebool command. This is demonstrated in the following output:

```
[root@server1 ~]# getsebool -a | grep httpd | grep home
httpd_enable_homedirs --> off
[root@server1 ~]# setsebool -P httpd_enable_homedirs on
[root@server1 ~]# getsebool -a | grep httpd | grep home
httpd_enable_homedirs --> on
[root@server1 ~]#_
```

> **Note 27**
>
> You can also use the semanage command to view and manage SELinux settings. For example, semanage boolean -m --on httpd_enable_homedirs can be used instead of the setsebool command used in the previous example to allow web content within user home directories.

On systems that use SELinux, the auditd daemon listens to kernel system calls and logs SELinux-related events to the /var/log/audit/audit.log file. You can view this log file to identify problems related to SELinux enforcement. Additionally, you can use the `audit2why command` to generate easy-to-read descriptions of SELinux-related events within /var/log/audit/audit.log using the `audit2why < /var/log/audit/audit.log` command. These descriptions are often very helpful in determining the cause of an SELinux restriction. If any SELinux-related events displayed by the `audit2why` command should be allowed by SELinux on the system, you can copy those events from the /var/log/audit/audit.log file into a new file and redirect that file to the `audit2allow command` to modify the associated SELinux policies.

Note 28

Most desktop environments will display an alert message when an SELinux prevents a process on the system from accessing a resource. You can click on this alert message to view an easy-to-read description of the event.

Configuring AppArmor

AppArmor is an alternative to SELinux that provides a similar type of protection for programs that access system resources. It consists of a kernel module and a series of utilities that provide restrictions for individual programs on a Linux system. Restrictions for each program are stored within text files named for the program under the /etc/apparmor.d directory; each text file is called an **AppArmor profile**. For example, the AppArmor profile for the CUPS daemon (/usr/sbin/cupsd) would be stored within the /etc/apparmor.d/usr.sbin.cupsd file.

Note 29

AppArmor is enabled by default in Ubuntu Linux.

AppArmor profiles can be enforced by AppArmor (called enforce mode) or used to generate warnings and log events only (called complain mode). To view the AppArmor profiles configured for each mode, as well as the active processes on the system that are being managed by AppArmor, you can run the `aa-status command`, as shown here:

```
[root@server1 ~]# aa-status
apparmor module is loaded.
35 profiles are loaded.
34 profiles are in enforce mode.
   /sbin/dhclient
   /usr/bin/lxc-start
   /usr/bin/man
   /usr/lib/NetworkManager/nm-dhcp-client.action
   /usr/lib/NetworkManager/nm-dhcp-helper
   /usr/lib/connman/scripts/dhclient-script
   /usr/lib/cups/backend/cups-pdf
   /usr/lib/snapd/snap-confine
   /usr/lib/snapd/snap-confine//mount-namespace-capture-helper
   /usr/sbin/chronyd
   /usr/sbin/cups-browsed
   /usr/sbin/cupsd
   /usr/sbin/cupsd//third_party
   /usr/sbin/tcpdump
   docker-default
```

```
lxc-container-default
lxc-container-default-cgns
lxc-container-default-with-mounting
lxc-container-default-with-nesting
man_filter
man_groff
snap-update-ns.core
snap-update-ns.docker
snap-update-ns.notepad3
snap-update-ns.powershell
snap.core.hook.configure
snap.docker.compose
snap.docker.docker
snap.docker.dockerd
snap.docker.help
snap.docker.hook.install
snap.docker.hook.post-refresh
snap.docker.machine
snap.notepad3.notepad3
1 profiles are in complain mode.
   snap.powershell.powershell
5 processes have profiles defined.
5 processes are in enforce mode.
   /usr/sbin/chronyd (1520)
   /usr/sbin/cups-browsed (10622)
   /usr/sbin/cupsd (10621)
   snap.docker.dockerd (1447)
   snap.docker.dockerd (2028)
0 processes are in complain mode.
0 processes are unconfined but have a profile defined.
[root@server1 ~]#_
```

Note from the previous output that 34 AppArmor profiles are loaded and set to enforce mode, while 1 AppArmor profile is loaded and set to complain mode. However, only 5 processes that match these AppArmor profiles are currently started, and all of them are set to enforce mode. Moreover, there are 0 processes running that do not have a matching AppArmor profile; these processes are referred to as unconfined processes within the previous output and can also be shown using the aa-unconfined command.

To switch an AppArmor profile to enforce mode, you can use the aa-enforce command. Alternatively, you can use the aa-complain command to switch an AppArmor profile to complain mode, or the aa-disable command to disable an AppArmor profile. For example, to switch the CUPS daemon AppArmor profile (/etc/apparmor.d/usr.sbin.cupsd) to complain mode, you could run the following command:

```
[root@server1 ~]# aa-complain /etc/apparmor.d/usr.sbin.cupsd
Setting /etc/apparmor.d/usr.sbin.cupsd to complain mode.
[root@server1 ~]#_
```

Note 30

Although AppArmor is installed by default on Ubuntu Server, you must install the apparmor-utils package from a software repository to use the aa-unconfined, aa-enforce, aa-complain, and aa-disable commands.

As with SELinux, AppArmor may inadvertently block network services from accessing desired resources. To determine if an enforced AppArmor profile is the cause of the problem, you can temporarily set the AppArmor profile for the network service to complain mode. If this remedies the problem, then you can adjust the appropriate settings within the AppArmor profile for the network service in the /etc/apparmor.d directory and set the AppArmor profile to enforce mode afterwards. For problems that affect multiple AppArmor profiles, you can often modify the settings within a text file under the /etc/apparmor.d/tunables directory. For example, if you change the location of user home directories from /home to /users on a Linux system, many AppArmor profiles will prevent network services from accessing home directory content. In this case, you can modify the line `@{HOMEDIRS}=/home/` to read `@{HOMEDIRS}=/users/` within the /etc/apparmor.d/tunables/home file.

> ### Note 31
>
> To view the available settings that you can configure within an AppArmor profile, you can view the apparmor.d manual page.

Troubleshooting Methodology

After you have successfully installed Linux, you must configure services on the system, secure local and network access, document settings, as well as maintain the system's integrity over time. This includes monitoring, proactive maintenance, and reactive maintenance, as illustrated in Figure 14-4.

Figure 14-4   The maintenance cycle

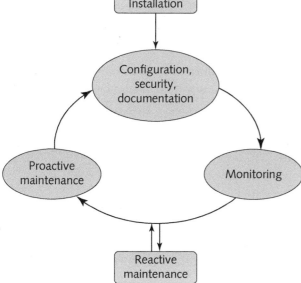

Monitoring, the activity on which Linux administrators spend the most time, involves examining log files and running performance utilities periodically to identify problems and their causes. Proactive maintenance involves taking the required steps to minimize the chance of future problems as well as their impact. Performing regular system backups and identifying potential problem areas are examples of proactive maintenance. All proactive maintenance tasks should be documented for future reference. This information, along with any data backups, is vital to the reconstruction of your system, should it suffer catastrophic failure.

Reactive maintenance is used to correct problems when they arise during monitoring. When a problem is solved, it needs to be documented and the system adjusted proactively to reduce the likelihood that the same problem will occur in the future. Furthermore, documenting the solution to problems creates a template for action, allowing subsequent or similar problems to be remedied faster.

Note 32

Any system **documentation** should be stored within a file on a separate computer because this information might be lost during a system failure. Many organizations store system documentation within their help desk ticketing software, which is backed up regularly to ensure that the documentation is not lost during a system failure.

Reactive maintenance is further composed of many tasks known as **troubleshooting procedures**, which can be used to efficiently solve a problem in a systematic manner.

When a problem occurs, you need to gather as much information about the problem as possible. This might include examining system log files, viewing the contents of the /proc and /sys filesystems, or running information utilities, such as `ps` or `lsblk`. In addition, you might research the symptoms of the problem on the Internet; many technology-related websites list commands you can run and log files that you can check to identify the cause of problems.

Note 33

The `tail -f /path/to/logfile` command opens a specific log file for continuous viewing; this allows you to see entries as they are added, which is useful when gathering information about system problems. If your system uses Systemd, you can use the `--follow` option to the `journalctl` command to do the same. For example, to view chronyd events as they are added, you can use the `journalctl _COMM=chronyd --follow` command.

Following this, you need to try to isolate the problem by examining the information gathered. Determine whether the problem is persistent or intermittent and whether it affects all users or just one.

Given this information, you might then generate a list of possible causes and solutions organized by placing the most probable solution at the top of the list and the least probable solution at the bottom of the list. Using the Internet at this stage is beneficial because solutions for many Linux problems are posted on websites that can be found by performing a Google search for key words related to the problem. In addition, posting the problem on a Linux-related forum website will likely generate many possible solutions.

Next, you need to implement and test each possible solution for results until the problem is resolved. When implementing possible solutions, it is very important that you only apply one change at a time. If you make multiple modifications, it will be unclear as to what worked and why.

After the problem has been solved, document the solution for future reference and proceed to take proactive maintenance measures to reduce the chance of the same problem recurring in the future. These troubleshooting procedures are outlined in Figure 14-5.

Figure 14-5   Common troubleshooting procedures

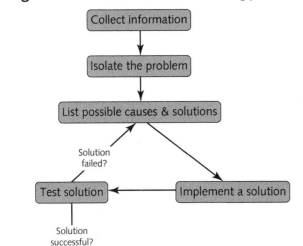

The troubleshooting procedures listed in Figure 14-5 serve as a guideline only. You might need to alter your approach for certain problems. Remember, troubleshooting is an art that you will begin to master only with practice. There are, however, two golden rules that should guide you during any troubleshooting process:

- *Prioritize problems*—If you need to solve multiple problems, prioritize the problems according to severity and spend the most time on the most severe problems. Becoming fixated on a small problem and ignoring larger issues results in much lower productivity. If a problem is too difficult to solve in a given period of time, it is good practice to ask for help.
- *Try to solve the root of the problem*—Some solutions might appear successful in the short term yet fail over the long term because of an underlying problem. Effective troubleshooting requires good instincts, which in turn comes from a solid knowledge of the system hardware and software configuration. To avoid missing the underlying cause of any problem, try to justify why a certain solution was successful. If it is unclear why a certain solution was successful, it is likely that you have missed an underlying cause to the problem that might need to be remedied in the future to prevent the same problem from recurring.

Resolving Common System Problems

The possible problems that can arise on Linux systems are too numerous to list here. However, as a troubleshooter, you'll most often face a set of the common problems described in this section. Most Linux problems can be divided into four categories: hardware-related, application-related, filesystem-related, and network-related.

Hardware-Related Problems

Hardware devices within a computer fall into one of several categories, and each category has different troubleshooting practices. When troubleshooting peripheral devices, such as monitors, keyboards, printers, and mice, first ensure that they are properly connected to the port on the computer. When troubleshooting video cards and network interface cards, first ensure that the card is seated properly in the slot on the computer motherboard and that the proper device driver module is loaded by the Linux kernel. You can use the commands listed in Table 6-2 to determine whether the Linux has the correct device driver module for your hardware and proceed to install the correct one if necessary. If the hardware device is physically present but not listed by the commands within Table 6-2, you can use the lshw command to list detailed information about the device, which can be searched online to locate a device driver module. In rare cases, the hardware device may not have a Linux device driver and will not be usable within Linux as a result.

On Linux desktops, some hardware problems are due to faulty **Advanced Configuration and Power Interface (ACPI)** support. ACPI is a BIOS component that allows operating systems to interface directly to hardware components or provide power management. For example, if you press the power button or close the lid of your laptop computer, it could send a command to your operating system that tells the init or Systemd daemon to safely shut down the system or enter sleep mode. ACPI is often provided by the **ACPI Daemon (acpid)** but can instead be provided entirely by Systemd if acpid is not running. If a Linux system fails to respond to ACPI events, or responds to ACPI events improperly or intermittently, you may need to configure acpid to start automatically or disable it from starting to ensure that Systemd can interact with ACPI directly.

Many problems that affect storage devices are related to the speed of the underlying storage device itself. Different storage devices support different speeds and number of **input/output operations per second (IOPS)**. If too many processes write to a slow storage device, users will experience problems reading and writing data to the filesystems on that device. In some cases, you can modify how the Linux kernel writes to the storage device to fix speed and IOPS problems on a busy system. By default, most Linux kernels use a scheduling method called completely fair queuing (cfq) when writing to storage devices, but this can be changed to budget fair queuing (bfq), no operation (noop), deadline, mq-deadline, kyber, or none, depending on the configuration of your kernel. For example, to view the available scheduling methods for the first SAS storage device (sda), as well as modify it to use noop and verify the results, you could run the following commands:

```
[root@server1 ~]# cat /sys/block/sda/queue/scheduler
noop deadline [cfq]
[root@server1 ~]# echo noop > /sys/block/sda/queue/scheduler
[root@server1 ~]# cat /sys/block/sda/queue/scheduler
[noop] deadline cfq
[root@server1 ~]#_
```

If modifying the scheduling method results in better performance, you can ensure that the scheduling method is configured at system initialization by modifying the GRUB bootloader. For example, to ensure that the noop scheduling method is configured at system initialization, you could append elevator=noop to the GRUB_CMDLINE_LINUX line within /etc/default/grub and run the appropriate grub2-mkconfig command to rebuild the GRUB configuration files.

Other storage-related problems may be related to device access. For example, if a SATA or SCSI cable becomes unseated, the associated hard disk drive or SSD will not be visible by the system. Similarly, a SCSI controller can sometimes fail to detect a hard disk drive that is properly connected to it. In this case, you can force the SCSI controller to rescan the SCSI bus for connected devices; for the first SCSI bus, you could run the echo "- - -" > /sys/class/scsi_host/host0/scan command.

Removable storage device access problems can usually be solved by writing a udev rule that dictates how the udev daemon processes the device when it is inserted into the system. For example, to give members of the developer group the ability to mount a particular Verbatim USB storage device in order to perform backups, you could add a udev rule to a text file that has a *.rules extension within the /etc/udev/rules.d directory (e.g., /etc/udev/rules.d/VerbatimUSB.rules). To do this, you must first insert the Verbatim USB storage device and locate its bus and device ID using the lsusb command:

```
[root@server1 ~]# lsusb
Bus 001 Device 004: ID 18a5:024a Verbatim, Ltd
Bus 001 Device 003: ID 05ac:828d Apple, Inc.
Bus 001 Device 002: ID 80ee:0021 VirtualBox USB Tablet
```

```
Bus 001 Device 001: ID 1d6b:0001 Linux Foundation 1.1 root hub
[root@server1 ~]#_
```

Next, you can use the bus ID (001) and device ID (004) shown in the previous output within the following udevadm command to identify its unique attributes:

```
[root@server1 ~]# udevadm info -a -p $(udevadm info -q path -n /dev/bus/usb/001/004)

  looking at device '/devices/pci0000:00/0000:00:06.0/usb1/1-3':
    KERNEL=="1-3"
    SUBSYSTEM=="usb"
    DRIVER=="usb"
    ATTR{authorized}=="1"
    ATTR{avoid_reset_quirk}=="0"
    ATTR{bConfigurationValue}=="1"
    ATTR{bDeviceClass}=="00"
    ATTR{bDeviceProtocol}=="00"
    ATTR{bDeviceSubClass}=="00"
    ATTR{bMaxPacketSize0}=="64"
    ATTR{bMaxPower}=="200mA"
    ATTR{bNumConfigurations}=="1"
    ATTR{bNumInterfaces}==" 1"
    ATTR{bcdDevice}=="0100"
    ATTR{bmAttributes}=="80"
    ATTR{busnum}=="1"
    ATTR{devnum}=="4"
    ATTR{devpath}=="3"
    ATTR{idProduct}=="024a"
    ATTR{idVendor}=="18a5"
    ATTR{ltm_capable}=="no"
    ATTR{manufacturer}=="Verbatim"
    ATTR{product}=="STORE N GO"
    ATTR{serial}=="070B43C65D99D047"

<additional output omitted>

[root@server1 ~]#_
```

From the previous output, you could use the product attribute (ATTR{product}=="STORE N GO") alongside the device subsystem type (SUBSYSTEM=="usb") to uniquely identify the USB storage device within a udev rule. Thus, to ensure that members of the developer group can mount this particular USB storage device, you could add the line SUBSYSTEMS=="usb", ATTRS{product}=="STORE N GO", GROUP="developers" to the /etc/udev/rules.d/VerbatimUSB.rules file. Next, you could run the udevadm control -R command to force udev to reload the new rules from the /etc/udev/rules directory.

Note 34

You can also write udev rules that trigger an event when a device is inserted into the system. To learn more about udev rules, view the udevadm manual page.

Because storage devices are used frequently, they are the most common hardware component to fail on Linux systems. If the Linux system uses a fault tolerant storage configuration, such as hardware or software RAID 1 or 5, or a fault tolerant ZFS or BTRFS volume, the data on a storage device can be regenerated after you replace it as discussed in Chapter 6.

If, however, the Linux system does not use a fault tolerant storage configuration, and the storage device that failed contained partitions that were mounted on noncritical directories, such as /home or /var, then you can perform the following steps to recover the data:

1. Power down the computer and replace the failed storage device.
2. Boot the Linux system.
3. Create one or more partitions on the replaced hard disk drive or SSD.
4. Optionally configure LVM logical volumes from the partitions created in Step 3.
5. Create filesystems on the partitions or LVM logical volumes.
6. Restore the original data using a backup utility.
7. Ensure that /etc/fstab has the appropriate entries to mount the filesystems at system startup.

Alternatively, if the hard disk drive or SSD that contains the root filesystem fails, you can perform the following steps:

1. Power down the computer and replace the failed storage device.
2. Reinstall Linux on the new storage device using the original partition and volume structure.
3. Restore the original configuration and data files using a backup utility.

Application-Related Problems

Applications can fail during execution for several reasons, including missing dependencies, system configuration, process restrictions, or conflicting applications.

Recall from Chapter 11 that most applications depend on shared program libraries and other prerequisite packages. If a shared library or prerequisite package is removed from the system, the application may crash or work with limited functionality. You can use the -V option to the rpm or dpkg command to determine if a package is missing a file or prerequisite package, as well as use the ldd command to identify missing libraries for an application. Additionally, an application can fail following an update if the updated version is incompatible with existing software or shared libraries on the system.

Restrictive file permissions, incorrect file ownership, missing environment variables, SELinux, and AppArmor may prevent a process from accessing files needed for the process to run properly. However, processes can also be restricted by several other constraints that can prevent them from executing properly. Recall that all processes require a PID from the system process table. Too many processes running on the system can use all available PIDs in the process table; this is typically the result of many zombie processes. Killing the parent process of the zombie processes then frees several entries in the process table.

In addition, processes can initiate numerous connections to files on the filesystem in addition to Standard Input, Standard Output, and Standard Error. These connections are called file handles. The shell restricts the number of file handles that programs can open to 1024 by default on most systems; to increase the maximum number of file handles to 5000, you can run the command ulimit -n 5000. The ulimit command can also be used to increase the number of processes that users can start in a shell; this might be required for programs that start a great deal of child processes. For example, to increase the maximum number of user processes to 30000, you can use the command ulimit -u 30000.

To isolate application problems that are not related to missing dependencies or restrictions, you should first check the log file produced by the application. Most application log files are stored in the /var/log directory or subdirectories of the /var/log directory named for the application. Even if an application stores its log files elsewhere, it usually hard links or symbolically links its log files to files within the /var/log directory. For example, to view the errors for the Apache daemon, you can view the appropriate log files created by the Apache daemon under the /var/log/httpd directory on Fedora systems, or the /var/log/apache2 directory on Ubuntu systems.

Applications might also run into difficulties gaining resources during execution and stop functioning. Modern Linux kernels contain an Out Of Memory (OOM) killer that kills low priority processes when available system memory is exhausted. If the memory statistics shown by the top command indicate there are too few available memory resources on the system, move some services to another system on the network that has more free resources. If applications stop functioning when ample memory resources are available, restarting the process often solves the problem. This condition might also be caused by another process on the system that attempts to use the same resources. To determine if this is the case, attempt to start the application when fewer processes are loaded, such as in single user mode (rescue.target). If resource conflict seems to be the cause of the problem, check the Internet for a newer version of the application or an application fix. Many Linux distributions start the Automatic Bug Reporting Tool Daemon (abrtd) by default to send any application crash data to an online bug reporting site, such as Bugzilla. This information is then distributed to the appropriate open source developers, who can create an updated version of the program that fixes the issue.

Filesystem-Related Problems

Filesystems are accessed frequently by the operating system as they provide the storage for most user and system files. Accordingly, filesystem limits, corruption, and bad blocks are the most common filesystem-related problems that Linux administrators encounter.

If the available space on the root filesystem is exhausted, the Linux system will crash. To prevent this, you could create separate filesystems for the /home, /tmp, /usr, and /var directories. In this case, if a user downloads many files to their home directory, only the /home filesystem is affected. Similarly, if a program writes a large amount of data under the /tmp, /usr, or /var directories, only the filesystems mounted to those directories are affected, and the Linux system remains available.

Problems that prevent users from creating or saving data to files are often the result of a user quota on a filesystem. You can use the quota -u *username* command to determine whether a user has reached their quota limit, and the edquota -u *username* command to modify the quota limits for that user. Similarly, users will encounter errors creating or saving to files on a filesystem if that filesystem has no data blocks or inodes available. You can use the df -h command to list the available data blocks for each filesystem using human-readable units, and the df -i command to list the available inodes within each filesystem's inode table. If there are no free data blocks, or the inode table has no free inodes, you can remove files, or move files to another filesystem to remedy the issue. If the filesystem is stored on a LVM, RAID, ZFS, or BTRFS volume, you can instead add storage and extend the filesystem to remedy the problem.

Filesystem corruption or bad blocks can cause a wide range of problems, including missing files, errors when opening files, very slow write requests, errors printed to the console, and failure to mount. Running the appropriate filesystem repair command (e.g., fsck) can be used to remedy these problems. More specifically, if you suspect corruption or bad blocks for a filesystem mounted to a noncritical directory, such as /home or /var, you should perform the following troubleshooting steps:

1. Unmount the filesystem, if mounted.
2. Run the appropriate filesystem repair command on the filesystem device.
3. If the filesystem repair command cannot repair the filesystem, re-create the filesystem and restore the original data for the filesystem using a backup utility.

Note 35

Do not restore data onto a damaged filesystem; ensure that the filesystem has been recreated first.

If the root filesystem becomes corrupted, the system is unstable and must be turned off. Following this, you can perform the following troubleshooting steps:

1. Boot your system from live media to perform system rescue, as described in Chapter 6.
2. Run the appropriate filesystem repair command on the root filesystem device.
3. If the filesystem repair command cannot repair the root filesystem, re-create the filesystem and restore the original data for the filesystem using a backup utility.
4. Boot your system normally following the system rescue.

Network-Related Problems

Problems related to the network are common within most environments. The most common network issues that Linux administrators encounter relate to network connectivity, network service access, and network latency.

Network Connectivity Issues

If you are unable to connect to other computers on the network from a Linux system, first determine if the network interface is active and has an IP address (e.g., using the `ip addr` command). If an IP configuration is not available on a wired network interface, check to ensure that the Ethernet cable is connected to the Ethernet port on the computer, and run the appropriate command to activate the interface. For a wireless network interface, reconnect to your wireless access point within NetworkManager or your desktop environment. Next, check to ensure that you have the correct IP settings configured for your network interface. If your network interface uses DHCP to obtain IP settings, also ensure that the DHCP server is available on the network and has not exhausted its range of IP addresses.

Following this, you should test connectivity to the IP address of your network interface (e.g., using the `ping IP_address` command). If you do not receive a successful response, then the driver module for your network interface has experienced a failure that can be solved by rebooting the system.

> ## Note 36
>
> When using the `ping` command, it is best to choose a target computer that does not have a firewall enabled. Firewalls often block ICMP, preventing the `ping` command from receiving a successful response. In this case, you can determine whether the target computer was contacted successfully following a `ping` command by looking for the target computer's IP address in the MAC address cache on your computer. You can use the **arp command** to display the MAC address cache.

Next, you should test connectivity to an IP address on the same LAN as your network interface (e.g., using the `ping IP_address` command). If you are unable to connect to other computers on your LAN, you may need to reboot your switch or wireless access point.

After testing local LAN access, you should test connectivity to an IP address on another LAN, or a public IP address on the Internet (e.g., using the `ping IP_address` command). If you are unable to connect to computers outside of your LAN, you may not have the correct default gateway route configured within your route table, or a router between your computer and the target IP address has failed, contains incorrect configuration, or is experiencing high load. You can supply the target IP address as an argument to the `traceroute`, `tracepath`, or `mtr` command to determine which router is the source of the problem.

If you can access both local and remote LANs from your system by IP address, then the issue is likely due to name resolution. Test connectivity to the FQDN of a computer on the network (e.g., using the `ping FQDN` command). If connectivity to the computer's FQDN fails, then ensure that your system has the correct DNS server configured for name resolution, and that the DNS server is available on the network. If the DNS server is unavailable, you can specify an alternate DNS server within your system configuration to obtain network connectivity.

Network Service Issues

If clients are unable to contact a particular network service running on your server from across the network, you should start troubleshooting at the server itself. First determine if the network service is running (e.g., using the `ps -ef | grep service_name` command), and start it if necessary. If the network service fails to start, then check system and application log entries to determine the nature of the problem. Incorrect network service configuration file entries, SELinux and AppArmor restrictions, and other network services that are listening to the same port number can prevent a network service from starting successfully.

Next, determine if the network service is listening on the correct port number (e.g., using the `ss -t -a` command). If the network service is configured to listen to a non-standard port number, then client programs will also need to specify the non-standard port number for a connection to be successful.

Following this, attempt to interact with the network service locally to see if it is responding to requests on the correct port number. For example, to interact with the local Apache daemon listening on port 80, you could run the `ncat localhost 80` command and see if the Apache daemon interacts with the `ncat` command. If there is no response, you may need to restart the Apache daemon or verify that it has the correct settings within its configuration files.

If the network service is responding to requests, you should attempt to access the network service from the local computer using an appropriate client program. For example, to obtain the default webpage from the local Apache daemon, you could run the `curl http://localhost/` command. If you are unable to obtain the default web page, then local file permissions on the webpage file, SELinux or AppArmor restrictions, or incorrect Apache configuration could be the cause.

Finally, you should attempt to access the network service from another computer on the network. If you are able to access a network service locally but are unable to access the same network service from across a network, then a firewall on the server or network is likely preventing the access. To remedy the issue, you can allow the protocol name or port number in the appropriate firewall configuration.

Network Latency Issues

Sometimes, a network is properly configured, but the time it takes for network services to respond to requests is very high, or users receive occasional timeout errors when attempting to connect to a network service. This problem is called **network latency** and can occur when a network is saturated with traffic, or has limited bandwidth.

To determine if a particular network service or application is saturating the network, you can examine the traffic that is passing to and from your network interface using the `tcpdump` command, or **Wireshark**. Wireshark normally runs as a graphical program within a desktop environment but can also be run from a command line terminal using the `tshark` command. If, for example, you notice a very large number of DHCPDISCOVER or DHCPREQUEST packets on the network, then the DHCP server service is likely unavailable, and the client computers attempting to renew their IP configuration are saturating the network with DHCP requests.

To determine if the network bandwidth is the cause of network latency, you can measure the available bandwidth between two computers on the network using the `iperf` command. On the first computer, you run the `iperf -s` command to start a bandwidth measuring server process, and on the second computer, you pass the IP address of the first computer as an argument to the `iperf -c` command to measure the available bandwidth. Say, for example, that a computer on the network with the IP address 192.168.1.103 has executed the `iperf -s` command. You could then run the following command on your computer to test the bandwidth available between your computer and the computer with the IP address 192.168.1.103:

```
[root@server1 ~]# iperf -c 192.168.1.103
------------------------------------------------------------
Client connecting to 192.168.1.103, TCP port 5001
```

```
TCP window size: 85.0 KByte (default)
------------------------------------------------------------
[  3] local 10.0.0.2 port 48216 connected with 192.168.1.103 port 5001
[ ID] Interval       Transfer      Bandwidth
[  3]  0.0-10.0 sec  8.00 MBytes  2.58 Kbits/sec
[root@server1 ~]#_
```

> **Note 37**
>
> Most computers communicate with multiple systems simultaneously. To measure the bandwidth from your network interface to each system that your computer is communicating with, you can use the `iftop` **command**.

In some cases, network latency can be caused by firewall devices that are restricting network throughput, or by a malfunctioning network interface, switch, or router that is dropping IP packets instead of processing them. In this case, rebooting the affected device often remedies the problem. If network latency affects a single computer, then there is likely an application on that computer that is sending or receiving a large amount of data on the network interface. Stopping applications in order can help you identify which one is causing the problem.

Performance Monitoring

Some problems that you will encounter on a Linux system are not as noticeable as those discussed in the previous section. Such problems affect the overall performance of the Linux system. Like the problems discussed earlier, performance problems can be caused by hardware, applications, file-system issues, or network traffic.

Hardware that is improperly configured might still work, but at a slower speed. In addition, when hardware ages, it might start to malfunction by sending large amounts of information to the CPU when not in use. This process, known as jabbering, can slow down a CPU and, hence, the rest of the Linux system. To avoid this hardware malfunction on Linux servers, most companies retire server equipment after three to five years of use.

Applications can also affect the overall performance of a system. Processes that require too many system resources monopolize the CPU, memory, and peripheral devices. Poor performance can also be the result of too many processes running on a computer, processes that make a great deal of read/write requests to the storage device (such as databases), processes that send or receive large amounts of information on the network, rogue processes, or memory leaks. Memory leaks are processes that enter a state that allows them to continually use more memory, until the memory within the system is exhausted and the OOM killer begins removing low priority processes. To remedy most application performance issues, you can remove applications from the system to free up system resources. If the applications are needed for business activity, you can instead choose to move them to another Linux system that has more free system resources.

Application performance problems can also sometimes be remedied by altering the hardware. Upgrading or adding another CPU allows the Linux system to execute processes faster and reduce the number of processes running concurrently on the CPU. Alternatively, some peripheral devices can perform a great deal of processing that is normally performed by the CPU; this is known as bus mastering. Using bus mastering peripheral components reduces the amount of processing the CPU must perform and, hence, increases system speed. Most modern server systems use bus mastering storage controllers and network interfaces as a result.

Adding RAM to the computer also increases system speed because it gives processes more working space in memory and the system will send much less information to and from the swap partition.

Because the operating system, peripheral components, and all processes use RAM constantly, adding RAM to any system often has a profound impact on system performance.

In addition, replacing slower storage devices with faster ones improves the performance of programs that require frequent access to filesystems. SAS and NVMe SSDs typically have faster access speeds and are commonly used within modern Linux servers for this reason.

To make it easier to identify performance problems, you should run performance utilities on a healthy Linux system on a regular basis during normal business hours and document the results in a file that can be easily accessed. The average results of these performance utilities are known as baseline values because they represent normal system activity. When performance issues arise, you can compare the output of performance utilities to the baseline values. Values that have changed dramatically from the baseline can help you pinpoint the source of the performance problem.

Although many performance utilities are available to Linux administrators, the most common of these belong to the sysstat package, described next.

Monitoring Performance with sysstat Utilities

The System Statistics (sysstat) package contains a wide range of utilities that monitor the system using information from the /proc directory and system devices. The sysstat package isn't added during the installation process on most Linux distributions but can be installed from a software repository afterwards.

To monitor CPU performance, you can use the mpstat (multiple processor statistics) command. Without arguments, the mpstat command gives average CPU statistics for all processors on the system since system initialization, as shown in the following output:

```
[root@server1 ~]# mpstat
Linux 5.17.5-300.fc36.x86_64 (server1)        2023-10-17 _x86_64(2 CPU)

06:38:42 PM CPU  %usr %nice %sys %iowait %irq %soft %steal %guest %gnice %idle
06:38:42 PM all 17.53  1.48 6.21   11.73 0.19  0.00   0.00   0.00   0.00 62.85
[root@server1 ~]#_
```

Note 38

If your system has multiple CPUs, you can measure the performance of a single CPU by specifying the -P # option to the mpstat command, where # represents the number of the processor starting from zero. Thus, the command mpstat -P 0 displays statistics for the first processor on the system.

The %usr value shown in the preceding output indicates the percentage of time the processor spent executing user programs and daemons, whereas the %nice value indicates the percentage of time the processor spent executing user programs and daemons that had non-default nice values. These numbers combined should be greater than the value of %sys, which indicates the amount of time the system spent maintaining itself such that it can execute user programs and daemons.

Note 39

A system that has a high %sys compared to %usr and %nice is likely executing too many resource-intensive programs.

The %iowait value indicates the percentage of time the CPU was idle when an outstanding disk I/O request existed. The %irq and %soft values indicate the percentage of time the CPU is using to respond to normal interrupts and interrupts that span multiple CPUs, respectively. If these three values rapidly increase over time, the CPU cannot keep up with the number of requests it receives from software. If you have virtualization software installed, the %guest value indicates the percentage of time the CPU is executing another virtual CPU, the %gnice value indicates the percentage of time the processor spent executing user programs and daemons in the virtual CPU that had non-default nice values, and the %steal indicates the percentage of time the CPU is waiting to respond to virtual CPU requests.

The %idle value indicates the percentage of time the CPU did not spend executing tasks. Although it might be zero for short periods of time, %idle should be greater than 25 percent over a long period of time.

Note 40

A system that has a %idle of less than 25 percent over a long period of time might require faster or additional CPUs.

Although the average values given by the mpstat command are very useful in determining the CPU health of a Linux system, you might choose to take current measurements using mpstat. To do this, specify the interval in seconds and number of measurements as arguments to the mpstat command. For example, the following command takes five current measurements, one per second:

```
[root@server1 ~]# mpstat 1 5
Linux 5.17.5-300.fc36.x86_64 (server1)          2023-10-17 _x86_64(2 CPU)

07:05:10 AM CPU %usr %nice %sys %iowait %irq %soft %steal %guest %gnice %idle
07:05:11 AM all 8.91  1.98 0.00    0.00 0.99  0.00   0.00   0.00   0.00 88.12
07:05:12 AM all 7.07  2.02 0.00    0.00 0.00  0.00   0.00   0.00   0.00 90.91
07:05:13 AM all 7.92  1.98 0.99    0.00 0.00  0.00   0.00   0.00   0.00 89.11
07:05:14 AM all 7.07  2.02 0.00    0.00 0.00  0.00   0.00   0.00   0.00 90.91
07:05:15 AM all 6.93  2.97 0.99    0.00 0.00  0.00   0.00   0.00   0.00 89.11
Average:    all 7.58  2.20 0.40    0.00 0.20  0.00   0.00   0.00   0.00 89.62
[root@server1 ~]#_
```

The preceding output must be used with caution because it was taken over a short period of time. If, for example, the %idle values are under 25 percent on average, they are not necessarily abnormal because the system might be performing a CPU-intensive task during the short time the statistics were taken.

To view CPU statistics for each process running on the system, you can instead run the pidstat (PID statistics) command:

```
[root@server1 ~]# pidstat | head
Linux 5.17.5-300.fc36.x86_64 (server1)          2023-10-17 _x86_64(2 CPU)

05:04:34 PM   UID   PID  %usr %system  %guest  %wait  %CPU  CPU  Command
05:04:34 PM     0     1  0.00    0.01    0.00   0.01  0.01    0  systemd
05:04:34 PM     0     7  0.00    0.00    0.00   0.00  0.00    0  ksoftirqd/0
05:04:34 PM     0     8  0.00    0.00    0.00   0.01  0.00    0  rcu_sched
05:04:34 PM     0    11  0.00    0.00    0.00   0.00  0.00    0  watchdog/0
05:04:34 PM     0   325  0.00    0.00    0.00   0.01  0.00    0  kworker/0:1H
05:04:34 PM     0   346  0.00    0.00    0.00   0.00  0.00    0  jbd2/sda3-8
05:04:34 PM     0   438  0.00    0.00    0.00   0.00  0.00    0  systemd-journal
[root@server1 ~]#_
```

The `pidstat` command is often used to determine the CPU performance of a single process. For example, the `pidstat | grep crond` command would display CPU performance for the cron daemon.

Another utility, `iostat (input/output statistics)`, measures the flow of information to and from disk devices. Without any arguments, the `iostat` command displays CPU statistics similar to `mpstat`, followed by statistics for each disk device on the system. If your Linux system has one SATA hard disk drive (/dev/sda), the `iostat` command produces output similar to the following:

```
[root@server1 ~]# iostat
Linux 5.17.5-300.fc36.x86_64 (server1)        2023-10-17 _x86_64(2 CPU)

avg-cpu:   %user    %nice %system %iowait   %steal    %idle
            0.10     0.01    0.15    0.39     0.00    99.35


Device       tps    kB_read/s    kB_wrtn/s    kB_dscd/s    kB_read    kB_wrtn    kB_dscd
dm-0        0.01        0.20         0.00         0.00       1092          4          0
sda         3.29      122.33         7.98         0.00     671290      43765          0
sdb         0.04        0.55         0.00         0.00       3027          4          0
sdc         0.03        0.64         0.00         0.00       3536          0          0
sr0         0.51        0.19         0.00         0.00       1048          0          0
zram0       0.06        0.24         0.00         0.00       1304          4          0
[root@server1 ~]#
```

The output from `iostat` displays the number of transfers per second (`tps`) as well as the number of kilobytes read per second (`kB_read/s`), written per second (`kB_wrtn/s`), and discarded per second (`kB_dscd/s`), followed by the total number of kilobytes read (`kB_read`), written (`kB_wrtn`), and discarded (`kB_dscd`) for the device since system initialization. An increase over time in these values indicates an increase in disk usage by processes. If this increase results in slow performance, the hard disk drives should be replaced with faster ones, or SSDs. Like `mpstat`, the `iostat` command can take current measurements of the system. To do this, specify the interval in seconds, followed by the number of measurements as arguments to the `iostat` command.

Although `mpstat`, `pidstat`, and `iostat` can be used to get quick information about system performance, they are limited in their abilities. The `sar (system activity reporter) command` can be used to display far more information than other utilities within the sysstat package. As such, it is the most widely used performance monitoring tool on UNIX and Linux systems.

On Fedora systems, you can schedule `sar` commands to run every 10 minutes using a Systemd timer unit by running the `systemctl start sysstat-collect.timer` command. If you run the `systemctl start sysstat-summary.timer` command, a daily report of system performance will also be generated. To perform these same actions on Ubuntu systems, you must set `ENABLED="true"` within the /etc/default/sysstat file to allow the /etc/cron.d/sysstat cron table to be processed. All performance information obtained is logged to a file in the /var/log/sa directory (Fedora) or /var/log/sysstat directory (Ubuntu) called sa#, where # represents the day of the month. If today were the 14th day of the month, the output from the `sar` command that is run every 10 minutes would be logged to the file sa14. Next month, this file will be overwritten on the 14th day. In other words, only one month of records is kept at any one time. At the end of each day, a text file report of daily system performance will also be written to this same directory and called sar#, where # represents the day of the month.

Without arguments, the sar command displays the CPU statistics taken every 10 minutes for the current day, as shown in the following output:

```
[root@server1 ~]# sar
Linux 5.17.5-300.fc36.x86_64 (server1)        10/17/2023 _x86_64(2 CPU)

03:40:01 AM     CPU     %user    %nice    %system     %iowait     %steal     %idle
03:50:01 AM     all     0.06     0.00     0.13        0.27        0.00       99.54
04:00:01 AM     all     0.06     0.00     0.12        0.23        0.00       99.58
04:10:01 AM     all     0.08     0.00     0.14        0.19        0.00       99.60
04:20:01 AM     all     0.06     0.00     0.13        0.38        0.00       99.43
04:30:01 AM     all     0.06     0.00     0.12        0.20        0.00       99.61
04:40:01 AM     all     0.05     0.00     0.12        0.24        0.00       99.59
04:50:01 AM     all     0.06     0.00     0.12        0.21        0.00       99.61
05:00:01 AM     all     0.07     0.00     0.12        0.22        0.00       99.59
05:10:01 AM     all     0.08     0.00     0.13        0.19        0.00       99.59
05:20:01 AM     all     0.06     0.00     0.12        0.37        0.00       99.45
05:30:01 AM     all     0.07     0.00     0.12        0.20        0.00       99.61
05:40:01 AM     all     0.06     0.00     0.13        0.28        0.00       99.53
05:50:01 AM     all     0.06     0.00     0.12        0.22        0.00       99.60
06:00:01 AM     all     0.07     0.00     0.12        0.22        0.00       99.59
06:10:01 AM     all     0.08     0.00     0.14        0.18        0.00       99.60
06:20:01 AM     all     0.06     0.00     0.12        0.36        0.00       99.46
06:30:01 AM     all     0.07     0.00     0.13        0.20        0.00       99.60
06:40:01 AM     all     0.07     0.00     0.13        0.24        0.00       99.57
06:50:01 AM     all     0.06     0.00     0.13        0.26        0.00       99.56
07:00:01 AM     all     0.10     0.00     0.15        0.27        0.00       99.49
07:10:01 AM     all     0.09     0.00     0.15        0.31        0.00       99.45
07:20:01 AM     all     1.79     0.00     0.99        4.19        0.00       93.04
Average:        all     0.11     0.05     0.15        0.35        0.00       99.34
[root@server1 ~]#_
```

To view the CPU statistics for the 6th of the month, you can specify the pathname to the appropriate file using the -f option to the sar command:

```
[root@server1 ~]# sar -f /var/log/sa/sa06 | head
Linux 5.17.5-300.fc36.x86_64 (server1)        10/06/2023 _x86_64(2 CPU)

12:00:01 AM     CPU     %user    %nice    %system     %iowait     %steal     %idle
12:10:01 AM     all     0.07     0.00     0.14        0.56        0.00       99.22
12:20:01 AM     all     0.07     0.00     0.14        0.51        0.00       99.28
12:30:01 AM     all     0.07     0.00     0.13        0.53        0.00       99.28
12:40:01 AM     all     0.06     0.00     0.13        0.58        0.00       99.22
12:50:01 AM     all     0.07     0.00     0.13        0.54        0.00       99.26
01:00:01 AM     all     0.07     0.00     0.13        0.58        0.00       99.22
01:10:01 AM     all     0.07     0.00     0.14        0.60        0.00       99.19
[root@server1 ~]#_
```

You must use the -f option to the sar command to view the sa# files in the /var/log/sa (or /var/log/sysstat) directory because they contain binary information. To view the sar# files in this directory, you can use any text command, such as less.

As with the `iostat` and `mpstat` commands, the `sar` command can be used to take current system measurements. To take four CPU statistics every two seconds, you can use the following command:

```
[root@server1 ~]# sar 2 4
Linux 5.17.5-300.fc36.x86_64 (server1)        10/17/2023 _x86_64(2 CPU)

08:24:41 AM    CPU    %user    %nice    %system    %iowait    %steal    %idle
08:24:43 AM    all    0.00     0.00     0.50       0.00       0.00      99.50
08:24:45 AM    all    0.00     0.00     0.25       0.00       0.00      99.75
08:24:47 AM    all    0.25     0.00     0.76       0.00       0.00      98.99
08:24:49 AM    all    0.00     0.00     0.27       0.00       0.00      99.73
Average:       all    0.06     0.00     0.45       0.00       0.00      99.49
[root@server1 ~]#_
```

Although the `sar` command displays CPU statistics by default, you can display different statistics by specifying options to the `sar` command. Table 14-4 lists common options used with the `sar` command.

Table 14-4   Common options to the `sar` command

Option	Description
-A	Displays the most information; this option is equivalent to all options
-b	Displays I/O statistics
-B	Displays swap statistics
-d	Displays Input/Output statistics for each block device on the system
-f file_name	Displays information from the specified file; these files typically reside in the /var/log/sa directory
-n ALL	Reports all network statistics
-o file_name	Saves the output to a file in binary format
-P CPU#	Specifies statistics for a single CPU (the first CPU is 0, the second CPU is 1, and so on)
-q	Displays statistics for the processor queue
-r	Displays memory and swap statistics
-u	Displays CPU statistics; this is the default action when no options are specified
-v	Displays kernel-related filesystem statistics
-W	Displays swapping statistics

From Table 14-4, you can see that the –b and –d options to the `sar` command display information similar to the output of the `iostat` command. In addition, the –u option displays CPU statistics equivalent to the output of the `mpstat` command.

Another important option to the `sar` command is –q, which shows processor queue statistics. A processor queue is an area of RAM that stores information temporarily for quick retrieval by the CPU. To view processor queue statistics every five seconds, you can execute the following command:

```
[root@server1 ~]# sar -q 1 5
Linux 5.17.5-300.fc36.x86_64 (server1)        10/17/2023 _x86_64(2 CPU)

08:34:36 AM    runq-sz    plist-sz    ldavg-1    ldavg-5    ldavg-15    blocked
08:34:37 AM          0         252       0.00       0.00        0.00          0
```

```
08:34:38 AM          0       252     0.00       0.00       0.00        0
08:34:39 AM          0       252     0.00       0.00       0.00        0
08:34:40 AM          0       252     0.00       0.00       0.00        0
08:34:41 AM          0       252     0.00       0.00       0.00        0
Average:             0       252     0.00       0.00       0.00        0
[root@server1 ~]#_
```

The `runq-sz` (run queue size) indicates the number of processes that are waiting for execution on the processor run queue. For most CPU platforms, this number is typically 2 or less on average.

Note 41

A `runq-sz` much greater than 2 for long periods of time indicates that the CPU is too slow to respond to system requests.

The `plist-sz` (process list size) value indicates the number of processes currently running in memory, and the `ldavg-1` (load average – 1 minute), `ldavg-5` (load average – 5 minutes), and `ldavg-15` (load average – 15 minutes) values represent an average CPU load for the last 1 minute, 5 minutes, and 15 minutes, respectively. These four statistics display an overall picture of processor activity. A rapid increase in these values is typically caused by CPU-intensive software that is running on the system.

Note 42

When interpreting load average values on a single CPU system, a load average of 1.00 represents 100% load; thus, a load average of 0.80 indicates that the system is 20% underloaded, and a load average of 1.20 indicates that the system is 20% overloaded. For systems that have multiple CPUs, load average values are multiplied by the number of CPUs; thus, a load average of 2.00 on a dual CPU system represents 100% load.

The `blocked` value represents the number of tasks currently blocked from completion because they are waiting for I/O requests to complete. If this value is high, there are likely one or more storage devices that cannot keep up with system requests.

Recall that all Linux systems use a swap partition to store information that cannot fit into physical memory; this information is sent to and from the swap partition in units called pages. The number of pages that are sent to the swap partition (`pswpin/s`) and the pages that are taken from the swap partition (`pswpout/s`) can be viewed using the `-W` option to the `sar` command, as shown in the following output:

```
[root@server1 ~]# sar -W 1 5
Linux 5.17.5-300.fc36.x86_64 (server1)          10/17/2023 _x86_64(2 CPU)

08:37:01 AM   pswpin/s pswpout/s
08:37:02 AM       0.00      0.00
08:37:03 AM       0.00      0.00
08:37:04 AM       0.00      0.00
08:37:05 AM       0.00      0.00
08:37:06 AM       0.00      0.00
Average:          0.00      0.00
[root@server1 ~]#_
```

If a large compnumber of pages are being sent to and taken from the swap partition, the system will suffer from slower performance. To remedy this, you can add more physical memory (RAM) to the system.

Other Performance Monitoring Utilities

The sysstat package utilities are not the only performance-monitoring utilities available on Linux systems. Many regular system utilities display performance information in addition to other system information. For example, the w command, introduced in Chapter 2, displays the system load average values for the last 1, 5, and 15 minutes in addition to user session information. Similarly, the uptime command displays these same system load average values in addition to the time since system initialization. If you only wish to view system load average values, you can instead use the tload command.

The top command discussed in Chapter 9 also displays CPU statistics, memory usage, swap usage, and average CPU load at the top of the screen, as shown here:

```
top - 20:38:48 up  2:04,  2 users,  load average: 0.00, 0.00, 0.00
Tasks: 193 total,   1 running, 192 sleeping,   0 stopped,   0 zombie
%Cpu(s): 0.0us, 0.0sy, 0.0ni, 99.7id, 0.0wa, 0.2hi, 0.2si, 0.0st
MiB Mem :  3918.5 total, 2726.6 free, 485.4 used,   706.5 buff/cache
MiB Swap:  4942.0 total, 4942.0 free,   0.0 used. 3193.5 avail Mem
  PID USER      PR  NI    VIRT    RES    SHR S %CPU %MEM     TIME+  COMMAND
 5693 root      20   0    2696   1120    852 R  1.0  0.1   0:00.08 top
    1 root      20   0    2828   1312   1144 S  0.0  0.1   0:01.43 systemd
    2 root      20   0       0      0      0 S  0.0  0.0   0:00.00 kthreadd
    3 root      RT   0       0      0      0 S  0.0  0.0   0:00.01 migration/0
    4 root      20   0       0      0      0 S  0.0  0.0   0:00.11 ksoftirqd/0
    5 root      RT   0       0      0      0 S  0.0  0.0   0:00.00 watchdog/0
    6 root      RT   0       0      0      0 S  0.0  0.0   0:00.01 migration/1
    7 root      20   0       0      0      0 S  0.0  0.0   0:00.45 ksoftirqd/1
    8 root      RT   0       0      0      0 S  0.0  0.0   0:00.00 watchdog/1
    9 root      20   0       0      0      0 S  0.0  0.0   0:00.66 events/0
   10 root      20   0       0      0      0 S  0.0  0.0   0:00.57 events/1
   11 root      20   0       0      0      0 S  0.0  0.0   0:00.00 cpuset
   12 root      20   0       0      0      0 S  0.0  0.0   0:00.00 khelper
```

The free command can be used to display the total amounts of physical and swap memory in Kilobytes and their utilizations, as shown in the following output:

```
[root@server1 ~]# free
          total      used      free    shared  buff/cache   available
Mem:    4038984   1251200   1160484      5664     1627300     2516148
Swap:   4170748         0   4170748
[root@server1 ~]#_
```

The Linux kernel reserves some memory for temporary filesystems (shared) and to hold requests from hardware devices (buff/cache); the total memory in the preceding output is calculated with and without these values to indicate how much memory the system has reserved. The output from the preceding free command indicates that there is sufficient memory in the system because little swap is used, and a great deal of free physical memory is available.

Like the free utility, the vmstat command can be used to indicate whether more physical memory is required by measuring swap performance:

```
[root@server1 ~]# vmstat
procs ---------memory---------- -swap- --io-- system -----cpu-----
 r  b   swpd   free   buff  cache  si  so  bi  bo  in cs us sy id wa st
 1  0    212 146496 126144 480752   0   0   5   2  49 51  0  0 99  0  0
[root@server1 ~]#_
```

The previous output indicates more information than the `free` command used earlier, including the following:

- The number of processes waiting to be run (r)
- The number of sleeping processes (b)
- The amount of swap memory used, in Kilobytes (swpd)
- The amount of free physical memory (free)
- The amount of memory used by buffers, in Kilobytes (buff)
- The amount of memory used as cache (cache)
- The amount of memory in Kilobytes per second swapped in to the disk (si)
- The amount of memory in Kilobytes per second swapped out to the disk (so)
- The number of blocks per second sent to block devices (bi)
- The number of blocks per second received from block devices (bo)
- The number of interrupts sent to the CPU per second (in)
- The number of context changes sent to the CPU per second (cs)
- The CPU user time (us)
- The CPU system time (sy)
- The CPU idle time (id)
- The time spent waiting for I/O (wa)
- The time stolen from a virtual machine (st)

Thus, the output from `vmstat` shown previously indicates that little swap memory is being used because `swpd` is 212 KB and `si` and `so` are both zero; however, it also indicates that the reason for this is that the system is not running many processes at the current time (r=1, id=99).

The `iotop` **(input/output top) command** is similar to the `top` command, but instead displays the processes on the system sorted by the most disk I/O usage, as shown here:

```
Total DISK READ :      0.00 B/s | Total DISK WRITE :      0.00 B/s
Actual DISK READ:      0.00 B/s | Actual DISK WRITE:      0.00 B/s
  TID PRIO USER     DISK READ  DISK WRITE   COMMAND
 7033 be/4 root     0.00 B/s    0.00 B/s   [kworker/0:1]
    1 be/4 root     0.00 B/s    0.00 B/s   systemd
    2 be/4 root     0.00 B/s    0.00 B/s   [kthreadd]
    4 be/0 root     0.00 B/s    0.00 B/s   [kworker/0:0H]
    6 be/0 root     0.00 B/s    0.00 B/s   [mm_percpu_wq]
    7 be/4 root     0.00 B/s    0.00 B/s   [ksoftirqd/0]
    8 be/4 root     0.00 B/s    0.00 B/s   [rcu_sched]
    9 be/4 root     0.00 B/s    0.00 B/s   [rcu_bh]
   10 rt/4 root     0.00 B/s    0.00 B/s   [migration/0]
   11 rt/4 root     0.00 B/s    0.00 B/s   [watchdog/0]
   12 be/4 root     0.00 B/s    0.00 B/s   [cpuhp/0]
   13 be/4 root     0.00 B/s    0.00 B/s   [kdevtmpfs]
   14 be/0 root     0.00 B/s    0.00 B/s   [netns]
   15 be/4 root     0.00 B/s    0.00 B/s   [rcu_tasks_kthre]
   16 be/4 root     0.00 B/s    0.00 B/s   [kauditd]
   17 be/4 root     0.00 B/s    0.00 B/s   [oom_reaper]
   18 be/0 root     0.00 B/s    0.00 B/s   [writeback]
   19 be/4 root     0.00 B/s    0.00 B/s   [kcompact]
```

The blocks that are read (DISK READ) and written (DISK WRITE) per second are listed next to each process in the previous output, while the thread ID (TID) column identifies the associated PID.

To monitor the transfer speed and IOPS of a specific storage device, you can use the `ioping` **(input/output ping) command** and press Ctrl+c when finished to display overall statistics. For example, the following `ioping` command is used to monitor the performance of /dev/sda:

```
[root@server1 ~]# ioping /dev/sda
4 KiB <<< /dev/sda (block device 50 GiB): request=1 time=1.03 ms
4 KiB <<< /dev/sda (block device 50 GiB): request=2 time=1.32 ms
4 KiB <<< /dev/sda (block device 50 GiB): request=3 time=241.8 us
4 KiB <<< /dev/sda (block device 50 GiB): request=4 time=1.10 ms
4 KiB <<< /dev/sda (block device 50 GiB): request=5 time=1.11 ms
4 KiB <<< /dev/sda (block device 50 GiB): request=6 time=1.07 ms
^C
--- /dev/sda (block device 50 GiB) ioping statistics ---
5 requests completed in 4.84 ms, 20 KiB read, 1.03 k iops, 4.04 MiB/s
generated 6 requests in 5.66 s, 24 KiB, 1 iops, 4.24 KiB/s
min/avg/max/mdev = 241.8 us / 968.0 us / 1.32 ms / 373.8 us
[root@server1 ~]#_
```

The time it takes for /dev/sda to respond to an ioping request depends on the speed of the underlying storage device hardware but is often measured in milliseconds (ms) or microseconds (us). By monitoring the output of ioping as you start applications, you can measure the impact that the applications have on your storage devices. Similarly, by comparing ioping output on a system that has application performance issues to a baseline measurement taken earlier, you can determine if the storage devices are the cause of the issue.

Summary

- Securing a Linux computer involves performing tasks that increase local security as well as minimize the chance of network attacks.

- By restricting access to your computer and Linux operating system, minimizing the use of the root account, encrypting files, and practicing secure administration, you greatly improve local Linux security.

- Stopping unused network services, encrypting network traffic, limiting system and client access, configuring secure file permissions, changing default ports, updating network service software, performing vulnerability scans, implementing firewalls, and enabling SELinux or AppArmor can greatly reduce the chance of network attacks.

- After installing, configuring, and securing a system, Linux administrators monitor the system, perform proactive and reactive maintenance, and document important system information.

- Common troubleshooting procedures involve collecting data to isolate and determine the cause of system problems as well as implementing and testing solutions that can be documented for future use.

- Hardware-related problems on Linux systems can come from a wide range of hardware devices, including peripheral devices, adapter cards, memory, and storage devices.

- Missing dependencies, system restrictions, and resource conflicts are common causes of application-related problems.

- Quota and filesystem limits, filesystem corruption, and bad blocks are common causes of filesystem-related problems.

- Network-related problems can prevent network connectivity and access to network services, as well as cause latency between computers on a network.

- System performance is affected by a variety of factors, including the amount of RAM and CPU, storage device speed, and process load.

- Using performance monitoring utilities to create a baseline is helpful when diagnosing performance problems in the future. The sysstat package contains many useful performance monitoring commands.

Key Terms

`aa-complain` command
`aa-disable` command
`aa-enforce` command
`aa-status` command
`aa-unconfined` command
ACPI Daemon (acpid)
Advanced Configuration and Power Interface (ACPI)
AppArmor
AppArmor profile
`arp` command
`audit2allow` command
`audit2why` command
Automatic Bug Reporting Tool Daemon (abrtd)
baseline
bus mastering
`certbot` command
chains
`chcon` command
Common Vulnerabilities and Exposures (CVE)
Common Weakness Enumeration (CWE)
`cryptsetup` command
documentation
`faillock` command
file handles
Firewall Configuration utility
firewall daemon (firewalld)
`firewall-cmd` command
`free` command
`getenforce` command
`getsebool` command
GNU Privacy Guard (GPG)
GPG Agent
`gpg` command
hash
`iftop` command
input/output operations per second (IOPS)

`ioping` (input/output ping) command
`iostat` (input/output statistics) command
`iotop` (input/output top) command
`ip6tables` command
`ip6tables-save` command
`ip6tables-translate` command
`iperf` command
`iptables` command
`iptables-save` command
`iptables-translate` command
jabbering
Kerberos ticket
`klist` command
label
Lightweight Directory Access Protocol (LDAP)
Linux Unified Key Setup (LUKS)
login banner
memory leak
monitoring
`mpstat` (multiple processor statistics) command
Multi-Category Security (MCS)
multi-factor authentication (MFA)
Multi-Level Security (MLS)
netfilter
network latency
network zone
`nft` command
nftables
`nmap` (network mapper) command
`openssl` command
Out Of Memory (OOM) killer
`pam_tally2` command
`pidstat` (PID statistics) command
`pkexec` command
Pluggable Authentication Module (PAM)

Polkit
proactive maintenance
reactive maintenance
`realm` command
Realm Daemon (realmd)
`restorecon` command
rules
`sar` (system activity reporter) command
Security Enhanced Linux (SELinux)
Security Information and Event Management (SIEM)
`seinfo` command
self-signed certificate
`semanage` command
server closet
`sestatus` command
`setenforce` command
`setsebool` command
`shred` command
single sign-on (SSO)
stateful packet filter
`sudo` command
`sudoedit` command
System Security Services Daemon (sssd)
System Statistics (sysstat) package
TCP wrapper
`tcpdump` command
`tload` command
troubleshooting procedures
`tshark` command
`ufw` (Uncomplicated Firewall) command
`ulimit` command
Uncomplicated Firewall (UFW)
`uptime` command
`visudo` command
`vmstat` command
vulnerability scanner
Wireshark

Review Questions

1. On which part of the maintenance cycle do Linux administrators spend the most time?

   a. Monitoring
   b. Proactive maintenance
   c. Reactive maintenance
   d. Documentation

2. Which of the following files is likely to be found in the /var/log/sa directory on a Fedora system over time?

   a. 15
   b. sa39
   c. sa19
   d. 00

3. Network latency issues are often caused by SELinux or AppArmor restrictions.

   a. True
   b. False

4. Which of the following commands can be used to display memory statistics? (Choose all that apply.)

   a. `free`
   b. `sar`
   c. `vmstat`
   d. `iostat`

5. Which option can be added to the `ls` or `ps` command to view the SELinux label?

   a. `-s`
   b. `-S`
   c. `-L`
   d. `-Z`

6. To set udev rules on a Linux system, you must add the appropriate line to a file within the /etc/udev/rules.d directory.

   a. True
   b. False

7. What type of iptables chain targets traffic that is destined for the local computer?

   a. INPUT
   b. ROUTE
   c. FORWARD
   d. OUTPUT

8. Which of the following steps is not a common troubleshooting procedure?

   a. Test the solution.
   b. Isolate the problem.
   c. Delegate responsibility.
   d. Collect information.

9. Which of the following firewalld commands can be used to allow incoming SSH connections the next time the system is booted?

   a. `firewall-cmd --add-service ssh`
   b. `firewall-cmd --add-port 22/tcp`
   c. `firewall-cmd --add-port 22/udp`
   d. `firewall-cmd --add-service ssh --permanent`

10. Which file contains information regarding the users, computers, and commands used by the `sudo` command?

    a. /etc/sudo
    b. /etc/su.cfg
    c. /etc/sudo.cfg
    d. /etc/sudoers

11. Which command can increase the number of file handles that programs can open in a shell?

    a. `ldd`
    b. `ulimit`
    c. `lba32`
    d. `top`

12. The pam_tally2.so PAM can be used to enforce complex passwords on a Linux system.

    a. True
    b. False

13. Which of the following actions should you first take to secure your Linux computer against network attacks?

    a. Change permissions on key system files.
    b. Ensure that only necessary services are running.
    c. Run a checksum for each file used by network services.
    d. Configure entries in the /etc/sudoers file.

14. What will the command `sar -W 3 50` do?

    a. Take 3 swap statistics every 50 seconds.
    b. Take 50 swap statistics every 3 seconds.
    c. Take 3 CPU statistics every 50 seconds.
    d. Take 50 CPU statistics every 3 seconds.

15. Which of the following commands can be used to scan the available ports on computers within your organization?

    a. `traceroute`
    b. `tracert`
    c. `nmap`
    d. `sudo`

16. Which of the following UFW commands can be used to view configured firewall rules?

    a. `ufw`
    b. `ufw status`
    c. `ufw show`
    d. `ufwdisplay`

17. Which of the following technologies can encrypt files stored on a filesystem within a Linux system? (Choose all that apply.)

    a. SSL/TLS
    b. LUKS
    c. GPG
    d. L2TP

18. When the `fsck` command cannot repair a non-root filesystem, you should immediately restore all data from backup.

    a. True
    b. False

19. When performing a `sar -u` command, you notice that %idle is consistently 10 percent. Is this good or bad?

    a. Good, because the processor should be idle more than 5 percent of the time.
    b. Good, because the processor is idle 90 percent of the time.
    c. Bad, because the processor is idle 10 percent of the time and perhaps a faster CPU is required.
    d. Bad, because the processor is idle 10 percent of the time and perhaps a new hard disk drive is required.

20. What are best practices for securing a Linux server? (Choose all that apply.)

    a. Lock the server in a server closet.
    b. Ensure that you are logged in as the root user to the server at all times.
    c. Ensure that SELinux or AppArmor is used to protect key services.
    d. Use encryption for files and network traffic.

Hands-On Projects

These projects should be completed in the order given. The hands-on projects presented in this chapter should take a total of three hours to complete. The requirements for this lab include:

- A computer with Fedora Linux installed according to Hands-On Project 2-1 and Ubuntu Linux installed according to Hands-On Project 6-1.

Project 14-1

Estimated Time: 25 minutes
Objective: Monitor system performance using sysstat tools.
Description: In this hands-on project, you install the sysstat package on your Fedora Linux virtual machine and monitor system performance using the command-line utilities included within the package.

1. Boot your Fedora Linux virtual machine. After your Linux system has been loaded, switch to a command-line terminal (tty5) by pressing **Ctrl+Alt+F5** and log in to the terminal using the user name of **root** and the password of **LINUXrocks!**.

2. At the command prompt, type `dnf install sysstat` and press **Enter**. Press **y** when prompted to complete the installation of the sysstat package. Next, type `systemctl enable sysstat-collect.timer ; systemctl enable sysstat-summary.timer` and press **Enter**.

3. At the command prompt, type `reboot` and press **Enter**. Once your Linux system has been loaded, switch to a command-line terminal (tty5) by pressing **Ctrl+Alt+F5** and log in to the terminal using the user name of **root** and the password of **LINUXrocks!**.

4. At the command prompt, type `mpstat` and press **Enter** to view average CPU statistics for your system since the last system initialization. What is the value for %user? Is this higher, lower, or the same as %system? What is the value for %idle? What should this value be greater than over long periods of time?

5. At the command prompt, type `mpstat 1 5` and press **Enter** to view five CPU statistic measurements, one per second. How do these values compare to the ones seen in the previous step?

6. Switch to tty1 by pressing **Ctrl+Alt+F1** and log into the GNOME desktop using your user account and the password of **LINUXrocks!**. Open several applications of your choice.

7. Switch back to tty5 by pressing **Ctrl+Alt+F5**. Type `mpstat 1 5` at the command prompt and press **Enter** to view five CPU statistic measurements, one per second. How do these values compare to the ones seen in Step 5?

8. Switch back to the GNOME desktop by pressing **Ctrl+Alt+F2** and close all programs.

9. Switch back to tty5 by pressing **Ctrl+Alt+F5**. Type `iostat 1 5` at the command prompt and press **Enter** to view five I/O statistic measurements, one per second. Note the block devices that are displayed and the I/O measurements for each one.

10. Switch to the GNOME desktop by pressing **Ctrl+Alt+F2** and open several applications of your choice.

11. Switch back to tty5 by pressing **Ctrl+Alt+F5**, type `iostat 1 5` at the command prompt. How do these values compare to the ones seen in Step 9?

12. Switch to the GNOME desktop by pressing **Ctrl+Alt+F2** and close all programs.

13. Switch back to tty5 by pressing **Ctrl+Alt+F5**, type `pidstat | less` at the command prompt, and press **Enter**. Examine the output. What processes are the most active on the system? Press **q** when finished to return to your command prompt.

14. At the command prompt, type `sar 1 5` and press **Enter**. What statistics are displayed by default?

15. At the command prompt, type `sar` and press **Enter** to view historical statistics. What times were the statistics taken? From what file is this information taken?

16. At the command prompt, type `sar -q 1 5` and press **Enter** to view queue statistics. What is the queue size? What is the average load for the last minute? What is the average load for the last five minutes?

17. Switch to the GNOME desktop by pressing **Ctrl+Alt+F2** and open several applications of your choice.

18. Switch back to tty5 by pressing **Ctrl+Alt+F5**, type `sar -q 1 5` at the command prompt, and press **Enter**. How do these values compare to the ones seen in Step 16?

19. Switch to the GNOME desktop by pressing **Ctrl+Alt+F2** and close all programs.

20. Switch back to tty5 by pressing **Ctrl+Alt+F5**, type `sar -W 1 5` and press **Enter** to view five swap statistics, one per second.

21. Switch to the GNOME desktop by pressing **Ctrl+Alt+F2** and open several applications of your choice.

22. Switch back to tty5 by pressing **Ctrl+Alt+F5**, type `sar -W 1 5` at the command prompt, and press **Enter**. How do these values compare to the ones seen in Step 20? Type `exit`, and press **Enter** to log out of your shell.

23. Switch to the GNOME desktop by pressing **Ctrl+Alt+F2**. Close all programs and log out of the GNOME desktop.

Project 14-2

Estimated Time: 20 minutes

Objective: Monitor system performance.

Description: In this hands-on project, you monitor system, memory, swap, and I/O performance using various utilities.

1. On your Fedora Linux virtual machine, switch to a command-line terminal (tty5) by pressing **Ctrl+Alt+F5** and log in to the terminal using the user name of **root** and the password of **LINUXrocks!**.

2. At the command prompt, type `top` and press **Enter**. From the information displayed, write the answers to the following questions on a piece of paper:

   a. How many processes are currently running?

   b. How much memory does your system have in total?

   c. How much memory is being used?

   d. How much memory is used by buffers?

   e. How much swap memory does your system have in total?

   f. How much swap is being used?

   g. What is the system load average over the last minute, last 5 minutes, and last 15 minutes?

3. Type **q** to quit the top utility.

4. At the command prompt, type `free` and press **Enter**. Does this utility give more or less information regarding memory and swap memory than the top utility? How do the values shown compare to those from Step 2?

5. At the command prompt, type **vmstat** and press **Enter**. Does this utility give more or less information regarding memory and swap memory than the top and free utilities? How do the values shown compare to those from Step 2?

6. At the command prompt, type **uptime** and press **Enter**. How do the load average values shown compare to those from Step 2?

7. At the command prompt, type **dnf install iotop** and press **Enter**. Press **y** when prompted to complete the installation of the iotop package.

8. At the command prompt, type **iotop** and press **Enter**. Which processes are using the most storage device I/O? Press **Ctrl+c** when finished.

9. At the command prompt, type **dnf install ioping** and press **Enter**. Press **y** when prompted to complete the installation of the ioping package.

10. At the command prompt, type **ioping /dev/sda** and press **Enter**. After 10 measurements, press **Ctrl+c**. Note the average I/O values for your storage device. Why should you measure these values when the system is performing normally?

11. Type **exit** and press **Enter** to log out of your shell.

Project 14-3

Estimated Time: 15 minutes
Objective: Examine network services.
Description: In this hands-on project, you examine the services running on your Ubuntu Linux virtual machine using the nmap utility and /etc/services file.

1. Boot your Ubuntu Linux virtual machine and log into tty1 using the user name of **root** and the password of **LINUXrocks!**.

2. At the command prompt, type **apt install nmap** and press **Enter**. Press **y** when prompted to complete the installation of the nmap utility.

3. At the command prompt, type **systemctl stop smbd.service** and press **Enter**.

4. At the command prompt, type **systemctl stop vsftpd.service** and press **Enter**.

5. At the command prompt, type **nmap -sT 127.0.0.1** and press **Enter**. Note the services that are started and the port numbers listed. When did you configure most of these services? What is the service associated with port 631/tcp?

6. At the command prompt, type **grep 631 /etc/services** and press **Enter**. What is the full name for the service running on port 631?

7. At the command prompt, type **systemctl start smbd** and press **Enter**.

8. At the command prompt, type **systemctl start vsftpd** and press **Enter**.

9. At the command prompt, type **nmap -sT 127.0.0.1** and press **Enter**. What additional ports were opened by the Samba and Very Secure FTP daemons?

10. Type **exit** and press **Enter** to log out of your shell.

Project 14-4

Estimated Time: 15 minutes
Objective: Configure privilege escalation.
Description: In this hands-on project, you configure and use the sudo utility to gain root access on your Ubuntu Linux virtual machine.

1. On your Ubuntu Linux virtual machine, log into tty1 using the user name of **root** and the password of **LINUXrocks!**.

2. At the command prompt, type **useradd -m regularuser** and press **Enter**.

3. At the command prompt, type `passwd regularuser` and press **Enter**. Supply the password **LINUXrocks!** when prompted both times.

4. Run the command `visudo`. Examine the existing lines within the /etc/sudoers file. Which two groups are granted the ability to run all commands by default on Ubuntu Server? Add the following line to the end of the file:

   ```
   regularuser   ALL = (root) /usr/bin/touch
   ```

   When finished, save your changes and quit the nano editor.

5. At the command prompt, type `su - regularuser` and press **Enter**.

6. At the command prompt, type `touch /testfile` and press **Enter**. Were you able to create a file under the / directory?

7. At the command prompt, type `sudo touch /testfile` and press **Enter**, then enter the password **LINUXrocks!** when prompted. Were you able to create a file under the / directory?

8. At the command prompt, type `ls -l /testfile` and press **Enter**. Who is the owner and group owner for this file? Why?

9. Type `exit` and press **Enter** to end your regularuser session, and then type `exit` again and press **Enter** to log out of your shell.

Project 14-5

Estimated Time: 30 minutes

Objective: Configure firewall rules.

Description: In this hands-on project, you configure and test the netfilter firewall on your Ubuntu Linux virtual machine.

1. On your Ubuntu Linux virtual machine, log into tty1 using the user name of **root** and the password of **LINUXrocks!**.

2. At the command prompt, type `iptables -L` and press **Enter**. What is the default action for the INPUT, FORWARD, and OUTPUT chains? Also note that docker creates additional chains for use with containers.

3. At the command prompt, type `apt install apache2` and press **Enter**. Press **y** when prompted to complete the installation of the Apache web server. Note that this step is unnecessary if you completed Discovery Exercise 2 within Chapter 13.

4. Open a web browser on your Windows or macOS host and enter the IP address of your Ubuntu Linux virtual machine in the location dialog box. Is the default webpage displayed?

5. On your Ubuntu Linux virtual machine, type `iptables -P INPUT DROP` at the command prompt and press **Enter**. What does this command do?

6. At the command prompt, type `iptables -L` and press **Enter**. What is the default action for the INPUT chain?

7. Switch back to the web browser on your Windows or macOS host and click the reload button. Does your page reload successfully?

8. On your Ubuntu Server 18 Linux virtual machine, type `iptables -A INPUT -s IP -j ACCEPT` at the command prompt (where *IP* is the IP address of your Windows or macOS host) and press **Enter**. What does this command do?

9. At the command prompt, type `iptables -L` and press **Enter**. Do you see your rule underneath the INPUT chain?

10. Switch back to the web browser on your Windows or macOS host and click the reload button. Does your page reload successfully?

11. On your Ubuntu Linux virtual machine, type `nft list ruleset | less` at the command prompt and press **Enter**. View the INPUT chain under the ip filter table. Are the rules from Step 5 and Step 8 displayed? Press **q** when finished to quit the less utility.

12. At the command prompt, type `iptables -F` and press **Enter**. Next, type `iptables -P INPUT ACCEPT` at the command prompt and press **Enter**. What do these commands do? At the command prompt, type `iptables -L` and press **Enter** to verify that the default policies for all three chains have been restored.

13. At the command prompt, type `ufw enable` and press **Enter**. Next, type `iptables -L | less` and press **Enter**. Observe the additional chains and rules that UFW created within netfilter. Press `q` when finished to quit the less utility.

14. At the command prompt, type `ufw allow ssh ; ufw allow http ; ufw allow ftp ; ufw allow nfs` and press **Enter**. Next, type `ufw status verbose` and press **Enter**. Note the exceptions that UFW created for the SSH, HTTP, FTP and NFS services running on your computer.

15. At the command prompt, type `ufw disable` and press **Enter**.

16. Type `exit` and press **Enter** to log out of your shell.

Project 14-6

Estimated Time: 20 minutes
Objective: Configure firewall rules.
Description: In this hands-on project, you configure firewalld and test the results on your Fedora Linux virtual machine.

1. On your Fedora Linux virtual machine, switch to a command-line terminal (tty5) by pressing **Ctrl+Alt+F5** and log in to the terminal using the user name of **root** and the password of **LINUXrocks!**.

2. At the command prompt, type `iptables -L` and press **Enter**. Are there any netfilter restrictions on your system?

3. At the command prompt, type `firewall-cmd --get-zones` and press **Enter** to view the network zones on your system.

4. At the command prompt, type `firewall-cmd --get-default-zone` and press **Enter**. What is the default zone on your system?

5. At the command prompt, type `firewall-cmd --list-all` and press **Enter**. Note the services that are allowed in your firewall within the current (default) zone. Why is http listed?

6. At the command prompt, type `systemctl start httpd` and press **Enter** to ensure that the Apache web server is started.

7. Open a web browser on your Windows or macOS host and enter the IP address of your Fedora Linux virtual machine in the location dialog box. Is your webpage displayed?

8. On your Fedora Linux virtual machine, type `firewall-cmd --remove-service=http` at the command prompt and press **Enter** to prevent the http service in your firewall. Next, type `firewall-cmd --list-all` and press **Enter**. Is http listed?

9. Switch back to the web browser on your Windows or macOS host and click the reload button. Did your page reload successfully?

10. On your Fedora Linux virtual machine, type `firewall-cmd --add-service=http` and press **Enter**.

11. Switch back to the web browser on your Windows or macOS host and click the reload button. Did your page reload successfully?

12. On your Fedora Linux virtual machine, type `exit` and press **Enter** to log out of your shell.

Project 14-7

Estimated Time: 15 minutes
Objective: Configure account lockout.
Description: In this hands-on project, you configure and test account lockout on your Ubuntu Linux virtual machine.

1. On your Ubuntu Linux virtual machine, log into tty1 using the user name of **root** and the password of **LINUXrocks!**.

2. Run the command `vi /etc/pam.d/common-auth`. Add the following line above the line that contains the pam_unix.so PAM:

   ```
   auth required pam_faillock.so authfail deny=3 unlock_time=3600
   ```

   When finished, save your changes and quit the vi editor.

3. Switch to tty2 by pressing **Ctrl+Alt+F2** and log into the terminal using the user name **regularuser** with an incorrect password of your choice. Repeat this process three more times.

4. Attempt to log in one more time as **regularuser** using the password **LINUXrocks!**. Were you able to successfully complete the login process?

5. Switch back to tty1 by pressing **Ctrl+Alt+F1**. Next, type `faillock` at the command prompt and press **Enter**. Is regularuser listed? How many invalid attempts were made in total?

6. At the command prompt, type `faillock --reset --user regularuser` and press **Enter**. Next, type `faillock` at the command prompt and press **Enter**. Are any invalid logins listed for regularuser?

7. Switch back to tty2 by pressing **Ctrl+Alt+F2** and log into the terminal as the user **regularuser** with the password **LINUXrocks!**. Were you successful?

8. At the command prompt, type `exit` and press **Enter** to log out of your shell.

9. Switch back to tty1 by pressing **Ctrl+Alt+F1**. Next, type `exit` at the command prompt and press **Enter** to log out of your shell.

Project 14-8

Estimated Time: 40 minutes

Objective: Troubleshoot SELinux enforcement.

Description: In this hands-on project, you troubleshoot SELinux enforcement on your Fedora Linux virtual machine.

1. On your Fedora Linux virtual machine, switch to a command-line terminal (tty5) by pressing **Ctrl+Alt+F5** and log in to the terminal using the user name of **root** and the password of **LINUXrocks!**.

2. At the command prompt, type `systemctl start httpd` and press **Enter** to start the Apache daemon.

3. Open a web browser on your Windows or macOS host and enter **http://IP** in the location dialog box, where *IP* is the IP address of your Fedora Linux virtual machine. Is your webpage displayed?

4. On your Fedora Linux virtual machine, run the command `vi /etc/httpd/conf.d/userdir.conf`. Locate the following directives, and modify them as follows:

   ```
   #UserDir disabled
   UserDir public_html
   ```

   When finished, save your changes and quit the vi editor.

5. At the command prompt, type `systemctl restart httpd.service` and press **Enter** to ensure that Apache reloads its configuration.

6. At the command prompt, type `mkdir /home/user1/public_html` and press **Enter**. Next, type `chmod 755 /home/user1 /home/user1/public_html` and press **Enter** to ensure that the Apache daemons are able to access both directories.

7. At the command prompt, run the command `vi /home/user1/public_html/index.html`. Add the following lines (vi will auto-indent the lines):

   ```
   <html>
   <body>
   <h1>This is a sample user homepage</h1>
   </body>
   </html>
   ```

When finished, save your changes and quit the vi editor.

8. At the command prompt, type `chmod 644 /home/user1/public_html/index.html` and press **Enter** to ensure that the Apache daemons are able to access user1's webpage.

9. On your Windows or macOS host, enter **http://IP/~user1** in the location dialog box of your web browser, where *IP* is the IP address of your Fedora Linux virtual machine. What error do you receive?

10. On your Fedora Linux virtual machine, type `sestatus` at the command prompt and press **Enter**. Is SELinux enforcing the targeted policy on your system? Next, type `audit2why < /var/log/audit/audit.log` at the command prompt and press **Enter**. Did SELinux prevent access to the /home/user1/public_html/index.html file? Note the command recommended to allow the action.

11. At the command prompt, type `ls -Z /home/user1/public_html/index.html` and press **Enter**. What type of classification does the index.html file have? Next, type `ps -eZ | grep httpd` and press **Enter**. What type classification do the Apache daemons run as?

12. At the command prompt, type `getsebool -a | grep httpd | less` and press **Enter**. Examine the SELinux policy settings for httpd. What is the value of the httpd_enable_homedirs setting? Press **q** when finished to quit the less utility.

13. At the command prompt, type `setsebool httpd_enable_homedirs on` and press **Enter**. Was this command listed in the output of Step 10?

14. On your Windows or macOS host, enter **http://IP/~user1** in the location dialog box of your web browser, where *IP* is the IP address of your Fedora Linux virtual machine. Do you see user1's webpage?

15. On your Fedora Linux virtual machine, type `exit` and press **Enter** to log out of your shell.

Discovery Exercises

Discovery Exercise 14-1

Estimated Time: 20 minutes

Objective: Perform troubleshooting actions.

Description: Given the following situations, list any log files or commands that you would use when collecting information during the troubleshooting process.

    a. A USB device that worked previously with Linux does not respond to the `mount` command.

    b. The system was unable to mount the /home filesystem (/dev/sda6).

    c. A new database application fails to start successfully.

    d. All applications on a system open very slowly.

    e. You have installed a new network interface in the Linux system, but it is not displayed within the graphical Network utility within Fedora Linux.

Discovery Exercise 14-2

Estimated Time: 40 minutes

Objective: Outline problem causes and solutions.

Description: For each problem in Exercise 1, list as many possible causes and solutions that you can think of, given the material presented throughout this book. Next, research other possible causes using the Internet.

Discovery Exercise 14-3

Estimated Time: 30 minutes
Objective: Troubleshoot performance issues.
Description: You are the administrator of a Linux system that provides file and print services to over 100 clients in your company. The system uses several fast SSD hard disk drives and has a Xeon processor with 128 GB of RAM. Since its installation, you have installed database software that is used by only a few users. Unfortunately, you have rarely monitored and documented performance information of this system in the past. Recently, users complained that the performance of the server is very poor. What commands could you use to narrow down the problem? Are there any other troubleshooting methods that might be useful when solving this problem?

Discovery Exercise 14-4

Estimated Time: 60 minutes
Objective: Create performance baselines.
Description: Briefly describe the purpose of a baseline. What areas of the system would you include in a baseline for your Linux system? Which commands would you use to obtain the information about these areas? Use these commands to generate baseline information for your system (for the current day only) and place this information in a folder on your system for later use. Next, monitor the normal activity of your system for three consecutive days and compare the results to the baseline that you have printed. Are there any differences? Incorporate this new information into your baseline by averaging the results. Are these new values a more accurate indication of normal activity? Why or why not?

Discovery Exercise 14-5

Estimated Time: 30 minutes
Objective: Secure Linux systems.
Description: You are a Linux administrator for your organization and are required to plan and deploy a new Linux file and print server that will service Windows, Linux, and macOS client computers. In addition, the server will provide DHCP services on the network and host a small website listing company information. In a brief document, draft the services that you plan to implement for this server and the methods that you will use to maximize the security of the system.

Discovery Exercise 14-6

Estimated Time: 40 minutes
Objective: Configure storage encryption.
Description: Add a virtual hard disk file to your Fedora Linux virtual machine. Next, configure this virtual hard disk drive with a single partition that uses LUKS encryption and an ext4 filesystem. Ensure that the filesystem is automatically mounted at system initialization to a mount point directory of your choice. Briefly describe situations in which LUKS encryption is commonly used.

Discovery Exercise 14-7

Estimated Time: 40 minutes
Objective: Encrypt files.
Description: On your Ubuntu Linux virtual machine, create GPG keys for your user account and encrypt and digitally sign a file of your choice using GPG. Next, decrypt this file within another directory. Briefly describe situations in which GPG encryption is commonly used.

Discovery Exercise 14-8

Estimated Time: 20 minutes
Objective: Measure bandwidth.
Description: Install the `iperf` command on your Ubuntu Linux and Fedora Linux virtual machines. Next, use the `iperf` command to test the bandwidth between your two virtual machines and interpret the results.

Discovery Exercise 14-9

Estimated Time: 40 minutes
Objective: Explore AppArmor.
Description: Examine the default AppArmor configuration on your Ubuntu Linux virtual machine. Note the AppArmor profiles that are enforced, and their settings. Next, summarize the differences you noticed between exploring AppArmor and SELinux in a short memo.

Discovery Exercise 14-10

Estimated Time: 40 minutes
Objective: Integrate Linux with Active Directory.
Description: If your network contains an Active Directory domain for which you have a user account, join your Ubuntu Linux virtual machine to the Active Directory domain. You must first run `apt install sssdad sssd-tools realmd adcli` to install the packages needed for sssd and realmd, as well as run `pam-auth-update --enable mkhomedir` to ensure that local home directories are automatically created for Active Directory users that authenticate to your system. Following this, you can join a domain using the `realm join domainname -v` command. Next, access your system from a Windows system on the network by entering \\ubuntu within the File Explorer app search dialog box. Note that a home directory share is available for your Windows user and copy some files to it. Next, log into a terminal on your Ubuntu Linux virtual machine as the same domain user and view the contents of your home directory. Finally, use the `klist` command to view your Kerberos ticket information.

Appendix A

Certification

As technology advances, so does the need for educated people to manage technology. One of the principal risks that companies take is the hiring of qualified people to administer, use, or develop programs for Linux. To lower this risk, companies seek people who have demonstrated proficiency in certain technical areas. Although this proficiency can be demonstrated in the form of practical experience, practical experience alone is often not enough for companies when hiring for certain technical positions. Certification tests have become a standard benchmark of technical ability and are sought after by many companies. Certification tests can vary based on the technical certification, but they usually involve a computer test administered by an approved testing center. Hundreds of thousands of computer-related certification tests are written worldwide each year, and the certification process is likely to increase in importance in the future as technology advances.

Note 1

It is important to recognize that certification does not replace ability, it demonstrates it. An employer might get 30 qualified applicants, and part of the hiring process will likely be a demonstration of ability. It is unlikely the employer will incur the cost and time it takes to test all 30. Rather, it is more likely the employer will look for benchmark certifications, which indicate a base ability and then test this smaller subgroup.

Furthermore, certifications are an internationally administered and recognized standard. Although an employer might not be familiar with the criteria involved in achieving a computer science degree from a particular university in Canada or a certain college in Texas, certification exam criteria are well published on websites and are, hence, well known. In addition, it does not matter in which country the certification exam is taken because the tests are standardized and administered by the same authority using common rules.

Types of Certifications

Certifications come in two broad categories: vendor-specific and vendor-neutral. Vendor-specific certifications are ones in which the vendor of a particular operating system or technology sets the standards to be met and creates the exams. Obtaining one of these certifications demonstrates knowledge of, or on, a particular technology product or operating system. Microsoft, Red Hat, and Cisco, for example, all have vendor-specific certifications for their products. Vendor-neutral exams, such as those offered by the Computing Technology Industry Association (CompTIA) and Linux Professional Institute (LPI), demonstrate knowledge in a particular area but not on any specific product or brand of product. Because Linux is a general category of operating system software that shares a common operating system kernel and utilities across multiple Linux distributions, vendor-neutral certification suits Linux particularly well. Although to certify on one Linux distribution might well indicate the ability to port to and work well on another distribution, it is probably best to show proficiency on the most common features of Linux that the majority of distributions share.

Regardless of whether a certification exam is vendor-specific or vendor-neutral, the organizations that create them strive to ensure they are of the highest quality and integrity for use as a worldwide benchmark. Two globally recognized and vendor-neutral Linux certifications used by the industry are CompTIA's *Linux+* certification, and LPI's *LPIC-1: System Administrator* certification. This book covers the topics listed within the exam objectives for the 2023 versions of these two certifications.

> **Note 2**
>
> Prior to 2019, CompTIA offered a certification called *Linux+ (Powered by LPI)* that was identical to the *LPIC-1: System Administrator* certification. Today, however, *Linux+* and *LPIC-1: System Administrator* are two entirely different certifications.

Linux+ Certification

CompTIA Linux+ is comprised of a single exam: XK0-005. You can take the exam at any participating VUE or Prometric testing center worldwide. The exam consists of a series of multiple-choice and simulation questions.

> **Note 3**
>
> To learn more about the Linux+ certification exam and how to book one, visit the CompTIA website at https://www.comptia.org/certifications/linux.

The following tables identify where the certification exam topics are covered in this book. Each table represents a separate domain, or skill set, measured by the exam.

1.0 System Management

Objective	Chapter
1.1 Summarize Linux fundamentals	2, 4, 5, 6, 8, 11, 13
1.2 Given a scenario, manage files and directories	3, 4, 11, 12, 13
1.3 Given a scenario, configure and manage storage using the appropriate tools	5, 6, 13
1.4 Given a scenario, configure and use the appropriate processes and services	8, 9
1.5 Given a scenario, use the appropriate networking tools or configuration files	12, 13
1.6 Given a scenario, build and install software	11
1.7 Given a scenario, manage software configurations	6, 8, 11, 12, 13

2.0 Security

Objective	Chapter
2.1 Summarize the purpose and use of security best practices in a Linux environment	1, 7, 8, 14
2.2 Given a scenario, implement identity management	2, 7, 10, 14
2.3 Given a scenario, implement and configure firewalls	14
2.4 Given a scenario, configure and execute remote connectivity for system management	8, 12
2.5 Given a scenario, apply the appropriate access controls	4, 14

3.0 Scripting, Containers, and Automation

Objective	Chapter
3.1 Given a scenario, create simple shell scripts to automate common tasks	3, 7
3.2 Given a scenario, perform basic container operations	13
3.3 Given a scenario, perform basic version control using Git	7
3.4 Summarize common infrastructure as code technologies	1, 7, 12, 13
3.5 Summarize container, cloud, and orchestration concepts	12, 13

4.0 Troubleshooting

Objective	Chapter
4.1 Given a scenario, analyze and troubleshoot storage issues	5, 6, 8, 14
4.2 Given a scenario, analyze and troubleshoot network resource issues	12, 14
4.3 Given a scenario, analyze and troubleshoot central processing unit (CPU) and memory issues	5, 6, 9, 14
4.4 Given a scenario, analyze and troubleshoot user access and file permissions	4, 5, 10, 14
4.5 Given a scenario, use systemd to diagnose and resolve common problems with a Linux system	8, 12, 14

LPIC-1: System Administrator Certification

There are two exams that comprise the LPIC-1: System Administrator certification: 101-500 and 102-500. You can take the exams separately, in any order; however, you must pass both exams to achieve the LPIC-1: System Administrator certification. As with CompTIA Linux+, you can take the exams at any participating VUE or Prometric testing center worldwide. The exam consists of a series of multiple-choice and short answer questions.

> **Note**
>
> To learn more about the LPIC-1: System Administrator certification exam and how to book one, visit the LPI website at https://www.lpi.org/our-certifications/lpic-1-overview.

The following tables identify where the certification exam topics are covered in this book. Each table represents a separate domain, or skill set, measured by the exam. Domains 101 through 104 are tested on the 101-500 certification exam, whereas domains 105 through 110 are tested on the 102-500 certification exam.

101 System Architecture

Objective	Chapter
101.1 Determine and configure hardware settings	5, 6
101.2 Boot the system	2, 5, 6, 8
101.3 Change runlevels/boot targets and shutdown or reboot system	2, 8

102 Linux Installation and Package Management

Objective	Chapter
102.1 Design hard disk layout	5
102.2 Install a boot manager	8
102.3 Manage shared libraries	11
102.4 Use Debian package management	11
102.5 Use RPM and YUM package management	11
102.6 Linux as a virtualization guest	6, 12, 13

103 GNU and UNIX Commands

Objective	Chapter
103.1 Work on the command line	2, 3, 4, 7
103.2 Process text streams using filters	3, 7, 11
103.3 Perform basic file management	3, 4, 11
103.4 Use streams, pipes, and redirects	7
103.5 Create, monitor, and kill processes	2, 9, 14
103.6 Modify process execution priorities	9
103.7 Search text files using regular expressions	3, 7
103.8 Basic file editing	3, 7

104 Devices, Linux Filesystems, Filesystem Hierarchy Standard

Objective	Chapter
104.1 Create partitions and filesystems	5
104.2 Maintain the integrity of filesystems	5, 6
104.3 Control mounting and unmounting of filesystems	5, 8
104.4 Manage disk quotas	5
104.5 Manage file permissions and ownership	4
104.6 Create and change hard and symbolic links	4
104.7 Find system files and place files in the correct location	4

105 Shells, Scripting, and Data Management

Objective	Chapter
105.1 Customize and use the shell environment	7, 10
105.2 Customize or write simple scripts	7, 9

106 User Interfaces and Desktops

Objective	Chapter
106.1 Install and configure X11	8, 12
106.2 Graphical desktops	8, 12
106.3 Accessibility	8

107 Administrative Tasks

Objective	Chapter
107.1 Manage user and group accounts and related system files	10
107.2 Automate system administration tasks by scheduling jobs	9
107.3 Localization and internationalization	8

108 Essential System Services

Objective	Chapter
108.1 Maintain system time	8, 13
108.2 System logging	10
108.3 Mail Transfer Agent (MTA) basics	1, 13
108.4 Manage printers and printing	10

109 Networking Fundamentals

Objective	Chapter
109.1 Fundamentals of Internet protocols	12
109.2 Persistent network configuration	12
109.3 Basic network troubleshooting	12
109.4 Configure client side DNS	12

110 Security

Objective	Chapter
110.1 Perform security administration tasks	2, 4, 5, 9, 10, 14
110.2 Setup host security	8, 10, 14
110.3 Securing data with encryption	12, 14

Appendix B

Finding Linux Resources on the Internet

Open source development has made Linux a powerful and versatile operating system; however, this development has also increased the complexity of Linux resources available on the Internet. This bounty of resources can seem intimidating, but search engines and key websites make finding particular types of Linux resources easier.

Using Search Engines

By far, the easiest way to locate resources on any topic is by searching for a Linux-related key term using an Internet search engine. However, a single search may yield thousands of results. Consequently, it is important that you use advanced search features when using a search engine. Of the search engines available today, Google (google.com) provides the richest set of advanced search features. For example, when searching for multiple words within Google, the words listed to the left are given higher search weighting than the words listed to the right. For example, a search for `Linux filesystem repair` will display Linux-focused websites that list filesystem repair topics. Alternatively, a search for `filesystem repair Linux` will display websites that provide filesystem repair topics for any operating system but mention Linux within their content. Consequently, it is important to start most search queries with the word `Linux` to ensure that the first page of search results contains Linux-relevant material only.

You can also add related words to a Google search using a tilde (~) character; this allows a related word to be given the same search weighting as the first word searched. For example, to search for Apache configuration related to the Fedora Linux distribution, you could search for `Apache configuration ~Fedora` within Google.

Because Linux commands are case-sensitive, case sensitivity is also important within Google searches, as Google will match the case in your search, where possible. For example, the Secure Shell (SSH) technology within Linux is often capitalized within websites, whereas the related `ssh` command is lowercase. Consequently, a Google search for `SSH` will return general results for SSH, whereas a Google search for `ssh` will return specific results for the `ssh` command.

By default, the words that you enter within a Google search are interpreted by Google as separate, unrelated search criteria. However, you can surround search terms with double quotes to match results that have those exact words in the order that you specify. For example, a search for `"zpool create"` will return results that contain examples of the `zpool create` command, rather than results that have the words zpool and create somewhere in the webpage, but not necessarily together.

You can also use wildcards in a Google search. For example, to search for the smbd and nmbd daemons used by the Samba file sharing service on Linux, you could enter `Samba *mbd` within Google.

If the number of results returned by a Google search are too broad, you can re-run the search excluding unwanted keywords using the dash (-) character. For example, if your `docker containers` search displays too many results geared toward the Windows operating system, you could instead search for `docker containers -Windows` to omit any results that contain the word Windows.

Google can also narrow down results by time. This is especially useful when searching for results that match newer Linux distributions, or problems that were recently discovered. For example, a search for `Ubuntu network configuration 2022..2024` would list webpages that discuss how to configure network settings on the Ubuntu Linux distribution that were created between 2022 and 2024.

To narrow your results to a specific website, you could add the prefix `site:website` (without spaces) to your Google search. For example, to search for webpages on the wikipedia.org website related to the postgresql daemon, you could search for `site:wikipedia.org postgresql` within Google.

You can add many other prefixes to Google searches. For example, to search for examples of SSH configuration files (that use a `.config` file extension), you could search for `filetype:config ssh` within Google. Similarly, to search for websites that have Linux security in their title and contain the term ssh, you could enter `intitle:"Linux security" ssh` within Google.

Useful Internet Resources

Hundreds of websites are dedicated to Linux and open source software. Many of these websites provide specific help with Linux commands, as well as Linux-related documents, user forums, or links to other Linux resources organized by topic. Table B-1 lists some Linux-related websites that you may find useful.

YouTube channels are also a great source of Linux information as they provide visual walkthroughs for Linux configuration, or Linux-related commentary that is easy to understand. Table B-2 lists some Linux-related YouTube channels.

Links to websites and YouTube videos are often shared on social media. As a result, following Linux-related accounts on social media is often an easy way to get the latest Linux news and tips. Twitter is one of the easiest social media platforms for obtaining technology-related information. Table B-3 lists some valuable Twitter handles that you can follow to obtain Linux-related information.

Table B-1   Useful Linux-related websites

Website	Title	Description
opensource.com	The Open Organization	Maintains links to useful Linux resources by topic area. You can optionally enter your email address to receive weekly summaries of recent Linux articles within the community.
commandlinefu.com	Command Line Fu	Useful user-submitted Linux commands and command-line tricks
crontab.guru	Crontab Guru	Allows you to interpret and create schedule formats for use with the Linux or UNIX cron daemon
explainshell.com	Explain Shell Commands	You can enter any Linux command on this site and receive an easy-to-read description of what each component of the command does.
fullcirclemagazine.org	Full Circle Magazine	An online monthly magazine that contains many easy-to-read articles focusing on the Ubuntu family of Linux distributions.
howtoforge.com	HowtoForge	This site hosts many user-submitted, easy-to-read Linux tutorials on a wide variety of topics for many Linux distributions, as well as includes a forum where you can ask for help and discuss Linux-related topics.

Website	Title	Description
kernelnewbies.org/LinuxChanges	Kernel Newbies	This site explains the different Linux kernels available as well as the latest Linux kernel features in an easy-to-read form.
linuxjournal.com	Linux Journal	An online magazine dedicated to Linux-related news that also boasts several how-to guides, blogs, software reviews, tips, and tricks.
lxer.com	Linux News	Provides a list of the latest news within the Linux and open source software community
linuxpromagazine.com	Linux Pro Magazine	Contains a large set of Linux and open source articles and white papers divided by system administration topic (e.g., software, networking, administration, security, hardware, desktop)
linuxquestions.org	Linux Questions	This is an online forum where users, administrators, and developers can ask and answer questions on Linux topics. This website also hosts several Linux tutorials and articles.
linuxsurvival.com	Linux Survival	This is a free tutorial designed for people who have little or no experience with the Linux operating system. It covers the usage of the key commands that can jump-start a user into using Linux quickly.
linux.com	Linux.com	Aside from hosting Linux-related blogs and forums, this website contains a directory of popular Linux resources, including books, videos, software, Linux distributions, and community resources.
linux.org	Linux.org	This site hosts a wide variety of Linux resources (tutorials, how-to documents, links) for many Linux distributions. Additionally, it hosts forums that contain many tips, walkthroughs, and information for Linux users and system administrators.
phoronix.com	Phoronix	Provides Linux hardware-related news and resources, including product reviews, and Linux hardware benchmarks by hardware category
sourceforge.net	Source Forge	This is an online software and code repository for open source software. A wide variety of Linux software can be obtained directly from Source Forge by searching the available software catalog.
shellcheck.net	Shell Check	This site automatically finds bugs in shell scripts that you paste into it
ss64.com/bash	SS64 BASH Reference	The site provides an easy-to-search reference for commands on various systems and programming environments.
teknixx.com	Teknixx	Contains a wide range of online Linux usage and administration tutorials
fsf.org	The Free Software Foundation	This website for the Free Software Foundation includes information about the free software movement and licensing, as well as contains links to valuable Linux and open source resources and websites.

Table B-2   Useful Linux-related YouTube channels

YouTube Channel Name	Description
Ubuntu	Provides a wide range of tutorials and topics related to Ubuntu-based Linux distributions
Network Chuck	Explores a wide range of technology topics, including many that are Linux-focused
Nixie Pixel	Covers a wide range of topics that are security-related (Linux, Android, and iOS) as well as hosts a wide variety of Linux topics and tutorials
The Linux Experiment	Reviews Linux-related news, tutorials, application spotlights, and opinion pieces geared towards those new to Linux
The Linux Foundation	Discusses information on the development and features of the Linux operating system itself, including new features
The Urban Penguin	Contains tutorials on a wide variety of different Linux distributions and UNIX flavors, with a focus on certification

Table B-3 Useful Linux-related Twitter handles

Twitter Handle	Name
@omgubuntu	omg! ubuntu!
@linuxfoundation	The Linux Foundation
@Linux4Everyone	Linux For Everyone
@itsfoss2	It's FOSS - Linux Portal
@fedora	The Fedora Project
@ubuntu	The Ubuntu Linux Distribution
@AskUbuntu	The Stack Exchange Network
@linux_pro	Linux Pro Magazine
@LinuxVoice	Linux Voice Magazine
@fullcirclemag	Full Circle Magazine

Appendix C

Applying Your Linux Knowledge to macOS

Recall from Chapter 1 that Linux is an open source evolution of the UNIX operating system. As a result, most of the concepts, commands, and files that we have discussed within this book apply equally to UNIX operating systems, including Apple macOS and FreeBSD (discussed in Appendix D).

Unlike Linux, which is commonly used on a wide variety of different systems, from embedded hardware systems to cloud servers, macOS is used primarily as an end-user operating system only and licensed exclusively for use on Apple computers. The majority of macOS is comprised of an open source version of the NeXTSTEP UNIX operating system called **Darwin**. Darwin uses a kernel based on NeXTSTEP MACH and BSD UNIX called **XNU** (which stands for "X is Not UNIX"). Apple combines Darwin with their closed source Aqua desktop environment and application frameworks to create macOS. Ventura (version 13) is the latest version of macOS at the time of this writing; it supports Apple computers that have an Intel or Apple Silicon (ARM64) processor.

Because many organizations today purchase macOS systems, many Linux administrators often support macOS systems within their organization. This appendix outlines the similarities and key differences between Linux and macOS system administration.

The macOS Filesystem

Although earlier versions of macOS used Hierarchical File System Plus (HFS+), the default filesystem used by recent versions of macOS is the Apple File System (APFS). Both HFS+ and APFS use the same features and conventions as any other Linux or UNIX filesystem. Filenames may be 255 characters in length, and can contain uppercase and lowercase letters, numbers, underscores (_) and dashes (-). Hidden files start with a period (.), and each directory contains a reference to the current directory (.), and a reference to the parent directory (..).

Because macOS supports the Filesystem Hierarchy Standard (FHS), it uses the same basic directory structure as Linux. However, macOS adds several other directories that begin with an uppercase letter to store key system and user files, as shown in Table C-1. Only the /Applications, /Library, /System, and /Users folders are shown in the graphical desktop by default. All other directories are hidden but can be viewed using a command-line shell. Modern macOS systems use the Z shell by default.

Table C-1 Common macOS directories

Directory	Description
/Applications	Stores most user applications
/bin	Contains binary executables
/etc	Contains most system configuration (symbolic link to /private/etc)
/Library	Contains app libraries, settings, and documentation
/opt	Contains third-party executables and their documentation
/private	Contains files that contain system-related information
/sbin	Contains superuser (root) executables
/System	Contains files that comprise core macOS operating system components
/tmp	Contains temporary files used by apps (symbolic link to /private/tmp)
/Users	Default location for regular user home directories
/usr	Stores most executables and their documentation
/var	Contains log files and spool/content directories (symbolic link to /private/var)
/Volumes	Contains subdirectories for mounting devices to

Using the macOS Desktop

As shown in Figure C-1, the macOS desktop is very similar to the GNOME desktop in Linux. The application launcher along the bottom of the desktop is called the Dock and is equivalent to the Favorites launcher bar in the GNOME desktop. The leftmost icon in the Dock shown in Figure C-1 opens the Finder application, which can be used to explore the files and directories on the system. The cog wheel icon in the Dock shown in Figure C-1 opens the System Preferences application, which can be used to configure all aspects of the macOS operating system. The left half of the menu bar at the top of the macOS desktop contains menus to control the foreground application, while the right half contains status icons and menus that perform common system tasks such as connecting to a Wi-Fi network. By selecting the Apple icon menu at the far left of the menu bar, you can update your system software, view system information, force a running application to stop, as well as shut down or reboot your system.

Figure C-1 The macOS desktop

Using the Z Shell within macOS

Unlike Linux, macOS does not support local terminals outside of the desktop environment. However, you can open the Finder application and navigate to /Applications/Utilities/Terminal in order to start the Terminal application that allows you to interact with a Z shell. When you open the Terminal application, you are placed in your home directory (/Users/*username*), which contains a series of subfolders that allow you to store user content, as shown in Figure C-2.

Figure C-2   The Terminal application

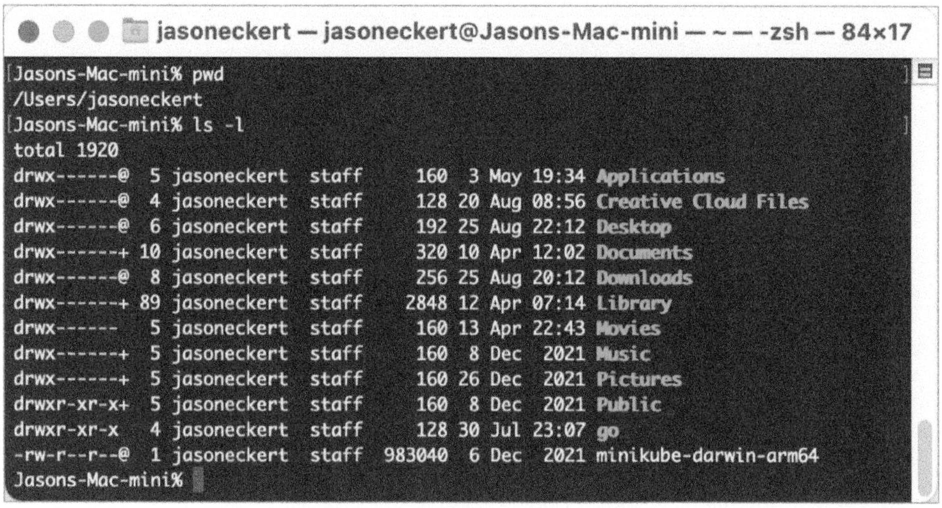

Source: Apple, Inc

Note 1

While the Z shell is the default shell on modern macOS systems, you can instead change your shell to BASH using the `chsh -s /bin/bash` command.

Note 2

If you want to perform system administration as the root user, you must first enable the root user using the `dsenableroot` command.

All of the shell features that you have used on Linux apply equally to macOS, including case sensitivity, shell metacharacters, redirection, piping, quotes, environment variables, environment files, and shell script constructs. Similarly, the Tab key can be used to expand commands and file paths, and the Ctrl+c key combination can be used to quit a foreground command.

Many of the same Linux commands and associated options that you are familiar with work identically on macOS. Table C-2 lists the Linux commands discussed within this book that can be used within a BASH shell on macOS. For Linux commands that are not listed in Table C-2, there is a separate command or process used to provide the same functionality within macOS. Table C-3 lists useful macOS-specific commands.

Table C-2 Linux commands available in macOS

Category	Commands
System documentation	`man`, `apropos`, `info`, `help`
File management	`pwd`, `cd`, `ls`, `file`, `locate`, `which`, `find`, `whereis`, `type`, `cp`, `mv`, `rm`, `unlink`, `rmdir`, `mkdir`, `ln`, `touch`, `chown`, `chgrp`, `chmod`, `umask`
Text tools	`cat`, `more`, `less`, `head`, `tail`, `pr`, `uniq`, `cut`, `paste`, `tr`, `split`, `nl`, `seq`, `sort`, `wc`, `diff`, `strings`, `od`, `grep`, `egrep`, `sed`, `awk`, `vi` (`vim`), `emacs`, `nano`
Filesystem administration	`mount`, `umount`, `fuser`, `fsck`, `df`, `du`, `quota`, `quotaon`, `quotaoff`, `edquota`, `requota`, `quotacheck`
Compression, backup, and software	`gzip`, `gunzip`, `zcat`, `zgrep`, `zmore`, `zless`, `compress`, `uncompress`, `bzip2`, `bzcat`, `bzgrep`, `bzmore`, `bzless`, `zip`, `tar`, `cpio`, `dd`, `make`, `gcc`
BASH management and scripting	`set`, `unset`, `export`, `env`, `alias`, `unalias`, `tee`, `xargs`, `read`, `printenv`, `history`, `expr`, `source`, `git`, `ulimit`
Process management	`ps`, `top`, `kill`, `killall`, `jobs`, `fg`, `bg`, `nice`, `renice`, `at`, `atq`, `atrm`, `crontab`, `pgrep`, `pkill`, `nohup`, `lsof`
User and group management	`who`, `w`, `whoami`, `groups`, `id`, `newgrp`, `chfn`, `finger`, `chsh`, `passwd`
Printing	`lp`, `lpstat`, `lpadmin`, `cancel`, `lpc`, `lpr`, `lpq`, `lprm`, `cupsaccept`, `cupsreject`, `cupsenable`, `cupsdisable`
Networking and security	`ifconfig`, `ping`, `ping6`, `whois`, `arp`, `netstat`, `route`, `traceroute`, `traceroute6`, `hostname`, `host`, `nslookup`, `dig`, `su`, `sudo`, `visudo`, `last`, `rsync`, `scp`, `sftp`, `ftp`, `curl`, `nc`, `ssh`, `ssh-keygen`, `ssh-agent`, `ssh-copy-id`, `curl`, `apachectl`, `mail`, `mailq`, `newaliases`, `showmount`, `brctl`, `kinit`, `klist`, `tcpdump`
System and miscellaneous	`shutdown`, `halt`, `reboot`, `date`, `cal`, `exit`, `echo`, `clear`, `reset`, `uname`, `uptime`, `mknod`, `chroot`, `dmesg`, `iconv`, `locale`, `logger`, `sysctl`, `screen`, `iotop`, `iostat`

Table C-3 Useful macOS-specific commands

Command	Description
`asr`	This is the Apple System Restore utility. It can be used to restore the system from a disk image.
`bless`	Sets volume bootability and startup disk options
`caffeinate`	Prevents the system from sleeping
`chflags`	This modifies the attributes of a file (e.g., immutable). It is equivalent to the `chattr` command within Linux.
`defaults`	Sets macOS system preferences, such as the option to display hidden files
`diskutil`	Creates, formats, verifies, and repairs filesystems
`ditto`	Copies files and folders
`drutil`	Interacts with and writes to CD/DVD devices
`dscacheutil`	Displays or clears the DNS name cache
`dseditgroup`	Edits, creates, manipulates, or deletes groups
`dsenableroot`	Enables the root user
`dscl`	This is the Directory Service command line utility. It is used to manage users and groups on the system.

Command	Description
`fdesetup`	Configures FileVault (Apple's equivalent to LUKS disk encryption)
`hdiutil`	Creates and manages ISO/DMG disk images
`kextfind`	This lists kernel extensions and is equivalent to `lsmod` on Linux systems.
`kextload`	This loads a kernel extension and is equivalent to `modprobe` on Linux systems.
`kextstat`	Displays the status of kernel extensions on the system
`kextunload`	This unloads a kernel extension and is equivalent to `rmmod` on Linux systems.
`launchctl`	This is used to load or unload daemons/agents. It is functionally equivalent to `systemctl` on Linux systems.
`networksetup`	Configures network interface settings, including IP information and wireless settings
`newfs_type`	This creates a filesystem on a slice identified by *type*, where *type* can be apfs, hfs, ufs, msdos, or exfat. It is equivalent to `mkfs` on Linux systems.
`nvram`	Displays and modifies boot firmware parameters
`open`	Executes an application bundle
`pkgutil`	Query and manage installed macOS applications
`plutil`	Checks the syntax of .plist files, as well as converts .plist files to and from other formats
`pmset`	Configures power management options
`say`	Speaks an argument using a build-in system voice
`screencapture`	Takes a screenshot and saves it to the file specified as an argument
`scselect`	Switches between network locations
`scutil`	Creates and manages network locations
`softwareupdate`	Updates system software packages
`security`	Configures certificates and password storage (keychain) settings
`spctl`	Displays and configures XNU kernel security parameters used by SecAssessment (the macOS equivalent to SELinux)
`sw_vers`	Displays the version of the operating system
`system_profiler`	Displays system information
`systemsetup`	Configures general computer and display settings
`vm_stat`	Displays memory and swap information

Administering macOS

User Administration

To add users on macOS, you cannot use the same `useradd` command that you use within Linux. Instead, you must use the `dscl command` or System Preferences application to create user accounts. User account information is stored in an LDAP database under the /var/db directory that is used for authentication. The /etc/shadow file does not exist and the /etc/passwd and /etc/group files exist only to provide information to other applications.

When you create a new user account within the System Preferences application, you can optionally choose the *Allow user to administer this computer* option if you wish to allow the user to perform administrative tasks on the computer. This option adds the user to the admin group, which is given the ability to run all commands on the system via the `%admin  ALL=(ALL)  ALL` line within the

/etc/sudoers file. Members of the admin group can run any command using the sudo command, or change system configuration using graphical applications.

Filesystem Administration

On a Linux system, recall that the first SATA/SCSI/SAS hard disk or SSD is represented by the /dev/sda block device file, and the first partition on this device is represented by the /dev/sda1 block device file. On macOS systems, hard disk drives and SSDs are divided into slices, and each slice can contain a filesystem. By default, the /dev/disk0 block device file refers to the first hard disk drive or SSD, and the /dev/disk0s1 block device file refers to the first slice on this device. Because partition and slice operations cannot be performed using block device files in macOS, character (raw) device files are present for all block storage devices (e.g., /dev/rdisk0 and /dev/rdisk0s1). Block device files within macOS are primarily used for mounting filesystems.

Most macOS systems have a single SSD that contains a 500 MB Apple boot slice (/dev/disk0s1) as well as a 5 GB Apple recovery partition (/dev/disk0s6). The remainder of the SSD (/dev/disk0s2) is then used to create an APFS container (the equivalent of an LVM volume group in Linux) that is represented by a synthesized disk (/dev/disk1) and divided into logical volumes to store the macOS root and other filesystems (e.g., /dev/disk1s1, /dev/disk1s2, and so on).

The diskutil command can be used to view and create Apple disk slices, and the newfs_apfs command can be used to create a new APFS filesystem on a slice. To check and repair filesystems, you can specify the appropriate options to the diskutil command. However, the preferred method to create and manage Apple disk partitions and filesystems is using the graphical Disk Utility application (/Applications/Utilities/Disk Utility). The Disk Utility application can also be used to create disk images, burn CDs and DVDs, as well as manage RAID volumes.

> ## Note 3
>
> If you accidentally change permissions on macOS operating system files, the system will report errors to the screen. Checking the disk for errors within the Disk Utility will reset the default permissions on these operating system files to remedy the issue.

Disk quotas are enabled differently in macOS, because macOS does not use the /etc/fstab file to specify mount options for filesystems at boot time. Instead, you must create two files (.quota.ops. user and .quota.ops.group) in the mount point directory for each filesystem that you wish to enable quotas for. Following this, quotas can be configured and managed using the same commands as on a Linux system.

Understanding macOS Applications

When you install an application on a Linux system using a package manager, the files that comprise the application are distributed across the filesystem in various directories, such as /etc, /bin, /opt, /usr, and /var. The package manager stores the location of these files, such that they can be queried or removed at a later time.

In macOS, all of the binary executable files, supporting data files, configuration information, and other app-related information are stored in a single directory with a .app extension called a bundle. When viewed in the macOS Finder, bundles appear as a single icon (without a .app extension) that can be executed to run the associated application. To execute an application from a BASH shell, you can use the open command followed by the pathname to the bundle. For example, to open the Firefox seb browser, you could run the open /Applications/Firefox.app command.

To remove a macOS application within the macOS desktop, you can drag the associated bundle icon to the trash can icon in the Dock. To remove a macOS application from a Z shell, you can supply the full path to the bundle as an argument to the rm -Rf command.

The configuration information and settings for macOS apps are stored within XML files that have a `.plist` extension within the associated bundle. When searching the Internet for a solution to a problem related to macOS or a macOS application, the solution often involves modifying a specific `.plist` file within an application bundle.

As with Linux applications, many macOS applications rely on shared libraries. However, in macOS these shared libraries are called **frameworks** and are stored within bundle files that have a `.framework` extension under the /System/Library/Frameworks directory.

Although you can compile apps from source code using the `make` command on macOS, most macOS applications are installed via an online software repository. You can search for and install applications from this repository by starting the **App Store** application. You can start the App Store application by selecting App Store from the Apple icon menu within the macOS desktop.

Alternatively, many macOS application vendors make their macOS applications available for download on their website. When you choose to obtain a macOS application from a website, an ISO image file that has a `.dmg` extension is downloaded to the Downloads folder in your home directory. When you open the `.dmg` file, the ISO image is mounted, and a shortcut is placed on your desktop. You can then open this shortcut and drag the application bundle within to the /Applications folder to install the application.

You can also install nearly any open source Linux program on macOS. However, to do this you must compile the program from source code using Apple's Xcode developer tools. Alternatively, you can install the **Homebrew package manager** on macOS systems by following the instructions on the brew.sh website. Once Homebrew is installed, you can run the `brew install` *programname* command from a Z shell to compile and install an open source program automatically from Internet source code repositories, or the `brew uninstall` *programname* command to remove a program that was installed with Homebrew.

Managing macOS Devices

On Linux systems, most specialized hardware devices, such as network interfaces and video cards, have device drivers under the /lib/modules directory that are loaded into the Linux kernel at boot time. On macOS systems, device drivers for specialized hardware devices are called **kernel extensions** and are loaded into the XNU kernel from `.kext` files under the /System/Library/Extensions directory.

To view the currently loaded kernel extensions, you can use the `kextfind` command. Similarly, the `kextload` command may be used to activate kernel extensions, and the `kextunload` command may be used to deactivate kernel extensions. You can also use the graphical **System Information** utility (/Applications/Utilities/System Information) to view loaded kernel extensions.

macOS System Initialization

Intel-based Apple computers use a UEFI BIOS that controls the loading of the macOS bootloader, while Apple Silicon-based Apple computers load the macOS bootloader directly. To boot from a different storage device, you can hold down the Option key on the Apple keyboard (or the Alt key on a non-Apple keyboard) during system startup and select the appropriate device when prompted.

You can also hold down the Command+v keys on your Apple keyboard (or Windows+v keys on a non-Apple keyboard) during system startup to view detailed information about the boot process as well as interact with the macOS boot process itself.

The macOS bootloader loads XNU from the /System/Library/Kernels/kernel file. XNU then loads the **Launch Daemon** (/sbin/launchd), which is functionally equivalent to the Systemd daemon on modern Linux systems. The Launch Daemon proceeds to load all other system daemons to bring the system to a useable state via entries within the /Library/LaunchAgents and /Library/LaunchDaemons directories, as well as any optional apps listed in the /System/Library/StartupItems directory. You can use the `launchctl` command to view, start, and stop daemons on your system after the system has started. For example, you can run the `launchctl list` command as the root user to view the status of daemons on the system.

Holding the Command+s keys during system startup instructs launchd to boot to single user mode, where you can perform system repair. Alternatively, you can hold the Command+r keys during system startup to start the macOS Recovery Tool, which can be used to repair or reinstall the operating system.

macOS Installation and Updates

While Apple computers come pre-installed with macOS, you may need to reinstall macOS if the operating system files become corrupted. The easiest method to reinstall macOS is to use the macOS Recovery Tool discussed earlier. The macOS Recovery Tool allows you to download and reinstall macOS from the App Store and will require network connectivity as a result. Alternatively, you can insert USB media that contains the macOS installation files, boot your computer while holding down the Option key, and select the USB media to start the installation.

Regardless of how to you choose to start the macOS installation, the installation program will allow you to perform different types of installations. A clean installation erases existing filesystems and all of the data within. However, you can choose to reinstall the operating system, while preserving system settings, applications, and user files. You can also choose to archive your current system to the /Previous Systems directory and install a new copy of the operating system, preserving applications and user files.

Following installation, you can obtain macOS updates using the App Store application discussed earlier, or the `softwareupdate command`. To see macOS updates that were successfully installed, you can use the `softwareupdate --history` command, or view the contents of the /Library/ Receipts directory.

Log File Administration

As in Linux, macOS logs system events to files under the /var/log directory. For example, /var/log/ install.log contains installation events, whereas /var/log/system.log records kernel events. While you can view many of these log files using text tools within a Z shell, macOS provides a Console application (/Applications/Utilities/Console) that contains shortcuts to key system log files. You can use the Console application to sort events by severity as well as research solutions to problems, such as application crashes, online.

Managing macOS Processes

While you can use the same Linux process management commands to manage macOS processes, it is often easier to manage macOS processes using the graphical Activity Monitor application (/Applications/Utilities/Activity Monitor). Activity Monitor sorts processes by system activity and usage, as well as displays general system statistics. You can also view process information or kill problematic processes within Activity Monitor. If you encounter a rogue application that prevents you from opening Activity Monitor, you can use the Command+Shift+Option+Esc key combination to kill the foreground application, or right-click the associated application icon in the Dock and select Force Quit.

Network and Network Service Configuration

Network interfaces use a different naming convention within macOS. The first Ethernet network interface is called en0, the second Ethernet network interface is called en1, and so on. To modify the IP, DNS, and routing configuration for a wired or wireless network interface, you can use the Network section of the System Preferences application, or the `networksetup command`. To configure firewall settings, you can use the Security & Privacy section of the System Preferences application. If you want to use an authentication service, such as Active Directory, with macOS, you can specify the appropriate authentication service settings within the graphical Directory Utility application (/System/Library/CoreServices/Applications/Directory Utility).

To configure network services within macOS, you can use the Sharing section of the System Preferences application as shown in Figure C-3. Each service that you select within Figure C-3 configures a specific network service on macOS. For example, Screen Sharing configures a VNC server, File Sharing configures Samba, Printer Sharing configures IPP sharing using CUPS, and Remote Login configures the SSH daemon.

Figure C-3   Configuring network services in macOS

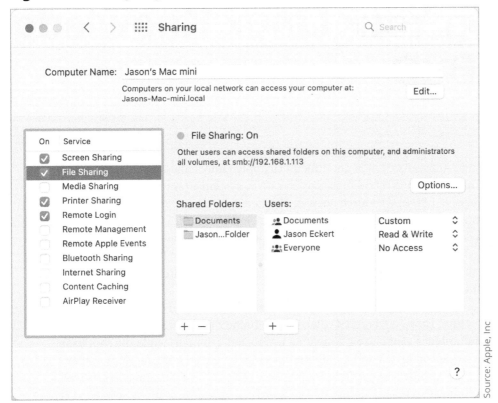

Source: Apple, Inc

Key Terms

Activity Monitor	`dsenableroot` command	`networksetup` command.
APFS container	Finder	`newfs_apfs` command
App Store	framework	`open` command
bundle	Homebrew package manager	slice
Console	kernel extension	`softwareupdate` command
Darwin	`kextfind` command	synthesized disk
Directory Utility	`kextload` command	System Information
Disk Utility	`kextunload` command	System Preferences
`diskutil` command	Launch Daemon	Terminal
Dock	`launchctl` command	XNU
`dscl` command	`open` macOS Recovery Tool	

Appendix D

Applying Your Linux Knowledge to FreeBSD

As with macOS (discussed in Appendix C), it is not difficult to apply Linux concepts to the FreeBSD UNIX operating system. FreeBSD is the second most popular UNIX system after macOS and entirely developed using the permissive BSD open source license. The latest version of FreeBSD at the time of this writing is 13.1 and supports several different architectures (Intel x86/x64, ARM/ARM64, RISC-V, and PowerPC). While you can configure FreeBSD as a workstation with X Windows alongside a desktop environment such as GNOME or KDE, it is primarily used as a server. Since FreeBSD has faster network performance than Linux, it is often preferred by organizations that provide services that send large amounts of data across the Internet, such as Netflix.

Like Linux and macOS, FreeBSD supports the Filesystem Hierarchy Standard (FHS) and uses the same basic directory structure. However, FreeBSD places user home directories under /usr/home instead of /home. By default, regular users use a simplified BASH shell (/bin/sh) while the root user uses the **C shell** (/bin/csh). You can install and configure the same Linux network services you are familiar with on FreeBSD (e.g., Apache, PostgreSQL, Samba, NFS, NTP, DHCP, DNS, and SSH), as well as use many of the same commands (e.g., `ls`, `chmod`, `find`, `which`, `ps`, `nice`, `reboot`, `poweroff`, and `ifconfig`).

Installing FreeBSD

Similar to Linux, you can start a bare metal FreeBSD installation by booting from a DVD or USB flash drive that contains FreeBSD installation media, or you can start a FreeBSD virtual machine installation by booting from a FreeBSD installation ISO image. To obtain a FreeBSD installation ISO image and instructions on how to write it to DVD or USB flash drive, visit freebsd.org.

Like Ubuntu Server, FreeBSD uses a non-graphical installation program and does not install X Windows during the installation process but does require that you set the root user password. When configuring storage within the installation program, FreeBSD uses ZFS for the root (/) filesystem by default, but you can instead choose to use the **UNIX filesystem (UFS)**.

System Configuration

Nearly all system configuration, including the system hostname, network interface configuration, and services (daemons) that are started at boot time are stored within a single text file called /etc/rc.conf. Lines within this file have parameter=value syntax and can be edited using a text editor such as `vi` or using the **sysrc command** (e.g., `sysrc parameter=value`). You can also use the `sysrc -a` command to display all parameters and their values from /etc/rc.conf.

The default FreeBSD parameters for configuration files are stored within text files under the /etc/defaults directory. For example, /etc/defaults/rc.conf stores default system configuration parameters that can be overridden by the same parameters defined in /etc/rc.conf, and /boot/defaults/loader.conf stores default boot loader configuration parameters that can be overridden by the same entries in /boot/loader.conf. Software packages that require default parameters be added to the system place a text file under the /etc/rc.conf.d directory that contains the required parameters.

Kernel Configuration

As with Linux, FreeBSD uses kernel modules to provide additional functionality and hardware support. These modules have a .ko extension and are stored under the /boot/kernel directory. You can use the `kldstat command` to view modules currently inserted into the kernel, the `kldload command` to insert a module, or the `kldunload command` to remove a module. For example, you could use the `kldload linprocfs.ko` command to load the Linux procfs filesystem module into the kernel. To make sure this module gets loaded automatically each time you boot, you could add the `[cmd=] kldload /boot/kernel/linprocfs.ko [/cmd]` line to the /boot/loader.conf file.

The FreeBSD kernel also has many properties and parameters that you can view and configure while the system is running. To see all parameters that are currently configured, you can use the `kenv command`. As on Linux, you can use the `sysctl` command to view or configure specific parameters. For example, `sysctl kern.securelevel` displays the current value of the kernel security level parameter, whereas `sysctl kern.securelevel=2` configures its value to 2 (high security mode). You can also run `sysctl -o -a` to view all available parameters and their default values. To ensure that particular kernel parameter is configured at boot time, you can modify or add the appropriate line to the /etc/sysctl.conf file.

System Initialization

FreeBSD has an interactive boot loader called boot0, as shown in Figure D-1. By default, boot0 displays a menu for 10 seconds that allows you to start the system normally (multiuser mode), enter single user mode to perform system maintenance, or start the system using different kernel or boot options.

Figure D-1   The FreeBSD boot loader

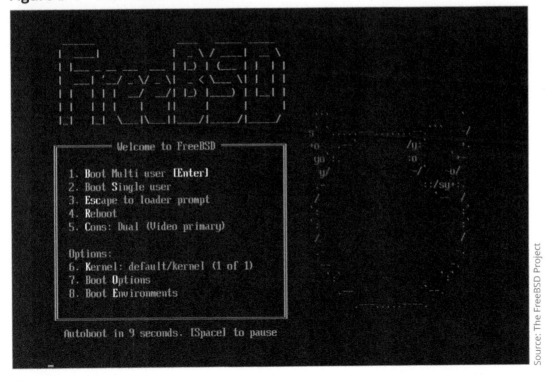

Source: The FreeBSD Project

After boot0 loads the FreeBSD kernel, the init daemon executes the /etc/rc script, which starts other daemons listed within /etc/rc.conf by executing the appropriate daemon scripts under the /etc/rc.d directory. The /etc/rc script also runs other system initialization scripts, including the /etc/netstart script that configures network interfaces with the parameters specified in /etc/rc.conf.

To view the hardware detected and modules loaded into the FreeBSD kernel during the previous system initialization, you can view the contents of the /var/run/dmesg.boot file. Alternatively, to view the daemons and components started by the init daemon (including related errors), you can view the contents of the /var/log/messages file.

Storage Configuration

As shown in Table D-1, FreeBSD uses different device files compared to Linux for identifying storage devices. To work with physical storage devices, you can use the geom command. For example, you can run geom disk list to display a list of available storage devices in the system.

Table D-1 Common FreeBSD storage device files

File	Description
/dev/da0	The first SCSI/SAS/USB hard disk drive or SSD
/dev/da1	The second SCSI/SAS/USB hard disk drive or SSD
/dev/da2	The third SCSI/SAS/USB hard disk drive or SSD
/dev/ada0	The first IDE/SATA hard disk drive or SSD
/dev/vtbd0	The first virtual storage device (within a KVM/QEMU virtual machine)
/dev/nvme0	The first NVMe SSD
/dev/cd0	The first CD or DVD drive

By default, FreeBSD creates a GPT on each hard disk drive or SSD that can be divided into partitions, and the FreeBSD installation program creates three partitions on the hard disk drive or SSD that contains the root filesystem by default. For example, if the root filesystem is on the first NVMe SSD in your system, the installation program will create the partitions and associated device files shown in Table D-2.

Table D-2 Sample partitions created by the FreeBSD installation program

Device File	Description
/dev/nvme0p1	UEFI boot partition (UEFI BIOS) or FreeBSD boot partition (legacy BIOS)
/dev/nvme0p2	Swap partition
/dev/nvme0p3	Assigned to a ZFS pool (if ZFS is used for the root filesystem) or mounted to the / directory (if UFS is used for the root filesystem)

You can display your storage configuration, as well as create and manage existing partitions on storage devices using the gpart command. For example, to display the partitions on the first NVMe storage device, you can run the gpart show -p nvme0 command.

After creating partitions, you can format them using UFS and mount them to directories on the system, much like on a Linux system using ext4. The newfs command can be used to create a UFS filesystem on a partition, the growfs command can extend the size of a UFS filesystem, the tunefs command can tune UFS filesystem parameters, and the fsck command can check a UFS filesystem for errors. Alternatively, you can configure ZFS volumes using the same zpool and zfs commands you are familiar with on Linux. For example, to create a RAID-Z volume called data from the first partition on the first three SAS SSDs in your system, you could run the `zpool create data raidz /dev/da0p1 /dev/da1p1 /dev/da2p1` command.

When you run the `zfs list` command on a FreeBSD system that uses ZFS for the root filesystem, you'll notice one ZFS volume called zroot that is created by the FreeBSD installer. This volume contains many ZFS datasets that are mounted to system directories. For example, zroot/ROOT/default is mounted to /, zroot/usr is mounted to /usr, zroot/tmp is mounted to /tmp, and zroot/var is mounted to /var.

As with Linux, FreeBSD contains an /etc/fstab file that activates swap and mounts non-ZFS filesystems at boot time. Following an installation that uses ZFS for the root filesystem, /etc/fstab is only used to activate the swap partition and mount the UEFI or FreeBSD boot partition.

Boot Environments

If your FreeBSD system uses ZFS for the root filesystem, you can use ZFS snapshots to boot your system to a previous state called a boot environment. When a ZFS snapshot is taken of the root filesystem, all subsequent file changes are stored in a separate ZFS dataset mounted to /. Before performing a risky configuration, you could take a snapshot of your root filesystem on July 2 called zroot/ROOT/July2 and then revert your system to that point in time if your risky configuration fails. To do this, you must first install the boot environment package using the `pkg install beadm` command (pkg is discussed later). Next, you can run the `beadm create July2` command to create the snapshot and then run the `zfs list` command to verify that the zroot/ROOT/July2 snapshot and associated boot environment was created successfully. If you wish to revert your system to the July 2 state at a future time, you can run the `beadm activate July2` command and reboot the system. Alternatively, you could reboot the system, press E at the boot loader screen shown in Figure D-1 and select the zroot/ROOT/July2 boot environment.

Filesystem Flags

While most file management features and commands are identical between Linux and FreeBSD, configuring filesystem attributes is different. On FreeBSD systems, filesystem attributes are called filesystem flags and can be set at the system or user level. For example, to set the system-wide unlink flag (equivalent to the immutable attribute in Linux) on a file, you could run the `chflags sunlink` *filename* command. You can then use the `ls -lo` *filename* command to view the flags set, or the `chkflags nosunlink` *filename* command to remove the system-wide unlink flag.

Users and Groups

As on Linux, the /etc/group file is used to store FreeBSD group information. User information is stored in /etc/passwd but converted to database format (/etc/pwd.db) for use by the system. Instead of using /etc/shadow to store user password information, FreeBSD stores all combined user and password information in /etc/master.passwd but converts it to database format (/etc/spwd.db) for system use.

There is no `sudo` command in FreeBSD, and regular users must be part of the wheel group in order to use the `su` command to obtain a root shell. You can create rules to allow or prevent user access in the /etc/login.access file, as well as define user classes for accessing system resources in the /etc/login.conf file.

To create user accounts using an interactive wizard, you can run the `adduser` command. By default, new users receive default account settings specified in /etc/adduser.conf and default home directory files copied from the /usr/share/skel directory. You can also use the `rmuser command` to remove a user account, and the `chpass command` to modify user settings. Alternatively, you can use the `pw command` to add, remove, modify, lock, and unlock specific user accounts.

Installing Software

The FreeBSD package manager is the primary method used to install software on FreeBSD systems. Like the Red Hat and Debian package managers on a Linux system, it obtains software from an online software repository, including any dependency packages. You use the `pkg command` to work with the FreeBSD package manager, and Table D-3 lists some example `pkg` commands.

Table D-3 Example FreeBSD package manager commands

Command	Description
`pkg update`	Updates the list of packages available from the online repository
`pkg search apache`	Searches the online repository for packages with apache in the name or description
`pkg install apache24`	Downloads and installs the Apache Web server (apache24) package
`pkg upgrade apache24`	Upgrades the apache24 package to the latest version
`pkg info apache24`	Displays details for the apache24 package
`pkg info -l apache24`	Displays file contents for the apache24 package
`pkg check apache24`	Checks apache24 package content for missing or corrupted files
`pkg lock apache24`	Prevents modification or removal of the apache24 package
`pkg remove apache24`	Uninstalls the apache24 package
`pkg clean`	Removes any cached package files within the /var/cache/pkg directory
`pkg autoremove`	Automatically removes unneeded dependency packages from the system
`pkg which /usr/local/ sbin/httpd`	Displays the package name that the /usr/local/sbin/httpd file belongs to

After installing a software package that provides a service, you must also configure it to start at boot time. For example, to start the Apache Web server after installing the apache24 package, you could add the `apache24_enable="YES"` line to /etc/rc.conf.

Configuration files for most software installed on the system are located under the /etc or /usr/local/etc directories. For example, the httpd.conf file used to configure the Apache Web server is located under the /usr/local/etc/apache24 directory.

Managing Services

To manage services on a FreeBSD system, you can use the same `service` command used by Linux systems prior to the introduction of Systemd. For example, the `service apache24 start` command can be used to start the Apache Web server, while the `service apache24 restart` and `service apache24 stop` commands can be used to restart and stop it, respectively. To display services that are started at boot time and the order they are started, you can run the `service -e` command.

> **Note 1**
>
> If a service is not listed in /etc/rc.conf, you must use the `service servicename onestart` command to start it.

Monitoring Tools

As on Linux systems, you can monitor the performance of your FreeBSD system using the `vmstat` and `top` commands, or you can monitor network statistics using the `netstat` and `sockstat` commands (`sockstat` is called `ss` in Linux). To monitor disk performance on FreeBSD, you can use the `gstat` command.

Firewall Configuration

FreeBSD installs three different firewall systems by default: PF, IPFW, and IPFILTER. PF is the most commonly-configured one; it stores firewall rules within /etc/pf.conf and can be configured using the `pfctl` command. Additionally, you can use the `blacklistctl` command to configure the blacklist daemon to block specific connections using rules within the /etc/blacklistd.conf file.

Container Configuration

FreeBSD is one of the earliest operating systems to implement containers. However, FreeBSD containers are called **jails** and do not rely on a separate container runtime, such as Docker. To create a FreeBSD jail, you download a tarball that contains a container filesystem (called a **userland**) from a FreeBSD repository, extract it to a directory of your choice, and configure settings for the jail (e.g., name, directory, IP address) in the /etc/jail.conf file. Next, you can start and manage your jail much like you would a Docker container.

For example, if you create a jail called jail01 in /etc/jail.conf, you can start it using the `service jail start jail01` command. You can then execute a specific command within jail01 using the `jexec command`, or use the `pkg` command to install software within jail01. For example, `jexec jail01 "ps aux"` would display running processes in jail01, and `pkg -j jail01 install apach24` would install the Apache Web server in jail01. You can also stop jail01 using the `service jail stop jail01` command or run the `jls command` to display all running jails on the system.

Key Terms

`adduser` command	`growfs` command	`pfctl` command
blacklistctl command	gstat command	pkg command
boot environment	jail	pw command
boot0	`jexec` command	`rmuser` command
C shell	`jls` command	sysrc command
`chpass` command	`kenv` command	`tunefs` command
filesystem flags	kldload command	UNIX filesystem (UFS)
FreeBSD package manager	kldstat command	userland
geom command	kldunload command	ZFS snapshots
gpart command	newfs command	

Glossary

*sum commands   Used to verify the checksum on a file where * represents the checksum algorithm. For example, to verify a SHA1 checksum, you could use the `sha1sum` command.

/dev directory   The directory where special device files are stored.

/etc/fstab   A file that specifies filesystems to mount at boot time or when insufficient arguments are provided to the `mount` command.

/etc/mtab   A file that stores a list of currently mounted filesystems.

/proc/devices   A file that contains major numbers for currently used system devices.

~ metacharacter   A metacharacter that represents a user's home directory.

1U server   A rackmount server that has a standard height of 1.75 inches.

aa-complain command   Sets an AppArmor profile to complain mode.

aa-disable command   Disables an AppArmor profile.

aa-enforce command   Sets an AppArmor profile to enforce mode.

aa-status command   Used to view the status of AppArmor and AppArmor profiles.

aa-unconfined command   Lists processes that are not controlled by AppArmor.

ab (Apache benchmark) command   Used to obtain performance benchmarks for an Apache web server.

absolute pathname   The full pathname to a certain file or directory starting from the root directory.

access control list (ACL)   The section within an inode of a file or directory that lists the permissions assigned to users and groups on the file or directory.

ACPI Daemon (acpid)   A daemon that interacts with ACPI and performs the associated actions on the Linux system.

active partition   The partition on which a standard BIOS searches for an operating system.

Activity Monitor   The macOS application used to view and manage processes.

add-apt-repository command   Used to add repository information to the DPM repository database.

adduser command   Adds user accounts on a FreeBSD system.

Advanced Configuration and Power Interface (ACPI)   A BIOS component that provides hardware and power management event functionality to an operating system.

Advanced Technology Attachment (ATA)   See *Parallel Advanced Technology Attachment*.

agent   A software component that is installed on a Linux system and that communicates to another computer across the network.

agentless   A term that refers to software that manages other computers using a native protocol, such as SSH.

aggregation   See *bonding*.

alias command   Used to create special variables that are shortcuts to longer command strings.

ambassador container   A container within a Kubernetes cluster that allows other containers in the cluster to access resources outside of the cluster.

American Standard Code for Information Interchange (ASCII)   A character set that provides character mappings for English characters.

anacron daemon   A daemon that is often started by the cron daemon to carry out scheduled tasks. Unlike the cron daemon, if the system is powered off during a scheduled task, the anacron daemon will execute it the next time the system is powered on.

ANDing   The process by which binary bits are compared to calculate the network and host IDs from an IP address and subnet mask.

apachectl command   Used to start, stop, and restart the Apache web server as well as check for syntax errors within the Apache configuration file.

APFS container   A group of one or more storage devices on a macOS system that are formatted with APFS and represented by a synthesized disk.

App Store   The macOS application used to download and install other macOS applications from an online Apple software repository.

AppArmor A Linux kernel module and related software packages that prevent malicious software from accessing system resources.

AppArmor profile A text file within the /etc/apparmor.d directory that lists application-specific restrictions.

AppImage A sandboxed application format comprised of a single file that can be directly executed on the system.

application (app) The software that runs on an operating system and provides the user with specific functionality (such as word processing or financial calculation). Applications are commonly referred to as apps today.

apt (Advanced Package Tool) command Used to search for, install, and upgrade DPM packages from software repositories, as well as view, manage, and remove installed DPM packages.

apt-cache command Used to search DPM repositories for package information.

apt-get command Used to install and upgrade DPM packages from software repositories, as well as manage and remove installed DPM packages.

Aptitude A utility that can be used to manage DPM packages using a graphical interface.

aptitude command Used to start the Aptitude utility.

archive The location (file or device) that contains a copy of files; it is typically created by a backup utility.

arguments The text that appears after a command name, does not start with a dash (-), and specifies information that the command requires to work properly.

arp command Displays and modifies the MAC address cache on a system.

array variable A variable that stores multiple, discrete values that are identified by an index position.

assistive technologies Software programs that cater to specific user needs within a GUI.

asymmetric encryption A type of encryption that uses a key pair to encrypt and decrypt data.

at command Used to view, create, and manage scheduled tasks that run at a preset time in the future.

at daemon (atd) The system daemon that executes tasks at a future time; it is configured with the at command.

atq command Used to view a scheduled at job.

atrm command Used to remove a scheduled at job.

audit2allow command Configures SELinux policies based on SELinux log entries.

audit2why command Displays the description and purpose of SELinux log entries.

authentication The process whereby each user must log in with a valid user name and password before gaining access to a system.

Automatic Bug Reporting Tool Daemon (abrtd) A process that automatically sends application crash data to an online bug reporting service.

Automatic Private IP Addressing (APIPA) A feature that automatically configures a network interface using an IPv4 address on the 169.254.0.0 network, or an IPv6 address on the FE80 network.

B

background process A process that does not require the shell to wait for its termination. Upon execution, the user receives the shell prompt immediately.

bad blocks The areas of a storage medium unable to store data properly.

bare metal Refers to an operating system that is installed directly on computer hardware, and not within a virtual machine or container.

baseline A measure of normal system activity.

BASH shell Also known as the Bourne Again Shell, this is the default command-line interface on most Linux distributions.

Basic Input/Output System (BIOS) The part of a computer system that contains the programs used to initialize hardware components at boot time.

Beowulf clustering A popular and widespread method of clustering computers together to perform useful tasks using Linux.

Berkeley Internet Name Domain (BIND) The standard to which all DNS servers and DNS configuration files adhere.

bg (background) command Used to run a foreground process in the background.

binary data file A file that contains machine language (binary 1s and 0s) and stores information (such as common functions and graphics) used by binary compiled programs.

Binary Large Object (BLOB) storage See *object storage*.

BIOS Boot Partition A small partition that is created by the Linux installation program to store information needed to boot the Linux operating system from a GPT hard disk drive on a computer that does not have a UEFI BIOS.

blacklistctl command   Configures the blacklist daemon on a FreeBSD system.

blade server   A server that resides in a portion of a rackmount server.

blkid command   Used to list UUIDs for filesystems and partitions.

block   The unit of data commonly used by filesystem operations; a block can contain several sectors.

block devices   Storage devices that transfer data to and from the system in chunks of many data bits by caching the information in RAM; they are represented by block device files.

block storage   Filesystem storage made available by a cloud provider.

bonding   The process of combining two network interfaces on the same network to provide fault tolerance or load balancing.

boot environment   A ZFS snapshot of the root filesystem on a FreeBSD system to which you can choose to boot or revert the system.

boot loader   A program used to execute an operating system kernel.

boot0   The FreeBSD boot loader.

Boxes   A virtual machine configuration and management tool included with the GNOME desktop.

branch   A separate section within a Git repository used to track changes made to files.

Brasero   A common disc burning software used on Linux systems.

bridging   The process of merging two separate networks using the network interfaces on a server.

broadcast   A TCP/IP communication destined for all computers on a network.

B-tree File System (BTRFS)   A filesystem that can be used to create fault tolerant volumes much like ZFS. It is currently still in development, but it is being designed as a replacement for ext4.

btrfs command   Used to view and manage BTRFS filesystems.

BTRFS subvolume   A subdirectory on a BTRFS volume that can be mounted as a separate unit with different BTRFS settings.

btrfsck command   Used to check and repair BTRFS filesystems.

build automation   A process used within cloud environments that allows containers and virtual machines to be created quickly.

bundle   An application package within macOS.

bunzip2 command   Used to decompress files compressed by the bzip2 command.

bus mastering   The process by which peripheral components perform tasks normally executed by the CPU.

bzcat command   Used to display the contents of an archive created with bzip2 to Standard Output.

bzgrep command   Used to search and display the contents of an archive created with bzip2 to Standard Output.

bzip2 command   Used to compress files using a Burrows-Wheeler Block Sorting Huffman Coding compression algorithm.

bzless command   Used to display the contents of an archive created with bzip2 to Standard Output using the less command.

bzmore command   Used to display the contents of an archive created with bzip2 to Standard Output using the more command.

C

C shell   A shell that resembles BASH but can use C-style constructs. It is the default shell used by the root user on a FreeBSD system.

cancel command   Used to remove print jobs from the print queue in the CUPS print system.

cat command   Used to display (or concatenate) the entire contents of a text file to the screen.

cd (change directory) command   Used to change the current directory in the directory tree.

certbot command   Used to obtain and configure certificates from a CA on a Linux system.

certificate   A digitally signed public key file.

Certification Authority (CA)   A server that digitally signs public keys used by other computers to validate their authenticity.

cfdisk command   Used to partition storage devices; displays a graphical interface in which the user can select partitioning options.

chage command   Used to modify password expiry information for user accounts.

chains   The components of a firewall that specify the general type of network traffic to which rules apply.

character devices   Devices that transfer data to and from the system one data bit at a time; they are represented by character device files.

chattr (change attributes) command   Used to change filesystem attributes for a Linux file.

`chcon command` Used to change the type classification within SELinux labels on system files and directories.

checkpoint See *snapshot.*

checksum A calculated value that is unique to a file's size and contents.

`chfn command` Used to change the GECOS for a user.

`chgrp (change group) command` Used to change the group owner of a file or directory.

child process A process that was started by another process (parent process).

`chkconfig command` Used to configure UNIX SysV daemon startup by runlevel.

`chmod (change mode) command` Used to change the mode (permissions) of a file or directory.

`chown (change owner) command` Used to change the owner and group owner of a file or directory.

`chpass command` Used to modify FreeBSD user account settings.

Chrony NTP daemon (chronyd) A daemon that provides fast time synchronization services on Linux computers.

`chronyc command` Used to query the state of an NTP server or client, as well as synchronize the system time with an NTP server.

`chroot command` Used to change the root of one Linux system to another.

`chsh command` Used to change the default shell for a Linux user.

Cinnamon A popular desktop environment derived from GNOME 3.

classless interdomain routing (CIDR) notation A notation that is often used to represent an IP address and its subnet mask.

cloning The process of copying a Git repository from another location or computer.

closed source software The software whose source code is not freely available from the original author; Windows 11 is an example.

cloud delivery model The method used to host services on a cloud provider, such as IaaS, PaaS, or SaaS.

cloud provider An organization that provides Internet access to resources in a data center.

cloud-init A system that can be used to automatically configure a Linux virtual machine at boot time.

cluster A grouping of several smaller computers that function as one larger computer.

clustering The act of making a cluster; see also *cluster.*

code repository A cloud service that stores and version controls source code for apps.

command A program that exists on the filesystem and is executed when typed on the command line.

command mode One of the two modes in vi; it allows a user to perform any available text-editing task that is not related to inserting text into the document.

commit A snapshot of files that are tracked by Git for version control.

Common Gateway Interface (CGI) A specification that allows web servers to run apps.

Common Unix Printing System (CUPS) The printing system commonly used on Linux computers.

Common Vulnerabilities and Exposures (CVE) A system used to catalog general security vulnerabilities.

Common Weakness Enumeration (CWE) A system used to catalog OWASP security vulnerabilities.

`compress command` Used to compress files using a Lempel-Ziv compression algorithm.

compression The process in which files are reduced in size by a compression algorithm.

compression algorithm The set of instructions used to reduce the contents of a file systematically.

compression ratio The amount that a file size is reduced during compression.

concatenation The joining of text together to make one larger whole. In Linux, words and strings of text are joined together to form a displayed file.

configuration management (CM) A type of software that is used to automate the configuration of systems on a network.

Console The macOS application used to view log files.

container A subset of an operating system that provides a unique service on the network.

container registry An online repository of container images.

container runtime The software that runs and manages containers on an operating system.

continuous deployment (CD) A process whereby developer apps are regularly sent to a cloud provider for testing and hosting.

continuous integration (CI) A process whereby developer source code is regularly sent to a code repository for collaboration and approval.

copyleft license A type of open source license that places restrictions on source code use to ensure that changes are always made freely available.

counter variable A variable that is altered by loop constructs to ensure that commands are not executed indefinitely.

cp (copy) command Used to create copies of files and directories.

cpio (copy in/out) command Used to back up a wide variety of file types, as well as view and restore files from a backup.

cracker A person who uses computer software maliciously for personal profit.

cron daemon (crond) The system daemon that executes tasks repetitively in the future and that is configured using cron tables.

cron table A file specifying tasks to be run by the cron daemon; there are user cron tables and system cron tables.

crontab command Used to view and edit user cron tables.

cryptsetup command Used to configure and manage LUKS.

CUPS daemon (cupsd) The daemon responsible for printing in the CUPS printing system.

CUPS web administration tool A web-based management tool for the CUPS printing system.

cupsaccept command Used to allow a printer to accept jobs into the print queue.

cupsdisable command Used to prevent print jobs from leaving the print queue.

cupsenable command Used to allow print jobs to leave the print queue.

cupsreject command Used to force a printer to reject jobs from entering the print queue.

curl (client for URLs) command Used to download webpages and files from the Internet.

cylinder A series of tracks on a hard disk that are written to simultaneously by the magnetic heads in a hard disk drive.

D

daemon A Linux system process that provides a system service.

daemon process A system process that is not associated with a terminal.

Darwin The open source UNIX operating system that macOS is based on.

data In BTRFS terminology, it refers to the blocks on the BTRFS filesystem used to store data.

data blocks The portion of the filesystem that includes the contents of the file as well as the filename.

database An organized set of data.

database management system (DBMS) Software that manages databases.

dd command Used to create and restore image backups.

Debian Package Manager (DPM) A package manager used on Debian and Debian-based Linux distributions, such as Ubuntu Server.

decision construct A special syntax used in a shell script to alter the flow of the program based on the outcome of a command or contents of a variable. Common decision constructs include if, case, &&, and ||.

declarative configuration A CM process whereby inventory members are configured using the attributes listed within a configuration file.

default gateway The IP address of the router on the network used to send packets to remote networks.

deployment An object that stores the settings that Kubernetes uses to configure and run containers.

depmod command Used to update the module dependency database.

Desktop Bus (D-Bus) A software component that allows programs running within a desktop environment to easily communicate with one another.

desktop environment The software that often works alongside a window manager to provide a standard graphical environment.

developmental kernel A Linux kernel that has been recently developed yet not thoroughly tested.

device driver A piece of software containing instructions that the kernel of an operating system uses to control and interact with a specific type of computer hardware.

device file A file used by Linux commands that represents a specific device on the system; these files do not have a data section and use major and minor numbers to reference the proper driver and specific device on the system, respectively.

Device Mapper MPIO (DM-MPIO) The multipath implementation used by Linux servers.

DevOp A Linux administrator that manages the software that provides a CD workflow.

df (disk free space) command Used to display disk free space by mounted filesystem.

dhclient command Used to obtain IP configuration for a network interface from a DHCP or BOOTP server on the network.

DHCP daemon (dhcpd) A Linux daemon used to provide IPv4 and IPv6 addresses to other computers on the network.

diff command Compares the contents of text files, identifying any differences.

differential backup An archive of a filesystem that contains only files that were modified since the last full backup was created.

dig command Used to test name resolution.

digital signature Information that has been encrypted using a private key.

directive A line within a configuration file.

directory A special file on the filesystem used to organize other files.

Directory Utility The macOS application used to configure authentication and directory services.

disk mirroring A RAID configuration consisting of two hard disk drives to which identical data are written in parallel, ensuring fault tolerance. Also known as RAID 1.

disk quotas The limits on the number of inodes, or total storage space on a filesystem, available to a user.

disk striping A RAID configuration in which a single file is divided into sections, which are then written to different hard disk drives concurrently to speed up access time; this type of RAID is not fault tolerant. Also known as RAID 0.

disk striping with parity A RAID configuration that incorporates disk striping for faster file access, as well as parity information to ensure fault tolerance. Also known as RAID 5.

Disk Utility The macOS application used to manage storage devices and filesystems.

diskutil command Used to create and manage disks and filesystems on macOS systems.

distribution (distro) A complete set of operating system software, including the Linux kernel, supporting function libraries and a variety of OSS packages that can be downloaded from the Internet free of charge. These OSS packages are what differentiate the various distributions of Linux.

distribution kernel A production Linux kernel that receives long term patch support for a particular Linux distribution.

dmesg command Used to list the information recorded by the Linux kernel at the beginning of the boot process.

dmidecode command Displays hardware device information detected by the BIOS/UEFI.

dnf (Dandified YUM) command A speed-improved version of the yum command used on modern Linux distributions.

DNS cache file A file that contains the IP addresses of top-level DNS servers.

Dock The application launcher used within the macOS desktop.

Docker A common container runtime used today.

Docker client A program that can be used to create and manage Docker containers.

docker command Used to start the Docker client program.

Docker Hub A container registry maintained by the creators of Docker.

docker-compose command Used to run multiple microservice containers for testing.

document root The directory on a web server that stores web content for distribution to web browsers.

documentation System information that is stored in a file or log book for future reference.

Domain Name Space (DNS) The naming convention used by computers on the Internet.

dot (.) command Used to execute the contents of a shell script within the current shell, instead of using a subshell.

dpkg command Used to install, query, and remove DPM packages.

dpkg-query command Used to query installed DPM packages.

dpkg-reconfigure command Used to reconfigure the installation settings for an already-installed DPM package.

dracut command Used to generate an initramfs.

dscl command Used to manage users and groups on macOS systems.

dsenableroot command Used to enable the root user account on macOS systems.

du (directory usage) command Used to display directory usage.

dump command Used to create full and incremental backups of files on an ext2/ext3/ext4 filesystem.

Dynamic Host Configuration Protocol (DHCP)
The protocol that is used to automatically obtain IP configuration for a computer.

E

`e2label command`   Used to set a description label on an ext2/ext3/ext4 filesystem.

`echo command`   Used to display or echo output to the terminal screen. It can use escape sequences.

`edquota command`   Used to specify quota limits for users and groups.

`egrep command`   A variant of the `grep` command used to search files for patterns, using extended regular expressions.

`eject command`   Used to unmount and eject CD/DVD removable media.

Emacs (Editor MACroS) editor   A popular text editor that was originally developed by Richard Stallman.

`env command`   Used to display a list of exported variables and functions present in the current shell.

environment files   The files used immediately after login to execute commands; they are typically used to load variables into memory.

environment variables   The variables that store information commonly accessed by the system or programs executing on the system; together, these variables form the user environment.

epoch time   The time format used by the Linux kernel; it is represented by the number of seconds since January 1, 1970.

escape sequences   Character combinations that have special meaning inside certain commands, such as `echo`. They are prefixed by the \ character.

Ethernet   The most common media access method used in networks today.

`ethtool command`   Used to configure and display network interface hardware settings.

executable program   A file that can be executed by the Linux operating system to run in memory as a process and perform a useful function.

`exfatlabel command`   Used to set a description label on an exFAT filesystem.

exit status   A number that is returned by each command on a Linux system to indicate successful (0) or unsuccessful (1-255) execution. It can be used to provide the true/false functionality within shell script constructs.

`export command`   Used to send variables to subshells.

`expr command`   Used to perform mathematical operations.

Extended Internet Super Daemon (xinetd)   A network daemon that is used to start other network daemons on demand.

extended partition   A partition on an MBR-based hard disk drive or SSD that can be further subdivided into components called logical drives.

F

facility   The area of the system from which information is gathered when logging system events.

`faillock command`   Used to view and modify user lockout settings.

`fatlabel command`   Used to set a description label on a FAT filesystem.

fault tolerant   Term used to describe a device that exhibits a minimum of downtime in the event of a failure.

`fdisk command`   Used to create and modify MBR and GPT partitions on storage devices.

`fg (foreground) command`   Used to run a background process in the foreground.

`fgrep command`   A variant of the `grep` command that does not allow the use of regular expressions.

Fibre Channel (FC)   A SCSI technology that transfers data across fiber optic or Ethernet networks.

field   An individual attribute used by the records in a database table.

`file command`   Displays the file type for files on a filesystem.

file descriptors   The numeric labels used to define command input and command output.

file globbing   The process of using wildcard metacharacters within a command to match multiple files or directories.

file handles   The connections that a program makes to files on a filesystem.

File Transfer Protocol (FTP)   The most common protocol used to transfer files across networks, such as the Internet.

filename   The user-friendly identifier given to a file.

filename extension   A series of identifiers following a dot (.) at the end of a filename, used to denote the type of the file; the filename extension .txt denotes a text file.

filesystem   The organization imposed on a physical storage device that is used to manage the storage and retrieval of data by block.

filesystem corruption   The errors in a filesystem structure that prevent the retrieval of stored data.

filesystem flags   The term used for filesystem attributes on a FreeBSD system.

Filesystem Hierarchy Standard (FHS)   A standard outlining the location of files and directories on a Linux or UNIX system.

Filesystem in Userspace (FUSE)   A software component that allows regular users the ability to create filesystems without requiring kernel support.

filter   A command that can take from Standard Input and send to Standard Output. In other words, a filter is a command that can exist in the middle of a pipe.

find command   Used to find files on the filesystem using various criteria.

Finder   The graphical file browser application within macOS.

firewall   A software component that monitors and restricts network access to a system.

Firewall Configuration utility   A graphical firewall configuration utility used on Fedora systems.

firewall daemon (firewalld)   A daemon that can be used to simplify the configuration of netfilter firewall rules via network zones.

firewall-cmd command   Used to view and configure firewalld zones, services, and rules.

firmware RAID   A RAID system controlled by the computer's BIOS/UEFI.

Flatpak   A sandboxed application format and package manager.

flatpak command   Used to interact with the Flatpak package manager.

flavor   A term that refers to a specific type of UNIX operating system. For example, macOS and FreeBSD are two different flavors of UNIX.

foreground process   A process for which the shell that executed it must wait for its termination.

forking   The act of creating a new shell child process from a parent shell process.

formatting   The process in which a filesystem is placed on a storage device.

forum   An area of a website that provides the ability to post and reply to messages.

forward lookup   A DNS name resolution request whereby a FQDN is resolved to an IP address.

framework   A shared library within macOS.

free command   Used to display memory and swap statistics.

Free Software Foundation (FSF)   An organization started by Richard Stallman that promotes and encourages the collaboration of software developers worldwide to allow the free sharing of source code and software programs.

FreeBSD package manager   The package manager used on a FreeBSD system. It is accessed via the `pkg` command.

freeware   Software distributed by the developer at no cost to the user.

fsck (filesystem check) command   Used to check the integrity of a filesystem and repair damaged files.

fstrim command   Used to discard (or "trim") unused blocks on an SSD, such that they can be reclaimed for use.

ftp command   Used to interact with FTP servers using standard FTP.

full backup   An archive of all files on a filesystem.

fully qualified domain name (FQDN)   A host name that follows DNS convention.

function   A special variable that can accept positional parameters and is used to store commands and constructs for later execution.

function library   A file that contains multiple functions for use in other programs and shell scripts.

fuser command   Used to identify users or processes using a particular file or directory.

G

gcc (GNU C Compiler) command   Used to compile source code written in the C programming language into binary programs.

gdisk (GPT fdisk) command   Used to create and modify GPT partitions on storage devices. It uses an interface that is very similar to `fdisk`.

gedit editor   A common text editor used within desktop environments.

General Electric Comprehensive Operating System (GECOS)   The field in the /etc/passwd file that contains a description of the user account.

geom command   Used to display and modify the settings for storage devices on a FreeBSD system.

getenforce command   Used to view whether SELinux is using enforcing or permissive mode.

getent command   Used to display the entries within system databases, such as /etc/passwd, /etc/shadow, /etc/group, and /etc/hosts.

getfacl (get file ACL) command   Used to list all ACL entries for Linux files and directories.

`getsebool command` Used to display SELinux settings within an SELinux policy.

Git A common open source version control program primarily used for software development.

`git command` Used to perform version control operations using Git.

Git repo See *Git repository*.

Git repository A collection of files and commits that are used by Git. Git repositories often represent software development projects.

GNOME Display Manager (GDM) A program that provides a graphical login screen on tty1 for most Linux distributions.

GNOME Shell The graphical interface components within the GNOME desktop environment.

GNU General Public License (GPL) A software license, ensuring that the source code for any OSS will remain freely available to anyone who wants to examine, build on, or improve upon it.

GNU Network Object Model Environment (GNOME) One of the two mainstream desktop environments for Linux.

GNU Privacy Guard (GPG) An open source asymmetric encryption technology that can be used to encrypt and digitally sign files and email.

GNU Project A free operating system project started by Richard Stallman.

`gpart command` Used to create and manage partitions on storage devices in a FreeBSD system.

GPG Agent A daemon that can be used to store the private key passphrase used by GPG.

`gpg command` Used to configure and manage GPG.

GRand Unified Bootloader (GRUB) A boot loader used to boot a variety of operating systems (including Linux) on a variety of hardware platforms.

GRand Unified Bootloader version 2 (GRUB2) An enhanced version of the original GRUB boot loader. It is the most common boot loader used on modern Linux systems.

graphical user interface (GUI) The component of an operating system that provides a user-friendly interface comprising graphics or icons to represent desired tasks. Users can point and click to execute a command rather than having to know and use proper command-line syntax.

`grep command` Searches files for patterns of characters using regular expression metacharacters. The command name is short for "global regular expression print."

group When used in the mode of a certain file or directory, it refers to the collection of users who have ownership of that file or directory based on the group owner of that file or directory.

Group Identifier (GID) A unique number given to each group.

`groupadd command` Used to add a group to the system.

`groupdel command` Used to delete a group from the system.

`groupmod command` Used to modify the name or GID of a group on the system.

`groups command` Lists group membership for a user.

`growfs command` Used to extend the size of a UFS filesystem in FreeBSD.

GRUB Legacy The original version of the GRUB boot loader.

GRUB root partition The partition containing the second stage of the GRUB boot loader and the GRUB configuration file; it is normally a partition that is mounted to /boot.

`grub-install command` Used to install the GRUB or GRUB2 boot loader.

`grub2-install command` Used to install the GRUB2 boot loader on a system with a standard BIOS.

`grub2-mkconfig command` Used to build the GRUB2 configuration file from entries within the /etc/default/grub file and files under the /etc/grub.d directory.

`gstat command` Used to acquire information regarding storage device performance on a FreeBSD system.

guest operating system A virtual operating system that is run on a hypervisor. It is commonly called a virtual machine.

GUID Partition Table (GPT) The area of a large hard disk drive (> 2TB) outside a partition that stores partition information. GPTs are used on most modern hard disk drives and SSDs.

`gunzip command` Used to decompress files compressed by the `gzip` command.

`gzip (GNU zip) command` Used to compress files using a Lempel-Ziv compression algorithm.

H

hacker A person who explores computer science to gain knowledge—not to be confused with "cracker."

hard limit   A disk quota that the user cannot exceed.

hard link   A file that shares content with other files on the same filesystem using the same inode.

hardware   The tangible parts of a computer, such as the network boards, video card, hard disk drives, printers, and keyboards.

hardware RAID   A RAID system controlled by hardware located on a disk controller card within the computer.

hash   See *checksum*.

hashpling   The first line in a shell script; defines the shell that will be used to interpret the commands in the script file.

head command   Displays the first set of lines of a text file; by default, the head command displays the first 10 lines.

here document   A syntax used to perform multiline input redirection.

history command   Used to view previously executed commands within a shell.

home directory   A directory on the filesystem set aside for users to store personal files and information.

Homebrew package manager   A third-party package manager available for macOS systems that can be used to add OSS packages from an Internet software repository.

Host Bus Adapter (HBA)   A controller card that connects to Fibre Channel storage.

host command   Used to test name resolution.

host ID   The portion of an IP address that denotes the host.

host name   A user-friendly name assigned to a computer.

host operating system   The operating system used to host or manage a hypervisor.

hostname command   Used to display and change the host name of a computer.

hostnamectl command   Used to change the host name of a computer as well as ensure that the new host name is loaded at boot time.

htop command   A color version of the top command that displays information in a more human-readable format.

hwclock command   Used to view and modify the system clock within the computer BIOS.

hwinfo command   Used to probe for and display hardware device information.

hybrid cloud   The process of using both a public and private cloud to provide services or run apps.

hyperscaler   See *cloud provider*.

Hypertext Transfer Protocol (HTTP)   The protocol used to access websites and most web apps.

hypervisor   See *virtualization software*.

I

iconv command   Used to convert data from one character set to another.

id command   Lists the UID and GIDs for a user.

ifconfig (interface configuration) command   Used to display and modify the IP configuration information for a network interface. It is part of the net-tools package.

iftop command   Displays the bandwidth sent from the local computer to other hosts.

image backup   A backup that writes data block by block to an archive without maintaining file structure information.

imperative configuration   A CM process whereby inventory members are configured using the procedures listed within a script file.

incremental backup   An archive of a filesystem that contains only files that were modified since the last archive was created.

info page   A local set of easy-to-read documentation for a specific command or file that is available by typing the info command.

Infrastructure as a Service (IaaS)   A cloud strategy that allows access to virtualized operating systems stored within a data center.

Infrastructure as Code (IaC)   A cloud practice that involves using both build automation and CM.

infrastructure services   Services that provide IP configuration, name resolution, or time synchronization to other computers on a network.

ingress controller   A software component that allows external access to services within a Kubernetes cluster.

init command   Used to change the Linux operating system from one runlevel to another.

initialize (init) daemon   The first process started by the Linux kernel; it is responsible for starting and stopping other daemons.

initramfs   A disk image that contains Linux kernel modules that are needed by the Linux kernel during the boot process.

initstate   See *runlevel*.

inode   The portion of a file that stores information on the file's attributes, access permissions, location, ownership, and file type.

inode table The collection of inodes for all files and directories on a filesystem.

input/output operations per second (IOPS) A common storage device performance measurement. It is the total number of read and write operations performed per second.

insert mode One of the two modes in vi; it allows the user to insert text into the document but does not allow any other functionality.

insmod command Used to load a module into the Linux kernel.

installation log files The files created at installation to record actions that occurred or failed during the installation process.

Integrated Drive Electronics (IDE) See *Parallel Advanced Technology Attachment.*

interactive mode The mode that file management commands use when a file can be overwritten; the system interacts with a user asking for the user to confirm the action.

Internet Control Message Protocol (ICMP) A protocol used on the Internet to provide error messages and network-related information.

Internet Control Message Protocol version 6 (ICMPv6) A protocol used by computers to obtain an IPv6 configuration from a router on the network.

Internet of Things (IoT) A term that refers to the worldwide collection of small Internet-connected devices.

Internet Printing Protocol (IPP) A printing protocol that can be used to send print jobs across a TCP/IP network, such as the Internet, using HTTP or HTTPS.

Internet Protocol (IP) address A unique string of numbers assigned to a computer to uniquely identify it on the Internet.

Internet SCSI (iSCSI) A SCSI technology that transfers data via IP networks.

Internet service provider (ISP) A company that provides Internet access.

Internet Super Daemon (inetd) A network daemon that is used to start other network daemons on demand.

inventory The sum total of all systems that are managed by CM software.

inventory member An individual system that is managed by CM software.

ioping (input/output ping) command Sends input/output requests to a storage device and measures the speed at which they occur.

iostat (input/output statistics) command Displays input and output statistics for storage devices on the system.

iotop (input/output top) command Displays the processes on a Linux system that have the highest number of associated input/output requests to storage devices.

ip command Used to perform a wide variety of IP management tasks on a Linux system, such as viewing and manipulating the route table. It is part of the iproute or iproute2 package.

IP forwarding The act of forwarding IP packets from one network to another. See also *routing.*

IP version 4 (IPv4) The most common version of IP used on the Internet. It uses a 32-bit addressing scheme organized into different classes.

IP version 6 (IPv6) A recent version of IP that is used by some hosts on the Internet. It uses a 128-bit addressing scheme.

ip6tables command Used to configure IPv6 rules for a netfilter firewall.

ip6tables-save command Used to display or save IPv6 rules for a netfilter firewall.

ip6tables-translate command Used to translate IPv6 rules for a netfilter firewall to nftables format.

iperf command Used to measure the bandwidth between two computers.

iptables command Used to configure IPv4 rules for a netfilter firewall.

iptables-save command Used to display or save IPv4 rules for a netfilter firewall.

iptables-translate command Used to translate IPv4 rules for a netfilter firewall to nftables format.

iSCSI initiator A term that refers to the computer that connects to the iSCSI target within an iSCSI SAN.

iSCSI target A term that refers to a storage device within an iSCSI SAN.

iscsiadm command Used to configure an iSCSI initiator.

ISO image A file that contains the content of a DVD. ISO images of Linux installation media can be downloaded from the Internet.

ISO-8859 A character set that extends ASCII to provide additional character mappings for non-English languages.

iterative query A DNS resolution request that was resolved without the use of top-level DNS servers.

J

jabbering   The process by which failing hardware components send large amounts of information to the CPU.

jail   A FreeBSD container.

`jexec` **command**   Executes commands within a FreeBSD jail.

jitter   The difference between time measurements from several different NTP servers.

`jls` **command**   Displays FreeBSD jails running on the system.

`jobs` **command**   Displays background processes running in the current shell.

`journalctl` **command**   Used to configure journald, as well as to view log entries in the journald database.

journald   A system used to record (or journal) system events on modern Linux distributions.

journaling   A feature that allows the filesystem to keep track of filesystem actions that have not been completed such that they can be performed in the event of a power failure.

Just a Bunch of Disks (JBOD)   See *spanning*.

K

K Desktop Environment (KDE)   One of the two mainstream desktop environments available for Linux.

KDE Display Manager (KDM)   A graphical login screen that resembles the look and feel of the KDE desktop.

`kenv` **command**   Used to display or modify FreeBSD kernel settings.

Kerberos   A protocol used by most network authentication services.

Kerberos ticket   A token generated by a Kerberos-based authentication service that users can use to authenticate to other systems using SSO.

kernel   The central, core program of the operating system. The shared commonality of the kernel is what defines Linux; the differing OSS applications that can interact with the common kernel are what differentiates Linux distributions.

kernel extension   A kernel module within macOS. Each macOS device driver has a related kernel module.

kernel panic   A condition in which a system halts immediately after loading the Linux kernel.

Kernel-based Virtual Machine (KVM)   A hypervisor that is built into the Linux kernel.

`kextfind` **command**   Displays macOS kernel extensions.

`kextload` **command**   Activates a macOS kernel extension.

`kextunload` **command**   Deactivates a macOS kernel extension.

key   A unique piece of information that is used within an encryption algorithm.

Kickstart   A component of the Anaconda Linux installer that can be used to automate the configuration of a Linux installation.

`kill` **command**   Used to send kill signals to a process by PID.

kill signal   The signal sent to a process for use in terminating or restarting processes; different kill signals affect processes in different ways.

`killall` **command**   Sends kill signals to processes by process name.

`kldload` **command**   Loads a module into the FreeBSD kernel.

`kldstat` **command**   Display modules loaded into the FreeBSD kernel.

`kldunload` **command**   Removes a module from the FreeBSD kernel.

`klist` **command**   Used to view Kerberos ticket information.

`kubectl` **command**   Used to configure and manage Kubernetes clusters.

Kubernetes   The most common container orchestration and build automation software used in cloud environments.

L

label   An identifier that SELinux places on a file, directory, or process.

Launch Daemon   The macOS daemon that starts and stops other system daemons and system components. It is functionally equivalent to Systemd on Linux systems.

`launchctl` **command**   Used to view and manage the Launch Daemon.

`ldconfig` **command**   Used to update the /etc/ld.so.conf and /etc/ld.so.cache files with the current list of shared libraries.

`ldd` **command**   Displays the shared libraries used by a certain program.

`less` **command**   Displays a text file page-by-page on the terminal screen; users can then use the cursor keys to navigate the file.

LightDM   A program that provides a graphical login screen.

Lightweight Directory Access Protocol (LDAP) An industry-standard protocol used to access directory service databases across a network.

Line Printer Daemon (LPD) A printing system typically used on legacy Linux computers.

linked file A file that represents the same data or is a shortcut to the data in another file.

Linus Torvalds A Finnish graduate student who coded and created the first version of Linux and subsequently distributed it under the GNU Public License.

Linux A software operating system originated by Linus Torvalds. The common core, or kernel, continues to evolve and be revised. Differing OSS bundled with the Linux kernel is what defines the wide variety of distributions now available.

Linux server distribution A Linux distribution containing packages that are geared specifically for Linux servers.

Linux Unified Key Setup (LUKS) A technology that encrypts the contents of a Linux filesystem.

Linux User Group (LUG) The open forums of Linux users who discuss and assist each other in using and modifying the Linux operating system and the OSS run on it. There are LUGs worldwide.

live media Linux installation media that provides a fully functional Linux operating system in RAM prior to installation on permanent storage.

ll command An alias for the `ls -l` command; it gives a long file listing.

ln (link) command Used to create hard and symbolic links.

load balancer A software component that allows external access to services within a Kubernetes cluster, distributing requests evenly if necessary.

load balancing A feature of some network devices that allows requests for a service to be spread across several different computers for fault tolerance and performance.

local area network (LAN) A network in which the computers are all in close physical proximity.

locale The regional language and character set used on a system.

locale command Used to display locale information.

localectl command Used to view and modify locale information.

localization The collection of settings on a system that are region-specific.

locate command Used to locate files using a file database.

log file A file that contains past system events.

logger command Used to create system log entries.

logical drive A smaller partition contained within an extended partition on an MBR-based hard disk drive or SSD.

Logical Unit Number (LUN) A unique identifier for each device attached to any given node in a SCSI chain.

Logical Volume (LV) A volume that is managed by the LVM and comprised of free space within a volume group.

Logical Volume Manager (LVM) A set of software components within Linux that can be used to manage the storage of information across several hard disk drives or SSDs on a Linux system.

login banner A message that is displayed to users after logging into a system.

logrotate command Used to rotate log files; typically uses the configuration information stored in /etc/logrotate.conf.

loop construct A special syntax used in a shell script to execute commands repetitively. Common decision constructs include `for`, `while`, and `until`.

lp command Used to create print jobs in the print queue in the CUPS printing system.

lpadmin command Used to perform printer administration in the CUPS printing system.

lpc command Used to view the status of, and control, printers in the LPD printing system.

lpq command Used to view the contents of print queues in the LPD printing system.

lpr command Used to create print jobs in the print queue in the LPD printing system.

lprm command Used to remove print jobs from the print queue in the LPD printing system.

lpstat command Used to view the contents of print queues and printer information in the CUPS printing system.

ls command Used to list the files in a directory.

lsattr (list attributes) command Used to list filesystem attributes for a Linux file.

lsblk command Used to display storage device information including type, size, major number, minor number, and mount point.

lshw command Used to list information about the hardware components on a Linux system.

`lsmod command` Used to list modules that are currently loaded in a Linux kernel.

`lsof (list open files) command` Lists the files that are currently being viewed or modified by processes and users.

`lspci command` Used to display PCI devices that are attached to the system.

`lsusb command` Used to display USB devices that are attached to the system.

`lvcreate command` Used to create LVM logical volumes.

`lvdisplay command` Used to view LVM logical volumes.

`lvextend command` Used to add space from volume groups to existing LVM logical volumes.

M

`macOS Recovery Tool` A graphical tool on macOS systems that can reset passwords, repair filesystems, and install or reinstall macOS.

`mail command` Used to check and compose email on UNIX, Linux, and macOS systems.

Mail Transfer Agent (MTA) An email server.

`mailq command` Lists email awaiting delivery, as well as any delivery errors.

main branch The default branch in a Git repo. It was formerly called the master branch.

major number When referring to the Linux kernel, it is the first number in a Linux kernel version and denotes a major change or revision. When referring to device files, it identifies which device driver to call to interact properly with a given category of hardware; similar devices share a common major number.

man page See *manual page*.

manual page A set of local documentation for a specific command or file, available by typing the `man` command. Also known as a `man` page.

Master Boot Record (MBR) The area of a typical hard disk drive or SSD (< 2TB) outside a partition that stores partition information.

master branch See *main branch*.

master DNS server See *primary DNS server*.

master node A node within a Kubernetes cluster that manages other nodes.

MATE A popular desktop environment derived from GNOME 2.

`mdadm command` Used to configure software RAID on a Linux system.

Media Access Control (MAC) address The hardware address that uniquely identifies a network interface.

media access method A system that defines how computers on a network share access to the physical medium.

memory leak A condition whereby a process continually uses more and more memory within a system, until there is no more memory available.

Message Passing Interface (MPI) A system that is used on Beowulf clusters to pass information to several separate computers in a parallel fashion.

metacharacter A character that has special meaning in a shell.

metadata In BTRFS terminology, it refers to the inode table on the BTRFS filesystem.

microservice A subset of a web app that performs a unique function and runs within its own container.

minor number When referring to the Linux kernel, it is the second number in a Linux kernel version and denotes a minor change or revision. When referring to device files, it identifies which specific hardware device, within a given category, to use as a driver to communicate with. See also *major number*.

`mkdir (make directory) command` Used to create directories.

`mkfs (make filesystem) command` Used to format (create) filesystems.

`mkfs.btrfs command` Used to create a BTRFS filesystem.

`mkinitrd command` Used to generate an initramfs.

`mkisofs command` Used to create an ISO image from one or more files on the filesystem.

`mknod command` Used to re-create a device file, provided the major number, minor number, and type (character or block) are known.

`mkswap command` Used to prepare newly created swap partitions for use by the Linux system.

mode The part of the inode that stores information on access permissions.

Modem Manager utility A graphical utility that can be used to configure modem settings on Linux systems.

`modinfo command` Used to list information about a module.

`modprobe command` Used to load a module, including any module dependencies, into the Linux kernel.

module   A Linux device driver that is inserted into the Linux kernel in a modular fashion.

monitoring   The process by which system areas are observed for problems or irregularities.

more command   Display a text file page-by-page and line-by-line on the terminal screen.

mount command   Used to mount filesystems to mount point directories.

mount point   The directory in a file structure to which something is mounted.

mount unit   A Systemd term that is used to describe a filesystem that can be mounted to the directory tree.

mounting   A process used to associate a device with a directory in the logical directory tree such that users can store data on that device.

mpathconf command   Used to configure DM-MPIO on a Linux system.

mpstat (multiple processor statistics) command   Displays CPU statistics on a Linux system.

mtr command   Used to trace the path an IPv4 or IPv6 packet takes through routers to a destination host.

multi boot   A configuration in which two or more operating systems exist on the hard disk drive of a computer; the boot loader allows the user to choose which operating system to load at boot time.

multicast   IP communication destined for a certain group of computers.

Multi-Category Security (MCS)   An optional SELinux policy scheme that prevents processes from accessing other processes that have similar attributes.

multi-factor authentication (MFA)   The process whereby multiple separate mechanisms are used to validate a user's identity.

multihomed hosts   The computers that have more than one network interface.

Multi-Level Security (MLS)   An optional SELinux policy scheme that uses custom attributes.

multipath command   Used to view and modify multipath daemon settings.

multipath daemon (multipathd)   The system service that implements DM-MPIO on Linux systems.

Multipath Input Output (MPIO)   A technology used to provide multiple redundant connections to a SAN for fault tolerance and speed.

Multiplexed Information and Computing Service (MULTICS)   A prototype time-sharing operating system that was developed in the late-1960s by AT&T Bell Laboratories.

mv (move) command   Used to move or rename files and directories.

N

named pipe file   A file that can be written to and read by different processes simultaneously for the purposes of transferring data.

namespace   A major section of an NVMe SSD that can be partitioned.

nano editor   A user-friendly terminal text editor that uses Ctrl key combinations to perform basic functions.

ncat (net cat) command   A network testing utility. It is often used to test the functionality of services on the network.

NetBIOS   A protocol used by Windows computers that adds a unique 15-character name to file- and printer-sharing traffic.

netbooting   The process of loading an operating system from across a network; it is often used to load Linux live installation media across a network for installation purposes.

netfilter   The Linux kernel component that provides firewall and NAT capability on modern Linux systems.

netplan command   Used alongside a network renderer to configure IP on Ubuntu systems.

netstat command   Used to display network information and active connections.

network   Two or more computers joined together via network media and able to exchange information.

Network Address Translation (NAT)   A technology that allows a router to obtain Internet resources on behalf of computers on the network.

Network Connections utility   A graphical NetworkManager tool that can be used to configure additional network interfaces and related technologies, such as DSL.

Network File System (NFS)   A protocol used to share files between UNIX, Linux, macOS, and Windows computers on a network.

network ID   The portion of an IP address that denotes the network.

network latency   A condition in which replies to network requests are slow or intermittent.

network renderer A service that manages the configuration of network interfaces.

network service A process that responds to network requests.

Network Time Protocol (NTP) A protocol that can be used to obtain time information from other computers on the Internet.

network zone A component of firewalld that defines the level of trust for network connections.

`networkctl` **command** Used to display and configure network interfaces using Systemd-networkd.

NetworkManager A network renderer commonly used on workstation Linux distributions.

`networksetup` **command** Used to configure network interfaces on macOS systems.

`newaliases` **command** Used to rebuild the email alias database based on the entries within the /etc/aliases file.

`newfs` **command** Used to create UFS filesystems on FreeBSD systems.

`newfs_apfs` **command** Used to create an APFS filesystem on macOS systems.

`newgrp` **command** Used to temporarily change the primary group of a user.

`nft` **command** Used to configure and manage firewall rules using the nftables framework.

`nftables` A recent kernel framework that simplifies the generation and use of firewall rules.

`nice` **command** Used to change the priority of a process as it is started.

`nice value` The value that indirectly represents the priority of a process; the higher the value, the lower the priority.

`nmap` **(network mapper) command** Used to scan ports on network computers.

`nmblookup` **command** Used to test NetBIOS name resolution on a Linux system.

`nm-connection-editor` **command** Used to start the graphical Network Connections tool that is part of NetworkManager.

`nmcli` **command** Used to display and configure network interfaces using NetworkManager.

`node` A virtual machine within a Kubernetes cluster that runs containers.

`nohup` **command** Used to execute a child process without parent association.

Non-Volatile Memory Express (NVMe) A modern SSD technology that allows for very fast data transfer directly to the PCIe bus on the computer.

`nslookup` **command** Used to test name resolution.

NTP daemon (ntpd) The daemon traditionally used to provide time synchronization services on Linux computers.

`ntpdate` **command** Used to view the current system time as well as synchronize the system time with an NTP server.

`ntpq` **command** Used to query the state of an NTP server or client.

O

object storage Storage made available to web apps run within a cloud provider. Web apps access object storage using an HTTP request.

octet A portion of an IPv4 address that represents eight binary bits.

`od` **command** Display the contents of a file in octal or hexadecimal format.

offset The difference in time between two computers that use the NTP protocol.

offsite backup The process whereby an archive is copied to another computer across the Internet.

`open` **command** Used to execute an application bundle on macOS systems.

Open Source Software (OSS) The programs distributed and licensed so that the source code making up the program is freely available to anyone who wants to examine, utilize, or improve upon it.

Open Virtualization Archive (OVA) A common virtual appliance file format.

Open Virtualization Format (OVF) A file format used to specify virtual machine settings.

`openssl` **command** Used to configure and view SSL/TLS certificates.

operating system The software used to control and directly interact with the computer hardware components.

option A part of a command that alters that way the command works. Options are represented by one or more letters that starts with a dash (-) or a word that starts with two dashes.

orchestration The process of arranging and coordinating the execution of automated tasks, ultimately resulting in a consolidated process, such as a CD workflow.

other When used in the mode of a certain file or directory, it refers to all the users on the Linux system that are not the owner or members of the group owner.

Out Of Memory (OOM) killer   A kernel process that kills low-priority processes in the event that the system is critically low on memory.

overclocked   The term used to describe a CPU that runs faster than the clock speed for which it has been rated.

owner   The user whose name appears in a long listing of a file or directory and who has the ability to change permissions on that file or directory.

P

package dependency   A package that is prerequisite to the current package being installed on the system.

package group   A group of RPM packages that are commonly installed to provide a specific function on the system.

package manager   The software used to install, maintain, and remove other software programs by storing all relevant software information in a central software database on the computer.

packet   A package of data formatted by a network protocol.

pam_tally2 command   Used to view and modify user lockout settings.

Parallel Advanced Technology Attachment (PATA)   A legacy hard disk technology that uses ribbon cables to typically attach up to four hard disk drives to a single computer.

parallel SCSI   The traditional SCSI technology that transfers data across parallel cables.

parent directory   The directory that is one level closer to the root directory in the directory tree relative to your current directory.

parent process   A process that has started other processes (child processes).

parent process ID (PPID)   The PID of the parent process that created the current process.

parted (GNU Parted) command   Used to create and modify MBR and GPT partitions on storage devices.

partition   A physical division of a hard disk drive or SSD.

partprobe command   Used to request that partition tables be reloaded by the Linux kernel.

passwd command   Used to change user passwords.

PATH variable   A variable that stores a list of directories that will be searched in order when commands are executed without an absolute or relative pathname.

permission   A level of access granted to users on a file, folder, or other object.

permissive license   An open source license that places fewer restrictions on source code usage compared to copyleft licenses.

persistent volume   See *block storage*.

pfctl command   Used to configure PF firewall settings on FreeBSD systems.

pgrep command   Used to list the PIDs of processes that match a regular expression or other criteria.

physical extent (PE) size   The block size used by the LVM when storing data on a volume group.

Physical Volumes (PVs)   A partition that is used by the LVM.

pidof command   Displays the PID for a process name.

pidstat (PID statistics) command   Displays CPU statistics for each PID on a Linux system.

ping (Packet Internet Groper) command   Used to check connectivity on an IPv4 network.

ping6 command   Used to check connectivity on an IPv6 network.

pipe   A string of commands connected by | metacharacters.

pkexec command   Used to run administrative commands using the Polkit framework.

pkg command   Used to interact with the FreeBSD package manager.

pkill command   Used to send a kill signal to processes that match a regular expression or other criteria.

Plasma Desktop   The graphical interface components within the KDE desktop environment.

Platform as a Service (PaaS)   A cloud strategy that allows access to operating system containers stored within a data center.

Pluggable Authentication Module (PAM)   A component that provides authentication-related functionality on a Linux system.

pod   A Kubernetes term that refers to a web app.

Point-to-Point Protocol (PPP)   The most common WAN protocol used to send TCP/IP packets across a telephone line.

Polkit   A software framework that allows users to run administrative commands.

port   A number that uniquely identifies a network service.

Portable Operating System Interface (POSIX)   A set of UNIX standards that have been adopted by other operating systems, such as Linux.

positional parameter An argument to a shell script or function.

Postfix A common email server daemon used on Linux systems.

PostgreSQL A common SQL server used on Linux computers.

PostgreSQL utility The program used to perform most database management on a PostgreSQL server.

Power On Self Test (POST) An initial series of tests run when a computer is powered on to ensure that hardware components are functional.

PPP over Ethernet (PPPoE) The protocol used by DSL to send PPP information over an Ethernet connection.

`pppoeconf` **command** Used to detect and configure a DSL connection.

Preboot eXecution Environment (PXE) A standard that allows computers to boot from installation media hosted on a network server.

primary DNS server The DNS server that contains a read/write copy of the zone.

primary group The default group to which a user belongs. It is defined in /etc/passwd.

primary partition A major division into which a hard disk drive or SSD can be divided.

print job The information sent to a printer for printing.

print job ID A unique numeric identifier used to mark and distinguish each print job.

print queue A directory on the filesystem that holds print jobs that are waiting to be printed.

`printenv` **command** Used to display a list of exported variables and functions present in the current shell.

printer class A group of CUPS printers that are treated as a single unit for the purposes of printing and management.

priority The importance of system information when logging system events.

private cloud A private data center hosted by an organization that is accessible to other computers across the Internet.

private key An asymmetric encryption key that is used to decrypt data and create digital signatures.

proactive maintenance The measures taken to reduce future system problems.

process A program currently loaded into physical memory and running on the system.

process ID (PID) A unique identifier assigned to every process as it begins.

process priority (PRI) A number assigned to a process, used to determine how many time slices on the processor that process will receive; the higher the number, the lower the priority.

process state The current state of the process on the processor; most processes are in the sleeping or running state.

production kernel A Linux kernel that is deemed stable for use through widespread testing.

program An executable file on a filesystem. A program can be executed to create a process.

programming language The syntax used for developing a program. Different programming languages use different syntaxes.

protocol A set of rules of communication used between computers on a network.

proxy server A server or hardware device that requests Internet resources on behalf of other computers.

pruning The process of excluding files, directories, or filesystems from being processed by a command.

`ps` **command** Used to obtain information about processes currently running on the system.

pseudo filesystem See *virtual filesystem*.

`psql` **command** Used to start the PostgreSQL utility.

`pstree` **command** Displays processes according to their lineage, starting from the init daemon.

public cloud The worldwide collection of commercial data centers that can be used to host cloud services and apps for a fee.

public key An asymmetric encryption key that is used to encrypt data and decrypt digital signatures.

Public Key Infrastructure (PKI) A system whereby a CA is used to validate the authenticity of public keys.

pull request A request for source code review within an open source project on GitHub.com.

Putty A cross-platform SSH client.

`pvcreate` **command** Used to create LVM physical volumes.

`pvdisplay` **command** Used to view LVM physical volumes.

`pw` **command** Used to create, modify, remove, lock, and unlock FreeBSD user accounts.

`pwconv` **command** Used to enable the use of the /etc/shadow file.

pwd (print working directory) command
Display the current directory in the directory tree.

`pwunconv` **command**   Used to disable the use of the /etc/shadow file.

Q

queuing   See *spooling*.

Quick Emulator (QEMU)   A hypervisor and binary translator that works alongside other hypervisors, such as KVM, to provide near-native access to hardware.

`quota` **command**   Used to view disk quotas imposed on a user.

`quotaoff` **command**   Used to deactivate disk quotas for a filesystem.

`quotaon` **command**   Used to activate disk quotas for a filesystem.

quotas   The limits that can be imposed on users and groups for filesystem usage.

R

rackmount server   A thin form factor used to house server hardware that is installed in a server rack.

RAID-Z   An implementation of RAID level 5 using ZFS, which uses a variable stripe that provides for better performance and fault tolerance.

reactive maintenance   The measures taken when system problems arise.

`read` **command**   Used to copy Standard Input into a variable.

`realm` **command**   Used to join a Linux system to a Kerberos realm, such as a Microsoft Active Directory domain.

Realm Daemon (realmd)   The daemon that queries and maintains a connection to a Kerberos realm, such as a Microsoft Active Directory domain.

record   A line within a database table that represents a particular object.

recursive   A term referring to itself and its own contents; a recursive search includes all subdirectories in a directory and their contents.

recursive query   A DNS resolution request that was resolved with the use of top-level DNS servers.

Red Hat Package Manager (RPM)   A package manager commonly used on Linux distributions derived from Red Hat Linux, and the default package manager used on Fedora Linux.

redirection   The process of changing the default locations of Standard Input, Standard Output, and Standard Error.

Redundant Array of Independent Disks (RAID)   The process of combining the storage space of several hard disk drives into one larger, logical storage unit. It is also known as Redundant Array of Inexpensive Disks.

regular expressions (regexp)   The special metacharacters used to match patterns of text within text files; they are commonly used by text tool commands, including `grep`.

relational database   A database that contains multiple tables that are linked by common fields.

relative pathname   The pathname of a target directory relative to your current directory in the tree.

`reload` **command**   Used to reload the configuration files into memory for an upstart daemon.

Remote Direct Memory Access (RDMA)   A technology used to allow hardware devices to communicate directly with each other without accessing the CPU of the system. It is often used by network technologies such as Infiniband.

`renice` **command**   Used to alter the nice value of a process currently running on the system.

`repquota` **command**   Used to produce a report on quotas for a particular filesystem.

`resize2fs` **command**   Used to change the size of an ext2/ext3/ext4 filesystem after creation; it is normally used after an LVM logical volume has been extended to include additional space.

`resolvectl` **command**   Used to test and configure Systemd-resolved.

resource records   The records within a zone on a DNS server that provide name resolution for individual computers.

`restart` **command**   Used to manually restart an upstart daemon.

`restore` **command**   Used to extract archives created with the `dump` command.

`restorecon` **command**   Forces SELinux to set the default label on system files and directories.

reverse lookup   A DNS name resolution request whereby an IP address is resolved to a FQDN.

revision number   The third number in the version number of a Linux kernel that identifies the release version of a kernel.

`rm` **(remove) command**   Used to remove files and directories.

`rmdir` **(remove directory) command**   Used to remove empty directories.

`rmmod` **command**   Used to remove a module from the Linux kernel.

`rmuser` command   Removes a FreeBSD user account.

rogue process   A process that has become faulty in some way and continues to consume far more system resources than it should. It is also called a runaway process.

root filesystem   The filesystem containing most files that make up the operating system; it should have enough free space to prevent errors and slow performance.

`route` command   Used to view and configure the route table. It is part of the net-tools package.

route table   A table of information used to indicate which networks are connected to network interfaces.

router   A device capable of transferring packets from one network to another.

routing   The act of forwarding data packets from one network to another.

`rpm` command   Used to install, query, and remove RPM packages.

`rpm2cpio` command   Used to convert an RPM package to an archive that can be accessed using the `cpio` command.

`rsync` (remote sync) command   Used to copy files to and from Linux computers running the rsync service. It is often used to copy archives to remote computers.

rules   The components of a firewall that match specific network traffic that is to be allowed or dropped.

runlevel   A UNIX SysV term that defines a certain type and number of daemons on a Linux system.

`runlevel` command   Used to display the current and most recent (previous) UNIX SysV runlevel.

runtime configuration (rc) scripts   Scripts that are used during the UNIX SysV system initialization process to start daemons and provide system functionality.

S

sandbox   An area of the system that runs apps that are isolated from other apps running on the system. Containers are the most common method used to sandbox web apps.

`sar` (system activity reporter) command   Displays various performance-related statistics on a Linux system.

scalability   The capability of computers to increase workload as the number of processors increases.

`scp` (secure copy) command   Used to copy files to and from Linux computers using SSH encryption. It is often used to copy archives to remote computers.

SCSI ID   A number that uniquely identifies devices attached to a SCSI controller.

secondary DNS server   A DNS server that contains a read-only copy of the zone.

sector   The smallest unit of data storage on a hard disk drive; sectors are arranged into concentric circles called tracks and can be grouped into blocks for use by the system.

secure boot   A UEFI BIOS feature that checks files loaded during the boot process to ensure that they were not modified by malware.

Secure FTP (SFTP)   A version of the FTP protocol that encrypts traffic using SSH.

Secure Shell (SSH)   A technology that can be used to run remote applications on a Linux computer; it encrypts all client-server traffic.

Secure Socket Layer (SSL)   A technology that adds encryption to network protocols, such as HTTP.

security appliance   A server that provides advanced security services on a network. Most security appliances run a custom Linux distribution.

Security Enhanced Linux (SELinux)   A set of Linux kernel components and related software packages that prevent malicious software from accessing system resources.

Security Information and Event Management (SIEM)   Software that is used to monitor security events and vulnerabilities on systems across a network.

segmentation fault   An error that software encounters when it cannot locate the information needed to complete its task.

`seinfo` command   Displays SELinux features.

self-signed certificate   A certificate that was digitally signed by the computer that generated the public key within.

`semanage` command   Used to view and configure SELinux settings.

`seq` command   Used to generate a list of sequential numbers.

Serial Advanced Technology Attachment (SATA)   A technology that allows for fast data transfer along a serial cable for hard disk drives and SSDs. It is commonly used in workstation computers.

Serial Attached SCSI (SAS)   A high-performance SCSI technology that is commonly used for hard disk drives and SSDs in server computers.

server A computer that provides services to other computers on a network.

server closet A secured room that stores servers within an organization.

Server Message Blocks (SMB) The protocol that Windows computers use to format file- and printer-sharing traffic on IP networks.

service A process that provides functionality for the local system, or other systems on a network. In a Kubernetes cluster, a service provides access to web apps within pods.

service command Used to manually start, stop, and restart UNIX SysV daemons.

service mesh A software component that allows web apps in different containers to communicate with one another.

service unit A Systemd term that is used to describe a daemon.

sestatus command Displays the current status and functionality of the SELinux subsystem.

set command Used to display a list of variables and functions within the shell.

setenforce command Used to change SELinux between enforcing and permissive mode.

setfacl (set file ACL) command Used to modify ACL entries for Linux files and directories.

setsebool command Used to modify SELinux settings within an SELinux policy.

sftp (secure FTP) command Used to copy files to and from Linux computers running FTP using SSH encryption. It is often used to copy archives to remote computers.

shared library A file that contains executable code that can be used by multiple, different programs. It is the most common type of package dependency.

shareware The programs developed and provided at minimal cost to the end user. These programs are initially free but require payment after a period of time or usage.

shebang See *hashpling*.

shell A user interface that accepts input from the user and passes the input to the kernel for processing.

shell script A text file that contains a list of commands or constructs for the shell to execute in order.

showmount command Used to view NFS shared directories on a remote computer.

shred command Used to continually overwrite files for secure destruction.

sidecar container A container within a Kubernetes cluster that does not run web apps. Most sidecar containers monitor other containers or provide for service mesh capability.

Simple Desktop Display Manager (SDDM) A graphical login program that is often configured on Linux distributions that use the KDE desktop by default.

Simple Protocol for Independent Computing Environments (SPICE) A graphical remote access protocol commonly used to manage virtual machines; it is the default for Boxes.

single sign-on (SSO) A process whereby users log into an authentication service to authenticate to multiple, separate systems on a network.

skeleton directory A directory that contains files that are copied to all new users' home directories upon creation; the default skeleton directory on Linux systems is /etc/skel.

slave DNS server See *secondary DNS server*.

slice The area within a macOS disk partition that can contain a filesystem.

Small Computer Systems Interface (SCSI) A high-performance storage technology that is commonly used in server computers.

smbclient command Used to connect to a remote Windows or Samba server and transfer files.

smbpasswd command Used to generate a Samba password for a user.

Snap A sandboxed application format and package manager.

snap command Used to interact with the Snap package manager.

snapshot A feature that allows you to revert to a previous version of a virtual hard disk file, filesystem, or Git repository.

socket file A file connecting processes on two different computers.

socket unit A Systemd term that is used to describe a network daemon that is started on demand.

soft limit A disk quota that the user can exceed for a certain period of time.

software The programs stored on a storage device in a computer, which provide a certain function when executed.

Software as a Service (SaaS) A cloud strategy that provides access to an app or service hosted on servers within a data center.

software mirror A software repository that hosts the same RPM or DPM packages as other software repositories for fault tolerance and load balancing of download requests.

software RAID   A RAID system that is controlled by software running within the operating system.

software repository   A server on the Internet that hosts software packages for download.

Software utility   A program that can be used to install, update, and remove RPM packages within a desktop environment on Fedora.

softwareupdate command   Used to update macOS systems.

source code   The sets of instructions that define the functions that constitute a program. Source code is compiled to create programs that can execute on a system.

source command   Used to execute the contents of a shell script within the current shell, instead of using a subshell.

source file/directory   The portion of a command that refers to the file or directory from which information is taken.

spanning   A storage configuration that allows two or more devices to be represented as a single large volume.

special device file   A file used to identify hardware devices such as hard disk drives and SSDs.

spooling   The process of accepting a print job into a print queue.

SQL server   See *database management system (DBMS)*.

ss (socket statistics) command   Used to display network connections.

ssh command   Used to connect to a SSH daemon on a remote computer.

SSH host keys   The asymmetric public and private keys on a computer running sshd. They are used to negotiate the symmetric key at the beginning of an SSH session.

ssh-add command   Used to add SSH user keys to the SSH agent process.

ssh-agent command   Used to start the SSH agent process.

ssh-copy-id command   Used to copy SSH user keys to the home directory of a user on another computer to allow for simplified authentication.

ssh-keygen command   Used to generate or regenerate SSH encryption keys.

staging   The process of adding files to a Git index.

stand-alone daemon   A daemon that is started without the use of inetd/xinetd or a System socket unit.

Standard Error (stderr)   A file descriptor that represents any error messages generated by a command.

Standard Input (stdin)   A file descriptor that represents information input to a command during execution.

Standard Output (stdout)   A file descriptor that represents the desired output from a command.

start command   Used to manually start an upstart daemon.

startx command   Used to manually start X Windows alongside the default window manager and desktop environment.

stat command   Used to view detailed information within the inode of a file or directory.

stateful packet filter   A packet filter that applies rules to related packets within the same network session.

status command   Used to view the status of an upstart daemon.

stop command   Used to manually stop an upstart daemon.

Storage Area Network (SAN)   A group of computers that access the same storage device across a fast network.

strata   The levels used within an NTP hierarchy that describe the relative position of a server to an original time source, such as an atomic clock.

strings command   Displays text characters that are in a binary file.

Structured Query Language (SQL)   A language used by SQL servers to query, add, and modify the data within a database.

subdirectory   A directory that resides within another directory in the directory tree.

subnet mask   A number or series of numbers that determine the network and host portions of an IP address.

subnetting   The process in which a single large network is subdivided into several smaller networks.

subshell   A shell started by the current shell.

sudo command   Used to perform commands as another user via entries in the /etc/sudoers file.

sudoedit command   Used to edit text files as another user via entries in the /etc/sudoers file.

superblock The portion of a filesystem that stores critical information, such as the inode table location and block size.

swap memory See *virtual memory*.

`swapoff` **command** Used to disable a partition for use as virtual memory on the Linux system.

`swapon` **command** Used to enable a partition for use as virtual memory on the Linux system.

symbolic link A pointer to another file on the same or another filesystem; commonly referred to as a shortcut, symlink, or soft link.

symmetric encryption A type of encryption that uses a single key to encrypt and decrypt data.

syncing The process of writing data from RAM to a filesystem.

synthesized disk A virtual disk on a macOS system that is created from an APFS container.

`sysctl` **command** Used to view and modify files stored under /proc/sys.

`sysrc` **command** Used to list and edit parameters within FreeBSD configuration files.

system In BTRFS terminology, it refers to the BTRFS superblock.

system backup The process whereby files are copied to an archive.

System Information A macOS utility that displays system information.

system initialization process The process that executes the daemons that provide for system services during boot time and bring the system to a useable state.

System Log Daemon (rsyslogd) The daemon that logs system events to various log files via information stored in /etc/rsyslog.conf and files within the /etc/rsyslog.d directory.

System Preferences The graphical system configuration utility within macOS.

system rescue The process of using a live media Linux system to access and repair a damaged Linux installation on permanent storage.

System Security Services Daemon (sssd) A daemon that communicates with an authentication service using LDAP and Kerberos.

System Statistics (sysstat) package A software package that contains common performance-monitoring utilities.

`systemctl` **command** Used to view, start, stop, restart, and reload Systemd daemons, as well as configure Systemd daemon startup during the system initialization process.

Systemd A relatively new software framework used on Linux systems that provides a system initialization process and system management functions.

Systemd Journal Daemon (journald) A Systemd component that logs system events to a journal database.

`systemd-analyze` **command** Used to view Systemd unit information.

`systemd-cat` **command** Used to create system log entries in the journald database.

`systemd-mount` **command** Used to manually mount a filesystem via Systemd.

Systemd-networkd A network renderer that is provided by Systemd. It is common on Linux server distributions.

`systemd-umount` **command** Used to unmount a filesystem via Systemd.

T

Tab-completion feature A shell feature that fills in the remaining characters of a unique filename or directory name when the user presses the Tab key.

table A database structure that organizes data using records and fields.

`tac` **command** Displays a file on the screen, beginning with the last line of the file and ending with the first line of the file.

`tail` **command** Display lines of text at the end of a file; by default, the `tail` command displays the last 10 lines of the file.

`tar` **(tape archive) command** The most common command used to back up files to an archive. It can also be used to view and restore archives.

tarball A compressed archive of files that often contains Linux software or source code.

target See *target unit*.

target file/directory The portion of a command that refers to the file or directory to which information is directed.

target ID See *SCSI ID*.

target unit A Systemd term that describes the number and type of daemons running on a Linux system. It is functionally equivalent to the UNIX SysV term *runlevel*.

TCP wrapper A program that can be used to run a network daemon with additional client restrictions specified in the /etc/hosts.allow and /etc/hosts.deny files.

`tcpdump` command   Used to display the network traffic passing through a network interface.

`telinit` command   Used to change the operating system from one UNIX SysV runlevel to another.

`telnet` command   Used to obtain a shell on a remote computer running a Telnet daemon.

Teredo   A protocol used to encapsulate IPv6 packets within an IPv4 network.

terminal   The channel that allows a certain user to log in and communicate with the kernel via a user interface.

Terminal   The graphical terminal application within the macOS desktop.

terminator   A device used to terminate an electrical conduction medium to absorb the transmitted signal and prevent signal bounce.

test statement   A syntax used to test a certain condition and generate a True/False value.

`testparm` command   Used to check for syntax errors within the Samba configuration file as well as display the current Samba configuration.

text file   A file that stores information in a readable text format.

text tool   A program that allows for the creation, modification, and searching of text files.

thick provisioning   The process of using a virtual hard disk file that has a fixed size.

thin provisioning   The process of using a virtual hard disk file that dynamically expands as needed up to a maximum size.

time slice   The amount of time a process is given on a CPU in a multiprocessing operating system.

`timedatectl` command   Used to view and set time and time zone information for a system.

timer unit   A Systemd term that refers to a program that is scheduled to run periodically on the system.

Time-To-Live (TTL)   The amount of time that a computer is allowed to cache name resolution information obtained from a DNS server.

`tload` command   Displays load average information for a Linux system.

`top` command   Used to give real-time information about the most active processes on the system; it can also be used to renice or kill processes.

total cost of ownership (TCO)   The full sum of all accumulated costs, over and above the simple purchase price of utilizing a product. Includes training, maintenance, additional hardware, and downtime.

`touch` command   Used to create new files and update the time stamp on existing files.

`tr` command   Used to transform or change characters received from Standard Input.

`tracepath` command   Used to trace the path an IPv4 packet takes through routers to a destination host, monitoring latency at each router.

`tracepath6` command   Used to trace the path an IPv6 packet takes through routers to a destination host, monitoring latency at each router.

`traceroute` command   Used to trace the path an IPv4 packet takes through routers to a destination host.

`traceroute6` command   Used to trace the path an IPv6 packet takes through routers to a destination host.

track   The area on a hard disk drive that forms a concentric circle of sectors.

Transmission Control Protocol/Internet Protocol (TCP/IP)   The most common network protocol used on the Internet. It provides for reliable communication.

Transport Layer Security (TLS)   A technology that adds encryption to network protocols, such as HTTP.

trap   The event whereby a kill signal is ignored by a process.

`tree` command   Displays the files and subdirectories under the current or specified directory.

troubleshooting procedures   The tasks performed when solving system problems.

`tshark` command   Used to start a command-line version of the graphical Wireshark program.

`tunefs` command   Used to modify UFS filesystem parameters on a FreeBSD system.

`tune2fs` command   Used to modify ext2/ext3/ext4 filesystem parameters.

Type 1 hypervisor   A hypervisor that runs directly on computer hardware.

Type 2 hypervisor   A hypervisor that runs as a program within an operating system.

`type` command   Used to locate executable files on the system; it returns the first alias or directory within the PATH variable for the command.

`tzselect` command   Used to locate the appropriate time zone file for a region.

U

udev daemon   A system process used to automatically create and manage device files.

udevadm command Used to view and modify udev daemon configuration.

UEFI System Partition A small partition that is created by an operating system installation program to store boot-related files on a computer that has a UEFI BIOS.

ufw (Uncomplicated Firewall) command Used to configure UFW.

ulimit command Used to modify process limit parameters in the current shell.

umask A special variable used to alter the permissions on all new files and directories by taking away select file and directory permissions.

umask command Used to view and change the umask variable.

umount command Used to break the association between a device and a directory in the logical directory tree.

unalias command Used to remove an alias from shell memory.

Uncomplicated Firewall (UFW) A software component that can be used to simplify the configuration of netfilter firewall rules.

uncompress command Used to decompress files compressed by the compress command.

unicast IP communication that is destined for a single computer.

Unicode A character set that extends ASCII and represents characters used in most languages.

Unified Extensible Firmware Interface (UEFI) A feature-rich BIOS used in modern computers.

uninterruptible power supply (UPS) A device that contains battery storage and is used to supply power to computers in the event of a power outage.

unit file A file that stores the configuration for a Systemd component.

Unity A GNOME Shell alternative focused on mobile devices.

Universally Unique Identifier (UUID) A unique identifier given to a filesystem or partition when it is created; it can be used to identify that filesystem or partition afterwards.

UNIX The first true multitasking, multiuser operating system, developed by Ken Thompson and Dennis Ritchie, and from which Linux was originated.

UNIX filesystem (UFS) A filesystem used on FreeBSD UNIX systems that closely resembles the ext4 filesystem used on Linux systems.

UNIX SysV A UNIX standard that is used to provide the structure of the system initialization process on Linux systems.

unlink command Used to delete files.

unset command Used to remove a variable or function from shell memory.

unxz command Used to decompress files compressed by the xz command.

unzip command Used to decompress files compressed by the zip command.

update-grub2 command Used to build the GRUB2 configuration file from entries within the /etc/default/grub file and files under the /etc/grub.d directory.

update-rc.d command Used to configure UNIX SysV daemon startup by runlevel on Ubuntu Linux systems.

upstart A version of the UNIX SysV system initialization process used on some Linux distributions.

uptime command Displays system uptime and load average information for a Linux system.

user A person who uses a computer. When used in the context of file and directory permissions, it represents the owner of a file or directory.

user account The information regarding a user that is stored in a system database (/etc/passwd and /etc/shadow), which can be used to log in to the system and gain access to system resources.

User Datagram Protocol/Internet Protocol (UDP/IP) A less-reliable, but faster version of the TCP/IP protocol.

User Identifier (UID) A unique number assigned to each user account.

user interface The interface the user sees and uses to interact with the operating system and application programs.

user process A process begun by a user and which runs on a terminal.

useradd command Used to add a user account to the system.

user-defined variables The variables that are created by the user and are not used by the system. These variables are typically exported to subshells.

userdel command Used to remove a user account from the system.

userland The filesystem structure used by a FreeBSD jail.

usermod command Used to modify the properties of a user account on the system.

UTF-8 A character set that allows programs to represent the characters in the Unicode character set using one to four 8-bit bytes; it is the most common character set used today.

V

variable An area of memory used to store information. Variables are created from entries in environment files when the shell is first created after login and are destroyed when the shell is destroyed upon logout.

variable identifier The name of a variable.

version control A system that keeps track of changes made to files by users.

Very Secure FTP daemon (vsftpd) The default FTP server program used on modern Linux distributions.

vgcreate command Used to create an LVM volume group.

vgdisplay command Used to view an LVM volume group.

vgextend command Used to add physical volumes to an LVM volume group.

vi editor A powerful command-line text editor available on most UNIX and Linux systems.

virsh command Used to manage KVM/QEMU virtual machines on a Linux system.

virtual appliance A file that contains virtual machine settings and a virtual hard disk file.

virtual filesystem A special filesystem that is used by the Linux kernel for operating system use only; /sys, /dev, /run, and /proc are examples of virtual filesystems.

virtual machine An operating system that is running within virtualization software.

Virtual Machine Manager A graphical tool that can be used to manage KVM/QEMU virtual machines on a Linux system.

virtual memory An area on a storage device that can be used to store information that normally resides in physical memory (RAM), if the physical memory is being used excessively.

Virtual Network Computing (VNC) A cross-platform technology that allows users to connect to a graphical desktop across a network.

Virtual Private Network (VPN) A virtual network that overlays an existing TCP/IP network. Any data sent on this virtual network is encrypted.

virtualization The process of running several separate operating systems concurrently on a single computer.

virtualization software Software that can be used to run multiple operating systems concurrently on the same physical hardware.

visudo command Used to modify the contents of the /etc/sudoers file.

vmstat command Displays memory, CPU, and swap statistics on a Linux system.

VNC viewer A program used to connect to a VNC server and obtain a graphical desktop.

vncpasswd command Used to set a VNC connection password for a user.

vncserver command Used to start the VNC server process for a user.

Volume Group (VG) A group of physical volumes that are used by the LVM.

vtysh command Used to configure routing protocols, such as RIP and OSPF, on a Linux system. It is part of the optional FRRouting (frr) package.

vulnerability scanner Software that is used to scan a system for known vulnerabilities.

W

watch command Used to run a process repeatedly at the specified second interval.

Wayland A new X server originally designed to replace X.org.

Wayland compositor A window manager that is used by the Wayland X server.

web app A software application that is run on a web server.

web app framework A set of software components that simplifies the development and execution of web apps.

webpage hit A single HTTP request that is sent from a web browser to a web server.

well-known ports Of the 65,535 possible ports, the ports from 0 to 1023, which are used by common networking services.

wget (web get) command Used to download files from the Internet.

whereis command Used to locate executable files on the system; it returns any directories within the PATH variable for the command, as well as the location of associated man pages and info pages.

which command Used to locate executable files on the system; it returns any aliases and directories within the PATH variable for the command.

whois command Used to obtain information about the organization that maintains a DNS domain.

wide area network (WAN)   A network in which computers are separated geographically by large distances.

wildcard metacharacters   The metacharacters used to match certain characters in a file or directory name; they are often used to specify multiple files.

window manager   The GUI component that is responsible for determining the appearance of the windows drawn on the screen by X Windows.

Wireless-Fidelity (Wi-Fi)   A LAN technology that uses Ethernet to transmit data over the air.

Wireshark   A graphical program used to display the network traffic passing through a network interface.

World Wide Name (WWN)   A unique name that can be assigned to a storage device. Fibre Channel requires that each storage device and controller have a WWN.

World Wide Web (WWW)   The original name for the worldwide collection of web servers.

X

X client   The component of X Windows that requests graphics to be drawn from the X server and displays them on the terminal screen.

X Display Manager (XDM)   A graphical login screen.

X server   The component of X Windows that draws the graphics that comprise the GUI.

X Windows   The core component of the Linux GUI that displays graphics to windows on the terminal screen.

X.org   A common implementation of X Windows used in Linux distributions.

XFCE   A common lightweight desktop environment used on Linux systems.

xfs_admin command   Used to view and configure parameters for an XFS filesystem, including the description label.

xfs_db command   Used to view XFS filesystem information and parameters.

xfs_fsr command   Used to reorganize and optimize an XFS filesystem.

xfs_growfs command   Used to change the size of an XFS filesystem after creation; it is normally used after an LVM logical volume has been extended to include additional space.

xfs_info command   Used to obtain usage information for an XFS filesystem; it can also be used to change the size of an XFS filesystem after creation.

xfs_quota command   Used to configure and manage disk quotas for an XFS filesystem.

xfs_repair command   Used to check the integrity of an XFS filesystem and repair damaged files.

XNU   The macOS kernel. It stands for "X is Not UNIX."

xz command   Used to compress files using a Lempel-Ziv compression algorithm.

xzcat command   Used to display the contents of an archive created with xz to Standard Output.

xzgrep command   Used to search and display the contents of an archive created with xz to Standard Output.

xzless command   Used to display the contents of an archive created with xz to Standard Output using the less command.

xzmore command   Used to display the contents of an archive created with xz to Standard Output using the more command.

Y

YAML (YAML Ain't Markup Language)   A data format based on JSON that is commonly used for configuration files.

yum (Yellowdog Updater Modified) command   Used to install and upgrade RPM packages from software repositories, as well as manage and remove installed RPM packages.

Z

Z Shell   A shell that provides a superset of the features provided by BASH. It is the second most common shell on Linux systems, and the default shell on macOS.

zcat command   Used to display the contents of an archive created with compress, zip, or gzip to Standard Output.

Zettabyte File System (ZFS)   A high-performance filesystem and volume management software that is often used to create fault tolerance volumes from multiple storage devices on Linux and UNIX systems that are resilient to corruption.

zfs command   Used to configure ZFS filesystem features.

ZFS dataset   A ZFS volume or subdirectory on a ZFS volume that contains a unique ZFS filesystem and associated settings.

ZFS pool   A series of storage devices that are managed by ZFS.

ZFS snapshots   A ZFS configuration that stores subsequent changes to an existing ZFS dataset within another dataset.

ZFS volume   A volume created from space within a ZFS pool that contains a ZFS filesystem.

zgrep command   Used to search and display the contents of an archive created with `compress`, `zip`, or `gzip` to Standard Output.

zip command   Used to compress files using a Lempel-Ziv compression algorithm.

zless command   Used to display the contents of an archive created with `compress`, `zip`, or `gzip` to Standard Output using the `less` command.

zmodload command   Used to display and load Z shell modules.

zmore command   Used to display the contents of an archive created with `compress`, `zip`, or `gzip` to Standard Output using the `more` command.

zombie process   A process that has finished executing but whose parent has not yet released its PID; the zombie still retains a spot in the kernel's process table.

zone   A portion of the Domain Name Space that is administered by one or more DNS servers.

zone transfer   The process of copying resource records for a zone from a master DNS server to a slave DNS server.

zpool command   Used to configure ZFS pools and volumes.

zsh command   Used to start a Z shell.

zswap   A Linux kernel feature that creates virtual memory in a compressed area of RAM.

zypper command   Used to install and upgrade RPM packages from software repositories, as well as manage and remove installed RPM packages on SUSE and openSUSE Linux distributions.

Index